THE OXFORD HANDBOO

MODERN IRISH HISTORY

The study of Irish history, once riven and constricted, has recently enjoyed a resurgence, with new practitioners, new approaches, and new methods of investigation. *The Oxford Handbook of Modern Irish History* represents the diversity of this emerging talent and achievement by bringing together 36 leading scholars of modern Ireland and embracing 400 years of Irish history, uniting early and late modernists as well as contemporary historians. The *Handbook* offers a set of scholarly perspectives drawn from numerous disciplines, including history, political science, literature, geography, and the Irish language. It looks at the Irish at home as well as in their migrant and diasporic communities.

The *Handbook* combines sets of wide thematic and interpretative essays, with more detailed investigations of particular periods. Each of the contributors offers a summation of the state of scholarship within their subject area, linking their own research insights with assessments of future directions within the discipline. In its breadth and depth and diversity, *The Oxford Handbook of Modern Irish History* offers an authoritative and vibrant portrayal of the history of modern Ireland.

Alvin Jackson is Sir Richard Lodge Professor of History at the University of Edinburgh. He was educated at Corpus Christi College and Nuffield College, Oxford, and has been Lecturer in Modern Irish History at University College Dublin and Professor of Modern Irish History at Queen's University Belfast. Among his books are *Ireland 1798–1998: War, Peace and Beyond* (2010) and *The Two Unions: Ireland, Scotland and the Survival of the United Kingdom, 1707–2007* (2012).

Praise for *The Oxford Handbook of Modern Irish History*

'what Alvin Jackson has done with this overview is to provide one of the most extensive overviews of Irish history, calling on 36 leading scholars from a wide range of disciplines…as such this is very much a handbook which should be in the possession of anyone studying and researching Irish history—not only does it offer a useful introduction to Irish history and historiography, it is also a crucial reference work'

English Historical Review

'it is likely to become an essential first port of call for anyone with a serious interest in Irish history for years to come'

Irish Catholic Books of the Year

'truly a blockbuster…36 chapters from leading scholars on a comprehensive range of topics, from thematic studies to more chronological accounts of Irish history since the late 16th century, cumulatively amounting to a panoramic prospectus of the current state of Irish historiography'

History Ireland

'the work is an excellent contribution to the field… [and] an excellent teaching tool'

Irish Studies Review

'fully up to the standard of the celebrated *Oxford Handbook* series…Jackson's fine opening essay draws on his widely admired archival research on the avatars of professionalism in the Irish historical scene—Robin Dudley Edwards, TW Moody and JC Beckett'

Paul Bew, *Irish Times*

'The OUP Handbook of Modern Irish History, ranging over the last five centuries, imaginatively and expertly edited by Alvin Jackson, offers a rich cornucopia of perspectives from the 36 contributors, skilfully blending the chronological with the thematic in summarising the most recent understanding of topics and periods, while frequently and fruitfully meditating on possible future directions of enquiry. It is essential reading for understanding both how Ireland has got here, and for pondering possible further approaches to the historiography of the past five centuries'

J.J. Lee, New York University

THE OXFORD HANDBOOK OF

MODERN IRISH HISTORY

Edited by

ALVIN JACKSON

OXFORD

UNIVERSITY PRESS

OXFORD
UNIVERSITY PRESS

Great Clarendon Street, Oxford, OX2 6DP,
United Kingdom

Oxford University Press is a department of the University of Oxford.
It furthers the University's objective of excellence in research, scholarship,
and education by publishing worldwide. Oxford is a registered trade mark of
Oxford University Press in the UK and in certain other countries

© Oxford University Press 2014

The moral rights of the authors have been asserted

First published 2014
First published in paperback 2017

All rights reserved. No part of this publication may be reproduced, stored in
a retrieval system, or transmitted, in any form or by any means, without the
prior permission in writing of Oxford University Press, or as expressly permitted
by law, by licence or under terms agreed with the appropriate reprographics
rights organization. Enquiries concerning reproduction outside the scope of the
above should be sent to the Rights Department, Oxford University Press, at the
address above

You must not circulate this work in any other form
and you must impose this same condition on any acquirer

Published in the United States of America by Oxford University Press
198 Madison Avenue, New York, NY 10016, United States of America

British Library Cataloguing in Publication Data
Data available

Library of Congress Cataloging in Publication Data
Data available

ISBN 978–0–19–954934–4 (Hbk.)
ISBN 978–0–19–876821–0 (Pbk.)

Links to third party websites are provided by Oxford in good faith and
for information only. Oxford disclaims any responsibility for the materials
contained in any third party website referenced in this work.

For Adam James Jackson

ACKNOWLEDGEMENTS

I am most grateful to Christopher Wheeler of Oxford University Press for the original invitation to edit this volume, and to Stephanie Ireland of OUP for helping to see the volume into print. My friends and colleagues at Edinburgh, Harry Dickinson, Frances Dow, and Owen Dudley Edwards, read and commented on much of the text, as did my friend and former colleague from University College Dublin, James McGuire. Other, anonymous, reviewers also helped greatly. I am most grateful to them, and to Laura Drummond, Niko Ovenden, and Lorraine Stewart: Niko, and latterly Laura and Lorraine, have offered critical support during my years as Head of the School of History, Classics and Archaeology at Edinburgh, and helped enormously with the editing of the Handbook.

Alvin Jackson,
Edinburgh, March 2013

CONTENTS

PART III   PERIOD STUDIES

THE THIRD KINGDOM: IRELAND, *c.*1580–1690

ASCENDANCY IRELAND (1691–1801)

BRITISH STATE AND CATHOLIC NATION (1800–1920)

DOMINION, REPUBLIC, AND HOME RULE: THE TWO IRELANDS, 1920–2008

List of Contributors

Robert Armstrong Associate Professor of History, Trinity College Dublin

Paul Arthur Emeritus Professor of Politics, University of Ulster at Magee

Toby Barnard Emeritus Fellow, Hertford College, Oxford

Thomas Bartlett Emeritus Professor of Irish History, University of Aberdeen

Timothy Bowman Senior Lecturer in History, University of Kent

Maurice J. Bric Associate Professor of History, University College Dublin

Nicholas Canny Emeritus Professor of History, National University of Ireland, Galway

Sean Connolly Professor of Irish History, Queen's University Belfast

Fintan Cullen Professor of Art History, University of Nottingham

Enda Delaney Professor of History, University of Edinburgh

David Dickson Associate Professor of History, Trinity College Dublin

Terence Dooley Associate Professor of History and Director of the Centre for the Study of Historic Irish Houses and Estates, National University of Ireland, Maynooth

Marianne Elliott Emerita Blair Professor and Director of the Institute of Irish Studies, University of Liverpool

Diarmaid Ferriter Professor of Modern Irish History, University College Dublin

Patrick Geoghegan Professor in Modern History, Trinity College Dublin

Brian Girvin Honorary Professor of Politics, University of Glasgow

Peter Gray Professor of Modern Irish History, Queen's University Belfast

D. W. Hayton Emeritus Professor of Early Modern Irish and British History, Queen's University Belfast

Stephen Howe Senior Research Fellow in History, Bristol University

Alvin Jackson Sir Richard Lodge Professor of History, University of Edinburgh

Margaret Kelleher Professor of Anglo-Irish Literature and Drama, University College Dublin

James Kelly Professor of History, St Patrick's College, Drumcondra

Matthew Kelly Professor of Modern History, University of Northumbria

Maria Luddy Professor of History, University of Warwick

Donald M. MacRaild Professor of British and Irish History, University of Ulster at Coleraine

Ted McCormick Associate Professor of History, Concordia University

Fearghal McGarry Professor of Contemporary Irish History, Queen's University Belfast

Éamonn Ó Ciardha Senior Lecturer in Irish Literary and Historical Studies, University of Ulster at Magee

Eunan O'Halpin Professor of Contemporary Irish History, Trinity College Dublin

Tadhg Ó hAnnracháin Senior Lecturer in History, University College Dublin

Jane Ohlmeyer Erasmus Smith's Professor of History and Director of the Long Room Hub, Trinity College Dublin

Philip Ollerenshaw Associate Professor of History, University of the West of England

Henry Patterson Emeritus Professor of Politics, University of Ulster at Jordanstown

Robert J. Savage Professor of the Practice of History, Boston College

Yvonne Whelan Senior Lecturer in Geography, Bristol University

Niall Whelehan Lecturer in Modern History, University of Strathclyde

PART I

INTRODUCTION

CHAPTER 1

....

IRISH HISTORY IN THE TWENTIETH AND TWENTY-FIRST CENTURIES[*]

....

ALVIN JACKSON

I. Introduction

....

In the first years of the millennium Irish history has been in flux, and the origins, form, and content of this fluidity are the central concerns of this introduction. The rise and fall, and strengths and weaknesses, of the once ascendant methodological model, supplied by the founding editors of the journal *Irish Historical Studies* (IHS), provide a critical starting point. One dimension of the 'fall' of the model has been the changing form of Irish history—the astonishing growth and subvention of the discipline, the fuller consequences (and stalling) of which demand investigation. Another dimension—affecting both form and content within the current writing of Irish history—has been the Northern Ireland Peace Process, culminating in the Good Friday (1998) and St Andrews (2006) Agreements. It is impossible to ignore either that the Northern Irish 'Troubles' has exercised varying levels of influence over the profession, or that the diminution of violence has supplied a liberation of sorts. The divination of future directions within the discipline has been a notoriously hazardous enterprise, distinguished in the past by hubristic, wrong-headed, and prescriptive imaginings; but, even with the wreckage of past enterprises firmly in view, it is possible to detect certain—sometimes countervailing—trends within the historiography.

II. The Reformers of *Irish Historical Studies*

....

As is well known, the dominant professional model for Irish historians for the half-century between the late 1930s and the late 1980s was supplied by the founders of

IHS through their 'Preface' to the journal (March 1938), and through the earlier constitutions of the Irish Historical Society and the Ulster Society for Irish Historical Studies
(1936).[1] The achievement of these patriarchs—the key figures included Robert ('Robin')
Dudley Edwards (1909–88), T. W. Moody (1907–84), and initially David Beers Quinn
(1909–2002)—was to define a professional standard for Irish historical scholarship, as
well as to identify and develop media through which this scholarship might be effectively communicated. There is, however, some disparity between what the reformers said
they were doing, and their impact, particularly their perceived impact, on the writing
and teaching of Irish history. Certainly by the 1980s, in the context of sustained violence
in Northern Ireland, and tense Anglo-Irish relationships, a range of critics ascribed
much that was deficient in modern Irish historiography—aridity, lack of emotional
range and empathy, contempt for the mainstream national tradition—to the failings of
the patriarchs and their scholarly 'revolution' of the 1930s. A particular allegation was
(in essence) that a combination of this restrictive scholarly culture together with the
impact of terror and counter-terror in Northern Ireland had frightened Ireland's liberal
scholarly establishment into an ever more skewed and anti-national posture.[2]

The debate between the reformers—labelled (belatedly) as 'revisionists'—and their
opponents burned fiercely in the last years of the twentieth century; but the primary significance, so far as the themes of this introduction are concerned, is less with the debate's
substance than with its eventual fall-out. Some of the embers of the conflagration are,
however, worth scouring. The founders of *Irish Historical Studies* were not, in fact, a
tightly knit, inward-looking group of disciplinary radicals who wanted to break with
the Irish revolution. They were engaged in what one of their number, R. B. McDowell
(1913–2011) of Trinity College Dublin, called 'an updating', rather than a revolution: the
new initiatives of the 1930s embodied much from an older, national historiography,
including some key figures such as Eoin MacNeill (first president of the Irish History
Society) and R. M. Henry (first president of the Ulster Society for Irish Historical
Studies).[3] They were personally a diverse group, a fact all too apparent in the squalls of
their relationships (Moody and Dudley Edwards ultimately broke with each other, while
younger reformers, such as J. C. Beckett (1912–96) of Queen's University Belfast, maintained their distance).[4] Nor were the reformers wholly distant from the achievements
of the revolution. It is true that Moody and McDowell were Belfast Protestants, though
of unconventional kinds (McDowell was from a Redmondite background); but Dudley
Edwards was educated briefly at St Enda's School, in the aftermath of the execution of its
founder, Patrick Pearse, and at a time when an educational choice of this kind was decidedly a cultural and political statement. Indeed, the decision-maker, and a dominant
influence on Dudley Edward's childhood, was his mother, Bridget MacInerney, a Clare
republican and an opponent of the Anglo-Irish Treaty of 1921. Young Robin was a member of the Fianna Éireann during the revolutionary years, and subsequently received the
Na Fianna medal (1959) for his membership of this republican youth movement.[5]

If they were diverse in temperament, then the shared Christianity of the *IHS* reformers has been mostly overlooked. It is true that Beckett's highly engaged Anglicanism is
now well known; but the faith of the two key reformers, Moody and Dudley Edwards,

less considered, was also highly significant as an influence on their lives and scholarship.[6] Beckett's correspondence with Moody deals occasionally with private spiritual themes, such as Moody's growing interrogation of 'institutional religion' after the Second World War: Moody (who was moving towards Quakerism) and Beckett discussed C. S. Lewis' *Screwtape Letters*, the Student Christian Movement in Ireland, and negotiated over the purchase of a Bible. Beckett (a lay reader in the Church of Ireland) also sermonized to Moody's son, David.[7] Dudley Edwards has passed into professional legend as an often outrageous iconoclast, but his archive suggests a different and more complex set of perspectives. He was a devout Catholic, and maintained a correspondence with a very large range of religious orders and congregations. He was an active advocate of the Irish Catholic Historical Committee (he served as Secretary between 1939 and 1980); and he was evidently thoroughly trusted by the tough-minded Archbishop of Dublin, John Charles McQuaid (McQuaid invited Dudley Edwards to serve on a commission to select candidates for beatification amongst the Irish Catholic martyrs). Dudley Edwards also scrupulously applied to McQuaid for permission to study 'communistic literature' (permission for three years was duly granted, excepting 'works which of set purpose propound heresy or schism, works which of set purpose aim at the overthrow of the very foundations of religion').[8]

In their 'Preface' to the first *IHS* of March 1938 Moody and Dudley Edwards stressed that their desire was to create a 'scientific' historiography (the imagery of science and of the laboratory permeates their document); but they also clearly sought to identify with an older, Catholic tradition of scholarship in ending their call with the traditional Irish dedication 'dochum Dé agus onóra na hÉireann' (to God and the honour of Ireland).[9] Despite allegations of exclusivity, they in fact strove to engage with the wider public, and laid some stress on communicating with schools and with schoolteachers. While sensitive to (what they saw as) the ignorance of Irish history then prevalent in English universities, they sought to emulate the innovations of English and continental European scholarship, and strove for a methodological rigour; but they were also attentive to the needs of a wider public, and keen not to create an unduly enclosed or cloistered academic clique. And, indeed, a study of the Dudley Edwards papers reveals the effort that he invested both in addressing teachers (through individual communication as well as conferences) and the wider Irish society (including consultation work on a succession of legal cases). Moody and other, younger, members of the *IHS* group (such as Beckett) devoted scarcely less effort in communicating their scholarship through both traditional popular media such as the press as well as relatively new media like radio and—eventually—television: Beckett, for example, has some claims to be regarded as the first Northern 'media don'.

The desire to connect with mainstream British and continental European scholarship encouraged an historiography which was not so much actively 'anti-national' as relatively unconcerned with national sensitivities. British historians from the 1960s deconstructed some of their country's favoured historical myths relating (for example) to the First World War, the Victorian 'golden age', or empire. Scottish historians sought to create a national historiography which firstly brought a liberation from the often uncritical Presbyterian and unionist meta-narratives of the nineteenth century, and which latterly has begun to transcend the nation, with emphases on supranational and transnational themes. In some senses the development of Irish history under the *IHS* reformers has been similar. Both Scottish and Irish historiographies (as well as the work of their critics) may occasionally have been subtly infected with the religious antagonisms of their wider societies. In Ireland there was certainly a movement away from a Catholic and nationalist meta-narrative to a more complex set of modern Irish stories.

But diversity was not the only attribute of the *IHS* reformers: there was a complex legacy, which brought both a professionalization as well as some less uplifting features. In the context of an exceedingly small and under-resourced Irish history enterprise in Ireland, the reformers sought to raise professional standards, and to link their enterprise more securely to a wider European scholarship. They raised the profile of Irish history both within and beyond Ireland: Moody at Trinity College Dublin (1939–77), Dudley Edwards at University College Dublin (1939–79), and Moody (1935–9), Quinn (1939–44), and eventually Beckett (1945–75) at Queen's University Belfast collectively oversaw the development of substantial graduate schools, with Masters' and (to a lesser extent) doctoral training. They were of course not the only Irish historians at work, but were part of a larger and diverse scholarly community spanning the United Kingdom, the USA, Canada, and other European and Commonwealth nations. However, they exercised a disproportionate influence in Ireland itself.

This was in fact the nub of the problem. This influence was critical, both in terms of patronage as much as scholarship. The group had an astonishing command over both the replication of the history profession within Irish universities, as well as over the community of history teachers in the schools of Ireland (Herbert Butterfield once wrote to Dudley Edwards, evidently sincerely, saying that he did 'not know any department that owes more to its professors than yours [at University College Dublin] owes to you and Desmond [Williams]').[10] The form of history which was communicated was very rigorously empirical, resistant to theorization, suspicious of the contemporary, and distinguished by a marked tendency to fetishize the archive and the manuscript primary source. It emphasized its 'scientific' credentials, but made few concessions to the social sciences. Despite the original claims, it was in fact a very literary historiography; history may have been produced in scholarly 'laboratories', but ultimately—in this definition—contained much artistry. It would of course be facile to depict an undifferentiated or homogeneous history profession in Ireland, or to imply that history and the wider academy beyond Ireland were uniformly distinguished by healthy diversity and disinterestedness. But the personnel of Irish history, and its intellectual content in the forty years after 1938 certainly owed much to Moody, Dudley Edwards, and (to a slightly lesser extent) lieutenants such as Beckett.

The fundamental difficulty with the *Irish Historical Studies* group was thus not that it was (as is sometimes implied) an anti-national conspiracy, but rather that it was (however well-meaning) a small and relatively closed elite, which remained in place for nearly forty years, and which ultimately was losing touch with its original ideals.[11] There was a tendency towards the end to enshrine the achievements of the scholarly 'revolution' of the 1930s, rather than to treat them as a starting point for debate; and there was an equally marked tendency to sanctify the authors of the 'revolution', particularly Moody, rather than to subject their achievement to regular testing and interrogation. This combination of excessive reverence and a failure to renew occasionally led Irish historians up some very odd or very difficult paths indeed, one example being (arguably) the Actonian 'New History of Ireland'.

Several factors coincided in the last third of the twentieth century to mitigate the *IHS* reformers' influence. The first, arguably, was the growth within the Irish and British (and US) university sector in the 1960s, stalling in the 1970s, which brought the creation of new lectureships, and some degree of intellectual and personal diversification. This growth was renewed in the 1990s in the context of the 'Celtic Tiger' economy, stalling again in 2008. The second was (what many regarded as) a revival of the revolutionary struggle against the British presence in Ireland after 1969. This essentially meant that what had looked to the reformers of the 1930s as the safely dead history of the revolution, and of Ireland's subjugation to English and British rule, now acquired a new political relevance, utility, and (thus) a new emotional charge. Moreover, violence in Northern Ireland not only stimulated a renewed popular appetite for a more reverential historiography, it also stimulated an export market for Irish history and Irish historians in Great Britain and further afield. This, again, encouraged the diversification of the enterprise. By the mid- and late 1980s criticism of mainstream Irish historiography was gathering apace, articulated by (inter alia) Desmond Fennell, the Belfast-born cultural commentator, and by Brendan Bradshaw, a Limerick-born early modern historian and priest working in Cambridge, and Brian Murphy, a Benedictine monk and historian at Glenstal Abbey, Limerick.[12] Whatever the justice of these successive assaults, there can be little doubt that they have helped to stimulate the single most serious and sustained reflection on the epistemology and teleology of Irish history since the 1930s.

III. THE SCHOLARLY CONSEQUENCES OF THE PEACE

Brendan Bradshaw, John Regan, and others critical of 'revisionism' have stressed the impact of the Northern Ireland 'Troubles' upon the historiography of modern Ireland, suggesting in particular that various forms of liberal, statist, or general 'establishment' bias were tolerated and encouraged in the context of the Provisional IRA's campaign in the North.[13] In this analysis the 'Troubles', at least indirectly, encouraged the conditions wherein debate and self-reflection on the state of Irish history might begin to flourish. But the corollary of these arguments about the impact of the 'Troubles' is of course the proposition that the ending, or diminution, of violence has also necessarily had an impact on the historiography of modern Ireland.

At present the full dimensions of this 'impact' can only be perceived in outline. A beginning may be made with the issue of content: if violence in the North implicitly encouraged some liberal academics to distance themselves from the insurgents, and from the tradition of insurgency, then it also encouraged a partial breakdown of the liberal self-confidence of the 1960s—a self-confidence eloquently expressed in several of the most influential texts of the decade, including J. C. Beckett's *The Making of Modern Ireland* (1966) and F. S. L. Lyons' *Ireland since the Famine* (written from the mid-1960s, but published in 1971). The emotional distance between Lyons' *Ireland since the Famine* and his sombre Ford lectures, *Culture and Anarchy* (1979), has often been noticed, but others of this era undertook a similar emotional and intellectual journey. Beckett combined a High-Church Christian spirituality with his historical enthusiasms, moving from a settled confidence in the existing order in the 1960s to (by the late 1970s and 1980s) an increasingly evangelical appeal to the mediating and reconciliatory value of his beloved Anglo-Irish tradition. Beckett's growing didacticism, and his emphasis on the diversity of Irishness, were important influences within the liberal historiography of the era and beyond; but there can be little doubt that a range of Irish historians, drawing upon a variety of religious and political traditions, sought to use their scholarship for what they saw as a higher moral purpose in the dark years of the Northern civil war.[14] Peace, of sorts, in 1994, with the ceasefires, and then more substantially with the Good Friday Agreement in 1998, brought an end to these quiet pleas and subtle moralizing; as Paul Arthur points out in his essay, an older confidence began then to reassert itself within the literature.[15]

For those distant by birth or inclination from the Anglo-Irish tradition, the peace of 1998 has brought an equal liberation and confidence. Historians with (for example) mainstream republican backgrounds or sympathies may now feel able to comment more freely upon an historiography which may hitherto have seemed in part alien or skewed. The fear of endorsing, or being seen to endorse, contemporary militancy seemingly no longer applies; and, while the political legacy of Good Friday and St Andrews will long be debated and disputed, there are grounds for believing that the peace settlement in the North was only ultimately attained through the republican 'armed struggle'. For republicans, the 'Long War' reveals yet again (as in 1919–21) the ruthlessness and divisiveness of British armed force in Ireland, and in this way further vindicates insurgency. The increasingly well-documented story of the 'Long War' also has much to say to republicans and others (as in 1919–21) about the long tentacles of British conspiracy and espionage. Little wonder, then, that since 1998 this combination of intellectual liberation, vindication, and revelation has stimulated some intensely hostile—even conspiracy-laden—critiques of revisionist historiography: the work of the late Peter Hart has been a particular focus of these assaults.[16]

Turning from questions of intellectual content to those of form and structure, there can be little doubt that in the aftermath of 1998 it has been possible to learn much more than formerly about the contemporary history of Ireland, and in particular of Northern Ireland. On the face of it, this is a matter of coincidence and timing as much as any other circumstance: the achievement of the Good Friday Agreement in 1998 coincided with the publication of key documentary evidence under the official thirty-year release rule—documents which (as it happened) related to the late 1960s, the era when the North was descending into prolonged political and military unrest.

Only speculation is possible at present, but the promulgation of the United Kingdom's Freedom of Information Act (2000) is hard to envision without the context of a cease-fire in Northern Ireland, and without the Good Friday Agreement; and the measure was clearly framed in the immediate context of the Agreement. More generally, in the context of politically and militarily more settled conditions in Northern Ireland, many of the protagonists of the conflict have begun to take a comparatively more relaxed attitude to issues of accessibility, whether in terms of archives or interviews and oral history. As Paul Arthur points out later in this volume, some of the most important academic work on republican paramilitarism (by for example Richard English) hinges upon access and interviews which are hard to imagine outside of the context of the Agreement.[17] Equally, much scholarship on Northern Ireland loyalism (by, for example, Christopher Farrington, Eric Kaufmann, and Rachel Ward) has also depended on the accessibility and volubility of historical witnesses—men and women who, in less relaxed political circumstances, might well have shied away from microphones and questionnaires.[18]

Kaufmann's work on Orangeism underlines the relatively greater accessibility of hitherto closed archival material, both in official and private hands. Political and religious organizations such as the Orange Order have granted access to their archives often—after 1998—for the first time, thereby facilitating an array of ground-breaking scholarship (the first fruits of David Fitzpatrick's work on Orangeism, based on this fresh archival access, are already evident, and Henry Patterson's work draws on similar material).[19] Official archives are also relenting: the thirty-year rule was in place until 2013, but a range of material deemed sensitive has hitherto been excepted, and—moreover—there have also been substantial redactions amongst those documents which have been released. Further, and more systematic, work on this theme is required, but it might be suggested as a starting point that both the level of redaction and the level of withholding have declined in the context of the more settled conditions in Northern Ireland. There is certainly some evidence to support this argument: the maintenance of the British state in Ireland has depended heavily upon espionage and intelligence, and the national archives have naturally tended to treat material on these themes with the greatest sensitivity. Occasionally, this has been carried to extremes. In the 1980s, for example, the (then) Public Records Office at Kew held the 'Secret Service Papers of Arthur Balfour, Chief Secretary for Ireland, 1887', which were closed for 100 years, an embargo which was subsequently extended, and which was then (as now) hard to understand except in the context of the disturbed condition of Northern Ireland. After 1998, however, these materials were at last released, and were used to some considerable effect by the journalist and historian Christy Campbell, particularly in the research for his work, *Fenian Fire* (2002).[20]

Of course, a comparatively more self-confident and self-critical, and a better documented, historiography is not the only scholarly consequence of peace in the North. The assumption that the Good Friday and St Andrews Agreements are definitive endings (rather than starting points, or nodal moments in a wider process) is as fraught in scholarly as it is in political terms. Enhanced accessibility to the protagonists of the 'Troubles', or to their papers, clearly may reflect not only the ebbing away of tension and suspicion but also a degree of political calculation. The war for the constitution of

Northern Ireland has been suspended; but the activists' battle for the historical record continues. The protagonists within the Northern conflict are clearly more keen than ever to cooperate with scholars in at least attempting to communicate their particular reading of the history of Northern Ireland. Christopher Farrington, author of a monograph on rejectionist Unionism, quotes the joking admonition of a Stormont MLA, Jim Wells: 'basically I want you to write the DUP's all singing, all wise perfection, and going from strength to strength...so anyone who reads this will join in the morning'. This is badinage, of course, but it reflects a wider concern for image and presentation, even within the electorally unpromising territory of the monograph.[21]

There are other problems, of course, as the case of the Boston College (BC) archives illustrate all too vividly. The 'Troubles' oral history archive at BC, which originated in the immediate aftermath of the Good Friday Agreement, was designed to capture first-hand accounts of the conflict, while many of the protagonists were still alive, well, and (perhaps in some cases) demob-happy. But the archive was soon associated with a protracted legal action, arising from the interest of the Police Service of Northern Ireland in its contents and in potential evidence for ongoing criminal investigations. The complex development of the lawsuits is not, however, a primary concern here. The BC case is relevant because its importance and resonance are such as to require a coda to some of the earlier arguments of this section. The cardinal points that the BC case illustrate are that the 'Troubles' have not wholly 'gone away', that they are still clearly legally and politically sensitive, and that the tendency to volubility and revelation, otherwise discernible since 1998, has now (certainly so far as certain sensitive aspects of the history of the 'Troubles' are concerned) hit the buffers.

From all this stems a wider and more fundamental point. The diminution of violence and the disappearance of Ireland from newspaper headlines has led, arguably, not only to the greater accessibility of some types of evidence (with the caveat of the Boston College affair); it has also brought a relative slackening of interest in Irish history in Britain, and the comparative relegation of the British-Irish relationship so far as both the British and Irish peoples and British and Irish historians are concerned. In these contexts, Ireland's relationships with continental Europe, with the Atlantic periphery, and with the Empire and its own diasporic communities are assuming a greater than ever significance (as the essays in this volume by Maurice Bric, Nicholas Canny, and Enda Delaney fully document).

IV. The Granular, the Gaelic, and the Global

The 'Troubles' and 'revisionism' have both (it seems) gone: a key context and a key mode for the writing of modern Irish history are no longer fully in place. Where, then, are Irish historians moving in the aftermath of the military and intellectual conflicts of the 1990s and before? The answers are (at least) threefold, and are evident in much of the work below: they are looking in a more detailed way at Ireland itself, they are looking to the international and to the supranational and to the theoretical, and they are looking not so much to Britain as to its constituent polities. A key aspect of all of this is indeed the condition of Northern Ireland; but it is important to recognize that the 'Long War' and its ending are only parts of a wider and more complex spectrum of influences. Ireland's developing relationship after 1973 with the European Union, formerly the EEC, and its brief blaze of rapid economic growth at the turn of the millennium, have also provided important contexts. The transnational (as distinct from the international) turn within Irish (and wider) historiography is of course also linked to the broad themes of economic, cultural, and political globalization.[22]

Taking the first of these, Irish historians are no longer so thoroughly preoccupied by the need to elucidate (sometimes to fret over) the story of the protracted relationship with 'Britain', and are instead looking partly to (what might be described as) the granular and the Gaelic. The origins of the granular—detailed case-study work, or micro-history—within Irish historiography are various, but include the *IHS* tradition (insofar as much of this work eschews the overtly theoretical in favour of the detailed and empirical), and the influences of continental European scholarship, as communicated through the Annaliste school and other sources. The efflorescence of social and economic history in the 1960s (led in Ireland at first by Kenneth Connell (1917–73) and Louis Cullen) expressed itself eventually through a flowering of work on the nineteenth-century land question, and in particular through a plethora of local case studies of the land war. This was complemented in terms of political and military history by David Fitzpatrick's pioneering *Politics and Irish Life, 1913–21* (1977), a case study of County Clare in the era of both the First World War and the Irish Revolution: at about the same time Don Akenson was working on an Annaliste-style case study of Islandmagee, County Antrim, over the longue durée (*Between Two Revolutions* (1979)). Case studies of both the land war and the revolution continue to emerge, and it is certain that these pointilliste approaches, often supported by newly digitised source materials, will continue to deliver insights into modern Irish history.

The micro-historical is one intellectual territory where the *IHS* tradition, continental intellectual influences, and both local historical as well as genealogical research productively (if sometimes tumultuously) intersect. Local history flourishes in Ireland, alongside a passion for the genealogical, and the two complement and inform professional historical work, creating new data and identifying new sources, as well as suggesting new approaches. That this is not always a harmonious relationship should not distract from the common ground shared by professional and amateur historians in the meticulous reconstruction of Irish history through detailed local study. It is certainly the case that perhaps the single most ferocious recent conflict within Irish historiography has been that between a local history society, the Aubane of Millstreet, Cork, and a professional historian, Peter Hart (who died in 2010), over the evidence and interpretation of the Irish revolution in its County Cork manifestations.[23] This, however, is an extreme case: the strengths and weaknesses of local work, and of the relationship between local historians and the academy are considered in different contexts (amongst much else) by Tim Bowman in his essay below.[24] Bowman's concern is not the Irish revolution, but rather the plethora of case studies of local communities in Ulster and their contribution to the Great War. But, whether 1914 or 1919 is the chosen starting point, the ferocity and importance of this widespread local engagement is unmissable; and, with the 'decade of anniversaries' (the centenaries of the Home Rule and revolutionary eras fall between 2012 and 2022), together with the many newly available online sources, it is more important than ever.

Another critical aspect of this local turn—this search for what might perhaps be deemed an essential Irish history—has been the growing body of work on the pre-Famine majority Gaelic tradition on the island. Three critical shifts in the constitutional relationship between Britain and Ireland—the constitution of 1782–3, independence, and the Northern crisis and its settlement—have each been complemented (or indeed anticipated) by advances in the development of an understanding of Gaelic literature and history. In terms of this most recent shift, the historiography of early modern Ireland has been significantly augmented by scholarship on the bardic and wider literary traditions of the Gaelic Irish. The starting point for much of this work remains the debates over Daniel Corkery's seminal *Hidden Ireland* (1924), a work first interrogated in the 1960s by Louis Cullen's researches into Munster society and culture; but there has been an efflorescence of more recent scholarship, spearheaded by (for example) Brendán Ó Buachalla's *Aisling Ghéar*. While one wider context for this work has been Ireland's shifting international relationships, and the consolidation of its international standing, it is unquestionably the case (as Éamonn Ó Ciardha argues below) that much remains to be done in terms of the exploration of Gaelic Ireland.[25]

This struggle to recover Gaelic Ireland is primarily a matter of correcting a grievous imbalance within the literature; but it is also perhaps about highlighting an essentialist vision of Irish history, liberated from the predominance of the English language and British politics and culture. Insofar as this is important as a context or reading, then it is complemented by both an international and a transnational thrust within recent Irish historiography. There has been a tendency within much recent work (particularly work stemming from Atlantic history) to emphasise the island's interlinkages with mainland Europe, the growing importance of Irish membership of the European Union (and the perceived success of this membership until 2008) being an obvious context for this work. Recent studies which might in theory have had much to say about the British-Irish (or the Irish-American) relationship alone, in fact now present a striking portrayal of the complex layers of relationships—British, continental European, North American, imperial—within which Irish history can successfully be cast.[26] Early modernists, concerned with Ireland's trading relationships with France and Spain, or with interlinkages generated by the Catholic reformation, or by comparisons between Ireland under the Stuarts and Central and Eastern Europe under the Habsburgs, have been the main pioneers of this turn within the literature; and the work of several of the key scholars—Nicholas Canny and Tadhg Ó hAnnracháin—is represented within this volume. Late modernists have been slower off the mark, though even here a range of stimuli (such as O'Connell's complex and resonant career, or the Northern 'Troubles') have stimulated an array of comparative or transnational work.

Though continental Europe and the European Union have been important recent focuses for this international 'turn' within Irish historiography, the internationalist impulse has more complex roots and flowerings. Irish historians are still criticized for their supposed insularity, and their faith in a supposedly exceptionalist history; but in fact they have been influenced by, and contributed to, successive ways of redefining their national history within wider, international, contexts. For example, the Atlantic history of the post-war era, cast by Bernard Bailyn and Jack Greene against the creation of NATO and of European integration, attracted significant contributions from a range of (again, in particular, early modern) Irish historians, beginning with D. B. Quinn, but also including Canny. Indeed, the emphasis by Atlantic historians upon the broad interplay between Europe and America has stimulated scholarly connections both with imperial history as well as (in the case of Canny) the history of Ireland's interconnections with continental Europe.

There has, perhaps, been greater suspicion in Ireland of both the new imperial and new British histories of the last decades of the twentieth century, but even here there have been marked contributions from Irish historians. Ireland's experience of British rule, and the interlinkages between its struggle for independence and those of other territories within the British Empire, might have predisposed Irish historians to regard empire as a major focus of enquiry; but in fact the predominantly anglocentric and metropolitan definitions of imperial history until the 1960s seem to have undermined any significant effort by Irish historians in this area. The subsequent emergence of a post-colonial theoretical literature, led by scholars such as Frantz Fanon and Edward Said in the era of European decolonization, has strongly influenced the work of Irish literary scholars on the history of the British-Irish relationship (as may be seen in Margaret Kelleher's essay below); but this, in combination with the emergence of a new imperial history, focusing on social and cultural relationships, and pioneered by scholars such as John Mackenzie, has liberated imperial history from the taint (however unmerited) of 'imperialism'. It has also stimulated a growing body of work on Ireland's complex interrelationships within the empire. Much of this is discussed in Stephen Howe's essay below.[27]

What of Ireland and British history? As has been argued, the end of the Troubles has had an historiographical fallout. But it would be a mistake to oversimplify, or to ignore the complexities and reciprocities within all this. Changes in Ireland, particularly Northern Ireland, have had a scholarly impact, but changes within the United Kingdom, both real and threatened over the past forty years, have also influenced the shape of Irish (and British) historiography. The rise of Celtic, Scottish, and Welsh nationalism, particularly from the 1960s onwards, has had diverse historiographical connotations: it has fed into the literature on the 'crisis of Britishness', or 'declinology', but it has also supplied an important context for J. G. A. Pocock's 'new British history' of the 1970s and afterwards. There has been some suspicion within Irish historiography of the new British history, despite Pocock's own sensitive response to Irish nationalism (expressed for example in his notion of the 'Atlantic archipelago', as against the 'British Isles'). But on the whole early modern Irish historians such as Jane Ohlmeyer have embraced the archipelagic ambitions of the new British history with zeal and considerable effect.[28]

The rise of 'Celtic' nationalisms and of the new British history have also been indirectly associated with the expansion of a comparative literature on Scotland and Ireland, pursued originally by late modern social and economic historians such as Louis Cullen and T. M. Devine, but developed lately by political historians.[29] There is also a slight, but growing, body of comparative work on Wales and Ireland, pursued in particular at present by the literary historian Claire Connolly and the Welsh historian Paul O'Leary. In other words, the rise of Scottish and Welsh nationalism at the end of the twentieth century has been complemented by a late modern historiography which has begun to examine the interrelationship between Ireland and the constituent nations of the United Kingdom, rather than between Ireland and 'Britain'.

But, late modernists have often been slower to ditch the insular and particular, and to embrace the international; and where they have done so (as with the history of empire) there has been evidence of hesitation or doubt: there are certainly countervailing pressures within the relevant literature. For example, recent work on the 1848 Rising demonstrates convincingly that the insurgents had a truly international hinterland, which reflected their political sophistication and impact, and which gave them at least potential strength (and which certainly scared the British authorities).[30] On the whole, however, the paradox of important recent arguments on the wider republican tradition is that, while they emphasize that (for example) Fenianism had very strong diasporic aspects, they also suggest that it bucked a variety of trends within international revolutionary politics and organization. Moreover, the fundamental impression left by the most recent assessments of the key Fenian, Michael Davitt, is that Davitt's internationalism was a source of weakness rather than strength in the wider nationalist politics of the 1880s and 1890s.[31]

But perhaps the most telling aspect of these works, particularly those on republican militancy, remains the complex set of wider circumstances in which they have been written. On the one hand, the peace settlements in Northern Ireland have helped here (again) to provide some scholarly breathing space, within which it has been possible to appraise revolutionary nationalism without endorsing its contemporary manifestations. On the other hand, the cataclysms of 9/11 and of 7/7, the London bombings, have encouraged a search for the origins of the 'War against Terror' and of international counter-terrorist strategies, which has led some scholars (such as Jonathan Gantt) back to Ireland and to Fenianism.[32] One scholarly hermeneutic within modern Irish history (the 'Long War') has therefore sometimes been replaced with another ('the War against Terror'). This has also created a set of scholarly reference points and a vocabulary which are very alien to the concerns of many Irish historians, however sensitive to international analogies and contexts.[33] In the end we may be left with an Irish historical scholarship which has transcended some of its local intellectual antagonisms, only to find them replaced with a much more bracing set of international challenges. It may be that the denouement to (late) modern Irish history's experiment in internationalization will be a vindication of its exceptionalist traditions and impulses.

V. THE POVERTY OF IRISH THEORY?

The present position of modern Irish historiography owes much not only to the revisionist debates of the late twentieth century, but rather to the conjunction of post-revisionist and post-structuralist assaults on the discipline. Post-revisionism, like revisionism itself, was and is a broad school, which drew upon older, patriotic, and historicist approaches within Irish historical scholarship; but its practitioners also took some of their emphases and concerns from the post-structuralist assault on the verities of the enlightenment and on the supposedly rational and scientific methodologies within western historiography. However, post-structuralism and the linguistic turn within western scholarship were more likely to impinge (generally indirectly) upon Irish history through Foucault and Derrida and Irish literary and philosophical scholars (such as Seamus Deane) rather than through (say) the mediating historiographical work of Hayden White. The impact of post-revisionist critiques was augmented arguably because Irish revisionists had (despite the precepts of the original reformers) fallen out of touch with wider, particularly theoretical, debates within European historiography. It is striking, for example, that easily the most sophisticated elaboration and defence of revisionist historiography, using a wide variety of continental European scholarly analogies and allusions, has come from beyond the Irish academy (in the work of Gkotzaridis).[34]

To what extent, then, has Irish history been under-theorized, and why? And to what extent is Irish historiography at present theoretically informed? It would in fact be a mistake to exaggerate the under-theorization of Irish history in the twentieth century, or to regard the *IHS* reformers as mere assemblers of 'facts'. The founding Professor of Modern History at University College Dublin was John Marcus O'Sullivan (1881–1948), a Heidelberg-trained Kantian philosopher, politically active but admittedly more prolific as a Cumann na nGaedheal politician than as an academic historian. To a considerable extent, the reformers of the 1930s and key intellectual precursors such as W. E. H. Lecky were influenced by Comtean positivism and its post-1918 derivatives, with their emphases upon scientific methodologies and grand historical patterns, if not 'laws' of history. Their repudiation of nationalist historicism fell within this broad theoretical position.[35] They earnestly desired to keep Irish historical scholarship in communication with wider British and continental European intellectual developments, though the close interconnections between Dublin and the University of Cambridge meant perhaps that the more conservative and empirical aspects of British historiography exercised too great an influence. This was particularly evident in the post-war era, with the influence of the Peterhouse, particularly Cowlingite, high-political methodologies over Irish historiography.[36]

There were also some interconnections between the great divisions of European political and intellectual life after 1945 and Irish historical scholarship: Ireland's strong Catholic tradition meant that Christian Democracy was a prevailing influence on the intellectual life of the country (for example, Michael Tierney, president of University

College Dublin (1947–64) claimed the Irish 'emancipator', Daniel O'Connell, as a patri-
arch of the movement).[37] Marxism and Marxian scholarship left an imprint on the historiography, though—excepting the tradition of the great Edinburgh-born socialist, James
Connolly—generally on work emanating originally from beyond Ireland: Paul Bew,
Peter Gibbon, and Henry Patterson's highly influential *The State in Northern Ireland,
1921–74* (1978) bore the imprint of Louis Althusser's thought, though Gibbon (then
working at Sheffield and subsequently at Copenhagen) has been primarily credited with
the theoretical frameworks of the book.

On the whole, therefore, Irish historical scholarship has not so much been
under-theorized as increasingly characterized by a set of conservative theoretical
models. Moreover, this state of affairs arose not because the reformers of the 1930s were
theoretically disengaged but rather because they and their successors subsequently
became detached from wider intellectual trends in a way that ran contrary to their published intentions. It is possible indeed to see this as a failure exclusively of the *IHS* tradition itself, a 'trahison des clercs'; but it is also the case that the wider conservatism
of post-war Irish society rendered it a peculiarly unpromising territory for the highly
influential Marxian or Marxisant philosophies rapidly gaining ground first in France
and then more broadly in the 1950s, 1960s, and after. However, it is also clear that, with
the systematic interrogation of the *IHS* reformers at the end of the twentieth century,
and the various challenges to the ascendancy of their achievement, the way has now
been opened for a redefinition of the relationship between mainstream Irish historiography and theory.

To an extent this volume embodies at least some of the theoretically informed
approaches current within a literature which (in the aftermath of Ireland's revisionist *Historikerstreit*) is now more open than before both to theoretical as well as interdisciplinary engagement. For example, the historical geographer Yvonne Whelan's
essay on landscape and politics draws upon both Foucault and the work of the Marxist
philosopher, Henri Lefebvre, on the production of social and political space in the city.
The literary historian, Margaret Kelleher, incorporates a range of theoretical readings into her essay on literary culture in English. Maria Luddy's work on gender draws
upon the work of Joan Scott and other feminist theorists. The contributions of several of the early modernists here represented (and others beyond this volume, such as
James Livesey) have been influenced by the theoretical work of Jürgen Habermas on
the growth and decay of the public sphere. Stephen Howe engages fully in his essay on
'Colonizers and Colonized' with the spectrum of post-colonial theorisation.[38]

The breakdown of the dominant *Irish Historical Studies* model of empirical, often
high political, scholarship has thus created a variety of possibilities, theoretical and
otherwise. Debate within Irish history flourishes, and Irish historians are more open
than ever to a range of wider influences and approaches. There is clearly a cost, however: the *IHS* manifesto of the 1930s created a strong sense of disciplinary identity and
cohesion, a sense of missionary purpose and confidence, all of which have long since
been lost. The suspicion arises, therefore, that Irish history has lost an empire, but not
yet found a role.

VI. Hubris

Irish history's modernist reformers held sway for nearly half a century after the creation of *Irish Historical Studies* in 1938, shaping an historiography very much in their own image. They were keen to link Irish history to wider European professional advances, but nervous about the impact of theory, whether Marxist or republican.[39] Eschewing theory, they were of course working within a set of implicit theoretical contexts, conservative, positivist, and empirical. While Moody had some leftward leanings (as a member of the not-very-leftist Irish Labour Party), the reformers were essentially taking a clear and conservative ideological stand in the context of a Europe whose political, religious, and intellectual life was perceived as being under threat from the Soviet Union. While they sought scientifically to transcend their circumstances, they were (despite their pretensions) very much men of their time—their 'time' being the aftermath of the Irish revolution and the wider challenge of totalitarian ideology.

The young reformers of the 1930s had become an entrenched professional establishment by the 1950s and 1960s, a fact noted self-critically by Dudley Edwards in 1957: 'while we may pride ourselves upon being in large part its creators,' he wrote of modern Irish historiography, 'we cannot regard it as our creation. To deny that younger scholars are fit to take our places is to refuse to a younger generation what [Edmund] Curtis did not refuse to us when we were younger...the chance of trial and error'.[40] This entrenchment, together with the relative smallness of the Irish history profession, and the relative conservatism of wider Irish society, tended to enshrine the historiographical model of the 1930s. Only with the wider political and intellectual shifts of the 1960s, particularly (in an Irish context) the Northern 'Troubles', were the circumstances created which facilitated the systematic questioning of the *IHS* achievement, partly as a consequence of professional growth and diversification. The reformist tradition had also now (in part) lost confidence, while for some the war in Northern Ireland was revalidating narratives of republican struggle.

While there are other influences, the 'end' of the Troubles has helped to stimulate a broadening of Irish history. Irish historians have been looking to redefine the geographical boundaries of their sub-discipline, but they have also been working creatively and imaginatively within the existing borders: if the present and the future of the Union are currently being re-imagined, then so, too, is its past. While the nature of the United Kingdom is changing, and the importance of Britain (as distinct from its constituent parts) for Ireland is slackening, Ireland's relationship with continental Europe, with empire, and with the global Irish diaspora, is assuming a greater political and historiographical significance than hitherto. If the imperium of the United Kingdom has weakened decisively, then that of the European Union is strikingly ascendant.

Thus, while there are grounds for celebrating the diversity and vitality of Irish history, it not yet time to put out the bunting. For, despite the evident failings and contingencies of an older historiography, much of the discipline (despite its fond imaginings) remains as influenced by wider social and political constructs as in the 1930s. Moreover, much that is supposedly novel in Irish historiography has in fact been foreshadowed in the thought and action of previous scholarly generations. Irish history's continental European 'turn' is not untouched by the Irish state's wider economic and political realignments, or by the funding structures of the European Union: it is also very much in keeping with the *IHS* reformers' agenda. Transnational and diasporic history reflects broader economic and cultural globalization, to say nothing of the embattled nation state's appeal for support to a diasporic audience (as in the 'homecoming' years of the early 21st century). Much scholarship remains tied to an agenda implicitly associated with the state, as in the 'decade of anniversaries' (2012–22) commemorating the achievement of independence at the beginning of the twentieth century. In the end, therefore, it would be ironic if the Irish historians of the twenty-first century, conscious of the 'progress' that they have achieved, were to reinvent both the achievements and the hubris of their predecessors in the 1930s.

Notes

* A draft of this introduction was presented to a colloquium on the 'State of Irish History' at the Keough-Naughton Institute for Irish Studies, the University of Notre Dame, Indiana, in September 2012. I am grateful to the staff and students of the Keough Center for Irish Studies for their questions and comments.

1. The text of the 'Preface' to *Irish Historical Studies*, i (1938–9), 1–3, is reproduced in Ciaran Brady (ed), *Interpreting Irish History: The Debate on Historical Revisionism* (Dublin, 1994), 35–8.

2. The argument of Brendan Bradshaw, 'Nationalism and Historical Scholarship in Modern Ireland', *Irish Historical Studies*, xxvi (1988–9), 329–51.

3. See David Dickson, 'Interview with R. B. McDowell', *History Ireland*, 1, 4 (Winter, 1993).

4. See, for example, Trinity College Dublin, T. W. Moody Papers, Ms.10048, f.86: Beckett to Moody, 19 March 1957 ('I will do my best with the probable result that in endeavouring to follow my conscience and common sense along a middle way I shall alienate both you and Edwards... I shall do no real good unless I made it clear that I wasn't coming in simply to provide two votes to one against Edwards').

5. University College Dublin Archives, Robert Dudley Edwards Papers, LA22/58: correspondence over the Fianna medal.

6. For a full discussion, see Alvin Jackson, 'J. C. Beckett: Politics, Faith, Scholarship', *Irish Historical Studies*, xxxiii, 130 (November 2002).

7. Moody Papers, Ms.10048, f.14: Beckett to Moody, 9 May 1946; Ms.10048, f.22: Student Christian Movement brochure for 'Ireland Awake! The National Conference of the Irish Universities and Training Colleges to be held in St. Columba's College, Rathfarnham, Dublin, 7–12 August 1950'; Ms.10048, f.35: Beckett to David Moody, 21 December 1951; Ms.10048, f.47: Beckett to Moody, 4 June 1953.

8. Dudley Edwards Papers, LA22/528-32, Correspondence on the Irish Catholic Historical Committee; LA22/611, Report on the Irish Martyrs; LA22/837, Fr. Christopher Mangan to Dudley Edwards, 22 September 1949.

9. Brady, *Interpreting Irish History*, 35. See also, for the promotion of scientific imagery: Dudley Edwards Papers, LA22/390/70: Ulster Society for Irish Historical Studies brochure, *c.* 1936 (members should be 'actively contributing to the scientific advancement of the subject'). Also, Dudley Edwards Papers, LA22/392/1: Constitution of the Irish Historical Society, 14 July 1937 ('its object shall be to promote scientific studies in Irish history and the publication of them') and LA 22/849/30: Prospectus for *Irish Historical Studies, c.* 1937 ('the lack of any periodical publication exclusively devoted to Irish history has been a serious handicap to the advancement of the subject on scientific lines').

10. Dudley Edwards Papers, LA22/739: Butterfield to Dudley Edwards, 8 December 1964. Thomas Desmond Williams (1921–87) was Professor of Modern History at University College Dublin (1949–84). See also Michael Bentley, *The Life and Thought of Herbert Butterfield: History, Science and God*, paperback edition (Cambridge, 2012), 240.

11. Though see Dudley Edwards Papers, LA22/381: Minute Book of the Irish Historical Society (1950–8), including R. D. Edwards' statement (20 May 1957).

12. See, for example, Desmond Fennell, *The Revision of Irish Nationalism* (Dublin, 1989); Brendan Bradshaw, 'Nationalism and Historical Scholarship', *Irish Historical Studies*, xxvi, 104 (November 1989).

13. John Regan, 'Southern Irish Nationalism as a Historiographical Problem', *Historical Journal*, 50, 1 (2007); John Regan, 'Irish Public Histories as a Historiographical Problem', *Irish Historical Studies*, xxxvii, 146 (November 2010).

14. Alvin Jackson, 'J. C. Beckett: Politics, Faith, Scholarship', *Irish Historical Studies*, xxxiii (November 2002).

15. See below, Paul Arthur, 'The Long War and its Aftermath: Northern Ireland, 1969–2006'.

16. See, for example, Meda Ryan, *Tom Barry: IRA Freedom Fighter* (Cork, 2005).

17. See below, Paul Arthur, 'The Long War and its Aftermath: Northern Ireland, 1969–2006'. See also, Richard English, *Armed Struggle: A History of the IRA* (London, 2003).

18. Christopher Farrington, *Ulster Unionism and the Peace Process in Northern Ireland* (Basingstoke, 2006); Eric Kaufmann, *The Orange Order: A Contemporary Northern Irish History* (Oxford, 2007); Rachel Ward, *Women, Unionism and Loyalism in Northern Ireland: From Tea-Makers to Political Actors* (Dublin, 2006). See also Alvin Jackson, ' "Divided hearts, united states": Historians, the Union and Unionists', *Irish Historical Studies*, xxxvi, 143 (May 2009), 419.

19. See below, Henry Patterson, 'Unionist Ireland, 1923–72'. See also Henry Patterson and Eric Kaufmann, *Unionism and Orangeism in Northern Ireland since 1945: The Decline of the Loyal Family* (Manchester, 2006).

20. Christy Campbell, *Fenian Fire—The British Government Plot to Assassinate Queen Victoria* (London, 2002).

21. Farrington, *Ulster Unionism and the Peace Process*, quoted in Alvin Jackson, ' "Divided hearts, united states": Historians, Unionism, and the Union', *Irish Historical Studies*, xxxvi, 143 (May 2009), 419.

22. Enda Delaney, 'Our Island Story?: Towards a Transnational History of Modern Ireland', *Irish Historical Studies*, xxxvii, 148 (2011).

23. See, for example, Ryan, *Barry*.

24. See below, Timothy Bowman, 'Ireland and the First World War'.

25. See below, Éamonn Ó Ciardha, 'Irish Language Sources for the History of Early Modern Ireland'.

26. Alvin Jackson, 'Widening the Fight for Ireland's Freedom: Revolutionary Nationalism in its Global Contexts', *Victorian Studies*, 54, 1 (Autumn, 2011), 96.

27. See below, Stephen Howe, 'Colonizers and Colonized'.

28. See below, Jane Ohlmeyer, 'Confederation and Union, 1641–1660'.

29. Alvin Jackson, *Two Unions: Ireland, Scotland and the Survival of the United Kingdom, 1707-2007* (Oxford, 2012).

30. Christine Kinealy, *Repeal and Revolution: 1848 in Ireland* (Manchester, 2009). See also Leon Litvack and Colin Graham (eds), *Ireland and Europe in the Nineteenth Century* (Dublin, 2006).

31. Fearghal McGarry and James McConnel (eds), *The Black Hand of Republicanism: Fenianism in Modern Ireland* (Dublin, 2009); Fintan Lane and Andrew Newby (eds), *Michael Davitt: New Perspectives* (Dublin, 2009).

32. Jonathan Gantt, *Irish Terrorism in the Atlantic Community, 1865–1922* (Basingstoke, 2010)

33. This point is argued by Máirtín Ó Catháin in McGarry and McConnel (eds), *The Black Hand of Republicanism*.

34. Evi Gkotzaridis, *Trials of Irish History: Genesis and Evolution of a Reappraisal, 1938–2000* (London and New York, 2006).

35. Donal McCartney, *W. E. H. Lecky, Historian and Politician* (Dublin, 1994).

36. Bentley, *Life and Thought of Herbert Butterfield*, 239–41.

37. Michael Tierney (ed.), *Daniel O'Connell: Nine Centenary Essays* (Dublin, 1949), 170.

38. See below, Yvonne Whelan, 'Landscape and Politics', Margaret Kelleher, 'Irish Literary Culture in English', Maria Luddy, 'Gender', Stephen Howe, 'Colonizers and Colonized'. See also James Livesey, *Civil Society and Empire: Ireland and Scotland in the Eighteenth Century Atlantic World* (New Haven, 2009).

39. Dudley Edwards Papers, LA22/850: Dudley Edwards to Moody, 16 February 1965 (copy) (where Dudley Edwards suggests that the greatest benefit of his recent trip to the USA has been to illuminate Irish history in a more European light).

40. Dudley Edwards Papers, LA22/381: Minute Book of the Irish Historical Society (1950-8), including R. D. Edwards' statement (20 May 1957). Edmund Curtis (1881–1943), Erasmus Smith's Professor of Modern History, Trinity College Dublin (1914–39) and Lecky Professor of History, Trinity College Dublin (1939–43).

Select Bibliography

Boyce, D. George and O'Day, Alan (eds), *The Making of Modern Irish History: Revisionism and the Revisionist Controversy* (London, 1996).

Bradshaw, Brendan, 'Nationalism and Historical Scholarship', *Irish Historical Studies*, xxvi, 104 (November 1989).

Brady, Ciaran, *Interpreting Irish History: The Debate on Historical Revisionism, 1938–94* (Dublin, 1994).

Clarke, Aidan, 'Robert Dudley Edwards, 1909-88', *Irish Historical Studies*, xxvi, 102 (November 1988).

Dickson, David, 'Interview with R. B. McDowell', *History Ireland*, 1, 4 (Winter, 1993).

Dunne, Tom (ed.), *The Writer as Witness: Literature as Historical Evidence (Historical Studies XVI: Papers Read at the Conference of Irish Historians at Cork, 1985)* (Cork, 1987).

Dunne, Tom, *Rebellions: Memoir, Memory and 1798* (extended edition: Dublin, 2010).

Dunne, Tom and Geary, Laurence (eds), *History and the Public Sphere: Essays in Honour of John A Murphy* (Cork, 2005).

Gkotzaridis, Evi, 'Irish Revisionism and Continental Theory: An Insight into Intellectual Kinship', *Irish Review*, 27 (Summer, 2001).

Gkotzaridis, Evi, *Trials of Irish History: Genesis and Evolution of a Reappraisal, 1938–2000* (London and New York, 2006).

Jackson, Alvin, 'J. C. Beckett: Politics, Faith, Scholarship', *Irish Historical Studies*, xxxiii, 130 (November 2002).

Jackson, Alvin, 'Unveiling Irish History', *Journal of Contemporary History*, 40, 4 (2005).

Jackson, Alvin, ' "Divided hearts, united states": Historians, the Union and Unionists', *Irish Historical Studies*, xxxvi, 143 (May 2009).

Jackson, Alvin, 'Widening the Fight for Ireland's Freedom: Revolutionary Nationalism in its Global Contexts', *Victorian Studies*, 54, 1 (Autumn, 2011).

Regan, John, 'Southern Irish Nationalism as a Historiographical Problem', *Historical Journal*, 50, 1 (2007).

Regan, John, 'Irish Public Histories as a Historiographical Problem', *Irish Historical Studies*, xxxvii, 146 (November 2010).

PART II

THEMATIC STUDIES

NATION, EMPIRE, AND LANDSCAPE

....

CHAPTER 2

PATRIOTISM AND
NATIONALISM

....

SEAN CONNOLLY

I. INTRODUCTION

....

ON 28 April 1916, as an offshoot of the armed rising taking place in the capital, a group of Irish Volunteers attacked a police station at Rath Cross, near Ashbourne in County Meath, then fought an action against a party of some sixty members of the Royal Irish Constabulary (R.I.C.) sent as reinforcements. Forty years later, one of their number, now minister for education and a former commander-in-chief of the Irish Army, recalled in an obituary tribute the subsequent experience of another Volunteer, a medical doctor:

> Later, after some hours fighting, on a road margined with death and pain and anguish, he tended the wounded. As I stood nearby an RIC man stretched out his arms impulsively to cry—'Oh, we are all Irishmen, Sir, we are all Irishmen. You know me, Sir, I am Glennon the boxer.'[1]

Glennon's words derive their poignancy partly from the circumstances, partly from the contrast between the formal diction of the period and the bewilderment and emotion they express. But they also highlight a more general point: the gap that existed between a clearly defined sense of national identity ('We are all Irishmen...') and a programme, executed in the name of that nation, of direct and in this case violent political action. These related but separate ways of identifying self and others— national consciousness on the one hand and nationalism on the other—provide the twin poles around which any history of early modern and modern Irish politics must be constructed.

II. Early Modern Origins

At the end of the Middle Ages, Ireland was a society in which ideas of national identity were already well defined. On one side there were the descendants of the English settlers who had colonized a large part of the island during the late twelfth and thirteenth centuries. As with other colonial populations, prolonged geographical separation and occasional bruising encounters with metropolitan indifference to their interests had, over time, created a sense of separate identity. In 1460 the Irish parliament had gone so far as to declare that Ireland was a land 'corporate of itself', bound only by laws made in its own parliament. Here, however, the appeal was not to any principle of national self-determination, but rather to corporate privileges, sectional and specific, of the kind enjoyed by individual cities, liberties, palatinates, guilds, and other associations throughout late medieval and early modern Europe.[2] It was also true that settler lords in outlying regions had, to a large extent, adopted the dress, language, and general lifestyle of their Gaelic counterparts; a few in more remote regions had been wholly absorbed into native society. But the majority continued to see themselves as Englishmen and as subjects of the English Crown. Meanwhile, in the core of the lordship—the major towns and the more intensively colonized east coast area known as the Pale—the settler community sought to preserve a cultural as well as a political Englishness, protecting themselves against contamination by laws against Gaelic dress and custom and by the periodic expulsion of native interlopers.

On the other side of the ethnic divide were the native or Gaelic Irish, inhabiting a patchwork of autonomous lordships, within which regional overlords claimed authority over lesser units. They shared a language and culture with Highland Scotland, which they recognized as the other part of a single Gaeldom. But there was also a sense of the island of Ireland as a territory, the land of *Éire* or *Banba*, politically fragmented but united by a single code of law, as well as by a common origin myth that identified the *Gaeil* with the Milesians or followers of the legendary warrior Míl. Native poets sometimes made rhetorical calls for the sons of Míl to unite in a crusade to free *Banba* of the English intruders, referred to as *Gaill*, or foreigners, who occupied part of its territory. But in practice native rulers pragmatically accepted the *Gaill* as one element in a system of competing polities to be fought or allied with as occasion demanded; Gaelic poets could even, when it suited, produce work praising English patrons for the valour with which their warrior ancestors had conquered their share of the island.

During the sixteenth century this well-established pattern of identity and allegiance was disrupted by two main developments. The establishment, under Henry VIII, of direct Crown control of a lordship formerly managed through local intermediaries forced the king and his successors to embark on progressively more ambitious strategies of conquest and plantation. Meanwhile, the failure of the Reformation to gain significant support introduced a new division between the Crown and its Irish subjects. The brutal conflicts that resulted were, for the most part, a defence of local autonomy by regional magnates, reinforced as the century progressed by an element of Counter-Reformation ideology. During 1595–1603, however, what began as a revolt by a group of Ulster Gaelic lords, led by Hugh O'Neill, expanded into a nationwide rebellion. O'Neill's propaganda called on 'Irishmen' of both Gaelic and English descent to join in a crusade to defend Catholicism and to liberate the island from the rule of 'a strange and foreign prince'. The appeal was still to religious solidarity and to the feudal notion of a just lord, rather than to the inherent legitimacy of the nation state. But the language of a shared Irishness, transcending long-standing ethnic divisions, has been seen as reflecting the introduction to Ireland of the new concept, recently recovered from classical sources by Renaissance scholars, of attachment to a *patria* or fatherland.[3]

The descendants of the medieval settlers, despite their shared religious allegiance, did not for the most part respond to O'Neill's appeal. However, their loyalty was poorly rewarded: already before 1603 these long-standing servants of the Crown had begun to find themselves shouldered aside by a new cohort of soldiers, administrators, and adventurers drawn to Ireland by the multiple opportunities opened up by war and conquest. Their change in status was reflected in the rise of a new term, 'Old English', to distinguish the obdurately Catholic heirs to a far distant conquest from the new arrivals, English by birth as well as blood, and Protestant in religion. Now the defeat of the last serious military challenge from Gaelic Ireland opened the way to a concerted assault on Catholic religious practice. Against this background of shared oppression, the early seventeenth century saw increased social contact, including intermarriage, between Old English and Gaelic Irish. One striking product of the reassessment of traditional divisions was the completion of Geoffrey Keating's *Foras Feasa ar Éirinn* in 1633. In what became a widely influential text, a Counter-Reformation clergyman, himself of Old English descent but writing in Irish, set out to give the two parts of the Catholic population a shared history, with the medieval English and the mythical Milesians each allocated an honourable role as warriors asserting by conquest their right to inhabit the land of Ireland.[4]

The long political crisis of the Old English reached its climax with the outbreak in 1642 of civil war in England. Faced with the prospect of a seizure of total power by the violently anti-Catholic English parliament, Old English leaders agreed to join forces with the Gaelic Irish in a Catholic Confederation. In doing so, they denied that they had departed from their allegiance to the English Crown. The motto of the Confederates proclaimed them to be 'Irishmen united for God, king and fatherland'. In practice this attempt to combine the defence of an Irish *patria* with support for a pan-British royalism proved fragile. The Confederates divided, and even fought one another, over the terms of any formal alliance with Charles I and his supporters. The conflict of interest was, in part, between those Catholics who had already lost everything in earlier wars and plantations, and those whose wealth and status inclined them to greater caution. But there was also an ethnic dimension, with the Old English desperate to return to an unambiguous loyalty while the Gaelic Irish were more disposed to make commitment to the king's cause conditional on his acceptance of their church's former privileges and estates.[5] To their Protestant opponents, however, the willingness of the Old English to ally themselves with rebellious natives was final confirmation that their disloyal Catholicism negated any claim to favour based on their ethnic origin. The extensive confiscations of Catholic land that took place in the 1650s, following the victory of the parliamentary forces, dispossessed Old English and native Irish alike. Over the next few decades the final obliteration of a centuries-old ethnic identity was reflected in a growing practice among Protestants of referring to all Catholics, regardless of ethnic origin, as 'Irish'.

On the Protestant side too, war and revolution brought new alignments and new definitions of identity. By 1641 the New English had successfully displaced the Old English at most levels of government. When civil war broke out in England in 1642, they were initially divided in their allegiances, but increasingly sided with parliament as the ally most likely to sustain them in their local fight for survival. Following the defeat and execution of Charles I, however, these established Protestant settlers found themselves resentfully subordinated to the unrestrained authority of a new cohort of military and civilian administrators imposed by the victorious English republic. In a further semantic shift the New English became the 'Old Protestants'. Following the restoration of the monarchy in 1660, on the other hand, Cromwellian and pre-1641 settlers joined forces to defend the recent land settlement, in which both had gained substantially at the expense of the Old English and Gaelic Irish. Their determination to assert their right to a say in their own political future has been seen as a turning point in the emergence of a united Protestant ruling class.[6]

Meanwhile, a further element had been added to Ireland's already complex ethnic and religious mix. The Scottish population established in some northern counties by the Ulster plantation—and augmented by subsequent immigration—had, up to 1641, remained uneasily contained within the established church. Thereafter, however, the breakdown of civil and ecclesiastical authority, combined with the arrival in Ulster of a Scottish army, had encouraged them to create their own Presbyterian network. In politics too they had pursued their own course, initially allying with parliament but later rising in arms against the English republic following the execution of Charles I. After 1660 they remained political outsiders, excluded from the Restoration church settlement and regarded as potentially disloyal. As late as 1705 the Dublin government expressed concern at the likely response of what it still saw as a Scottish population in Ulster to any military conflict between their homeland and England. The Scots themselves shared this sense of a separate identity. Ulster Presbyterians registering at the University of Glasgow in the first half of the eighteenth century continued to describe themselves as 'Scotus Hiberniae', on one occasion reacting with indignation to being described as 'Irishmen'.[7]

III. PATRIOTS AND JACOBITES

At the beginning of the eighteenth century the vocabulary of identity in Ireland continued to apply ethnic labels to what were in fact primarily religious distinctions. The ruling elite, made up of propertied members of the Church of Ireland, was overwhelmingly recruited from descendants of the New English of the Elizabethan and early Stuart eras, or of later Cromwellian settlers. But they also included a handful of Gaelic Irish families, like the O'Haras of Sligo or the O'Briens of Clare, as well as Scottish families that had abandoned Presbyterianism for the privileges that came with membership of the established church. In their own eyes this hybrid group were 'the English', while their Catholic and Presbyterian neighbours were the Irish and the Scots. (A brief attempt by Whig champions of Protestant unity in the reign of Queen Anne to introduce the term 'British' to cover both Protestant denominations had not taken hold.) Already by this time, however, this self-image had begun to bump up against hard political reality. The disastrous parliament of 1692 was the first of a series of occasions in which those who still saw themselves as the English of Ireland protested at what they regarded as the illegitimate intrusions on their rights of the government of England itself, while exasperated London ministers denounced them as 'Irishmen' seeking 'independence'.

This succession of constitutional disputes arose in part from practical grievances: the more systematic use of commercial restrictions to protect English economic interests, the increased share of Irish appointments going to well-connected English interlopers, and the growing tendency of English public opinion to include Protestants as well as Catholics in their stereotype image of an uncouth and backward Ireland. Equally, Irish Protestants, to some extent, were claiming their share in the constitutional liberties seen as having been achieved by the Revolution of 1688–9. At bottom, however, the cause of Irish discontent was that political dependence was no longer mediated through the person of a shared monarch. A succession of patriot writers, commencing with William Molyneux in 1698, continued doggedly to insist that Ireland's connection was to the Crown of England, and did not involve any subordination to the parliament or people of that kingdom. But that was to ignore the implications of the Revolution and its aftermath. Whatever fictional constructions of constitutional continuity had helped to make that settlement acceptable to conservative sensibilities, the reality was that to be ruled by George I or his successors was inescapably to be ruled by the British parliament, or rather by the faction within that parliament that formed the government of the day.

It would be misleading to interpret the succession of political crises that began with the parliament of 1692 in terms of a linear progression towards a new Irish political identity. The initial response of many Protestants to intrusions from London was not to stand on their rights as inhabitants of a separate kingdom, but rather to appeal to the people of Great Britain on the basis of their shared citizenship. Molyneux, celebrated by later generations as a champion of Irish liberty, was regarded by most contemporaries as a troublemaker.[8] In retrospect, indeed, the succession of conflicts that took place in the decades immediately following the Revolution can be seen as a period of transition, in which British ministers and members of the Irish Protestant elite alike attempted to discover the limits of their freedom of action in a transformed political environment. The outcome, following a disastrous conflict on the issue of a new copper coinage, the so-called Wood's Halfpence controversy, was a new equilibrium, founded on an agreed distribution of patronage and influence between the British executive and local parliamentary managers or 'undertakers', that survived for almost three decades.

The first stage in the breakdown of that equilibrium had its origins in factional competition. Between 1753 and 1756 Henry Boyle, head of a large Munster-based political connection, picked a quarrel with the government on the issue of London's interference with financial legislation. It was a pragmatic manoeuvre intended to head off a threat to Boyle's position as the leading undertaker. But the enthusiastic popular response to his assumption of patriot virtue marked an important new development: the emergence, in an increasingly literate and commercialized society, of an assertive out-of-doors opinion. From now on political controversies were acted out on the streets as well as inside the walls of the parliament house on College Green. One consequence was to strengthen the feeling, already gaining ground in British political circles, that a lack of effective central control over different parts of the empire, including Ireland, was putting the security of the whole structure at risk. Between 1767 and 1772 a new lord lieutenant, Viscount Townshend, reformed the management of Irish affairs, transferring day-to-day political management from local undertakers to a resident viceroy. Thereafter British government in Ireland no longer had a local face, and political grievances were more easily cast in national terms. Even then, it took the wider crisis of the American Revolution to allow the patriot element within the political elite, backed by a strong popular movement, to challenge the compliant majority within and outside parliament, and to mount a sustained campaign for a change in Ireland's constitutional status.

Protestant patriotism presents serious problems of definition. J. G. Simms, writing in 1976, borrowed the phrase 'colonial nationalism', originally applied to movements of self-assertion among the settler populations of the white dominions of the late nineteenth and early twentieth-century British Empire.[9] The term captures certain essential features. On the one hand there is the emergence of a new collective identity, as those who had originally thought of themselves as Englishmen transplanted to a new dominion of the Crown began to see themselves instead as the inhabitants of a separate territory. On the other there is the rejection of the indigenous culture of the new homeland as inferior if not barbarous, and the determined exclusion of the native inhabitants from the privileges claimed for the settler elite.

In other respects, the term is less satisfactory. 'Colonial' begs several questions about the relationship between Ireland and England, and between settler and native. The conjunction with 'nationalism' raises further difficulties. George Boyce sees the qualifying adjective as an exclusionary term, reflecting the reluctance of mainstream Catholic nationalism to acknowledge its debt to the Protestant elite of the eighteenth century.[10] For Joep Leerssen, on the other hand, it is the word 'nationalism' that implies too much, unfairly measuring the aspirations of an eighteenth-century political elite against the modern ideal of the nation, with its connotations of inclusiveness and its invocation of culture as well as political rights. Instead, Leerssen argues, 'patriotism' should be defined as something quite different from nationalism: the stance of an early modern community defending its own historically defined and frankly sectional liberties, in the same way that the *parlements* of contemporary France resisted the encroachments of the Crown, or Dutch patriots defended the forms of republican government against the monarchist pretensions of the House of Orange.[11]

Leerssen's definition of patriotism as the defence of explicitly sectional interests captures admirably the distinctive political outlook of early and mid-eighteenth-century Irish Protestants. It explains, for example, why Jonathan Swift could address one of his polemics against Wood's Halfpence to 'the whole people of Ireland', while insisting in the same text that opposition to the scheme had nothing to do with 'the Irish' but arose instead from among 'the true English people of Ireland'.[12] It becomes less convincing when applied to the late eighteenth century, when Protestants began to acquire an extravagant enthusiasm for the history and antiquities of early Gaelic Ireland, presented by Charles Vallancey and others as a literate and sophisticated society, whose origins lay in the advanced cultures of the ancient Mediterranean.[13] At this point it seems clear that patriotism, whatever its blind spots, amounted to more than the defence of a particular set of vested interests; those involved also felt the impulse to give themselves a history that would be a source of pride and an assurance of continuity. In the case of Gaelic antiquities the identification was an act of wholly imaginative appropriation. More direct continuities were asserted in the case of religion, where ecclesiastical historians elaborated on the idea, first advanced by Archbishop Ussher in the early seventeenth century, that the Protestant Reformation had merely restored Irish Christianity to the purity represented by the bibliocentric and non-Roman church created by St Patrick.

The culture of patriotism that thus took shape during the eighteenth century was exclusively and self-consciously Protestant. The political allegiance of the great majority of Irish Catholics, by contrast, was to the exiled Stuart dynasty. It was a commitment that incorporated them into a pan-British movement firmly rooted in the confessional and dynastic loyalties of *ancien régime* Europe. In this respect, attempts to establish a direct line of succession leading to the nationalism of the Victorian and Edwardian era are misconceived. At another level Irish Jacobitism, like its Scottish counterpart, can be categorized as an example of what has been described as 'proto-nationalism': a movement expressing and fostering a sense of collective identity, based on language, history, and in this case religion, in the era before it came to be generally assumed that the proper focus for such sentiments was the nation state. No common ground, however, could exist between Jacobitism, even so described, and the patriotism of the Protestant elite, for whom the ultimate source of the liberties they demanded derived from the overthrow of James II and his popish allies.[14]

IV. United Irishmen and Defenders

Protestant patriotism had its moment of triumph in April 1782, when disaster in America brought to power the Rockingham Whigs, committed by their rhetoric in opposition to meeting Irish constitutional demands. But victory proved to be illusory. In theory the 'constitution of 1782' ensured that Ireland would henceforth be governed solely by its king in parliament. In practice the lord lieutenant, exercising executive power in the name of the monarch, remained as before a nominee of the British cabinet.

Irish legislation no longer required prior approval under the provisions of Poynings's Law, but bills passed by both houses of parliament were still scrutinized by the British Privy Council before being returned under the Great Seal of England. Approval was almost never withheld, because Irish patriotism had demonstrated its limitations in other ways. The failure of the parliamentary reform campaign during 1783–5, and continued resistance to the admission of Catholics to full political rights, meant that the Dublin parliament, now liberated from Westminster control, remained largely unaccountable to any significant section of Irish opinion. Instead the way was open for successive Irish executives to use all the resources of patronage at their disposal to ensure that government business proceeded smoothly through the Irish parliament, and that further constitutional challenges were stillborn. The 1780s and 1790s, celebrated by later nationalists as a brief era of Irish self-government, were in reality the golden age of Irish political corruption.

Against this background the revolt against French absolutism that began in 1789 inspired a new movement that linked the demand for Irish autonomy to the cause of radical political reform. The resolutions of the Society of United Irishmen, founded in 1791, called for 'an equal representation of all the people in parliament' as the only way of remedying the system of corruption through which Ireland was ruled 'by Englishmen and the servants of Englishmen'. The precise degree of independence aimed at was not initially clear. Theobald Wolfe Tone, author of the resolutions, was by this time, according to his own later account, a separatist. On the other hand the Dublin United Irish leader William MacNeven continued even much later to insist that a connection of some kind would be for the benefit of both counties, and that the real problem was the resistance of the British government to reform.[15] In its public statements the new movement, anxious to maximize support, initially confined itself to the traditional patriot goal of an Ireland that would be a sister kingdom, enjoying equal status with Great Britain under a shared crown. During 1795, however, with Britain and Ireland now at war with revolutionary France, and political dissent a target for increasingly harsh repression, the United Irishmen reconstituted themselves as a clandestine movement committed to the establishment, with French military aid, of an independent Irish republic.

In another respect too the United Irishmen went well beyond the traditional patriot agenda. Some of those involved in the succession of agitations inspired by the American War had taken up the argument that any true assertion of national rights must also include the admission to political life of the Catholic majority. Many, however, had remained committed to the idea of an exclusively Protestant political community, and the issue had been shelved in the interests of unity. The United Irishmen, by contrast, aware of the need to maximize support for their radical agenda, committed themselves from the start to the abolition of all religious tests. Their overtures came at an opportune moment. By the 1740s, if not earlier, the Catholic middle and upper classes had largely abandoned their support for the exiled Stuarts. Their main tactic in the decades that followed had been to parade their deferential attachment to the Hanoverian establishment. Some, including the greater part of the Catholic clergy, continued this stance of ostentatious loyalty into the 1790s. But others, responding to a climate of enhanced radical expectations, and emboldened by the repeal of the main anti-Catholic laws, were ready to be more assertive. The leadership of the United Irishmen remained mainly Protestant, and its strongest base was in the predominantly Presbyterian counties of east Ulster. In Dublin, however, Catholics made up just over half of the members of the city's Society of United Irishmen between 1791 and 1794, and they were to be in a clear majority of those drawn in as the movement began to recruit in the surrounding counties over the next four years.

Changing Catholic political attitudes were also evident, in a more ambiguous form, in the rise of another movement. The Defender society is less fully documented than the United Irish movement with which it allied, and to some extent merged, from 1795; what evidence exists suggests a complex interaction of old and new political trad-itions. Laments for the overthrow of the native ruling class, preserved in the Gaelic literary tradition, fused with the new ideology of universal rights to create a myth of communal dispossession; the language of universal liberty blended with visions of the long-dreamt-of expulsion of 'Calvin's breed'. When the insurrection came in the sum-mer of 1798, the failure of secular republicanism to override long-standing sectarian animosities became brutally obvious. Yet in bundling together religious, economic, and political grievances in the language of a historic nation struggling for its freedom from foreign oppression the Defenders, as well as the United Irishmen, have some claim to have initiated Ireland's entry into the era of nationalism.[16]

V. Repealers and Republicans

By 1800 the journey to Rath Cross was half completed. No one any longer talked of the different parts of the island's population in terms of 'English' and 'Irish' (although the notion of a separate nation of Ulster 'Scots' retained a shadowy presence, and was to be given new life by unionist polemicists in the late nineteenth century). Instead, all concerned, regardless of political and religious affiliation, would have described them-selves as Irish, even if with varying degrees of emphasis and quite different implications. By this time too the constitutional structures, a separate but dependent kingdom, that had been the focus of Irish political aspirations for over a century had been replaced by incorporation into a unitary British state; working out attitudes to that incorporation would dominate the politics of the next 120 years.

There has been an understandable tendency to write the history of Ireland under the act of union backwards: an arrangement ending in a separation enforced by violence, is easily assumed to have been flawed from the start. More recent work suggests a less stark, indeed frankly contradictory, picture. The evidence for widespread rejection of the union settlement is undeniable; the campaigns of the 1830s and 1840s for repeal of the act of union, along with the home rule movement established in 1870 and elector-ally dominant from 1885, represented a level of challenge that had no parallel elsewhere within the new union of four nations. The risings of the Young Ireland movement in

1848 and of the Fenians in 1867, with the sporadic later activities of the Irish Republican Brotherhood (IRB), were an armed response even further outside the British norm. Yet popular attitudes were hardly consistent. Royal visits to Ireland, from George IV in 1821 onwards, attracted large and apparently enthusiastic crowds. Meanwhile the proportion of Irish-born soldiers in Crown forces remained consistently higher than Ireland's share of total population. By 1903, it is true, advanced nationalist principles had gained ground sufficiently for Dublin Corporation to withhold the customary loyal address to Edward VII, and there was also by this time a growing campaign against recruiting. But the popular response both to the royal visit and slightly earlier to the Boer War suggests that majority attitudes remained less rigid.[17] Overall there is a striking resemblance to conditions in the Habsburg Empire, another union that was contested by a nationalist vanguard but which retained at least the passive loyalty of the majority, until the strains of war on an unprecedented scale led government to impose greater demands on the non-dominant nationalities than they were willing to accept.

The most striking feature of nineteenth-century Irish nationalism, when set against its European counterparts, is the absence (until a late stage) of a significant cultural dimension. An association between political self-assertion and the cultivation of an exalted vision of past cultural glories existed from the late eighteenth century. But practical issues of linguistic equality played no part in either patriot or, until the end of the nineteenth century, nationalist agitation. Speakers of Irish, faced with marginalization, reacted not by demanding more equal treatment but by learning English. Already by the 1830s the proportion of children acquiring a knowledge of Irish as part of the process of growing up was only 28 per cent.

Rather than becoming a part of mainstream nationalist agitation, interest in Irish language and culture was for most of the nineteenth century largely the preserve of members of the Protestant middle and upper classes. For some, like Thomas Davis, an emphasis on the cultural basis of Irish national identity was a way of countering the growing association between nationalism and Catholicism, allowing the Protestant gentry and middle classes to recover their proper role as spokesmen for a united Irish nation. Others, like Standish O'Grady, saw the rediscovery of Gaelic culture as a similar means to a different end: by rediscovering their roots in Irish society, the Protestant gentry and intellectual elite could defend their religion, their social position, and the union against disaffected Catholic demagogues.[18]

It was only at the end of the nineteenth century that popular and Catholic, as opposed to elite and Protestant, nationalism acquired a significant cultural dimension. What was involved at this stage was very much an example of Hobsbawm and Ranger's celebrated 'invention of tradition'. When middle-class urban members of the Gaelic League defined their identity in terms of an idealized image of the Irish-speaking western seaboard, what took place was an act of imaginative appropriation as heroic as the enthusiasm with which, a century earlier, the descendants of the New English had embraced the idealized image of early Gaelic Ireland offered by Vallancey and Charlotte Brooke. The nationalist sporting culture of the Gaelic Athletic Association had a broader popular base; here too, though, what was involved was no simple revival of traditional pastimes. Both hurling and Gaelic football, as developed by the GAA, were essentially spectator sports of a new kind, exhibitions of skill laid on for the mass audiences made possible by the railway, the newspaper, and the spending power of an emerging consumer society.[19]

What then was the true basis of an Irish sense of separateness so deep as to make incorporation into a larger British state unacceptable? The main answer, although it was one that nationalists were generally reluctant to acknowledge explicitly, was religion. Catholic Emancipation—the right of Catholics to take seats in parliament and to hold certain high offices of state—was achieved in 1829. Yet to be a Catholic remained a significant disadvantage in terms both of access to public employment and of opportunity within large parts of the private sector. Religion, in consequence, played the part more commonly played by language in the development of nationalist politics: on the one hand as a badge of identity; on the other, as a frustrating check on the aspirations of those middle- and lower-middle-class groups, what Hobsbawm has called 'the lesser examination passing classes', that formed the backbone of nationalist movements everywhere.[20] Across the nineteenth century, the circle of opportunity open to Catholic talents widened steadily. Progress, however, consistently lagged behind Catholic aspirations, held back less by the prejudices of what proved to be remarkably pragmatic Victorian English statesmen than by the need to consider the impact of concessions on Ireland's other inhabitants. In this sense, as Vincent Comerford has argued, a wholly Catholic Ireland might in fact have been easier to accommodate within the United Kingdom than one that was one quarter Protestant.[21]

The link that was thus to develop between nationalist and specifically Catholic grievances was not immediately apparent. Opposition to the act of union during 1799–1800 had come overwhelmingly from sections of the Protestant population. Catholics, with a few exceptions such as the young Daniel O'Connell, had remained either indifferent or favourable. Fifteen of the thirty-five members returned in 1832 as members of O'Connell's Repeal party at Westminister were Protestants, as were thirty-five of the sixty-one who attended the launch of Isaac Butt's Home Government Association in 1870. But these apparently striking figures concealed some hard political realities. Opposition to the union during 1799–1800 had been a defence of an Irish parliament under exclusively Protestant control; for some, indeed, the argument had been that only such a body could be trusted to deal with the Catholic question. Already by the 1830s Catholic emancipation, electoral reform, and, most important of all, the mobilization of the Catholic electorate through the agency of their priests had between them ensured that any new Irish legislative body would have a very different composition. At this point it was still possible for those so minded to look to the influence of deference, and of continued Protestant social advantage, as a counterweight to Catholic numbers. But by the 1870s the age of deference was passing. The impressive level of initial Protestant interest in Butt's movement must be set against the speed with which this early support melted away once the movement began to acquire a mass base, and in doing so to attract the attention of members both of the Catholic clergy and of the IRB. Nationalist politics had clearly not wholly lost their appeal to Protestants. But that appeal was by now in inverse proportion to a movement's potential to achieve real political success.

A further powerful element in the body of nationalist political thinking that developed in the course of the nineteenth century was the conviction that the main explanation of Ireland's economic problems lay in the loss of political autonomy. The collapse in the mid-1820s of the wool and cotton manufactures that had seemed to herald Ireland's entry into the new world of large-scale, factory-based industry followed closely on the final removal, under the terms of the union, of protective tariffs on imports from Great Britain. Modern analysis suggests that continued protection would at best have postponed the collapse of small and uncompetitive local enterprises. To contemporaries it seemed otherwise: from O'Connell's Repealers in the 1830s and 1840s to the Home Rulers and Sinn Féin of the early twentieth century, it remained an article of nationalist faith that only self-government could reverse the country's long economic decline, and restore the prosperity it had enjoyed during the supposedly golden era between 1782 and 1800.

While nationalists of all shades of opinion shared a conviction of the malign economic impact of the union, however, they did not for the most part link the recovery of national self-determination with a specific programme of social reform. The obvious exception is the harnessing of agrarian protest to the cause of Home Rule achieved during 1879–82. But this was the product of a particular, and unrepeatable, phase in the development of rural Irish society. In pre-Famine Ireland, where a hard-pressed tenant farmer class confronted an even more desperate population of cottiers and labourers, land issues had been more likely to divide than to unite the potential supporters of a nationalist movement. By 1879–82, on the other hand, famine and emigration had drastically thinned out the ranks of the landless and land poor. Against this background of a much simplified rural social structure it became possible to make the latest round of agrarian conflict a national issue. The Catholic clergy, the urban middle and working classes, and the diminished ranks of the agricultural labourers could all unite in backing the cause of the tenant farmers against a small and isolated landlord class.

Even at this stage, however, the successful fusion of Home Rule movement and Land League depended on a central ambiguity. A rhetoric that traced the inequalities of the land system back to a history of conquest and unjustified confiscation recast the anti-landlord campaign as a struggle by the Irish people to recover lost ancestral rights. In practice, however, a settlement confined to controlling rents and preventing arbitrary evictions would benefit only the tenant farmer. The Land League slogan 'the land for the people' allowed urban radicals, along with the diminished but still significant underclass of smallholders and landless labourers, to believe that they were campaigning for a more radical restructuring of the rural social order. After the Land Acts of 1881 and 1885, however, and even more clearly after 1903, that illusion became more difficult to sustain. The United Irish League, Sinn Féin after 1917, and Fianna Fáil after 1926 were each for a time to reawaken the hopes of the landless and land poor. But the reality was that any further redistribution of land would be at the expense, not of a politically marginalized religious minority, but of large farmers and graziers who were for the most part both Catholic and nationalist.

If attempts to link nationalism and social revolution in the Irish countryside were doomed to failure, the same was even more clearly true of the towns and cities. Ireland's industrial proletariat was numerically small and economically weak. The final crisis of British rule, in 1919–21, saw a few exotic episodes, such as the short-lived Limerick Soviet of April 1919. Sinn Féin and IRA leaders welcomed the potential of industrial militancy to further undermine government authority, and were willing to offer vague assurances that political freedom would bring social change. But working-class protest that threatened the unity of the nationalist movement, or its accommodation with the Catholic Church, was quickly disowned and, where necessary, suppressed by force.

VI. Violence, Constitutionalism, and Ambiguity

The final step on the road to Rath Cross was the most dramatic. Between 1914 and 1918 the Home Rule movement that had dominated Irish politics for more than thirty years was displaced by a Sinn Féin whose goal was a wholly independent Irish republic, to be achieved, if necessary, by violence. The men who initiated the transition believed—or claimed to believe—that in doing so they reasserted an alternative tradition. 'Six times during the past three hundred years' Ireland had asserted its claim to nationhood in arms: so declared the proclamation that announced the Rising of 1916. If such an interpretation of the wars of 1641–52 and 1689–91 was a clear distortion, the presentation of the remaining two hundred years was only marginally more convincing. Fifty years separated the rebellion of 1798 from the feeble stand of the Young Irelanders at Ballingarry. The Fenian Rising of 1867 had somewhat greater credibility, but half a century more had passed since its suppression. In this perspective the Rising of 1916 can be seen less as the triumphant reassertion of an alternative strain of nationalism than as a last-ditch effort to breathe life into a fading revolutionary tradition.

As well as this somewhat tendentious narrative of past insurgency, the men of 1916 and their successors could draw on a rather more significant tradition of popular collective violence. This had been supplemented up to the 1870s, by the existence of the Ribbon societies, whose blend of social protest, sectarian solidarity and vague aspirations to an eventual war of national liberation continued the tradition of the Defenders. But the Ireland of the early twentieth century was a changing society: Ribbonism had by now disappeared, while from the 1880s murder and arson were displaced as the weapons of agrarian protest by the boycott, cattle driving, and other less violent forms of direct action. This change in methods, moreover, was only part of a broader shift in the incidence of violence. In the 1870s and 1880s Irish homicide rates stood at more than twice the level in England and Wales; by 1901–10 they were only 26 per cent higher. The state, too, had come to rely less on force to uphold its authority. In the years before the First World War the number of executions, in relation to population, was a quarter of what it had been in the 1840s, and marginally lower than in contemporary England and Wales.[22] If some military commanders continued to see themselves as guarding against potential internal subversion, others took it for granted that the primary role of army units stationed in Ireland, as elsewhere in the United Kingdom, was home defence.[23] In the case of the police, the transformation was more clear-cut: by the early twentieth century what had been a paramilitary constabulary had become a civilian police force largely integrated into local communities.[24] All this confirms the image of 1916 as a revolt less against British rule in Ireland than against the progressive normalization of Ireland's place within the United Kingdom—a process in which the granting of limited self-government might, in other circumstances, have been the final stage.

All this makes it difficult to account for the impact of the posthumous triumph of the men of 1916 in terms of a strong revolutionary tradition. An alternative explanation focuses instead on a mainstream nationalist mindset that was itself characterized by a markedly ambiguous approach to questions of both ends and means. The general lack of enthusiasm for revolutionary nationalism contrasts sharply with the retrospective glorification bestowed on its practitioners. In the 1840s, at the same time that the Young Irelanders were failing significantly to dent O'Connell's hold on the loyalty of the Catholic nation, the United Irishmen were being widely celebrated both in popular ballads and in the more literary work of R. R. Madden. The Fenians, after 1867, achieved a level of public support out of all proportion to what they had enjoyed before their defeat. Against this background the most successful nationalist leaders of the nineteenth century, O'Connell and Charles Stewart Parnell, were masters of the art of combining the rhetoric of militancy with a pragmatic commitment to the politics of the possible. Neither man, equally, cared to spell out too precisely the aims for which they mobilized their followers: O'Connell presented repeal as a restoration of Ireland's lost status as a self-governing kingdom, while being fully aware that any feasible modification of the union would involve some much more limited devolution of powers; Parnell famously declined to set a boundary to the march of a nation by specifying whether Home Rule was to be a final settlement of the Anglo-Irish relationship, or a step towards more complete separation.[25]

The post-Parnell parliamentarians continued, if with somewhat less flair, to cultivate the same political style. In 1898, less than a decade after they had abandoned their charismatic leader to save their party's alliance with the British Liberals, they shamelessly presided over of the centenary commemoration of the United Irish rebellion. It was precisely this comfortable ambivalence, however, that the self-imposed martyrdom of the 1916 leaders made it impossible to sustain. As with the Fenians after 1867, imprisoned and executed physical force nationalists disrupted the political world in a way that they had never succeeded in doing by their chosen method of armed struggle. The background of total war was likewise inimical to creative ambiguity. Whereas Home Rule had fudged the issue of how Irishness could be combined with incorporation into a British polity, the conscription issue raised in inescapably specific form the question of what demands that polity could legitimately make on its Irish subjects.

The virtual annihilation of the Home Rule party in the general election of 1918 is gen-erally seen as marking the triumph of revolutionary over constitutional nationalism. In fact ambiguity remained as important as ever. The loose coalition of elements that swept to power under the label of Sinn Féin appealed to the legitimacy conferred by the Easter Rising, but the strategy it held out to the electorate centred on the illusory potential for Ireland of the Paris peace conference rather than on any attempt at renewed insurrec-tion. That armed action did nevertheless become central was the decision of a militant minority, who were partly motivated by dismay at what they perceived as the beginnings of a regression to the compromises and half measures of political action. The efforts of this group to force the pace of political change were successful for a time. Between 1919 and the middle of 1921, as during the First World War, the nationalist majority, caught between the militants of the IRA and the increasingly indiscriminate violence of Crown forces, was forced to make clear-cut choices of the kind that its leaders had long excelled at evading. However, the revolutionary period was short-lived. The electoral triumph of 1918 must be set against the very different outcome four years later, when the largest sin-gle body of voters gave their support to candidates unconnected with either of the two wings of what was now a Sinn Féin divided over the Anglo-Irish treaty. In the civil war that followed, doctrinaire republicans conspicuously failed to mobilize mass support against the half-way house of dominion status within the British Empire. Instead that settlement was to be dismantled by another exercise in studied political ambiguity: a Fianna Fáil movement described by one of its own leaders, just four years before it took power, as 'a slightly constitutional party'.

VII. Nations and Nationalism

The origins of nationalism remain the subject of debate. One influential line of argu-ment looks back no further than the late eighteenth century. Nationalism, in this view, was the product of new concepts of legitimacy, according to which the inhabitants of a state—now citizens rather than subjects—should be joined both to it and to one another by something more than geographical or dynastic accident. There was also the need, in a mobile, increasingly urbanised society, to replace lost bonds of neighbourhood with the 'imagined community' of the nation, as well as the transport and communications revolution that made that act of imaginative identification possible. But this is to con-sider nationalism in its most highly developed form, as a universal doctrine presenting the nation as a political unit of a distinctive kind, with unique claims both to external recognition and to the allegiance of its inhabitants. An alternative analysis points to the evidence, from across a much longer period, that a sense of shared identity, based on language, culture, and historical memory, was capable of inspiring high levels of both solidarity and antagonism towards outsiders.[26]

An Irish case study reveals the strengths of both perspectives. On the one hand, the development of Irish nationalism as a fully fledged political ideology followed a pattern very much at odds with its own rhetoric. Its appeal was to a political and cultural tradition imagined as stretching backwards across the centuries. Its real origins lay, as elsewhere, in the era of the American and French revolutions. Its flowering as a mass movement came in the second half of the nineteenth century, in response to the new opportunities opened up by the mass circulation newspaper, the railway, and the electric telegraph. As in other cases, equally, the development of a nationalist tradition depended as much on what was forgotten as on what was remembered. Into this category came not just the separate world of the Old English of the seventeenth century and earlier, and the close relationship of Catholic Ireland with the house of Stuart, but also more recent aspects of Irish life, such as the long history of Irish service in the armies of the British Crown, up to and including the tens of thousands who responded to the call to arms in 1914 and the years that followed.

Alongside this emphasis on the modern origins of Irish nationalism, and its dependence on invention and selective amnesia, however, must be set an appreciation of its success in meeting the social needs out of which it grew. An analysis of the rise of the Home Rule movement, for example, must recognize how much its success owed to a background of agrarian crisis, and to the shameless sleight of hand by which Parnell linked the issues of land tenure and self-government. But it is also important to acknowledge the durability of the popular nationalist consensus thus created. Subsequent attempts by Conservative governments to reverse the process, by means of agrarian and other reforms designed to 'kill Home Rule with kindness', spectacularly failed to weaken the nationalist grip on the electorate. Across a longer period, the Irish experience provides useful clues to the reasons why nationalism was to prove so much more successful than other political ideologies in mobilizing large numbers across Europe and beyond. The elaborate constructs by which the Old English Geoffrey Keating, and later the patriot gentry of the eighteenth century, sought to appropriate an imagined Gaelic past with which their ancestry gave them no direct connection were not in either case an expression of nationalism in the modern sense. But they nevertheless displayed some of the features that were in a later age to make the nationalist narrative so compelling to so many: a past to which people could relate, a territory with which they could identify, and traditions in which they could take pride.[27] If Ireland provides an illustration of the constructed character of the nation, in other words, it also testifies to the seductive appeal which that imagined community has proven itself to possess.

Notes

1. Richard Mulcahy, Obituary of Richard Hayes, *Irish Sword*, 3 (1957–8), 210.
2. For a fuller discussion see S. J. Connolly, *Contested Island: Ireland 1460–1630* (Oxford, 2007), 10–51.
3. Hiram Morgan, 'Hugh O'Neill and the Nine Years War in Tudor Ireland', *Historical Journal*, 36 (1993).
4. Bernadette Cunningham, *The World of Geoffrey Keating: History, Myth and Religion in Seventeenth-Century Ireland* (Dublin, 2000).

5. Micheál Ó Siochrú, *Confederate Ireland 1642–1649: A Constitutional and Political Analysis* (Dublin, 1999), and Tadhg Ó hAnnracháin, *Catholic Reformation in Ireland: The Mission of Rinnuccini 1645–1649* (Cambridge, 2002).

6. T. C. Barnard, 'Planters and Policies in Cromwellian Ireland', *Past and Present*, 61 (1973).

7. A. T. Q. Stewart, 'The Harp New Strung: Nationalism, Culture and the United Irishmen', in Oliver MacDonagh and W. F. Mandle (eds), *Ireland and Irish Australia* (London, 1986).

8. Patrick Kelly, 'William Molyneux and the Spirit of Liberty in Eighteenth-Century Ireland', *Eighteenth-Century Ireland*, 3 (1988), 133–48.

9. J. G. Simms, *Colonial Nationalism 1698–1776* (Cork, 1976). For the origins of the term see David Hayton and Gerard O'Brien (eds), *War and Politics in Ireland 1649–1730* (London, 1986), xiii–iv.

10. D. G. Boyce, *Nationalism in Ireland* (London, 1982), 106–8.

11. J. Th. Leerssen, 'Anglo-Irish Patriotism in its European Context: Notes Towards a Reassessment', *Eighteenth-Century Ireland*, 3 (1988).

12. 'To the Whole People of Ireland', in Jonathan Swift, *Prose Works*, ed. Herbert Davis and others (Oxford, 1939–74), X, 67.

13. Norman Vance, 'Celts, Carthaginians and Constitutions: Anglo-Irish Literary Relations 1780–1820', *Irish Historical Studies*, 22 (1981).

14. E. J. Hobsbawm, *Nations and Nationalism since 1780: Programme, Myth, Reality* (Cambridge, 1990), ch. 2.

15. 'Memoir or Detailed Statement of the Origins and Progress of the Irish Union' (National Archives, Dublin, 620/44/1).

16. James Smyth, *The Men of No Property: Irish Radicals and Popular Politics in the Late Eighteenth Century* (London, 1992).

17. James H. Murphy, *Abject Loyalty: Nationalism and Monarchy in Ireland During the Reign of Queen Victoria* (Cork, 2001); Terence Denman, "The Red Livery of Shame": The Campaign against Army Recruitment in Ireland, 1899–1914', *Irish Historical Studies*, 29 (1994), 208–33.

18. David Cairns and Shaun Richards, *Writing Ireland: Colonialism, Nationalism and Culture* (Manchester, 1988), ch. 2.

19. W. F. Mandle, *The Gaelic Athletic Association and Irish Nationalist Politics 1884–1924* (Dublin, 1987); E. J. Hobsbawm and Terence Ranger (eds), *The Invention of Tradition* (Cambridge, 1983).

20. Hobsbawm, *Nations and Nationalism*, 117–18.

21. R. V. Comerford, 'Ireland 1850–1870: Post-Famine and Mid-Victorian', in W. E. Vaughan (ed), *New History of Ireland, vol. V: Ireland Under the Union, I: 1800–1870* (Oxford, 1989), 385–6.

22. S. J. Connolly, 'Unnatural Death in Four Nations: Contrasts and Comparisons', in S. J. Connolly (ed.), *Kingdoms United? Great Britain and Ireland since 1500* (Dublin, 1999).

23. Elizabeth Muenger, *The British Military Dilemma in Ireland: Occupation Politics 1886–1914* (Dublin, 1991), 121–4, 145–63.

24. W. J. Lowe and Elizabeth Malcolm, 'The Domestication of the Royal Irish Constabulary, 1836–1922', *Irish Economic and Social History*, 19 (1992), 27–48.

25. Oliver MacDonagh, 'Ambiguity in Nationalism: The Case of Ireland', in Ciaran Brady (ed.), *Interpreting Irish History: The Debate on Historical Revisionism* (Dublin, 1994).

26. Compare Hobsbawm, *Nations and Nationalism since 1780* and Benedict Anderson, *Imagined Communities: Reflections on the Origins and Spread of Nationalism* (rev. ed. London, 1991) with Adrian Hastings, *The Construction of Nationhood: Ethnicity, Religion*

and Nationalism (Cambridge, 1997) and A. D. Smith, *The Ethnic Origins of Nations* (Oxford, 1986).

27. For a useful discussion of the basis of nationalism's appeal, summed up in the terms community, struggle, and power, see Richard English, *Irish Freedom: The History of Nationalism in Ireland* (London, 2006), Introduction, ch. 7.

Select Bibliography

Comerford, R. V. *Inventing the Nation: Ireland* (London, 2003).

Jackson, Alvin. *Home Rule: An Irish History 1800–2000* (London, 2003).

Leerssen, J. Th. *Mere Irish and Fíor-Ghael: Studies in the Idea of Irish Nationality, its Development and Literary Expression Prior to the Nineteenth Century* (Cork, 1996).

McNally, Patrick. *Parties, Patriots and Undertakers: Parliamentary Politics in Early Hanoverian Ireland* (Dublin, 1997).

O'Halloran, Clare. *Golden Ages and Barbarous Nations: Antiquarian and Cultural Politics in Ireland c. 1750–1800* (Cork, 2004).

CHAPTER 3

....

LOYALISTS AND UNIONISTS

....

ALVIN JACKSON

I. Introduction

....

THE Union and Unionism became inescapable (if also deeply contested) features of
Irish politics and society in the nineteenth century. Ireland (like Scotland) was successfully infiltrated by the British state and British culture—and indeed, just as Scottish
historians commonly link the development of Scots national institutions in the nineteenth century to the condition and intrusiveness of the Union, so no assessment of
the revival or creation of Celtic political and cultural institutions in the late nineteenth
century is possible without an appreciation of the challenge posed by the Union to Irish
distinctiveness. In the constricted electoral circumstances of the nineteenth century,
where the practice of politics remained bound to the possession of property, Unionism
thrived. For much of the first three quarters of the century, Irish electoral politics were
dominated by parties, Whig and Tory, Conservative and Liberal, which were united
by a shared commitment to Union. Each of these traditions, but in particular the
Conservative, fed into the creation of an organized Unionist movement between 1884
and 1886. Drawing upon a formidable range of social, financial, and cultural resources,
this movement (though representing perhaps only 30 per cent of the Irish people) successfully delayed the implementation of any form of Home Rule until 1920–1; and it has
so far prevented the attainment of the historic nationalist goal of a united and autonomous Irish state congruent with the island.

II. Protestants, Patriots, and Loyalists

....

Irish Unionism was a confluence or a node: it was a religious, geographical, economic, and party political intermingling. Irish Unionism united different traditions of
Protestantism, drawing in particular upon proto-evangelical and loyalist subcultures

from the eighteenth century; but it also appealed for a time to a small minority of propertied Catholics, those who had been enfolded by schooling or profession within the Union and Empire, or whose economic standing depended on the stability of the British state. Irish Unionism was also, originally, an all-Ireland phenomenon, with perhaps 250 000 adherents outside the six counties of what would become Northern Ireland in 1920: a scattered and (allowing for the 'Big House' strain) predominantly urban, indeed metropolitan, and Anglican and propertied unionism characterized the south and west, while the North was simultaneously more industrial, more rural, and more Presbyterian in character.[1] Liberals and Conservatives, Presbyterians and Anglicans, once mutually antagonistic, came to cooperate in the context of the looming threat from Parnellite Home Rule.[2]

However, the rapidity of this unionist organization and coalescence in the mid-1880s was not simply a consequence of the enormity of the—Gladstonian and Parnellite—political threat, though it was certainly partly that. Unionism was created with speed and efficiency because it built upon existing institutions and ideologies and half-formed alliances. Much, therefore, of the framework for Unionist mobilization had been prefabricated in an earlier age. In particular, the success of Unionism in the mid-1880s rested upon the adaptability and strength of the Conservative tradition on the island, the focus of significant scholarly reappraisal.[3]

The 1790s were (as recent work affirms) critical years in terms of the formulation of the institutions and culture of Irish, as of Scots, loyalism. The 1830s were equally critical years in terms of the invention of modern Conservatism and unionism in Ireland, as in Scotland and the rest of the United Kingdom. In part, this reflected the need for fresh institutions to address the practical challenges of the new, reformed, British politics after 1829–32. Certainly in Ireland the imminent threat of reform stimulated the creation of the Irish Protestant Conservative Society (1831), designed to bolster local electoral registration and to raise funds through a 'Protestant rent' (an obvious borrowing from the earlier O'Connellite Catholic Association).[4] This was followed by the foundation of the Belfast Conservative Society in 1835 and, in 1836, of the Dublin Metropolitan Conservative Society, a body which had significant intellectual ballast in the form of Isaac Butt and other Dublin University heavyweights. But while the Metropolitan Society reflected some of the emphases and inclusivity of Robert Peel's new 'Conservatism' and of his Tamworth Manifesto, there were of course specifically Irish contexts and inflections.

The challenge of O'Connellite politics was critical, not just in terms of indirectly inspiring Conservative reorganization, but also through precipitating some more fundamental movement within Irish Protestant politics. Wider ideological shifts in Irish society from an emphasis on the 'ancient constitution' and 'limited kingship' and rights of conquest towards individual rights and liberties involved a supersession of traditional patriotism. J. R. Hill has made the case for understanding the national importance of patriotism within Dublin civic politics; and she has depicted a politics defined by support for the 'ancient constitution', constitutional balance, and Protestant libertarianism.[5] But this was, indeed, a politics characterized by Protestantism, and by the effective absence, through much of the eighteenth century, of any serious Catholic challenge: it was also the politics of the *ancien régime*—'aristocratic, corporatist and confessional'.[6] Irish patriots had always been intensely divided over the issue of political rights for Irish Catholics; and these divisions helped ultimately to propel some towards unionism.

These transitions towards unionism were facilitated by the evolving condition of Protestant spirituality in Ireland. Evangelicalism, with its emphases on personal salvation through faith, and on religious witness, had trickled into Irish Protestantism from England and from continental Europe in the mid eighteenth century; but it rapidly gained ground in Ireland in the first half of the nineteenth century.[7] The Revolution in France and O'Connell's 'velvet' revolution with Catholic emancipation stimulated this development of Irish evangelical Protestantism; for each, in their way, fundamentally challenged the existing political and religious order in Ireland. Thus, the 1820s saw the 'Second Reformation', an evangelical counter-attack on Catholic mobilization, designed to secure religious conversion and reawakening throughout Ireland, but particularly amongst the impoverished Catholic cottiers of Connacht.[8] This effective reinvention of Irish Protestantism, binding Anglicans and Presbyterians in a conservative theology, was occurring simultaneously with the reorganization of Conservatism as well as the first effective challenge—O'Connellite repeal—to the union settlement of 1801.

Evangelical religion was a useful cement through which Presbyterians would be bound to Conservatism: it was also an essential component of the leadership and culture of mid nineteenth century Irish Conservatism (and ultimately thereby of Irish Unionism). Belfast and Ulster, particularly the outer, or 'frontier' counties, were hotbeds of evangelical conviction; but even the South, and in particular Dublin, was not immune to its attractions. The extended Guinness family combined brewing, Conservatism, and evangelical religion in the nineteenth century: Sir Arthur Guinness (1768–1855), for example, was a contributor to the Waldensian church in Italy in the 1850s.[9] Setting aside great Victorian Tory clans such as the Abercorns, Downshires, and Londonderrys, the dominant figures in mid-century Conservatism, certainly bourgeois Conservatism, were a community of evangelical lawyers, Dublin University graduates, including Sir Joseph Napier (1804–82), James Whiteside (1804–76), and Hugh McCalmont Cairns (later first Earl Cairns) (1809–85).[10]

While intellectual leadership was provided by the evangelical and other Tories emanating from Trinity, recent work (linked to some of the concerns of Marxian scholarship in the 1970s) has also made the case for the contribution of a liberal conservative mercantile and professional community within Belfast in the first half of the nineteenth century. The focus of this included the wealthy Tennent and Emerson clans, with (for example) James Emerson Tennent, Conservative MP for Belfast and (later) Lisburn, a prolific author who identified with a range of 'advanced' causes, such as Greek nationalism.[11] The wider significance of this literate and outward-looking Conservatism may still be open to debate; but at the very least it represented a minor Britannic and metropolitan strain within the party, which was carried over (certainly in a vestigial manner) into Irish and Ulster unionism.

Aside from (or connected with) evangelicalism, the (still under-researched) Orange Order supplied an additional medium through which forms of Protestant association and solidarity could be built, and through which the different cultures of late eighteenth-century loyalism could be melded within nineteenth-century Unionism. Unionism ultimately drew strength from the forms of loyalism which were being defined in the era of the Revolutionary and Napoleonic Wars, of which the most important in Ireland was the Protestant loyalism that underpinned Orangeism.[12] Hereward Senior and David Miller have shown how Orangeism grew largely from Protestant combinations in south Ulster, with its nativity being dated to a fallout from a sectarian clash in North Armagh, the Battle of the Diamond, in September 1795. The Order functioned from the beginning as a binding agent within Irish Protestantism, amongst the Irish Protestant diaspora in Britain and North America, and between Irish Protestants and British sympathizers: Allan Blackstock has suggested that already by 1797 a militarized Orangeism had become the predominant (though certainly not the only) form of loyalist expression in Ireland.[13] Its numbers (about 100 000) are one measure of its significance, as was its kaleidoscopic popular culture (in particular Orange tracts, ballads, and poetry).[14]

III. TORIES AND WHIGS

Drawing on these different cultural strands, Irish Conservatism survived the challenge of Catholic mobilization, and indeed thrived. As with Scots Conservatism in Glasgow and the West, Irish Conservatism was well placed to channel popular urban reactions to Catholic growth and activism. However, Scots Conservative success in rural constituencies was much less marked than that achieved by their Irish counterparts, who had relatively strong roots in the landscape of the North of Ireland: Irish landlordism, and by extension Conservatism, benefited from a mild consolidation in the aftermath of the Great Famine. Both Scots and Irish Conservatives benefited, too, from an accession of Orange strength; but this was proportionately more significant for the Irish, who were also drawing upon a coalescent Protestantism (as opposed to the Scots, where the Kirk was, after the 'Great Disruption' of 1843, in a more than usually complete state of schism). Where Scottish Conservatism was overshadowed by the dominant Liberal tradition for much of the century, Irish Conservatives enjoyed consistent success, being the single largest party in Ireland at the general elections of 1835, 1841, and 1859; in 1859, boosted by Independent support, and by evangelical religious revival, they peaked with a majority of Irish seats (55 out of the 105 available).[15] Only in the context of a wider franchise and a more coherent Home Rule and farmer challenge did the Irish Conservative standing falter: these factors reduced the number of Conservative seats by roughly one half from their average in the 1832–85 era to between sixteen and twenty-two in the years between 1885 and 1918.

Like its Scottish counterpart, the Irish Conservative Party responded to the challenge of electoral reform through reorganization and relaunch, but the Irish were first in creating a national coordinating body: the Central Conservative Society of Ireland was founded in 1850, in the aftermath of the critical Irish Franchise Act.[16] The Central Conservative Society not only foreshadowed the creation of the Scottish National Union of Conservative Associations (in 1882), it also anticipated the emergence of a distinctive Irish Unionism in the mid 1880s: one of the Society's patrons, Joseph Napier, stressed 'the importance of having our Irish Party kept together', and indeed this was its principal purpose and achievement.[17] Specifically northern bodies were subsequently created in the shape of the Ulster Constitutional Union (1880) and the Ulster Constitutional Club (1883).[18]

Irish Conservatives shared a view of Union with their mid-century Scottish counterparts. Just as Scots Conservatives (and others) emphasized that the Union of 1707 was an international treaty, so, too, Irish Conservatives of the period defined the Union of 1801 in similar terms. In the 1850s and 1860s Irish Conservatives, highlighting their patriot ancestry, referred back to the ancient constitution and traditions of the kingdom of Ireland: in 1853 the Conservative *Dublin Daily Express* remarked that it had been forgotten that before the Union Ireland had been 'an ancient kingdom ... [with] her own army, her own treasury, her own fiscal arrangements, and peculiar system of taxation'.[19] Napier and Whiteside were keen advocates of the idea, familiar enough within mid-nineteenth-century Scottish political discourse, that the Union was a treaty and a contract, any aspect of which (if dishonoured) might bring the voiding of the whole.[20] The corollary of this deeply entrenched view was of course that Irish Conservatives, like their Scottish counterparts, reserved the right to revisit or even to reject the Union if it was altered by any British government.

All of these speculations were of course tied up with the question of the Church of Ireland establishment, which was coming to the fore in the 1860s, and which was a natural development of the tithe and church endowment questions of the 1830s, and the rise of a separatist nationalism. For both Ireland and Scotland, the rights and status of the national churches were effectively tied up with the Union establishment. In each country the question of disestablishment was linked, therefore, to the politics of Union. Indeed, the ferocious battle over the Irish Church in 1868–9 has been seen as a precursor to the Home Rule crisis, because disestablishment was an amendment of the terms of Union; and also because disestablishment brought to the fore individuals, attitudes and alliances, which would be soon redeployed, in 1885–6.[21]

The political confluence which created Irish Unionism in the mid-1880s also owed much to its Liberal tributary. Like its Scottish and wider British counterparts, Irish Liberalism had both Whig and radical strains, and a variegated ancestry: all looked back to a history of support for the 'Glorious Revolution' of 1688, limited monarchy, cautious reform, and parliamentary sovereignty. Whiggery was associated with Union, the Hanoverian succession, and the varieties of Protestantism: Scottish Whiggery was associated with an integrationist unionism, and with an idealized North Britain. Irish Whiggery in the eighteenth century was Protestant and patriotic, enlightened, aristocratic, and loyal.[22]

The Irish Whig tradition was sustained in the nineteenth-century parliament by landowning clans such as the Achesons (earls of Belmore), the Caulfeilds (earls of

Charlemont), Chichesters (marquesses of Donegall), Hills (marquesses of Downshire), and Saundersons. Most of these migrated to a unionist Liberalism, and thence to either Liberal Unionism or full-blooded Conservatism. But, in addition to this aristocratic and landed heritage within Whiggery, an urban variant of the tradition also thrived in Belfast. The capitalist class within early nineteenth-century Belfast was largely Whig, and rooted disproportionately in the textile industries.[23] The identification of Home Rule with moderate protectionism emphatically did not chime with the interests of this class, who often combined (in a characteristic mid-Victorian formulation) non-conformist, Liberal and free trade convictions. Of course, not all of these magnates were Presbyterian or Liberal: some enormously wealthy linen clans such as the Ewarts or Mulhollands were already, by the 1870s, Conservative, while Peter Gibbon has argued that the shipowners of the city were generally Conservative from the 1850s onwards.[24] But, even allowing for this drift towards Conservatism, there remained a significant tradition of free trade Liberalism within the Presbyterian (and Dissenting) business community.[25] Taking their lead from John Bright, this business elite carried their free trade convictions, and the commercial clout of their industry, into organized Unionism.

Landed and Belfast Whiggery were not the only forms of Liberal bequest to Unionism, however. If some landed Whigs were being swiftly compelled towards Conservatism and Unionism by the perceived pressure of popular Catholic activism, then other, more bourgeois and radical, forms of Irish Liberal initially identified different sources of political challenge. In addition, the aftermath of the Famine was characterized by a resurgence of landlordism, aided by a new class of incoming landlord, the actions of the land courts, and the ending of the old semi-feudal relationships binding landlord and tenant. Government legislation on the land question encouraged landlords to take a more legalistic view of their social and economic obligations, and this contributed to a cooling of agrarian relations even before the dramatic downturn of the later 1870s. By the 1860s there was a widespread suspicion that landlords were determined to destroy the customary rights of tenant farmers in the north of Ireland (the 'Ulster Custom').[26] This (in the event, temporary) landlord efflorescence fed into the electoral consolidation of Irish Conservatism, the party tradition which identified most unequivocally with the rights of Irish property.

This landed and Conservative growth provided a spur to Liberal party organization in Ireland, and also created an opportunity for electoral gain. On 4 August 1865 the Ulster Liberal Society was established (in the Royal Hotel, Belfast), to be followed by the Ulster Reform Club.[27] But, more important even than these organizational initiatives, was the realization that the otherwise formidable edifice of landed and Protestant Conservatism did not accommodate the needs of the influential farmer interest, particularly in Ulster. This permitted Irish Liberals to draw upon their traditions of radical agrarian reform—traditions most conspicuously represented by the radical landed MP for Dundalk (1835–7) and Rochdale (1842–52), William Sharman Crawford. The Liberals successfully underscored a commitment to tenant rights at the general elections of 1868 (when they won 66 out of the 103 seats) and 1874 (when their successful appeal to Ulster farmers staved off electoral annihilation by the Home Rulers).[28] The particular success of this appeal to Ulster farmers was highlighted by the fact that, outside the Northern province, their party performed abysmally in the elections of 1874 and 1880.[29] Even Ulster Liberalism stalled when (after the 1881 Land Act) Presbyterians feared once again that the Catholic threat to their consciences was greater than the threat posed by the Ascendancy to their livelihood: it stalled when Catholics found alternative (Home Rule) structures wherein they could lead themselves.

Irish Liberals were mostly shocked by Gladstone's conversion to Home Rule, for (in the words of Thomas MacKnight, editor of the *Northern Whig*), they looked upon 'any proposal to repeal the Act of Union, or to tamper with it, as not a Liberal policy at all, but retrogressive, dangerous, incredible and impossible.'[30] Gladstone, in other words, was challenging the fundamentals of Irish Liberal self-definition. On 30 April 1886, in the context of the introduction of the first Home Rule Bill, a large gathering of Liberals met in the Ulster Hall to declare their opposition; and shortly afterwards the Ulster Liberal Unionist Committee was formed, soon to be renamed the Ulster Liberal Unionist Association. The general election of July 1886 revealed a wholesale (and, in the event, lasting) electoral alliance between Irish Conservatives and Liberal Unionists.

The Liberal bequest to Unionism was complex, however; for it offered not only a small Catholic accession of strength, but also Whig legacies of patriotism, concern for property and aristocracy, cautious reformism, and support for the religious and political achievements of the 'Revolution' of 1688. In addition, Liberalism brought a radical strain, focusing on the immediate needs and aspirations of tenant farmers as well as (to a lesser extent) the living and working conditions of the urban working classes. There was certainly an unremitting danger that the unstable new alliance would cling to the lowest common (sectarian) denominators of the two traditions; there was also a very real danger that the effort of maintaining the alliance would emerge as a political end in itself. But, on the whole, while its legacy was certainly mixed, Liberalism brought to Unionism a breadth and social concern that might otherwise have been diminished or lacking.

IV. UNIONISTS

The organized Unionism of the Home Rule era drew upon these various strains within popular and high culture, within Irish Conservatism and Whiggery, and inherited many of their characteristics. Unionism combined the support of much of the industrial and landed capital on the island, and subsumed a popular Protestantism, bound by Orangeism, loyalism, and evangelical conviction. In addition, Unionism drew strength both from the consolidation and expansion of the British state, as well as from a tradition of Irish patriotism and anti-Catholicism. Unionism was simultaneously an expression of Enlightenment, economic ascendancy, and sectarian defensiveness.

Paradoxically, given the strength of the Conservative inheritance, and the formerly close relationship between British and Irish parties, a semi-autonomous Irish Unionist organization was precipitated in the context of British Tory 'betrayal' in 1884–5. The occasion of the apparent treachery was the parliamentary reform (1884) and constituency redistribution (1885) of those years; for, as Sir Stafford Northcote remarked (with some insouciance), the British Conservative leadership had 'forgotten Ulster' in the negotiations to establish the details of the third reform measure.[31] But, if British Tories 'forgot Ulster', then Ulster loyalists did not readily forget Tory 'betrayal', particularly in the context of the developing electoral challenge from Parnellite Home Rule. By January 1885 a semi-independent Irish Unionist Parliamentary Party (or 'Ulster Party') had emerged at Westminster, to be followed by local organizational initiatives such as the Loyal Irish Union and the Irish Loyal and Patriotic Union (each formed in August 1885).

This autonomy had its immediate roots in the politics of reform, but (as has been observed) there was also a longer history of Irish Conservative distinctiveness. One measure of the paradoxical and distinctive condition of Irish Unionist politics, was that, while Ireland and its Union conditioned some of the fundamental contours of British politics between 1885 and 1920, Irish Unionism remained largely separate and detached. For example, the challenge of Home Rule in 1886 and 1893 brought comprehensive Irish Unionist organizational activity, and the creation of (aside from the bodies already named) the Ulster Defence Union (1886), the Irish Unionist Alliance (1891), the Unionist Convention League (1892), and the Templetown Unionist Clubs movement (from 1893). The reality of internal, popular Unionist, dissent, and the renewed threat of devolution and Home Rule, brought a root-and-branch and localist reorganization of Ulster Unionism in 1904–5, in the shape of the Ulster Unionist Council. This in turn provided an essential platform for the distinctively particularist Ulster Unionist reaction against the third Home Rule Bill, in 1912–14.

The drift within Irish Unionist politics, unlike in Scotland, was towards a regional concentration and predominance (in Ulster). The explanations for this 'ulsterization' of Irish Unionism are manifold. Home Rule coincided with a major democratic thrust in British politics, with the achievement of the secret ballot (1872), the curtailment of corrupt electoral practices (1883), and the reform and redistribution measures of 1884–5: politics retained a vestigial aristocratic presence and exclusivity, but was more than ever about popular mobilization. In Ireland, given the sectarian and political demographics, popular Unionist mobilization could only be achieved in the North.

Moreover, while there were some urban concentrations, the fatal strength of southern Unionism lay in its disproportionate command over the landed classes. In fact, the strength of the South, even in the heyday of Union, rested with the landed classes and their financial, literary, and political influence over the island as a whole. They were not only wealthy, but also comparatively well-organized: they had their own, powerful lobbying organization, the Irish Landowners' Convention, dominated by old Ascendancy magnates such as the Beresfords, marquesses of Waterford.[32] The wealth of great landed clans fed into the representative organizations of southern Unionism (the Irish Loyal and Patriotic Union, the Irish Unionist Alliance), and from thence (in the 1880s and 1890s) into Ulster Unionist election campaigns.[33] Southern landlords were disproportionately well represented in the House of Lords and indeed in the House of Commons.[34] But land was, relatively, a declining asset in the late nineteenth century, and nowhere in

Europe at this time was the decline more precipitate than in Ireland, where the moral and legal title of the existing landlord class was subjected to a ferocious assault by the farming interest. Successive land legislation defined the tenants' title—their right to 'free sale', 'fair rent', and 'freedom from eviction'—and ultimately created the financial mechanisms by which they could buy their holdings outright. The incremental effect of this legislation was to consolidate farmers' legal rights at the expense of their landlords, to curtail landlord freedom to arbitrarily fix rent levels, and in the end to encourage landlords to sell up.

Complementing these economic and cultural developments, was the elaboration of a separate party structure in the North. Ulster Unionism was thoroughly reorganized in 1904–5, with the creation of an Ulster Unionist Council and (as in contemporary Scotland) the revitalization of local electoral machinery. By 1910–11 this local organizational machine, allied with a more middle-class leadership, was pushing Ulster Unionism not only towards a more particularist strategy, but also towards greater militancy. These thrusts were also encouraged by the condition of British politics, where a combination of Liberal electoral ascendancy and the cerebral but effete leadership supplied by Arthur Balfour to the Conservatives, meant that Ulster Unionists appeared to be increasingly dependent on their own local political resources. This was confirmed by the passage of the Liberals' Parliament Act in 1911, when one of the key obstacles to Home Rule—the House of Lords' veto—was converted into a mere suspensory power. Already by 1910 Unionists were importing small quantities of weapons into Ulster and adopting military formations: after 1911 this militarization accelerated towards civil conflagration.

The outlines of Ulster Unionist militancy in 1912–14 are familiar enough, though the central interpretative problems posed by this militancy still remain contentious: were the Unionists serious in their apparent determination to go to war, could they have been successful in resisting the might of a British state intent on enforcing Home Rule, and to what extent were leading Conservatives implicated in Ulster Unionist illegality? The creation of the Ulster Volunteer Force during the winter of 1912–13 certainly created a strong military capacity, for (at its peak, in 1914) perhaps 90,000 to 100,000 oath-bound Ulster Unionists were recruited within its ranks. There were several importations of weapons, undertaken with the cooperation of leading Conservative politicians, and culminating in the Larne gunrunning of 24–25 April 1914, when perhaps 25,000 rifles were landed: this was achieved, with the foreknowledge of the Conservative front bencher and leadership candidate, Walter Long, and probably (as my own research suggests) with that of the leader himself, Andrew Bonar Law.[35]

The strength of Ulster Unionist militancy lay, not only in its support within the Conservative elite, and in areas of traditional sympathy (such as the West of Scotland), but also more generally within popular British Conservatism. British organizations such as the Union Defence League (1907) or the British League for the Support of Ulster (1913) focused money and support for the Ulster militants: the UDL seems to have been the key conduit through which cash for the gunrunners was channelled. The British League was certainly the means by which the British Covenant of Support for Ulster was organized: this document, based on the Ulster Solemn League and Covenant of September 1912, was launched in March 1913 by an array of British luminaries. Dan Jackson's work on the Unionist campaign tours of 1912–14, from Liverpool (September 1912) to Hyde Park (April 1914), has dissected the elaborate rhetoric and organization of these events, with their skilful use of large public buildings, arc-light technology, scarcely concealed sectarian appeals, and manipulation of the press.[36]

The achievement of Unionists in 1912–14 was not so much that they created a paramilitary threat; it was rather that they succeeded in commodifying their political case, so that (by the summer of 1914) the images and messages of their militancy were virtually inescapable throughout British and Irish society. Despite this omnipresence, however, they did not wholly succeed in thwarting the passage of Home Rule onto the statute books of the British parliament—for this was achieved in September 1914. Nor did these militants create the partition issue, since this had been privately mooted within British high politics from the moment that Home Rule was accepted by part of the British political elite. All that had been established, by the summer of 1914, was that Asquith's Liberal government, in company with reluctant Irish Nationalists, had accepted that some form of exclusion from Home Rule might be granted, at least temporarily, to some of the counties of the North. It would take the real militancy and bloodshed of the Western Front, as opposed to the virtual wars of the Ulster countryside, to translate this acceptance into something approaching practical politics.

With both Scotland and Ireland, the First World War acted to reinforce national identities, though in the Scots' case national sentiment remained largely curtailed within the frameworks of Union and of cultural politics. In Ireland, the experience of war appears to have radicalized and trained a generation of separatists who subsequently served with the IRA in the War of Independence and the Civil War. In the north of Ireland, mass participation in the Great War coincided with, and advanced, a stronger Unionist sense of Ulster's distinctiveness. This was partly the point of the mythology surrounding the actions of the main Unionist fighting force on the Western Front, the 36th Ulster Division: on 1 July 1916, at the start of the epically bloody Somme offensive, (following the official narrative by Cyril Falls) the Division successfully stormed the German Front Line, where (with over 5,000 casualties sustained) they were stranded in a maelstrom of killing owing to the failure of other British units and of the high command.[37] In essence, the Somme offensive served as a metaphor for the wider Ulster Unionist condition and self-perception: in this reading the Ulstermen had done their duty, but in the end had fought and died on their own. This narrative of the war was woven into the wider history of Ulster Unionist struggle and political identity; and these were phenomena which were taking on an increasingly particularist hue.

The idea of separating out the counties of the north with the greatest concentrations of Protestant and Unionist population had been publicly mooted from June 1912 and by 1914 the principle of exclusion had begun to achieve a form of consensus, although deep disagreements remained over the physical and temporal extent of any practical scheme. In March 1914 it was fleetingly proposed that the six north-eastern counties of Ulster should be excluded temporarily but *en bloc*; and this idea was resurrected in the aftermath of the Easter Rising, in May 1916, when it briefly (but deceivingly) appeared to have won the agreement of both Unionists and Nationalists. The notion of six-county partition reappeared in 1919–20, however, when it was given a federalist inflection; and it was thus a two-parliament, two-polity Ireland which emerged in the legislative cladding supplied by the Government of Ireland Act. The celebrants of 'Ulster' had won a form of homeland, even if the newly minted 'Northern Ireland' did not do justice to the intensity of their historical and political vision. Moreover, 'Ulster' came at a cost: over half a million dissatisfied and vulnerable Nationalists were trapped within the new Unionist polity, while Ulster Unionism had effectively cast off one third of its provincial identity (three Ulster counties were excluded from 'Northern Ireland'), as well as the whole of 'southern' Unionism.

Unionism was now reduced to a north-eastern, and preeminently bourgeois, core, with the complex cultures of southern landed and academic Unionism largely dismissed and isolated. The plantation creed—the celebration of the achievement and travails of the Ulster colonists—now became the inadequate governing ideology of Northern Ireland, rather than a balancing counterpoint to the motifs of Catholic Gaeldom and Irish Irelandism. In sum, just as it was once said of the Scottish National Party in government at Holyrood that they 'don't believe they're a government. They are a campaign', Unionists had difficulty making the same leap in faith and belief in 1921.[38]

V. 'NORTHERN' IRISH

How, and with what success, did Ulster Unionism contribute to the survival of the Union after 1920? The most important aspect of this challenge involves revisiting Unionism's comprehensive failure regarding the Catholic and Nationalist population of Northern Ireland. In Scotland, the Labour Party came to function as a conduit through which Catholics of Irish descent, particularly in the West, were tacitly recruited to the politics of the Union. Scottish Conservatism and Unionism retained connections with the Orange Order, but also embraced a tame Jacobitism and patriotism which were evidently accessible to some Scots Catholics. The Ulster Unionist government of Northern Ireland exercised none of this appeal, and (while it would be wrong to make assumptions about the negotiability of identity) it never really sought to do so. It defined itself (despite the size and influence of the northern Catholic minority) as the Protestant complement to what it saw as the Catholic and Gaelic Irish state, centred on Dublin; and (as a later Ulster Unionist leader, David Trimble, would famously concede), 'Ulster Unionists... built a solid house, but it was a cold house for Catholics'.[39]

Both Ulster Unionism and Irish Nationalism were in fact partly ethnic mobilizations, originally based upon (at the very least) radically different readings of Irishness, and different cultural and religious emphases.[40] The two Irish polities created in 1921–2, the Irish Free State and Northern Ireland, were born out of civil war; and, particularly in the northern case, the civil war had strong ethnic overtones, given that (certainly after

1922) the Crown forces were primarily Protestant and Unionist, and the republican insurgents primarily Catholic. The association of Protestantism and Unionism with the new northern state was therefore inescapable; and this was reinforced both by the ongoing institutional connection between Unionism and the exclusively Protestant Orange Order and by the half-hearted elaboration of an 'Ulster' political identity in the 1920s and 1930s, accessible only to Protestants and partitionists.[41] Ulster Unionists saw a disjunction between Catholic and state interests (again, in Trimble's assessment, 'although they [Northern Nationalists] had a roof over their heads, they seemed to us as if they meant to burn the house down').[42] But these political perceptions were formed, and thrived, in a state where Catholics (and, broadly, Nationalists) were one third of the population, and growing in strength.

One expression of this ethnic mobilization rests upon the abiding concern within the Ulster Unionist party for solidarity, and its relative success in this respect until the early 1970s. The precarious nature of the Unionist majority in many areas of Northern Ireland, combined with a heritage of division in the Edwardian era over denominational, class and land questions, meant that successive Unionist leaders were willing to sacrifice any ecumenical gesture to the exigencies of political unity. The movement's leaders did not make any serious effort to accommodate Catholic opinion (at least until the late 1960s, when popular Catholic mobilization was in full spate): but they did, however, continually fret about striking a balance between maintaining civilized relations with Westminster and responding to the fissiparous and sometimes angrily defensive nature of their political base.[43] These expectations focused on a wide range of issues, including employment and housing, and also the educational and health reforms of the Attlee government; but from the 1940s onwards one key emphasis was upon the right to parade through areas where the local nationalist population had become, or always had been, hostile to perceived Orange triumphalism.[44] It is striking that when (after 1968) massive civil unrest forced Westminster to attend to the problems of Northern Ireland, the Ulster Unionist party was speedily compelled to strike a new balance between local and metropolitan pressures, and to resist 'ethnic autism': in 1971 this brought the fracturing of the Party, and the creation of Ian Paisley's Democratic Unionists.

It was not just that the Unionists were culpably introspective, however: political violence for long negated the likelihood of political accommodation. The IRA's bloody effort to overturn the Northern Irish state in 1921–2 was complemented by violence pursued by the Crown forces and loyalist terror gangs against Northern Catholics. The apparently unflagging tradition of republican insurgency (represented by campaigns conducted during the Second World War and between 1956 and 1962) also tended to heighten Ulster Unionist defensiveness and reaction. The bloody complexities of this violence were also distilled into particular episodes, or martyr cults, or (indeed, in some cases) mythologies. Anti-Catholic violence in the early 1920s was grimly epitomized by the murder of the McMahon Family in March 1922 apparently by the Crown forces; anti-Protestant or anti-Unionist violence in the same era was symbolized by the murders at Altnaveigh, County Down, in June 1922, orchestrated apparently at the hands of the leading republican and future Irish minister, Frank Aiken.[45] Nationalists accused

Unionists of engaging in pogroms; Unionists accused Nationalists of (in effect) ethnic cleansing. Nationalists sought to identify Unionism with fascism; Unionists recoiled from what they saw as republicanism's entanglement with National Socialism.

Northern Ireland's depressed industrial economy also tended to precipitate and heighten sectarian competition. This rendered the Unionist state politically vulnerable, both in terms of its relationship with Britain (which held the purse-strings, certainly in the inter-war years) as well as in terms of social unrest (evident in particular in the context of the depression of the early 1930s). The slow failure of key Northern industries such as textiles and shipbuilding, the absence of those 'new' and compensating industries which restored economic life to the midlands and south of England, had a variety of critical political dimensions. First, these failures represented the retreat of those local capitalists who had created Belfast industry (and Belfast Unionism) in the mid- and late nineteenth century: shipbuilding and linen manufacturing dynasties originally critical to both commerce and Unionism were now superseded (just as the great Unionist land-owning clans had been partly overturned by falling land values, land agitation, and legislation in the early twentieth century). But the failure of the traditional industries put increasing pressure on public employment, particularly within the area of local government, as well as on the dispensation of various forms of welfare entitlement, including public housing. Unionism's control of the state, allied with its relative political insecurity through much of Northern Ireland, led to electoral abuse and religious or political discrimination particularly in the fields of employment and housing. Indeed, there is some evidence to suggest that these abuses became worse, or at any rate more pressing, in the post-war era (just as the growth of the British state in late nineteenth-century Ireland had brought sectarian resentments and rivalries into sharper relief).

The continuing ethnic imperatives of Ulster Unionism owed much to the cultural significance of the 'frontier' within the mentality and structure of the movement. The 'frontier', in southern Ulster, between predominantly Protestant and predominantly Catholic Ireland, had produced networks of embattled landlords as well as popular sectarian bonding which had, in turn, fed significantly into organized Unionism in the mid-1880s. The vulnerability of border Unionists after 1921 emerges in recent scholarship more thoroughly than ever as a key determinant of the direction of wider Unionist strategy.[46] Their position, for example, was a vital consideration in the Unionist party's failure to reform the local government franchise after the Second World War, and to bring it into line with both the parliamentary franchise and British local government practice (as established in 1948). Extending the local government vote beyond the community of ratepayers would have weakened Unionism's already tenuous hold on local government authorities west of the Bann, and transferred control over to Nationalists. The price of appeasing border Unionists' fears and defensiveness was high: Nationalists were effectively robbed of votes and local government control (and patronage) in the west of Ulster, while in the east 'tens of thousands of working-class Protestants, including many members of the Unionist party' were also unenfranchised.[47]

Linked with all this was the wider paradox that one of Ulster Unionism's key problems arose from the devolved parliament, the institution which apparently defined its success. Created in 1921, the Northern Ireland parliament and government became the central institutions of Ulster Unionist power within the partition state, responsible for administering the limited authority which Westminster had ceded through the Government of Ireland Act. Stormont became an emblem of despair for Northern Nationalists; but it also proved, at best, a very mixed blessing even for those who were supposed to be the beneficiaries. Unionists, representing a community of less than one million people, alongside their Northern Nationalist compatriots, thinly distributed their available political talent from the lowest reaches of local government—the local and district councils—through the two chambers of the local parliament, and its executive, to the Houses of Parliament at Westminster. In practice, the available talent (such as it was) tended to concentrate within Stormont, where ministerial office and other perquisites were not only relatively accessible (for Unionists), but also relatively well rewarded.[48] The relatively small base of the Party, and its cliquish and nepotistic operations, had a reflection in the often poor calibre of leadership.

In practice, too, Stormont did not function as a multi-party democratic forum, but rather as a one-party political assembly, elected after 1929 on a winner-takes-all basis (Marc Mulholland has made the point that Unionist control of the parliament was so strong that gerrymandering or other malpractice was superfluous at this level); so the parliament not only stretched and diverted Unionist political resources, it also institutionalized the relative powerlessness of Nationalists, and enflamed a sense of political suppression which exploded in the mid-1960s through movements such as the Campaign for Social Justice and the Northern Ireland Civil Rights' Association.[49] Stormont effectively liberated Westminster from the compromises, diversions, and entanglements of Ulster politics; while it also purged the 'Imperial Parliament' of a strong and effective Unionist presence. For much of the half-century of its existence, Stormont served the short-term and local purposes of a Unionist elite; but the price of this parliamentary gravy train was the derailing of the Union (and the decoupling of Unionists) from British politics.

There have been other structural anomalies or difficulties within Ulster Unionism. After the Second World War the number of party members was relatively restricted: as with the Orange Order, so with the Unionist Party, scholars are arguing that the number of members was generally much lower than once thought.[50] They now depict a party which was organizationally weak in Belfast and in much of eastern Ulster, but which (like the Orange Order) was relatively better organized in the west and south of the Province (hence, partly, the disproportionate influence exercised by these areas in the Party's policies): related to its weakness in Belfast was the fact that the party was losing its working-class membership in the post-war period.[51] A further long-term challenge rested with the Party organization, which had been designed in 1905 to translate power from an overweening parliamentary party and to distribute it among the growing number of 'stake-holders' in the Edwardian Unionist movement. This inevitably made for party democracy and inclusivity, but hampered decisive or dynamic leadership. The Party's constitution was a particular problem for reforming leaders from the 1960s onwards, such as Terence O'Neill, Brian Faulkner, and David Trimble; but it also (ironically) made the task of competing with the more centralized and hierarchical Democratic Unionist Party relatively difficult.[52]

Yet, accepting the significance of all of these structural limitations and failures, Ulster Unionism has still helped to preserve an embattled and contested form of Union between 1921 and the present day. Ulster Unionism, though constrained both structurally as well as ideologically, has continued to draw upon other complex social and cultural resources. Many of the institutions which bolstered late-nineteenth-century Unionism survived and thrived well into the era of partition: the Orange Order, for example, has served as an important binding agent, particularly in the south and west of Ulster, although scholars have noted a falling off both in the numbers and social standing of the membership through the last thirty years of the twentieth century (membership of the Order being incompatible with new forms of mobility and sociability).[53] Work by Diane Urquhart and Rachel Ward, among others, indicates the rich variety of institutions which existed to incorporate women within organized Unionism.[54] The children's organizations which were created in the late Victorian and Edwardian eras (the Boys' Brigade, the Church Lads' Brigade, and the Boy Scouts), and which served effectively as adjuncts to Unionism, survived through the twentieth century.[55]

Linked with this is the suggestion that Unionism and Orangeism may have recently taken an intellectual 'turn' of sorts. Here the two critical epiphanies were supplied by the Anglo-Irish Agreement of 1985 and the disputed Orange marches at Drumcree, County Armagh, between 1995 and 1998. The apparent failure of a rejectionist strategy both before and certainly after the Agreement of 1985 was a setback for traditional constitutional Unionist strategies; and it created space for some alternative visions of Unionism and loyalism. Some of these were supplied by the loyalist paramilitaries, who embarked upon a bloody offensive in the late 1980s and early 1990s; but there was also a significant cultural turn within the movements from the mid-1980s onwards. Trimble, then a law lecturer at Queen's University, was a major influence, particularly in terms of the Ulster Society ('for the promotion of Ulster-British heritage and culture'), founded in June 1985, just before the publication of the Anglo-Irish Agreement. In a sense, the period witnessed the birth not just of the 'new' Unionism, but of an intellectually engaged Unionism, as evidenced by the 'higher number of young graduates who were prominent in writing for Unionist publications and working for Unionist politicians'.[56]

There was also, however, a darker, and militant, side to Unionism's ongoing defence of the Union. Ulster Unionists and British Conservatives had helped to bring the United Kingdom close to civil war in 1912–14, and stalled the promulgation of Home Rule in what has been called a 'coup d'état'.[57] The Ulster Volunteer Force was recreated in 1919, and seems to have underpinned a variety of loyalist vigilante and terror groups (such as the 'Imperial Guards') in the blood-strewn Belfast of the early 1920s: here the IRA faced both the forces of the Crown as well as loyalist paramilitarism, though sometimes the distinction was hard to perceive.[58] In the later twentieth century Unionist paramilitarism tended to benefit less from the sponsorship of constitutional Unionism (though there were some exceptions) than from its confusion and defeat: the brand-name 'UVF' was reinvented in loyalist West Belfast in 1966 against the background of the first cracks within mainstream Unionism; and an explosion of paramilitarism accompanied the retreat and meltdown within constitutional Unionism in the early 1970s, culminating in the creation of the Ulster Defence Association (UDA) and the associated Ulster Freedom Fighters in 1971. Paramilitarism thrived in the context of constitutional Unionism's discomfiture or failure: the UVF and UDA contributed to the Ulster Workers' Strike of May 1974, which brought down the Sunningdale Agreement and the related power-sharing Northern Ireland Executive, headed by Brian Faulkner. The humiliating failure of constitutional Unionism in 1985, over the Anglo-Irish Agreement, led to a reinvigoration of the memory of militant resistance to the third Home Rule Bill within Unionist culture; and there was an accompanying explosion of loyalist paramilitarism and an effort (mimicking the Larne gunrunning of April 1914) to smuggle weapons into Northern Ireland in 1987.[59] The attempt to recapture the spirit and strategies of 1914 was underlined by the association of some leading Unionist politicians with a new militant organization, Ulster Resistance, and with some of the older loyalist paramilitary bodies within Northern Ireland. The prelude to the first paramilitary ceasefires of 1994 was characterized by a furious bloodletting which saw loyalist paramilitaries kill more people than their republican enemies for the first time in the history of the 'Long War'.

If the vestigial union of the twenty-first century owes something to the intellectual reinvention of constitutional Unionism in the 1990s and after, then it also rests partly on the peace of exhaustion. If Ulster Unionism at the beginning of the twenty-first century was about Trimbleite intellectualism, or Paisleyite religious fundamentalism, then it was also about the bling culture and bloody machismo of loyalist paramilitarism and clubland.[60]

NOTES

1. An expanded version of the arguments in this chapter may be found in Alvin Jackson, *Two Unions: Ireland, Scotland and the Survival of the United Kingdom, 1707–2007* (Oxford, 2011), 281–333. A starting point for any discussion of Irish Unionism remains Patrick Buckland's *Irish Unionism I: The Anglo-Irish and the New Ireland, 1885–1922* (Dublin, 1972) and his *Ulster Unionism and the Origins of Northern Ireland, 1886–1922* (Dublin, 1973). A key starting point for any discussion of the origins of British Unionism is Douglas Kanter, *The Making of British Unionism, 1740–1848: Politics, Government and the Anglo-Irish Constitutional Relationship* (Dublin, 2009). The best work on early Irish loyalism is now Allan Blackstock, *Loyalism in Ireland, 1789–1829* (London, 2007). James Kelly's work on early Unionism and loyalism is also important: see (for example) his *Sir Richard Musgrave: Ultra-Protestant Ideologue* (Dublin, 2009).

2. Alvin Jackson, *The Ulster Party: Irish Unionists in the House of Commons, 1884–1911* (Oxford, 1989), 214–16.

3. Important work on mid-nineteenth-century Irish Conservatism includes K. T. Hoppen, *Elections, Politics and Society in Ireland, 1832–1885* (Oxford, 1984) and Andrew Shields, *The Irish Conservative Party, 1852–68: Land, Politics and Religion* (Dublin, 2006).

4. Hoppen, Elections, 280; Ian D'Alton, *Protestant Society and Politics in Cork, 1812–44* (Cork, 1980), 226–7.

5. Jacqueline Hill, *From Patriots to Unionists: Dublin Civic Politics and Irish Protestant Patriotism, 1660–1840* (Oxford, 1997), 385.

6. Ibid.

7. The starting point for discussion of the history of evangelical Protestantism in Ireland remains David Hempton and Myrtle Hill, *Evangelical Protestantism in Ulster Society, 1740–1890* (London, 1992).

8. For the 'Second Reformation' see Desmond Bowen, *The Protestant Crusade in Ireland, 1800–1870: A Study of Protestant-Catholic Relations between the Act of Union and Disestablishment* (Dublin, 1978); Irene Whelan, *The Bible War in Ireland: The 'Second Reformation' and the Polarisation of Protestant-Catholic Relations, 1800–40* (Chicago, 2005).

9. Danilo Raponi, *British Protestants, the Roman Question, and the Formation of Italian National Identity, 1861–75* (University of Cambridge PhD thesis, 2009), 92.

10. See Anon [Catherine Marsh], *Brief Memories of Hugh McCalmont, First Earl Cairns* (London, 1885); A. C. Ewald, *The Life of Sir Joseph Napier, Bart., Ex-Lord Chancellor of Ireland, From His Correspondence* (London, 1887); James Whiteside, *Essays and Lectures: Historical and Literary* (Dublin, 1868); James Whiteside, *Early Sketches of Eminent Persons* (Dublin, 1870).

11. See John Bew, *The Glory of being Britons: Civic Unionism in Nineteenth Century Belfast* (Dublin, 2008).

12. See the arguments of Blackstock, *Loyalism*. See also the classic account of early Orangeism in Hereward Senior, *Orangeism in Ireland and Britain, 1795–1836* (London, 1966).

13. Blackstock, *Loyalism*, 129.

14. Ibid., 270–1. D. W. Miller, 'The Armagh Troubles, 1784–1795,' in James Donnelly and Sam Clark (eds), *Irish Peasants: Violence and Political Unrest, 1780–1914*, (Madison, 1983), 155–91 and D. W. Miller, 'The Origins of the Orange Order in County Armagh' in A. J. Hughes and William Nolan (eds), *Armagh: History and Society* (Dublin, 2001), 563–608.

15. Ian Hutchison, *Political History of Scotland, 1832–1924: Parties, Elections and Issues* (Edinburgh, 1986), 59.

16. Hoppen, *Elections*, 284.

17. Ibid., 284–5.

18. Ibid., 286.

19. Quoted in Shields, *Irish Conservative Party*, 163, 211.

20. Whiteside (ed.), *Essays and Lectures*, 2–206.

21. D. C. Savage, 'The Irish Unionists, 1867–86', *Éire-Ireland*, 2 (1967). Recent work on the political resonance of the disestablishment debate includes James Golden, 'Protestantism and Public Life: The Church of Ireland, Disestablishment and Home Rule, 1868–74', D.Phil. thesis (Oxford University, 2011).

22. For Irish, particularly northern, Liberalism, see for example Gerald R. Hall, *Ulster Liberalism, 1778–1876* (Dublin, 2011); Frank Thompson, *The End of Liberal Ulster: Land Agitation and Land Reform, 1868–86* (Belfast, 2001). See also Brian M. Walker, *Ulster Politics: The Formative Years, 1868–86* (Belfast, 1989); and Frank Wright, *Two Lands on One Soil: Ulster Politics before Home Rule* (Dublin, 1996).

23. Peter Gibbon, *The Origins of Ulster Unionism: The Formation of Popular Protestant Politics and Ideology in Nineteenth Century Ireland* (Manchester, 1975), 105. For other important contributions to the political and religious history of nineteenth century Belfast see Catherine Hirst, *Religion, Politics and Violence in Nineteenth Century Belfast* (Dublin, 2002).

24. Gibbon, *Origins*, 106.

25. Ibid., 106.

26. Thompson, *Liberal Ulster*, 302.

27. Hoppen, *Elections*, 270.

28. Thompson, *Liberal Ulster*, 5 and chapter six; Walker, *Ulster Politics*, 116.

29. Hoppen, *Elections*, 274.

30. Thomas MacKnight, *Ulster as It is,* two vols (London, 1896), i, 170.

31. Jackson, *Ulster Party*, 25ff. For Lord Randolph Churchill's prolonged flirtation with Parnellism, see R. F. Foster, *Lord Randolph Churchill: A Political Life* (Oxford, 1981), 226.

32. See Adam Pole, 'Landlord Responses to the Irish Land War, 1879–82', PhD thesis (Trinity College Dublin, 2006). There is a growing literature on Irish landlordism at the end of the nineteenth century: see Terence Dooley, *The Decline of the Big House in Ireland* (Dublin, 2001); Devon McHugh, 'Family, Leisure and the Arts: Aspects of the Culture of the Aristocracy in Ulster, 1870–1925', Ph.D. thesis (University of Edinburgh, 2011); Olwen Purdue, *The Big House in the North of Ireland: Land, Power and Social Elites, 1868–1960* (Dublin, 2009).

33. See Jackson, *Ulster Party*, 198–211.

34. Buckland, *Anglo-Irish*; Jackson, *Ulster Party*.

35. Alvin Jackson, *Home Rule: An Irish History, 1800–2000*, paperback edition (London, 2004), 154–5. For a recent authoritative account of the UVF see Timothy Bowman, *Carson's Army: The Ulster Volunteer Force, 1910–22* (Manchester, 2008). See also Alan Parkinson, *Friends in High Places: Ulster Resistance to Irish Home Rule, 1912–14* (Belfast, 2012); and A. T. Q. Stewart's classic, *The Ulster Crisis* (London, 1967).

36. Daniel Jackson, *Popular Opposition to Irish Home Rule in Edwardian Britain* (Liverpool, 2009).

37. See Cyril Falls, *The History of the Thirty Sixth (Ulster) Division* (Belfast, 1922), 57, 61–2.

38. *Scotland on Sunday*, 1 February 2009.

39. Dean Godson, *Himself Alone: David Trimble and the Ordeal of Unionism*, paperback edition (London, 2004), 402. For wider accounts of Ulster Unionism after 1920, see Paul Bew, Peter Gibbon, and Henry Patterson, *Northern Ireland 1921–94: Political Forces and Social Classes* (London, 1995); Patrick Buckland, *The Factory of Grievances: Devolved Government in Northern Ireland, 1921–39* (Dublin, 1979) and the accounts in the general histories of Ulster Unionism by John Harbinson, *The Ulster Unionist Party, 1882–1873: Its Development and Organisation* (Belfast, 1973), Henry Patterson and Eric Kaufmann, *Unionism and Orangeism in Northern Ireland since 1945* (Manchester, 2007) and Graham Walker, *A History of the Ulster Unionist Party: Protest, Pragmatism and Pessimism* (Manchester, 2004).

40. For a recent defence of this position, see, for example, James Loughlin, 'Politics and Society, 1800–1960' in Liam Kennedy and Philip Ollerenshaw, *Ulster since 1800: Politics, Economy, Society* (Oxford, 2013), 238.

41. The best starting point for the political culture of Unionism is Gillian V. McIntosh, *The Force of Culture: Unionist Identities in Twentieth Century Ireland* (Cork 1999).

42. Godson, *Trimble*, 402.

43. Patterson and Kaufmann, *Unionism*, 15.

44. See Henry Patterson, 'Party versus Order: Ulster Unionism and the Flags and Emblems Act', *Contemporary British History*, 13, 4 (1999).

45. Timothy Wilson, '"The most terrible assassination that has yet stained the name of Belfast": The McMahon Murders in Context', *Irish Historical Studies*, xxxvii, 145 (September 2010).

46. In, for example, Patterson and Kaufmann, *Unionism*. There are older roots to this motif—for example, Frank Wright, *Northern Ireland: A Comparative Analysis* (Dublin, 1987).
47. Patterson and Kaufmann, *Unionism*, 57.
48. Nicholas Mansergh, *The Government of Northern Ireland: A Study in Devolution* (London, 1936), 176, 179.
49. Marc Mulholland, *The Longest War: Northern Ireland's Troubled History* (Oxford, 2002), 41–5.
50. Harbinson, *Ulster Unionist Party*; Patterson and Kaufmann, *Unionism*.
51. Patterson and Kaufmann, *Unionism*, 5.
52. Christopher Farrington, *Ulster Unionism and the Peace Process in Northern Ireland* (Basingstoke, 2006), 186.
53. See Eric Kaufmann, *The Orange Order: A Contemporary Northern Irish History* (Oxford, 2007).
54. Diane Urquhart, *Women in Ulster Politics, 1890–1940: A History Not Yet Told* (Dublin, 2000); Rachel Ward, *Women, Unionism and Loyalism in Northern Ireland: From Teamakers to Political Actors* (Dublin, 2006).
55. The civil society associated with Unionism, particularly Unionist 'youth', is relatively unexplored: for a starting point, see Alvin Jackson, 'Unionist Politics and Protestant Society in Edwardian Ireland', *Historical Journal*, 33, 4 (1990).
56. Arthur Aughey, *Under Siege: Ulster Unionism and the Anglo-Irish Agreement* (Belfast, 1989); Farrington, Ulster Unionism and the Peace Process, 17–19.
57. Iain McLean and Alastair McMillan, *State of the Union: Unionism and the Alternatives in the United Kingdom since 1707* (Oxford, 2005).
58. Wilson, 'The most terrible assassination'.
59. See Alvin Jackson, 'Unionist Myths', *Past & Present*, 136 (August, 1992).
60. These areas—the history of Unionist ideas, the movement's religious and other cultures, particularly material—have stimulated some recent work, but remain rich in research potential.

SELECT BIBLIOGRAPHY

Blackstock, Allan, *Loyalism in Ireland, 1789–1829* (London, 2007).
Bowman, Timothy, *Carson's Army: The Ulster Volunteer Force, 1910–22* (Manchester, 2008).
Buckland, Patrick, *Irish Unionism I: The Anglo-Irish and the New Ireland, 1885–1922* (Dublin, 1972).
Buckland, Patrick, *Irish Unionism II: Ulster Unionism and the Origins of Northern Ireland, 1886–1922* (Dublin, 1973).
Farrington, Christopher, *Ulster Unionism and the Peace Process in Northern Ireland* (Basingstoke, 2006).
Gibbon, Peter, *The Origins of Ulster Unionism: The Formation of Popular Protestant Politics and Ideology in Nineteenth Century Ireland* (Manchester, 1975).
Godson, Dean, *Himself Alone: David Trimble and the Ordeal of Unionism* (London, 2005).
Hoppen, K. Theodore, *Elections, Politics and Society in Ireland, 1832–1885* (Oxford, 1984).
Hoppen, K. Theodore, *Governing Hibernia: British Politicians and Ireland, 1800–1921* (Oxford, 2016)

Jackson, Alvin, *The Ulster Party: Irish Unionists in the House of Commons, 1884–1911* (Oxford, 1989).

Jackson, Alvin, *Colonel Edward Saunderson: Land and Loyalty in Victorian Ireland* (1995).

Jackson, Alvin, *Home Rule: An Irish History, 1800–2000*, paperback edition (London, 2004).

Kanter, Douglas, *The Making of British Unionism, 1740–1848: Politics, Government and the Anglo-Irish Constitutional Relationship* (Dublin, 2009).

Kaufmann, Eric, *The Orange Order: A Contemporary Northern Irish History* (Oxford, 2007).

McIntosh, Gillian V., *The Force of Culture: Unionist Identities in Twentieth Century Ireland* (Cork, 1999).

Mulholland, Marc, *Northern Ireland at the Cross Roads: Ulster Unionism in the O'Neill Years, 1963–69* (London, 2000).

Nelson, Sarah, *Ulster's Uncertain Defenders: Loyalist Paramilitary Political and Community Groups and the Northern Ireland Conflict* (Belfast, 1984).

Patterson, Henry and Kaufmann, Eric, *Unionism and Orangeism in Northern Ireland since 1945* (Manchester, 2007).

Senior, Hereward, *Orangeism in Ireland and Britain, 1795–1836* (London, 1966).

Shields, Andrew, *The Irish Conservative Party, 1852–68: Land, Politics and Religion* (Dublin, 2006).

Urquhart, Diane, *Women in Ulster Politics, 1890–1940: A History Not Yet Told* (Dublin, 2000).

CHAPTER 4

··

COLONIZED AND COLONIZERS

Ireland in the British Empire

··

STEPHEN HOWE

'My own origins are Irish and as you know we were colonized not colonizers'. British Secretary of State for International Development Clare Short to Zimbabwean Agriculture Minister Kumbirai Kangai, November 1997.

(*Mail and Guardian*, 22 December 1997)

I. INTRODUCTION

··

ALL communities develop histories, and for all groups large, self-conscious, and encompassing enough to think of themselves as a people, ethnic group, or nation, they are political histories. They are always, if only implicitly, both comparative and competitive—though this may become obvious only where the boundaries of community, or of sovereignty, are overtly and even violently contested. The community's homegrown histories become something considerably more elaborate, self-conscious, and often combative: histories of a nation which are also, more often than not, nationalist histories. Especially under circumstances of overt contestation, they may become different again and more constricted: what the veteran historian of Zimbabwean nationalism Terence Ranger calls patriotic history. 'It is different from and narrower than the old nationalist historiography, which celebrated aspiration and modernization as well as resistance. It resents the "disloyal" questions raised by historians of nationalism. It regards as irrelevant any history that is not political. And it is explicitly antagonistic to academic historiography'.[1] Yet patriotic history need not be seen as necessarily being so restricted, or so destructive as Ranger believes its Zimbabwean variant to be: it may as another distinguished Africanist, John Lonsdale, argues be a way—indeed the most powerful, available way—of consolidating community, celebrating civic virtue, and resisting arbitrary power.[2]

Ireland, despite its relative ethnic homogeneity on any comparative standard, exemplifies all these points very well, and its historians have debated the meanings and merits of competing patriotic histories still more fiercely than have Africa's. My central thrust in this chapter will be to investigate these debates, as they have been played out in relation to the question of Ireland's historical relationship with empire. It will begin with the very widespread presumption that there are historically two communities, or indeed two nations, on the island of Ireland, and these correspond to antithetical historical fates as colonizers and colonized. I shall proceed to question and complicate—without entirely abandoning—that perception and to suggest that a rapidly developing modern historiography reveals a somewhat different, more richly textured one.

As the foregoing implies, historical investigation of colonialism's place in Irish history—and vice versa—was long entangled with several other kinds of argument, including directly political ones. These have included the long-running dispute between so-called 'revisionists' and their opponents (some of whom surely corresponded rather closely to Ranger's conception of patriotic historians, or at least were so seen by 'revisionists'), over whether Ulster's Protestant community should be viewed as settler-colonialists or, perhaps, rather as a separate nationality, and whether the contemporary Irish Republic might aptly be analyzed as 'postcolonial' or even 'neocolonial'.[3] Some came to perceive Irish historical and cultural debate as simply, starkly divided between 'revisionists' and those who adhered to colonial and/or postcolonial models. Equally, therefore, much discussion seemed polarized over the deceptively straightforward question 'was Ireland a British colony or not?' Yet the alternative to a simplistic 'either-orism' often seemed to be a frustrated or frustrating, almost helpless consignment of Irish history, in its relations to empire, to a residual, ill-defined, or even undefinable category denoted or dismissed with such terms as 'hybrid', 'ambivalent', 'complex', 'exceptional', and 'anomalous'. Thus not only most general or synoptic works on the British Empire as such, but also almost all the vast recent outpouring of research on British (or archipelagic) identities and cultures in their relation to imperialism, either curtly announced or silently conceded that Ireland did not fit the patterns they were exploring, and said almost nothing further about it.

These intellectual battles also had a disciplinary dimension—for literary scholars and cultural historians were far more often receptive to colonial models for Ireland than were most political, social, or economic analysts.[4] They had, moreover, a geographical one, in that researchers in some locations, perhaps especially North American ones, seemed more enamoured of colonial frameworks than those in others, including a probable majority within Ireland itself. And there was a temporal dimension too, insofar as historians of some periods, like the sixteenth and seventeenth centuries, seemed more likely to find explanatory power in the concepts of imperialism and colonialism than did many of those studying the nineteenth or twentieth centuries. Much of the literature in these fields, moreover, seemed to unfriendly critics to be weak in comparative or even definitional awareness in its use of terms like 'colony' and 'empire'; to ignore or underrate the complex and changing character of 'English', 'British', and 'Irish' identities and state formations across time, unduly to homogenize Irish experience itself across time, space, and social class, often to be excessively 'culturalist' in orientation while neglecting socio-economic determinants, and—not least of its faults—frequently to involve strong but unargued-for value judgements whereby to label something 'colonial' was more to condemn than to explain it.

Unsurprisingly, therefore, some historians could come to believe, with Toby Barnard, that: 'In so far as "colony" has entered general usage as something more than a loose descriptive metaphor, it owes most to a bizarre fusion of Catholic nationalist teleology and the observations of Marx and Engels on mid-nineteenth-century Ireland, and is pejorative'.[5] Or like another distinguished historian of early-modern Britain and Ireland, Steven Ellis, they might feel that whether the British-Irish relationship was a colonial one is merely 'a matter of opinion, since colonialism as a concept was developed by its modern opponents and constitutes a value-judgement which cannot be challenged on its own grounds'.[6] Conversely, they might suggest—as, for instance, David Lloyd has repeatedly done—that only some combination of intellectual myopia and political bias could prevent analysts from perceiving Ireland's history as that of a victim of British colonialism.[7]

The present author, along with many others, has elsewhere written extensively and sometimes combatively on these contestations.[8] It is not proposed to pursue them much further in their own right, though reference to them is often inescapable even when engaging with more substantive historiographical developments. Some of the negative judgements offered above, however, have quite rapidly become less fully apt. A fast-growing literature on Ireland's place in the British imperial system, Irish attitudes to empire, Irish involvement in British and other global imperial formations, and related themes has explored many aspects of these relationships in unprecedented detail, with much augmented attention to complexity and nuance. There remain, as we shall see, both notable empirical gaps and significant conceptual problems in the scholarly literature on 'Ireland and Empire', but this intellectual landscape is being transformed with conspicuous speed. One may happily concur with the view of Michael de Nie and Joe Cleary that 'Ireland and empire is now one of the most vibrant fields of inquiry in Irish Studies'.[9]

II. From Strongbow to Sarsfield

Prehistoric, ancient, and medieval Ireland evidently experienced numerous waves of invaders—or, to adopt a more neutral term, incomers. Even if we leave out of consideration, as surely we should, all semi- or entirely mythical ideas about Firbolg, Milesians, and Pretani, many different groups of people from England, Scotland, Scandinavia and sometimes further afield arrived on its shores across several centuries, and some of them conquered and dispossessed earlier inhabitants, or tried to do so.

Quite clearly, though, the most lastingly consequential of all these incursions were those made by people who came gradually to think of themselves as 'English'—and some of them, much later, as 'British'. The first significant such arrival is conventionally seen as being that of Richard fitz Gilbert, nicknamed Strongbow, in 1170. Although Strongbow was actually 'invited' to Ireland by an exiled King of Leinster, his landing near Waterford came retrospectively to be viewed, in a venerable tradition of Irish historiography, as the beginning of English invasion and colonization. Yet as many historians have argued energetically, to project such national labels as 'English' and 'Irish' so far back in time, or to see twelfth-century events as ushering in an era or a plan of colonial conquest, may be anachronistic. Though some believe that a sense of English national identity was evident very early by comparison with its counterparts elsewhere in Europe or indeed beyond— and that conflict and conquest in Ireland strengthened and hastened its formation—it is much disputed whether, when, or how far ideas of profound national, cultural, even racial, difference characterized English actions and attitudes in Ireland. Were the latter, in important ways, different from those operating in other medieval and early-modern European 'ethnic frontiers' or zones of conquest (including perhaps even those within England itself), and usefully comparable to those which operated later in non-European zones of colonial conquest? Historians disagree sharply on these questions, and will surely long continue to do so.[10]

By the early sixteenth century the English Crown had a long established, even if dubiously legitimate, claim to sovereignty over Ireland, and English conceptions of lordship, language, and law held sway over significant parts of the island. Yet this remained an 'incomplete conquest', constantly under challenge and, near the end of the century, almost overturned by a combination of resistance under Hugh O'Neill and threat from Spain.[11] Religious conflict began to enter the picture, as the Protestant Reformation triumphed in England and Scotland but largely failed to take root in Ireland. With the Union of the English and Scottish Crowns in 1603, and the establishment of joint English-Scottish colonizing ventures, there began to take shape a change from 'English' to 'British' claims over, and attempts to dominate, Ireland. Yet that fusion was certainly not complete during the seventeenth century—some historians doubt whether it *ever* really became so, either in general terms or in relation to the Irish. Nonetheless this era, that of England's Tudor, then Britain's Stuart, monarchies, is the one for which we come closest to a consensus among historians about Ireland's colonial position—though even here there remain sceptics, and those like Ciaran Brady and Raymond Gillespie who note the continued coexistence of two quite distinct English images of Ireland: as a sovereign kingdom, and as an arena for colonial exploitation.[12]

Some question, too, whether early-modern colonization in Ireland was quite so radically transformative as its later analogues elsewhere in the 'Angloworld' of British conquest and settlement. Much here remains hotly debated. Should one emphasize continuity (following Estyn Evans), or rather a radical break (as most recently and impressively, William J. Smyth has done), as a result of plantation?[13] Should one see the expansion of originally English state power in Ireland as of a piece with that elsewhere in the archipelago (as does, for instance, Steven Ellis) or as having a dramatically

distinct, colonial character? Should one stress the 'incomplete conquest' and the failure of the project to 'make Ireland British' (à la Nicholas Canny) or more the sweeping, indeed traumatic, impact especially of Cromwellian conquest? Even Smyth's work
too shows much continuity—except in Ulster, the relative population densities of different Irish regions remained very similar across the various conflicts, conquests,
and settlements, and indeed areas of economic dynamism and modernization in the
seventeenth-eighteenth centuries were much the same as those in the twelfth or even
the fifth. Historians—and literary scholars, who have contributed considerably to the
debate via analyses of the views on Ireland of Spenser, Shakespeare, Milton, and many
lesser figures—have also disagreed widely over how far a coherent, powerful, purposeful
English/British Protestant ideology of colonization may be discerned in Ireland. Also
how closely it may have paralleled that which was developed for the North American
colonies, and indeed how far attitudes to the 'native Irish' were similar to or different
from those towards Native Americans and other non-white subject peoples.[14] In all this
a 'four nations' or 'archipelagic' historical approach, one taking the 'Atlantic world' as
its analytical focus, and a more traditional focus on a bipolar English-Irish relationship,
interact and sometimes clash.

There might, however, be merit in attempting a still broader picture than any of
these. Perhaps the boldest recent global analysis of Anglophone colonial expansion is that found in James Belich's *Replenishing the Earth*.[15] He suggests four types
or stages of British world colonization: Incremental; Explosive; Recolonization; and
Decolonization. The incremental stage was the relatively slow growth of settler population from the sixteenth century to the early nineteenth century. Explosive colonization then ensued, driven by multiple new pressures and opportunities. Explosive
colonization—in North America, Australasia, and southern Africa—though, was
marked by dramatic alternations of boom and bust. And it always ended with a bang,
usually a big one, after which the third type of colonization emerged. With this, both
economic and cultural reintegration with the 'motherlands' took place, only to be
succeeded by real decolonization far later than usually thought, well into the twentieth century. British colonization in Ireland clearly does not fit Belich's schemata at
all—the chronology is all wrong. It took incremental form, and never took off into
the explosive stage. Rates of growth were, in comparative perspective, very slow—and
were unlike almost anywhere else in the Angloworld in coming in so many, tempo-
rally widely separated, waves and in being repeatedly accompanied by great waves of
emigration. Ireland's Protestant population, especially in the seventeenth, eighteenth,
and earlier nineteenth centuries, was—in the classic image—like a bathtub with the
taps running full blast, but the plug out. Only nineteenth-century Belfast comes anywhere near fitting an 'explosive' image. Belfast's population doubled in twenty years
from 1851 to 1871—but Belich's acid test is of major settler cities' decennial doubling,
which very many urban centres in the Americas, Australasia, and southern Africa
experienced repeatedly. And at this time, of course, Ireland's population as a whole
was falling very sharply. The boom and bust model is also very hard to apply plausibly
to Irish history—Ireland was, perhaps, just too closely tied to Britain, never a separate

enough economic space for the paradigm to fit well, though maybe we could think of the Famine as an especially drastic and tragic bust. [16]

III. Settlements, Unions, and Revolts

By the end of the seventeenth century, the previously 'incomplete conquest' of Ireland had seemingly been made total, and the country transformed by repeated wars[17], by general—though never total—dispossession of both 'native Irish' and 'Old English' landowners, and by large-scale Anglo-Scottish settlement, especially in the north-east. The Irish language entered sharp decline, and adherents of the majority Catholic religion were marginalized, subordinated, or persecuted.[18] Social status and power were almost monopolized by those who could proclaim their Englishness, Britishness, and/ or Anglican Protestantism. Yet still, as Thomas Bartlett says, Ireland 'resembled not so much a model colony…but rather an unruly palimpsest, on which, though much rewritten and scored out, could be discerned in an untidy jumble "kingdom", "colony", "dependency" and, faintly, "nation".[19] Some historians see in all this a pattern of cultural colonialism, very like that later characteristic of Africa and Asia, though others emphasize not a straightforward opposition of colonizers and colonized but rather the many forms of cultural hybridity and syncretism which developed, and suggest that eighteenth-century Ireland resembled continental Europe's 'ancien régimes' more than it did the colonial societies either of that era or later.[20] With time, some among the Protestant elites, and even more among the poorer settlers' descendants in Ulster, clearly came ever more strongly to identify themselves as Irish, and to develop demands for self-government which some have seen as a 'colonial nationalism' like that simultaneously emerging in the Americas.[21] Yet there has, again, been much debate over how far this radicalization, even in its most militant manifestation as the United Irishmen, ever overcame confessional divisions—and whether the 1798 uprising was a nobly failed attempt to transcend these or rather a highly sectarian affair which made them worse. How far, too, was Ireland before the Union treated as an inferior colonial possession in either constitutional or economic terms?

On the constitutional level Ireland's ambiguous 'colonial' status ended with the Union. It was now—in theory, and in *some* aspects of practice—a full and equal part of the British Empire's core state, not of its subordinate or exploited periphery. Advocates of Union indeed urged that it would enable Ireland to play a fuller role in Britain's imperial ventures worldwide. Yet historians of the nineteenth century too have debated hotly over whether Ireland's position remained colonial, since in some respects and on some understandings it was a more fully subordinated part of the British imperial system under the Union than it had been hitherto. As Terrence McDonough has noted, echoing Joseph Ruane, the notion of Irish experience as colonial, widely accepted among historians dealing with periods from Norman invasions to the eighteenth century, had been far less often invoked in work on the more recent past—except in some highly polemical writings, and by a number of literary and cultural studies scholars. McDonough identifies two intensely political reasons for this: anxiety among historians not to give 'aid and comfort to the Provisional IRA' by adopting models which might seem uncomfortably congruent to the IRA's view of late-twentieth-century Ireland, and the 'turn to Europe' in Irish life from the 1970s, which predisposed many to 'establish modern Irish history as partaking of the European mainstream' rather than having 'Third Worldish' parallels.[22] As he suggests, though, more recent work has now 'cast a provisional rope bridge across the chasm of neglect of colonialism' in relation to Ireland's nineteenth century. The bridge has three cables, in the application of postcolonial and Marxist literary theory to Ireland, in the study of political institutions and British official policies, and in economic investigations using 'critical perspectives drawn from economic development theory'.[23] All, however, remain contentious, and not only on straightforward political grounds. The argument has, again, intermingled with several others: notably on the character of nineteenth-century Irish nationalism, on how British policies and 'official minds' treated Ireland, and on changing attitudes to 'race'.

Nineteenth- and early twentieth-century British discourse on empire involved multiple shifts and mixtures of language, with some influential historians being highly sceptical whether these amounted, as an ensemble, to an elaborated, coherent, or consequential imperialist ideology. If, as some thus suggest, there was no such ideology in general, it ceases to be meaningful to ask whether or how policies and attitudes towards Ireland fitted into it.[24] Moreover, the idea of empire in this period did not mean only subject territories outside the 'core' state, but—not least in debates on Irish Home Rule—embraced the 'core' as well and often had that mainly in mind. In some such rhetorics, the discourse of empire fused with that of nationality itself. Ideas about empire, in addition, were intermingled with others such as that of a global 'Greater Britain' or 'British World' (with much ambiguity as to whether Ireland, or the Irish abroad, were parts of these); while historians disagree sharply over how profound or pervasive the impact of empire was in reshaping 'domestic' British and Irish societies and cultures.[25] It might be suggested, however, that it was precisely Ireland's 'hybrid' position which made it an important hinge between debates on domestic politics and those on the future of the Empire. There has been a fast-growing literature too on Irish nationalists' international attitudes and contacts, including those with anticolonial movements elsewhere in the British imperial system. Analysts have differed over how much explicitly 'anti-imperialist' thought or writing is to be found in nineteenth- or early twentieth-century Irish nationalism; though the broad internationalist sympathies of some important individuals, from Daniel O'Connell to James Connolly, have been stressed.[26] The closest imperial links and sympathies tended to be with movements in colonies of white settlement, and sometimes revealed racially exclusivist or supremacist ideas—including complaints that Ireland's lack of self-rule was peculiarly intolerable precisely because the Irish were white. Yet contacts and mutual influences between Irish and Indian nationalists have also been investigated by several recent historians.[27] The 'anti-imperialism' of some earlier Irish notables, especially Edmund Burke, has also been much discussed,[28] whilst James Livesey, in an innovative argument, has seen

Ireland as a key site for the development of ideas of civil society. Although some think-ers of the time proclaimed that Irish Protestants were children of England and derived their liberties not from Ireland or being Irish but as transplanted 'Freeborn Englishmen', others were more optimistic that Catholics and Protestants could meld together, that the latter were truly Irish, and that a good claim could be staked for equality, federa-tion, or partnership of Ireland with Britain. The Catholic elites' evolving languages of virtue, moral order, and improvement across the century, though initially separate from Ascendancy ones and drawing on different sources, were little different from them in their upshot and their desired ends. Civic republican thought and its notions of civil society emerged in a specifically imperial context, 'as a concept designed to manage the relationships of elite provincials to the British Empire... Far from threatening the power of the empire, it articulated and amplified it'.[29]

Conversely, we still sorely lack a really close investigation of empire's place in the political and cultural life of Irish Unionism and loyalism, and of post-1921 Northern Ireland. It has often been asserted or assumed that this place was a central, immensely powerful one: more so (or so it is implied) than in English, Scottish, or Welsh life in the same times and social milieux.[30] But the assertion remains to be tested in any detail—while as previously noted, the recently proliferating studies of imperialism in 'domestic' British life mostly, albeit inexplicitly, exclude Ireland both north and south from their remit. The Protestant religion has widely been taken as a badge of British-colonial iden-tity and as providing a justification for colonization. Most influentially, Linda Colley has seen Protestantism as a vital element in the common British imperial identity, which developed 'at home' in the seventeenth and eighteenth centuries and was then glo-balized. However, as David Armitage, among others, has suggested, it may not be easy theologically to link Protestantism to colonization.[31] Whilst the link may seem strong for some earlier settler colonies, whether in Ulster or in New England, it applies far less powerfully even for that era elsewhere, as in the Caribbean. It's too often forgotten that a good half of British and Irish migrants in the seventeenth and eighteenth centuries went to the Caribbean, where they died like flies. If Ireland's story was, as some have argued, one of 'failed colonization', it was a far less spectacular failure than the West Indies. For the later and more explosive phases, there is much debate over whether Protestantism should be seen as at all ideologically important to settlement in Australasia, the American West, or the Cape. For Ireland, Presbyterian United Irishmen and, a century later, Anglican Gaelic Revivalists are just two among many phenomena complicating the association.

These exchanges have often been related to a broader, often heated one, about the place of racial attitudes in British-Irish-empire relations, including the roles of anti-Irish racism and of Irish people's own racial ideas. Some specialists see close parallels between anti-Irish and anti-black racisms in nineteenth- and twentieth-century Britain; and believe that these greatly strengthen the case for seeing Ireland's position as colonial.[32] Others are more sceptical, urging that the Irish were (despite the title of a much-cited but empirically weak book by Noel Ignatiev) after all, always 'white'.[33] A further aspect of these questions which has received important recent attention is the role of both slavery and Abolitionism in Irish history. There was little direct involvement of Irish ports or Irish-owned ships in actually transporting enslaved Africans across the Atlantic, but in multiple other ways Ireland's engagement with and profit from New World slavery was substantial. Irish agricultural and other export products fed and equipped slave ships and plantations. Numerous Irish individuals—certainly not all 'Anglo-Irish' or indeed Protestant, and rather disconcertingly including even some former United Irish revolutionaries—prospered as slave owners and dealers. It all contributed considerably to Irish urban and commercial development across the eighteenth century, and thus helped shape the country's political and cultural lives too. Yet at the same time there were numerous poor Irish emigrants to the slave colonies, including large numbers of 'bound servants' whose status is often analyzed as being one of semi-slavery, and who have sometimes been suggested to have had especially close interaction and fellow-feeling with enslaved Africans, deriving in part from Irish people's own experience of national, 'racial', and religious persecution. Ireland from the later eighteenth century and through the nineteenth century became a major arena for Abolitionist mobilization, and such leading Irish nationalist figures as Daniel O'Connell were in the forefront of Abolitionism—though some others, like John Mitchel, were firmly and fiercely on the other side.[34]

IV. Emigrants and Imperialists

Very large numbers of Irish settlers, administrators, traders, soldiers, and missionaries operated throughout the British Empire. The patterns of migration and settlement, and the special roles of such groups as indentured labourers, Catholic missionaries, Anglo-Irish Protestant families with their high representation among senior British army officers and colonial administrators, and conversely of émigré nationalists from United Irishmen to Fenians, have all attracted close study in the recent historiography. The earlier phases of Irish emigration to the colonies were, it seems, disproportionately heavy among Ulster Protestants—the later 'Scotch-Irish' of Britain's North American colonies. Recent estimates suggest that between 1700 and 1775, 66,100 migrants went from Ulster to the thirteen North American colonies, as against 42,500 from the rest of Ireland. To these must be added possibly another 30,000 emigrants to North America in 1775–1800, roughly 40,000 migrants, mainly as indentured servants, from Ireland to the Caribbean, and perhaps 10,000 convicts transported first to the Americas, later to Australasia.[35] Later, and especially after the Famine of the 1840s, the outflow increased massively and the patterns changed: emigrants became more likely to be southern, Catholic Irishmen and women (and indeed the proportion who *were* women increased radically), and destinations shifted too, with a majority of Irish emigrants settling in the United States or Britain. Still, there were roughly 300,000 Irish-born people in Canada in 1861, almost as many in Australia by the century's end. During the later nineteenth century, over a third of immigrants in Canada were Irish, as were over a quarter of those in Australia and almost one-fifth in New Zealand. Far smaller numbers—but still almost everywhere a significant proportion of all white migrants and settlers—moved to India, South Africa, and indeed throughout the Empire. Between 1820 and 1920, roughly a million Irish people settled in British colonies (as against at least four times as many in the United States, and perhaps 1.5 million in Britain).[36] As many historians have enumerated, there was always significant reverse migration too—and even more migrants always planned to return home, but never made it—but in many ways this mass exodus was surely the most important of all aspects of the relationship between Ireland and empire. It is also, naturally, one which troubles and complicates aspects of the ideologically charged debates in this field, or the simplistic view advanced by Clare Short, with which this chapter opened. Numerous issues have aroused tempers as well as attracted research among historians. How far may the sheer scale of Irish emigration itself be related to Ireland's own putatively oppressed colonial status? How far can one speak meaningfully of a distinctive 'Irish empire', in the sense of Irish settlers, soldiers, officials, and others in the colonies faring, behaving, or thinking differently from English, Scottish, or Welsh ones? How did Irish 'imperialism' relate, ideologically, politically, and perhaps psychologically, to an Irish nationalism which is so often seen as inherently anti-imperialist?

It is, as Don Akenson urges, misleading to generalize about 'the Irish' in the colonial diaspora.[37] One must at the least disaggregate the group into the four broad categories recognized by seventeenth-century contemporaries: 'native Irish', 'Old English', 'New English', and 'Ulster-Scots'. One must note religious divisions—from at least the 1640s until the 1840s, Protestants formed a significantly higher proportion of the emigrants from Ireland than they did of the island's population, while probably a majority of Irish settlers in Canada and New Zealand continued to be Protestant until a much later date. One should beware of over-stressing the roles, for instance, of the Anglo-Irish Protestant families whose contribution to Britain's imperial officer and senior administrator caste was especially great, from Wellington to Montgomery, or the minority of wealthy emigrant merchants and landowners—some of them also slave-traders and slave-owners. One should not exaggerate the Irish presence in British-imperial armed forces, as has sometimes been done: in the early nineteenth century the Irish-born were significantly overrepresented among both officers and other ranks in both the British and the Indian armies, but their proportion fell steadily thereafter, and they seem always to have been under-represented in the Royal Navy and merchant marine. Equally, it is necessary to guard against stereotypes (quite widespread even in serious historical writing) of all Irish emigrants as impoverished indentured servants, starving victims of Famine and eviction, or nationalists burning with indignation at Ireland's historic wrongs.[38]

Almost everywhere in the Empire the Irish—Catholic and Protestant—were minorities. They found their places, often, though certainly not always, disadvantaged or marginalized ones, within imperial and colonial systems whose dominant, and usually majority, element was English and whose political, legal, religious, and cultural structures were predominantly those of the English Crown and then the British state. In that sense, there was never truly an 'Irish empire': they were never and nowhere numerous or powerful enough to shape imperial projects according to their own desires. There were, some have suggested, just two intriguing exceptions: Ontario in Canada, where the

Irish were by some margin the largest population group until the end of the nineteenth century; and the tiny Caribbean island of Montserrat.[39] Although a few historians have written of an Irish 'spiritual empire', forged through distinctive religious institutions and indeed persisting after the end of Britain's political empire, the term is here clearly being used in a loose, semi-metaphorical way.[40] Yet as John MacKenzie argues, a 'four nations' approach to British imperial history is ever more on the agenda, including recognition of the ways in which the Irish modified the makeup of British imperialism—not least in its religious character. 'We are becoming increasingly aware of the manner in which empire could re-emphasise the looseness and heterogeneity of the British state. The Protestant Reformation ensured that the denominational affiliations of the peoples of the British Isles became highly varied...Nothing symbolised more strikingly the manner in which the English were doomed to failure in the Anglicisation of empire than in the realm of religion'.[41]

V. After 1918: Decolonization, Postcoloniality, or Eternal Imperialism?

After the Anglo-Irish Treaty of 1921, the country's ensuing partition and as what was initially called the 'Free State' gradually thereafter achieved the full, formal status of an independent Republic, discussion of Ireland's relationship with Britain's now-declining empire naturally took new forms. Equally, the ways historians and other analysts addressing these questions have done so is quite different for the post-1921 era than it is for earlier periods, and has also taken radically different paths in relation to the two parts of the divided island.

For the Free State and later Republic, the stance of most commentators came to be that, if 'empire' or 'colonialism' were to be considered as issues at all, they were ones belonging to the past—though this still left open the possibility of seeing independent Ireland, or important aspects of life there, as continuing profoundly to be shaped by empire's legacies and/or as distinctively 'postcolonial', in ways that meant it had more in common with formerly colonized countries in Africa or Asia than with most other European states. A vigorous minority current in the Republic's political, cultural, and intellectual life, however, argued that it remained subject to external domination—whether this was seen as being by the former British masters, by the USA, later by the European Union, by global capitalism, or even all of these—which made it still a victim of imperialism, or a 'neocolonial' rather than truly 'postcolonial' state and society.

The 'postcolonial' view has been advanced especially in the fields of literary and cultural studies, among which has been advanced probably the single most influential mode of argument over 'Ireland and imperialism' since the 1980s. Applying to Irish contexts the global ideas of postcolonial theory and its close intellectual relative, colonial discourse analysis, of which Edward W. Said was generally seen as the key pioneer,[42] Irish literary scholars and historians such as Seamus Deane, Luke Gibbons, Declan Kiberd, and David Lloyd argued that a 'Saidian' mode of historical and theoretical analysis—and/or one drawn from such earlier anticolonial intellectuals as Frantz Fanon—was fully applicable to Ireland.[43] Such claims drew much counter-fire—including some from the present author—especially on the grounds that they were allegedly weakly grounded in historical knowledge and in comparative analysis of imperial and colonial histories. Latterly, however, some younger exponents of Irish postcolonial studies, perhaps most notably Joe Cleary, have been stronger on those fronts.[44]

The 'still colonized' arguments about Ireland were more diverse in form. Some critics addressed patterns of economic development and social structure, suggesting that despite all the apparent structural changes and economic growth since the 1920s, Ireland remained dependent or neocolonial. Marxists especially advanced such a view—though by no means all Marxist analyses of Ireland adhered to it—and it came to be widely accepted among Republicans too: first in the 'Official' Sinn Féin current which became the Workers' Party and later among 'Provisionals' also.[45] Independent intellectuals like Raymond Crotty and Denis O'Hearn, influenced by Latin American dependency and underdevelopment theory, developed their own versions of the case.[46] Theirs remained very much a minority view, especially after Ireland entered a period of rapid economic growth—though one might speculate that the new economic crisis since 2008 may win it more adherents. Others suggested that the Republic's political system had characteristically postcolonial features,[47] that colonial legacies accounted for the alleged failure or incompleteness of cultural modernity in Ireland or had abiding and damaging effects on Irish psychological traits.[48]

In relation to Northern Ireland, two intertwined issues were at stake: whether the partition and the continuing Union with Britain should be seen as colonialist, and whether the structural position, or the dominant ideologies, of Ulster Protestants were settler-colonialist ones. Arguments over colonial models for understanding Northern Ireland after 1921 have, naturally, been the most politically contentious of all the relevant fields. They have given rise to a vast body of writing, albeit involving far more vehement polemics than detailed or historically informed analyses. That writing cannot be surveyed here, except rather peremptorily to register this author's own view that, as argued elsewhere at some length, it is not very helpful or illuminating to analyze the recent politics of Northern Ireland, or the identities of Ulster Unionism, under the rubric of settler colonialism. Important aspects of the region's past can be 'captured' through use of the concepts of the settler colony, and of course of the Plantation, but whatever the perceptions and even self-perceptions of some actors, the distinctively settler-colonial features of Northern Irish society largely eroded or were dismantled during the nineteenth century.[49]

VI. Conclusions

Colonial and postcolonial studies of Ireland, in their once-dominant literary and cultural, and unfortunately often ahistorical or anti-historical, mode, are little more than two decades old—emerging only from the late 1980s—but have already, I suspect, peaked and are fading. What were still quite recently sometimes stark, ill-tempered schisms between historians and cultural critics, empiricists and theoreticists, and revisionists and anti-revisionists, have at least partially been replaced by a more transdisciplinary, multidirectional and complex conversation about empire and colonialism in Irish history. The conflicts 'haven't gone away, you know', but they are no longer the sites either of such bitter contestation, or of the most productive new research. There are many signs that the former gulf between Irish and British Empire historical studies, which so many critics (including this one) had long lamented, is in considerable measure being overcome from both sides.

In part, specifically Irish intellectual and academic developments, including a mass of impressive new scholarship, some of which we have surveyed here, account for the change. But it might be ventured that a more global 'breakup' of, or sense of intellectual exhaustion within, postcolonial studies in its 1980s–90s high-theoretical and Saidian moulds, has also contributed. So too perhaps have wider economic and political developments within Ireland. The switchback of Ireland's economic fortunes in recent decades has, one may conjecture, alternately fuelled and dampened intellectual interest in the country's impoverished, 'Third Worldish' past. Politically, Northern Ireland's at least partially successful peace process, Sinn Féin's tacit abandonment of the colonial model, secularization and partisan realignment in the Republic, and (not least) a historically unprecedented wave of non-European migration to Ireland have shifted the whole landscape in which academic debates take place. Equally evidently, global developments since 2001 have also done so: 9/11, the 'War on Terror', and the 'new imperialism' of the USA. As always, new kinds of present and possible future engender new perceptions of the past. There has, as we have seen, long been a strong association between viewing the Irish past in colonial terms, and adopting not just national, but nationalist, assumptions or beliefs about it. That indeed accounts in great part for the highly politically charged atmosphere around these historiographical debates. There are many indications, however, that these bonds are now loosening. If politics in Ireland is slowly ceasing to be so much a matter of clashing nationalisms, Irish history-writing too need ever less be about rival varieties of nationalist historian—let alone 'patriotic' ones in Terence Ranger's pejorative sense.

NOTES

1. Terence Ranger, 'Nationalist Historiography, Patriotic History and the History of the Nation: the Struggle over the Past in Zimbabwe' *Journal of Southern African Studies*, 30, 2, June 2004, 215–34, quotation from p. 218.
2. John Lonsdale, 'Writing Competitive Patriotisms in Eastern Africa' in Derek R. Peterson and Giacomo Macola (eds) *Recasting the Past: History Writing and Political Work in Modern Africa* Athens, Ohio, 2009, 251–67.
3. The best surveys of these disputes remain D. G. Boyce and Alan O'Day (eds), *The Making of Modern Irish History: Revisionism and the Revisionist Controversy* London, 1996 and Ciaran

Brady (ed.), *Interpreting Irish History: The Debate on Historical Revisionism* (Dublin, 1994). An intriguing recent contribution, with a stronger comparative dimension than most, is Evi Gkotzaridis, *Trials of Irish History: Genesis and Evolution of a Reappraisal 1938-2000* (London, 2006).

4. See the critique by Linda Connolly, 'The Limits of 'Irish Studies': Culturalism, Historicism, Paternalism', *Irish Studies Review* 12, 2, 2004, 139–62.

5. T. C. Barnard, 'Crises of Identity among Irish Protestants, 1641–1685' *Past and Present* 127, 1990, 39–83; 40.

6. Steven G. Ellis, 'Writing Irish History: Revisionism, Colonialism, and the British Isles' *Irish Review* 19, 1996, 1–21; 9.

7. For instance Lloyd, *Anomalous States: Irish Writing and the Post-Colonial Moment* (Dublin, 1993); *Ireland After History* Cork, 1999 and 'Regarding Ireland in a Post-Colonial Frame' *Cultural Studies* 15 (1) 2001, 12–32.

8. *Ireland and Empire: Colonial Legacies in Irish History and Culture* Oxford, 2000; 'The Politics of Historical "Revisionism": Comparing Ireland and Israel/Palestine', *Past and Present* 168, August 2000, 227–53; 'Historiography' in Kevin Kenny (ed.), *Ireland and the British Empire* (Oxford, 2004); 220–50; 'On Questioning the Question: Was Ireland a Colony', *Irish Historical Studies*, XXXVI, 142, 2008, 138–52; 'Minding the Gaps: New Directions in the Study of Ireland and Empire', *Jnl. Of Imperial and Commonwealth History*, 37, 1, 2009, 135–49. The present chapter draws especially on some passages from the last of these.

9. 'Editors' Introduction' *Eire-Ireland* 42, 1 and 2, 2007, 5–10; 5.

10. See for instance John Gillingham, 'The Beginnings of English Imperialism' *Journal of Historical Sociology* 5, 4, 1992, 392–409; R. R. Davies, *The First English Empire* (Oxford, 2000); Brendan Smith, *Colonisation and Conquest in Medieval Ireland. The English in Louth, 1170–1330* (Cambridge, 1999), and for a case that *all* medieval European history can be seen as 'colonial', Robert Bartlett, *The Making of Europe: Conquest,Colonization and Cultural Change 950–1350* (London, 1993).

11. Colm Lennon, *Sixteenth-Century Ireland: The Incomplete Conquest* (Dublin, 1994); see also Jane H. Ohlmeyer, ' "ilizinge of Those Rude Partes" Colonization within Britain and Ireland, 1580s-1640s' in Nicholas Canny (ed.), *The Oxford History of the British Empire. Vol.1: The Origins of Empire. British Overseas Enterprise to the Close of the Seventeenth Century* (Oxford, 1998), 124–47; John Morrissey, 'Contours of colonialism: Gaelic Ireland and the early colonial subject' *Irish Geography*, 37 (1), 2004, 88–102; Brian Mac Cuarta (ed.), *Reshaping Ireland 1550–1700: Colonization and its Consequences* (Dublin, 2011).

12. Nicholas Canny is widely seen as the pre-eminent historian of these themes. Amidst his great body of relevant work, see especially *Making Ireland British 1580–1650* (Oxford, 2001). The leading 'colonio-sceptic' has perhaps been Steven Ellis—*Tudor Ireland: Crown, Community and the Conflict of Cultures, 1470–1603* (London, 1985). See also Ciaran Brady and Raymond Gillespie (eds), *Natives and Newcomers: The Making of Irish Colonial Society 1534–1641* (Dublin, 1986); and Karl Bottigheimer, 'Kingdom and Colony: Ireland in the Westward Enterprise, 1536–1660' in K. R. Andrews, N. P. Canny, and P. E. Hair (eds), *The Westward Enterprise: English Activities in Ireland, the Atlantic and America, 1480–1650* (Liverpool, 1978), 45–65.

13. Estyn E. Evans, *The Personality of Ireland: Habitat, Heritage and History* Belfast, 1981; William J. Smyth, *Map-making, Landscapes and Memory: A Geography of Colonial and Early Modern Ireland c. 1530–1750* (Cork, 2006).

14. On the general question of early 'imperial ideology', see David Armitage, *The Ideological Origins of the British Empire* Cambridge, 2000, and for comparative perspectives, Anthony Pagden, *Lords of All the World: Ideologies of Empire in Spain, Britain and France c. 1500–c. 1800* (New Haven and London, 1995).

15. James Belich, *Replenishing the Earth: The Settler Revolution and the Rise of the Angloworld, 1780–1930* (Oxford, 2009).

16. Among the few scholarly works seeking to place the Famine in an imperial frame, see especially David P. Nally, *Human Encumbrances: Political Violence and the Great Irish Famine* (Notre Dame, 2011).

17. It has been estimated that 3.7 per cent of England's and Wales's population died in the wars. For Scotland, it was more like 6 per cent, and in Ireland maybe a staggering 35–40 per cent.

18. Historians dispute how far the harsher provisions of the anti-Catholic 'Penal Laws' were enforced, and thus which of the above terms is most apt.

19. Thomas Bartlett, '"This Famous Island Set in a Virginian Sea": Ireland in the British Empire, 1690–1801' in P. J. Marshall (ed.), *OHBE vol.2: The Eighteenth Century* (Oxford, 1998), 253–75; 254.

20. Daniel Corkery, *The Hidden Ireland: A Study of Gaelic Munster in the 18th Century* (Dublin, 1925); Kevin Whelan, *The Tree of Liberty: Radicalism, Catholicism and the Construction of Irish Identity 1760–1830* (Cork, 1996); Breandán Ó Buachalla, 'Irish Jacobitism and Irish Nationalism: the literary evidence' in Michael O'Dea and Kevin Whelan (eds), *Nations and Nationalisms: France, Britain, Ireland and the Eighteenth-Century Context* (Oxford, 1995), 103–16; I. R. McBride, *Scripture Politics: Ulster Presbyterian Radicalism in the Late Eighteenth Century* (Oxford, 1998); Joep T. Leerssen, *Mere Irish and Fíor-Ghael: Studies in the Idea of Irish Nationality, its Development and Literary Expression Prior to the Nineteenth Century* Amsterdam, 1988; C. D. A. Leighton, *Catholicism in a Protestant Kingdom: A Study of the Irish Ancien Regime* (Dublin, 1994); S. J. Connolly, *Religion, Law, and Power: The Making of Protestant Ireland* (Oxford, 1992).

21. For a range of views see inter alia Nicholas Canny, 'Irish Resistance to Empire? 1641, 1690 and 1798' in Lawrence Stone (ed.), *An Imperial State at War: Britain from 1689 to 1815* (London, 1994), 288–321; Aidan Clarke, 'Colonial Identity in Early 17th-century Ireland' in T. W. Moody (ed), *Nationality and the Pursuit of National Independence. Historical Studies XI* (Belfast, 1978), 57–72; J. L. McCracken, 'Protestant Ascendancy and the Rise of Colonial Nationalism' in T. W. Moody and W. E. Vaughan (eds), *A New History of Ireland, Vol. IV: Eighteenth-Century Ireland, 1691–1800* (Oxford, 1986), 104–22; R. B. McDowell, *Ireland in the Age of Imperialism and Revolution 1760–1801* (Oxford, 1979); Charles Ivor McGrath, *Ireland and Empire, 1692–1770* (London, 2012); and Thomas McLoughlin, *Contesting Ireland: Irish Voices against England in the Eighteenth Century* (Dublin, 1999).

22. Terrence McDonough 'Introduction' in idem (ed.), *Was Ireland a Colony? Economics, Politics and Culture in Nineteenth-Century Ireland* (Dublin, 2005), vii–viii. For the earlier argument, see Ruane, 'Colonialism and the Interpretation of Irish Historical Development' in Marilyn Silverman and P.H. Gulliver (eds), *Approaching the Past: Historical Anthropology through Irish Case Studies* (New York, 1992), 293–323.

23. Ibid., viii.

24. For an overview of these debates, see Howe, 'Empire and Ideology' in Sarah Stockwell (ed.), *The British Empire: Themes and Perspectives* (Oxford, 2007), 157–76.

25. On Greater Britain, see Charles Dilke, *Greater Britain* (London, 1868); idem. *Problems of Greater Britain* 2 vols. (London, 1890); J. R. Seeley, *The Expansion of England* (London,

1883), Duncan Bell, *The Idea of Greater Britain: Empire and the Future of World Order, 1860–1900* (*Princeton, 2007), David Armitage, *Greater Britain, 1516–1776: Essays in Atlantic History* (Aldershot, and Burlington, VT, 2004). For the 'British World', a concept which has had recent renewed popularity among historians, Carl Bridge and Kent Fedorowich (eds), *The British World: Diaspora, Culture and Identity* (London 2003, Belich, *Replenishing the Earth* op.cit. On empire's metropolitan British impact, contrast for instance Catherine Hall, *Civilising Subjects: Metropole and Colony in the English Imagination 1830–1867* (Oxford, 2002) with Bernard Porter, *The Absent-Minded Imperialists: What the British really thought about empire*, (Oxford, 2004). Equivalent investigation on empire and Irish society remains comparatively scanty, but see several contributions to Keith Jeffery (ed), *'An Irish Empire'? Aspects of Ireland and the British Empire* (Manchester, 1996).

26. Matthew Kelly, 'Irish Nationalist Opinion and the British Empire in the 1850s and 1860s' *Past & Present*, 204, 1, 2009, 127–54; Paul A. Townend, 'Between Two Worlds: Irish Nationalists and Imperial Crisis 1878–1880' *Past and Present* 194, 2007, 139–74; Townend ' "No Imperial Privilege": Justin McCarthy, Home Rule, and Empire'; Niamh Lynch 'Defining Irish Nationalist Anti-Imperialism: Thomas Davis and John Mitchel', and Caoilfhionn Ní Bheacháin 'The Mosquito Press': Anti-Imperialist Rhetoric in Republican Journalism, 1926–39' all in *Éire-Ireland* 42: 1 and 2 (2007); Niall Whelehan, 'The Dynamiters: Irish Nationalism and Political Violence in the Wider World, 1867–1900' (Cambridge, 2012).

27. Tadhg Foley and Maureen O'Connor (eds), *Ireland and India: Colonies, Culture and Empire* (Dublin, 2006); Kate O'Malley, *Ireland, India and Empire: Indo-Irish Radical Connections, 1919–64* (Manchester, 2008); Michael Silvestri, *Ireland and India: Nationalism, Empire and Memory* (Basingstoke, 2009); Barry Crosbie, *Irish Imperial Networks: Migration, Social Communication and Exchange in Nineteenth-Century India* (Cambridge, 2012); Jill Bender, 'The Imperial Politics of Famine: The 1873–74 Bengal Famine and Irish Parliamentary Nationalism', *Eire-Ireland* special issue 42, 1 and 2, (2007), 132–56; Jennifer Regan-Lefebvre, *Cosmopolitan Nationalism in the Victorian Empire: Ireland, India and the Politics of Alfred Webb* (Basingstoke, 2009). Earlier work includes H. V. Brasted, 'Indian Nationalist Development and the Influence of Irish Home Rule, 1870–1886', *Modern Asian Studies* 14, 1, (1980), 37–63; idem. 'Irish Nationalism and the British Empire in the Late 19th Century' in Oliver MacDonagh, W. F. Mandle, and Pauric Travers (eds), *Irish Culture and Nationalism, 1750–1950* (Dublin, 1983), 83–103; and 'Irish Models and the Indian National Congress 1870–1922' *South Asia VIII*, 1–2, (1985), 24–45.

28. Consult, for example, Luke Gibbons *Edmund Burke and Ireland: Aesthetics, Politics and the Colonial Sublime* (Cambridge, 2003).

29. James Livesey, *Civil Society and Empire: Ireland and Scotland in the Eighteenth-Century Atlantic World* (New Haven, 2009), quotation from p. 218.

30. See, for example, Donal Lowry, 'Ulster Resistance and Loyalist Rebellion in the Empire' (191–215), though for a different view, see Alvin Jackson, 'Irish Unionists and the Empire, 1880–1920: Classes and Masses' (123–49), both in Jeffery (ed.), *Irish Empire?*; Pamela Clayton, *Enemies and Passing Friends: Settler Ideologies in Twentieth Century Ulster* (London, 1996).

31. Linda Colley, *Britons: Forging the Nation 1707–1837* New Haven, 1992; Armitage, *Ideological Origins* op.cit.

32. Major instances include L. P. Curtis, *Anglo-Saxons and Celts: A Study of Anti-Irish Prejudice in Victorian England* (Bridgeport, Ct., 1968); Luke Gibbons, 'Race Against Time: Racial Discourse and Irish History', *Oxford Literary Review* 13, 1991, 95–113; R. N. Lebow, *White*

Britain and Black Ireland: The Influence of Stereotypes on Colonial Policy (Philadelphia, 1976); and H. L. Malchow, *Gothic Images of Race in Nineteenth-Century Britain* (Stanford, CA, 1996).

33. Noel Ignatiev, *How the Irish Became White* (New York, 1995) and the more carefully argued David R. Roediger, *The Wages of Whiteness* London, 1991. Very critical views are espoused for instance by Sheridan Gilley, 'English Attitudes to the Irish in England, 1780–1900' in Colin Holmes (ed.), *Immigrants and Minorities in British Society* (London, 1978), 81–110, and G. K. Peatling, 'The whiteness of Ireland under and after the Union' (and the accompanying Roundtable discussion), *Journal of British Studies*, 44 (1), 2005, 115–66.

34. Nini Rodgers, *Ireland, Slavery and Anti-Slavery: 1612–1865* (Basingstoke, 2007).

35. James Horn, 'British Diaspora: Emigration from Britain, 1680–1815' (28–52) and Thomas Bartlett 'Famous Island' op.cit., both in P. J. Marshall (ed.), *The Oxford History of the British Empire. Vol. 2: The Eighteenth Century* (Oxford, 1998). For an overview of Irish emigration and empire, see Kevin Kenny, 'The Irish in the Empire' in Kenny (ed.), *Ireland* op.cit., 90–122. From a vast relevant literature, see also especially Andy Bielenberg (ed.), *The Irish Diaspora*, London, 2000; Nicholas Canny (ed.), *Europeans on the Move: Studies in European Migration, 1500–1800* (Oxford, 1994). For a less familiar aspect of Irish involvement in the empire, see Barry Crosbie, 'Ireland, Colonial Science, and the geographical construction of British rule in India, c. 1820–1870' *The Historical Journal*, 52, 4, 2009, 963–87.

36. Kenny 'Irish in the Empire,' 98.

37. *The Irish Diaspora: A Primer* (Toronto and Belfast, 1996).

38. For a salutary corrective, consult David Fitzpatrick, *Oceans of Consolation: Personal Accounts of Irish Migration to Australia* (Ithaca, NY, 1994).

39. Donald Harman Akenson, *If the Irish Ran the World: Montserrat, 1630–1730* (Liverpool, 1997).

40. See Edmund Hogan, *The Irish Missionary Movement: A Historical Survey, 1830–1980* (Dublin, 1990); Colin Barr 'Imperium in Imperio': Irish Episcopal Imperialism in the Nineteenth Century, *English Historical Review* CXXIII, 2008, 611–50; and Fiona Bateman, 'Ireland's Spiritual Empire: Territory and Landscape in Irish Catholic Missionary Discourse' in Hilary M. Carey (ed), *Empires of Religion* Basingstoke, 2008 pp. 267–87—but also John Wolffe, 'Anti-Catholicism and the British Empire, 1815–1914' in ibid., 43–63.

41. John M. MacKenzie, 'Irish, Scottish, Welsh and English Worlds? The historiography of a four-nations approach to the history of the British Empire' in Catherine Hall and Keith McClelland (eds), *Race, Nation and Empire: Making Histories, 1750 to the Present* (Manchester, 2010), 133–53; 138.

42. Initially in his *Orientalism* (London, 1978). There are many anthologies and general surveys of work in the field, of which the most historically detailed is Robert J. C. Young, *Postcolonialism: An Historical Introduction* (London, 2001).

43. See especially, amidst a vast body of related work, Deane's 'General Introduction' to vol.1 of *The Field Day Anthology of Irish Writing*, Deane 3 Vols, (Derry, 1991) and his Deane, *Strange Country: Modernity and Nationhood in Irish Writing Since 1790* (Oxford, 1997); Gibbons, *Transformations in Irish Culture* Cork, 1996; Kiberd, *Inventing Ireland: The Literature of the Modern Nation* (London, 1995); Lloyd, *Anomalous States* and *Ireland After History* op.cit.

44. Cleary, 'Misplaced Ideas? Locating and Dislocating Ireland in Colonial and Postcolonial Studies' in Crystal Bartolovich and Neil Lazarus (eds), *Marxism, Modernity and Postcolonial Studies* (Cambridge, 2002), 101–24; *Literature, Partition, and the Nation State: Culture and Conflict in Ireland, Israel, and Palestine* (Cambridge, 2002); 'Amongst Empires: A Short History of Ireland and Empire Studies in International Context' *Eire-Ireland* special issue 42, 1 and 2, 2007, 11–57.

45. Henry Patterson, *The Politics of Illusion: A Political History of the IRA* (London, 1997); Brian Hanley and Scott Millar, *The Lost Revolution: The Story of the Official IRA and the Workers' Party* (London, 2009).

46. *Ireland in Crisis: A Study of Capitalist Colonial Underdevelopment* (Dingle, 1986); O'Hearn, 'The Irish Case of Dependency: An Exception to the Exceptions?', American Sociological Review 54, 4, 1989, 578–96, and his *Inside the Celtic Tiger: Reality and Illusion in the Irish Economy* (London, 1998).

47. For example, Tom Garvin, 'The Destiny of the Soldiers: Tradition and Modernity in the Politics of De Valera's Ireland' *Political Studies* 26, 3, 1978, 328–47; *The Evolution of Irish Nationalist Politics* (Dublin, 1981).

48. For arguments about colonial legacies and modernity, Conor McCarthy, *Modernisation: Crisis and Culture in Ireland, 1969–1992* (Dublin, 2000). On colonialism's supposed psychic effects, Geraldine Moane, *Gender and Colonialism* (Basingstoke, 1999), and—as part of a much wider-ranging, more influential argument—J. J. Lee, *Ireland 1912–1985: Politics and Society* (Oxford, 1989).

49. See Howe, *Ireland and Empire*, 'Historiography' and 'Questioning' op.cit. Also Joseph Ruane and Jennifer Todd, *The Dynamics of Conflict in Northern Ireland: Power, Conflict and Emancipation* (Cambridge, 1996); Frank Wright, *Northern Ireland: A Comparative Analysis* (Dublin, 1987); *Two Lands on One Soil: Ulster Politics Before Home Rule* (Dublin, 1996).

Select Bibliography

Belich, James, *Replenishing the Earth: The Settler Revolution and the Rise of the Angloworld, 1780–1930* (Oxford, 2009).

Bell, Duncan, *The Idea of Greater Britain: Empire and the Future of World Order, 1860–1900*. (Princeton, 2007).

Bridge, Carl and Fedorowich, Kent (eds), *The British World: Diaspora, Culture and Identity* (London, 2003).

Canny, Nicholas, *Making Ireland British, 1580–1650* (Oxford, 2001).

—— (ed), *The Oxford History of the British Empire. Vol. 1: The Origins of Empire. British Overseas Enterprise to the Close of the Seventeenth Century* (Oxford, 1998).

Howe, Stephen, *Ireland and Empire: Colonial Legacies in Irish History and Culture* (Oxford, 2000).

Jeffery, Keith (ed), *'An Irish Empire'? Aspects of Ireland and the British Empire* Manchester, 2006.

Kenny, Kevin (ed), *Ireland and the British Empire* (Oxford, 2004).

Lennon, Joseph, *Irish Orientalism: A Literary and Intellectual History* (Syracuse, NY, 2004).

McDonough, Terrence (ed.), *Was Ireland a Colony? Economics, Politics and Culture in Nineteenth-Century Ireland* (Dublin, 2005).

Marshall, P.J. (ed.), *The Oxford History of the British Empire. Vol. 2: The Eighteenth Century* (Oxford, 1998).

Rodgers, Nini, *Ireland, Slavery and Anti-Slavery: 1612–1865* (Basingstoke, 2007).

Silvestri, Michael, *Ireland and India: Nationalism, Empire and Memory* (Basingstoke, 2009).

Wright, Frank, *Northern Ireland: A Comparative Analysis* (Dublin, 1987).

CHAPTER 5

···

LANDSCAPE AND POLITICS

···

YVONNE WHELAN

I. INTRODUCTION

···

IN the Autumn of 2007 hundreds of protesters gathered at the Hill of Tara in County Meath, a prehistoric site of Irish cultural heritage and one of Ireland's most venerated archaeological sites. There they assembled in the form of a giant human harp, not as part of an elaborate stunt to gain entry into the *Guinness Book of Records,* but instead to promote the burgeoning campaign to reroute the national M3 motorway. Designed to ease the traffic in towns along the Meath corridor which have become part of the Dublin commuter belt, the M3 will also cut through the Tara-Skryne Valley, coming within a couple of kilometres of the Tara site. The campaign against the motorway gained momentum throughout the year as hundreds joined the campaign to stop the destruction of the environment around this historic location. The Hill of Tara was subsequently listed among the world's 100 most endangered heritage sites and was added to the crisis list of the World Monument Fund, one of the leading non-governmental organizations for the protection of cultural heritage. The clash between the commercially minded with a developmental agenda and those with a desire to protect and preserve ancient aspects of the cultural landscape eventually escalated into a bitter dispute that captures in microcosm a much broader set of debates about the relationship between landscape, politics, heritage, identity, and memory.

For historical and cultural geographers in particular, landscape has long been a key preoccupation and approaches to its study have changed markedly over time. The opening section of this chapter, therefore, reflects on the development of the landscape concept in human geography, before exploring the rich nexus of inquiry that has coalesced around landscape and politics in more recent years. Of particular significance is an approach to landscape that foregrounds the symbolic or iconic significance of the spaces in which we live and underscores the significance of the relationship between the cultural landscape and the political realm. The chapter then goes on to probe more deeply aspects of this relationship in an Irish context by focusing in turn on two case studies, the first relating to public spectacle and performance, and the second to the overlapping relationship between landscape and memory. These case studies underscore the significance of the cultural landscape and show that landscape is much more than a passive backdrop for the representation of the past.

II. LANDSCAPE: THE CONCEPTUAL CONTEXT

> A landscape is a cultural image, a pictorial way of representing, structuring or symbolising surroundings. That is not to say that landscapes are immaterial. They may be represented in a variety of materials and on many surfaces. […] A landscape park is more palpable but no more real, no less imaginary, than a landscape painting or poem. […] And of course, every study of a landscape further transforms its meaning, depositing yet another layer of cultural representation.[1]

Historical and cultural geographers have long been concerned with the study of landscape in all of its various forms, from the cultural to the physical, the rural to the urban, and have followed a variety of paradigms in order to represent its complexity. In the late nineteenth century, for example, the term *landschaft* came into common parlance in German geography to describe the appearance of the earth's surface or a particular region. At the same time in France, geographers approached landscape or *paysage* as 'an expression of human activity, as a human imprint upon the land'.[2] In many ways this work foreshadowed the influential research of Carl Sauer that would follow in the 1920s. When Carl Sauer, a Professor of Geography at the University of California at Berkeley, introduced the concept into American cultural geography he drew to some extent on the German *landschaft* tradition and approached landscape as the 'unit concept' of geography. For Sauer and his many students at Berkeley, landscape was an object to be studied. He was centrally concerned with how natural landscapes were transformed into cultural landscapes and in his 1925 paper 'The Morphology of Landscape' argued that 'the cultural landscape is fashioned from a natural landscape by a culture group. Culture is the agent, the natural area is the medium, and the cultural landscape is the result'.[3]

At the heart of Sauer's scientific endeavour, therefore, was a concern with the morphology of landscape, and more particularly, with the ways in which people (or 'culture groups') left their mark on the landscape. Sauer's research interests ranged widely, but a key strand focused on the human forces that shaped landscapes and he placed particular emphasis on the material artefacts, such as house types, that defined specific regions, especially in pre-European America. Although his legacy in cultural geography is extensive, his conceptualization of landscape and culture has also been controversial.[4] Sauer's accounts of seemingly obvious, tangible, countable, and mappable phenomena evident in the landscape were later criticized for resulting in 'endless studies of house-types, field patterns, log-cabin construction methods, and place-imagery in music lyrics', and for creating a sub-field of cultural geography that was 'antiquarian, particularistic and socially irrelevant'.[5]

The publication of Donald Meinig's edited collection *The Interpretation of Ordinary Landscapes* in 1979 marked something of a watershed moment for landscape studies.[6] The essays in this book in many ways demonstrated Sauer's continuing legacy but they also signalled some of the new directions that would take hold in the 1980s, especially relating to ideas of landscape as text and symbol. As geographers became increasingly influenced by theoretical developments in the humanities and social sciences more broadly, conceptualizations of landscape and culture were reformulated. Out of this intellectual ferment emerged a diverse range of new cultural geographies which critiqued more traditional understandings of culture and landscape. In the late 1980s and into the 1990s geographers began to revise received views of the cultural landscape. Instead of seeing landscapes as sites of settlement, they sought 'to recover layers of meaning lying beyond (or "beneath") those surface remains and relict features'.[7] The work of geographers like Denis Cosgrove, Stephen Daniels, and James Duncan was especially influential in this regard.

In the seminal *Social Formation and Symbolic Landscape*, published in 1984, Cosgrove conceptualized landscape as 'an ideologically-charged and very complex cultural product' and demonstrated a reflexive, sympathetic approach to the nuances and tensions evident in the processes of landscape creation.[8] In their edited collection, *The Iconography of Landscape* (1988), Cosgrove and Daniels advanced the idea of landscape as 'a cultural image, a pictorial way of representing, structuring or symbolising surroundings'.[9] Making use of an iconographic approach borrowed from art history, the authors focused attention on the symbolic make-up of cultural landscapes and on how landscapes might embody relations of power. The iconographic method had originally been employed by art historians to 'probe meaning in a work of art by setting it in its historical context and, in particular, to analyze the ideas implicated in its imagery. [It] consciously sought to conceptualise pictures as encoded texts to be deciphered by those cognisant of the culture as a whole in which they were produced'.[10] The adaptation of this approach for the study of the cultural landscape demanded that geographers focus renewed attention on the symbolic geographies embedded in the construction and design of landscapes and look beneath the surface to reveal the politics, processes, and symbolic qualities written into it.[11] James Duncan, meanwhile, was instrumental in positing a view of landscape as text and as 'one of the central elements in a cultural system, [...] a signifying system through which a social system is communicated, reproduced, experienced and explored'.[12]

Metaphors of landscape as text, symbol, and 'way of seeing' were indicative of a more overtly interpretative set of approaches to the study of landscape. Many of the 'new cultural geographers' of the 1990s were especially attentive to the idea of landscape as a construction and site of emblematic representation, a 'particular way of composing, structuring and giving meaning to an external world whose history has to be understood in relation to the material appropriation of land'.[13] The idea of landscape as an ideological and dynamic entity, one that could 'endorse, legitimise, and/or challenge social and political control' paved the way for a whole range of innovative readings of symbolic city spaces, many of which emphasized the politics of landscape and paid particular attention to public monuments.[14] The cultural landscape came to be conceptualized as a 'whole mix of human activities, systems of meaning and symbolic forms within the physical setting of the city'.[15] Seemingly ordinary, everyday spaces were seen to 'reveal, represent and symbolise the relationships of power and control out of which they have emerged and the human processes that have transformed and continue to transform them'.[16]

These new approaches to landscape study spawned innovative research in the cultural and historical geography of Ireland. As the historical geographer Anngret Simms explains, one of the key conceptual developments that enabled and enlivened much of this research was the theorization of landscape as a multifaceted symbolic text to be interrogated and decoded: 'The intention is to understand the iconography of the landscape for what it can tell us about the politically, economically and culturally dominant group in society [...] settlement is both medium and message, site and symbol, terrain and text'.[17] A body of work has subsequently evolved which approaches cultural landscapes as emblematic sites of representation and as dynamic symbolic constituents of sociocultural and political systems. Much of this research is sensitive to the symbolism and ideological significance of the built form in the construction, mobilization, and representation of identity. The blurring of the boundaries between historical and cultural geography has further strengthened the theoretical rigour of this subfield and highlighted the spatial dimensions of the negotiation of social and communal identities in Ireland. This has produced more nuanced readings of Irish cultural landscapes which focus fresh attention on the politics of space.[18]

The remaining sections of this chapter examine two case studies which delve into aspects of the relationship between landscape and politics in Ireland. The first examines the performative power and potential of landscape by providing a reading of one of the most spectacular events to take place in Ireland in the twentieth century, the thirty-first Eucharistic Congress. An especially striking aspect of this event, which took place in Dublin over five days in June 1932, relates to the use and manipulation of the urban landscape in order to mediate the effects of the congress and cultivate a very specific image of Ireland to the wider world. From the erection of grand architectural structures, to the nightly illuminations of the sky above the city, and from the excessive decoration of the city's streets and thoroughfares, to the carefully routed processions that marked the start and finale of the congress, landscape was central to the success of proceedings. The second case study calls attention to the monumental, as opposed to the spectacular, aspects of the cultural landscape. It explores more fully the ways in which monumental aspects of landscape play a crucial role in the representation and reconstruction of Ireland's past. Those seemingly innocuous aspects of the landscapes in which we live, whether it be a monument in a city square or the name attached to a street, are anything but accidental or ornamental features. On the contrary, they are very often the signifying threads that make up the fabric of our cultural landscapes and in turn help to construct and consolidate narratives of identity at a variety of spatial scales. After all, 'all memories have a geography. We recall memories, in part, through specific sites and attach our recollections to particular places'.[19] In particular, this section examines some recent

attempts to commemorate the Great Famine which demonstrate a shift from highly figurative forms of commemoration to more abstract, open, and nuanced memorials that
combine landscape, memory, and heritage in quite complex and challenging ways.

III. LANDSCAPE, SPECTACLE, AND THE EUCHARISTIC CONGRESS IN DUBLIN, 1932

In exploring the relationship between landscape and politics, historical and cultural
geographers have often looked to the ways in which public spectacles, parades, and
public performances serve as rituals of remembrance, as well as choreographed expressions of both power and resistance. Many studies have focused attention on the politics
of ritual and spectacle in different international contexts.[20] Research has shown that as
'landscape metaphors', parades have a multifaceted impact which is mediated materially and militarily, as well as through pageantry, illuminations, fanfare, music, and the
skilful appropriation of aspects of the past and public memory. A recurring theme in
this growing body of work on the spectacle and spatiality of performance relates to the
significant role of parades in identity formation, legitimation, and expression. Goheen's
work on the social valuation of public space and spectacle in late nineteenth-century
Toronto draws attention to the symbolic centrality of the city's 1884 semi-centennial
celebrations of a large parade which 'constituted a deliberate strategy of incorporation'
and was designed to afford maximum opportunity for spectators.[21] His analyses reveal
that public space 'is now as it has always been a space of contention. It is the visible and
accessible venue wherein the public—comprising institutions and citizens acting in
concert—enact rituals and make claims designed to win recognition'.[22]

A wide range of studies have explored Irish commemorative parades as examples of
public spectacle in dramatic form, whereby 'collective memory is maintained as much
through geographical discourses as historical ones'.[23] Drawing on Barthes's discussion
of the cultural meaning of spectacle, Johnson argues that the spaces in which the Peace
Day and Remembrance Day celebrations were staged in Ireland in the aftermath of
the First World War, and the formal iconography which surrounded them, were central to the cultivation of public memory.[24] Her spatial approach is echoed in Busteed's
study of two sympathy parades organized in response to the execution of the three
'Manchester Martyrs' in 1867, which he reads as expressions of subaltern resistance that
skilfully exploited local circumstances of time, tradition, and place to counteract the
hegemonic force of an authoritarian regime.[25] By focusing on the organization, route,
and composition of the processions, as well as on the dress and behaviour of participants, his research demonstrates how processions express resistance and reveal local
power relationships. Trigger's reading of St Patrick's Day parades in nineteenth-century
Montreal and Toronto reveals that parades exposed a wide range of complex political
questions, especially relating to the question of loyalty to Canada and Ireland and in

terms of the relationship between Catholics and Protestants.[26] Sugg-Ryan's analysis of the Irish Historic Pageant in New York in 1913 also points to the political subtext embedded in parades. In her exploration of the ways in which the Irish Historic Pageant represented Ireland's past, she argues that 'the pageant put on a performance of Irish heritage to show not only the continuation and resilience of Irish culture in the face of upheaval and oppression by the British, but also its superiority. […] it made a case for Home Rule and spearheaded the Irish renaissance in America.'[27]

This body of research illustrates that there are a range of landscape-based attributes associated with parading and public spectacle which demand closer scrutiny and which can inform the work of both the historian and the geographer alike. Chief among these are the processional space that is the parade route, the role of the military, and the forms of theatrical display that are deployed, including the use of decorations, lighting, fireworks, music, and temporary structures. It is also important to consider the ways in which aspects of the past can be drawn into public spectacles, underlining the significance of public memory in the contemporary affirmation of identity narratives. The sense of a shared heritage and history often assumes a great deal of importance in spectacular contexts. As Azaryahu observes, 'national history is a prime constituent in national identity', while a sense of a shared past is crucial for the cultural viability and social cohesiveness of both ethnic communities and nation-states'.[28] The past therefore constitutes a mass of symbolic capital which can be drawn upon, often rather selectively, in order to shape place identities and underpin particular ideologies. The dynamic relationship between history and geography is underscored in the context of public spectacles when selective reworkings of past events are interwoven into public displays which act as spatializations of memory. Many of these aspects converged in one of the most spectacular events to take place in twentieth-century Ireland, the thirty-first International Eucharistic Congress which took place in Dublin in June 1932.

Although primarily a celebration of the Blessed Sacrament and of the 1,500th anniversary of St Patrick's mission in the country, the Eucharistic Congress of 1932 offered the fledgling state an opportunity to showcase to the world a vision of a new, independent, and overtly Catholic nation.[29] Over the course of five days Dublin's urban landscape served as the stage upon which spectacular displays were performed, gigantic temporary structures were erected, and decorations were unveiled. It was also the setting for large gatherings and the mass movement of thousands of people in carefully coordinated processions through city space. In ways that mimicked the ostentatious spectacle of royal visits at the turn of the twentieth century, the spectacle of the Eucharistic Congress ensured 'that the Irish State would be defined in large part according to the religious loyalties of the vast majority of its citizens'.[30] The spectacular elements of the congress—the street decorations, the erection of temporary structures, the soundscape created by military bands and church choirs, the pioneering floodlighting and audiovisual technology, the symbolic welcoming of the papal legate, the procession of the legate through the capital on his arrival into the city—combined to create a 'web of signification' that was skilfully spun by the state in order to cultivate a very singular image of Ireland.[31]

The events that took place in June bring some key aspects of this strategic appropriation of urban space into sharp focus. Especially noteworthy is the way in which space was claimed by the extensive decorations that were erected on the major public thoroughfares, in residential districts, and especially along the chief parade routes in order to give visual expression to Irish religious and national identity. The *Irish Times* noted in the lead-up to the event that:

> Throughout the city in virtually all the main thoroughfares workmen are busily engaged in erecting gaily coloured Venetian poles to carry flags and bunting, and generally preparing a scheme of decoration that will transform the appearance of the city. [...] From Killiney in the south to Howth in the north there will be an unbroken display of flags, bunting, flowers and plants, with countless coloured lights, transforming the whole city and coastal borough into a veritable fairyland.[32]

Before the Pope's representative, Cardinal Lorenzo Lauri, arrived in Ireland, over £15,000 was spent on the decorations for the capital. Fresh flowers and bunting, as well as papal and Congress flags were the order of the day as local committees in every parish of the city vied with each other in terms of the lavishness of their displays. It was especially noteworthy that Dublin's less salubrious tenement areas of the north inner city were extremely well bedecked, in sharp contrast to the visit of Queen Victoria in 1900:

> It is in the poor districts, however, in the lowly tenement areas and the tumbledown back streets, that one observes the most impressive tokens of the faith which animates the poor and needy. For every single flag in the better-class districts, there seem to be at least half a dozen in such humble districts as Cumberland Street, Gloucester Street, or Gardiner Street. [...] Shrines of the Sacred Heart and of the Blessed Virgin, pictures of Christ the King, St. Patrick, and Congress shields are plentifully displayed: there is the keenest, yet the friendliest, rivalry among the people.[33]

With the city suitably bedecked and festooned, the spectacle got under way when the Papal Legate arrived at Dún Laoghaire harbour on 20 June 1932 and began his ceremonial procession through the city.

When Cardinal Lauri's steamer arrived near Dún Laoghaire it was led safely into the harbour by a squadron from the Irish Army, flying in cruciform formation. After the formal greetings from the Archbishop of Dublin, Edward Byrne, the main sponsor of the congress, as well as Eamon de Valera and other dignitaries, the nine-mile processional route from Dún Laoghaire to the Pro-Cathedral on Marlborough Street got under way. This procession was very carefully crafted, moving initially through Dublin's more affluent southern suburbs to the Merrion Gates, where the streets were lined with rows of 36,000 cheering schoolchildren. The *Irish Times* records that:

> The procession from Dun Laoghaire to Merrion Gates was a triumphal one. In the glittering sunshine, tempered with a slight breeze, motor cars moved along at creeping pace through a route decorated on a lavish scale with Papal and Eucharistic flags. Overhead was a squadron of aeroplanes in the shape of a cross. [...] The picturesque

suburbs looked their best, the decorations being magnificent. Every vantage-point *en route* was lined with people; shops were closed while the procession was passing, and all windows were filled by interested spectators.[34]

When the cortège arrived at Merrion Gates, the symbolic entry point to the inner city, the Papal Legate was formally welcomed by the Lord Mayor of Dublin, Alfie Byrne, who had travelled to the gates in his ceremonial golden carriage. Forming the backdrop for this impressive ceremony were two ornamental pylons representing ancient city gates, and erected especially for the occasion. With their Romanesque detailing, the mock gates at Merrion tellingly evoked the architecture of Ireland *before* the Anglo-Norman invasion.[35] Indeed, this reference to a more ancient iconography was also evident in the use of St Patrick's Bell, which was taken from the National Museum for the pontifical mass on the final day of the congress, and in the adoption of the Cross of Cong as the chief emblem of the congress, 'a perfect example of Irish ecclesiastical art'.[36] At Merrion, the legate was formally presented with an address of welcome which had been printed on vellum and decorated with designs from the Book of Kells. In many ways this ceremony was a throw-back to the official welcome presented by Dublin Corporation to Queen Victoria during her visit in 1900, although then the decision of the Corporation to present an address of welcome to the visiting queen was highly contentious and met with fierce opposition.[37]

The papal cortège then proceeded through the 'city gates' and on into the south inner city, where the scenes of enthusiasm continued unabated. The *Irish Times* described the 'continuous wave of cheering' that emanated from those lining the route as the cortège neared College Green.[38] There, another of the gigantic temporary decorations came into view—a round tower, fifty-two feet high and clothed in living ivy that had been erected on the spot where the equestrian statue of King William III had stood until it was destroyed in an explosion in November 1928 (Figure 5.1).[39] This impressive showpiece was much more than decorative pastiche, however; rather it was part of the broader attempt to imbue the congress with a specifically Irish iconography, one that drew inspiration from an ancient, and significantly, *pre-colonial* Ireland. The procession then continued around College Green and Westmoreland Street 'to the great crowd gathered on O'Connell Bridge, where a large number of people had secured a vantage point on the temporary altar. [...] In O'Connell Street every point of vantage on roof and in window had been utilised, and a great crowd filled one of the widest thoroughfares in Europe'.[40] Following a blessing in the Pro-Cathedral, the papal legate continued his journey to the Archbishop's House in Drumcondra where, 'again there was remarkable demonstration on the part of the public, countless thousands of men, women and children lining the route and acclaiming the Papal ambassador'.[41]

Over the course of the five days that followed, Dublin's urban landscape continued to play a central role in the congress spectacle, both by day and especially by night. Most of the city's prominent public buildings were specially lit for the duration of congress week in a manner that skilfully harnessed the power of the night sky:

> From dusk to dawn the city will be illuminated. Skylights will play on the clouds with such messages as 'Adoremus te' and 'Hail Christ the King' and 'Laudamus te' and buildings will be flood-lighted or festooned with strip lights. In residential streets

FIGURE 5.1 Round Tower, College Green (National Library of Ireland)

Source: National Library of Ireland.

every window will have its lighted candle, symbolic of the Light of Faith and of welcome to visitors.[42]

After a week-long programme of events, the congress reached its spectacular finale on Sunday, 26 June when Pontifical Mass was celebrated in the Fifteen Acres of the Phoenix Park in front of an estimated congregation of one million people. Another impressive architectural structure formed the centrepiece for this event, John J. Robinson's Great Altar. Designed by one of the leading church architects of the period, the altar comprised a central pavilion, with two curving colonnades on either side that drew on the classical style and echoed St. Peter's in Rome. In so doing, the altar conformed to the commission guidelines which specified the use of classicism in order to celebrate the universality of the Catholic Church. So, in contradistinction to those other aspects of the congress which drew on a specifically Celtic iconography, Robinson's altar 'distanced the congress from purely nationalist manifestations'.[43] After the mass, which concluded with a live address from the Vatican, the congregation processed through the city centre to O'Connell Bridge for the final benediction. In another carefully crafted and highly organized operation, the congregants processed along four different routes for the fifteen-mile journey. Each of the processional routes left the park via the Parkgate Street exit where an imposing triumphal arch had been erected especially for the event. Along the length of each route some four hundred loud speakers had been installed so that the 'processionists and those lining the route may join in the singing of the hymns led by the special choir in the park'.[44] This effectively meant that in a very real and tangible way Dublin was almost completely claimed by the congress and its congregation:

> The chanting of the choir in the Phoenix Park and the recitation of their prayers, relayed by the loud speakers, was taken up by the crowds until the roar of hundreds of thousands of voices echoed through the streets transforming the city of Dublin into a vast cathedral, the gently fluttering flags overhead like the banners of a triumphant army hung in other and less spacious cathedrals throughout the world.[45]

As many as half a million people then crowded around O'Connell Bridge for the final blessing from the Papal Legate, which 'concluded the greatest day of ritual that Ireland had ever seen'.[46] The architectural centrepiece of this benediction was Robinson's high altar, a scaled-down version of his Phoenix Park altar, with an art deco twist.[47]

Described as 'the greatest celebration of Catholicism in the history of independent Ireland' the Eucharistic Congress of 1932 harnessed the power of the cultural landscape in ways that had never been witnessed before in order to present a triumphant spectacle of religious devotion and national identity.[48] This brief reading of the event seeks to augment traditional historical accounts by drawing attention to the material role of landscape, social space, and spectacular display in the mediation of state and religious power. It also seeks to show that the cultural landscape does not simply provide a passive backcloth for the enactment of spectacle, but is, in fact, a crucially important aspect of public spectacles.[49] The congress was designed to leave an indelible mark upon the popular consciousness by exploiting both the enchanting power of grand display and the latent symbolic capital of the cultural landscape. The spectacular processions through the city, the decorations and gigantic temporary structures that were erected, as well as the cutting-edge technology used throughout, all combined to spectacular effect, and played a crucial role in the construction of a very particular image of Dublin. The event was designed to attract maximum publicity and set out to incorporate many of the city's residential neighbourhoods in a manner that afforded maximum opportunity for local people to become participants in the event. Thousands of people were subsequently drawn into a spectacle which was then projected around the world and the spatialization of Catholicism that occurred during congress week ultimately helped to make this event 'the culminating and most visual expression of Irish national Catholic ideals'.[50]

IV. Landscapes, Politics, and Spaces of Memory

Alongside a burgeoning body of work on the spectacular aspects of landscape another especially fruitful area of landscape inquiry has coalesced around the nexus of landscape, memory, and identity, and focused attention on the iconographic meanings embedded in cultural landscapes. Many cultural and historical geographers have probed the politics of public memory in a wide range of geographical settings and historical contexts, and elaborated on the symbolic geographies of what is remembered in the public domain, as well as upon that which is forgotten.[51] As focal points of public memory, monuments have been shown to possess an enduring significance as identity resources and as spaces 'where memories converge, condense, conflict, and [which] define relationships between past, present, and future'.[52] The trajectories of memory work in historical and cultural geography have been many and varied, but an especially rich seam has exposed the ways in which monuments act as mnemonic devices that feed into constructions of identity and articulate strategies of resistance.[53]

A large body of memory work has subsequently emerged which foregrounds the ways in which 'memorials and monuments are political constructions, recalling and representing histories selectively, drawing popular attention to specific events and people and obliterating or obscuring others.'[54] In an Irish context, Graham's work on contested landscape representations among Northern Irish Protestants, for example, has been important in advancing the notion of the representative landscape, defined as 'an encapsulation of a people's image of itself, a collage, based upon the particularity of territory and a shared past which helps define communal identity.'[55] McDowell has shown that the remembrance of the past in the north of Ireland is about much more than the expression of grief and the acknowledgement of loss. On the contrary, she argues, memorialization is a political resource, used to claim territory and express power in the cultural landscape.[56] Representative landscapes have also been a feature of Nash's work on the gendered dimensions of literary and artistic configurations of place. For example, her analysis of the construction of the west of Ireland as an iconic landscape purposefully blends literary criticism and spatial interpretation to expose the multiplicity of meanings that give the west its symbolic power.[57] Johnson's research on the commemoration of World War I in post-partition Ireland further illuminates the emblematic power of landscape by foregrounding the constitutive role of space in the poetics and politics of remembrance. Building on her earlier work on the commemoration of the 1798 rebellion and nationalist memorials in Dublin, Johnson explores 'the 'civil war' of identity and memory' that underpinned the public remembrance of Ireland's war dead and the casualties of the Easter Rising.[58]

Ireland, therefore, has long provided a rich resource base for work on the overlapping relationships between landscape, memory, and identity, especially given the contested political relationship between Britain and Ireland which placed significant demands upon the symbolic fabric of the cultural landscape. This is particularly evident in the capital, Dublin, where before and after independence the cityscape became a highly contested site in which competing ideologies found symbolic representation in the city's monuments, street names, and architectural developments, and even in various urban planning proposals. The monuments that line Dublin's central thoroughfare, O'Connell Street, for example, illustrate some of the ways in which monuments make meaning in public space and how fluid those meanings are. Before 1922, the centre of this street, then known as Sackville Street, was dominated by a monument dedicated to Lord Nelson which had been unveiled in 1809, on the anniversary of the Battle of Trafalgar. This monument, alongside many others throughout the city dedicated to figures associated with the British military and monarchy, stood as a symbol of Ireland's status as a city of the British Empire.[59] But Dublin was also a highly contested space and, even before the achievement of independence in 1922, monuments dedicated to a swathe of figures broadly related to Irish nationalist politics were used to issue a 'challenge in stone'. So, Nelson was joined by statues dedicated to figures associated with different strands of nationalist politics, like, for example, Daniel O'Connell, William Smith O'Brien, Sir John Gray, and Charles Stewart Parnell, as well as the temperance reformer, Fr Theobald Mathew. The unveiling of these monuments in such prominent locations also signalled the power of the increasingly nationalist Dublin Corporation. It is also notable that this public body refused permission for monuments like that dedicated to Prince Albert, for example, to be erected on Carlisle (later O'Connell) Bridge, instead relegating it to the then private domain of Leinster Lawn.

This process gathered momentum after independence when memorial spaces became an important tool in the nation-building agenda. The commemoration of the 1916 Rising became an important trope of memorial landscapes, reaching a crescendo in the fiftieth anniversary celebrations of 1966.[60] Then, the opening of Daithí Hanly's Garden of Remembrance in Parnell Square, just north of O'Connell Street, further underscored the significance of landscape, material culture, and popular spectacle in the remembrance of aspects of Ireland's past.[61] It is also notable, of course, that many older monuments of empire were destroyed during this period, underlining the significance of forgetting and erasure in the process of building nations. So, the jubilant scenes that had prevailed in 1809 when Nelson's Pillar was unveiled stand in marked contrast to events that took place some years later in 1966. In the early morning of 8 March a bomb rocked O'Connell Street, badly damaging the column, and toppling the statue of Nelson.

The site then remained vacant until December 2000 when the Irish Government announced that a new monument known as the 'Dublin Spire' was to be erected on the site of the old pillar. This slender steel structure, 120 metres high and 3 metres in diameter at its base, was constructed 'in celebration of Ireland's confident future in the third millennium' and contrasts markedly with those earlier erected monuments of both empire and nation-building.[62] Designed by the London-based architect Ian Ritchie and unveiled in 2003, the Spire of Dublin is significant in that it suggests a fundamental shift in the ways in which monuments are used in our contemporary cultural landscapes. For one commentator, 'the fact that it commemorates no historical figure is surely one of its strengths. By simply reaching for the heavens, from a base of only three metres to a height fully twice that of Liberty Hall, this extraordinary edifice can be viewed as a monument to optimism and hope for the future.'[63] The Spire captures the movement from a figurative to a non-figurative aesthetic, from monuments that celebrate fixity and are associated with static, unyielding emplacement, to monumental spaces that frustrate the desire to fix a singular memory or meaning on the memorial. In many ways, such monuments force the viewer to make and take their own meaning and in so doing they offer an alternative to those more traditional monuments which, as Gibbons claims, 'do not embody memory but efface it, absolving the citizen of the burden of remembering by relocating it in static form'.[64] This trend is especially evident in some recent monumental initiatives that have taken place in landscapes of the Irish diaspora.

For emigrant communities the process of migration and displacement sharpens nostalgia and fosters a hunger for heritage.[65] As Lively argues, 'displaced persons are displaced not just in space but in time; they have been cut off from their own pasts. [...] If you cannot revisit your own origins—reach out and touch them from time to time—you are forever in some crucial sense untethered'.[66] For many diasporic communities, therefore, claiming spaces of the cultural landscape takes on particular significance and the desire to reimagine spaces of the homeland has engendered a variety of commemorative practices rooted in the cultural landscape. As Aplin points out, 'we need connections with both place and time to locate our present lives geographically and historically; heritage helps in both the temporal and spatial sense. It also helps us locate ourselves socially, in the sense that it is one of the things that binds communities and nations, giving a sense of group identity to both insiders and outsiders.'[67] Although a burgeoning body of literature has shed new light on the materiality of diasporic experiences, drawing particular attention to the role of literature in forging narratives of migrant identity, there is also much scope for a closer and more sustained analysis of the spaces of memory created overseas.

For those Irish people abroad who trace their ancestry to the three-quarters of a million Irish people who emigrated or died during and after the Famine of the mid-nineteenth century, the commemoration and representation of that past has a great deal of cultural and political significance. This was brought to the fore in recent years with the sesquicentenary of the Famine in the mid-1990s, an anniversary that marked the onset of a concerted effort by many Irish-Americans to commemorate the plight of their ancestors, through the development of sites of famine memory and cultural heritage.[68] Landscapes in various sites of the Irish diaspora came to act as important stages upon which scenes of the Great Irish Famine were represented in monumental form. Invariably, these sites represented the famine and migration experience as a triumphant journey from poverty to socio-economic success.[69] In their form and composition many famine memorials projected a rather fixed and sanitized version of the past, one which erased the rawness of the Famine trauma in favour of a celebration of an immigrant group's fortitude and triumph.[70]

A number of recent memorials, however, have succeeded in melding landscape, memory, and heritage in much more complex, challenging and less overtly figurative ways. The Irish Hunger Memorial in Battery Park City, New York, for example, takes the form of a reconstructed ruined stone cottage from Attymass in County Mayo on Ireland's west coast. Designed by Brian Tolle, this memorial space was planted with Mayo vegetation and strewn with thirty-two fieldstones, one from each Irish county, and a single carved pilgrim stone. One entry to the base of the memorial takes the viewer through a passageway that is redolent of a neolithic burial mound, the walls of which are lined with glass-covered strands of text that deliberately mingle Famine facts, statistics about world hunger and obesity today, and quotations from literature and song. An especially striking feature of the memorial is the way in which it defies easy explanation and frustrates the desire to fix a singular memory or meaning on the memorial. The antithesis of a traditional public monument, the Irish Hunger Memorial is open to multiple interpretations and as such draws the visitor into a deeper engagement with what it seeks to represent, remember, and even forget.

The self-reflexive qualities of the Irish Hunger Memorial are also in evidence at the Australian Monument to the Great Irish Famine at Hyde Park Barracks in downtown Sydney. This memorial remembers the young women who were selected from poorhouses in Ireland during the Famine and offered the opportunity of work in New South Wales. Unveiled in 1999, this memorial was designed by the artists Hossein and Angela Valamanesh. The main focus of their design centred on the dislocation of the Barracks southern wall: 'a section of this wall will be dismantled and rebuilt on a rotated axis. In the space of the demolished wall, two glass panels bearing sandblasted inscriptions of women's names will be installed, which intersects a bronze cast table projecting outwards in either direction.'[71] At one end of the split table they placed a bowl with a void in its base that continues through the table itself, and at the other end an institutional table setting, complete with utensils cast in bronze. For the designers:

> This further symbolizes the contrast between hunger and comfort, which underpinned the role of the Barracks as shelter. The suggestion of continuity in the two ends of the table represents the continuous and evolving relationships between the site and the lives of those who immigrated. The table and the more intimate spaces created within the rotated wall evoke the domestic nature of life and work for the majority of Irish women migrants while their simplicity and sparseness allude to the subject of the Famine.[72]

The Famine Memorial at Hyde Park Barracks, like that at Battery Park City in New York, challenges the very idea of monumentality. The design and layout of this memorial means that it is impossible to view in its totality. The rotated wall and the adjacent etched glass panels might allow the visitor to see through the memorial space but it also prevents them from walking through the artwork. This physical distance creates a measure of disruption, dislocation, even frustration, while the faint and faded etchings serve to mirror the frail and inconstant nature of memory itself. It ultimately draws the visitor into a more active engagement with the memorial as they seek to make their own meaning.

The more complex rendering of the famine narrative that is presented at the memorials in New York and Sydney is also evident at Ireland Park in Toronto, one of the most recent examples of Irish famine memory. Situated on the banks of Lake Ontario in downtown Toronto, this memorial occupies a small stretch of land, 45 metres by 25 metres, on the city's otherwise rather exclusive waterfront. Its origins date back to the late 1990s when the Toronto-based architect Robin Kearns first viewed a sculpture in Dublin called 'Famine' on the banks of the River Liffey. Rowan Gillespie's 'Famine', with its seven departing figures, was unveiled in 1997 to commemorate the 150th anniversary.[73] It had always been intended that the Dublin monument should have a companion piece, one that would embody the migrant experience and arrival in a new land on the other side of the Atlantic. Kearns proposed Toronto as the location for that companion piece and Ireland Park, designed by the Toronto-based architect Jonathan M. Kearns, was the result.

The memorial was opened by former Irish President, Mary McAleese, in June 2007 and necessitated the renaming of a small stretch of the nearby Queen's Quay to Éireann Quay. It is a striking space for a whole host of reasons, not least for the way in which it combines the figurative with the abstract to great effect (Figure 5.2). Located a short distance from Toronto's city airport and ferry terminal, Ireland Park lies west of Rees's Wharf where the majority of immigrants landed, and south of the immigrant sheds which were established to receive the 38,560 Irish that arrived in Toronto in 1847. To the north of the park lie the city-owned but now defunct silos of the Canada Malting Company. These giant silos loom large in the background and in their empty, neglected state unwittingly provide a very fitting backdrop for this site dedicated to famine memory. These gigantic circular drums were also the inspiration behind one of the symbolic focal points of Ireland Park, the glass tower that was built in front of them. Standing approximately 6 metres in height, the illuminated tower of stacked glass blocks was designed to be 'a symbolic beacon of the 'New World' and the immigrants' hopefulness for the future'.[74] The second key element of Ireland Park is the wall of imported Kilkenny limestone broken up into fourteen columns to form the western edge of the memorial and creating in the process 'a remarkable landscape-within-a-landscape'.[75] What is especially striking about this disjointed wall is the way in which the names of 675 of Toronto's 1,100 famine victims are inscribed between the crevices of each of these rough-hewn slabs.[76] Only partially exposed, however, the visitor is forced to physically engage with this space, to weave their way into and through these slabs of Irish rock in order to read the names that are etched into the fissures.

At the eastern end of the Park, facing the harbour and in full view of the Toronto skyline, stands the figurative element of this memorial, Rowan Gillespie's sculpture series, entitled, 'The Arrival'. At the head of the sculptural group stands the 'jubilant

FIGURE 5.2 Ireland Park, Toronto

Source: Yvonne Whelan.

man' with his arms outstretched, thankful to arrive in a new land. Behind him, the 'pregnant woman' clutches her swollen stomach and to her right stands the 'the apprehensive
man', modelled on Pius Mulvey a character from Joseph O'Connor's *Star of the Sea* and,
it has been suggested, 'the spiritual reincarnation of the dog in the Famine sculpture' in
Dublin.[77] Between them, lies the 'woman on ground', sprawled and seemingly in the final
throes of a long and agonizing death. At the rear of the sculptural group stands the figure
of a child, the 'orphan boy'. He 'is of uncertain origin and time and could easily hail from
Ethiopia or the Sudan today'.[78] In creating these five figures, it is notable that Gillespie
'felt the onus to portray not only the horrendous human suffering of the Irish people
during the potato famine, but also the continuing suffering of famine victims globally'.[79]
For the sculptor, the coffin ships of the nineteenth century that would have carried his
migrants to Canada have a close parallel in the container ships and trucks that transport
migrants for cheap labour in the twenty-first century. Kohn writes of how 'it is hard not
to be reminded of the crowded fishing boats attempting to reach the Canary Islands
from West Africa or the Pakistani boys found frozen in a jumbo jet's wheel compart-
ment'.[80] The stark elegance and haunting sculptures of Ireland Park combine to create an
almost sacred space amidst the din of downtown Toronto. Surrounded by the ruins of
Toronto's industrial past and the hopes of its waterfront future, this memorial successfully combines both figurative and more abstract components as well as straddling the
past, present, and future.[81]

V. Conclusion

Landscape remains at the heart of a great deal of research in both human and physical geography and it continues to be conceptualized in new and innovative ways. In exploring the spectacular geographies of Ireland's Eucharistic Congress in 1932, as well as the rich iconographies of diasporic famine memorials that have been created in spaces of the Irish diaspora, this chapter has sought to highlight the merits of a conceptual and methodological approach that is attentive to the political, symbolic significance of landscape in shaping narrative of Irish identity and in the construction and representation of Ireland. The many and various spectacular dimensions of the 1932 congress coalesced to create an image of Ireland that privileged Catholicism and projected this outwards to the wider world. Landscape played a key role in the cultivation of this vision and although a largely ephemeral event—not a trace of any of the grand architectural displays remains—it nonetheless created a powerful evocation of Ireland in the fledgling years of the new state and one that lingered long in the imaginations of those who experienced it.[82] By way of contrast, the statues and memorials erected in landscapes in and of Ireland serve to create more tangible and permanent symbols in the landscape. The recent memorials remembering the Irish Famine demonstrate, however, that the meanings attached to these monuments are far from fixed, static, and stable. On the contrary, they present multiple visions of Ireland's past and use landscape in an altogether different way. They manage to connect the past with the present and the future and in the process create quite complex sites of public memory. These thoughtful, nuanced, and open-ended memorials, not only commemorate Ireland's Famine of the mid-nineteenth century, but they also speak to a whole host of global and very contemporary concerns.

Notes

1. Denis Cosgrove and Stephen Daniels (eds), *The Iconography of Landscape* (Cambridge, 1988), 1.
2. Alan R.H. Baker, *Geography and History: bridging the divide* (Cambridge, 2003), 110.
3. Carl O. Sauer, 'The Morphology of Landscape', *University of California Publications in Geography* 2, no. 2 (1925), 19–53. Reprinted in J. Leighly (ed), *Land and Life: a selection from the writings of Carl Ortwin Sauer* (Berkeley, 1963), 315–50, 343.
4. Denis Cosgrove and Peter Jackson, 'New directions in cultural geography', *Area* 19, no. 2 (1987), 95–101; Derek Gregory and David Ley, 'Culture's geographies', *Environment and Planning D: Society and Space* 6, no. 1 (1988), 115–16; Marie Price and Martin Lewis, 'The reinvention of cultural geography', *Annals of the Association of American Geographers* 83, no. 1 (1993), 1–17.
5. Don Mitchell, *Cultural Geography. A Critical Introduction* (Oxford: Blackwell, 2000), xiv; Denis Cosgrove and Peter Jackson, 'New directions in cultural geography', *Area* 19, no. 2

(1987), 95–101; Lily Kong, 'A "new" cultural geography? Debates about invention and rein-vention', *Scottish Geographical Magazine*, 113, no. 3 (1997), 177–85.

6. Donald Meinig (ed), *The Interpretation of Ordinary Landscapes* (New York, 1979).

7. Derek Gregory, *Geographical Imaginations* (Oxford, 1994), 145.

8. Denis Cosgrove, *Social Formation and Symbolic landscape* (London, 1984), 11.

9. Denis Cosgrove and Stephen Daniels (eds), *The Iconography of Landscape*, 1.

10. Cosgrove and Daniels, *The Iconography of Landscape*, 2.

11. Iain Robertson and Penny Richards (eds), *Studying Cultural Landscapes* (London, 2003), 4.

12. James Duncan, *The City as Text: the Politics of Landscape Interpretation in the Kandyan Kingdom* (Cambridge, 1990), 184.

13. Cosgrove and Jackson, 'New directions in cultural geography', 96.

14. Kong, 'A "new" cultural geography? Debates about invention and reinvention', 24.

15. William S. Logan, *Hanoi. Biography of a City* (Sydney, 2000), 1.

16. Robertson and Richards, *Studying Cultural Landscapes*, 4.

17. Anngret Simms, 'Perspectives on Irish settlement studies' in Terry Barry, ed., *A History of Settlement in Ireland* (London, 2000), 228–47, 237.

18. See, for example, Patrick J. Duffy, *Exploring the History and Heritage of Irish Landscapes* (Dublin, 2007); Brian J. Graham (ed), *In Search of Ireland* (London, 1997).

19. Joseph Nevins, 'The abuse of memorialized space and the redefinition of Ground Zero', *Journal of Human Rights* 4, no. 2 (2005), 267–82.

20. Peter Goheen, 'Parading: a lively tradition in early Victorian Toronto' in Alan R.H. Baker and Gideon Biger (eds), *Ideology and Landscape in Historical Perspective* (Cambridge, 1993), 330–51; Neil Jarman and Dominic Bryan, *From Riots to Rights. Nationalist Parades in the North of Ireland* (University of Ulster, 1998); Mike Cronin and Daryl Adair, *The Wearing of the Green. A History of St. Patrick's Day* (London, 2001).

21. Peter Goheen, 'The assertion of middle-class claims to public space in late Victorian Toronto', *Journal of Historical Geography* 29, no. 1 (2003), 73–92, 80.

22. Peter Goheen, 'The public sphere and the geography of the modern city', *Progress in Human Geography* 22, no. 4 (1998), 479–96, 479.

23. Nuala Johnson, *Ireland, the Great War and the Geography of Remembrance* (Cambridge, 2003), 57.

24. Johnson, *Ireland, the Great War and the Geography of Remembrance*, 78.

25. Mervyn Busteed, 'Parading the Green. Procession as subaltern resistance in Manchester in 1867', *Political Geography* 24, no. 8 (2005), 903–33.

26. Rosalyn Trigger, 'Irish politics on parade: the clergy, national societies, and St. Patrick's Day processions in nineteenth-century Montreal and Toronto', *Histoire Sociale–Social History* 37, no. 74 (2004), 159–99.

27. Deborah Sugg-Ryan, 'Performing heritage: the Irish historical pageant, New York, 1913' in Mark McCarthy (ed), *Ireland's Heritages* (Aldershot, 2004), 105–22, 106.

28. Maoz Azaryahu, 'German reunification and the power of street names', *Political Geography* 16, no. 6 (1997), 479–93, 480.

29. David G. Holmes, 'The Eucharistic Congress of 1932 and Irish identity', *New Hibernia Review* iv (Spring 2000), 55–78. See also Gary Boyd 'Supernational Catholicity', *Early Popular Visual Culture* 5, no. 3 (2007), 317–33; *Pilgrims' Souvenir and Guide to Dublin during the Eucharistic Congress* (Dublin, 1932); *Thirty-first International Eucharistic Congress,*

Dublin 1932: Pictorial Record (Dublin, 1932); *Advance Programme of the Eucharistic Congress* (Dublin, 1932).

30. Rory O'Dwyer, *The Eucharistic Congress, Dublin 1932. An Illustrated History* (Dublin, 2009).

31. David Ley and Kris Olds, 'Landscape as Spectacle: World's Fairs and the Culture of Heroic Consumption', *Environment and Planning D: Society and Space* 6, no. 1 (1988), 191–212.

32. *Irish Times*, 7 June 1932, 8.

33. *Irish Times*, 25 June 1932, 15.

34. *Irish Times*, 21 June 1932, 7.

35. John Turpin, 'Visual culture in the Irish Free State, 1922–1949', *The Journal of Ecclesiastical History* 57, no.1, 55–77, 75.

36. *Advance programme of the Eucharistic Congress* (Dublin, 1932). The emblem was also inscribed with the words 'International Congress at Dublin' in Celtic script.

37. Yvonne Whelan and Liam Harte, 'Placing geography in Irish Studies', in Liam Harte and Yvonne Whelan (eds), *Ireland Beyond Boundaries. Mapping Irish Studies in the Twenty-first century* (London, 2007), 175–97.

38. *Irish Times*, 15 June 1932, 3.

39. See Yvonne Whelan, *Reinventing Modern Dublin* (Dublin, 2003), 193.

40. *Irish Times*, 25 June 1932, 15.

41. Ibid.

42. *Irish Times*, 7 June 1932, 8.

43. Turpin, 'Visual culture in the Irish Free State, 1922–1949', 74.

44. *Irish Times*, 7 June 1932, 8.

45. *Irish Times*, 27 June 1932, 9.

46. Ibid.

47. Turpin, 'Visual culture in the Irish Free State', 74.

48. Ronan Fanning, *Independent Ireland* (Dublin, 1983), 130.

49. See Lily Kong and Brenda Yeoh, 'The construction of national identity through the production of ritual and spectacle', *Political Geography* 16, no. 3 (1997), 213–39.

50. Turpin, 'Visual culture in the Irish Free State', 72.

51. See Kenneth E. Foote and Maoz Azaryahu, 'Towards a geography of memory: geographical dimensions of public memory and commemoration', *Journal of Political and Military Sociology* 35, no. 1 (2007), 125–44.

52. Natalie Zemon Davis and Randolph Starn, 'Introduction: memory and counter-memory', *Representations* 26, no. 1 (1989), 1–6, 3.

53. David Atkinson and Denis Cosgrove, 'Urban rhetoric and embodied identities: city, nation, and empire at the Vittorio Emanuele II monument in Rome', *Annals of the Association of American Geographers* 88, no. 1 (1998), 8–49; Martin Auster, 'Monument in a landscape: the question of 'meaning', *Australian Geographer* 28, no. 2 (1997), 219–27; Michael Heffernan, 'For ever England: the Western Front and the politics of remembrance in Britain', *Ecumene* 2, no. 3 (1995), 293–323; Nuala C. Johnson, 'Sculpting heroic histories: celebrating the centenary of the 1789 rebellion in Ireland', *Transactions of the Institute of British Geographers* 19, no. 1 (1994), 78–93; Nuala C. Johnson, 'Cast in stone: monuments, geography, and nationalism', *Environment and Planning D: Society and Space* 13, no. 1 (1995), 51–65.

54. Rae Frances and Bruce Scates, 'Honouring the Aboriginal dead', *Arena* 86 (1989), 72–80, 72.

55. Brian J. Graham, 'No place of mind: contested Protestant representations of Ulster', *Ecumene* 1, no. 3 (1994), 257–81, 258.

56. Sara McDowell, 'Armalite, the ballot box and memorialization: Sinn Féin and the state in post-conflict Northern Ireland', *The Round Table. The Commonwealth Journal of International Affairs* 96, no. 393 (2007), 725–38.

57. Catherine Nash, 'Embodying the nation: the west of Ireland landscape and Irish identity' in Michael Cronin and Barbara O'Connor (eds), *Tourism in Ireland: a Critical Analysis* (Cork, 1993), 86–114; Catherine Nash, 'Embodied Irishness: gender, sexuality and Irish identity' in Brian J. Graham (ed), *In Search of Ireland* (London, 1997), 108–27.

58. Nuala C. Johnson, *Ireland, the Great War and the Geography of Remembrance* (Cambridge, 2003), 168, 170.

59. Yvonne Whelan, 'Monuments, power and contested space: the iconography of Sackville Street, Dublin before independence (1922)', *Irish Geography* 34, no. 1 (2001), 11–33; Yvonne Whelan, 'Symbolising the state: the iconography of O'Connell Street, Dublin after independence (1922)', *Irish Geography* 34, no. 2, (2001), 135–56.

60. See Mary E. Daly and Margaret O'Callaghan (eds), *1916 in 1966 Commemorating the Easter Rising* (Dublin, 2007); Róisín Higgins, '"The constant reality running through our lives": commemorating Easter 1916', in Liam Harte, Yvonne Whelan, and Patrick Crotty (eds), *Ireland: Space, Text, Time* (Dublin, 2005), 45–56.

61. Whelan, *Reinventing Modern Dublin*, 177–85.

62. Ian Ritchie, *The Spire* (London, 2004).

63. *Irish Times*, 22 January 2003, 17.

64. Luke Gibbons, *Transformations in Irish Culture* (Cork, 1996), 145.

65. David Lowenthal, *The Heritage Crusade and the Spoils of History* (Cambridge, 1998), 9.

66. Penelope Lively, *Oleander, Jacaranda: A Childhood Perceived* (London, 1994), 175, cited in Lowenthal, *The Heritage Crusade and the Spoils of History*, 9.

67. Graeme Aplin, *Heritage: Identification, Conservation and Management* (Oxford, 2002), 16.

68. See Mary E. Daly, 'History à la carte? Historical commemoration and modern Ireland', in Eberhard Bort (ed), *Commemorating Ireland. History, politics, culture'* (Dublin, 2004), 34–55.

69. Margaret Kelleher, 'Commemorating the Great Irish Famine', *Textual Practice* 16, no. 2, 249–76; Brian J. Graham, 'The past and present of the Great Irish Famine', *Journal of Historical Geography* 33, no. 1, (2007), 200–6; Whelan and Harte, 'Placing Geography in Irish Studies'.

70. Jenny Edkins, *Trauma and the Memory of Politics* (Cambridge, 2003), 122.

71. Joanna Gilmour and Michael Bogle, *Australian Monument to the Great Irish Famine* (Sydney, Historic Houses Trust of NSW, 2001).

72. Gilmour and Bogle, *Australian Monument to the Great Irish Famine*.

73. See Fintan O'Toole, 'Turning the Famine into corporate celebration', The *Irish Times*, 16 October 1998; John Crowley, 'Constructing Famine memory: the role of monuments', in Niamh Moore and Yvonne Whelan (eds), *Heritage, Memory and the Politics of Identity* (Aldershot, 2007), 55–68.

74. www.irelandparkfoundation.com/index.php.

75. Christopher Hume, 'Irish famine memorial park offers direction for waterfront', *Toronto Star*, 22 June 2007.

76. The historical team, led by Mark McGowan of the University of Toronto recovered these names from cemetery ledgers, newspapers, and manuscript collections. See Mark McGowan, *Death or Canada* (Toronto, 2009).

77. Roger Kohn, *Rowan Gillespie. Looking for Orion* (Dublin, 2007), 150.

78. Roger Kohn, *Rowan Gillespie. Looking for Orion*, 143.
79. Ibid.
80. Ibid.
81. Hume, 'Irish famine memorial park'.
82. See O'Dwyer, *The Eucharistic Congress, 1932* for accounts of personal testimonies.

Select Bibliography

Baker, Alan R.H., *Geography and History: bridging the divide* (Cambridge, 2003).

Boyd, Gary, 'Supernational Catholicity', *Early Popular Visual Culture* 5, no. 3 (2007), 317–33.

Cosgrove, Denis and Daniels, Stephen (eds), *The Iconography of Landscape* (Cambridge, 1988).

Duffy, Patrick J., *Exploring the History and Heritage of Irish Landscapes* (Dublin, 2007).

Duncan, James, *The City as Text: the Politics of Landscape Interpretation in the Kandyan Kingdom* (Cambridge, 1990).

Foote, Kenneth E. and Azaryahu, Maoz, 'Towards a geography of memory: geographical dimensions of public memory and commemoration', *Journal of Political and Military Sociology* 35, no. 1 (2007), 125–44.

Goheen, Peter, 'Parading: a lively tradition in early Victorian Toronto' in Alan R.H. Baker and Gideon Biger (eds), *Ideology and Landscape in Historical Perspective* (Cambridge, 1993), 330–51.

Graham, Brian J., 'The past and present of the Great Irish Famine', *Journal of Historical Geography* 33, no. 1, (2007), 200–6.

Graham, Brian J. and Howard, Peter (eds), *The Ashgate Research Companion to Heritage and Identity* (Aldershot, 2008).

Holmes, David G., 'The Eucharistic Congress of 1932 and Irish identity', *New Hibernia Review*, iv (Spring 2000), 55–78.

Johnson, Nuala, 'Sculpting heroic histories: celebrating the centenary of the 1789 rebellion in Ireland', *Transactions of the Institute of British Geographers* 19, no. 1 (1994), 78–93.

Johnson, Nuala, 'Cast in stone: monuments, geography, and nationalism', *Environment and Planning D: Society and Space* 13, no. 1 (1995), 51–65.

Johnson, Nuala, *Ireland, the Great War and the Geography of Remembrance* (Cambridge, 2003).

Kelleher, Margaret, 'Commemorating the Great Irish Famine', *Textual Practice* 16, no. 2, 249–76.

Kong, Lily and Yeoh, Brenda, 'The construction of national identity through the production of ritual and spectacle', *Political Geography* 16, no. 3 (1997), 213–39, 220.

Mitchell, Don, *Cultural Geography. A Critical introduction* (Oxford, 2000).

Robertson, Iain M. and Richards, Penny (eds), *Studying Cultural Landscapes* (London, 2003).

Simms, Anngret, 'Perspectives on Irish settlement studies' in Terry Barry (ed), *A History of Settlement in Ireland* (London, 2000).

Whelan, Yvonne and Harte, Liam, 'Placing geography in Irish Studies', in Liam Harte and Yvonne Whelan (eds), *Ireland Beyond Boundaries. Mapping Irish Studies in the Twenty-first Century* (London, 2007), 175–97.

Whelan, Yvonne, *Reinventing Modern Dublin* (Dublin, 2003).

PEOPLE, CULTURE, AND THE ECONOMY

CHAPTER 6

....

LAND AND THE PEOPLE

....

TERENCE DOOLEY

I. INTRODUCTION

....

ON 11 November 1966, Kevin O'Shiel, for many years a high-ranking Land Commission official, wrote in the *Irish Times* that 'land is the most combustible subject in Ireland'. It could be argued with a degree of justification that it had been for the previous 800 years or so. Beginning with the Anglo-Norman conquest of the twelfth century, successive waves of new settlers meant that the land question became inextricably entwined with issues of nationality, religion, and politics and, for as long as Ireland remained a predominantly agricultural society, where access to land greatly determined political, economic, and social status, it became inevitable that rural society would be characterized by generations of inter-class and sometimes sectarian tensions.

II. CONFISCATION AND PLANTATION

....

The Anglo-Norman settlement redefined landownership in social, cultural, economic, and political terms. The new settlers, predominantly confined within a geographical area commonly referred to as the 'English Pale', began to replace the existing tenurial arrangements determined by Gaelic kinship with a feudal system centred upon a manor that would eventually evolve into an estate system centred on a country house. For almost four centuries they regarded themselves and were accepted as the upholders of English rule in Ireland.[1]

By the early sixteenth century the Tudor government's more ambitious plans to consolidate control of Irish affairs led it to adopt a twinned conciliation and coercion policy. While at one level it was prepared to enter into accommodations with the Old English ruling elite (largely descendants of the Anglo-Norman settlers) and to offer

English titles of nobility and landownership to any Gaelic lord prepared to renounce his Gaelic title, surrender his lands, recognize the king, and promise to promote English law and custom (an instrument of policy usually referred to as 'surrender and regrant'), it also proceeded simultaneously with military campaigns. The forfeiture of certain estates (Anglo-Norman as well as Gaelic) allowed for the implementation in the 1540s of the first plantation schemes aimed at encouraging the settlement of English and Scots Protestants on confiscated lands. This was perceived not only as an effective means to assert state control but also as a way to expedite religious conversion, and so religion became very much entangled with the land question.[2]

The most ambitious of these schemes resulted in the plantation of Munster in the 1580s (following upon the break-up of the huge Anglo-Norman Desmond estate in 1579–83) and then Ulster in 1607, following the end of the Nine Years' War and the subsequent flight of the Gaelic earls into exile. Scholarly debate on the Ulster plantation illustrates just how complex the whole logic and process of land transfer was: private entrepreneurs did not just exploit the vacuum created by the departure of the Gaelic elite, they also benefited from the increasing indebtedness of those who remained and who were having difficulties adjusting to the new capitalist environment.[3]

Between 1603 and 1641 an estimated 70,000 English and 30,000 Scots migrated to Ireland, particularly to the northern province of Ulster, independently encouraged by the opportunities on offer in a new frontier or else enticed by improving landlords who brought in craftsmen as well as agricultural tenants. Dispossession of the Gaelic Irish naturally caused resentment as the new settlers took control of around 40 per cent of the profitable lands; they frequently found themselves under attack, most notably in Munster in 1598, Ulster in 1615, and again in 1641. All of these uprisings, especially in 1641, were characterized by religious tensions and the desire of some of the old Gaelic families to have their lands restored, but economic considerations—the poor harvests in 1640 and 1641 for example—remained possibly the dominant motivation.

The military campaigns of the sixteenth and seventeenth centuries provided obvious opportunities for English soldiers, administrators, and land speculators to benefit from confiscation and redistribution. One of the earliest examples was Richard Boyle, first earl of Cork, who rose from a modest administrative position to become the wealthiest man in Ireland by the end of the sixteenth century. On the other hand, officers and administrators who served the defeated Confederate Catholic cause in the 1640s were forced to forfeit their lands and were banished to Connaught where they received much smaller allocations. The Cromwellian plantation which followed in the 1650s was ostensibly intended to meet the cost of large-scale military operations in Ireland during the previous decade. In lieu of wages around 7,500 Cromwellians eventually settled on confiscated estates while another 1,000 so-called Adventurers, who had invested almost £360,000 in the campaign, were rewarded with lands totalling 1.6 million acres. The plantation represented the most significant phase of social engineering to date; S. J. Connolly has concluded that it was 'to determine the overall shape of the Irish social order for the best part of two centuries'.[4]

When the Commonwealth fell in 1659, Catholics, buoyed by the restoration of the monarchy, began to question the legal efficacy of the redistribution scheme. In late 1660, a royal declaration announced that Catholics who had not involved themselves in rebellion in 1641 or who had served the Crown in exile were to have their lands restored. In 1662 the Act of Settlement gave legal force to the declaration and in early 1663 a court of claims began to hear representations from those seeking the restoration of their lands. S. J. Connolly points out: 'The issue of so many decrees of innocence, entitling their holders to reclaim confiscated lands while leaving current occupiers to await compensation from clearly inadequate resources, provided understandable alarm.'[5] The result was that before one-seventh of the claims had been heard the government suspended the court and in 1665 the Restoration land settlement was abandoned. Catholics had only marginally increased their share of land to a total of around 20 per cent.[6]

The same alarm was evident amongst old and new Protestant settlers in 1685 when the Catholic King James II began to devise a scheme which proposed that Cromwellian and post-Cromwellian grantees would be required to restore one-half of their estates to their former owners. Instead, James' defeat in 1690–91 by William III opened the way for the further confiscation of Catholic lands and prompted the introduction of a series of penal (or anti-popery) laws. Simply stated, these were a series of discriminatory measures which represented the culmination of previously ad hoc attempts to exclude Catholics from landownership and positions of political and administrative influence and to repress Catholic worship. An act of 1697, for example, provided that the lands of a Protestant heiress who married a Catholic should be forfeited to her Protestant next of kin. Under the Act to Prevent the Further Growth of Popery (1704), Catholics were prohibited from buying land, inheriting land from Protestants, or holding leases for longer than thirty-one years. The lands of a deceased Catholic landowner had to be divided equally amongst all of his male heirs if they remained Catholics. In order to avoid the dispersal of their estates, many Catholic owners converted to the Established Church. Allied to the progressive subdivision or sale of Catholic estates during the depressed 1720s and 1730s (when they could legally be bought only by Protestants), this resulted in the almost total erosion of Catholic ownership. The 5 per cent of land they retained thereafter was concentrated mainly in Connaught and to a lesser extent in counties such as Meath, Dublin, Louth, and Kerry.

There were anomalies. The reasons why some Catholic landocrats such as the earls of Kenmare, earls of Fingall, or viscounts Gormanstown were allowed to retain large estates require investigation: did, for example, certain Gaelic families hold on to their lands, while remaining openly Catholic, because it was perceived that their influence and social standing would bring stability to an outlying region? As Ian McBride has pointed out, some Catholic landed families were 'able to evade legal restrictions by a variety of strategies including reliance on trustees, the friendly legal action known as the "collusive discovery", and nominal conversations'.[7] However, the erosion of Catholic landownership did not mean a corresponding erosion in Catholic landed interest. The vast majority of tenants remained Catholics, at least outside of large portions of Ulster. A significant proportion of these operated as middlemen leasing large tracts of lands from head landlords and deriving their profits from subletting in much smaller plots to tenant farmers. Their new-found position allowed them to maintain gentry-type lifestyles.[8]

Moreover, in the towns, despite the penal laws, a prosperous Catholic middle class emerged in the eighteenth century. Many of these wealthy merchant and manufacturing families were later able to reinvest in land, firstly as substantial tenants and later as purchasers when, for example, the crisis of the Great Famine provided them with the opportunity to purchase land under the Encumbered Estates Act of 1849.[9]

III. Pre-Famine Ireland

The second half of the eighteenth century witnessed a dramatic growth in the Irish population from around 2 million in 1740 to 5 million in 1800. The increase was mainly concentrated at the lower end of the social scale. On the eve of the Great Famine which began in 1845, there were approximately 10,000 landlords who controlled access to the bulk of Irish land; around 50,000–100,000 comfortable farmers of 50 to 80 acres who between them cultivated half of the lands (and provided also a good deal of labour); about 2.5 million farmers who held around 20 acres (but who did not usually employ labour from outside the family), and at the very bottom there were about 1.3 million smallholders, labourers, and cottiers who strove to subsist.[10] A degree of industrial prosperity (brewing, distilling, and linen) took some pressure off the land but change and stratification also gave rise to a myriad of rural complexities and often extreme regional variations. In the pre-Famine period outrage and intimidation shaped the land system to a peculiar degree; in fact, every decade from the 1760s to the 1840s witnessed at least one major outbreak of agrarian unrest. Conflict between competing economic interests—most particularly between strong farmers and smallholders, farmers and cottiers and labourers—frequently led to outbreaks of agrarian unrest orchestrated by secret societies: for example, the Whiteboys in Tipperary and surrounding counties in the 1760s and in parts of Leinster in the 1770s; the Hearts of Steel in the predominantly Presbyterian areas of Antrim and Down in the early 1770s, previously untouched by agrarian agitation (which later spread into Armagh, Tyrone, and Londonderry); and the Rightboys in Cork and surrounding counties in the 1780s.

These societies ostensibly sought to protect smallholders against unaffordable rents, to resist eviction, to discourage landgrabbing, and particularly to prevent the encroachment of the graziers who wanted to replace the small tillage holdings with much larger ones for the rearing of stock that would inevitably result in the unemployment of labourers.[11] The background to the Steelboy revolt in east Ulster in the early 1770s points to the need to understand these insurrections in their wider contexts: this was not just the result of economic crisis caused by three successive crop failures in 1769–71, a simultaneous decline in the linen industry, and the falling in of existing leases on estates in north Antrim; as Ian McBride has put it, this 'was partly a revolution of rising expectations on the part of the under-tenant class who sought to acquire direct leases for themselves and believed that long occupation combined with the "improvements" made by them and their ancestors gave them a moral entitlement to do so'.[12] In the main, agrarian conflict was, therefore, as Maura Cronin has succinctly put it in her pamphlet on agrarian protest in Ireland: 'the product of tradition reacting with modernisation in agriculture and land tenure'.[13] Cronin's pamphlet acts as an introductory guide to the work done to date by historians on agrarian protests from 1750 right up to the 1960s and points to how much research potential there is for further study in this area. On that point, it is worth considering McBride's argument that the understanding of the politics of pre-Famine agrarianism might be greatly enhanced if the willing historian had proficiency in the Irish language to make use of some of the important primary sources available, including material passed down in the oral tradition.[14]

Outbreaks until the 1830s were further complicated by the tithe question, the payment of support to the Established Church that was a major grievance with Catholic smallholders (who also had to maintain their own Church). Moreover, in areas of Ulster where there existed strong regional concentrations of small Presbyterian farmers, religious divides gave rise to many an agrarian confrontation stained by sectarianism.[15] Amongst the upper classes there were also wider socio-political concerns that because agrarian societies 'tapped into traditional notions of communal revenge, custom and justice within Irish society', social revolution could lead to a reconfiscation and redistribution of lands.[16] Thus, in the pre-Famine decades, as the state exerted more organized control, different religious, cultural, and political persuasions at the upper end of the social scale united in the interests of social respectability and status to break agrarian societies intent on controlling the local economy.[17]

IV. THE GREAT FAMINE

As the population continued to grow to around 8.2 million by the early 1840s a number of economic and social factors left the majority of inhabitants in rural Ireland extremely vulnerable: these included commercial restrictions; unstable market conditions; the existence of an encumbered landlord class reluctant to invest capital in estate improvements; the continued subdivision of holdings into smaller and, by extension, economically less viable units; and the overdependence of the poorer classes on the potato crop. When potato blight struck in successive seasons from 1845 to 1848 the resulting famine became one of the great social catastrophes of modern Europe.[18]

It is remarkable that considerably more attention has not been given to individual estates during the Great Famine.[19] Such studies are likely to show that there was a curious mix amongst landlords and their agents of investment and neglect, solicitude and indifference, sympathy and apathy.[20] There were rapacious landlords who used the Famine as a pretext to rid their estates of paupers to make room for more profitable grazier holdings; many were absentees neglectful of their lands and their duties (although not all absentee estates were poorly managed); while others remained over-indulgent and wasteful as their tenants and their families died or were forced to emigrate. On the other hand, many more bankrupted themselves in their attempts to alleviate the plight of their tenants. If most had one thing in common it was probably that they were financially constrained and as rental income was reduced they did not have the necessary capital to carry them through. Famine estate records are relatively rare—a subject worthy of a study in its own right—but it has been suggested that a decline of more than 50 per cent in rental incomes on individual estates from 1845 to 1851 may not be improbable.[21] Indeed, as has been argued by O Gráda and Eiriksson, it is likely that 'the famine's true role was that of a catalyst: getting rid of landlords who were doomed in any case'. In relation to this, the same authors also rightly contend that: '... the ability of so many [landlords] to accumulate such debts [through borrowing] offers a paradoxical reminder that Ireland before the famine was not short of idle capital'.[22]

The British government had an exaggerated view of what Irish landlords could have done to prevent catastrophe, as exemplified in legislative changes to the poor law that made them liable for all rates on holdings valued at £4 or under.[23] As many were faced with the Encumbered Estates Court they became less sympathetic towards the plight of their impoverished tenants and so began to clear their estates. But it is difficult to generalize: there were regional variations in terms of clearances, famine hardships, and landlord estate management policy, all of which require more detailed enquiry and explanation. How, for example, did so many northern landlords emerge unscathed from the Famine with, as Paul Bew puts it: 'their social functions and prowess preserved, possibly even enhanced'?[24] What was the national extent of 'assisted migration schemes' and did these generate legacies of resentment in both the local and receiving communities with repercussions for the future?[25] More practically, what impact had remittances on the local estate economy in the decades that followed? To what extent did they fashion the Irish land question and sustain various agrarian movements, or simply ensure the retention of a family farm?

A 'taboo subject' yet to be systematically tackled is the role of the strong farmers many of whom saw the social calamity as an opportunity to make further gains at the expense of cottiers and labourers.[26] They were continuously criticized by the contemporary press for their often callous behaviour which, in turn, only served to antagonize what might have been a much more generous English public. Can their behaviour be explained in terms of the class conflict and agrarian agitation that had divided strong farmers and the classes below them for generations? If the pre-Famine writings of the likes of Amlaoibh Ó Súilleabháin (1780–1837) can be taken as a gauge of the wealthier classes' fear of the impoverished, then there was likely to have been a relief amongst many strong farmers in the post-Famine period that the majority of the restless poor had disappeared.[27] What is more certain is that the disappearance of the cottiers, the labourers, and the smallholders gave farmers more room for manoeuvre and greater freedom of action in the years which followed the Famine.

There were also plenty of strong farmers (and, as mentioned previously, merchants and manufacturers) who would have benefited from the sale of estates by becoming purchasers. From 1849 to 1857 there were 3 000 sales in the Encumbered Estates Court for £20 million. Only about 4 per cent of purchasers were from Britain and only £3 million came from outside Ireland. To date no systematic analysis has been undertaken to examine nationally who purchased estates or to map the transfer of ownership. Estates were not sold *en bloc* but in lots and, as a case study of Castle Hyde in County Cork reveals, purchasers came from a wide variety of backgrounds including local professionals, merchants, land agents (including Hyde's own), and established strong tenant farmers. Local landlords were represented as were members of the non-agricultural wealth elite such as Arthur Guinness, who was intent on establishing social respectability through land ownership.[28]

It would seem that after the Famine, the management of estates generally became much more vigorous as landlords attempted to make up lost ground by ensuring rents were paid in full and on time; they rigorously opposed subdivision and subletting; they looked less favourably on the middleman system and they became increasingly reluctant to grant long leases (by 1870 only about 20 per cent of 662 000 holdings were held on leases, most of them for terms of twenty-one or thirty-one years). Between 1845 and 1851, the total of land in holdings of more than 200 and less than 500 acres increased by one million acres, a rise of 45 per cent, while the number of holdings over 500 acres rose by 53 per cent, to an aggregate of around 700 000 acres.[29] In the medium term the increase in the size of holdings contributed to some extent to the economic upturn that was to follow in the decades after.

V. THE LAND QUESTION

In his *Ireland 1798–1998*, Alvin Jackson tellingly entitles one of his chapters 'The ascendancy of the land question, 1845–1891' pointing out that the Famine highlighted the profound problems with the Irish land system and forged the bond between land and the national question.[30] One of the main instigators of this policy was James Fintan Lalor, who simultaneously promoted a radical agrarian agenda and urged the revolutionary Young Ireland movement of the 1840s to lend their strength to the tenants' struggle against landlordism.

In the post-Famine era, the burning issue in agrarian politics was the provision as a fundamental right of the 'three Fs' (commonly referred to as 'the Ulster custom')—fair rents, fixity of tenure, and free sale. In 1850, as a means to achieving this goal, the Irish Tenant League was established in Dublin. While it appealed to tenants across the religious divide and was led by Catholic priests and Presbyterian ministers, it is interesting that the farmers of Connaught, who proved to be the most radically minded in the decades that followed, failed to take up the cause and remained largely inactive throughout.[31]

In 1852, two years after the extension of the Irish county franchise to occupiers of land valued at £12 and over, forty Irish M.P.s were returned on the Tenant League ticket, thereby giving rise to an independent Irish Parliamentary Party. However, they soon became embroiled in wider political controversies which did little to forward agrarian issues in Ireland. As the economy recovered, tenant agitation became less important and went into decline, eventually leading to the disbandment of the League.

Meanwhile, landlords, whether old or new, were not investing in estate improvements that might have radically changed the structure of rural society. From 1850 to 1865 expenditure on improvements hardly exceeded 3 per cent of the country's gross rental. Renewed economic depression in the early 1860s revived agrarian upheaval. While the depression had regional variations—the west and north-west were the worst affected areas while the north escaped relatively unscathed—the overall effect resulted once again in a significant increase in permanent evictions, averaging 1 230 families a year between 1861 and 1864.[32] This depression failed to produce the collective action of a decade and a half later but it did coincide with the early years of Fenianism. Although not primarily an agrarian movement—Fenian leaders believed agrarian change was subordinate to nationalist principles—it did espouse a radical agrarian tradition that denounced graziers and their attempts to replace tillage with pasture. For that reason it did not appeal to the strong farming class who felt threatened by social revolution that promised a redistribution of lands (the Fenian proclamation of 1867 declared that 'the soil of Ireland in the possession of an oligarchy belongs to us, the Irish people, and to us it must be restored').[33]

The Fenian threat was diluted by the economic growth that followed after 1864 and that lasted to around 1877. Prosperity was, of course, relative and while there was nationally a significant decline in the levels of evictions and agrarian outrages there remained the fact that not all farmers experienced the increased prosperity that it has become fashionable to assume. This was particularly true of small farmers in large areas of the west for whom rent reductions alone were of little benefit. One of Barbara Solow's most controversial conclusions emanating from her econometric analysis was that the low eviction rate of around 3 per cent between 1855 and 1880 was not conducive to good estate management.[34] However, the statistic may equally point to the financial stability of the more prosperous farming class which emerged after the Famine, who could afford to pay their rents in full and on time, so there was no need for widespread evictions. Or it may mean that landlords were more indulgent than nationalist orthodoxy would later claim, with a more considered sense of social responsibility towards their tenantry.

The British government began to take a more measured approach to the land question in Ireland and it came to parliamentary prominence in the 1870s as successive Liberal and Conservative governments attempted to negate nationalist aspirations by tackling agrarian issues. W. E. Gladstone's land act of 1870 was a beginning but it was far from the final solution. Long and technically complex, it created tensions even on traditionally peaceful estates as landlords tried to circumvent its provisions for the compensation of departing tenants, while the latter responded by forming tenants' defence associations (which were later to be subsumed into the National Land League of the late 1870s). More pertinently, the government's failure to come to terms with the precise nature of land tenure relationships in Ireland and to deal satisfactorily with them meant, as Philip Bull has contended, that 'the issue became so important in national life that it shaped the future of Irish nationalism and the shape of the society which emerged out of the nationalist struggle, creating between the issues of land and nationalism a nexus which was so strong that the one issue became effectively a metaphor for the other'.[35]

Agrarian crime rose moderately in the early years of the decade but then more steadily after 1876 as economic recovery slowed down, a disastrous run of bad harvests followed in 1877–9, English markets were flooded with more competitive foreign produce, and potato blight returned to many areas. For some reason levels of emigration fell from a two-year average of 90 000 per annum in 1875 to 37 000 in 1876 and 38 000 in 1877, leading Paul Bew to conclude that 'Ireland in the mid 1870s was a country which appeared to be reluctant to employ the traditional safety valve for social tensions—emigration—whilst at the same time becoming steadily more turbulent'.[36] There may, therefore, be interesting parallels between the agrarian outbreak that occurred in the Land War period of 1879 to 1881 and that which followed the closure of emigration outlets during the Great War of 1914–18.

Until the 1970s attempts to explain the outbreak of the Land War concentrated upon the worsening agricultural crisis and the simultaneous political realignment of Fenians, constitutionalists, and agrarian radicals. Traditional orthodoxy was then challenged by a new generation of scholars who placed developments in a much wider context.[37] It was contended that economic stability in the post-Famine period had created a new rural alliance of shopkeepers, publicans, and farmers who were economically dependent on each other (even to the extent that urban prosperity created an avenue for the younger sons of farmers to live out their social expectations). In their simultaneous desire to protect the economic gains made over the previous decades and to achieve political power, both at the expense of landlords, these social groups found common ground in the Irish National Land League established in November 1879. Catholic priests also played a pivotal role in the formation of rural attitudes during the Land War, perhaps not surprising given that they essentially came from two social backgrounds—the sons of prosperous farmers and the sons of shopkeepers—a fact that may be more significant in the alliances which were forged in the Land League than has been heretofore acknowledged.

The Land League was certainly different to any of the movements that had preceded it in terms of much wider community participation and the organization of a widespread network of local branches which drew various social groups together in political activity. It was a fact that could not be ignored by national political leaders. Charles Stewart Parnell was astute enough to recognize the potential of mass organization to promote the national question and as a vehicle to bolster his own political power in Ireland. Meanwhile, Fenian separatists in the west of Ireland were infiltrating local branches of the Land League, and the Clan na Gael leader in America, John Devoy, was advocating the more active involvement of the Fenian movement in agrarian radicalism. This gave rise to the so-called 'new departure', a loose alliance of constitutionalists, separatists, and agrarian radicals.[38] Parnell's astuteness allied to a degree of good fortune allowed him to steer a path towards the organization of mass protest, which enhanced his and his parliamentary party's political position while at the same time avoiding the type of social revolution that some of the more radical agrarians might have wished for. While Parnell believed in the possibility of radical land reform generously subsidized by the British taxpayer, he did not see it being accomplished on terms that were disadvantageous to his own landlord class. The alliance, however, alienated Protestant agrarian radicals in Ulster and the Home Rule crisis of 1885–6 irrevocably changed their outlook with the result that the land question became polarized along the same lines as the political question.[39]

Outrage and boycotting were initially the most potent strategies of the League but the rise to prominence of strong farmers in the leadership and the legal strategy of collecting rent 'at the point of the bayonet' inaugurated in Leinster and Munster in late 1880 may have undermined it as much as contributing to its effectiveness. While boycotting 'demanded remarkable self discipline and total communal participation' and 'fostered a widespread sense of personal involvement in the struggle',[40] there are still many questions to be addressed in terms of the success of rent strikes on individual estates. From a landlord perspective the rent of one large holder was as important as the cumulative rents of a number of smaller ones but to what extent were large farmers prepared to sacrifice their holdings? A systematic analysis of the social status of all those evicted would be enlightening, as indeed would be a study of their subsequent plight.

As in all conflicts the extended Land War produced winners and losers. The greatest losers came from opposite ends of the rural social spectrum—landlords and labourers. Behind the apparently united front of the Land League there were tensions between labourer and farmer, large and small occupiers. Large farmers and landless labourers did not have the same priorities and the latter had no chance of determining the policy of the Land League after the strong farmers took control. When the 1881 Land Act provided the latter with new benefits in the form of lower rents adjudicated by courts working through the Land Commission, they ultimately rejected the union with the classes below, whose future depended more on a redistribution of land in the case of smallholders or a rise in wages and improved working conditions in the case of the labourers.

Arguably landlords initially mounted an effective counter-attack through the Property Defence Association but the majority were too heavily encumbered to survive the long-term exigencies.[41] The fixing of fair rents, which invariably came to mean lower rents, broke them (psychologically as well as financially) more than land agitation. When they ran for shelter to the British government to preserve their position they found that, although composed of fellow landlords, it was prepared to ditch them (even with the prospect that the Irish case might set a precedent for developments in Britain). Moreover, the stereotyped hostile representation of landlords that grew out of the Land War alienated them forever more in Irish society.

As agricultural depression, tenant distress, and evictions continued throughout the 1880s, the onset of the second phase of the Land War from 1885 was accompanied by the adoption of the Plan of Campaign on at least 200 estates. Under the Plan, tenants were to offer landlords a 'fair' rent; if the latter refused, tenants were then to lodge their monies into an estate fund to be used in the event of their eviction, with further financial support coming when needed from the organizing body, the National League. The true extent of the success of the Plan is debatable and undoubtedly many tenants paid their rents behind the National League's back rather than forfeit their lands. However, in the wider scheme of developments, it was simply another stage in the decline of Irish landlords.[42] By now their growing indebtedness, the reluctance of financial institutions to lend to them on the collateral strength of their estates, and declining rental incomes meant that increasingly more were willing to sell under the land acts of 1885 and 1891 and many more were prepared to do so if better incentives were put in place.[43]

VI. THE END OF LANDLORDISM

After the Parnellite split in 1891, various elements within the parliamentary party, including future leader John Redmond, supported the view that agrarianism was a barrier to the achievement of Home Rule. While there were others such as John Dillon who perceived a need for further struggle in order to placate the interests of the smaller farmers and the landless, they were outplayed by those who feared that any attempts to address the land question might weaken Irish nationalism. Interpretative difficulties stem from the fact that in the aftermath of the Land War large farmers and graziers (a class that also included many of the urban power elite) benefited from the availability of extra lands created by the thousands of evictions that had taken place, and from the growing popularity of the conacre system under which landlords let evicted holdings and other untenanted lands on eleven-month contracts to circumvent the fair rent fixing terms of the 1881 act. The continued proliferation of graziers in areas of the west and midlands frustrated the smallholders and landless. Thus in 1898 the land movement began anew when William O'Brien, a veteran of the Land War, established the United Irish League. This was not merely another version of the Land League or the National League; it had different objectives and adopted different methods, but its central aim was to break up the large grazier farms and so it caused inevitable tensions once again amongst nationalists divided on social class grounds.[44]

The mass movement built around the United Irish League and the Russellite campaign in Ulster highlighted to politicians of all persuasions the continued power of the land movements.[45] In 1903 the Conservative government, in reaction to widespread agitation, the proposals of a joint landlord-tenant conference of the previous year, and as part of their 'killing Home Rule by kindness' policy, introduced a new land act that was steered through parliament by the then chief secretary of Ireland, George Wyndham. This act initially went some way to tempering the zeal of small farmers. There was a dramatic transfer of land ownership in the early years but soon lack of funding and bureaucratic delays due to logistical problems of coping with demand ground progress to a halt.

It also soon became apparent that proprietorship was not the sole solution to the Irish land question. Thousands of the newly purchased farms were too small and economically unviable. Congestion was much more widespread than in the designated congested districts along the western seaboard and so the demand for the break-up of grazier holdings manifested itself from around 1907 in the so-called ranch war. John Redmond, by then Irish parliamentary leader, procrastinated in light of the renewed agrarian agitation. He could not condone the methods of cattle drivers, even if he agreed with their objective, but in so doing he put constitutional nationalism in a precarious position at a time of growing radicalism. Redmond, a landlord like Parnell, shared the latter's view that once the land question was solved to the mutual interests of landlord and tenant alike landlords could contemplate a role for themselves in a Home Rule parliament. Perhaps both were naive given the hostility that had grown towards landlords in the Land League era.

Arguably, Redmond did well to tame the United Irish League—providing it with more of a political dimension than its predecessors. But this could not hide the great discrepancies in nationalist society whereby the local leadership of the UIL, drawn largely from the grazier class, were for political gain denouncing the very system that gave them existence. The 1909 land act went some way to deflating the ranch war and agrarian agitation but of probably more significance was the inevitability of Home Rule following the ending of the Lords' veto in 1911. The possibility was that the final solution to the Irish land question would shortly lie with a Dublin nationalist parliament. It is one of the great 'ifs' of Irish history that had Home Rule been enacted how would the new nationalist ruling elite, presumably comprised of strong farmers and graziers, have dealt with the plight of the smallholders and the landless? At any rate it was not to be. Redmond's political success in having Home Rule enacted in 1914, only to see it suspended until after the Great War, was soon to be overshadowed by dramatic change in the political landscape.[46]

VII. FINAL PHASES OF AGRARIAN AGITATION

When the Great War reinvigorated the long depressed Irish agricultural economy graziers and strong farmers (and some landlords) benefited disproportionately. In 1917 a genuine fear of a food shortage led to a popular demand for increased tillage in Britain and Ireland and so the government introduced a compulsory tillage order requiring all occupiers of arable land to cultivate 10 per cent more of it than they had done the previous year. The idea of compulsory tillage appealed to the smallholders and landless labourers: it meant that large graziers would have to set aside lands for tillage and employ more men to work them or else sublet portions of their lands in conacre that would allow for more freedom of access. As graziers procrastinated, demands for the break-up of lands became more intense. From the spring of 1917 the last significant phase of popular agrarian revolt was orchestrated in the west by alleged Sinn Féiners and shortly afterwards Sinn Féin began to promulgate that the 'true remedy for the land problem' was the 'exclusive control of our own resources which sovereign independence alone can win'.[47] The land and national questions were once again redefined, but in more radical terms.

One of the greatest challenges facing historians of the twentieth century, particularly of the revolutionary period, will be to determine the extent of social revolution fuelled by the land question in the period 1917–23, and to ascertain if there was a collective good at the heart of the agitation that enveloped significant parts of the country (especially in the west) from 1917 or whether the social anarchy bred in political chaos was merely used as a vehicle for individual gain.[48] It would hardly be surprising to find that traditional grievances of oppression and economic deprivation amongst smallholders and labourers focused on those who had benefited most from economic upturns and that when the opportunity presented itself in the midst of revolution many took advantage of it. Agitation may not have been nationally coordinated or systematic but it was certainly regional, sporadic, and at times brutal.[49] In essence the Volunteers (later the IRA) created something of a monster when they pronounced that those who participated in the Volunteers would share in the spoils of revolution: when agrarian agitation enveloped the west by the spring of 1920 tough methods had to be employed by the Dáil and the IRA against the land-hungry for fear that agrarian agitation would dilute political ambitions. The reaction of the Dáil and the deployment of the IRA possibly go a long way to explaining the lack of support for the war of independence in Connaught. When the Anglo-Irish treaty made no provision for the completion of land purchase or the redistribution of large untenanted estates, it may not be an exaggeration to suppose that for almost half a million occupiers of uneconomic holdings in rural Ireland access to more land may have been a more desirable commodity than independence, so that many of those who had been quiescent in the independence struggle looked towards the anti-Treatyites to fulfil the earlier promises of Sinn Féin for a radical redistribution of lands.[50]

By January 1923, after six months of Civil War, it was recognized within provisional government circles that the final settling of the land question through legislation was a necessary step towards the restoration of law and order. Given the historical precedents since the 1880s of defusing agrarianism with land legislation, this response was inevitable. In January 1923 the first tentative steps were taken towards the formulation of a new land bill as a matter of 'importance and urgency'.[51] The proposed bill promised the final transfer of land from landlords to tenants and a further redistribution of lands to alleviate congestion. Its revolutionary proposals in terms of compulsory acquisition were in part motivated by the provisional government's fear that the expanded electorate would vote on land issues instead of political issues in the forthcoming general election.

The formal introduction of the bill to the Dáil in May 1923 coincided with the ending of the Civil War (the ceasefire was announced on 14 May 1923 and published on 24 May) and may very well have significantly contributed to the decline in support for the anti-Treatyites' agrarian campaign.[52] In a powerful speech, Kevin O'Higgins, the minister for home affairs, warned against recalcitrancy. Anyone who continued to remain active in agitation: 'who go out in the defiance of the law and in defiance of the Parliament to press their claims by their own violence and their own illegalities [would] be placed definitely outside the benefits of this Bill'. In the long term this act and those which followed would redesign the social structure of Irish rural society; in the short term it contributed to the return to more peaceful ways in the Irish countryside at least as much as any other legislative measure introduced by the Free State government in the first eight months of 1923 had done.

In its very ambitious attempt to solve the land question once and for all, the 1923 Land Act gave the newly constituted Land Commission powers to compulsorily acquire and redistribute lands. It gave due recognition to the problem of congestion at a national level. However, the transfer of tenanted holdings under the 1923 act was slow and unsatisfactory and was hampered by legal constraints so that post-independence agrarian grievances continued to be underpinned by the prevalence of uneconomic holdings. For almost the first decade of independence the existence of aggrieved smallholders, landless, evicted tenants of the extended Land War period, and many IRA veterans who felt that their contribution to the independence struggle entitled them to farm grants, ensured that the land question did not disappear. The extension of the franchise in 1918 further meant that these groups assumed more significant electoral power. This was a fact not lost on the Fianna Fáil party that came to power in 1932 which was quick to point out that Cumann na nGaedheal rhetoric on the 1923 Land Act had been much more revolutionary in its expressed intent than was the actual process of acquisition and redistribution.

Under the Fianna Fáil land act of 1933 that closed many of the legal loopholes exploited by the (ex-)landlord class and graziers to retain large tracts of lands, acquisition and redistribution proceeded along dramatic lines. For the first five years of Fianna Fáil's administration (up to 31 March 1937) over 353 000 acres were divided among almost 26 000 allottees. It also undertook, under the aegis of the Land Commission, a remarkable piece of social engineering when it migrated over 14 500 western smallholders on to lands comprising 382 000 acres in the midlands and east.[53]

In the end who gained? This author has argued elsewhere that there is a need to reassess the centrality of the land question to both national and local politics in the post-independence period.[54] The full extent to which the traditional local power brokers—the farmers, shopocracy, professionals—manipulated the political process and in this way benefited disproportionately from political patronage at the expense of the smallholders and landless needs to be scrutinized at local level. Certainly rural societies remained in a state of flux as long as perceptions existed (and were deliberately and often cynically created) by politicians that they had the final say in who received parcels of land.

Similarly, the relationship between the operation of the land act of 1933—introduced by a Fianna Fáil government whose members promised to expedite land redistribution during their election campaigns—and the growth of the Blueshirt movement in rural Ireland needs to be satisfactorily elucidated. The significance of the 'economic war' to the growth of the Blueshirt movement is accepted but it is also worth considering to what extent the threat to the proprietorial security of large farmers further stimulated this growth.[55]

It is equally important to systematically assess the significance of the Irish Land Commission after 1923 to Irish rural life. This author has argued elsewhere that making available the millions of Land Commission records—title documents, maps, surveys, records of proceedings, correspondence, inspectors' reports, schedules of acquisition and distribution, and much more—would provide the material for a very large number of PhD theses and books which would illuminate much about nineteenth- and twentieth-century rural Ireland and its society. However, as long as the records—recently moved to Portlaoise from Dublin—remain difficult to access, our understanding of the social, economic, and political world of rural Ireland will remain deficient and incomplete.[56]

It is worth noting that some Irish Land Commission records made their way to the Public Records Office in Northern Ireland and are freely available for consultation, whetting all the more the appetite to have those in the Republic made more accessible.[57] As Olwen Purdue has shown, landlords in the newly established state of Northern Ireland fared much better under the 1925 Land Act than their counterparts in the south did under the 1923 and later Free State acts. That many were allowed to retain greater estates helped them in the long term to counter the economic difficulties felt by southern landlords. They were also more adaptable to economic change, probably facilitated by the fact that they remained politically active and to a large extent in control in Northern Ireland.[58] The industrial outlets there also meant that access to land was not the primary economic and social consideration that it was in the Free State/Irish Republic.

It was decades after independence before prominent politicians in the dominant Fianna Fáil party began to recognize the negative impact on the agricultural economy of breaking up the large farms. Paul Bew points out that it was only when T.K. Whitaker 'dismantled the last vestiges of the Irish agrarian radical tradition' by publishing his report *Economic Development* in 1958 that the importance of grassland to the Irish agricultural economy was accepted.[59] But it was to be at least fifteen years more—coinciding with Ireland's entry to the European Economic Community—before land reform issues began to dissipate.

NOTES

1. S. J. Connolly, *Contested Island: Ireland 1460–1630* (Oxford, 2007).
2. See Colm Lennon, *Sixteenth-century Ireland: the Incomplete Conquest* (Dublin, 1994).
3. For seventeenth century studies, see Toby Barnard, *A New Anatomy of Ireland* (New Haven and London, 2003); S.J. Connolly, *Divided Kingdom: Ireland 1630–1800* (Oxford, 2008); L. M. Cullen, *The emergence of modern Ireland* (London, 1981); David Dickson, *Old World Colony: Cork and South Munster 1630–1830* (Cork, 2005); Raymond Gillespie, *The Transformation of the Irish Economy, 1550–1700* (Dundalk, 1991). See also T.C. Barnard, 'Further reading' in Barnard, *The Kingdom of Ireland, 1641–1760* (Basingstoke, 2004).
4. Connolly, *Divided Kingdom*, 103.
5. Connolly, *Divided Kingdom*, 135.
6. S.J. Connolly, *Religion, Law and Power: the Making of Protestant Ireland, 1660–1760* (Oxford, 1992) 14–15; Toby Barnard suggests a lower figure of 14 per cent in Barnard, *The Kingdom of Ireland*, 4.

7. Ian McBride, *Eighteenth Century Ireland*: the Isle of Slaves' (Dublin, 2009), 216.

8. Dickson, *Old World Colony*, 188; T.P. Power, *Land, Politics, and Society in Eighteenth-century Tipperary* (Oxford, 1993).

9. See discussion below on sale of Castle Hyde, County Cork, under the Encumbered Estates Act.

10. Paul Bew, *Ireland: the Politics of Enmity, 1789–2006* (Oxford, 2007), 99.

11. As very good starting points, see Maura Cronin, *Agrarian Protest in Ireland: 1750–1960* (Dundalk, 2012), and Samuel Clark and J.S. Donnelly Jr. (eds), *Irish Peasants: Violence and Political Unrest, 1780–1914* (Manchester, 1983).

12. McBride, *Eighteenth Century Ireland*, 319.

13. Maura Cronin, *Agrarian Protest in Ireland: 1750–1960* (Dundalk, 2012), p. 57.

14. McBride, *Eighteenth Century Ireland*, 319, 340.

15. M.W. Dowling, *Tenant Right and Agrarian Society in Ulster, 1600–1870* (Dublin, 1999); K. T. Hoppen, *Elections, Politics and Society in Ireland, 1832–1885* (Oxford, 1984); B. Jenkins, *Irish Nationalism and the British State: from Repeal to Revolutionary Nationalism* (Montreal and London, Ithaca, 2006).

16. Bew, *Politics of Enmity*, 83.

17. Terence Dooley, *The Murders at Wildgoose Lodge: Agrarian Crime and Punishment in Pre-Famine Ireland* (Dublin, 2007).

18. For an excellent starting point, see John Crowley, W.J. Smyth, and Mike Murphy (eds), *Atlas of the Great Irish famine* (Cork, 2012).

19. Desmond Norton, 'On Lord Palmerstown's Irish estates in the 1840s' in *English Historical Review*, 119: 448 (November, 2004), 1254–74.

20. Bew, *Ireland*, 343; Desmond Norton, *Landlords, Tenants, Famine: the Business of an Irish Land Agency in the 1840s* (Dublin, 2006); Ciaran Reilly, *John Plunket Joly and the Great Famine in King's County* (Dublin, 2012).

21. James S. Donnelly Jr., *The Great Irish potato famine* (Stroud, Sutton, 2001), 136.

22. Cormac Ó Gráda and Andres Eiriksson, 'Bankrupt landlords and the Irish famine' in Cormac Ó Gráda, *Ireland's Great Famine: Interdisciplinary Perspectives* (Dublin, 2006), 58, 59.

23. Peter Gray, *Famine, Land and Politics: British Government and Irish Society, 1843–50* (Dublin, 1998).

24. Bew, *Politics of Enmity*, 237; see also Frank Wright, *Two Lands on One Soil: Ulster Politics before Home Rule* (Dublin, 1994).

25. See Gerard Moran, *Sending out Ireland's Poor: Assisted Emigration to North America in the Nineteenth Century* (Dublin, 2004).

26. In terms of more recent studies, see Enda Delaney, *The Curse of Reason: the Great Irish Famine* (Dublin, Gill and Macmillan, 2012); Ciaran Ó Murchadha, *The Great Famine: Ireland's agony 1845–52* (London, 2011).

27. Bew, *Politics of Enmity*, 206–7.

28. *Cork Examiner*, 8 December 1851; *Cork Advertiser*, 9 December 1851; *Freeman's Journal*, 8 December 1851; Terence Dooley, 'Castle Hyde and the Great Famine, 1845–51', *Irish Architectural and Decorative Arts*, vol. xii (2009), 54–71.

29. Bew, *Ireland*, 215; the most comprehensive study of landlord-tenant relations in post-Famine Ireland is W.E. Vaughan, *Landlords and Tenants in Mid-Victorian Ireland* (Oxford, 1994).

30. Alvin Jackson, *Ireland 1798–1998* (Oxford, 1999), 86.

31. D.E. Jordan, *Land and Popular Politics in Ireland: County Mayo from the Plantation to the Land War* (Cambridge, 1994).
32. J. S. Donnelly Jr., 'The Irish agricultural depression of 1859–64' in *Irish Economic and Social History*, vol. iii (1976), 33–54.
33. Alan O'Day, *Irish Home Rule* (Manchester, 1998), 8; On Fenianism and the Land League, see R.V. Comerford, *The Fenians in Context: Irish Politics and Society, 1848–82* (Dublin, 1985); Owen McGee, *The IRB: the Irish Republican Brotherhood from the Land League to Sinn Féin* (Dublin, 2005).
34. Barbara Solow, *The Land Question and the Irish Economy, 1870–1903* (Harvard, 1971), 53.
35. Philip Bull, *Land, Politics & Nationalism: a Study of the Irish Land Question* (Dublin, 1996), 4.
36. Bew, *Politics of Enmity*, 296.
37. Paul Bew, *Land and the National Question in Ireland, 1858–82* (Dublin, 1978); Samuel Clark, *Social Origins of the Irish Land War* (Princeton, 1979); R.V. Comerford, 'The Land War and the politics of distress, 1877–82' in W.E. Vaughan (ed), *A New History of Ireland vi: Ireland under the Union, II, 1870–1921* (Oxford, 1996), 26–52; James S. Donnelly Jr., *The Land and the People of Nineteenth-century Cork: the Rural Economy and the Land Question* (London and Boston, 1975); Emmet Larkin, *The Roman Catholic Church and the Plan of Campaign in Ireland, 1886–1888* (Cork, 1978); Barbara Solow, *The Land Question and the Irish Economy, 1870–1903* (Harvard, 1971); E.D. Steele, *Irish Land and British Politics: Tenant-Right and Nationality 1865–1870* (Cambridge, 1974); Vaughan, *Landlords and Tenants*.
38. T.W. Moody, *Davitt and the Irish Revolution, 1846–1882* (Oxford, 1982).
39. Brian M. Walker, 'The land question and elections in Ulster' in Samuel Clark and James S. Donnelly Jr. (eds), *Irish Peasants: Violence and Political Unrest 1780–1914* (Madison and Manchester, 1983), 230–70.
40. Joseph Lee, *The Modernisation of Irish Society, 1848–1918* (Dublin, 1973), 94.
41. See L. P. Curtis Jr., 'Encumbered wealth: landlord indebtedness in post-famine Ireland' in *American Historical Review*, 85: 2 (April, 1980), 332–67; Terence Dooley, *The Decline of the Big House in Ireland: a Study of Irish Landed Families 1860–1960* (Dublin, 2001), 99–102.
42. Laurence Geary, *The Plan of Campaign, 1886–1891* (Cork, 1986).
43. Dooley, *Decline of the Big House*, 102–7.
44. Paul Bew, *Conflict and Conciliation in Ireland, 1890–1910: Parnellites and Radical Agrarians* (Oxford, 1987); Bull, *Land, Politics & Nationalism*; Fergus Campbell, *Land and Revolution: Nationalist Politics in the West of Ireland, 1891–1921* (Oxford, 2005); David Seth Jones, *Graziers, Land Reform and Political Conflict in Ireland* (Washington, 1995).
45. Alvin Jackson, 'Irish Unionism and the Russellite threat, 1894–1906' in *Irish Historical Studies*, 25 (1987), 376–404; Patrick J. Cosgrove, 'The Wyndham Land Act 1903: the final solution to the Irish land question?' (PhD thesis, NUI Maynooth, 2008), 11–21.
46. Bew, *Conflict and conciliation*; David Seth Jones, *Graziers, Land Reform, and Political Conflict in Ireland* (Washington DC, 1995); Patrick Cosgrove, *The Ranch War in Riverstown, Co Sligo, 1908* (Dublin, 2012).
47. Labhrás MacFhionnghail [Laurence Ginnell], *The Land Question* (Dublin, n.d.), 18–19.
48. Paul Bew, 'Sinn Féin, agrarian radicalism and the war of independence, 1919–21' in D.G. Boyce (ed), *The Revolution in Ireland, 1879–1923* (Basingstoke, 1988), 217–35; Terence Dooley, 'The land for the people': the Land Question in Independent Ireland* (Dublin, 2004), 33–56.
49. See, for example, Peter Hart, *The IRA & its enemies: violence and community in Cork, 1916–1923* (Oxford, 1998), 273–92.
50. Dooley, 'The land for the people', 49–52.

51. *Dáil Debates*, vol. 2, 5 January 1923, 592.
52. Dooley, 'The land for the people'.
53. Dooley, 'The land for the people', 132–54.
54. Dooley, 'Land and politics in independent Ireland, 1923–48: the case for reappraisal' in *Irish Historical Studies*, xxxiv, no. 134 (November 2004), 175–97.
55. Mike Cronin, *The Blueshirts and Irish Politics* (Dublin, 1997); Dooley, 'Land and politics in independent Ireland, 1923–48', 192–4.
56. Dooley, 'Land for the people', 22–5.
57. Olwen Purdue, *The Big House in the North of Ireland: Land, Power and Social Elites, 1878–1960* (Dublin, 2009), 277.
58. Purdue, *The Big House in the North of Ireland*.
59. Bew, *Politics of Enmity*, 477.

SELECT BIBLIOGRAPHY

Barnard, Toby, *A New Anatomy of Ireland* (New Haven and London, 2003).

Bew, Paul, *Conflict and Conciliation in Ireland, 1890–1910: Parnellites and Radical Agrarians* (Oxford, 1987).

Bull, Philip, *Land, Politics & Nationalism: a Study of the Irish Land Question* (Dublin, 1996).

Campbell, Fergus, *Land and Revolution: Nationalist Politics in the West Of Ireland, 1891–1921* (Oxford, 2005).

Clark, Samuel, *Social origins of the Irish Land War* (Princeton, 1979).

Clark, Samuel and Donnelly, J.S. Jr. (eds), *Irish Peasants: Violence and Political Unrest, 1780–1914* (Manchester, 1983).

Comerford, R.V., 'The Land War and the politics of distress, 1877–82' in W.E. Vaughan (ed), *A New History of Ireland vi: Ireland under the Union, II, 1870–1921* (Oxford, 1996).

Connolly, S.J., *Contested Island: Ireland 1460–1630* (Oxford, 2007).

Connolly, S.J., *Divided Kingdom: Ireland 1630–1800* (Oxford, 2008).

Cronin, Maura, *Agrarian Protest in Ireland: 1750–1960* (Dundalk, 2012).

Crowley, John, Smyth, W.J., Murphy, Mike (eds), *Atlas of the Great Irish Famine* (Cork, 2012).

Delaney, Enda, *The Curse of Reason: the Great Irish Famine* (Dublin, 2012).

Dickson, David, *Old World Colony: Cork and South Munster 1630–1830* (Cork, 2005).

Donnelly, James S. Jr., *The Land and the People of Nineteenth-century Cork: the Rural Economy and the Land Question* (London and Boston, 1975).

Donnelly, James S. Jr., *The Great Irish Potato Famine* (Stroud, Sutton, 2001).

Donnelly, James S. Jr., *Captain Rock: the Irish Agrarian Rebellion of 1821–1824* (London, 2009).

Dooley, Terence, *The Decline of the Big house in Ireland: a Study of Irish Landed Families 1860–1960* (Dublin, 2001).

Dooley, Terence, 'The land for the people': the Land Question in Independent Ireland* (Dublin, 2004).

Dowling, M.W., *Tenant Right and Agrarian Society in Ulster, 1600–1870* (Dublin, 1999).

Geary, Laurence, *The Plan of Campaign, 1886–1891* (Cork, 1986).

Gillespie, Raymond, *The Transformation of the Irish Economy, 1550–1700* (Dundalk, 1991).

Gray, Peter, *Famine, Land and Politics: British Government and Irish Society, 1843–50* (Dublin, 1999).

Hoppen, K. T., *Elections, Politics and Society in Ireland, 1832–1885* (Oxford, 1984).

Jordan, D.E., *Land and popular politics in Ireland: County Mayo from the plantation to the Land War* (Cambridge, 1994).

Lyne, Gerard, *The Lansdowne estate in Kerry under the agency of William Steuart Trench 1849–72* (Dublin, 2001).

Macaulay, Ambrose, *The Holy See, British policy and the plan of campaign in Ireland, 1885–93* (Dublin, 2002).

Maguire, W.A., *The Downshire estates in Ireland 1801–1845* (Oxford, 1972).

Ó Gráda, Cormac, *Black '47 and beyond: the Great Irish Famine in history, economy and memory* (Princeton NJ, 1999).

Ó Murchadha, Ciarán, *The Great Famine: Ireland's agony 1845–52* (London, 2011).

Purdue, Olwen, *The big house in the North of Ireland: land, power and social elites, 1878–1960* (Dublin, 2009).

Jones, David Seth, Graziers, *Land Reform and political Conflict in Ireland* (Washington, 1995).

Solow, Barbara, *The land question and the Irish economy, 1870–1903* (Harvard, 1971).

Vaughan, W.E., *Landlords and tenants in mid-Victorian Ireland* (Oxford, 1994).

CHAPTER 7

MIGRATION AND DIASPORA

ENDA DELANEY

Ye gallant sons of Erin's Isle, come listen to my lay,
About what Irishmen have done, I have a word to say;
Not only in America, but in almost every clime—
The sons of good St Patrick's land have made their lives sublime.

Chorus:
Then fill your glasses to the brim and drink this toast I pray,
'Irishmen the world o'er' and good St Patrick's day.

God grant the day may soon draw near, when the Fenian band,
Will raise the green above the red, in their own native land;
And free her from the thraldom, in which she so long has laid.
Then on the good 'old sod' again, we'll wear the Green Cockade.[1]

I. INTRODUCTION

BALLADS can capture popular sensibilities like no other form of historical source, mixing past and present concerns, and fusing collective memories with future aspirations. One example, 'What Irishmen have done', chosen from the literally thousands of broadsheet ballads that have survived, was sung in the United States in the Reconstruction era (1865–77), and contains many of the tropes that featured prominently in this genre of diasporic popular song. It unashamedly celebrates Irish success in hostile political or physical environments, and underscores the worldwide nature of settlement in 'almost every clime'. It also makes the explicit connection between the diaspora and the political situation in the homeland: only when the 'green' is raised above the 'red' will the redemptive homecoming be possible. In short, the end of British rule in Ireland will facilitate the biblical return of the dispossessed sons and daughters of Erin. Ballads form part of what has been described as the 'vernacular histories' of the Irish diaspora, celebrating Irish achievement in the face of adversity across the globe, an unsophisticated yet still appealing interpretation that has its proponents up to the present day.[2]

Traditionally migration out of Ireland was 'characterised by a basic dualism', in the words of Patrick O'Farrell, provoking conflicting and contradictory views encompassing the traditional nationalist images of dispossession, exile, and portrayal as a long-standing social evil while, on the other hand, presenting a unique opportunity for political, social, and economic advancement of the exiled Irish.[3] The great dispersal of the Irish since 1600 created many possibilities: to extend the influence and power of a small country, to forge a global Catholicism or Protestantism with a distinctively Hibernian feel, and to mark out a role in the evolution of nations across the world, primarily in parts of the British Empire. When a Catholic cleric and scholar, the Rev. P. S. Dineen, spoke of a 'world-wide Empire of the Irish race' in 1910, he argued that the Irish were uniquely positioned to take advantage of the myriad of opportunities in the English-speaking world: 'Our race at home and abroad are marked out among the races of the earth by four great gifts, which are in the main the secret of their success. These are oratorical genius, political genius, military genius, and religious fervour.'[4] Even allowing for the blatant ethnocentrism of these sentiments, Dineen was reflecting the contemporary view that mass migration fostered Irish influence well beyond a small island. This was not unique to Irish Catholic consciousness. Protestant Scots-Irish in the United States have celebrated their role in the formative years of the fledgling American nation with equal pride. In historical writing what might be termed 'contribution' histories published in the later nineteenth century, many written by journalists, political propagandists, or clerics, presented uncritical accounts of the beneficial effects of Irish immigration on the development of the host countries and noted 'the growing successes of Irishmen abroad, and [lauded] the prospects for the future'.[5] It was no coincidence that many of these accounts were written at a time of political debates in Ireland about its future within the United Kingdom. The message was clear: the Catholic Irish were capable of self-government, as demonstrated by the contributions they had made to societies the world over.

In the twentieth century the scholarly writing on Irish migration was avowedly revisionist in its energies; that is 'revisionist' in its widest sense of interrogating and challenging received historical interpretations rather than the politically loaded Irish use of the term. Historians expanded the chronological, confessional, and geographical boundaries as to what constitutes the Irish diaspora. This has involved looking beyond the great mass migrations of the nineteenth century to the seventeenth and eighteenth centuries, into the period after the First World War. While North America still looms large, as indeed it should given its numerical and symbolic significance as a destination for the Irish, more attention is being paid to lesser-known components of the diaspora in Asia, South America, and the Pacific. What is certainly the most innovative element in recent work is the emphasis on global connections across the Irish diaspora.[6] Irish Protestants, once excluded from the diaspora, now represent an important dimension of its study. Gradually, a history of the global Irish is being constructed, interpreted, and revised. At the heart of this story is Ireland itself. At one time the history of Ireland and the Irish abroad constituted separate fields, yet now the integration of the study of the homeland and the diaspora is an overarching theme in recent work.

No account can do complete justice to the complexity of migration patterns to and from Ireland over the past four hundred years, and equally to the huge corpus of scholarly work that has been devoted to this subject.[7] Migration is about human beings whose actions, motivations, and life histories defy easy categorization; sometimes they were driven by rational decisions to leave Ireland, but for others they had little choice owing to political persecution, the threat of famine, or endemic poverty. That said, a basic chronological outline of the main waves of migration since 1600 will establish the broader context, before moving on to consider the areas in which historical writing has developed since the 1970s. Three distinctive phases are described: the seventeenth and early eighteenth centuries, during which Ireland witnessed both large-scale movement to mainland Europe and North America and immigration from Britain; the long nineteenth century from roughly the end of Napoleonic Wars in 1815 until the 1920s, characterized by a huge exodus to North America, Britain, Australasia, and other parts of the British Empire; and the twentieth century, when emigration continued at lower levels with varying degrees of intensity, and immigration again occurred in the final years. Finally, the overall shape of what constitutes a history of the global Irish is considered, outlining a potential framework and some suggestive lines of future inquiry.

II. Migration and Modern Ireland

Modern Irish history was profoundly shaped by the movement of people, primarily out of Ireland to other societies but also by those who settled on the island. The four hundred years between 1600 and 2000 were bookended by two waves of mass immigration. The ethnic composition of the Irish population was irrevocably altered at these two points in time, separated by centuries: the arrival of successive waves of English and Scottish settlers throughout the sixteenth and seventeenth centuries, and immigrants coming to Ireland in recent decades. These developments were, however, exceptional. The story of Irish migration essentially revolves around large-scale movement out of Ireland. As the historian of the American Irish, Kevin Kenny, has observed, mass emigration may be regarded as the 'single most critical development in Irish history...the *sine qua non* of modern Ireland'.[8]

More than 10 million people left Ireland after 1600, many destined for North America, but considerable numbers also travelled to mainland Europe, Australasia, Latin America, Britain, and other parts of the British Empire, such as the Indian subcontinent and the Anglophone Caribbean. In international terms, relative to the size of Ireland, this diaspora was the most significant population movement of people in European history. The sheer variety of destinations is breathtaking, as indeed is the longevity of this phenomenon which continued with differing intensity and different directions over four centuries, with cyclical peaks occurring in the 1650s, the 1760s, the 1770s, the 1850s, the 1880s, and the 1950s. Historical treatments invariably centre on the dramatic period that runs from the early nineteenth century until 1921, punctuated as it was by the terrible catastrophe of the Great Irish Famine (1845–52). This focus on the 'long nineteenth century', in which the United States was the destination of choice par excellence, tends to obscure the inherent diversity and manifest complexities within the history of the Irish diaspora. The Irish in the United States are an important dimension of the history of the global Irish, but this component was not, by any yardstick, wholly representative of the experiences of the millions of people who left after 1600.

Movement in and out of Ireland was a feature of life for as long as a written historical record exists from late antiquity. By 1600 migration out of Ireland or settlement in Ireland was not new. What was novel were the scale, context, and consequences of population movements. As the historical geographer R. A. Butlin observed, 'a striking aspect of the population geography of Ireland at this time [c. 1600] was the amount of migration and movement'.[9] From the late sixteenth century onwards the context of movement was radically transformed by patterns of European colonial expansion, political and religious conflicts within the Three Kingdoms, and the forging of a British imperial identity that linked Ireland, North America, and the West Indies. The Flight of the Earls in September 1607, when the defeated Catholic magnates of Ulster led by Hugh O'Neill left secretly for the continent, was a hugely symbolic event. O'Neill, like many members of the Irish Catholic aristocracy, sought refuge in mainland Europe and joined the considerable number of Irish exiles already located across the courts and cities of the great European powers (in the Low Countries, France, Spain, Italy, and elsewhere) engaged as they were in trade, sometimes conspiring against the English Crown, and training for the Catholic priesthood.[10] This exodus was primarily driven by religious and political persecution, especially after the Cromwellian conquest in the 1650s, but also by the economic dislocation caused by conflict and war. For another distinctive and well-known grouping, the 'Wild Geese', war was their stock in trade, and thousands of Irish troops served in the armies of continental Europe throughout the seventeenth and eighteenth centuries.[11] In the Caribbean, Irish settlement on the island of Montserrat occurred from the 1620s onwards with the beginning of English plantation schemes, also including Irish Catholic planters.[12] As Cullen has noted, for the younger sons of prosperous families the West Indies presented opportunities for those 'who wished to try their luck and venture their capital as planters and merchants'.[13] Even further afield, Irish settlement on the Amazon basin occurred as early as the 1610s.[14] Others had no choice, such as the Irish labourers forcibly transported to the West Indies during the tumultuous 1650s.[15] On arrival in Barbados, the Irish 'were derided by the negroes and branded with the epithet of white slaves'.[16] But these were not the first exiles of Erin to travel to the Caribbean. Indentured servants and freemen from Munster and Wexford had made the journey voluntarily before that. So numerous were they that, after a slave revolt in 1692 in the West Indies, such suspicion fell on the Irish role in acting as the focus for dissatisfaction that English planters refused to accept any more Irish servants.[17]

The Flight of the Earls paved the way for the ambitious scheme of state-sponsored colonization in Ireland, the Ulster Plantation. The official plantation itself achieved only modest success by the early seventeenth century, and it was the counties excluded from the scheme, Antrim and Down, that attracted significant numbers of British settlers, largely due to the energetic efforts of Sir Randal MacDonnell. Compared with the low number who travelled across the Atlantic to colonies in Virginia and New England, before the outbreak of the rebellion in 1641 roughly 100,000 British people had migrated to Ireland.[18] Indeed, a number of scholars have argued that Ireland and the New World offered different variations on the same theme of colonization: economic opportunity.[19] The second phase of large-scale British immigration occurred in the second half of the seventeenth century in the aftermath of the 1641 rebellion, the Cromwellian conquest, and especially the War of the Three Kings (1689–91).[20] The policy was based on the presumption that British settlers would invariably bring prosperity, peace, and 'civilization' to this troubled kingdom. The Protestant population of Ulster increased significantly over the course of the late seventeenth century, but this was a result of informal immigration from Scotland rather than being a planned or government-sponsored settlement. The 1690s witnessed an influx of Scots, partly to do with the availability of cheap land, though also caused by a series of bad harvests in Scotland and a famine in 1698–9. Contemporaries estimated that between 50,000 and 80,000 Scots arrived in that decade alone, causing concerns within the Anglican elite about the growing Presbyterian influence on trade and commerce, especially in the incipient linen industry in Ulster.[21] The traffic between Britain and Ireland was not just one way: in the aftermath of the 1641 rebellion thousands of refugees fled to Britain to escape the chaos that unfolded, causing a degree of panic among the British population.

Plantation schemes in the New World also needed people. The Irish were part of early colonial settlement in North America. The poor came mostly as servants who had signed an indenture or contract to sell their labour for a fixed period, routinely for three to four years. As Kenny has pointed out, 'bondage rather than freedom was the norm for most people, black or white, in the seventeenth-century Atlantic world'.[22] Irish servants arrived in Virginia and Maryland from the 1620s onwards and, notwithstanding a preference for Protestant settlers on the part of the colonial companies who controlled recruitment to the New World, Irish Catholics also made the long and arduous journey until restrictive legislation was introduced at the end of the seventeenth century.[23]

By the early seventeenth century the patterns of migration from modern Ireland were crystallizing. The diasporic Irish settled in a number of overlapping worlds radiating outwards from the 'old' European world, including the British Isles, to the 'new' colonial ones that were taking shape in the Americas, the Caribbean, and later Asia, Africa, and Australasia.[24] Short-term expedients, such as escaping famine, war, or religious persecution—or equally an unholy trinity of all these, as occurred in the mid-seventeenth century—combined with much wider factors, including taking advantage of economic opportunities in trade, land ownership, or military service, shaped the decisions of those who left. The variety of destinations, the length of distances travelled, as well as the frequency of multiple migrations to different places at different times underscore the inherent diversity of these flows. Some left because of the brutal nature of English colonization, others to become active agents of imperialism and conquest in the New World. Some left of their own free will; others had no choice, as indentured servants or prisoners. Perceived opportunities to exploit natural resources, especially land, spurred on those seeking to improve themselves, often with disastrous consequences for indigenous cultures in the Americas and the Caribbean. Within the context of the confessional conflicts of the sixteenth and seventeenth centuries, religious freedom and the possibilities for Christian evangelization initiated yet another series of migrations in the name of religious liberty to mainland Europe and the British Atlantic World.

At the vanguard of the forging of the First British Empire in North America were Ulster Presbyterians. Historians have paid considerable attention to the mass movement of Ulster Protestants from seventeenth- and eighteenth-century Ulster to the New World.[25] The Scots-Irish appropriately occupy a central place in both the historiography of eighteenth-century colonial and revolutionary America and the history of the diaspora, in part because of the distinctive nature of the context in which they left, as well as the long-lasting influence they had on the development of the British Atlantic world and the formation of the American nation.[26] Estimates as to how many left Ireland for the American colonies vary considerably, but one recent assessment indicates that as many as 250,000 left Ulster before the American Revolutionary War broke out in 1775.[27] What has attracted particular scholarly concern is the complex and malleable nature of the Scots-Irish identity in North America, especially with the arrival of large numbers of Irish Catholics from the 1830s onwards.[28] In proportional terms emigration had a higher incidence in Ireland before 1800 than it did in the following century.[29]

As more is known about the nineteenth- and twentieth-century diaspora, only the principal trends will be outlined here.[30] From the mid-nineteenth century until the First World War the massive exodus of Catholics to North America, Australasia, and other destinations dominates the historical consciousness of the Irish diaspora. Again total numbers are difficult to be certain about, but informed estimates suggest somewhere in the region of 8 million people migrated out of Ireland between the Act of Union in 1801 and partition in 1920. During the period of the Great Famine and its immediate aftermath nearly 2 million people left. After the famine large-scale emigration continued with peaks in the 1860s and 1880s. In the 1890s two-fifths of those born in Ireland were living outside the country, with 3 million people living overseas, in the United States, Britain, Canada, Australia, and many other places, including Latin America.[31] The scale of this movement was unprecedented. Understandably, the history of the American Irish has dominated the Irish abroad during the long nineteenth century, since roughly 5 million of these migrants arrived in the United States. However, studies of the Irish in Canada, Australia, New Zealand, South Africa, as well as many other lesser-known sites of settlement such as Argentina and Brazil, have proved equally important in challenging truisms of a homogeneous Irish diasporic experience.

Diversity rather than uniformity was the hallmark of the nineteenth-century Irish diaspora.[32] This is best illustrated by the accounts of Irish involvement in the expansion, governance, and administration of the Second British Empire. This involved the Irish of all classes, religions, and political persuasions in military service, colonial administration, and in service as clerics, missionaries, and religious leaders.[33] Other major themes that emerge in the huge corpus of work on the nineteenth-century Irish diaspora include reactions in the receiving countries, in particular anti-Catholicism and anti-Irish prejudice, the gendered nature of the migration experience, the differences between urban and rural settlement, the nationalist political activity of the Irish overseas, and the global role of the Irish Catholic Church.[34]

After the First World War, Britain became the destination of choice for Irish exiles, from north and south. From the mid-1930s until the end of the twentieth century over a million and a half people born on the island of Ireland left, some of whom subsequently returned.[35] The closing off of the American option with the introduction of immigration restrictions in the 1920s, as well as a preference for short-distance movement, resulted in Britain being the principal recipient of Irish migrants for most of the twentieth century. During the Second World War at least 100,000 Irish wartime workers travelled to Britain. Britain, at one time the least-favoured destination, was home to nearly one million people born in Ireland by the early 1970s. Yet long-distance migration to Australia, New Zealand, the United States, and Canada also took place in the 1950s and 1960s, and, in the case of Northern Irish migrants, with financial support from governments seeking to secure 'white' migrants. Throughout the 1980s and early 1990s the patterns of migration out of Ireland again diversified. The United States again became a popular destination, as did Australia, New Zealand and mainland Europe, reflecting by the end of the twentieth century the patterns of demand for skilled workers in the global labour market. The century closed with a new phenomenon: the arrival of large numbers of what were termed 'non-national' immigrants from Eastern Europe, Africa, and Asia.

III. Writing the Diaspora

In the last quarter of the twentieth century new approaches to the study of the past were reflected in the writings on the Irish diaspora. The most obvious area concerned using gender as a category of historical analysis to explore how the experiences of diasporic Irish females and males differed over time and space. Given the relative parity in gender terms of those who left Ireland after the Great Famine, older accounts that neglected the female experience—or did not even acknowledge that Irish women were part of the outward flow—captured only what was essentially a minority experience. Large numbers of Irish women living overseas became 'invisible' in the historical record. The scholarly work that has appeared in more recent times has tended to concentrate on the principal destinations during the post-Famine era, but there are other contributions which reach back into the seventeenth century.[36] Subjects that have proved especially fruitful include the position and experiences of Irish women in the nineteenth- and twentieth-century United States, Britain, Canada, and Australia.[37]

At the heart of the debates about the Irish diaspora is the complicated issue of race. Unlike the history of modern Ireland, where race has only featured as a marginal factor, scholars see racial images, some positive but predominantly negative, as the defining element of the reactions to the arrival and settlement of successive waves of Irish migrants. Across the four centuries the responses that the diasporic Irish provoked were

shaped by hierarchies of race. Whether it be attempts to limit the numbers of Irish arriving in the Caribbean in the late seventeenth century, nativist fears in the United States in
the antebellum era, or campaigns to restrict Irish immigration in interwar Scotland, the
underlying message was clear: the Irish were perceived as inferior, unlikely to ever make
a lasting contribution to the host society, and, for Irish Catholics, their political loyalty
was always open to question.[38] Anti-Irishness was often fed by and intermingled with
long-standing anti-Catholic prejudices. In the United States, being part of the white
'race' demarcated the Irish as different from African-Americans, and fostered a collective identity that socially constructed whiteness, hindering any effective cooperation
between the Irish and African-Americans in which might have been a powerful alliance
of the powerless. Historians have speculated on the potential, albeit never fulfilled, for
class solidarity between the poor Catholic Irish arrivals and African-Americans. The
failure to forge a common cause and the incorporation of the American Irish within
the 'white race' is not, however, without its critics, who see this approach as ahistorical,
forcing present-minded sensibilities on a more complex historical landscape.[39]

A related question that is only beginning to feature in current historical writing is the
relationship between the Irish and other migrant groups in the countries of settlement.
The tendency to record the Irish experience in almost total isolation from that of other
immigrants and ethnic groups is striking. Apart from a few pioneering studies predominantly located in the nineteenth- and twentieth-century United States, especially
New York City, relatively little is known about how the Irish interacted on a daily basis
with African-Americans, Asians, Eastern Europeans, and a whole host of other groups
located on the margins of society.[40] During the famous draft riots in New York City in
July 1863 working-class Irish immigrants attacked African-Americans indiscriminately
in a frenzy of violence initiated by the introduction of the draft, though also driven by
long-standing antagonisms with black workers.[41] The Irish in San Francisco were prominent in the campaigns to restrict Chinese immigration in the 1870s.[42] There is, however,
an understandable tendency to focus on the flashpoints when violence erupted or riots
broke out rather than the more mundane everyday encounters. In Britain too the Irish
experience is rarely conceptualized within a broader frame of reference, the most startling lacuna in knowledge being the absence of a wide-ranging comparative study of the
relations between the two largest migrant groups in nineteenth-century England and
Wales, the Irish and the Scots.[43] After the Second World War, the Irish shared social, economic, and geographical spaces with arrivals from the Caribbean and south-east Asia,
and only now is work emerging that not only compares experiences but seeks to chart
the encounters between the Irish and other incomers.[44] In other multi-ethnic societies
such as post-war Canada, New Zealand, and Australia the potential for such studies is
considerable. These would ideally concentrate on a particular region or urban locale
over a long period of time, charting and analyzing interactions and seeking to understand changing structures of power and authority as well as the more obvious issue of
the role of the Irish in initiating and perpetuating racial discrimination.

This raises a broader interpretative question about the Irish role in colonization,
subjugation, and the treatment of those lacking the power or resources to resist. That

the dispossessed could become the oppressors of other groups in other contexts is not altogether surprising. Moreover, such findings pose problems for postcolonialist interpretations of modern Irish history, much favoured by literary critics and cultural theorists. A recent major study recounts the role of the Paxton Boys, mainly of Ulster origin, in the massacre of the Conestoga Indians in Pennsylvania in 1763, raising important issues about the part played by the Scots-Irish, along with other European settlers, in forcibly extending the American frontier, with disastrous consequences for Native Americans.[45] A provocative exploration of the Irish settlers in the seventeenth and eighteenth centuries on the Caribbean island of Montserrat is at variance with nationalist self-identification with other 'victims' of British colonialism.[46] And the ever-increasing knowledge of Irish participation in late modern British imperialism in Africa, Asia, and the Pacific opens up a new vista. This could take many forms, from colonial administrators, to soldiers serving in the British military, and even missionary priests who worked to exploit the evangelical opportunities presented by the expansion of the Anglophone world.[47] But the Irish could also be the strongest critiques of colonial power; for instance the most vociferous critique of the brutal treatment of rebels in Ceylon's 1848 rebellion was produced by the Kilkenny-born Protestant medic and editor of the *Colombo Observer*, Christopher Elliott, who used his contacts in London to campaign successfully for a parliamentary inquiry into the response of the Governor, Lord Torrington, who was recalled in 1850.[48] At a more elevated level the sustained efforts to place Irish-born Catholic bishops in dioceses across the English-speaking world generated not entirely unfounded suspicions about the insidious power of the Irish 'hibernarchy'.[49]

Migrants brought with them material possessions and, after settling, exhibited patterns of consumption that provide an insight into aspects of self-identity and how they wished others to perceive them. A valuable and perhaps not widely known study of the du Pont Irish in nineteenth-century northern Delaware demonstrates the potential of a framework that explores how cultural and class identities were articulated through objects from linen tablecloths to lace curtains. Indeed, this intriguing account of the 'lace curtain' Irish, mostly Ulster Catholics, who worked in the du Pont gunpowder factory suggests the malleability of class identities and the significance of aspirations towards upward social mobility.[50] A related approach uses archaeological techniques to reconstruct the material cultures of Irish-Americans in the later nineteenth century, underlining the transnational dimension of Irish identity as well as yielding insights into the everyday existence of the working-class Irish in the United States.[51]

Using autobiographical literature to understand life experiences, identity construction, and perceptions of both the homeland and the countries of settlement demands sensitive handling of these first-hand and often highly stylized accounts. More than any other historical source, autobiographies and memoirs involve to a greater or lesser extent a degree of self-representation. First-hand published accounts have been used extensively by historians and other scholars to chronicle the experiences of the Irish overseas. Autobiographies can take many different forms, from narratives of self-improvement, celebratory chronicles of individual achievement, to somewhat unreflective accounts of Irish nationalist activities which naturally privilege the importance of the individual concerned over the wider collective. Taken together with other personal accounts such as migrant letters and oral histories, these first-hand testimonies provide insights into the natural fears, expectations, and emotions generated by moving to a new country— whether that be simply across the Irish Sea or to the other side of the world—and also into the varied nature of encounters with the host society. Within this genre, the classics of working-class Irish migrant autobiography are Michael McGowan's *The Hard Road to Klondike* (1962), Patrick MacGill's *Children of the Dead End* (1914), and Donall Mac Amhlaigh's, *An Irish Navvy: the Diary of an Exile* (1964). Scholars have also identified a wide range of lesser-known autobiographical texts from as early as the seventeenth century.[52] Two volumes written by Pat O'Mara (1901–83) confound traditional stereo-types, the first of which records his grim upbringing in an Edwardian Liverpool until he leaves for the United States in 1920. O'Mara's life history is an untypical rags to riches story: born to poor Irish parents in Liverpool, though with a mutable sense of his own identity, self-taught as a writer, he travelled across the Atlantic to pursue the 'American dream', settling first in Baltimore and then Arizona, serving in the US Marines during the Second World War, and eventually becoming an artist of some repute who apparently married a German baroness.[53]

By far the most valuable collection of original materials on how migration was conceived within post-Famine Irish society is that collected by the Irish Folklore Commission between 1935 and 1971. Geographically biased towards rural districts, and with all the interpretative challenges raised by the use of evidence collected retrospect-ively, folklore nevertheless provides uniquely rich and vivid insights into the place of migration in popular consciousness. In 1955 a special questionnaire was distributed by the Irish Folklore Commission to assist the work of the American scholar Arnold Schrier, and the accounts generated from across Ireland offer valuable insights into what may be termed the 'culture of migration'. Highly original and innovative accounts of the lives of temporary migrants who went to Britain, the famous 'tattie hokers', the image of America, as well as more wide-ranging accounts of the place of emigration within Irish society, deploy these ethnographic sources to great effect.[54] As has been argued in another context, folklore allows insights into the historical sense of the pow-erless individuals who, while being central to the process of migration, too often remain marginal subjects in accounts based on statistical and other traditional documentary sources.[55]

A crucial component of these identities was religion, and much of the writing on the history of the Irish overseas emphasizes the role of faith, practice, and belief in the evo-lution of ethnic identities. At one level, there are the migrations that were driven by the search for religious freedom, such as Ulster Presbyterians leaving Ireland for colonial America in the seventeenth and eighteenth centuries, or Catholic exiles fleeing to con-tinental Europe to avoid persecution. At a more institutional level historians have paid considerable attention to the export of clerical and lay personnel as missionaries across the world, and the subsequent emergence of the Irish-born in important leadership positions within the Anglophone Catholic world, often operating in a British imper-ial or colonial environment in Australasia, Asia, or Africa.[56] The anomalous position of Protestants within the broader schema of Irish diasporic identity, which until relatively recently was seen as essentially Catholic, has now been investigated across a wide range of geographical and chronological contexts.

While the significance of religion in framing individual and collective identities is not open to question, the role of religious belief and faith in shaping the everyday existence of the Irish overseas is less certain.[57] Many accounts are based on institutional sources such as the records of churches, charities, or quasi-political bodies such as the Ancient Order of Hibernians or the Orange Order. Inevitably, such sources tend to privilege very public manifestations of Catholic or Protestant religious identity, ranging from devotional activities to street preaching or indeed sectarian rioting. Yet religious piety was about more than simply being part of an institution, whatever form that might take. Reconstructing the widespread belief in a supernatural presence and the significance of often deeply held religious faith poses interpretative challenges for secular-minded historians. Pioneering accounts of popular Irish religious piety, based on locales as different as New York at the turn of the twentieth century and Victorian Manchester, underscore the complex layers of devotion and practice and how these were adapted to suit local circumstances and individual needs.[58] Religious piety thus served both to strengthen communal identity and act as a form of support to individuals when faced with the dislocation of migration.

IV. INTERPRETATIONS

M. A. G. Ó Tuathaigh, writing in the late 1970s, noted that there was a dramatic increase in studies of Irish emigration and the Irish overseas, which challenged many of the 'old assumptions' about movement from Ireland and settlement in North America, Britain, and Australasia.[59] Since the mid-1980s this field has expanded almost beyond recognition as the global study of Ireland and its diaspora has excited the interest of hundreds of scholars. Three distinguished and gifted historians have dominated the study of the historical Irish diaspora: D. H. Akenson, David Fitzpatrick, and Kerby A. Miller. Akenson, whose earlier scholarly work was on the education system in Ireland and Irish foreign policy, completed his major study of the Irish in rural Ontario in 1984, and thereafter broadened his conspectus over the next decade to comparative study of the Irish overseas in South Africa, New Zealand, and North America, culminating in his wide-ranging and perceptive overview of the history of the Irish diaspora published in 1993.[60] What Akenson has demonstrated beyond doubt is the requirement for strong statistical foundations, and the need to place the study of the Irish overseas in a comparative context, taking due account of the specific circumstances in each country or region of settlement rather than assuming an innate sense of Irishness. This intellectual trajectory was very different to that of Fitzpatrick, whose first book was an imaginative study of the Irish revolution in country Clare. Fitzpatrick's focus was anchored in nineteenth- and early twentieth-century Irish emigration and the Irish in Britain.[61] In the early 1990s he produced what is one of the masterpieces of Irish historical scholarship on

Irish movement to Australia, using migrant letters: *Oceans of consolation* (1994), a work widely regarded as being among the most innovative studies of global migration history published in recent decades. Finally, the best-known and most original scholarship on the Irish in the United States has come from Kerby A. Miller. Through a series of penetrating articles, but especially in his *magnum opus, Emigrants and exiles* (1985), Miller established the terms for understanding the massive transatlantic movement to North America over three centuries. More recently, Miller's collaborative volume of letters and memoirs of the Irish in colonial and revolutionary America confirmed his reputation as the leading interpreter of the Irish in the United States.[62] What is noteworthy about all three scholars is that they have also published extensively on the history of modern Ireland, and what underpins their approach to the history of the Irish overseas is a wide-ranging knowledge of the society from which these migrants originated. This was often lacking in older traditionalist accounts which essentially interpreted the history of the Irish overseas with little appreciation of Ireland itself.[63] Other seminal contributions to the history of the Irish diaspora are too numerous to list, but it is worth noting that some of the finest work has come from scholars whose work is located firmly in this transnational approach.

The next generation of scholars has capitalized on this work, and refined these approaches to the study of the Irish diaspora. Comparative and transnational frameworks have dominated recent studies of the Irish overseas. A whole host of scholars working on early-modern Ireland have located their findings within the broader Atlantic and British history contexts, emphasizing the connections between colonial activities in Ireland, the New World, and the integrated history of the Three Kingdoms. From the eighteenth century onwards the transnational framework dominates. For instance, one historian, Kevin Whelan, has described the links between Irish and American revolutionaries in the later eighteenth century as constituting a 'Green' Atlantic.[64] Kevin Kenny has completed a major reinterpretation of the Molly Maguires, using a transatlantic approach, locating the violence of this group as much in pre-Famine Ulster as the anthracite fields of antebellum Pennsylvania.[65] Kenny has also formulated what has been lacking: an overall conceptual framework for the history of the global Irish since 1700 that underlines the benefits and limitations of differing comparative and transnational methodologies.[66] Donald M. MacRaild has similarly stressed the importance of the transnational focus through his studies of the Protestant Irish in England, bringing a subject that was at one time located at the margins into the mainstream of the study of the Irish in modern Britain. MacRaild, like Kenny, has also explored the potential for the comparative study of the Irish overseas.[67]

Irish nationalism from the 1780s is the exemplar of a diasporic and transnational movement, involving ever-changing nodes of political activity in the United States, Canada, continental Europe, Australasia, and, of course, Britain.[68] Indeed, the domestic history of modern Ireland might well have been very different were it not for the funding, moral and physical support, and publicity generated by nationalist organizations of varying outlooks such as Clan na nGael, the Friends of Irish Freedom, and the National Brotherhood of St Patrick. The United Irishmen, Young Irelanders, Fenians, the United Irish League, as well as the early twentieth-century Irish Party and Sinn Féin had a diasporic dimension to their activities. Nationalist politics within Ireland itself was shaped by factors that reached far beyond the island, often seeking to invigorate communities of Irish descent overseas, and not just Irish Catholics. By enlarging the focus above the level of the nation state it is possible to reconstruct these interactions, marked as they were by concerns about the situation in the homeland and the country of settlement, fuelled by patriotism but also by practical considerations such as consolidating the ethnic base of support in national party politics in the new communities. Uncovering the global role of Irish Catholicism is another excellent example of a subject that lends itself to a transnational approach, a topic on which Sheridan Gilley completed pioneering work in the 1980s.[69]

The other major interpretative innovation developed from the study of what were essentially public and well-documented manifestations of migration, such as associational culture to essentially private or individual experiences. Understandably, much of the scholarly work has been on formal institutions such as the Orange Order or the Catholic Church, since such bodies generated extensive archival material, but increasingly scholars are seeking to reconstruct the everyday experiences of the diasporic Irish. Irish migrants were part of a multiplicity of networks, ranging from extended family members to formal political and religious institutions. This shift away from what were ostensibly public markers of adaptation and adjustment into the complex private worlds of migrants has demanded a more imaginative approach to the use of source materials. Use of these first-hand accounts, especially migrant letters, but also autobiographies, memoirs, and oral histories, has transformed the study of Irish migration and settlement in the United States, Australasia, Canada, Britain, and Latin America.[70] Genealogical techniques have also been exploited to piece together in a painstaking way the life histories of hundreds of individuals who left Ireland.[71]

Historiographical debates within the field of diaspora and migration history have centred around a number of specific issues.[72] The first relates to Kerby Miller's argument, based on an impressive array of source materials, especially migrant letters, memoirs, songs, and folklore, that the Irish in North America perceived themselves to be exiles, and that the 'concept itself reflected not the concrete realities of most emigrants' experiences but a distinctive Irish Catholic worldview rooted deeply in history and culture'.[73] This bold and wide-ranging interpretation attracted sharp criticism when his work was first published in the mid-1980s, especially from D. H. Akenson, but also from other scholars such as David Fitzpatrick.[74] Since then, however, Miller's thesis has both its supporters and its critics in almost equal measure. Accounts based on the Irish experience elsewhere, in particular Australia and New Zealand, have sought to underscore the diverse nature of sensibilities ranging from exile to the economic and social opportunities presented by leaving Ireland.[75] Yet others working on the Irish in the United States offer qualified support to the 'exile' interpretation.[76] In fact, some recent assessments of historical writing on the Irish diaspora single out Miller's arguments as being especially important and still being as relevant today as when his book first appeared over a quarter of a century ago.[77] One legitimate criticism that can be made of Miller's work relates to his overemphasis on structural factors, reflecting contemporary concerns about modernization theory in the 1970s and 1980s, which allowed little scope for individual agency or the power of people to influence their own life course. More recent scholarship on the American Irish gives equal weight to individual life-histories within a broader context of structural forces.[78]

Another area of controversy has focused on racial images of the Irish in the Victorian press in both Britain and the United States, and what this means for understanding the nature of anti-Irish prejudice. Such negative stereotypes and unashamedly racist images of the Irish have a long genealogy. L. P. Curtis pioneered this innovative approach in the late 1960s, generating much debate, which continues to the present day, about its significance. What Curtis demonstrates is that these racial prejudices were given greater potency during the later Victorian period when social Darwinism reached its apogee in the Anglo-American world. What made nineteenth- and early twentieth-century hierarchies of race different was that they were used to justify British policies in Ireland, since the Irish were perceived to be on the margins of human civilization, requiring strong and often coercive governance. Much of the debate relates to caricature, and the portrayal of the Irish with simian features in middle-class journals such as *Punch*. 'Paddy' was seen as a threatening monster and, according to Curtis, from the mid-nineteenth century onwards the Irish were presented as a subordinate and inferior race, prejudices that were given a pseudo-scientific respectability with the emergence of social Darwinism in the 1870s.[79] This argument as it relates to the Irish in nineteenth-century Britain has prompted a series of responses, including sustained critiques from R. F. Foster and Sheridan Gilley, as well as other work which develops and modifies Curtis' original conclusions, either in terms of the timing of the peak of anti-Irish prejudice in the United States and Britain.[80] Gilley, for instance, emphasizes the religious and national dimensions of anti-Irish prejudice as well as the ambiguous set of responses to the Irish with both positive and negative 'Paddy' stereotypes, whereas Foster underlines the class antipathies that underpinned the outlook of middle-class journals such as *Punch*.[81] Even allowing for the inherent ambiguity in the range of responses that the Irish generated in popular discourses, a measured and judicious assessment has concluded that 'on balance, from the 1840s immigrants benefited much less from the idealized and benign elements of the "Paddy" stereotype in cartoons and elsewhere than they suffered from its malign elements'.[82]

The conceptual framework that underpins historical writing about the Irish in modern Britain has been challenged by Mary Hickman in a number of closely argued contributions.[83] Hickman has questioned interpretations that seek to cast doubt on the existence of an Irish community, in particular the writings of David Fitzpatrick. For Fitzpatrick, the Irish in later nineteenth- and early twentieth-century Britain did not constitute a community and 'despite their persistently low social status, Irish settlers adopted patterns of residence, religious practice, political participation, and criminality that do not suggest a segregated population locked together in defensive ethnicity'.[84] The principal target of Hickman's critique is that historians, including Fitzpatrick but also many others, implicitly assume that homogeneity equates with sociological understandings of community that were prevalent in the 1970s. Equally, she argues that placing an overarching emphasis on uncovering degrees of segregation or assimilations fails to capture the inherent diversity and 'hybridity' of the Irish in Britain.[85] These criticisms of the 'segregation/assimilation' model were well judged, and timely, especially as Hickman also observed that 'many displaced populations are part of wider diasporic communities and that this is a significant determinant of communal identities'.[86] It is an indication of the well-developed state of the field that many scholars are seeking to move beyond simply documenting the Irish experience in an empirical manner, and raising important conceptual and interpretative issues about how this history is written.

V. Conclusion

By locating the Irish diaspora in wider analytical frameworks, such as Atlantic history or the transnational history of ethnicity, untested assumptions of Irish exceptionalism have been questioned and found wanting. Many other European countries experienced both large-scale emigration and immigration after 1600, and while the Irish case diverged in a number of key respects—for instance, the sheer scale of the outflow relative to the size of the population—the effects and consequences for both the sending and receiving societies were often comparable. Rigorous accounts of settlement in a range of locations serve to raise complex issues about what was distinctive, if anything, about the Irish diasporic experience. Studies that compare either the Irish in two different places or seek to assess how they fared relative to other migrants can often yield findings that otherwise would not emerge in accounts limited to one nation state or migrant group. Only through systematic comparison can the elements of diversity and similarity of the Irish diaspora ever be fully recovered.

As D. H. Akenson has argued, the scope of what actually constitutes the Irish diaspora should include people of Irish descent.[87] For defensible reasons, historians often delimit their focus to those who were actually born in Ireland, first-generation migrants, or second-generation migrants with at least one Irish parent, avoiding complicated issues of ethnic self-identification that arise when it comes to second and third generations of Irish descent. Histories of the Irish diaspora that do adopt such an approach demonstrate the malleable nature of Irish identity, and the complex set of mechanisms by which it was transmitted from generation to generation.[88]

One of the more notable developments in the past thirty years of writing on the diaspora has been the extension of the coverage from traditional countries and regions such as the United States, Canada, Australasia, and Britain to mainland Europe, South Asia, Africa, South America, and the Pacific World. Indeed a number of these regions are currently generating the most engaging and imaginative scholarship on the Irish diaspora. The neglect of Africa, for instance, was startling: as one historian argued in the early 1990s, 'the chroniclers of the Irish diaspora have until the late 1980s ignored the continent of Africa'.[89] Similarly, the study of the Irish in the Spanish-speaking countries of South America has generated important contextual questions about how the Irish interacted in a very different environment to that of the Anglophone world.[90] For scholars concerned with the interactions between Irish across the Pacific, this has opened up a whole new vista on the diaspora.[91] Little substantive work has been done on the Irish in Russia or China. Only when investigations of the relatively unknown dimensions of the Irish migrant experience are systematically integrated with the better documented sites of settlement can a truly global history of the Irish emerge. That this history is a polyphonal one with many different voices, identities, and variations over time and space serves to remind us that the diaspora, like the Irish in Ireland, was a complex group of people whose lives, outlooks, and experiences were shaped in divergent ways by class, region, gender, and religion.

Notes

1. 'What Irishmen have done', [c. 1870?], reproduced in Robert L. Wright (ed), *Irish Emigrant Ballads and Songs* (Bowling Green OH, 1975), 528. Capitalization and spelling as in original. My thanks go to Professor Malcolm Campbell for a critical reading of an earlier draft of this chapter.
2. For this term, see Guy Beiner, *Remembering the Year of the French: Irish Folk History and Social Memory* (Madison, WI, 2007), 12; Tim Pat Coogan, *Wherever Green is Worn: The Story of the Irish Diaspora* (London, 2000).
3. Patrick O'Farrell, 'Emigrant Attitudes and Behaviour as a Source for Irish History', in G. A. Hayes-McCoy (ed), *Historical Studies*, X (Galway, 1976), 113.
4. Quoted in ibid.
5. Alan O'Day, 'Revising the Diaspora', in D. George Boyce and Alan O'Day (eds), *The Making of Modern Irish History: Revisionism and the Revisionist Controversy* (London, 1996), 200.
6. See, for example, Malcolm Campbell, *Ireland's New Worlds: Immigrants, Politics, and Society in the United States and Australia, 1815–1922* (Madison, WI, 2008).
7. For assessments, see D. H. Akenson, *The Irish Diaspora: A Primer* (Toronto, 1993); Enda Delaney, Kevin Kenny, and Donald M. MacRaild, 'Symposium: Perspectives on the Irish Diaspora', *Irish Economic and Social History*, 33 (2006), 35–52; Patrick Fitzgerald and Brian Lambkin, *Migration in Irish History, 1607–2007* (Basingstoke, 2008); Mary Hickman, 'Migration and Diaspora', in Joe Cleary and Claire Connolly (eds), *The Cambridge Companion to Modern Irish Culture* (Cambridge, 2005), 117–36; J. J. Lee, 'The Irish Diaspora in the Nineteenth Century', in L. M. Geary and Margaret Kelleher (eds), *Nineteenth Century Ireland: A Guide to Recent Research* (Dublin, 2005), 182–222; Kevin Kenny, 'Writing the History of the Irish Diaspora', in Robert J. Savage Jr., (ed), *Ireland in the New Century: Politics, Culture and Identity* (Dublin, 2003), 206–26; Kevin Kenny, 'Diaspora and Comparison: the Global Irish as a Case Study', *Journal of American History*, 90 (2003), 359–98; O'Day, 'Revising the Diaspora'.
8. Kenny, 'Writing the History of the Irish Diaspora', 206.
9. R. A. Butlin, 'Land and People, c. 1600', in T. W. Moody, F. X. Martin, and F. J. Byrne (eds), *A New History of Ireland, III: Early Modern Ireland, 1534–1691* (Oxford, 1976), 148.
10. J. J. Silke, 'The Irish Abroad', in Moody, Martin, and Byrne (eds), *A New History of Ireland, III*, 593. See the chapter below by Nicholas Canny.

11. Harman Murtagh, 'Irish Soldiers Abroad', in Thomas Bartlett and Keith Jeffery (eds), *A Military History of Ireland* (Cambridge, 1996), 295–6, 307.
12. D. H. Akenson, *If the Irish Ran the world: Montserrat, 1630–1730* (Liverpool, 1997).
13. L. M. Cullen, 'The Irish Diaspora of the Seventeenth and Eighteenth Centuries', in Nicholas Canny (ed.), *Europeans on the Move: Studies on European Migration, 1500–1800* (Oxford, 1994), 126.
14. Ibid., 118.
15. Patrick J. Corish, 'The Cromwellian Regime, 1650–60', in Moody, Martin, and Byrne (eds.), *A New History of Ireland, III*, 364.
16. Quoted in ibid., 364.
17. Hilary McD. Beckles, ' "A Riotous and Unruly Lot": Irish Indentured Servants and Freemen in the English West Indies, 1644–1713', *The William and Mary Quarterly*, 3rd ser., 47 (1990), 503–22.
18. Jane Ohlmeyer, Civilizinge of Those Rude Partes': Colonization within Briain and Ireland, 1580s–1640s', in Nicholas Canny (ed), *The Origins of Empire* (Oxford, 1998), 138–9.
19. Nicholas Canny, 'Migration and Opportunity: Britain, Ireland and the New World', *Irish Economic and Social History*, 12 (1985), 7–32; idem, *Kingdom and Colony: Ireland in the Atlantic World* (Baltimore, 1988), 69–133.
20. L. M. Cullen, 'Population Trends in Seventeenth-Century Ireland', *Economic and Social Review*, 6 (1975), 157; T. C. Barnard, 'New Opportunities for British Settlement: Ireland', in Canny (ed), *The Origins of Empire*, 309–27.
21. L. M. Cullen, 'Economic Development, 1691–1750', in T. W. Moody and W. E Vaughan (eds), *A New History of Ireland, IV: Eighteenth-Century Ireland, 1691–1800* (Oxford, 1986), 133–4.
22. Kevin Kenny, *The American Irish: A History* (London, 2000), 9.
23. Silke, 'The Irish Abroad', 600–1; Kenny, *The American Irish*, 9.
24. See Cullen, 'Irish Diaspora' for an overview.
25. See the chapter below by Maurice Bric.
26. Patrick Griffin, *The People With No Name: Ireland's Ulster Scots, America's Scots Irish, and the Creation of a British Atlantic World, 1689–1764* (Princeton, 1999).
27. Kerby A. Miller, Arnold Schrier, Bruce D. Boling, and David N. Doyle, *Irish Immigrants in the Land of Canaan: Letters and Memoirs from Colonial and Revolutionary America, 1675–1815* (Oxford and New York, 2003), 657.
28. Kerby A. Miller, ' "Scotch-Irish" Myths and "Irish" Identities in Eighteenth- and Nineteenth-Century America', in Charles Fanning (ed), *New Perspectives on the Irish Diaspora* (Carbondale, 2000), 75–92, and idem, 'Ulster Presbyterians and the "Two Traditions" in Ireland and America', in J. J. Lee and Marion Casey (eds), *Making the Irish American: History and Heritage of the Irish in the United States* (New York, 2006) 255–70.
29. Cullen, 'Irish Diaspora', 112.
30. A concise and stimulating overview can be found in David Fitzpatrick, *Irish Emigration, 1801–1921* (Dublin, 1984).
31. Ibid., 5.
32. David Noel Doyle, 'Cohesion and Diversity in the Irish Diaspora', *Irish Historical Studies*, 31 (1999), 413–15.
33. Kevin Kenny 'The Irish in the Empire' in idem (ed), *Ireland and the British Empire* (Oxford, 2004), 90–122.
34. See the chapter below by Donald M. MacRaild.

35. Enda Delaney, *Irish Emigration since 1921* (Dublin, 2002).

36. For example, see Grainne Henry, 'Women "Wild Geese", 1585–1625: Irish Women and Migration to European Armies in the Late Sixteenth and Early Seventeenth Centuries', in Patrick O'Sullivan (ed), *Irish Women and Irish Migration* (London, 1995) 23–40.

37. See Janet Nolan, 'Women's Place in the History of the Irish Diaspora: A Snapshot', *Journal of American Ethnic History*, 28 (2009), 76–81.

38. Beckles, 'A Riotous and Unruly Lot'; Dale T. Knobel, *Paddy and the Republic: Ethnicity and Nationality in Antebellum America* (Middletown, 1986); Stewart J. Brown, ' "Outside the Covenant": The Scottish Presbyterian Churches and Irish Immigration, 1922–1938', *Innes Review*, 42 (1991), 19–45.

39. Kevin Kenny, 'Twenty Years of Irish American Historiography', *Journal of American Ethnic History*, 28, no. 4 (2009), 70–2; Timothy J. Meagher, *The Columbia Guide to Irish American History* (New York, 2006), 214–33.

40. Ronald H. Bayor, *Neighbors in Conflict: The Irish, Germans, Jews and Italians of New York City, 1929–1941* (2nd edn., Urbana, 1988); Graham T. Hodges, ' "Desirable Companions and Lovers": Irish and African Americans in the Sixth Ward, 1830–1870' in Ronald H. Bayor and Timothy J. Meagher (eds), *The New York Irish* (Baltimore, 1996), 107–24; John Kuo Wei Tchen, 'Ozuimbo Appo's Fear of Fenians: Chinese-Irish-Anglo Relations in New York City', in Bayor and Meagher (eds), *The New York Irish*, 125–52.

41. Kenny, *American Irish*, 125–6.

42. R. A. Burchell, *The San Francisco Irish, 1848–1880* (Manchester, 1979), 153.

43. A suggestive local study is John A. Burnett and Donald M. MacRaild, 'The Irish and Scots on Tyneside', in Robert Colls (ed), *Northumbria: History and Identity 547–2000* (Chichester, 2007), 178–93.

44. John Corbally, 'Shades of Difference: Irish, Caribbean, and South Asian Immigration to the Heart of Empire, 1948–1971' (unpublished PhD dissertation, University of California-Davis, 2009).

45. Kevin Kenny, *Peaceable Kingdom Lost: The Paxton Boys and the Destruction of William Penn's Holy Experiment* (New York, 2009).

46. Akenson, *If the Irish Ran the World*.

47. Kenny 'The Irish in the Empire', 102–21.

48. V. G. Kiernan, *The Lords of Human Kind: European Attitudes towards the Outside World in the Imperial Age* (London, 1969), 75.

49. Colin Barr, ' "Imperium in Imperio": Irish Episcopal Imperialism in the Nineteenth Century', *English Historical Review*, 123 (2008), 611–50.

50. Margaret M. Mulrooney, *Black Powder, White Lace: The du Pont Irish and Cultural Identity in Nineteenth-century America* (Hanover, 2002).

51. Stephen A. Brighton, *Historical Archaeology of the Irish Diaspora: A Transnational Approach* (Knoxville, 2009).

52. Liam Harte, *The Literature of the Irish in Britain: Autobiography and Memoir, 1725–2001* (Basingstoke, 2009).

53. Pat O'Mara, *The Autobiography of a Liverpool Irish Slummy* (London, 1934); idem, *Irish Slummy in America* (London, 1935).

54. Anne O'Dowd, *Spalpeens and Tattie Hokers: History and Folklore of the Irish Migratory Agricultural Worker in Ireland and Britain* (Dublin, 1991); Arnold Schrier, *Ireland and the American Emigration, 1850–1900* (Minneapolis, 1958); Grace Neville, 'Westward

Bound: Emigration to North America in the Irish Folklore Commission Archives', *Etudes Irlandaises*, 17 (1992), 195–208.

55. See Beiner, *Remembering the Year of the French*.
56. Barr, 'Imperium in Imperio'.
57. See the essays on the Irish abroad in Mervyn Busteed, Frank Neal, and Jon Tonge (eds), *Irish Protestant Identities* (Manchester, 2008).
58. Bernard Aspinwall, 'Catholic Devotion in Victorian Scotland', in Martin J. Mitchell (ed), *New Perspectives on the Irish in Scotland* (Edinburgh, 2008), 31–43; G.P. Connolly, 'Little Brother be at Peace: The Priest as Holy Man in the Nineteenth-Century Ghetto', in W. J. Shiels (ed), *The Church and Healing* (Oxford, 1992), 191–206; Hugh McLeod, 'Popular Catholicism in Irish New York, c. 1900', in W. J. Shiels and Diana Wood (eds), *The Churches, Ireland and the Irish* (Oxford, 1989), 353–73; Raphael Samuel, 'The Roman Catholic Church and the Irish Poor', in Roger Swift and Sheridan Gilley (eds), *The Irish in the Victorian City* (London, 1985), 267–300.
59. M. A. G. ÒTuathaigh, 'Ireland, 1800–1921', in Joseph Lee (ed), *Irish Historiography 1970–79* (Cork, 1980), 106.
60. Akenson, *The Irish Diaspora*.
61. Fitzpatrick, *Irish Emigration*; idem, 'Emigration, 1801–70' in W. E. Vaughan (ed), *A New History of Ireland, V: Ireland under the Union, 1 (1801–70)* (Oxford, 1989), 562–622; idem, 'Emigration, 1871–1921' in W. E. Vaughan (ed), *A New History of Ireland, VI: Ireland under the Union, 11 (1871–1921)* (Oxford, 1996), 606–52; idem, 'Irish Emigration in the Later Nineteenth Century', *Irish Historical Studies*, 22 (1980), 126–43; idem, ' "A Peculiar Tramping People": The Irish in Britain, 1801–70', in Vaughan (ed), *A New History of Ireland, V, 623–660*; idem, 'The Irish in Britain, 1871–1921', in Vaughan (ed), *A New History of Ireland, VI, 653–702*.
62. Miller et al, *Immigrants in the Land of Canaan*; see also his collection of essays, *Ireland and Irish America: Culture, Class, and Transatlantic Migration* (Dublin, 2009).
63. The best known example is Oscar Handlin's, *Boston's Immigrants, 1790–1865: A Study in Acculturation* (Cambridge MA, 1941).
64. Kevin Whelan, 'The Green Atlantic: Radical Reciprocities between Ireland and America in the Long Eighteenth Century', in Kathleen Wilson (ed), *A New Imperial History: Culture, Identity, and Modernity in Britain and the Empire, 1660–1840* (Cambridge, 2004), 216–38.
65. Kevin Kenny, *Making Sense of the Molly Maguires* (New York, 1998).
66. Idem, 'Diaspora and Comparison'.
67. Donald M. MacRaild, *Faith, Fraternity and Fighting: The Orange Order and Irish Migrants in Northern England, c. 1850–1920* (Liverpool, 2006); idem, 'Crossing Migrant Frontiers: Comparative Reflection on Irish Migrants in Britain and the United States during the Nineteenth Century', in idem (ed), *The Great Famine and Beyond: Irish Migrants in Britain in the Nineteenth and Twentieth Centuries* (Dublin, 2000), 40–70. For a suggestive indication of how transnational history might integrate both Ireland and the diaspora, see Enda Delaney, 'Our Island Story? Towards a Transnational History of Late Modern Ireland', *Irish Historical Studies*, 37 (2011), 83–105.
68. Kenny, 'Diaspora and Comparison', 158–9; for an assessment primarily concerned with Irish American nationalism but which contains many points of relevance more generally, see David Brundage, 'Recent Directions in the History of Irish American Nationalism', *Journal of American Ethnic History*, 28 (2009), 82–9.

69. Sheridan Gilley, 'The Roman Catholic Church and the Nineteenth-Century Irish Diaspora', *Journal of Ecclesiastical History*, 35 (1984), 188–207.

70. David Fitzpatrick, *Oceans of Consolation: Personal Accounts of Irish Migration to Australia* (Cork, 1994); Harte, *Literature of the Irish in Britain*; C. J. Houston and W. J. Smyth, *Irish Emigration and Canadian Settlement* (Toronto, 1990); Angela McCarthy, *Irish Migrants in New Zealand, 1840–1937: 'The Desired Haven'* (Woodbridge, 2005); Edmundo Murray, *Becoming Irlandés: Private Narratives of the Irish Emigration to Argentina, 1844–1912* (Buenos Aires, 2006); Patrick O'Farrell, *Letters from Irish-Australia* (Sydney, 1984).

71. Bruce S. Elliott, *Irish Migrants in the Canadas: A New Approach* (Kingston and Montreal, 1988); John Mannion and Fidelma Maddock, 'Old World Antecedents, New World Adaptations: Inistioge Immigrants in Newfoundland', in William Nolan and Kevin Whelan (eds), *Kilkenny: History and Society* (Dublin, 1990), 345–404.

72. For recent discussions of the historiography in the United States, Britain, and the British Empire, see Kenny, 'Twenty Years of Irish American History'; J. J. Lee, 'Introduction: Interpreting Irish America', in Lee and Casey (eds), *Making the Irish American*, 1–62; Timothy J. Meagher, 'From the World to the Village and the Beginning to the End and After: Research Opportunities in Irish American History', *Journal of American Ethnic History*, 28 (2009), 122–7; Roger Swift, 'Identifying the Irish in Victorian Britain: Recent Trends in Historiography', *Immigrants & Minorities*, 27 (2009), 134–51; Stephen Howe, 'Historiography', in Kenny (ed), *Ireland and the British Empire*, 220–50.

73. Miller, *Emigrants and Exiles*, 1.

74. D. H. Akenson, 'The Historiography of the Irish in the United States', in Patrick O'Sullivan (ed), *The Irish in the New Communities* (London, 1992), 99–127; David Fitzpatrick, 'The Irish in America: Exiles or Escapers?', *Reviews in American History*, 15 (1987), 272–8.

75. Fitzpatrick, *Oceans of Consolation*; McCarthy, *Irish Migrants in New Zealand*; Campbell, *Ireland's New Worlds*.

76. David Gleeson, *The Irish in the South, 1815–1877* (Chapel Hill, 2001); Matthew Frye Jacobson, *Special Sorrows: The Diasporic Imagination of Irish, Polish and Jewish Immigrants in the United States* (2nd edn., Berkeley, 2002).

77. On the enduring significance of Miller's book, see Kenny, 'Twenty Years of Irish American History', 67–8; Delaney, Kenny, and MacRaild, 'Symposium: Perspectives on the Irish Diaspora'.

78. Kenny, 'Twenty Years of Irish American History', 69.

79. L. Perry Curtis Jr., *Anglo-Saxons and Celts: A Study of Anti-Irish Prejudice in Victorian England* (Bridgeport CT, 1968); idem; *Apes and Angels: The Irishman in Victorian Caricature* (London, 1971).

80. Sheridan Gilley, 'English Attitudes to the Irish in England, 1780–1900', in Colin Holmes (ed.), *Immigrants and minorities in British society* (London, 1978), 81–110; R. F. Foster, 'Paddy and Mr Punch', in *Paddy and Mr Punch: Connections in Irish and English History* (London, 1993), 171–94; Richard Ned Lebow, *White Britain and Black Ireland: The Influence of Stereotypes on Colonial Policy* (Philadelphia, 1976); Paul B. Rich, 'Social Darwinism, Anthropology and English perspectives of the Irish, 1867–1900', *History of European Ideas*, 19 (1994), 777–85.

81. For an overview of the various strands in the debate, see Donald M. MacRaild, *Irish Migrants in Modern Britain* (1st edn., Basingstoke, 1999), 160–2.

82. M. A. G. Ó Tuathaigh, 'The Irish in Nineteenth-Century Britain: Problems of Integration', *Transactions of the Royal Historical Society*, 5th ser., 31 (1981), 161.

83. Mary J. Hickman, 'Alternative Historiographies of the Irish in Britain: A Critique of the Segregation/Assimilation model', in Roger Swift and Sheridan Gilley (eds), *The Irish in Victorian Britain: The Local Dimension* (London, 1999), 236–53; idem, *The Irish Commuity in Britan: Myth or Reality?* (London, 1996).

84. Fitzpatrick 'The Irish in Britain, 1871–1921', 687.

85. Hickman, 'Alternative Historiogaphies', 253.

86. Ibid., 236.

87. Donald H. Akenson, 'Irish Diaspora', in S. J. Connolly (ed), *The Oxford Companion to Irish History* (1st edn., Oxford, 1998), 257.

88. Timothy J. Meagher, *Inventing Irish America: Generation, Class and Ethnic Identity in a New England City* (Notre Dame, 2000).

89. Donal McCracken, 'Irish Settlement and Identity in South Africa before 1910', *Irish Historical Studies*, 28 (1992), 134.

90. Murray, *Becoming Irlandés;* Patrick McKenna, 'Irish Emigration to Argentina: A Different Model', in Bielenberg (ed), *The Irish Diaspora*, 195–212; idem, 'The Formation of Hiberno-Argentine', in Oliver Marshall (ed), *English-Speaking Communities in Latin America* (Houndmills, 2000), 81–103.

91. Malcolm Campbell, 'Irish Immigrants in the Pacific World', in Laurence M. Geary and Andrew J. McCarthy (eds), *Ireland, Australia and New Zealand: History, Politics and Culture* (Dublin, 2008), 3–13.

Select Bibliography

Akenson, D.H., *The Irish Diaspora: A Primer* (Toronto, 1993).

Campbell, Malcolm, *Ireland's New Worlds: Immigrants, Politics, and Society in the United States and Australia, 1815–1922* (Madison, WI, 2008).

Cullen, L.M., 'The Irish Diaspora of the Seventeenth and Eighteenth Centuries', in Nicholas Canny (ed.), *Europeans on the Move: Studies on European Migration, 1500–1800* (Oxford, 1994).

Delaney, Enda, *Irish Emigration since 1921* (Dublin, 2002).

Delaney, Enda, 'Our Island Story? Towards a Transnational History of late Modern Ireland', *Irish Historical Studies*, 37 (2011).

Fitzpatrick, David, *Irish Emigration, 1801–1921* (Dublin, 1984).

Fitzpatrick, David, *Oceans of Consolation: Personal Accounts of Irish Migration to Australia* (Ithaca, 1994).

Harte, Liam, *The Literature of the Irish in Britain: Autobiography and Memoir, 1725–2001* (Basingstoke, 2009).

Hickman, Mary, 'Migration and Diaspora', in Joe Cleary and Claire Connolly (eds), *The Cambridge Companion to Modern Irish Culture* (Cambridge, 2005).

Houston, C.J. and Smyth, W.J., *Irish Emigration and Canadian Settlement* (Toronto, 1990).

Kenny, Kevin, *The American Irish: A History* (London, 2000).

Kenny, Kevin, 'Diaspora and Comparison: the Global Irish as a Case Study', *Journal of American History*, 90 (2003).

Lee, J.J., 'The Irish Diaspora in the Nineteenth Century', in L. M. Geary and Margaret Kelleher (eds), *Nineteenth Century Ireland: A Guide to Recent Research* (Dublin, 2005).

MacRaild, Donald M., *The Irish Diaspora in Britain, 1750–1939* (2nd ed., Basingstoke, 2011).

McCarthy, Angela, *Irish Migrants in New Zealand, 1840–1937: 'The Desired Haven'* (Woodbridge, 2005).

Miller, Kerby A., *Emigrants and Exiles: Ireland and the Irish Exodus to North America* (New York, 1985).

Miller, Kerby A., Schrier, Arnold, Boling, Bruce D., and Doyle, David N., *Irish Immigrants in the Land of Canaan: Letters and Memoirs from Colonial and Revolutionary America, 1675–1815* (Oxford and New York, 2003).

O'Farrell, Patrick, *Letters from Irish-Australia* (Sydney, 1984).

CHAPTER 8

....

BUSINESS AND INDUSTRY

....

PHILIP OLLERENSHAW

I

....

THIS chapter considers the evolution of business and industry in Ireland from the eighteenth to the later twentieth centuries.[1] The secondary literature in this area is not large and, although there has been considerable discussion about some topics, such as the impact of the Act of Union on industrialization, or the significance of tariffs for industrial development in the Free State in the interwar period, rarely has this evolved into a debate. In particular, there has been no major debate on nineteenth- and early twentieth-century entrepreneurship of the kind that has generated such a substantial literature in Britain.[2] Even in such influential works as Mokyr's *Why Ireland Starved*, there is relatively little discussion of industrial and commercial entrepreneurship.[3] For Cullen, the doyen of modern Irish economic historians, no serious work was published on the economic and social history of eighteenth-century Ireland until Froude's *The English in Ireland in the Eighteenth Century* (1872–4) which was updated in 1881 to include the period up to 1880. Froude's work was influential in constructing an interpretation which quickly became orthodoxy until well into the twentieth century. It received powerful reinforcement from three substantial books on the economic history of Ireland from the seventeenth century to the Great Famine by O'Brien written in the period between 1918 and 1921. Just as Froude's work was influenced by the growing importance of the land question, so the revolutionary context of O'Brien's work profoundly influenced his interpretation of long-term economic change. The emergence of what is loosely described as a nationalist interpretation of Irish economic history saw English influence as a negative influence, intentionally destructive of Irish industry from the later seventeenth century and most of the eighteenth, as well as from the Act of Union to partition in the early 1920s.[4] In terms of recent historiography, there have been a number of attempts to continue this line of argument, most notably in O'Hearn's use of world systems theory to explain the 'subjugation' of the Irish cotton industry by English industrial interests, and in his view that the Irish linen industry remained 'semiperipheral' and failed to generate strong developmental links with the northern regional economy. This view has been strongly challenged.[5]

One of the first scholarly commissioned business histories was Lynch and Vaizey's study of Guinness's Brewery from its foundation in 1759 to 1876, published in 1960. Guinness is by far the most successful global brand to have emerged from Ireland and this pioneering volume marked a substantial step forward in Irish business history, not only in its discussion of entrepreneurship, organization, costs, and marketing, but also because of its attempt to set the firm in a national economic context. Unfortunately much of its value was overlooked as critics focused on the overly simplistic and schematic model of the eighteenth-century Irish economy outlined in less than ten pages at the start of the book. This was alleged to comprise an advanced, monetized, trading maritime zone containing about a quarter of the Irish population and a rural economy 'founded on subsistence farming and barter', where circulation of money was so limited that there was practically no demand for industrial products from outside this area.[6] Lynch and Vaizey acknowledged their intellectual debt to O'Brien personally and to his three surveys of Irish economic history, but their maritime/subsistence zone schema attracted powerful criticism from Cullen who also challenged the view that the first eighty years of the eighteenth century were years of unrelieved depression for Irish industry, recovering only as a result of policies introduced by the Irish Parliament after 1782. Amongst other indicators Cullen pointed to the five-fold growth in linen exports between the 1720s and 1770s, a further doubling in the next twenty years, and in general to the role of organizational change in industry quite separate from legislative changes. Cullen was also critical of Lynch and Vaizey's arguments about the role of banking and credit, noting that the banking system before the establishment of the Bank of Ireland in 1783 was more robust than they assumed, though it was by no means insulated from credit crises.[7] Cullen's wider point—that historians should distinguish general industrial activity from the experience of particular industries, some of which did decline— applies not only to the eighteenth but also to later centuries.

In the eighteenth and early nineteenth centuries, industrial activity in Ireland was substantial and geographically widespread. In the 1821 Census of Ireland, more than 40 per cent of men and women who stated their occupation were 'chiefly employed in trades, manufactures, or handicraft'. Of the provinces, Ulster had the highest percentage (55), followed by Connacht (43), Leinster (33), and Munster (24).[8]

From the 1820s to the end of the nineteenth century, however, the process of industrialization in east Ulster accelerated and this led, by the 1850s, to a much clearer industrial demarcation of this area from the rest of Ireland. Indeed, until the 1830s, Dublin and Cork led Belfast in a range of industries, most notably in brewing, distilling, flour milling, and shipbuilding, but also in others such as engineering and foundries, tanning, glass and paper-making. Cork was and remained much more a commercial than an industrial city and the nineteenth century was one of widespread stagnation. At the end of the eighteenth century Cork was still larger than Liverpool or Manchester, but its population of 76 000 in 1901 was some 5 per cent less than that of 1821. Even if nineteenth-century Cork lost its dynamism, it remains the case that at least 20 per cent of its male and female population was engaged in manufacturing. Before the development of large-scale brewing and distilling in the later eighteenth century, sugar-refining was Dublin's most significant capital-intensive industry where the firms catered for a countrywide market. In general terms, the industrial development of eighteenth-century Dublin evolved from commercial activity, where goods were manufactured for the home market from raw materials either from within Ireland itself (for example woollens), or imported (such as silk or iron). During the eighteenth century Dublin was the predominant economic and social centre for the whole of Ireland, although towards the end of that century this dominance began to look less secure.[9]

In Dublin, traditional industries like cabinetmaking and carriage manufacture declined, as did clothing, the latter apparently a victim of a determination to retain outdated techniques; few manufacturing industries developed to provide substantial employment in the 'deposed capital' during the nineteenth century. There was some growth in engineering, especially relating to the railways, as well as in food and drink. A small number of large firms stand out. Among these was Quaker biscuit manufacturer W and R Jacob, formerly of Waterford, who opened a factory in Dublin in 1851. The firm demonstrated early commitment to mass-production methods and became a public company in 1883; by the beginning of the twentieth century it employed more than 2000 workers.[10] Dominating the manufacturing sector in Dublin was Guinness, established in 1759, but in output terms still behind Beamish and Crawford of Cork in the early nineteenth century. The trend in Irish brewing was towards much larger units in a smaller number of urban centres. Guinness rose to prominence not only because of its distinctive product, but also through its high-quality management, technical innovation, and successful marketing. The firm exploited the British market and, as the transport system improved, the market within Ireland. In both markets consumers increasingly favoured high-quality stout.[11] Decades of expansion led to the conversion of Guinness into a public company in 1886. Firms such as Jacob and Guinness were very much the exception than the rule; indeed apart from food and drink much of the south and west of Ireland had relatively little industry by the early twentieth century.

Leading the industrialization process in the north of Ireland was linen. Within Ireland, linen production developed from a thoroughly rural and widespread activity into a much more localized but strikingly successful example of factory-based industry centred on the Belfast area, and a contraction in the south and west of the country. Linen was central to the debate on protoindustrialization which developed in Europe from the 1970s and research into the industry in Ireland made a significant contribution to that literature.[12] Factory techniques, however, did not become widespread in spinning until the 1830s and in weaving until the late 1850s and 1860s.

The influence of Huguenot immigrants who arrived in 1698 has been shown to have been exaggerated and in fact the industry had been growing for several decades before that. In the 1640s and 1650s, substantial surpluses of linen yarn were sent from Ulster to England to be woven. A combination of cheap land, the chance to take refuge from religious persecution and the opportunity to take advantage of the evident yarn surpluses all combined to attract migrants from the north of England and Scotland in the later seventeenth century. Recent important work by Jean Agnew has brought new insight into the emergence and growth of the Belfast mercantile community from 1660 to the early eighteenth century and has demonstrated the significance of linen in that growth. Agnew has shown how Belfast's economic potential, availability of land for building, and the Earl of Donegall's tolerance of Presbyterianism attracted Scots immigrants who went on to form the core of the town's merchant community. At any point before the 1690s there may have been no more than fifty individuals engaged in overseas trade, but nevertheless Agnew has demonstrated the complexity of kinship networks and a hierarchy reflecting 'wealth status and the ownership of land'. Very few indeed of these individuals abandoned commerce in favour of pure gentrification; rather, many of them became gentrified while continuing their mercantile interests.

Most important from a business history point of view are Agnew's conclusions about trading patterns, business techniques, and ethics. In the four decades from the mid seventeenth century, Belfast merchants moved from working principally on commission, loading cargoes on behalf of Dublin-based traders while at the same time taking shares in cargoes to spread expenditure and risk, to much more independent mercantile activity. The increasing use of bills of exchange permitted more complicated trading patterns to emerge. In the mid seventeenth century most of the factors used by Belfast merchants at the ports with which they traded were either expatriate Irish or foreign; by the end of the century they had been replaced by Scottish Presbyterians, many of them from Ulster. Members of Belfast mercantile families first settled in Dublin and in the West Indies in the 1660s; thirty years later they were established in Cork and Waterford as well as Bordeaux. The Belfast merchant community concentrated in the first instance on the provisions trade, but linen was of growing significance and the first generation of that community was responsible for Belfast becoming the leading Ulster port for both.[13]

Encouragement for Irish linen came with the formation in 1711 of the Trustees of the Hempen and Flaxen Manufactures of Ireland: the 'Linen Board'. The main tasks of the Board were to oversee and operate the regulations governing linen duties, promote quality control in production, and make determined efforts through financial incentives to spread the industry more widely outside Ulster. The Board continued to function until 1828, but it lacked the expertise to ensure that its grants were used in the most cost-effective way. Even so, the most balanced assessments of the Board's activities have judged it to be mildly positive, and linen dominated the manufacturing sector in both Ireland and Scotland by the later eighteenth century. During the course of that century a number of significant related developments can be identified, each of which contributed to the subsequent transition to factory production. These included changes in bleaching and finishing technology and the emergence of large-scale bleachers and drapers; the move away from Dublin as the main entrepôt in the Anglo-Irish trade and the associated switch to direct exports from Ulster; and the impact of the short-lived factory-based cotton industry whose appearance coincided with the final phase of domestic spinning in the linen industry. Changes in the scale and function of bleachers had fundamental long-term significance since bleachers-turned-drapers and linen merchants provided some of the earliest machine spinners and weavers.

The linen trade contributed much to the development of an embryonic credit structure based on bills of exchange. In the absence of formal banking facilities, credit networks evolved directly between northern bleachers and Dublin, and English merchants and bankers. As direct shipments from Ulster to Britain increased, the intermediate role of Dublin declined and this was reflected in the construction in 1785 of the White Linen Hall in Belfast. This led to a further decline in the proportion of linen sent to Dublin, even from such major markets as Armagh which had traditionally strong links with the capital.

Recent research into the later-eighteenth-century business community has shown that although the construction of the Linen Hall was originally advocated by drapers, other merchants quickly came forward and used the Hall's management committee in order to organise shipping arrangements and the discount of bills of exchange. The same group of merchants has also been identified as being the driving force behind the formation of the Belfast Chamber of Commerce in 1783 and of the Belfast Harbour Board two years later.[14] These developments contributed considerably to the emergence of Belfast as a leading commercial centre.

The role of Belfast as a centre of textile production was transformed in the later eighteenth and early nineteenth centuries by the cotton industry and its origins as a factory town may be said to date from this period. The need to import raw cotton, coal and machinery meant that the Ulster cotton industry tended to be concentrated in coastal towns such as Belfast, Bangor, Larne, and Carrickfergus, although it also spread inland. The region's cotton manufacturers were from a range of backgrounds, including haberdashery and, significantly, linen bleaching and drapery. The industry was stimulated by the wars with France and by grants from the Linen Board. The principal type of cotton produced in Belfast was muslin, a finer and lighter product than calico, though the latter was also made. Long experience with the manufacture of fine linens in the area provided a ready supply of skilled labour that could easily move into muslin production.

The Irish cotton industry has been described by Bielenberg and Solar as 'one of the great "might have beens" of Irish economic history'. These authors have emphasized the early initiatives in cotton spinning, often under landlord patronage, in the Cork region and east Leinster, including some large mills built in the 1780s. Hand weaving expanded at the same time. Specialization in coarse fabrics opened these regions up to British competition at an early stage, and the decades from the 1820s saw protracted decline, although there were a few exceptions to this, most notably the large scale Malcomson enterprise in Waterford which continued to grow until the 1870s. In east Ulster the cotton industry expanded in the late eighteenth and early nineteenth centuries, making important technical and other connections with industrializing British regions. Cotton was the first example of factory-based textile production in Ireland and it provided essential skills and infrastructure, including credit networks, on which mechanized linen production could draw in the decades from the 1820s and 1830s when cotton was eclipsed by linen.[15]

The advent of the wet-spinning process for flax provided cotton spinners with an attractive alternative in the years after 1825 when trade was depressed. Those with a great deal of fixed capital already committed in Ireland thus had an opportunity and a strong incentive to move into power spinning, which some of them did. By 1834, twelve mills had been built or converted and a further nine were in the process of construction. Provincial production of linen was responsible for the growth of industrial villages in many parts of Ulster, especially in the period 1830–70.[16] The major factor underpinning expansion of factory spinning (and, later, factory weaving) was the growth of export markets, especially the United States. Over 40 per cent of Ulster's linen exports went to the USA by the later 1850s. Mill construction continued apace, despite interruptions during commercial crises such as that of 1847–8, so that by 1850 there were 69 spinning mills in Ireland, the vast majority of them in Ulster.

Within the Chamber of Commerce by the 1820s, textile interests—cotton, linen, and wool—were dominant, although there were also representatives from shipbuilding and engineering, tanning, distilling, printing and, among many from the service sector, members drawn from accountancy, banking, and insurance. From the 1820s the Chamber lent support to the promotion of railways in Britain and Ireland as well as improvements in mail services between Belfast and the west of Ireland. It attached great importance to free trade across the Irish Sea and would later become a militantly unionist body. The mechanization of flax spinning was of fundamental importance in extending the industrialization process in north-east Ulster. The pressure to refine powerloom technology intensified during the 1850s and the necessary improvements had in fact been made just in time for Ulster to reap huge benefits from the unprecedented demand for linen occasioned by the 'cotton famine' during the American Civil War, 1861–5.

In many ways the American Civil War period was a crucial one for the linen industry, with much new investment. A number of spinning and bleaching firms integrated weaving into their operations, but there were now more opportunities for specialist, single-process, weaving enterprises to develop. In fact, the number of looms in both types of enterprise was almost exactly equal by 1875, though there was a marked tendency for the specialist firms to increase their share of weaving capacity during the later nineteenth and twentieth century. At the same time, a relatively small number of large, fully integrated firms developed and became the giants of the industry between the 1860s and 1914. This process was accelerated by the decision, first taken by the York Street Flax Spinning Company in 1864, and soon by many others, to adopt a joint stock form with limited liability, a development which contributed considerably to the extension of the stock market in Belfast. It was also aided by an immense expansion of bank credit, the availability of flax increasingly imported from Europe and by the development of a textile engineering sector which, by mid-century, also competed successfully in American and European markets. The linen industry became organized into a great variety of process-based trade associations in the later nineteenth century, the three most important of which catered for the interests of spinners, weavers, and merchants.[17]

The transition to factory production in the linen industry was the most significant feature of industrialization in nineteenth-century Ireland. The majority of workers in the linen industry as a whole were women, but the diversification of the economic base in Belfast meant that men increasingly found work, and relatively high wages, in engineering and shipbuilding. The two shipyards, Harland & Wolff (established in the late 1850s) and Workman Clark (in 1879), though subject to considerable short-term fluctuations in output, grew in internationally favourable economic conditions so that between the 1880s and the First World War they came to epitomize the success and self-confidence of industrial Belfast. On the eve of the First World War, employment at Harland and Wolff had reached 14 000. Other industries such as ropemaking and various branches of engineering developed as spin-offs and helped to sustain expansion when the rate of expansion of the linen industry slowed. By 1911 these areas, together with textiles, accounted for some 40 per cent of total employment in the city. Belfast was exceptional in Ulster terms. Derry, the province's second city, had no comparably dynamic industrial base; rather it developed a specialization in shirt- and collar-making and embroidery, mostly using female labour.

II

The evolution of business in Ireland involved not only manufacturing but transport and a range of financial services such as banking, accountancy, and stockbroking. The virtual absence of coal and iron was not only a profound influence on the location of modern industry but an equally strong influence on the development of canals and railways. In Britain many canals and railways were both cause and effect of the exploitation of coal deposits. The modern railway system in Ireland grew from slow beginnings in the 1830s, through mania in the mid 1840s to extensive and more solid growth from mid-century. The standard gauge system was supplemented from the 1880s by 'light' or narrow gauge lines mainly in the west and the total mileage reached about 3000 by the time of partition. A few of these, such as the Great Southern and Western Railway, the largest of the 'big four' railway companies with eventually about a thousand miles of track, had substantial capital, complex management, and were large employers of manual and clerical labour. On the system as a whole, the data on passengers and freight offer useful indicators of commercialization: passenger numbers increased fivefold from mid-century to 1912, while freight tonnage doubled in the forty years from the early 1870s.[18] The political conflict 1919–23 had a negative impact on the business of many railway lines and was the background to extensive government sponsored amalgamation in the Free State from which Great Southern Railways emerged in 1925; GSR would form one of the constituent parts of Córas Iompair Éireann (Irish Transport Company) from 1945.

The emergence of formal banking institutions in Ireland was preceded by the development of credit facilities in internal and cross-channel trade. The shortage of banks was to some extent offset by the fact that some important areas of economic activity, linen markets for example, functioned mainly on a cash basis, while much of the credit for cross-channel trade was provided by London merchants. An act of 1782, which established the Bank of Ireland by royal charter the following year, also limited all other banks to a maximum of six partners. Despite its large size, the Bank of Ireland did not open any branches until 1825 and proved itself highly conservative in the provision of credit, refusing to grant overdrafts on current accounts until the 1830s. In the north, the formation of three new banking partnerships, the Belfast Bank (1808), the Commercial Bank (1809), and Northern Bank (1809) indicated the extent to which religion and finance combined to produce a set of durable banking houses firmly rooted in Ulster's industrial and commercial development. Within a few years the banks established agencies in country towns and villages, the principal function of which was to increase note circulation through the discount of bills of exchange, thereby facilitating industrial and commercial development. They were the forerunners of the modern branch networks.

Financial instability in the decade following the end of the Napoleonic Wars, causing bank failures, was the most important factor leading to legislation in the mid 1820s which permitted the formation of banks with more than six partners. There were two main phases of joint stock bank promotion, 1824–1827 and 1834–1838, which greatly increased competition for customers. By the middle of the nineteenth century all banks, with the exception of the Dublin-based Royal Bank, operated branch networks.

Between 1850 and 1913 the Irish banking system continued to expand, from fewer than 200 offices to around 850. Of the many reasons driving this expansion, the main one was the need to maximize deposits, which was a key determinant of lending capacity and of profitability. By 1913 some 320 offices were open only on specified days of the week, particularly market or fair days, to cater for local need. Most of the deposits came from rural areas and branch networks enabled banks to utilize them to fund industrial expansion in larger towns, as well as to spread their risks. The great majority of banks were both stable and profitable. Bank failure was comparatively rare in Ireland. The most notable joint stock failures were the Tipperary Bank (1856) and the Cork-based Munster Bank (established only in 1864) in 1885, although from the latter emerged the successful Munster and Leinster Bank. In order to protect their shareholders, banks adopted limited liability, especially following the Companies Act of 1879. The First World War brought great prosperity to much of Irish agriculture and led to a huge increase in deposits which helped to provide financial stability for the country after partition.[19]

In addition to banking, the development of stockbroking and of three stock exchanges, in Dublin (1799), Cork (1886), and Belfast (1897), was an indication of higher levels of financial intermediation. Brokers dealing in government and bank stock emerged in Dublin in the later eighteenth century. Of thirteen licensed brokers in the original Dublin Stock Exchange, ten were public notaries, a reminder of the evolution and diversification of function that often characterized those involved in financial services. Similarly, in 1843 Josias Cunningham, a Belfast merchant, became the town's first share dealer. In Belfast, as in Dublin, the mania in railway shares in the mid 1840s did much to popularize share ownership and greatly increased the scope for specialist brokers, even if not all the projected railway schemes were successful. The coming of limited liability in the 1850s resulted in a number of linen firms taking advantage of the legislation during the linen boom of the mid 1860s and at the same time provided a further stimulus to the local share market. The pace of company formation accelerated towards the end of the century. Harland & Wolff did not become a public company until

1924, but the interwar depression was not a promising environment for its shares, or for those of local linen firms, many of which frequently failed to pay dividends and whose shares usually traded at a discount.[20] Rather better performance came from the shares of more resilient firms such as Gallaher's tobacco.

The teaching of bookkeeping was seen as an important part of the curriculum from the eighteenth-century hedge schools, through to National Schools after 1831 and a range of other schools, colleges, and universities in the later nineteenth and twentieth centuries. Bookkeeping skills were considered significant for a range of private businesses and increasingly for public sector employment. They might contribute to upward social mobility, not only for those within the country but also for those emigrating overseas. For example, in 1901 Rathmines Municipal Technical Institute ran courses in accounting and commercial subjects and more specialist courses for clerical staff in railways, banks, and insurance; University College Galway in 1914 established the first chair in the United Kingdom with 'accounting' or 'accountancy' in the title.[21]

A further important development in the later nineteenth century was the formation of the Institute of Chartered Accountants in Ireland (ICAI) in 1888. Of the small founding membership numbering 31 (27 of whom were Protestant), 13 were based in Dublin, 12 in Belfast, and 6 in Cork. The aims of the ICAI were to raise the professional status of accountants, strengthen connections with barristers, solicitors, bankers and merchants, and to act as an influential business lobby. Paseta has suggested that professions were seen as 'patently "un-Irish" constructs' and that the declaration of the ICAI early leadership to emphasize 'gentlemanliness', trust, and respectability led to criticism from the nationalist *Leader* that it was little more than an attempt to promote 'cringe and snobbery' and also a possible way to divert the rising middle class from Irish nationalism and culture.[22] The relative decline of industry in much of Ireland before 1914, and the business expansion of the north-east, was reflected in the growing importance of Belfast in the ICAI. By 1909 Belfast accountants represented 53 per cent of the membership, while articled clerks from the city registered with the Institute represented 71 per cent of the total. The Belfast membership was almost entirely Protestant.[23]

Within Ireland the uneven experience of industrialization generated a range of views in the nineteenth-century debate on free trade versus protectionism. The perception in nationalist Ireland that the Union had been a prime cause of deindustrialization was bound to lead to an espousal of protectionism in order to underpin industrial regeneration, not least as a way to stem emigration. Such views became more widespread with the Home Rule movement from the 1870s and especially with the emergence of Sinn Féin in the first decade of the twentieth century. Protectionist arguments always had to balance the possible restriction of consumer choice and the danger of inflation that came with tariffs, against the potential longer term benefit of growth of new and/ or older industries and the import substitution this would bring. Most nationalists in pre-partition Ireland never gave unequivocal support to protection and preferred instead to support selective and short-term tariffs. For example, Parnell, who saw the agricultural and industrial sectors as interdependent, argued that an industrial revival needed a Dublin parliament with powers to introduce tariffs. However, those tariffs

would not be, and would not need to be, either universal or permanent. He appreciated that Britain had comparative advantages but that there were certain industries in
Ireland which could develop behind temporary tariff barriers and it was the government's role to provide a cost-effective and appropriate infrastructure to enable this to
occur.[24] Some of Parnell's ideas would come to eventual fruition under Fianna Fáil in
the Free State of the 1930s, but before partition the most cogent of all advocates of industrial revival and protectionism was Arthur Griffith, notably at the first Sinn Féin Annual
Convention in 1905.

Nationalist Ireland saw protection in purely Irish terms, but in the predominantly
unionist north-east so many large firms depended upon overseas markets that the
debate on protectionism took on a different character. From the later nineteenth century, in textiles and in some other industries, the Belfast region faced increasingly serious competition from overseas. Mainly for this reason, there were a growing number
of businessmen and business organizations prepared to consider protectionism, not of
course in a purely Irish context, which they judged suicidal to their own British and
wider connections, but in a UK-wide or imperial framework. Although free trade would
remain official UK policy until 1931, in 1906 there was a clear majority of the Belfast
Chamber in favour of imperial preference, and a 'respected' minority who remained
committed to free trade.[25]

III

Although it is undeniable that much of the industry of the Belfast region depended upon
imported raw materials and export markets, it is also true that the region's links with the
rest of Ireland never disappeared and indeed remained significant for a range of manufacturing and service businesses, including many in retailing, wholesaling, and distribution. However, as is so often the case with inland trade, much of this was unrecorded and
has often been overlooked. In fact, much more research is required into the retail and
wholesale sectors of the economy in the period before and after partition. The nature of
links between the north-east and the rest of Ireland became temporarily more visible in
the early 1920s during the period of the 'Belfast boycott'. Boycotting had a long history
before 1920, even before the invention of the term during the Land War of the 1880s.

The boycott started in 1920 and was triggered by a mixture of anti-partitionism
and, more importantly, by the high-profile expulsion of thousands of mainly Catholic
employees from their workplaces and homes during the summer of that year. Members
of the Dáil who pressed that body to move against the north-east used the boycott from
August 1920 as an economic weapon against businesses in the manufacturing and service sectors with the hope of reinstating expelled workers and their families and to prevent partition.[26] That the boycott failed on both counts did not diminish its severity for
those firms which made or distributed goods, or provided services, for towns outside
the north-east. The boycott was wide-ranging, sometimes violent, had far-reaching

consequences for the conduct of local government in border areas, and also involved women as both activists and victims to an important extent.

Boycott activity declined, but did not end, after the Civil War and would resurface on a number of subsequent occasions. Thus, when De Valera was arrested in February 1929 and sentenced to 30 days' imprisonment, the RUC reported an increase in boycott activity as a reprisal. This included cancellation of orders by letter, harassment of commercial travellers, and 'a great deal of "barracking" from their customers, especially from shop hands who played a prominent part in the last Boycott'.[27] Later still, in 1957, the business boycott as a political weapon would be used in the famous example of Fethard-on-Sea in County Wexford when Protestant-owned businesses were boycotted for six months after a Protestant woman married to a Catholic man refused to allow her children to be educated in a local national school and for a time left her husband and took her children to Britain.[28] The Fethard boycott occurred during the IRA border campaign of 1956–62 and since partition business boycotting has been greatest at times of heightened political tension. In the mid 1990s, for example, there was a recurrence of boycott activity of Protestant businesses, especially in Fermanagh and Tyrone, over the Nationalist/Loyalist stand-off at Drumcree.[29]

The extent to which businesses were vulnerable to local boycotts depended on the degree to which they were patronized by customers of a religious denomination different from that of the owner. In some areas, especially where customers had a relatively convenient choice, shops might have an overwhelmingly single-denomination clientele. In her classic portrayal of the pseudonymous 'Ballybeg' in the 1950s, Rosemary Harris expressed surprise at the range of services provided in this village of 324 residents at the time of the 1951 census: nine grocers, five clothing shops, four pubs, two sweetshops, one newsagent/sweetshop, two butchers, two chemists, three hardware stores, one feed merchant, three part-time bank offices, three cafes, three garages, and two petrol stations. She explained this large number first by reference to the poverty of surrounding farms which made even the humble shopkeeper's lot preferable and, second, by the sectarian element in customer loyalty: 'The advantages offered by one shop over its rivals had to be very considerable before a Protestant owner could attract Catholic customers, or vice versa. One shop, no matter how good, could never monopolise the trade, and no matter how poor it could normally expect a number of faithful clients.' In this way, competition was limited and bankruptcy quite rare, although many shops did not do much business and ownership could change hands often, 'always to a co-religionist of the current owner'.[30]

Before partition, nationalist Ireland had assumed that the departure of the British would bring industrial regeneration. In the Free State from the 1920s, however, the formidable obstacles to this became all too obvious. In Northern Ireland, the assumption of much of unionist opinion that the British link would continue to underpin industrial progress proved to be similarly misplaced. In both parts of Ireland the political impact of such illusion was significant and, since partition, interventionist governments in both Dublin and Belfast have introduced a wide range of policies to attempt to stimulate business activity. Government intervention has taken place in old and new industries, sometimes privileging indigenous enterprise, sometimes with a strong emphasis on inward foreign investment, but always with mixed success, both north and south of the border.

In Northern Ireland the weakness of the traditional staple industries became obvious from the time of partition. Most of the members of the new Belfast government had business interests and there is no doubt that businessmen had easy access to ministers, including the prime minister, to an extent unknown in Britain.[31] Moreover, representatives of the staple industries of textiles and shipbuilding clearly had an advantage in seeking assistance. An early initiative designed to reduce the risks faced by private firms in a period of heightened market uncertainty was the Loans Guarantees Act, introduced in 1922 and extended on a number of occasions until 1946. Loans made by financial institutions to businesses could be guaranteed by the government so that the preferred private-enterprise framework of both business and government could be maintained. The principal beneficiaries of this legislation were the shipyards and it is no coincidence that there were detailed discussions between the region's premier industrialist, Viscount Pirrie of Harland & Wolff, and members of the government during the framing of the legislation. By 1925 about a quarter of Northern Ireland's insured population was unemployed, compared to 11 per cent in Britain, and in the general election of April the Unionist Party lost seven seats in Belfast, four to the Independent Unionists and three to the Labour Party, both of which became and remained critical of the government's responses to the emerging unemployment problem. This provided the critical motivation for supporting manufacturing industry and particularly the shipyards to try to maintain the support of the male Protestant working class. In Norton's phrase, the government was 'creating jobs, manufacturing unity'.[32] On a number of occasions during elections the east Belfast shipyard workers were reminded just how much their industry owed to government support. The problem of global excess capacity in shipbuilding hit both of Belfast's shipyards in the 1920s and Workman Clark, after a very difficult period, closed in 1935. Harland & Wolff in peacetime would never again achieve its pre-1914 position. The problems of UK shipbuilders between the wars are well known, and from 1922 Harland & Wolff began to build vessels for fixed prices which were virtually at cost.[33]

Although orders for passenger vessels helped Harland & Wolff in the 1920s and early 1930s the firm did not receive what it regarded as its fair share of rearmament work after 1935. Indeed, in a wider context Northern Ireland was remote from pre-war rearmament and wartime decision-making in London and this, together with relatively high transport costs and the predominance of small firms, put it at a disadvantage in securing government contracts as the UK prepared to fight a second world war. Moreover, unlike a number of depressed regions in Britain, Northern Ireland did not have 'Special Area' status after 1934 and this put the region at a further disadvantage during the rearmament period. In regional terms one of the most remote industries was the important shirt and collar manufacturing centred on Derry city. Only a very small number of large firms were successful in gaining contracts before the war and not until 1940 were most shirt factories working full time. Many firms in traditional industries barely survived the interwar years and did so only by cutting costs and dividends, short-time working, and increasing their dependence on bank credit. A good example was Belfast textile engineering firm Combe Barbour, which would have disappeared in the early 1930s without extensive support from the Ulster Bank and the agreement of debenture holders to postpone interest payments. Had firms like this been forced into bankruptcy the subsequent rearmament programme and wartime munitions production would have been very much more difficult.

Industry in Northern Ireland was slow to mobilize during the war and reached a peak of mobilization in 1943, after which government orders began to decline and familiar patterns of unemployment to re-emerge. Physical distance from decision-making in London disadvantaged the award of government contracts, as did the lack of Special Area status. As in the First World War, the linen industry was seriously affected by the severe shortage and high cost of raw materials. Industrial relations also deteriorated during the war, with organized labour in the strongest position it had enjoyed for a generation and strike action in war-related industry widespread. Even large firms on direct contracts, such as Harland & Wolff and Short & Harland aircraft manufacturers (established in 1936), faced very substantial obstacles to expanding production: labour immobility, skill shortages, trade disputes, production bottlenecks, managerial shortcomings, dispersal of production, endless changes to specifications and erratic ordering by government all contributed to this. Similarly, once the peak of the war effort was past, firms typically faced cuts in government contracts which could be immediate and severe, leading to disruption in production schedules and uncertainties which disrupted management of the transition to peace. In every industry, firms in Northern Ireland at the end of the war generally faced greater uncertainty than in other UK regions.[34]

IV

After the war, although there were few years to compare with the worst of the interwar period, business enterprise in Northern Ireland continued to face competitive pressures from outside which led the government to increase its support to established industries, especially shipbuilding and linen. There is, however, strong evidence to suggest that the nature of government-business relations in the post-war world were such that they militated against the modernization of the industrial base and that this was in turn a powerful reason why the region did not participate in the 'golden age' of economic growth in post-war Western Europe. Only with the election of the new Prime Minister Terence O'Neill from early 1963 did the reform of industrial policy mean that the region could increase its rate of business investment and development. Brownlow has argued that, up to the end of the premiership of Brookeborough in 1963, the lack of legislative control over conflicts of interest between politicians and business meant that those responsible for allocating grants and those receiving them were often one and the same.[35] The argument has important implications for the region's economic performance in the decades after partition.

In the second half of the twentieth century the vicissitudes of industrial policy in Northern Ireland reflected not only the impact of political violence from the later 1960s but also the suspension of the Stormont parliament in 1972 and the introduction of direct rule from Westminster. Between the mid-1950s and the end of the century, however, there were no fewer than eleven major policy documents which examined the Northern Ireland economy and more especially how industrial competitiveness might be improved. This large number of documents would not have been necessary had there been significant improvement in regional economic performance.[36] In fact, as Crafts has suggested, if the UK in general during the 'golden age' of post-war growth was disadvantaged compared to much of Europe in a number of ways, including capital markets, taxation, and labour relations, Northern Ireland as a peripheral UK region was still more disadvantaged. Crafts also suggests that government policy was, in some respects, of 'poor design' and may have inhibited innovation and productivity gain.[37] The oil crisis in the early 1970s was particularly serious for energy-intensive synthetic textile producers which had established themselves in the region, beginning with Courtaulds in 1945, and their closure in large numbers was one of the most visible indicators of later-twentieth-century deindustrialization. The persistence of political conflict gave Northern Ireland a negative image overseas, while some observers pointed to a low appetite for risk-taking within the region itself, perhaps strengthened by the large range of government assistance available. The Local Enterprise Development Unit, established in 1971 with an emphasis on assisting small enterprise, was one response to the region's problems. However, what has been called the 'grantrepreneur' culture of maximizing government financial aid may reflect weaknesses in the local propensity for risk-taking, and, in any case, in government policy the distinction between job creation and stimulating enterprise is sometimes blurred.[38]

Whatever the reasons, in the long run the extent of convergence of Northern Ireland GDP per capita with that of Britain has been disappointing and this was still more evident when compared with the performance of the Republic of Ireland. Expressed as a percentage of the UK figure, Northern Ireland GDP per capita was 71 in 1947 and 76 in 2000; the figures for the Republic were 46 and 112 respectively.[39] At the centre of explanations for this have been the relatively disappointing levels of productivity in most areas of manufacturing in Northern Ireland. In fact, productivity levels in several industries actually declined in the later twentieth century and there is little to suggest that the productivity gap will close in the foreseeable future. In Northern Ireland in the early twenty-first century the problems facing the region and its government seem as intractable as ever: how to balance assistance between local and foreign firms, between the relatively advantaged and disadvantaged areas within the region (especially the East versus the West), between small and larger firms, between creating new jobs and safeguarding old ones, between high skill and value added and lower skill activity, and between manufacturing and services. The predominance of small firms is regarded as one of the main reasons for the low expenditure on research and development compared to some British regions. With both wages and salaries and Gross Value Added at some 20 per cent lower than the UK average, there is clearly much work to do and a recognition that government alone cannot solve structural problems of a long-standing nature, especially during the adverse economic conditions of 2008 and 2009.[40]

V

In the Free State, industrial policy evolved slowly and cautiously under Cumann na nGaedheal and within the business sector there were still strongly free-trading elements in the years immediately following partition, usually from those firms with strong trading connections with Britain—these included Jacob's biscuit manufacturers and Jameson's distillers. Many of the directors of this type of enterprise would no doubt have been included in President William Cosgrave's summary description of Irish businessmen in 1926 as 'antique furniture'.[41] The new Ford plant in Cork, opened in that year, was an example of foreign investment, and the general issue of such investment, along with that of industrial finance, quickly became two of the most controversial areas for policy makers after partition. Even before this, British banks' takeover of the Belfast Bank and the Ulster Bank in 1917 had raised the question of whether control from London would restrict the flow of credit to Ireland. In contrast to those proponents of free trade, an increasing number regarded a more active protectionist policy as a badge of political independence. The formation of the protectionist Fianna Fáil in 1926, a continuing unemployment problem greatly exacerbated by the onset of the world economic crisis after 1929, more powerful lobby groups and a British move to protectionism in 1932 all contributed to far more numerous, systematic, and higher industrial tariffs when Fianna Fáil entered government with Labour support in 1932.[42] In the longer term, Irish industrial policy falls into two phases: the first between 1932 and 1958 which emphasized high levels of tariff protection, decentralization, and limited involvement of foreign firms and capital; the second from 1958, triggered by a number of economic problems in the early and mid-1950s, stressed much more outward-looking and liberal policies and a more determined effort to attract foreign investment.

For Ó Gráda, industrial policy during the 1930s made more of a contribution to the generation of short-term employment over a relatively wide geographical area than it did to creating a sustainable industrial sector. Even by the later 1940s those firms established under protection tended to be small and be characterized by low labour productivity: in fact labour productivity in the South remained static in the 1930s and was lower in the mid 1940s than it had been in 1932.[43] In protected industries, enterprises were typically small with low labour productivity and they were also characterized by limited success in export competitiveness. Apart from food, drink and tobacco—already established before the 1930s as Ireland's major manufactured exports—the remainder of the manufacturing sector exported only 6 per cent of output in 1951. The significance of this performance increases when it is recalled that the need to import domestically unavailable capital goods, industrial components, and raw materials led to severe balance-of-payments problems, deflationary budgets, recession, and increased emigration.[44] This was the essential context for a radical revision of industrial policy and particularly of the role of inward foreign investment as the basis for export growth. The revision included a reconsideration of traditional Fianna Fáil thinking on the desirability and effectiveness of protectionism, although as ever there were significant differences in outlook between, for example, the Department of Finance and the Department of Industry and Commerce. Among politicians Seán Lemass (himself a leading advocate of extensive protectionism after 1932) and among public servants T.K. Whitaker, especially in his *Economic Development* published in 1958, played key roles in the reorientation of policy.

During the 1960s and 1970s, the rate at which Irish industrial output expanded was more than three times greater than in the 1950s, with a particularly impressive export performance in manufactured products. The basis upon which this was achieved was the establishment of new foreign firms. Employment in manufacturing in 'new foreign industry' grew from just 3000 in 1960 to 61000 in 1980 while employment in indigenous manufacturing industry at the same dates was 169 000 and 182 000. By the early 1980s foreign-owned enterprises accounted for a third of manufacturing employment and about three-quarters of manufacturing exports—indicating the relatively sluggish performance of indigenous firms during the 1960s and 1970s. This dichotomy triggered some serious reflections about industrial policy and entrepreneurship. As Joseph Lee, one of the keenest critics of Irish industrial performance in these years, has written that after sixty years of political independence, wide-ranging protectionism since the 1930s, government initiatives such as the Committee on Industrial Organisation, a free trade agreement with Britain and EEC membership, 'a native entrepreneurial cadre of the requisite quality had failed to emerge. Irish industry could not compete internationally. It could not even compete on the home market'.[45] A notable result of the self-reflection on industrial policy, and one which in turn triggered much debate, was the Telesis report of 1982. This pointed to the frequently weak linkages between foreign firms and the host economy and made the case for a greater emphasis on indigenous firms.[46] At that time, few would have predicted the exceptionally strong industrial performance from the mid 1990s to 2007, manifested by greater European economic integration, a positive international image, a relatively low tax regime, currency stability following adoption of the euro in 2002, European aid and the location of many foreign multinationals using the country as a base for their European operations. The 'Celtic tiger' years were impressive but finite. The speed of decline after 2007 was just as dramatic and served as a reminder of the vulnerability of the industrial and financial sectors to global economic forces. In 2009 the Dell Corporation, the country's second-largest private sector employer and largest exporter, accounting for some 5 per cent of Irish GDP, announced the transfer of its manufacturing business from Limerick to the Polish city of Lodz.[47] The global credit crisis hit all Irish banks, none more so than Anglo-Irish Bank, which was nationalized early in 2009 and which suffered a loss of €12.7bn in the fifteen months to the end of December 2009, the largest corporate loss in Irish history.[48] The fallout from the crisis was bound to be severe. At the end of 2012, the *Irish Times* declared that if 2011 was all about reducing the number of banks in the Irish financial sector, 2012 was about reducing and repairing the size of those that remained. It reminded its readers that at the start of 2012 the €64 billion bailout for the banks, about 40 per cent of the country's GDP, was 'the most expensive bailout for any country in modern times'.[49] By early 2013 the Irish economy was described by *The Economist* as 'fitter but still fragile'. Aided by its low (12.5 per cent) rate of corporation tax, levels of new Foreign Direct Investment for 2012, especially in pharmaceuticals, IT, and financial services, were comparable to those of 2011, which itself was the highest for ten years.[50] However, if the continuing cost of the bank bailout, the structural problems and uncertainties in the Eurozone, and the implications of the UK decision in 2016 to leave the European Union complicate predictions, the grounds for optimism about the future of Irish business remain.

Notes

1. Parts of this essay draw on Philip Ollerenshaw 'Industry and Finance, 1780–1945', in Liam Kennedy and Philip Ollerenshaw (eds), *Ulster Since 1600: Politics, Economy, and Society* (Oxford, 2012).
2. The best summary is Andy Bielenberg, *Ireland and the Industrial Revolution: the Impact of the Revolution on Ireland, 1801–1922* (Abingdon, 2009).
3. Joel Mokyr, *Why Ireland Starved* (London, 1983), 212–13.
4. David Johnson and Liam Kennedy, 'Nationalist Historiography and the Decline of the Irish Economy: George O'Brien Revisited', in Sean Hutton and Paul Stewart (eds), *Ireland's Histories* (London, 1991).
5. Bielenberg, *Ireland and the Industrial Revolution*, 5, 178–9.
6. Patrick Lynch and John Vaizey, *Guinness's Brewery in the Irish Economy 1759–1876* (Cambridge, 1960), 12–13.
7. See especially L.M. Cullen, 'Problems in the Interpretation and Revision of Eighteenth Century Irish Economic History', *Transactions of the Royal Historical Society*, 5th Series, 17, (1967), 1–22.
8. Frank Geary, 'The Act of Union, British-Irish trade and pre-Famine deindustrialization', *Economic History Review*, 48 (1995), 68–88.
9. Andy Bielenberg, *Cork's Industrial Revolution, 1780–1880: Development or Decline?* (Cork, 1991); David Dickson, 'The Place of Dublin in the Eighteenth Century Irish Economy' in T.M. Devine and David Dickson (eds), *Ireland and Scotland, 1600–1850* (Edinburgh, 1983).
10. Mary Daly, *Dublin—The Deposed Capital: A Social and Economic History, 1860–1914* (Cork, 1984); Maura Murphy, 'The Economic and Social Structure of Nineteenth Century Cork' in David Harkness and Mary O'Dowd (eds), *The Town in Ireland* (Belfast, 1981).
11. Andy Bielenberg, 'The Irish Brewing Industry and the Rise of Guinness, 1790–1914' in R.G. Wilson and T.R. Gourvish (eds), *The Dynamics of the International Brewing Industry Since 1800* (Abingdon, 1998).
12. Marilyn Cohen (ed), *The Warp of Ulster's Past* (Basingstoke, 1997); Jane Gray, *Spinning the Threads of Uneven Development: Gender and Industrialization in Ireland during the Long Eighteenth Century* (Lanham, MD, 2005).
13. Jean Agnew, 'The Merchant Community of Belfast, 1660–1707', *Irish Economic and Social History*, 22 (1995), 91–2.

14. W.H. Crawford, 'The Evolution of the Linen Trade in Ulster Before Industrialisation', *Irish Economic and Social History*, 15 (1988), 32–53.

15. Andy Bielenberg and Peter Solar, 'The Irish Cotton Industry from the Industrial Revolution to Partition', *Irish Economic and Social History*, 37 (2007), 1–29.

16. D.S. Macneice, 'Industrial Villages of Ulster, 1800–1900', in Peter Roebuck (ed), *Plantation to Partition: Essays in Honour of J.L. McCracken* (Belfast, 1981), 172–90.

17. Brenda Collins and Philip Ollerenshaw 'The European Linen Industry Since the Middle Ages', in Brenda Collins and Philip Ollerenshaw (eds), *The European Linen Industry in Historical Perspective* (Oxford, 2003), 27–8.

18. Cormac O Gráda, *Ireland: A New Economic History, 1780–1939* (Oxford, 1994), 266.

19. Philip Ollerenshaw, 'The Business and Politics of Banking in Ireland, 1900–43', in P.L. Cottrell, Alice Teichova, and Takeshi Yuzawa (eds), *Finance in the Age of the Corporate Economy* (Aldershot, 1997), 52–78.

20. W. A. Thomas, *The Stock Exchanges of Ireland* (Liverpool, 1986), 51, 219–47.

21. Peter Clarke, 'The Teaching of Bookkeeping in Nineteenth Century Ireland', *Accounting, Business and Financial History*, 18 (2008), 21–33.

22. Senia Paseta, *Before the Revolution: Nationalism, Social Change and Ireland's Catholic Elite* (Cork, 1999), 89, 98–9; *The Leader*, 1 September and 29 December 1900, quoted in Philip O'Regan, '"Elevating the Profession": the Institute of Chartered Accountants in Ireland and the Implementation of Social Closure strategies', *Accounting, Business and Financial History*, 18 (2008), 36, 38.

23. Ibid., 46.

24. Liam Kennedy, 'The Economic Thought of the Nation's Lost Leader', in D. George Boyce and Alan O'Day (eds), *Parnell in Perspective* (London, 1991), 184–9.

25. Philip Ollerenshaw, 'Businessmen and the Development of Ulster Unionism, 1886–1921', *Journal of Imperial and Commonwealth History*, 28 (2000), 51–2.

26. Philip Ollerenshaw, 'Business Boycotts and the Partition of Ireland', in Brenda Collins, Philip Ollerenshaw, and Trevor Parkhill (eds), *Industry, Trade and People in Ireland, 1650–1950: Essays in Honour of W.H. Crawford* (Belfast, 2005), 205–27.

27. Public Record Office of Northern Ireland, HA/32/1/157, Police Report on Boycott of Belfast Goods in the Free State, 22 February 1929.

28. *Irish Times*, 30 June 2009.

29. See, for example, *Belfast Telegraph*, 18 September 1996 and 9 January 1997.

30. Rosemary Harris, *Prejudice and Tolerance in Ulster* (Manchester, 1972), 5–6.

31. Patrick Buckland, *The Factory of Grievances: Devolved Government in Northern Ireland, 1921–39* (Dublin, 1979), ch. 1.

32. Christopher Norton, 'Creating Jobs, Manufacturing Unity: Ulster Unionism and Mass Unemployment, 1922–34', *Contemporary British History*, 15 (2001), 1–14.

33. F. Geary and W. Johnson, 'Wages and Employment in Northern Ireland and Scotland Between the Wars: the Case of Shipbuilding', in S.J. Connolly, R.A. Houston, and R.J. Morris (eds), *Conflict, Identity and Economic Development: Scotland and Ireland, 1600–1939* (Preston, 1995), 245.

34. Philip Ollerenshaw, 'War, Industrial Mobilisation and Society in Northern Ireland, 1939–45', *Contemporary European History*, 16 (2007), 169–97.

35. Graham Brownlow, 'The Causes and Consequences of Rent-Seeking in Northern Ireland, 1945–72', *Economic History Review*, 60 (2007), 70–96.

36. Esmond Birnie and David Hitchens, 'Chasing the Wind? Half a Century of Economic Strategy Documents in Northern Ireland', *Irish Political Studies*, 16 (2001), 1–27.

37. N.F.R. Crafts, 'The Golden Age of Economic Growth in Postwar Europe: Why Did Northern Ireland Miss Out?', *Irish Economic and Social History*, 22 (1995), 5–25.

38. Sue Birley and Simon Bridge, 'Promoting Small Business in Northern Ireland', *Long Range Planning*, 20 (1987), 71–7.

39. Birnie and Hitchins, 'Chasing the Wind?', 3.

40. Invest Northern Ireland, *Performance Information Report, 2002–03 to 2007–08* (Belfast, 2009), 119.

41. Ó Gráda, *Ireland*, 396.

42. See the excellent discussion in Mary Daly, *Industrial Development and Irish National Identity, 1922–39* (New York, 1992), 13–57.

43. Ó Gráda, *Ireland*, 401.

44. Eoin O'Malley, 'The Problem of Late Industrialisation and the Experience of the Republic of Ireland', *Cambridge Journal of Economics*, 9 (1985), 141–54.

45. Joseph Lee, *Ireland 1912–85: Politics and Society* (Cambridge, 1985), 535–6.

46. Ibid., 531–7.

47. *The Observer*, 18 January 2009.

48. *The Guardian*, 31 March 2010.

49. *Irish Times*, 28 December 2012.

50. *The Economist*, 5 January 2013.

Select Bibliography

Bielenberg, Andy, 'The Irish Brewing Industry and the Rise of Guinness, 1790–1914' in R.G. Wilson and T.R. Gourvish (eds), *The Dynamics of the International Brewing Industry Since 1800* (Abingdon, 1998).

Bielenberg, Andy, *Ireland and the Industrial Revolution: the Impact of the Revolution on Ireland, 1801–1922* (Abingdon, 2009).

Birley, Sue and Bridge, Simon, 'Promoting Small Business in Northern Ireland', *Long Range Planning*, 20 (1987).

Birnie, Esmond and Hitchens, David, 'Chasing the Wind? Half a Century of Economic Strategy Documents in Northern Ireland', *Irish Political Studies*, 16 (2001).

Brownlow, Graham, 'The Causes and Consequences of Rent-seeking in Northern Ireland, 1945–72', *Economic History Review*, 60 (2007).

Clarke, Peter, 'The Teaching of Bookkeeping in Nineteenth Century Ireland', *Accounting, Business and Financial History*, 18 (2008).

Crafts, N.F.R., 'The Golden Age of Economic Growth in Postwar Europe: Why did Northern Ireland miss out?', *Irish Economic and Social History*, 22 (1995).

Cullen, L.M., 'Problems in the Interpretation and Revision of Eighteenth Century Irish Economic History', *Transactions of the Royal Historical Society*, 5th Series, 17, (1967).

Daly, Mary, *Dublin—The Deposed Capital: A Social and Economic History, 1860–1914* (Cork, 1984).

Daly, Mary, *Industrial Development and Irish National Identity, 1922–39* (New York, 1992).

Geary, Frank, 'The Act of Union, British-Irish trade and pre-Famine Deindustrialization', *Economic History Review*, 48 (1995).

Johnson, David and Kennedy, Liam, 'Nationalist Historiography and the Decline of the Irish Economy: George O'Brien Revisited', in Sean Hutton and Paul Stewart (eds), *Ireland's Histories* (London, 1991).

Lynch, Patrick and Vaizey, John, *Guinness's Brewery in the Irish Economy 1759–1876* (Cambridge, 1960), 12–13.

Norton, Christopher, 'Creating Jobs, Manufacturing Unity: Ulster Unionism and Mass Unemployment, 1922–34', *Contemporary British History*, 15 (2001).

Ó Gráda, Cormac, *Ireland: A New Economic History, 1780–1939* (Oxford, 1994).

Ollerenshaw, Philip, 'The Business and Politics of Banking in Ireland, 1900–43', in P.L. Cottrell, Alice Teichova, and Takeshi Yuzawa (eds), *Finance in the Age of the Corporate Economy* (Aldershot, 1997).

Ollerenshaw, Philip, 'Business Boycotts and the Partition of Ireland', in Brenda Collins, Philip Ollerenshaw, and Trevor Parkhill (eds), *Industry, Trade and People in Ireland, 1650–1950: Essays in Honour of W.H. Crawford* (Belfast, 2005).

O'Malley, Eoin, 'The Problem of Late Industrialisation and the Experience of the Republic of Ireland', *Cambridge Journal of Economics*, 9 (1985).

O'Regan, Philip, ' "Elevating the Profession": the Institute of Chartered Accountants in Ireland and the Implementation of Social Closure Strategies', *Accounting, Business and Financial History*, 18 (2008).

Thomas, W.A., *The Stock Exchanges of Ireland* (Liverpool, 1986).

CHAPTER 9

··

FAITH IN IRELAND, 1600–2000

··

MARIANNE ELLIOTT

'It is a peculiarity known only to Ireland, perhaps of all other countries, that its inhabitants are more distinguished from each other, on account of their religious opinions, than they are by any other criterion'.

George Cooper, *Letters on the Irish Nation*, 1799

I. INTRODUCTION

··

FOR the past four centuries Ireland has been the theatre of contesting politicized religions. The religious conflicts which accompanied the Protestant and Catholic Reformations made it imperative to know why you were one rather than the other (or so you were told by the religious and political elites). It is important therefore to know what was taught by the elites and the structures that developed in consequence. Does this mean that everyone in Ireland was as confrontational as their churches appeared to be? By no means. Nor were the churches continuously so. In reality, contrary to the stereotype, Ireland rarely experienced widespread religious-based conflict. People's 'faith' encompassed very much more than the elite ideal, and sometimes the churches themselves had to adapt. Above all, the institutions were man-made and could rarely take their people where they did not want to go. Until very recently Ireland has been an almost exclusively Christian country. I will therefore be concentrating on Ireland's two major faith systems, Protestantism and Catholicism.[1] Both terms are controversial. I use the term 'Catholic' because Irish Catholics prefer it to 'Roman' Catholic, which has all too often been used in insult. However, the term loosely referred to the whole of Christianity before the Reformations and its exclusive use by the Roman church has been resented by others.[2] Likewise, the collective noun 'Protestant' covers a very large number of different denominations. In England Protestants often prefer to identify themselves by the names of their churches. To a lesser extent this was also the case in Ireland in the early modern period. From the late eighteenth century the collective term was more often the norm. 'In Ireland,' wrote George Bernard Shaw in the preface to *John Bull's Other Island* (1904), 'Protestantism is really Protestant...all that the member of the Irish Protestant Church knows is that he is not a Roman Catholic...The clause in the Apostles' Creed professing belief in a Catholic Church is a standing puzzle to [Irish] Protestant children.'[3]

II. Structures: The Institutional Churches

(a) Seventeenth Century

From 1537 to 1871 the Church of Ireland (Episcopalian/Anglican) was the state church in Ireland. For much of this period its members dominated every aspect of state life and from the late seventeenth century possessed most of the landed property and the attendant social and political power. The Church itself operated as an effective department of state, collecting the equivalent of local taxes, peopling the magistracy, and mingling religious with state ceremonies. Unlike established churches elsewhere, however, it represented only 10 per cent of the population. In the highly confrontational nature of religious culture in these centuries (at least at leadership level), this failure to convert Ireland to Protestantism has been interpreted as proving the organic link between Irishness and Catholicism, which rather ignores the fact that every other country which adopted the reformed faith had been 'Catholic' too. Indeed James I's attorney-general in Ireland, Sir John Davies, thought Ireland could have been converted had the trouble been taken.[4] Part of the reason that it was not was the reluctance of successive English monarchs to enforce conformity. Another was the structural weakness of the Church outside the towns.

The net result was that the religious make-up of Ireland at the end of the sixteenth century was not very different from what it had been for centuries. There was much fluidity, and clergy from the old church continued to operate in the Church of Ireland into the seventeenth century. However, this started to change with a new supply of Protestant clergy coming out of Trinity College Dublin (established 1592), and the arrival of Protestant settlers from England and Scotland. A distinctly Calvinistic brand of Protestantism established itself in Ireland at this stage. Its equation of the Pope with the biblical Antichrist informed a belief that the Catholic Irish were damned in any event and further deterred any conversionary crusade. The Irish Church also gave a home to nonconformists fleeing persecution in England and Scotland and Presbyterian clergy continued to operate within it until the Restoration (1660). The legacy was the distinctly 'low church' nature of Irish Anglicanism.[5] Although separate from the Church of England (except in the years 1801–71) its upper reaches came to be dominated by Englishmen. Lord John Beresford's appointment to the primacy in 1822 was the first of an Irishman in 120 years.[6] This promotion of Englishmen to the top positions caused much bitterness. Indeed the relationship between the Irish and English established churches has been an uneasy one.

From the 1640s Ireland was pulled into the vortex of the religious wars, which tore through Europe and added more religious groupings to its population: Moravians, Palatines, Huguenots (from the 1670s), and, arriving with the parliamentary troops, Quakers, Baptists, and Presbyterians. English Presbyterians had been prominent in the Church of Ireland since the last decades of the sixteenth century. It was the Ulster Plantation from 1609, the arrival of General Monro's Scottish army to suppress the 1641 Ulster rebellion, and the huge influx of Scottish Presbyterians at the end of the seventeenth century which gave Irish Presbyterianism its particular Scottish character. Presbyterians saw themselves as a covenanted people, having made a covenant with God to fulfil his will as laid out in the Bible, particularly the Old Testament. They believed they had the only truly biblical church structure and in the Solemn League and Covenant— signed in 1643 with the parliamentarians against Charles I—and subsequent Westminster Assembly, they thought they had secured an agreement to establish Presbyterianism throughout England, Scotland, and Ireland. The Covenant's signees had pledged themselves to stamp out 'Popery, prelacy (that is, church government by bishops and "hierarchy")…superstition, heresy, schism, profaneness, and whatsoever shall be found to be contrary to sound doctrine and the power of godliness.'[7] The established churches in England and Ireland retained the hierarchical structure inherited from the Roman church, which Presbyterians saw as unscriptural and sinful. Thus began their strained relationship with government and church in Ireland and, despite a shared Protestantism, they were often seen as politically dangerous and experienced intermittent persecution.

Presbyterianism was the most complicated of all faith systems in Ireland in these centuries. Its democratic church structure involved each congregation choosing its minister and ruling elders, the elective system continuing upwards to presbyteries and synods (after 1690). In effect, congregations were largely self-governing. The result was numerous divisions as congregations split from structures which they believed had become too authoritarian. In the eighteenth century this produced the so-called New Light strain, which resisted subscription to the Westminster Confession of Faith (first required of those licensed to preach in 1698), as denying the right to private judgement, so fundamental to Presbyterianism. Historians once identified this more tolerant strain within Presbyterianism as a key element in the development of radicalism (and revolt) at the end of the eighteenth century. The work of David Miller and Ian McBride has fundamentally altered this view and sent us back to original Presbyterian principles: that is, the belief in a direct communion between man and God and the unbiblical nature of states and church structures headed by an uncovenanted king. Thus Miller and McBride located among the 1798 rebels significant numbers of more fundamental Presbyterians, Covenanters or Reformed Presbyterians and Seceders who had arrived from Scotland in the 1660s and 1740s respectively.[8]

The rise of political Catholicism in the nineteenth century, however, united most strands of this most anti-papist of religions. While flashes of old dissent could still be seen over issues such as tenant right (1850s–80s), the increasing participation of Catholic clergy in nationalist campaigns sent most Presbyterians into Unionism and was to give new life to the idea of a covenanted state in the creation of Northern Ireland in 1920. In his 1942 sermon to commemorate the tercentenary of Irish Presbyterianism, the Rev. R. L. Marshall recalled past persecution, but thought that they were now 'at ease in Zion'.[9] Few stopped to question how this most anti-establishment of faiths had become part and parcel of a new Protestant establishment.

Apart from a shared reverence for the Pope, the medieval Christian church had been anything but united. An older form of highly localized structures flourished in Gaelic areas. It had survived reforms introduced by the Anglo-Normans from the twelfth century, which tended only to apply to the anglicized areas. Despite the disputes which ensued, there was a major revival on the eve of the Reformation, largely driven by the friars and sponsored by the Gaelic elite. It is no accident that such friars were to become the main drivers of the Catholic Counter-Reformation and successfully laid the ground for the definition of Catholicism as Ireland's national religion. The old church in non-anglicized areas had not depended on the grand structures which characterized continental Catholicism, so was less affected by the Henrician dissolution of the monasteries. But the wanton destruction of the old church's property during the early Reformation, and the alienation of church land to private owners, left all churches weakened, including the Church of Ireland.[10] Possession of the older religious structures was to remain a contested issue between Catholic and Protestant churches into the future. At this point there was a chance of reconciling property owners to the new system, for Catholics too had acquired spoils from the Henrician dissolution.

As Monsignor Patrick Corish pointed out in his short and accessible survey of Catholicism in this period, the process by which people worked out whether they were Catholic or Protestant was slow.[11] The same barriers to the spread of the reformed religion deterred that of Tridentine Catholicism, after the Council of Trent (1545–63) established the parameters of the Catholic Reformation. In Ireland it would take over three centuries to achieve and even then significant compromises had to be made with the highly localized religion left over from pagan times. The ethnic divisions between Anglo-Norman (Old English) and Gaelic Irish (Old Irish) in the medieval church continued, in varying degrees, for much of the seventeenth century and played a part in the trumped-up charges against, and subsequent execution in 1681 of, Archbishop Oliver Plunkett. This was to change after the final resolution of the land question at the end of the century, which involved both in common ruin. My sense, nevertheless, is that the descendants of the Old English were more committed than the Old Irish to working out a *modus vivendi* with the Protestant state, though it would need more research over a longer time span to prove as much.

In the Catholic Church the organizational ideal, as set out by the Council of Trent, was of authority flowing from bishops through a parish structure. This was largely in place by the 1630s. However, the further one moved from the towns and areas where Old English landowners survived, the less a sense of 'conscious commitment' to Catholicism, and criticisms by Catholic clergy (particularly *emigré* English Catholic clergy) sound very similar to those being made by Protestants.[12] The turmoil of the 1640s–50s eroded these structural changes and there seems to have been a strengthening of the kind of 'abuses' and semi-pagan practices so denounced by Tridentine reformers. In the 1660s–70s there was a sense of having to start all over again. Catholics had expected much from the restoration of the Stuarts in 1660, though a proclamation forbidding meetings of 'papists, Presbyterians, Independents, Anabaptists, Quakers and other fanatical persons',[13] while testimony to the increased diversity of religious culture in Ireland also highlights the difficult climate in which all religions besides the established one operated. Despite King William's personal commitment to tolerance after the defeat of James II in 1690, his reign opened the period of the penal laws, when all religions besides the established church experienced restrictions. The Church of Ireland attained a more secure position as the established church and as an effective department of state, with some long-term negative consequences for its own spiritual development and national standing. Loyalty thereafter became synonymous with Protestantism.

(b) Eighteenth Century

The victory of King William resolved the land, religious, and political issues which had convulsed Ireland for the previous century in favour of the Church of Ireland. The various 'Popery Acts', passed after 1695, confined the political nation and landownership (its foundation) to its members. The seventeenth-century campaign to prove that Catholics could be loyal to a Protestant monarch continued through the eighteenth century and was just as strongly resisted by Protestant politicians who argued that they never could be. Successive Popes, by refusing to endorse an oath of loyalty and permitting the exiled Stuarts to nominate Catholic bishops for Ireland until 1766, did not help their case. They were still campaigning to be so recognized when in the 1790s the mood of the age grew tired of such unproductive supplication and identified the Catholic cause with that of the United Irishmen.

Confining power to those following the same religion as the ruler was not unusual in eighteenth-century Europe. Doing so to a religious minority was; and while many more Catholics than is generally recognized seem to have conformed to the state religion to preserve family property and power, the long-term impact on Ireland was utterly invidious. While a strong farmer class remained, a Catholic landed elite had all but disappeared and landownership (and the local and political patronage which went with it) remained in Anglican hands till the early twentieth century. Presbyterianism lacked a landed class for the same reasons, but Catholics (particularly in plantation areas, where the land and power transfer was more complete), were pushed down the social scale, giving some credence to political Protestantism's contempt for a faith that was seen as slavish and inferior. The loss of a landed elite effectively transferred social leadership of Catholics to the Catholic clergy.

The impact on the practice and structures of Catholicism, however, was less damaging than once thought and, free from state interference, the Catholic Church revived and reformed. Although bishops and regular clergy were banished by an act of 1697, the aim of the penal laws was not to abolish the Catholic religion, and secular clergy were recognized, provided they registered and gave securities. In 1703 some 1089 did so. But the refusal of most clergy in 1708 to take an oath of abjuration of Stuart rights to the throne—following its rejection by the Pope—effectively rendered the Catholic Church illegal. There followed two decades of great uncertainty and harassment. However, there are signs of considerable distaste at such religious intolerance among the Anglican divines and even members of the government. Moreover, there was simply not the mechanism to enforce such laws and priests were regularly rescued by angry crowds. After 1730 there was de facto toleration, provided Catholic clergy kept their heads down. A government 'Report on the State of Popery' in 1731 recorded 1445 priests and 254 friars, 892 mass-houses, 54 private chapels, 51 friaries, 9 nunneries, and 549 schools.[14]

Apart from a small number of temporary structures and 'movable altars', the report failed to mention mass-rocks, which for later generations of Catholics became the main symbol of penal persecution. They had originated during a short period of persecution under Cromwell, but on the whole such temporary places of worship were the result of impoverishment rather than outright persecution, and in poorer rural areas all denominations had inadequate provision for religious services. The 1731 Report records mass being said in sheds and a number of other temporary structures. It also reports new mass-houses being built, and overall the eighteenth century was to be a period of major recovery for the Catholic Church. Many mass-houses were built on land supplied by Protestant landlords.[15] From the 1740s the Irish Catholic Church experienced a large number of overdue regulatory measures. In 1751 bishops were ordered by papal decree to reside in their dioceses and submit regular reports. But it was the friars who experienced most regulation, for it was their independence from episcopal control and closeness to old ways which had figured most prominently in complaints to Rome. In 1751 Pope Benedict XIV ordered the closure of their novitiates in Ireland and their numbers declined sharply thereafter.[16] Predictably the reforms were earlier and more effective in the towns and more prosperous areas in Leinster and Munster, and here we see the early establishment of practices normally associated with the so-called 'Devotional Revolution' of the nineteenth century.[17] However, in Connacht and Ulster the decline of the friars left a real shortage of priests. For the past two centuries Ireland had been dependent on priests trained abroad. This in many ways had exacerbated the divide between the regulars and seculars, the former being trained in Spain and the Netherlands, the latter in France, and not all returned to Ireland.[18] In the 1780s the newly empowered Irish bishops started to set up diocesan seminaries, though the long-standing problem of seminary training was not resolved until the government established Maynooth in 1795. Not only had the French revolutionary crisis closed all the continental seminaries, but it had also brought home to government the importance of the Catholic Church as a counter-revolutionary force. The early years of Maynooth saw it stocked with very conservative professors, many of them having fled from the anticlerical activities of the French Revolution.

Although we do not know enough about the actual impact of the penal laws, their enforcement was patchy, with Ulster and Munster more affected than the other provinces.[19] On the whole there appears to have been a certain *modus vivendi* between the religious groupings, and more movement between the faiths than any would acknowledge. And while the jury is out on the issue of whether the penal laws did or did not aim to convert Catholics to Protestantism, the belief, once strong, that conversions to the established church were materially motivated is no longer sustainable.[20] Even so, social, political, and most of all proprietorial pressures largely succeeded in bringing the Catholic landed over to the established church. Among the rising middle class there was less enticement or need. But lower down the social scale there seems to have been considerable movement, despite the rulings of all churches and the government against 'mixed' marriages. So-called 'couple-beggars'—wandering friars or defrocked priests—made a living from conducting such marriages, and poorer Catholics and Protestants seem not to have been averse to using the services of clergy other than their own.[21]

(c) Nineteenth Century

The accommodating nature of the Irish Catholic Church towards the state in the late eighteenth century disappeared in the nineteenth. Among the reasons was the long-drawn-out campaign for Catholic emancipation (finally granted 1829). It had been expected, but was withheld at the Union (1801) and the subsequent campaign highlighted the anti-popery of the King, mobilized the local power of the priests, and terrified even Protestant liberals, who had been supportive until then. At the same time the development of the 'Second [Protestant] Reformation' alarmed the Catholic clergy.

Like so much of the eighteenth century, the story of the Church of Ireland is under-researched and the erastianism and lavishness of its princely bishops can be overplayed. Certainly recent work by Toby Barnard and Sean Connolly presents a more positive view of 'improving clergymen' and a clerical 'underclass', scraping a living in the provinces.[22] The story of the Church of Ireland in the nineteenth century was one of reform and a progressive reduction in its power and privileges, culminating in its disestablishment in 1871.[23] Its decoupling from the state was an inevitable consequence of growing democracy. Even though its members continued to dominate public positions, disestablishment nevertheless was a great shock when its members had considered themselves part of the governing structure. It also experienced spiritual renewal. Unfortunately for inter-faith relations, that renewal took a profoundly evangelical direction.

Evangelicalism came to Ireland with Methodism in the 1740s, and Methodism was introduced by junior officers in the military garrison, followed by the arrival of John Wesley in 1747 on the first of his twenty-one missions to Ireland. Methodism in England was critical of the establishment and saw itself as having a particular mission to the poor and underprivileged. It took a different form in Ireland, where the bulk of the lower order was Catholic. Very negative attitudes towards the Irish had characterized English accounts even before the Reformation. Anti-popery gave them a new edge. And such perceptions were reinforced by Protestant sects such as the Moravians, Palatines, and Huguenots, who had fled persecution by Catholic states in Europe. Methodism, therefore, was confined initially to the military garrison, to the southern ports, and to these European Protestant refugees. By 1815 its main presence was in Ulster, where the concentration of the evangelical revival—particularly after the Catholic Church's successful fightback elsewhere in Ireland—'helped reinforce the peculiar concentration of Protestantism in the north of the country and…sharpened its anti-Catholic characteristics'.[24] All Protestant denominations were changed by the evangelical revival or Second Reformation, as indeed was the Catholic Church. By the 1820s/30s the proselytizing activities of the evangelicals among Catholics had awakened a newly empowered Catholic clergy and the fightback helped create the Catholic Church of modern times.

The newly created Catholic Truth Society (1827) produced five million books in its first ten years. A series of synods, particularly the first national one since 1642 (Thurles, 1850), resulted in a greater regulation of priests, the introduction of distinctive clerical dress, and a raft of ordinances taking devotional practices out of the home and into the church. Although there were bitter disagreements among the bishops at the synod, it marked the arrival and future dominance of a new type of bishop whose name has become synonymous with the transformation of the Catholic Church thereafter. This was Archbishop Paul Cullen, who was firmly ultramontane and impatient of the idiosyncrasies which had characterized the Irish church. He was effective head of it 1849–78 and he appointed bishops in his own image, who carried his puritan sternness into the modern church. There was a new toughness towards the state and Protestantism generally, and while the new church structures were certainly desperately needed, they nevertheless vied with the Protestant ones obviously and consciously. There was less religious mixing than before as the Catholic Church—partly as a result of evangelical proselytizing—had established a firm hold on the education of its flock, a hold which it guards to this day. In 1972 Emmet Larkin coined the phrase 'devotional revolution' to describe these changes in Irish Catholicism. The idea has received some criticism, largely based on the fact that the changes were already under way in the eighteenth century and his study concentrated on 'orthodox' Catholic practice. It is still, however, a useful concept, for by the end of the nineteenth century the Irish Catholic Church had acquired almost all its modern characteristics: a highly visible organizational structure, a disciplined clergy, a high level of religious instruction and practice, Church control of Catholic education and social activities, and visible allegiance to Rome.[25]

All the other Irish churches had also undergone major reform and religious revival. Modern church structures and governance emerged in Presbyterianism in 1840, and in the Church of Ireland in 1871. The latter had been over-supplied with buildings, and the amalgamation of parishes which accompanied disestablishment also contributed to the significant decline of Anglicanism in rural areas.[26] In contrast, urban growth and improvements in transport made access to churches easier. While the growth in the number of gospel and mission halls—as well as that of smaller Protestant denominations, Baptists and Methodists in particular—testified to the continued success of evangelical revivalism.[27] By 1861 Catholics accounted for 78 per cent of Ireland's population, Anglicans 12 per cent, Presbyterians 9 per cent. However, this disguises the fact that Protestantism was increasingly concentrated in Ulster and Dublin (with clusters in parts of Leinster and Munster), against less than 5 per cent in Connacht, while outside Ulster Presbyterianism was negligible.[28]

(d) Twentieth Century

In 1912 the Solemn League and Covenant (and female Declaration) against Home Rule in Ireland was signed by over 400 000 Protestants in Ulster. All the Protestant churches were open for the occasion, religion reinforcing politics as so often before. Reluctantly the Church of Ireland had accepted Home Rule as a better alternative to partition. The most Protestant province in the country decided otherwise. Partition in 1921 and the withdrawal of Britain from the rest of Ireland saw a dramatic decline in the numbers of Protestants. Outside Dublin, Methodism and Presbyterianism (together accounting for only 1 per cent of the southern population by 1961) had all but disappeared—giving quite a different feel to northern and southern Protestantism. The Church of Ireland, accounting for 3.7 per cent of the population by 1961, was left as the dominant Protestant community in the South. But although its organizational centre remained in Dublin, it was now a predominantly northern church, accounting for 80 per cent of members by the 1970s. With the large decline of working-class Protestants in the South because of the withdrawal of the British garrison, here the Church of Ireland retained a somewhat privileged status.[29] In contrast, a more working-class (and evangelical) membership existed in Northern Ireland, where the strength of Orangeism was a shock to southern clergy taking up positions there.[30] On the whole Protestants in the South did not experience discrimination, as the Catholic minority did in the North. But they were now a tiny drop in a sea of triumphal Catholicism. Catholic religious services took over the public thoroughfares and while the Catholic Church itself may have interfered less in state affairs than once was thought, it did not need to when the ethos of that state was Catholic and public officials were culturally predisposed to act accordingly.[31]

For over three hundred years the Church of Ireland had seen itself as law-abiding, loyal to monarchy and constitution, a force for moderation and polite culture, and latterly a pillar of the empire. The sudden fall from such a position has been described as something of 'a psychological trauma'. Members closed in upon themselves and took little part in public life.[32] The progressive severing of ties with Britain and its empire (culminating in the establishment of the Irish Republic in 1949) was painful for Church of Ireland members. However, the Church was guided through these difficult decades by the pragmatism of Bishop, later Archbishop, John Gregg, and in 1949, when the Church replaced prayers for the Monarch with those for the Irish President and government, he argued: 'in our prayers, above all, there must be reality'.[33] That reality included almost unstoppable decline. The Catholic Church's strict rules about raising as Catholic the children of mixed marriages, was held largely responsible. By 1971 it had dropped to 3.3 per cent of the population, with figures of 1 per cent and less in some western counties.[34]

Despite the rhetoric about reunification of the island, partition suited the Catholic ethos of the new Irish state. From 74 per cent in the all-Ireland census of 1911, Catholics after partition formed 93 per cent of the southern population. The revolutionary generation which ran Ireland till the 1960s had been produced by that narrowing nationalism of the early twentieth century, which saw Ireland's history as that of suffering Catholicism. Visitors marvelled at the high levels of Catholic religious practice and packed churches—a church triumphant. Yet much of the rhetoric was still of the church suffering, persecution under communism and attacks on Catholics in the North providing new examples. There was little theological debate. The freedom from state interference, enjoyed for so long by the church, continued into the twentieth century, education in particular being considered its particular preserve. The Catholic Church in Ireland was leading 'a uniquely sheltered existence', observed one priest in 1966.[35] There was a movement for change coming from within the Church itself, notably from the Primate, Cardinal William Conway (Archbishop of Armagh, 1963–77). Even so the reforms of Vatican II (1962–5) came as quite a shock and old-style bishops such as the redoubtable John Charles McQuaid (Archbishop of Dublin, 1940–72) were slow to introduce the changes.[36] But they did transform the Catholic Church, in many ways reversing the long hold which the Counter-Reformation Council of Trent had exercised over it. In the process many of the elements which Protestants had long criticized disappeared. It should have heralded a new era of ecumenism—and so it did, in that regular meetings between the different churches started in 1964. However, the vexed issues of mixed marriages and how to bring up their offspring have continued and the Troubles in Northern Ireland reinvigorated the politico-religious prejudices which had shaped Ireland's faith communities in the first place.

In Northern Ireland the Catholic laity was even more uncritical of their church, for here Catholics were often under attack and the 'hotter' Protestantism, which dominated the Northern Ireland state, ensured that Catholics would consider their Church as part of their own struggle. At 34 per cent of the populace, after partition, and growing (41 per cent by 1991), they had less cause for pragmatism than southern Protestants, and, though never as 'disloyal' as portrayed by Unionists, there were few northern Catholics who did not want reunification with the rest of Ireland. Their religion *was* their politics. In the first decades they were poorly led by their church's hierarchy. Bishop (then Archbishop) MacRory made no secret of his hostility towards Protestantism and the northern state and tried (unsuccessfully) to have the southern government declare the Catholic Church as the only true church in its 1937 constitution. Northern Catholic churches were packed and pilgrimages, special confraternities, and masses attracted crowds in tens of thousands. Even more than south of the border, the northern Catholic's social, educational, and political life revolved around the Catholic Church. Such cohesion, identification with the southern state and intermittent republican violence, kept the fears of political Catholicism alive and Orange banners and murals recalled past persecutions of Protestants to urge constant vigilance.

In both parts of twentieth-century Ireland inter-communal relations have paid a high price for the success of politicized religion. The Troubles in Northern Ireland caused a rethink about such politicized religion, though not enough. And while the Presbyterian Church in Ireland has always been held back by a fear of how its individual congregations might react (the boasted democratic church structure), the Catholic laity, so long denied any say in church affairs, began to turn on their Church in fury at the abuses which it tolerated. Perhaps the Church of Ireland might finally be able to reassert its perceived moderating role. Indeed the halt in its declining numbers holds out that promise.

III. WHAT THE CHURCHES TAUGHT

The theology of all Christian churches in Ireland was defined in the highly oppositional climate of the Protestant Reformation and the Catholic Church's fightback (the Counter or Catholic Reformation). This meant that the fluidity of medieval religion was no longer acceptable. In essence Catholicism was centred on the sacraments, Protestantism on the scriptures. For the Protestant churches the Bible was the only source of God's word. As such the faithful should be given access to it without the mediation of priests, saints, or devotional aids. The Catholic Church believed the Bible needed interpreting and also taught that there were equally valid apostolic 'traditions' of which the Church was guardian. In Protestant teachings Christ was the true head of the church, the cross the only sacrifice. So the 'sacrifice' of the mass and the position of the Pope (denounced as the Antichrist in a number of documents) were considered unscriptural and blasphemous. While the Catholic Church believed in the intercession and veneration of the saints (including the use of images and relics), Protestants considered this idolatrous. And where the latter believed in justification by faith, the Catholic Church taught that in addition to faith, grace could be gained through the sacraments and good works.[37] It was political events in the seventeenth century which introduced more fervent religionists and forced people to decide what they were and what they were not. In time the competition for souls produced a more serious approach to instructing the faithful. But it was a long time coming and until the nineteenth century most churches' pastoral side was deemed negligent. In the seventeenth century there was widespread ignorance of the essentials of one's faith. 'The native Irish are very good Catholics,' noted French traveller Boulaye-le-Gouz in 1644, 'though knowing little of their religion.'[38] Nor did early seventeenth-century Protestant settlers have strong religious attachments.[39]

Although clergy of all denominations had reservations about giving the unlettered laity 'unfettered access to holy writ',[40] Protestantism was a religion of the word, with the Bible at its centre, and from quite early in the seventeenth century it was being identified by Catholics as a purely Protestant book. This made for a highly literate Protestant laity, particularly among the dissenters. When most of the Irish populace was Irish-speaking, however, the lack of an Irish-speaking Protestant clergy deterred conversion to Protestantism and also created problems for continental-trained Catholic clergy sent on mission to Ireland.[41] Both Elizabeth I and James I had recognized such a need for an Irish-speaking clergy and tried to supply it. There were intermittent efforts to reach the people in their own language by individual Church of Ireland clerics, such as Archbishop Ussher and Bishop Bedell in the seventeenth century and Cavan rector Dr John Richardson in the eighteenth century. However, the task was vast and not sustained, at least not by the established church, as Methodist preachers used the Irish language to good effect in the late eighteenth century.[42] Ireland also lagged behind in the production of vernacular versions of the Bible and Book of Common Prayer. While both appeared in Welsh in the 1560s, an Irish translation of the New Testament only appeared in 1602 (a full translation in 1685), and that of the Book of Common Prayer in 1608.

The Catholic Church did not see the Bible as the only word of God and favoured explanation in sermons above direct access. Indeed, it was not till the 19th century—in response to the proselytizing campaign by the various Bible societies—that it made the Catholic (Douai) version more widely available, though it had been in print since 1603. Although the bulk of books published in the eighteenth century were religious, efforts to turn the laity from inactive to active Catholics or Protestants remained a problem into the nineteenth century.

The Council of Trent, which laid the basis for the modern Catholic Church, sought instruction through catechism and education, and priests were obliged to provide instruction at mass. Bilingual Catholic catechisms were circulating in manuscript from the 1550s. However, there was a reluctance by the Gaelic literary elite to accept texts printed in Roman type or colloquial Irish, and the 'dangerous Popish books' circulating in the mid seventeenth century were issuing from the Franciscan printing press at Louvain.[43] Since the basics of the Catholic faith seem not to have been widely understood, the Catholic Church had the most heightened need to so instruct its faithful in the sixteenth and seventeenth centuries and the continental seminaries produced a number of catechisms for the Irish mission.[44] These were largely manuals for the clergy and it was not until the eighteenth century that the Catholic Church took seriously its responsibility to educate its laity. While a uniform catechism did not emerge until the twentieth century, the eighteenth-century catechisms had a lasting influence. They contain all the expected teachings about God, the sacraments and commandments, stern warnings about 'carnal knowledge' outside marriage, impure thoughts, drunkenness, and receiving communion in a state of sin. The 'holy Catholic Church' was 'the one true Church', the Pope its 'visible Head'. Given the long life of these catechisms (that of the Paris-trained and future Archbishop Michael O'Reilly remaining in use from the 1720s to the 1940s), we can already see all the obsessions of the modern church two centuries earlier.[45]

Although the Church of Ireland's 1634 canons called for instruction of its people 'in the body of the Christian religion',[46] Presbyterians were more advanced than other denominations, with good editions of catechisms from the 1640s and a system where catechesis was conducted in the houses of elders at least once a year.[47] The Church of Ireland's Book of Common Prayer informed its catechisms and was often bound in with the Bible, as was the Presbyterians' Confession of Faith. It was not till the end of the seventeenth century, however, that more sustained efforts were made to produce catechisms for use by children. In hindsight it is the common Christianity which strikes in the catechisms of the various denominations, though Presbyterian ones also identified their members as a 'pre-ordained elect'.[48] The main differences were ritual, with Catholic works aimed at preparing the faithful for its many more sacraments; while dissenting ones—much in the manner of Jack in Jonathan Swift's *A Tale of a Tub*, tearing away all adornments—contested those rituals remaining in the state church.[49] Far more important to Ireland's religious divisions were cultural differences and in this respect the fact that most Protestant spiritual works came from England or Scotland and most Catholic ones from the Continent was an important influence at this formative stage.[50]

Inability to read, of course, meant that such texts had to be read and interpreted by elites. But throughout the centuries there are contemporary reports of popular thirst for religious knowledge. Even in a period of unusual religious tension in the nineteenth century, the plucky American evangelical, Asenath Nicholson found that people of all faiths would ask her to read passages from the Bible. Irene Whelan also tells of popular Catholic bafflement turning to enthusiasm to hear travelling Protestant evangelists reading in Irish, once the listeners were sure their existing faith was not under attack. Like Nicholson, Presbyterian missionaries (so-called colporteurs) in the early twentieth century were happy enough to distribute Catholic editions of the Bible. By then, however, the idea of the Bible as something appropriated by Protestants had become ingrained in Irish Catholic culture. And while the experiences of these Presbyterian missionaries further demonstrates the thirst of people to hear and read the word of God, they also encountered lingering beliefs that the Bible was written by Luther and resistance from Catholic clergy to such reading without clerical approval.[51]

Far more important in the religious instruction of the laity was the sermon. In 1683 Edward Synge, rector of Summerhill in county Meath, reported that poor attendance at catechesis and evening prayer vastly improved once a sermon was introduced.[52] However, it would appear that complacency in the Church of Ireland caused sermons to become dry and formal. The Quakers, with no preaching or sacramental tradition, felt no need to ordain ministers. In general, preaching was more important in Dissenting than in other faiths and in Presbyterianism it could make the difference between entire congregations staying with a minister or calling in another. Congregations were encouraged to bring their own Bibles, to follow the preacher in his scriptural quotations and take notes on what they heard.[53] 'Presbyterian worship is meant to be a unity of PRAISE PRAYER and PROCLAMATION', advised a 1993 handbook for use in Sunday schools and Bible classes, 'with the Reading and Preaching of the Word of God having a central place'.[54] Preaching also determined the internal architecture of various Protestant places of worship, privileging pulpits over the central positions of altars in Catholic ones.[55] In the evangelical revival open-air preaching was a notable feature, particularly at fairs and markets. Such populist preaching was also a significant factor in the various revivals which occurred, particularly in Ulster. The most famous were the Sixmilewater revival of 1625 and the Great Revival of 1859, and while the emotionalism associated with religious revivals was an accepted part of Methodism, it was often frowned upon by the clergy of other denominations, who would then step in to direct it towards more orthodox channels. As with the miraculous visions in popular Catholicism, these revivals were also a form of criticism of the mainstream churches. It is perhaps no surprise that these two most famous of the revivals occurred within Presbyterianism, which so frowned on rituals and 'superstitions', or that, as in the case of the 1859 revival, such fervour was ultimately directed into new places of religious practice such as the mission halls and non-mainstream groupings like the Plymouth Brethren.[56] All churches mixed religion and politics in their sermons, though, as Ian McBride has shown in his aptly titled *Scripture Politics*, Presbyterians were particularly predisposed to 'apply biblical principles to current events'.[57]

In the Catholic Church, Trent had laid out the rulings for a priest and church-centred religion and various synods and other regulatory statements called for regular preaching at mass.[58] A mix of persecution and shortage of churches and priests meant that this was unattainable until the nineteenth century. However, missions conducted by professional preachers often substituted. The many devotional works issuing from Counter-Reformation divines were largely sermons for the use of the clergy and the best of these continued to be used in manuscript form well into the eighteenth century.[59] Notable among these were Geoffrey Keating's theological prose works, making available in Irish ideas hitherto only accessible in Latin. His sermons adapted scriptural themes and dramatic moral tales to emphasize the importance of confession and other sacraments.[60] Given the attachment to the friars in Irish-speaking areas, large crowds would rally to hear such preachers, and they continued to be politically suspect to the authorities into the eighteenth century. One such was captured, branded, and deported in 1725. However, the dangerous literature found on him turned out to be the Protestant Revd John Richardson's Irish translation of the celebrated sermons by Anglican Archbishop of Canterbury, John Tillotson.[61] Of course there was an element of the spectacle in clerical preaching and the Church of Ireland was critical of this performance element in Dissenting preaching. Reforming Catholic clerics were just as critical of this tendency among their own and this is the topic of a very funny seventeenth-century satirical poem, about an ill-educated priest, whose 'thunderous refrain' and frequent 'amens' disguised his lack of learning.[62] It was in the eighteenth century that here, as in other areas, the Catholic Church became more organized. Bishop Patrick Plunkett of Meath kept a diary (1787–90), itemizing the topics of sermons and 'exhortations' delivered in each parish during his annual visitations. These included the real presence, a good communion, repentance, charity to one's neighbour, the mass, Easter duty, the last judgement, and warnings against swearing, drunkenness, and rioting. These seem rather mundane and there is an occasional complaint suggesting that the audiences were not large.[63] It is likely that the enduring popularity of Bishop James Gallagher's sermons (1736) came from their hell-fire and brimstone character.[64] Indeed it has been suggested that the increasing orthodoxy associated with the nineteenth-century 'devotional revolution', and conveyed through printed sermons, was less influential in Gaelic than in English-speaking areas, preachers in the former accommodating older attitudes.[65]

IV. WHAT PEOPLE BELIEVED

Improved structures and education in time produced a more informed laity. However, ordinary people rarely left evidence about their beliefs. 'The Irish peasant...[is] not to be known by a passing glance, or conversation', wrote Dr Patrick Murray, professor of theology at Maynooth in 1852, and to outsiders of a different class or creed, 'he is absolutely impenetrable'.[66] Surviving devotional literature from the late middle ages testifies to a genuine popular spirituality. This did not always translate into doctrinal awareness and conscious commitment declined the further down the social ladder and the further removed from the towns. Indeed Thomas O'Connor has suggested that the reliance on preaching and underuse of printed aids in the seventeenth century 'facilitated the survival of folk practices and...a selective acceptance of reformed Catholicism'.[67] As in Europe generally, such popular spirituality was often poorly led. Bishops were distant figures; basic doctrine was not generally taught and critical Elizabethans were to pronounce the Irish ignorant of the commandments. Such apparent weaknesses were only structural and once remedied the old religion had centuries of experience in adapting to local traditions.

The success of early Irish Christianity was in a large part due to such adaptation of existing familial structures and pagan practices. It Christianized pagan festivals and deities and constructed early saints' lives to show it had ever been thus. The saints had acquired those gifts and virtues valued by that society, not least their role in providing hospitality and blessing the festivities which accompanied their special days (patrons' days or patterns) usually celebrated at local holy wells. These continued to attract vast crowds into the early nineteenth century, esteemed as much for entertainment as for any spiritual significance lost in the clouds of time. In times of political disturbance, these gatherings were targeted by the authorities as potentially subversive. However, before the dramatic alteration in the political climate from the 1790s onwards, they seem to have been accepted by Protestants, who were also reported as attending.[68] In a rare insight into daily life in rural Ireland, Nicholas Peacock's diary of estate management in mid-eighteenth-century Limerick regularly records tenants and servants' attendance at patterns and money he distributed to them to drink 'Patricks *(sic)* Pott' on such occasions.[69] Given the many booths and stalls which operated, patterns were also good business. A 1754 attempt to prevent 'the enormities and scandalous excesses' annually committed at one well, gave advance notice 'to prevent a disappointment to such publicans as usually erected tents or booths near said well'.[70] The Catholic Church—so influenced by Protestant criticisms—also singled them out for taming and the huge number of 'Holy Days'—when people resorted to such holy places—were significantly reduced from the 1750s onwards, 'as it will prevent drunkenness, profaneness and impiety, and make them more sober, industrious and useful to their country'.[71] Those remaining were adapted to celebrate official Catholic holy days, notably 15 August, feast of the Assumption of the Blessed Virgin Mary, and the booths and stalls of the patterns were replaced at later events by those selling holy pictures, rosary beads and other devotional aids.[72] Anthropologist Lawrence Taylor comments wryly on such churching of pagan survivals: 'It is difficult to find poor Brigid among the Marian images and Sacred Hearts...Then again, that is probably no more than what Brigid herself did to whatever goddesses preceded her...one is tempted to conclude that the once wild pilgrimage so often condemned by the clergy is now but an extension of the church.'[73] By the late nineteenth century the 'devotional revolution' had enhanced the status of the clergy. But in the previous century the Irish-language poets called on the local saint to rise and celebrate the death of the cleric who had tried to stop his pattern.[74]

Such reverence for sacred landscape owed much to the way in which the fifth-century Patrician church had worked through local secular dynasties. Early Christian monastic foundations had come from land donated by such families, their descendants retaining a special stewardship and, given that clerical celibacy (though pronounced by the Church in the twelfth century) was not universally practised even as late as the seventeenth century, such families continued to provide clerical leaders for many centuries. Such 'termon' lands have survived in many rural place names, their loss in the later plantations causing particular resentment. In the seventeenth and eighteenth centuries necessity often compelled clergy to live with their families and perform mass and other sacraments in private houses, drawing criticism from Church reformers and the secular authorities alike. Such practices, complained the papal legate to Ireland in the 1640s, meant that once mass was said 'on the very table from which the altar cloth has just been removed, playing cards or glasses of beer together with food for dinner are at once laid'.[75] These 'stations' were to survive into the twentieth century. As depicted in William Carleton's *Traits and Stories of the Irish Peasantry*, they were prized by some hosts as a particular honour, but also caused excessive expenditure and there were many real-life examples of the fictional priest who valued them as much for the food and drink as for their spiritual side.[76]

As elsewhere in Europe, such veneration for places and local saints shaded into magic and 'superstition'. Protestants thought Catholics particularly prone to such beliefs. Catholic divines went to considerable lengths to prove otherwise. In his history of Down and Connor the Revd James O'Laverty was at pains to prove that witchcraft, and a range of other superstitions, had been introduced by Scottish Presbyterians.[77] In fact most people in early modern Europe believed that the supernatural took many forms and Protestants were not immune.[78] Formal religion itself told of the endless battle between good and evil, and natural misfortunes were often given supernatural explanations. Were not the fairies, after all, the angels who had fallen with Lucifer? Even if your religious leaders denounced the cures and spells as popish, it made sense to take every precaution.[79]

The Catholic priest in particular was thought to possess magical powers. In 1771 the Catholic bishop Nicholas Sweetman denounced priests in Wexford, 'who read exorcisms, or gospels, over the already too ignorant...or act as fairy doctor in other shape...[or] who bless water to sprinkle sick persons, cattle, fields, with'.[80] The friars were held to have a special access to the other world and burial in ruined monasteries and in a monk's habit were still ideals as late as the mid twentieth century. Because of their apparent rootlessness they were also particularly feared by the Protestant authorities. A 1731 complaint reported 'stroling (sic) vagabond Friars', from Youghall, Kinsale, and Killarney doing 'much mischief' in Munster:

> For these Friars creep into the Houses of the weak and ignorant People, they confirm the Papists in their Superstition and Errors, they marry Protestants to Papists contrary to Law, they haunt the Sick Beds even of Protestants, they endeavour to pervert them from our holy religion...[81]

All denominations also subscribed to various prophecies and apocalyptic readings of unusual events. Protestants interpreted past, present, and future through the apocalyptic books of the Bible, seeing many happenings as examples of the relentless struggle with the Antichrist and Rome as its seat.[82] They were particularly strong among the Covenanters—strict Presbyterians who had fled persecution in Scotland—and the floods of prophecies being printed in Ulster in the 1790s contributed to the wave of millenarianism which underpinned the end-of-century crisis.[83] For Catholics, particularly in poorer, rural areas, the recurrent prophecy was that of the sixth-century saint, Colum Cille, which predicted their massacre at the hands of Protestants. At times of unusual social disruption and political tension this prophecy circulated, leading to attacks on Protestants in the 1640s, and the flight of hundreds of Catholics from their homes in the 1790s and 1840s. One of the strangest episodes of millenarian excitement occurred in the 1820s, when the prophecies of Pastorini, based on an English Catholic churchman's study of the Apocalypse of St. John, foretold the overthrow of Protestantism.[84] In fact this picked up recurrent themes in Irish-language poetry, saying much the same.

In medieval Christianity the real and the spiritual worlds were interwoven, the saints and holy people, the many devotional aids doing battle with evil spirits which took many forms. Most prominently it was the Virgin Mary who was invoked and devotion to Mary would remain a peculiarly Catholic thing. Mary, the representative of humanity and her particular prayer, the rosary, was already venerated in late medieval practices and spiritual texts.[85] In a continuation of medieval spirituality, the terrors of Judgement Day figure prominently in seventeenth and eighteenth-century religious verse and other works. But Mary will be there to reason with her son on behalf of humanity, is the theme of this eighteenth-century Irish-language poem (and many others):

> O Mary who art in heaven eternally,
> looking down continually,
> listen to my sighs every time,
> and lead strongly for my case[86]

Another told of Judgement Day, when:

> The only son will come to do justice...
> seated on a bench above the progeny of Eve,
> reading our crimes as we look up at Him.

Then 'the polite, courteous virgin will come', remind him of how she suffered for him in life, and bargain for those who had prayed to her.[87] Simon Macken, Fermanagh scribe and schoolmaster (active 1770s–1820s) routinely signed off with a request that the reader pray to Mary 'since she receives every request'.[88] Though in a version sanitized from the earthier medieval, Marian devotion was central to the modern Irish Catholic Church. The rosary would become something of a Catholic 'weapon' much as the Bible did for Protestants. But the belief in Mary's closeness to humanity meant that she might also be used against a church not always living up to what it preached and heightened devotion to the Virgin Mary (as well as miraculous appearances) very often represented a turning away from, or chastisement of the clergy.[89]

Although there was some confusion in early modern Protestantism (at least among some Church of Ireland laity)[90] about praying to the saints, this became peculiarly associated with Catholicism. It had already been a matter of contention in the late medieval church and was denounced by Calvin as idolatrous.[91] So images were removed, destroyed, or painted over. Protestants believed in the direct communion of man and God, Jesus alone the mediator. Indeed, an influential nineteenth-century evangelical attack on Catholic belief devoted most space to this particular issue.[92] As the nineteenth-century Oxford Movement introduced to Anglicanism some of the rituals and church adornments lost at the Reformation, they were denounced as 'trappings of popery';[93] while disputes within Presbyterianism about permitting any music whatsoever in church were not resolved until late in the twentieth century. 'The Charismatic movement and a widespread demand for greater informality in worship are changing the face of Irish Presbyterian worship,' wrote Finlay Holmes in 2000. 'Not only organs but choirs, often robed, and musical groups lead praise. Presbyterians of the past must be uncomfortable in their graves.'[94]

V. Conclusion

It has only been possible in this chapter to skim the surface of a complex topic. I have not been able to discuss inter-faith dialogue and inter-communal relations, the role of women, the missions, and a host of other related topics. The mass of published work on religion in Ireland has privileged discussion of its institutional aspects, its divisiveness, and contribution to contesting national cultures, rather than its spiritual dimensions. Recent historical scholarship, however, has moved away from narrow institutional studies, though the work of earlier scholars, sifting documents in Rome and elsewhere has laid the groundwork—even if the contemporary can, justifiably, wince at some of the underlying assumptions. There is a wealth of new findings appearing in scholarly collections, but no equivalent of those earlier masterly overviews by historians such as J. C. Beckett, A. T. Q. Stewart, R. B. McDowell, Patrick Corish, and Finlay Holmes. The future, one hopes, will focus on the laity, on the debate within the churches, particularly where new ideas and critics did not become mainstream. Perhaps, as D. H. Akenson once commented, the institutional churches and their leaders needed humbling before any reassessment could occur.

Notes

1. D.H. Akenson, *Small Differences. Irish Catholics and Irish Protestants, 1815–1922. An International Perspective* (Dublin, 1991), 3–14.
2. See good overview in Diarmaid MacCulloch, *Reformation. Europe's House Divided, 1490–1700* (London, 2003), xix–xx.
3. [Dan H. Laurence (ed)], *The Bodley Head Bernard Shaw Collected Plays with their Prefaces* (3 vols., London, 1971), ii, 821–3.
4. Henry Morley (ed), *Ireland under Elizabeth and James I* (London, 1809), 378.
5. Alan Ford, James McGuire, and Kenneth Milne (eds), *As by Law Established. The Church of Ireland since the Reformation* (Dublin, 1995), 67.
6. A.P.W. Malcolmson, *Archbishop Charles Agar: Churchmanship and Politics in Eighteenth-Century Ireland* (Dublin, 2002), 184. The foreignness can be overplayed: of serving clergy in Cork in 1837, most were local and only 1.6 per cent were English-born; Ian d'Alton, *Protestant Society and Politics in Cork 1812–1844* (Cork, 1980), 66. See D. H. Akenson, *The Church of Ireland: Ecclesiastical Reform and Revolution, 1800–1885* (New Haven, 1971), 166, for one of the many examples of English appointees being more dedicated than Irish ones.
7. J.P. Kenyon (ed), *The Stuart Constitution, 1603–1688: Documents and Commentary* (Cambridge, 1966), 264; R. Gardiner (ed), *The Constitutional Documents of the Puritan Revolution, 1625–1660*, 3rd edn (Oxford, 1906), no 58.
8. D.W. Miller, 'Presbyterianism and "Modernization" in Ulster', *Past and Present*, 80 (1978), 66–90; I.R. McBride, *Scripture Politics. Ulster Presbyterians and Irish Radicalism in the Late Eighteenth Century* (Oxford, 1998), 203, 235.
9. Patrick Mitchel, *Evangelicalism and National Identity in Ulster, 1921–1998* (Oxford, 2003), 236.
10. James Buckley (ed), 'A Tour in Ireland in 1672–4', *Cork Historical and Archaeological Society Journal*, x (1904), 97; Brian MacCuarta, *Catholic Revival in the North of Ireland, 1603–41* (Dublin, 2007), 26; Colman Ó Clabaigh, *The Friars in Ireland, 1224–1540*, (Dublin, 2012) for the pre-Reformation revival.
11. Patrick J. Corish, *The Catholic Community in the Seventeenth and Eighteenth Centuries* (Dublin, 1981).
12. Ibid., 31; MacCuarta, *Catholic Revival*, 145–9.
13. Ibid., 56.
14. 'Report on the State of Popery in Ireland, 1731', *Archivium Hibernicum*, i (1912), 11.
15. See, for example, Patrick J. Duffy, *Landscapes of South Ulster. A Parish Atlas of the Diocese of Clogher* (Belfast, 1993), 36, 44, 54; Rev. A. Cogan (ed), *The Diocese of Meath, Ancient and Modern*, 3 vols. (Dublin, 1862–70), ii, 242–3.
16. Hugh Fenning, *The Undoing of the Friars of Ireland. A Study of the Novitiate Question in Eighteenth-century Ireland* (Louvain, 1972); idem., 'A time of reform: from the "penal laws" to the birth of modern nationalism, 1691–1800', in Brendan Bradshaw and Dáire Keogh (eds), *Christianity in Ireland. Revisiting the Story* (Blackrock, Co. Dublin, 2002), 137.
17. idem., 'A time of reform', 142.

18. Ian McBride, *Eighteenth-Century Ireland. The Isle of Slaves* (Dublin, 2009), 246–9, on the continental life of the Irish Catholic clergy.

19. S.J. Connolly, *Religion, Law and Power. The Making of Protestant Ireland 1660–1760* (Oxford, 1992), 288.

20. See Michael Brown, Charles I. McGrath, and Thomas P. Power (eds), *Converts and Conversion in Ireland, 1650–1850* (Dublin, 2005), particularly essays by Betsey Taylor Fitzsimon and Thomas P. Power. Eileen O'Byrne and Anne Chamney (eds), *The Convert Rolls: the Calendar of the Convert rolls, 1703–1838: with Fr. Wallace Clare's Annotated List of Converts 1703–1708* (Dublin, 2005).

21. John Brady, *Catholics and Catholicism in the Eighteenth-Century Press* (Maynooth, 1965), 52; Marianne Elliott, *The Catholics of Ulster. A History* (London, 2000), 178–9; MacCuarta, *Catholic Revival*, 194, finds much temporary conformity among the poor, on whom recusancy fines fell heaviest.

22. Toby Barnard, 'Improving clergymen, 1660–1760', in Alan Ford et al, *As By Law Established*, 136–51; idem, *A New Anatomy of Ireland. The Irish Protestants, 1649–1770* (New Haven and London, 2003), 81–114; Connolly, *Religion, Law and Power*, 171–90; idem, 'The Moving Statue and the Turtle Dove: Approaches to the History of Irish Religion', *Irish Economic and Social History*, XXXI (2004), 15–16; idem, *Divided Kingdom. Ireland 1630–1800* (Oxford, 2008), 274–5; Alan Acheson, *A History of the Church of Ireland* (Dublin, 1997), 23.

23. The fullest account is Donald Harman Akenson, *The Church of Ireland. Ecclesiastical Reform and Revolution, 1800–1885* (New Haven and London, 1971), Donald Harman Akenson, *A Protestant in Purgatory. Richard Whately, Archbishop of Dublin* (Hamden, Conn., 1981); Jacqueline Hill, 'Protestant ascendancy challenged: the Church of Ireland laity and the public sphere, 1740–1869', in Raymond Gillespie and W. G. Neely (eds), *The Laity and the Church of Ireland, 1000–2000* (Dublin, 2002), 153.

24. David Hempton and Myrtle Hill, *Evangelical Protestantism in Ulster Society, 1740–1890* (London, 1992), 9.

25. Elliott, *Catholics of Ulster*, 269; Emmet Larkin, 'The Devotional Revolution in Ireland, 1850–75', *American Historical Review*, LXXVII (1972), 625–52; Larkin's thesis received endorsement from a very influential study by his former student, David Miller, 'Irish Catholicism and the Great Famine', *Journal of Social History*, IX (1975), 81–98, also his 'Mass attendance in Ireland in 1834', in Stewart J. Brown and David Miller (eds), *Piety and Power in Ireland 1760–1960* (Belfast and Indiana, 2000), 158–79. For Cardinal Cullen, see Daire Keogh and Albert McDonnell (eds), *Cardinal Paul Cullen and His World* (Dublin, 2011).

26. Liam Kennedy, *Colonialism, Religion and Nationalism in Ireland* (Belfast, 1996), 25–34; R. B. McDowell, *The Church of Ireland 1869–1969* (London, 1975), 26–70.

27. S.J. Connolly, *Religion and Society in Nineteenth-century Ireland* (Dundalk, 1985), 43–6.

28. Akenson, *Small Differences*, 155–6.

29. Though see Martin Maguire on the Protestant working class of Dublin, 'The Organization and Activism of Dublin's Protestant Working Class, 1883–1935', *Irish Historical Studies*, 29 (May 1994), 65–87, and idem., 'A Socio-economic analysis of the Dublin Protestant Working Class, 1870–1926', *Irish Economic and Social History*, 20 (1993), 35–61. McDowell, *Church of Ireland*, 119–24.

30. Daithí Ó Corráin, *Rendering to God and Caesar: The Irish Churches and the Two States in Ireland, 1949–73* (Manchester, 2006), 31–2.

31. For a very full account of how Church influence impacted, see John Cooney, *John Charles McQuaid. Ruler of Catholic Ireland* (Dublin, 1999), especially 243–5.

32. Kenneth Milne, 'The Protestant Churches in Independent Ireland', in James P. Mackey and Enda McDonagh, *Religion and Politics in Ireland at the turn of the Millennium* (Dublin, 2003), 69.

33. Kurt Bowen, *Protestants in a Catholic State. Ireland's Privileged Minority* (Dublin, 1983), 116; also Heather Crawford, 'Outside the glow': *Protestants and Irishness in independent Ireland* (Dublin, 2010) and Ian d'Alton, ' "A Vestigial Population"? Perspectives on Southern Irish Protestants in the Twentieth Century', *Eire-Ireland*, 44 (Fall/Winter, 2009), 9–42.

34. Bowen, *Protestants in a Catholic State*, 21–6. There is an excellent analysis of the decline in numbers in Coakley, 'Religion, Ethnic Identity and the Protestant Minority in the Republic', 88–93. Archbishop Gregg also blamed celibacy and late marriage; *Journal of the Church of Ireland General Synod* (1939), lxvii–lxviii.

35. Dónall Ó Moráin, 'Ireland and the Council, *The Furrow*, 17 (1966), 429.

36. The most comprehensive account of such changes is Louise Fuller, *Irish Catholicism since 1950. The Undoing of a Culture* (Dublin, 2002).

37. I look at this in some detail in *When God Took Sides. Religion and Identity in Ireland—Unfinished History* (Oxford, 2009), chapter 3, and there is a very good analysis of the doctrinal differences by Thomas P. Power, 'The theology and liturgy of conversion from Catholicism to Anglicanism', in Brown, McGrath and Power (eds), *Converts and Conversion*, 60–78. See also Rev V.G.B. Griffin, *Anglican and Irish. What we Believe* (Dublin, 1976).

38. T. Crofton Croker (ed), *The Tour of the French Traveller M. de la Boulaye le Gouz in Ireland in A.D. 1644* (London, 1837), 39; a similar observation was made by the Catholic Church in 1613, see John Hagan (ed), 'Miscellanea Vaticano-Hibernica', *Archivium Hibernicum*, iii (1914), 300.

39. M. Perceval-Maxwell, *The Scottish Migration to Ulster in the Reign of James I* (London, 1973), 273; K.S. Bottigheimer, 'Kingdom and Colony: Ireland in the Westward Enterprise', in K.R. Andrews et al (eds), *The Westward Enterprise: English Activities in Ireland, the Atlantic and America 1480–1650* (Liverpool 1978), 56–9.

40. Toby Barnard, 'Reading in eighteenth-century Ireland', in Bernadette Cunningham and Máire Kennedy (eds), *The Experience of Reading: Irish Historical Perspectives* (Dublin, 1999), 64, also Raymond Gillespie, 'Reading the Bible in seventeenth-century Ireland', in ibid., 26–8.

41. See, for example, Fenning (ed), *Fottrell Papers*, 23, 29; Revd P. Ó Gallachair, 'Clogherici. A Dictionary of the Catholic Clergy of the Diocese of Clogher (1535–1835)', *Clogher Record*, xi (1982), 55.

42. Myrtle Hill, 'Popular protestantism in Ulster in the post-rebellion period, c. 1790–1810', in W.J. Sheils and Diana Woods (eds), *The Churches, Ireland and the Irish* (Oxford, 1989), 194–5; Ian Green, ' "The necessary knowledge of the principles of religion": catechisms and catechizing in Ireland, c. 1560–1800', in Ford et al, *As By Law Established*, 71–2; Elliott, *Catholics of Ulster*, 129–30; Connolly, *Religion, Law and Power*, 298–301; Robert Dunlop (ed), *Ireland under the Commonwealth: Being a Selection of Documents Relating to the Government of Ireland, 1651–9*, 2 vols.(Manchester, 1913), i, 355–7 and ii, 517, a 'native' Presbyterian clergyman preaching the gospel in Irish; Thomas O'Connor, 'Religious change, 1550–1800', in Raymond Gillespie and Andrew Hadfield (eds), *The Oxford History of the Irish Book*, Vol. III: *The Irish Book in English 1550–1800* (Oxford, 2006), 173–4.

43. Dunlop, *Ireland under the Commonwealth*, ii, 695, 1659; O'Connor, 'Religious change', op.cit., 179; Green, 'The necessary knowledge', 70; Corish, *Catholic Community*,

61–4; Raymond Gillespie, *Devoted People. Belief and Religion in Early Modern Ireland* (Manchester, 1997), 151.

44. MacCuarta, *Catholic Revival*, 162–3.

45. Michael Tynan, *Catholic Instruction in Ireland 1720–1950* (Dublin, 1985); Edward Rogan, *Synods and Catechesis in Ireland, c.* 445–1962, 2 vols. (Rome, 1987), i, 38–47.

46. John McCafferty, *The Reconstruction of the Church of Ireland. Bishop Bramhall and the Laudian Reforms, 1633–41* (Cambridge, 2007), 105.

47. Raymond Gillespie, 'The religion of the Protestant laity in early modern Ireland', in Bradshaw and Keogh (eds), *Christianity in Ireland*, 119.

48. Green, 'The necessary knowledge', 79.

49. Raymond Gillespie, 'Lay spirituality and worship, 1558–1750: holy books and godly readers', in Gillespie and Neely (eds), *The Laity and the Church of Ireland*, 141.

50. Green, 'The necessary knowledge', 77; J.R.R. Adams, *The Printed Word and the Common Man. Popular Culture in Ulster 1700–1900* (Belfast, 1987), 43.

51. Presbyterian Church in Ireland. *G.A. Reports* (1916), 8, (1917), 6–7: Asenath Nicholson, *Ireland's Welcome to the Stranger*, ed. Maureen Murphy (Dublin, 2002), 160, 231, 251; Irene Whelan, *The Bible War in Ireland. The 'Second Reformation' and the Polarization of Protestant-Catholic Relations, 1800–1840* (Dublin, 2005), 118–19.

52. Gillespie, 'Religion of the Protestant laity', 120.

53. Raymond Gillespie, 'The reformed preacher: Irish Protestant preaching, 1660–1700', in Alan J. Fletcher and Raymond Gillespie (eds), *Irish Preaching 700–1700* (Dublin, 2001), 140.

54. [Revd Dr Finlay Holmes], *About Being a Presbyterian* (Presbyterian Church in Ireland, 1993).

55. Stephen Larmour and Stephen McBride, 'Church building, from medieval to modern', in Gillespie and Neely (eds), *Laity and the Church of Ireland*, 338.

56. W.T. Latimer, *A History of the Irish Presbyterians* (Belfast, 1893), 220–1, is very critical; Finlay Holmes, *Presbyterian Church in Ireland*, 106–113; Hempton and Hill, *Evangelical Protestantism*, 145–60; Marilyn J. Westerkamp, *Triumph of the Laity. Scots-Irish Piety and the Great Awakening 1625–1760* (Oxford, 1988), 21–34; Mark Doyle, 'Visible differences: the 1859 revival and sectarianism in Belfast', in Mervyn Busteed, Frank Neal, and Jonathan Tonge (eds), *Irish Protestant Identities* (Manchester, 2008), 141–54; J. Holmes, *Religious Revivals in Britain and Ireland, 1859–1905* (Dublin, 2000).

57. McBride, *Scripture Politics*, 119, also 11, 127–9; Adams, *Printed Word*, 176–202, for sermons and other religious works being sold 1700–1900.

58. Rogan, *Synods and Catechesis in Ireland*, i, 38–62 (seventeenth–nineteenth century synods); Fenning, *Fottrell Papers*, 5.

59. See, for example, Bernadette Cunningham, 'Seventeenth-century interpretations of the past: the case of Geoffrey Keating', *Irish Hist. Studies*, xxv (1986), 120.

60. Bernadette Cunningham, '"Zeal for God and for souls": Counter-Reformation preaching in early seventeenth-century Ireland', in Fletcher and Gillespie (eds), *Irish Preaching*, 119–25.

61. J. Larkin, '"Popish Riot" in South County Derry', *Seanchas Ard Mhacha*, viii (1975–6), 110; also *Report on the State of Popery, Archivium Hibernicum*, i, 17.

62. *Comhairle Mhic Clamha ó Achadh na Muilleann: The Advice of MacClave of Aughnamullen*, trans. S.Ó Dufaigh and Brian Rainey (Lille, 1981), 65–71.

63. Cogan, *Diocese of Meath*, ii, 196–226.

64. Elliott, *Catholics of Ulster*, 204–5.

65. David Ryan, 'Catholic preaching in Ireland, 1760–1840', in Raymond Gillespie (ed), *The Remaking of Modern Ireland 1750–1950. Beckett Prize Essays in Irish History* (Dublin, 2004), 90–2.

66. Tomás Ó Fiaich, 'Filíocht Uladh mar Fhoinse don Stair Shóisialta san 18ú hAois', *Studia Hibernica*, xi (1971), 80.

67. O'Connor, 'Religious change', 179.

68. Revd J. O'Laverty, *An Historical Account of the Diocese of Down and Connor, Ancient and Modern*, 5 vols. (Dublin, 1878–95), iii, 237; Gillespie, 'Religion of the Protestant laity', 115–16.

69. Marie-Louis Legg, *The Diary of Nicholas Peacock, 1740–1751. The worlds of a County Limerick farmer and agent* (Dublin, 2005), 199, also 60, 63, 65, 145, 157, 179.

70. Brady, *Catholics and Catholicism in the Eighteenth-Century Press*, 85.

71. Ibid., 89; Fenning, *Undoing of the Friars*, 168–9; Dunlop, *Commonwealth*, ii, 712, 1659, order to suppress patterns as riotous and debauched.

72. Emmet Larkin, 'The Parish mission movement, 1850–1880', in Bradshaw and Keogh, *Christianity in Ireland*, 202.

73. Laurence Taylor, *Occasions of Faith. An Anthropology of Irish Catholics* (Dublin, 1995), 66–7. For the tradition of Holy Wells, see also S.J. Connolly, *Priests and People in Pre-Famine Ireland, 1780–1845* (Dublin, 1982), 135–48, and Diarmuid Ó Giolláin, 'The Pattern', in J.S. Donnelly Jnr. and Kerby A. Miller, *Irish Popular Culture 1650–1850* (Dublin, 1999), 201–21, and Elliott, *Catholics of Ulster*, 45, 286.

74. Ó Gallachair, 'Clogherici', *Clogher Record*, vi (1966–8), 380.

75. Corish, *Catholic Community*, 42; *Report on the State of Popery*, 14, 18; for sacred landscape, see Alexandra Walsham, *The Reformation of the Landscape: Religion, Identity, and Memory in Early Modern Britain and Ireland* (Oxford, 2011).

76. William Carleton, *Traits and Stories of the Irish Peasantry*, 2 vols. (Gerrards Cross, 1990), ii, 145–79; Connolly, *Priests and People*, 50, 67.

77. O'Laverty, *Diocese of Down and Connor*, iii, 394–7.

78. Raymond Gillespie, 'Popular and Unpopular Religion: A View From Early-Modern Ireland', in Donnelly and Miller (eds), *Irish Popular Culture*, 32; E. M. Johnston, 'Problems common to both Protestant and Catholic churches in eighteenth-century Ireland', in O. MacDonagh, W.F. Mandle and P. Travers (eds), *Irish Culture and Nationalism, 1750–1950* (London, 1983), 22.

79. Elliott, *Catholics of Ulster*, 287–8; Gillespie, *Devoted People*, 107–22; idem, 'Religion of the Protestant laity', 115–16.

80. P.J. Corish, 'Two centuries of Catholicism in County Wexford', in Kevin Whelan and William Nolan (eds), *Wexford: History and Society: Interdisciplinary Essays on the History of an Irish County* (Dublin, 1987), 242.

81. 'Report on the State of Popery in Ireland, 1731', *Irish Culture and Nationalism, 1750–1950* (London, 1983), 127.

82. Elliott, *When God Took Sides*, 54–67; Alan Ford, *James Ussher: Theology, History, and Politics in Early-Modern Ireland and England* (Oxford, 2007), 76–84; Crawford Gribben and Andrew R. Holmes (eds), *Protestant Millennialism, Evangelicalism and Irish Society, 1790–2005* (Basingstoke, 2006), various essays particularly those by Gribben, Hill, Whelan, Holmes, and Mitchel; Phil Kilroy, 'Sermons and pamphlet literature in the Irish reformed church, 1613–34', *Archivium Hibernicum*, 33 (1975), 116–17.

83. Adams, *The Printed Word*, 86–90; McBride, *Scripture Politics*, 195–201.

84. The fullest account is James S. Donnelly Jr, 'Pastorini and Captain Rock: Millenarianism and Sectarianism in the Rockite Movement of 1821–4', in Samuel Clark and James S. Donnelly Jr

(eds), *Irish Peasants. Violence and Political Unrest 1780–1914* (Madison, Wisconsin, 1983), 102–39.

85. Elliott, *Catholics of Ulster*, 67–8; Peter O'Dwyer, *Mary. A History of Devotion in Ireland* (Dublin, 1988), 23–7.

86. Énrí Ó Muirgheasa, *Dánta Diadha Uladh* (Dublin, 1936), 143.

87. Ibid., 126.

88. Séamus P.Ó Mórdha, 'Simon Macken. Fermanagh Scribe and Schoolmaster', *Clogher Record*, ii (1957), 439.

89. Eugene Hynes, *Knock: The Virgin's Apparition in Nineteenth-Century Ireland* (Cork, 2008), 219–21.

90. Gillespie, 'Lay spirituality and worship', 136.

91. MacCulloch, *Reformation*, 248–9.

92. Revd Charles Stuart Stanford, *A Handbook to the Romish Controversy: Being a Refutation in Detail of the Creed of Pope Pius the Fourth on the Grounds of Scripture and Reason* (Dublin, 1864), 89–130; also useful summary of the various Protestant churches' objections to Catholic teaching and practices in *Sectarianism. The Report of the Working Party on Sectarianism* (Irish Inter-Church Meeting, Belfast 1993), 131–45.

93. Paul Larmour and Stephen McBride, 'Buildings and faith: church building from medieval to modern', in Gillespie and Neeley (eds), *Laity and the Church of Ireland*, 345.

94. Finlay Holmes, *The Presbyterian Church in Ireland: A Popular History* (Blackrock, 2000); W. T. Latimer, *A History of the Irish Presbyterians* (Belfast, [1893]), 227, 132–3.

Select Bibliography

Akenson, D.H., *Small Differences. Irish Catholics and Irish Protestants, 1815–1922. An International Perspective* (Dublin, 1991).

Barnard, Toby, *A New Anatomy of Ireland. The Irish Protestants, 1649–1770* (New Haven and London, 2003).

Brown, Stewart J. and Miller, David (eds), *Piety and Power in Ireland 1760–1960* (Belfast and Indiana, 2000).

Brown, Michael, McGrath, Charles I., and Power, Thomas P. (eds), *Converts and Conversion in Ireland, 1650–1850* (Dublin, 2005).

Connolly, S.J., *Priests and People in Pre-Famine Ireland, 1780–1845* (Dublin, 1982).

Connolly, S.J., *Religion, Law and Power. The Making of Protestant Ireland 1660–1760* (Oxford, 1992).

Corish, Patrick J., *The Catholic Community in the Seventeenth and Eighteenth Centuries* (Dublin, 1981).

Elliott, Marianne, *The Catholics of Ulster. A History* (London, 2000).

Elliott, Marianne, *When God Took Sides. Religion and Identity in Ireland–Unfinished History* (Oxford, 2009).

Ford, Alan, McGuire, James, and Milne, Kenneth (eds), *As by Law Established. The Church of Ireland since the Reformation* (Dublin, 1995).

Fuller, Louise, *Irish Catholicism since 1950. The Undoing of a Culture* (Dublin, 2002).

Gillespie, Raymond and Neely, W.G. (eds), *The Laity and the Church of Ireland, 1000–2000* (Dublin, 2002).

Hempton, David and Hill, Myrtle, *Evangelical Protestantism in Ulster Society, 1740–1890* (London, 1992).

Hempton, David, *Religion and Political Culture in Britain and Ireland. From the Glorious Revolution to the Decline of Empire* (Cambridge, 1996).

Holmes, Finlay, *The Presbyterian Church in Ireland: A Popular History* (Blackrock, 2000).

McBride, I.R., *Scripture Politics. Ulster Presbyterians and Irish Radicalism in the Late Eighteenth Century* (Oxford, 1998).

Mackey, James P. and McDonagh, Enda, *Religion and Politics in Ireland at the turn of the Millennium* (Dublin, 2003).

Malcolmson, A.P.W., *Archbishop Charles Agar: Churchmanship and Politics in Eighteenth-Century Ireland* (Dublin, 2002).

Mitchel, Patrick, *Evangelicalism and National Identity in Ulster, 1921–1998* (Oxford, 2003).

Ó Corrain, Daithí, *Rendering to God and Caesar: The Irish Churches and the Two States in Ireland, 1949–73* (Manchester, 2006).

Sheils, W.J. and Woods, Diana (eds), *The Churches, Ireland and the Irish*, (Oxford, 1989).

CHAPTER 10

GENDER AND IRISH HISTORY

MARIA LUDDY

IRISH women are now much more visible in Irish historical studies than they have ever been before. It was in the 1970s that the first modern scholarly treatments of Irish women came to be written. The landmark was the broadcast, between October and December 1975, of a Thomas Davis lecture series on the position of women in Irish society. This series was published in 1978 as *Women in Irish Society*, edited by Margaret Mac Curtain and Donnchadh O'Corráin.[1] The end of the 1980s boasted three edited collections and three monographs directly concerned with women in Ireland in the nineteenth century. By the end of the 1990s there were in the region of 60 articles and 43 books dealing with, or at least containing, substantial information on women in Ireland in this period. The number of articles and books that relate directly to Irish women's history now numbers in the hundreds. The focus of these works is primarily on women's history as distinct from gender history.

Gender history has yet to have any real impact on the writing of Irish history though aspects of women's history are beginning to be incorporated into general histories.[2] There are few works that focus on gender in Irish history[3] and the explicit study of women's history predominates over gender history. It is worth noting the evolution of women's history more generally and its connection with gender history. Women's history was 'created', though there were earlier studies, primarily in the 1970s within the context of the rise of 'second-wave feminism' and under the impact of the 'new' social history. During the 1970s, especially in the United States and in Britain, women historians began to question the exclusion of women from historical studies and argued, with justification, that the dominant narratives of political and economic history saw history as a male phenomenon.[4] At the same time the 'new social history', in its insistence that historians seriously consider the poor, workers, and the marginalized, further challenged the ways in which history had been written. Historians also broadened the range of sources that could be utilized for historical purposes, moving away from a reliance on those state documents and papers that elite men had left behind. It now sought out prison records, the records of institutions, poor law records, etc, which documented the experiences of the marginalized where women were as evident as men.

Women's history thus emerged as a major research field, though it was not without its problems. For many years women's history endured a lack of academic status. This history was most often written by women who were not necessarily working in academic history departments. 'Women's history' as an academic subject was often marginalized and left as a 'special study'. Even social historians often relegated women to a chapter in a book rather than integrating their story into the fabric of a monograph, or women's history became subsumed into 'family history' where it was thought, erroneously, to have a natural place. Much of the early writing on women's history was concerned with locating women in the past; it often saw women as victims of patriarchy and feminist historians of the 1970s emphasized the 'separate spheres' theory, where men's history was primarily located in the public sphere of politics and work and women's history was associated within the sphere of the home, the domestic world. Here women's work was primarily reproductive and nurturing. However, by the end of the 1970s the writing of women's history was beginning to move beyond the recovery of women's lives and more sophisticated views with new theoretical visions were emerging. Feminist theory was a rapidly developing and evolving field and historians such as Joan Scott began to argue for a more theoretical view of history that would take 'women's history' from the margins and transform male-centred history. In 1986 Scott published her much-cited article 'Gender: A Useful Category of Historical Analysis'[5] where she argued that 'gender', the social and cultural construction of sexual difference, must become the central category of historical analysis. For Scott the ways in which different societies and cultures interpret and understand male and female sexual difference signifies how 'power' lies in the ability to name, define, and categorize. She argued that in the effort to deconstruct 'absolute categories of gender differences' historians would be able to 'attack normative rules…linked to gender and the power attached to gender discourse'. Gender history thus advocated that both men and women needed to be studied together as the history of one group could not be understood without the history of the other. Gender history has of course evolved since the 1980s and has been further influenced by postmodernism and the linguistic turn, exemplified particularly again in the work of Joan Scott. Here there was an emphasis on the ways in which language determines what we experience and how we experience it. Some historians, of the postmodern bent, argued that our understanding of ourselves and our societies comes to us through language and that our understanding, determined as it is by language, is in constant flux. Gender identity, for instance, can only be understood through an analysis of discourse. Attention then must be given to the structured systems of language by which human beliefs and perceptions are expressed and constrained. Ideas around masculinity, for instance, could not be understood fully unless there was an equal understanding of the construction of femininity. Political theorists, such as Judith Butler, argued that 'gender' itself is a process, something that is performed in everyday life.[6] Whether gender history has succeeded in providing a new and integrative history of society is very much questioned by historians who continue to explore and write about women in history. 'Women's history', 'feminist history' and 'gender history' remain vibrant sub-fields within history, though in Ireland, as far as we have come in the writing of history, the significant evolution has been in the writing of women's history. Irish historians, or those who write about Ireland's history, rarely utilize gender theory or postmodernism to understand that history. It is for this reason that this chapter focuses attention on women's rather than gender history.

Irish women's history of the nineteenth and twentieth centuries dominates our knowledge of women's pasts. Few historians work on periods earlier than the eighteenth century though the notable exceptions provide us with a rich, general, and sometimes detailed focus on our ancestors. Women in early modern Ireland left no texts to tell their stories, but they were written about by men, who defined women and their place and role in society in secular and canon laws, penitentials, the martyrology of saints, sagas, and poems. Women were always subordinate to men and their status depended upon that of their male guardians. A variety of complex female characters was to be found in the surviving writings of the period. As Bitel has shown in one epic poem alone the *Táin Bó Cúailnge* (The Cattle Raid of Cooley), 'a parade of voracious Amazons, passive sex kittens, androgynous prophetesses with otherworldly powers, and goddesses passed through'.[7] Queens were often held in high esteem and the twelfth-century list of Irish Queens, the Banseanchas, is unique in medieval Europe.

Though in reality women were never the political or social equals of men, they did participate in early Irish society and developed economic strategies and social networks that helped them advance in a male-centred culture. They aligned themselves within their extended families to exert influence in politics and to advance their family's economic interests. Archaeological and other evidence throws light on the existence of convents where communities of women dwelt. Amongst the earliest recorded lives of three Irish saints, written in Latin towards the end of the seventh century, the only female was St Brigit. She is possibly the greatest Irish female saint and her major foundation was at Cill Dara (Kildare), where her convent attracted recruits and donations from across Ireland. According to one source her cult flourished and her life appears to have been the most frequently copied of all early medieval saints' lives.[8]

There is evidence of noblewomen playing a role in politics in medieval Ireland. In 1315, for instance, it was recorded that Aodh O'Donnell, King of Tirconnell, ravaged Carbury after 'being advised thereto by his wife... She herself, with all her gallowglasses and men of the Clan Murtagh that she could obtain, marched against the churches... and plundered many of its clergy'.[9] In a letter to Thomas Cromwell in 1535 John Alen wrote that Lady Janet Eustace had played a key role in the Kildare rebellion. She was described as the 'Earl of Kildare's aunt, and... she was the chief councilor and stirrer of this inordinate rebellion'.[10] Grainne O'Malley (*c.* 1530–*c.* 1603) had been born into the Gaelic aristocracy and acquired great wealth, land, and castles through marriage and piracy. She was deemed by Sir Henry Sidney to be 'a terror to all merchantmen that sailed the Atlantic'.[11] However, wealthy women could also be the source of much envy. In 1324 Alice Kyteler, together with accomplices, was accused, by her stepchildren, of sorcery. It appears that Kyteler's wealth was a major cause of the conflict and the charge was compounded by contemporary political and religious conflict in England and Ireland. While Alice was found not guilty of the charges one of her maidservants, Petronella de Mida, was found guilty and became the first woman in Europe to be burnt at the stake on charges of witchcraft.[12]

For nobles marriage played a significant role in forming political alliances. Gerald, earl of Kildare (c.1456–1513) had six daughters whom he married off to strengthen alliances or win political support. Such marriages often allowed women political power otherwise denied them. For instance, Margaret Fitzgerald, who married the chief governor in Ireland in the early sixteenth century, was described by a contemporary as so 'politic, that nothing was thought substantially debated without her advice'.[13] Not only could noblewomen engage in warfare, and be politically active, they were also often literate and sometimes learned. A fifteenth-century woman, Margaret O'Reilly, for instance, was noted as a 'woman that was learned in Latin and in English and in Irish'[14] and many noblewomen played a significant role in patronage of the arts.[15]

From the thirteenth to the seventeenth centuries there were, as O'Dowd notes, considerable changes in Irish women's legal, economic, and political status.[16] There were major differences in the status allowed women under Irish customary law and English Common Law.[17] Under the English law women could, under certain conditions, inherit property, while under Irish law women could not do so. In the sixteenth and seventeenth centuries the ways in which women might inherit or hold on to property allowed them greater social and sometimes political power in society. In merchant families providing a woman with an inheritance often allowed for the survival of a business. At the landed level marriage settlements and inheritance were not just about forming political alliances but also ensuring the expansion of a family's estate. New settlers arriving in Ireland in the sixteenth and seventeenth centuries were sympathetic to women inheriting property, and thus marriage to an heiress became the means by which many families expanded their estates.[18] Women from poor families, especially single women, began to find employment as domestic servants in the more anglicized households and the demand for women servants expanded as English landlords began to build large houses on their estates. Peddling and dealing, and prostitution, formed the occupations of single women in urban areas. Married women's work depended very much on the status of their husbands. In estate houses they managed servants, amongst other chores. For those who did not live in the tower house or the estate house, home was often a 'cabin' made of mud or clay. Women often brought animals and household utensils as part of their dowry. They would milk the cow, produce butter, cook and also brew ale for the family.[19]

The eighteenth century saw greater economic opportunities available to women. Increasingly women found employment as domestic servants, shopkeepers, in the food and clothing businesses, and as farm workers. Women with some resources opened millinery and mantua-making businesses. In the Temple Bar area of Dublin a high proportion of women operated businesses independent of men.[20] For the poorer women huckstering, working as washerwomen or charwomen were amongst the occupations available. Prostitution continued to be an option for women. Margaret Leeson ran the most famous brothel in Dublin, attended by members of the Irish establishment. The concern with the extent of the problem of prostitution can be seen by the opening of the first Magdalen Asylum in Dublin in 1767 by Lady Arabella Denny who sought to rescue and reform young women who had become, or were in danger of becoming, prostitutes.[21] The emergence of a strong philanthropic tradition amongst middle- and upper-class women, which Denny exemplified, was to continue into the early years of the twentieth century, and has its origins in the eighteenth century.

Marriage remained a significant institution for women and it is a subject that has received attention from historians of Ireland. Most recently, Deborah Wilson, in an exploration of twenty landed families in Ireland between 1750 and 1850, considers the legal, social, and familial imperatives that shaped the experience elite women had of property.[22] Much of the literature on Irish marriage focuses on aristocratic marriage and tends to record it as a financial arrangement within which there could be some leeway for a choice of partner.[23] The social and domestic life of the eighteenth century has been opened up by the publication of collections of letters. The Synge letters, from Edward Synge to his daughter Alicia, and the letters of William Drennan and his sister, Martha McTier, offer an insight into family and individual life from eighteenth- and early nineteenth-century Ireland.[24] Through these letters we can explore the world of domesticity, investigate the intimacy of personal relationships, marriage and parenthood. These letters also offer us insight into attitudes to servants, to health, and the roles expected of women and men in society. Marriage is a major theme in both sets of correspondence. The best kind of wife to have, as evidenced in the correspondence, was a 'sensible' one; this implied a wife who would be 'prudent' in her expenses, and who would support the endeavours of her husband, and care for him and their children, an ideal that remained powerfully influential up to the present day.

While we now have some degree of insight into the private and domestic world of women, new studies also reveal how women remained politically active in the eighteenth century. As O'Dowd notes, the major difference between the politics of the sixteenth and seventeenth centuries and the politics of the eighteenth century was the role and status of parliament.[25] Elite women could exercise political influence by acting as hostesses, by receiving important political figures at their homes, by socializing within their class and political groups, even by attending social gatherings where they could hear and pass on political gossip.[26] Women, unlike their counterparts in England, frequented the public gallery of the Irish House of Commons where it was noted that the front row of the gallery was 'generally occupied by females of the highest rank and fashion'.[27] The evolution of patriot politics in late eighteenth-century Ireland also had a place for women. Supporting Irish trade through 'buy Irish' campaigns was one form of political protest. Women were among the crowds cheering for the Irish Volunteers in the 1780s.[28] They were participants in, and witnesses to the violence of, the 1798 rising.[29]

The possibilities for how women might choose to live their lives were broadened by the expansion of convents from the late eighteenth century. The last decades of the eighteenth century saw a revival in Catholicism, in which the Catholic laity played a distinct role evidenced by the beginnings of the expansion of native religious foundations and the rise of men's and women's philanthropic endeavours. While the penal

laws prevented the endowment of Catholic charities and education many Catholic philanthropists worked round the legislation. Thus Nano Nagle, for example, later founder
of the Presentation Order of nuns, began voluntarily, and illegally, to educate the poor
in Cork city in the 1750s. At the same time in Dublin, Teresa Mulally also began to
educate poor Catholic girls and Edmund Ignatius Rice formed the Catholic teaching order of Christian Brothers in 1802. From the eighteenth century an identifiable
Catholic middle class began to emerge. It was the Catholic merchant and professional
classes who began to challenge their inferior political status under Protestant rule and
the Catholic charitable and philanthropic revival was spearheaded by men and women
of these classes.[30]

In 1750 there were four religious orders of nuns, with twelve houses in Ireland. By
1800 that had grown to eighteen houses and six orders, and 120 nuns; by 1901 there were
thirty-five religious orders or congregations consisting of 6642 nuns living in 368 convents. This increase occurred at a time when the Irish population itself had declined
from the 6.5 million, noted in the 1841 census, to 3.3 million recorded in the 1901 census.
There was thus an extraordinary expansion of female religious communities throughout
the nineteenth century.[31] In 1800 nuns made up approximately 6 per cent of the Catholic
Church's workforce; by 1851 they made up about 38 per cent and were 64 per cent of that
workforce by the end of the nineteenth century.[32] New congregations and orders were
formed, for example the Ursulines arrived in Cork in 1771, the Presentation convents
were formed from 1775, the Sisters of Charity were founded in 1815 by Mary Aikenhead,
and the Sisters of Mercy established by Catherine McAuley in 1831. A large number of
European communities, such as the French Sisters of the Good Shepherd, and the St.
Louis Sisters, also established houses in Ireland.

Recent discussion of convents and nuns has revolved around issues of autonomy
and control, of the practical impact of female religious communities on the social and
cultural development of Irish society since the late eighteenth century.[33] The work of
Magray argues that women were central to the emergence of convents from the late
eighteenth century in spite of the credit for this expansion often being given to clerics.[34] It was women themselves who generated the momentum for convent foundation,
providing financial support for these communities. While social, demographic, and cultural changes have been given as reasons for convent expansion, Magray argues that it
was also the nature of convent life itself which proved a powerful attracting force for
many women. Communal life offered not only a spiritual but also an emotional and
material experience for women. Magray focuses attention upon the personal relations
that existed within religious communities where loyalty to the community was often
encouraged through personal devotion to the leadership. She makes a strong case for
the role of nuns in revitalizing the Catholic Church as allies of the reforming bishops
appointed from the 1830s. Magray argues convincingly that it was the development of
women's religious communities and the work they carried through that made possible
the transformation of the Irish church and Irish society in the nineteenth century. She
shows that women religious were central to the evolution of social and cultural life in
nineteenth-century Ireland and to ignore their influence is to misunderstand a major

historical force in Irish society. They were instrumental in extending the welfare infra-structure of the Catholic Church though much of their work had, by the end of the nine-teenth century, become rigid and institutionalized.

Nuns describe and have described their entries as a 'vocation'. This rhetoric was approved and accepted by society and should not blind us to the more realistic expecta-tions which nuns, as women, might have had for convent life. From a social perspective, women's religious communities provided a viable and esteemed alternative to marriage and motherhood in a society that seemed to value women only for their procreative ability. The extent of convent networks in the nineteenth century also allowed women to choose the type of work which best suited their needs and abilities. Within a convent women could create their own sense of rank and status, dependent though it was on a class background, and also organize, devise, and even create their own systems of labour. The wealthier Choir nuns enjoyed the possibility of rising to a position of authority and power unmatched by women in nineteenth-century secular society.[35]

Another aspect of nineteenth-century society that had an important bearing on women's lives was the availability of employment. It is clear from the limited research completed to date that the nature and extent of women's work was tremendously varied. Women engaged in a host of occupations, including begging, rag-picking, laundress-ing, huckstering, taking lodgers, keeping inns and small hotels, teaching, nursing, etc. It is also clear that women of the poorer classes contributed to the family income in an essential way and their contribution often made the difference between survival and destitution.

The participation of women in the Irish workforce, and the economic significance of their labour, has been obscured in historical inquiry until relatively recently though there is, as yet, little sustained analysis of women's working lives. We know little about the impact of gender roles on women's employment or the factors—economic, regional, or personal—that affected women's working lives. In the pre-famine period it seems clear that a woman's domestic contribution was not confined to cooking, cleaning, and child-rearing alone; women also made a vital contribution to the family economy by working alongside men. Mary Cullen has estimated that what labourers' wives' earned from spinning—and, when times were really difficult, begging—accounted for at least 15 per cent of the families' income and this could rise to 35 per cent at times.[36]

The role of women in the textile trades has received some relatively substantial treat-ment. Marilyn Cohen, in a 'micro-history' of the parish of Tullylish, surveys the devel-opment of the linen industry over two centuries, in part by exploring the intersections between gender and class. The extent of women's employment in the sewing trades and the links between outwork and homework with women's domestic work, social and domestic organization, and migration have been broadly explored.[37] The strengths of these works lie in the fact that they are regionally based, charting the changing relation-ships between family members and the world of paid work. They acknowledge the vari-ety of employment opportunities that went into family survival and reveal new insights into the cultural understanding of work and gender that operated in the sewing and textile industries.

Joanna Bourke has argued that women in post-famine Ireland voluntarily withdrew from the paid workforce to return to the household.[38] Bourke attributes the decline in women's employment to a boom in the rural economy that allowed women to opt out of paid work in favour of unpaid domestic duties within the family. Women, she argues, thus made a choice to return to domestic work. The idea that this was a choice or a strategy on the part of women, however, is difficult to sustain in light of the fact that employment opportunities for women were declining and emigration was a substantial feature of the life cycle of young Irish women by the end of the century. The number of women in employment fell steadily from 29 per cent in 1861 to 19.5 per cent by 1911.[39] Bourke's various studies concentrate on the period between 1890 and 1914 and so we get little sense of the development of women's attitudes to, or their participation in work, prior to 1890. However, Bourke's research is especially strong in revealing the vital role of women in household agriculture, particularly through poultry rearing. She also shows how the spread of creameries affected women's role in dairying. This was an example of the way in which the introduction of technology often resulted in women workers being displaced by men. The co-operative movement, which was responsible for encouraging creameries, attempted, without success, to encourage women to organize poultry rearing on a co-operative rather than on an individual basis. It was also the case that most of the efficiency schemes, like those advocated by the co-operative movement, tended to transfer managerial power to the male members of the family or to male organizers. Women objected to selling eggs to creameries because the money was added to the milk account, which was paid to the man, rather than coming directly to the woman.[40]

There were other women who did not engage in formally recognized employment and who suffered the brunt of society's odium by being classified as 'outcasts'. First among the 'outcasts' were prostitutes, who obviously caused moral outrage. Prostitution can be looked upon as an occupation that gave a number of women the means of securing economic survival in a society that provided them with few other opportunities. It is impossible to tell how many women engaged in this occupation in either the nineteenth or twentieth centuries, though thousands were arrested for soliciting or on vagrancy charges.[41] How these women were treated by society and how prostitution became politicized in twentieth-century Ireland by both nationalists and suffragists, and later by Irish politicians, has been the focus of some recent attention. What has become evident is that by the twentieth century women were seen as central to understanding how immorality could 'harm' society. There was a strong condemnation of unmarried motherhood and increasing legislation to curtail any expression of sexuality and to curb the consumption of sexuality. The policing of sexual activity was to become a feature of Irish life for much of the twentieth century and, allied as it was with familial and community surveillance, exerted its greatest force on women.

One way in which Irish society sought to deal with 'outcast' women was to create an institutionalized space where they could be kept from interaction with the public. One such institution, the Magdalen Asylum, has received considerable publicity and some scholarly attention in recent years. Magdalen asylums were so named after the sinner Mary Magdalene, follower of Jesus, and a woman who repented her sinful life.

The first Magdalen asylum was established in Ireland in 1765; by the mid nineteenth century at least forty such establishments had existed in the country. Catholic female religious congregations ran the majority of Magdalen asylums that survived into the twentieth century. Originally these asylums were intended to care for and protect 'fallen' women, women who worked as prostitutes or who were in danger of doing so. All of the Protestant-run homes had either closed or cared for unmarried mothers by the early twentieth century. Asylums managed by Catholic nuns continued to take in prostitutes, unmarried mothers, or women who had been convicted of criminal acts until at least the 1960s. Many of these women stayed for long periods of time in these institutions and when the last Magdalen asylum closed in 1996 the remaining inmates were placed in sheltered accommodation. Life within these institutions was harsh and the women engaged, without payment, in laundry work to ensure the financial viability of the institution. The current popular image of these institutions, advanced most strongly by Peter Mullan's 2003 film, *The Magdalene Sisters*, is that they were inhuman institutions of confinement. However, from their inception until at least the first decade of the twentieth century these institutions were 'flexible' ones, which the majority of inmates entered and left voluntarily. With the harsher moral climate of independent Ireland from the 1920s these institutions appear to have become much less accommodating to women leaving.[42]

Unmarried motherhood was as problematic in Ireland as it was in most other European countries. Reflecting badly on the 'moral character' of the woman, unmarried motherhood carried a stigma that was almost impossible to shake. An unmarried mother's child was more likely than a legitimate child to die in infanthood; the mother, once her status was known, found it difficult, if not impossible, to find respectable employment and was often shunned by her family. As an issue unmarried motherhood had become firmly problematized in Ireland by the end of the nineteenth century. Representing possible immorality, a drain on public finances, and someone in need not only of rescue, but also of institutionalization, the unmarried mother had become, by the foundation of the Irish Free State in 1922, a symbol of unacceptable sexual activity and a problem that had the potential to blight the reputation not only of the family but of the nation. The poor law, introduced into Ireland in 1838, was the first comprehensive relief system made available to the poor of the country.[43] Workhouses, wherein people sought relief, became a magnet for the destitute and among these were many unmarried mothers. From the beginnings of the workhouse system unmarried mothers, and especially their 'bastard' children, as well as other outcast women such as prostitutes, were believed to be a considerable problem for both the management and financial health of these institutions. Mother and baby homes were established by philanthropists from the late nineteenth century and similar institutions were formed by Catholic nuns from the 1920s. As Shephard has shown, the Legion of Mary played a significant role in the care of unmarried mothers in Belfast in the mid-twentieth century.[44] Despite the variety of establishments available to unmarried mothers, many women eschewed all such provision and made their own arrangements. Some were to find their way to England. Reports available from the early 1920s onwards indicate the concern of English and Scottish charitable organizations with the numbers of Irish women utilizing their services. These women became known as PFIs (Pregnant from Ireland). Attempts were made as early as the 1930s to repatriate these women to Ireland and this was still being carried out in the 1970s. The introduction of the 1967 Abortion Act in England was to bring a new anxiety to those Catholic agencies concerned with Irish unmarried mothers travelling to England.[45] Now the fear was that such women were availing themselves of this new service.[46]

Allied to the problem of unmarried motherhood was that of infanticide, a subject that has now gained the serious attention of historians of Ireland. Recent studies reveal the factors that led to this crime, which included the stigma of illegitimacy, the shame of unmarried motherhood, and the practical problems of financially supporting illegitimate children. Attitudes to those who committed infanticide changed over the period and the crime itself, while often punished by execution in the eighteenth century, and remaining a capital offence until 1949, saw perpetrators dealt with more leniently from the nineteenth century. Studies of infanticide also reveal how the courts system and medical practitioners sought to minimize sentences in these cases, arguing for medical impairment, or other circumstances to evoke sympathy for the accused. Such cases reveal the extent of illicit sexual activity outside marriage and can also tell us much about family relationships and the importance of 'gossip' in shaping and controlling women's sexual behaviour.[47]

Despite the numbers of Irish who migrated from Ireland there is still no substantial study of Irish women in nineteenth-century Britain. Women migrants have also tended to be marginalized in important studies of Irish migration to America in the last century. There is still no agreement among historians on which motives were most important in encouraging women to migrate. Was it a lack of employment opportunities, poor marriage prospects, an expectation within the family that emigration was inevitable? Were Irish women knowingly prepared for emigration through the educational system? A number of the 'pull' factors associated with women's emigration, such as the wish to marry, have been recently queried. Much detailed archival and statistical work needs to be completed before some of these questions can be adequately answered. We know something of the successes and also of the tribulations of some emigrant women. But the experiences of Irish women in nineteenth-century Britain have still to be systematically examined. Emigration offered women opportunities and disappointments and held out all kinds of promises for a fulfilling life, just as entering a convent did for many women in nineteenth–century Ireland.

In the early nineteenth century women's political activism took a number of forms. Women were politicized through their engagement with O'Connellite politics and played an active role in the Catholic Association.[48] The Young Irelanders of the 1840s, like many other politically motivated groups, thought in terms of gender-specific roles for women. For many nationalists women's place was deemed to be in the home. However, women played a role in nationalist politics, especially through their literary output. Women wrote numerous ballads that appeared in the Young Ireland paper *The Nation*; Jane Elgee, for instance, wrote extensively for the paper.[49] Ellen O'Leary and Fanny Parnell contributed poetry to the *Irish People*, the newspaper of the Fenian movement.[50] Other women formed their own newspapers; Anna Johnston and Alice Milligan, for example, founded the weekly journal the *Shan Van Vocht* (The Poor Old Woman), which ran from 1896 to 1899. This paper focused its support particularly on the commemoration of the 1798 rebellion.[51] Women also had a symbolic role in Irish nationalism. Ireland was long represented as a woman in Irish songs and ballads. But not all nationalist women accepted the limited symbolic constraints imposed on them by male-run organizations. Women did involve themselves in the practical aspects of revolutionary organizations. For example, when the male Young Irelanders were arrested or on the run Anne Elgee and Margaret Callan virtually ran *The Nation* newspaper in the summer of 1848. The Fenian Sisterhood was formed in 1865 as an auxiliary to the Fenian Brotherhood. Its principal function was in fundraising, prisoner support, and social organization. Women were also used to carry mail and according to one informer in 1865 all Fenian correspondence between the United States and Ireland was sent through the Sisterhood.[52] The kind of work carried through by the Fenian Sisterhood was to be echoed in the work of the Ladies' Land League.

The Land War and the formation of the Ladies' Land League, established in New York in October 1880 for the purpose of collecting funds for Davitt's Land League, provided a significant opportunity for women to become involved in national politics. On 31 January 1881, Anna Parnell presided over the first official meeting of the Ladies' Land League in Dublin. From that time to its formal dissolution on 10 August 1882, the women of the League raised funds, oversaw the rehousing of evicted tenants, and took a very visible role in the public and political life of the country. Much of the attention devoted to the Ladies' Land League focuses on Anna Parnell and unfortunately we have as yet little information on how this League operated in the various counties. It does appear, however, that the leadership within the branches was confined to the middle classes but it is also clear that peasant women did play some role in protests organized by the League.

Feminist activism remained a strong strand in women's political engagement in the nineteenth century and education was a major preoccupation of these activist women. Before the 1830s, the range of education available to girls in Ireland, as in other European countries, was haphazard. Some were educated in mixed pay-schools where the emphasis was on reading, writing, and arithmetic. The introduction of the national school system of education in 1831 eventually opened up education to the majority of children in the country. The curriculum drawn up for the national schools was strongly gendered with emphasis being placed on the acquirement of domestic skills for girls, and they were expected also to learn knitting and sewing. While there were special subjects for girls there were also special readers for them. The Commissioners of National Education believed that the education of girls was exclusively to prepare them for their domestic role within the home. Their textbooks emphasized dairy management, laundry work, the duties of female servants, the care of the sick and so on.[53]

Only a small proportion of the population had access to secondary education in the nineteenth century. Nuns led the way in catering to the needs of the emerging Catholic middle classes who wanted their daughters educated. The kind of education available in these schools laid stress on the 'accomplishments'; while subjects such as arithmetic, French, Italian, and history formed part of the curriculum, girls were also taught music, singing, and drawing. While convents provided the most extensive secondary education available, it was women from Protestant backgrounds who fought for improvements in the education available for middle-class girls. Female activists had to fight to have girls included in the benefits of the Intermediate Education Act and they also had to fight for access to university education. O'Connor argues that the introduction of the Intermediate Education (Ireland) Act of 1878 'revolutionized' girls' secondary education. It was religious as well as academic rivalry that increased the numbers of females studying at second and third level. Catholic middle-class parents urged for changes to the education their daughters were receiving in the convent schools. Competition among lay and convent schools forced convent schools to meet the new demands.[54] Again it was women of Protestant and nonconformist backgrounds who led the campaign for access to universities in Ireland.[55] Many activists argued that education would make women better wives and mothers, and enable them to fulfil their social and moral duties better. But in effect it was these newly educated middle-class women who were to be an important shaping force in early twentieth-century Ireland.

The demand for suffrage was the principal means whereby women fought for political involvement on the same terms as men in the late nineteenth and early twentieth centuries. A sizable majority of those women who originated the suffrage campaign in Ireland had activist roots in various philanthropic organizations: people like Isabella Tod, who established the first suffrage society in the north of Ireland in 1872 a number of years before Anna and Thomas Haslam organized a similar society in Dublin.[56] The methods used by members of these societies were 'genteel'. Drawing-room meetings, petitions, letters, etc. were the means preferred to lobby politicians or win public favour. It was not until the establishment of the Irish Women's Franchise League in 1908 that more vigorous or militant methods were entertained. Hanna Sheehy-Skeffington and Margaret Cousins were instrumental in setting up this organization that in 1913 instituted a 'strenuous policy of heckling', breaking windows, and raising false fire alarms. Some of their members suffered imprisonment and brought militancy into the prison system. They brought to Ireland a tool that was, as Murphy notes, to 'become synonymous with Irish political imprisonment from [Thomas] Ashe to Bobby Sands: the hunger strike'.[57] While Catholic women were active in the suffrage campaign it was not until 1916 that the first Catholic suffrage organization was founded, named the Irish Catholic Women's Suffrage Association. It augmented the numerous other national and local societies that existed by this time.

There were other campaigns that claimed the support of women. By the end of the nineteenth century, through vigorous campaigning, mainly by women involved in the suffrage movement, success in ensuring their places as Poor Law Guardians was guaranteed with the passage of the Irish Women Guardians Act in 1896. In 1897 there were thirteen women PLGs; in 1898 there were twenty-two and by 1899 over eighty had been elected. From 1898 women could vote in municipal elections and sit as councillors. By 1899 four women had been returned as urban district councillors and more than twenty-six as rural district councillors.[58]

From 1886 there was a unionist campaign against Home Rule. The chief instigator of this campaign among women was Isabella Tod. In 1886 she herself campaigned vigorously in Ireland and England against Gladstone's Home Rule proposals. In 1893 a memorial against Home Rule with 103 000 female signatures was addressed to Queen Victoria. Another petition sent at the same time from Ulster women had over 145 000 signatures. The ladies committee of the Irish Unionist Alliance insisted that their role in preventing the passage of Home Rule was as significant as that of the men. On 23 January 1911, the Ulster Women's Unionist Council was established and soon developed into a strong, active, and democratically elected organization. It bound unionist women together in one common aim, the resistance to Home Rule for Ulster. During the first month of its existence over 4000 women joined the west Belfast branch and within a year the UWUC's membership numbered between 40 000 and 50 000. In 1911, in response to the *Ne Temere* decree of Pope Pius X, (which declared that marriages between Catholics and Protestants were null and void unless solemnized according to the rites of the Catholic Church) the UWUC prepared a petition to the House of Commons. Their opposition to this decree can be easily explained as Ulster Unionists saw it as a clear example of the fate that would befall Protestants under a Home Rule Parliament. The Ulster Covenant on 28 September 1912 was signed by 234 000 women.[59]

The turn of the twentieth century also saw the development of different kinds of organizations and movements, many of which were to add to the nationalist cause. The Gaelic League was the first male organization to offer membership on the same terms to women. The establishment of Inghinidhe na hÉireann (Daughters of Ireland) in 1900 was significant as it was the first autonomous nationalist women's organization which supported both nationalist and feminist principles. Later, in 1914, it merged with Cumann na mBan (Women's Council). While religious affiliation made it impossible for philanthropic women to work together in the nineteenth century, political developments and the growth of a separatist movement in the early twentieth century divided women just as religion had in the nineteenth century. Disagreements arose eventually amongst nationalist, unionist, and suffragist women, not so much on whether women should be granted the vote but on how and when the vote should be achieved. Constance Markievicz and Mary MacSwiney were two nationalist women who had their roots in the suffrage movement. For MacSwiney, republicanism came before feminism. In her 1921 tour of the United States, she remarked that 'a feminist movement is not necessary in our country. The women of Ireland are on full equality with the men and are comrades in everything.'[60]

In Ireland the campaign for the suffrage became more popular and more controversial in the twentieth century, in contrast to the rather rarefied nature of the nineteenth-century debate. The movement, which was always small, tended to be overshadowed by the nationalist and labour questions. Irish women played an active role in the fight for Irish independence through their involvement in the Easter Rising of 1916, the War of Independence 1919–1921, and the Civil War 1922–1923. The opening of the

Bureau of Military History records has allowed historians access to the detail of men's and women's involvement in separatist organizations in the period before 1923 and has enormous potential to provide us with a gendered history of the period.[61] Some interesting work on the performative aspects of gender suggests how subversive women's role was in 1916. For instance, in order to take up arms and fight alongside the men Weiman notes that 'the women at the Royal College of Surgeons reportedly changed from skirts to trousers…in order to hold a gun they had to wear pants'.[62] This type of transgression caused confusion, particularly amongst men, with one noting he could have nothing to do with the Volunteers as he had a 'horror of ladies being in uniform and masquerading as soldiers'.[63]

The winning of the vote was generally perceived as the greatest triumph of the equal-rights feminists: the franchise, it was believed, would demolish nineteenth-century ideas, by making women into autonomous political actors. Moreover, the liberal belief persisted that enfranchisement and parliamentary representation would provide the key to equality and an end to the discrimination experienced by all women. Equal citizenship had been guaranteed to Irish men and women under the Proclamation of 1916. Irish women over the age of thirty who filled particular property requirements won the right to the parliamentary franchise in 1918. Active lobbying, particularly by women, saw all Irish citizens over the age of twenty-one enfranchised under the Irish Free State Constitution enacted in June 1922. In the period 1918 to 1922 Irish women enjoyed limited but significant success at the polls. This is noteworthy considering the widespread opposition to women's suffrage prior to the 1918 Act. The Irish Parliamentary Party and the Unionist Party indeed opposed the extension of the act to Ireland but Sinn Féin saw women voters as a crucial factor in the 1918 election. The well-documented case of Constance Markievicz has tended to obscure other successes. Winifred Carney, who also stood for election in 1918, did not have the same spectacular success in Belfast but she went on to become prominent in trade union and Northern Irish labour politics. Six women were among the 128 deputies returned unopposed to the Second Dáil in the May 1921 election held under the Government of Ireland Act which allowed for parliaments in Dublin and Belfast. All of these women—Kathleen Clarke, Dr Ada English, Mary McSwiney, Constance Markievicz, Kathleen O'Callaghan, and Margaret Pearse— were intimately connected with the struggle for independence. As Knirck notes, these women became the guardians of memory, their authority to speak for the dead derived from their suffering.[64] All of these women opposed the Anglo-Irish treaty and within a short space these 'brave girls' of the War of Independence had been transformed into what P..S..O'Hegarty called the 'implacable and irrational upholders of death and destruction'.[65] There is no doubt that women lost formal political influence after 1922 and in some part that may be due to women T.D.s' (Teachta Dála: Member of the Irish Parliament) response to the treaty. From 1922 it became increasingly difficult for women to be elected to the Dáil and from 1922 between two and five were elected until the breakthrough of the 1981 general election that saw eleven women win seats.

Wartime conditions, whether in World Wars or nationalist and unionist struggles in the twentieth century, had the potential to shift accepted views on women's roles in society. In World War I, Irish women joined nursing organizations such as the Voluntary Aid Detachments (VADs), and aided the war effort by joining the Women's Legion, founded by Edith, seventh Marchioness of Londonderry. Efforts to establish a Women's Land Army in Northern Ireland during the Second World War challenged accepted views on appropriate farm work for women, believed to be butter and egg production. The outbreak of 'the troubles' in Northern Ireland in the late 1960s saw female republicans challenge the place of women within the Provisional republican movement, and a number sought to place feminist issues on the republican agenda.[66]

It would appear that Irish women were well placed to benefit from the roles they had played in the fight for Irish independence. However, women did not retain a high profile in the political affairs of the country and from the foundation of the Free State women's political, economic, and social rights were gradually eroded. The implementation of restrictive legislation in the economic and political spheres found echoes in the social sphere. For instance, divorce became illegal from 1925. The 1927 Juries Act made it very difficult for women to sit as jurors. The 1929 Censorship of Publications Bill prohibited the advertisement of contraceptives. Other legislation also had repercussions on how women could live their lives in Ireland. There was a marriage bar in place and women were subjected to lower salary and pension rates to men. The 1936 Conditions of Employment Act allowed the Minister for Industry and Commerce to control the employment of women in industry. The view that women should be wives and mothers and not workers was a powerful force in Irish society. Such a view rarely took on board the fact that many women had to work in order to help or fully support their families. The problems faced by women workers, the personal satisfaction that women gained from work, their guilt at leaving children to 'minders', their desire to have some financial independence from their husbands, their attempts to develop careers, or to progress at work, or even their desire to stay at home and not, through financial necessity, be forced to enter the world of paid work, are factors that complicate how women related to the job market.[67] The 1937 Constitution, though challenged by strong feminist objections, defined women's primary roles as wife and mother. But women did remain politically active, with the Joint Committee of Women's Societies and Social Workers (1935) fighting consistently for the advance of women's citizenship rights. The Irish Housewives Association (1942) helped to shape government policy in a number of areas, especially in relation to consumerism and women's rights.[68] The IHA was instrumental in establishing, for instance, the Council for the Status of Women (1973). Throughout the period from the 1920s women remained active in republican politics and communist organizations and were also immersed in radical activism. Women's activism, for example, in Northern Ireland from the 1960s saw them engage in civil disobedience, street protest, and militant action, as well as organize a range of pressure groups and support organizations among nationalists, republicans, unionists, and loyalists.[69]

Clear details the hard physicality of home life in Ireland from the 1920s to the 1960s and argues that middle-class feminist activists were largely irrelevant to poor working women.[70] However, those feminist activists did help to change society through their campaigning, their impact on government, and their relentless pursuit of equality. After the stagnation of the 1940s and 1950s change became evident in the 1960s. Changing attitudes to the role of women evolved over the period, assisted by a complex range of factors. New media such as television helped to create a more open society. The Irish economy began to thrive and by the 1970s the Women's Liberation movement was beginning to have an impact.[71] An allowance for unmarried mothers was introduced in 1973; in the same year the marriage bar was removed for women in the civil service, local authorities, and health boards. In 1976 a Juries act was passed which deemed that the conditional exclusion of women from jury lists was unconstitutional. The first Rape Crisis Centre opened in Dublin in 1974, the same year that equal pay legislation was introduced. Ireland's entry into the European Union in 1973 assisted in the development of legislation that advanced women's position in society. The issues of divorce and abortion were debated divisively from the 1980s, with divorce legislation finally being adopted in 1996. Ireland's first woman president, Mary Robinson, was elected in 1990.

Irish women's history has extended and expanded our understanding of Irish history more generally. It has been most influential in opening up Irish social history where subjects such as sexuality, motherhood, infanticide, welfare, emigration, and institutional care have now become a part of our investigated history, which problematizes our understanding of the nature of Irish society in the past and adds to the complexity of our history. There are young scholars developing new projects on women's criminality, family life in Ireland, and marriage, among other subjects.[72] Biographies of women continue to be written, a genre that sells especially well for publishers.[73] There are still a myriad of subjects that need to be explored relating to Irish women's history: we still know little, for instance, of women who ran their own businesses, of the place of servants, whether in the 'Big House' or as farm or domestics in rural and urban Ireland. The lives of widows and single women in Ireland remain hidden. We know relatively little of the day-to-day life of women of the aristocracy in Ireland. We have not yet had studies of the aspirations or preoccupations of Irish women over the centuries, whether social, political, economic, or personal, the detail of their daily struggles, their small triumphs, their tragedies, their solace and their happiness. But given the strong interest among scholars in Irish women's history, I have no doubt but that these studies will emerge.

NOTES

1. Margaret Mac Curtain and Donnchadh O'Corráin (eds), *Women in Irish Society: The Historical Dimension* (Dublin, 1978).
2. See, for instance, Diarmaid Ferriter, *The Transformation of Ireland, 1900–2000* (London, 2004) and R.F. Foster, *Luck and the Irish: A Brief History of Change, 1970–2000* (London, 2007). The space allocated for this chapter does not allow me to engage with the vast cultural heritage that women have contributed to Irish history and society as artists, writers, scholars, actors, dancers, and musicians.
3. See, for example, Maryann Gialanela Valiulis (ed), *Gender and Power in Irish History* (Dublin, 2008).

4. These included historians such as Gerda Lerner and Nathalie Zemon Davis. See Ann Curthoys and John Docker, *Is History Fiction?* (Sydney, 2006), 154–79, for a general overview of the rise of women's history and Sue Morgan (ed), *The Feminist History Reader* (London, 2006), for a collection of significant writings in the field.

5. Joan W. Scott, 'Gender: A Useful Category of Historical Analysis' in Joan Wallach Scott, *Gender and the Politics of History* (New York, 1988).

6. Judith Butler, *Gender Trouble: Feminism and the Subversion of Identity* (New York, 1990).

7. Lisa M. Bitel, *Land of Women: Tales of Sex and Gender from Early Ireland* (Ithaca, N.Y., 1998).

8. Máirín Ni Dhonnachadha, 'Mary, Eve, and the Church, *c*. 600–1800' in Angela Bourke et al (eds), *The Field Day Anthology of Irish Writing: Irish Women's Writing and Traditions*, iv, (Cork, 2002), 45–57.

9. Cited in Mary McAuliffe, 'The lady in the tower: the social and political role of women in tower houses' in C.E. Meek and M.K. Simms (eds), *'The Fragility of Her Sex'?: Medieval Irish Women in Their European Context* (Dublin, 1996), 159.

10. Cited in Elizabeth McKenna, 'Was there a role for women in medieval Ireland?: Lady Margaret Butler and Lady Eleanor MacCarthy', in Meek and Simms, *'The Fragility of Her Sex'?*, 165.

11. Cited in J.C. Appleby, 'Women and piracy in Ireland; from Grainne O'Malley to Anne Bonny' in Mary O'Dowd and Margaret Mac Curtain (eds), *Women in Early Modern Ireland* (Edinburgh, 1991), 57.

12. Bernadette Williams, '"She was usually placed with the great men and leaders of the land in the public assemblies"—Alice Kyteler: a woman of considerable power' in Christine Meek (ed), *Women in Renaissance & Early Modern Europe* (Dublin, 2000), 67–83.

13. Mary O'Dowd, 'Property, work and home: women and the economy, *c*. 1170–1850' in Bourke, *Field Day Anthology*, 467.

14. Cited in Elizabeth McKenna, 'Was there a role for women in medieval Ireland?: Lady Margaret Butler and Lady Eleanor MacCarthy', in Meek and Simms, *'The Fragility of Her Sex?'*, 164.

15. Bernadette Cunningham, 'Women and Gaelic literature, 1500–1800' in Mary O'Dowd and Margaret Mac Curtain (eds), *Women in Early Modern Ireland* (Edinburgh, 1991), 147–59.

16. Mary O'Dowd, 'Property, work and home: women and the economy, *c*. 1170–1850' in Bourke, *Field Day Anthology*, 464–71. Mary O'Dowd, *A History of Women in Ireland, 1500–1800* (Harlow, 2005).

17. See Gillian Kenny, *Anglo-Irish and Gaelic Women in Ireland c. 1170–1540* (Dublin, 2007).

18. O'Dowd, *History of Women in Ireland*, 9–42, 73–113.

19. O'Dowd, *History of Women in Ireland*, 86–9.

20. Catherine Cox, 'Women and business in eighteenth-century Dublin: a case study' in Bernadette Whelan (ed), *Women and Paid Work in Ireland, 1500–1930* (Dublin, 2000), 30–43.

21. David Fleming, 'Public attitudes to prostitution in eighteenth-century Ireland', *Irish Economic and Social History*, 31 (2005), 1–18; Maria Luddy, *Prostitution and Irish Society, 1800–1940* (Cambridge, 2007).

22. Deborah Wilson, *Women, Marriage and Property in Wealthy Landed Families in Ireland, 1750–1850* (Manchester, 2009).

23. A.P.W. Malcomson, *The Pursuit of an Heiress: Aristocratic Marriage in Ireland* (Belfast, 2006); Toby Barnard, *The Abduction of a Limerick Heiress: Social and Political Relations in Mid-Eighteenth Century Ireland* (Dublin, 1998).

24. Marie-Louise Legg (ed), *The Synge Letters: Bishop Edward Synge to His Daughter Alicia, Roscommon to Dublin 1746-1752* (Dublin, 1996) and Jean Agnew and Maria Luddy (eds), *The Drennan-McTier Letters, 1776-1807*, 3 vols (Dublin, 1998-2001).

25. O'Dowd, *A History of Women in Ireland*, 43.

26. O'Dowd, *A History of Women in Ireland*, 47.

27. Cited in O'Dowd, *A History of Women in Ireland*, 52.

28. O'Dowd, *A History of Women in Ireland*, 55-61.

29. Daire Keogh and Nicholas Furlong (eds), *The Women of '98* (Dublin, 1998); John D. Beatty (ed), *Protestant Women's Narratives of the Irish Rebellion of 1798* (Dublin, 2001).

30. L. M. Cullen, *The Emergence of Modern Ireland: 1600-1900*, (Dublin, 1981).

31. Tony Fahey, 'Nuns and the Catholic church in Ireland in the nineteenth century', in Mary Cullen (ed), *Girls Don't Do Honours: Irish Women in Education in the 19th and 20th Centuries* (Dublin, 1987), 7.

32. Mary Peckham Magray, *The Transforming Power of the Nuns: Women, Religion & Cultural Change in Ireland, 1750-1900* (New York, 1998), 9.

33. Caitriona Clear, *Nuns in Nineteenth-Century Ireland* (Dublin, 1987).

34. Magray, *The Transforming Power of the Nuns*.

35. For a valuable study of Irish women who joined religious communities in the twentieth century, see Yvonne McKenna, *Made Holy: Irish Women Religious at Home and Abroad* (Dublin, 2006).

36. Mary Cullen, 'Breadwinners and Providers: Women in the Household Economy of Labouring Families, 1835-36' in Luddy and Murphy, *Women Surviving*, 98-111.

37. See, for instance Brenda Collins, 'The organisation of sewing outwork in late nineteenth-century Ulster' in Maxine Berg (ed), *Markets and Manufacture in Early Industrial Europe* (London, 1991), 139-56; Marilyn Cohen, *Linen, Family, and Community in Tullylish, County Down, 1690-1914* (Dublin, 1997); Kevin James, *Handloom Weavers in Ulster's Linen Industry, 1815-1914* (Dublin, 2007); Margaret Neill, 'Homeworking in Ulster' in Holmes and Urquhart, *Coming Into The Light*, 2-32.

38. Joanna Bourke, *Husbandry to Housewifery: Women, Economic Change and Housewifery in Ireland 1890-1914* (Oxford, 1993).

39. Mary Daly, *Women and Work in Ireland* (Dundalk, 1997), 19-24.

40. Bourke, *Husbandry to Housewifery*, passim.

41. Luddy, *Prostitution and Irish Society*.

42. For studies of Magdalen asylums, see F. Finnegan, *Do Penance or Perish: Magdalen Asylums in Ireland* (Piltown, Co. Kilkenny, 2001); L. McCormick, *Regulating Sexuality. Women in Twentieth-Century Northern Ireland* (Manchester, 2009); J.M. Smith, *Ireland's Magdalen Laundries and the Nation's Architecture of Containment* (Notre Dame, 2007); Luddy, *Prostitution and Irish Society*, chapter 3.

43. Virginia Crossman, 'Viewing women, family and sexuality through the prism of the Irish poor law', *Women's History Review*, 15 (September 2006), 541-50.

44. Christopher Shepard, 'The Legion of Mary, unmarried mothers and the expansion of the welfare state in Northern Ireland, 1940-55' in S. O'Connor and C. Shepard (eds), *Women, Social and Cultural Change in Twentieth-Century Ireland: Dissenting Voices* (Newcastle, 2008), 124-47.

45. The number of women citing Irish addresses in British abortion clinics rose from 64 in 1968 to 577 in 1971.

46. For works on unmarried mothers, see: L. Earner-Byrne, *Mother and Child: Maternity and Child Welfare in Dublin, 1922-60* (Manchester, 2007); idem., 'The Boat to

England: an Analysis of the Official Reactions to the Emigration of Single Expectant Irishwomen to Britain, 1922–1972', *Irish Economic and Social History*, 30 (2003), 2–70. M. Luddy, 'Moral Rescue and Unmarried Mothers in Ireland in the 1920s', *Women's Studies: An Interdisciplinary Journal*, 30, 6 (2001), 809–813. P.M. Garrett, 'The Abnormal Flight: Migration and Repatriation of Irish Unmarried Mothers', *Social History*, 25, (2000), 330–43; idem., *Social Work and Irish People in Britain: Historical and Contemporary Responses to Irish Children and Families* (Bristol, 2004); J. Redmond, 'In the family way and away from the family: examining the evidence for Irish unmarried mothers in Britain, 1920s-1940s', in E. Farrell (ed), *'She Said She Was in the Family Way': Pregnancy and Infancy in Modern Ireland* (London, 2012), 163–85.

47. See J. Kelly, 'Infanticide in 18th-century Ireland', *Irish Economic and Social History*, 19 (1992), 5–26; idem., 'Responding to infanticide in Ireland, 1680–1820' in Farrell (ed), *'She Said She Was in the Family Way'*, 189–203; C. Rattigan, *'What else Could I do?': Single Motherhood and Infanticide, Ireland 1900–1950* (Dublin, 2012); E. Farrell, 'A very immoral establishment': the crime of infanticide and class status in Ireland, 1850–1900', in Farrell (ed), *'She Said She Was in the Family Way'*, 205–222; idem., *Infanticide in the Irish Crown Files at Assizes 1883–1900* (Dublin, 2012).

48. Mary O'Dowd, 'O'Connell and the lady patriots: women and O'Connellite politics, 1823–1845' in Allan Blackstock and Eoin Magennis (eds), *Politics and Political Culture in Britain and Ireland, 1750–1850: Essays in Tribute to Peter Jupp* (Belfast, 2007), 283–303.

49. She wrote under the pen name of Speranza and was the mother of Oscar Wilde. See Karen Sasha Anthony Tipper, *A Critical Biography of Lady Jane Wilde, 1821?-1896, Irish Revolutionist, Humanist, Scholar and Poet* (Lampeter, Wales, 2002).

50. Rose Novak, 'Ellen O'Leary: a bold Fenian poet', *Éire-Ireland*, 43: 3 and 4 (Fall/Winter 2008), 59–84.

51. Karen Steele, *Women, Press and Politics During the Irish Revival* (New York, 2007).

52. Fenian Papers: File A40, National Archives of Ireland, Dublin.

53. Deirdre Raftery and Susan M. Parkes, *Female Education in Ireland, 1700–1900* (Dublin, 2007).

54. Anne V. O'Connor, 'Influences Affecting Girls' Secondary Education in Ireland, 1860–1910', *Archivium Hibernicum*, 141, (1986), 83–98.

55. Judith Harford, *The Opening of University Education to Women in Ireland* (Dublin, 2008).

56. Carmel Quinlan, *Genteel Revolutionaries: Anna and Thomas Haslam and the Irish Women's Movement* (Cork, 2002).

57. William Murphy, 'Suffragettes and the transformation of political imprisonment in Ireland, 1912–1914' in Louise Ryan and Margaret Ward (eds), *Irish Women and the Vote: Becoming Citizens* (Dublin, 2007), 130.

58. See Mary Cullen, 'Women, emancipation and politics' in J.R. Hill (ed), *A New History of Ireland VII, Ireland 1921–1984* (Oxford, 2003), 826–91.

59. Diane Urquhart, *Women in Ulster Politics, 1890–1940* (Dublin, 2000). Rachel Ward, *Women, Unionism and Loyalism in Northern Ireland: From 'Tea-Makers' to Political Activists* (Dublin, 2006).

60. Charlotte H. Fallon, *Soul of Fire: a Biography of Mary MacSwiney*, (Cork, 1986), 69.

61. Eve Morrison, 'The Bureau of Military History and female republican activism, 1913–1923' in Valiulis, *Gender and Power*, 59–83. The Bureau of Military History Witness Statements are now available online at http://www.bureauofmilitaryhistory.ie.

62. Lisa Weiman, ' "Doing my bit for Ireland": transgressing gender in the Easter Rising', *Eire-Ireland*, 39, 3 and 4 (Fall/Winter 2004), 228–49.

63. Very Rev. Fr. T. O'Donoghue, Bureau of Military History, Witness Statement 1666, National Archives of Ireland, Dublin.

64. Jason Knirck, *Women of the Dáil: Gender, Republicanism and the Anglo-Irish Treaty* (Dublin, 2006).

65. P.S. O'Hegarty, *The Victory of Sinn Féin* (Dublin, 1924), 104.

66. For work on these various subjects, see the following essay collections: G. McIntosh and D. Urquhart (eds), *Irish Women at War: The Twentieth Century* (Dublin, 2010); L. Ryan and M. Ward (eds), *Irish Women and Nationalism: Soldiers, New Women and Wicked Hags* (Dublin, 2004).

67. E. Kiely and M. Leane, *Irish Women at Work 1930–1960: An Oral History* (Dublin, 2012).

68. Hilda Tweedy, *A Link in the Chain: The Story of the Irish Housewives' Association, 1942–1992* (Dublin, 1992).

69. Tara Keenan-Thomson, *Irish Women and Street Politics 1956–1973* (Dublin, 2010); Myrtle Hill, *Women in Ireland: A Century of Change* (Belfast, 2003).

70. Caitriona Clear, *Women of the House: Women's Household Work in Ireland 1922–1961* (Dublin, 2000).

71. See L. Connolly and T. O'Toole, *Documenting Irish Feminisms: The Second Wave* (Dublin, 2005).

72. Forthcoming work by Sarah-Anne Buckley, Elaine Farrell, Diane Urquhart, Maria Luddy, and Mary O'Dowd will address some of these subjects.

73. Among the best of recent biographies is Leeann Lane, *Rosamond Jacob: Third Person Singular* (Dublin, 2010), which situates the life of writer and activist Jacob, firmly within the social and moral worlds of twentieth-century Ireland.

SELECT BIBLIOGRAPHY

Bitel, Lisa M., *Land of Women: Tales of Sex and Gender from Early Ireland* (Ithaca, N.Y., 1998).

Bourke, Angela et al (eds), *The Field Day Anthology of Irish Writing: Irish Women's Writing and Traditions*, iv and v, (Cork, 2002).

Bourke, Joanna, *Husbandry to Housewifery: Women, Economic Change and Housewifery in Ireland 1890–1914* (Oxford, 1993).

Cullen, Mary, 'Women, emancipation and politics' in J.R. Hill (ed), *A New History of Ireland VII, Ireland 1921–1984* (Oxford, 2003).

Cullen-Owens, Rosemary, *A Social History of Women in Ireland, 1870–1970* (Dublin, 2005).

Earner-Byrne, Lindsey, *Mother and Child: Maternity and Child Welfare in Dublin, 1922–60* (Manchester, 2007).

Farrell, Elaine (ed), *'She Said She Was in the Family Way': Pregnancy and Infancy in Modern Ireland* (London, 2012).

Ferriter, Diarmaid, *Occasions of Sin: Sex and Society in Modern Ireland* (London, 2009).

Finnegan, Richard B., and James L. Wiles, *Women and Public Policy in Ireland: A Documentary History* (Dublin, 2005).

Hill, Myrtle, *Women in Ireland: A Century of Change* (Belfast, 2003).

Kiely, Elizabeth and Maire Leane, *Irish Women at Work 1930–1960: An Oral History* (Dublin, 2012).

Luddy, Maria, *Women and Philanthropy in Nineteenth-Century Ireland* (Cambridge, 1995).

Luddy, Maria, *Prostitution and Irish Society, 1800–1940* (Cambridge, 2007).

MacPherson, D. A. J., *Women and the Irish Nation: Gender, Culture and Irish Identity, 1890–1914* (Basingstoke, 2012).

Magray, Mary Peckham, *The Transforming Power of the Nuns: Women, Religion & Cultural Change in Ireland, 1750–1900* (New York, 1998).

Matthews, Ann, *Renegades: Irish Republican Women 1900–1922* (Cork, 2010).

O'Dowd, Mary, *A History of Women in Ireland, 1500–1800* (Harlow, 2005).

Quinlan, Carmel, *Genteel Revolutionaries: Anna and Thomas Haslam and the Irish Women's Movement* (Cork, 2002).

Rattigan, Cliona, *'What Else Could I Do?': Single Motherhood and Infanticide, Ireland 1900–1950* (Dublin, 2012).

Valiulis, Maryann Gialanella (ed), *Gender and Power in Irish History* (Dublin, 2009).

CHAPTER 11

....

IRISH LITERARY CULTURE IN ENGLISH

....

MARGARET KELLEHER

I. INTRODUCTION

FOR much of the twentieth century, the reputation of Irish literary writers (beyond the acknowledged 'greats' of Yeats, Joyce, or Beckett) suffered from their treatment by critics as failed, or partly successful, imitators of literary forms successfully realized in the mainstream English tradition. In the past decade, a contrasting critical tendency has been towards the celebration, and at times the valorization, of Irish writers' innovations in genre, theme, and form. Such reappraisals, supported by significant literary and cultural retrieval projects, in turn have enlivened older debates as to what are the distinctive, common, and enduring features of an 'Irish' literary tradition. An analysis of Irish literary culture from 1550 to the present day, in the specific context of the *Oxford Handbook of Modern Irish History*, offers a welcome opportunity to reassess the relationships between history and literature in the light of recent research. The following discussion will therefore prioritize such issues as: the changing status of literature as a historical source; the emergence of diverse literary genres and their implications for the periodization of Irish literary history; and the complex and contested trajectory of Irish literary historiography.

II. LITERATURE AND POLEMIC: 1550–1690

Recent investigations into the writings of the early modern period (1550–1690) have challenged earlier notions of its literary culture as 'fitful' or lacking substantial aesthetic interest. That a highly populated terrain of literature in English exists between the landmark figures of Edmund Spenser and Jonathan Swift has been convincingly argued by Deana Rankin in her study of seventeenth-century Ireland, which she characterizes as 'a noisy, scribbling world': 'In Ireland, as in England, both pen and sword were at insistent work as successive waves of recent settlers and returning exiles, soldiers and administrators, old hands and new arrivals moved through the country'.[1] Andrew Carpenter's anthology *Verse in English from Tudor and Stuart Ireland* (2003) presents the diversity and range of material which has survived from an age which, he notes, was 'much more accustomed to the sound of verse than our own and one in which verse was regarded as accessible to all, the illiterate and the literate'.[2] This increased interest in literary production has further challenged and complicated the overly schematic categories previously employed with regard to early modern Ireland; as Anne Fogarty has demonstrated, 'complex generic interconnections' exist between texts written by Irish writers from a diversity of ethnic backgrounds, authors writing of Ireland from England, and English travellers, military, settlers, and colonists.[3] Fogarty's attentive readings reveal the lines of affiliation and patronage often subtly present in early modern texts and also the tendency of the more significant of such writings to 'straddle boundaries, whether geographical, artistic, ideological or political'; hence Spenser's *The Faerie Queene* (1596) may be read 'at once as a veiled rendering of the anxieties of the New English planter in late sixteenth-century Ireland and as a product of the charged, self-fashioning aesthetics of the Elizabethan court'.[4]

A welcome trend in such studies, and one with important wider ramifications, is the increased attention to the literariness of writings previously mined for narrowly interpreted historical information. The work of Patricia Coughlan has been especially pioneering in this regard, underlining the importance of investigating the various writings of the early modern period 'in themselves as symbolic representations (as distinct from seeing them as relatively inert and transparently readable pieces of evidence for the views or political positions of various factions)'.[5] Such attention to the fictive and discursive aspects of sixteenth- and seventeenth-century texts from and about Ireland includes analysis of the expressive opportunities provided by specific literary forms, most notably satire, anti-pastoral, tragicomedy, and memoir. Work by Marie-Louise Coolahan and others has elucidated the tropes, language, and rhetorical stances employed by female and male authors in the many testamentary and autobiographical narratives that were produced in the seventeenth century, most especially in the aftermath of conflicts such as the Nine Years' War and the 1641 Rebellion.[6] Such analyses in turn help to illuminate the discursive and ideological potency of eyewitness accounts, depositions, and testimonies as deployed within the highly contested historiography of the early modern period.

Relatedly, the interrelationships of orality and literacy, and of oral, manuscript, and print cultures in early modern Ireland have become an especially rich field of enquiry. Gillespie's *Reading Ireland*, a history of print, reading, and social change in early modern Ireland, is the first in-depth study of the 'world of print as a vantage point from which to observe the shifts in early modern Irish society', deploying in very stimulating ways both the material history of printed commodities and their role in social change.[7] The 2006 publication of *The Irish Book in English 1550–1800*, edited by Gillespie and Andrew

Hadfield in the Oxford History of the Irish Book series, is a landmark in intellectual history of early modern Ireland, with extensive studies of the print trade, collectors, readers, and the impact of print.[8] The existence of this comprehensive history of print culture has in turn enabled a more nuanced history of print's impact on the manuscript traditions of English- and Irish-language literature, a complex and multidirectional process which includes—as Lesa Ní Mhungaile has shown in her work on Charlotte Brooke's *Reliques of Irish Poetry*—instances of borrowing from print by manuscript scribes as late as the early nineteenth century.[9]

III. Irish Writing and the Development of Literary Genres: 1690–1800

For writing from the period 1690–1800, clearer categorizations are possible in generic terms. While the more esteemed and formal genres of poetry, drama, and fiction begin to emerge at this time, their less aesthetically refined predecessors—verse, theatrical performance, and prose writing—are of considerable interest and have been the subject of some fascinating investigations in research published since the late 1990s. In compiling his anthology *Verse in English from Eighteenth-Century Ireland* (1998), Andrew Carpenter unearthed a remarkable quantity of verse material from broadsheets, printed volumes, chapbooks, manuscripts, and newspapers from the eighteenth century.[10] Many of these writings evocatively convey the marginalized voices of the rural and urban poor, through a variety of ballads, elegies, and 'Dublin underworld' poems. Carpenter's findings also reveal a striking number of female authors, including some sixty Irish women who 'published verse under their own names in the eighteenth century' and 'scores of others' who 'composed songs which were printed, anonymously, in chapbooks and broadsheets'.[11]

The retrieval of this literary material has in turn highlighted the extent of linguistic contact in the society of the time, a cultural dynamic with rich and complex implications for an understanding of eighteenth-century social interaction. As evidenced by Carpenter's anthology, the 'cross-pollination of form, syntax and vocabulary between the cultures and languages of eighteenth-century Ireland' includes significant cross-pollination between English and Irish, and also Scots influence on the language of Ulster (notable examples include Ulster-Scots poets Samuel Thomson, James Orr, Hugh Porter, and Olivia Elder). The numerous macaronic or mixed-language songs uncovered by his invaluable research—songs which required a knowledge of English and Irish not only for their performance but also for a full comprehension of their humour and innuendo[12]—further attest to the prevalence of practical bilingualism or some bilingual comprehension during this period. The orthographical and other irregularities in the printing of such texts further suggest that the authors and the compositors who set the type may have had little formal schooling in English, while the purchasers, and future singers, were not expected to be able to read Irish. Consequently, the Irish passages were printed 'as an English speaker would spell them out if he heard them; thus when they are read aloud by someone who can read English, an Irish speaker should be able to understand them as Irish'.[13]

The significance of eighteenth-century Irish theatre in the staging of Irish identity and the multifold conflicts inherent in such a term have been well documented by Chris Morash, Helen Burke, and Christopher Wheatley, among others. Their focus on theatre history, rather than drama, has brought into view the previously neglected importance of performers and the sites of performances in this period. Helen Burke has extensively researched the occurrence of 'riotous performances' in the Irish theatre between 1712 and 1784, events which illustrate both the contested nature of the eighteenth-century Irish theatre and also the 'politically generative' significance of these conflicts.[14] Infamous occasions include the Patriot protests which disrupted the staging of *Tamerlane* at Dublin's Smock Alley in 1712 and the Patriot riots which greeted Thomas Sheridan's restaging of Voltaire's *Mahomet the Imposter* in 1754. With regard to the former, Burke argues that 'the unauthorized stagings of these patriots blurred the boundaries between Irish Protestant and Irish Catholic and opened up a space for the latter subject to speak', while the mid-century stage was, by contrast, the site of 'an intense struggle between Catholic-identified gentry reformers and Protestant-identified populist reformers'.[15]

The relationship between the London and Dublin stages is a central and fascinating aspect of the history of Irish theatre in the eighteenth century. Chris Morash observes that '[t]he same factor that made it so difficult to keep a theatre financially afloat in Dublin—the proximity to London—helped to give the Irish theatre its political edge'. While '[p]lays about liberty in London could be absorbed as platitudinous in any but the most disturbed periods, in Dublin they continually opened up uncomfortable questions about the position of the vast majority of the population whose liberty was so severely curtailed'.[16] The financial lure of London, and the widening gap between it and the Dublin market, led to the departure from Ireland of many successful playwrights, Mary Davys, Arthur Murphy, Frances and Thomas Sheridan, and Hugh Kelly being some examples. These migratory trends compound the difficulties in answering what can be a deceptively simple question: in what meaningful sense can authors such as William Congreve, Richard Steele, Susannah Centlivre, or even Oliver Goldsmith be termed Irish playwrights?[17] While most of these writers (excluding Congreve) were born in Ireland, few spent a significant part of their adult lives in Ireland, fewer engaged directly with Irish subjects in their plays, and all wrote primarily for London audiences. Yet, as Morash (who poses this question most constructively) persuasively argues by way of answer, the performance, publication, and reception-history of their work show that all of these writers 'were part of eighteenth-century Irish theatre culture, extending from the stage of Smock Alley to the booksellers in the streets surrounding the theatre, to the drawing rooms around the country where plays were read'.[18] Critical analyses have thus moved fruitfully away from the more problematic issue of Irishness as a biographical designation to a rich engagement with the history of performance and the material culture of eighteenth-century Irish theatre.

Prose writings from 1690 to 1800 are less easy to demarcate along lines which are familiar to students of literature today. Among the key categories identified by literary critic Ian Ross, who has led recent scholarship in this field, are Enlightenment and Counter Enlightenment writings, biography and memoir, prose fiction, and the suggestive thematic area of 'literary cosmopolitanism' (exemplified for Ross by Oliver Goldsmith), which he suggests may be understood 'as a reaction to the growing interest in *national* literatures within these islands, which encompassed work in English, Irish, Welsh or Scots Gaelic'.[19] Meanwhile historians have re-emphasized the cultural significance of antiquarian writings of the period, including the close relationship of such writings not only to the political culture of Ireland but also to European antiquarianism in the seventeenth and eighteenth centuries.[20] O'Halloran's vivid study of these relationships, entitled *Golden Ages and Barbarous Nations*, explores the origins, debates, and golden-ages myth current in Irish cultural discourse in the eighteenth century, along with their influence on political affiliations and alignments. Joep Leerssen's influential analysis of Patriot politics and Protestant antiquarianism is in turn part of a larger and illuminating study of imagology and the construction of a national self-image in Irish literary and historical scholarship through to the late nineteenth century.[21]

The genealogy of the Irish novel has been traced back to the late seventeenth and early eighteenth centuries through the scholarship of Siobhán Kilfeather, Aileen Douglas, Ian Ross, Moyra Haslett, and others. The 2006 publication of the Loebers' *Guide to Irish Fiction: 1650–1900* dramatically increased the known size of the field, with a listing of over 5000 fiction titles relating to Ireland, published prior to 1900; the Loebers' work also points to the fascinatingly complex history of the circulation of Irish fiction, with publishing locations ranging from Ireland and Great Britain to North America, Australia, and India.[22] While a comparatively small number of novels appear to have been published in the period before 1800, many display a richness of formal experimentation and diversity of thematic content.[23] Important examples include politician and soldier Robert Boyle's six-volume heroic romance *Parthenissa* (1654–1665), the anonymous *Vertue Rewarded; or, the Irish Princess* (1693), and Sarah Butler's *Irish Tales* (1716).[24] A compelling feature of such prose fictions, and one which would continue in their nineteenth-century successors, is their explicit engagement with earlier accounts of Ireland (Spenser's *A View of the State of Ireland* being most frequently cited) and their consequent self-positioning within a developing historiographical tradition of writing about Ireland. The towering figure of Jonathan Swift continues to command critical attention, with newly detailed investigations of the complexity and longevity of his engagement with Irish society, economics, and culture, from the early 1690s to the late 1730s. The 'Irish' Swift is itself an example of a trend in late twentieth- and early twenty-first-century historiography which has focused also on the 'Irish' Edmund Burke, 'Irish' Maria Edgeworth, and others; the more sophisticated of these studies, Luke Gibbons' study of Edmund Burke being the most notable,[25] involve, as critic James Chandler has identified, a productive complication not only of 'the question of what the "Irishing" of an author might mean, but also that of how to locate an "Irish author" on a larger cultural map'.[26]

IV. LITERARY CULTURE AND THE CRISES OF REPRESENTATION: 1800–1890

Irish literary history does not fit easily or neatly into the periodizations frequently employed for the English literary tradition, such as Romanticism, Victorianism, or Modernism, though the awkwardness of the fit is often telling and revealing. In the case of Romanticism, Irish literature has typically been seen to exemplify 'the late flowering of a Romantic sensibility' in comparison to its neighbours, with the writings of the 1840s *Nation* poets or even the early Yeats as exemplars.[27] However, 'Irish Romanticism' has recently been reclaimed as a meaningful, distinctive, and early phenomenon by the work of Claire Connolly and Luke Gibbons. In her influential analysis of the decades 1800 to 1830, Connolly argues that 'Ireland emerged from this period with a renovated reputation as a naturally distinct national culture; this is turn fostered and supported new theories of nationality and nourished the cultural nationalism of the 1830s and 1840s'. 'Strongly marked by a sense of grievance', Irish romantic literary culture existed alongside 'persistent calls to mould civil society in a more progressive shape', the result of this being that the literature of the period bears and assumes 'the burden of reform and change'.[28] To date, the literary genres which have received most attention in this new critical context are, firstly, the national tale, frequently authored by women (Maria Edgeworth and Sydney Owenson, Lady Morgan being the best-known examples), and, secondly, the body of writing now recognized as Irish Gothic, whose representatives extend from Charles Robert Maturin to later nineteenth-century writers such as Joseph Sheridan LeFanu, Charlotte Riddell, and Bram Stoker.

The term 'Anglo-Irish', which appeared more and more frequently in post-Union discourse, in turn came to be used as a designation for many early nineteenth-century writers although, as a number of commentators have suggested, their identity is more accurately understood as 'negative' rather than 'syncretic', that is, 'neither Irish nor English' rather than '*both* Irish and English'.[29] To support this view, Ina Ferris quotes the revealing line from Maturin's dedicatory letter to *The Wild Irish Boy* (1808): 'I am an Irishman, unnoticed and unknown'.[30] The national tale, Irish Gothic, and other subgenres from the early decades of the nineteenth century have, in consequence, returned to critical prominence as literary forms which refract the historical issues of the time and thus expose key political and social fissures: in Ina Ferris's pithy terms, they constitute 'a writing *around* rather than within history, and it is precisely because of this position of not-quite-belonging that they estrange foundational narratives of history and gender'.[31]

Moving to the mid century, the field of Irish famine literature has, over the last two decades, become the subject of wide-ranging investigation, much of which was prompted by the sesquicentennial commemoration in the mid- to late 1990s. Morash's 1989 anthology *The Hungry Voice* gathers over 100 poems, written between 1845 and 1850, in response to the Great Famine; their authors include Jane Wilde 'Speranza', Aubrey De Vere, Samuel Ferguson, and most notably James Clarence Mangan, whose poem 'Siberia', first published in the *Nation* 18 April 1846, is one of the most evocative literary treatments of the famine, made all the more powerful by the obliqueness of its representation.[32] The retrieval of contemporary literary responses has also had important implications for wider historiographical debates about governmental responsibility. One such example is the novel most frequently associated with the 1840s famine, William Carleton's *The Black Prophet*; although Carleton's text takes for its subject matter the earlier famines of 1816–7 and 1821, its publication in the *Dublin University Magazine* between May and December 1846 gave it an urgent contemporary significance. In the preface to the single-volume edition in 1847, which he dedicated to Prime Minister Lord John Russell, Carleton claimed a direct interventionist role for his novel, 'calculated to awaken those who legislate for us into something like a humane perception of a calamity that has been almost perennial in this country', and forcefully criticized the British legislature for its 'long course of illiberal legislation and unjustifiable neglect'.[33] Almost a century later, the fiercer arguments of Carleton's contemporary John Mitchel as to extensive food exports and a policy of deliberate governmental neglect would be given novelistic form in Liam O'Flaherty's *Famine* (1937) which remains a strong seller. In recent years the famine has also been deployed as the subject of historical fiction for children, most popularly in the work of author Marita Conlon-McKenna.[34]

These examples notwithstanding, it has been common for cultural critics to argue that a 'repression or evasion' has been at work with regard to literary responses to the Great Irish Famine—the event straining 'at the limits of the articulable' or marking 'the threatened death of the signifier' in Terry Eagleton's terms.[35] Such generalizations as to the 'silence' of literary writers, while powerful in emotive terms, had the effect of delaying a detailed engagement with the body of literature that does survive and deflecting a much-needed analysis of its influence. Recent studies of Irish-language material in the nineteenth century have pointed to the existence of a significant body of famine literature, written contemporaneously or soon after,[36] while Cormac Ó Gráda's research into the folklore and folk song of the period has made available a number of popular songs, one of which, 'Amhrán na bPrátaí Dubha' (Song of the Black Potatoes), is believed to have been composed in the 1840s. Among the striking features of this song is its sharp refutation of contemporary views of the famine as providential or 'God-given' and, as a result, it was said to have generated the disapproval of local clergy:

> *Ní hé Dia cheap riamh an obair seo,*
> *Daoine bochta a chur le fuacht is le fán,*
> *Iad a chur sa phoorhouse go dubhach is glas orthu,*
> *Lánúineacha pósta is iad scartha go bás.*[37]

A large body of eyewitness accounts of the famine also exists, many of which were republished during the 1990s commemorative period; these include the writings of American visitor Asenath Nicholson and of the British journalist Alexander Somerville, along with the monumental *Transactions of the Central Relief Committee of the Society of Friends during the Famine in Ireland in 1846 and 1847* (1852, republished 1996). Historians of the famine have tended to treat these sources with considerable ambivalence, rightly noting that their privileged status reveals 'more about the assumptions of the observer than the experience of those observed'.[38] The best-selling *The Great Hunger* (1962) by Cecil Woodham-Smith was one of the first histories to make detailed use of contemporary testimonies, in contrast to her revisionist predecessors and successors who considered them unduly emotive; her study in turn proved influential for a new generation of writers who took the famine as literary subject, including poet Seamus Heaney ('At a Potato Digging' and 'For the Commander of "The Eliza"'), dramatist Tom Murphy (author of *Famine*), and poet Eavan Boland, whose poems 'That the Science of Cartography is Limited' and 'Quarantine' are now anthologized in the influential *Norton Anthology of English Poetry*. The 2012 publication of the magisterial *Atlas of the Great Irish Famine* has greatly advanced historiography regarding famine mortality and famine's regional impact; in contrast, its analysis of the cultural impact of the Famine and its mapping of the diversity of cultural responses is much less satisfactory. What this suggests is that a full integration of literary and cultural source-material into famine historiography—and within Irish historiography more generally—has not yet been achieved, nor have the diverse aesthetic and symbolic dimensions of literary representations fully been explored.

Far from avoiding the burden of the actual, nineteenth-century Irish literary fiction—in particular in the post-1850 period—it is distinguished by a direct engagement with contemporary social and political events. One example of the prevalence of such 'factual fictions'[39] is that of the land agitation and land wars of the late 1870s and 1880s concerning which at least fifteen novels were published in the period 1881 to 1890 alone, nine written by women. The most famous of these are Anthony Trollope's *Landleaguers* (1883) and George Moore's *A Drama in Muslin* (1886), while Emily Lawless's *Hurrish* (1886) has also received critical attention. Other notable works include Letitia McClintock's strongly anti-League novel *A Boycotted Household* (1881), Rosa Mulholland's *Marcella Grace* (1886), *The Plan of Campaign* (1888) by English historian and novelist Frances Mabel Robinson, and *When We Were Boys* (1890) by parliamentarian William O'Brien, written during his periods of imprisonment in the 1880s.

The critical neglect of these works is itself part of a more general underestimation of the role played by domestic and sentimental fiction in the nineteenth century. These 'factual fictions' employ standard plots from sentimental fiction (social and economic obstacles to lovers' relationships, mistaken identities, wrongful accusations, etc.) yet in their depiction of contemporary politics they also take on a substantial burden of representation involving political agitation, contemporary class antagonisms, and social change. A considerable number of the land war novels belong to the categories of 'Catholic upper middle-class fiction' or 'Catholic gentry novels', reflecting the outlook and aspirations of this class.[40] Ultimately such novels generally serve to reinforce a social order of private property and landed ownership, and the marriages with which they typically conclude are designed to resolve anxieties concerning legal title and inheritance. However such legitimizing gestures barely contain the social instabilities which form much of the narrative interest; it cannot have been lost on readers that the transfer of land ownership, once countenanced, could occur again and, in class terms, elsewhere.

Nor was the subject matter without danger for its authors: an intriguing case is that of Elizabeth Owens Blackburne Casey, whose accomplished novel *The Heart of Erin* was published in 1882. Born in County Meath in 1848, Casey was then at the height of her career as a successful novelist and writer based in London. Her novel, subtitled *An Irish Story of Today*, presented itself as a vehicle for better understanding between England and Ireland and castigated contemporary newspapers for their ignorance and misrepresentation of Irish news. However in a review which appeared on 20 May 1882, two weeks after the Phoenix Park murders, the *Athenaeum* sharply criticized Casey as 'a thoroughgoing partisan of the Land League'; this proved to be her last published novel and she died in penury in Dublin in 1894.

The history of nineteenth-century Irish literary anthologies offers a useful perspective on the role and influence of cultural representations in the period; landmark anthologies such as *The Spirit of the Nation* (1843) or *The Cabinet of Irish Literature* (1879–1880), published at times of political transition, offered the literary means to articulate and disseminate a shared cultural identity.[41] In addition, these collections played a key role in the consolidation of 'Anglo-Irish' literature from the mid nineteenth century onwards and, with significant exceptions, in the related occlusion of the tradition of Irish-language writing. A printed tradition in the Irish language did develop in the early decades and co-existed for the first half of the century with a continuing manuscript tradition. Consequently, and as noted earlier, considerable evidence exists of manuscript scribes borrowing and copying from printed texts, Charlotte Brooke's *Reliques of Irish Poetry* (1789) and John Daly and Edward Walsh's 1844 *Reliques of Irish Jacobite Poetry* being some examples.[42] James Hardiman's *Irish Minstrelsy, or Bardic Remains of Ireland with English Poetical Translations* (1831) was quickly eclipsed by Samuel Ferguson's infamous *Dublin University Magazine* reviews (1834). Yet *Irish Minstrelsy* is worth further examination in its own right, usefully summarized by Matthew Campbell as an 'O'Connellite project conceived during the struggle for Catholic emancipation', in contrast to Ferguson's articles which 'sought to provide a literary service for unionist readers, while not challenging their politics'.[43]

Even less well recognized is the prevalence in the mid century of bilingual collections, for example, *Reliques of Irish Jacobite Poetry*, Edward Walsh's *Irish Popular Songs* (1847), and John O'Daly and James Clarence Mangan's *Poets and Poetry of Munster* (1849). As late as 1866, when the second edition of *Reliques* appeared, O'Daly chose to include seventeen ballads without Irish translations, arguing that 'the generality of our purchasers, we suspect, will be those who are more or less acquainted with their native tongue; and therefore will not have much difficulty in reading the same'.[44] Such editorial choices underline the complex reception-history of bilingual poetry anthologies in nineteenth-century Ireland: too often dismissed as language primers, both by contemporary reviewers and by later literary historians,[45] or condescended to as antiquarian pursuits, these collections performed a variety of functions for contemporary readerships with mixed linguistic and educational competences.[46] The two 'best sellers' of the nineteenth century were, however, published fully in English: *The Spirit of the Nation* (1843, expanded in 1845) and Charles Gavan Duffy's *Ballad Poetry of Ireland* (1845). By 1874, *The Spirit of the*

Nation had reached its fifty-seventh edition, and as late as 1895 W.B. Yeats reported that it was to be seen 'on the counter of every country stationer'.[47] By its thirty-ninth edition in 1866, Duffy's anthology of ballad poetry had sold an estimated 76 000 copies. Dismissed for much of the twentieth century—partly as a result of its contemporary popularity— mid nineteenth-century poetry in English would attain a new critical status within post-colonial historiography, chiefly through David Lloyd's writings on Mangan, Davis, and Duffy in which Lloyd, following the work of Deleuze and Guattari, reclaims the term 'minor literature' as the mark of political contestation and opposition.[48]

In the post-1850 period many Irish-born authors and journalists found significant professional opportunities and some success in London; this still-neglected genera-tion of migrant authors included many female writers, such as Charlotte Riddell, Annie Hector, Frances Cashel Hoey, and the aforementioned Elizabeth Owens Blackburne Casey, as well as male writers Justin McCarthy, Edmund Downey, and Richard Dowling. One of the most ambitious publishing ventures of the period was the four-volume *Cabinet of Irish Literature* (1879–1880), the work of journalist and novelist Charles Read and of journalist and parliamentarian T.P. O'Connor who completed the project following Read's death in 1878. The correlation between the *Cabinet*'s publication and the developing Home Rule movement may be traced between the lines of the editors' stated rationale for the anthology, which they presented as 'primarily necessary for the purpose of enabling the literary history of Ireland to be traced in a systematic manner; and not the literary history only, but also the historical and social development of the people'.[49] In addition, the preface included a firm assurance that the editors had sought the avoidance 'of anything that has become hackneyed or that could wound the feelings or offend the taste of any class or creed'. Instead, in all four volumes, the criteria upon which the 'Irishness' of a selection is determined are markedly broad and the inclu-siveness of genre is a notable feature of the project, ranging from political and religious oratory to philosophical, scientific, and orientalist writings. Katharine Tynan's 1902 revised edition of the *Cabinet* would see a regrettable narrowing of genres which was itself exemplary of a general tendency in literary studies of the time; however, her revi-sions did include the addition of a new fourth volume featuring contemporary writing, with enlightened choices of Revival writers such as Emily Lawless, W.B. Yeats, Douglas Hyde, Somerville and Ross, and George Bernard Shaw. Of the ninety-one authors fea-tured by Tynan in this volume, forty-three are female—a ratio of inclusion unique in the history of Irish anthologies.

V. Irish Literary Historiographies: 1890–1920

As discussed above, the migration of many Irish-born writers to London, as well as the cultural bilocation or translocation of much of Irish writing from the eighteenth and nineteenth centuries, renders difficult an immediate differentiation between 'English' and 'Irish' writing in many cases. Such cultural hybridity can all too easily be equated with aesthetic inferiority, an assumption made by the young W.B. Yeats whose objections to the nineteenth-century novel lay in what he termed the impossibility of dividing 'what is new, and therefore Irish, what is very old, and therefore Irish, from all that is foreign, from all that is an accident of imperfect culture'.[50] Although initially a voracious reader of nineteenth-century poetry and prose, Yeats had, by the first decade of the twentieth century, assumed the role of self-begetter in terms of cultural inheritance. This autochthonous position itself exemplified a deep ambivalence among Revival writers towards cultural tradition; as Colin Graham has argued, the Revival 'had to be its own point of origin. In being a revival it had not quite done away with literary history, but it had started from the assumption that almost nothing was in place'.[51]

A highly engaging narrative history of the key texts of the Irish Revival is provided by Declan Kiberd in his *Inventing Ireland: The Literature of the Modern Nation* (1995), loosely inflected by the post-colonial theory of Frantz Fanon and Ashis Nandy, and supplemented by his study of Irish-language and English-language writers in *Irish Classics* (2000). The history of the Northern Revival between 1890 and 1920, previously occupying an 'uncertain place in twentieth-century Irish literary history',[52] has been illuminated by Richard Kirkland in his biography of Cathal O'Byrne, and by Eugene McNulty in his study of the Ulster Literary Theatre.[53] Even the recalcitrant James Joyce has been repatriated, at least in part, to an Irish narrative and variously resituated within a national, post-colonial, or 'semi-colonial' context by the work of Emer Nolan, Enda Duffy, Derek Attridge, and Marjorie Howes.

Whether an 'Irish Modernism' existed, and if so to what extent, are questions that have increasingly vexed scholars of Irish studies over the past decade, the most frequent critical stance being the positioning of Irish revivalism and international modernism as largely unrelated, even opposed, cultural forces. However, as Paige Reynolds has persuasively demonstrated in her study of drama and Irish spectacle in the early twentieth century, 'cultural production in late nineteenth- and early twentieth-century Ireland was rich with overlaps between the seemingly antipathetic ideals espoused by these two movements'.[54] Reynolds's tracing of such interconnections further supports a significant re-envisioning of the potential of both movements: the recognition of Irish revivalism's 'thematic innovation and formal experimentation' and the underscoring of Irish modernism's 'dynamic relationship between cultural producers and their audiences'.[55]

The literary genealogies conventionally ascribed to Irish twentieth-century writing also contain some revealing fractures and disjunctions: while Irish fiction for much of the century has been dwarfed by the towering figure of Joyce,[56] he, rather than Yeats, tends to be seen as the enabling figure of later Irish poetry, as suggested by the title of Dillon Johnston's study *Irish Poetry after Joyce*. Meanwhile those few figures allowed entry to the Irish modernist assembly are almost exclusively male (Samuel Beckett, Denis Devlin, Thomas MacGreevy, Brian Coffey) and generally exiles from Ireland. Some of the newer historiographies of Irish writing have usefully challenged earlier categorizations, with sustained critical attention being paid to the work of Elizabeth

Bowen, Kate O'Brien, and Blanaid Salkeld, for example.[57] Other works of criticism have attempted new mappings of cultural preoccupations, for example Edna Longley's support of archipelagic studies of history and literature or Joe Cleary's situation of Irish partition narratives in the context of other 'colonial' partitions;[58] however, with some notable exceptions, the comparative impulse remains greatly undeveloped in studies of Irish literary culture.

The prominence accorded Ireland in one recent 'world literature' study, Pascale Casanova's *World Republic of Letters* (1999), offers a cautionary example. Casanova, closely following Kiberd, presents the Irish Revival in markedly heroic terms: 'Thus between 1890 and 1930, in a literarily destitute country under colonial rule, there occurred one of the greatest literary revolutions—the "Irish miracle"—marked by the appearance of three or four of the most important writers of the twentieth century.'[59] Yet this valorization—attractively and compellingly phrased—is in turn supported by a highly reductive and damaging simplification of the earlier Irish-language tradition as the barren ground upon which the 'miracle' appears. 'Even though Irish had ceased to be a language of intellectual creation and communication, at least since the early seventeenth century', Casanova notes, 'it was still spoken by more than half of the population until 1840'.[60] That a language could continue to be spoken by millions of people centuries after it had 'ceased to be a language of intellectual creation and communication' might be termed a level of wilful cultural achievement unique on the global stage.

Moving to the close of the twentieth century, the publication of the much-awaited *Field Day Anthology of Irish Writing* in 1991 would lead to one of the most contentious episodes in the history of Irish cultural criticism. Compiled by a team of scholars under the general editorship of Seamus Deane, the anthology was produced within the auspices of the Field Day group; first established as a theatrical company in Derry in 1980, Field Day had emerged as an important forum for cultural debate in the 1980s and published an influential series of pamphlets on literary, cultural, and intellectual history. The three large volumes constituted a monumental act of retrieval of Irish 'writing' (a term preferred over the narrower sense of 'literature'), ranging from Latin writing in Ireland to Oliver Cromwell's letters from Ireland to twentieth-century political writings and speeches, and implicitly located within a post-colonial methodology of cultural reclamation and recovery. In his general introduction, Deane sought a delicate balance between assertions of cultural authority and definitiveness: 'There is no attempt here to establish a canon. Instead, what we show is an example of the way in which canons are established and the degree to which they operate as systems of ratification and authority ... Therefore, we consider ourselves to be engaged in an act of definition rather than in a definitive action'.[61] Other parts of his preface convey an overall ambition in less tentative terms, namely, the construction of 'a meta-narrative, which is, we believe, hospitable to all the micro-narratives that, from time to time, have achieved prominence as the official version of the true history, political and literary, of the island's past and present'.[62]

Given Deane's acknowledgement that 'this anthology, like the works it presents to the reader, is at the mercy of the present moment and, also like them, derives its authority (such as it is) from that moment',[63] it might have been predicted that such ambition would be most carefully scrutinized in the context of 1980s Northern politics. However, the storm of protest that immediately greeted the publication centred on two other issues: the scarce representation of writing by women, and the gapped selection of Irish-language writing. On the highly contentious issue of women's writing, while the inclusion of thirty-nine female authors was deemed as 'by no means lamentable',[64] critics focused not only on the overall head-count (under 10 per cent of the total) and the omission of many celebrated writers (historical and contemporary), but also on the overall neglect of gender and sexuality as categories of discourse in the project. The many such reviews which appeared in the early 1990s provide a fascinating insight into contemporary views on cultural politics and underlying expectations of literary culture. Read at a distance, what is especially striking is the division between reviewers who welcomed the anthology's detailed inclusion of diverse Northern political traditions, and commentators who sharply criticized the relative exclusion of the Irish Republic and its concerns.[65]

In 2002, two further Field Day volumes appeared, dedicated to 'Irish Women's Writing and Traditions' and compiled by a team of over fifty contributing scholars, under the general editorship of eight leading feminist critics and historians. The thematic organization of the volumes enabled the redress of various areas of under-representation in the preceding volumes: for example, the section 'Medieval to Modern, 600–1900' (edited by Máirín Ní Dhonnchadha) covers a rich diversity of Irish-language source material that includes medical literature, medieval law texts, and court literature. In this and other sections, the question of women's participation in literary culture is suggestively expanded to include the history of women as readers, auditors, patrons, sponsors, and recipients of oral and literary production, as well as female authorship of religious, scientific, theological, and ethical writings (the latter sections edited by Margaret Mac Curtain). The section on 'Sexuality, 1685–2001' (under the general editorship of Siobhán Kilfeather), read in conjunction with the impressive contributions on women and politics, 1500–2000, and women in Irish society, 1200–2000 (edited by Mary O'Dowd and Maria Luddy respectively), uncovers a startling wealth of archival source material—personal and institutional—to be further explored. Similarly, the anthologization of women's writings, from 1700 to 1960 (general editor Gerardine Meaney), and from 1960 to 2000 (Clair Wills), together with the landmark section 'Oral Traditions' (Angela Bourke), have radically altered the known landscape of Irish women's literary and cultural production.

One of the many benefits allowed by the scale of Field Day Volumes IV and V is an avoidance of the orthodoxies invoked by some earlier feminist retrieval projects, which understandably but regrettably tend to prioritize the return to attention of texts marked by their transgressive, subversive, or otherwise demonstrably oppositional character.[66] Yet the size of the Field Day project has also limited the extent of its dissemination; as one reviewer remarked, the volumes are 'far less an anthology, in even the modified current understanding of that term, than a database that assembles a vast quantity of material and affords the possibility of multiple cross-connections'.[67] The full extent of such rich cross-connections and interrelationships, including with the preceding three volumes, remains however largely unmapped while the volumes exist only in printed form.

Large-scale literary initiatives are now the domain of digital humanities whose potential as a discipline to support complex intertextual studies also brings a welcome opportunity to combine bio-bibliographical research with theoretical/critical appoaches—activities sometimes separated in the sphere of Irish literary studies.[68] The critique of digital humanities for its failure to date to engage meaningfully with cultural context, as advanced by Alan Liu and others,[69] underlines both the challenges and opportunities for a national literature in deploying digital modes of dissemination. More specifically, the comparative studies that are facilitated by new data mining and data modelling methods may in turn facilitate a release from the discourse of exceptionality which can limit, as well as stimulate, an understanding and appreciation of Irish literary culture. 'What assumptions enable us to take an adjective derived from a territorial jurisdiction and turn it into a mode of literary causality, making the latter reflexive of and indeed coincidental with the former?' asks American critic Wai Chee Dimock.[70] It is striking that some of the richest investigations and reformulations of these assumptions are emerging from locations outside of Ireland: in Brazil, the United States and Canada, Japan, Australia, and in a range of locations in Europe. In this context, and looking to the future, 'transnational' Irish literary studies offer an especially vibrant perspective on historical and contemporary writing, and digital technologies one means of transforming international connections.

Notes

1. Deana Rankin, *Between Spenser and Swift: English Writing in Seventeenth-Century Ireland* (Cambridge, 2005), 3.
2. Andrew Carpenter, *Verse in English from Tudor and Stuart Ireland* (Cork, 2003), 1.
3. Anne Fogarty, 'Literature in English, 1550–1690: from the Elizabethan settlement to the Battle of the Boyne' in Margaret Kelleher and Philip O'Leary (eds), *The Cambridge History of Irish Literature* (Cambridge, 2006), I, 140.
4. Ibid., 141.
5. Patricia Coughlan, ' "Cheap and Common Animals": the English anatomy of Ireland in the Seventeenth Century', in Thomas Healy and Jonathan Sawday (eds), *Literature and the English Civil War* (Cambridge, 1990), 206.
6. See Marie-Louise Coolahan, ' "And this deponent further sayeth": orality, print and the 1641 Depositions', in Marc Caball and Andrew Carpenter (eds), *Oral and Print Cultures in Ireland 1600–1900* (Dublin, 2010), 69–84; also Coolahan, *Women, Writing and Language in Early Modern Ireland* (Oxford, 2010).
7. Raymond Gillespie, *Reading Ireland: Print, Reading and Social Change in Early Modern Ireland* (Manchester, 2005), 6.
8. Raymond Gillespie and Andrew Hadfield (eds), *The Irish Book in English 1550–1800*, Oxford History of the Irish Book, Volume III (Oxford, 2006).
9. See Lesa Ní Mhungaile, 'The intersection between oral tradition, manuscript, and print cultures in Charlotte Brooke's Reliques of Irish Poetry (1789)', in Caball and Carpenter (eds), *Oral and Print Cultures*, 14–31.
10. Andrew Carpenter (ed), *Verse in English from Eighteenth-Century Ireland* (Cork, 1998).

11. Ibid., 31.

12. For an analysis of examples of such songs, see Carpenter, 'Poetry in English, 1690–1800', in Kelleher and O'Leary (eds), *Cambridge History of Irish Literature*, I, 307–9. The subject of macaronic verse from the perspective of the Irish-language tradition has been examined by Liam Mac Mathúna in *Béarla sa Ghaeilge. Cabhair Choigríche: An Códmheascadh Gaeilge/Béarla i Litríocht na Gaeilge 1600–1900* (Dublin, 2007).

13. Ibid., 307.

14. Helen Burke, *Riotous Performances: The Struggle for Hegemony in the Irish Theatre, 1712–1784* (Indiana, 2003), 3.

15. Ibid., 16–17.

16. Christopher Morash, *A History of Irish Theatre 1601–2000* (Cambridge, 2002), 54.

17. See Morash, 'Theatre in Ireland, 1690–1800', in Kelleher and O'Leary (eds), *Cambridge History of Irish Literature*, I, 374.

18. Ibid., 374–5.

19. See Ian Ross, 'Prose in English, 1690–1800', in Kelleher and O'Leary (eds), *Cambridge History of Irish Literature*, I, 232–81, 259.

20. Clare O'Halloran, *Golden Ages and Barbarous Nations: Antiquarian Debate and Cultural Politics in Ireland, c. 1750–1800* Field Day Critical Conditions series (Cork, 2004), 5.

21. See Joep Leerssen's two volumes in the Field Day Critical Conditions series: *Mere Irish and Fíor-Ghael: Studies in the Idea of Irish Nationality, Its Development and Literary Expression prior to the Nineteenth Century* (1986; republished Cork, 1996) and *Remembrance and Imagination: Patterns in the Historical and Literary Representation of Ireland in the Nineteenth Century* (Cork, 1996).

22. Rolf and Magda Loeber, with Anne M. Burnham, *A Guide to Irish Fiction, 1650–1900* (Dublin, 2006). Electronic version available at http://www.lgif.ie.

23. Siobhán Kilfeather, 'Sex and Sensation in the Nineteenth-Century Irish Novel', in Margaret Kelleher and James H. Murphy (eds), *Gender Perspectives in Nineteenth-Century Ireland: Public and Private Spheres* (Dublin, 1997), 83–92, and Kilfeather, 'The Profession of Letters, 1700–1810', in Angela Bourke et al (eds), *Field Day Anthology of Irish Writing Vol. V: Irish Women's Writing and Traditions* (Cork, 2002), 772–832; see also Ian Ross, 'Irish fiction before the Union', in Jacqueline Belanger (ed), *The Irish Novel in the Nineteenth Century* (Dublin, 2005), 34–51.

24. The series of new editions of early Irish fiction, inaugurated by Four Courts in 2010, is a highly welcome initiative and its first publications have included Butler's historical romance, Thomas Amory's *The Life of John Buncle, Esq.*, and the anonymously published *Vertue Rewarded*. See also the special issue of the *Irish University Review* (Spring/Summer 2011) on the subject of 'Irish Fiction, 1660–1830'.

25. Luke Gibbons, *Edmund Burke and Ireland: Aesthetics, Politics, and the Colonial Sublime* (Cambridge, 2003).

26. James Chandler, 'A Discipline in Shifting Perspective: Why We Need Irish Studies', *Field Day Review*, 2 (2006), 19–39, 31.

27. Claire Connolly, 'Irish Romanticism, 1800–1830', in Kelleher and O'Leary (eds), *Cambridge History of Irish Literature*, I, 408. See also Connolly, *A Cultural History of the Irish Novel, 1790–1829* (Cambridge, 2012).

28. Ibid., 408–10. See also Luke Gibbons, 'Romantic Ireland: 1750–1845', in James Chandler (ed), *The Cambridge History of English Romantic Literature* (Cambridge, 2009), 182–203.

29. Patrick J. O'Farrell, *Ireland's English Question: Anglo-Irish Relations 1534–1970* (London: Batsford, 1971), 17; cited by and elaborated upon by Ina Ferris, *The Romantic National Tale and the Question of Ireland* (Cambridge, 2002), 15.

30. Ferris, *The Romantic National Tale*, 15.

31. Ibid., 15.

32. James Clarence Mangan, 'Siberia', reproduced in Chris Morash (ed), *The Hungry Voice: The Poetry of the Irish Famine* (Dublin, 1989), 143–4.

33. William Carleton, *The Black Prophet* (1847; Shannon, 1972), author's preface and dedication. See Margaret Kelleher, *The Feminization of Famine* (Cork and Durham, 1997), 29–39.

34. Celia Keenan, 'Narrative Challenges: the Great Irish Famine in Recent Stories for Children', in Ann Lawson Lucas (ed), *The Presence of the Past* (Westport, CT, 2003), 113–20; reprinted in Christian Noack, Lindsay Janssen, and Vincent Comerford (eds), *Holodomor and Gorta Mór: Histories, Memories and Representations of Famine in Ukraine and Ireland* (London, 2012), 189–96.

35. Terry Eagleton, *Heathcliff and the Great Hunger: Studies in Irish Culture* (London, 1995), 11–13.

36. See Antan Mac Lochlainn, 'The Famine in Gaelic Tradition', *The Irish Review* 17/18 (1995), 90–108; Neil Buttimer, ' "A Stone on the Cairn": The Great Famine in Later Gaelic Manuscripts', in Chris Morash and Richard Hayes (eds), *Fearful Realities: New Perspectives on the Famine* (Dublin, 1996), 93–109; Máirín Nic Eoin, 'Ar an Trá Fholamh—an Gorta Mór in Litríocht Ghaeilge na hAoise seo', in Cathal Póirtéir (ed), *Gnéithe den Ghorta* (Dublin, 1995), 107–30.

37. Cormac Ó Gráda, *An Drochshaol: Béaloideas agus Amhráin* (Dublin, 1994), 59. Translation by Ó Gráda: 'This business was no part of God's plan,/Scattering the poor in grief and pain,/The poorhouse gates clanging closed on them,/And married couples separated for life'; cited in Peter Gray, *The Irish Famine* (London, 1995), 162–3.

38. David Fitzpatrick, 'The Failure: Representations of the Irish Famine in Letters to Australia', in E.M. Crawford (ed), *The Hungry Stream: Essays on Famine and Emigration* (Belfast, 1997), 161.

39. The phrase is that of Lennard J. Davis: 'The novel is a factual fiction which is both factual and factitious. It is a report on the world and an invention that parodies that report'; see his *Factual Fictions: The Origins of the English Novel* (1983; Philadelphia, 1996), 212.

40. James H. Murphy, *Catholic Fiction and Social Reality in Ireland, 1873–1922* (Westport, CT, 1997), 8, 20–2, 66–8. See also Murphy, *Irish Novelists and the Victorian Age* (Oxford, 2011).

41. As Leah Price observes, it is 'in the process of recognizing commonplaces' that 'readers learn to recognize themselves within a common culture'; see her *The Anthology and the Rise of the Novel: From Richardson to George Eliot* (Cambridge, 2000), 104.

42. See Meidhbhín Ní Úrdail, *The Scribe in Eighteenth- and Nineteenth-Century Ireland: Motivations and Milieu* (Münster, 2000).

43. Matthew Campbell, 'Poetry in English, 1830–1890' in Kelleher and O'Leary (eds), *The Cambridge History of Irish Literature*, I, 511–12.

44. John O'Daly, *Reliques of Irish Jacobite Poetry, with metrical translations by the late Edward Walsh*, 2nd edition (1844; Dublin, 1866), 90.

45. Niall Ó Ciosáin, 'Creating an Audience: Innovation and Reception in Irish Language Publishing, 1880–1920', in Clare Hutton (ed), *The Irish Book in the Twentieth Century* (Dublin, 2004), 14.

46. For a fuller treatment of this subject, see Kelleher, 'The Anthology and the Duanaire in Nineteenth-Century Ireland', in James H. Murphy (ed), *The Irish Book in English 1800–1891*, Oxford History of the Irish Book Volume IV (Oxford, 2011), 448–60.

47. W.B. Yeats, 'Irish National Literature, IV', *Bookman*, October 1895; reproduced in John P. Frayne (ed), *Uncollected Prose by W.B. Yeats Vol. I: First Reviews and Articles, 1886–1896* (London, 1970), 383.

48. David Lloyd, *Nationalism and Minor Literature: James Clarence Mangan and the Emergence of Irish Cultural Nationalism* (Berkeley, 1987); Lloyd, 'Adulteration and the Nation', in *Anomalous States: Irish Writing and the Post-Colonial Moment* (Dublin, 1993), 88–124.

49. Charles A. Read and T.P O'Connor (eds), *The Cabinet of Irish Literature Selections from the Works of the Chief Poets, Orators and Prose Writers of Ireland* (London, Glasgow, Edinburgh, and Dublin, 1879–80), preface by T.P. O'Connor. See Kelleher, 'The Cabinet of Irish Literature: A Historical Perspective on Irish Anthologies', *Éire-Ireland*, 38, nos 3 and 4 (2003), 68–89.

50. W. B. Yeats, 'First Principles', *Samhain*, 7 (November 1908), 8.

51. Colin Graham, 'Literary Historiography', in Kelleher and O'Leary (eds), *Cambridge History of Irish Literature*, II, 568.

52. Richard Kirkland, 'Dialogues of Despair: Nationalist Cultural Discourse and the Revival in the North of Ireland, 1900–1920', *Irish University Review*, 33, no. 1 (Spring/Summer 2003), 64–78, 64.

53. See Richard Kirkland, *Cathal O'Byrne and the Cultural Revival in the North of Ireland, 1890–1960* (Liverpool, 2006), and Eugene McNulty, *The Ulster Literary Theatre and the Northern Revival* (Cork, 2008).

54. Paige Reynolds, *Modernism, Drama, and the Audience for Irish Spectacle* (Cambridge, 2007), 8.

55. Ibid., 8, 14.

56. For an important corrective to this view, see the work of John Wilson Foster, including *Fictions of the Irish Literary Revival: A Changeling Art* (Syracuse, 1987) and his extensive survey of popular and minor literature in the first decades of the twentieth century, *Irish Novels 1890–1940: New Bearings in Culture and Fiction* (Oxford, 2008).

57. See Walshe, Eibhear (ed), *Ordinary People Dancing: Essays on Kate O'Brien* (Cork, 1993); Sinead Mooney, Kathryn Laing, and Maureen O'Connor (eds), *Edna O'Brien: New Critical Perspectives* (Dublin, 2006); Moynagh Sullivan, '"The Woman Gardener": Transnationalism, Gender, Sexuality and the Poetry of Blanaid Salkeld', *Irish University Review*, 42.1 (Spring/Summer 2012), 53–71.

58. Joe Cleary, *Literature, Partition and the Nation State: Culture and Conflict in Ireland, Israel and Palestine* (Cambridge, 2002).

59. Pascale Casanova, *The World Republic of Letters* (first published in 1999 as *La République Mondiale des Lettres*; Cambridge, Mass, 2004), 84.

60. Ibid., 308.

61. Seamus Deane, 'General Introduction', *The Field Day Anthology of Irish Writing*, 3 vols (London, 1991), I, xix–xx.

62. Ibid., xix.

63. Ibid., xxi.

64. Siobhán Kilfeather, 'The Whole Bustle', *London Review of Books*, 9 January 1992, 20.

65. For examples of the latter viewpoint, see Edna Longley, 'Introduction: Revising "Irish Literature"', in Longley, *The Living Stream: Literature and Revisionism in Ireland* (Newcastle-Upon-Tyne, 1994), 9–68.

66. See Kelleher, 'Writing Irish Women's Literary History', *Irish Studies Review*, 9.1 (Spring 2001), 5–14.
67. Anne Fogarty, 'Challenging Boundaries', *Irish Literary Supplement*, 22, no. 1 (Spring 2003), 3.
68. For a database of recent Irish-related digital humanities projects, see http://www.dho.ie/drapier/home.
69. Alan Liu, 'Where is Cultural Criticism in the Digital Humanities?', in Matthew K. Gold (ed), *Debates in the Digital Humanities* (Minneapolis, 2012), 490–509.
70. Wai Chee Dimock, *Through Other Continents: American Literature across Deep Time* (Princeton, 2006), 3.

SELECT BIBLIOGRAPHY

Bourke, Angela et al (eds), *The Field Day Anthology of Irish Writing Volumes IV and V: Irish Women's Writing and Traditions* (Cork and New York, 2002).
Campbell, Matthew (ed), *The Cambridge Companion to Contemporary Irish Poetry* (Cambridge, 2003).
Carpenter, Andrew (ed), *Verse in English from Eighteenth-Century Ireland* (Cork, 1998).
Carpenter, Andrew (ed), *Verse in English from Tudor and Stuart Ireland* (Cork, 2003).
Connolly, Claire, *A Cultural History of the Irish Novel, 1790–1829* (Cambridge, 2012).
Coolahan, Marie-Louise, *Women, Writing and Language in Early Modern Ireland* (Oxford, 2010).
Deane, Seamus (ed), *The Field Day Anthology of Irish Writing Volumes I-III* (Derry, 1991).
Douglas, Aileen, Moyra Haslett, and Ian Campbell Ross (eds), *Irish Fiction, 1660–1830*, special issue of *Irish University Review*, 41.1 (Spring/Summer 2011).
Foster, John Wilson, *Irish Novels 1890–1940: New Bearings in Culture and Fiction* (Oxford, 2008).
Gillespie, Raymond and Andrew Hadfield (eds), *The Irish Book in English 1550–1800*, Oxford History of the Irish Book Volume III (Oxford, 2006).
Kelleher, Margaret, 'Writing Irish Women's Literary History', *Irish Studies Review*, 9.1 (Spring 2001), 5–14.
Kelleher, Margaret and Philip O'Leary (eds), *The Cambridge History of Irish Literature* (Cambridge, 2006), 2 vols.
Kiberd, Declan, *Inventing Ireland: The Literature of a Modern Nation* (London, 1995).
Loeber, Rolf and Magda Loeber, with Anne M. Burnham, *A Guide to Irish Fiction, 1650–1900* (Dublin, 2006). Electronic version available at http://www.lgif.ie.
Lloyd, David, *Anomalous States: Irish Writing and the Post-Colonial Moment* (Dublin, 1993).
Morash, Christopher, *A History of Irish Theatre 1601–2000* (Cambridge, 2002).
Murphy, James H., *The Irish Book in English 1800–1891*, Oxford History of the Irish Book Volume IV (Oxford, 2011).
Palmer, Patricia, *Language and Conquest in Early Modern Ireland: English Renaissance Literature and Elizabethan Imperial Expansion* (Cambridge, 2001).
Rankin, Deana, *Between Spenser and Swift: English Writing in Seventeenth-Century Ireland* (Cambridge, 2005).
Reynolds, Paige, *Modernism, Drama, and the Audience for Irish Spectacle* (Cambridge, 2007).

CHAPTER 12

....

VISUAL ARTS

....

FINTAN CULLEN

THE art that survives from seventeenth-century Ireland is nearly all portraiture and portraits, which would remain the dominant form of artistic expression in Ireland for another two hundred years. Not surprisingly, such images are symbols of power and ownership and, again not surprisingly given the history of the island, they often represent men and women who were not necessarily Irish and are often the work of artists from a variety of cultural backgrounds. This is not to say that portraits of Irish-born men and women are hard to find; on the contrary, there are many. What it does suggest is that in tracing the story of art from 1600 to 2000 in Ireland, we must always be aware of the foreign element: that Ireland has always attracted non-native personalities both as patrons of art and practitioners of artistic production. It must also be said that the formal concerns of the art produced, both in terms of style and appearance, have invariably been greatly influenced by trends in Britain and continental Europe.

Dating from the first half of the seventeenth century, it is doubtful whether the portraits of such individuals as Máire Rúa O Brien of Leamaneh, County Clare (private collection), or George FitzGerald, the sixteenth Earl of Kildare, also known due to his small stature as the 'Fairy Earl' (private collection), were done by Irish hands. Despite the fact that both individuals are clearly associated with Irish locations and that the canvases may well have been produced in Ireland, the actual creators of the paintings were probably foreign-born. Seventeenth-century Ireland was not the training ground for a home-grown pictorial tradition. As research into the great collection of the Ormonde family has begun to show, the 'seventeenth-century ducal collection [in Kilkenny Castle and other Butler properties] was certainly the largest and finest of its time in Ireland, but it was by no means wholly Irish in content'.[1]

In terms of native production, things begin to change after the Restoration. The establishment in 1670 of the Guild of Dublin Cutlers, Painter-Steyners and Stationers (also known as the Dublin Guild of St Luke), created a record of artists working in the city, the majority of whom were probably heraldic and sign painters. Artists continued to visit, as George Vertue, a valuable chronicler of artistic happenings in London was later to record:

> Mr Michael Wright painter was in Ireland several years where was in great esteem...Wright is said in his first year of coming there he gain'd nine hundred pounds. He had ten pounds a head—Smith & he were always at strife which was the best painter.[2]

It has been convincingly suggested that this gossipy note refers to John Michael Wright who was in Dublin in 1679 and stayed for about four years. Vertue's 'Smith' is most probably Caspar Smitz, a Dutch artist who became a member of the Dublin Guild of St Luke in 1681. The Scottish-trained Wright is a major artist whose Irish work is truly spectacular. A Roman Catholic, it has been suggested that he fled London to escape anti-Catholic legislation[3] and his sympathies may thus have led him to receive the patronage of Sir Neill O'Neill of Killelough, County Antrim. By 1700, his wonderful full-length portrait of O'Neill painted in 1680 (figure 12.1), in the costume of an Irish chieftain, is known to have been hanging in Ormonde House, St James's Square, London, where a few years later it is referred to as a portrait of 'an *Irish Tory* in his Country Dress'.[4] Despite the specificity of this identification, the full-length portrait offers the puzzling inclusion of some Japanese armour in the lower left of the picture. A possible explanation for the representation of the armour suggests that:

> It is of a style called 'Do-Maru', meaning 'round the body'; worn during the period *c.* 1350–1530, it was of a type kept as gifts for eminent people. O'Neill was an uncompromising Roman Catholic, who was to become a Captain of Dragoons in the army of...James II...The Japanese were perceived in the West as persecutors of Catholics, so the armour may have been included in order to represent O'Neill as a defender of his faith, treading on the deflated armour of its enemies.[5]

Despite the existence of powerful full-length portraits of Catholic noblemen such as O'Neill, the Irish visual history of the eighteenth century is the story of an Anglican elite that had its own parliament and confidently carved its own cultural furrow. Following the second Duke of Ormonde's support for the Jacobite cause, the great Ormonde picture collection suffered major dispersal in 1719. The history of Irish portraiture that followed for the rest of the eighteenth century was a celebration of the power of a settled and confident *ancien régime*. The great houses built in Ireland from the early decades of the century, in combination with their interior decoration, created an image of a prosperous and assured culture that lasted until at least the Union of the Parliaments in 1801.

Portraiture dominated artistic production, with native-born artists receiving indigenous patronage, although after the mid 1740s Irish artists did begin to receive training in Dublin. A decade after the foundation of the Dublin Society in 1731, Robert West (d. 1770) was employed to act as first master of a drawing school that was to become the training ground of an impressive array of artists well into the nineteenth century.

FIGURE 12.1 John Michael Wright, Sir Neill O'Neill, 1680.

Copyright Tate Gallery, London.

Students were not taught oil painting; instead, the focus was on drawing, design, and ornament. With its emphasis on skills that could then be utilized in manufactures, a highly practical ethos dominated the schools. Although artists continued to produce portraits, the existence of the Dublin Society Schools was a key ingredient in the supply of talented craftsmen who contributed to the decoration of Irish houses and public buildings, both urban and rural, in the eighteenth century. Art in eighteenth-century Ireland was taught in order to serve the economy.

One of the pupils of the early years of the Dublin Society Schools was Hugh Douglas Hamilton (1740–1808). Trained by West, Hamilton soon began producing impressive small portraits in pastel and like so many of his fellow artists, both in the eighteenth and nineteenth centuries, he eventually left Dublin for the more lucrative patronage to be found in London. As a pastellist, Hamilton excelled in capturing an accurate likeness mixed with a dexterous use of the fragile medium of chalks. After succeeding in London, he travelled to Italy where he lived and worked for well over a decade. Given such an international workbase, a list of Hamilton's patrons between the 1760s and his return to Dublin c. 1791, becomes a who's who of the European elite. His Irish sitters included landed families such as the Conollys of Castletown, County Kildare, the extended family of the first Duke of Leinster at nearby Carton, as well as the wealthy banking family of La Touche. In England, he received royal commissions and produced innumerable portraits of members of the family of the first Duke of Northumberland, while in Italy, Hamilton's clientele included many travelling Irish, English, and Scottish gentlemen who wished to have their visits to Rome recorded for posterity standing amidst the stones of the eternal city. In time, Hamilton befriended fellow artists including the celebrated sculptor Antonio Canova. Hamilton's double portrait in pastel of Canova and the Irish artist Henry Tresham is perhaps the single most accomplished chalk drawing of the late eighteenth century (c. 1788–9; figure 12.2). Produced towards the close of Hamilton's Italian sojourn, the pastel can be read as an elaborate and technically masterful personal memento of a close friendship and a stimulating period in the Irish artist's career. One of the most technically innovative aspects of this large pastel is that Hamilton drew Canova's and Tresham's portraits on separate pieces of paper from the surrounding composition. This may have been done so that the artist could maintain an up-to-date representation of his associates, a further indication of Hamilton's determination to record an important series of friendships. On returning to Ireland, Hamilton wrote a number of letters to Canova in which he frequently lamented having left Italy and the friends and companions he had known there. The Canova-Tresham pastel can thus be seen as a statement of an international friendship forged by at least two Irishmen and a leading Italian artist of the late eighteenth century. The cool linearity of Hamilton's control of the pastel pencil combined with the cosmopolitan air of its execution and its sitters makes this piece a major contribution to international neoclassicism.

Despite Hamilton's great dexterity in portraiture, according to the academic tradition established in the sixteenth century, history painting was the only true activity for an artist of merit. On occasion portraiture could reflect heroism and the high ideals of its sitters, but it was fundamentally a base depiction of the visible and lacked imagination.

FIGURE **12.2** Hugh Douglas Hamilton, Antonio Canova in his Studio with Henry Tresham, *c.* 1788–9.

Copyright Victoria & Albert Museum, London.

In terms of Irish artistic productivity in the eighteenth century, the only artist actively to answer the call of the academic tradition, as laid down in Florence and Bologna and then in Paris, was the Cork-born James Barry (1741–1806). After some rudimentary training in Cork and Dublin, Barry left Ireland in his early twenties, never to return. A few years in Paris and Rome gave him the confidence to turn himself into a committed historical artist, one who criticized portraiture and ignored the genre of landscape painting. While Ireland occasionally features in his works, his real contribution to European art is as a large-scale muralist whose steadfast dedication to the ideals of ancient Greece lies behind his series of canvases that decorate the Great Room of the Royal Society of Arts in London. His theme was human progress from a primitive state, epitomized by the introduction of the arts by Orpheus to the wealth and power of eighteenth-century London.

Barry concludes his cycle with a vast celebration of human endeavour (1777–84), which contrasts the Elysium of intellectual achievement with the 'State of Final Retribution' where the insincere meet their doom. In many ways, this last painting in the series is an asymmetrical Enlightenment version of the medieval depiction of the Last Judgement, with far more attention given to positive achievements than selfish preoccupations.

Barry had little or no influence on the visual arts in Ireland during his lifetime. The monumentality of James Barry's works and their unwavering loyalty to a classical ideal allowed some, at least, to speculate on the possibility of the existence of an Irish school of painting. In 1854, in his account of the art on display at the 1853 Dublin Industrial Exhibition, John Sproule saw Barry and a few other Irish artists (William Mulready and Daniel Maclise) as inspirational. In discussing Barry's *Entombment* (untraced) which was on exhibition in the Dublin Exhibition of 1853, Sproule was ecstatic in his praise:

> Viewed merely as a triumph of power in drawing, this work is a production quite wonderful, and merely as a study is deserving of the most careful attention, more especially as few, if any, masters of modern times, except this singular Irish genius, have approached or attempted to approach the style of Michael Angelo's designs of this nature, and probably no one of them possessed the extraordinary power of James Barry. Those who have seen his great finished paintings at the Society of Arts, London, are well aware that his powers of execution were not inferior, and that in his perfect works no one was more capable of grace and expression than this extraordinary Master.[6]

Although he only ever exhibited one work in Ireland during his lifetime, *The Baptism of the King of Cashel by St Patrick,* shown at the Dublin Society in 1763 (Terenure College, Dublin), other paintings by Barry were repeatedly on display in various Irish cities throughout the nineteenth century. As an excellent engraver, Barry had produced both original prints and reproductions of his painted *oeuvre.* These prints played a still relatively under-researched role in broadcasting his work to a larger public and to future generations.

James Barry had despised the genre of landscape painting. Yet this section of artistic practice had enjoyed a sustained patronage in Ireland from at least the late seventeenth century. As with the development of landscape painting in England, the story of landscape art is a movement from topographical exactitude strongly influenced by Flemish and Dutch precedence to a more classically composed composition with stylistic effects borrowed from Italian-based art of the sixteenth and seventeenth centuries. A visual comparison focusing on country seats between these different mid eighteenth-century approaches to landscape highlights the attractions of these two styles. The *View of Westport House* of 1760 (private collection) by George Moore shows both the house itself and describes a vast landscape that includes Croagh Patrick and Clare Island, while Thomas Roberts' canvas of just one small section of the demesne at Carton, County Kildare (1775–7; private collection), indulges in a growing concern in landscape art with the evocation of mood. In the Moore, the focus is on a northern European concern with topography and a need to show all that is under the power of the patron. We get a vista that extends far beyond the capacity of the human eye. By contrast, in Roberts' much more focused representation of a section of the elegantly manicured property of the second Duke of Leinster, one is asked to consider the pleasures of ownership with an emphasis on exclusive access to that land. The scene is elegantly framed by a dominant overhanging tree on the left and newly planted trees and shrubs on the right.[7] In the Mayo scene, the landscape is productive: we see animals and evidence of river widening and the creation of a lake leading into Clew Bay. In the Kildare landscape, the demesne is for leisure, the Duke and Duchess of Leinster (who had married in November 1775) stroll and consider

FIGURE 12.3 James Barry, Death of Adonis, *c.* 1775.

Copyright National Gallery of Ireland, Dublin.

a boat ride, while their surroundings are well maintained: in the foreground we see two men pulling a garden roller.

To an artist such as Barry, landscape painting lacked intellectual punch; it ignored the enduring struggle of the human condition. Ironically, in his *Death of Adonis* (figure 12.3), he himself could create a highly elegiac backdrop to a scene of tragic love. Venus mourns her lover in a calm and dignified manner while the surrounding trees bend and writhe in sympathy with the theme of heedless death. By the end of the eighteenth century such emotive ingredients in nature had become commonplace in landscapes produced in Ireland. The work of the English-born William Ashford (1746–1824) is a case in point: his views of the *Dargle Valley* (Dublin: Royal Hibernian Academy) in County Wicklow or his evocative scene of *Tourists visiting Cloghoughter Castle, Co. Cavan* (Fota House, Cork), delight in the less-ordered landscape made fashionable by a preoccupation with the picturesque.

An important event in the history of art in Ireland in the second half of the eighteenth century was the instigation of public exhibitions. Public art exhibitions began in Dublin in 1765 under the auspices of the Society of Artists with a display at Napper's Room, George's Lane. Exhibitions continued almost annually until 1780. After a twenty-year lapse, in 1800, the renamed Society of Artists of Ireland organized a series of annual exhibitions, but Dublin was now a changed place: parliamentary Union was in the air, a rebellion had recently been crushed, and the city was altogether a more muted capital. As the nineteenth century progressed, exhibitions continued but aristocratic patronage declined. The creation of the Royal Hibernian Academy in 1823 was the culmination of many years of haphazard organization and finally allowed artists to organize training and display. Its annual exhibitions, which continue to this day, became a vital part of Dublin's artistic scene. Other loan exhibitions also took place throughout the century culminating in the great Irish Industrial Exhibition of 1853, held in a purpose-built glass-roofed complex on Leinster Lawn. Unlike the precedent set by the so-called Crystal Palace Exhibition in Hyde Park, London, in 1851, the Dublin show exhibited sculpture and painting, both old-master works and a huge collection of contemporary European art. Such activity might imply a healthy artistic culture in Dublin, but that was not the case. Patronage was now no longer the preserve of the landed classes, but of the emerging middle and professional classes who were slow to patronize Irish visual culture. As with the examples of Hamilton and Barry in the eighteenth century, Irish-born artists continued to emigrate to London and elsewhere. Important names such as Martin Archer Shee (1760–1850), Daniel Maclise (1806–70), John Henry Foley (1818–74), through to John Lavery (1856–1941) found success in London. Although all of those mentioned enjoyed a modest degree of patronage from their Irish contemporaries, none of them returned to live in Ireland, although Lavery did visit frequently in the 1920s and actually died in Kilkenny.

This migration of artistic talent left Ireland susceptible to a barrage of non-native display. It could be said that the story of art in Ireland in the nineteenth century is one of English art made more publicly available. In this regard, nineteenth-century Dublin was seen by the British art establishment as a provincial city in need of occasional exposure to cosmopolitan taste. Works by major and not-so-major artists were on continuous display in Dublin, Belfast, and Cork; panoramas of recent imperial victories were brought over from England, and the British representation at the many international industrial exhibitions was always large. The RHA and the establishment of the National Gallery of Ireland and the Museum of Science and Art (later the National Museum of Ireland) all followed well-established London patterns for the democratization of culture. And yet, as John Sproule had said in the catalogue of the 1853 exhibition, the creation of art in mid nineteenth-century Ireland was a victim of 'poverty and ignorance'. Native artists who did use the RHA and pursued a career in their home country did so without much financial reward.

The Irish work of Maclise and Foley must be understood within the context of their successful careers in London. Maclise's large painting, *The Marriage of Strongbow and Eva* (1854; figure 12.4), with its array of defeated Irish in the foreground, has, for obvious reasons, been read by many as coming from a 'nationalist' viewpoint. It could be a celebration of a lost culture or a cultural lamentation. The prominence of the gold torcs, erroneously placed on the wrists and upper arms of the defeated Irishmen in the right foreground, and the old bard with a broken harp on the far left of the paintings, do indeed suggest an effort by Maclise to explore his nation's past. But, given that the painting was originally planned as part of the redecoration of the Palace of Westminster and that it neatly fitted into a deeply colonial schema of moments from the ancient history of the various nations that made up the United Kingdom, its 'Irishness' is in need of serious

FIGURE 12.4 Daniel Maclise, The Marriage of Strongbow and Eva, 1854.

Copyright National Gallery of Ireland, Dublin.

questioning. Maclise's painting shows a defeated Ireland about to enter into a marriage of convenience. Indeed, the London *Art Journal* of 1854 recognized this only too well. Its critic praised the painting as displayed at the Royal Academy 'as one of the best productions of the modern schools', adding that it is 'the duty of government to secure [it]' given that it is 'so well suited for a national property'.[8] That nation is not Ireland alone, but the United Kingdom; Irish history, to the mid nineteenth-century writer in the *Art Journal*, is also imperial history.

Like many Irishmen, John Henry Foley benefited from working at the heart of the British Empire. In the 1850s and 1860s, with a studio in London, he produced an impressive array of equestrian monuments, destined for India, which celebrated military heroes of the Raj, such as Lord Viscount Hardinge (now in a private collection in Cambridgeshire) and Sir James Outram (Victoria Memorial Hall Gardens, Kolkata). Commissioned to produce the prominent figure of *Asia* for the Albert Memorial in Hyde Park, London, Foley also worked on the figure of the Prince Consort himself after the sudden death of Carlo Marochetti in 1867. It thus came as quite a shock to Dublin when, in 1867, given that he was seen as a London artist, Foley was chosen to produce that city's monument to Daniel O'Connell (1864–82; Dublin: O'Connell Street).[9] Foley's depiction of the great nationalist hero at the apex of a tiered arrangement of four winged Victories, a figure of Erin, and a representative group of nineteenth-century Irish men and women in contemporary costume is one of the great set pieces of public sculpture in Ireland. It celebrates the man and makes reference to religion, education, civic reform, and a host of relevant O'Connellite issues, all within a highly detailed figurative language. At the same time, as with Maclise in his *Strongbow and Eva,* the artistic vocabulary is conservative. Wide of girth and looking tired, O'Connell, high on his pedestal, is recognizably himself. Yet such realism is juxtaposed by the winged allegories and the multitude of types on the circumference of the drum. Although Dublin objected to a London-based artist and Unionists objected to a monument to the Liberator of Roman Catholicism, what the city got was a standard piece of European celebratory sculpture.

Moving into the twentieth century, the major contemporary event in the history of art in Ireland was the establishment by Hugh Lane (1875–1915) of a Municipal Gallery of Modern Art in Dublin in 1908. A key ingredient in the development of Lane's plans for a gallery of modern art was a patriotic desire to build a collection for Ireland. In the opening paragraph of his Prefatory Notice to the 1908 *Illustrated Catalogue* of the Dublin Gallery, Lane stated that he planned to hand over his 'collection of pictures and drawings of the British Schools...and Rodin's Masterpiece, "L'Age d'Airain"...a group of portraits of contemporary Irishmen and women...[and] my collection of pictures by Continental artists'.[10]

Exhibited in a Georgian terraced house, formerly known as Clonmell House, on Dublin's Harcourt Street, the paintings were arranged in distinct sections—Irish Painters, British Schools, French Barbizon School, and French Impressionists. They included Edouard Manet's *Eva Gonzalès* and Auguste Renoir's *Umbrellas (Les Parapluies),* which were only on loan to the new gallery. Other exhibits were unconditional Lane gifts, with examples of work by Irish, British, and American artists. On the staircase Lane hung a selection of portraits, mainly by John Butler Yeats and William Orpen. The former was represented by portraits of his son, W. B. Yeats, and John Millington Synge, while Orpen's subjects ranged from the Fenian Michael Davitt to the Unionist J. P. Mahaffy.[11] It was an eclectic collection and to all intents and purposes it was an exercise in cultural reconciliation. Its aim was to bring contemporary Ireland and Europe closer together.

The fact that Lane's attempt at cultural reconciliation did not succeed is evidenced by the saga of his thirty-nine continental pictures which are still shared by Dublin and London. Lane himself died in 1915 and, annoyed by Dublin's Corporation's failure to provide 'a suitable building' for his paintings in the city,[12] he bequeathed all thirty-nine works to London's National Gallery. Controversially, however, after Lane's death an unwitnessed codicil to his will reversing this decision was found in his desk in the National Gallery of Ireland. Despite this 'codicil of forgiveness', as his aunt Lady Augusta Gregory represented it, the paintings are still legally owned by London.[13]

Lane collected contemporary Irish artists and was supported in his campaigns by many of the key figures in the Irish Revival. At the same time, it comes as a surprise to discover that the original 1908 Municipal Gallery in Dublin exhibited only one small drawing by the artist who was to become the single most important name in Irish visual arts in the first half of the twentieth century, Jack B. Yeats (1871–1957). That drawing was presented to the Gallery by the artist himself and represented one of his archetypal themes of his early period, *The Day of the Sports.* A decade and a half later, post-1916, after the Treaty and the establishment of the new state, Yeats's subject matter had become more obviously political. His *Patriotic Airs* (National Gallery of Ireland) of 1923, shows an Irish nineteenth-century interior, either Dublin's Gaiety Theatre or the Empire Theatre of Varieties, later known as the Olympia Theatre.[14] Shortly after painting this small canvas, Yeats chose to include it in an exhibition of thirty-six of his works, which he entitled *Pictures of Irish Life*, in the Gieves Art Gallery in London's Mayfair in January 1924. This exhibition of Irish themes included loosely painted landscapes of scenes in Galway and Sligo, the evocative *A Westerly Wind* (1921, private collection) and an archetypal Yeats subject, *Market-day, Mayo* or *The Long Car* (1920, private collection) which shows a cart and horses with a distant watery horizon.[15] The inclusion of a painting in this London exhibition with such a provocative title as *Patriotic Airs* only a few years after the creation of the Irish Free State was a bold move on Jack Yeats's part. The songs or airs alluded to in the title of the painting would no doubt have included nationalist or separatist tunes that here entertain the Dublin bourgeoisie as they await the start or resumption of the evening's entertainment in a well-known music theatre.

To exhibit such a painting in a London gallery in 1924 may have been a bold move, but a closer examination of the small canvas shows that it was not necessarily a move aimed, as one might be excused for thinking, at provoking anti-British sentiment. As Yeats's characters listen to the sentimental airs possibly derived from such a source as Tom Moore's 'Irish Melodies' of a hundred years earlier, we notice the bent heads and somewhat sullen expressions on the faces of this middle-class audience.[16] The scene in *Patriotic Airs* is not one of urban merriment or a record of independence achieved; rather it is the opposite. Instead of being a celebration of the achievement of independence, the painting is a reprimand to the new emerging Ireland by a man who did not side with the creation of the Irish Free State. In *Patriotic Airs*, the audience sits in silence, wrapped in winter coats with one woman wearing a high-collared fur. The comfortable Dublin theatre-goers convey the antithesis of Yeats's independent Irish spirit as represented in so many of his west of Ireland sketches and oils.

As an academician with the RHA, Jack Yeats exhibited at its annual shows but by the 1940s these exhibitions were becoming stale. In 1942, concerned, as she claimed, that the Academy 'must not shut its doors to life, otherwise it will of necessity die of senile decay', the artist, Mainie Jellett (1897–1944), was instrumental in founding an alternative to the RHA.[17] The other founding members of the newly created Irish Exhibition of Living Art, which held its first display in the National College of Art in Dublin in 1943, included Evie Hone (1894–1955), Norah McGuinness (1903–80), Fr Jack Hanlon (1913–68), and Louis le Brocquy (1916–2012). This mere list of names reveals something new about art developments in Ireland in the first half of the twentieth century. Three of those named were women and indeed at least two further women artists were on the original IELA committee. Moreover, all those listed, apart from Le Brocquy, had previously studied in Paris with the artist Andre Lhote (1885–1962) and were well-versed in avant-garde ideas. The introduction of European Modernism to Ireland by a group of women artists is an important moment in the maturing process of Irish art. By turning away from a dependency on the English academic system and the equally powerful late nineteenth- and early twentieth-century preoccupation with a native cultural background (as suggested by the works of Jack B. Yeats), Jellett and her companions introduced what one disgruntled critic of the 1943 exhibition referred to as a 'strange foreign-ness' into the Irish visual experience.[18]

The appearance of women artists in post-Independence Ireland is of major significance. Although Jellett died a year after the founding of the IELA, still only in her forties, her inspiration was important. In 1950, two women artists, Nano Reid (1905–81) and Norah McGuinness, represented Ireland at the international Venice Biennale, the first time Ireland had appeared in the 55-year history of the exhibition.[19] In time, future generations of Irish women would forge influential careers in the visual arts and represent Ireland at leading art events. At the São Paulo Bienal between 1985 and 1996, Ireland was represented by no fewer than five women—Mary FitzGerald (b. 1956), Anne Carlisle (b. 1956), Eilis O'Connell (b. 1953), Alice Maher (b. 1956), and Alanna O'Kelly (b. 1955)—while at recent Venice Biennales, Ireland chose to display more works by women than by men—1993: Dorothy Cross (b. 1956) and Willie Doherty (b. 1959); 1995: Kathy Prendergast (b. 1958) and Shane Cullen (b. 1957); 1997: Alastair MacLennan (b. 1943) and Jaki Irvine (b. 1965); 2001: Grace Weir (b. 1962) and Siobhán Hapaska (b. 1963). Prendergast gained the added prestige of winning the Premio 2000 Award at the 1995 Biennale.[20]

The contribution of many of the above-named artists undermines the patriarchal stranglehold that masculinity has held on Irish life. In two works of 1994, *Berry Dress* (Figure 12.5) and *Bee Dress* (Collection of the Arts Council of Northern Ireland, Belfast), Alice Maher pinned two miniature girls' dresses with natural objects and, through wire framing, allowed the skirts of the dresses to expand. In displaying the dresses, Maher asks that these small objects (the *Berry Dress* is the taller of the two but still only comes to 30 cm) be displayed high on a glass shelf. The viewer may thus, if inclined, peer up into the frock and act like a naughty boy indulging in a voyeuristic experience. Maher's use of ordinary material such as a cotton frock, organic substances like rosehip berries (which have severely wilted over time), and such everyday sexual experiences as youthful voyeurism act as a potent commentary on how the feminine is endlessly subjected to masculine dominance. Similarly, the frequent placement by Dorothy Cross in the 1990s of cow's udders in unusual places questions the male hold on a whole range of professions and experiences. In covering a day-bed with cowhide and placing four udders on the pillow and naming it *Freud's Couch* (1993, private collection), Cross subverts male supremacy in psychotherapy through echoes of Surrealism and witty juxtapositions. To strengthen the quiet deliberateness of her argument, Cross places a Waterford-crystal phallus on the body of the couch, pointing towards the udders.[21]

Such a rich output by women does not imply that male artists in Ireland in recent decades have been inactive or ignored. On the contrary, it could be argued that male artists have dominated two major areas of artistic production in the past century: landscape and expressionism. In landscape, the expansion of the railway in Ireland to the far reaches of the western seaboard greatly aided the development of this particular genre. The many visits of the artist Paul Henry (1876–1958) to Achill and Connemara began in 1910 and, as his biographer points out, 'after only a couple of days he made the third great

FIGURE 12.5 Alice Maher, Berry Dress, 1994.

Copyright Irish Museum of Modern Art, Dublin. Reproduced with the permission of the artist.

decision of his life, and, taking his return railway ticket out of his pocket, in his own words, he "tore it into small pieces and scattered the fragments into the sea"; he would settle on Achill Island'.[22] Henry proceeded to create the archetypal Irish landscape image of the thatched cottage, a brooding mountain backdrop, a winding road, or perhaps a glittering lake. He even returned the favour to the railway companies who had taken him originally to Achill Sound; in the mid 1920s, as Ireland struggled to create a viable tourist industry, one of his Connemara scenes received huge international exposure on a poster published by the London Midland and Scottish Railway Company.[23]

Developments in landscape since Henry, that is, since at least the Second World War, have been read by one critic as being founded in 'agricultural roots, conservatism, an obsession with the past, and a passion for indirect statement'.[24] The works of such artists as Barrie Cooke (b. 1931), Camille Souter (b. 1929), and Brian Bourke (b. 1936) have been said to celebrate the natural environment and all with the aid of such natural media as oil paint, watercolour, and fired clay. Combined with such naturalness, Irish artists of the mid century have been praised for their individualism, their personal integrity. As Tom Duddy has astutely discussed, so much of this commentary is tinged with a romantic mystification which, as he argues, needs to be balanced by a more historically driven, ideologically inquisitive, and economically aware criticism.[25]

The expressionist tendency in Irish art has to some extent been a male preserve. From the colourful exuberance of the late Jack B. Yeats in the 1940s and 1950s to the brooding menace of Brian Maguire's vision (b. 1951), Irish art has moved from a romantic reverie to what Donald Kuspit has called 'a battlefield between superego and impulse—a place of violent emotion and angry intimacy'.[26]

One would be forgiven for expecting artistic reaction to the Troubles in Northern Ireland over the past few decades to be another area of male preserve.[27] Fortunately this is not the case. Artists both male and female have reacted to the violence and dislocation from the 1960s to the 1990s with innovative use of film and photography (Anne Carlisle, b.1956; Willie Doherty, b. 1959), sound and material objects (Philip Napier, b. 1965), or etched metal (John Kindness, b. 1951), while others continue to use long-established media such as oil on canvas or board. Two such painters are Dermot Seymour (b. 1956) and Rita Duffy (b. 1959). Both have used humour to focus on irrational behaviour. Sometimes the humour plays on the bizarre: in Seymour's case, animals such as domestic cows are placed in incongruous settings; in Duffy's case, a grotesque delight in facial expression asks us to realize that political and cultural differences are merely skin deep.

Back in 1908, Hugh Lane had endeavoured to bring modern European art to Dublin. In exhibiting Manet, Degas, and Renoir, he hoped his gallery would show its influence 'in the next generation of artists, and of their critics'.[28] A hundred years later, Dublin and the other big cities such as Belfast, Cork, and Limerick are rich in contemporary Irish art. Admittedly, one can truthfully say that only Dublin, Belfast, and Cork offer the year-round selection of European (and world) art that Lane envisaged being available, but by exhibiting at international gatherings such as the Venice Biennale or the São Paulo Bienal, Irish-based artists are no longer at a disadvantage. The foreign element, mentioned at the beginning of this essay, is still there but it does not dominate; instead it interacts constructively with the indigenous.

NOTES

1. Jane Fenlon, *The Ormonde Picture Collection* (Kilkenny, 2001), 11.
2. George Vertue, 'Notebooks', vol. I, *Walpole Society*, 18 (1930), 31. See also Jane Fenlon, ' "A good painter may get good bread" Thomas Pooley and Garret Morphey, two gentlemen painters' in *Irish Provincial Cultures in the Long Eighteenth Century. Making the middle sort. Essays for Toby Barnard*, Raymond Gillespie and R.F. Foster (eds), (Dublin, 2012), 221–2.
3. Anne Crookshank and the Knight of Glin, *Ireland's Painters 1600–1940* (New Haven and London, 2002), 20.
4. Jane Fenlon, 'John Michael Wright's "Highland Laird" identified,' *Burlington Magazine*, 130, no. 1027 (October 1988), 767.
5. Karen Hearn, tate.org.uk (Collection: Wright, short text).
6. *The Irish Industrial Exhibition of 1853; a detailed catalogue of its contents*, J. Sproule (ed), (Dublin: 1854), 452, 455. Barry's *Entombment* is not listed in William L. Pressly, *The Life and Art of James Barry* (New Haven and London, 1981).
7. The painting in question is entitled, 'The Sheet of Water at Carton, with the duke and duchess of Leinster about to board a rowing boat'; see Crookshank and Glin, 148, Finola O'Kane, *Landscape Design in Eighteenth-Century Ireland* (Cork, 2004), 110– 11 and William Laffan

and Brendan Rooney, *Thomas Roberts. Landscape and Patronage in Eighteenth-Century Ireland* (Tralee, 2009), 277, 294–7, 398–9.

8. *Art Journal* (1854), 166; for other reviews, see Nancy Weston, *Daniel Maclise, 1806–1870. Irish Artist in Victorian London* (Dublin, 2001), 214–15. See also Fintan Cullen, *Ireland on Show. Art, Union, and Nationhood* (Farnham, 2012), 64.

9. For the story of the O'Connell monument, see Homan Potterton, *The O'Connell Monument* (Ballycotton, 1973); Judith Hill, *Irish Public Sculpture: A History* (Dublin, 1998), 93–7; Paula Murphy, 'John Henry Foley's O'Connell Monument', *Irish Arts Review*, 11 (1995), 155–6 and her book, *Nineteenth-Century Irish Sculpture. Native Genius Reaffirmed* (New Haven and London, 2010), ch. 8.

10. Hugh Lane, *Illustrated Catalogue of the Municipal Gallery of Modern Art* (Dublin: 1908), ix. See also Cullen, *Ireland on Show*, ch. 5.

11. On Lane's portrait commissions, see Fintan Cullen, *The Irish Face: Redefining the Irish Portrait* (London, 2004), 65–9.

12. The term 'a suitable building' appears in the famous codicil, written in 1915, in which Lane bequeathed the pictures to Dublin. See Thomas Bodkin, *Hugh Lane and his Pictures* (Dublin, 1956), 43.

13. Lady Gregory, *Hugh Lane's Life and Achievement, with some account of the Dublin Galleries* (London: 1921), ch. 17.

14. Adele M. Dalsimer and Vera Kreilkamp (eds), *America's Eye. Irish Paintings from the Collection of Brian Burns* (Chesnut Hill, MA, 1996), 133. While it is often identified as being an interior of the Gaiety Theatre (1871), Róisín Kennedy has shown that several contemporary reviews state that Yeats's painting is of the Empire Theatre (1897), see her essay in *A Century of Irish Painting. Selections from the Brian P. Burns Collection*, Thomas J. Loughman (ed), (Phoenix, AZ, 2007), 21.

15. Bruce Arnold, *Jack Yeats* (New Haven and London, 1998), 227; *A Westerly Wind* is illustrated in Arnold, 209; *Market Day, Mayo* is illustrated in Hilary Pyle, *Jack B. Yeats: A Catalogue Raisonne of the Oil Paintings*, 3 vols (London, 1992), III, 261.

16. Yeats was to paint a comparable subject in oils in 1923, *Singing the Minstrel Boy*, Sligo County Museum and Art Gallery, see Pyle, *Yeats. A Catalogue Raisonné*, I, 190.

17. Mainie Jellett, 'The RHA and Youth', *Commentary*, 7 May 1942; quoted in S.B. Kennedy, *Irish Art & Modernism* (Belfast, 1991), 116.

18. Mairin Allen, 'Irish Post-Impressionism', *Father Mathew Record* (November 1943), 10, quoted in Kennedy, *Irish Art & Modernism*, 122.

19. See Fionna Barber, 'Excavating Room 50: Irish painting and the Cold War at the 1950 Venice Biennale', in *A Shared Legacy. Essays on Irish and Scottish Art and Visual Culture*, Fintan Cullen and John Morrison (eds), (Aldershot, 2005), 207–23.

20. See *Irish Museum of Modern Art: Shifting Ground. Selected Works of Irish Art 1950–2000*, Brenda McParland (ed), (Dublin, 2000), 70–8.

21. Enrique Juncose, *Dorothy Cross* (Dublin, 2005), 14.

22. S.B. Kennedy, *Paul Henry* (New Haven and London, 2000), 41; Kennedy is quoting from Henry's *An Irish Portrait* (London, 1951), 6.

23. Kennedy, *Henry*, 94–5.

24. Frances Ruane, quoted in Tom Duddy 'Irish Art Criticism—A Provincialism of the Right?', in *Sources in Irish Art. A Reader*, Fintan Cullen (ed), (Cork, 2000), 92.

25. Duddy, 'Irish Art Criticism', 99.

26. See Donald Kuspit, *Brian Maguire* (Dublin, 1988).

27. See Brian, McAvera, *Directions Out. An Investigation into a selection of artists whose work has been formed by the post-1969 situation in Northern Ireland* (Dublin, 1988), an exhibition which was much criticized for ignoring women artists. For a more complete overview, see Luke Kelly, *Thinking Long. Contemporary art in the north of Ireland* (Kinsale, 1996).
28. Lane, *Illustrated Catalogue,* ix.

SELECT BIBLIOGRAPHY

Arnold, Bruce, *Jack Yeats* (New Haven and London, 1998).

Bodkin, Thomas, *Hugh Lane and his Pictures* (Dublin, 1956).

Crookshank, Anne and the Knight of Glin, *Ireland's Painters 1600–1940* (New Haven and London, 2002).

Cullen, Fintan, *Sources in Irish Art. A Reader* (Cork, 2000).

Cullen, Fintan, *The Irish Face: Redefining the Irish Portrait* (London, 2004).

Cullen, Fintan and R.F. Foster, *'Conquering England'. Ireland in Victorian London* (London, 2005).

Cullen, Fintan and Morrison, John (eds), *A Shared Legacy. Essays on Irish and Scottish Art and Visual Culture* (Aldershot, 2005).

Cullen, Fintan, *Ireland on Show. Art, Union, and Nationhood* (Farnham, 2012).

Dalsimer, Adele M. and Kreilkamp, Vera (eds), *America's Eye: Irish Paintings from the Collection of Brian Burns* (Chesnut Hill, MA, 1996).

Dawson, Barbara (ed), *Hugh Lane. Founder of a Gallery of Modern Art for Ireland,* (London, 2008).

Gillespie, Raymond and Foster, R.F. (eds), *Irish Provincial Cultures in the Long Eighteenth Century. Making the middle sort. Essays for Toby Barnard* (Dublin, 2012).

Henry, Paul, *An Irish Portrait* (London, 1951).

Hill, Judith, *Irish Public Sculpture: A History* (Dublin, 1998).

Hodge, Anne (ed), *Hugh Douglas Hamilton (1740–1808): A Life in Pictures* (Dublin, 2008).

Kelly, Luke, *Thinking Long. Contemporary art in the north of Ireland* (Kinsale, 1996).

Kennedy, S.B., *Irish Art & Modernism* (Belfast, 1991).

Kennedy, S.B., *Paul Henry* (New Haven and London, 2000).

Laffan, William and Rooney, Brendan, *Thomas Roberts. Landscape and Patronage in Eighteenth-Century Ireland* (Tralee, 2009).

Lane, Hugh, *Illustrated Catalogue of the Municipal Gallery of Modern Art* (Dublin, 1908).

McConkey, Kenneth, *Sir John Lavery* (Edinburgh, 1933).

Murphy, Paula, *Nineteenth-Century Irish Sculpture. Native Genius Reaffirmed* (New Haven and London, 2010).

O'Byrne, Robert, *Hugh Lane 1875–1915* (Dublin, 2000).

O'Kane, Finola, *Landscape Design in Eighteenth-Century Ireland* (Cork, 2004).

Pressly, William L., *The Life and Art of James Barry* (New Haven and London, 1981).

Pyle, Hilary, *Jack B. Yeats. A Catalogue Raisonné of the Oil Paintings,* 3 vols (London, 1992).

Pyle, Hilary, *Jack B. Yeats, A Biography* (London, 1989).

Weston, Nancy, *Daniel Maclise, 1806–1870. Irish Artist in Victorian London* (Dublin, 2001).

CHAPTER 13

MATERIAL CULTURES

TOBY BARNARD

I

MATERIAL culture concerns the essentials for living: shelter, warmth, food, and drink. Yet, quickly enough, human needs moved beyond necessities to accessories. If many possessions had utilitarian purposes, some were valued chiefly as symbols. They expressed status and wealth. Also they could link makers, owners, and users with imagined or invisible worlds. Accordingly, reconstructions of material life throw light on the prosaic realities of daily existence and the struggle to exist. In addition, understanding how highly some objects were valued can elucidate attitudes, of both individuals and communities.

In Ireland, as elsewhere, the stuff of material life exists in bewildering variety. Before the eighteenth century, surviving artefacts are few. Archaeology has unearthed some, but usually in fragments. Furthermore, the survivals are often weighted towards the exceptional; especially the further back in time the enquirer goes. The dearth of objects is compensated by other kinds of documentation. Travellers, administrators, reformers, painters, novelists, and poets in describing what they saw give insights into the way in which the Irish lived. Other sorts of written records bring greater precision to these impressions. Accounts, receipts, and bills tell of what was bought and sold. Imports and exports through Irish ports are also recorded for some periods. Individuals sometimes listed what they owned and even how it was distributed through the rooms in their houses. By the eighteenth century, advertisements were printed in the newspapers. Again, these reveal an enlarged choice and new techniques to persuade purchasers.

This evidence, although patchy, allows classification of what was available, its first appearance and gradual popularization in Ireland and, sometimes, estimates of quantities. Much of this information is uncertain and inferred. Nevertheless, it has encouraged interpretations of material culture along the lines of studies that have multiplied in continental Europe, Britain, and North America. Fundamental in these studies are economic factors. The acquisition of objects reflected spending power. It also told of technological and commercial innovations. More, and more complicated, articles were being made. Also, the markets for them expanded. Traffic, which had first brought into Ireland goods from Europe's Atlantic seaboard, the Baltic, and Mediterranean, lengthened into Africa, Asia, and the Americas. Ireland, while neither populous nor wealthy, offered potential profits to traders.

Important to understanding the growing complexity of material cultures is the irrational element. The goods to be bartered might be few and the amount of money to spare small, but these considerations did not always restrain purchasers from impulsive and apparently unnecessary indulgences. Their choices might speak of a wish to display status or simply to savour the unfamiliar. Manufacturers and traders in any case had a powerful motive to teach more in the population to consume. They implanted desires for need-nots and luxuries, and unscrupulously inflamed them. The sellers identified specific groups from whom they could profit: women were regarded as particularly rewarding. In time, too, materials were aimed at children. Blatant economic calculations lay behind many innovations. The receptiveness of the Irish, as of most populations, to these blandishments provoked strictures over the moral as well as financial damage. Simplicity and self-sufficiency, it was argued, had been supplanted by a craving for the outlandish. In Ireland too, a patriotic worry—the draining of money into the coffers of foreign merchants and manufacturers—took another twist. An indigenous material life based on the pastoralism and frugality of the native Irish, seemingly 'natural', had been corrupted as successive generations of immigrants introduced their strange tastes. By the later eighteenth century, injunctions to curb sybaritic pleasures and so to arrest the resulting enfeeblement were linked with calls for Ireland to throw off its dependence on England. Powerful as the patriotic slogans were, they could not insulate Ireland against a material culture that had long been international and which was now global. Like it or not, the materials of Irish life were hybrids. In this situation, a more constructive response was for Irish producers to stamp their wares with recognizably Hibernian features.

The often fraught relationship between Ireland and its nearest neighbour affected the nature of, and attitudes towards, material culture. Further complications arose from religious confession. Catholics and Protestants diverged over the theological significance and the liturgical uses of icons and objects. In general, Catholic worship required more physical accessories. In Ireland, however, this trait was offset by the poverty of the church, its adherents and—during the eighteenth century—the legal disabilities under which services were conducted.

II

Excavations have unearthed traces from the Neolithic era in the fourth millennium. Even at this early stage, diversification in forms and decoration suggest seemingly simple pots and implements meant something more to their makers and owners than austere functionality. Thereafter the urge to decorate, together with the appeal of particular patterns and colours, remain constant themes in material culture. Once the first millennium after Christ is reached, more objects survive. The most spectacular were generated by, and owe their preservation to, the Christian church. Settings and furnishings associated with religious rituals range from the remnants of buildings—the Gallarus Oratory on the Dingle Peninsula—to sacred objects. The latter include bells, shrines, crosses, reliquaries, hand-written and elaborately decorated versions of the Bible, and even covers for the holy books, sometimes of stamped leather, but more often of wood overlaid with precious metals and stones. Chalices needed for the celebration of the sacraments, such as that from Ardagh, exhibit the technical dexterity and inventiveness of the craftworkers. So too does a unique belt shrine of bronze, silver, glass, and enamel from Moylough, County Sligo. Made in the eighth century, it is now at the Country Life Museum at Turlough Park. Most of these articles owe their survival to the special renown they have long enjoyed. In turn their fame reflected rare and costly materials and the expertise that went into their fabrication. These told of the prestige of the establishment for which they were created. But the degree to which they were venerated—important in their preservation—arose also from association. They proclaimed the power of the family which had commissioned them; they were linked with the cults of local, regional, and transnational holy figures.

The religious rituals in which many of these objects were featured were common across much of Europe. Accordingly, the functions and forms of the artefacts that have been recovered in Ireland resemble those found elsewhere within Christendom. Close inspection does, however, show variations. How these are best explained is one of the consistent threads in systematic studies of material culture. Some idiosyncrasies point to particular local conditions and traditions. Many suggest linkages between apparently remote and isolated Irish places and other parts of the island, or further afield, with Scotland, England, and continental Europe. In this way, the objects yield clues about the movement of individuals, ideas, and styles as much as of the articles themselves.

Ireland, never subject to Roman invasion and conquest (except in the minds of a few eccentric antiquarians), was affected by the arrival of Christianity, with its notionally standardized and international culture. In assessing its impact on the material cultures of Ireland, interpreters differ in the weighting to be given to the local and the imported. Similar disagreements recur throughout the assessment of the cultural effects of the invasions that followed: first the Vikings; then the Cambro-Normans; next the English and Scots; and, between the sixteenth and eighteenth centuries, smaller contingents of refugees from France and the Rhineland. Whether these contributions to material, as to other aspects of Irish life, are regarded as fruitful or harmful often depends on political outlook. Newcomers frequently belittled what they encountered in Ireland. Settlers from Britain were committed to replacing alleged backwardness—evident in housing, clothing, and diet—with the modes to which they were accustomed. Industry would supplant idleness; civility, barbarism; and improvement would banish primitivism. These attitudes expressed cultural superiority. Equal contempt was directed onto those who dwelt in remote upland districts of the west and north of England, Wales, and Scotland.

In their turn the English, on the western margins of Europe, were seen as uncouth and backward by visitors from Mediterranean Europe.

The aggression with which these objectives were pursued in Ireland provoked local resistance. At the same time, the interactions between natives and newcomers produced hybrids. Sometimes there has been a reluctance to acknowledge their distinction, a reluctance which has even extended to systematic study and conservation of what could be retrieved. The best-publicized example was the destruction of the site of Viking Dublin after it was exposed before the building of new civic offices on Wood Quay in the 1970s. Fortunately, enough was excavated and saved to reconstruct a much more detailed account of Viking and medieval Dublin. The prevalence of imports and the gradual and selective adoption of foreign styles were clarified. Once settlers from England and Wales arrived after 1172, material life was profoundly affected. Some of their ways were copied, especially in the areas around Dublin and the eastern and southern seaboards where they were concentrated. Also, these coastal belts were open to shipments, either from Britain or continental Europe. On the other hand, aspirations to turn Ireland into a replica of England ran up against ecological realities. Materials that abounded locally in Britain—building stones, clays, and timber—were more sparsely scattered in Ireland. Moreover, designs and techniques in Ireland had evolved to exploit what there was. Immigrants necessarily adjusted to the conditions. A tension existed between the desire to hang on to what spoke of their origins and to succeed in the different environment of Ireland. Regional variants of the international Gothic fashionable throughout Western Europe appeared. In Dublin and the adjacent Pale, the contribution of masons from the west of England was seen in prestigious structures, such as cathedrals. West of the Shannon, in the friaries and abbeys, it was connections with France and the Iberian Peninsula that showed in the tracery of windows.[1] Tower houses, favoured as the residences of the heads of Gaelic septs and of anglicized barons, resembled those which punctuated the contested marches between England and both Scotland and Wales.

What survives or can be reconstructed of these buildings, once again, throws light chiefly on the houses of the elites. How these residences were furnished and used has largely to be guessed. The makeshift housing of the majority, along with their buried possessions, is being excavated. Since wealth and status were largely embodied in perishables—livestock and their by-products—the strongest impression is of material deprivation. It is modified by the occasional recovery of archaeological deposits and, more substantially, by the fifteenth century, by the records of imports and exports. A dazzling array of consumer durables—glass, pottery, fabrics, metalwares, and haberdashery—was shipped in. This upsurge in demand within Ireland for the materials of a more comfortable and refined life predates the influx of settlers from England and Wales in the later sixteenth and early seventeenth centuries.[2] It suggests, contrary to some popular assertions, that those already long settled in Ireland had a taste for novelties and the means to purchase them. Furthermore, if already there was a brisk market for such goods, then the incentives for locals to supply it were strong. Local production of textiles was certainly common. More shadowy are enterprises in metalworking and ceramics.

They existed—for example, souterrain pottery in the north-east—but the Irish regional wares were hard to identify with certainty.

Customs records offer evidence about the volume, value, and nature of imported commodities. The growth reflects the diversification of what was on offer, especially as producers throughout Britain and continental Europe innovated in designs and forms. Also, the documentation tells of the dramatic expansion in the sources of the goods.

To long-established trade with Asia and Africa was added, from the late fifteenth century, rapid exploitation of the riches of America. Textiles, ceramics, precious and semi-precious metals and stones, and exotic timbers were the most eye-catching additions. But the introduction of tobacco, unfamiliar vegetables, and plants with culinary or medicinal applications also affected material lives. Disposable clay pipes allowed tobacco to be smoked. Such was their popularity that potters within Ireland tried to cash in.[3]

Similarly, the preparation and storage of drugs and foods required suitable vessels. Initially, price and scarcity kept many of these items from the majority of the population. Its desires were satisfied with cheaper, locally manufactured versions. In the case of fine porcelain, usually decorated in blue and white, arriving in Europe from the Orient, potteries in the Low Countries (notably the eponymous Delft), along the Rhineland, in France, the Iberian Peninsula, and England improvised their own earthenware equivalents. Efforts were renewed to set up local manufactures in order to reduce dependence on the foreign. The lack of the necessary raw materials and of technological expertise hampered these initiatives. It was mostly cruder wares that were made within Ireland. Nevertheless, a few experienced in ironworking, glass-blowing, potting, spinning, and weaving were encouraged to settle in order to teach locals. The ventures seldom lasted long. Perennial problems were the high costs of materials, labour and transport, uncertain quality, and the fickleness of consumers.

III

The precise date at which Ireland was exposed to this internationalized and ultimately global world of goods is subject to argument. Geography meant that it limped behind many countries more advantageously placed to participate. However, as trade with the West and East Indies quickened, southern Ireland in particular was well situated. Vessels bound for the Orient or the Caribbean were regularly supplied from ports such as Kinsale, Cork, and Waterford. Yet trade was inhibited by the restrictions introduced by a series of English navigation acts. From the 1650s onwards, Ireland was forbidden to trade directly with the growing empire. Instead, it was obliged to receive the goods only after they had been landed in England. These prohibitions encouraged circumvention. Contraband was smuggled into the many creeks and havens around the long coasts of Ireland. Wrecks, sometimes engineered by those living near the coast, also brought the desired objects unexpectedly within reach.

Against these opportunities to enjoy what the globe yielded have to be set the obstacles. Some, as has been suggested, were created by the English government. Others arose from the location of Ireland. Most, arguably, came from the meagre spending power of the bulk of the inhabitants. The prevalent poverty stunted the development of consumerism. For most, life was stripped down to the fundamentals. Even these—food, shelter, clothing—were not always there. Furthermore, features thought to be intrinsic to the organization of Irish life militated against sophisticated material cultures. Nomadism discouraged the acquisition of goods; so too, apparently, did barter. In practice, these habits did not automatically stop the production and acquisition of inessentials or investing objects with symbolic value.

Those who wrote to justify English conquest and British settlement in Ireland contrasted—and often misrepresented—the indigenous and imported systems. Profound differences did exist. Yet, both the indigenous and imported systems were structured hierarchically. Status was communicated visually: through what was owned and worn as well as what was eaten and drunk. The unfamiliar, especially if costly, enhanced prestige. Because the upsurge in spending on non-essentials in England, sometimes dramatized into a consumer 'revolution', coincided with the more intensive settlement of Ireland by emigrants from England, Scotland, and Wales, it is easy to assume that the newcomers introduced similar preferences into Ireland. Recent analysis of the customs records indicates that the process was already under way before the later sixteenth century. Even so, there are two ways in which this larger number of recent arrivals affected the material cultures of Ireland. The first was the strengthening of existing physical and cultural linkages with the distinct regions of the neighbouring island. Fusing with and modifying localized vernacular traditions within Ireland, the arrangement and detail of housing, wooden furnishings, farming, and household tools varied. The variants were entrenched more deeply thanks to regular trade. Bristol and the smaller ports around the Bristol Channel offered the most direct crossings to south Munster, Waterford, and Wexford. Dublin and Drogheda were supplied mainly from Chester, Liverpool, the harbours of North Wales, and Whitehaven. Further north, Newry, Carrickfergus, Coleraine, and Derry all trafficked with western Scotland. The movement of people and goods perpetuated idiosyncrasies. Immigrants from these areas had landed with practices and preferences in building, furniture, diet, clothing, cultivation, and recreation that persisted in their new settings. Official prescriptions and proscriptions aimed to spread uniformity. Laws decreed who should wear what; other edicts stipulated the materials for housing. In the end, most were obliged to work with what was available. In some places, reeds rather than straw thatched roofs; walls were built of mud or turf rather than brick; utensils were fashioned from bone and horn, not wood.

Before the eighteenth century, the sparse artefacts that have survived have to be supplemented with other information. Inventories, fewer than those for Britain and continental Europe, list and frequently value possessions. As elsewhere, they tend to survey the prosperous who owned goods in plenty and of value. Much in these listings is too bald to allow anything other than an impression of how a few houses were equipped: 'a table', 'six chairs', 'lattin ware', 'old tapestry'. Specialists were sometimes summoned (and paid) to inventory particular types of goods: silver; paintings; books. There were occasions, too, when women were asked to appraise. A particular female province was clothing and textiles. Despite their shortcomings, the catalogues of household effects can pinpoint the first appearance and gradual spread of particular items. Looking-glasses, clocks, the equipment for serving tea, coffee, and hot chocolate, glasses for syllabub and sweetmeats, fish or oyster knives can be traced. Furthermore, altering tastes in fabrics, their textures, colours, and patterns are retrievable. Then, too, the names given to rooms are signs of specialized functions having reserved spaces, such as dining and later breakfasting, sleeping, reading, and for children and servants. Such differentiation was practicable only in the largest houses and may have broken down in the face of daily realities.[4] Once more, unfortunately, the resulting insights leave the middling and lower orders in almost total darkness.

In trying to penetrate that obscurity, there are a few helps. Contemporary commentators censure more often than they praise the material circumstances of the Irish peasantry. Customs returns, printed advertisements, bills, receipts, and account books, coupled with occasional information about the stock of traders in Dublin and the provinces, hint at the spread of more goods beyond the prosperous elite. The proliferation and vitality of fairs and markets similarly suggest wider opportunities to participate in the alluring material world. The calculated magnetism of retailing premises, included in the prestigious redevelopments of Dublin in the 1780s and 1790s, wooed shoppers. Equally innovative and perhaps more important in increasing demand was the opening of shops in provincial towns. Some protested against these developments. They signified the luxury and effeminacy that were said to be weakening Britain and Ireland. In addition, patriots attacked the extravagances as yet another consequence of Ireland's subordination to Britain. The manly simplicity of the Irish was being corrupted through exposure to the artificially stimulated tastes from abroad. In this way, moral damage was added to the more obvious financial implications. Intermittent but regular injunctions to buy and dress Irish, patronized at the highest level by the Lord Lieutenant and his entourage, could mutate into uglier manifestations of xenophobia. Importers and even wearers of foreign goods were attacked periodically and the offending articles, especially fabrics, destroyed.[5]

Economic nationalism, although endorsed by reformers, improvers, and moralists, had to contend against the irrational appetites for the smart and uncommon. Moreover, buoyant consumerism was defended. Theorists like Bernard Mandeville and Adam Smith argued that it brought economic gains. Less remarked, although sometimes a cause of concern to misogynistic observers, were the greater opportunities for women to exercise choice as they equipped themselves, their families and households. Moreover, things allowed their possessors—even humble ones—to project their personalities.[6]

At best, the poor participated fitfully in this brisk consumerism. Yet the bleak picture can be lightened a little. Among tenants, craftworkers, and artisans there were variations in earnings and circumstances. The middling sorts, more visible in towns, were not missing from the countryside. Even when they did not utilize the itinerant peddlers and journeymen, the fairs, markets, and booths at religious patterns, or the emerging general stores, they had other chances to enjoy something of the material plenty. Gifts and legacies were one device. The well-to-do frequently favoured dependants and servants with gifts of particular articles: clothing was most common, but sometimes pieces of silver, wooden furniture, timepieces, and paintings. Auctions dispersed the contents of both grand and modest establishments. Squires and their wives did not disdain the second-hand. But the public sales were also an occasion when the desirable, useful, and unusual could be bought by those lower on the social scale. More ubiquitous still were dealers in the second-hand, unredeemed pawnbrokers' pledges, and the stolen. Through these channels much was recirculated or recycled.

Just as customers might spend scarce resources on what looked like fripperies, so the chances of descent and resale allowed once valuable items to reappear in incongruous settings. These processes are glimpsed rarely and briefly. Clearest are specific developments that occurred in the eighteenth century: the making of furniture, glass, silver, pottery, and fabrics. Again, much of what has been painstakingly uncovered and analyzed concerns consciously fashionable articles. Individually and in aggregate, the findings indicate a widening and strengthening of demand. Professionals, town-dwellers, and prospering members of the middling sorts were sharing many of the commodities conventionally associated with, even reserved for, the most elevated stratum of peers and squires.[7]

Those able to afford it ordered some of their showiest furnishings from Dublin or London. But many also purchased everyday items locally. Fairs and auctions were ready sources. Owners of estates had employees who could turn their talents from fencing and gates to built-in dressers, bedposts, cupboards, and tables. Furthermore, there were travelling specialists who, moving from house to house, would stay as long as it took to construct a table, wooden bowls and plates, or pairs of breeches and flashy coats. Payment was partly in kind—board and lodging—and in money.[8]

Common to all the goods is an unpredictable and constantly changing amalgam of styles copied from elsewhere with those originating in Ireland itself. Designs could be taken easily from outside Ireland. Printed books of patterns, engravings, and drawings rapidly spread what was in vogue on the continent of Europe or metropolitan Britain into Ireland. Accomplished cabinetmakers in Dublin would be commissioned to make a prototype chair, which was then used as the template by carpenters in County Galway or County Down. Entrepreneurs seized the chance to profit from the vigorous demand. On the Wentworth estate in south Wicklow, plentiful timber was turned into prefabricated legs, arms, stretchers, and splats for chairs. These were then sold in Dublin.

This mobility—of the artefacts and the artificers—frustrates efforts to identify distinctively Irish features. Stylistic oddities have been proposed: a liking for bold animal masks on the aprons of tables and hairy paws for pad-feet of chairs, stools, and tables. Greater confidence in attributing pieces to Irish makers comes from written orders and payments. Occasionally an item retains the printed label of the supplier. Not until the nineteenth century does it become more common to stamp into the wood the name of its manufacturer or retailer. Provenance—an accurate record of the descent of a piece from one owner to the next and across many generations—occasionally makes good the deficiency. Then, too, 'tradition' can be invoked: families or recent owners sometimes retell tales about the commissioning and subsequent fate of the table or bureau. As with most traditions, separating the authentic from the invented is taxing.[9]

Silver poses fewer difficulties in identifying the authentically Irish. It is also possible to quantify domestic output at certain times. Because of the intrinsic and lasting value of the metal itself, it was widely used both to advertise wealth and as a secure investment. Its production was subject to official control. Silver (and gold) objects had to have their metallic content verified. Assay offices certified it by stamping marks (assay marks) on the products. These amounted to an inbuilt certificate of authenticity. Also, the marks recorded the year and place of making, and frequently the maker. These signs, employed also for silver made outside Ireland, enable pieces to be identified conclusively as Irish.

Silver continued to be hallmarked outside Dublin: at Cork, Waterford, Limerick, and Galway.[10] Some connoisseurs have isolated traits that characterize the different areas. Even so, the essential forms of both utilitarian and decorative articles permitted relatively little deviation. Moreover, just as what was in demand in the capital was readily reproduced in the provinces, so patterns popular outside Ireland were quickly adopted in Dublin and then in the regions. Customers also moved about, enabling them to order directly from specialists in France and England.[11] Certain utensils seem to have been particularly liked in Ireland—for example, piggins (for holding cream or butter), butter tubs, and dish-rings (to lift hot dishes off the surface of a table). Again, as in wooden carving, a penchant for grotesque animals can be detected.[12] Towards the close of the eighteenth century, the most common articles to be fashioned from silver were teaspoons.[13] Replacing horn, tin, pewter, and improvised stirrers, the cutlery denoted refinement and substance. Frequently, spoons were bequeathed to offspring and friends.

Ceramics and glass catered to more mundane needs than did silverwares. Pottery had long been made in Ireland, but much also was shipped in. The art of making glass, in contrast, eluded the Irish. Whether for windows, mirrors, or drinking vessels, crates and cribs arrived from Bristol, London, the Low Countries, and, via intermediaries, Venice. By the early seventeenth century, several landowners, such as the Parsons in County Offaly (King's County), sponsored the building of glasshouses on their lands. These enterprises were typically overseen by immigrants with knowledge acquired elsewhere. Most ambitious was the enterprise which functioned towards the end of the seventeenth century in Dublin's quayside district. The glass met some of the local demand, but was not highly esteemed.[14] Still the imported enjoyed a cachet, partly snobbish but also practical, with those who could afford it. Glass plates for the pier-glasses that were becoming *de rigueur* in smart Dublin town houses by the middle of the eighteenth century simply could not be produced in Ireland.[15] More systematic efforts to correct these deficiencies were directed towards factories in Waterford and Cork. These succeeded in popularizing the Irish makes as a cheaper (and therefore inferior) substitute for the imported. The increased demand for the accoutrements of what was considered to be polite living sustained the Irish manufactures.[16]

Similar features underlie the episodic history of ceramics in Ireland. Local kilns potted rudimentary vessels. But archaeological findings suggest large volumes were routinely imported from north Devon, Saintonge, Iberia, and the Rhineland.[17] By the sixteenth century, these traditional sources of supply were challenged as the craze for the oriental spread into Ireland. At first, few could afford the exotic wares coming from the East. Instead, they acquired cheaper versions pioneered in the Low Countries. These earthenwares, typically painted in blue and white, but sometimes with brighter ochres and manganese, were swiftly plagiarized in France and England. They were soon included in loads consigned for Ireland.

Potential profit and the patriotic desire to curb the outward flow of bullion combined to promote local potteries. The vivid designs were readily imitated and adapted, but the recipes for bodies and glazes proved more challenging to Irish experimenters. A pot-house was established in Dublin by Henry Delamain. Throughout the 1740s and 1750s, it competed against the dishes baked in Staffordshire, London, Rouen, and the United Provinces. Delamain's triumph was brief.[18] During the 1770s, manufacturers claimed to have introduced into Dublin the making of light, durable, and attractive pottery to match the creamware or queensware that Josiah Wedgwood was marketing in Ireland. The Dublin enterprises never eclipsed the highly esteemed imports. Wedgwood opened an outlet in Dublin between 1772 and 1777. This fed the craving that he had stimulated, including 'a violent vase madness' that was raging in Dublin. One resident of the city acquired a suite of five vases from Wedgwood in 1773, for which he paid £3 11s.[19] Despite the taste for imports, those with nearby deposits of china clay, mindful of the artistic and technical skills available within Ireland or hopeful of enriching themselves, renewed the attempts to create an Irish ceramics industry. Notable among them was the Marquess of Downshire in Belfast.[20]

Technical weaknesses, inadequate capital, and wayward customers explain why so many domestic ventures foundered. Indicative of the ambiguities, if not contradictions, in the attitude of fervent patriots is the failure of local manufacturers to cash in on the demand for material emblems of the political campaigns of the last quarter of the eighteenth century. Those wishing to proclaim their allegiance to movements such as Volunteering did so by buying jugs potted in Staffordshire and Liverpool and then transfer-printed with Hibernian images.[21] English manufacturers applied Irish subjects to their wares in the same way as other heroes and villains—Frederick of Prussia, the elder Pitt, Wilkes, Lafayette, Franklin, Washington, Nelson, Wellington, and Napoleon—in order to render them topical and saleable. Since non-Irish subjects sold well in Ireland, the souvenirs became a further method through which identification with Britain or the rebels in North America could be announced. One effect was clearly to dilute any distinctively Irish taste in material culture. This paradox persisted. James Donovan established himself as a seller of the smartest ceramics in early nineteenth-century Dublin. Donovan, the 'emperor of China', bought decorated pieces and blanks from Staffordshire potteries. The undecorated were then painted by the proficient artists who had been trained in Ireland, but seldom with scenes with any obvious Irish resonances. Later in the same century, attempts were made in Dublin to emulate the art pottery coming into vogue across Europe. The result, 'Vodrian ware', although it had a following, never displaced imports.[22] Indeed, recent excavations suggest that the cheap products from Staffordshire were permeating the Irish midlands by the nineteenth century.[23] Vodrian remained an oddity for the arty.

Among the prime targets to reduce Irish dependence on costly imports were textiles. Warmth and convention demanded that humans cover themselves. In time, the law required the abandoning of the Irish mantle, a loose plaid that enveloped the head as well as much of the body. It is uncertain the extent to which the injunction was obeyed. Irish cloaks and shawls seem often to have been draped around the person in much the same manner as the forbidden mantle. Laws, common throughout much of Europe, tried to link what was worn—and especially its cost—with rank. However, those with enough money bought the furs and thick, dark broadcloths that were intended only for the grand. Heavy materials never lost their allure, but they were joined by lighter fabrics with gaudy patterns, either from the Orient or copying oriental designs. There was much complaint about the seekers after these vanities. From time to time, there were drives, backed by governors and grandees in Dublin, to dress and buy Irish. It was quickly realized that they would succeed only when the Irish-made competed in value and design. These causes were taken up in the eighteenth century by bodies in receipt of public moneys, notably the Linen Board and the Dublin Society. The former through stricter regulation of standards and the latter by encouraging greater sophistication in dyes and patterns raised the repute of linens and poplins. Other fabrics—damask, silk velvet, woollens, and cottons—struggled harder to defeat foreign competitors.

IV

Two other developments, concurrent but at best only loosely linked, deserve attention for possible effects on Irish lives. The vitality and prosperity which led to the physical expansion and embellishment of Dublin during the second half of the eighteenth century were threatened and (some would argue) well-nigh destroyed in 1801. The Act of Union abolished the Irish Parliament. Without the regular influx of parliamentarians (a group of about 450), the capital, if not turned into a ghost town, was emptied of its most prodigious spenders. However, Dublin continued to act as a magnet for provincials, thanks to its unique educational, recreational, legal, medical, commercial, and social attractions. It remained the prime shopping centre in Ireland. Moreover, its residents (numbering around 182 000 in 1800), economically and occupationally diversified, created enough demand to sustain a rich variety of manufactures and services.[24] In any case, the city had long contended with the rivalry of London, Bath, and Paris.

One element increasing in numbers and prosperity, particularly in Dublin but across most of the island, was the Catholic majority. Even before being freed from the most irksome legal restraints, some Catholics had joined in and profited from the buoyant consumerism. Reticent about display in their own homes, reflecting either prudence or penury, restraint was less apparent in their places of worship. Initially it was in the interiors and furnishings of chapels and convents, not in the austere and self-effacing exteriors, that material splendour blazed. The utensils required for worship allowed opportunities for ostentation and invention. Donors turned sometimes to locals to make the necessary vessels. Similarly, vestments might be woven and embroidered, statues carved, and canvases painted in the locality. Parishioners were exhorted to contribute particular objects, to which their or their forbears' names would be attached in perpetuity. For those who had left their native places and prospered elsewhere, this was a device through which sentimental pride and subsequent success could be trumpeted. In the eighteenth century, churches in Waterford had gained from the generosity of members of local families who had prospered in Spain. Already, worshippers were being habituated to styles fashionable outside Ireland.[25]

What was needed by churches, Protestant as much as Catholic, differed so greatly from domestic needs that their splendour and novelties may be thought irrelevant to the material culture of the laity. Yet, the sacred and secular were not altogether discrete spheres, one public, the other private. Church attendance, if far from universal, nevertheless habituated many to imagery and accoutrements contrived to impress. During the nineteenth century, the Catholic Church paraded a distinctive material culture. As early as the 1780s, processions on Corpus Christi day (11 June) threaded through the streets of Tullow (County Carlow). From the 1830s, new churches, often grandiose in scale, replaced the humbler makeshifts. A modest classicism, deriving from the continent and ultimately from early-Christian Rome, was superseded by an aggressive Gothic. The separate churches were slower to associate themselves with Celtic motifs. In time, the latter would be invoked as the physical manifestations of a creed unpolluted by the subsequent accretions and an island uncorrupted by invaders.[26]

Parishes and their priests vied with one another to fill the buildings with sumptuous decorations. Worshippers were thereby introduced to an iconography which, in simpler forms, might be adopted in their homes. Statues and pictures, reproduced through engraving, oleograph, and even photography, followed themes unknown in austere Protestant churches and houses. Personal piety also required accessories. They ranged from workaday missals and catechisms to much more highly decorated ones: rosaries, decade rings (to assist in the recitation of the decades of the rosary), religious medals, souvenirs from pilgrimages, amulets, and tokens. Some commemorated trips to shrines; others were tossed into holy wells as offerings or in propitiation. Patterns, the annual veneration of a local saint, also generated artefacts. In some cases, the objects were sanctified versions of similar objects that had been used in calendar customs that elided the Christian and the pagan. Before the possibility of mass manufacture in the nineteenth century, the devices were constructed locally. Wooden and base-metal crucifixes from the sixteenth to the eighteenth century have survived, thanks to their durable materials and the value (not just monetary) with which they were invested.[27] Rosaries from this period have also been preserved. More ephemeral are the crosses and *asperges* of straw that were plaited together for celebrations such as St Bridget's Eve or the celebration of Mass within a private house (the stations).

The greater confidence of the Catholic Church manifested itself in its physical arrangements. It told of the relaxation and eventual lifting (in 1829) of legal disabilities. It further revealed a more assertive and prosperous Catholic laity. The latter were important in sustaining other developments in the material cultures of nineteenth- and twentieth-century Ireland. Just as the bijouterie accompanying Catholic rituals was commercialized and mechanized, so too were the products necessary for daily routines. Especially in the larger towns, the well-to-do in the professions and trades and among *rentiers*, could buy comforts. The tastes of this group have so far attracted less analysis than those of landowners. By the nineteenth century, the spending power of successful Catholics enabled them to accumulate and relish material possessions. Thanks to confession, familial and trading links, education, and travel, they might be oriented more towards continental Europe than to Britain.

Cheaper, mass-produced goods flooded into Ireland. Worries about the financial and moral consequences recurred. Unavailing efforts were made to free consumers from enslavement to the foreign by encouraging domestic industries. However, Irish producers were slow to adopt the methods of rivals in Britain, continental Europe, and North America. In addition, innovations in transport—steam power, then the railways, and ultimately motor and air transport—eased the import into, and distribution throughout, Ireland of the mass-produced. Strategies of selling were also altering. Advertising showed greater skill in making both blatant and subliminal appeals. By the mid nineteenth century, department stores beguiled those who entered their halls. Much of their magnetism came from gathering under one roof a galaxy of goods. Since they were drawn from across the globe, shops such as Clerys, Arnotts, Switzers, and Brown Thomas further internationalized the materials on offer to the refined and respectable.

Easier access to worldwide markets, and particularly to those within the extensive British Empire, was an incentive to Irish producers. Goods distinctive in look or superlative in quality commanded a premium. To achieve these objectives, it was thought important to offer more education in art and design. This continued the thinking of some within the eighteenth-century Dublin Society. It was rooted in the belief that continental European competitors were helped by their attractive designs. By the middle of the nineteenth century, training was offered outside Dublin. Belfast, Cork, Limerick, Clonmel, and Wexford acquired their own technical colleges. Frequent national and international exhibitions offered opportunities to show off Irish materials. The Dublin Society continued to organize displays: for example, in 1834 and 1835. At Cork in 1853, then in Dublin in 1865, 1882, and 1907, and again in Cork in 1903, extravaganzas exhibited Irish staples and novelties. More lucrative markets were courted by showing goods outside Ireland. There was an Irish presence at the Great Exhibition in the Crystal Palace in 1851. Valuable too were shows at Paris in 1855, Chicago (1893), and St Louis (1904). As a result, Ireland became firmly associated with specialities: lace from Muckross and Limerick; fine porcelain from Belleek; linen from Lisburn. All were rarefied commodities.

V

A few conspicuous ventures divert attention away from the basics in material culture. Domestic production and sales have yet to be quantified. Moreover, throughout the nineteenth century, despite the physical and demographic growth of towns, Ireland's economy remained overwhelmingly an agricultural one. Farming and rural communities suffered several blows: the famine of 1848 and the depression in prices later in the century. The poverty in which many lived prevented wholehearted participation in the world of goods. As a consequence, the increasingly variegated material culture was experienced unevenly. The poor, living in cramped quarters, were forced to improvise. Materials were salvaged, in coastal areas from wrecks, and ingeniously re-used. Many pieces had to serve dual purposes: beds would be turned during the day into tables; dressers which shelved the Delftware had, in their lower sections, coops in which hens could be housed. The forms of the cottages themselves and their rudimentary wooden furnishings reflected not only the materials at hand locally but also told of tenacious traditions. Of perishable materials and low monetary value, little has survived and even less in their original locations. Because the simplicity of these articles announced penury, they tended to be swept away as reminders of unhappy times best forgotten. Only recently have the naïveté and evidence of regional traits come to be valued. Collections of such materials have been assembled in the National Museum in Dublin, its outpost at Turlough Park, County Mayo, the Agricultural Museum at Johnstown Castle, County Wexford, and the Folk Museum at Cultra in County Down.

Finances and utility dictated much in material culture. However, attitudes continued to have an impact. Town-dwellers wished still to differentiate themselves from rustics. Catholics, too, might be distinguished from Protestant neighbours in occasional details of their possessions. Feelings about the British connection also prompted gestures. The smart proclaimed attachment to Ireland through small pieces of furniture veneered with the arbutus and other woods which grew around Killarney. Hence, these pieces were marketed as 'Killarney ware'. Bog oak (sections of oak long sunk into bogs but hardened and preserved) lent itself to the making of small souvenirs. They declared sentimental feelings for the old country. They rang the changes on well-worn symbols: round towers, wolfhounds, and the abbey at Muckross near Killarney. More costly objects—prints, textiles, and jewellery—looked back to early Christian Ireland. In particular, the interlacing and stylized human and animal figures in illuminated manuscripts, metal caskets, torcs, and book shrines inspired late nineteenth-century designers. At the same time, the stereotyped repertoire of round towers, wolfhounds, giant elks, harps, Hibernia, or Cathleen Ni Houlihan supplied motifs.

The resulting Celtic revival in both its aesthetic and political manifestations affected material culture. Its impulses and forms reflected comparable aspirations elsewhere in Europe—for example, in Austria, Scotland, and Belgium—and often looked like an Irish variant of the international arts and crafts movement. Its fullest expressions tended to be in public places—such as the Honan Chapel at University College Cork and Loughrea Cathedral in County Galway—rather than in ordinary houses.[28] Not all strove to revive the artistic glories of distant times and went back for their inspiration no further than the eighteenth century. Dublin cabinetmakers, notably James Hicks, based their own pieces on Georgian prototypes. Demand for mementoes from that era, revered as the heyday of Irish Protestant achievement, was also felt by silversmiths and glass-makers.

The emblems associated with William III, the great deliverer, and the Volunteers as patriots were again engraved on drinking glasses. At the same time—at the turn of the nineteenth and twentieth centuries—exuberant rococo figures reappeared on silver teapots and cream jugs. The traditional gave reassurance in uncertain times.

Public spaces continued to offer the most visible manifestations of material culture. The churches and institutions, rather than the state, were most active as patrons. Traditionalism in their requirements and preferences was offset by an ideological craving to harness Irish talents. Standardized fittings and ornaments—confessionals, sanctuary lamps, statues, even stained-glass windows and Stations of the Cross—could be ordered from catalogues. A few firms within Ireland specialized in these artefacts, but many had to be ordered from Britain and continental Europe.[29] Oppenheimer's, a firm in Manchester, supplied mosaics for churches in the Galway diocese. The ambitious church erected at Midleton (County Cork) late in the nineteenth century boasted metalwork and mosaics from Dublin specialists, such as McGloughlin and George Smyth. The principal stained-glass light came from the London office of the Munich Mayers. However, much of the woodwork was made by the nearby Murray and Sons of Youghal.[30] Comparable eclecticism about the origins of their furnishings appeared in nineteenth-century Protestant churches. At Castlerock (County Londonderry), £100 was spent on stained glass from Newcastle, encaustic tiles came from the prominent Shropshire firm of the art potters Maws, and the bells from Loughborough, also in England.[31]

Developments in the domestic sphere remain harder to uncover. So, too, is the extent to which innovative ideas in the decoration of churches filtered into the homes of laypeople. Evolving attitudes towards comfort, privacy, conjugality, women, and children have yet to be connected with the material cultures of nineteenth- and twentieth-century Ireland. From the 1920s, the straitened conditions of the Free State circumscribed what most could buy. Also, the regime was reluctant to have scarce money spent on imports. Efforts were made to promote ventures which would simultaneously proclaim the excellence of Irish goods and earn foreign orders. As a result, glass-making in Waterford, pottery at Arklow, tweeds in Donegal, and carpets at Youghal were favoured. Modernism found little official backing. Yet the adventurous, familiar with styles current in America, continental Europe, and even Britain, lightened the prevailing drabness and conservatism. Muriel Gahan encouraged appreciation of vernacular methods and styles, and opened an outlet—The Country Shop on St Stephen's Green in central Dublin—where they were sold. Gahan set up her own bodies to forward the cause. One, The Crafts Council, continues. Occasional entrepreneurs, like Stephen Pearce at Ballycotton, Nicholas Mosse of Bennetsbridge, and the Jerpoint glass works, have attracted both commercial and critical success. Workshops at Kilkenny have also promoted simpler design, often deriving from Scandinavia.[32]

Given that many dwellings were still waiting for indoor sanitation, electricity, and piped—not pumped—water, the reach of such inventive products was short. Money inevitably constrained what could be bought. Even so, conventions about respectability and expectations about comfort justified spending on what the ascetic dismissed as inessentials. Purchasing was also determined by what was available, with producers and sellers artificially exciting wants. Emblematic of these desires was the enthusiasm in the middle of the twentieth century for the acme of improved living, the O'Dearest mattress.[33]

During spells of financial buoyancy, the fortunate have increased their stocks of material goods, often heedless of injunctions to favour the Irish-made. The distinctive material cultures of Ireland have been heavily diluted since the phases of prosperity have frequently coincided with aggressive marketing of goods from elsewhere. Indeed, prosperity has allowed more to savour the non-Irish. At the very moment when Irish styles have acquired a cachet internationally, at home they are shunned as dull. Of course, not all have forsaken Irish products. But what have tended to be sought most avidly are the rare survivals from earlier centuries. This demand for authentically Irish furniture, glass, silver, and pottery has encouraged more systematic study of what survives from the past. The portable, saleable, and collectable have benefited. Humbler objects seldom excite the same enthusiasm. As a result, much in the vernacular material culture has been destroyed. This rapid and unthinking destruction affects the public and private alike. Locations in which an exotic material world was sampled—churches and chapels, shops, public houses, restaurants, and hotels—when not simply swept away as relics of a past age, have been modernized according to transient commercial and ideological whims. Unpretentious and humble houses, together with their furnishings, have virtually vanished. During the years of late twentieth-century affluence, Irish material culture has been homogenized at an alarming pace.

NOTES

1. H.G. Leask, *Irish churches and monastic buildings*, 3 vols (Dundalk, 1960), iii, 4–5, 14, 21; R. Stalley, 'The architecture of the cathedral and priory buildings, 1250–1530' in K. Milne (ed), *Christ Church Cathedral Dublin: a history* (Dublin, 2000), 71–4.
2. S. Flavin and E. Jones, *Bristol's trade with Ireland and the continent, 1503–1601: the evidence of the Exchequer customs accounts* (Dublin, 2009).
3. J. Norton and S. Lane, 'Clay tobacco-pipes in Ireland, *c.* 1600–1800' in A. Horning, R. Ó Baoill, C. Donnelly, and P. Logue (eds), *The post-medieval archaeology of Ireland 1550–1850* (Dublin, 2007), 435–52.
4. The fullest treatment is now Patricia McCarthy, 'The planning and use of space in Irish houses, 1730–1830', unpublished PhD thesis, Trinity College Dublin, 2 vols (2008).
5. S. Foster, ' "An honourable station in respect of commerce as well as constitutional liberty": retailing, consumption and economic nationalism in Dublin, 1720–85' in G. O'Brien and F. O'Kane (eds), *Georgian Dublin* (Dublin, 2008), 30–44; M.J. Powell, *The politics of consumption in eighteenth-century Ireland* (Basingstoke, 2005).
6. Male and female hemispheres in the world of goods: M. Finn, 'Men's things: masculine possession in the consumer revolution', *Social History*, 25 (2000), 133–55; A. Vickery, 'His and Hers: gender, consumption and household accounting in eighteenth-century England' in R. Harris and L. Roper (eds), *The art of survival: gender and history in Europe, 1450–2000* (Oxford, 2006), 12–38; C. Walsh, 'Shops, shopping and the art of decision-making in

eighteenth-century England' in J. Styles and A. Vickery (eds), *Gender, taste and material culture in Britain and North America, 1700–1830* (New Haven, 2006).

7. A. Moran, 'Merchants and material culture in early nineteenth-century Dublin: a consumer case study', *Irish Architectural and Decorative Studies*, xi (2008), 140–65.

8. T. Barnard, *Making the Grand Figure: lives and possessions in Ireland, 1641–1770* (New Haven and London, 2003), 251–81; M-L. Legg (ed), *The diary of Nicholas Peacock, 1740–1751: the worlds of a County Limerick farmer and agent* (Dublin, 2005), 103, 116, 132, 138, 141, 159, 196.

9. D. Fitzgerald, Knight of Glin, and J. Peill, *Irish furniture* (New Haven and London, 2007).

10. F. Ahern, 'Jane Williams, an outstanding Cork silversmith and her work', *Journal of the Cork Historical and Archaeological Society*, 117 (2012), 31–6; J.R. Bowen and C. O'Brien, *A celebration of Limerick's silver* (Cork, 2007); J.R. Bowen and C. O'Brien, *Cork silver and gold: four centuries of craftsmanship* (Cork, 2005); A. FitzGerald, 'Fighting for a "small provincial establishment": the Cork goldsmiths and their quest for a local assay office' in R. Gillespie and R.F. Foster (eds), *Irish provincial cultures in the long eighteenth century* (Dublin, 2012), 170–80; The Hunt Museum, Limerick, *North Thomond church silver, 1425–1820* (Limerick 2000); J. Mulveen, 'Galway goldsmiths, their marks and ware', *Journal of the Galway Archaeological and Historical Society*, 46 (1994), 43–64; C. O'Brien, 'The goldsmiths of Waterford', *Journal of the Royal Society of Antiquaries of Ireland*, 133 (2002), 111–29.

11. A. Fitzgerald, 'Oliver St George's passion for plate', *Silver Studies*, 19 (2007), 33–43.

12. J. Teahan, *The Dr Kurt Ticher donation of Irish silver* (Dublin, no date), 45; J. Teahan, *National Museum of Ireland: Irish silver, recent additions* (Dublin, 1980), plate 5.

13. A. Fitzgerald and C. O'Brien, 'The production of silver in eighteenth-century Dublin', *Irish Architectural and Decorative Studies*, iv (2001), 8–47; T. Sinsteden, 'Surviving Dublin assay records: part 2 (1708–48)', *Silver Studies*, 16 (2004), 87–101.

14. T.L. Cooke, *The early history of the town of Birr, or Parsonstown* (Dublin, 1875), 41–3; P. Francis, 'The development of lead glass', *Apollo* (February 2000), 47–53.

15. A. Moran, 'From factory floor to fine dining: making, selling and using glass in Ireland, c. 1730–c. 1830', PhD thesis, University of Warwick (2011); N. Roche, 'Irish eighteenth-century looking glasses: makers, frames and glasses' in B. Austen (ed), *Irish furniture* (London, 2000), 20–1; Roche, 'The manufacture and use of glass in post-medieval Ireland' in Horning et al (eds), *The post-medieval archaeology of Ireland*, 405–20.

16. A. Moran, 'Selling Waterford glass in early nineteenth-century Ireland', *Irish Architectural and Decorative Studies*, vi (2003), 56–89.

17. Horning, et al (eds), *The post-medieval archaeology of Ireland*, 98, 110–11, 124, 137, 142, 153, 155, 207, 396–401.

18. P. Francis, *Irish delftware: an illustrated history* (London, 2000).

19. G. Cockburn, inventory of furniture, Rutland Row, Dublin, 1763, with later additions, BL, Additional Ms. 48, 314, 19; M. Reynolds, 'Wedgwood in Dublin, 1772–1777', *Irish Arts Review*, i, no 2 (1984), 36–9.

20. P. Francis, 'The Belfast pothouse, Carrickfergus clay and the spread of the delftware industry', *Transactions of the English Ceramic Circle*, xv (1994), 267–82; P. Francis, *A pottery by the Lagan: Irish pottery from the Downshire pottery, Belfast, 1787–c. 1806* (Belfast, 2001).

21. Stephen O'Connor, 'The Volunteers, 1778–1793: iconography and identity', unpublished Ph.D. thesis, NUI, Maynooth (2008).

22. A. Molloy, 'Vodrian Pottery', *Irish Arts Review*, iv, no 1 (1987), 33–6; M. Reynolds, 'James Donovan, "the emperor of China"', ibid., ii, no 3 (1985), 28–36.

23. C.E. Orser Jr (ed), *Unearthing hidden Ireland: historical archaeology at Ballycline, County Roscommon* (Bray, 2006).

24. D. Dickson, 'The place of Dublin in the eighteenth-century Irish economy' in T.M. Devine and D. Dickson (eds), *Ireland and Scotland, 1600–1850* (Edinburgh, 1983), 177–92; D. Dickson, 'Death of a capital? Dublin and the consequences of the Union' in P. Clark and R. Gillespie (eds), *Two capitals: London and Dublin, 1500–1840, Proceedings of the British Academy*, 107 (2001), 111–31; Moran, 'Merchants and material culture', 140–65.

25. T. Barnard, 'Fabrics of faith: the material worlds of Catholic Ireland and Protestant Ireland, 1500–1800' in R. Ó Floinn (ed), *Franciscan faith: sacred art in Ireland, A.D. 1600–1750* (Dublin, 2011), 31–41; E. McEneaney (ed), *Waterford treasures* (Waterford, 2004), 158–9; M. Murphy, 'Varieties of Irishness in eighteenth-century Seville: Wisemans and Whites' in T. O'Connor and M.A. Lyons (eds), *Irish communities in early-modern Europe* (Dublin, 2006), 312–21; P. O'Flanagan and J. Walton, 'The Irish community at Cádiz during the late eighteenth century' in H.B. Clarke, J. Prunty, and M. Hennessy (eds), *Surveying Ireland's past* (Dublin, 2004), 353–84.

26. E. McParland, 'Chapel or Church? The case of St Mary's, Pope's Quay, Cork' in Gillespie and Foster (eds), *Irish provincial cultures*, 231–42; A. Rowan, 'Irish Victorian churches: denominational distinctions' in B. Kennedy and R. Gillespie (eds), *Ireland: art into history* (Dublin, 1994), 207–30.

27. A.T. Lucas, *Penal crucifixes* (Dublin, 1958); J. McDonnell, 'Art and patronage during the penal era' in Maynooth College, *Ecclesiastical art of the penal era* (Maynooth, 1995).

28. P.K. Egan, *St Brendan's Cathedral, Loughrea* (Dublin, 1986); V. Teehan and E. Wincott Heckett, *The Honan Chapel: a golden vision* (Cork, 2004).

29. F. Blom, J. Blom, F. Korsten, and G. Scott (eds), *The correspondence of James Peter Coghlan (1731–1800)*, Catholic Record Society (2007), 395.

30. T.M. May, *Churches of Galway, Kilmacduagh and Kilfenora* (Galway, 2000); B. Troy, *Church of Our Lady of the Most Holy Rosary Midleton . . . Centenary Celebration* (Midleton, 1996).

31. H. Caskey, *Castlerock and its Anglican church* (Coleraine and Ballycastle, 2003), 66, 69, 73–4.

32. J. Addis and N. Marchant, *Kilkenny design: twenty-one years of design in Ireland* (Kilkenny, 1985); G. Mitchell, *Words and deeds: the life and work of Muriel Gahan* (Dublin, 1997); J. Quinn, *Designing Ireland: a retrospective exhibition of the Kilkenny Design Workshops 1963–1988* (Cork, 2005).

33. M.J. Andrews, *The life and work of Robert Gibbings* (Bicester, 2003), 292–3; J. Ballantyne, *Lismore: autobiography of an Irish town* (London, 2008), 29–30.

SELECT BIBLIOGRAPHY

Addis, J. and Marchant, N., *Kilkenny design: twenty-one years of design in Ireland* (Kilkenny, 1985).

Austen, B. (ed), *Irish furniture* (London, 2000).

Barnard, T., 'The worlds of goods and County Offaly in the early eighteenth century' in W. Nolan and T.P. O'Neill (eds). *Offaly: history and society* (Dublin, 1998), 371–92.

Barnard, T., *A guide to sources for the history of material culture in Ireland, 1500–2000* (Dublin, 2005).

Barnard, T., *Making the Grand Figure: lives and possessions in Ireland, 1641–1770* (New Haven and London, 2003).

Barnard, T., 'The artistic and cultural activities of the Caldwells of Castle Caldwell, 1750–1783', *Irish Architectural and Decorative Studies*, x (2007), 90–111.

Bennett, D., *Irish Georgian silver* (London, 1992).

Bowe, N.G., *The arts and crafts movements in Dublin and Edinburgh, 1885–1925* (Dublin, 1998).

Bowen, J.R. and O'Brien, C., *Cork silver and gold: four centuries of craftsmanship* (Cork, 2005).

Bowen, J.R. and O'Brien, C., *A celebration of Limerick's silver* (Cork, 2007).

Boyle, E., *The Irish flowerers* (Belfast, 1971).

Crawford, W.H., 'A Ballymena business in the late eighteenth century' in J. Gray and W. McCann (eds), *An uncommon bookman: essays in memory of J.R.R. Adams* (Belfast, 1996), 23–33.

Dunlevy, M., *Ceramics in Ireland* (Dublin, 1988).

Dunlevy, M., *Dress in Ireland* (London, 1989; reprinted Cork, 1999).

Fenlon, J., *Goods and Chattels: a survey of early household inventories in Ireland* (Dublin, 2003).

Fitzgerald, A. and O'Brien, C., 'The production of silver in eighteenth-century Dublin', *Irish Architectural and Decorative Studies*, iv (2001), 8–47.

Fitzgerald, A., 'The production and consumption of goldsmiths' work in eighteenth-century Dublin', unpublished PhD thesis, Royal College of Art, London (2005).

Fitzgerald, D., Knight of Glin, and Peill, J., *Irish furniture* (New Haven and London, 2007).

FitzPatrick, E. and Kelly, J. (eds). Domestic Life in Ireland, *Proceedings of the Royal Irish Academy, 111*, C (2011).

Francis, P., *Irish delftware: an illustrated history* (London, 2000).

Francis, P., *A pottery by the Lagan: Irish pottery from the Downshire pottery, Belfast, 1787–c. 1806* (Belfast, 2001).

Hall, D., *Irish pewter: a history* (Welshpool, 1995).

Hall, D., *Types of Irish pewter* (Welshpool, 2005).

Hearne, J.M. (ed), *Glassmaking in Ireland: from the medieval to the contemporary* (Dublin, 2010).

Horning, A., Ó Baoill, R., Donnelly, C., and Logue, P. (eds), *The post-medieval archaeology of Ireland 1550–1850* (Dublin, 2007).

Johnston, M.M., *Hidden in the pile: the Abbey Leix carpet factory, 1904–1912* (Portlaoise, 1997).

Kinmonth, C., *Irish country furniture, 1700–1950* (New Haven and London, 1993).

Kinmonth, C., *Irish rural interiors in art* (New Haven and London, 2006).

Laffan, W., 'A Dublin sampler book of 1832: Dorothy Tyrrell' in W. Laffan (ed), *A year at Churchill* (Tralee, 2003), 304–5.

Larmour, P., *The arts and crafts movement in Ireland* (Belfast, 1992).

McDonnell, J., *Maynooth College Bicentenary Art Exhibition: Ecclesiastical art of the penal era* (Maynooth, 1995).

Moran, A., 'Merchants and material culture in early nineteenth-century Dublin: a consumer case study', *Irish Architectural and Decorative Studies*, xi (2008), 140–65.

Moran, A., 'From factory floor to fine dining: making, selling and using glass in Ireland, c. 1730–c. 1830', D. Phil. thesis, University of Warwick (2011).

O'Connor, Stephen, 'The Volunteers, 1778–1793: iconography and identity', unpublished PhD thesis, NUI, Maynooth (2008).

Ó Floinn, R. (ed), *Franciscan faith: sacred art in Ireland, A.D. 1600–1750* (Dublin, 2011).

Orser Jr, C.E. (ed), *Unearthing hidden Ireland: historical archaeology at Ballycline, County Roscommon* (Bray, 2006).

Parkhill, T., and Pollock, V., *Made in Belfast* (Stroud, 2005).

Roche, N., *The legacy of light: a history of Irish windows* (Bray, 1999).

Rothery, S., *The shops of Ireland* (Dublin, 1978).

Sheehy, J., *The rediscovery of Ireland's past: the Celtic revival 1830–1930* (London, 1980).

Siggins, B., *The Great White Fair: the Herbert Park exhibition of 1907* (Dublin, 2007).

Warren, P., *Irish glass: Waterford, Cork, Belfast, in the age of exuberance* (London, 1970).

Westropp, D., *Irish glass: an account of glass-making in Ireland from the XVIth century to the present day* (London, 1920), M. Boydell (ed) (Dublin, 1978).

CHAPTER 14

···

FILM AND
BROADCAST MEDIA

···

ROBERT J. SAVAGE

I. INTRODUCTION

···

JUST a few days before Christmas 1909, *The Freemans Journal* reported that Ireland's first cinema, the Volta, had opened to a capacity crowd with a 'most interesting cinematograph exhibition'. The manager of the new cinema was none other than James Joyce, who chose three films for an opening that received mixed reviews. The concluding film, 'The Tragic Story of Beatrice Cenci', struck one viewer as a rather odd choice given it was screened in Christmas week. Although the film was described as 'very excellent', the reviewer observed it 'was hardly as exhilarating a subject as one would desire on the eve of the festive season'.[1] The film told the unhappy story of Beatrice Cenci and her father Francesco, an aristocrat who met an untimely death in sixteenth-century Italy. Francesco's family decided to dispatch their abusive father after the courts refused to prosecute him for his many violent and cruel indiscretions, including a sexual assault on his young daughter Beatrice. After poisoning Francesco failed, his wife and children bludgeoned him to death with a hammer and threw his body over a balcony in an attempt to disguise his death as accidental. The papal police were not convinced an accident had occurred; the family was tried, convicted, and publicly executed. For the Roman people, Beatrice became a heroic symbol of resistance to an arrogant and contemptible aristocracy. Legend has it that she haunts the Sant'Angelo Bridge where she was beheaded for patricide.

It is unclear whether Joyce's continued choice of film features undermined the finances of the Volta, but it soon failed as a commercial enterprise. Unsurprisingly, Joyce proved to be a man ahead of his time; Dublin witnessed a cinema boom as audiences flocked to see a steady diet of mostly American and British productions. By 1922, just twelve years after the Volta had closed its doors, thirty-seven cinemas were operating in Dublin.[2] The Irish developed a famously voracious appetite for film in the succeeding years. By 1950, there were 41.6 million admissions to Irish cinemas and, in 1954, the number had reached 54.1 million.[3] The cinema was one of many twentieth-century innovations that found a wide and enthusiastic audience throughout Ireland.

Ireland's geographic position, situated in the north Atlantic between Britain, Europe, and the Americas, enabled Irish society to benefit from the technological revolution that transformed western societies in the twentieth century. Transatlantic cables linking North America and Britain came through Ireland, literally connecting the island to two of the world's most technologically sophisticated societies. Ireland was drawn into a dynamic Atlantic community where technological innovation resulted in quicker and more manageable means of travel and communication. The enormous English-speaking Irish Diaspora that emerged out of Ireland helped shape this growing Atlantic world. The rapid movement of people, goods, and services within this trans-national community and the expansion of printed and electronic media enabled an unrelenting Anglo-American culture to become dominant.

As the twentieth century progressed, innovations in film, radio, and television helped the Irish, both at home and abroad, to engage fully with a more modern and secular world. Although these innovations threatened to overwhelm a frail, indigenous Irish culture, they also provided the tools its supporters needed to protect and nurture what they defined as a rich and diverse culture. When developing a film culture and establishing indigenous radio and television networks, advocates were influenced by exposure to the American and British institutions that surrounded them. Politicians, civil servants, clerics, and cultural activists looked to American and British models when deciding how initiatives in cinema and the broadcast media should be developed, structured, and funded and when thinking of how they might serve the public. This chapter will address how a film and broadcast culture emerged through the twentieth century and enabled Ireland to be part of a more modern and interconnected world.

II. Radio

The Irish Free State's first radio station, designated '2RN', began broadcasting in January 1926 via a fairly primitive, low-power transmitter based in Dublin.[4] The Dublin station went on the air after a drawn-out debate in the Dáil that wrestled with the question of how an Irish radio service should be structured, operated, and financed. A special parliamentary committee was established to consider these questions after the excitable James Joseph Walsh, a Cumann na nGaedheal Minister and Postmaster-General, tried to seize the initiative and organize what he referred to as the Irish Broadcasting Company. Walsh, a native of Cork and a veteran of the 1916 Easter Rising, headed a department which by default assumed responsibility for broadcasting.[5] On his own initiative, and to the consternation of many Dáil deputies, Walsh placed advertisements in the national press in the summer of 1923 requesting parties interested in being part of a proposed Irish Broadcasting Company to contact his department.

Walsh later distributed to deputies what was to become known as the Post Office White Paper on Broadcasting. The white paper argued that the relatively short history of radio revealed the challenges inherent in establishing broadcast stations; it also illustrated that the competing models examined by Walsh and his department were American and British. It stated: 'In America, and elsewhere, where broadcasting has been conducted as a private enterprise, a multiplicity of companies has been found to lead to chaos and confusion and to inefficient service.'[6] Walsh viewed the American model of broadcasting as a debacle to be avoided at all costs and instead advocated a centralized system loosely modelled on the recently established British Broadcasting Company. He argued that 'all experience has proven that there must be unified control in broadcasting if the public are to get an efficient service' and later explained that his proposal 'follows as closely as circumstances will permit the English model'.[7] He informed deputies that, based on these findings, 'negotiations were opened up with various firms interested and after many conferences...constituent firms have agreed to join together in a scheme to work out a system of broadcasting in the Irish Free State under licence from the post office'.[8]

Walsh seemed to have convinced some people, certainly himself, that his scheme was a workable one and he wanted it implemented quickly. The white paper however was considered seriously flawed by many deputies, who were annoyed by what was defined as the postmaster-general's 'hole in the corner' approach to the subject. Complicating matters further were rumours in the national press of 'influence peddling' by a member of the Dáil, Darrell Figgis, who was accused of supporting a dubious application from one of the constituent companies of the proposed Irish Broadcasting Company.[9] Walsh became frustrated by the appointment of the lethargic, but thorough, Special Committee on Wireless Broadcasting that examined and debated his scheme, item by item. The committee called dozens of witnesses before issuing a six-hundred-page final report that rejected the central principles of Walsh's proposal. The committee concluded that radio was much too important to be entrusted to a private company, even if that company was licenced and overseen by a government department. Instead, the committee endorsed the concept of a service that would be owned and operated by Walsh's department, Posts and Telegraphs. The Cumann na nGaedheal government accepted the recommendations of the Special Committee and instructed Walsh to make arrangements for establishing a national radio service.

Walsh was furious, angry that his own proposal had been rejected and upset that his department should be burdened by operating a national radio service. He warned the Dáil: 'If this house determines that the Post Office must differentiate between rival organ grinders, rival tenors and people of that kind and even rival politicians who want to get control and preferential treatment, we will be able to do it at a price and it will be a very dear price.'[10] Walsh believed the Dáil had made a serious mistake and was also concerned that political interference in broadcasting would be inevitable. As minister, he insisted radio should avoid any and all political and religious broadcasting, advising the first director 'that it would be safe to steer clear as far as possible of religion and politics'.[11]

On 1 January 1926 Douglas Hyde, co-founder of the Gaelic League and future president of Ireland, opened the station by extolling the richness of Irish culture and emphasizing the need to promote the Irish language. Hyde, who in 1892 had advocated the de-anglicization of Ireland in the foundational polemic of the Gaelic Revival, remarked that the new radio service 'was a sign to the whole world that a great change has come about when we can take our place among the nations of the world and make this wireless instrument work in our own language like every other country'.[12] He once again cautioned against anglicization, telling listeners:

> There were two tides in Ireland—one of them coming in on this side of Ireland and the other going out on the west coast. The tide of Gaelic was ebbing there and leaving behind a bare, cold, ugly beach in its wake. The fine, Gaelic water had ebbed away and was replaced by the mud, slime and filth of English.[13]

An interview committee that included John Reith, later Lord Reith, the director general of the BBC, appointed the first director of the station, Séamus Clandillon, in November 1925.[14] The new director was a talented traditional singer and in radio's formative years he performed regularly with his wife, Maighréad Ní Annagáin, to the annoyance of some listeners. The national service that emerged in 1932 as Radio Éireann continued to be staffed by civil servants and operated by the Department of Posts and Telegraphs until the 1960 Broadcasting Act created an independent public authority responsible for overseeing both radio and television. In its early years, Irish radio operated under considerable financial constraints as a resource-starved government enterprise. Between 1927 and 1932, the Minister of Finance, the notoriously frugal Ernest Blythe, was also Minister for Posts and Telegraphs, and radio was not one of his priorities. After his departure, radio was overseen by a number of ministers from different political parties, many of whom had little interest in broadcasting.

During this time Radio Éireann's programming supported the conservative ethos of the state, emphasizing that Ireland possessed a unique culture that had to be appreciated. In supporting the Gaelic Revival with lectures, concerts, and Irish-language broadcasts, Radio Éireann generally reinforced an identity that cultural nationalists were keen to promote. When Fianna Fáil came to power in 1932, a modest effort was made to improve the service. A new director, T. J. Kiernan, was appointed and by 1937 the number of licences purchased had exceeded one hundred thousand. Under Kiernan, a number of new initiatives were developed, outside broadcasts were increased, and there was a concerted effort to improve coverage of Gaelic games. The station tried to improve Irish-language broadcasts by introducing short plays and lessons, but these met with mixed results. Taoiseach Éamon de Valera recognized radio as an important resource for the government and used it successfully on a number of occasions. His St Patrick's Day address, 'The Ireland that we dreamed of', broadcast on Radio Éireann in 1943, is perhaps his best known and most often quoted speech.[15] After Winston Churchill denounced Ireland's policy of neutrality at the conclusion of World War II, de Valera replied by addressing the nation on Radio Éireann, making an impassioned and popular defence of Ireland's position. His government's effort to find a wavelength for short-wave broadcasts to the United States, though not successful, demonstrates that de Valera appreciated the power of the medium. The additional resources devoted to Radio Éireann during this time meant that, by 1947, the service was becoming more professional. That year, Kiernan was able to hire a news staff, a symphony orchestra, and a number of scriptwriters. He was also able to appoint staff to travel the countryside to collect traditional music and folklore. The additional resources enabled the quality of broadcasts to improve dramatically.

In 1940, León Ó Broin became Secretary of the Department of Posts and Telegraphs and quickly established himself as a resourceful and powerful civil servant with a keen interest in broadcasting. Ó Broin later emerged as a critical voice in the debates concerning television and his ideas concerning its structure were influential; one could even argue that he was the architect of the Irish television service.[16] The Secretary was an also important intermediary between broadcasters and a powerful political player in the state, the Catholic hierarchy. While Ó Broin was settling into his role in Posts and Telegraphs, John Charles McQuaid, a close confidant of Éamon de Valera, was taking up his appointment as Archbishop of Dublin. McQuaid proved a deeply conservative and highly controversial archbishop, who shared Ó Broin's interest in broadcasting. As Dublin's archbishop, he was comfortable intervening in the political, social, and cultural affairs of the nation when he believed issues of faith and morals were at stake. Although Ó Broin may have bristled at some of the decisions of the authoritarian archbishop, he enjoyed a quiet, constructive relationship with McQuaid, who valued Ó Broin's advice, especially on broadcasting matters.

While Radio Éireann remained a government enterprise, it was susceptible to pressure from a number of sources, including the Catholic Church. Archbishop McQuaid quietly worked through his contacts in government to arrange the introduction of the Angelus in daily radio broadcasts. This was inaugurated at his direction on the Feast of the Assumption, 15 August 1950. The ease by which the Angelus made its way into the daily programming of Radio Éireann underscores the very comfortable unofficial relationship between Radio Éireann and the Catholic Church. This new initiative was not in any way controversial in a country that was overwhelmingly Catholic and deeply conservative.[17] The programming featured on the national radio service during this period mirrored the conservative society it served.

While controversy involving the Catholic Church and Radio Éireann was unheard of, the relationship between advocates of the Irish language and the radio service was more complicated. The language was an important part of programming on Radio Éireann from its origins as 2RN in 1926 through the 1950s, in spite of the fact that it struggled to gain a wide audience. In the early decades, the concerted effort made to develop programmes that embraced Gaelic culture and the Irish language met with mixed results. The station certainly failed to impress the leader of the Irish Free State, William Cosgrave, who considered it simply a vehicle for Irish-Ireland propaganda. Cosgrave complained about monotonous programming and of a general assumption that '2RN is an Irish-Ireland institution and that there is only abuse awaiting any criticism'.[18]

Irish-language broadcasts on Radio Éireann were unpopular according to the station's own surveys, which indicated that the numbers of listeners to Irish programmes were embarrassingly low. In March 1953, a confidential listener survey conducted by Radio Éireann revealed that few people were listening to these broadcasts. A cabinet meeting later that year rejected demands made in the Dáil and in the national press to publish the report 'in light, particularly, of the very poor showing of programmes in the Irish language'.[19] One has to keep in mind that the quality of the Irish-language programmes was an issue for supporters, who complained of the low standards of the material broadcast. The Irish language only found a comfortable home in radio when the Irish language station, Raidió na Gaeltachta, began broadcasting from County Galway in 1972.

In 1953, Erskine Childers became Fianna Fáil Minister of Posts and Telegraphs and quickly exhibited a keen interest in improving the national radio service. He appointed a professional broadcaster, Maurice Gorham, as director and tried to give the service a degree of independence by establishing a committee to operate radio, Comhairle Radio Éireann. This met with mixed results as the Comhairle enjoyed limited autonomy; its members were incorporated into the civil service and were answerable directly to the Department of Posts and Telegraphs. Gorham, an Irishman who worked for the BBC before taking up his position in Dublin, tried to improve educational programming and enjoyed some success. He was responsible for the inauguration of the popular Thomas Davis Lectures in 1953, lectures that brought some of Ireland's best historians into the studios to deliver informed and accessible talks on Ireland's contested history. In spite of these initiatives, however, the service remained chronically underfunded, enjoyed limited autonomy, and struggled to deliver imaginative programmes that could capture and hold an audience.

Radio came to Northern Ireland in 1924 when the province's first station, 2BE, went on the air. This became BBC Northern Ireland when a Royal Charter established the BBC a few years later, in 1927. Initially, BBC Northern Ireland transmitted the national programme from London, and in Belfast it was overseen by a small, mostly English, staff. Although relations between the governments in Belfast and Dublin were non-existent, this did not preclude cooperation between the two broadcasters on the island. BBC Northern Ireland enjoyed a more substantial budget than its Dublin counterpart and often featured guests from the Irish Free State, including actors from the Abbey Theatre and the director of Radio Éireann, Séamus Clandillon, and his wife, Maighréad Ní Annagáin, both talented singers.

During the inter-war years, the Unionist establishment came to appreciate the importance of the BBC, seeing it as a critical link to a British culture they considered their own. Cooperation between the two radio stations declined during this period, especially when George Marshall became the new director of the Belfast station in 1932. As Rex Cathcart and Michael Muldoon have pointed out, Marshall arrived in Belfast at a difficult time. Tension between Belfast and Dublin increased when Fianna Fáil came to power in 1932, and the fierce sectarian rioting that scarred Belfast in 1935 underscored divisions within the province and between the two jurisdictions.[20] As relations between Belfast and Dublin deteriorated, some Unionists became concerned with overtures made by BBC Northern Ireland to Dublin. When the unionist press learned Marshall was in Dublin, to talk with broadcasting officials there, it 'forcefully condemned this collaboration', prompting Marshall to deny that any collaboration was being planned. Some Unionist officials remained so concerned that they called for the government of Northern Ireland to take over the BBC. A wary Marshall therefore endeavoured to keep politics off the air, determining 'broadcasting should not precipitate civil strife'.[21] BBC Northern Ireland became overly sensitive to the concerns of the unionist community and this alienated the Catholic minority in the province. For instance, BBC officials in Belfast acquiesced to Prime Minister Lord Craigavon's demand that it stop reporting results of Gaelic Athletic Association games in the province. Broadcasting officials accepted his complaints that the Sunday broadcasts 'were hurting the feelings of the large majority of people in Northern Ireland'.[22]

In spite of concerns expressed by the Unionist government, BBC Northern Ireland eventually made a modest effort to develop more inclusive regional broadcasts. In the post-war period, the station carefully began to increase regional programming, recruiting Ulster writers, who included Sam Hanna Bell and John Hewitt. A concerted effort was also made to increase the number and range of outside broadcasts. Although Irish-language programming remained beyond the Pale, there was 'extensive use of recordings of everyday life, folklore, and traditional music'.[23] Gillian McIntosh's study of unionist identities, *The Force of Culture*, points out that 'the influx of locals did bring the station closer to the indigenous population'.[24] These initiatives were intended to make the service more inclusive, but many nationalists in the province still tended to view BBC Northern Ireland as overly sympathetic to the unionist community and focused on representing a culture that was not their own. Unionists worked to marginalize the nationalist community and its culture, and were determined that the image of Ulster presented to the outside world should be a British one. Well into the 1950s, the station employed few Catholics and featured little cultural programming that could be defined as Gaelic or Irish.[25] This deference to the Unionist establishment came under tremendous pressure in the 1960s when television took hold in the province, proving subversive in destabilizing archaic political and social structures that failed to gain cross-community support.

III. FILM

One of the first companies to make films in Ireland was the American Kalem Film Company. Canadian-Irish director Sidney Olcott made a number of films in Ireland for Kalem between 1910 and 1914, including the adaptation of two Dion Boucicault plays, *The Colleen Bawn* (1911) and *The Shaughraun* (1912). He also made a number of films that were sympathetic to the nationalist cause, including *For Ireland's Sake* and *Bold Emmet, Ireland's Martyr* (1914). Another foreign initiative, the short-lived Film Company of Ireland, started by Irish-American James Mark Sullivan, also experienced success in the country by producing both romantic material and rousing nationalist films. An adaptation of Charles Kickham's *Knocknagow* (1917) was followed by an adaptation of William Carleton's *Willy Reilly and His Dear Colleen Bawn* (1920) before the civil strife engulfing Ireland forced the company to close. These films found enthusiastic audiences in Ireland and within the Irish Diaspora in the United States. The few indigenous films made in the decades after independence were financed with small budgets and focused on the country's recent past. This included *Irish Destiny* (1926), a silent film set during the war of independence that was made by an Irish cinema owner, Dr Isaac Eppel. Denis Johnston's remarkable adaptation of Frank O'Connor's short story, *Guests of the Nation* (1935), was a silent film made on a shoestring budget. *The Dawn* (1936), another film about the war of independence, though fairly primitive, was also received warmly by Irish audiences. Other endeavours by a host of foreign film-makers gained critical international acclaim, including Robert Flaherty's iconic *The Man of Aran (1934)*, a film that emphasized the primitive nature of life in the Aran Islands. The more successful of these foreign films include *The Informer* (1935), *The Odd Man Out* (1947), and *The Quiet Man* (1952). These award-winning films tended to project an image of a country either mired in a pre-modern rural idyll or a nation challenged by a legacy of political violence. These depictions of Ireland found enthusiastic audiences both at home and abroad and helped construct an identity in popular culture for independent Ireland.

Martin McLoone addresses the emergence of a film culture in Ireland by pointing out that the improving economic climate of the 1960s and 1970s enabled a number of young men and women to start making short films while students in universities and art colleges in Ireland and the United Kingdom. These included Joe Comerford, Thaddeus O'Sullivan, and Pat Murphy who, together with film-makers from RTÉ, including Bob Quinn and Tommy McArdle, produced high-quality short fiction and documentary films. Much of this early work was funded by British sources, including the British Film Institute and, later, Channel 4. For Irish film-makers, an important initiative was the establishment of the Irish Film Board in 1980 for funding indigenous film. It financed Neil Jordan's film *Angel* in 1982, encouraging a director who went on to become Ireland's best known film-maker over successive decades. The Film Board succeeded in helping support ten feature films, twenty short fiction films, and numerous documentaries for television, as well as a number of experimental projects, before being suspended in 1987 due to cutbacks in government spending.[26]

A fledgling film industry developed, in spite of the recession and economic turbulence that characterized 1980s Ireland. The Irish Arts Council took an interest in film, leading to the expansion of the Irish Film Institute and the eventual establishment of the Irish Film Centre in 1992. The Irish Film Centre provided critical educational and archival resources that were a key ingredient to a viable film culture. Film historian Kevin Rockett points out that there was a major boost to Irish filmmaking when a coalition government came to power in 1992 and the portfolio of Minister for Arts, Culture, and the Gaeltacht fell to Labour's Michael D. Higgins.[27] A poet, academic, and left-leaning intellectual, Higgins proved an advocate of the arts and especially the film industry. He restarted the Irish Film Board and succeeded in revising tax codes to encourage small-scale investment in film production. Higgins was elected President of Ireland in 2011.

The Irish Screen Commission was established in 1998 to encourage foreign companies to film in Ireland and this was complemented by the establishment of Screen Training Ireland, set up to provide training for those interested in the film industry. As McLoone has argued, these initiatives enabled the development of a coherent 'film strategy that catered for the commercial development of Ireland as a base for film-making and at the same time provided for indigenous film-making and the nourishment of young film talent'.[28] This established a foundation for the building of a film culture that witnessed uneven, though often impressive, results in succeeding decades.

Northern Ireland also struggled to secure state support for film production until it was able to avail itself of British Lottery funds in 1995 and European money in 1997. The Northern Ireland Film Council, formed in 1998 to support film-making in the province, was renamed the Northern Ireland Film Commission and charged with encouraging the development of a Northern Irish film industry. This included developing strategies to lure filmmakers to Northern Ireland, introducing training courses, and developing initiatives to encourage film production. The Council has succeeded in supporting a range of projects, often working with the Irish Film Board to support co-productions. In fact, a defining feature of recent 'Irish' films from both sides of the border today is the variety of producers involved from different countries. Irish, British, French, and German production companies backed one of the more successful 'Irish' films, *The Wind that Shakes the Barley*, made by Englishman Ken Loach in 2006.

IV. TELEVISION

Not unlike the experience with radio, questions concerning the establishment of a television service proved controversial. In the Irish Republic, this resulted in the establishment of a parliamentary committee that explored options open to the state, concentrating on established American and British models. As Secretary of the Department of Posts and Telegraphs, Leon Ó Broin emerged as a critical voice in the debates that shaped Irish television. Throughout the 1950s, he waged a protracted battle with the Department of Finance over how an indigenous service should be structured and financed. He was an advocate of public service television and looked to the BBC as the best model for Ireland to follow. Given Ireland's dire economic situation, however, it is not surprising that the Department of Finance did not regard television as a priority. Finance remained adamantly opposed to underwriting an Irish public television service.

The question remained lively because of television broadcasts making their way into Ireland from Britain and later from Northern Ireland. Signals from British transmitters could be picked up along Ireland's east coast in the 1950s, as viewers erected aerials to capture British programmes. In 1953, the BBC built a temporary transmitter in Belfast, enabling citizens to witness the coronation of Queen Elizabeth II. The range of these broadcasts increased when the Divis mountain transmitter became operational in 1955. This enabled approximately 80 per cent of the people of Northern Ireland and many people south of the border to view BBC programmes.[29] These broadcasts from Britain and Northern Ireland created discomfort for political, religious, and cultural elites, who grew increasingly concerned at the content of programmes, which they regarded as objectionable.[30] Church leaders believed that British programmes that raised issues of adultery, single mothers, or even featured semi-nudity were inappropriate for Irish viewers. Political and cultural elites resented broadcasts that concentrated on the lives of the royal family, extolled the richness of English culture, or addressed the accomplishments of the British Empire. In 1958, when it was estimated that there were between 20 000 and 22 000 sets in the Irish Republic, the government established a Television Commission to consider how an indigenous television service should be established. This commission heard evidence from a wide range of cultural and political organizations, and sorted through proposals from domestic and foreign companies interested in gaining an exclusive licence to operate a television station in Ireland. Many of the proposals were from foreign companies, some with subsidiaries in Ireland, although the Irish-language organization Gael-Linn submitted one of the more comprehensive applications. The Gael-Linn application made it clear that it viewed television primarily as a didactic tool to revive the Irish language.

Given the small size of the Irish population and the relative poverty of the country, Ó Broin understood that, for financial reasons, the public service model he preferred would not be accepted. He therefore reluctantly proposed an alternative, a state-owned service that combined the two seemingly incompatible models. This proposal was much more palatable to the Department of Finance, which in the end offered reluctant support. In 1959, the Lemass government decided to accept this proposal and create a state-owned, commercial public television service that would be financed by both advertising revenue and licence fees and overseen by a public authority.

Although he had reluctantly supported the creation of a state-run service, Seán Lemass was apprehensive about the new medium. Much like his predecessor, Éamon de Valera, Lemass was uncomfortable with the advent of Irish television. Both men believed that the state should have a strong voice in determining what should and should not be broadcast by an Irish service. Lemass wrote to the Secretary of his department and instructed him to convey to the new television authority his belief that 'stage-Irishisms (and) playboyisms' should be avoided. In language that captured his vision of a native service, he stressed that the station should produce an 'image of a vigorous progressive nation, seeking efficiency'.[31] With regard to social and economic problems that challenged the country, he emphasized that television should 'encourage objective presentation of facts and constructive comment. The "God-help-us" approach should be ruled out'.[32] The Taoiseach cautioned: 'objectivity should not be allowed to excuse the undue representation of our faults. What you should aim to present is a picture of Ireland and the Irish as we would like to have it, although our hopes and aims may well be helped by the objective presentation of facts in association with constructive comment'.[33] He made it clear that Irish television needed to avoid coverage or comment about Northern Ireland that might upset the Stormont Government and maintained that the issue of partition should be addressed only with the greatest of care. According to the Taoiseach, the new authority had to act with prudence when dealing with other sensitive topics such as sex, religion, and education.

An American, Edward Roth, was named the first director-general of Telefís Éireann and during his tenure the broadcaster featured countless American Westerns; thus 'cowboys and Indians' became regular visitors in Irish homes, as the station cultivated a following that succeeded in delivering revenue to the fledgling service. John Doyle, in his memoir, *A Great Feast of Light, Growing Up Irish in the Television Age*, recalls the excitement in his home when his father brought home a television in May 1963. For a six-year-old growing up in Nenagh, Tipperary, the arrival of television and especially *Bat Masterson* was a special event. Although he had seen older westerns in a crowded, noisy, local cinema, television delivered a special hero from the American west into the intimacy of his home. 'This man Bat Masterson was different. He was a rebel, you could tell by the cut of him, and he was in my own house where I could watch everything he was doing, without the bother of screaming children and the fear of somebody pulling my hair.'[34]

But Telefís Éireann was not all American westerns and crime dramas; slowly, indigenous programming made its way onto the screen. As the 1960s progressed, a number of impressive and very popular drama serials were produced, and current affairs programming also found a wide audience. *The Late Late Show*, *The Riordans*, *7-Days* and later *Glenroe*, *Fair City*, and *Ros na Rún* all became important programmes as current affairs and entertainment programming began to find extensive and engaged viewers. Current affairs programmes upset the deference that many political elites expected from the press and the public. As public broadcasting services, both radio and television began to challenge the status quo, much to the chagrin of government officials. In 1966, a young Minister of Agriculture, Charles Haughey, was incensed by a news report that juxtaposed his statement as minister with a contradictory one by the president of the National Farmers' Association. He called the RTÉ newsroom directly to complain, resulting in the news programme editing a subsequent report. This created a controversy in the press as accounts of ministerial censorship and interference in the affairs of RTÉ were reported extensively in the print media. In the Dáil, a short time later, an angry Taoiseach Seán Lemass declared:

> Radio Telefís Éireann was set up by legislation as an instrument of public policy and as such is responsible to the government. The government have overall responsibility for its conduct and especially the obligation to ensure that its programmes do not offend against the public interest or conflict with national policy as defined in legislation. To this extent the government reject the view that Radio Telefís Éireann should be, either generally or in regard to its current affairs and news programmes, completely independent of Government supervision.[35]

Lemass's pronouncement has often been quoted as proof of the government's ambivalence to the freedom of the press. The declaration is indeed extraordinary and illustrates the extent of suspicion held by many senior political leaders who were convinced broadcasters were enemies out to subvert government policy. His successor as Taoiseach, Jack Lynch, also had deep misgivings about current affairs programming at RTÉ. In 1967, a current affairs team was prevented from travelling to North Vietnam to report on the war for fear of upsetting the American government. A short time later, another team was prevented from travelling to Biafra to report on the Nigerian civil war. The Department of Foreign Affairs maintained it was concerned that such a programme might put at risk the lives of Irish missionaries working in the country. When the current affairs programme *7-Days* screened a programme on illegal moneylending in Dublin, the government took offence, believing that the programme makers were unfairly critical of the police and the Department of Justice. An expensive tribunal was established, which put RTÉ through the proverbial wringer, sending a chill through RTÉ and illustrating just how menacing and hostile the Fianna Fáil government could be. In November 1972, with violence spiralling out of control in Northern Ireland, the Lynch Government took the extraordinary step of firing the entire RTÉ Authority for broadcasting material it defined as seditious. The hostility of Fianna Fáil to public service broadcasting did not end in the 1970s. Later, the extensive deregulation of television broadcasting was considered a direct attack on a public service broadcaster that throughout its history had demonstrated a pronounced lack of deference to the political elites of the country.

Other critics emerged to challenge the television service well beyond the 1960s and 1970s. The language lobby grew increasingly frustrated with the television service, lambasting Telefís Éireann for failing to produce quality Irish-language programming. Supporters of the language had been hopeful that the 1960 Broadcasting Act would require television and radio to make a concerted effort to feature a significant amount of material in Irish. Officials in government and broadcasting were convinced that many of the demands of the language lobby were simply unreasonable and therefore not acceptable. Supporters of Irish were dismayed by this attitude and by the paltry amount of Irish-language broadcasting that made its way into RTÉ broadcasts, especially television. Their concerns were constant until the government relented and set up an Irish language television service in the west of Ireland in 1996.

The 1960 Broadcasting Act also upset the quiet informal networks that characterized church-state relations. The archbishop of Dublin, John Charles McQuaid, was successfully kept at arm's length in the formative years and Irish radio and television resisted direct overtures from the Irish hierarchy. As television evolved and gained a sense of independence, a number of incidents provoked the Catholic Church to complain about broadcasts it regarded as offensive or indecent. These have been chronicled over the years by a number of historians and cultural critics.[36] Perhaps the most famous incident occurred in 1966 and is simply known as the 'bishop and the nightie' episode. This unfolded on the iconic *Late Late Show*, hosted by Gay Byrne, when a contestant in a quiz revealed that she might not have been wearing a nightdress on her wedding night. The subsequent criticism emanating from Dr Thomas Ryan, Bishop of Clonfert, denouncing the episode as indecent, received widespread coverage in the national and regional press. The station issued an apology and, although some viewers may have been upset by the incident, the bishop was widely ridiculed for his awkward intervention.

Byrne's programme proved to be one of the most provocative features on Irish television and deserves much of the credit it has received for helping to open up Irish society. He was a master performer and mediator who provided a popular and accessible forum for the discussion of a wide array of often controversial topics that had previously been taboo in a public setting.[37] Cultural historian Lance Pettitt notes that the programme helped pro-voke 'legislative changes and shifted the boundaries of taboos in Irish social discourse on a variety of topics including unmarried mothers, Travellers' rights, infanticide, different kinds of sexuality, marriage and clerical celibacy'.[38] Byrne also hosted a popular daytime call-in radio programme on RTÉ that addressed a wide array of sensitive subjects, break-ing down barriers that had kept a range of controversial topics out of the public sphere.

Slowly, the Irish Catholic Church became more comfortable with the medium. A new generation of priests with engaging personalities who were interested in develop-ing innovative programmes made their way into television. In spring 1967, the radical Dominican Austin Flannery presented a series of *Outlook* programmes that addressed poverty and the housing crisis in Dublin. One of the more remarkable broadcasts included four guests: a Jesuit priest, two members of Sinn Féin, and Michael O'Riordan, general secretary of the Irish Workers Party, the official Irish Communist party. While the broadcast created unease among politicians and members of the clergy, it illustrated that Ireland was changing. Another iconic programme, *Radharc*, emerged in 1962 and quickly gained a reputation for developing innovative documentaries about Irish life. F Joseph Dunn, Desmond Forristal, Peter Lemass, and Dermot McCarthy were Dublin priests who formed an independent production company and produced remarkable documentaries that addressed issues of social justice both at home and abroad.

V. TELEVISION IN NORTHERN IRELAND

As noted above, television formally came to Northern Ireland in the spring of 1953 when a small temporary transmitter began relaying BBC programmes to viewers in the Belfast metropolitan area. The BBC was especially keen to transmit the coronation of Elizabeth II, believing that the event would be popular with many viewers and hoping the coro-nation would spur demand for televisions and licences. In Northern Ireland, as in the Irish Republic, the arrival of television proved transformative, challenging a conserva-tive society and ultimately undermining the status quo. Its arrival particularly upset the political and cultural hegemony that Unionist elites had worked hard to cultivate and that had defined the state since its creation in 1920.

Rex Cathcart's seminal study of the BBC in Northern Ireland, *The Most Contrary Region, the BBC in Northern Ireland 1924–1984*, points out that BBC television made a number of programmes about Northern Ireland in the 1950s that were for the most part complimentary. This created unrealistic expectations from political leaders within the province who thought that complimentary features such as *The Pattern of Ulster* and a feature in the series *About Britain* would be typical of future programmes.[39] There was certainly a degree of naiveté in official thinking that BBC television would continue to provide positive publicity for an audience throughout the UK. Cathcart notes that the Unionist government and the Unionist majority never thought that television would have 'anything other than a positive, promotional role'.[40] This was partly due to the evolution of the BBC's radio service in Northern Ireland, which timidly avoided upsetting or challenging the Unionist-controlled government at Stormont.

When the Northern Ireland Civil Rights Association was established in February 1967, it soon became clear that its members were watching the campaign for African-American civil rights in the United States. NICRA was influenced by the strategies of Martin Luther King Jr and began a series of marches in the spring of 1968 showing that it understood the power of television to gain national and international attention. The campaign for civil rights in Northern Ireland hoped to use television to force London to intervene in order to redress many long-held grievances of the Catholic community. In the autumn of 1968, one particular march gained the civil rights campaign international attention and sympathy, while profoundly damaging the image of the Stormont government. On 5 October 1968, civil rights leaders announced that they would march in Derry, ignoring a ban issued by the hard-line Minister of Home Affairs, William Craig. During the demonstration, the Royal Ulster Constabulary attacked the demonstrators, viciously beating helpless marchers with batons. Gerry Fitt, M.P. for West Belfast, and three other Labour M.P.s, who had travelled from England for the march, experienced police violence first hand. A bloodied Gerry Fitt had to be transported to the hospital in an ambulance for medical treatment.

What made the event extraordinary was the fact that an RTÉ cameraman, Gay O'Brien, and sound technician Eamon Hays captured the violence on film as it unfolded. This sensational footage made its way into the BBC programme, *Twenty-Four Hours*, causing uproar. After the incident, O'Neill's government issued a statement 'supporting in a firm way the decisions of the Minister (William Craig) and the actions of the police in Londonderry'.[41] The juxtaposition of truncheon-wielding policemen attacking unarmed civil rights marchers and the statement of the government heavily damaged its credibility. In London, the British government grew increasingly alarmed and embarrassed at developments in the province and began to put pressure on Stormont to speed up long-overdue reforms.

A short time after the Derry melee, O'Neill wrote a long, insightful memorandum for his Cabinet addressing the crisis that was threatening the stability of the province. He argued that it was critical that members of the government understand that difficult decisions had to be made about reform. The Prime Minister told his colleagues that his government was already under tremendous pressure from London to initiate substantial reforms in the province. According to O'Neill, the unflattering publicity from the Derry march meant that the British government would be more aggressive in demanding reforms in the province.

> I would be failing in my duty if I did not make it clear to you that, in my view, Londonderry has dramatically altered this situation to our great disadvantage.

Whether the press and T.V. coverage was fair is immaterial. We have now become a focus of world opinion; indeed we know through official channels that the Embassy and B.I.S. in America have been under intense pressure from the American press.[42]

O'Neill announced a set of sweeping reforms on 22 November designed to mollify both the British Prime Minister and moderates in the civil rights organization. Confronting opposition within his own party, O'Neill decided to address the province on television, appearing both on the BBC and the independent Ulster Television (UTV). O'Neill's famous 'Ulster at the crossroads' speech told civil rights leaders 'your voice has been heard, and clearly heard. Your duty now is to take the heat out of the situation.' It was perhaps the only time the Unionist government at Stormont had taken advantage of the power of television. It would be the last.

Although many moderate leaders of the civil rights movement heeded O'Neill's call to give his reforms a chance, a more confrontational group, People's Democracy, decided to embark on a contentious march from Belfast to Derry on New Year's Day 1969. Once again television played a critical role, capturing the ensuing violence, including an attack on the marchers by loyalists at Burntollet Bridge. Jonathan Bardon's history of the BBC Northern Ireland points out that these images were broadcast internationally, as 'television footage vividly recorded history in the making and not only vied with reports about the Vietnam War but also played its part in giving Northern Ireland a sharp push towards the precipice'.[43] O'Neill resigned a short time later to be replaced by the ineffective James Chichester-Clarke.

Ulster Television and the BBC continued to follow events in Northern Ireland through the darkest years of 'the Troubles'. Images of bombings, shootings, the imposition of internment, Bloody Sunday, the Ulster Workers Strike, the 1981 Hunger Strikes, the 1985 Anglo-Irish Accord, and eventually the 1998 Belfast Agreement chronicled thirty years of murder, mayhem, controversy, political paralysis, then compromise and an uneasy peace. Governments in Dublin, Belfast, and London tried with varying degrees of success to control, shape, and censor broadcasts during these years, provoking serious questions about censorship in democratic societies. Although dissident republicans have been responsible for additional carnage since 1998, 'the Troubles' seem over. Television in Northern Ireland has settled back into a more traditional role of trying to entertain and inform viewers of news from around the world, while reporting on more mundane events at home.

VI. Conclusion

Television became ubiquitous throughout Ireland and a major source of news and entertainment in the closing decades of the twentieth century. The traditional television networks came under increasing pressure from market forces as the Dublin government introduced greater competition, licensing TV3 and the Irish language station TG4 while the advent of satellite television increased the options available to the viewing public throughout the island. The same is true for radio as listeners have more options today than ever before. The media landscape in Ireland has changed and changed dramatically since audiences flocked to the cinema at the start of the century and began listening to the broadcasts of 2RN and 2BE.

Our understanding of Irish media history has been enhanced by the pioneering work of John Horgan, John Bowman, Christopher Morash, Richard Pine, and the late Rex Cathcart. All have helped define a new field in Irish history and contributed much to our understanding of the role of both radio and television in transforming Irish society. But there is still much work to be done. Areas within Irish media history that require research include the role of women in shaping television and radio as well as their representation in programmes broadcast. Education, drama, music, health, sport, labour relations, children's programming, audience, and advertising also require more scholarly investigation. With more archival material coming into the public domain in Ireland, Northern Ireland, and Great Britain there is tremendous potential to address this void and to enhance our understanding of the recent past.

Over the past twenty-five years there has been an extraordinary amount of work done by innovative scholars in the field of Irish film studies. Kevin Rockett, Luke Gibbons, John Hill, Lance Pettitt, and Martin McLoone have produced valuable studies that have defined the field. Their work has been supplemented by a number of other scholars who have published important books and articles, including Brian McIlroy, Ruth Barton, Harvey O'Brien, and Diane Negra.[44] All have explored the complex evolution of an Irish film culture from the start of the twentieth century to the very recent past. These scholars have also explored the challenges confronted by many talented filmmakers who began to make a national and international impact in the 1980s. Film studies has emerged as an exciting and popular academic field and Irish film enables rich interdisciplinary scholarship to address the intersection of film, history, and literature. It appears certain that there will be a continuing exploration of this evolving medium.

In his *History of the Media in Ireland,* Christopher Morash instructively addresses how a very broadly defined media has transformed Ireland over the past five hundred years.[45] He does this by pointing out that in 1500 there were over 160 printing presses in operation in Germany, France, and Italy whereas in Ireland there were none. While the pioneering Johannes Gutenberg published his first Bible in 1456, the first Irish book would not be printed until 1551. That was the year when a London bookseller, Humphrey Powell, produced *The Boke of Common Praier* of the Anglican Communion. Ireland was on the European periphery in more ways than one. This he contrasts with a remarkable survey completed in 2004 by the journal *Foreign Policy* that lists Ireland as the most globalized country in the world, ahead of such highly developed and technologically sophisticated nations as Singapore, Sweden, the United Kingdom, and the United States. It is hard to imagine what the Irish media landscape might look like ten years from now and impossible to conceive what shape it might take over the course of this new century. The constant revolution in communications that has brought us the Internet and portable mobile and satellite technology among a host of other innovations, guarantees however that Ireland will continue to participate in and be part of a truly globalized world.

Notes

1. Kevin Rockett, *Irish Film Censorship, a Cultural Journey from Silent Cinema to Internet Pornography* (Dublin, 2004), 29.
2. National Archives of Ireland, Department of Justice, H 84/7. See http://www.national-archives.ie/topics/jjoyce/Image_pages/DJ.htm.
3. Lance Pettitt, *Screening Ireland: Film and Television Representation* (Manchester, 2000), 37.
4. The British Post Office gave the designation 2RN to the Irish Free State. See Richard Pine, *2RN and the Origins of Irish Radio* (Dublin, 2002), 39–40.
5. Broadcasting fell under the remit of the Irish Post Office, following the British example.
6. White Paper on Wireless Broadcasting (1923), quoted in Robert Savage, *The Origins of Irish Radio*, unpublished MA thesis, University College Dublin (1982), 32.
7. Robert Savage, *Irish Television, the Political and Social Origins* (Cork, 1996), 2.
8. Ibid., 2–3. There were differences: the companies that joined to form the BBC were all involved in the broadcasting industry; this was not the case for the proposed IBC.
9. Ibid., 3–4, also Richard Pine, *2RN and the Origins of Irish Radio*, 79–94.
10. Robert J. Savage, *Irish Television*, 5.
11. See Brian Lynch, 'Steering Clear: Broadcasting and the Church, 1926–1951', *New Hibernia Review*, 4 (2000), 28.
12. Opening address of 2RN, Douglas Hyde, 1 January 1926. Thanks to Nollaig Mac Congáil for the translation.
13. Ibid.
14. Desmond Bell, 'Proclaiming the Republic: Broadcasting Policy and the Corporate State in Ireland' in *Broadcasting Policy and Politics in Western Europe*, 8 no. 2 (1985), 27, and Richard Pine, *2RN and the Origins of Irish Radio*, 138.
15. Maurice Moynihan (ed), *Speeches and Statements by Éamon de Valera 1917–1973* (Dublin, 1980), 466.
16. Robert Savage, *A Loss of Innocence, Television and Irish society 1960–1972* (Manchester, 2010), 14.
17. Ibid., 170.
18. Ronan Fanning, *Independent Ireland* (Dublin, 1983), 79.
19. National Archives of Ireland, Department of Taoiseach, SP15580, report and minute, 25 September 1953.
20. H.R. Cathcart with Michael Muldoon, 'The mass media in twentieth century Ireland', in *A New History of Ireland, VII, Ireland 1921–1984*, J.R. Hill (ed), (Oxford, 2003), 685.
21. Ibid., 685.
22. Gillian McIntosh, *The Force of Culture, Unionist Identities in Twentieth-Century Ireland* (Cork, 1999), 82–3.
23. H.R. Cathcart with Michael Muldoon op.cit.
24. Gillian McIntosh, *The Force of Culture*, 94.
25. Ibid., 80.
26. Martin McLoone, *Irish Film, the Emergence of a Contemporary Cinema* (London, 2000) 111–13.
27. Kevin Rockett, *The Irish Filmography* (Dublin 1996), 150.

28. Ibid., 115.
29. Savage, *Irish Television*, 146, n 12.
30. Ibid., 46.
31. National Archive of Ireland, DT S14996D, Lemass to Moynihan, 30 March 1960.
32. Ibid.
33. Ibid.
34. John Doyle, *A Great Feast of Light, Growing Up Irish in the Television Age* (London, 2005), 15.
35. Quoted in Savage, *A Loss of Innocence*, 83–4.
36. See especially. John Horgan, *Broadcasting and Public Life* (Dublin, 2004); Louise Fuller, *Irish Catholicism Since 1950* (Dublin, 2002); and Gay Byrne with Deirdre Purcell, *The Time of My Life* (Dublin, 1989).
37. *The Corkman*, 12 December 1969.
38. Pettitt, *Screening Ireland*, 169–70.
39. See John Hill, *Cinema and Northern Ireland* (London, 2006), 152–3.
40. Rex Cathcart, *The Most Contrary Region, The BBC in Northern Ireland 1924–1984* (Belfast, 1984), 174.
41. Public Records Office, Northern Ireland, Cab/4/1406, memorandum by the Prime Minister, 14 October 1968.
42. Ibid. (B.I.S. is the British Information Service).
43. Jonathan Bardon, *Beyond the Studio, A History of BBC Northern Ireland* (Belfast, 2000), 29–30.
44. See Brian McIlroy, *Shooting to Kill, Filmmaking and the 'Troubles' in Northern Ireland* (Trowbridge, 1988); Harvey O'Brien, *The Real Ireland, the Evolution of Ireland in Documentary Film* (Manchester 2004); Ruth Barton, *Irish National Cinema* (London, 2004); and Diane Negra, 'Irishness, Anger and Masculinity in Recent Film and Television', in *Screening Irish-America: A Reader* (Dublin, 2009).
45. Christopher Morash, *A History of the Media in Ireland* (Cambridge, 2010).

Select Bibliography

Bowman, John, *Window and Mirror, RTÉ Television 1961–2011* (Cork, 2011).
Cathcart, Rex, *The Most Contrary Region, The BBC in Northern Ireland 1924–1984* (Belfast, 1984).
Cathcart, Rex with Muldoon, Michael, 'The mass media in twentieth-century Ireland', in *New History of Ireland, Vol. VII, Ireland 1921–1984*, J. R. Hill (ed) (Oxford, 2004), 671–710.
Crowley, Tony, *War of Words, The Politics of Language 1537–2004* (Oxford, 2004).
Doolan, Lelia, Dowling, Jack, and Quinn, Bob, *Sit Down and Be Counted, The Cultural Evolution of a Television Station* (Dublin, 1969).
Dunn, Joseph, *No Tigers in Africa* (Dublin, 1986).
Foster, R.F., *Luck and the Irish, a Brief History of Change from 1970* (Oxford, 2008).
Fuller, Louise, *Irish Catholicism since 1950; the Undoing of a Culture* (Dublin, 2002).
Garvin, Tom, *Preventing the Future, Why was Ireland so poor for so long?* (Dublin, 2004).
Girvin, Brian and Murphy, Gary, *Sean Lemass and the Making of Modern Ireland* (Dublin, 2006).
Gorham, Maurice, *Forty Years of Irish Broadcasting* (Dublin, 1967).
Hill, John, *Cinema and Northern Ireland* (London, 2006).
Horgan, John, *Broadcasting and Public Life* (Dublin, 2004).

McIntosh, Gillian, *The Force of Culture, Unionist Identities in Twentieth-Century Ireland* (Cork, 1999).

McLoone, Martin, *Film, Media and Popular Culture in Ireland* (Dublin, 2008).

Morash, Chris, *A History of the Irish Media* (Cambridge, 2010).

O'Brien, Harvey, *The Real Ireland, The Evolution of Ireland in Documentary Film* (Manchester, 2004).

Ó Broin, León, *Just Like Yesterday* (Dublin, 1985).

Ó Tuathaigh, Gearóid, 'The State and the Language: An Historical Perspective', in Caoilfhionn Nic Pháidín and Seán Ó Cearnaigh, *A New View of the Irish Language* (Dublin, 2008).

Pine, Richard, *2RN and the Origins of Irish Radio* (Dublin, 2002).

Pettitt, Lance, *Screening Ireland, Film and Television Representation* (Manchester, 2000).

Quinn, Bob, *Maverick, a Dissident View of Broadcasting Today* (Dingle, 2001).

Rockett, Kevin, *Irish Film Censorship* (Dublin, 2004).

Rolston, Bill and Miller, David (eds), *War and Words, The Northern Ireland Media Reader* (Belfast, 1996).

Savage, Robert J., *Irish Television, The Political and Social Origins* (Cork, 1996).

Savage, Robert J., 'Constructing/deconstructing the image of Sean Lemass's Ireland' in *Ireland in the New Century, Politics, Culture and Identity*, Robert J. Savage (ed) (Dublin, 2003), 151–62.

Savage, Robert J., *A Loss of Innocence? Television and Irish Society 1960–1972* (Manchester, 2010).

Watson, Iarfhlaith, *Broadcasting in Irish* (Dublin, 2003).

PART III

PERIOD STUDIES

THE THIRD
KINGDOM: IRELAND,
C.1580-1690

CHAPTER 15

PLANTATION, 1580–1641

TADHG Ó HANNRACHÁIN

I. INTRODUCTION

PLANTATION is a key theme, and in the eyes of some historians *the* key theme, in the history of early modern Ireland, but what is comprehended under that term is less self-evident than might seem apparent at first glance.[1] Policies of plantation grew out of, and in tandem with, other state-sponsored schemes to pacify and settle the island of Ireland. Contemporaries, for instance, were quite happy to style settlers who had occupied former monastic sites as 'planters', although such centres of immigration were clearly not comprehended in what Sir Francis Blundell referred to in 1622 as the 'six plantations made in Ireland since the memory of man'.[2] Moreover, as they evolved, plantation settlements were inevitably influenced by 'colonial spread' as settlers tended to abandon less desirable plantation sites to move to more attractive estates and prime locations.[3] The geographical and ideological coherence which distinguished the planning of first the Munster and then, pre-eminently, the Ulster plantation thus rapidly dissolved under the pressure of economic reality. When viewed in this light, it might be suggested that, rather than representing a discrete theme in the history of early modern Ireland, plantation might perhaps be better seen as a vital component in the wider topic of British settlement in the island during the sixteenth and seventeenth centuries.[4]

The chronology of the process is also somewhat problematic. A sustainable case can certainly be made that the period 1580–1641 represented a particular era of plantation in Ireland. Contemporary perceptions, however, tended to link this era to earlier developments. Towards the end of King James VI and I's reign, an attempt was made to compile a general set of directions, comparable to those relating to the settlement of the church and the Irish revenue, to deal with the various plantations.[5] In a very similar fashion to Blundell, the directions noted:

> in our kingdom of Ireland, there have been (of late years) six several plantations made, whereof two were in the time of Queen Elizabeth (of famous memory) and four have been since the time of our reign over England and Ireland.

The first of the plantations considered was 'of the counties of Leix in the Queen's county and Offaly in the King's county', the second and third were in Munster and Ulster, fourth was the plantation of Wexford, fifth was Longford and Ely O'Carroll, and last was the plantation of Leitrim and 'other small territories'.[6] Catholic contemporaries, however, were eager to subsume much older processes of settlement under the rubric of plantation. Thus, on 29 May 1622, while carefully lauding the plantation of Ulster, a petition from the nobility and gentry of the realm of Ireland subtly laid claim to the title of plantation for the Anglo-Norman conquest and identified the Old English as the heirs of 'plantators' noting:

> The ancient plantation established upon the conquest hath fixed deep and firm roots for growth and life of the government of this kingdom ... wherein the heirs and off-springs of those worthy plantators, by loss of life and effusion of their blood, gave invincible proof of their faithful obedience befitting the issue of some memorable progenitors.[7]

The traditional historiography of the early modern period tended to echo the Jacobean state perception of 1622, with the line of plantations studied generally commencing with Laois-Offaly in the 1550s. The term plantation was also frequently used with regard to Sir Thomas Smith's adventure in the Ards peninsula in 1570 and the earl of Essex's failed settlement of Antrim in 1572–3. More recent studies of Tudor Ireland, however, have tended to anchor the Laois-Offaly plantations, and even those of Smith and Essex, within a more complex network of contemporary governmental policy rather than emphasizing their status as the harbingers of a new approach to the settlement of Ireland. As Ciarán Brady has identified, the first plans for plantation in Laois-Offaly were actually begun by Anthony St Leger, the principal architect of the imaginative scheme—generally termed Surrender and Regrant—to assimilate the Gaelic elites of the island into a new Kingdom of Ireland. Indeed, St Leger's original plans were actually more radical than those eventually executed by the Earl of Sussex since he had envisaged a settlement confined exclusively to planters either from England or the older colonial community.[8] More generally, Brady suggests that down to 1579 plantation projects in Ireland were fundamentally influenced by the unwillingness of the Crown to countenance the complete removal of the native population from anything other than a restricted area. Consequently, colonizing enterprises were largely based around the notion of nuclear fortified sites and such schemes therefore were not necessarily at odds with the avowed governmental intention to promote internal reform of the Gaelic lordships.[9] For his part, although he acknowledges the importance of the Laois-Offaly plantations as a 'template' for all later plantations,[10] Rolf Loeber has also noted how the suppression of the monasteries acted as a forerunner of later plantations, particularly through the allocation of properties in strategic locations to New English military officers such as Kilbeggan in 1550.[11] Kilbeggan, indeed, was to be revived as a private plantation in 1606 through a grant to Sir Oliver Lambert. The confiscation of monastic land was also key to the English settlement of Roscommon in the 1570s and 1580s, where Sir Nicholas Malby assembled a vast estate of over 17 000 acres with several dozen settlers, mostly of English stock.[12] Hand in hand with the plans for plantation in Laois-Offaly was the revival of governmental subsidies for the building of castles in border areas which had previously been encouraged by the statue of 1427,[13] a policy which mutated in later plantations into a requirement that undertakers undertake extensive and onerous building in return for the generous nature of their land grants.

The terminus of the era of plantation is in some respects as elastic as its starting date. In addition to the six schemes already mentioned, there is little historiographical debate about the use of the term plantation to describe the plans floated for Upper Ossory, Ormond, and Connacht in the reign of Charles I and Nicholas Canny has argued cogently against the notion that, during this period, plantation was of less importance than beforehand. The post-Wentworth era, however, is historiographically more problematic. In Canny's interpretative schema the Interregnum settlement represented the culmination of the policy of plantation and he makes unambiguous use of the term Cromwellian plantation in his monumental study of British settlement in early modern Ireland.[14] This is not uniform practice, however: frequently the great land confiscations of the Cromwellian period are not analyzed under the rubric of plantation or indexed under that heading in histories of seventeenth-century Ireland, despite the substantial similarities in terms of ideology, planning, uneven execution, and unintended outcomes which linked that national land-settlement to the plantations of the previous period.[15] The study of plantation in early modern Ireland, therefore, necessitates a certain caution about the term itself. Plantation evolved both from and into wider patterns of settlement and the process resists an easy pigeon-holing either of time or of place. Yet its significance is undoubted, perhaps, most of all, because of its destabilizing effect on the pre-Elizabethan elites of the island.

II. Plantation in Marian and early Elizabethan Ireland

Although it began before Elizabeth's accession, the plantation of Laois-Offaly remains germane to the examination of the topic in the period 1580–1641 for three principal reasons. First, contemporaries identified the Laois-Offaly settlement as a plantation and analysis of the area materially affected the planning and evaluation of the outcomes of other plantations which began after 1580. Second, the plantation of Laois-Offaly continued to evolve in the course of the period under review. Lastly, renewed plantation in these counties in the Jacobean period was affected by the contours and the understanding of the previously planted portions of the counties.[16]

In the course of the 1540s, the difficult midland terrain west of Kildare—the lordships of the O'Moores and O'Connors, whose threat to the Pale had formerly been contained by the influence of the earls of Kildare—came to assume an increasing salience in English governmental thinking. In 1546–8 two garrisons, Fort Governor (later Philipstown) and

Fort Protector (later Maryborough) were established. In line with conventional colonial thinking, the initial plan was to confiscate only the land in the immediate environs of the garrisons.[17] The arrival in Ireland in 1556 of Thomas Lord FitzWalter, later earl of Sussex, saw a major attempt to reinvigorate the colonization of the midlands. In 1557 the two lordships were formally shired but effectively no further progress was made and no land grants were implemented.[18] By 1561 very few of the original leases were occupied. In the three years following, eighty-eight new leases were issued, although roughly half of the county of Laois and close to two-thirds of County Offaly were not included in the grants, which ultimately was to leave space for a new round of plantation in the seventeenth century. The plantation estates were grouped heavily around the forts of Philipstown and Maryborough and the two settlements were largely separate from each other.[19] Forty-four of the grants were to soldiers and one detailed investigation has suggested a population of possibly five hundred English, although this would appear somewhat inflated.[20] Indeed, one contemporary noted that English grantees preferred to populate their holdings with native Irish tenants who were attracted by the possibility of military protection.[21] The climate of war contributed to this development as up to eighteen risings occurred in the forty years after 1563. Maryborough and Philipstown were incorporated in 1569–70 and at this stage the walled area of Maryborough amounted to about 145 000 square feet.[22] But land was already becoming concentrated into the hands of a number of individuals such as Francis Cosby, the seneschal of Maryborough, in Offaly, and the Cowley family in Laois. Cosby was later to be accused of having 'devoured' other Englishmen.[23] From the late 1560s, Cosby developed a relationship with Rory Óg O'Moore which apparently protected his own estates while those of his English neighbours were ravaged. Such behaviour evidently allowed Cosby to attract more native tenants than his competitors and the attendant ruin of their lands probably facilitated his swallowing them up. Native Irishmen also came to play a significant role. Sir Barnaby Fitzpatrick, for instance, not only became the lieutenant of Laois, but his important role as a military bulwark against the dispossessed clans evidently contributed to the survival of the MacGiollapadraig (Macgillapatrick) lordship in its traditional form, complete with Brehon law and an army maintained by the traditional Gaelic billeting system of coyne and livery down to the end of the Tudor period.[24]

In 1573, Rory Óg O'Moore launched a serious rebellion in Laois which engulfed both counties for several years. Rory was eventually killed by Sir Barnaby FitzPatrick in 1578; later that year Cosby and Robert Harpole engineered a horrific massacre of much of the remainder of the O'Moore clan at Mullaghmast.[25]

By 1584, the earl of Ormond attempted to use the apparent failure of the midlands plantations, in particular the insufficient means of the planters, as part of his argument that the proposed settlement of Munster should reward native lords who had stood by the government in the conflict with the earl of Desmond.[26] Ten years later, a novel scheme, which apparently originated with the O'Moores themselves, emerged with the notion that the entire clan would be transplanted to an unoccupied area of Munster.[27] During the Nine Years' War (1594–1603) the rebellious midland septs continued to pose a problem both to the local planter population and to the government. Owny O'Moore emerged as a significant rebel figure who played a major role in the overthrow of the Munster plantation. Yet the midlands plantation survived and regenerated with surprising speed in the wake of the conflict. The transplantation scheme was revived by Sir Piers Crosby who engineered the removal of the Gaelic clans to County Kerry. In the event, this proved of limited success as many filtered back over the following decades, yet by 1610 there was evidence of agricultural activity by English tenants. Most of the plantation grants were still in the possession of the families of the original recipients. The commissioners of the 1622 enquiry were even more positive, noting:

> this plantation in the King's and Queen's counties as it was well begun so it hath prosperously continued, and is for the most part well built and peopled by the English and a great strength to the country and ready for your majesty's service and their own defence.[28]

In particular the commissioners were delighted to note that the 'owners of the said lands are most of them such as dwell and inhabit upon their plantations, which were to be wished and pursued in all other places of the plantations'. The chief focus of governmental discontent in the aftermath of this investigation was evidently the alteration of the nature of the patents by which lands were held. This was originally intended to be through knight service *in capite* with a condition of residence and no right to alienate. Many of these grants, however, had been converted to socage tenure, which was less advantageous to the state, and the Crown was eager to prevent any further incidences of this procedure.[29] The restrained nature of governmental criticism was thus a recognition that, from its unpromising beginnings, the Laois-Offaly plantation had come to be seen as a success through the installation of a loyal settler community and the military neutralization of a previously endemically rebellious area.

III. TUDOR PLANTATION IN ULSTER

Plantation in Ulster during the sixteenth century sits at somewhat of a tangent to the traditional narrative line. The various enterprises in Ulster during Elizabeth's reign were not, for instance, considered by the 1622 commission under the rubric of plantation. Yet, at Newry, Carrickfergus, the Ards Peninsula, and south Antrim, a variety of projects involving the transfer of English settlers to Ireland were launched. The most successful of these was the Bagenal settlement of Newry, but the evolution of this outpost corresponds uneasily to the notion of plantation, since most of the population of the town was Irish, even though the principal residences were evidently held by English people. In the rural hinterland of the town, the traditional pattern of occupancy was even less disturbed. Nevertheless, for all its continuities the Bagenal lordship was clearly an 'anglicising outpost'.[30] Like the Malby settlement in Roscommon, which it resembled in many details, the core of Bagenal's position in Newry rested on the granting of church lands in the period 1550–2. Carrickfergus had once been the centre of the earldom of Ulster but in 1575 only six householders of any significance apparently remained. Gradually, however, the town recovered, partially because of government patronage to favour the port over Drogheda, where the issue of recusancy was creating increasing friction between local community and government. The town government was gradually taken over by New English figures such as William Piers.[31] The most ambitious schemes of colonization attempted for Ulster during the Tudor period were by Sir Thomas Smith in the Ards Peninsula and the earl of Essex in Antrim. Both, however, found local resistance insurmountable, despite assistance from the Queen and the use of often savage violence.[32]

Two principal effects of these various ventures can be observed. First, English intrusion into East Ulster became a major factor in the evolving politics of the local lordships. The rise of the Bagenal nexus at Newry was ultimately a crucial influence on Hugh O'Neill's rebellion against the crown.[33] Smith and Essex failed to secure Antrim from MacDonnell immigration and settlement but they did materially contribute to the weakening of the Clandeboye lordship, and the eventual opening of the area to Hugh O'Neill's influence.[34] Moreover, the credibility of English reform projects was necessarily diminished by the savagery displayed by the colonizers and the evident inconsistency of approach towards the Gaelic population.[35] Second, the experience of failure, in particular with regard to Smith's and Essex's ill-fated projects, materially contributed to the planning of later plantations, especially in Munster and the Jacobean plantation of Ulster.

IV. THE PLANTATION OF MUNSTER

The plantation of Munster has been the subject of detailed historical enquiry which has produced a rich pool of conclusions.[36] In many respects, it can be regarded as the watershed event in the history of plantation in Ireland.[37] Like the later Ulster and Cromwellian projects, it occurred in the wake of ruinously expensive conflict which had resulted in widespread devastation and depopulation of the area to be settled and was the product of careful and very ambitious planning in both the Irish and English administrations. The proximate cause for the plantation was the suppression of the great Desmond revolt of 1579–83, although previously plans had been advanced for extensive confiscation and settlement of land in the late 1560s and in 1573.[38] While the Desmond revolt was still raging, Sir Francis Walsingham encouraged the development of plans of colonization and a variety of figures tendered their opinions about how best to effect them.[39] The earl of Ormond (on his own behalf and that of other loyal native landholders) and a variety of servitors offered conflicting views on the best mode of proceeding. In the event, Ormond successfully cast doubt on the ability of army captains and resourceless officials to undertake a primary role in the plantation. Eventually, the dominant view in the English privy council came to emphasize the idea of a hierarchical settlement in which the undertakers were to be men of substance who could afford an estimated initial investment of £2577 before beginning to reap profits from their grants. Planters were to receive seignories of 12 000 acres of profitable land, on which they were to settle ninety-one families. In the case of smaller grants of 8 000, 6 000, and 4 000 acres, a correspondingly lesser number of settlers was expected, but in every instance the obligation lay on undertakers to introduce colonists of exclusively English origin. This massive undertaking was legitimized not only on the grounds of justifiable reward for the trouble and expense of repressing the rebellion but also because land was underpopulated and underutilized. It was also anticipated that the plantation would have an educational and ameliorative effect on the native population who would be forced to learn from and imitate the more civilized and dominant newcomers.[40]

In reality, this grandiose scheme suffered many setbacks and revisions. The process of surveying revealed less land available than had been envisaged. Encouraged by the earl of Ormond, a series of lawsuits launched by local interests reduced the pool of land still further by proving that land from which the attainted earl of Desmond had drawn rent was not necessarily his property and by asserting the rights of mortgage holders to compensation. By 1611, it has been estimated that 94 000 acres originally assigned to undertakers had been reclaimed.[41] This served notably to diminish the enthusiasm of many would-be planters and of the eighty-six original volunteers only fifteen ultimately took out patents, although these were supplemented by another twenty individuals not associated with the initial scheme.[42] These additions, including twelve military officers and sundry officials, ensured a certain revival of the servitor interest and the military dimensions of the new settlement were enhanced by the government's utilization of undertakers as commanders of horsemen maintained at the Crown's expense.[43] It is surmised that the total English population in the colony stood at c.4000 at the time of its first overthrow in 1598. This was well short of the 11 375 people that the original plans had envisaged but, as Nicholas Canny has argued, it still represented a substantial inflow of settlers in the context of the contemporary European pattern of colonial migration.[44]

By this date, however, the plantation showed marked differences from the idealized and hierarchical settlement originally devised. The Irish predilection for pasture, and in particular the widespread practice of transhumance,[45] was conventionally linked to their inferior cultural status and it was a stable assumption that the promotion of English civility through plantation would lead to an increase in tillage. The economic reality of Munster, however, dictated that greater profits were available from pastoralism and the new English colony was apparently more likely to convert arable land to grazing than the reverse.[46] Economic dispersal of the settlement community also followed as tenants consistently sought better land in preference to less desirable plantation estates. This created significant economic difficulties for some undertakers whose tenants simply deserted them for more attractive situations. It also militated against the creation of compact model settlements along the lines envisaged, a process which was further impeded by the nature of the confiscated land, which did not lend itself to orderly division into seignories and which became even more incoherent as native landowners successfully regained large swathes of territory through legal processes. Moreover, while conscientious undertakers certainly existed, many of those granted estates simply lacked the economic resources to fulfil the conditions under which they had been granted land. As a consequence, they were prepared to retain Irish tenants on their lands, often on exploitative terms, and looked for further occasions of profit at the expense of local proprietors, even in highly unscrupulous ways.[47] Such behaviour was evidently legitimized by the conviction that the loyalty of the entire native elite was suspect, and was materially assisted by the administration's willingness to confer the offices of sheriff and justice of the peace on planters and the use of the Munster provincial council to buttress the influence of the new colony.[48] The nascent colony, therefore, was both ill-organized for defence and the subject of a festering native resentment which culminated in its swift and brutal overthrow in October 1598.[49] The ease with which the English settlers were swept away ultimately was to have a significant impact on the planning of future projects, for it exposed the vulnerability of isolated plantation settlements and their failure to act as a 'civilizing' influence on the native population. As a result, the notion that plantation needed to be applied across the entire country gained greater currency among the administrative elite.[50]

After 1603, the plantation of Munster was gradually revived. The undertakers retained the right to their estates although many changed hands. By 1611, it has been estimated that the English population was close to 5000; in 1622 it had almost tripled and possibly stood at around 14 000, while twenty years later it probably amounted to over 20 000.[51] This represented a very sizeable movement of population, drawn especially from south-western England, but settlement in Munster reflected less the realization of the original plantation ideal than its adaptation to the economic possibilities of the province. In 1622, it was noted that most of the undertakers were not resident on their seignories, that some were actually tenants of others, and the fact that individuals frequently held land from different undertakers gave a falsely inflated figure of English inhabitants. The English tenants largely did not build in villages or towns but were scattered on their estates and inadequately furnished with arms. By a multitude of different contracts and devices, and in flagrant breach of the original articles, large amounts of plantation land now housed native Irish inhabitants. The planters were also held responsible for a major depletion of timber stands, particularly through ironworks and the making of pipestaves. There was also evidence of a widespread shortfall in the rents which were due to the Crown from the various seignories.[52]

The central figure in the seventeenth-century plantation was undoubtedly Richard Boyle, who in 1602 purchased Sir Walter Raleigh's three and a half seignories: by 1629 he had acquired the bulk of the land confiscated in the province in the aftermath of the Desmond rebellion.[53] Intensive study of Boyle's estates has revealed the multitude and spread of his commercial contacts and activities and indicates that the high density of Protestant settlement on his better estates and those of other settlers was the result of determined recruitment and a keen awareness on the part of both landowners and tenants of the commercial value of any given parcel of land.[54] The result was that areas such as the south-west and the north of County Cork and the towns of Kinsale and Youghal attracted particularly large numbers of settlers in a process of colonial spread.[55]

V. The Ulster Plantation

The seventeenth-century plantation of Ulster was the most ambitious of the state-sponsored schemes for British settlement of Ireland during this period.[56] In the first years of James VI and I's reign it was the area east of the Bann which was most open to penetration from Britain. Grants to the Lord Deputy Sir Arthur Chichester, James Hamilton, and Hugh Montgomery laid the foundations for what developed into significant migration of English and Scottish settlers into Counties Antrim and Down.[57] The flight of the earls, however, in 1607 and the foolhardy insurrection of Sir Cahir O'Doherty in the following year opened the door to a massive colonization project in six counties, as the government turned from an attempt to assert the rights of native tenants and freeholders within the western lordships of Ulster to the decision to treat the entire area as escheated to the Crown through the treason of the ruling lords. A multitude of conflicting opinions and priorities influenced the planning of the project. In particular, divisions existed between, on the one hand, the servitor interest in Ireland eager to ensure that those who had already made careers in the island should direct the plantation and, on the other, prominent figures at court who believed that only men of significant resources should be allowed a leadership role. The king's personal enthusiasm for the plantation as a 'British' project in which both his Scottish and English subjects should have a role was also a critical influence. The result was a scheme which reflected compromise and accommodation rather than the fulfilment of a single vision of plantation. While the design of the plantation went through many mutations, Nicholas Canny has argued that five principal factors provided the theoretical underpinnings to the planning of the project. First, classical notions of a hierarchical and exemplary colony continued to exert a profound influence, which dictated that the leadership cadre—the undertakers—should rely entirely on British and Protestant tenants to inhabit and work their lands. Second, the plantation was intended to create an urban network of towns and fortified dwellings which would foster economic development as well as provide a conduit for an improving example to be delivered to the native population. Third, a genuine desire to establish the state church with the economic and structural foundations to undertake the religious reformation of the area resulted in a generous provision of land to support the clergy. In addition to the 9240 acres of bishops' demesne land which was discovered in the six escheated counties of the plantation, it was decided that the far larger amount of territory classified as termon and erenagh land, which had helped to underpin the Gaelic ecclesiastical system and which legal inquisition found to be escheated to the Crown, should also be granted to the bishops of the established church.[58] Fourth, the experience of the Munster plantation dictated the inadvisability of scattering English colonies over a wide area among a native population which still outnumbered them and where local lords retained their traditional seats and influence. It was planned, therefore, that even those natives who were to receive estates in the plantation would be forced to designated areas of the province where they could be kept under military surveillance. Finally, in the fulfilment of a civilizing function, the plantation was planned to allow for the compensation of blameless natives forced off the undertakers' proportions under the comforting notion that plenty of vacant or underutilized land was available to satisfy their needs.[59]

Although the native Irish were singularly absent from the process of planning, Gaelic structures and the spatial system of the area also bequeathed an important legacy to the settlement, as to previous colonization projects. The existing Gaelic pattern of land division into units known as Ballyboes (or tates, or polls) and Ballybetaghs reflected a keen awareness of agrarian value as opposed to mere acreage and this mode of classification was adopted by the newcomers, with the ballyboe becoming the basis of the townlands which undertakers leased to their tenants. In the plantation, ballyboes were generally assumed to contain sixty acres of profitable land (with sufficient bog and woodland attached to provide fuel) but their actual size in statute acreage varied depending on the fertility of the soil. Plantation estates of 1000 acres generally equated to sixteen ballyboes, which in turn reflected the existing divisions of ballybetaghs, the area traditionally controlled by a sept within a lordship, such as the O'Quinns or O'Hagans in Tyrone. As with the smaller unit of the ballyboe, the correspondence of these 1000-acre parcels to modern statute acres, however, was extremely erratic. Philip Robinson has noted, for instance, the disparity between the two supposedly 1000-acre plantation estates at Gortaville and Eden: the former actually contained 1851 statute acres of largely fertile soil while the latter comprised 46 814 statute acres of much poorer quality.[60] At a higher level, the baronies and precincts of the plantation corresponded to the 'countries' of Irish chieftains of the pre-plantation era.[61]

In escheating the six counties of Armagh, Cavan, Coleraine, Donegal, Fermanagh, and Tyrone, it was assumed that 459 110 acres of land would be redistributed.[62] 162 500 acres were granted to English and Scottish undertakers and a further 45 520 acres to a corporate body of London companies, whose resources were seen as vital to the commercial success of the project and in particular to the development of two towns in Derry and Coleraine. In recognition of their contribution, they were offered an area with optimum possibilities for commercial development which was redesignated as Londonderry.[63] Land allocated to the church amounted to 74 852 acres while 54 632 acres, over a third of which lay in County Cavan, were granted to servitors. Another 27 593 acres were assigned to Trinity College and to provide for schools, towns, and forts. 94 013 acres were allotted to native proprietors, although in several instances this grant was for life only and could not be passed to the grantee's heirs.[64]

The undertakers and the London companies were expected within three years of the grant to plant twenty-four adult British males 'conformable in religion' for every 1000-acre proportion which they received. They were to be resident, were not allowed to retain Irish tenants, and were to build strong houses for themselves and to cause their tenants to build in villages near the principal house. Their lands were granted in free and common socage at a rent of £5 6s 8d per annum. Servitors were charged the same level of rent for lands which they let out to English or Scottish tenants but were allowed to retain native Irish on their estates on payment of a higher rate of £8 per 1000 acres.

The native Irish proprietors were charged the highest rents at £10 13s 4d, exactly double those required of the undertakers.[65] Despite the rent discrimination in their favour, the requirements which the undertakers faced were very onerous and costly. Government practice in the sixteenth century had included the offer of subsidies for the construction of castles on the frontiers of the Pale. The expectation that the undertakers would cover this cost themselves, however, was frankly unrealistic. Even the London companies experienced difficulties in meeting the building requirements despite the advantages which they enjoyed in terms of wealth, and access to shipping, materials, and artisans.[66] It has been estimated, for instance, that in less than thirty years the companies had spent £62 000 on the towns of Derry and Coleraine, together with at least another £22 000 in construction projects within the county of Londonderry. By 1622, Derry already contained four paved principal streets, with room for six more, and a 200-foot-square paved marketplace. There were 102 houses of lime and stone with slated roofs, with room for an additional 300. The wall of the town was twenty feet high and six feet thick.[67]

The lack of realism demonstrated by the devisers of the scheme with regard to the costs of building was replicated in the requirement to clear large portions of the planted area of all Irish inhabitants. Those natives who were granted lands in almost all cases were expected to transplant to new places of residence, thus breaking the traditional nexus of influence and patronage. The 'inferior sort', to whom nothing had been allotted, were ordered in chilling terms in 1611 to move from the precincts of the undertakers and the London companies into the lands of the servitors or of the church 'in no less numbers than the same will conveniently bear, both in respect of grazing and manureance. And concerning the surplus of the common people…they must prepare themselves to depart with their goods and chattels, at or before the first day of May next, into what other parts of this realm they please.'[68] This was not only notably harsh towards the Gaelic population, who were to be forced from their areas of residence irrespective of any consideration of culpability other than their ethnic origin, but it added considerably to the economic difficulties of the incoming undertakers.

Attracting English tenants, particularly with farming expertise, to Ulster proved difficult for all undertakers since the province was relatively unattractive compared to other possible areas of immigration open to English settlers.[69] Economically, it was far more attractive to retain Irish tenants in defiance of the plantation articles and this practice proved endemic. Indeed, the majority of the British population who settled in Jacobean Ulster was not English but Scots. Scottish enthusiasm for settlement in Ireland was reflected by heavy migration to Antrim and Down prior to the flight of the earls. The Privy Council of Scotland took a keen interest in the idea of planting the western counties of Ulster and fifty-nine Scots eventually became undertakers for 81 000 acres of land. Although the number of Scottish undertakers exceeded their English counterparts, who numbered only fifty-one, the latter were on average wealthier and acquired slightly more and evidently rather better land (81 500 acres).[70] Not surprisingly, the rate of failure among Scottish undertakers was even greater than with their English counterparts: by 1619, thirty-three of the original names had surrendered their interest in their plantation properties.[71]

Because of the pattern of Scottish debt guarantee, however, most defaulting undertak-ers of Scottish origin passed their holdings to their fellow countrymen, while Scots also sometimes acquired estates from English undertakers and servitors who were unable to make them a going concern.[72] Scots too were evidently often the only British tenants available to English landowners on some holdings. It has been estimated that 6 545 adult Scots inhabited the plantation area by 1622, about a thousand more than the English population of the escheated counties. Moreover, the proximity of what was probably an even higher Scottish population in Antrim and Down gave a distinctly Scottish over-tone to the British population of Ulster. As Nicholas Canny has argued, by contem-porary European standards this rate of immigration was a substantial achievement, particularly as the adult female component of the population was equivalent to per-haps three-quarters of the male.[73] Moreover, a surprising lack of rancour seems to have existed between the Scottish and English components of the new 'British' population of the province, despite some notable and high-profile incidents.[74]

The personal involvement of the king and the fact that the settlement was intended as a great project of social engineering, rather than merely colonization for defence and security purposes, help account for the consistent disappointment which all surveys of the plantation revealed. Undertakers were constantly shown to be in breach of their arti-cles, particularly in terms of clearing their lands of Irish tenants. New deadlines were set for this to be achieved on a number of occasions before it was finally accepted in 1621 that residence by Irish tenants would be allowable on one quarter of the under-takers' estates. This acceptance of the failure of the original plan to create zones free of native Irish settlement went hand in hand with a failure to achieve uniform British set-tlement across the areas which had been designated. In common with all other planta-tions, it was the quality of land and its proximity to desirable resources, such as ports, which determined the attractiveness of a given location to prospective tenants. Similarly to Munster, the English and Scottish population clustered in particular areas of Ulster, especially south and west of Lough Neagh and the Foyle and Erne basins, together with the Clogher and lower Bann valleys, mid-Cavan, and the north-east of the new county of Londonderry.[75] By contrast, with the exception of the Scottish precinct of Portlough (the Laggan), Lifford, and the barony of Kilmacrennan, there was little British settle-ment of Donegal: in the barony of Boylagh and Banagh the earl of Annaghdale amassed a vast estate including the holdings granted to the original undertakers, but the popu-lation was almost entirely native Irish and remained an active security worry for the government.[76]

Even more serious was the plantation's failure to contribute to the exemplary and assimilative purpose for which it was originally designed. Ironically, the most costly war which the early modern English state was to endure in Ireland was precipitated by the rebellion in 1641, not of the dispossessed native nobles of the plantation, but by 'men of broken fortune' from the deserving Irish who received land grants but who proved poorly equipped to adapt to the new conditions of plantation Ulster. The difficulties which afflicted this cohort were many. Although 280 grants were made to native Irish figures, few of them exceeded 2000 acres, which left families with slender resources to draw on in a period of rapid economic change.[77] Even successful economic adaptation, however, did not guarantee smooth relations within the new dispensation. The outstanding Gaelic figure in plantation Donegal was evidently Turlogh O'Boyle, the recipient of 2000 acres in Doe and Fanad barony. By 1641, partly by renting to English tenants, he had increased this holding to over 4000 acres. Nevertheless, in 1628, O'Boyle was arrested on suspicion of collusion for an invasion of Ireland by Gaelic exiles and spent an uncomfortable period in Lifford gaol before he was released.[78]

Not least of the plantation's failures was the manner in which the generous provision for the state church resulted in little or no effective evangelization of the native population of the escheated counties, despite the initial willingness of large numbers of the Gaelic clergy to conform. Economic motivations undoubtedly contributed largely to this pattern of conformity but it did not last. The wives and children of conforming clergy, many of whom were members of the hereditary ecclesiastical families, often remained Catholics and, in many cases, the clerics themselves eventually returned to the church of Rome. A major contributory factor to this development was undoubtedly the pattern of displacement of native by settler clergy in the most desirable livings of the province of Ulster which was visible in every diocese by the 1630s, with the partial exception of Kilmore, where Bishop William Bedell fought against the common assumption among the settler clergy that they were free of pastoral responsibilities in parishes devoid of British inhabitants.[79] From the perspective of the bishops who appointed them, the new English and Scottish clergy far outstripped the undereducated and dubiously motivated native clerics as representatives of a movement of religious reform which was intrinsically anglicizing as well as Protestantizing. Nevertheless, the new clergy showed little sense of pastoral responsibility towards the Gaelic population, although they were often rapacious in trying to exploit the pecuniary possibilities, not only of the traditional entitlements which the Gaelic clergy had enjoyed, but also the tithe system which the plantation had established, and the imposition of recusancy fines which it enabled. Their activity in this regard was probably particularly resented because the endemic chaos of the preceding period had meant that much of the population had been freed from even traditional ecclesiastical payments and consequently resented the novelty of the clergy's demands to an even greater extent.[80] Thus, rather than providing a secure base for the evangelization of Ulster as was originally envisaged, the plantation directly contributed to a wide popular resentment of the clergy of the established church, which was to be made very evident in 1641 when they became particular targets of fury.[81] In addition, as Brian Mac Cuarta has recently noted, the plantation seems to have contributed to the Catholic revival in the north in other ways. In this regard, the under-researched presence of Catholic families in the plantation, most notably the Hamiltons of Strabane, seems to have served as an important conduit for the arrival and maintenance of elite Catholic clergy in the province.[82]

The great disappointment which was constantly expressed in governmental circles at the failure of the Ulster plantation can partly be related to the bloated expectations with which it was saddled. Although responsible for the advent of a very sizeable British population into what had previously been the least anglicized area of the island, the plantation came to be perceived as not having accomplished significantly more than the lesser plantations[83] of the Jacobean era.

VI. The Plantations of Wexford, Longford, Leitrim, Offaly (Ely O'Carroll, Ferricall, Delvyn, Montcragan, Clincolman), Laois (Iregan and Upper Ossory), and Westmeath (Portion of Clincolman)

These lesser plantations of Jacobean and early Caroline Ireland have traditionally been treated as something of a footnote to the greater enterprises of Munster and Ulster. More recent historiography has tended to highlight the key role which they played in helping to determine the political atmosphere of the period and the alienation of the native population. The actual scale of the confiscations, however, is often underestimated. In these various plantations, undertakers received almost 110 000 plantation acres, more than half of the total undertaker acreage in Ulster.[84] Moreover, while in Ulster the native proprietors were not necessarily assigned the worst land available, the level of corruption, partly as a result of very dubious surveying, in these lesser plantations was evidently very considerable.[85] In Upper Ossory, for instance, it has been noted that the vast Villiers grant comprised mostly profitable arable and pastoral land in contrast to the marginal territories assigned to many native grantees.[86] The basis for most of this plantation activity was laid in the Lord Deputyship of Sir Arthur Chichester (1605–16). Chichester's sponsoring of additional plantation settlements outside the great enterprise of Ulster would appear to have been driven by two main considerations. The first was to provide for the servitor interest which had been relatively unrewarded in Ulster. Second, the plantations were intended to fulfil a social and defensive remit as the aim was evidently to break up lordships and redistribute land among a greater number of freeholders.[87] Chichester's plans, however, met with significant opposition. The plantation of Wexford, where a major compensation of servitors was planned, rapidly ran into such a degree of difficulty that the implementation of other plantations in the midlands was seriously delayed or, as in the case of Carbery in Cork, entirely abandoned. Between 1612 and 1618, four different schemes were partially implemented in Wexford to the ongoing frustration of the Lord Deputy.[88] A significant reason for the level of opposition to the plantation project was the degree to which it threatened Old English as well as native Irish landowners, which resulted in Old English support and legal advice for the Gaelic Irish of the area. By the close of James I's reign, while the Old English position in the county had been maintained to a considerable degree,[89] it was becoming apparent that significant amounts of fraud had occurred.

The basic thrust of the final scheme for the area was that a quarter of the land was to be assigned to undertakers with the remainder to be re-granted back to the natives. Yet the manner in which this was done, similar to the process in Longford, Leitrim, Offaly, and Laois, was highly suspicious.[90] The investigations of 1622 later estimated that 30 000 acres in these plantations (exclusive of Upper Ossory) had been 'misemployed', or granted wrongly as a result of corruption or lack of skill in the surveyors. Lands had been granted to individuals who were neither undertakers nor natives. Some native landholders, presumably as a reward for collusion in corruption, received augmented holdings, while others saw their entitlements diminished or at times entirely removed. In the immediate aftermath of the commission's work, more than 500 petitions of grievance were presented, evidently chiefly by native proprietors, the principal victims of the process.[91]

Unlike the Munster and Ulster plantations, these lesser settlements, which did not bind undertakers to introduce British families, were not responsible for major inflows of population into Ireland. In the main, the undertakers seem to have been casual in fulfilling their responsibilities; the 1622 investigations found less than 10 per cent of the undertakers in Leitrim to be resident, for instance. Nor was this surprising, as many of the undertakers were state officials who presumably had never intended to settle.[92] These plantations were characterized by a predatory venality which prioritized the enrichment of a New English caste. Whereas a case could be made that the Munster and Ulster settlements were based on justifiable forfeitures of rebellious nobles, the Leitrim, midlands, and Wexford projects operated on a different logic. The expropriation of Leitrim, for instance, was a particularly unsavoury exercise in state bullying.[93] In seeking to prevent the extension of plantation further into Connacht in 1621, the lord president of the province noted the importance of distinguishing between the lands of the loyal and disloyal in designating lands for plantation and warned of the dangers which ignoring such distinctions could bring.[94] Increasingly, however, such logic was contested by the servitor interest of Ireland who felt free to question the loyalty of almost all native interests on religious grounds and who aspired to reap the benefits of ongoing plantation. The level of grievance which they created was profound, as Richard Bellings was later to note.[95]

Most of the land confiscated in this series of plantations was at the expense of native Gaelic Irish figures, but the logic of continuous confiscatory plantation also posed a deadly threat to Old English proprietors. Two forces, however, combined to slow the momentum towards what Nicholas Canny has described as 'a plantation society'.[96] The first was the conjunction of forces in London in the early 1620s, strengthened by the findings of the 1622 commission, which brought back into consideration the idea that the government's interests might be better served by conciliating native landholders rather than by risking their alienation by plantation. Second was the outbreak of war in the second half of the 1620s, which allowed the landed elite of Ireland to extract concessions, termed the Graces, from their monarch in return for financial support. One of their central objectives was a statute of limitations which promised to protect their holdings from future plantation. The ending of the war with Spain and the failure to ratify the Graces, however, meant that plantation was to continue to dominate the politics of Ireland down to the rebellion of 1641. In 1628, failure in a court case between Phelim O'Byrne and Sir Richard Graham exposed the O'Byrne lordship of Ranelagh to a plantation which Viscount Falkland attempted to implement.[97] In 1629–30, following Falkland's recall, the earl of Cork, as one of two lords justice, energetically put the case for the plantation of Ormond, by which he hoped to establish a precedent for further plantations in Connacht. Such plans caused enormous alarm, not merely in Ormond but to other Catholic proprietors conscious of the weakness of their title against the Crown.[98] In the event, Cork's plans did not come to fruition and it was to be under Lord Deputy Wentworth's government that the full threat of plantation was brought home to the Catholic landowners of Ireland.

VII. Plantation under Wentworth

The plantations which Wentworth attempted to implement in the 1630s offer a direct contrast with the plantation of Munster in the 1580s. Rather than the punishment of convicted rebels, these projects clearly established the notion that even those who had demonstrated their loyalty in the great convulsions of the late sixteenth century were also liable to plantation. Wentworth himself was clearly animated both by the desire to increase Crown revenue (in tandem with his personal profit) and by a determination to create a mechanism to bridle Irish recusancy, but his relatively clear-sighted objectives became vulnerable also to a more naked opportunism from other court interests.

While the Lord Deputy himself was to acquire substantial portions of planted land in Wicklow,[99] and while his policy had implications for much of the rest of Leinster, Monaghan, and unplanted Munster, it was in Connacht, and particularly in the county of Galway, where the crux of his plantation strategy lay. Plans for plantation in Connacht long predated Wentworth's arrival in Ireland. In 1615 an attempt was begun to formalize the composition arrangements of the 1580s, which were essentially a system of taxation rather than recognition of land title, but this was eventually defeated by a shadowy coalition of interests who correctly realized that the enrolment of patents along these lines would frustrate any plantation of the province.[100] By 1624, unease about the situation in Connacht was evidently feeding into a more general Old English anxiety about the threat to Irish land titles in general.[101] As a result, Article 25 of the Graces was intended to allow for the enrolment of the disputed Connacht titles in Chancery, while Article 24 articulated the idea of a more general protection against plantation through a statute of limitations on the English model.[102] Similar to the Ormond territories, however, the failure of the Graces to pass into law allowed for the plantation of Connacht to come once again onto the agenda.

By 1631, Lord Justice Cork was lobbying for a plantation of the province, excluding County Galway, where Old English interests were most strongly entrenched.[103]

This presumably was tactical: it was clear to all parties that the plantation of Galway would signal that no recusant land titles in Ireland, even in the Pale, would be free of threat. In the months following his appointment as Lord Deputy, however, Wentworth duplicitously exploited the recusant interest in Ireland in order to secure parliamentary support for the subsidies which would convey freedom of action on his government. Having achieved this, he then shocked the Catholic political community by refusing to endorse either article 24 or 25 of the Graces. Instead he proceeded with the implementation of plans for the plantation of the entire province of Connacht, including County Galway. Juries in Roscommon, Mayo, and Sligo found for the Crown with relatively little difficulty in 1635. In Galway, however, he faced very stern resistance from the earl of Clanricard which was mounted both at local level and in court in England.[104] Wentworth was well aware of the anxieties in the Pale and elsewhere at this overt commitment to re-plantation of Old English areas and this reinforced his determination to secure victory and set a binding precedent. By April 1637, Wentworth seemed to have achieved a complete triumph as two inquisitions found for the king's title: in contrast with the more amenable counties to the north, a vindictive and exemplary procedure of confiscating half the county and all properties below 134 acres in size was to be instituted which would have resulted in the loss to the existing landholders of around 80 per cent of the area.[105] Within months, the landowners of Clare were admitting the king's title in a demonstration of abject fear of the Lord Deputy and an agreement concerning royal title had also been reached in the baronies of Ormond.[106] Wentworth's objective was evidently to continue piecemeal plantation until nearly all land in Catholic possession throughout the island had been dealt with.[107] The Lord Deputy was clearly optimistic that this process would deal a mortal blow to Irish recusancy. While natives would generally retain three-quarters of their original lands in plantation grants, they would be subject to close superintendence by new Protestant proprietors. Moreover, by granting plantation estates to the existing landowners under the conditions of knight service, the heirs of the original grant would be forced to conform in order to succeed to the property. The curtailment of the power and numbers of the Catholic elite would then provide the opportunity for effective evangelization of the general population by the refurbished Church of Ireland, which the Lord Deputy was determined to establish on a firm financial footing.[108]

In the event, Wentworth's ambitious plantation schemes stalled almost before they had begun. It proved difficult to attract settlers to Ireland, not least because of the new restrictiveness in religion which Wentworth promoted in the established church. More pertinently, the crisis of the Prayer Book in Scotland and the Bishops' Wars of the late 1630s began to engulf the Lord Deputy from the moment of his apparent triumph in Clare in August 1637.[109] Nevertheless, Wentworth's practice of plantation proved of considerable long-term significance. It is certainly true that the negotiations for the Graces in the 1620s revealed the extent of Old English as well as Gaelic Irish fears about the momentum of plantation policy. However, the ease with which Wentworth duped the Catholic party in the parliament of 1634 was itself a testament to the existence of a remaining reservoir of trust between that community and the Crown. Wentworth's government did much to erode that trust: it is difficult to disagree with Hugh Kearney's assertion that the participation of the Old English in rebellion in 1641 was crucially influenced by Wentworth's pursuit of plantation.[110] By the 1640s, not even the vast prestige of the earl and first marquess of Ormond could persuade the Confederate Catholics of Ireland to align their forces with the king against the mutual enemy of parliament until they had been convinced that the terms of peace would make the future prosecution of Wentworth's plantation strategy impossible.[111] Without the poisonous legacy of Wentworth, it is conceivable that the entire course of the Wars of the Three Kingdoms might have been different.

VIII. Conclusion

The Cromwellian plantations, which effectively operated on the assumption of the guilt and untrustworthiness of the entire Catholic population, represented the intensification of the policy which Wentworth had attempted to implement in the 1630s and the culmination of more than a century's initiatives by the English state to tranquillize Ireland and thus to guarantee English security. It was during the 1650s that the majority of the land of Ireland passed for the first time into the ownership of Protestants, who were (rightfully) perceived as more politically reliable. Yet even these massive confiscations failed to secure the island. Catholic irredentism remained a smoking fire which once again was to erupt in the War of the Three Kings following the deposition of James II in 1688. From this wide perspective, plantation represents an important aspect of the general failure of the policies of the English state in Ireland, providing neither security nor leading to assimilation and anglicization. Moreover, the alienation, rebellion, and ultimate dispossession of existing elites was a hugely expensive as well as a bloody process. Taking this into account, during this period, the state's long-term failure to incentivize the native stakeholders of the island (whether Gaelic Irish or Old English) to act as trustworthy collaborators is a truly remarkable phenomenon. Plantation was not the only reason for this failure, but as George Carew perceptively noted in 1614 in the wake of the Ulster settlement, it was a potent force in uniting both the Gaelic Irish and Old English of Ireland against the state.[112] Why did Ireland differ to such an extent from England and Scotland where, despite the manifold temptations for the state, it was realized that widespread resumptions of land were simply too costly in political and financial terms?[113] The critical difference in this regard was evidently the recusancy of the existing elite of early modern Ireland which weakened their political power. Rather than merging with existing interests, therefore, as had happened to many previous waves of English settlement and as occurred with the Catholic English and Scottish immigrants of this era,[114] the New English of Ireland could aspire to replace the existing elite. The engrossing of political power, but not complete economic or social dominance by the Protestant minority in the period 1580–1641, was thus at the root of what might be termed the structural instability of early modern Ireland. Inevitably, this group, which insisted on the identity of its interests with those of the state,[115] cast hungry eyes upon the land of the existing elites and thus created a situation which would have been destabilizing in any early modern polity. Plantation ultimately became the preferred vehicle to redress this instability but with ultimately catastrophic effects for both the English state, which during this period not only was forced to subvent the Irish administration but also eventually had to foot the bill for four ruinously expensive conquests in the long century after 1580, and for the pre-Plantation elites. On the other hand, the clear winners of the game were the New English community for whom plantation proved a key mechanism in their emergence as the political nation of Ireland by the eighteenth century. It was not merely that a significant portion of New English settlement derived from plantation but the justification and implementation of continuing plantation became crucial in underpinning this community's self-understanding and in the development of their political culture.[116]

NOTES

1. With regard to the perceived salience of plantation note, for instance, James Lyttleton and Colin Rynne (eds), *Plantation Ireland: Settlement and Material Culture* c. *1550–c. 1700* (Dublin, 2009): despite the title of the book, many of the essays have only a tenuous connection to actual plantations.
2. Victor Treadwell (ed), *The Irish Commission of 1622: An Investigation of the Irish Administration 1515–22 and its Consequences 1623–4* (Dublin, 2006), 41.
3. Nicholas Canny, *Making Ireland British 1580–1650* (Oxford, 2001), 152.
4. Canny, *Making Ireland British* offers an example of such contextualized analysis; for a historical geographical approach, see Rolf Loeber, *The Geography and Practice of English Colonisation in Ireland from 1534 to 1609* (Athlone, 1991); see also Raymond Gillespie's critique of over-concentration on plantation in, 'Material Culture and Social Change in Early Modern Ireland' in Lyttleton and Rynne, *Plantation Ireland*, 43–60.
5. Treadwell, *Irish Commission*, 727.
6. Ibid., 727–32.
7. Ibid., 102–3.
8. Ciarán Brady, *The Chief Governors: the Rise and Fall of Reform Government in Tudor Ireland, 1536–1588* (Cambridge, 1994), 52–3.
9. Ibid., 248–51.
10. Loeber, *English Colonisation*, 22, 28.
11. Ibid., 12–13.
12. Ibid., 35.
13. Ibid., 15.
14. Canny, *Making Ireland British*, 285, 558–9.
15. David Edwards implies a closing date of 1641 to the 'Age of Plantation': see David Edwards, 'The MacGiollapadraigs of Upper Ossory, 1532–1641' in Pádraig G. Lane and William Nolan (eds), *Laois History and Society: Interdisciplinary Essays on the History of an Irish County* (Dublin, 1999), 327–75, at 331; for the slackening of plantation after the 1650s, see Toby Barnard, 'Last stages of plantation' in Lyttleton and Rynne, *Plantation Ireland*, 265–85.
16. Ivan Cosby, 'The English settlers in Queen's county, 1570–1603' in ibid., 283–322, at 292.
17. Loeber, *English Colonisation*, 16–17.

18. D.G. White, 'The Tudor Plantations in Ireland before 1571' (PhD thesis, University of Dublin, 1968), i. 422.
19. Loeber, *English Colonisation*, 26–7; Steven Ellis, *Ireland in the Age of the Tudors 1447–1603: English Expansion and the End of Gaelic Rule* (London, 1998), 278.
20. White, *Tudor Plantations*, ii, 406.
21. Canny, *Making Ireland British*, 78.
22. Loeber, *English Colonisation*, 28.
23. Sir Charles Willmott to Lord Deputy Mountjoy, 22 March 1603 (*Calendar of the Carew Manuscripts 1601–03, London, 1870*), 448–9.
24. David Edwards, 'Collaboration without Anglicisation: The MacGiollapadraig Lordship and Tudor Reform' in Patrick J. Duffy, David Edwards, and Elizabeth Fitzpatrick (eds), *Gaelic Ireland: Land, Lordship and Settlement c. 1250–1650* (Dublin, 2001), 77–97.
25. Vincent Carey, 'The End of the Gaelic Political Order: The O'More Lordship of Laois 1536–1603' in Lane and Nolan, *Laois: History and Society*, 225–46.
26. Canny, *Making Ireland British*, 128–9.
27. Vincent Carey, 'Gaelic Political Order', 213–56, at 247.
28. Treadwell, *Irish Commission*, 461.
29. Ibid., 728.
30. Canny, *Making Ireland British*, 79–80.
31. Loeber, *English Colonisation*, 30.
32. Colm Lennon, *Sixteenth Century Ireland: The Incomplete Conquest* (Dublin, 1994) 279–83; Hiram Morgan 'The colonial venture of Sir Thomas Smith, 1571–75', *Historical Journal*, xxviii (1985), 261–78.
33. Lennon, *Sixteenth Century Ireland*, 292–3.
34. Ciaran Brady, 'The MacDonalds and the provincial strategies of Hugh O'Neill, earl of Tyrone, 1585–1603' in William Kelly and John Young (eds), *Scotland and the Ulster Plantations: Explorations in the British Settlements of Stuart Ireland* (Dublin, 2009), 41–61.
35. Lennon, *Sixteenth Century Ireland*, 282–3.
36. Robert Dunlop, 'The Plantation of Munster, 1584–89', *English Historical Review*, iii (1888); D.B. Quinn, 'The Munster Plantation: problems and opportunities' *Cork Historical Society Journal*, lxxi (1966); Michael McCarthy Morrogh, 'The English Presence in Seventeenth-Century Munster' in Ciaran Brady and Raymond Gillespie (eds), *Natives and Newcomers: The making of Irish colonial society 1534–1641* (Bungay, 1986), 171–90; idem, *The Munster Plantation* (Oxford, 1986); Canny, *Making Ireland British* and idem, *The Upstart Earl* (Cambridge, 1982); David Dickson, *Old World Colony: Cork and South Munster, 1630–1830* (Cork, 2006).
37. Canny, *Making Ireland British*, 129.
38. Loeber, *English Colonisation*, 37; Brady, *Chief Governors*, 254.
39. Canny, *Making Ireland British*, 124–5.
40. MacCarthy-Morrogh, *Munster Plantation*, 50–1; Canny, *Making Ireland British*, 129–34.
41. Anthony Sheehan, 'Official Reaction to Native Land Claims in the Plantation of Munster', *Irish Historical Studies*, 23 (1985), 303–13.
42. MacCarthy-Morrogh, *Munster Plantation*, 69, 290–2.
43. Canny, *Making Ireland British*, 143–4.
44. Ibid., 146–7.
45. Seasonal movement of livestock and their herders.
46. Ibid., 148.

47. Terence Ranger, 'Richard Boyle and the Making of Irish fortune, 1588–1614', *IHS* X (1957), 257–97.

48. Canny, *Making Ireland British*, 158.

49. John McGurk, *The Elizabethan Conquest of Ireland: The Burdens of the 1590s Crisis* (Manchester, 1997).

50. Canny, *Making Ireland British*, 164.

51. MacCarthy-Morrogh, *Munster Plantation*, 146–9, 295–6.

52. BL Add. Ms 4756 ff. 88r-97v.

53. Canny, *Making Ireland British*, 309.

54. Ibid., 317.

55. MacCarthy-Morrogh, *Munster Plantation*, 151–69.

56. A core study for the plantation of Ulster remains Philip Robinson, *The Plantation of Ulster: British Settlement in an Irish Landscape 1600–1670*, 2nd edition (Belfast, 1994); a crisp discussion of the plantation conditions can be found in Aidan Clarke, 'Pacification, Plantation and the Catholic Question, 1603–23' in T.W. Moody, F.X. Martin, and F.J. Byrne (eds), *A New History of Ireland, iii, Early Modern Ireland 1534–1691* (Oxford, 1976), 187–232, especially 197–202; Canny, *Making Ireland British*, 165–401 offers an indispensable interpretation of British settlement in seventeenth-century Ireland, including many new findings on Ulster. See also R.J. Hunter, 'The Ulster Plantation in the counties of Armagh and Cavan, 1608–1641' (PhD thesis, University of Dublin, 1969); many of the most important documents relating to the plantation have now been collected in Treadwell, *Irish Commission*.

57. M. Perceval-Maxwell, *The Scottish Migration to Ulster in the Reign of James I* (Belfast, 1990), 48–56; Peter Roebuck, 'The Making of an Ulster Great Estate: the Chichesters, Barons of Belfast and Viscounts of Carrickfergus 1599–1648' *PRIA*, C, 79 (1979); Raymond Gillespie, *Colonial Ulster: the Settlement of East Ulster, 1600–41* (Cork, 1985).

58. Robinson, *Plantation of Ulster*, 69–70.

59. Canny, *Making Ireland British*, 202–5.

60. Robinson *Plantation of Ulster*, 86; for the analysis of another 1000-acre parcel, see R.J. Hunter, 'The Bible and the Bawn: an Ulster planter inventorised' in Ciaran Brady and Jane Ohlmeyer (eds), *British Interventions in Early Modern Ireland* (Cambridge, 2005), 116–34, at 122.

61. Robinson, *Plantation of Ulster*, 89–90.

62. The six counties actually comprise 3 690 714 statute acres but this discrepancy is explained by the huge variation in the size of the Irish territorial measurements which were used as a basis of the grants: see Robinson, *Plantation of Ulster*, 85–7.

63. Ibid., 80–1.

64. Ibid., 77–86.

65. BL. Add MS 4756 ff. 97–8.

66. Canny, *Making Ireland British*, 218–26.

67. Treadwell, *Irish Commission*, 622–3; T.W. Moody, *The Londonderry Plantation, 1609–41: The City of London and the Plantation in Ulster* (Belfast, 1939), 270.

68. Warrant for removing the natives by the Lord Deputy and Council, 22 August 1611 (*Calendar of Carew Mss*), 87–8.

69. Canny, *Making Ireland British*, 229.

70. R.J. Hunter, 'The English Undertakers in the Plantation of Ulster', *Breifne,,* iv (1974), 471–500; Canny, *Making Ireland British*, 208.

71. Robinson, *Plantation of Ulster*, 80.

72. Canny, *Making Ireland British*, 234.

73. M. Percevall-Maxwell, *Scottish Migration*, 217–28, 126; Canny, *Making Ireland British*, 211–12.

74. Raymond Gillespie, *Seventeenth Century Ireland* (Dublin, 2006) 50–2.

75. Robinson, *Plantation of Ulster*, 92–5.

76. Darren McGettigan, *The Donegal Plantation and the Tír Chonaill Irish, 1610–1710* (Dublin, 2010). I am deeply indebted to Dr McGettigan for allowing me access to the unpublished manuscript of his text.

77. Although not a study of the plantation area, analysis of debt in County Monaghan provides a valuable insight into the mechanisms which were probably at work in the escheated counties: see Pilib Ó Mórdha, 'The MacMahons of Monaghan (1603–40)', *Clogher Record*, ii (1957–58), 148–69, 311–27.

78. McGettigan, *Donegal Plantation*.

79. E. Shuckburgh (ed), *Two Biographies of William Bedell, Bishop of Kilmore: with a Selection of his Letters and an Unpublished Treatise* (Cambridge, 1902), 40–2.

80. Brian Mac Cuarta, *Catholic Revival in the North of Ireland 1603–41* (Dublin, 2007), 37–70; Ford, *Protestant Reformation in Ireland*, 138–47; Phil Kilroy, 'Protestantism in Ulster, 1610–41' in Mac Cuarta, *Ulster 1641*, 25–36.

81. Brian Mac Cuarta, 'Religious violence against settlers in south Ulster, 1641–2' in Edwards, *Age of Atrocity*, 154–175.

82. MacCuarta, *Catholic Revival*, 102–7; see also BL Add. MS 4756 fo. 118r which notes the presence of recusants among those granted servitors' proportions.

83. Canny, *Making Ireland British*, 240–2.

84. This calculation is based on the documents in Treadwell, *Irish Commission*, 643–60, 670–89. The general reckoning for the Ferricall, Delvyn, Montcragan, Clincolman, and Iregan on p.671 seems to underestimate the undertakers' share.

85. Ibid., 693–700, 742–3.

86. Edwards, 'MacGiollapadraigs of Upper Ossory', 365–6.

87. John McCavitt, *Sir Arthur Chichester: Lord Deputy of Ireland 1605–16* (Belfast, 1998), 160–1.

88. Henry Goff, 'English Conquest of an Irish Barony: the changing patterns of landownership in the barony of Scarawalsh, 1540–1680' in Kevin Whelan (ed), *Wexford: History and Society* (Dublin, 1987), 122–49, at 138; McCavitt, *Sir Arthur Chichester*, 163–7.

89. Goff, 'English Conquest', 140.

90. Treadwell, *Irish Commission*, 697.

91. Ibid., 742–3.

92. Clarke, 'Pacification, plantation and the Catholic question', 221; Treadwell, *Irish Commission*, 675.

93. Victor Treadwell, *Buckingham and Ireland 1616–1628: A Study in Anglo-Irish Politics* (Dublin, 1998), 140–1.

94. Canny, *Making Ireland British*, 255.

95. John Thomas Gilbert, *A History of the Confederation and War in Ireland* (Dublin, 7 vols., 1882–91), i, 1–5.

96. Canny, *Making Ireland British*, 255.

97. Hugh Kearney, *Strafford in Ireland: A Study in Abolutism, 1633–41* (Cambridge, 1989), 174–8.

98. Canny, *Making Ireland British*, 273–4.

99. Kearney, *Strafford in Ireland*, 174–8; Canny, *Making Ireland British*, 281–2.

100. Treadwell, *Buckingham*, 264–7; Clarke, 'Pacification, plantation and the Catholic question', 222.
101. Kearney, *Strafford in Ireland*, 87.
102. Aidan Clarke, *The Graces, 1625–41* (Dundalk, 1968).
103. Ibid., 88.
104. Clarke, 'The Government of Wentworth, 1632–40' in *NHI*, 243–69.
105. The subsequent exemption of the earl of Clanricard's lands in 1639 saw much of five baronies escape the process, to Wentworth's great anger: see Canny, *Making Ireland British*, 284; Kearney, *Strafford in Ireland*, 102.
106. Clarke, 'Government of Wentworth', 262–3.
107. Canny, *Making Ireland British*, 283.
108. Ibid., 280, 285–6.
109. Kearney, *Strafford in Ireland*, 99–103.
110. Ibid., 90.
111. Confederate negotiations with the royalist party are best followed in Micheál ó Siochrú, *Confederate Ireland: A Constitutional and Political Analysis* (Dublin, 1999).
112. A discourse of the present Estate of Ireland, 1614 (*Cal. Carew papers*), 306.
113. Treadwell, *Buckingham*, 272.
114. David Edwards, 'A haven of popery: English Catholic migration to Ireland in the age of plantations' in A. Ford and John McCafferty (eds), *The Origins of Sectarianism in Early Modern Ireland* (Cambridge, 2005), 95–126.
115. Aidan Clarke, 'The Genesis of the Ulster Rising of 1641', in Peter Roebuck (ed), *Plantation to Partition* (Belfast, 1981), 29–45, at 42–3.
116. For the evolution of these attitudes after 1641, see Robert Armstrong, *Protestant War: The 'British' of Ireland and the Wars of the Three Kingdoms* (Manchester, 2005), 232–5.

SELECT BIBLIOGRAPHY

Canny, Nicholas, *Making Ireland British 1580–1650* (Oxford, 2001).
Clarke, Aidan, 'Pacification, Plantation and the Catholic Question, 1603–23' in T.W. Moody, F.X. Martin, and F.J. Byrne (eds), *A New History of Ireland, iii, Early Modern Ireland 1534–1691* (Oxford, 1976), 187–232.
Gillespie, Raymond, *Colonial Ulster: the Settlement of East Ulster, 1600–41* (Cork, 1985).
Goff, Henry, 'English Conquest of an Irish Barony: the changing patterns of landownership in the barony of Scarawalsh, 1540–1680' in Kevin Whelan (ed), *Wexford: History and Society* (Dublin, 1987), 122–49.
Hunter, R.J., 'The Ulster Plantation in the counties of Armagh and Cavan, 1608–1641' (PhD thesis, University of Dublin, 1969).
Hunter, R.J., 'The Bible and the Bawn: an Ulster planter inventorised' in Ciaran Brady and Jane Ohlmeyer (eds), *British Interventions in Early Modern Ireland* (Cambridge, 2005), 116–34.
Kearney, Hugh, *Strafford in Ireland: A Study in Absolutism, 1633–41* (Cambridge, 1989).
Loeber, Rolf, *The Geography and Practice of English Colonisation in Ireland from 1534 to 1609* (Athlone, 1991).
Lyttleton, James and Colin Rynne (eds), *Plantation Ireland: Settlement and Material Culture c. 1550–c. 1700* (Dublin, 2009).
McCarthy-Morrogh, Michael, *The Munster Plantation* (Oxford, 1986).

McCavitt, John, *Sir Arthur Chichester: Lord Deputy of Ireland 1605–16* (Belfast, 1998).

McGettigan, Darren, *The Donegal Plantation and the Tír Chonaill Irish, 1610–1710* (Dublin, 2010).

Moody, T.W., *The Londonderry Plantation, 1609–41: The City of London and the Plantation in Ulster* (Belfast, 1939).

Ó Siochrú, Micheál and Ó Ciardha, Éamonn (eds), *The Plantation of Ulster* (Manchester, 2013).

Perceval-Maxwell, M., *The Scottish Migration to Ulster in the Reign of James I* (Belfast, 1990), 48–56.

Robinson, Philip, *The Plantation of Ulster: British Settlement in an Irish Landscape 1600–1670*. 2nd edition (Belfast, 1994).

Treadwell, Victor, *Buckingham and Ireland 1616–1628: A study in Anglo-Irish politics* (Dublin, 1998).

Treadwell, Victor (ed). *The Irish Commission of 1622: An Investigation of the Irish Administration 1515–22 and its Consequences 1623–4* (Dublin, 2006).

White, D.G., 'The Tudor Plantations in Ireland before 1571' (PhD thesis, University of Dublin, 1968).

CHAPTER 16

....

CONFEDERATION AND UNION, 1641–60

....

JANE OHLMEYER

I. INTRODUCTION

....

THE 1640s and 1650s were defining decades in Irish history. The 1641 rebellion was a central military event, which played a crucial role in shaping the triple Stuart monarchy during the seventeenth century and triggered the onset of a decade of civil war in Ireland. Though Catholic Ireland failed to win lasting political autonomy, the 1640s was the only time before 1922 that Ireland enjoyed legislative independence and Catholics worshipped freely. By contrast, during the 1650s, England dramatically reasserted control over Ireland. Cromwellian military victory after 1649, followed by English reconquest, paved the way for another round of expropriation on a scale that not even Edmund Spenser would have imagined possible. The Instrument of Government (December 1653) created, albeit for a brief period, a unitary British state with a single parliament at Westminster. A decade of warfare had effected a political integration of the three kingdoms, which would not be achieved again until the parliamentary union of 1800–1.

From a historiographical perspective, this chapter takes as a point of departure a review, published in 1995, of the state of research on Ireland during the 1640s and 1650s: pioneering scholarship dating from the 1930s and 1940s by Donal Cregan and Hugh Hazlett featured, alongside seminal studies (largely dating from the 1970s and early 1990s) by Toby Barnard, Karl Bottigheimer, Nicholas Canny, Aidan Clarke, Michael Perceval-Maxwell, Conrad Russell, and David Stevenson.[1] Yet back in 1995 much work remained to be done that did justice to the richness of the extant primary materials relating to mid-century Ireland. This chapter draws on the wealth of scholarship that has been produced since then, especially on the 1641 rebellion, the course and conduct of the civil wars, and the Cromwellian land settlement, and suggests avenues for future research. Given the complexity of events, particularly during the 1640s, this

chapter takes a chronological approach but this should not obscure the forces of continuity, especially social and cultural ones, which transcend a period otherwise characterized by intense change and upheaval. Finally, space precludes a full discussion of the
'three kingdoms' context or of the intimate links during these years between Ireland and
continental Europe and the Atlantic world. These wider contexts infused every aspect of
the histories of mid-century Ireland and their significance cannot be overstated.[2]

II. 1641

On 22 October 1641, the authorities thwarted an attempt to seize Dublin Castle but
could not prevent Catholic insurgents from capturing strategic strongholds in Ulster.
Over the winter of 1641 and spring of 1642, the rebellion spread to engulf the rest of
the country. The rising was accompanied by incidents of extreme violence as Catholics
attacked, robbed, and murdered their Protestant neighbours. The Protestants retaliated
with equal force in what became one of the most brutal periods of sectarian violence in
Irish history. The total number of men, women, and children who lost their lives in the
aftermath of the rebellion or subsequent war will never be known. Yet it is likely that
more people died during the course of the 1640s than in the rebellion of 1798 or in the
civil wars of the twentieth century.

The '1641 depositions', which provide a unique insight into this particularly traumatic
period of Irish history, record the events that surrounded the outbreak of the 1641 rebellion primarily from the perspective of the Protestant community.[3] In all, about 8 000
depositions or witness statements, examinations, and associated materials, by thousands of men and women of all social classes, amounting to 19 010 pages and bound in
thirty-one volumes, are extant in Trinity College Dublin.[4] The depositions record the
names of over 90 000 victims, assailants, bystanders, and observers and include references to nearly every county, parish, and barony in Ireland. They document losses of
goods and chattels, military activity, and the alleged crimes committed by the Irish
insurgents, including assault, imprisonment, the stripping of clothes, and murder. In
short, they reveal as much about debt as they do about death and recapture the biographies, hopes, and fears of ordinary folk, as well the extraordinary.

The depositions vividly recapture life in colonial Ireland: the land transfers and the
settlement patterns of the newcomers as they built fortified mansions, villages, schools,
and churches, cut down woods, drained and enclosed land, and nurtured the development of urban settlements and proto-industry (tanning, iron-making, glass-making,
cloth-making, and so on).[5] A handful of depositions mention the Ulster plantation as
a cause of the rebellion.[6] For example, Sir Phelim O'Neill, one of the leaders of the 1641
rebellion, allegedly chastised George Creighton, a minister and a Scotsman who had
settled in Virginia in County Cavan, for bringing 'Plantacions into our Landes'.[7] The
extent to which plantations contributed to the outbreak of the 1641 rebellion is debatable, with many historians suggesting that short-term political factors remained the

primary reason why rebellion erupted in October 1641.[8] The 1641 depositions also constitute the chief evidence for the sharply contested allegation that the rebellion began
with a general massacre of Protestant settlers, something that Aidan Clarke has—after
centuries of bad-tempered debate—finally disproved in a recent article.[9] Many others,
including a new generation of scholars, have analysed this and subsequent 'massacres'
by Protestants against Catholics and Catholics against Protestants and have situated
these mass killings in wider chronological and geographic contexts.[10]

What is immediately clear is the rapidity and extent to which law and order broke
down and people, who had previously been neighbours, acquaintances and even friends,
engaged in acts of violence against individuals and communities. The depositions capture the distress, fears, and anxieties of those caught up in the insurrection and highlight
how the war tore families apart and shattered livelihoods. As far as the English state was
concerned, they illustrated the great cruelties acted against the Protestant community
by the Catholics and formed the basis for convictions in the war crimes tribunals of the
early 1650s. In this sense they must be seen, as William Smyth reminds us, 'as documents of conquest'.[11] Yet the depositions also record acts of toleration, friendship, and
compassion, where Catholics protected the local Protestants from the excesses of the
insurgents. During the 1650s, and especially after the restoration, testimonies recount-
ing these kindnesses proved important in securing the survival and restoration of many
families, especially Catholic ones.

III. 1640s

Complexity and confusion remain the hallmarks of the 1640s, but our understanding of
the conflict that was variously known as the 'Irish Civil Wars', the 'Eleven Years' War', the
'Wars of Religion', and the 'Confederate Wars' has been transformed since 1995 by the
publication of a number of important monographs and collections of essays, many of
which are discussed below. The Irish Civil Wars fall into three reasonably well-defined,
chronological phases: 1641–3, 1643–7, and 1647–53.[12] With the exception of seven battles
there were few set-piece encounters; instead uncoordinated 'small wars' or 'guerrilla tactics' dominated the military proceedings. These aimed to destroy the enemy's economic
base but also resulted in massacres and atrocities, especially during the early 1640s and,
again, later in the decade.[13]

The first phase of the war began with the outbreak of the rebellion (October 1641) and
ended with the conclusion of a ceasefire (September 1643) between the Irish Catholic
confederates and the predominantly Protestant, Irish royalist forces, under the command of the marquis of Ormond. The arrival of 2600 foot from England, over the winter
of 1641 to 1642, reinforced the inadequate Protestant standing army, initially a pitiful
force of 2297 foot and 943 horse, and allowed the government to hold Dublin and much
of the Pale. The landing, in April 1642, of an army of 10 000 Scots helped the government
to regain control over much of central and east Ulster. But the outbreak of civil war in

England in August 1642 had an immediate and destabilizing impact since it reduced the amount of money and the quantity of supplies and soldiers available for the Irish war effort and put pressure on the uneasy Protestant alliance.

The outbreak of civil war in England also enabled the Catholic insurgents to put their war effort on a more permanent footing. As early as December 1641, leading Catholics temporarily sank their economic, cultural, and religious differences and the Old English lords concluded an uneasy alliance with the Ulster insurgents. Then in May 1642, the Catholic clergy and laity met at Kilkenny in order to set up an alternative form of government. The architecture of government and the exercise of power closely resembled pre-1641 structures and processes. Aside from the important difference that the general assembly was a unicameral body and, very significantly, that the executive (or the supreme council) was subordinate to the legislature, the general assembly was modelled on parliament. On 24 October, the confederates held their first general assembly at Kilkenny and elected a supreme council, which was a committee of twenty-four members (six representatives from each province), twelve of whom were supposed to sit permanently and run the confederation. An 'oath of association' which bound together the Catholic Confederates, as they were now known, called for full toleration for the Catholic religion and the restoration of the clergy to their pre-Reformation properties and privileges.

The second phase of the war, between September 1643 and autumn 1647, was particularly complex and was characterized by tortuous negotiations for peace between the royalists and the confederates. The ceasefire of 15 September 1643, known as the 'cessation of arms', heralded a new departure in Anglo-Irish relations. After much haggling it was agreed that, in return for troops, supplies, and cash for the English war effort, the king would consider repealing the anti-recusancy laws and granting the confederates considerable political independence, freedom of worship, and security of land tenure. Yet the cessation achieved nothing. In the long term this temporary end of hostilities proved disastrous for the confederates, for instead of pursuing their strategic advantages and focusing their efforts on driving their Parliamentary and Scottish opponents out of Ireland, they became involved in lengthy negotiations with the king (it was January 1649 before a lasting peace settlement was reached). Had the Catholics concentrated on domestic victory, the English reconquest of Ireland in 1649–52 would have been more difficult and the course of the 'Wars of the Three Kingdoms' might have been very different.

The cessation immediately shattered the already strained anti-Catholic alliance because many Protestants could not stomach the king's concessions. It also intensified the war: first in Ulster (by driving, as Kevin Forkan and others have shown, the Scots deep into the Parliamentary camp)[14] and then in Munster (by alienating, in July 1644, the earl of Inchiquin and his Protestant army from the royalist cause). One of the greatest guardians of the Protestant interest in Ireland during these years was Roger Boyle, Lord Broghill and later earl of Orrery. Patrick Little's political biography offers a thorough account of Broghill's contribution to the war effort in Munster and his politicking in London as a leader of the 'Irish independents'.[15] Robert Armstrong develops this in

Protestant War as he reconstructs warring Protestant communities from Ireland (royalist, Parliamentarian and covenanter) in their exploits across the three kingdoms and especially at Westminster and Oxford.[16]

Works such as these have transformed our understanding of the Protestant war effort just as the publications of Tadhg Ó hAnnracháin, Micheál Ó Siochrú, and Pádraig Lenihan have done for the Catholic war effort. Military defeat in England strengthened Charles I's resolve to secure immediate and substantial support from Ireland. In January 1645, he instructed the earl of Glamorgan, a prominent Catholic noble, to secure Irish troops for royalist service in return for religious concessions. These ultimately came to nothing because the more extreme Catholics led by the papal nuncio, Giovanni Battista Rinuccini, refused to compromise with the king, machinations which Ó hAnnracháin explores in his fulsome account of Rinuccini's mission.[17] In a masterly study of confederate Ireland, Ó Siochrú deftly recovers the intricacies of confederate politics during these years. As Ó Siochrú shows, three loose groupings predominated—and played havoc with—Kilkenny politics: the 'war' faction, led by Rinuccini and leading clerics, the 'peace' faction, comprised of supporters of Ormond, and the 'neutral' faction.[18] Despite these internal divisions, the confederate armies enjoyed considerable successes, most notably the battle of Benburb (5 June 1646) when Owen Roe O'Neill and his Catholic army of 5 000 at last routed the Scottish army. Lenihan analyses these (and the failures) and situates them in the context of the wider military developments associated with the Military Revolution.[19]

Throughout this four-year period, the confederates had been aware of the need to prevent the English Parliament, their implacable enemy, from becoming so powerful that it could invade and destroy them. To achieve this, two options had been open to them: either they could aid Charles I with all their might in return for the best political, religious, and tenurial concessions they could extort, and hope for a royalist victory in Britain; or they could abandon the king altogether and make Catholic Ireland, with the aid of foreign powers, impregnable to invasion from England. By failing to decide between these equally viable but totally incompatible options, the confederates failed to achieve their principal objective and thus safeguard their own survival. Ormond's decision in June 1647 to hand over Dublin to Parliament and the confederates' subsequent failure to take the capital by force simply underscored their political and military impotence.

The third phase of the conflict, between autumn 1647 and the completion of the Cromwellian conquest of Ireland in April 1653, witnessed the political and military dismemberment of both the Catholic and royalist armies at the hands of an army controlled by the English Parliament. It began with confederate defeat on the battlefield at the battle of Dungans Hill (8 August 1647) and at the battle of Knockanauss, County Cork (13 November 1647). Predictably, battlefield defeat further exacerbated confederate political divisions. Matters reached crisis point in the spring of 1648 when, on 27 May, Rinuccini excommunicated those who supported the truce negotiated between Lord Inchiquin and the confederates (20 May 1648). The supreme council immediately appealed to Rome against the excommunication. A brief period of intense and bitter civil war followed until Ormond finally managed to conclude, in January 1649, an uneasy peace treaty which paved the way for the dissolution of the confederate association and the creation of a pan-archipelagic royalist coalition.[20]

Any successes that this royalist coalition enjoyed in the spring of 1649 were short-lived and the rout of Ormond's army by the Parliamentarians under Michael Jones at Rathmines on 2 August 1649 enabled Oliver Cromwell and his force of 12 000 veterans, armed with heavy artillery, to land unmolested near Dublin. Micheál Ó Siochrú's *God's Executioner* provides the definitive account of the ensuing conquest of Ireland.[21] Having decimated the royalist army at Drogheda (11 September), Cromwell set out to destroy the Irish fleet of privateers, which had plagued English shipping from the early 1640s. On 11 October, Wexford fell, affording Cromwell control of the all-important sea-lanes, which were, as Elaine Murphy's work has demonstrated, so critical to the continued success of his land campaigns in Ireland and elsewhere.[22] For his part, Ormond had managed to offset some of the disastrous losses by persuading Owen Roe O'Neill and the army of Ulster to join him; but O'Neill's death (6 November), less than three weeks after the treaty had been signed, created a power vacuum and helped to pave the way for the capture of Kilkenny (27 March 1650), Clonmel (10 May), Carlow (24 July), and Charlemount (14 August), together with the defeat of the army of Ulster at Scarrifhollis in County Donegal (21 June 1650).

On 11 December 1650, Ormond sailed back into continental exile, leaving the marquis of Clanricarde, who took over as Lord Deputy, and his erstwhile confederate allies to fall out amongst themselves and to negotiate the surrenders of Limerick (27 October 1651) and finally of Galway (12 April 1652). On 12 May 1652, the army of Leinster agreed terms with the Cromwellians at Kilkenny. The war in Ireland was over. The physical, economic, and demographic devastation was complete. The need to support the war effort had bankrupted the country; years of intense guerrilla fighting had scarred the physical landscape and reduced to ruins great houses, castles, churches, mills, and villages; and disease and bouts of famine and plague had decimated the population. In fact, Lenihan has suggested that the destruction and loss of life in Ireland was comparable to the devastation in Bohemia caused by the Thirty Years' War.[23]

IV. 1650s

With the completion of the military conquest, England subjected Ireland to a level of control that was unprecedented.[24] During the early 1650s, the Cromwellians conducted war crimes trials and, as the recent publication of the records of the courts martial show, a number of Catholics died as a result.[25] Others faced transplantation to Connacht. The land settlement of the 1650s represented the most ambitious attempt to plant Ireland at any point in the island's history. The Adventurers' Act (March 1642) began the process of expropriation by offering Protestant speculators 2.5 million acres belonging to Irish delinquents. Legislation the following year allotted Parliamentary soldiers serving in Ireland land in lieu of their pay on the same terms as the adventurers. In order to recompense these soldiers and adventurers, the English parliament stipulated in the Act of Settlement (August 1652) that virtually all land held by Catholics should be confiscated and that many of the dispossessed should be transplanted to Connacht. The following year, the Act of Satisfaction (26 September 1653) reserved the greater part of Connacht and Clare for the transplanted Irish and a further act (30 November 1654) ordered all transplantable people to move by 1 March 1655. In December 1654, parliament appointed commissioners to sit at Athlone and Loughrea to decide on the claims of the transplanted Irish. In a path-breaking study, John Cunningham has shown how these commissioners granted settlements to 1800 claimants from thirty counties (of these, 1205 transplanters came from west of the Shannon and were assigned 40 per cent of the land earmarked for redistribution). The process of land allocation comprised, in the words of Cunningham, a complex and messy combination 'of truncation, redistribution, transfer and consolidation'.[26]

A small number of Catholics did reach an accommodation with the new regime. The terms under which they surrendered to the Cromwellians often determined their fate and, as Cunningham has shown, Oliver Cromwell insisted—against the advice of the regime in Dublin—that the terms of the agreement be honoured.[27] In other instances, English connections and a legitimate jointure claim appear to have saved a number of prominent titled Catholic families.[28]

It was easier for Protestants to survive and by the mid 1650s even those who had been loyal to the Stuarts had reached compromises much as the royalists did in England. Henry Cromwell, who arrived in Ireland in July 1655, was eager to secure political stability and promoted policies of reconciliation that often involved restoring the 'Old Protestants' (as they were now termed) to positions of authority and local influence and of minimizing the influence of religious radicals.[29] In the absence of a paid bureaucracy and a standing army to coerce the population, the Cromwellians instinctively turned to these traditional power brokers in order to rule the more remote regions of Ireland. The example of the Boyles of Cork illustrates this. The second earl had not been a particularly prominent royalist but claimed benefit of the Dublin articles (negotiated by Ormond in 1647) when he returned to Ireland in May 1651. By the mid 1650s, the situation had improved dramatically; Cork compounded for his English estates and recovered his Irish lands. By 1658, he took an active role in local affairs and that summer welcomed the Lord Deputy to his estates. Cork's ability to recover his patrimony stemmed in large part from the prominence his brother, Lord Broghill, enjoyed with the ruling regime. In 1655, Broghill headed the civil government in Scotland and, in 1657, he was one of a small group that offered the crown to Oliver Cromwell. Throughout these years, Broghill, as Patrick Little has shown, watched over the interests of the wider Boyle lineage.[30] He also played an important role in securing the restoration of Charles II to the throne of the three kingdoms.[31]

V. SOCIETY

Research on the mid seventeenth century tends to focus on the issues that divided the body politic, especially racial and religious differences, and in so doing obscures the vertical bonds—attitudes towards marriage and death, concepts of honour, religious toleration, social status and wealth, economic interdependence, indebtedness, literary and cultural patronage—that linked communities.[32] Often, local studies recapture these vertical linkages in a way that other studies do not. In fact some of the most exciting recent research on the 1640s and 1650s takes the form of county or regional studies. Aoife Duignan's account of war and revolution in Connacht, Charlene McCoy's careful examination of events between 1640 and 1666 in County Fermanagh, Maighréad Ní Mhurchadha's forensic analysis of the communities living in north County Dublin, and David Dickson's masterly overview of mid-century south Munster provide powerful insights into how the long and brutal war impacted on communities and how forces of continuity, especially kin patronage links and mutual indebtedness, often moderated those of change.[33]

The voices of women and children living in Ireland during the mid seventeenth century are rarely heard despite the fact that sources like the 1641 depositions contain a remarkable amount of material relating to ordinary lives as well as to the horrors of war experienced by wives, widows, spinsters, and children. What is known is largely thanks to Mary O'Dowd's pioneering work on women's history.[34] This needs to be read alongside more specialist works like that of Eleanor O'Keeffe who has analysed the marriages contracted by the house of Ormond during the 1640s and 1650s.[35] In the pre-war years, marriages across religious boundaries, which helped to forge economic, social and cultural assimilation, occurred regularly, especially amongst members of the nobility.[36] In 1651 and 1653, the Cromwellian authorities prohibited intermarriage between Catholics and Protestants and, in 1658, the Catholic synod did likewise. This suggests that mixed marriages continued to be widespread. Certainly the synod conceded that, when mixed marriages occurred, the Catholic spouse should have liberty to practice their faith and that any children resulting from the marriage should be raised as Catholics.[37]

The methodologies developed by early-modern English gender historians provide more general insights that might be of value to Irish scholars. For example, the recent literature on manhood and masculinities in early modern England, especially Alex Shepard's monograph on *Meanings of Manhood in Early Modern England*, is particularly stimulating.[38] Shepard moves away from a concept of gender 'defined exclusively in terms of a male-female dichotomy' and thereby complicates and enriches our understanding of patriarchy and the social relations of power. A history of early modern Irish masculinity awaits its historian, as do studies of the social and cultural constructions of maleness, manhood, and manliness and what these meant in the context of wartime Ireland.

Closely linked to discussions of manhood and womanhood are those of honour. There has been healthy analysis of honour by early modern English historians.[39] Influenced by this, the literature on honour in early modern Ireland is growing and the scholarship of Brendan Kane is particularly important.[40] However, the complexities inherent in the operation of 'honour politics' and the varying interpretations of what 'honour' actually meant to individuals of different religious, ethnic, and cultural backgrounds remain to be fully explored. Honour was also highly gendered, with female honour being inextricably linked to chastity, sexual purity, and obedience. How did 'honour communities' form? How did considerations around race, religion, and rank influence their development and what impact did the events of the 1640s and 1650s have on them?

VI. Culture

The themes of honour and dishonour featured in the Irish, English, and Latin verse, literature, and histories of the mid seventeenth century and—along with patronage and kin links—shaped how a writer represented an individual or an event. Once again, rigorous study of representation and literary patronage is limited, especially for the 1640s and 1650s, despite the proliferation of contemporary works. An analysis of Lord Broghill's literary output might bring into sharper focus issues of honour and representation and help to recapture the complexities and nuances of Broghill's mindset.[41] Over a period of forty years, Ormond assembled a remarkable 'literary scrap book' (now housed in the Beinecke Library in Yale) of fifty-nine manuscripts that includes copies of verse, anagrams, satires, elegies, panegyrics, prose, speeches, pictorial, and other addresses.[42] Of these Yale verses, twenty-two are in Latin, one is in French, one in Irish (a panegyric written by an Irish Franciscan in 1680) and the remainder are in English. Interestingly, two-thirds of the items that Ormond collected date from the period before 1660. The collection includes verse by the confederate 'lawyer-poets' who used poems to trumpet their loyalty to the Stuart cause and to the Ormond dynasty. The Catholic verse of the 1640s in the Ormond scrapbook also documents key political and military episodes: the battle of Benburb (1646), the First and Second Ormond Peaces (1646 and 1649), and the execution of Charles I (1649). Given that so little verse has survived from Ireland in the 1640s and many of these manuscripts appear to be unique (and certainly never appeared in print), these items are of particular significance, yet very little is known about Ormond's literary patronage or how he used writers to create and sustain his reputation.[43]

Closely linked to discussions of patronage and representation are debates around print and oral culture. Once again, the stimulating studies produced by scholars of early modern British and continental print and oral culture have shaped how Irish scholars have written about these.[44] Andrew Carpenter's *Verse in English from Tudor and Stuart Ireland* embraces high and low culture: almanacs, anthems, ballads, carols, and ditties are reproduced in his anthology alongside anagrams, elegies, funerary inscriptions, panegyrics, and conventional poetry.[45] Our understanding of reading and print and oral culture has been transformed by the work of Raymond Gillespie and others.[46] Eamon Darcy's recent research explores how the oral communication of news of the insurrection and its appearance in manuscript sources, namely the 1641 depositions, made its way into print. Darcy's construction of the initial memory of the 1641 rebellion and its effect on contemporary politics and identity formation builds on the foundations laid by others interested in exploring how the events and witness testimonies of 1641 shaped politics and attitudes across the three kingdoms.[47]

Of course, when compared with England, the total printed output (259 works) from the Irish presses, for the years between 1640 and 1660, was tiny (37 000 items were published in London during the same period).[48] But the modest scale of domestic production should not suggest that Ireland did not enjoy a vibrant print culture during the early modern period, especially when one remembers the easy access Irish people had to thousands of texts published in London. Moreover, many Irish writers, intent on reaching a wider audience or influencing political opinion at Westminster, preferred to publish their work with an English press. These publications bristled with Irish news. In fact, many of the 4600 newsbooks published between November 1641 and September 1649 contained stories about events in Ireland.[49] Some, such as James Cranford's *The Tears of Ireland* (London, 1642), contained grisly atrocity woodcuts, which were remarkably similar to images reproduced in Philip Vincent's *The Lamentations of Germany* (London, 1638). The 1641 rebellion dominated English print during the winter of 1641 and spring of 1642, with nearly 25 per cent of all pamphlets devoted to the insurrection and its aftermath.

As Ethan Shagan and Kathleen Noonan have demonstrated, these cheap newsbooks (costing a penny each for the smaller ones) and pamphlets, profoundly shaped popular opinion in England.[50] Tracts such as Henry Jones's *Remonstrance of Diverse and Remarkable Passages* (London, 1642) helped, as Joseph Cope has shown, to persuade the English parliament and people to support relief projects for the victims of the 1641 rebellion, especially the *Act for a speedy contribution and loan* (1643).[51] One of the most significant publications was Sir John Temple's *The Irish Rebellion*, which appeared in London in 1646.[52] Temple's hyperbole immediately impacted on Westminster politics and government propagandists imbibed Temple's prejudices and maintained that the barbarism and incivility of the Irish denied them individual rights and liberties.[53] The anti-Catholic and anti-Irish rhetoric of the majority of these publications, together with the atrocity stories they printed, also inflamed deep-rooted English fears that the apparent resurgence of Catholicism in Ireland was part of a wider international conspiracy intended to subvert godly England to popery.[54]

VII. New Departures

Mid-century Ireland is blessed with the survival of a remarkable amount of material relating to landholding and the development of new technologies is allowing us to interrogate theses sources like never before. Of particular importance are the various maps and surveys associated with the revolution in landholding: the Strafford Survey of Connacht (1636–40), Sir William Petty's 'Down Survey' (1654–9), the 'Civil Survey' (1654–6), and the Books of Survey and Distribution, which are the equivalent of the Domesday Book (a great English land survey dating from 1086) and record the names of landholders in 1641 and again in *c.* 1670/5, together with the number of plantation acres (profitable and non-profitable) and the county, barony, and parish where the land was held.

The recently completed 'Down Survey of Ireland Project', led by Micheál Ó Siochrú, has created a consolidated digital atlas of the Down Survey by overlaying all extant Down Survey maps and related cartographic material onto an Ordnance Survey 1:25 000 base.[55] The project has created a geo-referenced town land index and a historical Geographic Information System (GIS). When combined, these can be used to consolidate a wide range of seventeenth-century source materials, including the Books of Survey and Distribution, the 1641 depositions, and the 1659 Census. The survival of records like these is rare and, thanks to the development of the appropriate technologies, offers historians a fascinating opportunity to examine (amongst other things) the revolution in landholding that so profoundly shaped modern Ireland.

With time, the 'Down Survey of Ireland Project' will spawn new historical research in much the same way that the '1641 Depositions Project' has.[56] The availability of the depositions in digital format has also led to related technology initiatives. The 'Language and Linguistic Evidence in the 1641 Depositions' was an AHRC-funded (2010–11), multidisciplinary project that aimed to develop new ways of interacting with, analyzing, and visualizing the depositions. It used forensic and critical linguistic analysis to investigate how language was used in the period to serve legal, political, and religious agendas, and sought to understand the language of conflict encountered in the corpus.[57] In 2011, the 1641 Depositions Project also attracted intensely competitive European funding under the guise of CULTURA (CULTivating Understanding through Research and Adaptivity).[58] The development of social network analysis tools as part of CULTURA allows for sophisticated interrogation of the relationships that connected people, places, and events. The full extent to which this analysis will change or enrich our knowledge of the course of the 1641 rebellion and the conduct of the war will become clearer in due course.

When viewed from the perspective of a historical researcher, the possibilities that technology offers are truly exciting. The fact that the 1641 depositions are now freely available in digital form and many of the printed pamphlets and histories relating to the rebellion are accessible electronically (albeit at a considerable price) on Early English Books Online (EEBO) and Eighteenth Century Collections Online (ECCO) could, for instance, allow for the identification of key phrases that appear in both the manuscript folio and on the printed page. Of course for this to happen, these digital resources need to inter-operate in a way that is currently not possible. However, imagine the research possibilities if electronic resources like the 1641 depositions, EEBO and ECCO could be linked to other digital resources, such as the *Dictionary of National Biography*, the *Dictionary of Irish Biography*, the Irish State Papers, the records of the Irish Statute Staple, and the military migration datasets that document the Irish soldiers who fought in the armies of Scandinavia, Spain, and France in the early modern period.[59] As emphasis shifts from the generation of digital data to how these resources can be interrogated and as technology becomes increasingly sophisticated and user-friendly, historians—together with literary scholars, historical geographers, linguists, computer scientists, and other researchers—will be able to interrogate their sources and represent their findings in ways currently unimaginable.[60]

Notes

1. Jane Ohlmeyer, 'Introduction: a failed revolution?' in Jane Ohlmeyer (ed), *Ireland from Independence to Occupation, 1641–1660* (Cambridge, 1995; reprinted in paperback, 2002).

2. J.G.A. Pocock, *The Discovery of Islands: Essays in British History* (Cambridge, 2005) and Nicholas Canny, 'Writing Early Modern History: Ireland, Britain, and the Wider World', *Historical Journal*, 46 (2003), 723–47; Nicholas Canny, 'Moving Forward from the "New British History"' in Claudia Schnurmann and Hartmut Lehmann (eds), *Atlantic Understandings: Essays on European and American History in Honor of Hermann Wellenreuther* (Hamburg and London, 2006), 405–16; Jane Ohlmeyer, Review article: 'The "Old British History" and the early modern period', *Historical Journal* (2007), 499–512; 'Seventeenth-century Ireland and the New British and Atlantic Histories', *American Historical Review*, 104: 2 (1999), 446–62; and 'Literature, Identity, and the New British Histories' in David Baker and Willy Maley (eds), *British Identities and English Renaissance Literature* (Cambridge, 2002).

3. The 1641 Depositions Project aimed to conserve, digitize, transcribe, and make the depositions available online at http://1641.tcd.ie/ in a fully TEI-(Text Encoding Initiative) compliant format. It was a collaborative project between Trinity College Dublin, the University of Aberdeen, and the University of Cambridge working in partnership with IBM LanguageWare and Eneclann. The principal investigators on the project (2007–11) were Professors Jane Ohlmeyer, Thomas Bartlett, Micheál Ó Siochrú, and John Morrill. Professor Aidan Clarke edited the transcriptions. The researchers on the project were Dr Edda Frankot, Dr Annaleigh Margey, and Dr Elaine Murphy. The Irish Manuscripts Commission is publishing serially a twelve-volume edition of the 1641 depositions; edited by Aidan Clarke; vols 1–3 are scheduled for publication in 2014.

4. The best introduction to the 1641 depositions remains Aidan Clarke, 'The 1641 depositions' in P. Fox (ed), *Treasures of the Library, Trinity College Dublin* (Dublin, 1986).

5. Nicholas Canny, *Making Ireland British, 1580–1650* (Oxford, 2001) and William Smyth, *Map-making, Landscapes and Memory. A Geography of Colonial and Early Modern Ireland c. 1530–1750* (Cork, 2006).

6. Éamonn Ó Ciardha and Micheál Ó Siochrú (eds) *Plantation of Ulster: Ideology and Practice* (Manchester, 2012); Annaleigh Margey, *Mapping Ireland, c. 1550–1636: a Catalogue of the Early Modern Manuscript Maps of Ireland* (Irish Manuscripts Commission, Dublin, forthcoming 2013). Also see C. Rynne and J. Lytellton (eds), *Plantation Ireland: Settlement and Material Culture, c. 1550–1700* (Dublin, 2009).

7. TCD, MS 833, fol. 233.

8. For example, see chapters by Bríd McGrath and Jane Ohlmeyer in Ciaran Brady and Jane Ohlmeyer (eds), *Making Good: British Interventions in Early Modern Ireland* (Cambridge, 2005).

9. Aidan Clarke, 'The 1641 Massacres' in Jane Ohlmeyer and Micheál Ó Siochrú (eds) *Ireland, 1641. Contexts and Reactions* (Manchester, 2013).

10. See the chapters by John Walter, Judith Pollman, Mark Greengrass, and Ben Kiernan in Ohlmeyer and Ó Siochrú (eds) *Ireland, 1641*; Charlene McCoy, 'War and Revolution: County Fermanagh and its borders, *c.* 1640–*c.* 1666' (unpublished PhD thesis, Trinity College Dublin, 2007); Inga Volmer, 'A comparative study of massacres during the wars of the three kingdoms, 1641–1653' (PhD thesis, Cambridge, 2007); the chapters by Brian MacCuarta, Kenneth Nicholls and Mark Clinton, Linda Fibiger and Damian Shiels in David Edwards, Padraig Lenihan, and Clodagh Tait (eds), *Age of Atrocity. Violence in Political Conflict in Early Modern Ireland* (Dublin, 2007); Joseph Cope, 'The experience of survival during the 1641 Irish rebellion', *Historical Journal*, 46 (2003), 295–316. See also Brendan Scott, 'Reporting the 1641 rising in Cavan and Leitrim' in Brendan Scott (ed), *Culture and Society in Early Modern Breifne/Cavan* (Dublin, 2009) and Jason McHugh, '"For our owne defence": Catholic insurrection in Wexford, 1641–2' in Brian MacCuarta (ed), *Reshaping Ireland 1550–1700. Colonization and its Consequences* (Dublin, 2011).

11. Smyth, *Map-making*, 115.

12. For a basic overview of the war, see Jane Ohlmeyer, 'The Wars of Religion, 1603–60' in Thomas Bartlett and Keith Jeffery (eds), *A Military History of Ireland* (Cambridge, 1996); 'The civil wars in Ireland' in Jane Ohlmeyer with John Kenyon (eds), *The Civil Wars: A Military History of England, Scotland and Ireland, 1638–1660* (Oxford University Press, 1998; reprinted, 2002) and 'The baronial context of the Civil War in Ireland' in John Adamson (ed), *The Civil Wars* (London, 2008).

13. Micheál Ó Siochrú, 'Atrocity, Codes of Conduct and the Irish in the British Civil Wars 1641–1653', *Past and Present*, 195 (2007), 55–86 and the works cited in note 10 above.

14. Kevin Forkan, 'Ormond's alternative: the lord lieutenant's secret contacts with Protestant Ulster, 1645–6', *Historical Research*, 81 (2008), 610–35; 'The Ulster Scots and the Engagement, 1647–8', *Irish Historical Studies*, 35 (2006–7), 455–76; 'The south Ulster borderland as a political frontier in the 1640s', *Breifne*, 10 (2004), 270–89; 'Inventing a Protestant icon: the strange death of Sir Charles Coote, 1642' in Edwards, Lenihan, and Tait (eds), *Age of Atrocity*, 204–18; and '"The fatal ingredient of the covenant": the place of the Ulster Scottish colonial community during the 1640s' in MacCuarta (ed), *Reshaping Ireland*. Also see Kevin McKenny, *The Laggan Army in Ireland 1640–1685: the Landed Interests, Political Ideologies and Military Campaigns of the North-west Ulster Settlers* (Dublin, 2005).

15. Patrick Little, *Lord Broghill and the Cromwellian Union with Ireland and Scotland* (Woodbridge, 2004); 'The first unionists?: Irish Protestant attitudes to union with England, 1653–9', *Irish Historical Studies*, 32 (2000), 44–58; 'The English Parliament and the Irish Constitution, 1641–1649' in Micheál Ó Siochrú (ed), *Kingdoms in Crisis: Ireland in the 1640s* (Dublin, 2001), 106–21; and 'An Irish governor of Scotland: Lord Broghill, 1655–6' in A. MacKillop and Steve Murdoch (eds), *Military Governors and Imperial Frontiers c. 1600–1800* (Leiden, 2003).

16. Robert Armstrong, *Protestant War: The 'British' of Ireland and the Wars of the Three Kingdoms* (Manchester, 2005).

17. Tadhg Ó hAnnracháin, *Catholic Reformation in Ireland. The Mission of Rinuccini 1645–1649* (Oxford, 2002). See also 'Lost in Rinuccini's shadow: the Irish clergy, 1645–9' in Ó Siochrú (ed), *Kingdoms in Crisis*, 176–91; '"In imitation of that holy patron of prelates the blessed St Charles": Episcopal activity in Ireland and the formation of a confessional identity, 1618–1653' in Alan Ford and John McCafferty (eds), *The Origins of Sectarianism in Early Modern Ireland* (Cambridge, 2005), 73–94.

18. Micheál Ó Siochrú, *Confederate Ireland 1642–1649: A Constitutional and Political Analysis* (Dublin 1999). See also Donal Cregan, 'The Personnel of the Confederation of Kilkenny', *Irish Historical Studies*, 29 (1995), 490–512; Bríd McGrath, 'Ireland and the third university attendance at the inns of court, 1603–1649' in David Edwards (ed), *Regions and Rulers in Ireland 1100–1650: Essays for Kenneth Nicholls* (Dublin, 2004), 217–36; Jane Ohlmeyer, 'Irish Recusant Lawyers during the Reign of Charles I' in Siochrú (ed), *Kingdoms in Crisis*, 63–89.

19. Pádraig Lenihan, *Confederate Catholics at War, 1642–49* (Cork, 2001); 'Confederate military strategy, 1643–7' in Ó Siochrú (ed), *Kingdoms in Crisis*; 'Conclusion: Ireland's military revolution(s)' in Lenihan (ed), *Conquest and Resistance: Irish Warfare in the Seventeenth Century* (Leiden, 2001).

20. Barry Robertson offers a structural account of Irish royalism over the course of the war and assesses who the royalists were, what it meant to be a royalist and a loyalist, and how this changed over time, *Royalists at War in Scotland and Ireland, 1638–1650* (London, 2014). See also Jane Ohlmeyer, 'For God, King and Country: Political Thought and Culture in seventeenth-century Ireland' in Ohlmeyer (ed), *Kingdom or Colony?*; Micheál Ó Siochrú, 'Catholic Confederates and the Constitutional Relationship between Ireland and England, 1641–1649' in Brady and Ohlmeyer (eds), *Making Good*; Tadhg Ó hAnnracháin, 'Conflicting Loyalties, Conflicted Rebels: Political and Religious Allegiance among the Confederate Catholics of Ireland', *English Historical Review*, 119 (2004), 851–72.

21. Micheál Ó Siochrú, *God's Executioner. Oliver Cromwell and the Conquest of Ireland* (London, 2008) and 'Propaganda, rumour and myth: Oliver Cromwell and the massacre at Drogheda' in Edwards, Lenihan, and Tait (eds), *Age of Atrocity*, 266–82. See also John Morrill, 'The Drogheda massacre in Cromwellian context' in Edwards, Lenihan, and Tait (eds), *Age of Atrocity*, 242–65.

22. Elaine Murphy, *Ireland and the War at Sea 1641–1653* (London, 2012) and 'Atrocities at sea and the treatment of prisoners of war by the parliamentary navy in Ireland, 1641–1649' in *Historical Journal*, 53 (2010), 21–37. See also Elaine Murphy, 'The English navy and intelligence in the 1640s' in Eunan O'Halpin, Robert Armstrong, and Jane Ohlmeyer (eds), *Intelligence, Statecraft and International Power: Papers read before the 27th Irish Conference of Historians held at Trinity College, Dublin, 19–21 May 2005* (Dublin, 2006), 35–47; Elaine Murphy (ed), *A Calendar of High Court of Admiralty material relating to Ireland, 1641–1660* (Irish Manuscripts Commission, Dublin, 2011); and Kevin Costello, *The Court of Admiralty of Ireland, 1575–1879* (Dublin, 2011).

23. Pádraig Lenihan, 'War and population, 1649–52', *Irish Economic and Social History*, 24 (1997), 1–21.

24. A minority of Catholics joined the king in exile on the continent, J.J. Cronin, 'The Irish Royalist Elite of Charles II in Exile, c. 1649–1660' (PhD thesis, European University Institute, Florence, 2007).

25. Ian Gentles, Heather Mclean, and Micheál Ó Siochrú, 'Minutes of courts martial held in Dublin 1651–53', *Archivium Hibernicum*, 64 (2011).

26. John Cunningham, 'Transplantation to Connacht, 1641–1680: Theory and Practice' (Unpublished PhD thesis, Galway, 2009), 212–19. See also John Cunningham, 'The transplanters' certificates and the historiography of Cromwellian Ireland', *Irish Historical Studies*, 37 (2011), 376–95; 'A secret unlimited power? transplantation policy in Cromwellian Ireland' in Anthony McElligott, Liam Chambers. and Ciara Breathnach (eds), *Power in History: From Medieval Ireland to the Post-Modern World* (Historical Studies XXVII) (Dublin, 2011).

27. Cunningham, 'Transplantation to Connacht, 1641–1680'.

28. Jane Ohlmeyer, *Making Ireland English: the Irish Aristocracy in the Seventeenth Century* (New Haven and London, 2012).

29. The definitive work remains T.C. Barnard, *Cromwellian Ireland. English Government and Reform in Ireland 1649–1660* (Oxford, 1975). See also Crawford Gribben, *God's Irishmen. Theological Debates in Cromwellian Ireland* (Oxford, 2007) and Ted McCormick, *William Petty and the Ambitions of Political Arithmetic* (Oxford, 2010).

30. See note 15 above.

31. Aidan Clarke, *Prelude to Restoration in Ireland: The End of the Commonwealth, 1659–1660* (Cambridge, 1999).

32. For notable exceptions, see Raymond Gillespie, *Devoted People. Belief and Religion in early modern Ireland* (Manchester, 1997) and Clodagh Tait, *Death, Burial and Commemoration in Ireland, 1550–1650* (London, 2002).

33. Aoife Duignan, ' "All in confused opposition to each other". Politics and War in Connacht, 1641–9' (unpublished PhD thesis, University College Dublin, 2006) and 'Shifting allegiances: the Protestant community in Connacht, 1643–5' in Armstrong and Ó hAnnracháin (eds), *Community in Early Modern Ireland*; McCoy, 'War and Revolution'; Maighréad Ní Mhurchadha, *Fingal, 1603–60 Contending Neighbours in North Dublin* (Dublin, 2005), 229–84; David Dickson, *Old World Colony. Cork and South Munster 1630–1830* (Cork, 2005), 29–52.

34. Mary O'Dowd, *A History of Women in Ireland, 1500–1800* (London, 2005) and Margaret Mac Curtain and Mary O'Dowd, 'An Agenda for Women's History in Ireland, 1500–1900, pt. 1: 1500–1800', *Irish Historical Studies*, 28:109 (1992), 1–19.

35. Eleanor O'Keeffe, 'The Family and Marriage Strategies of James Butler, 1st Duke of Ormonde, 1658–1688' (unpublished Cambridge PhD thesis, 2000).

36. Jane Ohlmeyer, 'Making Ireland English: the seventeenth-century Irish peerage' in MacCuarta (ed), *Reshaping Ireland; Making Ireland English: the Irish Aristocracy in the Seventeenth Century* (New Haven and London, 2012), especially chapter 6.

37. Alison Forrestal, *Catholic Synods in Ireland, 1600–1690* (Dublin, 1998), 105.

38. Alexandra Shepard, *Meanings of Manhood in Early Modern England* (Oxford, 2003); 'Manhood, Credit and Patriarchy in Early Modern England c. 1580–1640', *Past and Present*, 167 (2000), 75–106.

39. See particularly Mervyn James, *English Politics and the Concept of Honour, 1485–1642* (first published in 1978); Richard Cust, 'Honour and Politics in early Stuart England', *Past and Present*, 149 (1995), 57–94; and Cynthia Herrup, ' "To Pluck Bright Honour from the Pale-Faced Moon": Gender and Honour in the Castlehaven Story', *Transactions of the Royal Historical Society*, sixth series, VI (1996), 137–60.

40. Brendan Kane, *The Politics and Culture of Honour in Britain and Ireland, 1541–1641* (Cambridge, 2010) and 'Making the Irish European: Gaelic Honor Politics and Its Continental Contexts', *Renaissance Quarterly*, 61 (2008), 1139–66. See also William Palmer, 'That "Insolent Liberty": Honor, Rites of Power, and Persuasion in Sixteenth-Century Ireland', *Renaissance Quarterly*, 46 (1993), 308–27, James Kelly, *That Damn'd Thing Called Honour: Duelling in Ireland, 1570–1860* (Cork, 1995); Bernadette Cunningham, 'Colonized Catholics: perceptions of honour and history in Michael Kearney's reading of "Foras Feasa ar Éireann" ' in Vincent P. Carey and Ute Lotz-Heumann (eds), *Taking Sides: Colonial and Confessional Mentalities in Early Modern Ireland* (Dublin, 2003); Raymond Gillespie, 'The social thought of Richard Bellings' in Ó Siochrú (ed), *Kingdoms in Crisis*; and Ohlmeyer, 'The baronial context' in Adamson (ed), *The Civil Wars*.

41. John Kerrigan, 'Orrery's Ireland and the British Problem' in Baker and Maley (eds), *British Identities*.

42. Andrew Carpenter, 'A Collection of Verse Presented to James Butler, First Duke of Ormonde', *The Yale University Library Gazette*, 75: 1–2 (2000), 64–70.

43. Michael Perceval Maxwell, 'Sir Robert Southwell and the duke of Ormond's reflections on the 1640s' in Ó Siochrú (ed), *Kingdoms in Crisis*, 229–47; Jane Ohlmeyer and Steven Zwicker, 'Patronage and Restoration Politics: John Dryden and the House of Ormond' in *Historical Journal* (2006), 677–706.

44. See, for example, Roger Chartier (ed), *The Culture of Print: Power and Uses of Print in Early Modern Europe* (Cambridge, 1989) and Roger Chartier, *The Cultural Uses of Print in Early Modern France* (Princeton, 1987); Adam Fox, *Oral and Literate Culture in England 1500–1700* (Oxford, 2000); Adam Fox and Daniel Woolf (eds), *The Spoken Word. Oral Culture in Britain 1500–1850* (Manchester, 2002); and Margaret Spufford, *Small Books and Pleasant Histories. Popular Fiction and its Readership in Seventeenth-century England* (Athens, GA, 1981).

45. Andrew Carpenter, *Verse in English from Tudor and Stuart Ireland* (Cork, 2003) and Andrew Carpenter, 'Circulating ideas: coteries, groups and the circulation of verse in English in early modern Ireland' in Martin Fanning and Raymond Gillespie (eds), *Print Culture and Intellectual Life in Ireland, 1660–1941* (Dublin, 2006), 1–23. See also Tony Sweeney, *Ireland and the Printed Word. A Short Descriptive Catalogue of Early Books, Pamphlets, Newsletters and Broadsides relating to Ireland. Printed: 1475–1700* (Dublin, 1997).

46. Raymond Gillespie, *Reading Ireland: Print, Reading and Social Change in Early Modern Ireland* (Manchester, 2005); Raymond Gillespie and Andrew Hadfield (eds), *The Oxford History of the Irish Book. III. The Irish Book in English 1550–1800* (Oxford, 2006); Bernadette Cunningham and Máire Kennedy (eds), *The Experience of Reading: Irish Historical Perspectives* (Dublin, 1999), 10–38.

47. Eamon Darcy, 'Pogroms, Politics and Print: The 1641 rebellion and contemporary print culture' (PhD thesis, Trinity College Dublin, 2009) and *The Irish Rebellion of 1641 and the Wars of the Three Kingdoms* (London, 2013). See also John Gibney, *The Shadow of a Year: The 1641 Rebellion in Irish History and Memory* (Madison, 2013) and David O'Hara, *English Newsbooks and Irish Rebellion 1641–1649* (Dublin, 2006).

48. Jane Ohlmeyer, 'Society: the changing role of print—Ireland (to 1660)' in Joad Raymond (ed), *The Oxford History of Popular Print Culture. Vol 1. Cheap Print in Britain and Ireland to 1660* (Oxford, 2011).

49. Joad Raymond, *Making the News. An Anthology of the Newsbooks of Revolutionary England 1641–1660* (Moreton-in-Marsh, 1993), 16.

50. Kathleen Noonan, '"The Cruell Pressure of an enraged, barbarous people": Irish and English Identity in seventeenth-century Propaganda', *Historical Journal*, 41 (1998), 151–77; Ethan Howard Shagan, 'Constructing Discord: Ideology, Propaganda, and English Responses to the Irish Rebellion of 1641', *Journal of British Studies*, 36:1 (1997), 4–34.

51. Joseph Cope, *England and the 1641 Irish Rebellion* (London, 2009) and 'Fashioning victims: Dr Henry Jones and the plight of Irish Protestants, 1642', *Historical Research*, 74 (2001), 370–91.

52. Sir John Temple, *The Irish Rebellion ... Together with the barbarous cruelties and bloody massacres which ensued thereupon* (London, 1646); Raymond Gillespie, 'Temple's fate: reading The Irish Rebellion in late seventeenth-century Ireland' in Brady and Ohlmeyer (eds), *British Interventions*.

53. John Adamson, 'Strafford's ghost: the British context of Viscount Lisle's lieutenancy of Ireland' in Ohlmeyer (ed), *Ireland from Independence to Occupation*.
54. Raymond Gillespie, 'Temple's Fate: Reading The Irish Rebellion in late seventeenth-century Ireland' in Brady and Ohlmeyer (eds), *Making Good*; Cope, 'Fashioning Victims'.
55. I am grateful to Micheál Ó Siochrú and his team for sharing their findings with me in advance of publication.
56. Discussed in note 3 above. For some of this recent research on society and culture in pre-war Ireland, the nature of warfare during the 1640s, print culture, and cultural memory, see Eamon Darcy, Annaleigh Margey, and Elaine Murphy (eds), *The 1641 Depositions and the Irish Rebellion* (London, 2012).
57. The website, the 1641 Collaborative Linguistic Research and Learning Environment, http://kdeg-vm-15.cs.tcd.ie/omeka-1.2.1/about. Mark Sweetnam, 'Natural Language Processing and Early Modern Dirty Data: IBM LanguageWare and the 1641 Depositions', *Linguistic and Literary Computing* (2011; doi: 10.1093/llc/fqr050).
58. CULTURA is an EU FP7-funded, three-year (2011–14) Specific Targeted Research Project (STReP) held in partnership with the universities of Sofia, Padua, Gratz, IBM (Haifa and Dublin), and Commetric, an SME based in Sofia and London, http://www.cultura-strep.eu/home.
59. For Early English Books Online, see http://eebo.chadwyck.com/homeand; for Eighteenth-century Collections Online, see http://gdc.gale.com/products/eighteenth-century-collections-online/; for the *Dictionary of National Biography*, http://www.oxforddnb.com/; for the *Dictionary of Irish Biography* http://dib.cambridge.org/; for the Irish State Papers, http://gale.cengage.co.uk/state-papers-online-15091714.aspx; for the 1641 depositions, see note 3 above; Jane Ohlmeyer and Éamonn Ó Ciardha (eds), *The Irish Statute Staple Books, 1596–1687* (Dublin, 1998); Steve Murdoch and Alexia Grosjean have compiled a relational database profiling 'British' (English, Scottish, and Irish) officers serving largely in the Scandinavian forces (including hundreds of men of Scottish provenance but resident in Ireland and a few Irish Catholics), 'Scotland, Scandinavia and Northern Europe 1580–1707' database [www.st-andrews.ac.uk/history/ssne/].
60. Mark Greengrass and Lorna Hughes (eds), *The Virtual Representation of the Past* (London, 2008).

Select Bibliography

Armstrong, Robert, *Protestant War: The 'British' of Ireland and the Wars of the Three Kingdoms* (Manchester, 2005).
Barnard, T.C., *Cromwellian Ireland. English Government and Reform in Ireland 1649–1660* (Oxford, 1975).
Brady, Ciaran and Ohlmeyer, Jane (eds), *Making Good: British Interventions in Early Modern Ireland* (Cambridge, 2005).
Canny, Nicholas, *Making Ireland British, 1580–1650* (Oxford, 2001).
Clarke, Aidan, 'The 1641 depositions' in P. Fox (ed), *Treasures of the Library, Trinity College Dublin* (Dublin, 1986).
——, *Prelude to Restoration in Ireland: The end of the Commonwealth, 1659–1660* (Cambridge, 1999).
Cope, Joseph, 'The experience of survival during the 1641 Irish rebellion', *Historical Journal*, 46 (2003), 295–316.

——, *England and the 1641 Irish Rebellion* (London, 2009).

Cunningham, John, *Conquest and Land in Ireland: the Transplantation to Connacht, 1649–1680* (London, 2011).

Darcy, Eamon, Margey, Annaleigh, and Murphy, Elaine (eds), *The 1641 Depositions and the Irish Rebellion* (London, 2012).

Darcy, Eamon, *The Irish Rebellion of 1641 and the Wars of the Three Kingdoms* (London, 2013).

Edwards, David, Lenihan, Padraig, and Tait, Clodagh (eds), *Age of Atrocity. Violence in Political Conflict in Early Modern Ireland* (Dublin, 2007).

Gibney, John, *The Shadow of a Year: The 1641 Rebellion in Irish History and Memory* (Madison, 2013).

Lenihan, Pádraig, *Confederate Catholics at War, 1642–49* (Cork, 2001).

Little, Patrick, *Lord Broghill and the Cromwellian Union with Ireland and Scotland* (Woodbridge, 2004).

McCormick, Ted, *William Petty and the Ambitions of Political Arithmetic* (Oxford, 2010).

McCoy, Charlene, 'War and Revolution: County Fermanagh and its borders, *c.* 1640–*c.* 1666' (unpublished PhD thesis, Trinity College Dublin, 2007).

Murphy, Elaine, *Ireland and the War at Sea 1641–1653* (London, 2012).

Ó hAnnracháin, Tadhg, *Catholic Reformation in Ireland. The Mission of Rinuccini 1645–1649* (Oxford, 2002).

Ohlmeyer, Jane, 'The Wars of Religion, 1603–60' in Thomas Bartlett and Keith Jeffery (eds), *A Military History of Ireland* (Cambridge, 1996).

Ohlmeyer, Jane (ed), *Ireland from Independence to Occupation, 1641–1660* (Cambridge, 1995; reprinted in paperback, 2002).

——, 'The civil wars in Ireland' in Jane Ohlmeyer with John Kenyon (eds), *The Civil Wars: A Military History of England, Scotland and Ireland, 1638–1660* (Oxford University Press, 1998; reprinted, 2002).

——, 'The baronial context of the Civil War in Ireland' in John Adamson (ed), *The Civil Wars* (London, 2008).

——, 'Society: the changing role of print—Ireland (to 1660)' in Joad Raymond (ed), *The Oxford History of Popular Print Culture. Vol 1. Cheap Print in Britain and Ireland to 1660* (Oxford, 2011).

Ohlmeyer, Jane, *Making Ireland English: the Irish Aristocracy in the Seventeenth Century* (New Haven and London, 2012).

Ohlmeyer, Jane and Ó Siochrú, Micheál (eds), *Ireland, 1641. Contexts and Reactions* (Manchester, 2013).

Ó Siochrú, Micheál, *Confederate Ireland 1642–1649: A Constitutional and Political Analysis* (Dublin, 1999).

Ó Siochrú, Micheál (ed), *Kingdoms in Crisis: Ireland in the 1640s* (Dublin, 2001).

Ó Siochrú, Micheál, *God's executioner. Oliver Cromwell and the Conquest of Ireland* (London, 2008).

Robertson, Barry, *Royalists at War in Scotland and Ireland, 1638–1650* (London, 2014).

Smyth, William, *Map-making, Landscapes and Memory. A Geography of Colonial and Early Modern Ireland c. 1530–1750* (Cork, 2006).

Volmer, Inga, 'A comparative study of massacres during the wars of the three kingdoms, 1641–1653' (PhD thesis, Cambridge, 2007).

CHAPTER 17

....

IRELAND AND CONTINENTAL EUROPE, C.1600–C.1750

....

NICHOLAS CANNY

I. INTRODUCTION

....

WHILE most historians of Ireland writing today insist that the country they have chosen to study is European, they select for their interpretative framework a national grand narrative that allows little scope for broader contextualization. The only serious challenge to this approach over the past several decades has come from advocates of what was once known as the 'New' British History, but these are doubly insular since they contend that interactions between the various populations occupying the two islands of Britain and Ireland were more potent in shaping the destinies of all than any contacts beyond the confines of the two islands.[1]

Arguments can be advanced for the relative appropriateness of competing interpretative frameworks for the study of the history of Ireland at particular times, and it does seem that links between Ireland (or between Ireland and Britain collectively) and the European continent were more sporadic and tentative at the close of the medieval period than for earlier or later historical periods. However, even in the late medieval period, some contacts were maintained between Ireland and the Continent, not all of them mediated through Britain. Moreover, some of these contacts contributed to the forging of the altogether stronger links that would bind experiences in Ireland closely to those in continental Europe from the early seventeenth to the mid eighteenth century.

II. THE POLITICAL DIMENSION

....

The course of political events in Ireland, as in Britain and in much of Europe, during the late medieval period was determined principally by dynastic conflicts. Despite, or perhaps because of, the resultant political instability, Irish merchant communities strove to maintain some degree of autonomy behind their walls, and maintained trading contact with ports on the western coast of France and southwards to the Iberian coast. At the same time, continental fishermen, particularly Basques, fished regularly off the Munster coast, sometimes even landing to dry, cure, and barrel their catches with the sanction of local lords. Also, Irish clerics, particularly from the Gaelic parts of the country, made occasional visits to Rome when seeking to outmanoeuvre their rivals for appointment as bishops. That some Irish people knew something of more significant developments is suggested in the secular sphere by the adventurer from Galway who sailed to the coast of Guinea in the employ of Prince Henry the Navigator and was rewarded with a lion as a gift for his native city, while one Michael Donquan, an Irish resident of St Malo, accompanied the locally based Jacques Cartier in 1535 on his second exploratory voyage to North America.[2] In the religious sphere, while Irish clergy—particularly those who held positions in Gaelic lordships—seemed to stand aloof from spiritual and intellectual movements in Europe, some of them, and particularly the Observant Friars, were alert to the implications of the breach between King Henry VIII and Rome.[3] Then, in the later decades of the sixteenth century, it was Catholic bishops from Gaelic Ireland who were persistent in advocating a transfer of allegiance by Catholics from the heretical Queen Elizabeth to the Catholic King of Spain whom they would have had as protector of Ireland.[4]

The resort to an extreme political position in the 1590s by some Irish Catholic bishops, and by those lords who took advantage of whatever continental contacts the bishops could make for them, may have been in reaction to the efforts of the agents of the English Crown in Ireland to assert the authority of that government in all parts of Ireland and to compel the population to reject the Pope as their spiritual leader in favour of the English monarch as head of a state-defined Protestantism. If so, Irish dalliance with the continental enemies of the English Crown elicited, in the later 1590s, a counter-reaction that led to the utter overthrow of those in Ireland—and those Spaniards who had come to their assistance—who, it was perceived in England, had collectively threatened the English monarchy itself. Many of the 20 000 troops who were deployed by the English Crown in Ireland to effect a conclusion to the Nine Years' War (1594–1603) had seen previous service in continental Europe, either in the Netherlands or in Brittany, as part of a combined Protestant effort to curtail the efforts of successive Kings of Spain, and the Catholic League in France, to reverse the gains that had been made by the Protestant Reformation in the Netherlands, in France, and in England. Many of these English soldiers, or at least their officers with continental experience, thought, as did the Irish Catholic bishops, that conflict in Ireland was but one dimension of a continuing opposition between Catholicism and Protestantism to achieve religious, political, and moral dominance over Europe.[5]

Since those who had opposed the Crown in Ireland had gambled all by combining with England's continental enemies, they cannot have been surprised at the outcome that befell them after their defeat. Those in the province of Munster who had associated with the Spanish expeditionary force that had landed at Kinsale suffered an immediate loss of property and power. Therefore, some Munster lords who had survived the conflict, and also the Ulster lord Hugh O'Donnell, took ship for Spain in the vain hope of persuading the Spanish crown to mount a second expedition. Then, as the English military took control of Munster, large numbers of the ordinary inhabitants also fled the province to become unwanted destitute exiles in the provinces of Galicia and Brittany, to which they travelled either through England or by securing passage in the many trading and fishing vessels that sailed directly to those destinations.[6] Many of the Ulster lords who had been prime leaders in the insurrection against Crown authority persisted in arms until the death of Queen Elizabeth in March 1603, but the apparently generous terms that were then conceded by King James VI of Scotland (who had succeeded Elizabeth as James I of England) to the leaders of the insurgency did not prove durable. Therefore, in September 1607, these lords also opted for continental exile in preference to living under British and Protestant rule. As had happened in Munster, these were soon followed by many of their immediate followers (although not by a mass exodus), both those who had fought with them as officers and soldiers and members of the learned orders in Gaelic Ulster society, including many Catholic clergy. Their departure left their territories open to an officially government-sponsored plantation in the province of Ulster, designed to make the previously most recalcitrant province in Ireland both loyal to the Crown and Protestant in religion.[7]

This outcome proved both salutary and inspirational for all would-be leaders of rebellion in Ireland to the mid eighteenth century and beyond. It was salutary because, from this point forward, all landed proprietors in Ireland proceeded cautiously in their dealings with the government in full knowledge of the risks associated with challenging the established authority in Ireland. It proved inspirational because whenever Irish lords believed that they had no option but to take up arms to defend their interests, they had a better appreciation of the need to secure prior support from some of England's enemies on the continent of Europe. Thus, from the early seventeenth to the mid eighteenth century, all conflicts or proto-conflicts in Ireland had a European dimension. Those lords who professed that they had been forced to take up arms in 1641 did so in the knowledge that they, like the Covenanters in Scotland a few years previously, could count on military support from their kinsmen who had made careers as soldiers in continental armies; the Irish hoped also for assistance from Catholic powers on the continent, including the Pope. Then, in 1688, those lords in Ireland, who would uphold King James VII and II as their legitimate king after his daughter Mary and her husband William of Orange had ousted him from the throne in England, were assured that Louis XIV of France would augment their support for King James. And whenever insurrection in, or an invasion of, Ireland was contemplated, or feared, during the first half of the eighteenth century it was always assumed that this would only happen if Irish regiments were free to return from France after the French army and its allies had defeated Britain's armies on the continent.[8]

If conflict in Ireland always had a European dimension for Irish Catholic leaders, so it did for their Protestant opponents, whether these were based in Ireland or were witnessing events in Ireland from an English or Scottish perspective. Several English adventurers who had been involved with Ireland in Elizabethan times, as has been mentioned, had previous continental experience and frequently depicted events in Ireland in European terms. Matters were no different as the seventeenth century progressed when the Protestant presence in Ireland came to include Scots as well as English. Several of the Scottish families who took estates in the plantation of Ulster had themselves had experience fighting alongside some of the Protestant rulers of northern Europe or had close kin involved there. Thus, when war beset Ulster after the insurrection of 1641, George Monro, commander of the army sent by the Scottish Covenanters to assist their besieged kin in Ulster, was an old Protestant adversary (from the Thirty Years' War) of Owen Roe O'Neill. Like Monro, O'Neill had returned from military service on the continent (in his case with the Spanish army based in Flanders) to assist the discontented Catholic gentry of Ulster to recover their lost power, property, and religious freedom.[9]

Protestants of English ancestry who rose to prominence in Ireland during the first half of the seventeenth century may not have had the amplitude of experience of their Scottish counterparts, but their more successful members took to sending their sons to Europe on the Grand Tour with the particular purpose of placing them for a time in the continental centres of Protestant learning, particularly Geneva, Leiden, and Saumur.[10] Some of the emerging elite maintained correspondence with English political figures who were known to be acquainted with events on the continent. In this way, and through similar contacts, a great many of the emerging Protestant elite in Ireland remained informed of political events on the continent, knowing that every reverse suffered by the Protestant interest during the course of the Thirty Years' War in Europe weakened their own position in Ireland. They showed particular concern for the fate of Protestants in Bohemia and the Palatinate, possibly suggesting that the fate of the Winter King, Frederick V Elector of the Palatinate, and Elizabeth, his queen, who was sister to King Charles I, presaged what might befall themselves.[11] On the positive side, Irish Protestants took satisfaction from the precocious reputation gained by Trinity College Dublin as a seat of Protestant learning, and of the international scholarly standing of James Ussher, one of that college's first students, who became a professor of divinity before being appointed Bishop of Meath and then Archbishop of Armagh.[12]

The previous experience of those commanding the Parliamentary armies that achieved the Cromwellian reconquest of Ireland (1647–52) was primarily insular. However, they, like their Elizabethan predecessors in Ireland, saw all military conflict as part of the universal struggle between the forces of good and evil. Therefore, they, no less than their Catholic opponents in Ireland, readily identified the prolonged conflict in Scotland, England, and Ireland as part of the military continuum that was disturbing all of Europe, and they frequently likened the efforts of Oliver Cromwell to those of Gustavus Adolphus of Sweden. It seemed logical therefore that they, unlike their royalist predecessors in Ireland, should invite Protestant refugees from disturbed areas of the continent both to take up residence in the country and to apply their intelligence to convert it into a stable and prosperous condition. *Ireland's Naturall History*, published in 1652 for the Dutch scientists Gerard and Arnold Boate, was thus designed not only to guide the reform of Ireland, but to serve as a template for the improvement of all countries of Europe once their resources had also come under the control of enlightened Protestant rulers. The work was so recognized by Samuel Hartlib, a refugee from Habsburg oppression in the Baltic region, who had come to enjoy enormous respect in English scientific circles during the middle decades of the seventeenth century.[13] The ambition of Sir William Petty to have Ireland mapped more scientifically than any other country of Europe as a precursor to a comprehensive plantation and re-plantation was also considered exemplary, and while the inspiration for his approach is usually attributed to the empirical method promoted in England by Sir Francis Bacon, it owed a good deal also to the influence of the French savant René Descartes, with whose works Petty was familiar from his early schooling in France.[14]

The desire of Cromwellian reformers to advance the programme of making Ireland Protestant by introducing some Protestant refugees from Europe fell short of expectations because of the insufficiency of confiscated Irish land to meet the demands of even British and Irish claimants. Despite the fact that the new Protestant element introduced to Ireland in the course of the Cromwellian settlement was primarily English, albeit representing a wider spectrum of Protestant opinion—including Quakers, Independents and Baptists—than had previously existed in the country, the idea of augmenting these with continental Protestants was never out of sight. Consequently, all future Protestant programmes for settling Ireland encouraged first Bohemians, Dutch, and Flemings to take up residence there, followed by French Huguenots and Rhineland Palatines, who came to be considered victims of continuing Catholic tyranny dispensed this time by King Louis XIV of France.

Irish Royalists who had opposed the Cromwellians soon became as adept as their opponents in addressing Irish issues in pan-European terms because, after the Parliamentary armies had defeated their efforts to uphold Crown authority in Ireland, the principal leaders of the royalist cause (like their English and Scottish counterparts) abandoned their estates and fled Ireland to join the exiled Charles Stuart (Charles II) and his mother, Henrietta Maria (aunt to Louis XIV of France). Those who did so (Protestant and Catholic alike) were forced to spend the years from the late 1640s until the early 1660s either as servants or hangers-on of the exiled King and Queen Mother in the varying locations in which they were offered frugal hospitality, or as soldiers of fortune in various military campaigns of the French army, or, after 1661, in defending Tangiers, which was offered by the King of Portugal as a dowry when his daughter Catherine of Braganza married King Charles II.[15] After their decades in exile, many of these royalists, or their heirs, returned to Ireland to play prominent roles in the Irish administrations appointed respectively by King Charles II (1660–85) and by King James II (1685–91). Those who were from the highest rank of nobility, those who were Protestant, and those connected with James Butler, marquis (soon to be duke) of Ormond, enjoyed the best prospects of recovering their estates in Ireland after 1660. On the other hand, many of those from Catholic gentry backgrounds were tardy about returning to Ireland because they were offered but limited prospects of compensation; of those who did return, many remained discontented when they received, at best, but a partial recovery of what had been taken from them by the Cromwellians.[16]

The return of royalist exiles to Ireland meant that very many of those who became involved with the Irish administration in the decades after 1660 had lived for a considerable time in various parts of the continent, but especially in France, the Netherlands, and Flanders. These had first-hand knowledge of continental politics and military affairs. Those who were Protestant were acquainted with continental Protestants and the circumstances in which they lived: both in the Netherlands and in several German principalities where Protestants were dominant; and in France where Protestants endured as a politically resented minority until 1685 when, with the Revocation of the Edict of Nantes, they were forced to choose between conforming to Catholicism or leaving France. Ormond displayed an interest from the outset in what was initially a Cromwellian idea of making Ireland more secure for Protestantism by settling continental Protestants there.

Those associated with Ormond were particularly interested in inviting to Ireland continental Protestants who were masters of particular skills, such as tapestry making, linen production, agronomy, and interior decorating, considered conducive to the improvement of the country.[17] The Irish Protestant community was also more generally concerned about the fate of French and other continental Protestants who faced persecution, and believed that Ireland should become a place of refuge for them. Some continentals did settle there, but the largest injection of French Protestants occurred after William of Orange, who enjoyed the support of a strong Huguenot military following, had ousted King James from Ireland. This influx resulted not only in the elevation of some French Protestant followers of King William to the ranks of the Irish nobility (notably Henri Massue de Ruvigny, earl of Galway), but also to the establishment of French Huguenot communities in Ireland, both in Dublin and in some nucleated outlets such as Portarlington. The same process was repeated a few years later after the armies of Louis XIV crossed the Rhine and invaded the Palatinate, thus causing another Protestant refugee problem, which was partly resolved by having some Palatine communities settle in Ireland.[18]

Catholic royalists who had also been in exile and who, after 1660, became the principal upholders of the Catholic interest in Ireland were opposed to bringing continental Protestants there, most particularly since their own dogged efforts to recover their lost estates from the hated Cromwellians was making scant progress. As they despaired of having their grievance resolved by King Charles II, their hopes focused on his younger brother and likely successor, James, Duke of York, who, in 1685, succeeded as King James VII and II. They pinned their hopes on James because many Catholic swordsmen had fought with him in military campaigns on the continent while Ormond and his associates had been closeted at the court-in-exile of King Charles. They were also aware that James was more sympathetic to Catholics than his older brother, even before 1673 when James openly admitted to Catholicism.

James's Irish supporters and their followers were correct in thinking that he was well disposed to Catholics, to the extent that he believed that Catholics of proven loyalty should not be precluded from holding office or military commissions in any of the jurisdictions of the British monarchy. In Ireland, however, the new king's supporters expected that the norms of continental Europe should obtain and that the succession of a Catholic to a previously Protestant monarchy would result in Catholics taking control of government as a first step to having Catholicism displace Protestantism as the religion of the state.

The haste with which Richard Talbot, who was created earl of Tyrconnell in 1685 and appointed King James's Lord Deputy of Ireland in November 1686, proceeded to make Irish Catholic expectations a reality by appointing Catholics to military and civil positions gave Protestant leaders in England another reason to invite William and Mary to intervene in James's dominions soon after James's queen bore him a son in June 1688. To the extent that Tyrconnell and his associates precipitated this action, they can be held responsible for bringing a continental war to Ireland (1689–91) as the Jacobite/Williamite conflict in Ireland became an insular dimension of the War of the League of Augsburg, in which a formidable alliance, spearheaded by William of Orange, strove to impose limits on the expansionist ambitions of Louis XIV.[19]

The force that fought on the side of King James in Ireland was the official royal army in Ireland, albeit now commanded mostly by Catholic officers, augmented by troops raised by the Irish Catholic gentry from among their tenants, and supported significantly by the military personnel and munitions supplied by Louis XIV. The opposing army of King William was composed of English, Scottish, and Irish Protestant officers and men who had joined William's continental force of Dutch, French-Huguenot, and Danish officers and men, together with smaller representations from other parties to the League of Augsburg. The outcome, as is well known, was an ignominious defeat for the Jacobite army in two battles—the Boyne and Aughrim—and the eventual negotiation of terms by those who remained in arms after a sequence of sieges at Athlone, Galway, and Limerick. The principal concession was that the Jacobite soldiers still in arms, together with their French allies, could withdraw from Ireland to join a continental army of their choosing. As many as 19 000 took advantage of this opportunity in what became known romantically in Catholic nationalist historiography as the Flight of the Wild Geese.[20]

The departure of the Wild Geese made it possible for the followers of William and Mary in Ireland to make the country more secure for the Protestant interest. While the various legal and military stratagems they pursued certainly achieved that objective, they fell short of eliminating Catholicism, which persisted as the religion of the majority population. Whether this shortfall can be attributed to a lack of resolution on the part of those in authority in Britain and in Ireland or to the exceptional resilience of Irish Catholicism is a debate that is unlikely to be resolved. However, the survival of Catholicism in Ireland certainly owed a great deal to the support that it obtained from the European continent in its hour of greatest need.

Many of the soldiers who opted for European service in 1691, like the Huguenots who left France in 1685, departed their ancestral homes expecting to return when political circumstances turned in their favour.[21] In the Irish Catholic case, the hope was that the French army, which soon employed as many as seven Irish regiments, would prevail over King William and his supporters in Europe. This expectation was disappointed, and after the death in 1714 of Queen Anne (the last reigning Stuart monarch), the dream of return became linked to the hopes of restoring a Stuart pretender to displace the Hanoverian princes who had succeeded to the British throne. However, after 1746 and the destruction at Culloden of the Scottish Jacobite army that had actually attempted to bring the Stuart pretender to the throne, even this hope was forlorn, and the descendants of most of those who had gone into exile came to accept that their future would be on the continent.

It transpired that British forces on the continent did not suffer any major defeat between the 1690s and 1763, but even if the British had been defeated, it is unlikely that the army of France (as had been proven in the case of Spain at the outset of the seventeenth century) would have had an interest in any further direct involvement in Ireland. In effect, European powers who took an interest in Irish affairs to the point of providing, or sponsoring, military aid to combatants, were concerned primarily to further their own larger ambitions. Thus, King Philip III of Spain in the interlude 1598–1602 and Louis XIV of France during the years 1689–91 were interested primarily in dispersing the military prowess of their opponents, and invested in Irish adventures principally in the hope that this would divert the English/British monarchy from military engagement on the continent.[22] Even the papacy which, by its standards, invested heavily in Ireland when the Catholic Confederacy was dominant there, and appointed Gian Battista Rinuccini as Nuncio to the Confederacy (1645–9), was more interested in recovering Britain for the Catholic fold than in upholding Catholicism in Ireland. Moreover, in the course of his negotiations in Ireland, Rinuccini was always concerned lest any settlement there would compromise the position for Catholicism within a divided Europe which was being simultaneously negotiated in the lead-up to the Peace of Westphalia of 1648.[23] A second factor, not always appreciated by historians of Ireland, is that no European power ever contemplated establishing itself in Ireland as a preliminary to invading England, if for no other reason than this would have been a strategic nonsense. The idea of holding Ireland as a protectorate, and having Britain encircled by hostile powers, was attractive to some continental rulers at particular moments, but anyone planning an English invasion would, as with Spain in 1588, have attempted it directly from a power base on the continent rather than from a tenuous toehold in Ireland.

Such realities explain why the so-called Flight of the Wild Geese, unlike the departure of royalists from Ireland at the end of the 1640s, led to permanent rather than temporary exile. In this respect, the romantically named Wild Geese were more like the post-Kinsale exiles, and they were to respond to their host communities much as this earlier group had done. Also, like those earlier exiles, they continued to interact with their communities and kin at home long after they had departed Ireland.

III. The Human Dimension

The first sizeable group of exiles from Ireland, initially from Munster and somewhat later from Ulster, departed in the aftermath of defeat in the Nine Years' War, and headed, for the most part, to Spain and Flanders.[24] A significant number of poorer exiles also found their way to France, especially Brittany,[25] while Hugh O'Neill, earl of Tyrone, the prime leader of the insurrection, lived out his exile in Rome as a pensioner of the King of Spain. The next significant exit of refugees were those royalists who left Ireland towards the close of the 1640s, who were to spend most of their time abroad in France, the Netherlands, Spain, and Flanders before many of them returned to Ireland after 1660.[26] These were soon to be followed to the continent by the survivors of those—mostly Ulster Irish—who persisted in arms to fight the Cromwellian forces to the bitter end. After their defeat and surrender, these were conveyed by ships of the victorious Cromwellian army to Spain where they entered the service of the Spanish monarchy and fought on its behalf, mostly in Portugal.[27] And the Wild Geese, as was to be expected, took refuge in France with smaller numbers resorting to various parts of the Austrian empire and eventually even to Russia.[28]

The stimulus for each major departure from Ireland to the continent was defeat in battle, and by far the largest number of emigrants on each occasion comprised soldiers and their officers. These were as anxious to seek military service abroad as were the victorious British to rid Ireland of fighting men. The desire of the government to restore ordered conditions to the country explains why, on each occasion, they permitted, or even conveyed, Irish soldiers to serve with Britain's continental enemies. Each major outflow also involved the exodus of dependants who sometimes travelled in the wake of the departing soldiers, and also the departure from Ireland of many of the poor whose livelihoods in Ireland had been destroyed by war. Another category to leave Ireland on each occasion of major migration was composed of professionals. These included gentlemen who had been officers in the defeated armies hoping to receive commissions in continental armies; Catholic clergy (ranging from bishops and priests to nuns and brothers) sometimes fleeing for their lives, but determined to live out their vocations abroad until they might return home; members of Gaelic learned families (particularly conspicuous in the first great migration) whose support base in Ireland had vanished with the death, or departure for Europe, of their former patrons; and finally merchants (especially numerous in the departures of the mid seventeenth century) whose property and opportunity to trade had been taken from them by the new dominant group in Ireland.[29]

Of those who departed, information is most readily available on the professionals, and it is clear that, whenever these succeeded in establishing careers in their adopted countries, they fostered further migration from Ireland either to support family members and former dependants at home, or, as in the case of officers and clergy, because fresh recruits were necessary to sustain their respective missions. Thus, while the moments of major exits from Ireland to the continent are readily identifiable, these, in turn, stimulated migration flows from Ireland to the continent during the interludes of peace. Follow-on migration of this kind persisted to the 1740s or beyond. Given the uncertainty of data for the early modern centuries, it is impossible to state precisely how many from Ireland went into exile abroad during our period, but it can hardly have been less than a gross figure of 200 000 (ignoring Irish migration to Britain, but not to the

Americas) when the total population of the country fluctuated between 1 and 2.5 million inhabitants.

Until relatively recently, scholarly writing on the Irish (and the descendants of the Irish) on the continent has given attention to the clergy who contributed to the preservation of Catholicism in Ireland, and to those of them who achieved scholastic reputations in the countries of their adoption; to the officers who rose to positions of high command in various military services, or to those such as Alejandro O'Reilly or Bernardo O'Higgins who gained fame in European adventures overseas, particularly in central and South America; to the merchants who established wine, sherry, and brandy houses, some of which survive to the present day; and to the very few, most famously Ricardo Wall, who gained prominence as civil administrators in governments in Europe and in European dominions overseas. Such narrations of achievement were especially important to Catholic/Nationalist grand narratives composed in the nineteenth and twentieth centuries, to sustain the argument that Ireland would have enjoyed an altogether higher standing among the nations of Europe if only circumstances had enabled Irish people (or at least Irish Catholic people) to give of their talents for the improvement of their own country.[30]

While one can sympathize with this perspective, it tells us little about the migrations themselves and recent scholarship has made it clear that the seventeenth-century exodus from Ireland, like all largely forced migrations, was a harsh, inelegant business. This scholarship has alluded to migrants drawn from the ranks of the poor and destitute in Ireland, including women, children, and elderly people, who either fell by the wayside or, after perhaps two decades in penury, won a reluctant acceptance in their host societies by studiously conforming to their norms in religious and social comportment. Attention is also being drawn to the harsh, impecunious, frequently short, and forgotten lives of the soldier migrants who numerically constituted the most significant component within the continental migration in each generation.[31] We now also understand something of the menial positions that fell to many of the clerical migrants who served as army chaplains, as priests on vessels trading with the East Indies, as missionaries in the Caribbean, as dogmatic upholders of orthodoxies in European seminaries and universities—at a time when such institutions were looked upon with disdain by proponents of enlightened ideas—and as ill-paid understudies to well-beneficed continental prelates of high social standing who assigned them responsibility to execute the spiritual duties to which they themselves could not attend because of their involvement with civic or state affairs.[32] It is also becoming clear that continental emigrants who succeeded in business were more often involved with the slave trade than with the brandy trade, and that the majority made their way as privateers or pirates, or acted as smugglers and freebooters using their linguistic talents (and claims to multiple nationalities) to good effect in negotiating between the various trading empires of the Atlantic and particularly in the Caribbean where there were Irish communities settled on islands dominated by Britain, France, Spain, and Denmark.[33] It is now also increasingly clear that while the vast majority of exiles can be associated with France, Spain, and Flanders, some adventured as far afield as the Baltic countries and Russia.[34] Besides advancing such additions and correctives to received wisdom, this recent scholarship also shows that success was reliant upon the acquisition of patrons as well as upon the mutual-help networks that the migrants themselves created.

Those who found patrons most readily were clerical exiles and people of high social rank. Once they arrived at their destinations, these tended to make the case that they had lost their fortunes in Ireland either because of the principled stand they had taken on behalf of Catholicism or because they had supported the interests of the monarch in whose kingdom they now sought refuge. Petitioners for support glossed over the fact that they had been fighting primarily to secure, or recover, their lands and power in Ireland. Exiles of high social rank were always few in number and, depending on age and experience, were usually paid off with a pension, or a military commission, or by being placed in command of a regiment; some were even granted a title of nobility that would have currency in the host community.[35] Those of them who sought access to the royal court in the host country were usually denied that privilege and had to negotiate their causes through noblemen or clergy who were sympathetic to their plight and who had good connections at court. Irish supplicants were usually chastened to discover that there were strict limits to the largesse dispensed by any ruler, and that their petitions had to compete with similar requests from others of their countrymen or from other foreigners, or with solicitations from those at the upper reaches of the host society itself. Under these circumstances those who were anxious and able for military service found that advancement in the ranks came most readily to those who volunteered for, and survived, service in war zones or in overseas territories where mortality rates were high.[36]

Clerical exiles secured their most steadfast support from influential members of the church in the host society, with whom contact had usually been established by earlier Irish priestly exiles.[37] Such patronage could deliver individual appointments within the church, or access to educational institutions, while the most coveted concession—the sanction and support to establish an Irish college or residence—required royal and sometimes papal approval, as well as financial backing. Such support was secured with dramatic rapidity and in each generation resulted in a chain of continental Irish colleges stretching from Spain, Portugal, and Flanders, to France, Rome, and Prague.[38] The multiplication of Irish college foundations, particularly in Spain, sometimes resulted from rivalries between religious orders (and particularly between the Franciscans and Jesuits), but we also note that each was located either in a place associated with the Habsburg effort to advance its dynastic ambitions and suppress Protestantism in Europe, or with those parts of France where the Catholic League had been influential. The ambition of each founder was to create a place of refuge and training for incoming clerics and seminarians from Ireland, and to establish a training programme that would equip clergy to resume missionary activity in Ireland at an opportune moment. And when return eluded those trained in seminaries, they became part of an Irish intellectual community in exile working to uphold papal orthodoxies against succeeding challenges, just as Protestant religious exiles from Bohemia or France pronounced in favour of a Protestant international to oppose the tyranny of Rome. Then, when some clergy did manage to return to Ireland, those in the colleges supported their work of evangelization from a distance, even to the extent of translating into Irish and English from a variety of European languages, and adapting, for use in Ireland, several of the catechisms and spiritual texts that had been found appropriate for evangelization by Counter Reformation clergy in various parts of Europe. Once established, colleges also provided an orientation for Irish lay students wishing to attend secular courses in the universities with which the colleges were affiliated, as well as for recent arrivals intent on taking up positions as junior officers in Irish regiments.[39] More generally, the Irish colleges also supplied material and spiritual help for the poor and destitute, and supplied information and even financial services for a community that became dispersed as vocational opportunities presented themselves across Europe. The colleges also boosted the morale of the Irish Catholic community, whether in Ireland or in exile, by promoting pseudo-historical writing on Ireland's recent and antique past which insisted that the traditional inhabitants of Ireland, whether of Gaelic or Anglo-Norman ancestry, had been exemplary Catholics and that those Irish of recent times who had suffered loss of life or property for religion's sake were following in a well-established tradition.[40]

This description may be thought to summarize activities at St Anthony's College in Leuven, chartered in 1606, which was one of the more dynamic of the early colleges and that most dedicated to using the Irish language in print to promote its mission. However, each passing group of missionaries was convinced that theirs was the generation that had suffered most for the faith, and we find that John Lynch, the author of *Cambrensis Eversus* in 1662, was no less concerned than Seathrún Céitinn (Geoffrey Keating) in the 1630s to counter the malign view of the Gaelic Irish population being spread by their Protestant critics who still cited the twelfth-century author, Giraldus Cambrensis, as the prime authority on the depravity of the Irish.[41] While the colleges certainly cultivated a sense of community among the Irish abroad, and sustained links with the Irish at home, so also did the emerging clusters of Irish merchants in the western port towns of the European continent ranging from Dunkirk to Cadiz, and also the officers in charge of the Irish regiments initially in the Spanish army but subsequently also in that of France.

Commanders of the Irish regiments, as was previously mentioned, sustained contact with Catholic Ireland if for no other reason than officers without soldiers in the ranks lacked credibility with potential employers. Therefore, the continued existence of Irish regiments on the continent meant that agents were employed in Ireland to enlist recruits. Such recruitment, sometimes with the approval of the Dublin government and sometimes conducted against official orders, was most active during periods of intense warfare in Europe when soldiers were at a premium, and ensured that a steady outflow of migrants to the continent persisted even during peacetime in Ireland. Enlistment in continental armies thus provided a continuing source of employment (however ill-paid it might have been) to the Irish Catholic male poor, which tapered off only after 1713 when the wars of Louis XIV finally concluded. Even as soldier recruitment eased, the French government countenanced Irish regiments commanded by Irish officers but with few Irish men in the ranks. This meant that opportunities to become officers in continental armies continued to be available to the younger sons of surviving Catholic landed families in Ireland, and these were particularly cherished by the minor Catholic gentry families in the west and the south of the country. This is one reason why familial connections at this level were sustained across distance and across generations. Service in the army was also of interest to members of the Irish merchant community in exile, if for no other reason than that some officers who survived service and accumulated savings invested in a business partnership (frequently with Irish traders or producers) and thus established a permanent stake in the host society.[42]

Such examples were exceptional since most Irish merchant families on the continent, and throughout the Atlantic world, came from previous backgrounds in trade. Attention has already been drawn to resident Irish traders who established themselves essentially as factors in continental Atlantic ports with which Irish towns had traditionally conducted business. Such ports also became places of refuge for Irish merchant families whose trading activity was threatened or closed down by a hostile government, as particularly happened in Galway, Waterford, and Wexford when the Cromwellian regime sought to sever Irish Catholic contact with the continent. Sometimes the dispersed trading families re-constituted themselves in foreign locations stretching from London, the Canary Islands, and Antwerp, to French west-facing ports and Cadiz. Their presence became increasingly evident in Nantes and Bordeaux as well as in Cadiz and the Canaries, which locations, as the eighteenth century proceeded, became increasingly involved in burgeoning Atlantic trade.[43] Merchants, like the officers, who proved themselves successful, maintained contact with family members in Ireland and in other European locations, and were regularly called upon to place Irish-born relatives in employment. Members of what were now dispersed merchant families also sometimes pooled their resources to recover some of their former family property in Ireland that had fallen into Protestant hands.

Merchants also made their identification with the wider Irish community evident by supporting particular Irish colleges. For example, the rise of the college at Nantes from obscure beginnings to becoming the second most important Irish college in France (after that in Paris), and its subsequent rapid decline, can be related to the rise of the Irish merchant community in Nantes and the later transfer of interest by some of its members to Bordeaux, and lesser cities further south along the French coast, in pursuit of better commercial opportunity. The prosperity of the community in eighteenth-century Nantes resulted principally from involvement of its members with the slave, sugar, and other Atlantic trades, at the point when Nantes was the most dynamic French (and indeed European) port in those domains.[44] There is evidence in the archives in Nantes that slave traders in that city fell into two categories: those who were freemasons and those who were of Irish descent. This suggests that Irish Catholic merchants could operate independently of freemasonry because they had access to a ready-made international support network of their own devising located in European ports, along the coast of Africa, in the Caribbean, and in Colonial British America. But while Catholicism was as important to the merchants as it was to any other element of the Irish community abroad, they did not allow religion to stand in the way of promoting business. Thus, as was previously mentioned, Irish Catholic traders frequently had contacts with, and even established partnerships with, Protestant (including British and Irish Protestant) business people in London, in the islands of the West Indies, and in the ports of British North America.[45] Moreover, successful Irish traders and planters in the Atlantic sometimes sent their sons to be educated in continental colleges with English Catholic rather than Irish Catholic associations.[46] Also, a few Irish families (notably the Bartons) who succeeded in business in eighteenth-century France were Protestant from the outset.

This brief conspectus suggests that one golden age of an Irish community on continental Europe was from the early seventeenth to the mid-eighteenth century. Quite clearly it was British military success in the wars in Ireland, linked to associated plantations and discriminatory laws and practices that provoked a disproportionate exodus of Irish Catholics to the continent, and it may be more than coincidental that the tapering off in migration to the continent occurred when overt disempowerment of Catholics in Ireland began to ease. There are, however, other factors which explain the reduction of Irish Catholic interest in the continent as a place in which to pursue a career. The first was the sharp decline in the demand for soldiers in the armies of Western Europe after 1713 when conditions became more peaceful. While nominal Irish regiments commanded by Irish officers persisted in the French army, they were perceived as increasingly anomalous, until even the final two Irish regiments were disbanded when the French revolutionary army displaced the French royal army. At the same time, any Catholics in Ireland wishing to pursue a career in military service had increasing opportunities open to them in the British navy, or even openly in the British army after 1792 when the ban on Irish Catholics serving in British forces was formally lifted due to the government's desperate need for troops to send against the French revolutionary armies. Alternative career opportunities were also available to potential Irish emigrants in the increasingly prosperous British colonies of mainland North America, and transport from all major ports of Ireland to Philadelphia and New York became readily available.[47] There were also greater employment opportunities in Ireland itself as its economy expanded steadily from the 1740s forward to the later eighteenth century, while a growing economy in Britain created an increased demand for Irish labour.

The drop-off in the number of soldier emigrants, with their dependants, meant that the size of the Irish-born community on the continent shrank rapidly, thus also curtailing the demand for priests to meet the pastoral needs of a resident community. The number of Irish colleges on the continent decreased correspondingly, but their primary function remained constant so long as it was not possible to train priests in Ireland, either because it was forbidden by law or because there were no facilities available. Both of these constraints were removed in 1795 when the Royal College of St. Patrick was established at Maynooth with the sanction of, and a grant from, the British government as a seminary to train priests to meet the spiritual needs of Catholic Ireland. Most of those who took up professorial positions in Maynooth had themselves been trained in Irish colleges abroad which meant that continental Europe continued to exert an indirect intellectual influence on Catholic Ireland for one further generation. However, this happened when traditional institutions in France, and much of Europe, were being cast down by the forces of the French Revolution, a movement that may have been hailed as a liberating force by Irish radicals but not so by Irish Catholic leaders who were quick to realize that the Revolution was destroying the organizations that had sustained many of themselves and their families for most of two centuries.

IV. Conclusion

Now that our story has come full circle, it remains to assess the historical significance of Ireland's relations with continental Europe, 1600–1750. In practical terms, the continent provided a place of refuge and opportunity for tens of thousands of Irish Catholics (and some Protestants) just as Ireland became a home for a significant number of Protestant refugees from the continent. The scale of Irish emigration to the continent and to European territories in the Atlantic world, relative to the size of the Irish population, means that Ireland at this time was suffering a loss of its population—particularly its adult male population—greater in percentage terms than that experienced by most countries in Europe (other than Portugal and Scotland). What renders the Irish experience unique in the history of migrations is that the number of Catholics who left Ireland was matched by the number of Protestants welcomed into the country, including some from continental Europe. The composition of the Protestant population in Ireland, added to their knowledge of continental affairs, made them keenly conscious of the need for Protestants everywhere, regardless of denomination, to stand guard against a relentless persecuting foe. Their attitude was matched on the Catholic side where it was widely accepted that Irish Catholics, having suffered uniquely for their faith, were certain to be rewarded ultimately by a providential recovery of what had been taken from them unjustly. The co-existence in Ireland of these clearly irreconcilable political aspirations rendered the governance of the country more complex, most particularly because there were actors on either side throughout the period 1600–1750 who believed that an Irish presence on the continent increased the possibility of foreign intervention in domestic politics.

The other unique consequence of the continental relationship was that it made it possible for Catholic Ireland to maintain a Catholic priesthood by having clerics trained and ordained on the continent at a time when the maintenance of seminaries and bishops in Ireland was prohibited by law. The survival of Catholicism as the majority religion in Ireland owed much to the pastoral endeavours of those who returned as bishops, priests, and members of religious orders, but they, in turn, would have had difficulty in functioning in Ireland without the support of Catholic merchant and landed families whose survival, as was noted, also owed much to continental contacts and opportunities. Both parties to this survival-against-the-odds were conscious that their achievement was exceptional, and they were deeply impressed by the version of Ireland's historical past, and of the role attributed to Catholicism in the formation of an Irish Catholic nation, that had been formulated and propagated within the seminaries on the continent. There was every reason why memories of the continental experience, and of the persecution that had necessitated it, came to be cherished by Irish priest historians, and by lay nationalist historians, of the nineteenth and twentieth centuries. This too may explain why the counter grand narrative of Ireland's past favoured by their Protestant counterparts took the continental experience of their ancestors into account: firstly to explain that Irish Protestants were cosmopolitan survivors from several persecutions; and secondly, to reiterate how they and their ancestors had served willingly as officers and men in successive continental and extra-European campaigns to uphold the interests of Protestantism and the British monarchy.

Notes

1. For example, Hugh Kearney, *The British Isles: a History of Four Nations* (Cambridge, 2nd edition 2006).
2. On the lion gift, see Gomes Eanes de Zurara, *Crónica dos Feitos de Guiné* vol., 2 Texto (Lisbon, Agência Geral das Colónias, 1959), 410; for evidence on Donquan, see Mary Ann Lyons, 'The Emergence of an Irish Community in Saint-Malo, 1550–1710', in Thomas O'Connor (ed), *The Irish in Europe, 1580–1815* (Dublin, 2001), 110.
3. Brendan Bradshaw, *The Dissolution of the Religious Orders in Ireland under Henry VIII* (Cambridge, 1974), 208–14. Colmàn Ò Clabaigh OSB, *The Friars in Ireland 1224–1540* (Dublin, 2012), especially 326-9.
4. J.J. Silke, 'The Irish appeal of 1593 to Spain; some light on the genesis of the Nine Years War', *Irish Ecclesiastical Record*, 92 (1959), 279–90, 362–71; Silke, *Ireland and Europe, 1559–1607* (Dundalk, 1966); Hiram Morgan, *Tyrone's Rebellion: the Outbreak of the Nine Years War in Tudor Ireland* (Woodbridge, 1993), 139–66; Declan M. Downey, 'Irish-European Integration; the legacy of Charles V', in Judith Devlin and Howard Clarke (eds), *European Encounters; Essays in Memory of Albert Lovett* (Dublin, 2003), 97–117; Colm Lennon, 'Political Thought of Irish Counter-Reformation churchmen: the testimony of the "Analecta" of Bishop David Rothe', in Hiram Morgan (ed), *Political Ideology in Ireland, 1541–1641* (Dublin, 1999), 181–202.
5. Nicholas Canny, *Making Ireland British, 1580–1650* (Oxford, 2001), 1–167.
6. J.J. Silke, *The Spanish Intervention in Ireland at the End of the Elizabethan Wars* (Liverpool, 1970); Hiram Morgan (ed), *The Battle of Kinsale*, (Bray, 2004); Ciaran O'Scea, 'The significance and legacy of Spanish intervention in west Munster during the battle of Kinsale', in Thomas O'Connor and Mary Ann Lyons (eds), *Irish Migrants in Europe after Kinsale, 1602-1820* (Dublin, 2003), 32–63; Karin Schüller, 'Irish migrant networks and rivalries in Spain', in O'Connor and Lyons, *Irish Migrants*, 88–103; Éamon Ó Ciosáin, 'A hundred years of Irish migration to France, 1590–1688', in O'Connor, *Irish in Europe*, 93–106; Óscar Recio Morales, *España y la pérdida del Ulster: Irlanda en la estrategia política de la monarquía hispánica, 1602–1649* (Madrid, 2003); Óscar Recio Morales (ed), *Redes de nación y espacios de poder: La comunidad Irlandesa en España y la América Española; Power Strategies Spain and Ireland, 1600–1825* (Valencia, 2012).
7. Canny, *Making Ireland British*, 165–242.
8. Breandán Ó Buachalla, *Aisling Ghéar, na Stíobhartaigh agus an tAos Léinn* (Dublin, 1966); Eamonn Ó Ciardha, *Ireland and the Jacobite Cause, 1685–1766: a fatal attachment* (Dublin, 2002).
9. Jerrold Casway, *Owen Roe O'Neill and the Struggle for Catholic Ireland* (Philadelphia, 1984).

10. Jane Ohlmeyer, 'Seventeenth-century Ireland and Scotland and their wider worlds' in Thomas O'Connor and Mary Ann Lyons (eds), *Irish Communities in Early-Modern Europe* (Dublin, 2006), 457–84.

11. Nicholas Canny, *The Upstart Earl; A Study of the Social and Mental World of Richard Boyle, first Earl of Cork, 1566–1643* (Cambridge, 1982), for that earl's interest in the Grand Tour, 71, 96, 99, 105; and in European politics, 29, 163, n. 38.

12. Elizabethann Boran (ed), *The Correspondence of James Ussher, 1600–1656* (Dublin, 2015); Alan Ford, *James Ussher: Theology, History and Politics in Early Modern Ireland and England* (Oxford, 2007).

13. Gerard Boate, *Ireland's Naturall History* (London, 1652), reprinted in *A Collection of Tracts and Treatises Illustrative of the Natural History, Antiquities...of Irelan*d (Dublin, 1860), 1–148; Hartlib's dedication, 3–7.

14. Ted McCormick, *William Petty and the Ambitions of Political Arithmetic* (Oxford, 2009).

15. John Cronin, 'The Irish Royalist Elite of Charles II in exile, *c.* 1649–1660', (PhD thesis, EUI, Florence, 2007).

16. Coleman A. Dennehy (ed), *Restoration Ireland: always settling and never settled* (Aldershot, 2008); Jane Ohlmeyer, *Making Ireland English: The Irish Aristocracy in the Seventeenth Century* (New Haven, CT., 2012), 301–36.

17. Jane Fenlon, 'Episodes of Magnificence: the material worlds of the Dukes Of Ormonde', in Toby Barnard and Jane Fenlon (eds), *The Dukes of Ormonde, 1610–1745* (Woodbridge, 2000), 137–60.

18. C.E.J. Caldicott, H. Gough, and Jean-Paul Pittion (eds), *The Huguenots and Ireland: Anatomy of an Emigration* (Dun Laoghaire, 1987); Raymond Hylton, *Ireland's Huguenots and Their Refuge: an Unlikely Haven* (Brighton, 2005); V. Hick, 'The Palatine settlement in Ireland: the early years', *Eighteenth-century Ireland: Iris an dá chultúr*, 4 (1989), 113–32; Vivien Hick, 'Palatine settlement in Ireland' (PhD thesis, UCD, 1994).

19. J.G. Simms, *Jacobite Ireland, 1685–91* (London, 1969); Pádraig Lenihan, *1690: Battle of the Boyne* (Stroud, 2003); Lenihan, 'The impact of the battle of Aughrim (1691) on the Irish Catholic elite', in Brian Mac Cuarta (ed), *Reshaping Ireland, 1550–1700: Colonization and its Consequences; Essays Presented to Nicholas Canny* (Dublin, 2011), 300–25.

20. Nathalie Genet Rouffiac, 'The Irish Jacobite Exile in France', in Barnard and Fenlon, *Dukes of Ormonde*, 195–210; Colm James Ó Conaill, 'The Irish Regiments in France: an overview of the presence of Irish soldiers in French Service, 1716–91', in Eamon Maher and Grace Neville (eds), *France-Ireland: Anatomy of a Relationship* (Frankfurt am Main, 2004), 327–42.

21. Susanne Lachenicht 'Huguenot Immigrants and the Formation of National Identities', in *Historical Journal*, 50 (2007), 309–31.

22. Enrique García Hernán, 'Philip II's forgotten Armada', in Morgan (ed), *Kinsale*, 45–58.

23. Tadhg Ó hAnnracháin, *Catholic Reformation in Ireland: The Mission of Rinuccini, 1645–1649* (Oxford, 2002).

24. Ciaran O'Scea, 'In Search of Honour and A Catholic Monarchy: the assimilation and integration of an Irish minority in early modern Castile', (PhD thesis, EUI, Florence, 2007); O'Scea, 'Irish emigration to Spain and its dominions; from resistance to integration', in *Los Irlandeses y la Monarquía Hispánica (1529–1800): Vínculos en espacio y tiempo* (Simancas, 2012), 51–60; María Begoña Villar García, 'Irish migration and exiles in Spain: refugees, soldiers, traders and statesmen', in O'Connor and Lyons, *Irish Communities*, 172–99; Óscar

Recio Morales, 'Irish émigré group strategies of survival, adaptation and integration in seventeenth- and eighteenth-century Spain', in O'Connor and Lyons, *Irish Communities*, 240–66; Karin Schüller, 'Irish migrant networks and rivalries in Spain, 1575–1659' in O'Connor and Lyons, *Irish Migrants*, 88–103; Gráinne Henry, *The Irish Military Community in Spanish Flanders, 1586–1621* (Dublin, 1992); Clare Carroll, 'Irish and Spanish cultural and political relations in the work of O'Sullivan Beare', in Hiram Morgan (ed), *Political Ideology in Ireland*, 229–53; Thomas O'Connor and Mary Ann Lyons, eds., *The Ulster Earls and Baroque Europe* (Dublin, 2010); Igor Pérez Tostado and Enrique García Hernán (eds), *Irlanda el Atlántico Ibérico: movilidad, participación e intercambio cultural, 1580–1823* (Valencia, 2010); Óscar Recio Morales, *Ireland and the Spanish Empire, 1600–1825* (Dublin, 2010); Igor Pérez Tostado, *Irish Influence at the Court of Spain in the Seventeenth Century* (Dublin, 2008); R.A. Stradling, *The Spanish Monarchy and Irish Mercenaries; The Wild Geese in Spain, 1618–68* (Dublin, 1994)

25. Mary Ann Lyons, *Franco-Irish Relations, 1500–1610: Politics, Migration and Trade* (Woodbridge, 2003); Éamon Ó Ciosáin, 'A hundred years of Irish migration to France, 1590–1688', in O'Connor, *Irish in Europe*, 93–106; Alain le Noac'h and Éamon Ó Ciosáin (eds), *Immigrés Irlandais au xviie siècle en Bretagne* (2 vols., Rennes, 2009).

26. Cronin, 'The Irish Royalist Elite of Charles II in exile, c. 1649–1660'; John Cronin, 'Representing exiled royalists to the Spanish: the Irish courtiers of the exiled Caroline Stuart Court and the Spanish Alliance of 1656–1660' in Pérez Tostado and García Hernán (eds), *Irlanda el Atlántico Ibérica*, 165–76; Phillip Williams, The Irish in the Spanish Royal Armada, 1650–1670; Community and Solidarity in the Irish tercio', in Óscar Recio Morales (ed), *Redes de nación*, 171–82.

27. Stradling, *The Spanish Monarchy and Irish Mercenaries*.

28. Nathalie Genet Rouffiac, 'The Irish Jacobite Exile in France'; Colm James Ó Conaill, 'The Irish Regiments in France'; *Die wildgänse: The Wild Geese: Irische soldaten im dienst der Habsburger* (Vienna, Heeresgeschichtliches Museum, 2003); Declan M. Downey, 'Whether Habsburgs or Bourbons: some reflections on the alignments of nobles of Irish origin in the War of the Spanish Succession, 1713–23', in Pérez Tostado and García Hernán (eds), *Irlanda el Atlático Ibérica*, 243–52.

29. L.M. Cullen, 'The Irish Diaspora of the Seventeenth and the Eighteenth Centuries', in Nicholas Canny (ed), *Europeans on the Move; Studies on European Migration, 1500–1800* (Oxford, 1994), 113–52; Cullen, 'Galway merchants in the Outside World, 1650–1800', in Diarmuid Ó Cearbhaill (ed), *Galway: Town and Gown, 1484–1984* (Dublin, 1984), 63–89; Cullen, 'The Irish merchant communities of Bordeux, La Rochelle and Cognac in the eighteenth century', in P. Butel and L.M Cullen (eds), *Négoce et industrie en France et en Irlande aux xviii et xix siècles* (Paris, 1980); David Dickson, Jan Parmentier and Jane Ohlmeyer (eds), *Irish and Scottish Mercantile Networks in Europe and Overseas in the Seventeenth and Eighteenth Centuries* (Gent, 2007); Carmen Lario de Oñate, 'Irish integration in eighteenth century maritime mercantile city of Cadiz', in Óscar Recio Morales (ed), *Redes de nación y espacios de poder*, 183–90.

30. For an example of this older literature exuding pride in Irish achievement in foreign service, see Christopher Duffy, *The Wild Goose and the Eagle; a Life of Marshal von Browne* (London, 1964); the most effective nineteenth-century Catholic exponent of the contribution made by clerical exiles to the survival of Irish Catholicism was the Rev. P.F. Moran, nephew of Cardinal Paul Cullen, who researched and published from the Irish college in Rome before becoming Bishop of Ossory and later Cardinal Archbishop of Sydney.

31. It is now possible to trace the careers of Irish soldiers (and soon also sailors) in continental service in the data base being compiled jointly by research teams at NUI Maynooth and Trinity College, Dublin, in cooperation with colleagues in Spain http://irishineurope.ie/vre/search/index.

32. For examples, see Jason McHugh, ' "Soldier of Christ": The Political and Ecclesiastical Career of Nicholas French, Catholic Bishop of Ferns (1603–78)'(PhD thesis NUI Galway, 2005); Liam Chambers, *Michael Moore, c 1639–1726: Provost of Trinity, Rector of Paris* (Dublin, 2005).

33. See, for example, Orla Power, 'Irish Planters and Atlantic Merchants at St.Croix, Danish West Indies' (PhD thesis NUI Galway, 2011); Thomas M. Truxes, 'Irish interloping trade and colonial warfare in the 18th century', in Pérez Tostado and García Hernán (eds), *Irlanda el Atlántico Ibérico.* 59–68; the various essays in Dickson, Parmentier and Ohlmeyer (eds), *Irish and Scottish Mercantile Networks in Europe and Overseas.*

34. Steve Murdoch, 'Irish entrepreneurs and Sweden in the first half of the eighteenth century', and Jan Parmentier, 'The Ray dynasty: Irish mercantile empire builders in Ostend, 1690–1790' each in O'Connor and Lyons, *Irish Communities,* 348–66, and 367–82.

35. Downey, 'Whether Habsburgs or Bourbons'.

36. Igor Pérez Tostado, ' "Mártires de profesión": estudio de caso de los conflictos de las comunidades inglesa e irlandesa en la Andalucía a finales del XVII', in Villar Garcia and Pezzi Cristobal (eds), *I Coloquio Internacional 'Los Extranjeros en la Espana Moderna'* (Madrid, 2003), 645–55; Igor Pérez Tostado, *Irish Influence at the Court of Spain,* 118–33; Óscar Recio Morales, *Ireland and the Spanish Empire,* 48–166.

37. Enrique García Hernán, 'Irish clerics in Madrid, 1598–1665', in O'Connor and Lyons, *Irish Communities,* 267–93; Igor Pérez Tostado, *Irish Influence at the Court of Spain,* 88–117; Benjamin Hazard, *Faith and Patronage: The Political Career of Flaithrí Ó Maolchonaire, c. 1560–1629* (Dublin, 2010).

38. Patricia O'Connell, 'The early-modern Irish college network in Iberia, 1590–1800', in O'Connor, *Irish in Europe,* 49–64; Enrique García Hernán, 'The Irish College at Valencia (1623–1680): historical consequences', Benjamin Hazard, 'Saint Isador's Franciscan College, Rome: From centre of influence to site of memory', Linda Kiernan, 'Cloister and community; A comparative view of the roles of Irish women in the convents of early modern Flanders, France, Spain and Portugal' each in Óscar Recio Morales (ed), *Redes de nación y espacios de poder,* 93–102, 103–16, 221–34.

39. Patrick Ferte, 'Étudiants et professeurs irlandais dans les universités de Toulouse et de Cahors (XVIIe-XVIII siècles): les limites de la mission irlandaise', in O'Connor and Lyons, *Irish Communities,* 69–84; Joeroen Nilis, *Irish Students at Leuven University, 1548–1797* ((Leuven, 2010); Brian Mac Cuarta, *Catholic Revival in the North of Ireland, 1603–41* (Dublin, 2007), 149–58.

40. Mícheál Mac Craith, 'The political and religious thought of Florence Conry and Hugh McCaughwell' in Alan Ford and John McCafferty, *The Origins of Sectarianism in Early Modern Ireland* (Cambridge, 2005), 183–202; Edel Bhreatnach and Bernadette Cunningham (eds), *Writing Irish History: The Four Masters and their World* (Dublin, 2007); Bernadette Cunningham, *The Annals of the Four Masters: Irish History, Kingship and Society in the Early Seventeenth Century* (Dublin, 2010).

41. Bernadette Cunningham, *The World of Geoffrey Keating: History, Myth and Religion in Seventeenth-Century Ireland* (Dublin, 2000); Ian W. S. Campbell, 'Alithinologia: John Lynch and seventeenth-century Irish political thought' (PhD thesis, Trinity College Dublin,

2008); Bernadette Cunningham, 'Representations of king, parliament and the Irish people in Geoffrey Keating's *Foras Feasa ar Éirinn* and John Lynch's *Cambrensis Eversus* (1662)', in Jane H. Ohlmeyer (ed), *Political Thought in Seventeenth-Century Ireland: Kingdom or Colony* (Cambridge, 2000), 131–54.

42. L.M. Cullen, 'Apotheosis and crisis: the Irish diaspora in the age of Choiseul', and Patrick Clarke de Dromantin, 'L'insertion des réfugiés jacobites dans la société francaise du dIx-huitième siècle' each in O'Connor and Lyons, *Irish Communities*, 6–31 and 130–44; L.M. Cullen, *The Irish Brandy Houses of Eighteenth-Century France* (Dublin, 2000).

43. L.M. Cullen, *The Brandy Trade under the Ancien Régime: Regional Specialisation in the Charente* (Cambridge, 1998); Agustín Guimerá Ravina, *Burguesía extranjera y comercio atlántico: la empresa commercial irlandesa en Canarias (1703–1771)* (Santa Cruz de Tenerife, 1985); Dickson, Parmentier and Ohlmeyer (eds), *Irish and Scottish Mercantile Networks in Europe and Overseas*.

44. Guy Saupin has shown how this community was already concentrating on West Indies trade during the seventeenth century in Saupin, 'Les réseaux commerciaux des irlandais de Nantes sous le règne de Louis XIV' in Dickson, Parmentier, and Ohlmeyer (eds), *Irish and Scottish Mercantile Networks in Europe and Overseas*, 115–46.

45. Thomas M. Truxes, 'London's Irish merchant community and North American commerce in the mid-eighteenth century', in Dickson, Parmentier, and Ohlmeyer (eds), *Irish and Scottish Mercantile Networks in Europe and Overseas*, 271–310; see the essays by Craig Bailey on the Nesbitts and by L.M. Cullen on the two George Fitzgeralds of London in the same volume, 231–50 and 251–70.

46. Power, 'Irish Planters and Atlantic Merchants at St.Croix'; Ronald Hoffman, *Princes of Ireland, Planters of Maryland; A Carroll Saga, 1500–1782* (Williamsburg, 2000), 101, 143–5, 153–4; for a similar choice by an Irish Catholic family with English, French, and Portuguese associations, see Toby Barnard, 'Sir Richard Bellings: a Catholic courtier and diplomat from seventeenth-century Ireland', in Brian Mac Cuarta (ed), *Reshaping Ireland*, 326–47.

47. Marianne Wokeck, *Trade in Strangers; The Beginnings of Mass Migration to North America* (University Park, Pa., 1999); Maurice J. Bric, *Ireland, Philadelphia and the Re-invention of America, 1760–1800* (Dublin, 2008).

SELECT BIBLIOGRAPHY

Bibliographic note on Ireland in Europe

This is a subject that is still in the making, and Ireland has, as yet, no counterpart to Tom Devine, *Scotland's Empire, 1600–1815* (London 2003). The absence of such a synthetic work does not mean that interest in Ireland in the overseas endeavours of its peoples lags behind that in Scotland. The essential difference is an archival one. Scots who proved successful in foreign parts and endured their ordeal tended to retire to country houses or urban residences in Scotland or England, where they frequently left detailed records of the businesses that had contributed to their fortunes. In the case of Ireland, where most who ventured overseas were Catholic, those who prospered in exile were prohibited by the laws against Catholics from purchasing estates in Ireland to which they might retire. The result is that whatever relevant records have survived are as scattered as the migrants themselves. On the positive side, the large number of recently published conference proceedings on the Irish who made their careers abroad during these centuries, points to scholarly awareness of a neglected subject. So also does the concern in Spain, Belgium, France, Austria, as well as in Ireland, to compile databases on Irish people who served in various capacities in European host communities during the seventeenth and eighteenth centuries. The most accessible of those compiled to date is that sponsored jointly by researchers at NUI Maynooth and at Trinity College Dublin with support from colleagues in Spain. (http://irishineurope.ie/vre/search/index)

There have also been a significant number of doctoral theses completed in recent years on various dimensions of Irish service in Europe and overseas and we can look forward to publications from these scholars in the years ahead.

General Bibliography

The subject has been pioneered by L.M. Cullen, three of whose published papers provide an essential context to the subject; these are:

Cullen, L.M., 'Galway merchants in the Outside World, 1650–1800', in Diarmuid Ó Cearbhaill (ed), *Galway: Town and Gown, 1484–1984* (Dublin, 1984), 63–89.
Cullen, L.M., 'The Irish Diaspora of the Seventeenth and the Eighteenth Centuries', in Nicholas Canny (ed), *Europeans on the Move; Studies on European Migration, 1500–1800* (Oxford, 1994), 113–52.
Cullen, L.M., 'Apotheosis and crisis: the Irish diaspora in the age of Choiseul', in O'Connor and Lyons, *Irish Communities*, 6–31.

The following may also prove useful:

Canny, Nicholas (ed), *Europeans on the Move; Studies on European Migration, 1500–1800* (Oxford, 1994).
O'Connor, Thomas (ed), *The Irish in Europe, 1580–1815* (Dublin, 2001).
O'Connor, Thomas and Lyons, Mary Ann (eds), *Irish Migrants in Europe after Kinsale, 1602–1820* (Dublin, 2003).
O'Connor, Thomas and Lyons, Mary Ann (eds), *Irish Communities in Early-Modern Europe* (Dublin, 2006).
Tostado, Igor Pérez and Hernán, Enrique García (eds), *Irlanda el Atlático Ibérico: movilidad, participación e intercambio cultural, 1580–1823* (Valencia, 2010).
Morales, Óscar Recio, *Ireland and the Spanish Empire, 1600–1825* (Dublin, 2010).

Irish Political Background

Canny, Nicholas, *Making Ireland British, 1580–1650* (Oxford, 2001).
Connolly, S.J., *Religion, Law and Power: The Making of Protestant Ireland, 1660–1760* (Oxford, 1992).
Ó hAnnracháin, Tadhg, *Catholic Reformation in Ireland: The Mission of Rinuccini, 1645–1649* (Oxford, 2002).
Ohlmeyer, Jane, *Making Ireland English: The Irish Aristocracy in the Seventeenth Century* (New Haven, CT., 2012).

Spanish Political Background

Morgan, Hiram (ed), *The Battle of Kinsale*, (Bray, 2004).

Tostado, Igor Pérez, *Irish Influence at the Court of Spain in the Seventeenth Century* (Dublin, 2008).

Silke, J.J., *The Spanish Intervention in Ireland at the End of the Elizabethan Wars* (Liverpool, 1970).

The Military Dimension

Cronin, John, 'The Irish royalist elite of Charles II in exile, *c*. 1649–1660' (PhD thesis, EUI, Florence, 2007).

Henry, Gráinne, *The Irish Military Community in Spanish Flanders, 1586–1621* (Dublin, 1992)

Hick, Vivien, 'Palatine settlement in Ireland' (PhD. thesis, UCD, 1994).

Hylton, Raymond, *Ireland's Huguenots and their Refuge: an Unlikely Haven* (Brighton, 2005).

O'Scea, Ciaran, 'In Search of Honour and a Catholic Monarchy: the assimilation and integration of an Irish minority in early modern Castile' (PhD thesis, EUI, Florence, 2007).

Le Noac'h, Alain and Ó Ciosáin, Éamon (eds), *Immigrés Irlandais au xviie siècle en Bretagne* (2 vols., Rennes, 2009).

Ó Conaill, Colm James, 'The Irish Regiments in France: an overview of the presence of Irish soldiers in French Service, 1716–91', in Eamon Maher and Grace Neville (eds), *France-Ireland: Anatomy of a Relationship* (Frankfurt am Main, 2004), 327–42.

Rouffiac, Nathalie Genet, 'The Irish Jacobite Exile in France', in Toby Barnard and Jane Fenlon, *The Dukes of Ormonde, 1610–1745* (Woodbridge, 2000), 195–210.

Stradling, R.A., *The Spanish Monarchy and Irish Mercenaries; The Wild Geese in Spain, 1618–68* (Dublin, 1994).

Die Wildgänse: The Wild Geese: Irische Soldaten im dienste der Habsburger (Vienna, Heeresgeschichtliches Museum, 2003).

The Scholarly Dimension

Campbell, Ian W.S., 'Alithinologia: John Lynch and seventeenth-century Irish political thought' (PhD thesis, Trinity College, Dublin, 2008).

Chambers, Liam, *Michael Moore, c 1639–1726: Provost of Trinity, Rector of Paris* (Dublin, 2005).

Cunningham, Bernadette, *The Annals of the Four Masters: Irish History, Kingship and Society in the early seventeenth century* (Dublin, 2010).

Craith, Mícheál Mac, 'The political and religious thought of Florence Conry and Hugh McCaughwell' in Alan Ford and John McCafferty, *The Origins of Sectarianism in Early Modern Ireland* (Cambridge, 2005), 183–202.

McHugh, Jason, '"Soldier of Christ": The Political and Ecclesiastical Career of Nicholas French, Catholic Bishop of Ferns (1603–78)' (PhD thesis, NUI Galway, 2005).

Nilis, Jeroen, *Irish Students at Leuven University, 1548–1797: a Prosopography* (Leuven, 2010).

The Business Dimension

Lyons, Mary Ann, *Franco-Irish Relations, 1500–1610: Politics, Migration and Trade* (Woodbridge, 2003).

Cullen, L.M., *The Irish Brandy Houses of Eighteenth-Century France* (Dublin, 2000).

Ravina, Agustín Guimerá, *Burguesía extranjera y comercio atlántico: la empresa commercial irlandesa en Canarias (1703–71)* (Santa Cruz de Tenerife, 1985).

Parmentier, Jan and Ohlmeyer, Jane (eds), *Irish and Scottish Mercantile Networks in Europe and Overseas in the Seventeenth and Eighteenth Centuries* (Gent, 2007).

Power, Orla, 'Irish Planters, Atlantic Merchants: The Development St. Croix, Danish West Indies, 1750–1776' (PhD thesis, NUI, Galway, 2011).

CHAPTER 18

....

RESTORATION IRELAND, 1660–88

....

TED MCCORMICK

I. INTRODUCTION: THE RESTORATION'S IRISH PROFILE

WELL-DEFINED and much studied by historians of England, as a chapter in Irish history, the Restoration lacks a clear profile of its own. Though it has attracted a new degree of attention over the past fifteen or twenty years, it is still most often viewed from the perspective of adjacent periods or transcendent processes: a drawn out but ultimately inevitable elaboration of the Cromwellian conquest and settlement of the late 1640s and 1650s, or a pregnant pause between two brief moments of Catholic resurgence in 1641–9 and the late 1680s (each ending in calamitous reconquest); the last act of 'the heroic period of Irish history', or else a foretaste of the Protestant 'Ascendancy' of the eighteenth century.[1] The developments that dominate accounts of the period—the transfer of land on a massive scale from Catholic to Protestant proprietors, deepening fissures between and within confessional and national subpopulations on the island, the role of English and Continental connections and imperatives in shaping or distorting Irish politics and economic life, and the formation of a new and more exclusively Protestant landowning elite, together with its material and intellectual trappings—all began earlier or matured later. The spatial boundaries of 'Restoration Ireland' pose another set of problems. Successive lords lieutenant found their authority and initiatives hamstrung by backstairs dealings in Whitehall or politicking at Westminster; different segments of the Protestant population took their cultural cues from England or Scotland; much of Catholic Ireland, meanwhile, sustained body, spirit, and community through commercial, political, religious, and familial ties to Continental Europe and, increasingly, the wider Atlantic world.[2]

Despite all this, recent work suggests the usefulness of thinking in more positive terms about a quarter-century that witnessed the erection of a new and lasting order—briefly threatened during the reign of James II, but surviving intact—on the ashes of the old.[3] Indeed, the very fluctuations of political fortune, the hazardous loose ends to be tied up, and the unpredictable interventions from afar that characterized the Restoration era in Ireland may be seen to have generated both concrete developments and more intangible possibilities unique to the period. If it makes little sense to treat Restoration Ireland as an autonomous political, social, or cultural unit, there is nevertheless much in the label 'Restoration' that signals decisive and distinct change for Ireland, whether in common with or in contrast to its neighbours. Most obvious is the consolidation of the post-war land settlement, perhaps the greatest and most systematic expropriation in early modern European history and an event decisive for Ireland's future.[4] Neither simply the end of Gaelic Ireland nor merely the prelude to an inevitable era of Penal Laws, the new dispensation's tangled origins and lingering fragility effectively set the terms of political debate between 1660 and 1689 for the various groups concerned. Considered from a wider angle, the events of the period quickly brought visible changes across the social, economic, and physical landscape of the country as rural improvement, regional specialization, and the expansion of trade linked Irish market towns and port cities to European and transatlantic markets while new kinds of community—denominational, urban, literary, and even scientific—took shape under the watchful eye of a more and more self-consciously provincial Protestant landed elite.

II. THE LAND SETTLEMENT

From the outset, anxiety about the fate of the Cromwellian land settlement, and about the security of confiscated Catholic estates purchased in the lively land market created thereby in the later 1650s, was fundamental to the Restoration in Ireland.[5] Henry Cromwell's removal from the lord deputyship in June 1659, and his replacement by more radical army commissioners, alienated many Old (or pre-Cromwellian) Protestants— the main gainers from the settlement, though by no means convinced Cromwellians themselves.[6] The result was a bloodless coup on 13 December, led by Theophilus Jones, which put proponents of the recall of the English Parliament in charge. The ensuing Dublin Convention, in session between March and May 1660, helped galvanize a common 'English' interest around the land question, uniting Old Protestants with Cromwellian newcomers and identifying a strong English government—likely, following the failure of Hardress Waller's attempted coup in February, to mean a restored monarchy—as their best bulwark against a restive and resentful Catholic majority.[7] By the time word of Charles's restoration in England reached Dublin, the leading representatives of the Protestant interest, Sir Charles Coote and Roger Boyle, Baron Broghill, had already made contact with both the English Convention Parliament and the royal court.[8] On 14 May, the Dublin Convention proclaimed the king's restoration.

The fact that the restoration of the monarchy in Ireland was effected in large part by the beneficiaries of Cromwellian confiscations made a return to the *status quo ante bellum* impossible, whatever the merits of the case; this basic fact goes a long way towards explaining Ireland's distinctive politics in the decades to come.[9] More immediately, it confronted Charles with the challenge of satisfying the incompatible claims of dispossessed Catholics and royalists on the one hand and the composite Protestant interest— 'the natural leaders of Irish society', as they perhaps saw themselves—on the other.[10] His response was the 'Gracious Declaration' of November 1660, setting out the key terms of the Restoration settlement. First, those claiming land were to be classified according to 'qualifications' reflecting their behaviour during the 1640s.[11] Second, Catholics who qualified as 'innocent' of rebellion, 'ensign-men' who had served Charles abroad, '49 Officers' (royalists serving before the 'Ormond peace' of 1649), and individual 'nominees' of the king were to be restored or granted estates, but only after Cromwellian 'adventurers' and soldiers, regicides excepted, had been confirmed in their holdings as of 7 May 1659.[12] As James Butler, duke of Ormond and Lord Lieutenant from early 1662, observed, 'a new Ireland' would be needed to satisfy everyone.[13]

A struggle ensued between rival groups of lobbyists as the principles of the Declaration took legislative form between the summer of 1661 and the spring 1662. However, agents of the Protestant interest, led initially by Coote (now Earl of Mountrath; he died in December 1661) and Broghill (now Earl of Orrery) had little trouble beating out a Catholic interest ethnically divided, poorly represented by the overbearing Richard Talbot, and tainted by the radicalism of the Confederacy. Orrery's revelation of a 1647 letter from the then-Confederate Nicholas Plunkett offering the crown of Ireland to various European monarchs in return for military support was the final blow.[14] The impossible task of implementing the resulting Act of Settlement (1662) was, however, further complicated by the king's overgenerous grants to favourites, notably his brother, the duke of York, to whom went the regicide lands—a large portion of the land immediately usable for redistribution.[15] When a Court of Claims convened to evaluate putative 'innocents' in January 1663, it was clear that the stock of available land was inadequate to the demands placed upon it. As decrees of innocence—how many genuine, how many illicitly procured remains subject to debate—piled up by the hundreds through the spring and summer, the scale of the mismatch became still more apparent.[16] After an explosive parliamentary session and the discovery of two Protestant plots to seize Dublin Castle, the Court shut down in August, the majority of claims as yet unheard.[17]

A compromise that did something to quieten Protestant complaints while restoring an innocent, fortunate, or favoured few was worked out by Orrery, Arthur Annesley, Earl of Anglesey, and others associated with the Protestant interest—over the objections of Talbot and Plunkett, lobbying through the duke of York—during the next two years.[18] The resulting Act of Explanation, pushed through the Irish Parliament in late 1665 by Ormond and Orrery, called for a 'retrenchment' by one third of estates held by Interregnum grantees, creating a fund of land for 'reprisals' to innocents and nominees. A second Court of Claims sat between January 1666 and January 1669, but as new claims of innocence were excluded, the vast majority of the dispossessed were now doomed to remain so.[19] As the legislative phase of the settlement came to an end, land continued to change hands and lawsuits dragged on, but the overall character of the shift was unmistakable. Even in County Dublin, which, owing to the connections of its largely Old English proprietors, saw an unusually high number of restorations, Catholics now held just 65 per cent of what they had in 1641.[20] In Donegal, by contrast, only one Gaelic Irish Catholic landowner remained in 1660, and none by 1710.[21] Nationally, Catholic landownership has now been shown to have declined from about 66 per cent of productive land in 1641 to 29 per cent *c.* 1675—a nearly exact reversal along sectarian lines.[22]

III. Confessional Politics

The land settlement's confirmation of Cromwellian expropriation and transplantation came as a bitter disappointment to Catholic observers who recalled the 1649 Ormond peace's promise of 'oblivion' for wartime acts, and who may even have hoped for a Catholic Church settlement.[23] A strand of clerical polemic represented by Nicholas French, Bishop of Ferns, and emanating from Continental presses in English, Latin, and other languages, dwelt upon the earl of Clarendon and his friend Ormond's perfidious role in 'the settlement and sale' of Ireland and looked first to France and Spain and then to Rome for support.[24] Meanwhile, patronage-starved poets such as Dáibhí Ó Bruadair lamented in vernacular Irish the rise of the uncouth and grasping and the disappearance of a worthy aristocracy.[25] Not all Catholics fared alike, however, and differences persisted not merely between Old English and Gaelic Irish or between those 'vested' and those 'devested', as Sir William Petty put it, of their lands, but also over what constituted proper objects and limits of political ambition now that monarchy was restored.[26]

In this light, the first Catholic political project of the period was the most revealing. This was the 'loyal formulary' or 'Remonstrance' composed in December 1661 by the former Confederate Sir Richard Bellings, an oath meant to defend Catholic clergy accused of plotting by a Protestant parliament exercised over the land settlement.[27] Proclaiming loyalty in secular matters, the Remonstrance and its fate exemplified the conflict between temporal and spiritual allegiance and the impossibility of any decisive resolution.[28] Promoted by Bellings and the Franciscan Peter Walsh, the document garnered signatures from twenty-four clerics in Dublin in January 1662, and then, in a new version, from ninety-eight Irish nobles and gentry in London. Both versions were well received by the king, while the appended signatures provided Ormond with a guide to Catholics who could be shown favour; from Walsh's Gallican perspective, the document suggested the possibility of regaining the terms of the 1649 peace, and even of a reunified national church, while signalling that the Crown's real enemies were Calvinist.[29] Opposition from Catholic quarters was immediate and mounted with time, notwithstanding the alternative formulation produced by a general congregation of Catholic clergy in Dublin in 1666.[30] After the Act of Settlement, the Remonstrance served no practical purpose in recovering estates; its implications for papal authority, meanwhile, ensured attacks from Rome, Louvain, and local leaders such as Peter Talbot and Oliver Plunkett (Archbishops of Dublin and Armagh, respectively, from 1669).[31] Paradoxically, the reconstruction of a Catholic hierarchy after Ormond's removal, the rise of the Cabal ministry in England, and Charles's pursuit of toleration and a French alliance together doomed the possibility, opened up by the peculiar politics of the early 1660s, of 'a more distinctive Anglo-Irish Catholic identity' bound to the Stuart state and detached from continental patronage, institutions, and commitments.[32]

Nor were many Protestants enthusiastic about the device. The Lord Lieutenant, with his Old English family background—as wary of Presbyterian as of Catholic disaffection—might see the Remonstrance as a litmus test of Catholic political reliability. But for those like Orrery, Anglesey, and more recent arrivals, 'Irishness was the attribute that had tainted and inspired their Catholic adversaries' in 1641, and no oath could change this.[33] Parliament's reaction to the first court of claims in 1663 and two Presbyterian-linked plots against Dublin Castle in the same summer reveal the anger aroused by the least sign of concession. Frustration with retrenchments of land after 1665 and turf battles between the Lord Lieutenant and Orrery (Lord President of Munster until the post's abolition in 1672) ensured that each new political crisis brought fresh accusations of 'indifference' to popery and counter-accusations of insubordinate meddling.[34] While factional antipathies were genuine, however, individual motives were mixed, and rivals cooperated where the common interest of Protestant Ireland was perceived to be at stake—as, for example, in the unsuccessful attempt to resist the passage in England of the Cattle Acts in 1663 and 1667.[35] Indeed the Parliament of 1661–6 concluded on a conciliatory note, voting Ormond £30 000 and settling the civil and military list not merely for the king's life but those of his heirs as well. Parliament itself never became a site of organized or sustained opposition—the Popish Plot and Exclusion Crisis nullified preparations for a new parliament in 1678—and after 1666 no alternative forum for such criticism appeared.[36]

One reason for this was that English political pressures were so often decisive. Recent work has qualified rather than reversed J.C. Beckett's judgment that Irish concerns 'had little independent force' in the formation of policy.[37] Orrery succeeded in casting doubt on Ormond's management of finances, but the latter's removal in 1669 depended on the fall of Clarendon in 1667, the machinations of Orrery's ally, Buckingham, and Charles's own shift towards a French alliance and a dilution of the church settlement Ormond backed.[38] Ormond's successors—the Presbyterian John Robartes from 1669 to 1670; John Berkeley, close to Peter Talbot and married to a Catholic, from 1670 to 1672; and finally the earl of Essex, from 1672 until 1677—took their cues from this more tolerant dispensation, capped in England by the 1672 Declaration of Indulgence and manifested in Ireland by the relaxation of laws excluding Catholics from towns, the bar, and certain local offices and by the provision of a *regium donum* (a small sum of money, conferring no official recognition) to Presbyterian ministers.[39] So far had the ground shifted that, when Richard Talbot took a petition signed by fifty-two nobles and gentry to London in December 1670, a committee of enquiry halted further grants.[40] Even before Essex's appointment, a second committee was reviewing the settlement itself, so that the new Lord Lieutenant found himself the unlikely champion of the dispossessed and the local agent of the King's dispensing power.[41] From here on, a renewed struggle over the settlement loomed, galvanizing confessional divisions.[42] Essex's other major challenge was the 'Ranelagh undertaking', a revenue farm that privatized the exchequer from 1671 to 1682 and resulted in the transfer of fiscal control to Whitehall. Again, court politics decided the matter: Richard Jones, viscount Ranelagh, was both Orrery's brother-in-law and a client of the rising earl of Danby. In 1677, Essex departed and Ormond returned in his place.[43]

The major event of Ormond's second Restoration viceroyalty further illustrates the disruptive effects of English politics, for the Popish Plot fabricated by Titus Oates in 1678 was, in Ireland, a non-event. Yet, beyond causing a firestorm in England over the succession, it generated anxiety both in and about Ireland, whose weak government and lack of parliamentary ventilation gave Protestant imaginations ample opportunity to run wild.[44] Ormond's foes raised the spectre of Irish rebellion, abetted by the publication of Edmund Borlase's history of 1641 and the reprinting of Sir John Temple's.[45] By early 1680, with Whig hopes at their height, Oliver Plunkett had been imprisoned and rumours of an 'Irish Plot' and French invasion proliferated. As the tide turned in England, these lost momentum. Plunkett was hanged at Tyburn in July 1681, but the Plot's chief legacy in Ireland was to lash Protestant identity still more tightly to the memory and commemoration—in histories like Temple's, sermons marking the anniversary of the 23 October 1641 rising, and violent public festivities—of popish rebellion, while showing how easily Irish realities and viceregal concerns went by the board in England.[46]

Restoration politics in Ireland ended, as they had begun, with the land settlement. The great initiative of Ormond's second term was a Commission of Grace for remedying defective land titles, designed to finalize the settlement, finally granted by Charles in 1684. But with James II's accession in February 1685, Ormond's replacement by Clarendon and the subsequent rise of Richard Talbot, now earl of Tyrconnell, the commission was abandoned.[47] At Tyrconnell's direction, Protestant army officers were purged and Catholics appointed. Though the civil administration could not be so quickly transformed, Catholics began to be commissioned as judges and to serve as sheriffs. Clarendon was recalled in early 1687, and with Tyrconnell as Lord Deputy (and Richard Nagle, whose 1686 'Coventry Letter' attacked the land settlement, now Attorney-General) the pace of change quickened.[48] Finally, draft legislation revising the land settlement itself appeared. Initially this took the form of a new round of retrenchments; but by the time the 'patriot' Jacobite parliament sat in 1689, this was not nearly radical enough for a Commons dominated by unrestored proprietors. With numbers of Protestants leaving or gone and James himself in desperate straits, the demand for repeal of the settlement overrode both Protestant protest and the fugitive king's commitment to 'English' interests.[49] Significantly, repeal also overrode the claims of a 'new interest'—the Catholic proprietors who owned, through restoration or purchase, fully 30 per cent of the country's profitable land, and who feared the economic effects of Tyrconnell's policies.[50] War decided the question, and the settlement endured.

IV. ECONOMIC AND SOCIAL CHANGE

If the land settlement continues to structure the political history of the Restoration in Ireland, economic development and various social changes loom much larger than before. Once seen simply as a colonial victim of English mercantilism, Ireland's economy was in fact undergoing complex change and rapid, if uneven, growth.[51] This had relatively little to do with the dramatic improvements preached by colonial projectors: William Petty's ambitious plans for an ironworks and fisheries on his vast Kerry estates created little other than headaches and expense, though a rival foundry in a more promising location at Enniscorthy in Wexford achieved modest success, supplying Dublin as well as Liverpool, Bristol, and forges in the Forest of Dean.[52] Rather, a growing population after 1660 (1.7 million in 1672, 2.2 million by 1687), a longer-term trend towards consolidated estates accompanied by a shift from arable to pasture in certain areas, and the growth of port cities—Dublin and Cork especially—and smaller regional entrepôts marked out the main lines of development, inflected but never wholly driven by English legislation and ideology.[53]

No sustained work examines the whole of Irish economic life in the period, but regional and local studies suggest the prominence of certain shifts.[54] Chief among these is the growth of export trade. Following a slump in the 1660s and the imposition in 1663 and 1667 of prohibitions on the export of live cattle to England, a staple of trade to that point, butter and beef emerged as major export commodities, the former sent to northern France and Flanders and the latter to English and, later, French colonies in the West Indies. Alongside dairying, encouraged over grazing by improving landlords, and colonial provisioning, wool gradually grew in importance. In each business, English markets rendered harder of access by tariffs and navigation laws occupied a decreasing share of the trade: while England received 74 per cent of Irish exports in 1665, it took only 30 per cent by 1683, though the end of the century, disrupted by war, saw a moderate reversal of this trend.[55] With the rise of trade came new regional specialization and new losers as well as winners. For example, Cork's role as a depot for colonial sugar, tobacco, and provisions and later in shipping finished wool and salted butter vaulted it over its nearby rivals, Youghal and Kinsale, and made it Ireland's second port as early as the mid 1660s.[56] While exceptional in the scale of its achievement (its population grew more rapidly than Dublin's, tripling between 1659 and 1685, when it numbered roughly 20 000), Cork's experience reflects Ireland's integration into a widening world of trade.[57] By 1686, only 25 per cent of the port's trade was with England, the rest divided almost evenly between France, Holland, and the Caribbean and North American colonies, with Iberia slightly behind.[58]

In most of these shifts, neither the land settlement—which largely spared Cork and Kerry, already in New English hands in 1641—nor even mercantilist legislation, a product as much of clamorous lobbies as of imperial planning, played more than a proximate role. One net effect, however, was a more, or perhaps a different, 'Atlantic' Ireland by the 1680s, tied to coastal Europe and the Caribbean by elaborate commercial networks, exile, forced migration, family ties, and individual mobility, and no longer simply as the laboratory of empire imagined by the likes of Petty.[59] Forced to the margins by war and hostile legislation, Catholic merchants forged new links or joined existing Irish communities on the Continent while others found themselves recruited by a labour-hungry French state or 'integrated as outsiders' in England.[60] Another effect was a gradual transformation in the conditions of economic life in many parts of Ireland itself. In rural areas, relations between chief tenants and landlords were monetized on paper, if not always in practice. Specialization in staples meant dependence on markets for other goods, and the expansion of trade introduced a new, if still modest, world of goods.[61] In towns and on improving estates, crafts multiplied as populations grew. The Ulster town of Strabane, swelled by Scottish migration and natural increase and home to a merchant class with links to Dublin, supported multiple glovers and wigmakers catering to a local demand for luxury, besides more lowly weavers, tailors, bakers, shoemakers, and so on.[62] Few merchants made large fortunes, and nowhere did many abandon the cities for landed life; but at the upper end a mixture of trade and agriculture facilitated contact and even intermarriage with the gentry.[63] The leaders of the new elite, meanwhile, ensconced themselves in country houses built to impress—sometimes, as with Orrery's seat at Charleville, at unsustainable expense—filled with fashions received from London, decorated with taste cultivated on the Grand Tour, and surrounded by carefully landscaped gardens and hunting grounds.[64]

The scale of change was most visible in the larger cities, and most impressively in Dublin, whose population reached 45 000 in 1685 and over 60 000 two decades later, making it the 'second city' of the empire.[65] Host to literary circles centred in Dublin Castle, to a rickety Theatre Royal in Smock Alley (built 1662; rebuilt following a balcony collapse in 1671), and to a succession of rival, if hardly overactive, printers, the capital was the focus of an expanding anglophone cultural life.[66] Thanks in part to the role of Dublin courts in the land settlement and the disappearance of provincial courts in Munster and Connacht in 1672, it was also the centre of legal business. Conforming Protestants dominated political and economic life. There was no Irish answer to the English Corporation Act of 1661, but the 1665 Act of Explanation prohibited Catholics from owning land in towns, and for most of the period the oaths of allegiance and supremacy excluded them from the guilds that controlled urban trades. Only temporarily in 1672 and then again under James II in 1686 were civic privileges restored to Catholics, although the economic inconvenience of total exclusion led to the compromise of 'quarterage', by which Catholics as well as Dissenters such as the Quaker merchant Anthony Sharp paid a fee to do business unmolested as 'quarter-brothers'.[67] Despite persistent ties between confessional politics and corporate privileges, total exclusivity in Dublin, as in other towns, was impracticable, made nonsense by economic interest and demography, fluctuating royal imperatives, as well as the Dublin administration's attempts to attract dissenting 'strangers' with valuable skills.[68] Indeed, despite the programme of transplantation and expropriation that preceded the Restoration and the strict episcopalian settlement that accompanied it, the outstanding characteristic of the period is arguably the formation and conjugation of distinct confessional and cultural communities in the midst of a commercializing provincial society.

V. Plural Communities

The social history of Ireland in the later seventeenth century remains underdeveloped.[69] One point few doubt, however, is that this was a society fractured along confessional lines. The restoration of the monarchy led almost immediately to the restoration of an episcopalian church settlement, and half a dozen vacant bishoprics were hastily filled with candidates for the most part sympathetic to the goals of Laudian reform, with eleven bishops being consecrated in St Patrick's in January 1661.[70] Yet, neither the full panoply of repressive English legislation nor the demographic dominance of conformity applied in Ireland, while shifts in royal policy and later in the religion of the monarch limited the viceroy's room for manoeuvre, to say nothing of the bishops'. Ormond's reputation for tolerance had come under scrutiny, and certainly his response to Blood's Plot in 1663 (having bishops round up Presbyterian ministers) and his initial belief both in the pursuit of uniformity and in the political threat posed by Presbyterianism set him apart from the likes of Orrery, who tarred him as a Catholic sympathizer, as well as from his own successors in Dublin Castle.[71] Neither Irish circumstances nor English policy allowed for the thoroughgoing enforcement of conformity the bishops sought, however, and on a local level nonconformist preaching might even be permitted in parish churches.[72] Particularly under James, printed polemic gave vent to tensions obscured by Charles's policy but now brought into the open with toleration: William King, chancellor of St Patrick's cathedral and later bishop of Derry and archbishop of Dublin, and Anthony Dopping, bishop of Meath, took on all comers, confronting Presbyterians, Quakers, and Catholics alike in defence of an embattled Anglican settlement.[73] Yet, with respect to attitudes prevalent in the wider population before and after the cataclysm of 1688–91, the more revealing image may be that of the 23 October charivari in Athlone in 1685: a celebration, or a riot, implicitly emphasizing Protestant unity by invoking the Catholic crimes upon which the Restoration settlement was predicated.[74]

The experiences of the hibernophone and Catholic majority remain least known and hardest to get at using traditional sources and methods. Catholic Ireland was cross-cut both by slowly fading ethnic enmities between Old English and Gaelic Irish and by intra-confessional rivalries of more recent vintage—as well as by conflicting stakes in the land settlement.[75] Studies of Irish literary and historical sources draw heavily on the early seventeenth century or the Cromwellian period rather than its aftermath, but they suggest the intellectual response of the learned and their readers to the changing political situation.[76] For example, the contrast between Geoffrey Keating's prewar manuscript 'best-seller', *Foras Feasa ar Éirinn*, which saw the establishment of Anglo-Norman rule following the papal bull *Laudabiliter* as essentially continuous with Ireland's earlier history, and John Lynch's 1662 *Cambrensis Eversus*, which appealed instead to the right of conquest, reveals tensions in Old English political thought while indicating that for some a defensible Irish identity should be articulated in non-ethnic terms.[77] Studies of survivors such as the marquis of Antrim, his cousin Daniel O'Neill, or those slightly further down the social scale, such as the earl of Carlingford's agent John Bellew, shed light on the confessional flexibility of court politics and the local mechanics of the land settlement.[78] But the mass of 'poor Irish' gestured at in the writings of Petty and others remain visible chiefly as statistics. One promising step is the sort of regional study undertaken by David Dickson for Cork and South Munster; another is the historical-geographical approach taken by William Smyth to the Irish landscape as a whole.[79] Such long-term views, however, often preclude precise judgments about this period in particular.

The consolidation of Dissenting communities and denominational churches presents a very different case, appearing as a distinct product of the Restoration.[80] Independents and Baptists who had flourished in the army under Fleetwood suffered with his replacement and the subsequent return of monarchy.[81] Prominent individuals such as Richard Lawrence survived and even found limited patronage (Ormond put him in charge of the textile works at Chapelizod), but numbers declined and wider proselytizing went by the board.[82] Quakers, too, entered the 1660s with diminished expectations. Owing to a 'solid base in the middling social ranks', however, they succeeded in surviving sporadic persecution—mobilizing networks of Friends in Ireland, England, and America to gather and disburse aid in times of trouble—and in maintaining a common identity visible in dress and conduct and policed through the travels and teaching of public Friends, regular local meetings, home visitations, procedures for correction and disownment, and certificates marking communal permission for activities such as marriage or relocation.[83] Given their small numbers, Quaker progress was impressive, expanding from just over thirty meeting places in 1660 to over fifty by 1701. William Edmundson's work setting up 'six-weekly' meetings around the country during the 1660s was capped by George Fox's visit in 1669, which saw the establishment of men's and women's meetings in major cities and the first General Meeting in Dublin.[84] Friends like Anthony Sharp came to play major parts in the economic life of the cities, and the public roles of Quaker women— including the Irish-born Katherine McLoughlin—attracted attention from outside.[85] At the same time, the erection of systems of surveillance and sanction combined with a new attention to denominational history, involvement in printed polemic, and attention to the problem of education to keep communal boundaries fairly well defined.

Presbyterianism, divided between populous Scottish settlements in Ulster and an attenuated English community centred in Dublin, faced still other challenges. While English Presbyterians sustained themselves by sharing ministers and meetings with Independents, the Ulster community—thanks both to its proximity to Scotland and to the legacy of the Solemn League and Covenant—bore the brunt of official mistrust.[86] Repression loomed at moments of crisis, in the early 1660s and again around the brief rebellion that ended in the battle of Bothwell Brig in 1679, and after the Rye House Plot of 1683; the crackdown in Scotland following the 'Apological Declaration' of 1684 (a renewal of the Covenant) brought an influx of refugees who rejected the Restoration altogether.[87] Furthermore, the restoration of the Church of Ireland brought financial difficulties that the *regium donum* from 1672 only partly alleviated. Yet, as with the Quakers, this was in general a period of consolidation; the large meetings of the Interregnum disappeared, along with formal visitations, in the 1660s, but returned later on; by the 1670s, purpose-built meeting houses were increasingly common and meetings policed the behaviour of their members, commissioned communal histories, and even set fast days without interference.[88] Even if public meetings were sometimes suppressed, as in 1682–6, Presbyterianism was now a denominational church enjoying considerable *de facto* toleration.

VI. Cultural and Intellectual Formations

The cultural and intellectual histories of these various communities and of Restoration Ireland as a whole invite further exploration. Instruments of high politics are best known: constitutional thinking from Patrick Darcy before the Restoration, through William Domvile's 1660 'Disquisition' on the application of English statute law to Ireland to the celebrated arguments of Domville's son-in-law, William Molyneux; various strands already noted of Old English politico-historical thought; Continentally inflected Catholic responses to the cruel ironies of the Restoration settlement; pot-stirring Protestant histories of 1641 and its aftermath; and Irish-language laments for an extinguished world of Gaelic lordship and patronage.[89] Recent years have also seen innovative attempts to grasp wider and deeper changes in manuscript and print production, circulation, and consumption, and to capture something more of the texture of religious life than simply the details of belief and the structures of discipline.[90] If Ireland was divided between denominational churches and confessional communities, much of it, high and low, was also united in a fundamentally providential world view that shaped responses to major crises and to the incidents of everyday life. In cities and towns, meanwhile, Catholics, Dissenters, and conformists alike felt the incursions of print culture and experienced—unevenly, to be sure—new forms and spaces of sociability: the print shop, the coffeehouse, the theatre. The emergence of a full-fledged public sphere is usually reckoned to have occurred only in the eighteenth century, but the crucial structures and materials were in place before 1688.[91]

Perhaps less obvious at first glance are the new strains of political and economic thinking, natural history and philosophy, and aspirational social engineering—tied in various ways to the wide-ranging ideology of 'improvement'—that animated contemporary thinking about the changes planned or hoped for on the ground.[92] Yet these, too, distinguish the Restoration from earlier phases of Irish plantation and, in some respects, from Ireland under William III and his successors. In economic writing, Ireland's potential operated as a foil to hallowed Dutch achievements and a spur to predacious colonial projectors and framers of patriotic policy, even as the social problems of commercialization loomed ever larger.[93] Whether or not these years saw Ireland 'belatedly overtaken by the scientific age', they certainly witnessed a qualitative transformation in the pursuit of practical natural knowledge by experimental means, capped by the creation of the Dublin Philosophical Society, offspring of the Royal Society and sibling to the Oxford Philosophical Society, in 1683.[94] Both the articulation of an Irish economic interest distinct from England's and the enthusiastic study of specifically Irish natural phenomena were aspects, in turn, of the emergence of a self-conscious provincial elite, a fusion of the settlement's Old and New Protestant winners that embraced and promoted new forms of improvement, economic, social, scientific, religious, and moral.[95] One question posed by this web of material and intellectual concerns is not whether Ireland was a kingdom or a colony but rather how its experience as the site of an endless succession of putatively transformative projects, imposed from within as well as without, compares to, or connects with, contemporaneous developments on both sides of the Atlantic.

VII. Gaps and Departures

A striking characteristic of Restoration Ireland as a historical subfield is the dearth of book-length studies devoted specifically to it. This impression is heightened, but not explained by, the period's proximity to such rich historiographical soil as the Interregnum and the war of 1688–91. The lion's share of monographs focus on the origins, mechanisms, and effects of the land settlement, or on the political battles fought around it. To this, the last two decades have added examinations of the growth of Dissenting churches and events such as the Popish Plot, as well as several biographies and a host of essay collections and conference proceedings that cast diffuse light on other features of the period. Mary O'Dowd's *History of Women in Ireland, 1500–1800* explores, among much else, the implications of late-seventeenth-century religious and political developments for the position of women and hence the shape of society in general; similarly, expansive surveys of early modern reading and religiosity, of local and regional economic change, and of the material culture and social world of the Protestant elite all indicate the Restoration's considerable importance in long-term perspective. As many of these works suggest, this was not simply in confirming the end of Gaelic society, grounding what would become a Protestant Ascendancy or securing the island's colonial subservience to England, but also in initiating Ireland's own transition to 'modernity', whether this is conceived of in terms of settled provincial status within an expanding British Empire, the spread of agricultural improvement, urban growth and commercial links to Europe and the Atlantic world, changes in the legal standing and social roles of women, the transfer of the burden of social reform from the monarchical state and missionary church to civil society, or the emergence of print culture and a public sphere. At the same time, several scholars have described the peculiar intellectual, material, and political contingencies of the time in ways that warn against its reduction to a chapter in the making of any one future state. If 'big pictures', new or old, are to be scrutinized properly and elaborated in detail, many more fine-grained examinations of Restoration Ireland will be needed.

Notes

1. Donal F. Cregan, 'Early Modern Ireland', *Irish Historical Studies*, 20:79 (1977), 272–85:272. See Toby Barnard, 'Conclusion: Restoration Ireland', in Coleman A. Dennehy (ed), *Restoration Ireland: Always Settling and Never Settled* (Aldershot, 2008), 179–93:179.
2. See Jane Ohlmeyer, 'Seventeenth-century Ireland and the new British and Atlantic histories', *American Historical Review*, 104:2 (1999), 446–62; Thomas O'Connor, 'Ireland and Europe 1580–1815: some historiographical remarks', in O'Connor (ed), *The Irish in Europe, 1580–1815* (Dublin, 2001), 9–26; Tim Harris, 'Restoration Ireland—Themes and Problems', in Dennehy (ed), *Restoration Ireland*, 1–17.
3. There is no comprehensive, single-author study of 'Restoration Ireland'. Valuable surveys are offered in David Dickson, *New Foundations: Ireland 1660–1800* (Dublin, 1987), 1–28, Raymond Gillespie, *Seventeenth-Century Ireland: Making Ireland Modern* (Dublin, 2006), 215–98, and S.J. Connolly, *Divided Kingdom: Ireland 1630–1800* (Oxford, 2008), 119–72. See also J.G. Simms, 'The restoration, 1660–85', in T.W. Moody, F.X. Martin, and F.J. Byrne (eds), *A New History of Ireland*, vol. 3: *Early Modern Ireland, 1534–1691* (hereafter *NHI*), 420–53.
4. See Michael Perceval Maxwell, 'The Irish Land Settlement and Its Historians', in Dennehy (ed), *Restoration Ireland*, 19–34:19. No monograph covers every aspect of the settlement. Important studies include Karl S. Bottigheimer, 'The restoration land settlement in Ireland: a structural view', *Irish Historical Studies*, 18:69 (1972), 1–21, Kevin McKenny, 'The Restoration Land Settlement in Ireland: A Statistical Interpretation', in Dennehy (ed), *Restoration Ireland*, 35–52, and L.J. Arnold, *The Restoration Land Settlement in County Dublin, 1660–1688: A History of the Administration of the Acts of Settlement and Explanation* (Dublin, 1993).
5. Aidan Clarke, *Prelude to Restoration in Ireland: The End of the Commonwealth, 1659–1660* (Cambridge, 1999), 316–17.
6. S.J. Connolly, *Religion, Law and Power: the Making of Protestant Ireland 1660–1760* (Oxford, 1992), 5–8.
7. Bottigheimer, 'Restoration land settlement', 5–6; Connolly, *Divided Kingdom*, 126–8.
8. Arnold, *Restoration Land Settlement*, 37.
9. Connolly, *Religion, Law and Power*, 12–17.
10. Ibid., 6.
11. This idea has now been shown to have originated in the wartime policy of Henry Ireton; see John Cunningham, *Conquest and Land in Ireland: The Transplantation to Connacht, 1649–1680* (Woodbridge, 2011), 18–21.
12. Arnold, *Restoration Land Settlement*, 41–2; Connolly, *Divided Kingdom*, 133. On the '49 officers', see Kevin McKenny, 'Charles II's Irish Cavaliers: The 1649 Officers and the Restoration Land Settlement', *Irish Historical Studies*, 28:112 (1993), 409–25.
13. Thomas Carte, *An History of the Life of James the First Duke of Ormonde, from his Birth in 1610, to his Death in 1688*, 2 vols. (London: Printed by J. Bettenham for J.J. and P. Knapton, 1736), 2:240. On Ormond, see more recently J.C. Beckett, *The Cavalier Duke: A Life of James Butler—1st Duke of Ormond* (Belfast, 1990), and various essays included in Toby Barnard and Jane Fenlon (eds), *The Dukes of Ormonde, 1610–1745* (Woodbridge, 2000).

14. Arnold, *Restoration Land Settlement*, 45–7.

15. Ibid., 50.

16. Ibid., 53–70. Harold O'Sullivan argues that 'considering the legal and socio-political pressures brought to bear upon them, they appear to have done their work with a remarkable degree of fairness'; O'Sullivan, 'The Restoration Land Settlement in the Diocese of Armagh, 1660 to 1684', *Seanchas Ardmhacha: Journal of the Armagh Diocesan Historical Society* 16:1 (1994), 1–70:20. But Connolly suggests that the 'high rate of acquittals' may simply reflect corruption; Connolly, *Divided Kingdom*, 135.

17. On Parliament and the 1663 plots, see Coleman A. Dennehy, 'The Restoration Irish Parliament, 1661–6', in idem (ed), *Restoration Ireland*, 53–68:58–60.

18. Arnold, *Restoration Land Settlement*, 71–85; Connolly, *Divided Kingdom*, 136–8.

19. Arnold, *Restoration Land Settlement*, 86–108.

20. Ibid., 109. For case studies of Old English survival or (partial) recovery, see Joseph Byrne, *War and Peace: The Survival of the Talbots of Malahide, 1641–1671* (Dublin, 1997), and Harold O'Sullivan, *John Bellew: A Seventeenth-Century Man of Many Parts, 1605–1679* (Dublin, 2000), especially 123–39. Jane Ohlmeyer's recent *Making Ireland English: The Irish Aristocracy in the Seventeenth Century* (New Haven, 2012) greatly extends and deepens knowledge of this.

21. Darren McGettigan, *The Donegal Plantation and the Tír Connaill Irish, 1610–1710* (Dublin, 2010), 58.

22. McKenny, 'Restoration Land Settlement', 39.

23. On the transplantation to Connacht and its legacy, John Cunningham's *Conquest and Land in Ireland* supersedes earlier studies; on related debates, see also Sarah Barber, 'Settlement, transplantation, and expulsion: a comparative study of the placement of peoples', in Ciaran Brady and Jane Ohlmeyer (eds), *British Interventions in Early Modern Ireland* (Cambridge, 2005), 280–98. On the wider context of forced migration, see Patrick J. Duffy, 'Introduction: migration management in Ireland', in idem (ed), *To and from Ireland: Planned Migration Schemes c. 1600–2000* (Dublin, 2004), 1–15.

24. Jason McHugh, 'Catholic Clerical Responses to the Restoration: The Case of Nicholas French', in Dennehy (ed), *Restoration Ireland*, 99–121; *A Narrative of the Earl of Clarendon's Settlement and Sale of Ireland* (Louvain, 1668) is often attributed to French, though McHugh argues against this; see Perceval Maxwell, 'Irish Land Settlement', in Dennehy (ed), *Restoration Ireland*, 20–1.

25. See T.J. Dunne, 'The Gaelic Response to Conquest and Colonisation: The Evidence of the Poetry', *Studia Hibernica*, 20 (1980), 7–30:18–20; Allan Macinnes, 'Gaelic culture in the seventeenth century: polarization and assimilation', in Steven G. Ellis and Sarah Barber, *Conquest and Union: Fashioning a British State, 1485–1725* (London, 1995), 162–94; Nicholas Canny, 'The Formation of the Irish Mind: Religion, Politics and Gaelic Irish Literature 1580–1750', *Past and Present*, 95 (1982), 91–116; Margo Griffin-Wilson, 'Ó Bruadair, Dáibhidh (Dáibhí)', *DIB*.

26. William Petty, *The Political Anatomy of Ireland* (London, 1691), 42.

27. Anne Creighton, 'The Remonstrance of December 1661 and Catholic Politics in Restoration Ireland', *Irish Historical Studies*, 34:133 (2004), 16–41:24–5.

28. McHugh, 'Catholic Clerical Responses', 114.

29. Creighton, 'Remonstrance of December 1661', 28–31.

30. Anne Creighton, '"Grace and Favour": the Cabal Ministry and Irish Catholic Politics, 1667–1673', in Dennehy (ed), *Restoration Ireland*, 141–60:148; Vincent Morley, 'Walsh, Peter', *DIB*.

31. Ibid., 141–4.

32. Creighton, 'Remonstrance of December 1661', 19.

33. Toby Barnard, 'The Protestant Interest, 1641–1660', in Jane Ohlmeyer (ed), *Ireland from Independence to Occupation, 1641–1660* (Cambridge, 1995), 218–40:240; James McGuire, 'Ormond and Presbyterian Nonconformity, 1660–1663', in Kevin Herlihy (ed), *The Politics of Irish Dissent, 1650–1800* (Dublin, 1997), 40–51.

34. Toby Barnard, 'Conclusion: Settling and Unsettling Ireland: The Cromwellian and Williamite Revolutions', in Ohlmeyer (ed), *Ireland from Independence to Occupation*, 265–91:284–5.

35. Carolyn A. Edie, 'The Irish Cattle Bills: A Study in Restoration Politics', *Transactions of the American Philosophical Society*, New Series, 60:2 (1970), 1–66.

36. Dennehy, 'Restoration Irish Parliament', 64–8; see James Kelly, *Poynings' Law and the making of Law in Ireland, 1660–1800* (Dublin, 2007).

37. J.C. Beckett, 'The Irish Viceroyalty in the Restoration Period', *Transactions of the Royal Historical Society*, Fifth Series, 20 (1970), 53–72:56.

38. James McGuire, 'Why Was Ormond Dismissed in 1669?', *Irish Historical Studies*, 18:71 (1973), 295–312.

39. Phil Kilroy, *Protestant Dissent and Controversy in Ireland, 1660–1714* (Cork, 1994), 233–4; Creighton, 'Grace and Favour', 150–1; John Miller, *Charles II* (London, 1991), 149–54; Jim Smyth, *The Making of the United Kingdom, 1660–1800* (London, 2001), 77–107. On legal practice, see T.C. Barnard, 'Lawyers and the Law in Later Seventeenth-Century Ireland', *Irish Historical Studies*, 28:111 (1993), 256–82; Hazel Maynard, 'The Irish Legal Profession and the Catholic Revival, 1660–89', in James Kelly, John McCafferty, and Charles Ivar McGrath (eds), *People, Politics and Power: Essays in Irish History 1660–1850 in Honour of James I. McGuire* (Dublin, 2009), 28–50.

40. Arnold, *Restoration Land Settlement*, 120–1.

41. Creighton, 'Grace and Favour', 150–8; Cunningham, *Conquest and Land*, 119–49, draws attention to Essex's role in supporting the claims of transplantees; see especially 148.

42. See Arnold, *Restoration Land Settlement*, 120–34.

43. Dickson, *New Foundations*, 14–17; Gillespie, *Seventeenth-Century Ireland*, 258–9; Miller, *Charles II*, 224–6.

44. Work on the Popish Plot and the Exclusion Crisis abounds, but the only dedicated account of its Irish dimension is John Gibney, *Ireland and the Popish Plot* (Basingstoke, 2009).

45. Ibid., 41–52, 66–98, 120; Alan Ford, 'Past but still present: Edmund Borlase, Richard Parr and the reshaping of Irish history for English audiences in the 1680s', in Brian Mac Cuarta, S.J. (ed), *Reshaping Ireland, 1550–1700: Colonization and Its Consequences* (Dublin, 2011), 281–99:287–8.

46. Gibney, *Ireland and the Popish Plot*, 149–55; T.C. Barnard, 'The Uses of 23 October 1641 and Irish Protestant Celebration', *English Historical Review* 106:421 (1991), 889–920; James Kelly, ' "That Glorious and Immortal Memory": Commemoration and Protestant Identity in Ireland 1660–1800', *Proceedings of the Royal Irish Academy* 94C:2 (1994), 25–52; Raymond Gillespie, 'Reading Print, 1550–1700', and Kelly, 'Political Publishing, 1550–1700', both in Gillespie and Hadfield (eds), *Irish Book in English*, 135–45 and 194–214:144, 206–7. On the related dispute between Ormond, Anglesey, and the Earl of Castlehaven over the events of the 1640s, see Michael Perceval-Maxwell, 'The Anglesey-Ormond-Castlehaven dispute, 1680–1682: taking sides about Ireland in England', in Vincent P. Carey and Ute Lotz-Heumann (eds), *Taking Sides? Colonial and Confessional Mentalities in Early Modern*

Ireland: Essays in honour of Karl S. Bottigheimer (Dublin, 2003), 213–30, and Jane Ohlmeyer and Steven Zwicker, 'John Dryden, the House of Ormond, and the Politics of Anglo-Irish Patronage', *The Historical Journal*, 49:3 (2006), 677–706, especially 680–7.

47. Arnold, *Restoration Land Settlement*, 131–3; Eoin Kinsella, ' "Dividing the Bear's Skin before She is Taken": Irish Catholics and Land in the Late Stuart Monarchy, 1683–91', in Dennehy (ed), *Restoration Ireland*, 161–78:163–70.

48. J.G. Simms, *Jacobite Ireland, 1685–1691* (London: Routledge and Kegan Paul, 1969), 19–36; John Miller, 'The Earl of Tyrconnel and James II's Irish Policy', *The Historical Journal*, 20:4 (1977), 803–23.

49. Arnold, *Restoration Land Settlement*, 132–4; Simms, *Jacobite Ireland*, 31–2, 81–4.

50. Kinsella, 'Dividing the Bear's Skin', 170–8; see also John Miller, 'Thomas Sheridan (1646–1712) and his "Narrative" ', *Irish Historical Studies*, 20:78 (1976), 105–28:119–20; Toby Barnard, 'Sir Richard Bellings, a Catholic courtier and diplomat from seventeenth-century Ireland', in Mac Cuarta (ed), *Reshaping Ireland*, 326–47:333–40.

51. L.M. Cullen, 'Economic Trends, 1660–91', in *NHI*, 387–407. See, for example, Edie, 'Irish Cattle Bills'; Michael Hechter, *Internal Colonialism: The Celtic Fringe in British National Development, 1536–1966* (London, 1975), especially 91–109. Raymond Gillespie, *The Transformation of the Irish Economy, 1550–1700* (Dundalk, 1998), includes an overview of Restoration developments.

52. See T.C. Barnard, 'Sir William Petty, Irish Landowner', in Hugh Lloyd-Jones, Valerie Pearl, and Blair Worden, *History and Imagination: Essays in honour of H.R. Trevor-Roper* (London, 1981), 201–17; 'Sir William Petty as Kerry Ironmaster', *Proceedings of the Royal Irish Academy* 82C:1 (1982), 1–32; and 'An Anglo-Irish Industrial Enterprise: Iron-Making at Enniscorthy, Co. Wexford, 1657–92', *Proceedings of the Royal Irish Academy* 85C:1 (1985), 101–44.

53. Gillespie, *Transformation of the Irish Economy*, 41–49; see also David Dickson, *Old World Colony: Cork and South Munster 1630–1830* (Cork, 2005), 72.

54. The most thorough by far is Dickson, *Old World Colony*; see also William J. Roulston, *Restoration Strabane, 1660–1714: Economy and society in provincial Ireland* (Dublin, 2007).

55. Gillespie, *Transformation of the Irish Economy*, 43–7.

56. Dickson, *Old World Colony*, 113–48.

57. Mark McCarthy, 'The forging of an Atlantic port city: socio-economic and physical transformations in Cork, 1660–1700', *Urban History*, 28:1 (2001), 25–45:38.

58. Dickson, *Old World Colony*, 117.

59. See Thomas M. Truxes, *Irish-American Trade, 1660–1783* (Cambridge, 1988), 7–28; McCarthy, 'Forging of an Atlantic port city'. See also Nicholas Canny, *Kingdom and Colony: Ireland in the Atlantic World, 1560–1800* (Baltimore, 1988); Canny, 'The Origins of Empire: An Introduction', in idem, *The Origins of Empire: British Overseas Enterprise to the Close of the Seventeenth Century* (*The Oxford History of the British Empire*, vol.1) (Oxford, 1998), 1–33:22–3; Duffy (ed), *To and from Ireland*; Frances Harris, 'Ireland as a Laboratory: the Archive of Sir William Petty', in Michael Hunter (ed), *Archives of the Scientific Revolution: The Formation and Exchange of Ideas in Seventeenth-Century Europe* (Woodbridge, 1998), 73–90; Patrick Carroll, *Science, Culture, and Modern State Formation* (Berkeley, 2006), 52–80. On Irish settlement in the Caribbean, see Donald Harman Akenson, *If the Irish Ran the World: Montserrat, 1630–1730* (Montreal, 1997), and most recently Kristen Block and Jenny Shaw, 'Subjects without an Empire: The Irish in the Early Modern Caribbean', *Past and Present* 210:1 (2011), 33–60; for Europe, see O'Connor (ed), *Irish in Europe*.

60. See Éamon Ó Ciosáin, 'A hundred years of Irish migration to France, 1590–1688', and Mary Ann Lyons, 'The emergence of an Irish community in Saint-Malo, 1550–1710', both in O'Connor (ed), *Irish in Europe*, 93–106 and 107–26; McCarthy, 'Forging of an Atlantic port city', 35; Helen Burke, '"Integrated as Outsiders": Teague's Blanket and the Irish Immigrant Problem in Early Modern Britain', *Éire-Ireland* 46:1–2 (2011), 20–42.

61. Dickson, *Old World Colony*, 191.

62. Roulston, *Restoration Strabane*, 19–22, 38–45.

63. Compare ibid., 38–45, and Dickson, *Old World Colony*, 80–1.

64. See Barnard, *Making the Grand Figure*; on Charleville, see Dickson, *Old World Colony*, 50; on Michael Boyle's seat at Blessington, see Brian de Breffny, 'The Building of the Mansion at Blessington, 1672', *GPA Irish Arts Review Yearbook* (1988), 73–7.

65. Gillespie, *Seventeenth-Century Ireland*, 245; see also Jacqueline Hill, *From Patriots to Unionists: Dublin Civic Politics and Irish Protestant Patriotism, 1660–1840* (Oxford, 1997), 19–24.

66. See Christopher Morash, 'Theatre and Print, 1550–1800', in Gillespie and Hadfield (eds), *Irish Book in English*, 319–34.

67. Hill, *From Patriots to Unionists*, 31–9, 46–59; Richard L. Greaves, *Dublin's Merchant-Quaker: Anthony Sharp and the Community of Friends, 1643–1707* (Stanford, 1998), 68–104.

68. See Hill, *From Patriots to Unionists*, 32–9; Gillespie, 'Planned migration', 46–55; compare T.C. Barnard, 'Athlone, 1685; Limerick, 1710: Religious Riots or Charivaris?', *Studia Hibernica* 27 (1993), 61–75.

69. Mary O'Dowd, *A History of Women in Ireland, 1500–1800* (London, 2005), 3.

70. Connolly, *Divided Kingdom*, 139. See James McGuire, 'Policy and Patronage: The Appointment of Bishops 1660–61', in Alan Ford, J.I. McGuire, and Kenneth Milne (eds), *As by Law Established: The Church of Ireland since the Reformation* (Dublin, 1995), 112–19; John McCafferty, 'John Bramhall's Second Irish Career, 1660–3', in Kelly et al. (eds), *People, Politics and Power*, 16–27.

71. See James McGuire, 'Ormond and Presbyterian Nonconformity, 1660–1663', in Herlihy (ed), *Politics of Irish Dissent*, 40–51.

72. Kilroy, *Protestant Dissent and Controversy*, 26–7.

73. Andrew Carpenter, 'William King and the Threats to the Church of Ireland during the Reign of James II', *Irish Historical Studies*, 18:69 (1972), 22–8; Raymond Gillespie, 'Irish print and Protestant identity: William King's pamphlet wars, 1687–1697', in Carey and Lotz-Heumann (eds), *Taking Sides?*, 231–50. In general, see Kilroy, *Protestant Dissent and Controversy*, 169–262, and Richard L. Greaves, *God's Other Children: Protestant Nonconformists and the Emergence of Denominational Churches in Ireland, 1660–1700* (Stanford, 1997), 88–158.

74. See Barnard, 'Athlone, 1685; Limerick, 1710', and idem, 'Uses of 23 October'.

75. Compare McKenny, 'Restoration Land Settlement', and Kinsella, 'Dividing the Bear's Skin'.

76. On literary sources in Irish, see L.M. Cullen, 'The Hidden Ireland: Re-Assessment of a Concept', *Studia Hibernica*, 9 (1969), 1–47; Dunne, 'The Gaelic response to Conquest and Colonisation'; Canny, 'The Formation of the Irish Mind'; T.C. Barnard, 'Historiographical Review: Farewell to Old Ireland', *Historical Journal* 36:4 (1993), 909–28, especially 927; Breandán Ó Buachalla, 'Review Article: Poetry and Politics in Early Modern Ireland', *Eighteenth-Century Ireland*, 7 (1992), 149–75; and most recently Michelle O'Riordan, 'Ireland 1600–1780: New Approaches', in Mary McAuliffe, Katherine O'Donnell, and Leeann Lane (eds), *Palgrave Advances in Irish History* (London, 2009), 49–83, especially 50–1.

RESTORATION IRELAND, 1660–88   373

77. Bernadette Cunningham, 'Representations of king, parliament and the Irish people in Geoffrey Keating's *Foras Feasa ar Eirinn* and John Lynch's *Cambrensis Eversus* (1662)', in Jane H. Ohlmeyer (ed), *Political Thought in Seventeenth-Century Ireland: Kingdom or Colony* (Cambridge, 2000), 131–54; see also idem, *The World of Geoffrey Keating: History, Myth and Religion in Seventeenth-Century Ireland* (Dublin, 2004), and 'Historical Writing, 1660–1750', in Gillespie and Hadfield (eds), *Irish Book in English*, 264–81.

78. See Jane H. Ohlmeyer, *Civil War and Restoration in Three Stuart Kingdoms: The Career of Randall MacDonnell, Marquis of Antrim, 1609–1683* (Cambridge, 1993); Donal F. Cregan, 'An Irish Cavalier: Daniel O'Neill in Exile and Restoration, 1651–64', *Studia Hibernica*, 5 (1965), 42–77; O'Sullivan, *John Bellew*.

79. Dickson, *Old World Colony*; William J. Smyth, *Map-Making, Landscapes and Memory: A Geography of Colonial and Early Modern Ireland c. 1530–1750* (Cork, 2006).

80. See especially Kilroy, *Protestant Dissent and Controversy*, and Greaves, *God's Other Children* (Stanford, 1997). Greaves emphasizes structural factors, arguing against Kilroy that only Quakers and Presbyterians exited the period as denominational churches (rather than sects). Kevin Herlihy has edited several volumes of conference proceedings devoted to Protestant Dissent; see, for example, *The Religion of Irish Dissent, 1650–1800* (Dublin, 1996); *The Politics of Irish Dissent; Propagating the Word of Irish Dissent, 1650–1800* (Dublin, 1998).

81. Greaves, *God's Other Children*, 25–7.

82. Ibid., 249–68; Toby Barnard, 'Interests in Ireland: the "fanatic zeal and irregular ambition" of Richard Lawrence', in Brady and Ohlmeyer (eds), *British Interventions in Early Modern Ireland*, 299–314; Kevin Herlihy, ' "A Gay and Flattering World": Irish Baptist Piety and Perspective, 1650–1780', in Herlihy, *Religion of Irish Dissent*, 48–67.

83. Greaves, *God's Other Children*, 269–376; Kilroy, *Protestant Dissent and Controversy*, 82–108.

84. Kilroy, *Protestant Dissent and Controversy*, 90–1.

85. Greaves, *Dublin's Merchant-Quaker*; Kilroy, *Protestant Dissent and Controversy*, 93; O'Dowd, *History of Women in Ireland*, 175–6.

86. Kilroy, *Protestant Dissent and Controversy*, 15–59.

87. Ibid., 111–38; Greaves, *God's Other Children*, 88–132.

88. See Greaves, *God's Other Children*, 159–248.

89. Besides work cited above, see in general essays collected in Ohlmeyer (ed), *Political Thought in Seventeenth-Century Ireland*, and Brady and Ohlmeyer (eds), *British Interventions in Early Modern Ireland*. On Domville and Molyneux, see especially Patrick Kelly, 'Recasting a Tradition: William Molyneux and the Sources of the Case of Ireland ... Stated (1698)', in Ohlmeyer (ed), *Political Thought*, 83–106; Hazel Maynard and Patrick H. Kelly, 'Domvile (Domville), Sir William', *DIB*; William Domvile (Patrick Kelly (ed)), 'A Disquisition Touching That Great Question Whether an Act of Parliament Made in England Shall Bind the People and Kingdom of Ireland Without Their Allowance and Acceptance of Such Act in the Kingdom of Ireland', *Analecta Hibernica*, 40 (2007), 17–72.

90. Besides work cited above, see especially Raymond Gillespie, *Devoted People: Belief and Religion in Early Modern Ireland* (Manchester, 1997), and idem, *Reading Ireland: Print, Reading and Social Change in Early Modern Ireland* (Manchester, 2005).

91. James Kelly, 'Political Publishing', 212.

92. See Toby Barnard, *Improving Ireland? Projectors, Prophets and Profiteers, 1641–1786* (Dublin, 2008).

93. Compare Barnard, 'Interests in Ireland', and Ted McCormick, *William Petty and the Ambitions of Political Arithmetic* (Oxford, 2009), 168–208.

94. Cregan, 'Early Modern Ireland', 275; K.T. Hoppen, *The Common Scientist in the Seventeenth Century: A Study of the Dublin Philosophical Society, 1683–1708* (London, 1970). See also Hoppen (ed), *The Papers of the Dublin Philosophical Society, 1683–1709*, 2 vols. (Dublin, 2008).

95. See Barnard, *New Anatomy of Ireland*; Michael Hunter, 'Robert Boyle, Narcissus Marsh and the Anglo-Irish intellectual scene in the late seventeenth century', in Muriel McCarthy and Ann Simmons, *The Making of Marsh's Library: Learning, Politics, and Religion in Ireland, 1650–1750* (Dublin, 2004), 51–75; Connolly, *Religion, Law and Power*, 1–40.

SELECT BIBLIOGRAPHY

Arnold, L.J., *The Restoration Land Settlement in County Dublin, 1660–1688: A History of the Administration of the Acts of Settlement and Explanation* (Dublin, 1993).

Barnard, Toby, *A New Anatomy of Ireland: The Irish Protestants, 1641–1770* (New Haven, 2004).

——, *Making the Grand Figure: Lives and Possessions in Ireland, 1641–1770* (New Haven, 2006).

——, *Improving Ireland? Projectors, Prophets and Profiteers, 1641–1786* (Dublin, 2008).

Brady, Ciaran, and Jane Ohlmeyer (eds), *British Interventions in Early Modern Ireland* (Cambridge, 2005).

Canny, Nicholas, *Kingdom and Colony: Ireland in the Atlantic World, 1560–1800* (Baltimore, 1988).

Carey, Vincent P., and Ute Lotz-Heumann (eds), *Taking Sides? Colonial and Confessional Mentalities in Early Modern Ireland: Essays in honour of Karl S. Bottigheimer* (Dublin, 2003).

Clarke, Aidan, *Prelude to Restoration in Ireland: The End of the Commonwealth, 1659–1660* (Cambridge, 1999).

Connolly, S.J., *Divided Kingdom: Ireland 1630–1800* (Oxford, 2008).

Cunningham, John., *Conquest and Land in Ireland: The Transplantation to Connacht, 1649–1680* (Woodbridge, 2011).

Dennehy, Coleman A. (ed), *Restoration Ireland: Always Settling and Never Settled* (Aldershot, 2008).

Gibney, John, *Ireland and the Popish Plot* (Basingstoke, 2009).

Gillespie, Raymond, *Devoted People: Belief and Religion in Early Modern Ireland* (Manchester, 1997).

——, *The Transformation of the Irish Economy, 1550–1700* (Dundalk, 1998).

——, *Reading Ireland: Print, Reading and Social Change in Early Modern Ireland* (Manchester, 2005).

—— and Andrew Hadfield (eds), *The Oxford History of the Irish Book, vol. 3: The Irish Book in English, 1550–1800* (Oxford, 2006).

Greaves, Richard L., *God's Other Children: Protestant Nonconformists and the Emergence of Denominational Churches in Ireland, 1660–1700* (Stanford, 1997).

Hoppen, K.T., *The Common Scientist in the Seventeenth Century: A Study of the Dublin Philosophical Society, 1683–1708* (London, 1970).

Kilroy, Phil, *Protestant Dissent and Controversy in Ireland, 1660–1714* (Cork, 1994).

Ohlmeyer, Jane H. (ed), *Ireland from Independence to Occupation, 1641–1660* (Cambridge, 1995).

—— (ed), *Political Thought in Seventeenth-Century Ireland: Kingdom or Colony* (Cambridge, 2000).

Simms, J.G., *Jacobite Ireland, 1685–1691* (London, 1969).

CHAPTER 19

··

THE WAR OF THE THREE KINGS, 1689–91

··

ROBERT ARMSTRONG

I

··

'DERRY, Aughrim, Enniskillen and the Boyne': the roll-call from the Orange ballad 'The Sash My Father Wore' is at once a reminder of the mythological element in the history of the Jacobite era in Ireland and an indication of the centrality of conflict to these years. This was war on a grand scale, conflict where the true scope and horror of contemporary European warfare was visited upon Ireland. The study of warfare has dominated the modern historical writing on this period, pushing even political history into its shade.[1] Little has been done to examine the economic effects or social impact of the war, or even the unfolding of religious developments. Indeed, the period as a whole has not generated the same quantity of detailed study as other periods of Irish history, notably the confederate and Cromwellian years of the 1640s and 1650s.[2] Popular images of the period have, perhaps, lent an air of inevitability to the years 1689–91, that of the final act of a drama whose key moments had already been played out, a long-drawn contest of Protestant and Catholic (leading, now, to victory at the Boyne), or of Irish and English (culminating in defeat at Aughrim). That Ireland was caught up in a grand struggle for European dominance has also tended to a perception, among some of the Irish public, that what was taking place in Ireland was no more than a series of battles between two 'foreign' kings in which Irish people were unfortunately, and presumably misguidedly, involved. Yet, these could be considered years not only of war, but of revolution. Future generations in England and Scotland would look back on the events of 1688–9 as giving shape to the 'Revolution principles' upon which the British constitution would rest; however, the term has been more contested in Ireland. Some historians have denied the applicability of the term 'revolution' altogether; others have seen a multiplicity of revolutions tumbling one after another.

The present brief consideration of Jacobite Ireland will draw upon a sequence of 'mythological moments' to raise questions about these years. Above all, it will seek to ask whether war was indeed accompanied by, or led to, revolution, and how far the Irish experience can be better understood when read against the upheavals not only in destabilized Britain but across war-torn Europe.

II

On 7 December 1688, a detachment of the royal army neared the walled city of Derry, en route to take up garrison duties, only to find the city gates shut before them. Refusal of entry was the result of direct action by a batch of young men, immortalized as the thirteen 'apprentice boys'. Their action precipitated a stand-off with the military, then the lengthy siege of the city, only ended in July 1689. Little over a week after the event in Derry, armed defiance had emerged at Enniskillen, and soon armed associations sprang up among the Protestant population elsewhere in Ulster and beyond, in Sligo and County Cork. Protestant Ireland had for a generation defined itself against the potential disaffection and disloyalty which it ascribed to the Catholic population, earlier witnessed in the great rising of 1641, deliverance from which was commemorated annually.[3] Now at Derry and elsewhere, Protestant, not Catholic, disaffection had arisen, indicative not least of the changes to the regime against which defiance was being made.

James II had succeeded to his Irish throne, alongside those of England and Scotland, upon the death of his brother, Charles II, in February 1685. It had been clear for some years not only that he was heir apparent, but that he was a convert to Catholicism poised to inherit the rule of three legally Protestant kingdoms. Such a situation had prompted political upheaval in England, especially in the years after 1678, yet James came to power not only with the rights and powers enjoyed by his brother, but with a healthy financial balance and apparently compliant parliaments in England and in Scotland. Few historians seem inclined to dissent from the notion that he threw away these advantages in a series of actions which undermined the loyalty of many, maybe most, of the subjects of his two British kingdoms, who regarded his promotion of the interests of his fellow Catholics as merging into an 'endeavour to Subvert and extirpate the Protestant Religion, and the Lawes and Liberties of this Kingdome'.[4]

If subversion occurred anywhere, it was in Ireland: subversion, that is, of a political order which the three Stuart kingdoms had shared since 1660 as Protestant monarchies, sustained by episcopal churches under royal supremacy, and cooperating, if uneasily, with resurgent noble and landed power secured by law, property, and parliamentary privilege. This shared order jarred against some of the realities of the Irish kingdom. Exclusion of the majority of the population from significant political power was apparent across all of the three kingdoms, while substantial popular rejection of the established religion was widespread not only in Ireland but in Scotland, where it more readily prompted armed resistance. But in Ireland there was also a mismatch between political power and social prestige, and tensions generated by sectarian and ethnic division which cut jaggedly across social ranks. A Catholic social elite remained in existence despite a drastic reordering of economic and social power to its disadvantage, undertaken most dramatically in the 1650s, and seen particularly in landownership, and the continuing reality that access to power, profit, and patronage in Ireland, a 'dependent' kingdom not the equal of Scotland or England, left the country open to the ambitions of Englishmen, and a few Scots. It was a diminished Catholic elite, but one which extended across the seas to embrace elements of exile communities in Continental Europe. And it was accompanied by a Catholic clerical power structure painstakingly re-created over much of the island, in contrast to the patchy presence in Britain, and usually able to function, if discountenanced and intermittently harassed by authority. The English polity, upon which the Irish was designedly modelled, was one with a high degree of non-elite participation, deep into the structures of power at every level from the parochial to the national.[5] But, in Irish conditions, such incorporation meant that division cut deeply too, with participation often restricted to Protestants, or liable to generate competing claims of partiality.[6]

James's efforts to elevate the position of his fellow Catholics differed less in form than in degree across his three kingdoms. There is general agreement as to the principal components of 'Catholicization' in Ireland; less as to its implications.[7] A Catholic share of such civil offices as judgeships or Privy Council membership, and of local government positions as justices of the peace, sheriffs, or members of urban corporations, was replicated, most strikingly, in the army. In Ireland, that share had become a majority stake within two years and culminated in the appointment of a Catholic lord deputy in the person of Richard Talbot, earl (later duke) of Tyrconnell, a man already seen by many as the driving force for such changes. Lacking the equivalent of the English Test Act, designed to exclude Catholics from office, exclusion in Ireland had generally been a consequence of the requirement that office-holders swear an oath of supremacy which acknowledged the monarch as 'supreme governor' in matters 'spiritual or ecclesiastical' as well as 'temporal' and repudiated the authority of any 'foreign prince, person, prelate, state, or potentate', a claim which Catholics could not square with papal authority. The oath had been dispensed with before, but not on the scale now applied. Prevailing rules for the regulation of corporations (bodies responsible for urban government) allowed the oaths to be set aside,[8] enabling numbers of Catholic merchants and townsmen to regain a place in urban life. Yet greater changes were now afoot, as towns faced the recall of the corporate charters from which they drew authority, reissued with greater power conferred on the chief governor.[9] Dublin, for instance, lost its charter despite its 'spirit of submission and compliance' as regards the admission of Catholics, its new charter coming with a slate of appointees to city government (thereby securing a significant Catholic majority), but also permanently trimming the powers of the city authorities while empowering the chief governor to prune future nominees for city office.[10] Changes locally would have implications nationally in any attempt to convene an Irish parliament.

'Catholicization', at its simplest, offered the prospect of a reconnection between the Catholic elite and the structures of the state, bridging a gap which had been growing over the century but which might still—just—be overcome in the 1680s. Reversal was partial, in more senses than one: Protestants remained entrenched in some key posts of the administration, Tyrconnell was accused of favouring 'old English' Catholics over the Gaelic 'old Irish', and James remained intent on upholding elements of the 'dependent' position of the Irish kingdom.[11] The Catholic Church could be open and free, but would not be the new establishment, for James insisted on a principled commitment to 'liberty of conscience' in religion alongside the maintenance of the existing Protestant establishment. More telling was the question whether such changes would last. Surely, as Tyrconnell's close associate Richard Nagle argued, most offices, civil and military, would 'determine with our sovereign's life', and would hardly be sustained by a Protestant successor. Rather 'nothing can support Catholick religion in that kingdom, but to make Catholicks there considerable in their fortunes as they are considerable in their number', a resolution which would aid James, too, for the Catholics of Ireland were 'the only body of people of that persuasion that the king hath in his three kingdoms'.[12] Nagle argued for the overturning of the 'settlement' of landed property, and land has, at times, come to be seen as the defining issue of the Catholic cause in these years. If the proportion of land in Catholic hands had increased during the reign of Charles II, it still remained a minority stake, perhaps as little as one third, where it had been more like two thirds in 1641.[13]

A wholesale or even large-scale overturning of land ownership affected more than the private fortunes of individuals or families; for its proponents it meant the restoration of what we might term a fitting moral order appropriate to a properly functional kingdom. James's critics in England or Scotland accused him of flouting legality in pursuit of his objectives. In Ireland, it was over land that the sharpest challenge to the legal order was posed, given that attachment to common law was inextricably bound up with the protection which it offered to property, and that in Ireland 'property rights derived largely from recent acts of conquest'.[14] To challenge the present distribution of property, validated by statute and the processes of the courts, was to challenge the values underlying those undoubtedly legal actions. Catholic spokesmen like Nagle instead appealed to James to use the instruments which shaped statute (parliament) and case law (the courts) in order to redefine legality in a manner which would uphold deep-seated moral values of justice (towards those deemed innocent who had earlier forfeited their property) and honour (towards those who had served, or died, for James and his predecessors). Royal approval of such far-reaching change was not readily granted, and the debate over property was far from resolved at James's fall.[15] But the debate over the land settlement epitomized an emergent new order in Ireland. In all his kingdoms, James's desire was to entice conversion to Rome through removing disabilities and disfavour: this reflected both his conviction that the duty and privilege of service to the monarch overrode any barriers erected on confessional difference, even legal ones, and also his growing belief that he could only fully rely upon those of his own faith. The results were magnified in Ireland. The legal and political order there could be reconstructed upon the primordial bond of monarch and subject, strengthened by common faith and shared values, into a Catholic monarchy which, for all James's abhorrence of 'bargaining' with his subjects, might in practice allow for an informal compact securing the truly loyal in the properties and privileges which would allow them to duly serve their King.

Would the result be a king strengthened as well as secured in his position; in short, one moving more towards an Irish 'absolutism'? The whole notion of 'absolutism' might be found less useful than once it was, whether in terms of wider European or narrower English developments;[16] it has barely been raised as applicable to Irish conditions.[17] Any assessment is problematic given the necessarily ramshackle nature of the Jacobite regime as it was tipped precipitately into massive war on its own soil. But, tellingly, assessments of a possible absolutism in James's other kingdoms have made much of the military and of parliaments, in the latter case perhaps as part of a 'three-pronged strategy' to 'secure a pliant legislature' in each of his realms.[18] Some readings suggest that in England parliament might have become permanently tamed, a vehicle for a more authoritarian monarchy. J.R. Jones's interpretation instead considers James's plans for a 1688 English parliament as 'a one-off' to break the barriers to full Catholic participation in national life,[19] a perspective which could fit readily with an Ireland that had barely experienced parliaments in the last generation, but where a parliament might now act to recast the kingdom of Ireland as a Catholic kingdom.

The army in Ireland was not subject to the inflation of numbers seen in England, but its alteration from a Protestant monopoly to a predominantly Catholic institution was of profound importance at all levels from the local to the multi-national.[20] The military potential of Protestant Ireland extended beyond the army to the semi-professional militia: what Protestants lacked in numbers they made up for in having 'far more Soldiers and Soldier-like men'.[21] Thus the impact of Tyrconnell's disarming of the militia and of other Protestants, and the redeployment of weapons to newly enlisted Catholics was profound. David Hayton notes that Irish language poetry 'suggests that it was the disarming of the Protestants and the recruitment of Catholic troops which gave the greatest satisfaction', allowing at least some Catholics to celebrate 'the opportunity to protect themselves and perhaps enjoy some reprisals of their own'.[22] The jolt involved in the redistribution of power can hardly have been effected without some disarray in the upholding of 'law and order'. The scale of disorder is one of many issues where reliance upon Protestant testimony renders assessment tricky. But it is likely that the interplay between structural change and ethnic-sectarian social fractures prompted instances and even cycles of local tensions, score-settling, and violence, if not on a scale like that unleashed in 1641–2. Whether a more long-established Catholic regime could have reasserted itself to curb such patterns or not is moot, for outside developments would render this impossible. Instead, Ireland would spiral down into years marred not only by battles and sieges but by sustained brutality as conflicting armies and their hangers-on inflicted abuse on the population. It was in such a fear-fuelled atmosphere that Protestant mobilization occurred.[23]

While it has been made clear that many, maybe most, Protestants in Ireland sustained their allegiance to their monarch despite their dislike of his actions, that even the flight of Protestant persons and capital from the country during James's reign had been less than post-revolution accounts might suggest;[24] nonetheless, the stirring of Protestant armed engagement had been taking place by 1688. Disarming had, from

Tyrconnell's perspective, produced the worst of all worlds—not full-scale implementation but widespread alarm, allowing the organization and assembly of armed bodies, pledged to the prevention of disorder and 'the Preservation of our selves, our Religion, Laws, Lives and Liberties, by Repelling Force with Force', and to mutual protection of 'each other in the Suppression of all that shall molest us' in promised 'Obedience to the established and known Laws of the Land'.[25] Intensely local circumstances soon connected with processes of international importance. Derry's defiance had begun on 7 December, just over a month after William of Orange had landed in England—not, he insisted, to challenge James's crown, but to uphold Protestantism, the laws, and free parliaments—and four days before James's first attempt to flee to France. The early resolution of the Derry citizenry was to bar all papists, yet to maintain 'our Duty and Loyalty to our Sovereign Lord the King [James], without the least breach of Mutiny, or Seditious Opposition to his Royal Commands'.[26] In the short term, accommodation was patched up, involving the admission of a royal (but Protestant) garrison, and amnesties.

Understanding such events might be advanced by paying more attention to the case made for an 'Anglican revolution' in England, set in train before William's arrival, which 'very nearly succeeded' in its design not to overthrow James but rather his ministers and his policies,[27] and to efforts, after William's invasion, to promote admittedly more far-reaching change whilst yet retaining James as king.[28] Raymond Gillespie's case for the persistence of discontented loyalty among Protestants in Ireland might usefully be set against this sense that some challenge to James's designs might prove compatible with upholding his throne. In the north-west, any such moment passed relatively rapidly. By January, the Enniskillen garrison were appealing to William as 'the happy Instrument, under God, of our Delivery from Popery and Arbitrary Power'[29] but as opinion in London moved towards the acknowledgment of the new monarchs, so such tendencies filtered through to various Protestant bodies in the northern parts of Ireland.[30] However militarily significant such outposts—and claims have been advanced as to the strategic marginality of the north-west[31]—they were vital political bridgeheads, bringing the clash of allegiance directly onto Irish shores. Whether any negotiated submission to the new English King on the part of the Dublin regime appointed by James was likely or even possible, or whether a direct request for protection of the mighty French monarch Louis XIV, now James's guardian, was more probable, such options were forestalled by the arrival in Ireland of James himself in March 1689. As he made his way to Dublin, cheered by enthusiastic crowds, his army was engaging more closely with the besieged population of Derry.

III

Summoned by the King on the day after his arrival in Dublin, a new Irish parliament assembled on 7 May, the first since the dissolution of 1666. Where its immediate predecessor had had an exclusively Protestant House of Commons, this parliament was predominantly Catholic: Catholic peers, barred as a result of the mid century wars, were restored and new peerages created; only six Protestants are known to have been returned to the Commons, and though the bishops of the Church of Ireland, not their Catholic equivalents, were summoned, only four attended.[32] It was an active assembly and may be reckoned to have passed thirty-five known pieces of legislation.[33] Its reputation has been mixed. Some post-mortems, Jacobite and Williamite, inclined towards the sense of the parliament as a distraction, in which parliamentarians would 'spend their time in wrangling about Settling the Kingdom, and disposing Estates, before they had reduced it'.[34] But, one hundred years on, it was winning plaudits, from Henry Grattan to Wolfe Tone—who saw 'a body of men whose wisdom, spirit and patriotism reflect no discredit on their country or their sect'[35]—and by 1843 had received its first detailed assessment from the Young Irelander Thomas Davis.[36]

That Davis's articles were published posthumously under the title *The Patriot Parliament of 1689* is indicative of the emphasis placed upon the constitutional activities of the 1689 assembly, notably 'An Act declaring that the Parliament of England cannot bind Ireland'. Its significance becomes clearer when set alongside the first enactment of the session, the 'Act of Recognition of the Just and Most Undoubted Right of His Majesty's Imperial Crown',[37] expressive of 'the classic theories of indefeasible hereditary right and divinely ordained, irresistible monarchy'.[38] Its importance should not be over-played: Scottish parliaments in 1681 and 1685 had proclaimed an 'indefeasible' hereditary succession in equally thoroughgoing terms, and even articulated a notion of an ancient 'absolute' monarchy, only to see such ideas roundly overthrown with the removal of James in 1689. But neither should it be diminished. In one sense, the act of recognition complemented the rejection of English parliamentary authority, in that both cleared the ground for a complete and permanent alignment of the Irish kingdom with its rightful King, despite attempts to incorporate Ireland into the English revolution.[39] Loyalty to the Stuart kingship was more than a vessel in which to carry national, religious, or political aspirations. In a Europe still fixated on the idea of monarchy, it enabled Catholic Ireland to take its place within a natural order, a moral and theologically correct ordering of the world, and one which enabled a re-conceptualization of the subjects, their past as well as their present standing. The 1660s land settlement was addressed in terms which presented the 'Roman Catholic subjects of this kingdom' as having 'for several years, to the apparent hazard of their lives and estates, under the royal authority defended this kingdom', only to have failed of favour from 'contrivances...contrary to justice and natural equity'; now, once again, they had 'eminently manifested their loyalty to His Majesty against the usurper, the prince of Orange'.[40] Disloyalty was re-defined through the mass attainder of over two thousand named individuals, on the grounds of giving allegiance, overt or covert, to William. A further act was secured to remove 'incapacities on the natives of this kingdom', bars to property or office based on ethnic as well as religious identity. Catholic 'old English' constitutional statements from the early seventeenth century had blended internal and external considerations, the recalibration of English-Irish institutional arrangements interlocking with a reordering of relations between a king of Ireland and his Irish subjects.[41] The same was true now. The repudiation of English parliamentary authority, exercised to 'the great oppression of the people here, and to the overthrow of the fundamental constitutions of this realm'[42] was a necessary protection of an Irish monarchy now enabled to act for the protection of its loyal subjects.

The act of recognition had made explicit claims underlying James's earlier actions as ruler of three kingdoms, that 'as it is against the law of nature to hinder or deprive Your Majesty's subjects of your royal protection, so it is directly against the same law, and the laws and statutes of this realm thereon grounded, to hinder or deprive Your Majesty from the service of your subjects in peace or war (being inseparably annexed to and inherent in your royal person), of what persuasion in religion soever they be'. Translating such aspirations into specific terms, reconnecting the monarchy to the elite of Catholic Ireland, could be hard. James's continued concern for the impact of Irish measures upon possible support in England and Scotland was not unreasonable—any enduring Jacobite order would require the restoration of James to his other kingdoms, unless Ireland were to become in effect a French protectorate. But it could involve severe tussles. If James was reluctant to enact the rejection of English parliamentary authority, he refused to budge on the repeal of Poynings's Law, the fifteenth-century statute which required prior scrutiny of Irish legislation by the Privy Council of England. As well as this defence of royal executive authority, it is notable that no measures were passed to ensure a greater future role for parliaments, whether through more regular meetings, or enhanced powers. Yet, James can appear often on the back foot during the session. His distaste for the full overthrow of the land settlement had apparently seen him collude with those who opposed the measure, at least in part because of the damage it would inflict on the Catholic 'new interest' (purchasers of property since the 1660s).[43] In exile, he would later commit himself to upholding the older, 1660s, settlement.[44] All the indications are that it was the 'land question' which generated most conflict within parliament itself, though the internal politics of the assembly and indeed its place within the political evolution of the Jacobite movement, have been little studied, and, given the limited survival of source material, this seems fated to continue.

It was in matters religious that James most clearly staked out his position, notably the enactment of a bill for 'Liberty of Conscience'. Even as parliament gathered, he proclaimed to his 'loving subjects' of England his continued protection both of members of the established church and Protestant Dissenters in Ireland and his determination to persuade parliament to 'settle...Security and Liberty, both in Spiritual and Temporal matters, as may put an End to these Divisions, which have been the Source of all Our Miseries'.[45] His insistence that such 'was always Our design' indeed matches with his offers, before his ouster in England, to press a forthcoming parliament there both towards confirmation of the act of uniformity and of religious liberty.[46] It was precisely this policy which was now enacted in Ireland, despite some apparent pressure to move further to disestablish the Protestant episcopal church, or secure property and rights to the Catholic Church. It would appear that a bill was drafted to remove the royal supremacy and all 'penal laws', perhaps reopening a very old debate as to what that latter phrase entailed, but this did not pass the Lords, presumably with James's approval.[47] The concession that all should pay tithes only to clergy of their own persuasion was the furthest that legislation proceeded. James's other actions propped up the principle of religious liberty: he issued a proclamation condemning the seizure of church buildings into Catholic hands, a practice undoubtedly occurring, and made much of by later Protestant writers, though its extent remains uncertain. What does seem undoubted is that the open practice of Catholicism brought its own dilemmas, exposing the complications for the Catholic ecclesiastical system of an interventionist Catholic king, most especially his insistence upon his rights of nomination, not only of bishops (granted by Rome) but to other clerical posts.[48]

Legislation was passed relating to the remedy of deficiencies in the legal system, and for the promotion of trade—the latter the assertion of Irish claims against damaging limitations imposed by association with the stronger English economy, though there were limits here, too. Measures were passed to open access for Ireland to colonial trade while blocking coal imports from Britain, and 'for the encouragement of strangers and others to inhabit and plant in Ireland'. The latter, it seems, was James's preferred alternative to a plan to naturalize French subjects in Ireland which, alongside a measure to transfer the monopoly on wool exports from England to France, passed the Commons, but was blocked in the Lords, with James's approval.[49]

France has barely featured in the present discussion, yet all the events across the Stuart kingdoms were played out against a slide into general European war centred on the question of French power, of Louis XIV's determination to protect his position in a perilous international order or what his enemies saw as a determination to dominate and 'enslave' Europe.[50] Louis and William of Orange were protagonists in a war which would place Ireland as one campaign zone alongside Flanders, the Rhineland, Catalonia, and northern Italy. The web entangling France and Ireland was multi-stranded, strategic considerations being to the fore of French governmental concerns, though with some awareness of the economic potential of Ireland, too.[51] Nor should Louis's support for James as the principled upholding of a lawful monarch be underestimated. Irish involvement with France had multiplied and diversified in recent decades, not only in terms of trade but in the increasing tilt towards the education of Irish clergy in French seminaries.[52] Louis's ambassador extraordinary, the comte d'Avaux, was a key player in James's Irish regime in 1689–90; his extensive surviving reports have proved a vital source for historians seeking to reconstruct the events of these months.[53] Yet, much remains to be unravelled about Franco-Irish connections, the tensions generated by the presence of French troops on Irish soil, or the agendas pushed by French diplomats and generals, as well as the identity or ambitions of those in Ireland ready to promote commercial or political ties.

If the Irish war has been depicted, for the most part, in 'national' terms, and the English revolution in constitutional ones,[54] Louis's wars are often seen as balance-of-power European geopolitics. Of late, the categories have become somewhat more blurred: events in England have been pictured as both a 'godly revolution' and a 'nationalist revolution'.[55] Strikingly, there has also been a reappraisal of the role of 'religion' in the end-of-century struggles across Europe. Rather than a draining away of confessional content from international conflict, it has been argued that 'from the 1680s on religious strife was unequivocally on the rise throughout Europe'.[56] Scrupulous efforts have been made to demonstrate not only the power but the variety of 'religious' language as applied to war and politics, to national identity and international alliance in these years.[57] If the Irish war has been little discussed in such terms,[58] David Hayton long since pointed out how English anti-popery retained its potency, but across a spectrum from speaking as the handmaid of liberty to articulating 'traditional prejudices' which accorded Irish Catholics 'a streak of barbarity, even of bestiality'.[59] The French presence did little to aid sectarian accommodation—in Cork, the French governor closed churches and 'commandeered' goods as if the Protestants 'were a conquered community'.[60]

For the moment, whatever else a Jacobite Irish parliament needed to do, it needed to furnish funds for conflict already engaged and set to escalate. It proved not ungenerous in its tax measures, drawing local notables further into the business of governance as county tax commissioners,[61] but such votes could not in themselves be adequate to the needs of what was becoming a 'war society' faced with massive mobilization of resources if it was to survive.

IV

On 30 June 1690, little under a year after the end of the parliamentary session, something of the order of 60 000 troops had assembled in opposing armies on the banks of the river Boyne. The largest land battle in Irish (and possibly also British) history would be fought a day later. While scouting the terrain, William of Orange was struck, in the shoulder, by the 'glancing blow' of a Jacobite cannon shot. A difference of inches separated a superficial wound from the death of the leader of an international coalition and the claimant to the thrones of the three kingdoms.[62] Military history has a considerable capacity for the contingent: the 'what if' of the missed shot, the misunderstood order, and the failed cavalry charge, but there is an undertow of inevitability to considerations of the war in Ireland. Once England was fully engaged, the sheer weight of resources which could be mobilized by the new regime in London can seem to render inexorable its capacity to crush resistance principally dependent upon Irish resources, and especially in the context of an age of 'military revolution' in European warfare, of growing tactical and strategic complexity, inflated armies, escalating costs, and comparatively rapid technological change. Such an analysis can be folded into a reading of the pattern of warfare in Ireland across the seventeenth century.[63] Of course, each conflict was at least as much determined by its particular political context and in 1688–91 by the unparalleled degree of integration of the Irish conflict into a struggle for supremacy at European level. The implications ranged from the most tangible—the presence on Irish soil of French engineers, Danish grenadiers, and the whole lethal equipage of modern war—to the calculations, speculations, and motivations of the participants.

The gloomy analysis which one Jacobite historian would attribute to Tyrconnell in the summer of 1690, that 'if the prince of Orange should be beaten in a pitched battle, England, with the assistance of Holland, would send another army, and another after that...'[64] had grounds in the events of the preceding year.[65] July 1689 had seen the relief of Derry—'a near-run thing'[66]—and the subsequent Jacobite defeat at Newtownbutler by the forces of the Enniskillen garrison. The following month witnessed the arrival at Bangor of English and allied forces under Marshal Schomberg, bringing Williamite numbers to around 20 000, and heralding the almost total collapse of the Jacobite position in Ulster. Schomberg would achieve little: dogged by logistical troubles, poor weather conditions, and the travails of raw recruits, and unable to face down his Jacobite opponents, his advance towards Dundalk turned into a sodden retreat in the autumn. By spring he had lost perhaps half his numbers to disease and poor conditions, without fighting any major engagement.[67] Yet the spring brought a yet greater army to Ulster, better resourced, more experienced and under the direct and decisive command of William himself. Brisk advances southwards brought the two armies to confrontation at the Boyne.

Jacobite efforts had been immense. With the depletion of numbers through the despatch of trained troops to England in 1688, energetic recruitment gathered perhaps 36 000 troops by 1689, most of them raw recruits, but with experienced officers, munitions, and all the paraphernalia of war in desperately short supply. French assistance, delivered by a succession of eight significant convoys in 1689–91, met some of the shortfall, and training and experience remedied some of the deficiencies, though the 6500-strong veteran French brigade, which served for only a few months in 1690 and was then withdrawn, won few plaudits.[68] English warships consistently failed to halt French intervention. The only major naval engagement, at Bantry Bay in May 1689, was large scale by Irish standards, but, though both sides celebrated their alleged success, no ships had actually been lost by either navy. French actions in Irish waters continued unimpeded, and the very day that William narrowly escaped death in Ireland, the combined Anglo-Dutch fleets went down to a major defeat off Beachy Head, near the south coast of England. The argument has been made that France failed to exploit fully its naval superiority both in terms of the Irish war, particularly with regard to hindering English operations and communications, and more widely in terms of the war as a whole.[69] The nature and extent of French intervention could not but be bound up with the debates concerning the relative value of the multiple fronts upon which war was being waged; perhaps not irrelevant, too, was the fact that in 'seventy-seven years Louis only saw ships three times' and, if 'impressed' by and supportive of his navy, was not inclined to accord it the importance he gave his army.[70] French assistance came with a price tag. Recruits drawn from Ireland for Louis XIV's campaigns elsewhere outnumbered—and out-performed—the veterans shipped into the country, and French priorities intruded into strategic decision-making in Ireland.

Even with French aid, Ireland's economic base and infrastructure have been reckoned as simply inadequate to the needs of the wartime Jacobite regime. Particular problems proved pressing—the lack of indigenous arms production, too few horses, a shortage of currency, the latter prompting the 'brass money' or 'gun-money' initiative to reduce the desperate need for low-value coins.[71] As war ground on, escalating, and at times systematic, destruction, undertaken by both sides, further depleted the base from which the Jacobites could draw sustenance, while William could more readily ship in supplies from England. The difficulties he faced should not be underestimated. William, like James, needed to draw upon the most advanced war-making skills and equipment, in his case including formidable Dutch artillery, specialist transport ships, and hundreds of wagons, as well as 13 000 Dutch troops and a further 7000 hired from the king of Denmark.[72] England in the 1690s would proceed through massive governmental expansion, driven by the ravening needs of war, growing its tax resources alongside the credit capacities of a burgeoning financial sector. But this was only beginning. Schomberg in 1689 faced systematic corruption as well as structural inadequacies in sustaining his troops. Things had improved a year later, when William reached Ireland, yet by now large sums were also required to support troops fighting in the Low Countries, and to sustain the navy.[73] The capacity to sustain war on this scale was not a given, not at any rate without immense political will. The presence of James in Ireland, a direct threat to the new regime in Britain, and the prospect of Ireland as an outpost of French power, would steel English resolve.[74] Events in Ireland would, in turn, supply part of the propulsion for the great military-fiscal leap forward in England.

The battle at the Boyne was but the beginning of a sequence of full-scale pitched battles and sieges, at least comparable to those scarring much of the rest of Europe, larger and more densely clustered than in any other Irish conflict. The major engagements have offered plenty of options for historians willing to weigh their relative significance, even to venture to put their finger on a 'decisive' moment or 'turning point'. At the same time, a second, 'small war' was constantly waged, a war of skirmish, ambush, and plunder. Encompassing the less extensive but also less regular actions of opposing armies, such activities also drew in the mobilized or self-selected irregulars and, inescapably, the civilian population. The numerous 'tories' and 'rapparees' on the Jacobite side covered the spectrum from 'criminals, bandits, deserters and aggrieved persons intent on plunder',[75] through to those endorsed by James himself who, though 'not enlisted in our standing army' yet had 'armed themselves...for the defence of our kingdom' or perhaps of themselves and their communities.[76] Their closest counterparts, the Protestant volunteers of 1689 in Derry and Enniskillen, had been reorganized and sometimes demobilized following the arrival of English professionals, but a new Protestant militia was being created by the summer of 1690, particularly charged to meet the rapparee challenge.[77] Together their actions contributed to the contours of the conflict—sapping advancing armies, preventing secure control of territory gained, denying resources and eliminating outposts—and added much to the sheer destruction, atrocity, and intimate brutality of the war.

If the battle of the Boyne would form the centrepiece of the Orange reading of the war, then Jacobite—and later nationalist—traditions instead elevated the battle of Aughrim to the status of the great disaster. The Boyne may have led to defeat and retreat, and the departure of James from Ireland, but it was Aughrim which saw the destruction of the

Jacobite forces, with an estimated 7000 of them killed as against perhaps a thousand in the earlier battle. The Boyne has been the subject of sustained scrutiny, and mistakes and shortcomings on both sides have been uncovered. William's success was real, but with an army perhaps half as large again as James's, his was 'not an overwhelming victory', given the failure to cut off and destroy the defeated forces.[78] Yet the outcome at the Boyne resonated widely across Europe; more practically it delivered Dublin and much of the east of Ireland into Williamite hands. The prospect of outright defeat for William seems unlikely thereafter. Less certain was the nature of victory. The aftermath of the Boyne saw a failure to capitalize upon military triumph by securing a negotiated end to the war. Eager to end the war swiftly but buoyed by success, and aware of the potential of confiscated Irish property to offset his war costs, William's peace offers were so framed as to prove deeply unattractive even to the more reluctant of his enemies.[79]

Jacobite readiness to resist was only strengthened when William's army trudged to Limerick but failed to take the city by siege or storm (August 1690). Some compensation for the Williamites was obtained through the swift and startling seizure of Cork and Kinsale by that rising star John Churchill, Earl of Marlborough. Where the fall of Kinsale showed up the limitations of even relatively modern fortifications (albeit directed towards the sea rather than landward) Limerick, its defences heavily strengthened over the course of 1690–1, demonstrated the application of advanced techniques of fortification and siegecraft, and endowed the city with a strategic significance comparable to that enjoyed, or endured, by fortified cities elsewhere in Europe.[80] William's commander, the Dutchman Ginckel, entered the campaigning season of 1691 under pressure to end the war quickly, but boosted by fresh supplies and a much enhanced artillery train. Athlone was to feel its force, battered with 12 000 cannonballs and six hundred bombs in ten days to be judged 'the most bombarded town in the British Isles' at any time.[81] Its fall meant the breach of the Shannon line, a valuable, but overestimated defensive position sustainable, Pádraig Lenihan has convincingly argued, only in conjunction with French commitment to an extensive and prolonged seaborne support of the Jacobite cause, a 'blue water strategy', otherwise leaving it reliant upon the inadequate resources which could be generated within the west of Ireland.[82]

A major resupply had been conveyed from France by a convoy over eighty strong in May 1691, along with the ill-fated general St Ruth, who would command at Aughrim. The responsibility for the decision to give battle, on fairly equal terms, had been his, though the Jacobites surely had more to lose by defeat than they could have gained from victory. St Ruth was killed by the cannon shot which struck him on the field of battle, though his loss, if severe, was not fatal as William's would have been for his cause a year earlier. Where Jacobite resistance to Williamite assault had been staunch, lack of co-ordination and cavalry failures—later interpreted as treachery—saw the battle turn decisively in Ginckel's favour, then into a rout. Galway surrendered soon after, leaving the Jacobite forces concentrated, once more, upon Limerick. Preparations for a further restocking from France were hastened. In the event, the fleet only left port after the treaty of Limerick had brought the Irish war to a close. From the uncertain days before the Boyne to those of intense debate amongst the Jacobites boxed in to besieged Limerick, decisions could not be taken without weighing local conditions against what was known, hoped, or dreaded concerning the wider war. Though marked at once by local campaigns and isolated conflicts, the war was at once more 'national' than other comparable Irish wars, with major encounters serving as stages in securing or losing control of the kingdom as a whole, and more international.

V

On 3 October 1691, Ferdinand-Wilhelm, duke of Württemberg-Neustadt, commander of the Danish contingent in the Williamite army, hosted senior Jacobite officers to dinner in his tent outside Limerick. Fed and wined, they repaired to General Ginckel's quarters to sign the terms of the 'treaty of Limerick'. If hardly 'a treaty in the normal modern usage of the term' it has rightly been said that it 'was surrounded by controversy and opprobrium' from the time of its signing, not least through 'its reputation as a broken treaty'.[83] Yet, as Patrick Kelly has noted, the revolution in Ireland 'did not produce any central revolutionary document such as the Declaration of Rights [England] or the Claim of Right [Scotland]. By default, therefore, the central document of the Revolution in Ireland was the treaty which ended the Jacobite War...'[84] Historians of Scottish and especially English events have sought to assess the constitutional statements of 1688–90 alongside the changes experienced by both war-stricken nations throughout the 1690s, where the real 'revolution' could be seen as the entrenchment of parliament due to the needs of war finance, and the transformation of government into a 'military-fiscal state'. So with Ireland the treaty must be set within subsequent developments which produced a 'settlement' at least partly determinative of how the eighteenth century Irish kingdom would operate.[85]

The talks process was short-run. There was no replication of the tortuous negotiations of the 1640s culminating in far-reaching schemes for a redesigned Irish kingdom. Indeed, the timing and the terms of the articles prompted surprised responses from within both camps. Ginckel may have had Limerick cut off, but he admitted that he was in no position to take the city by assault, the campaigning season was drawing to an end, Jacobite numbers remained high, and French aid, if delayed, was on the way. The Williamites had made the running in terms of a negotiated end to war[86] and with primary direction lying in the hands of three Dutchmen—William, his close advisor Bentinck, and Ginckel—the tug of Continental commitments proved strong, and flexibility replaced the unpromising terms offered by William after the Boyne. Over the winter of 1690–1, though, matters seemed to have stalled. With Tyrconnell, hitherto open to negotiation, turned advocate of resistance, then absent in France (September 1690–January 1691), those most responsive to the renewed Williamite overtures were isolated, in some cases dismissed from office, even temporarily arrested. Meanwhile, William had locked horns with some members of his English parliament over the confiscation and disposal of Irish land, seen as offering compensation for the costs of war and an issue which would dog

English politics for years ahead. By the spring of 1691, though, the new administration in Dublin had drafted terms which would prove substantially similar to the final articles, trading some degree of amnesty, of religious freedom, and of the retention of property in return for a swifter end to war. Publicized, in modified form, after Athlone's fall, the proposed deal encountered hostility in some quarters in England and Protestant Ireland for its supposed leniency, even while Ginckel complained that every month's war out-weighed the total value likely to accrue from all forfeitures.

The political profile of wartime Irish Jacobitism has been less thoroughly surveyed than that of the mid-century confederates. The earlier movement was more structur-ally complex, with its councils, assemblies, and provincial armies. The Jacobite cause was moulded to the forms of royal governance. This was a gain in terms of international credibility and had potential to incorporate diversity, but the price was paid in terms of the accessibility and accountability of the Jacobite leadership.[87] The internal tensions afflicting the Jacobites, filtered through the reports of French allies and Williamite ene-mies, or their own bitter post-war reflections, have mostly been presented in terms of a 'war party' and a 'peace party'. Motives were sometimes ascribed on the basis of differing stakes in the existing distribution of land and wealth, recent purchasers of land being seen as 'only too anxious to submit',[88] as evidenced by the rapidity with which Galway, with a disproportionate concentration of propertied Catholics, sued for surrender in July 1691. Alternatively, different sectional interests were identified, with the Catholic clergy being presented as supporters of continued resistance, or the civilian leadership in Limerick depicted as struggling to 'over-rule the remonstrances for a surrender of the great officers of the army'.[89] The maverick Hugh Balldearg O'Donnell, while admitting a degree of unity between the English-descended 'nouveaux Irlandois' ('new Irish') and the Gaelic 'anciens Irlandois' ('old Irish'), read the peace terms as slanted towards the former, and resisted by the latter.[90] Then there was the gravitational pull of personal-ity, whether that of the massively experienced Tyrconnell or the charismatic Sarsfield. The stance of the former was certainly not uncomplicated, and no doubt reflected not only his ongoing reading of the situation, national and international, but a carefully cul-tivated talent for securing his political position and his hold on power. Sarsfield only apparently presents a more straightforward case as the unrelenting opponent of surren-der and the champion of the army. Denied the formality of a commanding office, civil or military, it was he who took the lead in the final negotiations, to the puzzlement of Williamite generals and some later historians, if only to the delight of the former.[91]

At most, the Jacobites sought a situation no worse than in 1688; at the least they were willing to accept a return to conditions prevailing in 1685, if only for those still holding out. The final terms included both civil and military articles, the latter of obvious impor-tance to the Jacobite officers but relatively uncontentious and not ungenerous, permit-ting those troops who wished to remove themselves to France, Ginckel even offering shipping. The terms allowed the self-justification that, 'by passing them into France we may be in a condition not only to oppose the common enemy but also to make a descent into England or Scotland . . .'.[92] But it was more than mere special pleading. French power seemed formidably placed in the wider war, Louis XIV still insisted on the restoration of

James to his three kingdoms as part of any peace settlement, and twice, in 1692 and 1696, assembled formidable bodies of troops and shipping for a planned invasion of England in James's interest. In 1692, the exiled Irish troops, reordered and refreshed, formed the majority of the intended expeditionary force.[93]

The civil articles began with the commitment that Catholics should 'enjoy such Privileges in the Exercise of their Religion as are consistent with the Laws of Ireland; or as they did enjoy in the Reign of King Charles the second' with the monarchs offering to seek 'farther Security' through an Irish parliament (article one). Subsequent articles were more restricted, applying only to those still in arms and 'all such as are under their protection' in five western counties—on the basis of an oath of allegiance to William and Mary, all such could be guaranteed the retention of their property and the exercise their 'Professions, Trades and Callings' (article two), and secure amnesty from lawsuits for wartime actions (article six). The suggestion that what was being forged was seen by Jacobites as a 'temporary truce' ahead of a future Jacobite restoration seems very likely to be correct;[94] as such, criticism of the Jacobite negotiators for not holding out for more extensive terms seems misplaced.

Reports had suggested that some Jacobites had earlier entertained 'surmises of the parliament not making...good'[95] on a prospective deal, prefiguring the later reputation of the 'broken treaty'. Partly this relates to the 'missing clause' dropped from article two, probably in scribal error, whereby the terms were to apply to civilians in Jacobite quarters and not just the military; restored by William, it was deliberately cut when the articles were ratified by the parliament of Ireland in 1697. The results may have been of limited effect, at least in terms of property. There would be no repetition of the 1650s revolution in landownership—that would have required Jacobite victory, not defeat.[96] Not only was there so much less property available for seizure, but the wrangles of English domestic politics meant the lack of a blanket legislative enactment, resort being had to individual legal process to secure condemnation and confiscation. While over 2000 persons were outlawed, most were not landowners, and of the 1.7 million acres yielded up, a combination of pardons and claims made under the various surrender articles (virtually all of which were upheld) saw 848 500 acres restored. If, as seems likely, the Crown also chose not to pursue cases against some landholders in the protected counties, then the claim that most of those who might have been entitled to protection of property duly secured their position seems plausible.[97] Much more serious were other alterations to the articles undertaken by the Dublin parliament in 1697, especially the removal of the first clause, which extended religious benefits to all Irish Catholics. It was framed in very ambiguous terms, since any 'Privileges in the Exercise of their Religion' which Catholics might have enjoyed under Charles II were by virtue of governmental restraint rather than legal protection. Even so, there was little doubt that the Dublin parliament, reassembled in 1692, and again in 1695, was set to increase rather than diminish the restrictions placed upon Catholics, in the latter case actually enacting 'popery laws' or 'penal laws', in several subsequent sessions.

The outworking of the post-war settlement is beyond the scope of this chapter. The new order, like the war itself, was shaped both by the distinctive Irish historical experience and by the international order of unstable power politics and confessional strife. The security of the regime from perceived external and internal threats was a significant concern, whether that be read in terms of an age-old war 'from the first settling an English colony in this country, to this very day',[98] or of the immediate, international Jacobite threat,[99] which, for all the varying assessments as to its endurance, was clearly real and present in the 1690s, as real anyway as the contemporary fears of Louis XIV about his 'nouveaux convertis', the French Protestants 'newly converted' by repression.[100] It was hardly surprising, given the persistent entanglement of the institutional Catholic Church both with James and his successors, and with Continental Catholicism, and especially, now, that of France, that it should be corralled into a limited and closely monitored existence in post-war Ireland, though clearly Catholic political and economic power was the primary target of the new order, not Catholic worship. It can prove too easy to contrast 'penal law' Ireland with 'revolutionary' England, constitutionally invigorated and legislatively, if partially, 'tolerant'. Both countries saw continued espousal of the confessional state, especially in terms of the exclusion of religious dissidents from much of public life, notably political office (enforced on Protestant Dissenters in Ireland from 1704). Both countries still nurtured individuals with a fulsome commitment to the role of the established church in the life of the nation: in Ireland, above all, the future Archbishop of Dublin, William King, whose vision of his preferred 'constitution in church and state' had been distilled during the war years.[101] Both saw a post-war order characterized by a state at once more extractive of national resources, and more constitutional in controlling that extraction through regular parliamentary sessions.

Ireland had seen the Protestant state consolidated at the expense of the Catholic monarchy. War, in this case on home soil, had, as in the British kingdoms, contributed to making that state sturdier institutionally and constitutionally,[102] yet in Ireland more detached from its host society. In so far as events like the siege at Derry had papered over divisions among Protestants, any such unity was soon lost.[103] Presbyterian numbers and geographical stretch increased with mass Scottish immigration in the 1690s, leaving a substantial and well-integrated but partially detached community within the island.[104] It remained to be seen how far the Protestant state could become a vessel in which to incubate a nation, even a 'Protestant nation' equivalent to the old Catholic elite in its harnessing of parliament and the language of patriotism to defend its interests, and possibly the 'common good'. The brief but real alternative of a Catholic monarchy had been premised upon alignment of Catholic king, Catholic Church, and Catholic nation. The interplay between them would continue within post-war Jacobitism, the role of the king becoming ever more nebulous, the idea of the 'nation' being stretched to encompass wider social interests and the position of the church becoming more central to the social experience of the Catholic population as that of a Catholic nobility receded.[105] Ireland's experience of the wars of Louis, William, and James would prove formative in shaping not just the structures but also the myths of the Catholic nation and the Protestant kingdom.

NOTES

1. Both political and military history were considered in the lucid and understated studies of J.G. Simms; see especially his narrative *Jacobite Ireland, 1685–91* (1969; reprinted Dublin, 2000), and his collected essays *War and Politics in Ireland 1649–1730* D.W. Hayton and Gerard O'Brien (eds) (London, 1986). Full-length monographs published since Simms have been military histories: Piers Wauchope, *Patrick Sarsfield and the Williamite war* (Blackrock, Co. Dublin, 1992); Richard Doherty, *The Williamite War in Ireland, 1688–1691* (Dublin, 1998); Pádraig Lenihan, *1690: Battle of the Boyne* (Stroud, 2003); John Childs, *The Williamite Wars in Ireland 1688–1691* (London, 2007).

2. Valuable interpretations have been offered, notably by Patrick Kelly, 'Ireland and the Glorious Revolution: from Kingdom to Colony', in Robert Beddard (ed), *The Revolutions of 1688* (Oxford, 1991), 163–90 and D.W. Hayton, 'The Williamite revolution in Ireland, 1688–91', in Jonathan I. Israel (ed), *The Anglo-Dutch Moment* (Cambridge, 1991), reprinted in revised form in Hayton, *Ruling Ireland, 1685–1742* (Woodbridge, 2004), 185–213, as well as in a number of essays by James McGuire and John Miller (referenced below) and the relevant chapters of Tim Harris, *Revolution: the Great Crisis of the British Monarchy, 1685–1720* (London, 2006). The impact of the war has recently received attention in Alan J. Smyth, 'A social and economic history of the Williamite war in Ireland, 1689–91' (PhD, University of Dublin, 2013). See now also the important study of Tyrconnell by Pádraig Lenihan, *The last cavalier: Richard Talbot (1631–91)* (Dublin, 2014), unfortunately received after the completion of this essay.

3. T.C. Barnard, 'The uses of 23 October 1641 and Irish Protestant celebrations', *English Historical Review*, 106 (1991), 889–920.

4. The statement comes from the 'Declaration of Rights' adopted by the parliamentary convention in England in February 1689.

5. Mark Goldie, 'The unacknowledged republic: officeholding in early modern England', in Tim Harris (ed), *The Politics of the Excluded, c. 1500–1850* (Basingstoke, 2001), 153–94.

6. Toby Barnard, *The Kingdom of Ireland, 1641–1760* (Basingstoke, 2004), ch. 5.

7. John Miller, 'The earl of Tyrconnel and James II's Irish policy, 1685–1688' *Historical Journal*, 20 (1977), 803–23.

8. James McGuire, 'James II and Ireland 1685–90' in W.A. Maguire (ed), *Kings in Conflict: the Revolutionary War in Ireland and its Aftermath 1689–1750* (Belfast, 1990), 45–57 at 54–5.

9. Harris, *Revolution*, 134–6.

10. Jacqueline Hill, *From Patriots to Unionists: Dublin Civil Politics and Irish Protestant Patriotism, 1660–1840* (Oxford, 1997), 59–60.

11. Miller, 'Tyrconnel', 804–5, 808–10. Miller presents James as having to choose between two irreconcilable policies, an 'English' and an 'Irish', though cf. Hayton *Ruling Ireland*, 14–15. Tyrconnell's favouring of 'old English' over Gaelic Irish has been challenged in Lenihan, *The last cavalier*, 119–20.

12. John T. Gilbert (ed), *A Jacobite Narrative of the War in Ireland* (Dublin, 1892: reprinted, Shannon, 1971), 194–5. See James McGuire, 'A lawyer in politics: the career of Sir Richard Nagle *c.* 1639–1699' in Judith Devlin and Howard B. Clarke (eds), *European Encounters: Essays in Memory of Albert Lovett* (2003), 118–31.

13. As calculated by Kevin McKenny, Catholic landownership stood at 66 per cent of the total in 1641, and 29 per cent *c.* 1675, though regional variations were considerable: McKenny, 'The Restoration land settlement in Ireland: a statistical interpretation', in Coleman A. Dennehy (ed), *Restoration Ireland: Always Settling and Never Settled* (Aldershot, 2008), 39, 43–4.

14. J.R. Jones, 'The Revolution in context' in Jones (ed), *Liberty secured? Britain before and after 1688* (Stanford, 1992), 47.

15. Eoin Kinsella, ' "Dividing the bear's skin before she is taken": Irish Catholics and land in the late Stuart monarchy, 1683–91' in Dennehy (ed), *Restoration Ireland*, 161–78.

16. Though a case has been mounted for James seeking to 'establish Catholic absolute monarchy across his three kingdoms' in Harris, *Revolution*.

17. Cf. Hayton, *Ruling Ireland*, 9.

18. Harris, *Revolution*, 134.

19. J.R. Jones, 'James II's revolution: royal policies, 1686–92', in Israel (ed), *Anglo-Dutch Moment*, 47–71 (quoted at 70).

20. John Childs, *James II, the Army and the Glorious Revolution* (Manchester, 1980).

21. Sir William Petty, quoted in S.J. Connolly, 'The defence of Protestant Ireland', in Thomas Bartlett and Keith Jeffery (eds), *A Military History of Ireland* (Cambridge, 1996), 231–46 at 236.

22. Hayton, *Ruling Ireland*, 18.

23. Harris, *Revolution*, 122–5, 426–31; Éamonn Ó Ciardha, *Ireland and the Jacobite Cause, 1685–1776: a Fatal Attachment* (Dublin, 2001), 54–8.

24. Raymond Gillespie, 'The Irish Protestants and James II, 1688–90' *Irish Historical Studies*, 28 (1992–3), 124–33.

25. *The Declaration of the Protestant Nobility and Gentry of the Province of Munster in Ireland* (London, 1689).

26. George Walker, *A True Account of the Siege of London-Derry* (3rd ed., London, 1689), 47.

27. Mark Goldie, 'The political thought of the Anglican Revolution' in Beddard (ed), *Revolutions of 1688*, 107–8.

28. Robert Beddard, 'The unexpected Whig revolution of 1688', in Beddard (ed), *Revolutions of 1688*. Clearly England, however seething with discontent in some quarters, had not seen disorder akin to that in Ulster. For an illuminating comparison, see the study of one regional uprising, W.A. Speck, 'The revolution of 1688 in the north of England', *Northern History*, 25 (1989), 188–204.

29. Andrew Hamilton, *A True Relation of the Actions of the Inniskilling-men* (London, 1690), 56.

30. Gillespie, 'Irish Protestants', 131.

31. Pádraig Lenihan reckons the 'peripherality' of north-west Ulster rendered the encounters of 'relative unimportance': 'Introduction' to Lenihan (ed), *Conquest and Resistance: War in Seventeenth-century Ireland* (Leiden, 2001) 18.

32. J.G. Simms, *The Jacobite Parliament of 1689* (Dundalk, 1966), reprinted in Simms, *War and Politics*, 65–90; Brian Farrell, 'The patriot parliament of 1689', in Farrell (ed), *The Irish Parliamentary Tradition* (Dublin, 1973), 116–27.

33. Its records were subsequently destroyed. Crucial for understanding the 1689 Parliament is the edition of its legislation: John Bergin and Andrew Lyall (eds), *The acts of James II's Irish parliament, 1689* (Dublin, 2016).

34. William King, *The state of the protestants of Ireland under the late King James's government...* (1691), 148.

35. Quoted in Simms, *War and Politics*, 80.

36. In a series of articles in 1843, edited and published by Charles Gavan Duffy as *The Patriot Parliament of 1689* (Dublin, 1893).

37. Conveniently printed in Browning (ed), *English Historical Documents 1660–1714*, 746–9. Bergin and Lyall (eds), *Acts of James II's Irish parliament*, 3–6.

38. Harris, *Revolution*, 439.
39. Under the act declaring Henry VIII king of Ireland, passed by the Irish parliament in 1541, the king of England was recognized as *ipso facto* king of Ireland. James, of course, continued to maintain his claim to be king of England. William and Mary were proclaimed rulers of England and of Ireland by the parliamentary convention in London, while a separate Scottish convention had confirmed the settlement of the crown of Scotland.
40. Preamble to 'An Act for repealing the Acts of Settlement and Explanation...', in Browning ed., *English Historical Documents 1660-1714*, 717–18. Bergin and Lyall (eds), *Acts of James II's Irish parliament*, 21–2.
41. Aidan Clarke, 'Patrick Darcy and the constitutional relationship between Ireland and Britain', in Jane H. Ohlmeyer (ed), *Political Thought in Seventeenth-century Ireland* (Cambridge, 2000), 35–55.
42. An Act declaring that the Parliament of England cannot bind Ireland, 1689, in *A List of such of the names of the nobility, gentry and commonalty of England and Ireland... attainted of high treason together with the true and authentick copies of several of the acts of the said pretended parliament...* (London, 1690), 5–6. Bergin and Lyall (eds), *Acts of James II's Irish parliament*, 54–7.
43. The act repealing the 1660s settlement was not only damaging to recent purchasers (the attainder legislation may have freed property for their compensation) but made no provision for losers under confiscation or plantation prior to 1641. The threat to property has been seen as alienating the remnant of Protestant loyalists.
44. *His majesties most gracious declaration to all his loving subjects* (1693) offers to remit it to a future English parliament to 'establish the late Act of Settlement of *Ireland*', albeit with some room to 'recompense such of that Nation as have followed us to the last...'.
45. *A declaration of his most sacred majesty, King James II, to all his loving subjects in the Kingdom of England.*
46. Jones, 'James II's revolution', 56, 61–5.
47. Harris, *Revolution*, 440–1.
48. Liam Chambers, *Michael Moore c. 1639–1726: Provost of Trinity, Rector of Paris* (Dublin, 2005), chapter two, provides a valuable account of such developments.
49. Simms, *Jacobite Ireland*, 92–3.
50. John C. Rule, 'France caught between two balances: the dilemma of 1688', in Lois G. Schwoerer, *The Revolution of 1688–1689* (Cambridge, 1992), 35–51.
51. René Pillorget, 'Louis XIV and Ireland' in Bernadette Whelan (ed), *The Last of the Great Wars: Essays on the War of the Three Kings in Ireland 1688–91* (Limerick 1995), 1–16.
52. Éamon Ó Ciosáin, 'The Irish in France 1660–90: the point of no return', in Thomas O'Connor and Mary Ann Lyons (eds), *Irish Communities in Early Modern Europe* (Dublin, 2006), 85–102.
53. James Hogan (ed), *Négiciations de M. le comte d'Avaux en Irlande, 1689–90* IMC (Dublin, 1934, 1958).
54. Hayton, *Ruling Ireland*, 8–11.
55. Tony Claydon, *William III and the Godly Revolution* (Cambridge, 1996); Steven Pincus, '"To protect English liberties": the English nationalist revolution of 1688–9' in Tony Claydon and Ian McBride (eds), *Protestantism and National Identity* (Cambridge, 1998), 75–104. See now Pincus's important reassessment of the revolution, *1688: the First Modern Revolution* (New Haven, 2009).

56. David Onnekink, 'Introduction: the "dark alliance" between war and religion' in Onnekink (ed), *War and religion after Westphalia, 1648-1713* (Farnham, 2009), 1–16 (quoted at 8).

57. For England, see Tony Claydon, 'Protestantism, universal monarchy and Christendom in William's war propaganda, 1689-1698', in Esther Mijers and David Onnekink (eds), *Redefining William III: the Impact of the King-stadholder in International Context* (Aldershot, 2007), 125–42; Andrew C. Thompson, 'After Westphalia: remodelling a religious foreign policy', in Onnekink (ed), *War and Religion*, 47–67.

58. Though see Tim Harris, 'Politics, religion and community in later Stuart Ireland' in Robert Armstrong and Tadhg Ó hAnnracháin (eds), *Community in Early Modern Ireland* (Dublin, 2006), 51–68.

59. David Hayton, 'The propaganda war', in Maguire (ed), *Kings in Conflict*, 106–21.

60. David Dickson, *Old World Colony: Cork and South Munster 1630-1830* (Cork, 2005), 56.

61. Listed in the Act of Supply, printed as *Anno Regni Jacobi II. Regis…At the Parliament begun at Dublin…* (Dublin, 1689). Bergin and Lyall (eds), *Acts of James II's Irish parliament*, 6–19.

62. Lenihan, *Boyne*, 120–7.

63. See, for example, James Scott Wheeler, 'The logistics of conquest' in Lenihan (ed), *Conquest and resistance*, 177–210. The volume as a whole is a valuable collection of essays which sets events in Ireland in these years within the wider European context, and a longer chronological span.

64. Gilbert (ed), *Jacobite Narrative*, 110.

65. For Tyrconnell's reflections upon war and strategy, and much else, see Lilian Tate (ed), 'Letter-book of Richard Talbot', in *Analecta Hibernica* iv (1932), 99–138.

66. Simms, *Jacobite Ireland*, 112.

67. Childs, *Williamite Wars*, 179.

68. Harman Murtagh, 'The Irish Jacobite army, 1689-1691', in Whelan (ed), *Last of the Great Wars*, 69–82.

69. A.W.H. Pearsall, 'The war at sea' in Maguire (ed), *Kings in Conflict*, 92–105; Paul M. Kerrigan, 'Ireland in naval strategy 1641-1691' in Lenihan (ed), *Conquest and Resistance*, 151–76.

70. John A. Lynn, *The Wars of Louis XIV 1667-1714* (London, 1999), 35–6, and passim for useful comments on the relative importance of the navy in Louis's wars.

71. Robert Heslip, 'Brass money' in Maguire (ed), *Kings in Conflict*, 122–35.

72. Jonathan I. Israel, 'The Dutch role in the Glorious Revolution' in Israel (ed), *Anglo-Dutch Moment*, 150–1.

73. Childs, *Williamite Wars*, 18–20; Wheeler, 'Logistics of conquest', 204–5.

74. John Miller, 'William III: the English view', in Whelan (ed), *Last of the Great Wars*, 17–38.

75. Childs, *Williamite Wars*, 27. Childs's account is alert to these aspects of the war throughout.

76. Quoted in Ó Ciardha, *Ireland and the Jacobite Cause*, 69.

77. Childs, *Williamite Wars*, 137–8, 155–6, 282.

78. Simms, *Jacobite Ireland*, 147, 152. See especially Lenihan, *Boyne*, for the significance of the battle.

79. J.G. Simms, 'Williamite peace tactics, 1690-1', *Irish Historical Studies*, 8 (1952–3), 303–23, reprinted in Simms, *War and Politics*, 181–201.

80. James Burke, 'Limerick in the golden age of siege warfare', in Whelan (ed), *Last of the Great Wars*, 83–107.

81. Wauchope, *Patrick Sarsfield*, 212.

82. Lenihan, 'Strategic geography, 1641-1691' in Lenihan (ed), *Conquest and Resistance*, 139–48.

83. James McGuire, 'The Treaty of Limerick' in Whelan (ed), *Last of the Great Wars*, 126–38 at 126, 132. Another important assessment of the treaty can be found in J.G. Simms, *The Treaty of Limerick* (Dundalk, 1961), reprinted in Simms, *War and Politics*, 203–24.

84. Kelly, 'Ireland and the Glorious Revolution', 163.

85. Only brief consideration can be given to developments after 1691, but see David Hayton's chapter in the present volume.

86. Simms, 'Williamite peace tactics' remains the fullest account, and is drawn upon here.

87. One exception might be the short-lived attempt, made during Tyrconnell's absence in France, to challenge his authority by mobilizing a more representative form of government—the authority of the returning Tyrconnell, now Lord Lieutenant, and of his king, was swiftly reasserted: Childs, *Williamite War*, 277–9.

88. Charles O'Kelly, quoted in Simms, *Jacobite Ireland*, 191.

89. Gilbert (ed), *Jacobite Narrative*, 176.

90. Hugh Balldearg O'Donnell to D'Avaux, 4 November 1690, in Gilbert (ed), *Jacobite Narrative*, 267–72. For O'Donnell, see Simms, *Jacobite Ireland*, 165, 192, 195, 236–9, 260.

91. For Sarsfield, see Liam Irwin, 'Patrick Sarsfield: the man and the myth' in Whelan (ed), *Last of the Great Wars*, 108–26; Wauchope, *Patrick Sarsfield*, 257–67.

92. Gilbert (ed), *Jacobite Narrative*, 310–1.

93. Guy Rowlands, *An army in exile: Louis XIV and the Irish forces of James II in France, 1691–1698*, Royal Stuart Society paper LX (London, 2001).

94. Patrick Kelly, 'Lord Galway and the penal laws', in C.E.J. Caldicott, H. Gough and J.-P. Pittion (eds), *The Huguenots and Ireland* (Dun Laoghaire, 1987), 239–54 at 254, note 51; Wauchope, *Patrick Sarsfield*, 266–7.

95. Quoted in Simms, *War and Politics*, 196. Article twelve pledged ratification of the articles by the monarchs within a year, and that Ginckel and the lords justices would 'use their utmost endeavours that the same shall be ratified and confirmed in parliament', Gilbert (ed), *Jacobite Narrative*, 301.

96. W.A. Maguire, 'The land settlement', in Maguire, *Kings in Conflict*, 139–56; J. G. Simms, *The Williamite Confiscation in Ireland, 1690–1703* (London, 1956). See also Eoin Kinsella, 'In pursuit of a positive construction: Irish Catholics and the Williamite articles of surrender, 1690–1701', *Eighteenth-century Ireland*, 24 (2009), 11–35.

97. Simms, *War and Politics*, 213–5; McGuire, 'Treaty', 136–7.

98. Bishop Anthony Dopping, sermon of 1691, quoted in S.J. Connolly, *Religion, Law and Power: the making of Protestant Ireland 1660–1760* (Oxford, 1992), 264.

99. C.I. McGrath, 'Securing the Protestant interest: the origins and purpose of the penal laws of 1695', *Irish Historical Studies*, 30 (1996–7), 235–49.

100. For plans to use Huguenot exiles to invade France, perhaps in association with domestic insurrection, see Matthew Glozier, 'Schomberg, Miremont and Huguenot invasions of France', in Onnekink (ed), *War and Religion*, 121–53.

101. Philip O'Regan, *Archbishop William King of Dublin (1650–1729) and the Constitution in Church and State* (Dublin, 2000), especially chapter two; Christopher J. Fauske (ed), *Archbishop William King and the Anglican Irish Context, 1688–1729* (Dublin, 2004).

102. As argued in detail in C.I. McGrath, 'Parliamentary additional supply: the development and use of regular short-term taxation in the Irish parliament, 1692–1716', *Parliamentary history*, 20 (2001) 27–54.

103. Ian McBride, *The Siege of Derry in Ulster Protestant Mythology* (Dublin 1997).

104. Patrick Griffin, 'Defining the limits of Britishness: the "new" British history and the meaning of the Revolution Settlement in Ireland for Ulster's Presbyterians', *Journal of British
   Studies*, 39 (2000) 263–87; Kathleen Middleton, 'Religious revolution and social crisis in
   southwest Scotland and Ulster 1687–1714' (PhD, University of Dublin, 2010).
105. There are valuable comments in Patrick Kelly, 'Nationalism and the contemporary historians of the Jacobite war in Ireland', *Studies on Voltaire and the eighteenth century*, 335 (1995),
   89–102. See also Ó Ciardha, *Ireland and the Jacobite Cause*.

SELECT BIBLIOGRAPHY

Barnard, Toby, *The Kingdom of Ireland, 1641–1760* (Basingstoke, 2004).

Bergin, John and Lyall, Andrew (eds), *The acts of James II's Irish parliament, 1689* (Dublin, 2016).

Childs, John, *The Williamite Wars in Ireland, 1688–1691*, (London, 2007).

Connolly, S.J., *Religion, Law and Power: the making of Protestant Ireland 1660–1760* (Oxford,
   1992).

Dennehy, Coleman A. (ed), *Restoration Ireland: always settling and never settled* (Aldershot,
   2008).

Fauske, Christopher J. (ed), *Archbishop William King and the Anglican Irish Context, 1688–1729*
   (Dublin, 2004).

Gillespie, Raymond, 'The Irish Protestants and James II, 1688–90' *Irish Historical Studies*, 28
   (1992–3), 124–33.

Harris, Tim, *Revolution: the great crisis of the British monarchy, 1685–1720* (London, 2006).

Hayton, D.W., *Ruling Ireland, 1685–1742* (Woodbridge, 2004).

Kelly, Patrick, 'Ireland and the Glorious Revolution: from Kingdom to Colony', in Robert
   Beddard (ed), *The Revolutions of 1688* (Oxford, 1991), 163–90.

Kinsella, Eoin, 'In pursuit of a positive construction: Irish Catholics and the Williamite articles
   of surrender, 1690–1701', *Eighteenth-century Ireland*, 24 (2009), 11–35.

Lenihan, Pádraig, *1690: Battle of the Boyne* (Stroud, 2003).

Lenihan, Pádraig, *The last cavalier: Richard Talbot (1631–91)* (Dublin, 2014).

Maguire, W.A. (ed), *Kings in Conflict: the revolutionary war in Ireland and its aftermath
   1689–1750* (Belfast, 1990).

McBride, Ian, *The Siege of Derry in Ulster Protestant Mythology* (Dublin 1997).

McGrath, C.I., 'Securing the Protestant interest: the origins and purpose of the penal laws of
   1695', *Irish Historical Studies*, 30 (1996–7), 235–49.

Miller, John, 'The earl of Tyrconnel and James II's Irish policy, 1685–1688' *Historical Journal* 20
   (1977), 803–23.

Ó Ciardha, Éamonn, *Ireland and the Jacobite Cause, 1685–1776: a fatal attachment* (Dublin, 2001).

O'Regan, Philip, *Archbishop William King of Dublin (1650–1729) and the Constitution in Church
   and State* (Dublin, 2000).

Simms, J.G., *War and Politics in Ireland 1649–1730* (D.W. Hayton and Gerard O'Brien, eds)
   (London, 1986).

Simms, J.G., *Jacobite Ireland, 1685–91* (1969; reprinted Dublin, 2000).

Wauchope, Piers, *Patrick Sarsfield and the Williamite War* (Blackrock, Co. Dublin, 1992).

Whelan, Bernadette, (ed), *The Last of the Great Wars: essays on the war of the three kings in
   Ireland 1688–91* (Limerick 1995).

ASCENDANCY IRELAND (1691–1801)

CHAPTER 20

EARLY HANOVERIAN IRELAND, 1690–1750

D. W. HAYTON

I. INTRODUCTION

THE half-century following the Battle of the Boyne was once commonly portrayed as a period of consolidation and stability, almost of stasis, in political and social development. In this traditional picture, the 'Protestant Ascendancy' class, dependent on an English military guarantee, lay supine under viceregal government. Occasional outbursts of a type of colonial patriotism, inspired by the writings of disgruntled intellectuals like William Molyneux or Jonathan Swift, were thought to lack the vehement self-assertion of later transatlantic revolutionaries, and to have subsided almost as quickly as they arose. The Irish economy, a victim of English discriminatory legislation, remained stagnant, while the most memorable achievement of the period was the erection of a code of 'penal laws' against Catholics (and to a lesser extent) Protestant Dissenters, that created a uniquely oppressive confessional state.

Historical scholarship over the past thirty years has transformed this picture. Instead of a caricature of torpor, we see a changing, indeed a dynamic, society. The first steps were taken by economic historians, whose research demonstrated that Ireland enjoyed a healthy balance of trade (legal and illegal) in spite of the restrictions imposed by English statute, and a spurt of economic growth beginning in the second quarter of the century.[1] Work on parliament and the press has uncovered a vibrant political culture, and a more complex relationship between the Irish Protestant elite and the imperial British state.[2] The history of Irish society has been rewritten, to question the teleological imperative that interpreted developments in the relatively stable first half of the eighteenth century, in the light of the more turbulent period that followed, and to set early Hanoverian Ireland in its contemporary context, so that the monopoly of power by the propertied class and the institutionalizing of religious discrimination no longer appear as peculiar features of the Irish condition.[3] This thoroughgoing 'revisionism' has not been to everyone's taste: historians unable to embrace an *ancien régime* Ireland in which the ascendancy of the Protestant landed gentry was accepted by a deferential Catholic populace, the privilege of the established church was a familiar aspect of the legal fabric, and the 'confessional state' merely an expression of economic realities, have re-emphasized what they regard as the essentially colonial nature of Irish society.[4]

II. A CONSTITUTIONAL REVOLUTION

In the controversy over the extent to which eighteenth-century Ireland was a 'colony', a distinction must be made between, on the one hand, the constitutional relationship with England, which did resemble that of colony and mother country, and on the other, the position and self-image, of the Irish governing elite. The fact that Ireland was ruled by a viceroy; that its parliament was supervised by the English Privy Council; and that the Westminster parliament determined the succession to the Irish crown, regulated Irish trade with the empire and occasionally interfered in Irish domestic affairs: all this resembled the government of the American colonies. However, Irish Protestants saw themselves as different from New Englanders or Virginians.[5] Their self-image was more complex, and it was also undergoing change in this period. In 1690, there was ambivalence. Some described themselves as 'the king's English subjects of Ireland', or simply 'the English in Ireland'; this was particularly useful when claiming the political rights of 'free-born Englishmen'. Some were unequivocally 'Irish', but many were capable of switching between the two national identities in different circumstances: 'English' to distinguish them from the native Catholic Irish; 'Irish', when their own vested interests clashed with those of England. Eventually, with the passage of generations, a clearer sense of 'Irishness' emerged, partly because of repeated Anglo-Irish friction, partly because the English themselves began to treat members of the Protestant elite as Irish, and to use traditional 'stage Irish' stereotypes to make fun of them in a fashion formerly reserved for mere 'Teagues'.[6]

A growing sense of Irish 'patriotism' did not stiffen Protestant attitudes to their constitutional subordination so much as might be supposed, largely because the implications of the Anglo-Irish relationship were less stark in practice than in theory. While Charles II's parliament, through a grant of 'additional' taxation for the king's lifetime, had effectively voted itself out of existence, M.P.s after 1691 were keenly aware of the consequences of over-generosity. The fragile financial position of the Irish treasury after the war, exacerbated by the continuance of a large-scale military budget, a consequence of the English government's preference for maintaining its standing forces on Irish soil, made the Dublin government dependent upon parliamentary supply, which was only given for short periods. The result was what has been called a 'constitutional revolution', transforming the Irish parliament into a permanent institution.[7] By 1715, a pattern of biennial sessions was established and a small national debt had appeared, to provide the capstone on this new construction. Poynings' Law still limited legislative autonomy, but its provisions were circumvented by the 'heads of bills' procedure, which meant that most statutes began as draft bills in the Irish parliament.[8] In particular the Commons had secured recognition, *de facto* if not *de iure*, of their supposed 'sole right' to initiate supply bills.[9]

Of course, this system was not perfect and there were still occasions for grievance. Both Irish and English privy councils possessed a power to interfere in legislation, amending or suppressing bills they did not like. Moreover, the 'heads of bills' procedure was cumbersome, and the fact that sessions of the Irish parliament were biennial rather than annual (as in England) compounded the difficulty of securing a prompt legislative response to personal, local, or national problems. Nonetheless, Irish Protestants accepted the disadvantages of a system which nevertheless gave them some influence over government. The key episode was the lord deputyship of Lord Capel in 1695–6, which followed an abject failure of parliamentary management in 1692. Capel reached an understanding with the leaders of the opposition which brought them into office, afforded them a share in patronage, and allowed them a say in the direction of policy.[10] Thus was born the so-called 'undertaker system'—contracting out responsibility for management to Irish politicians who could 'undertake' the satisfactory completion of parliamentary business—that would subsist until the 1770s.

The recruitment of 'undertakers' did not mean the end of all difficulties in political management. A viceroy might still select the wrong managers, or fail to support his 'undertakers' with sufficient clarity. And it was possible for the English government or parliament to provoke resentment by meddling in Irish affairs. The most serious example in this period occurred soon after the end of Capel's viceroyalty, when a series of decisions taken at Westminster infuriated Protestant Irishmen. First the English House of Lords claimed the right to act as a final court of appeal in Irish legal cases; then Westminster passed the Woollen Act of 1699, which denied Irish manufacturers the opportunity to export their cloth, and permitted exports of yarn only to provide raw material for English weavers. Finally in 1700 came an act to take back the forfeited Jacobite estates given away by King William, for resale to raise funds to compensate the English taxpayer for the reconquest of Ireland in 1689–90. These were all major issues: the loss of the appellate jurisdiction removed from Ireland the final decision in lawsuits over land; the restrictions on the woollen trade threatened a staple of the Irish economy; while the resumption of the forfeited estates affected not only the immediate beneficiaries of William's largesse, English and Dutch courtiers, but Irish Protestants who had purchased from them. The debate over wool inspired Molyneux's assertion of Irish legislative autonomy, *The case of Ireland...stated* (1698), which the English parliament condemned. Two years later, the Forfeitures Act prompted not only a 'paper war' between pamphleteers but a country-wide petitioning campaign.

So febrile was the political atmosphere that no Irish parliament was summoned between 1699 and 1703, despite financial exigencies, and some at the English court as well as in the press came to believe that Irish Protestants were determined on independence.[11] This was, however, a serious misreading. Molyneux's largely historical arguments for the sovereignty of the Irish parliament did not enjoy vocal support in Ireland

and even the petitioners against the Forfeitures Act were quick to stress that what they wanted was fair treatment, not independence. Interest was expressed in the possibility that Ireland might be drawn into a parliamentary union with England, but historians differ as to how seriously it should be taken, and in any case, the English were not interested.[12] Ultimately, what is more revealing about the episode is not how angry Irish Protestants became, but how their anger was stifled without significant concessions, beyond a promise from the Westminster parliament to promote the linen industry in Ireland as an alternative to wool.

III. The 'Penal Laws'

Where Irish interests and English interests did not clash directly, it was possible for the Irish parliament to make its own decisions. This was particularly true in relation to issues of domestic politics and security. The best example is provided by the 'penal laws' against Catholics, which derived from initiatives in the Irish parliament. King William was personally tolerant of differences in religious belief, wishing to keep the promises his general, Ginkel, and his lords justices had made to the Jacobites in the treaty of 1691, and was embarrassed in dealings with Catholic European allies by the persistent intolerance of his Irish Protestant subjects.[13] The most important of the penal laws were enacted between 1695 and 1709, though supplementary bills were proposed throughout the period.[14] They attacked the Catholic Church and the surviving Catholic political classes, banishing bishops and members of religious orders, making Catholic education illegal, depriving Catholics of the opportunity to hold office or participate in public life, insisting that their estates were divided up among their children, preventing Catholics from purchasing freehold land and excluding them from the legal profession. Later advocates of Catholic relief, notably Edmund Burke, condemned this 'code' as uniquely repressive in terms of its scope, a view some historians have endorsed.[15] Burke was also sceptical of the justification advanced by contemporaries, that the laws were necessary for the security of the Protestant interest. Instead, he described them as the fruits of Protestant supremacist arrogance, principally intended to reduce Catholics to the position of second-class citizens. This argument too has found echoes in the commentaries of historians, who have emphasized the patchiness of enforcement, and the fact that the most effective laws were those preserving Protestant control of land.[16]

'Revisionist' analysis has made a number of important modifications to this interpretation, through a detailed re-examination of the laws themselves and the circumstances in which they were introduced.[17] First and most important, the notion that the laws constituted a 'code' has been questioned; they were not enacted en bloc, but piecemeal over time, in different contexts and for different reasons. Nor were they the work of a single mindset, but the result of a complex process of legislation in which various parties were involved. This argument can be overstated, however, and the extreme view, that the laws were no more than a 'rag-bag' of miscellaneous measures, plays down their incremental nature. Attention has been drawn to the contours of the European scene as a genuine explanation for Protestant insecurities: the retraction of Protestantism to the fringes of northern Europe in the face of a resurgent Catholic Church, and the ever-present Jacobite threat to the Revolution settlement, aided by foreign powers. It is also clear that many of the laws, though appearing to modern eyes to be petty manifestations of religious bigotry, in fact related to specific issues of security; as, for example, the notorious act to prevent Catholics owning horses worth more than £5, intended to forestall the recruitment of native Catholic cavalry to assist a Jacobite invasion. Finally, those historians who have compared Ireland with other states of the *ancien régime* have pointed out, *contra* Burke, that the Irish situation was not unique. Many, if not most, European states restricted political rights to those of the established religion, while maintenance of the legal authority of a minority established church constituted an equally familiar defence of corporate privilege.

The Burkean explanation of the uneven pattern of enforcement has also been challenged, namely the argument that the Protestant landed classes were primarily interested in maintaining their own near-monopoly over landownership and in the symbolic effect of the 'penal code' in degrading Catholics. In practice the eighteenth-century state lacked the means systematically to enforce the laws against Catholic clergy. It was easier to ensure that Catholics did not take office, did not purchase land, or inherit undivided estates. Even in those cases, however, the law could be evaded through collusion with friendly Protestants, or by the nominal conversion of Catholics who remained privately committed to their old faith.[18] Certainly there was much suspicion of facile conversion, and many of the supplementary laws of the period after 1715 were designed to make the process harder.

IV. RELIGION AND POLITICS

Despite the broad popularity of anti-Catholic legislation, which was rarely opposed in the Irish parliament before 1707 and only cautiously criticized thereafter, differences of opinion began to emerge over the extent to which the laws should be strengthened and enforced. This was not simply a matter of personal connexion—whether an individual M.P. had Catholic relatives or friends—but of political outlook. The hotter Williamites never abated their fears of a 'popish' restoration—engineered by Jacobite conspirators, supported by the disaffected Catholic population, and backed by foreign aid. Any declaration of confidence could be rapidly unhinged by rumours of Catholic plotting. A candidate at the general election of 1713, hearing that he was being opposed by local Catholic interests, observed that 'his adversary being set up by a popish interest, he cannot lie *couchant* under it till the knife comes to his throat, or he be led to the stake'.[19]

Some responded differently, however, and concluded that the danger of a Catholic counter-revolution had receded with the defeat of James II and the expropriation and exile of Catholic landowners, the 'natural rulers' whose leadership was crucial to the success of an insurrection. Substantial Catholic proprietors remaining in Ireland sometimes lobbied against penal legislation, but preferred discretion. It was thus possible to believe that continuing anti-Catholic hysteria was overdone. In part this attitude resulted from an objective appraisal, both of the economic and social profile of the Catholic community and of the strategic thinking of the Jacobites and their European backers, neither of whom gave Ireland a priority. It also reflected the fact that there was now another source of fear: Protestant Dissent, in particular the concentration of Scottish Presbyterians in Ulster.

Ever since 1660, the Dublin government had been wary of Protestant Nonconformity, given the demographic weakness of the established church. Attention focused on Ulster, whose Presbyterian community was roused by the armed conflict that broke out in Scotland in 1678 between 'Covenanter' radicals and the episcopalian establishment. The precautions taken by the Irish government during the 'Covenanter' rising were followed in the aftermath of its suppression by equally heavy-handed measures, to ensure that Ulster remained quiet. Recent scholarship has shown how the brutalities of religious conflict in Scotland reverberated across the three kingdoms and agitated opinion in Ireland.[20] The effects could be seen even in the darkest days of the Jacobite war: in Derry, Anglicans and Presbyterians did not put aside their animosities despite sharing the privations of the siege.[21]

The process was accelerated by the events of the Glorious Revolution. Churchmen in Ireland looked on with horror as Presbyterian activists in Edinburgh exploited the Williamite victory to recover control of the Church of Scotland, abolish episcopacy, purge the universities, and expel from parishes ministers deemed sympathetic to episcopalianism. They could be forgiven for thinking the same fate might await Church of Ireland parsons, especially when Ulster Presbyterians organized themselves into a General Synod, along the lines of the reconstituted General Assembly in Scotland.[22] The Ulster Presbyterian clergy—trained in Edinburgh and Glasgow—were in close touch with their co-religionists and a number, including one of the most aggressive polemicists, John McBride, minister of Belfast congregation, had taken refuge in Scotland during the Jacobite period and had been present during the coup of 1688–9.

The new regime did little to allay these fears. The King's personal preferences were suspect: although Queen Mary was a staunch Anglican, William was a Calvinist. Moreover, among the early fruits of his victory had been recognition of the General Synod of Ulster and the restoration of the royal pension to Irish Presbyterian ministers; the *regium donum*. When the Irish parliament met in 1692, the English administration pushed for a toleration bill, an equivalent of the controversial Toleration Act passed at Westminster in 1689 which in the view of High Church clerics had grievously damaged the prestige and authority of the Church of England. Irish bishops successfully resisted this first attempt, but the issue did not disappear and Lord Deputy Capel raised it, again unsuccessfully, in 1695. (Eventually a limited toleration was enacted in 1719, though in very different circumstances, and in the eyes of Presbyterians, poor compensation for a continued restriction of their rights to participate in politics and government.)

Anglican anxieties were already acute in the early years of William III's reign, and tensions between the established church and the General Synod were running high—manifested in bad-tempered exchanges in print, with bishops challenging the entitlement of Dissenters to toleration and even questioning the validity of Presbyterian orders.[23] A succession of bad harvests in Scotland after 1694 prompted a further rush of economic refugees to Ulster from the 'Covenanter' heartlands of the Scottish south-west. Without accurate shipping records, it is impossible to arrive at an accurate figure for the extent of this migration; contemporary observers put it as high as 80 000 families in five years, though the number may have been less than half that.[24] The effect on the Anglican clergy was dramatic. In sermons and pamphlets, intemperate clergymen like William Tisdall, vicar of Belfast, inveighed against the religious, political, and even social practices of Presbyterians, who were accused of operating as a 'state within a state', encroaching on the corporate privileges of the church, presuming to discipline their congregations in ways that infringed upon the authority of ecclesiastical courts, and conspiring to expand their influence beyond Ulster. Tisdall even accused Presbyterian merchants of refusing to trade with Anglicans or take them as apprentices.[25] But it was not just the hot breath of clerical denunciation that Presbyterians were obliged to suffer and which they were perfectly capable of returning in kind. In the absence of a legal toleration, church authorities exerted their legal powers to curb the spread of Dissent, summoning Presbyterians to ecclesiastical courts on various charges including fornication if they had been married by a Presbyterian minister contrary to law.

The virulence of the Anglican reaction was accentuated by the difficulties under which clergy were labouring. Never financially robust, the Church of Ireland suffered acutely from the alienation of tithe and glebe to lay proprietors. The devastating effects of war resulted in further loss of income. In these circumstances, clerical pluralism—the holding of more than one benefice—was rife, with the obvious consequences for pastoral provision. Historians differ over the extent to which the clergy were failing to meet their obligations and one persuasive modern commentary has argued that, if judged by their capacity to minister to their own denomination, they were doing a good job and certainly no worse than their counterparts elsewhere.[26] But this was not the way many influential churchmen viewed clerical performance. This sour view was perhaps unduly affected by notorious cases of dereliction of duty, such as the English bishop Hackett, whose chronic absenteeism earned him the sobriquet 'the bishop of Hammersmith', or Dean Matthews of Down, deprived for simony. Equally, it may have been disappointment that the church was unable to capitalize on the political defeat of Catholicism, which seemed to afford an unparalleled opportunity to change the confessional balance.

A powerful lobby emerged in the episcopate in King William's reign, bent on reform to reinvigorate the church.[27] This co-existed uneasily with a concurrent movement for religious revival, deriving from the influence of German pietism, that attracted a number of influential laymen into prayer-groups, societies 'for the reformation of manners', and the foundation of schools, hospitals, and poorhouses. But with the exception of the charity-school movement, the bishops concentrated their energies on parliamentary initiatives to restore lay impropriations and enforce clerical residence.[28] In this effort they encountered only frustration. The unhelpfulness of government and parliament drove them to seek alternative methods and by 1700 reformers were urging the recall of convocation, the clerical equivalent of parliament, as an engine for ecclesiastical improvement independent of secular influence.

A similar approach was adopted in England, but there the campaign was driven by clergymen with different ambitions, the so-called 'High Church party', allied with the Tories. Their intention was not constructive reform so much as the recovery of corporate authority. There were men of this type in Ireland, where the priority for parochial clergy was to strike against Dissent. Initiatives to oblige parsons to reside, or to rebuild churches and rectories, were far from welcome; indeed, they resented such episcopal interference. When the Irish convocation was summoned in 1703, it was 'high-flyers' who predominated. Bishops tried to induce restraint, in order to get business done, but only antagonized the lower house and created factions that took the colour of English clerical politics, with debates a battleground between 'High' and 'Low Church'.[29]

The conflict in the church mirrored a secular political scene that was becoming polarized, in imitation of the existing English 'party' structure. The time lag in following the English example may be ascribed to the absence of a tradition of cavalier loyalism in Protestant Ireland, such as underlay the rise of the Tory party in England. Moreover, recent experience did not incline many to hanker after James II's return. The ethos of the parliament that met in Dublin in 1692 was strongly Williamite and the principal disputes were between 'court' and 'country'—as far as the leading figures were concerned, 'ins' against 'outs'. Slowly, however, these factions crystallized into 'parties' on the English model. To some extent this was a natural consequence of the Anglo-Irish political nexus. The presence in the Dublin government of front-rank English politicians created alliances with local politicians. But issues were also important. At first, accusations that elements in the Castle administration were favouring Catholics in the land settlement inspired an ultra-Williamite faction that identified with the English Whigs. Later, the perceived danger from Ulster Presbyterianism created a principle around which an Irish Tory interest could at last coalesce. The rise of a 'High Church' faction among the clergy equipped these proto-Tories with an auxiliary army of propagandists and electoral canvassers, and the political re-emergence of the Ormonds in the person of the highly respected, if unintelligent, second duke, gave it a native leadership.

V. THE RAGE OF PARTY

These developments came together with Ormond's appointment as viceroy at the beginning of Queen Anne's reign. His first parliament saw the final kicks of the 'patriot' campaign against the Woollen and Forfeitures Resumption Acts, as opposition members attempted to mobilize popular fear of economic depression. One of their tactics was a campaign for the inclusion of Ireland in the projected Anglo-Scottish union, a move some historians interpret as genuine and others as opportunistic.[30] More important was the imposition in 1704 of a sacramental test, designed to exclude Dissenters from participation in government and politics, by obliging holders of crown and municipal office to take communion annually in the established church. Ulster Presbyterians, unlike their English counterparts, refused to compromise by conforming 'occasionally' and resigned *en masse*. The greatest impact was felt in borough corporations, with Presbyterian strongholds like Belfast and Derry falling to Anglican domination. Thereafter the maintenance of the test became the focus of parliamentary debate, alongside the strengthening of the penal laws against Catholics, as religion, rather than the economy, preoccupied members.[31] It was a question of strategic preference: Whigs harped on the danger from papists and the need for Protestant unity; Tories began to regard the existing penal laws as sufficient and focused instead on the defence of the church.

Equally significant, in the development of a two-party *system*, was the way in which Ormond responded to the opposition given to his administration by the Speaker of the Commons, Alan Brodrick. Though indisputably Whiggish in his political beliefs and friendships, Brodrick had held office since 1695, under viceroys of both parties. Ormond supported his election as Speaker in 1703, in a misguided attempt at conciliation, only to find Brodrick opposing him at every turn.[32] When the session was over, Brodrick was dismissed as Solicitor-General, and the Irish administration remodelled on party lines. This was the first in a series of purges: Wharton, a Whig, returned Brodrick and his friends to power in 1708; Ormond reversed the process in 1710, and Sunderland in 1714–15 shifted power back to the Whigs. Every time the tide turned, it was with greater force, and the incoming Whig politicians in 1714 expected every Tory to be removed.[33] From the highest office to the lowest, a spoils system was in operation.

The most important effect of this two-party system was to restrict the viceroy's freedom of manoeuvre. Neither Wharton in 1708, nor Ormond in 1710, had any choice in the Irish politicians they employed. Those who did mistakenly seek a balance between the parties and a 'mixed' administration, notably the hapless Shrewsbury in 1713, saw their hopes founder in confusion. The existence of a spoils system also devalued the currency of patronage. This was seen most clearly in the aftermath of the Hanoverian succession, when it became impossible for any politician, English or Irish, to secure the retention of an adherent of the outgoing administration.

The heyday of party, while brief, demonstrated that the integration of Irish with English politics was the most effective way in which the self-government enjoyed by the Irish Protestant landowning class could be enhanced. It was, of course, self-government within limits: Irish politicians were subject to the same kinds of restriction as their English masters, and in 1714 Irish Whigs were no better able to save Tory friends than was the viceroy. The situation changed with great suddenness, however, after the triumph of the Whigs on the Hanoverian succession.

The rapid collapse of the Tories as a political force after 1714 demonstrated that the party had sunk only shallow roots in Irish society. Irish Protestants were bound to be wary of the element of Stuart loyalism that was central to the party's ethos, since their own title to property depended on the Revolution settlement. Significantly, the more vocal—and more extreme—representatives of the party were English imports: clergymen like

Thomas Lindsay, who rose to the primacy in the last days of Queen Anne, and lawyers like the fiery Jacobite sympathizer Sir Constantine Phipps, Lord Chancellor 1710–14. There is fragmentary evidence of an indigenous Tory interest below the level of the elite: in the volume of cheap print produced for electoral purposes, the vicious infighting in borough corporations, and the partisan behaviour of election mobs in Dublin and other large towns. But as yet this kind of 'public opinion' seems to have mattered little. From what we know of the Irish electoral system (and much more research could, and should, be done) the voters were highly susceptible to the influence of property, with most boroughs still being dominated by landed patrons. Despite the frequency of general elections in the first decades of the century (as many as five between 1692 and 1715 as compared to two between 1716 and 1760), parliament essentially represented the landowning class.[34] And it was the gentry who turned their backs on Toryism after 1714. The indiscretions of the previous ministry (Phipps's intervention to protect a Dublin printer from prosecution for publishing a pro-Jacobite tract; and the official permission granted to French recruiting agents to canvass Irish Catholics) had already resulted in a Commons majority for the Whig opposition in the 1713 parliament. Ormond's flight to the exiled court in 1715 completed the identification of the Tory cause with the Pretender.

VI. PATRIOTISM AND POLITICS

Moderate Tories began to change sides before the new parliament met in 1715; others followed. A remnant survived, in irreconcilable opposition, but the changing parameters of political debate undermined a sense of group identity. Not even when English ministers canvassed a repeal of the test could Tories recapture their former impetus, for the fact that a full-scale repeal (as distinct from palliative measures) was always unpopular with a majority of M.P.s robbed the issue of its divisive quality. Outside parliament, Whig and Tory factions continued to operate in counties and boroughs, but within a decade had discarded party labels for locally based identities.[35]

As for the churchmen whose visceral hatred of Presbyterianism had animated the Tory cause, the discontinuance of convocation deprived them of a platform, and the attenuation of the Tory element on the episcopal bench weakened their voice in parliament. Careerism drew aspiring clerical politicians into a more comfortable relationship with the Whig ascendancy. Moreover, the sense of crisis for Irish churchmen was diminishing. Scottish Presbyterian immigration had stopped, and by the late 1710s the demographic balance was beginning to tilt in the opposite direction, as distress propelled the first of a series of waves of emigration from Ulster to North America.[36] The doctrinal divisions which increasingly plagued the General Synod also made Presbyterians appear less formidable, especially when a major controversy arose in 1719 over the question of ministerial subscription to the Westminster Confession, which resulted in congregations splintering off to form the semi-independent Presbytery of Antrim.

As 'party' divisions receded, the pattern of allegiances in parliamentary politics acquired a new fluidity. 'Connexions' based on kinship and patronage took the place of the broader-based parties of Queen Anne's reign. Families like the Gores, of whom there were at one time as many as nine in the Commons, operated as political units. The more successful built outwards from a central core of kinship networks, using different forms of political cement. Alan Brodrick's lengthy political career enabled him to construct a substantial personal following from members of his extended family, from others who owed their election to his recommendation or their preferment to his influence, or who simply admired his ability and trusted his judgment.[37] His great rival, William Conolly, could command an even larger squadron. His great strengths were his electoral empire, based in the north-west, and the patronage at his disposal through membership of the revenue commission, which controlled the largest and fastest-growing department of state in eighteenth-century Ireland.[38] The supporters of 'the two great men', were sometimes described in regional terms: Brodrick's 'Munster squadron' and Conolly's 'Ultonians', after their leader's Ulster origins. But while Brodrick's influence does indeed seem to have been concentrated in the south-west, his rival was by no means a regional figure and drew a significant following from aspiring politicians in other provinces, especially from the world of Dublin officials and men of business.[39]

A shift from ideology to 'interest' as the prevailing currency of politics brought a change in the tone and direction of parliamentary discourse. Politicians playing the game of opposition looked to a different set of issues: corruption in government, especially financial scandals, such as brought down the treasury official John Pratt in 1725; interference with the liberties of parliament, usually by the over-zealous application of conciliar powers under Poynings' Law; and the defence of Irish economic interests. Similar concerns agitated M.P.s at Westminster and representative institutions in other European monarchies; they were the natural stock-in-trade of 'patriots', in the usual sense of those defending the public interest against the selfishness of courtiers. But in Ireland 'patriotism' inevitably had national connotations. Corrupt office-holders were appointed by English ministers; interference with the working of the Irish parliament originated in Whitehall as much as with the Dublin government; while the greatest threat to the Irish economy came from the jealousy of English vested interests.

The essential pragmatism of Irish Protestant 'patriots' kept protests against constitutional subordination in a low key. When they did become strident, in 1717–19, in the revived jurisdictional dispute between the Irish and British House of Lords over Westminster's claim to act as a final court of appeal, this was largely because of the implications for the security of Irish landholding, always a tender point. It was also the case that the 'patriot' majority in the Lords, which pressed the jurisdictional issue so far as to imprison three Irish judges for giving unwelcome legal opinions, was composed of die-hard Tories, and Irish-born bishops (the heart of the so-called 'Irish party') resentful of the appointment of Englishmen to lucrative sees and despairing of preferment themselves. When the British parliament responded with the Declaratory Act of 1720, not only stating bluntly the superiority of its own appellate jurisdiction, but gratuitously adding a clause to affirm its right to legislate for Ireland, there was some puffing in the Dublin press, but a shattering silence in the Irish parliament.

Economic issues, on the other hand, could arouse passions of a very different order. The best-known example is the furore in 1722–5 against Wood's Halfpence, in which Swift, whose disappointing reward for service to the English Tory ministry in 1710–14 had been a return to his native land in 1713 as dean of St Patrick's cathedral in Dublin, established his reputation as a 'patriot' hero. The affair of the halfpence combined the old story of casual English exploitation of Ireland's resources with the stench of corruption in high places, since Wood had obtained his patent for an Irish copper coinage through George I's mistress, the duchess of Kendal. Swift's pamphlets on the affair, the *Drapier's letters*, exploited the popular belief that Ireland's bullion would be drained away, to be replaced by Wood's worthless copper. The ferment engendered in the populace, manifest in violent attempts to prevent the landing of ships carrying the halfpence, was enough to intimidate the authorities in Dublin Castle, and to force Walpole to withdraw the patent.

There was, however, an alternative political history of the affair of the halfpence. While the violence of popular reaction should not be underestimated, English government was more concerned with what seemed to be an acute failure of Irish political management. At the root of the failure lay a smouldering rivalry between Alan Brodrick and William Conolly. Brodrick had found that by taking the prestigious post of Lord Chancellor in 1714 he had removed himself from the Commons, where the real business of parliament—the granting of taxes—was carried on, and where Conolly reigned supreme. While Brodrick did not oppose government directly, he watched from the sidelines as his son, St John, led the attacks on the ministry in the lower house. This pattern was repeated in every parliamentary session, with Conolly seeking to accommodate viceroys and their political bosses and the Brodricks joining the Tories on popular issues. By 1720, the English ministry decided on Brodrick's dismissal, but lost its nerve. The affair of Wood's Halfpence brought matters to a head. Walpole blamed over-reliance on Irish parliamentary managers for the pusillanimity of the Dublin administration and determined on action. He sent to Dublin a new viceroy, Carteret, who would have to choose between Conolly and Brodrick, and at the same time he set in motion a scheme to limit dependence on Irish 'undertakers' by appointing senior English officials who would act as watchdogs for Whitehall's interests. Carteret completed the first task, opting for Conolly, but the second plank in Walpole's strategy failed, since Carteret was not prepared to sustain a serious attempt to undermine 'undertaker' authority.[40]

The differences between Conolly's party and Brodrick's were personal rather than ideological. Nor indeed was there a deep gulf of principle between those who spoke in parliament on behalf of the Castle and those portraying themselves as 'patriots'. The private correspondence of members of Conolly's circle[41] shows that they were equally committed to the 'improvement' of Ireland but saw the opportunity for achieving this through cooperation with English ministries and the English parliament rather than by raging impotently against the inevitable.[42] The same could be said of those politicians who followed after. When Conolly died in 1729, he was replaced as Speaker by his closest collaborator, Sir Ralph Gore, who maintained business as usual. Gore's death only two years afterwards left no obvious successor, and the new viceroy, the duke of Dorset, after a feeble attempt to take the reins of power into his own hands, entrusted management to a former oppositionist, Brodrick's political heir, Henry Boyle. Much was made publicly of the new Speaker's principles, and doubtless some of those—'patriot' Whigs and former Tories—who had followed him in opposition hoped for a change of direction, but none was forthcoming. Boyle's prime concern was to secure English ministerial endorsement of his recommendation for a lucrative appointment in the revenue.

VII. Protestant Ireland in Crisis

These high-political manoeuvres did not reflect public debates on the great issues of the day. The years 1727–34 were in fact marked by a widespread perception of profound national crisis and by significant efforts to change the direction of economic and social development. The underlying problem was understood to be the backwardness of the Irish economy; ironically, since modern historians have identified the second third of the eighteenth century as a period of economic 'take-off' on which later prosperity was based. Contemporary commentators bemoaned the weakness of Irish agriculture—in particular the preference for large-scale pastoral farming over tillage—the absence of a strong manufacturing base, the inadequacies of inland communications and transport, the limitations of the banking system, and the chaotic state of the coinage. These issues were brought to a head in the late 1720s by a succession of bad harvests which reduced sections of the population, especially in Ulster, to near-starvation. Worse still, the response of many northern communities was to seek a better life across the Atlantic and this second wave of emigration, stronger than the first, was a significant diminution of the Protestant interest, even if the majority of those leaving were Presbyterian.

At the same time, the realization was growing that the penal laws, and other initiatives to seek the conversion of Catholics, were not working. The charity-school movement, in which philanthropists had invested time and money, had run into the ground.[43] Several *causes célèbres* drew public attention to the Catholic question: complaints of Catholics voting in the 1727 election; rumours that a Catholic peer, Clancarty, was using the English parliament to impugn the land settlement; and news that French recruiting agents were again beating drums among the Catholic populace. When the Irish House of Lords initiated an inquiry in 1731 into 'the state of popery', they discovered that the number of priests in the kingdom had actually risen.[44]

The progress of the Reformation in Ireland had long been synonymous with the spread of English 'civility'; in social relations, respect for the law, and the organization of economic activity. Thus the poverty, lawlessness, and disorder that Swift and others saw as disfiguring Irish life, especially in the expanding capital, were interpreted as symptoms of spiritual and economic dereliction. The response of the ruling elite to this growing danger to the stability of Protestant Ireland was twofold: attempts to reinforce the penal laws and reinvigorate Protestant proselytism and renewed emphasis on modernization of agriculture and manufacture. Not all those involved shared the belief that religious and economic regeneration were inseparable, but there was a strong overlap between the two enterprises.

Between 1727 and 1733, eight bills were introduced into the Irish parliament to tighten up the corpus of penal legislation, only two of which (including an act to prevent Catholics from voting) reached the statute book. More significant in the long run was the establishment, by royal grant, of the Incorporated Society for Promoting English Protestant Working Schools—the so-called 'charter schools'—which revived the principle of the charity schools by founding a network of elementary schools for the children of the poor that would combine education in basic literacy, the established religion, and the 'habits of industry'.[45] At the same time, the Irish parliament enacted measures to encourage agricultural improvement and the building of roads and canals. The one bright light in the encircling economic gloom had been the growth of the linen manufacture, especially in east Ulster, under the supervision of the statutory Linen Board (set up in 1711). Parliament sought to repeat this success by encouraging other industrial developments, including mining and fishing as well as cloth manufacture, through grants and bounties.

These initiatives tapped into what had become a fashion—almost a mania—for the economic, social, and moral 'improvement' of Ireland. The press buzzed with schemes, some sensible, some inevitably hare-brained; and the establishment of the Dublin Society in 1731 brought together wealthy enthusiasts in this common purpose, to exchange ideas and publicize pet projects.[46] This was precisely the kind of pompous social engineering satirized by Swift, most notably in his *Modest Proposal* of 1729 which recommended the raising of Irish Catholic children as livestock for the butchery market. In recent years historians have paid considerable attention to the craze for 'improvement', some seeing it as a key to open up the mental world of the Irish Protestant elite, others more sceptical of the extent of its magnetic power over thought and behaviour.[47] Undoubtedly commitment among the landowning class varied. Nor should every aspect of material 'improvement' necessarily be seen as a reflection of social theory: the employment of fashionable architects and garden designers and the importation of foreign luxuries was as much about conspicuous consumption as national regeneration.[48] But while the active participants in the Dublin Society were a minority, they did include many leading political figures, office-holders, and oppositionists, across different factions.

The drive for 'improvement', although sometimes accompanied by a strong evangelical purpose, came to work against the interests of the established church. Members of the clerical estate had always been suspicious of the attitude of the gentry to ecclesiastical reform, especially when proprietorial interests were affected. They now witnessed a movement of opinion against their corporate privileges. Noted 'improvers' began to depict the church as a drag anchor on economic progress.[49] The pressure of tithe bore heavily on the rural poor, while the insistence on allowing only short leases of church land, to preserve ecclesiastical incomes, was seen as stifling the enterprise of tenants. In parliament, in the press, and in the countryside, controversy raged over tithe: a decision of the Commons in 1736 to exempt some lands provoked Swift into his bitterest satire on what he saw as the weak intellects and corrupt morals of Irish M.P.s: the *Legion Club*.[50] Infuriated clergymen presumed that the Irish parliament had contracted the virus of anticlericalism from its English counterpart and indeed the church was placed on the defensive by a series of bills designed to curb its authority. Conversely, Presbyterian hopes were raised, and although two English-inspired initiatives to repeal the sacramental test were dismissed out of hand in 1731 and 1733, some relief was finally afforded in 1737 on the marriage question, by an act sponsored by economic 'improvers'.

VIII. A Changing Scene

By the 1740s, the contours of Irish politics had changed. The principal issues that had agitated Irish politics in the early decades of the century seemed to have been settled. Even if the Catholic Church had not been destroyed, Catholic political interests were quiescent and, despite the survival of a popular Jacobite sentiment, manifested most clearly in Irish-language poetry of a traditional kind, the rebellion in Scotland in 1745 produced no significant response.[51] Some of the heat had also gone out of the Presbyterian question with changing demographics and theological ruptures; the maintenance of the sacramental test had been confirmed and its effects were seen in the reduction of the Presbyterian landowning class through gradual conformity. And Irish Protestant opinion seemed to have accepted the practical advantages of limited legislative autonomy. A pragmatic approach prevailed, government and opposition sharing a 'constructive' patriotism with economic growth as its objective. In terms of day-to-day political management, viceroys had developed a system in which they relied on local politicians, or 'undertakers', to do their business.

Of course, the effectiveness of the 'undertaker' system depended on a continuing appreciation of its value, an understanding of its dynamics. There were worrying signs that complacency had caused some British ministers to forget the principal political lesson of the preceding half-century: that when the viceroy was only present in Ireland for a parliamentary session every two years, what was needed was to select a single Irish politician or political grouping to manage, and to give those managers unequivocal support. Although Boyle had been settled as the chief 'undertaker' by 1735, his monopoly of influence was short-lived. For the next viceroy, Devonshire, adopted just the kind of 'divide-and-rule' strategy which had failed repeatedly in the past, and one of Conolly's former lieutenants, Brabazon Ponsonby, rose to prominence as a rival to Boyle. Boyle's problems were then compounded by the appointment as archbishop of Armagh in 1747 of the Englishman George Stone, an incurably meddlesome priest who used his influence at Whitehall to advance his own position in the Dublin government.[52]

At the same time, the 'patriot' element in Irish politics was showing a harder edge, evident in the willingness of some M.P.s to challenge the once impregnable position of the established church. A more forthright concern for Irish interests was only to be expected in times of distress, as occurred in the early 1740s, but it was certainly enhanced by long-term developments: a more emphatic sense of Irish national identity, and perhaps also frustration at the limitations of Irish legislative processes as a means of solving social and economic problems. 'Patriotism' had also found a broader constituency. Extra-parliamentary opinion was an increasingly important factor, as politicians sought 'popularity' through orchestrating campaigns in the press, or presenting themselves as opponents of elitism.[53] Much of this story remains to be written, but current scholarship has at least clarified the outlines. Champions of electoral 'independence' appeared in the larger borough corporations, and in some counties. Not all were genuine and in some instances the 'independent interest' may have served only to cloak more traditional forms of electoral campaigning against established patrons. But the most renowned opponent of 'oligarchy', the Dublin apothecary Charles Lucas, did undeniably represent a popular movement of the capital's freemen, against the self-perpetuating authority of the aldermen.[54]

Below the surface, more profound changes were beginning. Despite the jeremiads of political economists, and the suffering caused by the savage winter of 1740–1, the Irish economy was improving. There were significant regional variations, but in Munster the Atlantic trade had boosted agricultural production. In Ulster, the nascent linen industry was beginning to transform the lives of farmer-weavers in the countryside and the urban commercial and professional elites in towns like Belfast and Newry. In due course the appearance of a wealthy Catholic mercantile class would result in pressure for the relaxation of the penal laws,[55] while the economic strengthening of the Presbyterian communities in the north would create a similar demand for political change.

These new pressures were felt as early as 1749, with the first appearance of what was to become a major constitutional issue. The accumulation of revenue surpluses in the Irish treasury raised a new constitutional question with which governments and M.P.s had to grapple: competing claims as to whether Crown or parliament had the authority to dispose of these funds. In the following decade, government and parliament would again be in dispute over money bills, in ways that recalled the conflicts of the 1690s. In an equally familiar way, posturings over constitutional principle were accompanied by, and to some degree served as a cover for, what was in essence a duel for power between rival Irish politicians. But the appeals made to opinion 'out of doors', the use of the press, and the mobilization of non-voters in a 'patriotic' cause, were all indications that Irish Protestants had entered a new, uncertain political world.

Notes

1. See L.M. Cullen, *Anglo-Irish Trade 1660–1800* (Manchester, 1968); idem, *An Economic History of Ireland since 1600* (London, 1972).
2. See, for example, Patrick McNally, *Parties, Patriots and Undertakers: Parliamentary Politics in Early Hanoverian Ireland* (Dublin, 1997); Eoin Magennis, *The Irish Political System 1740–1765: the Golden Age of the Undertakers* (Dublin, 2000); D.W. Hayton, *Ruling Ireland*

1685–1742: Politics, Politicians and Parties (Woodbridge, 2004); T. C. Barnard, 'Considering the inconsiderable: electors, patrons and Irish elections 1659–1761' in *Parliamentary History*, xx (2001), 107–27.

3. See especially, S.J. Connolly, *Religion, Law and Power: the Making of Protestant Ireland 1660–1760* (Oxford, 1992), and, for a more specific discussion of the 'corporatist' ethos of Irish institutions, J.R. Hill, 'Corporate values in Hanoverian Edinburgh and Dublin' in S.J. Connolly, R.A. Houston, and R.J. Morris, *Conflict, Identity and Economic Development: Ireland and Scotland, 1600–1939* (Preston, 1995), 114–24.

4. See, for example, Kevin Whelan, *'The Tree of Liberty': Radicalism, Catholicism, and the Construction of Irish Identity 1760–1830* (Cork, 1996); Vincent Morley, *Irish Opinion and the American Revolution, 1760–1783* (Cambridge, 2002).

5. D. G. Boyce, *Nationalism in Ireland* (London, 1982), 106–8.

6. D.W. Hayton, 'Anglo-Irish attitudes: changing perceptions of national identity among the Protestant Ascendancy in Ireland, ca. 1690–1740', in *Studies in Eighteenth-Century Culture*, xvii (1987), 145–57; idem, 'From barbarian to burlesque: English images of the Irish, *c.* 1660–1750', in *Irish Economic and Social History*, xv (1988), 7–31; Jim Smyth,. ' "Like amphibious animals": Irish Protestants, ancient Britons, 1691–1707' in *Historical Journal*, xxxvi (1993), 785–97.

7. C. McGrath, *The Making of the Eighteenth-century Irish Constitution: Government, Parliament and the Revenue, 1692–1714* (Dublin, 2000).

8. The legislative output of the Irish parliament awaits a systematic study, but the raw materials have been assembled in E.M. Johnston-Liik, *History of the Irish Parliament 1692–1800* (6 vols, Belfast, 2002), i, 405–581; and the online 'Irish Legislation Database' (www.qub.ac.uk/ild). Preliminary attempts at analysis have been made in Johnston-Liik, *History of the Irish Parliament*, i, 2-09-404; D.W. Hayton, 'Patriots and legislators: Irishmen and their parliaments' in Julian Hoppit (ed), *Parliaments, Nations and Identities in Britain and Ireland, 1660–1850* (Manchester, 2003), 103–23; and D.W. Hayton, James Kelly, and John Bergin (eds), *The Eighteenth-century Composite State: Representative Institutions in Ireland and Europe, 1689–1800* (Basingstoke, 2010).

9. James Kelly, *Poynings' Law and the Making of Law in Ireland, 1660–1800* (Dublin, 2007), chs. 2–3.

10. C.I. McGrath, 'English ministers, Irish politicians and the making of a parliamentary settlement in Ireland, 1692–5' in *English Historical Review*, cxix (2004), 585–613.

11. *The Private Diary of William, first Earl Cowper*, E.C. Hawtrey (ed) (Eton, 1833), 37.

12. James Kelly, 'The origins of the act of union: an examination of unionist opinion in Britain and Ireland, 1650–1800' in *Irish Historical Studies*, xxv (1986–7), 236–63; D. W. Hayton, 'Ideas of union in Anglo-Irish political discourse, 1692–1720: meaning and use' in D.G. Boyce, R.R. Eccleshall, and Vincent Geoghegan (eds), *Political Discourse in Seventeenth and Eighteenth-century Ireland* (London, 2001), 142–68; A.I. Macinnes, 'Union failed, union accomplished: the Irish union of 1703 and the Scottish union of 1707' in Dáire Keogh and Kevin Whelan (eds), *Acts of Union: the Causes, Contexts and Consequences of the Act of Union* (Dublin, 2001), 67–94; C. I. McGrath, 'The union representation of 1703 in the Irish House of Commons: a case of mistaken identity' in *Eighteenth-Century Ireland*, xxiii (2008), 11–35.

13. Wouter Troost, 'William III and Ireland' in C.C. Barfoot and Paul Hoftijzer (eds), *Fabrics and Fabrications: the Myth and Making of William and Mary* (Amsterdam, 1990), 225–58.

14. The most detailed account is to be found in James Kelly, 'Sustaining a confessional state: the Irish parliament and Catholicism' in Hayton, Kelly, and Bergin (eds), *Composite State*, 44–77.

15. The older literature is surveyed in R.E. Burns, 'The Irish penal code and some of its historians' in *Review of Politics*, xxi (1959), 276–99; and S.J. Connolly, 'Religion and history' in *Irish Economic and Social History*, x (1983), 66–80.

16. The most sophisticated exposition of this view may be found in *Catholic Ireland in the Eighteenth Century: Collected Essays of Maureen Wall*, G.O'Brien (ed) (Dublin, 1989).

17. R.E. Burns, 'The Irish popery laws: a study of eighteenth-century legislation and behavior [sic]' in *Review of Politics*, xxiv (1962), 485–508; S.J. Connolly, 'The penal laws' in W.A. Maguire (ed), *Kings in Conflict: the Revolutionary War in Ireland and its Aftermath, 1689–1750* (Belfast, 1990), 157–72; Thomas Bartlett, *The Fall and Rise of the Irish Nation: the Catholic Question, 1690–1830* (Dublin, 1992), chs. 1–2; C.I. McGrath, 'Securing the Protestant interest: the origins and purpose of the penal laws of 1695' in *Irish Historical Studies*, xxx (1996–7), 25–46.

18. T.P. Power, 'Converts' in. T.P. Power and Kevin Whelan (eds), *Endurance and Emergence: Catholics in Ireland in the Eighteenth Century* (Dublin, 1990), 101–27; C.I. McGrath, 'The provisions for conversion in the penal laws, 1695–1750' in Michael Brown, C. McGrath, and T. P. Power (eds), *Converts and Conversion in Ireland 1650–1850* (Dublin, 2005), 35–59. This is a subject on which a great deal more might be written.

19. Sir Richard Cox to Edward Southwell, 24 December 1711, quoted in Hayton, *Ruling Ireland*, 171.

20. Tim Harris, *Restoration: Charles II and his Kingdoms, 1660–1685* (London, 2005), chs. 6–7.

21. Ian McBride, *The Siege of Derry in Ulster Protestant Mythology* (Dublin, 1997), 15–32.

22. Raymond Gillespie, 'The Presbyterian revolution in Ulster, 1660–1690' in W.J. Sheils and Diana Wood (eds), *The Churches, Ireland and the Irish* (Oxford, 1989), 159–170.

23. Ian McBride, 'Ulster Presbyterians and the confessional state, c. 1688–1733' in D.G. Boyce, Robert Eccleshall, and Vincent Geoghegan (eds), *Political Discourse in Seventeenth- and Eighteenth-century Ireland* (Basingstoke, 2001), 176–8; Philip O'Regan, 'William King as bishop and parliamentarian, 1691–7' in C.J. Fauske (ed), *Archbishop William King and the Anglican Irish Context, 1688–1729* (Dublin, 2004), 85–7.

24. William Macafee and Valerie Morgan, 'Population in Ulster 1660–1760' in Peter Roebuck (ed), *Plantation to Partition: Essays in Ulster History in Honour of J.L. McCracken* (Belfast, 1981), 46–63; S.J. Connolly, *Divided Kingdom: Ireland 1630–1800* (Oxford, 2008), 206.

25. William Tisdall, *The conduct of the Dissenters of Ireland, with respect both to church and state* (Dublin, 1712), 23–7.

26. Connolly, *Religion, Law and Power*, 180–6.

27. J. C. Beckett, 'The government and the Church of Ireland under William III and Anne' in *Irish Historical Studies*, ii (1940–1), 280–302; Philip O'Regan, *Archbishop William King of Dublin (1650–1729) and the Constitution in Church and State* (Dublin, 2000), chs. 3, 5.

28. T. C. Barnard, 'Reforming Irish manners: the religious societies in Dublin during the 1690s' in *Historical Journal*, xxxv (1992), 805–38; D. W. Hayton, 'Did Protestantism fail in eighteenth-century Ireland? Charity schools and the enterprise of religious and social reformation, c. 1690–1730', in Alan Ford, James McGuire, and Kenneth Milne (eds), *As By Law Established: the Church of Ireland since the Reformation* (Dublin, 1995), 166–86; idem, 'Bishops as legislators: Marsh and his contemporaries' in Muriel McCarthy and Ann Simmons (eds), *Marsh's Library: a Mirror on the World* (Dublin, 2009), 62–87.

29. S.J. Connolly, 'Reformers and highflyers: the post-Revolution church' in Ford et al (eds), *As By Law Established*, 152–65; Hayton, *Ruling Ireland*, ch. 4.

30. See above, n. 12.

31. Hayton, *Ruling Ireland*, ch. 6.

32. C.I. McGrath, 'Alan Brodrick and the Speakership of the Irish House of Commons, 1703–4' in James Kelly, John McCafferty, and C. I. McGrath (eds), *People, Politics and Power: Essays in Irish history 1660–1850 in Honour of James I. McGuire* (Dublin, 2009), 70–93.

33. Patrick McNally, 'The Hanoverian accession and the Tory party in Ireland' in *Parliamentary History*, xiv (1995), 263–83.

34. But see 'Considering the inconsiderable'; and D.W. Hayton, 'Voters, patrons and parties: parliamentary elections in Ireland, 1692-*c.* 1727' in Clyve Jones, Philip Salmon, and R.W. Davis (eds), *Partisan Politics, Principle and Reform in Parliament and the Constituencies, 1689–1880: essays in memory of John A. Phillips* (Edinburgh, 2005), 44–70.

35. For example, Barnard, 'Considering the inconsiderable', 81. See also David Fleming, *Politics and Provincial People: Sligo and Limerick, 1691–1761* (Manchester, 2010), chs. 1–3.

36. R. J. Dickson, *Ulster Emigration to Colonial America, 1718–1775* (New York, 1966).

37. D.W. Hayton, *The Anglo-Irish Experience, 1680–1730: Religion, Identity and Patriotism* (Woodbridge, 2012), 76–103.

38. McNally, *Parties, Patriots, and Undertakers*, ch. 5; Patrick Walsh, *The Making of the Eighteenth-century Protestant Ascendancy: the Life of William Conolly 1662–1729* (Woodbridge, 2010), chs. 6–7.

39. Hayton, *Anglo-Irish* experience, 124–48.

40. Patrick McNally, 'Wood's Halfpence, Carteret, and the government of Ireland, 1723–6' in *Irish Historical Studies*, xxx (1996–7), 354–76; Hayton, *Ruling Ireland*, chs. 7–8.

41. For example, *Letters of Marmaduke Coghill, 1722–1738*, D.W. Hayton (ed) (Dublin, 2005).

42. Hayton, *Anglo-Irish Experience*, 104–48.

43. Hayton, *Anglo-Irish Experience*, 149–73.

44. 'Report on the state of popery, Ireland, 1731' in *Archivium Hibernicum*, i (1912), 10–27; ii (1913), 108–56; iii (1914), 124–59; iv (1915), 131–77.

45. Kenneth Milne, *The Irish Charter Schools 1730–1830* (Dublin, 1997).

46. Terence De Vere White, *The Story of the Royal Dublin Society* (Tralee, 1955); James Livesey, 'The Dublin Society in eighteenth-century Irish political thought' in *Historical Journal*, xlvii (2004), 615–40.

47. Andrew Sneddon, *Witchcraft and Whigs: the Life of Bishop Francis Hutchinson, 1660–1739* (Manchester, 2008), ch. 8; Toby Barnard, *Improving Ireland? Projectors, Prophets and Profiteers 1641–1786* (Dublin, 2008); Andrew Sneddon, 'Legislating for economic development: Irish fisheries as a case study in the limitations of "improvement"' in Hayton, Kelly, and Bergin (eds), *Composite State*, 136–59.

48. Toby Barnard, *Making the Grand Figure: Lives and Possessions in Ireland, 1641–1770* (New Haven, 2004).

49. For example, Arthur Dobbs, *An essay on the trade and improvement of Ireland* (Dublin, 1729).

50. L.A. Landa, *Swift and the Church of Ireland* (Oxford, 1954), 135–150; Jonathan Swift, *Poetical works*, Herbert Davis (ed) (London, 1967), 601–8.

51. Éamonn Ó Ciardha, *Ireland and the Jacobite Cause: a Fatal Attachment* (Dublin, 2002), chs. 4–5; David Dickson, 'Jacobitism in eighteenth-century Ireland: a Munster perspective' in *Éire-Ireland*, xxxiv (2004), 38–99.

52. J.L. McCracken, 'The conflict between the Irish administration and parliament, 1753–6' in *Irish Historical Studies*, iii (1942–3), 159–79; Declan O'Donovan, 'The money bill dispute of 1753' in Thomas Bartlett and D. W. Hayton (eds), *Penal Era and Golden Age: Essays in Irish History, 1690–1800* (Belfast, 1979), 55–87.

53. Bob Harris, *Politics and the Nation: Britain in the mid-eighteenth century* (Oxford, 2002), ch. 5; David Fleming, 'Patriots and politics in Navan, 1753–5' in *Irish Historical Studies*, xxxvi (2008–9), 502–21.

54. Sean Murphy, 'Charles Lucas and the Dublin election of 1748–1749' in *Parliamentary History*, ii (1983), 93–111; J.R. Hill, *From Patriots to Unionists: Dublin Civic Politics and Irish Protestant Patriotism 1660–1840* (Oxford, 1997), ch. 3.

55. For many years the standard interpretation remained that of the late Maureen Wall, whose various contributions were gathered together in *Catholic Ireland in the Eighteenth Century: Collected Essays of Maureen Wall*, Gerard O'Brien (ed) (Dublin, 1989). For a significant revision, see David Dickson, 'Catholics and trade in eighteenth-century Ireland: an old debate revisited' in Power and Whelan (eds), *Endurance and Emergence*, 85–100.

Select Bibliography

Barnard, Toby, *A New Anatomy of Ireland: the Irish Protestants, 1649–1770* (New Haven and London, 2003).

Barnard, Toby, *Irish Protestant Ascents and Descents, 1641–1770* (Dublin, 2004).

Barnard, Toby, *Making the Grand Figure: Lives and Possessions in Ireland, 1641–1770* (New Haven and London, 2004).

Boyce, D.G., Eccleshall, Robert, and Geoghegan, Vincent (eds), *Political Discourse in Seventeenth- and Eighteenth-Century Ireland* (Basingstoke, 2001).

Connolly, S.J., *Religion, Law and Power: The Making of Protestant Ireland 1660–1760* (Oxford, 1992).

Cullen, L. M., *The Emergence of Modern Ireland 1600–1900* (London, 1981).

Dickson, David, *Old World Colony: Cork and South Munster 1630–1830* (Cork, 2005).

Fleming, D. A., *Politics and Provincial People: Sligo and Limerick, 1691–1761* (Manchester, 2010)

Ford, Alan, McGuire, James, and Milne, Kenneth (eds), *As By Law Established: The Church of Ireland since the Reformation* (Dublin, 1995).

Hayton, D. W., *Ruling Ireland, 1685–1742: Politics, Politicians and Parties* (Woodbridge, 2004).

Hayton, D.W., Kelly, James, and Bergin, John, *The Eighteenth-Century Composite State: Representative Institutions in Ireland and Europe 1690–1800* (Basingstoke, 2010).

Hayton, D.W., *The Anglo-Irish Experience, 1680–1730: Religion, Identity and Patriotism* (Woodbridge, 2012).

Magennis, Eoin, *The Irish Political System, 1740–1765* (Dublin, 2000).

McBride, Ian, *Eighteenth-Century Ireland: The Isle of Slaves* (Dublin, 2009).

McGrath, Charles Ivar, *The Making of the Eighteenth-Century Irish Constitution: Government, Parliament and the Revenue, 1692–1714* (Dublin, 2000).

McGrath, Charles Ivar, *Ireland and Empire, 1692–1770* (London, 2012).

McNally, Patrick, *Parties, Patriots and Undertakers: Parliamentary Politics in Early Hanoverian Ireland* (Dublin, 1997).

O'Brien, Gerard (ed), *Catholic Ireland in the Eighteenth Century: Collected Essays of Maureen Wall* (Dublin, 1989).

Ó Ciardha, Éamonn, *Ireland and the Jacobite Cause, 1685–1766: A Fatal Attachment* (Dublin, 2002).

O'Regan, Philip, *Archbishop William King of Dublin (1650–1729) and the Constitution in Church and State* (Dublin, 2000).

Power, T.P. and Whelan, Kevin (eds), *Endurance and Emergence: Catholics in Ireland in the Eighteenth Century* (Blackrock, Co. Dublin, 1990).

Walsh, Patrick, *The Making of the Irish Protestant Ascendancy: The Life of William Conolly, 1662–1729* (Woodbridge, 2010).

CHAPTER 21

....

FAMINE AND ECONOMIC CHANGE IN EIGHTEENTH-CENTURY IRELAND

....

DAVID DICKSON

THE death rattle of the Irish parliament in 1800 coincided with a more tangible crisis in the world outside: the aftermath of rebellion and two disastrous harvests had forced food prices to record levels and famine beckoned. The government reacted with unprecedented speed, importing food and banning grain exports, and the crisis passed. Nevertheless, deaths directly associated with the scarcity probably surpassed those associated with the rebellion. Does such an episode prove the exceptional vulnerability of Irish society to environmental shock, despite a hundred years of peace and the huge growth of trade? Or is the more telling point the contrast between the outcome in 1800 and the harsh seasons of the late 1720s and early 1740s, when much larger-scale famine, pestilence, and migration ensued?

The first and highly influential economic history of eighteenth-century Ireland, George O'Brien's survey of 1918, presented a narrative of endemic depression, with a brief, politically inspired moment of expansion after 1782. More than a generation passed before archives-based, statistically grounded research, informed by economic theory, told a more sophisticated story.[1] The key contributor here was Louis Cullen: in an extraordinary range of books and essays appearing between the 1950s and the 1990s, he has provided a far subtler reading of the economy and of accompanying cultural changes, setting Irish patterns in European and Atlantic contexts. Cullen's eighteenth-century Ireland was still exceptional in many respects, but not with the simplistic exceptionalism that earlier writers had postulated. The morbid political framework of English mercantilism and Irish penal laws which O'Brien had assumed to be all-important now receded, and in their place war, weather, and the invisible hand defined the story.[2]

Cullen's first monograph appeared in 1968. Its primary concern was the evolution of Anglo-Irish trade between the Restoration and the Union, but without announcing the fact that it worked over a much broader canvas. It was immediately recognized as a 'marvellous riposte' to O'Brien's history.[3] It emerged at a time when the origins of the industrial revolution on the neighbouring island were being re-interpreted and when deeper commercial, agrarian, and financial processes were being revealed as central to Britain's take-off. The implications of Cullen's arguments for these cross-channel debates were slow to register, but in Irish historiography his work brought about a paradigm shift. He reinstated economic factors—external markets and internal factor endowments—to account for the long-run growth of Irish foreign trade, and he emphasized the centrality of that trade in the material transformation of the country. Conventional assumptions as to the perennially depressed state of the population and the persistence of an overwhelmingly subsistence economy were forcefully rebutted, and the importance of economic cycles, strongly related to the pattern of harvests and maritime war, was emphasized. The appearance shortly afterwards of his general survey of Irish economic history since 1660 and of a number of other synoptic essays meant that this fundamental reinterpretation of eighteenth-century Ireland had considerable impact.[4] Cullen's work set a number of hares running—from a new interest in estate history, harvests, and trade cycles to a new recognition of the value of regional economic history.

The advance of knowledge on the eighteenth-century economy however was, and still is, held back by the thinness of the quantitative evidence. Compared with the extraordinary abundance of statistical data on Irish agriculture, settlement, inland trade, demography, social structure, and public health after 1820, statistical sources for the eighteenth century are too modest to allow any estimation of national income. The one branch of state administration that since the 1680s had been large, active, and relatively efficient was the revenue service, specifically the collection of excise and customs, an activity that was absolutely critical to the civil and military functioning of the state. Pre-Union standards of accounting and record-keeping were relatively advanced, with the management of customs collection in the main ports executed with particular care. It is this data which now provide us with the longest and most robust time series relating to the changing composition and levels of economic activity. Import and export returns, expressed by volume but with official valuations attached, are available for each designated port for four years in the 1680s and then in a continuous annual series from 1698 to the customs union of 1825. Surviving in British but not Irish archives, the customs accounts were neglected until Cullen so comprehensively exploited them. They have their faults and their limitations—the history of smuggling has remained a subsidiary theme in Cullen's work—and only when they come to be digitized and rigorously collated with comparable British data will their reliability be more precisely determined.[5]

The evidence of the ledgers suggests a pattern of stuttering growth with several false dawns in the early eighteenth century, and then from the late 1740s a powerful expansion of Irish exports, both in volume and value, which was sustained until the 1790s and beyond, implying unprecedented commercial momentum. There were setbacks, most obviously in the late 1770s, but a simple comparison of foreign trade in the years

1696–8 and 1795/6–1797/8 reveals the magnitude of change: between these two sets of years the value of Irish exports at official prices rose more than sevenfold, the value of imports by more than ninefold (admittedly this comparison is between years of post-war recovery and a pre-rebellion cyclical peak). Even in the 1790s, foreign trade as a proportion of national income remained at modest levels,[6] but it is striking that, for all the dynamism of the British economy, the growth in the official value of English and Welsh exports over the eighteenth century was significantly less than that from Ireland.[7] It was, however, the dynamism of the British-dominated Atlantic economy, the increasingly positive impact of Anglo-French warfare on the Irish economy, and the strengthening domestic British demand for Irish foodstuffs that underlay the striking Irish performance.

There were two groups of commodities that, between them, explain most of the growth in exports: cattle products and linen. A number of other categories that had been important in the seventeenth century—salted fish, timber, and wool—were now eclipsed, reflecting diminished Irish supplies and the workings of comparative advantage. Cereal exports, intermittently important in the seventeenth century, were virtually non-existent in the eighteenth until the last quarter of the century when international price trends once again favoured the grain farmer. Rather it was the trades in beef, butter, and linen which from the 1720s determined the health of the Irish economy. The produce of cattle and sheep accounted in all for about 84 per cent of Irish exports in 1700, with beef, butter, tallow, and cow hides preponderant. By mid century, the combined figure had fallen to 47 per cent, and slipped to 36 per cent by 1797, by which time sheep-derived products had almost vanished from the schedules. Balancing good and bad harvests, the country had been a net importer of cereals until the 1760s, but by 1797 grain-based products then accounted for some 6 per cent of Irish exports, and their share was to grow to over 30 per cent by the 1840s.[8]

It was, however, the cultivation of flax that underpinned the great success story of the eighteenth-century economy; even George O'Brien had had to concede that much. Exports of white linen cloth amounted to a mere 305 000 yards in 1700, but they were already rising, thanks to the concession of duty-free access to the English market in 1696 and the progressive exclusion by Westminster of rival sources of supply from France and northern Europe. Handicraft linen manufacture accelerated from the 1720s, receiving substantial and recurring parliamentary support (no doubt much of it wasteful and misdirected). But while a positive institutional environment was important in creating the initial critical mass of producers, the long-term cycle of growth reflected the reinforcing effects of strong metropolitan and transatlantic demand and favourable factor endowment. Linen's share of Irish exports rose from about 8 per cent in 1700 to just under 50 per cent at mid century, a share it held or slightly improved on during the following fifty years of overall Irish export growth. In the peak year of 1795/6, some forty-seven million yards of bleached linen cleared Irish ports, a quarter of which was destined for North America.[9]

At first sight these were regional stories, with the Munster ports handling the lion's share of beef, butter, and woollen yarn exports, and east and central Ulster remaining the heartland of the linen trade. But this was only partly the case. It is true that Cork city, witnessing an annual cull of up to eighty thousand cattle in its northside shambles by the 1760s, had no rival in Europe, and that its prosperity rested on the unique diversity of markets for its provisions trade products. Indeed, the dependability of livestock supplies made the Cork region a most valuable asset during the many episodes of European naval warfare, when ready access to high-quality provisions was a critical operational factor.[10] But the supply chain that ended up in the Munster ports stretched far across three provinces, and the long growth in pastoral exports and commercial dairying would have been impossible without the widespread adoption of improved strains of cattle and the intensification of grassland farming across Ireland.

Cullen was the first to recognize that revolutions both in the man-made landscape and in inland trade were essential ingredients in the expansion of Irish foreign trade. Agricultural output for much of the century was almost certainly rising faster than population.[11] The advancement of field enclosure and upland reclamation (whether because of, or despite, proprietorial policies) was critical to the growth of the national herd, and the overall quality of livestock was improving. The inter-regional trade in cattle, sheep, and wool led to the integration of wholesale markets and a measure of regional specialization within farming. Symptomatic of this was the collective enthusiasm to improve the road network and the great growth in the number of fairs: in the 1680s there were around 500 privately sponsored fairs advertised in the country, 43 per cent of which were in Leinster; by the 1770s there were nearly 3000 such fairs, with only 27 per cent held in Leinster. Some fairs were almost national events, notably the great wool fair at Ballinasloe, County Galway, which had only got going in the 1750s.[12] For much of the century, the losers in this process were the secondary ports (such as Wexford and Galway) as the commercial and financial muscle of the merchant communities in the larger ports—Cork, Waterford, Limerick, and Belfast—undermined wholesale business in formerly autonomous centres of trade. Dublin was of course the chief beneficiary: its position as principal distribution point for high-value imports entering Ireland—already achieved by the late seventeenth century—went unchallenged until the nineteenth century, and its crucial role in providing working credit for most regional trade intensified, at least up until the late eighteenth century. Long before the creation of the Bank of Ireland in 1783, Dublin's private bankers provided a large share of the seasonal credit which lubricated inland wholesale exchanges.[13]

Dublin credit was certainly vital to the international success of Ulster linen, but there were several factors at work in sustaining the growth of the industry. Production greatly expanded in those districts of north Armagh, south Antrim, and west Down where commercial weaving had first developed in the seventeenth century thanks to the progressive withdrawal of rural families from farming and farm-labouring and into a life at the loom. These were districts of early and sustained population growth, and as they became richer and more exclusively focused on linen weaving and processing, they became dependent on all the surrounding areas for raw materials (principally linen yarn) and food supplies (principally oatmeal). This demand was felt across the rest of Ulster and neighbouring counties, and in coastal districts further afield.

The huge growth in output was also achieved by the enlargement of the linen heartland, with fine weaving and bleaching spreading across most lowland districts in north
and west Ulster, and outlying pockets and enclaves in each of the other provinces. By the
end of the eighteenth century there was significant employment in linen weaving and/
or flax spinning in nineteen of the thirty-two counties.[14] The evolution of the industry in its east Ulster heartland is now well understood, thanks in particular to the work
of W.H. Crawford, but its history elsewhere less so.[15] Unlike the situation in the nineteenth century, when Belfast emerged as a great factory city and regional financial hub,
eighteenth-century Ulster looked to Dublin as its commercial centre. The multiplier
effects of the linen industry's extraordinary growth were thus felt across the whole island
to a greater or lesser extent.

Who then were the beneficiaries of this long growth in Irish trade? O'Brien's answer
would have been simple: England and English interests in Ireland—the landed gentry and the state who between them cornered all surplus value through punitive rents
and heavy taxes. Weren't most landowners absentees anyway, spending their disposable income in England or beyond? Such a gloomy picture of course echoes some of the
greatest eighteenth-century writers on the Irish condition—from Swift to Goldsmith—
not to mention the many lesser pamphleteers who came to life at times of economic
recession, notably in the 1720s and 1770s.[16] But import patterns, seen in a century-long
perspective, give a more ambiguous answer: sugar, silks, wines, and tobacco imports
soared between the 1680s and 1790s, far ahead of population growth, as did raw silk and
many categories of finer textiles. The pessimists would argue that this soaring demand
for discretionary goods merely indicated a profoundly unequal society and reflected
the conspicuous consumption by a wealthy elite in the cities and their rural mansions,
as the great majority (so it was assumed) had no discretionary spending power to
indulge in foreign commodities. Modern work, particularly that by Toby Barnard, has
revealed an emerging and complex non-elite world, one in which the consumption of
non-traditional material goods was progressively diffused in the course of the century.[17]
The old binary world of a wealthy high-spending landlord class lording it over a sea of
impoverished self-sufficient tenants is now long discredited. There was quite obviously
a rising eighteenth-century tide which lifted a great many boats. But were there losers
as well?

First, let us take the situation in the towns. Urban Ireland in 1700 was a collection
of small maritime communities, with the biggest centres growing disproportionately.
Dublin and Cork roughly doubled between 1700 and 1750; the former, with around
125 000 inhabitants by mid century, was then in the top twelve of European cities by population, and Cork, at 40 000, around number forty.[18] Some twenty-two Irish ports were
involved in foreign or cross-channel trade in 1700, but in the next half century, maritime commerce gravitated towards the big five—Cork, Waterford, Limerick, Belfast,
and Dublin itself—and their populations expanded broadly in line with the growth in
overseas trade; of the inland centres, only Kilkenny grew noticeably at this time. The
citizenry of these larger towns were more Protestant than their hinterlands; most male
adults were trained in a skill and were fairly mobile. Against older assumptions about

risk aversion and defective entrepreneurship, modern work on individual towns and business communities has revealed networks of merchants drawn from all religious denominations, opportunistic if not innovative in their business behaviour and adaptable to a fickle commercial environment, not so unlike their contemporaries across the water. But no Irish-based merchant accumulated great commercial wealth in the course of the century to rival the most successful of their compatriots in London or Paris. Therein lies an issue to be teased out. The great new fortunes of eighteenth-century Ireland were either professional or landed, with the most successful traders and bankers becoming landowning magnates within two generations, or else fading away.[19]

In the second half of the century, the physical appearance of the big five cities changed greatly thanks to public building projects, port improvement, and speculative domestic property development. Social divisions were, however, becoming more sharply etched and the opportunities for upward social mobility in the artisanal world were lessening as it became more visibly Catholic. The great demonstration of 'thousands' of Dublin city carpenters in the Phoenix Park in April 1792 against proposed statutory restrictions on journeyman clubs was a sign of the future.[20] The teeming poverty of the streets, once a feature of the hungry seasons of harvest failure, was now endemic. Meanwhile, the secondary ports and many inland centres were coming back to life after the 1740s and growing faster than the larger cities, a trend that continued up until the mid nineteenth century; indeed, some towns in Connacht and west Munster only began to grow after the turn of the century, linked to incremental improvements in the road network. Such trends reflected the gradual reorientation of Irish foreign trade away from southern Europe and the Atlantic and towards short-distance Anglo-Irish exchange, giving secondary ports a chance to compete on more equal terms with the big five, and in due course they and the hundred or so inland market towns developed a greater diversity of shops and professional services, suggesting a trickle-down of wealth within their hinterlands. But with the growth of aggregate population in the countryside, many of these towns developed labouring ghettoes, first in their suburbs and later within the obsolescent housing stock in the urban core.

The towns by their nature drew in the countryside, and urban ways and fashions were there to be copied. Some of the material goods brought from over the horizon, most obviously tobacco, had not required the mediation of the town to become popular in the countryside, but most new fashions did. Admittedly, many town goods were first sold across the countryside by itinerant pedlars and dealers at fairs, but townsfolk set new standards and the new demands, whether for goods or services. Bishop Berkeley in the 1730s had argued that the greatest weakness in the economy was the absence of incentives among poorer families to earn more than the minimum necessary to cover costs: their appetites had to be whetted to boost demand and draw the economy forward.[21] And towns, as they grew, did have that role. In addition, the growth of literacy, of reading and of doing business through English, was also strongly related to the slow ascendancy of urban values. We know most about the social structure of Armagh and Carrick-on-Suir in the late eighteenth century, but the wider issue of winners and losers in the towns remains tantalizingly opaque. We can assume that for most owners of urban assets, even down to the long lease of a backyard, there was a perceptible growth in wealth, but for craftworkers it was a fractious battle to retain purchasing power from the 1760s. Ó Gráda has concluded that, between the 1780s and the end of the French wars, the general rise in nominal wages only 'just about kept pace with rising prices'.[22]

To determine who was on the rising tide in the countryside, we have to go back to Sir William Petty, the first to speculate on the actual shape of Irish society, in search of an answer. Writing in 1686 just before the Jacobite wars, he suggested that 'above 100 000' houses, containing perhaps 40 to 45 per cent of the population, were worth less than ten shillings each, which would have been the equivalent of about a month's wages of a manual labourer. The owners of such cabins, he suggested, would be possessed of no more than two or three head of cattle and no land to speak of; in other words, the heads of household were labourers, herdmen, servants, and suchlike. Petty's rough estimate is not so different from one for contemporary England by Gregory King, who calculated that 47 per cent of the population there was headed by a labourer, a servant, a cottager, or a pauper. However, the similarity is perhaps deceptive: the landless class in late seventeenth-century England was more settled, had the benefit of a parish poor-law system (and thus protection against years of food shortage and times of family adversity), and enjoyed better material standards of clothing and housing (but perhaps not of heating) than their peers in Ireland. Petty had suggested in 1672 a (rather conservative) average per capita income of 60 shillings p.a. for no less than 86 per cent of the Irish population—embracing his near-landless families plus small farmers, and an average per capita income of 240 shillings for the residual 14 per cent of the population; by comparison, in King's estimates for England in 1688 the poorer 47 per cent of the population had an annual per capita income of nearly 75 shillings, and 53 per cent averaged just over 300 shillings. On this admittedly flimsy evidence, it would seem that Ireland was entering the eighteenth century with a much larger proportion of its inhabitants with little or no reserves than was the case in England, and in absolute terms a significantly poorer society. And, subsequently, the years of soaring food prices in eighteenth-century England had, it now appears, very little impact on the death rate, whereas in Ireland the ebb and flow of typhus, dysentery, and other epidemics remained only too obviously correlated with food prices.[23]

For the situation at the end of the eighteenth century, we have some tantalizing evidence based on household sampling by hearth-tax officials, which is slightly less impressionistic than Petty's data: their investigations published in 1792 implied that some 11 per cent of the Irish population had a gross per capita income of 480 shillings p.a., while 59 per cent were surviving on less than 120 shillings, some much less. There was thus a huge underclass embracing at least half the population, and even though nominal incomes would appear to have risen substantially since Petty's day, the cost of living in the 1790s was substantially higher at that time (and rising fast). But the significant new element was an increase of those strata in Irish society who were neither at the minimum subsistence level nor demonstrably wealthy: the 1790s data suggests that some 30 per cent of the population had a gross per capita income between 120 and 480 shillings p.a.[24]

This group—amounting to substantially more than a third of the population in some districts—included craftworking families who sold their product into the market (for example linen weavers) and land-holding families who owned cattle and traded livestock, butter, or grain. Net income of groups involved in the commercial economy was always going to depend on whether their principal overhead—rent—was tied to short-term price movements or was relatively insulated from them. All modern work on eighteenth-century estate history has confirmed Cullen's revisionist argument that it was generally the latter situation—that most tenant farmers enjoyed relatively long tenancies in the eighteenth century, that rents generally lagged behind the seemingly inexorable rise in Irish land values, and that the agricultural lease was a world apart from the unwritten yearly contracts enjoyed by most Irish labourers (or for that matter, the sharecropping arrangements in many Continental peasant societies).[25] In other words, the great bulk of Irish tenant farmers taking formal leases for twenty-one or (more commonly) thirty-one years from the 1720s onwards stood to benefit from a rising market, interrupted it is true by clusters of bad years that occurred in every decade, whether war-induced depression that deadened fairs and markets, or malign weather that hit crops, livestock, or a mixture of both. This was most starkly exposed as we shall see in the 1740s, when war and weather crippled the rural economy on two sets of occasions.

In a number of modern estate studies, trends in eighteenth-century land values have been reconstructed. The most revealing are those estates with a record of leasing transactions stretching over half a century or more. Crawford's reconstruction of new rent settings on the Brownlow estate in north Armagh is particularly robust; this district, the epicentre of linen manufacture, might seem hardly typical, what with rent levels soaring by just under eightfold between the first and final decades of the eighteenth century, in effect a doubling every thirty years. But other estates far outside the linen heartland suggest similar rates of growth: rent movement on the Perceval estate in north Cork over precisely the same period was slightly higher, at somewhat *over* eightfold. The long-term upward movement of commodity prices in the late eighteenth century explains much of this rise in rents, but there was also some redistribution of income from tenant to landowner as large middleman tenants were displaced by *bona fide* farmers.[26] But the salient point is that, as long as tenancies were being negotiated for multiple decades at rents fixed at the commencement of the contract, and as long as the expectation of future farm income was not being too heavily factored into the rents agreed, then tenants could in the course of the lease term enjoy an increasing share of the surplus. Crawford's studies of Ulster estate management reveal a pattern, subsequently confirmed elsewhere, of many landowners being prepared to take the long view in dealings with their tenants, quite consciously recognizing the value of incentivizing tenants to invest in their farms during their tenancies; the motive for tenants to 'improve' their lands was not so much a greater expectation of the renewal of tenancy as the expectation of attractive returns on such expenditure during the course of the lease. And while there was a great variety of management practices across regions, there were it seems many landlords who recognized the value of a settled tenantry over one that was denied any prospect of retaining a share of farm profits. Peter Solar has estimated the movement of *average* rents (as opposed to new settings) on a number of estates between the 1780s and early 1810s and has produced a composite price series for Irish agriculture over the same period: this provides a statistical basis for claiming that 'the average farmer was prospering' during that time.[27]

One of the key developments of the century was therefore the emergence of a composite layer of leaseholding, usually cattle-owning, farmers with an economic stake in the soil, however impermanent their legal status as leaseholders may have been. Some were what Kevin Whelan has called the 'underground gentry', descendants of lineage families whose freeholds had been confiscated at some point in the seventeenth century and who still held leaseholds on parts of the patrimony. But there were much larger numbers of farming families who were in effect upwardly mobile dynasties—escaping from partnership tenancy and sub-tenancy and through a mixture of luck and fortitude, improving their material and tenurial status over two or three generations.[28] The emergence of this 'middle peasantry' in the later eighteenth century, commercialized and acquisitive in outlook but often very shy consumers in terms of new housing or personal display, remains an opaque process requiring further research on those rare estates where there is adequate documentation.

If such petty leaseholders were among those who eventually rose with the tide, what then of the boats which foundered? If the history of small-farm families is poorly documented, the *direct* evidence on the fortunes of the labouring class below them, the cottiers, is almost totally hidden. But, like the Higgs boson particle, just because they are well hidden in the documentary record does not mean they were not everywhere. The ambiguity of the term 'cottier' (or 'cottar') has itself contributed to the confusion: in the first half of the century the label was attached more to a style of living than to membership of a social class. A cottier in 1700 lived in a mud house, wore brogues, and was probably an Irish-speaking partnership farmer sharing responsibility for the rent of a townland with a handful of other households, maybe as a yearly tenant but more likely holding a lease for a term of up to thirty-one years from a landlord or a middleman tenant; rent was fixed in money terms with an element of labour services included. A cottier in 1800 was generally a tied labourer, one who hired an acre of potato ground and perhaps grass for a few head of livestock, from a farmer by verbal agreement for twelve months, the rent for which was paid for by labour at an agreed *per diem* rate. There were many cottiers in this sense whose parents had been small farmers, but very few who in 1800 could look forward to their children becoming leaseholders again. And beneath the tied labourers were the unattached poor—the rootless *spailpíní*, the professional beggars, the widowed, and the infirm. Precarious as always, their relative numbers were already probably growing.[29]

It should not be a surprise that the recent regional studies of eighteenth-century Ireland are revealing strong differences as to the timing and character of the process of social differentiation—between, for example, areas of persistent and enduring large grazing farms and areas where there was a long tradition of cereal production for the market. But the terms of trade for all classes of male labourer were worsening by the 1790s, although the growth of opportunities for cottier women to make money (for example by spinning, pig-rearing, and egg production) were cancelling out, or certainly dulling, the impact of the fall in the real wage of male labourers. Gathering more evidence on these defensive adaptations at the regional level, in particular plotting the role of female earnings, is vital if we are to establish when the overall standard of living for labouring families began its long decline. In some areas it was probably the 1790s, but for others, not least in districts where the demand for common crafts remained strong, or where fishing or wartime farming expanded, it may not have been until after Waterloo.[30]

This decline in real wages reflected, of course, profound changes in the underlying labour supply, which leads us to the wider question of the causes and chronology of rural population growth. The once dominant and logically elegant model developed by Kenneth Connell in the 1940s put great emphasis on a population spurt in the final years of the century, arising he argued from a sharp rise in Irish fertility, prompted in turn by the new opportunities for farm sub-division and family formation that arose with the boom in tillage farming. His model has been severely questioned and his extreme scepticism of the hearth-tax evidence which informed all his pre-censal population estimates has been reassessed. Indeed, thanks to a number of separate but complementary projects, there has been considerable advance in eighteenth-century demographic history since Connell's day.[31] Several of the dominant strands in this debate have particular relevance here: the timing of the demographic take-off; the relationship between population growth and food supply; and the regional contrasts and their implications.

Modern work has suggested that the potential for high growth was present in the country long before the late eighteenth century, that female age at first marriage was low by English standards since the seventeenth century, and that Irish nuptiality rates were high. In addition, it is clear that the immigrant communities, the last of which only arrived in the 1690s, had initial high fertility.[32] Thus we can speculate that there were several strong pulses of growth since the early seventeenth century (some regionally defined), with a nationwide trough in the second quarter of the eighteenth century. It is clear that recent growth was cancelled out by the heightened virulence of killer epidemics, particularly in the 1720s and 1740s, which swept away children particularly. The epidemics took their rise from the highly abnormal weather, bad harvests, and recurring breakdowns in public health. The crises of 1727–9 (particularly in Ulster), 1740–1 (everywhere but Ulster), and 1744–5 (worst in the north-west) were the most traumatic, both in terms of the human devastation caused and the economic costs arising from massive livestock fatalities. Then, despite wretched harvests in the mid 1750s, mid and late 1760s, late 1770s, and early 1780s, rural Ireland seems to have developed a new ability to cope with these shocks, and child survival rates in particular seem to have improved. Connell's assumption that rapid population growth was only a reality from the 1780s to the 1830s quite missed the step change in the late 1740s, which in retrospect can be seen as the beginning of the longest demographic surge in Irish history.[33]

The potato's role in raising Ireland's population from less than two million in 1700 to close to five million in 1800 has remained controversial ever since R.N. Salaman's classic 1949 survey of the social impact of the tuber in world history, where he argued that its adoption in Ireland as the principal food of the poor was exceptionally rapid by European standards, largely in place by the mid seventeenth century, thereby setting the stage for Irish's long population growth and eventual Malthusian crisis in the 1840s. Several writers have sought to modify this argument, with Cullen completely rejecting Salaman's chronology and his assumption that the potato drove Irish population growth, others suggesting novel ways in which the adoption of the potato could have impacted on Irish fertility.[34]

There is just about enough evidence to sustain this long debate but not enough to close it. Building on the work of Austin Bourke, the present author has argued that, for the south Munster counties at least, Salaman was probably correct: by the 1660s the potato had become the standard winter food grown in gardens of the majority—the small landholders and the poor—cushioning them from the full impact of grain shortages. Then, as land values crept up, the potato helped drive land reclamation, being used to break in poorly drained land in preparation for regular grazing, and to regenerate soils at the start of a rotation on in-land that was being heavily cropped. Oatmeal as the dominant popular foodstuff was eclipsed in the second half of the eighteenth century, once longer-keeping varieties of potato became available and the potato's high calorie/acreage ratio made an exclusive potato diet economically attractive. At the same time, its potential as animal provender, especially for pigs, was realized as the external demand for pork strengthened, thus allowing smallholders a means of converting surplus potatoes into profit.[35] But what applies to Munster clearly did not apply with equal force to other parts of the country, and much of the controversy over the diffusion of the potato has arisen because historians were insufficently sensitive to regional difference. Munster was clearly first in the progressive adoption of the potato, with lowland Leinster and most of Ulster much later. It is tempting to link the early adoption of the potato as staple winter food in Munster with signs of early population growth there, but this is speculative. Detailed studies of other regions may help to throw more light on the chronology of the two processes and their causal relationship. The relevance of the potato in explaining the vigour of Irish population growth will not, however, go away.

Cullen's trade studies revealed the scale of food imports into Ireland in the bad-harvest episodes between the 1720s and 1760s—from England, the Baltic, and the American colonies. At first sight, this inflow of wheat and flour can be seen as pathological evidence of Ireland's dangerous switch to pastoral farming at the expense of the plough. While there was such a shift in some districts, this was exaggerated and the more important point is the evidence it provides of the relative facility with which overseas food could be secured for the port cities when needed, a sign of Ireland's fuller integration into the European and north Atlantic trading world. The operation of comparative advantage may indeed have caused the depopulation of quite a few 'sweet Auburns' as graziers played the market, but without this access to Atlantic markets the trades in beef, butter, and linen would have been stifled. It was only when war interrupted commerce or when an extreme hemispheric aberration hit international food reserves that Ireland's food security was seriously breached.

This is indeed what happened in 1740 and 1741, a time of war and weather extremes, when imports were not forthcoming and when a full-scale famine crisis hit the country.

Worst in the midlands and the south, where a frost of unprecedented intensity in the last days of 1739 decimated potato stocks, the freak weather profoundly affected the whole country. By the time weather patterns returned to normalcy in late summer of 1741, the 'year of slaughter' had killed between 12 to 15 per cent of the population in most Irish counties. As John Post's comparative study of the crisis across Europe has shown, mortality levels in Ireland were proportionately worst (or worst equal with Norway) despite the country not experiencing the greatest climatic shock in metereological terms. Post has persuasively argued that the weakness of the public institutions of poor relief in Ireland and the patchy and informal nature of private philanthropy go a long way towards explaining the appalling Irish death toll—amounting to at least a quarter of a million people. There was a learning process here, with heightened state monitoring and intervention in the scarcities of 1756, 1765, and 1783/4.[36] And when another great crisis was looming in 1799, prompt and energetic action by the state secured adequate international supplies and averted what might have been a minor version of 1741.

If the south Munster pattern of extended demographic growth from the early seventeenth century, with the longest slow-down in the second quarter of the eighteenth, is fairly clear, the pattern for other regions remains opaque. Brian Gurrin's tantalizing work on County Wicklow suggests the existence of strong contrasts in medium-term population behaviour between lowland, heavily commercialized farm zones and the poorer districts where tenancy patterns were slower to change. More demographic work on the midlands and the hinterland of Dublin during the century will help to determine the capital's impact, both on farming patterns and on population change.[37]

The demographic history of eighteenth-century Ulster is particularly intriguing, and not just because there is now a greater body of quantitative research at parish level available. It is apparent that for much of the eighteenth century the counties of most rapid population growth in Ireland were in Ulster. This was not because of immigration—the last wave from Scotland had passed over the province in the 1690s. And it was despite very substantial emigration: there was a precocious propensity in times of economic difficulty, first evident in the late 1710s, to emigrate to the American colonies (the latest estimate of Ulster emigration from the 1710s to 1775 claims that it 'may have ranged up to 250 000 or more').[38] Clearly of central importance was the distinctive rural economy that evolved around linen, built on the expectation that family income could be maintained or enhanced despite the progressive fragmentation of farms. We probably have to look to other European zones of rural proto-industrialization, from Lancashire to Flanders, to find parallels for the high-fertility family structures that drove population growth in the linen counties. The major episodes of Atlantic migration came about at times of depression in the linen trade (notably in the 1720s and early 1770s), and the rise of this passenger traffic westwards was directly linked to the very substantial eastward trade in flaxseed from Connecticut to the Ulster ports, with the latter intially subsidizing the former. It has yet to be determined how far there were clear differences in the demography of Anglican, Presbyterian, and Catholic families in the province, but recent work confirms that emigration was overwhelmingly Presbyterian, with a north and west Ulster bias. Crawford and Elliott have suggested a distinct economic trajectory for

Catholic Ulster, at least until the late eighteenth century: a very gradual emergence out of the shadows and a delayed involvement in the more lucrative parts of the linen manufacture, but then signs of rapid change by the end of the century.[39] Economic factors—'population pressure' or the 'pressure on land'—have often been given as the catalyst for the wholesale expulsion of several thousand Catholic artisan families in Down and Armagh by plebeian Protestants in the 1790s, but in fact these were still good times for all involved in handicraft linen: an explanation for the campaign of intimidation lies more in the political sphere, but one factor stirring up communal tensions may well have been the relatively recent emergence of wealthy Catholics in the linen trade, at a time when skill hierarchies were being upset—in other words an insecurity of status more than of livelihood.[40]

The massive and sustained growth in the eighteenth-century linen economy was predicated on an abundant labour supply: the heartland districts provided much of this for the skilled processes, the slightly later take-off of population in poorer parts of west Ulster and north Connacht facilitating the massive growth in flax cultivation, yarn spinning, and the weaving of coarser counts of cloth. Lower labour costs than in the traditional linen districts in England were crucial to the ongoing success of the overall trade. The threat to its future, what with the rise of cotton, water-powered spinning, and wider mechanization, was not yet appreciated in the 1790s, when the transplantation of handicraft linen manufacturing to other parts of the country remained the foremost policy aim of parliament and government.

The role of public bodies in shaping eighteenth-century economic development was modest by comparison with the following century or with some contemporary continental regimes. This reflected the prevailing English norms of limited public involvement in the productive economy: Westminster's regulation of British and colonial foreign trade, done for both fiscal and strategic economic ends, remained the principal way in which purposive political decisions had direct economic consequences, and in this trade-shaping activity the Irish parliament had very limited room for independent manoeuvre until 1782. However F.G. James demonstrated long ago that there was a vigorous Irish trade lobby present at Westminster from early in the century which notched up a number of victories in modifying regulations that constrained Irish trade within the empire.[41] The opponents of the Union in 1799 failed to see this and argued that the recent bounce in the economy had come about as a result of legislative 'independence'. It is true that there were big parliamentary economic initiatives after 1782—to establish a national bank, to encourage the grain trade (Foster's corn law of 1784), to sponsor the fledgling cotton industry and the west-coast fisheries—and that much higher import duties were introduced in the early 1790s. The latter action was, however, driven by fiscal pressure at the start of the French wars and was not designed as a popular measure. As for parliamentary economic initiatives, these had deep roots—notably the establishment of the Linen Board in 1711, the encouragement of agricultural improvement and afforestation (principally via the Dublin Society) from the 1730s, and of the milling industry and the Irish grain trade from the 1750s. And as for the birth of the Bank of

Ireland, the idea was in the air before 1782 and had quiet Castle support before Grattan's moment of glory.

The College Green parliament had devoted more of its time to drafting legislation promoting economic improvement throughout the century than was once thought. And the allocation of revenue surpluses by the Irish parliament to infrastructural development, however arbitrary or (by later standards) corrupt such decision-making may have been, did have lasting local impact, the building of the Newry Canal being perhaps the best example.[42] But one can search in vain for evidence that Irish parliamentary or government policy directly altered the strategic evolution of the economy. What did of course matter profoundly in shaping Irish destinies was the political-military commitment in Britain to the defence and successful consolidation of its Atlantic empire, based on London and shaped not a little by the interests of London, and the participation of Ireland in that empire, albeit with some limitations, was central to the country's eighteenth-century development. However, we cannot completely discount the long-term economic impact of local political action. The policies of the ruling class in Dublin (the parliament, church, courts, and Castle) shaped the evolution of civil society and the formation of social capital in many important if unquantifiable ways—in the high esteem accorded to those who championed 'improvement', in the rigorous defence of private property rights, in the pursuit of policies that had the cumulative effect of promoting bilingalism and literacy in English. But there were also all the negative consequences of the penal legislation that had emanated from College Green on the investment of Catholic wealth in town and countryside, and of the distorted priorities that went with buttressing the confessional state. And while the country that entered the Union in 1801 was unprecedentedly populous, bilingual, monetized, and exercised as never before about matters that lay far beyond local horizons, the demotic sectarianism, deepening class divisions, and structural poverty of the new century turned out to be a high price to pay for those advances.

Notes

1. George O'Brien, *The Economic History of Ireland in the Eighteenth century* (Dublin, 1918). Cf. Conrad Gill, *The Rise of the Irish Linen Industry* (Oxford, 1925); E.R.R. Green, *The Lagan Valley 1800–1850: A Local History of the Industrial Revolution* (London, 1949); K.H. Connell, *The Population of Ireland 1750–1845* (Oxford, 1950).
2. See 'Bibliography of L.M. Cullen', in David Dickson and Cormac Ó Gráda (eds), *Refiguring Ireland: Essays in Honour of L.M. Cullen* (Dublin, 2003), 386–92.
3. Review by Michael Drake of *Anglo-Irish Trade 1660–1800* (Manchester, 1968), *Eng. Hist. Rev.*, lxxxv (1970), 673.
4. 'Problems in the re-interpretation and revision of eighteenth-century Irish economic history', *Trans. Royal Hist. Soc.*, 5th ser., xvii (1967), 1–22; 'The re-interpretation of Irish economic history', *Topic: A Journal of the Liberal Arts*, xiii (1967), 68–77; *An Economic History of Ireland since 1660* (London: Batsford, 1972); 'Economic development, 1691–1750' and

'Economic development 1750–1800', in T.W. Moody and W.E. Vaughan (eds), *A New History of Ireland*, IV (Oxford, 1986), 123–95.

5. For 1683/4-1686/7: Brit. Lib., Add. MS 4759, and for 1698/9-1824/5: NA/CUST/15. See also Cullen, *Anglo-Irish Trade*, 216–20; ibid., 'The Irish smuggling trade in the eighteenth century', *Proc. Royal Ir. Acad.*, lxvii, C (1968–9), 149–75.

6. Arthur Dobbs, *An Essay on the Trade and Improvement of Ireland* (Dublin, 1729–31), 5; Edward Wakefield, *An Account of Ireland, Statistical and Political* (London, 1812), ii, 45, 53; David Dickson, *New Foundations: Ireland 1660–1800* (Dublin, 2000), 100, fn. 4.

7. Dickson, *New Foundations*, 114; John McCusker, 'The current value of English exports, 1697 to 1800', *William and Mary Quarterly*, 3rd ser., xxviii (1971), 620–1.

8. Peter Solar, 'Growth and distribution in Irish agriculture before the Famine' (PhD dissertation, Stanford University, 1987), 206–7; Dickson, *New Foundations*, 114.

9. O'Brien, *Economic History*, 200–7; Cullen, *Anglo-Irish Trade*, 58–66; R.C. Nash, 'Irish Atlantic trade in the seventeenth and eighteenth centuries', *William and Mary Quarterly*, xlii (1985), 338.

10. Dickson, *Old World Colony: Cork and South Munster 1630–1830* (Cork, 2005), 135–47, 369–75.

11. For the case *against* labour productivity growth in Irish agriculture between the 1770s and the 1840s: Solar, 'Growth and distribution', ch. 10.

12. *New Foundations*, 110; W.J. Smyth, *Map-making, Landscapes and Memory...* (Cork, 2006), 386–7.

13. Dickson, 'The place of Dublin in the eighteenth-century Irish economy', in T.M. Devine and Dickson (eds), *Ireland and Scotland 1600–1850 ...* (Edinburgh, 1983), 177–92; Cullen, 'Landlords, bankers and merchants: The early Irish banking world 1700–1820', in A.E. Murphy (ed), *Economists and the Irish Economy from the Eighteenth Century to the Present Day* (Dublin, 1984), 25–44.

14. F.H.A. Aalen, Kevin Whelan, and Matthew Stout (eds), *Atlas of the Irish Rural Landscape* (Cork, 1997), 79.

15. W.H. Crawford, *The Impact of the Domestic Linen Industry in Ulster* (Belfast, 2005). For a bibliography of Crawford's work: Brenda Collins, Philip Ollerenshaw, and Trevor Parkhill (eds), *Industry, Trade and People in Ireland 1650–1950: Essays in Honour of W.H. Crawford* (Belfast, 2007), 277–80.

16. Cullen, 'The value of contemporary printed sources for Irish economic history in the eighteenth century', *Ir. Hist. Stud.*, xiv (1964–65), 142–55; Patrick Kelly, 'The politics of political economy in mid-eighteenth-century Ireland', in S.J. Connolly (ed), *Political Ideas in Eighteenth-century Ireland* (Dublin, 2000), 83–104.

17. Toby Barnard, *Making the Grand Figure: Lives and Possessions in Ireland 1641–1770* (New Haven, 2004). Cf. Cullen, 'Economic development 1750–1800', 186.

18. Jan de Vries, *European Urbanization 1500–1800* (London, 1988), 270–8; Dickson, *Old World Colony*, 662.

19. L.M. Cullen and Paul Butel (eds), *Cities and Merchants: French and Irish perspectives on urban development 1500–1900* (Dublin, 1986); David Dickson, Jan Parmentier, and Jane Ohlmeyer (eds), *Irish and Scottish Mercantile Networks in Europe and Overseas in the Seventeenth and Eighteenth Centuries* (Gent, 2007).

20. *Walker's Hibernian Magazine*, March 1792, 287; Brian Henry, *The Dublin Hanged...* (Dublin, 1994), 60–76.

21. Kelly, 'Political economy', 123–7.

22. L.A. Clarkson, 'The demography of Carrick-on-Suir, 1799', *Proc. Royal Ir. Academy, C*, lxxxvii (1987), 2–36; 'Armagh town in the eighteenth century', in Collins et al., *Industry, Trade and People in Ireland*, 51–68; Cormac Ó Gráda, *Ireland: A New Economic History 1780–1939* (Oxford: Clarendon Press, 1994), 16–17; Liam Kennedy and M.W. Dowling, 'Prices and wages in Ireland, 1700–1850', *Ir. Econ. Soc. Hist.*, xxiv (1997), 66–8.

23. Jona Schellekens, 'Irish famines and English mortality in the eighteenth century', *Jnl. Interdisciplinary History*, xxvii (1996), 29–42; Dickson, *New foundations*, 111–12.

24. Op.cit.; ibid., *Old World Colony*, 316–18.

25. Thomas P. Power, *Land, Politics and Society in Eighteenth-century Tipperary* (Oxford, 1993), 119–73; Dickson, *Old World Colony*, 181–90.

26. Crawford, 'Landlord-tenant relations in Ulster 1609–1820', *Ir. Econ. Soc. Hist.*, ii (1976), 13–14; Dickson, *Old World Colony*, 644. Cf. Peter Roebuck, 'Rent movement, proprietorial incomes and agricultural development 1730–1830', in Peter Roebuck (ed), *Plantation to Partition: Essays in Ulster History in Honour of J.L. McCracken* (Belfast, 1981), 82–101.

27. Ó Gráda, *Ireland*, 28–9.

28. Kevin Whelan, *The Tree of Liberty* . . . (Cork, 1996), 7–31.

29. Cullen, 'Economic development', 167–9; Dickson, *Old World Colony*, 197–203, 311–18, 341–3; S.J. Connolly, *Divided Kingdom: Ireland 1630–1800* (Oxford, 2008), 358–9.

30. Cullen, 'Economic development', 161, 170–1; Mary O'Dowd, 'Women and paid work in rural Ireland *c.* 1500–1800', in Bernadette Whelan (ed), *Women and Paid Work in Ireland 1500–1930* (Dublin: Four Courts Press, 2000), 21–5; Peter Connell, *The Land and the People of County Meath 1750–1850* (Dublin, 2004), 78–83, 133–41; Dickson, *Old World Colony*, 311–18.

31. Michael Drake, 'Population growth and the Irish economy', in L.M. Cullen (ed), *The Formation of the Irish Economy* (Cork, 1969), 65–87; L.A. Clarkson, 'Irish population revisited', in J.M. Goldstrom and L.A. Clarkson (eds), *Irish Population, Economy and Society: Essays in Honour of the late K.H. Connell* (Oxford, 1981), 13–35; David Dickson, Cormac Ó Gráda and Stuart Daultrey, 'Hearth tax, household size and Irish population change 1672–1821', *Proc. Royal Ir. Academy*, lxxxii, C (1982), 125–81; Joel Mokyr and Cormac Ó Gráda, 'New developments in Irish population history, 1700–1850', *Econ. Hist. Rev.*, 2nd ser., xxxvii (1984), 473–88; Liam Kennedy and L.A. Clarkson, 'Birth, death and exile: Irish population history, 1700–1921', in B.J. Graham and L.J. Proudfoot (eds), *An Historical Geography of Ireland* (London, 1993), 158–9.

32. Cullen, 'Economic development', 162–3; Ó Gráda *Ireland*, 8–11; Colin Thomas, 'Family formation in a colonial city: Londonderry 1650–1750', in *Proc. Royal Ir. Academy, c, C* (2000), 87–111; William Macafee, 'The pre-Famine population of Ireland', in Collins et al., *Industry, Trade and People in Ireland*, 78–81.

33. Dickson et al., 'Hearth tax', 169–173; R.T. Vann and David Eversley, *Friends in Life and Death: The British and Irish Quakers* (Cambridge: UP, 1993), 192–5, 200–10, 248; Macafee, 'Pre-famine popuation', 76–8.

34. Cullen, 'Irish history without the potato', *Past and Present*, xl (July 1968), 72–83; R.N. Salaman, *The History and Social Influence of the Potato* (2nd. ed., Cambridge, 1985), xvi–xix; Austin Bourke, '*The Visitation of God?*': The Potato and the Great Irish Famine* (Dublin: Lilliput Press, 1993), 9–29; Jona Schellekens, 'The role of marital fertility in Irish population history, 1750–1840', in *Econ. Hist. Rev.*, 2nd ser., xlvi (1993), 369–78.

35. L.A. Clarkson and E.M. Crawford, *Feast and Famine: A History of Food and Nutrition in Ireland 1500–1920* (Oxford, 2001), 61–7; Dickson, *Old World Colony*, 236–40, 301–3.

36. John Post, *Food Shortage, Climatic Variability, and Epidemic Disease in Preindustrial Europe...* (Ithaca, 1985), 174–83; David Dickson, 'The gap in famines: A useful myth?', in E.M. Crawford (ed), *Famine: The Irish experience...* (Edinburgh, 1989), 96–111; James Kelly, 'Scarcity and poor relief in eighteenth-century Ireland: The subsistence crisis of 1782–1784', in *Ir. Hist. Stud.*, xxviii (1992–3), 38–62; Dickson, *Arctic Ireland...* (Belfast, 1997); Brian Gurrin, *A Century of Struggle in Delgany and Kilcoole...1666–1779* (Dublin, 2000), 34–42.

37. Gurrin, *A Social History of the Wicklow Uplands* (Dublin, 2006), 59–63.

38. Kerby Miller, Arnold Shrier, B.D. Boling and D.N. Doyle, *Irish Immigrants in the Land of Canaan...* (New York, 2003), 657. This is a much higher figure than the conventional estimate of around 100 000.

39. Crawford, 'The Ulster Irish in the eighteenth century', *Ulster Folklife*, xxviii (1982), 24–32; Marianne Elliott, *The Catholics of Ulster* (New York, 2001), 186–92; Miller et al., *Irish Immigrants*, 656–73.

40. Elliott, *Catholics*, 225–7.

41. F.G. James, 'The Irish lobby in the early eighteenth century', *Eng. Hist. Rev.*, lxxxi (1966), 543–57.

42. Eoin Magennis, 'Coal, corn and canals: Parliament and the dispersal of public moneys, 1695–1772', in D.W. Hayton (ed), *The Irish Parliament in the Eighteenth Century: The Long Apprenticeship* (Edinburgh, 2001), 71–86; B.M.S. Campbell, 'Economic progress in the canal age: A case study from Counties Armagh and Down', in Dickson and Ó Gráda, *Refiguring Ireland*, 63–93. For an overview of public and private improvement initiatives: Toby Barnard, *The Kingdom of Ireland, 1641–1760* (Basingstoke, 2004), 79–89.

SELECT BIBLIOGRAPHY

Aalen, F.H.A., Whelan, Kevin, and Stout, Matthew (eds), *Atlas of the Irish Rural Landscape* (2nd ed., Cork, 2012).

Barnard, Toby, *Making the Grand Figure: Lives and Possessions in Ireland 1641–1770* (New Haven, 2004).

Connolly, S.J., *Divided Kingdom: Ireland 1630–1800* (Oxford, 2008), ch. 9.

Crawford, W.H., *The Impact of the Domestic Linen Industry in Ulster* (Belfast, 2005).

Cullen, L.M., *An Economic History of Ireland since 1660* (London, 1972).

——, 'Economic development, 1691–1750', and 'Economic development 1750–1800', in T.W. Moody and W.E. Vaughan (eds), *A New History of Ireland*, IV (Oxford, 1986), 123–95.

——. *Economy, Trade and Irish Merchants at Home and Abroad 1600–1988* (Dublin, 2012).

Dickson, David, *New Foundations: Ireland 1660–1800* (Dublin, 2000), ch. 4.

——, *Old World Colony: Cork and South Munster 1630–1830* (Cork, 2005).

Graham, B.J. and Proudfoot, L.J. (eds), *An Historical Geography of Ireland* (London, 1993).

Kennedy, Liam and Solar, Peter, *Irish Agriculture: A Price History from the Mid-eighteenth century to the Eve of the First World War* (Dublin, 2007).

Ó Gráda, Cormac, *Ireland: A New Economic History 1780–1939* (Oxford, 1994).

Roebuck, Peter (ed), *Plantation to Partition: Essays in Ulster History in Honour of J.L. McCracken* (Belfast, 1981).

CHAPTER 22

IRISH-LANGUAGE SOURCES FOR THE HISTORY OF EARLY MODERN IRELAND

ÉAMONN Ó CIARDHA

THE neglect of early modern Irish-language material by historians has been a constant refrain among scholars and a key theme in Irish letters. Francis John Byrne, a leading authority on early Irish history, suggested that the sympathetic historian 'must at least pay the subjects of his study the elementary courtesy of learning their language'.[1] James Lydon, one of the doyens of medieval Ireland, stressed the importance of Irish for any Irish historian working up until the modern period, and highly commended the endeavours of the English-born, Irish medievalist Edmund Curtis, who took the trouble to learn the language.[2] Similarly, Louis Cullen, the most productive eighteenth-century historian of his generation, remarked that 'it is distressing that under-graduates now are unwilling or incompetent to read Irish language material'.[3] Kevin Whelan considered it remarkable that there is 'no conception that an understanding of the majority language of the island until the nineteenth century might be a necessary qualification for an Irish historian'.[4] On the matters of historical consciousness, of nationhood and nationality, its antiquity and manifestations, Gearóid Ó Tuathaigh, one of Ireland's leading modern historians, stated that 'it is difficult to see how a discussion of cultural or "national" consciousness in Ireland in the early modern period can be conducted very sensibly by those who cannot comfortably handle sources'.[5] Tomás Mac Símóin, the Irish writer and critic has railed against the cultural colonization and post-colonial linguistic apartheid inherent in much Irish history, deeming it 'a serious lack in our current dominant historical narratives'. Indeed, he stated that 'the linguistic dimension of this process suffers particularly in this regard, being pretty much a 'no-go area' as far as the generality of historians is concerned'.[6]

This brief survey will outline the changing nature of the Irish literary tradition in the early modern period and assess the efficacy of Irish-language sources as a window on the socio-economic, political, and cultural history of the period through an appraisal of the Irish support for the exiled House of Stuart, Irish Catholicism, and Irish popular politics, with specific emphasis on the Irish outlaw. Finally, it will suggest that while a great deal has been done in recent years to uncover Gaelic Ireland in the early modern period, much more editorial and interpretative work needs to be completed before scholars can properly appreciate its usefulness in illuminating the period.

However, it is first necessary to examine the catastrophic impact of the Tudor conquest and subsequent plantations on Gaelic Ireland and the literary tradition which it had sustained for nearly a thousand years. The five decades after the 'Flight of the Earls' (1607) and the Plantation of Ulster (1609) saw a decline in the fortunes of the professional learned classes such as poets, scribes, brehons, genealogists, and chroniclers.[7] A wholesale destruction of manuscripts and the carelessness of subsequent generations has deprived us of much evidence with which historians and literary scholars might tabulate the extent and influence of the 'aos dána' (learned classes). Nevertheless, the surviving material vastly outstrips that for contemporary Scotland or Wales and sheds much light on Irish society. Thousands of manuscripts, some catalogued and many unedited, have survived the ravages of time to provide a unique and invaluable corpus of primary source material for Gaelic Ireland. Scribes and scholars transcribed these manuscripts, sometimes in very difficult circumstances, and often in the employ of a wealthy lay or clerical patron who still valued the native, literary heritage.[8]

Prior to the Tudor Conquest and subsequent plantations, the organization of Irish learning had changed little since the middle ages. In addition to the monasteries and monastic schools, secular academies of poetry, genealogy, history, medicine, and law operated under the control of an 'ollamh' (professor), a leading scholar of the highest social status.[9] Successive Tudor and early Jacobean administrations made concerted attempts to curb the activities of harpers, rhymers, chroniclers, and bards. In a letter to Thomas Cromwell in 1537, Robert Cowley complained that 'harpers, rymours, Irish cronyclers, bardes and isshallyn [aos ealadhan/an t-aos ealaín, the literati] commonly goo with praises to gentilmen in the Englishe Pale, praysing in rymes, otherwise callod danes (dánta, poems) their extorcioners, robberies and abuses, as valiauntes, which reyoysith theim in that their evell doines…'. Statutes such as those passed in 1534 decreed that 'no Yryshe minstrels, rymours, shannaghes [seanchaithe, storytellers], ne bardes, unchaghes [óinsigh, silly women], nor messengers, come to desire any goods of any man dwellinge within the Inglysherie, upon peyne of forfayture of all theyr goods, and theyr bodyes to prison'.[10] Furthermore, Sir Henry Sidney's Discourse for the Reformation of Ireland (1585) proposed that all 'brehons, carraghes, bards rhymers, friars, monks, Jesuits, pardoners, nuns and such like, be executed by martial law', thereby copper-fastening an association between language, literature, religion, and outlawry which would continue throughout the early modern period.[11]

Much of the surviving poetry, contained in manuscripts transcribed in the sixteenth century or later, would suggest that these attempts proved largely ineffective.

A large number of 'Duanairí' (poem-books)[12] date from the period, including collections for the Mhic Shadhbhráin (MacGaughrans),[13] Uí Dhomhnaill (O'Donnells),[14] Uí Eadhra (O'Hara),[15] Uí Chonchubhair Donn (O'Connor Donn),[16] Uí Rathallaigh (O'Reilly),[17] Búrcaigh (Burkes),[18] Buitléirigh (Butlers),[19] Uí Néill (O'Neill), Clan Aodha Buidhe (O'Neills of Clandeboy),[20] Branach/Uí Bhroinn (O'Byrnes)[21] and Mac Uidhir (Maguires).[22] Likewise, the position of the 'ollamh taoisigh' (chief poet), the subject of excellent studies by Osborne Bergin, Brian Ó Cuív, and Pádraig Breatnach,[23] continued to be maintained across large parts of the island for most of the sixteenth century. Particular learned families remained associated with specific lordships and clans: Mac an Bhaird (Ó Domhnaill), Ó hEódhasa (Mac Uidhir), Ó Gnímh (Ó Néill), Ó Dálaigh (Mac Cárthaigh, Mac Gearailt, Ó Caoimh) and Mac Bruaideadha (Ó Conchobhair).[24] In spite of this familial structure many prominent poets such as Aonghus Fionn Ó Dálaigh,[25] Godfraidh Fionn Ó Dálaigh,[26] Tadhg Dall Ó hUigínn,[27] Fearghal Óg Mac an Bhaird,[28] Eoghan Rua Mac an Bhaird,[29] Eochaidh Ó hEódhasa[30] and Tadhg Mac Bruaideadha[31] also penned verse for a host of different patrons, both in Ireland and Gaelic Scotland.[32]

The traditional conservatism of the poets, as manifest in the strict mandarin metres, literary motifs, allusions, and concepts, often masked their appreciation of, and reaction to, contemporary events. These included the rapid expansion of English power, the onset of the Protestant Reformation and the subsequent introduction of English law, language, dress, and mores, and the manner in which these changes impacted on Gaelic Ireland. Early seventeenth-century Irish poems and prose works often carried a stark message of impending doom at Ireland's sorry plight and despair at the continual scattering of her native aristocracy, gentry, and clergy, while bearing testimony to an emerging cult of loyalty to the House of Stuart.[33] Although the Irish language had still not lost its dominant position in Ireland's literary culture, the successive plantations, confiscations, and emigrations of the sixteenth and early seventeenth centuries had left the door ajar for rapid anglicization. In spite of this, and the incessant wars and political turmoil of the early modern period, the country showed a remarkable vitality in poetic, literary, and scribal activity. The Franciscan order, operating from the Counter-Reformation power-houses of Louvain, Salamanca, and Rome, utilized scions of the traditional learned families such as the Uí Ghnímh,[34] Uí Chléirigh,[35] Uí Eódhasa,[36] Uí Mhaoil Chonaire,[37] and Uí Dhuibhgheannáin,[38] in a two-pronged effort to stem the tide of Protestantism and promote the emerging Catholic nation's antiquity and literary heritage.[39] Throughout the Jacobean, Caroline, Cromwellian, and Restoration periods, a stream of confessional and theological works, religious primers, and catechisms emanated from these colleges, directed towards the clergy as opposed to the largely illiterate laity.[40] Reflecting both the continental and native bardic training of many of their authors and drawing heavily on contemporary post-Tridentine, Counter-Reformation works in Spanish, French, Latin, and Italian, they included such canonical texts as Giolla Brighde Ó hEódhasa's *An Teagasg Críostaithe*/The Teaching of Christ (1611),[41] *Suim Riaghlachas Phroinnsias*/The rule of St Francis (1610–14), Aodh MacAingil, *Scathán Shacramuinte na h-Aithrithe*/

Mirror of the Sacrament of Confession (1618),[42] and Flaithrí Ó Maoil Chonaire, *Sgathán an Chrábhaidh*/Desiderius (1616).[43]

Latin was taught, studied, and readily understood in sixteenth-century Ireland but a great flowering of Hiberno-Latin learning would be fuelled by the Counter-Reformation. The language had remained the medium of religion, politics, and government in the middle ages and continued to be important in the immediate pre-Reformation period, facilitating Irish communication with the European Catholic world.[44] Various testaments from the English Jesuit Edmund Campion, a survivor of the Spanish Armada, and Archbishop Giovanni Battista Rinuccini, Papal Nuncio to the Confederate Catholics in the 1640s, point to a widespread knowledge of vulgar Latin across the country.[45] However accurate these testimonies, it is possible to trace a vibrant early modern Hiberno-Latin tradition from north-west Donegal to Vienna and from Naples to Lisbon in the sixteenth and seventeenth centuries. In his *Zoilomastix*, the exiled Irish writer Philip O'Sullivan Beare listed eighty-six continental-based Irish Catholic writers and the full extent of this literary diaspora awaits the completion of various ongoing research projects.[46]

The schools and academies that flourished in a number of major towns in the fifty years after the onset of the Protestant Reformation further fuelled this learning. For example, Kilkenny Grammar School, presided over by Peter White, one-time graduate of Oriel College, Oxford, boasted alumni of the calibre of the Jesuit writer Richard Stanihurst and Archbishop Peter Lombard of Armagh, who would chair the first committee which tried Galileo for heresy.[47] Galway Academy, founded by Dominic Lynch, produced scholars of learning and renown such as the genealogist Dubhaltach Mac Fir Bhisigh and Archdeacon John Lynch of Tuam, author of *Cambrensis Eversus* (1662) and *Alithinologia* (1662–4), two vigorous rebuttals of the twelfth-century Anglo-Norman polemicist Giraldus Cambrensis,[48] as well as a hagiographical portrait of Bishop Francis Kirwan and a Latin history of the Irish episcopate. Roderick O'Flaherty, another eminent past-pupil and associate of Sir Thomas Molyneux, physician and renowned natural philosopher, and the eminent Welsh Celticist Edward Lhuyd. O'Flaherty's famous work *The Ogygia* (1685) presented a learned exposition of Irish Catholic loyalty to the House of Stuart and a vigorous assertion of the antiquity of the Kingdom of Ireland.[49] Throughout the course of the seventeenth century, Luke Wadding,[50] Peter Lombard,[51] Philip O' Sullivan Beare,[52] David Rothe,[53] Richard Creagh,[54] Cornelius O'Deveney, Richard Stanihurst,[55] Richard O'Ferell, Robert O'Connell,[56] and the prolific Franciscan friars of St Anthony's Louvain enhanced a long and eminent tradition of Hiberno-Latin history, hagiography, theology, and genealogy.

Archbishop James Ussher, Sir James Ware, and Bishop William Bedell provided the main Protestant contribution to Irish historical, antiquarian, and Latin learning.[57] The former collaborated with Gaelic scholars such as Dubhaltach Mac Fir Bhisigh, the 'celebrated antiquary', and Mícheál Ó Cléirigh, the leading evangelist of the 'Annála Ríoghachta Éireann' (Annals of the Kingdom of Ireland, otherwise 'The Annals of the Four Masters'), while Ware collected manuscripts and compiled numerous compendia on Irish bishops, writers, scribes, anchorites, and evangelists.

Pivotal to the ongoing efforts to promote Catholicism and preserve the Irish Catholic nation's literary heritage was 'The Annals of the Four Masters' assembled with the support of the Franciscan Order and the patronage of Fearghal Ó Gadhra, a Sligo nobleman.[58] Paul Walsh's *The Four Masters and their Work* (Dublin, 1944) has Mícheál Ó Cléirigh, the leading luminary among the quartet, depicted as the 'minstrel boy' of later Romantic literature.[59] In fact, Ó Cléirigh should instead be viewed as a renaissance man going back 'ad fontes' (to the sources), and listing the time and place where he found them. He did not seek to build a shrine to the past, Roy Foster's 'monument to a dead civilisation',[60] but rather to set down the basic source materials which he believed would be crucial to the new emerging Ireland.[61] Ó Cléirigh also produced the Martyrology of Donegal and a revised version of the Leabhar Gabála (Book of Invasions).[62] Seathrún Céitinn's (Geoffrey Keating) 'Foras Feasa ar Éirinn' (Compendium/Foundation of Wisdom on Ireland), another foundation-text in this genre, attacked those anti-Irish writers such as Giraldus Cambrensis, Edmund Spenser, William Camden, Richard Stanihurst, Edmund Campion, Meredith Hamner, and Fynes Moryson whom he deemed to be 'dall aineolach i dteangaibh na tíre' (blind and ignorant in the language of the country).[63] This monumental work proved immensely popular, the last 'best seller' in the European manuscript tradition, the first book of the old testament of an emerging Irish Catholic national identity, and a key reference work for Irish poets until the nineteenth century.[64] In the 'dionbhrollach' (foreword) Céitinn justified his extensive use of poetry, 'the bones and marrow of history' (Cnáimh agus smior an tSeanchusa) as a source for his work, a pronouncement which should not be lost on historians who wish to assess the importance of Irish literary sources.[65]

The first decades of the seventeenth century also witnessed a proliferation of historical texts, hagiographical works, biographies, diaries, and social commentaries. Tadhg Ó Cianáin, author of 'Imeacht na nIarlaí (The Departure of the Earls), accompanied the fugitive Ulster earls from Lough Swilly in 1607 and provides an invaluable eyewitness account of their travels through France, Flanders, and the Swiss Cantons to Rome.[66] Lughaigh Ó Cléirigh's 'Beatha Aodha Rua Uí Dhomhnaill' (The Life of 'Red' Hugh O'Donnell) comprises a hagiographical, heroic biography of the warrior-prince of Tír Chonaill,[67] while Cinn Lae Uí Mhealláin (Friar Mallon's Diary) provides a unique account of the military campaigns of General Eoghan Rua Ó Néill's Ulster army in the 1640s.[68] 'Pairlement Chloinne Tomáis' (The Parliament of Clann Thomas), a bitter invective from the learned classes at the effects of the social revolution which occurred in the aftermath of the Ulster Plantation/Cromwellian conquest, attacked Oliver Cromwell as king of churls who had established every boor and upstart. It proceeded to scurrilously lampoon his main beneficiaries, the vile, diabolical progeny of 'Clann Tomáis', who aped the manners, dress, and language of the English settlers.[69] In the religious realm, the Franciscan Seán Mac Colgáin reinvigorated the cult of Ireland's patron saints, Patrick, Brigit and Colum Cille,[70] Seathrún Céitinn penned two key counter-reformation tracts on the mass and mortality,[71] Anthony Gernon wrote on the soul,[72] Bernard Conny on the rule of St Francis,[73] while Teabóid Gállduff produced an Irish-Latin catechism.[74]

Poetic composition witnessed a general loosening of the traditional metres in the first half of the seventeenth century. The decline of the bardic schools system and collapse of the tradition of hereditary literary families also heralded the arrival of a new literary caste, some of whom sprang from the ranks of the Old English descendants of the original Anglo-Norman colonizers. Seathrún Céitinn,[75] Piaras Feiritéar,[76] Pádraigín Haicéad,[77] Muiris Mac Dháibhí Dubh Mac Gearailt,[78] Dáibhí Ó Bruadair,[79] and the named and anonymous Gaelic Irish authors of five long narrative political poems (subsequently edited by Cecile O'Rahilly)[80] continued the venerable traditions of eulogy and satire. Composing their verse in a more popular, accessible 'amhrán' (song) metre for a wider audience, these poets provide authoritative commentary on the unprecedented suffering of the Irish, massacres, transportations, and transplantations, and note their cataclysmic effects on the Irish language, aristocracy, gentry, and clergy.

This literature has been edited and translated by a whole host of scholars such as Osborn Bergin, Pádraig Breatnach, James Carney, David Greene, William Gilles, Eleanor Knott, Seosamh Laoide, Sean Mac Airt, John MacErlean, Lambert McKenna, Cuthbhert Mhag Craith, Canice Mooney, Rois Ní Ógáin, Breandán Ó Buachalla, Tómas Ó Cléirigh, Tómas Ó Concheannain, Brian Ó Cuív, Breandán Ó Doibhlin, Tadhg Ó Donnchadha, Cecile O'Rahilly, Thomas F. O'Rahilly, and Paul Walsh.[81] It has also engendered much lively debate in the realms of historical discourse and literary criticism, as evidenced in the writings of Brendan Bradshaw,[82] Marc Caball,[83] Nicholas Canny,[84] Bernadette Cunningham,[85] Anne Dooley,[86] Tom Dunne,[87] Andrew Hadfield,[88] Micheál Mac Craith,[89] Willy Maley,[90] Richard McCabe,[91] Breandán Ó Buachalla,[92] Breandán Ó Doibhlin,[93] Diarmaid Ó Doibhlin,[94] Tadhg Ó Dúshláine,[95] Nollaig Ó Muraíle,[96] Michelle O'Riordan,[97] Patricia Palmer,[98] and Katharine Simms.[99] Although the Gaelic literati had lost much of their time-honoured social status and political clout, the poet remained one of the great reflectors and, to a lesser extent, moulders of public opinion in Irish-speaking Ireland until the close of the eighteenth century. Through the accumulating social, economic, and political disasters of Reformation, Tudor centralization and anglicization, the collapse of the Nine Years' War (1594–1603), the Flight of the Earls (1607), the Plantation of Ulster (1609), the 1641 rebellion, the Cromwellian Conquest (1649–58), Caroline Restoration (1660–85), and the Jacobite Wars (1689–91), the poet remained close to the heart of Irish political life and retained his role as political chronicler and conscience of the nation.[100]

Eighteenth-century Irish political poetry has support for the exiled House of Stuart at its core. This is no great surprise, given that Jacobitism remained the ascendant political ideology in Irish Catholic society between the Battle of the Boyne (1690) and the French Revolution (1789) and one of the main languages of disaffection throughout the three kingdoms. Indeed, the thematic and ideological similarities between Irish, Scots-Gaelic, and English Jacobite literature give credence to Howard Erskine-Hill's 'rhetoric of Jacobitism'. Common themes on around the questions of hereditary succession, the right of the lawful prince, disdain for the corrupting influence of foreigners, and the inevitability of a Stuart restoration as the only solution to the nation's problems. Like its English or Scottish counterparts, however, Irish Jacobitism involved far more than a blind loyalty to the House of Stuart. Many Irish Jacobites looked to their exiled king to restore their confiscated lands, reverse the political dominance of Protestantism, and to rehabilitate the Catholic Church and the Irish language. The poets tailored Jacobitism to suit their community's particular needs: evoking the cause to demand the right to bear arms, to inherit lands, to take out leases, and vote in elections. Seventeenth-century confiscations and the subsequent political decimation of the Irish Catholic landed interest ensured that the Irish tradition was not characterized by a gentry-led or clan-inspired movement as in England and Scotland. It became closely associated with the surviving Catholic aristocracy, Whelan's so-called 'Underground Gentry', the Irish Brigades in France and Spain, and the Irish Continental colleges in Europe and was vigorously promoted at home by the Catholic clergy and Jacobite literati.[101]

In spite of this, Irish Jacobite poetry, particularly the 'aisling' [allegorical vision poem] has often been dismissed as lacking substantive political content, the stylized output of a literary caste. Careful examination and contextualization of this material shows that it did not flourish in a political vacuum. Compared thematically and ideologically with Scots-Gaelic and English Jacobite writings, and with contemporary Whig and anti-Jacobite rhetoric, Irish poetry showed an astute awareness of the workings of local, 'British', and European politics and their possible ramifications for the Stuart cause. The recent work of Ó Buachalla, Mac Craith, Morley, and Ó Ciardha has sought to contextualize this huge corpus of literary material and bring Irish Jacobitism and its vibrant literary culture to a similar level of serious scholarly engagement.[102] Ó Buachalla has argued that Irish historians have paid too much attention to official state documents, to the neglect of literary works, newspapers, and ballads. Ó Tuathaigh, in turn, takes the view that these poems 'deserve closer scrutiny as they are, in many ways, all that we have of the voice of Gaelic Ireland in the eighteenth and early nineteenth century'.[103] Indeed, the former's close re-readings and contextualizations have rescued Irish Jacobite poetry and prose from 'Charlie over the Waterism' and the literary nostalgia which plagued it for nearly two hundred years. Unfortunately, the inability of many Irish historians to engage with the massive corpus of source material surveyed in *Aisling Ghéar*, his *magnum opus*, means that the book is more referenced than read. David Hayton recently addressed what he considered the narrow source-base of the work: he claims that Ó Buachalla 'feasts extensively on one particular form of evidence (namely literature), and has nibbled around the edges of other sources'. But even a cursory perusal of its one-hundred-page bibliography bears testimony to a staggering range of manuscript, newspaper, and printed primary and secondary sources in Irish, Scots-Gaelic, English, French, Spanish, German, Welsh, Italian, and Latin.[104]

The Irish literary tradition became much more democratically minded in the eighteenth century and the poet increasingly functioned as the spokesman of his peers. This 'democratization' has numerous manifestations: Irish poetic culture adopted a toasting and drinking component; poets regularly addressed their verse to Ireland in her various female forms, or to her aristocracy, gentry, clergy, and people. Moreover, they often based their popular political verse on news gleaned from English-language newspapers, thereby acting as media for the transmission of European, North American, or Asian political and military affairs to a monoglot Irish-speaking public.[105] In addition, the messianic Jacobite literary tradition regularly sought authority from a popular prophetic, folkloric, and pre-'Devotional Revolution' religious tradition. The dramatic quality of the 'aisling' resembled an embryonic form of street theatre or the modern 'agallamh beirte' (dialogue of two), while the convergence of Gaelic elite and folk culture is also borne out by the employment of a more popular metre in contemporary composition and its survival and popular and widespread transmission in manuscript, folkloric, and oral sources. Murray Pittock noted 'those who wished to defend a particularly Scottish (or Irish) high culture were forced to surrender to the standards of the British state'.[106] Ó Buachalla utilized the memorable hierarchical analogy of 'trí ghluain ó rí go ramhainn' (three generations from a king to a spade) to represent the socio-economic decline of the Gaelic literati in seventeenth and eighteenth-century Ireland—from Dáibhí Ó Bruadair through Aogán Ó Rathaille and Séamas Dall Mac Cuarta to the hedge-school masters, scribes, and 'spailpíní' (casual labourers) Peadar Ó Doirnín, Art Mac Cumhaigh, Seán Ó Tuama, and Eoghan Rua Ó Súilleabháin.[107]

Furthermore, Irish poets regularly employed imported English and Scottish Jacobite airs such as 'The White Cockade', 'The King shall enjoy his own again', 'Bonnie Dundee', 'Charlie come over the water', and 'Over the hills and far away'. Wading through dusty manuscripts in the National Library of Ireland, the Royal Irish Academy, or any other major collection of eighteenth-century manuscripts in Ireland, Britain, continental Europe, or North America, or perusing the numerous edited volumes of Irish or Scots-Gaelic Jacobite poetry and song, it is easily forgotten that these literary works were not composed as historical source material but for public performance or recitation. In editing two hundred Ulster songs, Énrí Ó Muirgheasa rightly remarked that they were not composed for reading but for recital and they are now without the music as a widow is without her husband.[108]

That popular songs are worthy of examination for political content is demonstrated in Zimmermann's collection of political ballads, or indeed by the popular ballad-culture of the nineteenth and twentieth-century loyalist and nationalist traditions.[109] The Scottish writer, politician, and patriot commentator Andrew Fletcher of Saltoun famously commented that 'if a man were permitted to make all the ballads, he need not care who should make the laws of the nation'.[110] Thomas Crofton-Croker, the nineteenth-century Irish antiquarian, also observed that 'the songs of the people are always worthy of attention and it appears to me extraordinary that the most positive treason should for so long have been published without notice'.[111] Ó Muirgheasa attacked those who dismissed the political content of Irish poetry and song when he stated that the person who cannot see in these songs anything but harmless 'come all yes' is not only blind, but blind as the sole of their boot.[112] Moreover, he believed that 'the person who would try to understand the life and mentality of Gaelic Ireland during the eighteenth century must put aside the histories, forget all about the Irish parliament, and come to live in spirit with McCooey (Art Mac Cumhaigh) and his contemporary poets'.[113] Irish poets usually ignored Dublin and London and their parliaments, focusing instead on 'James III' and his confederates and prospective allies in Paris, Rome, and Madrid and on the battles and sieges of the dynastic wars which ravaged Europe in the first half of the eighteenth century. They believed that it was here, and not in Dublin, Edinburgh, or London, that the House of Stuart would be restored.

John Lorne Campbell highlighted a similar neglect of Scots-Gaelic sources by Scottish historians in his introduction to his *Highland Songs of the '45*: 'it is astonishing that any historian should feel himself properly equipped to write the history of his country while remaining ignorant of the language spoken over half its area'.[114] He pointed out that Scots-Gaelic literature had not been particularly well edited. This has been more than rectified in the last fifty years through the efforts of the Scottish Gaelic Texts Society, as well as through the prolific editing and translating work of scholars such as Donald Meek, Colm Ó Baoill, Cathair Ó Dochartaigh, and Meg Bateman. The same gap could not be said to exist in Irish literature due to the Trojan endeavours of Risteard Ó Foghludha, Tadhg Ó Donnchadha, Pádraig Ua Duinnín, Énrí Ó Muirgheasa, Rois Uí Ógáin, and a host of editors of the Irish Texts Society, An Gúm, Éigse Oirialla, and Field-Day.[115] Crucially, however, the bulk of this poetry has never been translated, and there has, until recently, been little understanding of, or engagement with, its contemporary political, literary, and historical contexts. Thus, for instance, R.A. Breatnach apologized in the 1960s for even discussing the historical background in his survey of eighteenth-century poetry.[116] As late as the early 1990s, Cornelius Buttimer noted that 'the period 1700–1850 is the best documented phase of the Gaelic literary, tradition', but added that 'it is the least understood' and lacks 'the informed critical commentary which one might expect for such a significant era'.[117] Ó Tuathaigh also lamented the lack of an integrated narrative of Irish poetry.[118]

This is a major lacuna in our understanding of eighteenth-century Ireland, not least because the greater Catholic populace had little access to other aspects of the popular Jacobite media and iconography such as newspapers, pamphlets, prints, medals, coins, touch-pieces, art, and ceremonial drinking-glasses. Internal and continental communication had obvious dangers. Therefore, poetry provided the principal medium through which they could articulate and disseminate their political sentiments with relative impunity. In spite of the allegorical nature of the verse and the protection afforded by the language itself, three poets were prosecuted in the eighteenth century for composing seditious verse, and a number of others expressed fears of prosecution. Like its Scottish and English counterparts, Jacobite poetry in Ireland operated at two levels, and the educated ear knew exactly who the poet meant when he referred to 'The Blackbird', 'The Young Steward', 'The Shepherd', 'The Little Branch', or 'The White-backed Heifer'. That the bilingual poet based much of his political verse on material from local news-sheets shows his key role in the diffusion of international war news to an Irish-speaking public. The fact that Jacobitism provides the dominant theme in eighteenth-century Irish poetry has obvious implications for its survival among Irish Catholics. Ó Buachalla has made the same point, noting that while the Jacobite ideology utilized many media in Britain, in pamphlets, sermons, orations, books, ballads, or indeed through iconography glass and touch-pieces, it manifested itself in Ireland through the exclusive medium of poetry.[119]

Paul Monod,[120] Paul Chapman,[121] and Murray Pittock[122] have all stressed the importance of the street-singer in the Jacobite ideology of Scotland and England. It is unlikely that eighteenth-century Ireland would have been different, particularly in view of the importance of the Irish oral tradition and because of the fact that it was one of the few media at their disposal for the articulation of Jacobite sentiment. However, the utilization of Irish poetry as a historical source presents some difficulties. Monod underlined the lack of interest shown by historians in English political poetry. Having considered its advantages and disadvantages as a reflection of the 'voice of the people', he argued that 'to be silent on the subject of Jacobite poetry is to ignore a whole industry'. Its use in eighteenth-century Ireland is even more pertinent, given the dearth of sources for Gaelic Ireland. Tomas Ó Fiaich made a similar point in his 1973 edition of Art Mac Cumhaigh's poetry, noting that the Gaelic-Irish public left little by way of a written record behind them apart from their poetry, and much of the English-language documentation pertaining to them perished in the Four Courts conflagration in 1922. Furthermore, many accounts left by visitors are disadvantaged by confessional and linguistic barriers between writer and subject.[123]

The difficulties which arise in assessing the political content of Irish poetry and the inherent dangers of utilizing it as historical source material are best exemplified by the long-running scholarly controversy surrounding Daniel Corkery's *Hidden Ireland*. Corkery penned his influential thesis in the 1920s as a belated response to what he deemed a major lacuna in W.E.H. Lecky's writings on eighteenth-century Ireland, namely his total neglect of its Gaelic-speaking populace.[124] Irish scholarship unequivocally accepted Corkery's unity of purpose between hovel and big house until Cullen's timely, critical reappraisal (below) and Corkery's work 'remains perhaps the most influential book to have informed the prevailing image of eighteenth-century Ireland'.[125] However one might stand on this long-running controversy, most participants in this rather protracted scholarly debate would concede that a failure to engage with one of the only major sources for Irish-speaking Ireland magnifies the dangers of reading Irish history from exclusively, English-language sources. According to Cullen, Corkery's thesis has been 'long established as an aspect of the interpretation of the eighteenth-century economic and social history of Ireland'.[126] However, Cullen's own reappraisal has been modified, particularly in the light of the general consensus among many English, Scottish, and Irish historians regarding the significance of Jacobitism as a political ideology until at least 1750. Difficulties do arise in assessing the real level of political alienation outlined in Jacobite 'aislingí' and political verse. Nevertheless, a failure to utilize this literature as a means of exploring the eighteenth-century Irish Catholic mentality magnifies the dangers of reading Irish history from exclusively English-language sources and state papers. Indeed, Cullen himself later conceded that 'in a fresh look at the Hidden Ireland, politicization would merit more attention than it received in my 1969 paper'.[127]

Cullen's claim that many well-to-do Catholics disassociated themselves from the Stuart cause must be balanced against the real fears of those Catholics who struggled to retain their lands in the face of penal laws, Protestant discoverers, and the opportunism of those who converted to Protestantism.[128] The suspect political loyalty of the members of latter group fascinated their Whig and Jacobite contemporaries and has come under the scholarly scrutiny of none other than Cullen himself. His choice of the work of Peadar Ó Doirnín, Piaras Mac Gearailt, and Eoghan Rua Ó Súilleabháin as representative examples of Irish diffidence towards the Stuart prince cannot be taken as sufficient to undermine the political dimension of the 'aisling'. Despite Ó Doirnín's apparent disparagement of the Stuarts, they feature in many of his poems, which shows the extent to which they retained the attention of his peers. Even his satirical 'Tá Bairéad i Londain' (There is a hat in London) appreciated the workings of European politics and the obligation of Ó Doirnín to address the Jacobite issue. Similarly, Piaras Mac Gearailt's retrospective criticism of the 'aisling' in 1767, eight years after Quiberon Bay (the last threatened Stuart invasion in 1759) runs counter to his earlier zeal for the fallen dynasty. Eoghan Rua's indications that the messianic dimensions of the 'aisling' should not be taken seriously reacted against the not entirely misplaced confidence of his predecessors that deliverance was at hand. Eoghan Rua himself straddles the period between the Jacobite twilight and the explosion of the United Irishmen onto the political scene. By this time, Irish literary figures such as Mícheál Óg Ó Longáin, Miles Byrne, and Charles Teeling finally managed to divert the attentions of 'Gráinne Mhaol' (Ireland) from her 'Buachaill Bán' (Charles Edward).[129]

A close perusal of the 'aislingí' and other Jacobite poetry composed in the eighteenth century, particularly in the context of Irish, British, and European politics, reveals that its Jacobite content was more than vacuous literary rhetoric. Although Cullen noted that the verse yearned for restoration and not revolution, a return of the Stuarts represented the only realistic option for Irish Catholics until the 1760s. Cullen's other main criticism of the 'Hidden Ireland' rests on his assessment of the 'aisling' as merely a literary motif, lacking substantive political significance. This criticism, however, leaves some questions unanswered. If this poetry was void of political content and confined to the upper classes of the literati, how does one explain its utilization of the popular 'amhrán' metre, its transmission throughout Ireland in the oral and scribal traditions, and its employment of imported Jacobite airs?

The 'Hidden Ireland' thesis has also been subjected to criticism by Nicholas Canny. He contends that 'enthusiasts', eager to trace Ireland's nineteenth and twentieth-century 'restless dominion' status back through the seventeenth and eighteenth centuries, have used 'a Hidden Ireland of Irish literary and spiritual leaders to cultivate the concept of an Irish independence to attain these objectives by political means'. Canny correctly warns against the teleological tendencies of the later republican and nationalist traditions, and questions the utility of nineteenth-century ballads and songs as historical sources. His commendation of recent revisionist historiography as disinfecting the received historical wisdom does not warn of the dangers of falling into the same trap as the 'enthusiasts'.[130] The 'Hidden Ireland' and the historical usefulness of seventeenth and eighteenth-century Irish poetry cannot be ignored by historians of early modern Ireland. Furthermore, a close examination of the covert political activities and seditious rhetoric of key members of an Irish episcopate and clergy, who owed their ecclesiastical dignities and secular allegiance to their Stuart master in Rome, shows that they did not cultivate Irish 'independence' but loyalty to the regal rights and pretensions of the exiled Stuart.

The neglect of poetry by Irish historians has also been compounded by an overemphasis on its most despairing and unrealistic aspects. Canny, for instance, has judged it as being 'deeply pessimistic in its outlook'.[131] There is certainly evidence of dejection in some of the poetry but it is more than offset by an optimism centred upon the exiled Stuarts and Irish Brigades in the service of France and Spain between the conclusion of the Williamite wars and the 1760s. This literary conceit reflected a political ideology which, although often idealistic or unrealistic, remained central to the politics of the former Stuart kingdoms until the 1760s. Jacobitism dimmed and flickered rhythmically with the ups and downs of the diplomatic fortunes of the House of Stuart. The tradition was never totally extinguished but smouldered until it was transformed by the explosive conflagrations of the 1790s. By this time, Irish popular political consciousness made the transition from Jacobite to Jacobin and 'Bony' (Bonaparte), and later Daniel O'Connell replaced the 'Bonny Prince' as the darling of the popular political consciousness.

The lack of a comprehensive study of the Catholic Church's relationship with the House of Stuart is another chasm in eighteenth-century Irish historiography. The close ties between Jacobitism and Catholicism had been firmly established at the outset of James II's accession to the throne. Immediately after his elevation, the new king successfully petitioned Pope Innocent XI for the right to nominate Catholic bishops in his three kingdoms. James retained this right after his deposition and he, his wife Mary of Modena (acting as regent for her son), and the future 'James III' (the 'Old Pretender') regularly exercised their prerogative. Indeed, of the 129 bishops and coadjutors appointed to Irish sees between 1687 and 1765, all but five were chosen by the Stuart king.[132] It is no surprise, therefore, that the exiled Stuart retained his role as political conscience of the Irish Catholic clergy. As a result of this hold, Jacobitism remained relevant for Catholic Ireland. Although the Stuart claimant never got the opportunity to show his appreciation and affection to those Irish who had sacrificed everything in his cause, he jealously guarded and judiciously exercised this right of nomination. Rome rarely refused any of his nominees and the Irish Catholic clergy understood that it was to the Stuart court and not the Holy See that episcopal hopefuls had to make their representations. In return for his patronage, Irish bishops and clergy such as Sylvester Lloyd, Stephen McEgan, and Ambrose O'Connor acted as the eyes and ears of the Stuart king and his allies in Europe, keeping them informed of the strength of the English/British garrison within the country and suggesting ports, towns, and regions which would be most suitable for a Jacobite descent. This commitment, in addition to official Vatican policy, meant that they continued to inculcate a loyalty to the exiled monarchy in their flocks.

The close relationship between Irish Jacobite poets and the Catholic clergy has obvious implications for the links between Jacobitism, Catholicism, and the penal laws.[133]

Priest-poets such as Liam Inglis, Seán Ó Briain, Conchubhar Ó Briain, Domhnall Ó Colmáin, and Uilliam Mac Néill Bhacaigh Ó hIarlaithe promoted the Stuart cause, which remained an intrinsic feature of Irish Catholic national identity until at least 1760. The Catholic Church stepped into the breach created by the effective destruction of the Catholic aristocracy to patronize the Jacobite literati. Poets, for their part, steadfastly supported their exiled king and proscribed church. The church appreciated their loyalty and, as Fr Conchubhar Mac Cairteáin recorded in his preface to the unpublished 'Agallamh na bhFioraon', held it to be a 'national' and 'spiritual' duty to patronize the native culture. The Irish Catholic clergy's influence on the main themes and the diffusion of literary output throughout the greater Catholic community had consequence for the popularization of the sentiments expressed in Irish literature.[134] However, much more work needs to be done to properly evaluate this relationship. A reconsideration of the links between the Irish literati, Catholic clergy, and Jacobite ideology might be well served by a quantitative, geographical stock-take of surviving Irish-language manuscripts, a comprehensive study of Irish Catholic institutional and clerical links with the exiled court and its ambassadorial networks, and an extensive prosopographical examination of the Irish Catholic episcopate, higher clergy, and the chaplaincy of the Irish Brigades in the French and Spanish service.

Finally, it is no great surprise that the 'Hidden Ireland' provides suitable cover and an alternative interpretative context for the Irish outlaw, an often illusive actor on the early modern Irish political stage. A whole series of factors from the proliferation of woods, marshes, bogs, and mountains and the nature of traditional Gaelic society (incessant warfare, raiding, a glorification of military prowess, and an ambivalent attitude towards English law) helps account for toryism and rappareeism and other forms of outlawry in the early modern period. The political, military, and economic collapse of O'Neillite, Royalist, Confederate, and Jacobite opposition to the Elizabethan, Cromwellian, and Williamite regimes respectively, usually heralded the start of 'a tory/rapparee war', where small groups of disbanded, disgruntled soldiers and dispossessed Irish aristocrats, gentry, and impoverished tenants used the relative safety of woods, bogs, and mountains to wage a 'war of the flea' against the superior forces of the government, the new planters, and their tenants. Through time, woodkerne, tory, and rapparee activity degenerated to banditry, localized thuggery, and extortion.

In spite of this de-politicization, and perchance as a consequence of their proclamation, liquidation, and impaling by the authorities, the tories and rapparees and their predecessors were often lionized in contemporary Irish poetry, folklore, and in eighteenth-century chapbooks. Described as 'vermin' by Sir Henry Sidney in the 1580s, Feagh Mac Hugh O'Byrne and his forebearers patronized the writers who contributed to the Leabhar Branach, one of the great poem-books of the Irish literary tradition. Furthermore, Edmund Spenser's 'View of the State of Ireland' bristled with impotent rage and indignation at Feagh's insolent outrages and spoils but, as Richard McCabe notes, the Leabhar Branach represented his attacks on the Pale as an heroic gesture which would have been disconcertingly familiar to readers of *The Faerie Queene*.[135] Aonghus Mac Doighri Ó Dálaigh's 'Dia libh a laochraidh Gaoidhiol' (God be with you, heroes of the Gael) lamented that Ireland's royal chiefs (ríoghradh Fhódhla) were now being dismissed as lowly woodkernes (ceithearn chúthail choilleadh). In 1658, the Munster poet Éamonn Mac Donnchadha Mac Cárthaigh observed that the Cromwellian regime used 'tory' as a term of abuse for all Irish Catholics and to facilitate a broad policy of persecution and liquidation.[136] Catholics, in turn, politicized tory activity by portraying their depredations as a response to the Cromwellian regime, linking their actions to their aspirations for political rehabilitation following Charles II's restoration in 1660. It was no coincidence, therefore, that 'Éamonn an Chnoic' (Ned of the Hill), the solitary outlaw on the mountainside who aspired to regain his ancestral lands, became one of the tory heroes of modern Irish literature. Similarly, 'Seán Ó Duibhir an Ghleanna', ' (John O'Dwyer of the Glen), which has as its hero the dispossessed heir of the Uí Dhuibhir of Kilnemanagh, County Tipperary, resonates with the themes of dispossession, de-afforrestation, transportation, transplantation, and the stimulus they provide to toryism. Dudley Costello, Redmond O'Hanlon, Pádraig Fléimoinn, Cathal MacAoidh, Muircheartach Ó Súilleabháin Béara, Dónall Ó Conaill, Séamas Mac Mhuirchidh, and Art Ó Laoghaire became the subjects of popular eulogies and laments, ascending the nationalist pantheon along with the exiled Stuart, 'Wild Geese' poet, and persecuted priest.[137]

These heroic eulogies, laments (caointe, tuirmh, ochláin, marbhnaí), for dead and executed outlaws provide a counter to the 'gallows speech' which became a staple of popular literature in the eighteenth century.[138] These two traditions coexisted and coalesced in popular, song culture from the late eighteenth century onwards, and the 'Gallows Speech or 'Speech from the Dock' became a key text in the Irish Republican discourse from Drennan's 'Wake of William Orr' through Robert Emmet's 'Speech from the Dock' to the scaffold defiance of the 'Manchester Martyrs' in the 1860s.

While a great deal of archival research, editorial recovery, and close literary and antiquarian reading has been completed, much more remains to be done before we can fully evaluate both the Jacobite legacy, the relationship between Jacobitism, popular Catholicism, and Irish-language literature and song, as well the emergence of the 'Outlaw Rapparee' as an important nationalist icon. Morley's seminal study of Ireland and the American Revolution has both influenced and supported my own remarks on the Jacobite 'Twilight'.[139] As well as stifling the emergence of a popular Hanoverian royalism, Jacobitism was crucial to the ease with which American and French-inspired republicanism penetrated Irish society in the 1790s. Similarly, Ó Tuathaigh's, Ó Buachalla's, and Ríonach Uí Ógáin's theses show that a messianic Jacobite residue survived the collapse of United Irish republicanism and manifested itself in the popular cult of O'Connell.[140] These relationships merit further investigation, in view of the fact that the long eighteenth century has now reached the 1830s. An examination of the residual Jacobite influence on, and the motivation behind, late-eighteenth and nineteenth-century literature, folklore, and antiquarian investigations might also shed light on its political, literary, and cultural legacy. This would necessitate a thorough investigation of the published works, writings, manuscripts, airs, libraries, and cultural milieux of Charlotte Brooke, her Irish evangelist Muiris Ó Gormáin, his peers and successors Peadar Ó Gealcháin, Art Mac Bionaid, and Nicholas Ó Cearnaigh, John O'Daly, Edward Walsh, Thomas Davis, Emily Lawless, Thomas Moore, James Clarence Mangan, and Douglas Hyde, among others. There is obvious scope for comparison with English and Scottish poets and writers such as Samuel Johnson, James Boswell, Robert Burns, Joseph Ritson, James Hogg, Lady Carolina Nairne, and Sir Walter Scott; indeed, recent research and lively scholarly exchanges across the Irish Sea have provided fruit-ful avenues of enquiry for scholars of English, Irish, and Scottish Jacobitism. A cursory perusal of Rolf and Magda Loeber's *Guide to Irish Fiction, 1650–1900* (2006) raises the subconscious literary spectres of Wild Goose, smuggler, outlaw, and ruined Jacobite houses and families—illusive Irish versions of Scott's *Redgauntlet* and *Waverley* or Stevenson's *Master of Ballantrae*.[141] Guy Beiner's groundbreaking intellectual rehabilita-tion and contextualization of Irish folk history and memory of the Year of the French and Breandán Mac Suibhne's splendid reconstruction of the fractured political land-scape of post-rebellion Ulster from the Gothic writings of John Gamble provide obvious templates for such scholarly endeavours.[142]

The scholar who examines the eighteenth century through both English- and Irish-language sources will invariably encounter two Irelands. The Protestant Nation survived the trauma of the seventeenth century and marched confidently, if some-times fitfully, through the eighteenth before sleepwalking into rebellion at its end. Its Catholic counterpart had been defeated, humiliated, and alienated in the same period but remained attached to the Stuarts and looked optimistically to Europe for mili-tary succour, in the manner of their royalist predecessors and republican successors. Subsequently fractured between Hanoverian accommodationists and those seduced by the new republican ideologies of the late eighteenth century, Catholic Ireland became the problem child of the British Empire. Indeed, the Hanoverian dynasty to which they had never been reconciled would sacrifice Pitt the Younger and Henry Dundas and defy the 'Iron Duke' (Wellington) before the laurels of Catholic Emancipation, the wages of union, would be snatched by Daniel O'Connell, the 'Uncrowned King' and the ultimate inheritor of the messianic Stuart mantle. However, the liberator's broken heart would be deposited in Rome, the mausoleum of the exiled Stuarts, after his failure to rene-gotiate Ireland's relationship with her sister kingdom, a failure which had also dogged James II and rendered Ireland as a fifth wheel in subsequent Jacobite politics. The Young Irelanders, Fenians, and Irish Volunteers, the inheritors of Tone's Republican mantle, would repudiate the Stuarts' royalist legacy but not the messianic message with which it had been associated since the early seventeenth century.

NOTES

1. Quoted in S. Duffy, *Ireland in the Middle Ages* (Dublin, 1997), 4.
2. S. Duffy, 'A real Irish historian: interview with James Lydon', in *History Ireland,* iii, no 1 (1995), 11–14.
3. K. Whelan, 'Watching the detective: interview with Louis Cullen', in *History Ireland,* ii (1994), 10–13.

454 ÉAMONN Ó CIARDHA

4. Idem, 'The recent writing in Irish history', in *UCD History Review*, i (1991), 27–35.
5. G. Ó Tuathaigh, 'Irish historical revisionism', in C. Brady (ed), *Interpreting Irish History: the Debate on Historical Revisionism* (Dublin, 1994), 317–24.
6. T. Mac Síomóin, 'The colonized mind—Irish language and society', in D. Ó Ceallaigh (ed), *Reconsiderations of Irish History and Culture. Selected papers from the Desmond Greaves Summer School 1989–1993* (Dublin, 1994), 44.
7. D. Finnegan, É. Ó Ciardha, and M.C. Peters (eds), *The Flight of the Earls: Imeacht na nIarlaí* (Derry, 2010); É. Ó Ciardha and M. Ó Siochrú (eds), *The Plantation of Ulster: Ideology and Practice* (Manchester, 2012).
8. The best single survey is Breandán Ó Buachalla, *Aisling Ghéar: na Stíobhartaigh agus an t-aos léinn 1601–1788* (Dublin, 1996). See also B. Ó Cuív, 'The Irish language in the early modern period', in T.W. Moody, F. X. Martin, and F.J. Byrne (eds), *A New History of Ireland*, iii (Oxford, 1976), 509–42; M. Caball, *Poetry and Politics: Reaction and Continuity in Irish Poetry, 1558–1625* (Cork, 1998); V. Morley, *Ó Chéitinn go Raiftearaí: Mar a cumadh stair na hÉireann* (Dublin, 2011).
9. M. Caball and K. Hollo, 'The literature of medieval Ireland, 1200–1600: from the Normans to the Tudors', in M. Kelleher and P. O'Leary (eds), *The Cambridge History of Irish Literature*, 2 vols (Cambridge, 2006), i, 74–139; M. Mac Craith, 'From the Elizabethan Settlement to the Battle of the Boyne: Literature in Irish, c. 1550–1690', in ibid., 191–231; A. Dooley, 'Literature and society in early seventeenth-century Ireland: the evaluation of change', in C.J. Byrne, M. Harry, and P. Ó Siadhail (eds), *Celtic Languages and Celtic Peoples: Proceedings of the Second North American Congress of Celtic Studies* (Halifax, Nova Scotia, 1992), 513–34.
10. Ó Cuív, 'The Irish language in the early modern period', 520.
11. T. Crowley, *The Politics of Language in Ireland, 1366–1922* (London, 2000), 38.
12. B. Ó Cuív, *The Irish Bardic Duanaire or Poembook* (Dublin, 1973).
13. L. McKenna (ed), *Leabhar Meig Shamhradháin* (Dublin, 1947).
14. T. Ó Cléirigh, 'A poembook of the O'Donnells', in *Éigse, i* (1939–40), 51–61, 130–42.
15. L. McKenna (ed), *The Book of O'Hara, Leabhar Í Eadhra* (Dublin, 1951).
16. D. Hyde, 'The Book of O'Connor Don', in *Ériu*, viii (1916), 78–99.
17. J. Carney (ed), *Poems on the O'Reillys* (Dublin, 1950).
18. T. Ó Raghallaigh, 'Seanchus na mBúrcach', in *Journal of Galway Historical and Archaeological Society*, xiii (1924–7), 50–60, 101–38; xiv (1928–9), 30–51, 142–671.
19. J. Carney (ed), *Poems on the Butlers of Ormond Cahir and Dunboyne, AD 1400–1650* (Dublin, 1945); A. O'Sullivan and P. Ó Riain (eds), *Poems on the Marcher Lords* (London, 1987).
20. T. Ó Donnchadha (ed), *Leabhar Cloinne Aodha Buidhe* (Dublin, 1931).
21. S. Mac Airt (ed), *Leabhar Branach* (Dublin, 1944).
22. D. Greene (ed), *Duanaire Mhéig Uidhir: the Poembook of Cúchonnancht Mág Uidhir, Lord of Fermanagh* (Dublin, 1972).
23. O. Bergin, *Irish Bardic Poetry*, introduction; B. Ó Cuív, *The Linguistic Training of the Mediaeval Irish Poet* (Dublin, 1983); P.A. Breatnach, 'The chief poet', in *Proceedings of the Royal Irish Academy*, 83, c. 3 (1983), 37–79.
24. M. Caball, 'Notes on an Elizabethan Kerry bardic family', in *Ériu*, xliii (1992), 177–92.
25. L. McKenna (ed), *Dánta do chum Aonghus Fionn Ó Dálaigh* (Dublin, 1919).
26. L. McKenna, 'Historical poems of Godfraidh Fionn Ó Dálaigh', in *Irish Monthly*, i–v (1919a), 102–7, 160–70, 224–8, 283–6, 341–4, 397–403, 455–9, 509–14, 563–9, 622–6, 679–82.
27. E. Knott (ed), *The Bardic Poems of Tadhg Dall Ó Huiginn, 1550–1591*, 2 vols (London, 1922), 26.

28. C. Ó Baoill, 'The Mac An Bhaird family (c. 1400–1695)', at http://www.oxforddnb.com/view/article/70043/72771.

29. Ibid.

30. M. Caball, 'Eochaidh Ó hEodhusa', in J. McGuire and J. Quinn (eds), *Dictionary of Irish Biography*, 9 vols (Cambridge, 2009), vii, 553–5.

31. V. Morley, 'Tadhg Mac Bruaideadha', in ibid., v, 746–7.

32. Ó Cuív, 'The Irish language in the early modern period'; Ó Buachalla, *Aisling Ghéar*, passim.

33. Caball, *Poetry and Politics*, passim; Ó Buachalla, *Aisling Ghéar*, passim.

34. B. Cunningham and R. Gillespie, 'The east Ulster bardic family of Ó Gnímh', in *Éigse*, xx (1984), 106–14.

35. P. Walsh, The O'Clerys of Tir Connell', in *Studies*, xxiv (1935a), 244–62.

36. C. McGrath, 'Í Eodhusa', in *Clogher Record*, ii (1957), 1–19.

37. E. Curtis, 'The O'Maolchonaire family', in *Journal of the Galway Historical and Archaeological Society*, xix (1941), 118–46.

38. P. Walsh, *The Four Masters and Their Work* (Dublin, 1944), passim.

39. J. Silke, 'The Irish abroad, 1534–1691', in Moody, Martin, and Byrne (eds), *New History of Ireland*, iii, 587–632; M. Mac Craith, 'Printing in the vernacular: the Louvain project', in Kelly and Ó Ciardha (eds), *History Ireland*, xv, no. 4 (July–August 2007), 27–32; 'idem., '"…the false and crafty bludsukkers, the Observauntes": na súmairí bréagacha beartacha: na hObsarvaintigh', in Finnegan, Ó Ciardha, and Peters (eds), *The Flight of the Earls*, 208–21.

40. J.J. Silke, 'The Irish abroad, 1534–1691', 587–632; B. Millet, 'Irish literature in Latin, 1550–1700', 561–86; M. Mac Craith, 'The Louvain book initiative: manuscript into print', in É. Ó Ciardha, F. Sewell, and A. Titley (eds), *History of the Irish Book: The Printed Book in Irish since 1567* (forthcoming, Oxford, 2015).

41. B. Ó hEodhasa, *An Teagasc Criosdaidhe* (Antwerp, 1611).

42. A. Mac Aingil, *Scáthán shacramuinte na haithridhe* (Louvain, 1618); C. O Maonaigh (ed), *Scáthán Shacramuinte na hAithridhe* (Dublin, 1952).

43. F. Ó Maolchonaire, *Sgáthán an Chrábhaidh* (Louvain, 1616); T.F. O'Rahilly (ed), *Desiderius, otherwise called Sgáthán an Chrábhaidh by Flaithrí Ó Maolchonaire* (Dublin, 1941); Mac Craith, 'The Louvain book initiative: manuscript into print'; B. Hazard, *Faith and Patronage: the political career of Flaithrí Ó Maolchonaire, c. 1560–1629* (Dublin, 2009).

44. B. Millet, 'Irish literature in Latin, 1550–1700, in Moody, Martin and Byrne (eds), *New History of Ireland*, iii, 561–86.

45. Ibid., 562.

46. http://www.irishineurope.com/publications.html.

47. E. McMullin, 'Galileo Galilei, Robert Bellmarine and Peter Lombard', in Finnegan, Ó Ciardha, and Peters (eds), *The Flight of the Earls*, 147–56.

48. N. Ó Muraíle, *The Celebrated Antiquary, Dubhaltach Mac Fhirbhisigh* (Maynooth, 1996); J. Lynch, *Cambrensis Eversis* (St. Malo, 1662); idem, *Alithnologia* (St. Malo, 1664); idem, *Supplementum Alinithinologiae* (St. Malo, 1667).

49. R. O'Flaherty, *Ogygia, or a chronological account of Irish events collected from very ancient documents: written originally in Latin by R. O'Flaherty; translated by the Rev J. Hely*, 2 vols (Dublin, 1793); V. Morley, 'Roderick O'Flaherty', in Mc Quire and Quinn (eds), *Dictionary of Irish Biography*, vii, 469–70.

50. The Franciscan Fathers (eds), *Father Luke Wadding Commemorative Volume* (Dublin, 1957); B. Millet, *The Irish Franciscans, 1651–65* (Rome, 1964).

51. P. Lombard, *De regno Hiberniae sanctorum insula commentarius* (Louvain, 1632).

52. P. Osulleuano Bearro Iberno, *Historiae Catholicae Iberni Compendium* (Lisbon, 1621); T. O'Donnell (ed), *Selections from the Zoilomastix of Philip O'Sullivan Beara* (Dublin, 1960).

53. C. Lennon, 'David Rothe', at http://www.oxforddnb.com/view/article/24147; T. O'Connor, 'Rothe, David', in Mc Guire and Quinn (eds), *Dictionary of Irish Biography*, viii, 620–1.

54. Idem, 'Richard Creagh, at http://www.oxforddnb.com/view/article/6658; C. Lennon, 'Creagh, Richard', in Mc Guire and Quinn (eds), *Dictionary of Irish Biography*, ii, 982–3.

55. Idem, 'Richard Stanihurst, at http://www.oxforddnb.com/view/article/26294. C. Lennon, 'Stanihurst, Richard', in Mc Guire and Quinn (eds), *Dictionary of Irish Biography*, ix, 6–8.

56. S. Kavanagh (ed), *Commentarius Rinuccianus*, vols i–vi (Dublin, 1932–49).

57. J. Leerssen, 'Archbishop Ussher and Gaelic culture', in *Studia Hibernica*, xxii–xxiii (1982), 50–8; E. Boran (ed), *The Correspondence of James Ussher* (Irish Manuscripts Commission, 3 vols, Dublin, 2013) shows the range of Ussher's scholarly contacts.

58. Ó Buachalla, '*Annála Ríoghachta Éireann* is *Foras Feasa ar Éirinn*: an comhthéchs comhaimseartha', in *Studia Hibernica*, xxii–xxiii (1982–3), 59–105; B. Cunningham, *The Annals of the Four Masters: Irish History, Kingship and Society in the Early Seventeenth Century* (Dublin, 2010).

59. P. Walsh, 'The work of a winter, 1629–30', in N. Ó Muraíle (ed), *Mícheál Ó Cléirigh, His Associates and St. Anthony's College, Louvain* (Dublin, 2008), 146–55; D. Ó Doibhlin, 'The plantation of Ulster: aspects of Gaelic letters', in Ó Ciardha and Ó Siochrú (eds), *The Plantation of Ulster*, 198–218; B. Ó Buachalla. '*Annála Rioghachta Éireann* is *Foras Feasa ar Éirinn*: an Comhthéacs Comhaimseartha', 59–105.

60. Ó Buachalla, *Aisling Ghéar*, 97.

61. Ó Doibhlin, 'The Plantation of Ulster: Aspects of Gaelic Letters', in Ó Ciardha and Ó Siochrú (eds), *The Plantation of Ulster*, 198–218.

62. R.A.S. Macalister, *Lebor Gabhála Érenn*, 5 vols (Dublin, 1938–56); R. Macalister and J. Mac Neill (eds), *Leabhar Gabhála: the book of the conquests of Ireland: the Recension of Mícheál Ó Cléirigh*, part 1 (Dublin, 1916).

63. S. Céitinn, *Foras Feasa ar Éirinn*, ed. by D. Comyn (London, 1902), i, 42.

64. Ó Buachalla, '*Annála Ríoghachta Éireann* is *Foras Feasa ar Éirinn*: an Comhthéachs Comhaimseartha', 59–105.; B. Cunningham, *The World of Geoffrey Keating: History, Myth and Religion in Seventeenth-century Ireland* (Dublin, 2000); P. Ó Riain (ed), *Geoffrey Keating's Foras Feasa ar Éirinn: Reassessments* (Dublin, 2008).

65. 'Do bhrígh gurab i nduantaibh atá cnáimh agus smior an tseanchusa, measaim gurab oircheas dam cinneadh mar ughdardhás air, ag tráchtadh ar an seanchus', quoted in C. O'Rahilly (ed), *Five Seventeenth-century Political Poems* (Dublin, 1952), vii.

66. N. Ó Muraíle (ed), *Turas na dTaoiseach nUltach as Éirinn: From Ráth Maoláin to Rome: Tadhg Ó Cianáin's contemporary narrative of the so-called 'Flight of the Earls'* (Dublin, 2008); Finnegan, Ó Ciardha and Peters (eds), *The Flight of the Earls/Imeacht na nIarlaí*.

67. P. Walsh (ed), *Beatha Aodha Ruaidh Uí Dhomhnaill*, 2 vols (London, 1948–57); M. Caball, 'Politics and religion in the poetry of Fearghal Óg Mac an Bhaird and Eoghan Rua Mac an Bhaird', in P. Ó Riain (ed), *Beatha Aodha Ruaidh: The Life of Red Hugh O Donnell: Historical and Literary Contexts* (London, 2002), 74–97.

68. M. Nic Cathmhaoil, 'Cin Lae Uí Mhelláin', in *Seanchas Ard Mhacha* (2006), 35–54.
69. N. J. A. Williams (ed), *Pairlement Chloinne Tomáis* (Dublin, 1980).
70. J. Colgan, *Triadis Thaumaturgae, seu Divorum Patricii, Columbae, er Brigidae...Acta* (Louvain, 1647; repr. with introduction by P. Ó Riain, Dublin, 1997); T. O'Donnell, *Father John Colgan OFM, 1592–1658* (Dublin, 1959).
71. S. Céitinn, *Eochair-Sgiath an Aifrinn*, P. O'Brien, ed. (Dublin, 1898); idem, *Trí bíor-ghaoithe an bháis*, O. Bergin, ed. (Dublin, 1931).
72. A. Gernon, *Parrthas an anma* (Louvain, 1645), ed. by A. Ó Fachtna (Dublin, 1953).
73. B. Conny, *Riaghuil Threas Uird S. Froinsias* (Louvain, 1641).
74. T. Gállduff, *Cathechismus* (Brussels, 1639).
75. E. Mac Giolla Eáin, *Dánta, amhráin is caointe Sheathrúin Céitinn* (Dublin, 1900): B. Cunningham, 'Seathrún Céitinn', at http://www.oxforddnb.com/view/article/15224; B. Cunningham, 'Keating, Geoffrey', in Mc Guire and Quinn (eds), *Dictionary of Irish Biography*, v, 42–4.
76. P. Ua Duinnín (ed), *Dánta Phiarais Feiritéir* (Dublin, 1934).
77. M. Ní Cheallacháin (ed), *Filíocht Phádraigín Haicéad* (Dublin, 1986); M. Hartnett (trans.), *Haiceád* (Oldcastle, 1993).
78. N. Williams (ed), *Dánta Mhuiris Mhic Dháibhí Dhuibh Mhic Gearailt* (Dublin, 1979).
79. J. MacErlean (ed), *Duanaire Dháibhidh Uí Bhruadair*, 3 vols (London, 1910, 1913, 1917).
80. O'Rahilly (ed), *Five Seventeenth-century Political Poems*.
81. Ó Buachalla, *Aisling Ghéar*, bibliography.
82. B. Bradshaw, 'Native reaction to the westward enterprise: a case study in Gaelic ideology', in K. Andrews, N. Canny, and P. Hair (eds), *The Westward Enterprise: English Activities in Ireland, the Atlantic and America, 1480–1650* (Liverpool, 1978), 65–80; idem, 'The bardic response to conquest and colonisation', in *Bullán*, i, no 1 (1994), 119–22.
83. Caball, *Poetry and Politics*, passim.
84. N. Canny, 'The formation of the Irish mind: Religion, politics and Gaelic Irish literature, 1580–1750', in *Past and Present*, xlv (1982a), 91–116.
85. B. Cunningham, 'Native culture and political change in Ireland, 1580–1625', in C. Brady and R. Gillespie (eds), *Natives and Newcomers* (Dublin, 1986), 148–70.
86. A. Dooley, 'Literature and society in early seventeenth-century Ireland: the evaluation of change', in C. Byrne et al (eds), *Celtic Languages and Celtic Peoples* (Toronto, 1992), 513–54.
87. T. Dunne, 'The Gaelic response to conquest and colonization: the evidence of poetry', in *Studia Hibernica*, xx (1980), 7, 30.
88. A. Hadfield, *Strangers to that Land. British Perceptions of Ireland from the Reformation to the Famine* (Buckinghamshire, 1994); idem., *Literature, Politics, National Identity. Reformation to Renaissance* (Cambridge, 1994); idem., *Literature, Travel and Colonial Writing in the English Renaissance 1545–1625* (Oxford, 1998); idem, *Edmund Spenser's Irish Experience* (Oxford, 1997).
89. M. Mac Craith, *Lorg na hIasachta agus litríocht na Gaeilge* (Dublin, 1989).
90. W. Maley, *Salvaging Spenser: Colonialism, Culture and Identity* (London, 1997); W. Maley, B. Bradshaw and A. Hadfield (eds), *Representing Ireland: Literature and the Origins of Conflict* (Cambridge, 1993).
91. McCabe, Richard A., *Spenser's Monstrous Regiment. Elizabethan Ireland and the Poetics of Difference* (Oxford, 2002).
92. B. Ó Buachalla, *Aisling Ghéar*, passim.
93. B. Ó Doibhlin, *Manual de Lítriocht na Gaeilge*, fasc i–v (B.Á.C., 2003–09); idem, *Aistí Critice agus Cultúrtha* (B.Á.C, 2009).

94. D. Ó Doibhlin, 'Gan tuisle gan teibeadh: gnéithe den litríocht na Gaeilge sa seachtú haois déag', in Finnegan, Ó Ciardha and Peters (eds), *The Flight of the Earls/Imeacht na nIarlaí*, 196–204; idem, 'The plantation of Ulster: aspects of Gaelic letters', in Ó Ciardha and Ó Siochrú (eds), *The Plantation of Ulster*, 198–218.

95. T. Ó Dúshláine, *An Eoraip agus litríocht na Gaeilge* (Dublin, 1987).

96. N. Canny, 'The formation of the Irish mind', 91–116.

97. M. O'Riordan, *The Gaelic Mind and the Collapse of the Gaelic World* (Cork, 1991); M. Caball, 'The Gaelic mind and the collapse of the Gaelic world: An appraisal', in *Cambridge Medieval Celtic Studies*, xxv (1993), 87–96; B. Ó Buachalla, 'Poetry and politics in early modern Ireland', in *Eighteenth-century Ireland*, vii (1992), 149–75.

98. Palmer, Patricia, *Language and Conquest in Early Modern Ireland* (Oxford, 2001).

99. K. Simms, 'Bardic poetry as a historical source', in T. Dunne (ed), *Writer as Witness: Literature as Historical Evidence* (Cork, 1987), 58–75; idem, *From Kings to Warlords* (Woodbridge, 1987).

100. B. Ó Buachalla, 'Anocht is uaigneach Éire', in B. Kelly and É. Ó Ciardha (eds), *History Ireland*, xv, no. 4 (July–August 2007), 32–4; M. Caball 'Dispossession and reaction: the Gaelic literati and the Plantation of Ulster', in É. Ó Ciardha and M. Ó Siochrú (eds), *History Ireland: Ulster Plantation, Special Issue* (November–December 2009), 24–8; idem, 'Responses to transformation: Gaelic poets and the plantation', in Ó Ciardha and Ó Siochrú (eds), *The Plantation of Ulster*, 176–98.

101. K. Whelan, 'An underground gentry? Catholic middlemen in eighteenth-century Ireland', in J. Donnelly and K. Miller (eds), *Irish Popular Culture, 1650–1850* (Dublin, 1998), 118–73.

102. Ó Buachalla, *Aisling Ghéar, passim*; Ó Ciardha, *Ireland and the Jacobite Cause, passim*; V. Morley, 'Idéeolaíocht an tSeacaibíteachas in Éirinn agus in Albain', in *Oghma*, ix (1997), 14–24; idem, 'Catholic disaffection and the oath of allegiance of 1774, in J. Kelly, J. McCafferty, and C. McGrath (eds), *People, Politics and Power: Essays on Irish History 1660–1850 in Honour of James I. McGuire* (Dublin, 2009), 122–43; idem, 'The idea of Britain in eighteenth-century Ireland and Scotland' in *Studia Hibernica*, xxxiii (2004–5), passim; M. Mac Craith, 'Filíocht Sheacaibíteachas na Gaeilge: ionar gan uaim?', in *Eighteenth-century Ireland*, ix (1994), 57–75; idem, 'Review article, Breandán Ó Buachalla, Aisling Ghéar: Na Stíobhartaigh agus an tAos léinn, 1603–1778 (Dublin, 1996), in *Eighteenth-Century Ireland*, xiii (1998), 166–71; Ó Ciardha, *Ireland and the Jacobite Cause, 1685–1766, passim*.

103. Ó Tuathaigh, 'Gaelic Ireland, popular politics and Daniel O'Connell', in *Journal of Galway Historical and Archaeological Society*, xxxiv (1974–5), 29.

104. Jackie Hill has cited Ó Buachalla's 800-page tome and appears to use my own 500-page monograph by way of a translation; J. Hill, 'Convergence and conflict in eighteenth-century Ireland', in *The Historical Journal*, xl, 4 (2001), 1039–63, 1042. D.W. Hayton, 'Review of Éamonn Ó Ciardha, Ireland and the Jacobite Cause, 1685–1766: A Fatal Attachment (Four Courts Press, 2002)', in *Eighteenth-Century Ireland*, xviii, (2003), 155. For the enormous flexibility of Irish poetry as a source, see M. Mac Craith, 'Review Article', 166.

105. For example, see Mac Craith, 'Filíocht Shecaibíteach na Gaeilge: ionar gan uaim', 57–75; Ó Buachalla, *Aisling Ghéar*; passim; Ó Ciardha, *Ireland and the Jacobite Cause*, passim.

106. M. Pittock, *Poetry and Jacobite Politics in Eighteenth-century Britain and Ireland* (Cambridge, 1994), 6, 37.

107. B. Ó Buachalla (ed), *Peadar Ó Doirnín: amhráin* (Dublin, 1970), 25.

108. 'Chan le h-aghaidh léightheoireachta act le h-aghaidh ceoltóireachta a cumadh na h-amhráin seo, agus níl ionnta mar tá siad annseo ná fochla gan na fuinnach mar bheadh

baintreabhach ann a mbéadh a céile pósta caillte aicí', É. Ó Muirgheasa (ed), *Dhá chéad de cheoltaibh Uladh* (Dublin, 1974), réamhra.

109. G. Zimmermann, *Songs of Irish Rebellion. Political Street-ballads and Rebel Songs* (Zürich, 1967).

110. E. Knowles (ed), *The Oxford Dictionary of Quotations* (Oxford, 1999), 317.

111. T. Crofton-Croker, *Researches in the south of Ireland illustrative of the scenery, architectural remains and the manners and superstitions of the peasantry, with an appendix containing a private narrative of 1798* (London, 1824), 329.

112. 'Agus an duine nach dtig leis féiceáil ins na ceoltaí seo ach cineál 'come all ye', tá sé níos mó ná bheith caoch tá sé chomh dall le bun do bhróige', Ó Muirgheasa (ed), *Dhá chéad de cheoltaibh Uladh*, réamhra.

113. É. Ó Muirgheasa (ed), *Amhráin Airt Mhic Chobhthaigh* (Dundalk, 1926), xxv.

114. J.L. Campbell (ed), *Highland Songs of the '45* (Edinburgh, 1984), xviii.

115. Ó Buachalla, *Aisling Ghéar*, bibliography; Ó Ciardha, *Ireland and the Jacobite Cause*, bibliography.

116. R. Breatnach, 'The end of a tradition': A survey of eighteenth-century Gaelic literature', in *Studia Hibernica,* i (1960), 129.

117. C. Buttimer, 'An Irish text on the war of Jenkins' Ear', in P. de Brún and M. Ó Murchú (eds), *Celtica: Essays in honour of Brian Ó Cuív* (Dublin, 1990), 75.

118. G. Ó Tuathaigh, 'Hyde and the Hidden Ireland: Interpreting Irish History', paper delivered at ESB Lecture series, 29 Fitzwilliam St, 12 November 1994.

119. 'Ní hionadh sin freisin, mar bíodh gur saothraíodh an reitric Sheacaibíteach i bhfoirmeacha difriúla (paimfléid, seanmóirí, óráideanna, leabhair, bailéid etc.) sa Bhreatain; in Éirinn bhí an reitric sin taobh, ar an mhórgóir, le haon mhéan amháin—véarsaíocht', Ó Buachalla, *Aisling Ghéar*, 333.

120. P. Monod, *Jacobitism and the English People, 1688–1788* (Cambridge, 1993), 47.

121. P. Chapman, 'Jacobite political argument in England, 1714–1766' (PhD. Cambridge, 1983), 175, 203–4.

122. Pittock, *Poetry and Jacobite Politics*, 5.

123. Ó Fiaich, *Art Mac Cumhaigh: Dánta*, 51.

124. D. Corkery, *The Hidden Ireland: a study of Gaelic Munster in the Eighteenth Century* (Dublin, 1925), introduction; P. Maume, *'Life that is exile': Daniel Corkery and the Search for Irish-Ireland* (Belfast, 1993); D. McCartney, 'W. E. H. Lecky', in McGuire and Quinn (eds), *Dictionary of Irish Biography*, v, 390–1.

125. S. Connolly, *Divided Kingdom: Ireland 1630–1800* (Oxford, 2008), 327. Recent work by Ó Buachalla (B. Ó Buachalla, 'An mheisiasacht agus an aisling' in P. De Brún, S. Ó Coileáin and P. Ó Riain, P., (eds), *Folia Gadelica* (Cork, 1983), 72–87); O'Riordan (M. O'Riordan, 'Historical perspectives on the Hidden Ireland' in *Irish Review*, iv (1988), 73–82) and Ó Ciardha (Ó Ciardha, *Ireland and the Jacobite Cause*, introduction) has not sought, neither explicitly or implicitly, to 'rehabilitate' Corkery (ibid., 328). Moreover, to suggest that scholars who have questioned Cullen's 'classic exposition' have sought to explicitly or implicitly rehabilitate the concept is to throw out the baby of eighteenth-century Irish literature with the bath-water of Corkery's imagined, shared common culture between big house and peasant's hut. A similar misunderstanding of their arguments pervades I. McBride, *Eighteenth-Century Ireland* (Dublin, 2009), 8.

126. L. Cullen, *The Hidden Ireland: the reassessment of a concept* (Gigginstown, 1988), vii, 1.

127. Cullen, *The Hidden Ireland: the Reassessment*, 48.

128. For an opposite view, see V. Morley, 'Catholic disaffection and the oath of allegiance of 1774', in Kelly, McCafferty, and McGrath (eds), *People, Politics and Power. Essays on Irish History, 1660–1850*, 122–43.

129. L. Cullen, *The Emergence of Modern Ireland* (London, 1981), 198; Ó Ciardha, *Ireland and the Jacobite Cause*, postscript.

130. N. Canny, 'Irish resistance to empire, 1641, 1689 and 1798', in L. Stone (ed), *An Imperial State at War, 1689–1815* (London, 1994), 288–9.

131. Canny, 'Formation of the Irish mind', 111.

132. C.Giblin, 'The Stuart nomination of Irish bishops, 1685–1765', in *Irish Ecclesiastical Record*, lv (1966), 35–47.

133. T. Ó Fiaich, 'Irish poetry and the clergy', in *Leachtaí Cholmcille, iv* (1975), 30–56; A. Heussaff, *Filí agus cléir san ochtú haois déag* (Dublin, 1993).

134. C. Mac Cairteáin, 'Preface to Agallamh na bhfíoraon', in *Iris leabhar Muighe Nuadhad* (1913), 35.

135. McCabe, *Spenser's Monstrous Regiment. Elizabethan Ireland and the Poetics of Difference*, 41–2.

136. O'Rahilly (ed), *Five Seventeenth-century Political Poems*, 89–90.

137. É. Ó Ciardha, 'The early modern Irish Outlaw: the making of a nationalist icon', in Kelly, McCafferty and McGrath (eds), *People, Politics and Power: Essays on Irish History 1660–1850*, 51–70.

138. J. Kelly, *Gallows Speeches from Eighteenth-century Ireland* (Dublin, 2001); É. Ó Ciardha, 'Review of J. Kelly, Gallows speeches from eighteenth-century Ireland (Dublin, 2001)', in *History Ireland*, Autumn, 2001.

139. Morley's comprehensive collection of the Irish-language poems of the American Revolution, *Washington i gceannas a ríochta* (Dublin, 2005) is a shining example of the untold riches which await the intrepid explorer in the uncharteted, unedited collections of Irish mss in Ireland, Britain, Europe, and North America. See also idem, *Irish Opinion and the American Revolution, 1760–1783* (Cambridge, 2002); Ó Ciardha, *Ireland and the Jacobite Cause*, 324–78.

140. B. Ó Buachalla 'From Jacobite to Jacobin', in T. Bartlett, D. Dickson, D. Keogh and K. Whelan (eds), *1798: A Bicentenary Perspective* (Dublin, 2003), 75–96; idem, *The Crown of Ireland* (Galway, 2006), 36–48; Ó Tuathaigh, 'Gaelic Ireland, popular politics and Daniel O'Connell', 21–34; R. Uí Ógáin, *Immortal Dan: Daniel O'Connell in Irish Folklore* (Dublin, 1995).

141. R. and M. Loeber, *A Guide to Irish Fiction, 1650–1900* (Dublin, 2006). See also J.M. Cahalan, *Great Hatred, little Room: the Irish Historical Novel* (Syracuse, 1983), passim.

142. G. Beiner, *Irish Folk History and Social Memory* (Madison, 2007); G. Ó Tuathaigh, 'Once upon a time in the West', in *Field Day Review, iv* (2008), 315–25; B. Mac Suibhne, 'Afterworld: the Gothic travels of John Gamble (1770–1831)', in *ibid.*, 63–113. See also L. Ní Dhonnchadha, *"An Míleannachas agus Meisiasachas i litríocht na Gaeilge idir 1780-1820"* (NUI, Galway, MA, 2005).

Select Bibliography

Breatnach, P., 'The chief poet', in *Proceedings of the Royal Irish Academy, 83*, c. 3 (1983), 37–79.

Caball, M., *Poetry and Politics: Reaction and Continuity in Irish poetry, 1558–1625* (Cork, 1998).

Caball, M. and Hollo, K., 'The literature of medieval Ireland, 1200–1600: from the Normans to the Tudors', in Kelleher, M. and O'Leary, P. (eds), *The Cambridge History of Irish Literature*, 2 vols (Cambridge, 2006), i, 74–139.

Cullen, L., *The Hidden Ireland: the Reassessment of a Concept* (Gigginstown, 1988).

Cunningham, B., *The World of Geoffrey Keating: History, Myth and Religion in Seventeenth-century Ireland* (Dublin, 2000).

Cunningham, B., *The Annals of the Four Masters: Irish History, Kingship and Society in the Early Seventeenth Century* (Dublin, 2010).

Finnegan, D., ÓCiardha, É., and Peters, M.C. (eds), *The Flight of the Earls: Imeacht na nIarlaí* (Derry, 2010).

Hadfield, A., *Strangers to that Land. British Perceptions of Ireland from the Reformation to the Famine* (Buckinghamshire, 1994).

Mac Craith, M., 'Review article, Breandán Ó Buachalla, Aisling Ghéar: Na Stíobhartaigh agus an tAos léinn, 1603–1778 (Dublin, 1996), in *Eighteenth-Century Ireland*, xiii (1998), 166–71.

Mac Craith, M., 'From the Elizabethan Settlement to the Battle of the Boyne: Literature in Irish, *c*. 1550–1690', in Kelleher, M. and O'Leary, P. (eds), *The Cambridge History of Irish Literature*, 2 vols (Cambridge, 2006), 191–231.

Maley, W., Bradshaw, B. and Hadfield, A. (eds), *Representing Ireland: Literature and the Origins of Conflict* (Cambridge, 1993).

McCabe, R. A., *Spenser's Monstrous Regiment. Elizabethan Ireland and the Poetics of Difference* (Oxford, 2002).

Morley, V., *Irish Opinion and the American Revolution, 1760–1783* (Cambridge, 2002).

Morley, V., *Ó Chéitinn go Raiftearaí: Mar a cumadh stair na hÉireann* (Dublin, 2011).

Ó Buachalla, B., 'Poetry and politics in early modern Ireland', in *Eighteenth-century Ireland*, vii (1992), 149–75.

Ó Buachalla, B., *Aisling Ghéar: na Stíobhartaigh agus an t-aos léinn 1601–1788* (Dublin, 1996).

Ó Buachalla, B., 'From Jacobite to Jacobin', in Bartlett, T., Dickson, D., Keogh, D., and Whelan, K. (eds), *1798: A Bicentenary Perspective* (Dublin, 2003), 75–96.

Ó Ciardha, É., 'The early modern Irish Outlaw: the making of a nationalist icon', in Kelly, McCafferty, and McGrath (eds), *People, Politics and Power: Essays on Irish History 1660–1850* (Dublin, 2009), 51–70.

Ó Ciardha, É., *Ireland and the Jacobite Cause, 1685–1766: A Fatal Attachment* (Dublin, 2002).

Ó Ciardha, É. and Ó Siochrú, M. (eds), *The Plantation of Ulster: Ideology and practice* (Manchester, 2012).

Ó Cuív, B., 'The Irish language in the early modern period', in Moody, T.W., Martin, F.X., and Byrne, F.J. (eds), *A New History of Ireland*, iii (Oxford, 1976), 509–42.

Ó Doibhlin, B., *Manual de Lítriocht na Gaeilge*, fasc i–v (B.Á.C., 2003–09).

Ó Riain P. (ed), *Geoffrey Keating's Foras Feasa ar Éirinn: Reassessments* (Dublin, 2008).

Palmer, P., *Language and Conquest in Early Modern Ireland* (Oxford, 2001).

Simms, K., *Medieval Gaelic Sources* (Dublin, 2009).

CHAPTER 23

IRELAND AND THE ATLANTIC WORLD, 1690–1840

MAURICE J. BRIC

By the middle of the seventeenth century, the first empire was well established. It also had a clear sense of 'civility' that was suggested by the supposed superiority of English laws as well as an established Church which reinforced its polity. In Ireland, an act of the Irish parliament known as Poynings' Law (1494–5) officially limited the ability of that assembly to initiate legislation, while the Declaratory Act, passed by the British meetings of Parliament in 1720, copper-fastened the subordinate status of the Irish assembly within the imperial framework. However, neither act prevented regular meetings of Parliament in Ireland from the 1690s onwards, when that assembly also established its right to initiate legislation by exercising its powers over the voting of the financial supply.[1] In America, colonial assemblies were not constitutionally circumscribed in the same ways and although their laws had to be sanctioned by the English Privy Council, this was after they had been discussed and passed at colonial level.[2] The empire was also a commercial entity. In 1696, what in time evolved into the Board of Trade issued instructions to governors, appointed agents, and received reports on how the colonies could enrich the metropolis.[3] Neither the commercial nor the political aspects of the empire diminished after the 'War of the Two Kings' (1688–90). However, the empire of William III received not only a new monarch; it would also promote what in the later eighteenth century would be called the 'Protestant Ascendancy'.[4] In Ireland, one of the more conspicuous aspects of the new regime was set out in the penal laws—enacted from 1695 onwards—the 'design' of which, as Archbishop Edward Synge of Tuam put it in 1731, was 'to lessen their [Catholic] number or break their power, that, they may be no longer formidable to those whom they are justly suspected to have good inclination to destroy'. Here Synge was suggesting that the laws would ensure that, as well as being victorious on the battlefield, the new ascendancy would not be challenged from other platforms. Most historians accept that these laws—with the exception of those which applied to land—were not applied consistently or rigorously after the 1720s and then usually only when Dublin Castle thought that the security of the state was being threatened by supporters of the exiled Stuarts.[5] However, there was another reality: the laws defined the polity in confessional terms and this remained the case until the campaign to repeal them gathered pace during the final decades of the eighteenth century. They also influenced how Ireland and colonial America interacted until the outbreak of the American Revolution.

Penal laws similar to those which had been passed in Ireland were also enacted in the American colonies and, while they did not loom as large there as they did in contemporary Ireland, they shaped the nature of the polity in both places. This was not immediately obvious in colonies which did not attract high numbers of Catholic immigrants. However, this was not the case in Maryland, which had been planted by the Catholic Calvert family in the 1630s. The response of the Calverts to these laws mirrored what happened in similar circumstances in eighteenth-century Ireland: in order to secure its influence within the polity, the family came to divide into Catholic and Anglican branches. Thus, as the penal laws were used to promote a religiously defined polity as well as to define political power, they did not encourage Irish Catholics to consider colonial America as a congenial place.[6] This was less true of Ulster Presbyterians, who emigrated there in considerable numbers during the eighteenth century.

The emigrant trade was also influenced by the patterns of transatlantic commerce and in particular by the fortunes and interrelationships of the linen and flaxseed trades. The direct export of Irish linen (from 1705) and the direct importation of American flaxseed (from 1731), as well as the decision by the Linen Board to award bounties to encourage that industry, led to a dramatic rise in Ireland's linen export to America.[7] While these developments underlined that Ireland and colonial America were part of a common commercial area, for all the formalities of law, the Atlantic trade was managed as a matter of fact by people: merchants, traders, brokers, and ship captains. It was the extended networks of such people which facilitated emigration to colonial America and determined the most popular routes. The fact that the linen industry was concentrated in Ulster and consequently attracted most of the flaxseed ships provided emigrants from that part of Ireland with incomparable opportunities to travel to America. Given that, for the most part, the owners of these vessels returned to Philadelphia and New York—through which most of the flaxseed export had been processed in the first place—their involvement in the emigrant trade ensured that the Delaware and the Hudson became the primary landing places of Irish emigrants to eighteenth-century America. These owners were happy to secure dependable and profitable 'freights' on the return journey to America '& is *all paid down at Shipping*'.[8] The Derry-born Blair McClenachan did not need to be told this. Before 1776, he was one of over thirty Philadelphia merchants who shipped flaxseed to Ireland and sought emigrants for the return journey, through agents whom he maintained in a number of towns and villages in Ulster. As merchants pushed and pulled prospective Irish emigrants towards America, they stressed what America had to offer to those who were willing to work hard. As a result, while it is a stretch to depict them as the more benign personalities of empire, the merchants of the later eighteenth century encouraged a positive view of America. This was particularly important as Catholic merchants turned to the lucrative transatlantic trade and, especially after 1750, they encouraged their fellow-communicants to view the colonies in a new light.[9]

Merchants were so anxious to encourage Irish emigration that occasionally they concocted favourable narratives. However, of far more influence were the accounts in which emigrants offered their own experiences, usually in the form of letters to their relatives in Ireland. Such letters often described their new surroundings and opportunities as well as the 'liberty' which they enjoyed in the new 'land of Canaan': freedom from the excessive demands of the landlord, his agents, and the hated tithe proctor but, above all, freedom to earn a living and to keep the proceeds of their labour. They also had a 'liberty' to develop an independence which they could not achieve in Ireland. While critics suggested that even such private accounts were often rose-tinted, others argued that even where they were, America offered undoubted opportunities. Immigrants could avail of them or not.[10] The push to do so was especially strong from the later 1760s when the linen industry slumped. Some years earlier, Primate Hugh Boulter of Armagh (1724–42) made the relevant point to the duke of Newcastle: 'the least obstruction in the linen manufacture, by which the north subsists, must occasion great numbers following' to America.[11] This observation again underlined the ways in which the linen trade and emigration complemented each other. Moreover, from the middle of the eighteenth century, emigration was being managed with the same kind of efficiency that merchants and brokers applied to other areas of profit. While the flow of emigrants was still dominated by Scots-Irish, the growing numbers who were leaving from outside Ulster— and especially from Dublin and Cork—suggested that both the typology and points of departure of emigrant ships were beginning to change. While in the past, potential emigrants had been reluctant to leave parts of Ireland that were predominantly Catholic, the increasingly specialized organization of the emigrant trade as well as the push that was provided from the 1750s by increasing economic distress, especially in Munster, led them to change their attitudes to America. As a result, while an estimated 100 000 sailed from non-Ulster ports between 1700 and 1776, the majority did so after 1750.[12]

At about a quarter of the number who left from contemporary Ulster, this figure suggests the general features of Irish emigration to colonial America: that, in denominational terms, it was predominantly non-Catholic and largely of Ulster origin and was mainly processed through the Delaware ports of Newcastle and Philadelphia. Although some Irish Quakers had settled in the Carolinas, the majority headed for these ports from the 1680s onwards.[13] Ulster emigration to the Delaware Valley did not slow down after 1729, and during its highest peak before the American Revolution—between 1771 and 1774—of some 26 320 who left for colonial America, 18 600 did so for the Delaware Valley. Only about 3400 arrived from non-Ulster ports.[14] These patterns did not change between 1783 and 1800 when at least 66 000 Irish emigrants entered the Delaware Valley. Between 9000 and 12 000 came to New York and an estimated 5000 landed in Baltimore.[15] The Delaware remained the most attractive destination for Irish immigrants after 1783, just as it had been during the colonial period.

Despite the undoubted appeal of the Delaware, the history of the first great surge of the eighteenth century—between 1717 and 1720—is a reminder that this had not always been the case. Most of the estimated 4000 people who left Ireland during these years sailed from Ulster to New England. They had been invited there by Cotton Mather who hoped that 'much may be done for the Kingdom of God in these Parts of the World by this Transportation'.[16] Mather's hopes highlighted the comparative ease with which Ulster Presbyterians could move within the Anglo-American world as well as the importance of their church networks and ministers in facilitating this. A similar point can be made with respect to Irish emigration to Charleston during the 1730s and 1760s which, as had been the case earlier in New England, was often organized and led by ministers in response to official encouragement from colonial authorities. Some of the Irish who answered Mather's call were disappointed with their reception in Boston and moved towards the frontiers of Massachusetts and New Hampshire, 'not finding their acc[oun]t in the project'.[17] As a result, Boston figured only infrequently as an attraction for Irish emigrants until the nineteenth century. Even organized settlement schemes such as those of Robert Edwards and Samuel Waldo failed to attract potential Irish settlers to New England during the 1730s.

The Scots-Irish who landed in Charleston did not have the same experience, in part because most of them moved further inland. As they took advantage of various programmes of assisted emigration and favourable terms for buying and holding land, they found themselves dotting the frontiers of the Carolinas, Georgia, and Virginia.[18] As a people who had reputedly tamed the 'wild Irish' frontier of Ulster, there were no better people to do the same in America. It was for such reasons that William Galliland sought 'considerable numbers of Irish pioneers...especially Scotch-Irish pioneers' when his 60 000 acre tract in upper New York was opened for settlement after the French and Indian War. Logan had expressed a similar preference in 1720:

> At the time we were apprehensive from the Northern Indians [in Pennsylvania]...I therefore thought it might be prudent to plant a settlement of such men as those who formerly had so bravely defended Londonderry and Iniskillen [in 1689] as a frontier in case of any disturbance.[19]

In moving from Ireland to America, the Scots-Irish received crucial support from their church and this gave their communities a level of stability that would have been difficult to develop otherwise. This was no small factor in the success of their settlements beyond the Cumberland Gap in Tennessee, Kentucky, and the Shenandoah, in the lower part of which as many as twenty of the twenty-three churches were Presbyterian by the outbreak of the American Revolution.[20]

While historians have given some attention to the flow of Irish emigrants across the Atlantic, we have a relatively poor sense of how many moved towards the frontier. Such adventures were not always a matter of choice. While those who arrived as indentured servants usually remained close to where they landed, as servitude declined during the 1780s, the more substantial 'new Irish' had more freedom to move wherever they wanted. However, we need a more detailed socio-economic analysis of the 'types' of Irish who were emigrating after 1783, not just as part of the narrative of emigration but as part of the commentary on why certain immigrants moved further inland. Studies such as that of Edward J. O'Day suggest one way in which this can be done. Using

naturalization records, O'Day has quantified the movements of 8854 Irish-born to analyze the nature and settlement patterns of the Irish community in New England between
1784 and 1825. In doing so, he has echoed the advice of Edward Carter II: that, despite the
paucity of official immigration records before the 1820s, there are other sources which
can be used to map the dispersal of Irish emigrants.[21]

Nonetheless, despite the lack of research, it is clear that both before and after 1800 not
all Irish immigrants settled near where they had landed. Only about half of those who
landed in Delaware before 1800 travelled upriver to Philadelphia. The remainder went
to other places, causing Maryland's assembly, for example, to worry about 'the great
Number of Irish Papists [being] imported into this Province by way of' Delaware. As
a result, the colony passed a law in 1755 to prevent such indirect traffic into its jurisdiction.[22] Regional studies—such as those of George W. Franz on Paxton, Judith Ridner on
Carlisle, Eric Hinderaker and Peter Mancall on the Ohio Valley, and A. Roger Ekirch on
the frontier Carolinas, also make it clear that there was a vibrant Irish presence beyond
the established immigrant *entrepôts* of Philadelphia and New York and that these frontier communities were not carbon copies of older settlements along the eastern seaboard.[23] The Irish presence in the western counties of colonies such as Pennsylvania was
often highlighted only when it became politically threatening. However, while this suggests that the number of Scots-Irish settlers was increasing in those parts, this 'inland'
culture has not been fully quantified, presented, or related to what might be termed the
earlier 'first settlement' which for the most part, had hugged the coast of the Atlantic.[24]

Some Irish immigrants also contributed to the unfolding American Revolution.
However, they did so less as a discrete group than as citizens of the common world of
Anglo-American *Patriotism* which for several years had been questioning how the
empire was governed.[25] In both Ireland and America, *Patriots* stressed that they were
not opposing the empire per se but rather the arbitrary ways in which Whitehall seemed
to be disregarding their traditional liberties. The rhetoric of opposition had already
been enunciated by William Molyneux whose argument that the Irish were 'bound only
by such [laws] to which the community had given its consent' not only reinforced the
pretensions of their own parliament—and by extension, those of the colonial assemblies—but inspired one of the more enduring mantras of revolutionary protest.[26]
Nonetheless, as Vincent Morley has concluded, Ireland's reaction to the American
Revolution was complex.[27] On 18 February 1766, the *Freeman's Journal* suggested that
the Townshend Acts might be 'part of a plan of humiliation nearer home'. As a result,
while Benjamin Franklin might be forgiven for thinking in 1773 that there were 'many
Points in Similarity' between Ireland and America, these would be blurred by the decision to grant 'free trade' and an 'independent' parliament to Ireland in 1779–80 and 1782,
respectively. The leaders of Irish Catholicism were also led to expect further repeal of the
penal laws as a *quid pro quo* for their loyalty. Thus, Bishop John Troy of Ossory (1776–
86) advised his communicants in February 1779 to 'be loyal' and condemned revolutionary Americans as 'rebels... [who had been] seduced by specious notions of liberty'.
For Troy, supporting a revolution three thousand miles away would bring little that was

tangible, whereas supporting Dublin Castle, especially after France and Spain entered the war on the side of the Americans, in 1778 and 1779 respectively, would.[28]

On the American side of the Atlantic, despite the often-quoted quip of a Hessian officer in 1778 that the American Revolution was 'nothing more or less than a Scotch-Irish Presbyterian rebellion', those of Irish origin who involved themselves in the revolutionary cause did so for varying reasons that included the personal, the pragmatic, the practical, and the patriotic. While historians can list men of Irish background who signed the Declaration of Independence, who sat in Congress and helped to frame the U.S. Constitution, the reality was that, aside from an ancestry on the island of Ireland, such men often had little in common. In any event, colonial protest was often driven by the politics of place rather than by some grand revolutionary scheme. For example, the history of the Scots-Irish in revolutionary Pennsylvania partly reflected the divisions that had been growing in that colony since the 1750s between the older eastern elite and the emerging leaders of the west. The protests which were generated by the American Revolution merely presented these divisions in a different way. Something similar happened in North Carolina where the bitterness of the Regulator Movement was incorporated into the rhetoric of the revolution.[29] Once the new republic had been established, men of Irish background took positions that were rarely informed by ethno-cultural identity. As the disputes on the 'first party system' raged during the 1790s, the Ballymena-born James McHenry, as Adams' Secretary for War, became the antithesis of everything espoused by his fellow Scots-Irishman, Thomas McKean, Thomas Jefferson's leading advisor in Pennsylvania and later governor of the state.[30] Persons of Irish background were also among the ranks of Loyalism, especially in New York. As the nerve centre of the British administration in North America until 1783, it is not surprising that the city would have a relatively high quota of Loyalists and that these would include Irish merchants such as Hugh Wallace and Robert Alexander. However, there has been no detailed study of Irish-born Loyalists in America—including imperial administrators and military officers—and the extent to which they served the empire on both sides of the Atlantic, especially during the pivotal years before the American Revolution. While the *Patriotic* relationship between Ireland and British America is clear, the complementary nature of Loyalism is less so.

After 1783, feeling that they had rescued their polity from the 'corruptions' of Lord North's government, America's Founding Fathers began to decide how their new republic would best reflect the 'virtue' with which they broken the link with London.[31] They also wanted to promote harmony. For John Adams, harmony was a *sine qua non* for the new republic and as increasing numbers of Irish emigrants travelled to America after 1783— most notably to Philadelphia, the nation's capital until 1800—he wondered whether they would turn out to be a troublesome asset.[32] He was not reassured by the growing vehemence of partisan politics during the 1790s in which Irish immigrants were prominent. At their most populist, political differences were often presented as being between Adams's admiration of the British polity and its deference to 'natural leadership' on the one hand, and Jefferson's less equivocal trust in the 'awakened democracy' on the other. To this extent, as one Congressional candidate noted in 1794, Jefferson could appeal to the recently arrived Irish for the same reasons that Adams could not. As a result, Jeffersonian candidates were strongly supported in the 'Irishtowns' of outer Philadelphia and New York as they challenged the Adams Federalists. The depiction of the Irish as a disruptive element was enhanced by a fiercely partisan press as well as by the presence in those cities of Irish leaders, many of whom had recently arrived in America from the popular protest movements of contemporary Ireland and who, as a result of their experiences there, could attract and organize an 'Irish vote'.[33] As Federalists saw it, the republic had to be secured from these 'wild Irish' who were *deliberately* trying to compromise it, not least by indulging their own 'national prejudices' as well as trying to drag America into the 'calamities' and bloodshed of Napoleonic Europe. Set in this context, Irish immigrants became a catalyst for the debate on what it meant to be 'truly American' after the break with Britain.[34]

Such considerations were less pointed after Jefferson became president in 1801. His inaugural address on 4 March set the new tone:

> every difference of opinion is not a difference of principle. We have called by different names brethren of the same principle. We are all Republicans, we are all Federalists . . . Let us, then . . . restore to social intercourse that harmony and affection without which liberty and even life itself are but dreary things.

In Jefferson's view, one should celebrate 'the minority' as well as 'the majority'; each had rights which 'to violate would be oppression'.[35] Thus, while the 'cult' of the United States was marked in more assertive ways after 1800, so was the celebration of the 'national day' of the Irish—St Patrick's Day (17 March)—as well as the heroes of Irish history and the political and cultural issues of contemporary Ireland. Irish ethno-cultural societies also became more public about themselves and their traditions than they had been before 1800.[36] Moreover, the fact that within older Irish communities in Philadelphia and New York, St Patrick's Day was sometimes marked by two and three different groups reflected the increasingly diverse nature of the Irish presence in early nineteenth-century America. Particularly in the south, this presence also had a multi-religious character.[37] However, the importance of these celebrations and, more particularly, their festive toasts and songs (which were often composed specially for the occasion and location) would benefit from the type of analysis which historians such as Albrecht Koschnik have applied to voluntary associations at large. It would also clarify the place of Irish immigrants in defining the public sphere of the early national republic.[38]

While Jefferson's election may have peacefully affected a 'second revolution' in the United States, contemporary Europe was deciding its future by military means. In 1793, the United States announced that it would not interfere. However, American neutrality was not always respected and it was a brave emigrant who risked impressment by crossing the Atlantic before 1815. In 1811–12, for example, as many as 200 passengers were impressed by the British navy off the coast of America. In any event, the 'push' to leave Ireland was not particularly strong during the war years. The booming Irish economy saw to that. As the boom led to the bust of the post-war years, America again loomed as a haven for the poor and distressed of Ireland. As 'everything was going to the bad' there, the contrast with the United States could not have been more stark. As Pádraig Cúndún wrote from upstate New York where he 'owned outright a farm of land':

> [N]o one can demand rent of me…[m]y family and I can eat our fill of bread and meat, butter and milk any day we like throughout the year…[with] no established churches nor Popes nor Bishops nor Fryers nor even Rectors to pay Tithes for.[39]

While such descriptions of America were not new, post-Waterloo emigration was to show unfamiliar as well as familiar characteristics. From Ireland, emigrants were leaving in the main from Protestant Ulster and most of them were financially solvent. Catholics still constituted a minority of emigrants although this began to change from the 1820s as did the increasingly prominent role of Liverpool and, to a lesser extent, Bristol and Cardiff in transatlantic emigration. The flow also varied over time: from an estimated 20 000 during 1815–16, to a drop by more than half to two-thirds during the first half of the 1820s. From 1827 or so, the figures began to rise again, from 20 000 to some 50 000 in 1831–2, to over 58 000 in 1838.[40] By 1840, the essential features of what was to be a lengthy period of high emigration from Ireland had been established. On the American side of the Atlantic, the familiar also blended with the unfamiliar: the rise of New York and the reappearance of Boston as ports of reception, the decline of the Delaware from its hitherto dominant position in the Irish emigrant trade, and, above all, the dramatic rise in the numbers who sailed for Canada.

The place of Canada in Irish emigration was particularly significant, especially when it is set amid contemporary debate. Especially after the Quebec Constitutional Act was passed in 1791, British leaders viewed Canada as an important commercial driver of their renewed empire and, as such, as a place which had to be protected from competition from the United States.[41] A series of passenger acts were passed after 1803 which ensured that, for emigrants, it would be twice as costly to sail to the United States and less lucrative for brokers to manage them if they did. After all, why should His Majesty's subjects be given leave to build up the rival American economy? As an alternative, Whitehall inaugurated a series of official programmes to direct them to Canada where it hoped to make 'the redundant labour and curse of the mother country, the active labour and blessing of the colonies' as well as a vehicle towards enhanced prosperity at home. As put by a parliamentary select committee on the poor laws on 4 July 1817,

> It seems not unnatural that this country should, at such a time, recur to an expedient which has been adopted successfully in other times, and in other countries, especially as it has facilities for this purpose which no other state has perhaps enjoyed to the same extent, by the possession of colonies affording an extent of unoccupied territory in which the labour of man assisted by a gentle and healthy climate would produce an early and abundant return.[42]

In practical terms, these views led to sponsored emigration schemes from north Cork (1824, 1825) and the establishment of land companies which would fund passage and provide 'cheap' land, together with agricultural tools, a house, and food for a year. Thus, they complemented the passenger acts: the one designed to attract by assisted emigration; the other to discourage persons from going to the United States by increasing the cost of travelling there. The structures of transatlantic commerce encouraged these developments because as the British demand for Canadian timber grew during the early nineteenth century, so did the need to engage emigrants for the return journey to the St Lawrence. It echoed the linen/flaxseed roundabout of the previous century. As a result of such factors, of the estimated 20 000 who left Britain and Ireland in 1818, up to 15 000 sailed for Canada while of the 400 000 or so Irish who emigrated to North America between 1828 and 1837, some 65 per cent landed in Quebec, the major port of Upper (Ontario) as well as Lower Canada (Quebec). However, while it is clear that Canada loomed large in Irish eyes, it is estimated that between a quarter and a third of those who went there later travelled to the United States.[43] Thus, Canada emerges not just as a new destination for Irish emigrants but as a new gateway into places such as Missouri, Illinois, and Iowa that were being opened up for settlement at the time. This backdoor into the United States has received little attention from historians.

In the United States, there were other attempts to settle Irish emigrants beyond the traditional 'Irishtowns' of the eastern cities. In 1817, New York's Irish Emigrant Association announced that, together with the Hibernian Societies of Philadelphia and Baltimore, it would petition Congress for 'for a grant of land in the Illinois territory suited to the settlement of Irish emigrants'. In their view, such a grant—especially if it offered easy terms—would ease the 'uncertainty' that settlement towards the west often involved. It would also attract immigrants who would otherwise remain 'necessitous' in the east where they would be 'a burden too heavy for private generosity, and a tax too generous even for public compassion'. Congress denied the petition, believing that, if allowed, it would 'foster peculiarities and prejudices…and…a state of segregation from their fellow citizens'.[44] However, it also highlighted the fact that some of the older Irish networks believed that their services should not be confined to assisting the recently arrived in their own cities and that they should also encourage them to settle in the developing states and territories further to the west. This point was made in 1816 when America's first 'Irish' newspaper, the New York-based *Shamrock*, published its *Hints to Irishmen Who Intend with their Families to Make a Permanent Residence in America*. In a country that was no longer limited to the founder states, Irish-Americans were being advised to engage with an expanding country.

The construction of canals such as the Erie (1817–25), Ohio-Erie (1825–32), and Illinois-Michigan (1836–44) offered specific opportunities to do so, especially for unskilled labourers. Some of these workers were recruited in Ireland as well as from the American ports where they landed. In 1818, 3000 Irishmen were already working on the Erie Canal. In 1826, over 5000 were doing so on three other projects. Thus, for all the efforts of New York's Emigration Association as well as similar promotions to settle the 'virgin frontier' with farmers, the movement of the Irish westwards—at least in organized groups—was often driven by factors other than land. For the Irish who went to Wisconsin's lead mines after 1820, agriculture was also 'a secondary pursuit' as it was for those who settled near the galena deposits in the town of the same name in Illinois. While some canal workers took up plots that were owned by their projects, most moved towards prospective urban centres such as Cincinnati, Buffalo, Detroit, Chicago, St Louis, and Milwaukee that were appearing on the horizons of 'mid-America'. Each of these places owed its initial importance to strategic connections with the canals and the ways in which the upper mid-west was being linked to the Great Lakes and Hudson Valley. Chicago had only thirty inhabitants in 1829. By 1837 (the year in which it was incorporated), it had some 4 000 including a 'great influx of Irish' who had arrived largely as a result of the canal and other public projects in the wider region of the Great Lakes.[45]

At the southern tip of the mid-west, the increasing traffic of steamboats on the Mississippi, as well as the peopling of the Louisiana Purchase, reinforced the long-established importance of New Orleans. As a pivotal place within the old French empire, New Orleans had long complemented the capitals of the British colonies of the eastern seaboard—albeit at a cultural and political remove. Its importance was now enhanced as the Mississippi became a more useable gateway into the centre of the country as well as to Texas where the Irish became leaders of Hispanic society both before and after the region was declared a republic in 1836.[46] New Orleans also had a settled and vibrant Irish community which acted as cultural mediators, first between Francophone and Anglophone, and later between 'old' and 'new' immigrants. As such, they traced a history that was different from that of their kin in New England and the former middle colonies. In the inclusive ways in which the Irish presented themselves and celebrated their history and even with respect to building schools and churches, it was, as Andrew Stern has argued, 'co-operation, not conflict, [that] dominated relations between Catholics and Protestants' in the antebellum South. One of the more notable indications of this culture of inclusivity were the ways in which the death of Charleston's first Catholic bishop (1820–42), the Cork-born John England, was marked in that city in 1842:

> Across the city, church bells tolled, ships in the harbor flew their flags at half mast, and politicians, journalists, and religious leaders added their voices to the chorus of dismay.[47]

As the southern states never attracted large numbers of Irish immigrants, it is easy to dismiss the significance of such reports. However, they stress that for all the ways in which the Irish, both in the south and the developing mid-west, were influenced by their more established cousins in places such as New York and Philadelphia, they developed their communities as they saw fit. Neither were they willing to have the ways in which they saw themselves, in relation to either the United States or Ireland, determined by the patriarchs of these other places. In many ways, their sense of identity developed in reaction to these older Irish communities as well as from a sense of alienation which they felt from what the Whiskey rebels had termed so sarcastically in 1793 'the great seat of information' in the east.[48] Instead, they focused on where they actually were and acted and spoke accordingly. As Andrew Cayton and Peter Onuf have put it so succinctly, this was not unusual: 'The South and New England were different from the rest of the country, but the Midwest was distinctive because it *was* the United States'.[49] Irish settlers took little time to feel no differently.

Despite the westward movement of Irish immigrants, the more established Irish networks in New York, Philadelphia, and Baltimore continued to see themselves as the anchors of the Irish presence in the country at large. Their role in the election of Andrew Jackson in 1828 reinforced this sense of self-importance. Also, it was to Thomas Addis Emmet, William Sampson, and William James MacNeven—the 'United Irish exiles' who had settled in New York after the collapse of the rebellion of 1798—that Daniel O'Connell initially looked for American support when he launched his campaign for Catholic Emancipation. The first chapter of his 'Friends of Ireland' was established in New York in July 1825 and it was from the same city that an appeal was issued to other parts of the United States. As a result, twenty-nine chapters of the Friends had been established by 1828 in various parts of the country, including twelve outside the original thirteen states. As altruistically as the Friends presented themselves, not everybody was convinced. On a number of levels, the objections were telling. When some of the friends equated the drive for Catholic Emancipation with the abolition of slavery, many Irish-Americans baulked at the comparison. For them, O'Connell's campaign was a movement which could be argued in terms of morality and civil and human rights. On this basis, they promoted O'Connell's cause across religious, class, and ethno-cultural lines and attracted support from the French of New Orleans, the Anglicans of Montreal and the Presbyterians of Savannah, in whose church they also held their local meetings. But even with such good will, there were lingering questions about whether Americans (whether Irish-born or not) should be interfering in 'the local concerns of the British empire'. As the *New York Morning Herald* put it in April 1829, 'Catholic Emancipation is no concern of ours and we shall do wisely to let it alone'.[50] While such arguments did not impede the development of the Friends, they did raise a crucial issue which would impact directly on American support for O'Connell's second campaign: the repeal of the Act of Union between Britain and Ireland.

As had been the case with Catholic Emancipation, O'Connell put his case for Repeal in the language of natural justice. As a result, he came into contact with similar causes—including abolitionism—for which he also became a champion. In America, O'Connell's views on slavery were read with particular interest, not least because they became increasingly uncompromising. Although he had already addressed anti-slavery societies in Dublin, Cork, and London and contributed to the parliamentary debates on the abolition of slavery in the British West Indies (1833), it was not until the World's Anti-Slavery Convention met in London in June 1840 that O'Connell's views became controversial in America. It was one thing to describe slavery as 'a hideous tyranny'. It was another to suggest that by indulging slavery, Americans were 'hypocrites, tyrants and unjust men' or that their flag was 'stained with the deep, foul blot of human blood'.[51]

While such comments were part of the familiar discourse of the anti-slavery movement, they were given another currency when O'Connell drew on them in the *Address from the People of Ireland, to their Countrymen and Countrywomen in America*. In this address, written towards the end of 1840, O'Connell implicitly challenged Irish networks and clubs in America 'to unite with the abolitionists, as the only consistent advocates of liberty'. By 1843, as 'the representative of the virtues of the people of Ireland', he was asking the Irish

> over the broad Atlantic ... [not to] dare countenance the system of slavery that is supported there, [for otherwise] we will not recognize you as Irishmen no longer.

Such language dismayed Irish-Americans not least because O'Connell effectively accused them of being 'less moral' than their 'cosines [*sic*] at home' if they did not follow his lead on this matter. Many of them also stressed that slavery was an 'American issue' which had to be addressed by 'Americans'. For Irish-American societies, to involve themselves with the anti-slavery movement—at least in a formal way—would be ungrateful and unpatriotic, especially at a time of growing nativism when abolitionists were sometimes being represented as the 'allies of foreign tyrants'. Set in this context, a second point was also important: that while American Repealers were willing to assist O'Connell in any way they could, this did not imply that they would accept his leadership blindly and without comment. If needs be, they were also willing to withdraw their support and in 1843 some of them did.[52] Such actions, and the attitudes which they reflected, suggested that by the 1840s Irish-Americans did not see themselves as uncritical appendages to Irish-based causes, however benevolent or just they were. They also underlined that, if nothing else, the Irish presence in America was less an integrated entity than the sum of its parts. In 1775, Charles O'Hara had suggested to Edmund Burke that 'Our [Irish] people, are so heterogeneously classed, we are no nation'.[53] This was no less true on the other side of the Green Atlantic.[54]

NOTES

1. The author wishes to thank Charles Ivar McGrath as well as the anonymous reviewers for their comments on an earlier draft of this paper. While the literature on the place of Ireland within the first British empire is extensive, most of the relevant writings are cited in Nicholas P. Canny (ed), *The Oxford History of the British Empire, vol. I: The Origins of Empire* (Oxford, 1998) and *Making Ireland British* (Oxford, 2001). For assessments of the Irish Parliament in both domestic and imperial settings, see Charles Ivar McGrath, *Ireland and Empire, 1692–1770* (London, 2012), 37–68 and James Kelly, '"Era of Liberty": The Politics of Civil and Political Rights in Eighteenth-Century Ireland' in Jack P. Greene (ed), *Exclusionary Empire: English Liberty Overseas, 1600–1900* (Cambridge, UK, 2010), 77–111.
2. See Jack P. Greene, *Peripheries and Centre: Constitutional Development in the Extended Polities of the British Empire and the United States 1607–1788* (Athens, GA., 1986).

3. For the ways in which mercantilism developed after the Restoration, see Thomas M. Truxes, *Irish-American Trade, 1660–1783* (Cambridge, UK, 1988), 7–13. For colonial America, see also John J. McCusker and Russell R. Menard, *the Economy of British America, 1607–1789* (Chapel Hill, NC, 1985).

4. For the evolution of the term 'Protestant Ascendancy', see Maurice J. Bric, 'Mathew Carey, Ireland and the "Empire for Liberty" in America' in *Early American Studies* , 11:3 (Fall, 2013), 403–30.

5. J.L. McCracken, 'The Rise of Colonial Nationalism' in T.W. Moody and W.E. Vaughan (eds), *Eighteenth-Century Ireland* (Oxford, 1986), 106. For the Penal Laws, see Thomas Bartlett, *The Fall and Rise of the Irish Nation: The Catholic Question, Catholic Ireland, 1660–1760* (Dublin, 1992).

6. Francis X. Curran, *Catholics in Colonial Law* (Chicago, 1963) and Ronald Hoffman, *Princes of Ireland, Planters of Maryland: A Carroll Saga, 1500–1782* (Chapel Hill, NC, 2000). For the attitudes of Irish Catholics to colonial America, see Maurice J. Bric, *Ireland, Philadelphia and the Re-Invention of America 1760–1800* (Dublin, 2008), 1–9, 20–21 et passim.

7. Truxes, *Irish-American Trade*, 34, 24–5, 154, 176 and R.C. Nash, 'Irish Atlantic Trade in the Seventeenth and Eighteenth Centuries' in *William and Mary Quarterly* (*WMQ*) 42:3 (1985), 329–56. The Linen Board had been founded in 1711.

8. Maurice J. Bric, 'Ireland and Colonial America: The Viewer and the Viewed' in Judith Devlin and Howard B. Clarke (eds), *European Encounters. Essays in Memory of Albert Lovett* (Dublin, 2003), 145–7; Washington, DC, Library of Congress, Blair McClenachan Papers, John and Robert Ogle (Newry) to McClenachan (Philadelphia), 15 August 1774.

9. Bric, *Re-Invention of America*, 37–8. For the similar networks of the New York firm of Greg & Cunningham—which corresponded with as many as fifty-five brokers in Ireland during the late 1750s—see Thomas M. Truxes, *Letterbook of Greg & Cunningham 1756–57. Merchants of New York and Belfast* (Oxford, 2001), 59. McClenachan is quoted in Bric, 'Ireland and Colonial America', 145.

10. See Kerby A. Miller, Arnold Schrier, Bruce D. Boling, and David N. Doyle (eds), *Irish Immigrants in the Land of Canaan. Letters and Memoirs from Colonial and Revolutionary Americas, 1675–1815* (Oxford, 2003). For the ways in which these letters encouraged more public commentaries, including what Kerby Miller calls 'the first emigrant guidebook' for America, see 'Revd James MacSparran's *America Dissected* (1753): Eighteenth-Century Emigration and Constructions of "Irishness" ' in *History Ireland*, 11:4 (2005), 17–22.

11. Boulter is quoted from his letter to the Duke of Newcastle, 16 July 1728, as in J.C. Beckett, *Protestant Dissent in Ireland* (London, 1948).

12. Bric, *Re-Invention of America*, 29 and David Noel Doyle, *Ireland, Irishmen and Revolutionary America, 1760–1820* (Cork and Dublin, 1981), 61.

13. Albert Cook Myers, *Immigration of the Irish Quakers into Pennsylvania, 1680–1750* (Swarthmore, PA., 1902), 81–2, estimated that 2 500 Irish Quakers emigrated to America.

14. Bric, *Re-Invention of America*, 28, 40, 41. While this work discusses how different figures for Irish emigration to the Delaware Valley have been estimated, it does not include comparable data for other colonial destinations, including New York. In his analysis of the Annapolis (Maryland) port books, Leroy Eid noted—perhaps recalling the Catholic origins of the colony—that only 764 of the 5 868 who arrived there between 1769 and 1775 came from Ulster; see Leroy V. Eid, ' "No Freight Paid So Well": Irish Emigration to Pennsylvania on the Eve of the American Revolution' in *Eire-Ireland*, 27 (1993), 48, n. 39, 46, n. 34.

15. For Irish emigration to the Delaware Valley between 1783 and 1800, see Maurice J. Bric, 'Patterns of Irish Emigration ro America, 1783–1800' in Kevin Kenny (ed), *New Directions in Irish-American History* (Madison, Wisc., 2003), 17–35.

16. Graeme Kirkham, 'Ulster Emigration to North America, 1680–1720' in H. Tyler Bethen and Curtis Wood, *Ulster and North America* (Tuscaloosa, AL., 1997), 76–117; Patrick Griffin, *The People With No Name. Ireland's Ulster Scots, America's Scots Irish, and the Creation of a British Atlantic World, 1689–1764* (Princeton, 2001), 90. Mather is quoted in ibid.

17. R.J. Dickson, *Ulster Emigration to Colonial America, 1718–1775* (London, 1966), 49–57. See also Jean Stephenson, *Scotch-Irish Migration to South Carolina, 1772* (Strasburg, 1971). Mather is quoted in Bric, *Re-Invention of America*, 35.

18. For the establishment of Queensborough with official support from colonial Georgia, see E.R.R. Green, 'Queensborough Township: Scotch-Irish Emigration and the Expansion of Georgia, 1763–76' in *WMQ*, 17:2 (1960), 183–99. For the spread of similar Scots-Irish settlements along the frontier, see James G. Leyburn, *The Scotch-Irish. A Social History* (Chapel Hill, NC, 1962), 184–222.

19. Galliland is quoted in Richard J. Purcell, 'Irish Contributions to Colonial New York' in *Studies* 29:6 (1960), 603 and Logan in Leyburn, *The Scotch-Irish*, 191.

20. Elizabeth I. Nybakken, 'New Light on the Old Side: Irish Influences on Colonial Presbyterianism' in *Journal of American History*, 68:4 (1982), 813–32, and Gregory H. Nobles, 'Breaking into the Backcountry: New Approaches to the Early American Frontier, 1750–1800' in *WMQ* 46:4 (1989),651. For the Scots-Irish, see Kerby A. Miller, '"Scotch-Irish" Myths and "Irish" Identities in Eighteenth and Nineteenth Century America' in Charles Fanning (ed), *New Perspectives on the Irish Diaspora* (Carbondale, Ill., 2000), 75–92. The best review of the historiography of the Scots-Irish is M.A. Jones, 'The Scotch-Irish in British America' in Bernard Bailyn and Philip Morgan (eds), *Strangers within the Realm: Cultural Margins of the First British Empire* (Chapel Hill, 1991), 284–313.

21. Edward J. O'Day, 'The "Second Colonization of New England" Revisited: Irish Immigration before the Famine' in Fanning, *New Perspectives*, 93–116, and Edward C. Carter II, 'A "Wild Irishman" under Every Federalist's Bed: Naturalization in Philadelphia, 1789–1806' in *Proceedings of the American Philosophical Society*, 133:2 (1989), 178–89.

22. Bric, *Re-Invention of America*, 39.

23. George W. Franz, *Paxton: A Study of Community Structure and Mobility in the Colonial Pennsylvania Backcountry* (New York, 1989); Judith Ridner, *A Town In-Between: Carlisle, Pennsylvania, and the Early Mid-Atlantic Interior* (Philadelphia, 2010); Eric Hinderaker, *Elusive Empires: Constructing Colonialism in the Ohio Valley, 1673–1800* (Cambridge, UK, 1997) and (with Peter Mancall), *At the Edge of Empire: The Backcountry in British North America* (Baltimore, 2003); A. Roger Ekirch, *'Poor Carolina': Politics and Society in Colonial North Carolina 1729–1776* (Chapel Hill, NC, 1981). For the sectional tensions within some colonies, see Richard Beeman, *Varieties of Political Culture in Eighteenth Century America* (Philadelphia, 2004), especially chapters 6 and 7.

24. Kevin Kenny, *Peaceable Kingdom. The Paxton Boys and the Destruction of William Penn's Holy Experiment* (Oxford, 2009), Thomas P. Slaughter, *The Whiskey Rebellion: Frontier Epilogue to the American Revolution* (Oxford, 1988) and 'The Friends of Liberty, the Friends of Order, and the Whiskey Rebellion: A Historiographic Essay' in Stephen R. Boyd (ed), *The Whiskey Rebellion: Past and Present Perspectives* (Westport, CT., 1985), 9–30 and Ekirch, *'Poor Carolina'*. On this point, see also David Noel Doyle, 'The Regional Bibliography of Irish-America, 1800–1930: A Review and Addendum' in *Irish Historical Studies (IHS)*,

23:91 (1983), 254–83. For the wider historiography, see the pioneering Seamus Metress and Donna Hardy-Johnston, *The Irish in North America: A Regional Biography* (Toronto, 1999).

25. I am using the capitalized words 'Patriot' and 'Patriotism' to refer to those commentators in Ireland and America who stressed the legislative independence of their respective assemblies, unrestricted trade, and political reform; see S.J. Connolly, *Religion, Law and Power. The Making of Protestant Ireland, 1660–1770* (Oxford, 1995).

26. William Molyneux, *Case of Ireland's Being Bound by Acts of Parliament in England Stated* (Dublin, 1698), J.G. Simms (ed) (Dublin, 1977), 127 and Patrick Kelly, 'William Molyneux and the Spirit of Liberty in Eighteenth-Century Ireland' in *Eighteenth Century Ireland (ECI)*, 3 (1988), 136. For the wider worlds of Anglo-American Patriotism, see Maurice J. Bric, 'Ireland, America and the Reassessment of as Special Relationship, 1760–1783' in *ECI*, 11 (1996).

27. Vincent Morley, *Irish Opinion and the American Revolution 1760–1783* (Cambridge, UK, 2002).

28. Franklin is quoted from J.G. Simms, (Cork, 1976), 63, and Troy in Bric, 'Ireland, America, and the Reassessment of a Special Relationship', 101, 100.

29. Leyburn *Scotch-Irish*, 299–312, James H. Hutson, *Pennsylvania Politics, 1746–1770: The Movement for Royal Government and its Consequences* (Princeton, 1972); James C. Leyburn, 'Presbyterian Immigrants and the American Revolution' in *Journal of Presbyterian History*, 54 (1976), 9–32, A.R. Ekirch, 'The North Carolina Regulators on Liberty and Corruption' in *Perspectives in American History*, 11 (1977–8), 199–256. The Hessian officer is quoted from Leyburn, *Scotch-Irish*, 305.

30. Doyle, *Ireland, Irishmen and Revolutionary America*, 186–8. Earlier in the century, McKean's parents had emigrated from Ballymoney—about twenty miles from Ballymena—and settled in Chester County, Pennsylvania.

31. See Gordon S. Wood, *The Creation of the American Republic, 1776–1787* (Chapel Hill, NC, 1969).

32. For attitudes to early-national immigration, see Marilyn C. Baseler, *'Asylum for Mankind'. America, 1607–1800* (Ithaca, 1998).

33. Bric, *Re-Invention of America*, 185–6 et passim; Richard G. Miller, *Philadelphia. The Federalist City: A Study of Urban Politics, 1789–1801* (Port Washington, 1976), 58–60; Alfred Young, *The Democratic Republicans of New York: The Origins, 1763–1797* (Williamsburg, 1967). For the press, see Jeffrey L. Palsey, *'The Tyranny of Printers': Newspaper Politics in the Early American Republic* (Charlottesville, 2001).

34. See Maurice J. Bric, 'The United Irishmen, International Republicanism and the Definition of the Polity in the United States of America, 1791–1800' in *Proceedings of the Royal Irish Academy*, 104:4 (2004), 81–106.

35. Joyce Appleby and Terence Ball (eds), *Jefferson. Political Writings* (Cambridge, UK, 1999), 173–4.

36. See David Waldstreicher, *In the Midst of Perpetual Fetes. The Making of American Nationalism, 1776–1820* (Chapel Hill, 1992), and Mike Cronin and Daryl Adair, *The Wearing of the Green. A History of St Patrick's Day* (London, 2002).

37. David Gleeson, ' "Scotch-Irish" and "Real Irish" in the Nineteenth-Century American South' in *New Hibernian Review*, 10:2 (2006), 68–91, and *The Irish in the South 1815–1877* (Chapel Hill, 2001).

38. Albrecht Koschnik, *'Let a Common Interest Bind Us Together': Associations, Partisanship, and Culture in Philadelphia, 1775–1840* (Charlottesville, VA., 2007).

39. Thomas Meagher, *The Columbia Guide to Irish American History* (New York, 2005), 44. Cúndún is quoted in Kerby A. Miller, *Emigrants and Exiles. Ireland and the Irish Exodus to North America* (Oxford, 1985), 215, 204.

40. While Meagher has estimated that in 1834, as many as 80 per cent of Irish emigrants came *via* Liverpool to New York, Miller puts the figure at a third; see Meagher, *Columbia Guide*, 53 and Miller, *Emigrants and Exiles*, 195. For the overall figures, see Miller, *Emigrants and Exiles*, 197, 195, 199 and David Noel Doyle, 'The Irish in North America, 1776–1845' in W.E. Vaughan (ed), *Ireland Under the Union I, 1801–70* (Oxford, 1989), 683, 195, 199. See also the classic William F. Adams, *Ireland and Irish Emigration to the New World from 1815 to the Famine* (New York, repr. 1967).

41. For Irish emigration before 1791, see C.J. Houston and W.J. Smyth (eds), *Irish Emigration and Canadian Settlement: Patterns, Links and Letters* (Toronto, 1990).

42. The quotations are from Helen I. Cowan, *British Emigration to British North America. The First Hundred Years* (Toronto, 1961), 86, 33. For the passenger acts, see Oliver MacDonagh, *A Pattern of Government Growth. The Passenger Acts and Their Enforcement* (London, 1961).

43. Miller, *Emigrants and Exiles*, 197, 195. For the Cork schemes, see James S. Donnelly Jr, *Captain Rock: The Irish Agrarian Rebellion of 1821–1824* (Madison, WI., 2009).

44. [New York] *National Advocate*, 9 February 1818; [Norfolk] *American Beacon*, 4 March 1818. For the text of three petitions, see *Niles Weekly Register*, 23 May 1818. The quotations are from the Baltimore and Philadelphia petitions.

45. John B. Duff, *The Irish in the United States* (Belmont, CA., 1971) 64; Grace McDonald, *History of the Irish in Wisconsin in the Nineteenth Century* (New York, 1976), 47. Michael Funchion, *Chicago's Irish Nationalists, 1881–1890* (New York, 1976), 8, 10. For the early history of Galena, see Samuel Augustus Mitchell, *Illinois in 1837* (Philadelphia, 1837), 44.

46. See Earl F. Niehaus, *The Irish in New Orleans, 1800–1860* (Baton Rouge, LA., 1965). For the early movement of Irish emigrants into Texas, see Graham Davis, *Land! Irish Pioneers in Mexican and Revolutionary Texas* (College Station, TX., 2002).

47. Andrew Stern, 'Southern Harmony: Catholic-Protestant Relations in the Antebellum South' in *Religion and American Culture*, 17:2 (2007), 165, 168, 165. See also Gleeson, *The Irish in the South: 1815–1877*.

48. Quoted in François Furstenberg, 'The Significance of the Trans-Appalachian Frontier in Atlantic History, c1754–1815' in *American Historical Review*, 113:2 (June, 2008), 666.

49. Andrew R.L. Cayton and Peter S. Onuf (eds), *The Midwest and the Nation: Rethinking the History of an American Region* (Bloomington & Indianapolis, 1990), xviii.

50. [New York] *Truth Teller*, 6 December 1828. This list did not include two branches in Pennsylvania. 23 July 1825. See also Thomas F. Moriarty, 'The Irish American Response to Catholic Emancipation' in *Catholic Historical Review*, 66:3 (1980), 353–73, from which this paragraph has been drawn in part. The *Herald* is quoted from page 362.

51. Maurice J. Bric, 'Daniel O'Connell and the Debate on Anti-Slavery, 1820–50' in Tom Dunne and Laurence M. Geary (eds), *History and the Public Sphere* (Cork, 2005), 70, 74–7, and "Debating Slavery and Empire: the United Staters, Britain and the World's Anti-Slavery Convention of 1840' in William Mulligan and Maurice J. Bric (eds), *Abolition and Empire. A Global History of Anti-Slavery Politics in the Nineteenth Century* (London, 2013). See also Anon. (comp.), *Daniel O'Connell upon American Slavery* (New York, 1860), 7, 21, 12. For a recent analysis of O'Connell's views on slavery in America, see Angela Murphy, *American Slavery, Irish Freedom: Abolition, Immigrant Citizenship and the Transatlantic Movement for Irish Repeal* (Baton Rouge, LA., 2010).

52. *Daniel O'Connell upon American Slavery*, 38–40; Bric, 'Daniel O'Connell and the Debate on Anti-Slavery', 80, 78, 81.
53. Quoted in Morley, *Irish Opinion and the American Revolution*, 1.
54. For this theme, see David Doyle, 'Cohesion and Diversity in the Irish Diaspora' in *IHS*, 31:123 (May, 1999), 411–34.

SELECT BIBLIOGRAPHY

Adams, William F., *Ireland and Irish Emigration to the New World from 1815 to the Famine* (New York, new ed., 1967).

Bric, Maurice J. *Ireland, Philadelphia and the Re-Invention of America, 1760–1800* (Dublin, 2009).

Bric, Maurice J. 'The United Irishmen, International Republicanism and the Definition of the Polity in the United States of America, 1791–1800' in *Proceedings of the Royal Irish Academy* 104 (2004), 81–106.

Dickson, R.J. *Ulster Emigration to Colonial America 1718–1785* (Belfast, new ed., 1976).

Doyle, David Noel *Ireland, Irishmen and Revolutionary America 1760–1820* (Dublin & Cork, 1981).

Doyle, David Noel 'The Irish in North America, 1776–1845' in W. E. Vaughan (ed), *Ireland Under the Union I, 1801–70* (Oxford, 1989), 682–725.

Griffin, Patrick *The People with No Name: Ireland's Scots Irish, America's Scots Irish, and the Creation of a British Atlantic World, 1689–1764* (Princeton, 2001).

McGrath, Charles Ivar, *Ireland and Empire, 1692–1770* (London, 2012).

Metress, Seamas and Johnston, Donna Hardy, *The Irish in North America: A Regional Bibliography* (Toronto, 1999).

Miller, Kerby A., Schrier, Arnold, Boling, Bruce D., and Doyle, David N. (eds), *Irish Immigrants in the Land of Canaan: Letters and Memoirs from Colonial and Revolutionary America* (Oxford, 2003).

Morley, Vincent, *Irish Opinion and the American Revolution* (Cambridge, 2002).

Murphy, Angela, *American Slavery, Irish Freedom: Abolition, Immigrant Citizenship and the Transatlantic Movement for Repeal* (Baton Rouge, LA., 2010).

Truxes, Thomas M., *Irish-American Trade, 1660–1783* (New York, 1988).

CHAPTER 24

PATRIOT POLITICS, 1750–91

JAMES KELLY

I

ON 8 December 1759, Nathaniel Clements, the deputy vice-treasurer for Ireland, reported to the prime minister, the duke of Newcastle, that he had delayed paying the pensioners on the Irish establishment lest he 'incurred the displeasure of our Patriots, *as they are pleased to call themselves*'.[1] Clements' unhappiness at the appropriation by a vocal political faction of the term 'patriot' is noteworthy; first, because his words echoed those uttered earlier in the decade by John Ryder, the Church of Ireland Archbishop of Tuam; second, and more indicatively, because they attest to the emergence in the 1750s of a distinct patriot political interest in the House of Commons.[2] The term 'patriot' was neither new nor unfamiliar, of course. The foundation text of Irish patriotism, William Molyneux's *The case of Ireland...stated*, first published in 1698, was one of the most influential titles of the early eighteenth century, having been reprinted on four occasions between 1706 and 1725, while the argument it advanced in support of the entitlement of Irish Protestants to the same rights and liberties as Englishmen had been influentially affirmed in the mid-1720s by Jonathan Swift.[3] Moreover, opponents of what was portrayed as an unjustifiable attempt by the British government during the late 1710s and early 1720s both to confine the authority of the Irish parliament and to administer Ireland as a dependent kingdom gloried in the appellation,[4] though the political edge associated with its usage then was blunted thereafter by the equation of patriotism and improvement, and by the political and social consensus in the wake of the difficult economic environment of the late 1720s that improvement was an object behind which all could unite.[5] The ensuing marginalization of the constitutional questions posed by Molyneux as to the rights and liberties of Irish Protestants was facilitated by the prioritization by the undertaker system, which dominated domestic politics in the quarter century after the Wood's halfpence crisis (1724–5), of issues of power, patronage, and personality, though it is notable that the preoccupation of a majority of M.P.s and peers with these matters provided those of a more principled, and confrontational, frame of mind with an incentive to embrace a different agenda.[6] This was strikingly revealed in Dublin in the late 1740s when the ebullient Charles Lucas spearheaded an unsuccessful challenge to the manner in which the aldermen of Dublin Corporation used their dominant position to favour oligarchical self-interest. Lucas appealed, albeit with some diffidence, to the language and rhetoric of patriotism in support of his position,[7] but it is notable that his actions had the effect of prompting a number of more focused interventions on what it meant to be a patriot.[8] They also served to encourage a number of young M.P.s (Edmond Sexten Pery, most notably), who were uneasy at the way the country was being governed, to make a more assertive stand.[9] Though their efforts were the subject of approving comment, they were essentially symbolic, and it required the seismic shock of the Money Bill dispute (1753–6), which for a time deprived the Irish administration of a majority in parliament and, as a result, of the capacity to shape law, to foster an environment in which an identifiable 'patriot party', with Pery to the fore, could develop.[10]

II

Guided by Henry Grattan's seminal, and much cited, apostrophe of 16 April 1782—'spirit of Swift, spirit of Molyneux, your genius has prevailed, Ireland is now a nation'—it was long the practice in Irish historiography to conceive of patriotism as a seamless tradition spanning the eighteenth century, and to portray the 'quest for constitutional rights' as a historical constant from its inauguration in the 1690s to its eclipse as a result of the Act of Union.[11] The identification by Richard Koebner in the 1950s that the collected edition of Grattan's speeches does not mirror the contemporary report of what he actually uttered in the House of Commons has prompted some not only to question the legitimacy of Grattan's efforts to elevate himself into the pantheon of patriots who carried the torch that had been lit by Molyneux, but also to query the suggestion that there was a continuous Patriot tradition.[12] As a result, modern historians are disposed to emphasize the contingent, discontinuous, and individualistic character of patriot politics. Still more significantly, guided by developments in the history of political thought, and by the discrediting of the long-influential point of view that conceived of eighteenth-century patriotism in proto-nationalist terms, the recognition that the underlying *raison d'être* of patriotism was neither ethnic, cultural, nor linguistic has prompted modern scholarship seriously to qualify, if not always unconditionally to discard, previous constructions and interpretations. We do not yet possess a full or integrated modern assessment, but enquiries into its philosophical and ideological basis by Leersen, McBride, and Small;[13] its politics by O'Connell, Mansergh, and Morley;[14] its metropolitan dimension by Hill;[15] its critics by Connolly;[16] some of its leading personalities by Kelly and McDowell,[17] and the impact of Volunteering by Smyth, McBride, Kelly, Higgins, and Mac Suibhne,[18] permit a more secure, if not always an agreed or consensual, reconstruction.

Arguably, the most significant development has been the identification of the fact that, as elsewhere in Europe, the ideological foundation of Irish patriotism in the eighteenth century was, in the words of Ian McBride, provided by 'polity (the myth of an ancestral constitution) and religion (a sense of chosenness [sic])'.[19] This conclusion can be sustained by reference both to the enduring intellectual appeal of Molyneux's historicist argument (four editions of his *ur*-text were published in the 1770s and early 1780s[20]), and by the persistence of anti-Catholicism. It is noteworthy in this context that while most patriots were prepared by the late 1770s to concede to Catholics the entitlement to freedom to worship and to participate fully in economic life, few were disposed to admit them to the political process.[21] Still more importantly, the breaking of the link, once assumed, between eighteenth-century patriotism, which embraced the ideal of love of country, and nineteenth-century ethnic nationalism, has obliged historians not only to revise fundamentally their perceptions of patriotism but also to forsake some terms long in favour when it comes to describing it. The main casualty has been the term 'colonial nationalism', which was influentially propounded by J.G. Simms in 1966, and ostensibly confirmed as the accepted term by its employment by various authors in the monumental *New History of Ireland: the eighteenth century* which was published in 1986.[22] Its adoption was inappropriate, both because of the obvious indebtedness of the term to the nationalist historiographical tradition that the *New History* was conceived to supplant, and because it implicitly failed to acknowledge that the patriots did not aspire either to cultural or political separation from Great Britain. Yet, since the alternatives then in use—Protestant nationalism and Anglo-Irish nationalism—were no more problematical, the terminological lack of clarity then obtaining, and the ongoing loose usage of 'nationalist' and 'nationalism' to describe and to define the patriots' efforts, continued unaltered until Joep Leerssen's decisive intervention in 1988.[23] This has taken some time to be absorbed, but encouraged by theoretical and comparative examinations of the phenomenon by Viroli and Leerssen,[24] which have highlighted the ideological distinction between patriotism and nationalism, and by the recognition that 'patriot' is more apt than the alternatives adopted in the twentieth century, political historians have reverted to employing the contemporary term.[25] McBride's nuanced account of Protestantism and patriotism and Stephen Small's forensic exploration of 'the five languages that formed the classic expression of Irish patriotism in the era of the American Revolution' have provided a rationale for this reversion. Yet, the fact that two recent examinations of the Volunteers have concluded that they promoted and fostered a sense of a distinct 'Irish nation' in the body politic, and that others continue to find 'Anglo-Irish nationalism' a useful analytical tool, suggests that this historical debate is not entirely resolved.[26]

However it evolves, it is now well established that the ideology of Irish patriots was shaped by a combination of the ideal of an 'ancient constitution' and classical republicanism, Protestant superiority, and the enduring adherence to the principle articulated by Molyneux that Protestants in Ireland were entitled to the same political, constitutional, and commercial rights as Englishmen. It would also seem, though this is a subject that would repay further investigation, that in common with many English Whigs and American patriots, Irish patriots had arrived at the conclusion by the mid eighteenth century that their political system was tainted by corruption and that it was incumbent on them to return it to its original purity. The ideal of a recoverable ancient constitution was an illusion, but it was compelling for many for whom patriotism was 'the voice of nature and reason'.[27] There were others, of course, for whom the politics of patriotism was nothing less than a means to wealth and power, and still more whose commitment was tempered by pragmatic calculation and personal concerns. It is thus not surprising that the question of whether those who presented themselves as patriots were 'true', 'real', 'pretended', 'pseudo', or 'mock' should excite ongoing animated debate,[28] because it mirrored the conviction and the passion patriots brought to Irish political life during the four decades of the second half of the eighteenth century, when they were an influential presence on the political landscape.

III

When it emerged in the early 1750s that the Lord Lieutenant, the duke of Dorset, the Chief Secretary, George Sackville, the English-born Primate, George Stone, and the Ponsonby interest sought, in order to return government to Dublin Castle, to replace Henry Boyle, the Speaker of the House of Commons, who had dominated domestic politics since his emergence as the leading political undertaker in 1733, Boyle was faced with a major decision.[29] Unwilling for a variety of reasons, personal and financial as well as political, to fade into the background, the Speaker determined to take the battle to his opponents. As the most accomplished parliamentary manager of his generation, and the acknowledged leader of a strong coalition of largely family-based political connections—or 'parties' as contemporaries misleadingly termed them—he was both a forbidding and a formidable target, and he cannily determined to make the task still more difficult for his rivals and opponents by appealing to the distinct and expanding identification with Ireland that the Protestant interest had embraced since the 1690s.[30] Though he was encouraged to take this action by allies such as Thomas Carter and Anthony Malone, whose Irishness was commonly held to be more advanced than his own, Boyle was not simply being calculating. Like all of those who pursued this power struggle, he had no wish, as his ally Thomas Pakenham (the MP for Longford) explained at considerable length, to alter the fundamentals of the Anglo-Irish connection as they were currently grounded, and no interest at all in pressing for independence. 'Independency is a word of offence, and I believe never entered the thoughts of any man in his senses,' Pakenham observed, but he was no less categorical in affirming that there were 'men of spirit, ability and resolution that will go as far as ever their ancestors did in defence of their just rights'—meaning the rights of the kingdom of Ireland.[31] As 'a staunch Whig', Boyle may not have been in the vanguard of those whom Pakenham had in mind when he ventured this opinion, but the Speaker had no difficulty conceiving of himself as Irish.[32] Certainly, his conclusion that 'no other mother country in the world received so much advantage from any dependent province or its colonies than England does from Ireland', persuaded him that Irish Protestants were not simply justified in refusing to accede to a system of government that must serve to accentuate Ireland's unwarranted 'dependency…upon the crown of England'; they were entitled to more 'favourable' treatment.[33]

Having determined to make a stand, and to do so in the name of the 'Irish interest', Boyle contrived to seize the initiative.[34] He might have been embarking on a lost cause had he not secured a crucial morale-boosting victory over the so-called 'English interest' in the division on the money bill on 17 December 1753 that gave the ensuing dispute its name,[35] but, having prevailed in parliament, the newly fledged patriots made a further crucial strategic decision when they decided to take the contest into the fast-expanding public sphere. One of their most critical decisions was to found a newspaper—the *Universal Advertiser*—since this not only assured them of a conduit for their views, but also gave them a palpable advantage over the Irish administration, which did not then appreciate the usefulness of a newspaper.[36] The administration was more aware of the importance of the pamphlet as a barometer of public opinion, but try as they might they were unable to neutralize the impact of the patriots' propagandists. The advantage the patriots secured, and maintained in the public sphere, can be exemplified by the broadside of the crucial division of 17 December which relayed the names of the 124 M.P.s who had opposed the money bill in red ink, and the 118 who had supported it in black. Printed division lists were not uncommon in the eighteenth century, but what is remarkable about this example is not only that it served explicitly to identify which sides M.P.s were on, but also that the colour of the ink in which names were printed became a sort of political shorthand for their public reputation. This was epitomized by the raising of toasts at patriot assemblies to 'The Glorious Red List', and 'A perpetual place in the hearts of Irishmen to every Black that becomes a Red'.[37] Indeed, it became such 'a mark of distinction' to have a place on the 'red list' that 'several…patriot members' chose in normal correspondence to 'write their names in red ink'.[38]

Though actions such as these were aspersed as an undignified manifestation of the 'party rage' to which the money bill dispute gave rise, they were of no more than symbolic import.[39] Of much greater consequence, both for the politics of the dispute and its legacy, was the establishment of a national network of patriot clubs, which served the dual purpose of minimizing defections from the ranks of 'the 124 patriots' that had distinguished themselves in December 1753 and of rallying public opinion. This was especially important in the winter of 1753–4, when copious toasts were drunk extolling 'those illustrious Patriots who distinguished themselves' in voting down the money bill, and 'illuminations, bonfires, [the] firing of guns' and other public displays were hosted in urban centres throughout the kingdom.[40] Such events were appropriate to this moment when attention was focused on generating a patriotic mood, but it is a testament to the appeal of the patriot clubs that they managed to sustain the patriot spirit so strongly in evidence in the winter of 1753–4 over the two years that the dispute raged.[41] However, once Boyle and the Irish administration reached a settlement in the spring of 1756, both the number of patriot clubs and the public interest in their activities underwent a sharp decline.[42]

One of the major achievements of recent scholarship on the 1750s has been to establish the importance of the press and the appreciating associational impulse to the emergence of political patriotism.[43] It is also apparent that, once released, there was no putting this genie back in its bottle. This was made clear in the by-election fought in King's County in 1757, when the independent freeholders, who had taken an active part in the money bill dispute, pursued a vigorous campaign in the name of returning 'honest and able men to parliament'.[44] They were unsuccessful, but despite this outcome, 'independent electors' and other groups in Counties Antrim, Westmeath, Galway and elsewhere continued to manifest their intrinsic patriot convictions by publishing occasional declarations in support of political reform.[45] They were encouraged in such actions by the example of the small but energetic 'patriot party', which emerged as a distinct presence in the House of Commons in the mid and late 1750s. Guided by Sexten Pery, these patriots had an impact palpably greater than their modest number might suggest because of their willingness to challenge the prevailing political consensus by presenting 'popular bills', and advancing motions on issues that the Irish administration did not want animated and most M.P.s reflexively avoided. Given their modest number, the patriots seldom prevailed in the division lobbies. Yet, the impact of a bill presented in 1755 that sought to extend the provisions of *habeas corpus* obtaining in England to Ireland was reinforced by motions critical of the size of the pension list and Poynings' Law, and calls for greater probity in the allocation of public money. By raising these issues they contrived successfully to ensure that the embryonic 'patriot party' was an acknowledged (if not universally welcomed) feature of the political landscape as the 1750s and the reign of George II drew to a close.[46]

IV

Building on the foundations already laid, the patriot interest achieved still greater visibility and influence during the 1760s. Their improved profile in the House of Commons was due in large part to the emergence of a more ideologically motivated generation of politicians, a significant proportion of whom were returned to parliament for the first time in 1761. The best known was Charles Lucas, the pugnacious advocate of municipal reform, whose election to represent Dublin city was crucial in establishing a bridgehead to the guilds, voluntary associations, and radical activists in the capital that were to play a crucial role both in articulating and sustaining patriot politics over the next three decades.[47] He was joined by three country gentlemen—William Osborne (Carysfort), Lucius O'Brien (Ennis), and Alexander McAuley (Thomastown)—who were also elected for the first time in 1761, and whose presence in the Commons reinforced Pery, Robert French, and William Brownlow, who had assumed the burden of making the patriot case until this point.[48] However, the most important addition to their ranks was Henry Flood, because his oratorical abilities (which exceeded those of the impressive

Pery) provided the patriots with a voice able not only to challenge the administration, but also to command the chamber.[49]

This proved especially valuable, both because the expanded patriot interest was committed to presenting its programme for improved and reformed government with greater vigour, and because the continuing rapid expansion of the public sphere meant that there was a fast-growing audience outside parliament, which looked to the House of Commons for leadership. To be sure, many of the issues that the patriots agitated—the increasing size of the pension list, which they opposed, responsible financial government, and *habeas corpus*, which they demanded, and the modification of Poynings' Law, which was emblematical of Ireland's constitutional subordination[50]—were pursued with no more success in the 1760s than was the case in the 1750s, because no matter what tactic or argument they deployed they 'seldom equall[ed] half of the majority'.[51] However, they did achieve an occasional morale-boosting victory, which combined with their generally enhanced profile and the visible commitment of a majority of patriot M.P.s, to persuade the public that the patriots aspired to a style of government that was inherently more virtuous than that practised by those in power. They were helped by the fact that the reforms they aspired to advance dovetailed in several important respects with the burgeoning aspirations of the increasingly politically aware middling sort. The most striking instance of this is provided by their embrace of the demand, articulated by a number of trade guilds during the 1761 general election, for a septennial act that would provide for regular general elections.[52] The hostility with which this prospect was regarded by a majority of M.P.s and officials ensured that successive septennial bills failed during the early and mid 1760s, but it did not inhibit belief in the merits of the proposition, or support for further municipal reform in Dublin.[53] The public was less taken by the proposal to establish a citizen militia (one of Flood's priorities) or by the attempt to enhance the independency of the judiciary by amending the terms on which judges were appointed, but the fact that these and other reforms sought by the patriots were addressed in the popular press from the mid 1760s was indicative of a broader acceptance of the legitimacy of the patriots' programme.[54]

The emergence of a vigorous popular press was, as this suggests, crucial to the percolation of patriot principles into all arenas of public and political discourse during the 1760s and early 1770s. Pamphlets meanwhile continued to function as a conduit of considered opinion, and patriot M.P.s such as Alexander McAuley, Henry Flood, and Lucas, of course, did not hesitate to employ this medium.[55] However, the major innovation in the public sphere during this period, initiated by the *Universal Advertiser* in the 1750s and taken a step further in the 1760s and 1770s, was the establishment of avowedly political newspapers. The *Freeman's Journal*, which commenced publication in 1763, represented an important step on this journey, since unlike most earlier papers, which did not seek overtly to encourage political debate, it allotted space in every issue to commentators and correspondents who were encouraged to debate theoretical as well as topical issues from an explicitly patriot position.[56] The reaction of readers requires investigation, but the fact that the *Freeman's Journal* outsold its rivals, and that the discussion of ideas and issues appertaining to the nature of patriotism as well as quotidian politics was imitated by others, sustains the conclusion that the newspaper exerted a formative influence. This is reinforced by the popularization of a view that true patriots were more principled and more nobly motivated than their critics; it was epitomized by the opinion articulated in the *Freeman's Journal* that since 'all patriots… [were] champions for liberty and their country', to be a patriot was an ideal to which all virtuous men, and all governors particularly, ought to aspire.[57] Saliently, these were sentiments that were promoted with more, rather than less, fervour in the 1770s, when the *Freeman's Journal* was joined by the *Hibernian Journal*, founded in April 1771, which replicated the former in the warmth of its endorsement of patriot politics.[58]

With the backing first of one and then of two popular newspapers, and a visible presence in other media, the patriots were assured from the mid 1760s that their political point of view did not want for public advocacy. This facilitated the dissemination of an increasingly elaborate patriot response to events. More importantly for the future, it dovetailed with the opposition's reading of events elsewhere—specifically in Great Britain where John Wilkes' mistreatment by the political elite had stirred enormous controversy, and in the North American colonies, where the polities pursued in respect of the colonies were still more unpopular—that disposed Irish patriots to accept the conclusion embraced across the anglophone world that the British government was embarked on an attempt to undo the Glorious Revolution and to restore Stuart despotism.[59]

Although Ireland did not want for political Cassandras before that date who warned that the 'venality and corruption [that] were the ruin of the Roman Commonwealth' would bring about the same doleful result in Ireland if politicians were not guided in their actions by patriot principles, this viewpoint became more widely accepted during the viceroyalty of George, Viscount Townshend (1767–72).[60] As a former soldier, who was instinctively repelled by the self-interest of the Irish undertakers, it might have been anticipated that Townshend and the patriots in the House of Commons would forge a productive working relationship. The enactment in 1768 of an octennial act, providing for general elections every eight years, was clearly something the patriots welcomed, but they rejected Townshend's plan to augment the army as contrary to one of the fundamental principles of patriotism, and they were no less troubled by his personal deportment and general political demeanour. As a result, when the lord lieutenant prorogued parliament following the rejection by M.P.s in December 1769 of a money bill that, in accordance with the provision of Poynings' Law, had taken its rise in the Irish Privy Council, patriot opinion was roused to greater animation than at any point since the money bill dispute was at its height. Guided by Henry Flood, Charles Lucas, and Robert French, the patriots concluded that they had to strain every sinew to resist the lord lieutenant's policies if they were to prevent the triumph of the despotism they perceived the British government aspired to achieve.[61]

As the dominant patriot voice, Henry Flood was the effective leader of the opposition to Townshend's plan to increase the administration's authority in the House of Commons in the early 1770s. However, the inherent instability of the coalition of interests opposed to the lord lieutenant ensured that Flood was always engaged in a rearguard action.[62] To make matters worse, although the rejection of the money bill in 1769 had prompted a number of significant interventions on the subject of Poynings' Law (by Lucas and French) and a new edition of Molyneux's *Case of Ireland* to which Flood provided a learned preface, the patriots in parliament experienced a number of high-profile defections. The decision of Edmond Sexten Pery to accept the speakership of the House of Commons, and the defection of a number of others, not only weakened the patriots in the House of Commons but also caused Flood to conclude, following Townshend's departure late in 1772, that he could better advance the programme of political reforms to which patriots aspired in tandem with the Irish administration.[63]

This conclusion prompted Flood to embark on an immensely convoluted negotiation with the Irish administration, which proved a turning point in his career from which he was never fully to recover.[64] The remaining patriots, angry at what they interpreted as Flood's betrayal, contrived to maintain some form of political coherence, but it proved difficult. They could muster fifty votes with some regularity in the division lobbies during the mid 1770s, but the lack of strong leadership and the readiness of the Harcourt administration (1772–6) to employ the extensive patronage at its disposal to detach the needy and less principled was still more telling. David Lammey has suggested that the patriots contrived to counter the tendency towards individualism that always diminished their effectiveness in the Commons by adopting some of the attributes of a party organization during the 1770s, but this is to misinterpret the significance of the label 'party', which continued to be employed in the loose manner in which it had been used since the 1750s.[65] In reality, though more M.P.s were—and were content to be described as—patriots in the parliamentary lists that were assembled in the mid 1770s, they possessed neither the numbers, a coherent programme, nor a workable strategy.[66] Indeed, there are good grounds for concluding that the patriot pulse then beat more strongly outside parliament, where the combination of a vigorous press, an expanding associational culture, typified by the Society for Free Citizens in Dublin, and the example of both John Wilkes and the American colonists stimulated reform-minded interests to prepare a 'test' inviting aspiring M.P.s to support a programme of parliamentary reform that had the potential to transform the political system.[67]

V

Given this background, it is reasonable to surmise that, had relations between Great Britain and the colonies not broken down, the late 1770s might have witnessed a sustained attempt to reform the representative system, in the guise of restoring the ancient constitution. Instead, as Great Britain sought militarily to bring the colonists to heel, many patriots chose not only to side with the colonists on the grounds that their aspirations were more in keeping with the principles of the ancient constitution than ministerial policy, but also to take advantage of the opportunity to press for the redress of those commercial and constitutional grievances that were the most obvious badge of their continuing subordination. Thus, though much effort and energy was devoted in 1775 and in 1776 to debating whether it was proper to send troops on the Irish army establishment to support the war in America, the outcome of the 1776 general election, which saw the return to the House of Commons of Henry Grattan, John Forbes, and others who were to re-energize the patriots in parliament, was pregnant with implications for the future. Their cause was assisted by changes at the head of the Irish executive that resulted in the replacement of the sinuous Earl Harcourt with the ineffectual Earl of Buckinghamshire; this was a critical matter since the implication of the decision taken during Townshend's administration to require lords lieutenant to reside in the kingdom for the duration of their appointment meant they were de facto leaders of the Castle party.[68]

The shift in the balance of influence in the House of Commons was hardly apparent during the 1777–8 session when the administration's majority was generally secure, though the patriots' ability to provide minorities of seventy was a significant improvement on recent sessions. Two events transformed the situation. The first, stimulated by the entry of France into the war on the side of the colonists and the absence of an official militia, was a surge of enthusiasm among the Protestant population to join in Volunteer corps. The second was the refusal of the Westminster parliament in 1778 to respond in a generous manner to the demand emanating from Ireland for the relaxation of the various mercantilist restrictions that limited the kingdom's capacity to trade. Exasperated by what was conceived as calculated insult, the more outspoken patriots in parliament and activists at local level capitalized on 'the general decay of out trade and manufacture' to persuade the Volunteers, which, as Ian McBride has best illustrated, corresponded to the patriot ideal of an armed citizenry, to support an assertive campaign for 'free trade'.[69] This development had a profoundly transformative impact. Whereas in 1778 an attempt by the patriots, spearheaded by Denis Daly, to secure approval for an address to the king 'pointing out…the necessity of some further extension of our trade' had been neutralized by the Castle phalanx, this was no longer possible when parliament resumed in the autumn of 1779.[70] Emboldened by an unprecedented display of public support, spectacularly manifested by the Volunteers' politicization of the annual celebration of William of Orange's birthday on 4 November, the patriots seized the initiative in the House of Commons. Led by Henry Grattan, who had assumed the mantle of oratorical leadership previously worn by Pery and Flood, the patriots convinced a majority of M.P.s to vote supplies for six months, instead of the usual two years, in order to compel the British government to concede a 'free trade'. They were assisted by the near-complete breakdown in discipline in Castle ranks, as officer-holders and previously dependable country gentlemen deserted in droves, by a surge in radical patriot print, and by the unprecedented concert of the patriot leadership, influenced and guided by a shadowy but effective political club, the Monks of the Order of St Patrick (better known as the Monks of the Screw). Fearful that the country would become ungovernable 'if an effectual extension of trade is not granted', and that this might encourage hotheads to seek to follow the example of America and press for independence, the prime minister Lord

North bowed to the demand, and in the spring of 1780 Ireland was permitted to trade within the empire on the same terms as England.[71]

The removal of the long-despised restrictions on trade was a resounding triumph for the patriots, who were encouraged by what John Forbes identified in February 1780 as 'the fixed determination' of 'persons of all ranks, descriptions and religions' to 'assert the natural rights of Ireland be the consequences ever so hazardous', and to turn their attention to still more emblematical legal and constitutional restrictions.[72] Forbes' assessment notwithstanding, political opinion was far from unanimous as to the wisdom of agitating these ultra-sensitive issues, which were crucial to the maintenance of a secure Anglo-Irish nexus. As a result, the patriots made less headway in 1780 and 1781 than the advocates of 'a free constitution' anticipated, but one of the results of recent work has been to identify the vital role played by bodies such as the Monks of the Screw and individuals such as John Forbes and Francis Dobbs in convincing Volunteer corps and political activists to offer their support.[73] The re-energizing of the Irish administration as a consequence of replacements at the helm in Dublin Castle presented a further obstacle, but once the alliance of patriot M.P.s and Volunteers agreed a programme of reforms at Dungannon in February 1782, and this received backing countrywide, it was only a matter of time before major constitutional concessions were forthcoming. The fact that the changes implemented addressed, and largely met, the patriots' concerns on all the points they identified was due in large part to the accession to power in Britain of the Rockingham Whigs. Like the government of Lord North which they replaced, these Whigs aspired to conclude a 'compact' with Ireland, which would define the nature of the Anglo-Irish nexus for the future, but those patriots towards whom they made overtures—Henry Grattan and Lord Charlemont—were unyielding in their unwillingness to negotiate on what they contended were matters of 'right'. Moreover, they were able to bring the House of Commons with them in an exemplary demonstration of unity on 16 April 1782. Obliged once more to yield to the superior forces arrayed against them, the government consented to the repeal of the Declaratory Act (1720), to the amendment to Poynings' Law (1494), the alteration of the terms on which judges were appointed, and the assertion of parliamentary control over the army.[74]

The achievement in 1782 of what is generally (if hubristically) termed 'legislative independence' was not only a moment of particular triumph for patriot politics within as well as without parliament, it brought the patriots close to the ultimate prize of an equality of rights and liberties with Britain identified by William Molyneux in the 1690s. Political realists of the calibre of John Forbes and Henry Grattan were happy to conclude 'that this country is settled', but there were others with different ideas.[75] Prominent among their number was Henry Flood. He concluded that the failure of Britain formally to renounce its authority to legislate for Ireland left the kingdom vulnerable to the reassertion by the Westminster parliament of this disputed claim. There was little likelihood of this happening, but Flood's cogently articulated case struck a chord with the rank and file of the Volunteers and the government of Lord Shelburne was obliged reluctantly to concede the point.[76] Welcome though this clarification was, many middle-class political activists perceived that the constitutional concessions were also incomplete without an equivalently decisive reform of the representative system. They were encouraged in this conviction by comments from experienced proponents of parliamentary reform in England, but the main impetus in support of the campaign that ensued came in 1783 from the Volunteers of Ulster and, in 1784, from the nexus of radical political activists in Dublin. Visceral antipathy within the elite to the very thought of sharing power with social interests that possessed neither the property nor the education required to make law dovetailed with unconcealed prejudice to frustrate an ambitious plan of reform emanating from the Grand National Convention of Volunteer delegates that assembled in Dublin in 1783, and decisively to repulse the still more radical plans advanced by James Napper Tandy in 1784.[77]

The rejection of the demand for parliamentary reform had profound implications for the once-formidable coalition of peers, M.P.s, activists, and Volunteers that had dominated the political landscape in Ireland since the late 1770s. It was improbable in any event that this would continue unaltered once the American War of Independence had concluded, since the cessation of hostilities provided an ideal opportunity for many who were unhappy at the political role taken by the Volunteers to withdraw. However, the unedifying class tensions exposed by the campaign to secure parliamentary reform, and the religious suspicions revealed when it was proposed to admit Catholics to the franchise in 1783 and 1784, were not only politically debilitating, but also hastened the disintegration of the most remarkable undertaking in popular politics in eighteenth-century Ireland. It certainly presented a clear and decisive answer to the question Henry Grattan had posed in 1782 when, with legislative independence all but achieved, he invited his listeners to consider 'whether we shall be a Protestant settlement or an Irish nation'.[78] The answer as far as most Irish Protestants were concerned in 1784 was 'a Protestant settlement'.

VI

Having surrendered the political impetus that had enabled them to achieve much in a short time, the much reduced and internally divided patriot interest faced an uncertain future. Henry Grattan perceived that he could continue to pursue a patriot programme by promoting an agenda of economical reform, but he was soon to realize that the generation of able but ideologically conservative officeholders that were ushered into power in the mid 1780s were unsympathetic, and that he did not have the skills required to progress such a plan.[79] The principles of patriotism remained popular notwithstanding but, having achieved the holy grail of commercial and constitutional reform, they no longer possessed the big idea that would provide them with purpose, and a reason to cling together. They did demonstrate their capacity to draw on the deep reservoirs of public good will in 1785 to resist William Pitt's sophisticated scheme to neutralize the impact of legislative independence by means of a commercial union, and they were able to successfully rally sufficient support in the winter of 1788–9 to secure approval for the idea of offering the crown of Ireland to the Prince Regent.[80] However, their essentially reactive position, epitomized by the commitment entered into by the Whig Club on its foundation in 1789, to safeguard and to secure legislative independence, was regarded with mounting cynicism by the beginning of the 1790s by ambitious young men such as Theobald Wolfe Tone (for a time a member of the Whig Club), who believed that the constitution of 1782 was elitist and insufficient. His departure to found the United Irishmen was as eloquent a statement of his priorities as the continuing devotion of the membership of the Whig Club to the constitution of 1782 was to the now essentially conservative ambitions of the surviving patriots.[81] This attachment was amply in evidence once more in 1799–1800 when the Irish parliament and public debated the merits of an Anglo-Irish union. Its ratification, in the teeth of their determined resistance, effectively signalled the end for the flickering embers of patriot politics, which in reality had not burned brightly since the mid 1780s.

In the half century that spanned its emergence, growth, climacteric, and decline, patriotism had exerted a formative influence on Irish politics. The patriots did not proffer an intrinsically radical agenda, but they did hold out the prospect that the Protestant elite in Ireland would have full access to the advanced constitutional rights conferred on their English cousins by the Glorious Revolution. They cannot be said to have quite succeeded in this aim because of their reluctance to press for the internal reform of the Irish political system and the re-shaping of the Anglo-Irish nexus relationship with Great Britain. But their pursuit of commercial, constitutional, and legal equality was a manifestation of the commitment to the principles of liberty that was integral to popular politics across the anglophone world in the eighteenth century.[82]

NOTES

1. Clements to Newcastle, 8 December 1759 (BL, Newcastle papers, Add. Ms 32899 ff 385–8), my emphasis.
2. John to Dudley Ryder, 30 November 1754, 15 December 1755 in A.P.W. Malcomson (ed), *Irish official papers in Great Britain* (2 vols, Belfast, [1973]-90), ii, 54, 58.
3. William Molyneux, *The case of Ireland's being bound by acts of parliament in England, stated* (Dublin, 1698); J.R. Hill, 'Ireland without union: Molyneux and his legacy' in John Robertson (ed), *A Union for Empire: Political Thought and the British Union of 1707* (Cambridge, 1995), 280–1; Ian McBride, '"The common name of Irishman": Protestantism and patriotism in eighteenth-century Ireland' in Tony Claydon and Ian McBride (eds), *Protestantism and National Identity: Britain and Ireland, c. 1650-c.1850* (Cambridge, 1998), 243–5; J.A. Downie, *Jonathan Swift, Political Writer* (London, 1984), 240–3.
4. Examples of the use of the term in the 1720s can be located in the letters of Bishop Nicolson of Derry: Dublin Public Library, Wake papers, Ms 27, f. 365; also F.G. James, 'The Church of Ireland and the patriot movement in the late eighteenth century', *Éire-Ireland*, 17 no 2 (1982), 47.
5. Acheson to Dodington, 23 October 1735 in HMC, *Reports on various collections, vi: Eyre Matcham mss* (8 London, 1901–14), 64–5; James Kelly, 'Jonathan Swift and the Irish economy in the 1720s', *Eighteenth-Century Ireland*, 6 (1991), 7–36.

6. R.E. Burns, *Irish Parliamentary Politics in the Eighteenth Century, 1714–60* (2 vols, Washington, 1989–90), ii, 1–120; David Hayton, *Ruling Ireland, 1685–1742: Politics, Politicians and Parties* (Woodbridge, 2002).

7. Jacqueline Hill, *From Patriots to Unionists: Dublin Civic Politics and Irish Protestant Patriotism, 1660–1840* (Oxford, 1997), 103–4.

8. George Berkeley, *Maxims Concerning Patriotism* (Dublin, 1750); Henry St John, Viscount Bolingbroke, *Letters, on the spirit of patriotism on the idea of a patriot king: and on the state of parties, at the accession of King George the First* (Dublin, 1749).

9. John Digby to Robert French, 10 December 1751 (French papers, PRONI, T/3444/2).

10. Edward Willes' Legal and political reminiscences, 8–9 (Warwickshire Record Office, Willes papers). These papers are no longer in the Warwickshire Record Office.

11. The most recent engagement in this tradition is Neil Longley York, *Neither Kingdom nor Nation: the Irish Quest for Constitutional Rights 1698–1800* (Washington, 1994).

12. Richard Koebner, 'The early speeches of Henry Grattan', *Bulletin of the Institute of Historical Research* 30 (1957), 102–14; Gerard O'Brien, 'The Grattan mystique', *Eighteenth-Century Ireland*, 1 (1986), 177–94.

13. J.T. Leerssen, 'Anglo-Irish patriotism and its European context: notes towards a reassessment', *Eighteenth-Century Ireland*, 3 (1988), 7–24; McBride, ' "The common name of Irishman" ', 236–60; Stephen Small, 'The twisted roots of Irish patriotism: Anglo-Irish political thought in the late eighteenth century', *Éire-Ireland*, 35 (2001–1), 187–216.

14. M.R. O'Connell, *Irish Politics and Social Conflict in the Age of the American Revolution* (Philadelphia, 1965); Vincent Morley, *Irish Opinion and the American Revolution 1760–83* (Cambridge, 2002); Danny Mansergh, *Grattan's Failure: Parliamentary Opposition and the People in Ireland, 1779–1800* (Dublin, 2005).

15. Hill, *From Patriots to Unionists*.

16. S.J. Connolly, 'Precedent and principle: the patriots and their critics', in idem (ed), *Political Thought in Eighteenth-century Ireland* (Dublin, 2000), 130–58.

17. James Kelly, *Henry Flood: Patriots and Politics in Eighteenth-century Ireland* (Cork, 1998); idem, *Sir Edward Newenham MP, 1734–1814: Defender of the Protestant Constitution* (Dublin, 2006); idem, *Henry Grattan* (Dundalk, 1993); idem, 'Lord Charlemont's political career' in Michael McCarthy (ed), *Lord Charlemont and His Circle* (Dublin, 2002), 7–37; R.B. McDowell, *Grattan: a Life* (Dublin, 2001).

18. Ian McBride, *Scripture Politics: Ulster Presbyterians and Irish Radicalism in the Late Eighteenth Century* (Oxford, 1998), 123–33; James Kelly, 'The politics of Volunteering, 1779–93', *Irish Sword*, 22 (2000), 139–56; Padhraig Higgins, 'Bonfires, illuminations, and joy: celebratory street politics and uses of 'the nation' during the Volunteer movement', *Eire-Ireland* (2007), 173–206; B. Mac Suibhne, 'Whiskey, potatoes and true-born patriot paddies: Volunteering and the construction of the Irish nation in northwest Ulster, 1770–89' in Peter Jupp and Eoin Magennis (eds), *Crowds in Ireland, c. 1720–1920* (Basingstoke, 2000), 45–82.

19. McBride, 'The common name of Irishman', 237.

20. See Patrick Kelly, 'William Molyneux and the spirit of liberty in eighteenth-century Ireland', *Eighteenth-Century Ireland*, 3 (1988), 133–48.

21. McBride, 'The common name of Irishman', 248–53; Kelly, 'Interdenominational relations and religious toleration in eighteenth-century Ireland', *Eighteenth-Century Ireland*, 3 (1988), 39–67.

22. J.G. Simms, *Colonial Nationalism, 1698–1776* (Cork, 1976); T.W. Moody and W. E. Vaughan (eds), *A New History of Ireland, vol 4: the Eighteenth Century* (Oxford, 1986), chapters by Simms, McCracken, and McDowell.

23. For instances of the problematical usage of these and allied terms see J.C. Beckett, 'Literary life in eighteenth-century Ireland' in S. Dyrvik et al. (eds), *The Satellite State in the Seventeenth and Eighteenth Centuries* (Bergen, 1979), 159–60; Sean Murphy, 'The Dublin anti-union riots of 3 December 1759' in Gerard O'Brien (ed), *Parliament, Politics and People* (Dublin, 1988), 50.

24. Maurizio Viroli, *For Love of Country: an Essay on Patriotism and Nationalism* (Oxford, 1995); Joep Leerssen, *National Thought in Europe: a Cultural History* (Manchester, 2008).

25. As, for example, Kelly, *Henry Flood*.

26. Mac Suibhne, 'Volunteering'; Higgins, 'Bonfires, illuminations and joy'; Thomas Bartlett, 'A people made rather for copies than originals': the Anglo-Irish 1760–1800', *International History Review*, 12 (1990), 16–18.

27. Rev J. Burrows, Journal of a journey … to Ireland (PRONI, T/3551).

28. *Freeman's Journal*, 1 June 1765, 30 September 1766, 11 December 1770, 8 May, 12 June 1773, 21 April 1774, 18 February, 23 December 1777; *Londonderry Journal*, 13 July 1776.

29. For an authoritative account, see Eoin Magennis, *The Irish Political System 1740–1765: the Golden Age of the Undertakers* (Dublin, 2000), chapter 3.

30. D.W. Hayton, 'Anglo-Irish attitudes: changing perceptions of national identity among the Protestant ascendancy in Ireland, c. 1690–1750', *Studies in Eighteenth-Century Culture*, 17 (1987), 146–57.

31. Pakenham's essay on Ireland, [4] September 1755 (PRONI, Chatsworth papers, T/3158/852).

32. John to Dudley Ryder, c. February 1754 in Malcomson (ed), *Irish Official Papers*, ii, 52.

33. Quoted in Declan O'Donovan, 'The money bill dispute of 1753' (PhD thesis, UCD, 1973), 304.

34. The terms 'Irish interest', and its corollary 'English interest' are cited from the informative commentary on events provided by Bishop John Ryder: John to Dudley Ryder, 13 April 1752, February 1754, Dudley Ryder's diary, 29 November 1754 in Malcomson (ed), *Irish Official Papers*, ii, 33–4, 52, 54.

35. The so-called 'money bill dispute' that defined the power struggle between Boyle and his allies on the one side, and the duke of Dorset, Lord George Sackville, Primate Stone and the Ponsonbys on the other, took its name from the refusal of Boyle and his allies to countenance that the Crown could spend the surplus money in the Irish exchequer without parliamentary approval. It was a classic whig/county/patriot issue, and Boyle had chosen his ground carefully. He was enabled as a result to present himself as upholding national honour, without challenging the administration on a mainstream financial issue, which would be palpably less popular. For a full account see O'Donovan, 'The money bill dispute of 1753', passim; Magennis, *The Irish Political System 1740–1765*, chapters 3 and 4.

36. See James Kelly, 'Political publishing, 1700–1800' in Andrew Hadfield and Raymond Gillespie (eds), *The Irish Book in English, 1550–1800* (Oxford, 2006), 226–7.

37. *Universal Advertiser*, 23 September 1755.

38. John to Dudley Ryder, 20 May 1755 in Malcomson (ed), *Irish Official Papers*, ii, 55–6.

39. Ibid.

40. *Universal Advertiser*, 17 November, 4, 8, 11, 15, 22, 26, 29 December 1753, 1, 3, 4, 8, 19, 22, 26 January, 7, 14, 16 February, 1754.

41. Claims that 'no less than 300 different Patriot Clubs participated in the first anniversary celebrations of the defeat of the money bill must be taken at a severe discount, but the press reports do suggest they possessed general appeal (*Universal Advertiser*, 3, 7, 14, 21 December 1754, 4, 7, 25 January, 26 April, 3 May, 8 July, 5, 30 August, 2, 9, 13, 16, 23 September, 4 October, 15 November, 6, 30 December 1755).

42. Magennis, *The Irish Political System*, ch. 4.

43. Bob Harris, *Politics and the Nation: Britain in the Mid-eighteenth century* (Oxford, 2002), ch. 5; idem, 'The patriot clubs of the 1750s' in James Kelly and Martyn Powell (ed), *Clubs and Societies in Eighteenth-century Ireland* (Dublin, 2010), 224–43; Kelly, 'Political publishing', 225–6.

44. *Universal Advertiser*, 5, 30 August 1755, 4 June, 24 September, 15 October 1757.

45. *Universal Advertiser*, 24 December 1758, 29 September 1759, 6 December 1760; *Pue's Occurrences*, 13 January 1759.

46. Conway to Wilmot, 26, 29 October, 3 November 1755, 29 April 1756 (PRONI, Wilmot papers, T3019/2696, 2698, 2705, 2809); John to Dudley Ryder, 15 December 1755 in Malcomson (ed), *Irish Official Papers*, ii, 58; Willes's Legal and political reminiscences, 7–9.

47. Hill, *From Patriots to Unionists*, 124–37; Bedford to [?], 12 March 1761 (NAI, Index of departmental letters and papers 1760–89, ii, 20).

48. See E.M. Johnston-Liik, *History of the Irish Parliament 1692–1800* (6 vols, Belfast, 2002), sub nom; *Universal Advertiser*, 1 November 1760.

49. James Kelly, *Henry Flood*, 89ff; Pery was described as 'one of the best speakers in the House of Commons' in 1763 (Malcomson, (ed), *Irish Official Papers*, ii, 64).

50. John to Dudley Ryder, 17 November 1761, 17 November 1763 in Malcomson (ed), *Irish Official Papers*, ii, 63–4.

51. Ibid., 63.

52. *Public Gazetteer*, 3 January, 10 March 1761.

53. Kelly, *Henry Flood*, 88, 104; Seamus Cummins, 'Extra-parliamentary agitation in Dublin in the 1760s' in R.V. Comerford et al. (eds), *Religion, Conflict and Co-existence in Ireland* (Dublin, 1990), 118–33; *Freeman's Journal*, 21 January 1766, 22 December 1767; John to Dudley Ryder, 15 March 1766 in Malcomson (ed), *Eighteenth-century Irish Official Papers*, ii, 66–7.

54. Kelly, *Henry Flood*, 104–5; *Freeman's Journal*, 27 May 1766.

55. Alexander McAulay, *An inquiry into the legality of pensions on the Irish establishment* (Dublin, 1763); Kelly, *Henry Flood*, 138–41; Charles Lucas, *The rights and privileges of parliaments asserted upon constitutional principles: against the modern anti-constitutional claims of chief governors* (Dublin, 1770).

56. James Kelly, 'Political publishing, 1700–1800', 227–8.

57. *Freeman's Journal*, 17, 20, 24 September 1763, 3 July 1764, 1 June, 19 October 1765, 30 September 1766.

58. Kelly, 'Political publishing, 1700–1800', 228; Kelly, *Sir Edward Newenham MP, 1734–1814*, ch. 3; *Freeman's Journal*, 17 April, 8 May, 17 June 1773.

59. See Kelly, *Sir Edward Newenham*, ch. 3 for the fullest account to date of this attitude in Ireland.

60. *Freeman's Journal*, 19 October 1765.

61. Thomas Bartlett, 'The Townshend viceroyalty, 1767–72' in idem and D.W. Hayton (eds), *Penal Era and Golden Age* (Belfast, 1979), 88–112: Kelly, *Henry Flood*, 141–5; Lucas, *The rights and privileges of parliaments asserted*, passim.

62. Thomas Bartlett, 'Opposition in late eighteenth-century Ireland: the case of the Townshend viceroyalty', *Irish Historical Studies*, 22 (1981), 313–30.
63. Kelly, *Henry Flood*, ch. 4.
64. Ibid., ch. 5.
65. David Lammey, 'The growth of the 'Patriot Opposition' in Ireland during the 1770s', *Parliamentary History*, 7 (1988), 257–81.
66. James Kelly (ed), 'Review of the House of Commons, 1774', *Eighteenth-century Ireland*, 18 (2004), 163–210.
67. *Freeman's Journal*, 25 February 1775; James Kelly, 'Parliamentary reform in Ireland politics, 1760–90' in David Dickson et al. (eds), *The United Irishmen* (Dublin, 1993), 76–7.
68. James Kelly, 'Residential and non-residential lords lieutenant—the viceroyalty, 1703–1790' in Peter Gray and Olwen Purdue (eds), *The Irish Lord Lieutenant c. 1541–1922* (Dublin, 2012), 77–83.
69. St George to Hardwicke, 10 August 1778 (BL, Hardwicke papers, Add. MS 35615 f. 16); McBride, *Scripture politics*, 123–33.
70. St George to Hardwicke, 10 August 1778 (BL, Hardwicke papers, Add. MS 35615 f. 16).
71. Forbes to Shelburne, 2 December 1779 (BL, Bowood papers, B33 ff 9–12); Morley, *Irish Opinion*, 223–5, 231–40; Kelly, 'Elite political clubs'.
72. Forbes to Shelburne, 2 December 1779 (BL, Bowood papers, B33 ff 9–12).
73. Forbes to Shelburne, 4 February 1780 (BL, Bowood papers, B33 ff 13–20); Mansergh, *Grattan's Failure*, 45–6; Kelly, 'Elite political clubs'
74. James Kelly, *Prelude to Union: Anglo-Irish Politics in the 1780s* (Cork, 1992), ch. 2.
75. Forbes to Shelburne, 15 June 1782 (BL, Bowood papers, B33 f. 23).
76. Kelly, *Henry Flood*, 324–36; Peter Jupp, 'Earl Temple's viceroyalty and the question of renunciation', *Irish Historical Studies*, 17 (1971–2), 299–317.
77. Kelly, 'Parliamentary reform', 78–86.
78. *The Speeches of Henry Grattan* (4 vols, London, 1822), i, 102.
79. Kelly, *Henry Grattan*, 22–3.
80. Kelly, *Prelude to Union*, ch. 5; R.B. McDowell, *Ireland in the Age of Imperialism and Revolution, 1760–1801* (Oxford, 1979), 339–42.
81. Kelly, 'Elite political clubs'.
82. A theme discussed in James Kelly, "Era of liberty': the politics of civil and political rights in eighteenth-century Ireland' in Jack P. Greene (ed), *Exclusionary Empire: English Liberty Overseas, 1600–1900* (New York, 2010), 77–111.

Select Bibliography

Bartlett, Thomas 'Opposition in late eighteenth-century Ireland: the case of the Townshend viceroyalty', *Irish Historical Studies*, 22 (1981), 313–30.
Connolly, S.J., 'Precedent and principle: the patriots and their critics', in idem (ed), *Political Thought in Eighteenth-century Ireland* (Dublin, 2000), 130–58.
Harris, Bob 'The patriot clubs of the 1750s' in James Kelly and Martyn Powell (eds), *Clubs and Societies in Eighteenth-century Ireland* (Dublin, 2010), 224–43.
Higgins, Padhraig, *A Nation of Politicians: Gender, Patriotism, and Political Culture in Late Eighteenth-century Ireland* (Madison, WI, 2010).

Hill, J.R., 'Ireland without union: Molyneux and his legacy' in John Robertson (ed), *A Union for Empire: Political Thought and the British Union of 1707* (Cambridge, 1995), 271–96.

Kelly, James, *Prelude to Union: Anglo-Irish Politics in the 1780s* (Cork, 1992).

Kelly, James, *Henry Flood: Patriots and Politics in Eighteenth-century Ireland* (Cork, 1998).

Kelly, James, 'The politics of Volunteering, 1779–93', *Irish Sword*, 22 (2000), 139–56.

Kelly, James, *Sir Edward Newenham MP, 1734–1814: Defender of the Protestant Constitution* (Dublin, 2006).

Kelly, James, 'Elite political clubs' in James Kelly and Martyn Powell (ed), *Clubs and Societies in Eighteenth-century Ireland* (Dublin, 2010), 268–72.

Kelly, James, '"Era of liberty": the politics of civil and political rights in eighteenth-century Ireland' in Jack P. Greene (ed), *Exclusionary Empire: English Liberty Overseas, 1600–1900* (New York, 2010), 77–111.

Kelly Patrick, 'William Molyneux and the spirit of liberty in eighteenth-century Ireland', *Eighteenth-Century Ireland*, 3 (1988), 133–48.

Lammey, David, 'The growth of the "Patriot Opposition" in Ireland during the 1770s', *Parliamentary History*, 7 (1988), 257–81.

Leerssen, J.T., 'Anglo-Irish patriotism and its European context: notes towards a reassessment', *Eighteenth-Century Ireland*, 3 (1988), 7–24.

McBride, Ian *Scripture Politics: Ulster Presbyterians and Irish Radicalism in the Late Eighteenth century* (Oxford, 1998).

McBride, Ian '"The common name of Irishman": Protestantism and patriotism in eighteenth-century Ireland' in Tony Claydon and Ian McBride (eds), *Protestantism and National Identity: Britain and Ireland, c. 1650-c. 1850* (Cambridge, 1998), 236–61.

McDowell, R.B., *Grattan: a Life* (Dublin, 2001).

Mansergh, Danny, *Grattan's Failure: Parliamentary Opposition and the People in Ireland, 1779–1800* (Dublin, 2005).

Morley, Vincent *Irish Opinion and the American Revolution 1760–83* (Cambridge, 2002).

Simms, J.G. *Colonial Nationalism, 1698–1776* (Cork, 1976).

Small, Stephen 'The twisted roots of Irish patriotism: Anglo-Irish political thought in the late eighteenth century', *Éire-Ireland*, 35 (2001-1), 187–216.

CHAPTER 25

···

RISING AND UNION, 1791–1801

···

PATRICK GEOGHEGAN

SPEAKING at Bodenstown, County Kildare, by the grave of Theobald Wolfe Tone, on Sunday, 17 October 2004, the Taoiseach Bertie Ahern linked the principles of the United Irishmen with the democratic republicanism of the modern Irish state. He noted correctly that the United Irishmen had started out as constitutional nationalists, and had only become revolutionaries when forced underground and when 'all meaningful reform was refused'.[1] Thus he attempted to argue that its republicanism had been inherently democratic and, 'so too, is our republicanism'. It was a nuanced speech, which attempted to unite two of the competing traditions on the island—the constitutional nationalist and the revolutionary republican—and bring an end to the false dichotomy between them. But Ahern was also keen to include a third tradition, often ignored in nationalist analyses, by linking Tone with Irish unionism. He noted that Tone was critical of the papacy and of certain of the formal aspects of Catholicism, a viewpoint which was 'more typical of a perspective of unionism'. Tone, the man who had attempted to substitute the names of Catholic, Protestant, and Dissenter for the common name of Irishman, was the perfect person to highlight the complexity in the Irish political experience. And it was the turbulent final decade of the eighteenth century that these complexities first became apparent in Ireland, as the differing traditions emerged formally, clashed violently, and then rested uneasily.

The formation of the United Irishmen in 1791 is rightly seen as marking a major turning point in Irish history. And the role of Tone is central to that story. As Sean Ó Faolain noted in his biography of Tone in 1937, 'If Tone did not, in his lifetime, achieve greatly, he started much. Without him, republicanism in Ireland would virtually have no tradition'.[2] It was he who gave the name to the society, and it was his pamphlet, *An argument on behalf of the Catholics of Ireland,* which did so much to generate public interest in the issues the society believed in. Tone considered his pamphlet to be his greatest contribution to Irish history, as he set out to show why reform in Ireland would fail, and would deserve to fail, unless it included the Catholics of Ireland. Since 1690, Ireland had been governed in part by playing the different religious denominations off against each other, exploiting existing suspicions and prejudices. Protestants feared Catholics bearing arms and any threat to their civil superiority; Presbyterians despised popish authoritarianism and believed Catholics were mentally enslaved. Completing the fear triangle, there was the Protestant belief that Presbyterianism represented fanaticism and disloyalty, and this explained why some of the penal laws were also extended to include Dissenters. Tone's mission was to undermine these divisions and show why 'an edifice of freedom' could never be built 'on a foundation of monopoly'.[3] His genius lay in how he developed the idea that Catholics had a capacity for liberty, and in how he popularized it.

Completed on 1 August 1791, and published three weeks later, Tone's pamphlet was written in a conversational style and was on sale for only a shilling. By the end of the year it had sold 6000 copies, making it an instant bestseller. Dr Hugh McDermot, a leading Catholic activist, declared that he had never read a better pamphlet and insisted 'It should become the manual of every person who is worthy of being an Irishman.'[4] An official in Dublin Castle sent a copy to Whitehall as 'a pretty specimen of the sentiments of Irish reformers'.[5] More importantly, it was read widely and discussed. Tone's anti-Catholic prejudices were evident in the pamphlet, despite his claims on their behalf. He argued that political freedom would lead Irish Catholics to abandon their religion, and their petty superstitions would gradually die away. He discussed how French Catholics had burned the pope in effigy and wondered 'who will now attend to the rusty and extinguished thunderbolts of the Vatican?'[6] By raising this question he either deliberately or accidentally appealed to a prophetic strain in Presbyterianism which believed that events in France might someday result in the downfall of the pope and the entire Catholic religion.

On Tuesday, 18 October 1791, the inaugural meeting of the United Irishmen was held in Belfast, with the Dublin society formed a few weeks later on 9 November. Dublin, in this period, was a city of clubs. There were so many opportunities for socialization and engagement, with clubs for drinking, eating, hunting, gambling, smoking, singing, and politics. Lawyers flocked to join the United Irishmen, and one-fifth of the original membership was from that profession. When the United Irishmen was declared illegal in 1795 and forced underground, it continued by using these other clubs for its own objectives, infiltrating and colonizing them. There were so many different pretexts which could be used for meetings: cockfights, horse races, wrestling matches, dinner parties, turf-cuttings, Masonic lodges. Indeed, the organization of a secret United Irishman lottery was seen as undermining the official state lottery and, as a result, the institutions of the state.[7] It has been estimated that Dublin had as many as 1300 pubs in the 1790s, and these were also used to discuss political events and recruit. United Irishmen orders forbade excessive drinking and visible signs of drunkeness and these orders were largely obeyed, confirming government fears that discipline was good, and that they were well organized. The loyalist M.P. Sir Richard Musgrave became increasingly anxious in 1798 precisely because the people seemed to be remaining sober.[8] However, the United Irishmen's belief that a cultural reawakening would undermine support for the government never materialized and seemed to demonstrate that there was more support for the state than they believed.

Confusion over the meaning of this cultural reawakening was also reflected in the confusion over what the French Revolution had meant for Ireland. For Thomas Addis

Emmet, a prominent United Irishman, the revolution was important as an example rather than for anything practical. This was because the revolution seemed to contradict the Whig idea that the Catholics were incapable of appreciating liberty. For others, the revolution had annihilated history, therefore the United Irishmen felt confident to repudiate the past and ask whether they were 'forever to walk like beasts of prey over the fields which these ancestors stained with blood?'[9] The enlightenment notion that knowledge, intelligence, truth, and reason were transforming the people was prevalent; as an editorial in the *Northern Star*, the newspaper of the United Irishmen, claimed: 'The present is an age of revolution. Everything is changing, every system is improving and mankind appears to become more wise and virtuous as they become more informed.'[10]

The influence of the American as well as the French Revolution was also clear, but again there was no certainty over what republicanism meant in general or what it meant for Ireland in particular. Tone's career epitomized these tensions and confusions, and these tensions have been reflected in the historiography. As a young Dublin Protestant, Tone was enamoured of the military life and attempted to get out of studying at Trinity College Dublin in the early 1780s so that he could enlist in the British Army and fight against the American colonists. Training as a lawyer in London, he was still attracted to the military life and wrote to the British Prime Minister, William Pitt the Younger, offering to establish a military colony in the South Seas Island (Hawaii) and embark on a privateering war with Spanish America. This has led Tom Dunne to argue that Tone was merely a frustrated imperialist, a man in search of a mission who would have been as content in a British uniform as a French (or Irish) one.[11] Pitt never responded to the letter, and Tone returned to Ireland attempting (and failing) to make an impression at the bar and becoming a political adviser and pamphleteer for the newly formed Irish Whig party. But here he became disillusioned with the slow pace of political reform, his failure to be offered a safe seat in the 1790 general election, and the widespread opposition to Catholic relief. Thomas Bartlett has offered a different way of understanding Tone's actions in this period, suggesting that his actions reflected a commitment to a more classical republicanism. He has also challenged the view of Tone as an inconsistent, self-interested romantic by arguing that, as Irish politics changed in the 1790s, so too did Tone, and to expect otherwise is to misunderstand the evolution of an individual's political thinking in reactions to events.[12] Republicanism and separatism were the almost inevitable consequences of his thinking, as evidenced in his 1790 pamphlet *Spanish War!* which challenged the idea of Ireland's foreign policy necessarily matching Britain's, and which represented a viewpoint that prompted Sir Henry Cavendish, a founder of the Whig Club, to exclaim that, if the author was serious, he ought to be hanged.[13]

Part of the problem in understanding Tone is that he attempted to rewrite his own political biography, and by leaving extensive journals and memoirs for publication, he helped create his own myth. At his trial for treason in 1798, he claimed to have been a separatist from his earliest days, and from his youth to have 'regarded the connection between Ireland and Great Britain as the curse of the Irish nation'.[14] This was clearly not the case, but it became easier to cast Tone as 'the father of Irish republicanism' without teasing out his role in its conception.[15]

While the French Revolution weakened important cultural barriers in the 1790s, there were also political implications. Britain's declaration of war with France in 1793 brought it into a long and costly war with what it considered to be a rogue state, and this accelerated the demands for both constitutional and radical reform in Ireland. It also prompted the British government to bring in another Catholic relief bill, as it had done in previous wartime crises such as 1778 and 1782, to purchase the loyalty of the Irish Catholics and encourage Catholic recruitment in the war effort. The problem was that the Irish parliament, which since 1782 considered itself to be legislatively independent, resented this obvious demonstration that Britain still decided how Ireland was governed. The 1793 relief bill, which gave Catholics with a forty-shilling freehold the right to vote but not to sit in parliament, passed in the Irish parliament despite the opposition of the influential Speaker of the House of Commons, John Foster, who spoke and voted against it, and the Lord Chancellor, John FitzGibbon, who spoke against it but voted for it. In a chilling speech in the House of Lords on 10 January 1793, FitzGibbon argued that, if Catholics were given full political rights, it would endanger the connection with Britain and ensure that the matter must 'once more be put to the issue of the sword'.[16] The 1793 measure had the unintended result of alienating the Protestant establishment from the British government, convincing it that it would have to look to itself for its protection, without gaining the loyalty and gratitude of the Irish Catholics. Recognizing this in London, Pitt conceded privately in 1792 that there was no 'ultimate solution' but a union of the two countries and he repeated in 1793 that 'the idea of union' was something that had been long on his mind.[17] The granting of relief in 1793, though necessary because of imperial considerations, meant a massive loss of prestige for the Irish parliament, a loss which eventually was to prove fatal. The breakdown of order began soon after. A Militia Act was passed in 1793 which allowed Catholics to join and assist in the defence of the country, but there was a fear that, as during the American War of Independence, the regular army would be sent abroad in times of crisis. Anti-militia riots raged in every county, and there was a hardening of political attitudes.

The problem was that there was no agreement about what constituted the Irish nation. For some Irish Protestants, it meant defending the Irish parliament and the measure of legislative independence which had been won in 1782. For others, the key thing was the connection with the British Crown no matter what the cost in terms of domestic prestige. The Irish Protestants knew they were a minority, but they claimed to be the Irish nation and the people of Ireland and knew that these claims depended on destruction of Catholic power. As the political crisis escalated in the 1790s, there was increasing unease about what this meant for the Protestant nation and what sacrifices would have to be made to survive. For Henry Grattan, the leading Whig M.P. the solution was limited rights for Catholics, and recognition of the legislative dominance of the Irish parliament. For John FitzGibbon, the Lord Chancellor and leading government supporter in the country, the solution was a stronger connection with Britain (he gradually became a supporter of union in the 1790s) and a resolution to do whatever it took to prevent annihilation at the hands of the Catholics.[18]

FitzGibbon's investigation into the United Irishmen, the Defenders (a radical agrarian society with connections to the United Irishmen), the Catholic Committee, and any other organization which seemed to pose a threat to the existing order eventually resulted in the suppression of the society in 1795. The Rev Jackson had been sent on a mission by the French government to investigate the possibility of opening a new front in Ireland, but he was betrayed by a spy and captured in early 1794. A memorandum on Ireland, prepared by Tone, was found on his person, and Tone was implicated in his treason. Avoiding prosecution by agreeing to leave the country, Tone went first to the United States before heading in secret to France. The United Irishmen were suppressed soon after. This marked the point that Tone became a fully-fledged separatist. Before leaving Ireland, he went to McArt's Fort, overlooking Belfast, and made a vow 'never to desist in our efforts until we had subverted the authority of England over our country and asserted her independence'.[19]

In 1794, political events in Britain changed the power balance in Ireland. To strengthen his ministry, Pitt decided to form a coalition with those Whigs who had split with Charles James Fox over the war with France. The duke of Portland was installed as home secretary and a sympathetic peer with no political experience, Earl Fitzwilliam, was named as Lord Lieutenant for Ireland. The Fitzwilliam viceroyalty lasted less than two months, but it has been credited with further polarizing events in Ireland. W.E.H. Lecky described it as 'a tragic turning point' in Irish history, but the reality is that the crisis was merely a catalyst which speeded up the disintegration of the political structures which had been coming for some time. Studies of the Fitzwilliam viceroyalty have usually looked at the crisis from the point of view of Fitzwilliam and the British Whigs, or the key Irish figures on both sides, and there remain many questions that need to be answered about what Pitt's ministry was thinking in this period.[20]

Certainly it can be argued that Fitzwilliam was correct in his boasting that his appointment represented a major shift in policy towards the Irish Catholics. The problem is that Fitzwilliam believed that this shift was explicit, whereas Pitt chose to see it as a more cautious and implicit signalling to the Catholics that something would be done for them. In other words, Pitt believed that appointing Fitzwilliam was enough in the short term to placate the Catholics, and that a decision on emancipation could be postponed indefinitely, and certainly until peacetime. But change was not only dramatic; it was immediate. Fitzwilliam arrived in Ireland on 4 January 1795, and when parliament resumed on 22 January all the major opposition figures, Henry Grattan, John Philpot Curran, and George and William Ponsonby, took their seats on the treasury benches. Everyone assumed that Grattan was the spokesman of the new administration, so when he introduced a new Catholic Relief Bill a few weeks later, it was seen as having the support of the Lord Lieutenant. Certainly Fitzwilliam had done nothing to dampen expectations, noting on his arrival that he 'trembled about the Catholics'. Inexperienced and naive, Fitzwilliam fell victim to the flattery and insinuations of the Irish Whig circle (which included his relations) and moved too quickly to implement his agenda of bringing in emancipation and rooting out corruption. This meant sacking office-holders who were loyal to the British government and replacing them with Irish Whigs, in the belief that if you controlled the patronage of the country you could make the parliament do whatever you wanted. Arthur Wolfe, the Attorney General, was persuaded to resign in return for a promise of a peerage for his wife and a judgeship for himself, allowing George Ponsonby to succeed him. John Beresford, a key member of the inner cabinet which had advised previous administrations, was dismissed, as was Edward Cooke, the Castle under-secretary whose expertise and influence was enormous. Showing all the judgement that Fitzwilliam lacked, Cooke did not respond publicly, but sent a letter to Lord Westmorland, the former Lord Lieutenant, which he knew would be shown to Pitt, describing how the changes represented, 'in two words, a complete revolution'.[21] Watching in horror from London, George Canning, the friend and protégé of Pitt, described it as one 'continued job, covered with the thin pretence of punishing jobbers'.[22]

However, it was the decision to raise the Catholic question, without consulting the British government, that killed Fitzwilliam's career. In one of the most misjudged acts in Irish political history, Fitzwilliam wrote to the cabinet to explain that he could not defer the Catholic Relief Bill and that if he did not hear back immediately he would assume that this silence represented support for the measure. It normally took four days for a letter to reach Dublin from London, so a response would have taken time in any case, but a storm delayed communications and the delay was fatal. Fitzwilliam learned too late that he was acting without any support and his position became untenable. He was dismissed on 24 February, with Pitt leaving the decision to Portland, who had no hesitation making it. Returning to London, humiliated and feeling betrayed by his former friends, Fitzwilliam incautiously published two justifications of his actions which only provided further proof of his inadequacies.

It was in the wake of the Fitzwilliam debacle that Pitt wrote of having to renew 'acquaintances with the unlucky subject of Ireland'.[23] In years to come this sound bite would be gladly seized upon by scholars of the period to demonstrate that Pitt had no interest in Irish affairs and avoided this 'unlucky subject' whenever he could.[24] But the letter was written in the heat of an agonizing political crisis (he considered Fitzwilliam's actions to be 'the strongest instance of the breach of political faith which had ever occurred to him') and it did not reflect the amount of time he had committed to Irish affairs since the beginning of his premiership in December 1783.[25] True, it only represented a small fraction of his energies, but that was only as it should have been, given that he was prime minister of Britain and was required to deal with a range of domestic as well as imperial concerns. The Pitt archive in Cambridge University, much neglected, offers a way of examining Pitt's priorities in this period, and within a context of wider national and international concerns.

Pitt was certainly aware that appointing Fitzwilliam meant putting Catholic emancipation on the table. In late 1794, he met with Fitzwilliam, Grattan, and the Ponsonbys at Portland's house and afterwards discussed matters in private with Grattan. Grattan later claimed that he left this meeting convinced that Catholic emancipation would be granted in the new administration, though not on the initiative of the ministers, and that the government would yield if pressed. But it is more likely that Pitt left the meeting concerned that Fitzwilliam would act precipitously, for on 15 November 1794 he arranged for a formal agreement on what would happen, insisting that FitzGibbon would not be dismissed, and that there would be no new system for Ireland. The disjuncture between Pitt's understanding of this meeting and Fitzwilliam's was at the heart of the crisis, and it is still not clear whether Fitzwilliam had just heard what he wanted to hear, or if he was sacrificed when the new policy ran into difficulties. Fitzwilliam never forgave Portland and claimed that either he had been 'the most wild, rash, unfaithful servant' or else he had been abandoned 'in the most shameful manner [by] his friend'.[26] But what was certain was that the time for compromise had passed, and the age of action had arrived.

The first attempt to establish an independent Irish republic was also the most dramatic. Tone himself claimed that the failed Bantry Bay invasion was the nearest English escape since the Spanish Armada, and it certainly represented one of the greatest gambles in Irish history. The plan was to send a French fleet in the middle of winter to Ireland, evading the British blockade, and land with a French army. Following this, the expectation was that the United Irishmen would join the French, the Catholics in the militia would defect, and Dublin would be captured. Ireland would then be used as a base to invade Britain, knocking it out of the war or forcing a peace treaty. These expectations were considerable, but the French were convinced by the persuasive Wolfe Tone, who spoke with a greater confidence about conditions in Ireland than he must have felt. For their part, the British were convinced that the French would never have the audacity to launch a winter invasion, and, even after the fleet left Brest, remained convinced it was heading for Portugal. Tone had wanted to land in Leinster or Ulster, where there were most Defenders, while the French preferred Galway Bay, but Bantry Bay was chosen in the end, its proximity to Cork which supplied the British navy a key advantage.[27]

The invasion fleet comprised seventeen ships of the line, thirteen frigates, and twenty transports, with 13500 experienced troops under General Lazare Hoche, the twenty-eight-year-old general who was considered France's brightest military prospect. A fog helped the fleet evade the British blockade at Brest when they set sail on 15 December 1796, but once at sea French naval ineptitude, coupled with French suspicions of their own commanders, combined with the weather to disastrous effect. Hoche's own ship, the *Fraternité,* sailed into the Atlantic and was lost for the engagement, with Tone's 'Addresses to the people of Ireland' onboard. An indication of how little faith the military had in its own admirals is that they were all put on the same ship, and to make matters worse it was one of the ships that sailed off in the wrong direction. It is also an indication of Tone's inferior position that he was put on board the *Indomitable* with the majors, not alongside Hoche on the flagship. By the time Tone reached Bantry Bay on 23 December, the ship had been separated from the fleet four times, and only thirty-five ships and approximately 6400 soldiers had made it there. The weather had proven to be both friend and foe, but at Bantry it offered no help. Storm conditions— compared to a hurricane by one English officer in Limerick who had experience of the West Indies—prevented a landing as the French waited impatiently for the weather to turn. On 27 December, the mission was abandoned and the ships set sail for France. For the entire period the fleet had been in the bay not a single British ship had attempted to intercept them, and no soldiers had arrived on land. The lack of a response did not inspire confidence. General Dalrymple in Cork admitted that he would not have put up a fight, but would just have made a diversion to allow his army to escape. General Carhampton, the commander-in-chief, conceded that both Cork and Limerick would have fallen to the French. But the truth is that it was as much an escape for the French as it was for the British. If the British fleet had arrived, it would have blockaded the French in the bay and would have destroyed or captured the thirty-five ships which had made it there, striking a massive blow to the French war effort. But instead, the focus was on how close the French had come to landing, and it encouraged a genuine sense of terror among loyalists.

It is still unclear about how many of Tone's predictions would have come true had the landing been successful. Following the near escape of Bantry, the government clamped down on the militia, flogging any suspected troublemakers and terrorizing the regiments until their loyalty was in no doubt. But December 1796 was a very different time, and it is possible that the French force could have been added to considerably by Irish defections. Whether the French promises to Tone would have been honoured is a different question and much of the debate around 1798 also centres on this question.[28] A direct consequence of the failed invasion was a decision taken by the French to wait in future until an Irish rebellion had broken out before getting involved.[29]

Earlier in the year, in March 1796, the cabinet had considered asking the king to veto the Insurrection Act which Lord Camden, Fitzwilliam's reactionary successor, had directed through parliament. This was an extraordinary step, but there was a feeling that Camden had gone too far, making oath-administering a capital crime, and oath-taking a transportable offence, and allowing courts and magistrates to proclaim martial law and send men to the fleet on suspicion alone. At the time, Portland expressed his astonishment 'that this was necessary', but, following Bantry, any hesitation was removed and the Irish administration was given a free hand to terrorize the country into tranquillity.[30] The big question surrounding the 1798 rebellion, and which has still not been satisfactorily answered, is whether this policy of terror in 1797–98 provoked the country into a series of mass uprisings, or whether it succeeded in limiting the extent of the violence and preventing a larger, more effective rebellion.

The role of the Defenders in this increasingly radicalized world remains a complex one. They had their origins in County Armagh in the 1780s, but spread throughout the rest of the country in the following decade. They were vocal in complaining about tithes, taxes, and rents, with their anti-Protestant slogans and support for Revolutionary France terrifying Dublin Castle. The belief that the Defenders had found common cause with the United Irishmen, and perhaps had even become subsumed into their membership, created further demands for counter-insurgency measures to be taken.[31] This security dilemma created a momentum for harsh action in the wake of the failed Bantry Bay landing.

General Gerard Lake, an experienced campaigner in the French wars, was given responsibility in 1797 to pacify Ulster, the most troublesome province. Infamous for his cruelty, he was ordered by Camden, the Lord Lieutenant, to do whatever was necessary to disarm Ulster, and advised not to allow the 'cause of justice to be frustrated by delicacy'.[32]

The crackdown on the militia proved particularly effective. To make a public example, four Catholics in the Monaghan militia, whose loyalty was questioned, were paraded in a wagon for ten miles around Belfast and then shot by firing squad. Determined to prove it could now be trusted, the very next day the Monaghan militia raided the offices of the *Northern Star* in Belfast and destroyed its printing press. The United Irishman paper never reopened. During all of this, the United Irishmen attempted to keep their heads down and wait for a French invasion. A policy of assassination was adopted and informers and magistrates were targeted. One informer in Wexford was murdered, as were his wife and daughter, and, to emphasize the point, his dog.[33] The Orange Order, which had been founded in 1795, was also used to terrify Catholics. Fake oaths were distributed as propaganda, claiming that its members wanted to exterminate all the Catholics of Ireland. 1798 became the year of the great fear in Ireland. For Protestants, it heralded a return to 1641 and the portents of a Catholic conspiracy to massacre them in their beds. For Catholics, it seemed that there was no escape from the terror of torture, house burnings, and death. In this context, the atrocities on both sides in the 1798 rebellion are more easily understood, as the fears on both sides intersected at the point of pre-emptive and retaliatory violence.

Loyalists demanded a free hand and the declaration of martial law, but General Abercromby, the new commander-in-chief, refused. Matters came to a head following the rape of a Catholic witness by two officers. Disgusted with the brutality of his own troops, Abercromby issued a general order on 26 February 1798 declaring that the army was in a state of licentiousness which rendered it formidable to anyone but the enemy. He was immediately dismissed and replaced by Lake. This was a misjudgement by Pitt, who mistakenly believed that Lake was 'brave, active and I believe, popular'.[34] The change meant that Lake's Ulster policy was now extended throughout the whole country. There were two major problems with the British strategy. The first was that viewing Ireland in the context of what was happening on the Continent meant the adoption of a strategy that was to prove disastrous; in the words of one of Lake's subordinates, it meant 'namely spreading devastation through the most disaffected parts'.[35] This meant indiscriminate pitch-capping, house burnings, floggings, and mass arrests, all aimed at recovering weapons and intimidating the population into submission. As Pitt admitted to some Irish visitors, 'terror could only be suppressed by the strongest terror'. The second problem with the British strategy was that it sought to provoke an open eruption of violence, believing that this was the only way of crushing the rebellion once and for all. For this reason it would be a mistake to see the 1798 rebellion as only beginning on the night of 23 May. As far as Dublin Castle was concerned, the country was in a state of rebellion from March and open conflict was welcomed as an opportunity to bring it to an end. As Edward Cooke insisted, 'If you look at the accounts that 200 000 men are sworn in a conspiracy, how could that conspiracy be cleared without a burst?'[36]

The United Irishmen directory was arrested on 12 March and martial law was declared throughout the country on 30 March. Lord Edward Fitzgerald, the only major leader still free, was captured and fatally wounded on 19 May, his death a massive blow for the rebellion. It was believed that his name alone would raise an army, and his death probably ensured that Dublin remained quiet. A question can then be asked about why the rebellion was limited to three distinct geographical areas: Ulster; the south-east of Ireland; and, later, the west of Ireland. This could be read as a reflection of the success of the government's policy of open terror and intelligence gathering, which prevented violence in every county. The alternative view is that the rebellion was forced on the people, bore little resemblance to the aims of the United Irishmen, and perhaps should not even be called a United Irishmen rebellion. Thomas Pakenham's *The Year of Liberty*, which remains the standard sole-authored, single-volume study of the rebellion despite being first published in 1969, developed this thesis and suggested that brave, fanatical, and undisciplined mobs joined in the fighting as a reaction to the government's policy of terror.[37] This was challenged by L.M. Cullen in 1987, who suggested that the most active areas in Wexford in 1798 were the areas which were most politicized and which had the largest degree of United Irishmen activity.[38] Despite being developed by Daniel Gahan and Kevin Whelan, this thesis is still unproven and the motivations of the rebels in 1798 remain indistinct.[39]

In Wexford, the rebels won some important initial victories, notably at Oulart Hill on 27 May, Enniscorthy on 28 May, and right up to the capture of Wexford. Some historians like Kevin Whelan and Brian Ó Cleirigh have claimed that a Wexford Republic was established following this victory, but others like Tom Dunne and Roy Foster have challenged this view, pointing to the lack of a single piece of documentary evidence.[40] The failure to capture New Ross proved costly as it would have spread the rebellion to the south. By the time an attempt was made, the town had been fortified and the attack was repulsed. It was following this defeat that the rebel atrocity at Scullabogue took place, with the rebels murdering one hundred Protestant prisoners (and their Catholic servants) by piking some and burning the majority in a barn. On 21 June, the rebels met Lake's army at Vinegar Hill and crumbled under the heavy artillery barrage in a two-hour battle. This brought an end to the rebellion in the south. Afterwards, a second rebel atrocity was committed, with seventy prisoners piked to death at Wexford Bridge.

One of the great ironies of the rebellion is that in Ulster the rebels were mainly Presbyterian and it was the largely Catholic militia which defeated them. Following the end of the 1798 rebellion, and thanks in part to the propagandizing of Musgrave who devoted only a small fraction of his massive history of the 1798 rebellion to the events in Ulster (twelve pages on Ulster, six hundred on the rest of the country), it was easy to portray the rising as a largely Catholic and sectarian affair.[41] As reports of Scullabogue and clerical involvement in the rebellion were circulated, the Ulster Presbyterians came to reject the principles of the United Irishmen altogether. Their subsequent support for the connection with the Crown crystallized around the Act of Union and all that it represented.

Upon hearing news of the outbreak of the rebellion, on 28 May 1798, Pitt made two important decisions. The first was to remove Earl Camden as Lord Lieutenant and replace him with someone who could control the violence of the loyalists as well as crush the rebellion. The second was to press immediately for a legislative union. The rebellion had confirmed his view that the experiment of legislative independence had failed and that the Irish parliament had proven itself incompetent to govern the country and keep things tranquil. Pitt's chosen successor was Lord Cornwallis, the imperial trouble-shooter who had surrendered at Yorktown in 1781, and who had twice turned down the job because of his sympathies for the Catholics. His willingness to accept the double role of Lord Lieutenant and commander-in-chief in 1798 showed that British policy had shifted on the Catholic question and that something would now be done on the issue. As far as Pitt was concerned, there was little danger in granting full emancipation within an imperial parliamentary framework, and the union represented a perfect opportunity to bring about long-term and long desired change in Ireland.[42] When Cornwallis arrived in Ireland, he put an immediate end to the house burnings and murders that had virtually become official policy, earning himself the derisory nickname of 'Croppy Wallis' because of his alleged sympathies for the rebels ('the Croppies'). He was horrified that 'universal rape and robbery' seemed to be legal throughout the whole country, and admitted that if putting an end to this was a crime, then 'I freely acknowledge my guilt'.[43]

The final phase of the rebellion began on 22 August, when a small French force under General Humbert landed near Killala in County Mayo. Humbert had hoped to be joined by further French forces, but was to be disappointed, and he was disappointed further by the small amount of native support. Disgusted with the Irish who did join, Humbert was reported to have said that he would have kept one third of them and shot the rest. Encountering Lake's army at Castlebar, Humbert famously put the British Army to rout (this soon became known as 'the races of Castlebar') but, although some Irish militia deserted and joined the French, the country did not re-ignite into rebellion. Cornwallis immediately set out with 20 000 men to intercept the French and the two mismatched armies met at Ballinamuck, in County Leitrim, on 8 September. After a short exchange of fire the French surrendered, leaving their Irish allies to be hunted down and killed where they stood. The French had expected to find a country in open rebellion and were disillusioned to find 'only ragamuffins', which explained their reluctance to prolong the campaign.[44]

Before news of Humbert's surrender reached France, Wolfe Tone and an even smaller French force set out for Ulster. Once again bad weather disrupted his plans, and his ship, the *Hoche,* arrived three weeks late at Lough Swilly, off the coast of Donegal. After a furious six-hour battle at sea, where Tone refused repeated offers to escape, he was captured. Upon being put in chains on shore he is alleged to have claimed that 'Mr Pitt is mad if he does not attempt a Union; and the French are mad if they don't invade before it is achieved.'[45] Brought to Dublin, he was tried by court martial on 10 November 1798 and found guilty of treason. Refused permission to be executed by firing squad, as befitted an officer in the French Army, he was sentenced to be hanged and beheaded. Taking a blade to his own throat in his prison cell, he committed suicide, though the attempt was botched and it took him a full week to die. His final words were, 'What should I wish to live for?'[46]

At his trial, Tone had spoken of his regret that atrocities had been committed during the rebellion. But in years to come, this would be the most disputed part of the entire history of the rebellion. Nationalist historians attempted to downplay the rebel atrocities, such as Scullabogue and Wexford Bridge, and instead create a narrative of an heroic struggle against foreign oppression. Revisionist historians for their part overplayed the significance of these atrocities and attempted to view the rebellion as a bloody, sectarian embarrassment. In the contested ground of the 1798 rebellion the real story was lost. 1798 represented a double conflict, superimposed on a single island. It was both a civil war, with loyalists fighting against nationalists, and also part of an international conflict, with Britain and France continuing their titanic conflict on Irish soil.

The role of religion in the conflict is an area which still divides. In the nineteenth century, the 'faith and fatherland' interpretation of Fr Patrick Kavanagh, which had priests like Fr John Murphy leading the rebellion in Wexford, rested uneasily enough alongside the sectarian histories of arch-loyalists like Richard Musgrave.[47] But for the bicentenary of the rebellion, in 1998, both these interpretations were neglected by nationalists in favour of an idealized account of national self-determination which downplayed any clerical involvement. It was emphasized that only 70 priests, out of 1800 in the country, had sided with the rebels, and these had been described by the Bishop of Ferns 'as the very faeces of the church'.[48] But given that the rebellion was confined to a relatively narrow geographical area, this figure of seventy could be considered remarkably high, and it is certainly plausible that a nationwide rebellion would have seen significant clerical involvement.

The rebellion failed because the counties did not act in unison, were easily sealed off, and because, by and large, Catholic Ireland sided with the government. But the terror of the rebellion was seized upon by the government to persuade the Irish Protestant elite to support a union, knowing that Catholic Ireland, broken and subdued, would be unable to resist. The original idea was to appoint commissioners in both countries to treat for a union, along the lines of the Scottish union of 1707, with Catholic emancipation a part of the arrangement. The British exchequer was already stretched to breaking point by the demands of the war with France so reckless expenditure was discouraged, and the union was to pass with as little extra expense as possible.

This meant no compensation for borough proprietors, who viewed the seats they controlled as property, and made gaining their support unlikely. Circumstances were to derail these good intentions. First, after a meeting between Pitt and the Lord Chancellor, the Earl of Clare (formerly John FitzGibbon), in October 1798, the Catholic component of the union was dropped after Clare made it clear that it would otherwise be opposed and rejected. Next, when the Irish House of Commons met on 22 January 1799, there was a concerted attack on the principle of union, which had been mentioned in the king's address. Government support haemorrhaged as M.P.s deserted through a mixture of self-interest, national pride, and because the arguments in favour of a union had been so badly presented. All the best speakers were on the opposition side, with William Plunket and George Ponsonby taking turns to taunt and humiliate the youthful chief secretary, Lord Castlereagh, whose inexperience had exposed the weakness in the government's position. Mobs took to the street in Dublin to celebrate the defeat of the union, unionists had their windows broken, and there were so many bonfires that only heavy rainfall prevented serious damage to the city after they began to spread.[49]

Regrouping after the humiliating defeat, the British government considered dismissing Cornwallis (whose unpopularity with the loyalists ever since the rebellion hampered discussions) and Castlereagh (whose coldness and inexperience were serious deficiencies in someone who was responsible for creating and managing a majority in the commons). Instead it was decided to give them one more chance to get things right, postponing the union for a year to allow for a majority to be won over to the union cause. All the hesitation about spending money was abandoned and it was decided to do whatever was necessary to win. Borough compensation was quickly conceded, which meant that the big magnates lost much of their motivation for opposing and were now prepared to allow their M.P.s to vote as they wished, or vacate their seats if they chose. Because compensation had not been part of the original plan, it soon came to be viewed as part of the general corruption which the opposition railed against.

Until 1793, M.P.s in Ireland had been unable to vacate their seats unless through death or taking holy orders, but the passing of a Place Act changed all that. M.P.s could now accept an escheatorship for one of the provinces, a nominal office, and the seat would automatically fall vacant, forcing a by-election. Between January 1799 and June 1800, the Place Act became the means by which the government constructed its majority. It was difficult to persuade M.P.s to switch sides, but it was relatively easy to persuade them (following some inducement) to accept escheatorships and thus withdraw from parliament, allowing more malleable M.P.s to replace them. This saved the M.P from any embarrassment about changing sides, or voting for a measure he did not agree with, but did not interfere with the construction of a majority. Sixty-six seats were represented by 106 different M.P.s in the first six months of 1800, as anti-unionists were persuaded to withdraw, and supporters of the measure were moved like chesspieces across the electoral board. For example, Thomastown Borough in County Kilkenny had five M.P.s (for two seats) in 1800 as unionists were brought in to support the measure. In Clogher, County Tyrone, the great future chronicler of union corruption, Jonah Barrington, was forced out of his seat, as indeed was his constituency colleague, Thomas Burgh, to allow for two unionists to replace them.[50]

Patronage was also dispensed liberally to build a majority. Many realized that this would be the last opportunity to get a serious raise in the Irish peerage, or strike terms for a British peerage, and much of the debate behind closed doors was over terms, not the merits of the argument. Nevertheless, by the autumn of 1799, Cornwallis and Castlereagh were still not convinced the union would pass. Their doubts centred on the position of the Irish Catholics. Even though no Catholic sat in parliament, there was still a general belief that no measure could pass if there was clear popular opposition to it in the country, whether because of fear of violent reaction or because M.P.s had a belief they were virtually representing them. At a cabinet meeting in November 1799, Castlereagh was given assurances that if the success of the union hung in the balance, then Cornwallis could make explicit promises to the Catholics that emancipation would quickly accompany the passing of the measure. In the event, no explicit promises were made, partly because Cornwallis wanted emancipation to be seen as a gift which had been given freely, and partly because such a declaration would have united much of the

Protestant nation against the union. But he did have negotiations with the Catholic hierarchy and let it be understood that emancipation would soon follow, thus neutralizing any attempts to rally an opposition outside of parliament.

The biggest debate surrounding the passing of the union has centred on the role of corruption. In nationalist historiography, there was never any doubt that illegal practices had been used, but the lack of available evidence prevented academic scholars from agreeing. The stretching of patronage to breaking point and the use of borough compensation could all be considered part of parliamentary management, acceptable and understood within the conventions of the time. But the discovery of a second set of secret service records in the 1990s shattered the consensus about how the union was passed.[51] These showed that a government slush fund had been established that illegally diverted money from the civil list, the secret service funds, and from any other available source, to help secure the parliamentary majority. Few direct bribes were given to persuade M.P.s to switch sides (although as many as twenty appear to have changed between 1799 and 1800); the real purpose of the money was to placate people until a legal sinecure, peerage, or some other kind of office could be secured for them. In other words, the slush fund allowed for a majority to be constructed; legal resources allowed for it to be maintained. Cornwallis grew increasingly disillusioned with the trading and trafficking he had to take part in during this period, and took to quoting from Swift, 'and then at Beelzebub's great hall, complains his budget is too small'.[52] There is now little disagreement about how the union was passed, but it is still not clear how many votes were purchased by hard cash in the period, how many were persuaded by promises of patronage, and how many were genuine statements of support for the legislative union.

When the Irish parliament met on 15 January 1800, the union was again introduced. As in the previous year, much of the finest oratory was to be heard coming from the opposition benches, especially after the dramatic return of Henry Grattan to the chamber. But whenever a division was called, the government was able to produce a majority, and that majority held throughout the three readings of the bill. Unable to make much of an impression inside parliament, the opposition considered various strategies for delaying the measure, varying from the practical (attempting to rally the yeomanry and the Catholics against the measure) to the outlandish (setting up a duelling club to wound or kill unionist M.P.s), but none got very far. The final reading of the bill took place on 7 June, and two-thirds of the opposition M.P.s walked out of the House rather than remain and witness their defeat.

The union came into effect on 1 January 1801, but far from being the unifying security mechanism that Pitt had intended, it became the focus of further division. King, George III refused to consider the question of granting Catholic emancipation, forcing the resignation of Pitt and ensuring that the Catholic question became the dominant issue in Irish politics until 1829. Few of the claims about the union were fulfilled. The benefits to the Irish economy were never obvious and were always disputed, and it was never clear how Ireland was able to play a greater part in the empire as a result of the measure. The union was seen as the great ending point for Irish nationalists, and the great starting point for Irish loyalists. Much work remains to be done on what exactly changed under the terms of the union, apart from having 100 Irish M.P.s at Westminster instead of 300 in Dublin. The Dublin Castle administration remained as before, with a lord lieutenant and chief secretary, and there was no real attempt to create a new set of structures to reflect the new dispensation. Instead, the union became a symbolic superstructure that was to cast its shadow over the entire nineteenth century, as politics became increasingly dominated by attempts to defend or destroy it.

NOTES

1. Speech by Bertie Ahern, then Taoiseach (Irish Prime Minister), at the Wolfe Tone Commemoration, Bodenstown, County Kildare, Sunday, 17 October 2004, http://cain.ulst.ac.uk/issues/politics/docs/dott/ba171004.htm.
2. Thomas Bartlett (ed), *Life of Theobald Wolfe Tone* (Dublin, 1998), xxxviii.
3. T.W. Tone, 'Reasons why the question of parliamentary reform has always failed in the Irish legislature' (unfinished, 1793) in ibid., 391.
4. James Quinn, *Soul on Fire: a Life of Thomas Russell* (Dublin, 2002), 45.
5. Bartlett (ed), *Life of Theobald Wolfe Tone*, xvii.
6. T.W. Tone, *An argument on behalf of the Catholics of Ireland*, in Bartlett (ed), *Life of Theobald Wolfe Tone*, 290.
7. Kevin Whelan, *The tree of Liberty: Radicalism, Catholicism and the Construction of Irish Identity, 1760–1830* (Cork, 1996), 236.
8. Ibid., 91.
9. Nancy J. Curtin, *The United Irishmen: Popular Politics in Ulster and Dublin, 1791–1798* (Oxford, 1994), 21.
10. Whelan, *Tree of Liberty*, 62.
11. Tom Dunne, *Theobald Wolfe Tone, Colonial Outsider* (Cork, 1992); see also Marianne Elliott, *Wolfe Tone: Prophet of Irish Independence* (London, 1989).
12. Thomas Bartlett, *Theobald Wolfe Tone* (Dundalk, 1997).
13. Bartlett (ed), *Life of Theobald Wolfe Tone*, 30.
14. Ibid., 367.
15. Leo McCabe, *Wolfe Tone and the United Irishmen, For or against Christ* (Dublin, 1937), 177.
16. John FitzGibbon, *Substance of the speech of the Rt Hon Lord FitzGibbon, lord chancellor of Ireland, on 10 January 1793 respecting the catholic delegates and the popery laws of Ireland* (London, 1793), 18.
17. John Ehrman, *The Younger Pitt* (3 vols., London 1969–96), iii, 171.
18. See James Kelly, *Henry Grattan* (Dundalk, 1993); D.A. Fleming and A.P.W. Malcomson (eds), *'A Volley of Execrations': the Letters and Papers of John FitzGibbon, Earl of Clare, 1772–1802* (Dublin, 2005).
19. Bartlett (ed), *Life of Theobald Wolfe Tone*, xxx.
20. E. A Smith, *Whig Principles and Party Politics: Earl Fitzwilliam and the Whig Party, 1748–1833* (Manchester, 1975); Deirdre Lindsay, 'The Fitzwilliam episode revisited' in David Dickson, Dáire Keogh, and Kevin Whelan (eds), *The United Irishmen: Republicanism, Radicalism and Rebellion* (Dublin, 1993); David Wilkinson, 'The Fitzwilliam episode, 1795: a reinterpretation of the role of the duke of Portland', *Irish Historical Studies*, 29 (1995), 315–39.

21. Ann C. Kavanaugh, John FitzGibbon, *Earl of Clare: Protestant Reaction and English Authority in Late Eighteenth-century Ireland* (Dublin, 1997), 308.
22. Dorothy Marshall, *The Rise of George Canning* (London, 2007), 100.
23. Ehrman, *Pitt*, iii, 165.
24. James Kelly, *Prelude to Union* (Cork, 1992), 232; P.M. Geoghegan, 'The making of the union' in Dáire Keogh and Kevin Whelan (eds), *Acts of Union* (Dublin, 2001), 35.
25. John Ehrman, *The Younger Pitt* (3 vols., London 1969–96), ii, 239.
26. E.A. Smith, *Whig Principles and Party Politics* (Manchester, 1975), 200.
27. See John A. Murphy (ed), *The French are in the Bay: the Expedition to Bantry Bay, 1796* (Dublin, 1996).
28. See Brendan Simms, 'Continental analogies with 1798: revolution or counter-revolution' in Thomas Bartlett, David Dickson, Dáire Keogh, Kevin Whelan (eds), *1798: a Bicentenary Perspective* (Dublin, 2003).
29. Marianne Elliott, *Partners in Revolution: the United Irishmen and France* (New Haven, 1982), ch. 6, especially 165–6.
30. Roger Wells, *Insurrection: the British Experience, 1795–1803* (Gloucester, 1983), 56.
31. See Jim Smyth, *The Men of No Property: Irish Radicals and Popular Politics in the Late 18th Century* (London, 1998).
32. David Dickson, *New Foundations: Ireland, 1660–1800* (2nd ed., Dublin, 2000), 210.
33. Thomas Bartlett, Kevin Dawson, and Dáire Keogh, *The 1798 Rebellion* (Dublin, 1998), 82.
34. Thomas Bartlett, 'Counter insurgency and rebellion' in Thomas Bartlett and Keith Jeffrey (eds), *A Military History of Ireland* (Cambridge, 1997), 297.
35. Ibid., 270.
36. Curtin, *United Irishmen*, 259.
37. Thomas Pakenham, *The Year of Liberty: the History of the Great Irish Rebellion of 1798* (London, 1969).
38. L.M. Cullen, 'The 1798 rebellion in Wexford: United Irishmen organisation, membership, leadership' in Kevin Whelan (ed), *Wexford: history and society* (Dublin, 1987).
39. Daniel Gahan, *The People's Rising: Wexford, 1798* (Dublin, 1995); Kevin Whelan, *Fellowship of Freedom: the United Irishmen and 1798* (Cork, 1998).
40. For a discussion of the controversy, see R.F. Foster, 'Remembering 1798' in R.F. Foster, *The Irish Story* (London, 2001).
41. Richard Musgrave, *Memoirs of the Different Rebellions in Ireland* (Dublin, 1801).
42. See P.M. Geoghegan, *The Irish Act of Union* (Dublin, 1999).
43. Ibid., 79.
44. Pakenham, *Year of Liberty*, 328.
45. Quoted by Kevin Whelan in 'The other within, Ireland, Britain and the Act of Union' in Keogh and Whelan (eds), *Acts of Union*, 15.
46. Bartlett (ed), *Life of Theobald Wolfe Tone*, 739.
47. Patrick Kavanagh, *A Popular History of the Insurrection of 1798* (Dublin, 1870).
48. Whelan, *Tree of Liberty*, 150; see also Thomas Bartlett, David Dickson, Dáire Keogh, Kevin Whelan (eds), *1798: a Bicentenary Perspective* (Dublin, 2003).
49. See P.M. Geoghegan, *Lord Castlereagh* (Dundalk, 2002).
50. P.M. Geoghegan, 'The Irish House of Commons, 1779–1800' in Michael Brown, P.M. Geoghegan, and James Kelly (eds), *The Irish Act of Union, 1800: Bicentennial Essays* (Dublin, 2003).

51. See David Wilkinson, 'How did they pass the Union?" Secret service expenditure in Ireland, 1799–1804', *History*, lxxxii (1997), 223–51.
52. Geoghegan, *Irish Act of Union*, 85.

SELECT BIBLIOGRAPHY

Bartlett, Thomas, *The Rise and Fall of the Irish Nation: the Catholic Question* (Dublin, 1992).
——, *Theobald Wolfe Tone* (Dundalk, 1997).
Bartlett, Thomas, Dickson, David, Keogh, Daire, and Whelan, Kevin (eds). *The 1798 Rebellion: a Bicentenary Perspective* (Dublin, 2003).
Bew, Paul, *Ireland: the Politics of Enmity 1789–2006* (Oxford, 2007).
Bolton, G.C., *The Passing of the Irish Act of Union* (Oxford, 1966).
Brown, Michael, Geoghegan, Patrick, and Kelly, James (eds), *The Irish Act of Union: Bicentennial Essays* (Dublin, 2003).
Curtin, Nancy, *The United Irishmen* (Oxford, 1994).
Dickson, David, *New Foundations: Ireland, 1660–1800*, 2nd ed. (Dublin, 2002).
Dickson, David et al (eds), *The United Irishmen* (Dublin, 1993).
Elliott, Marianne, *Partners in Revolution: the United Irishmen and France* (London, 1988).
——, *Wolfe Tone*, 2nd ed. (Liverpool, 2012).
Geoghegan, P.M., *The Irish Act of Union* (Dublin, 1999).
Hayton, David (ed), *The Irish Parliament in the Eighteenth Century: the Long Apprenticeship* (Edinburgh, 2001).
Keogh, Daire and Whelan, Kevin (eds), *Acts of Union* (Dublin, 2001).
McBride, Ian, *Eighteenth-century Ireland: the Isle of Slaves* (Dublin, 2009).
——, *Scripture Politics* (Oxford, 1998).
McDowell, R.B., *Ireland in the Age of Imperialism and Revolution, 1760–1801* (Oxford, 1979).
Smith, Jim (ed), *Revolution, Counter-revolution and Union* (Cambridge, 2000).
Smyth, Jim, *The Men of No Property* (Dublin, 1992).
Whelan, Kevin, *The Tree of Liberty: Radicalism, Catholicism and the Construction of Irish Identity* (Cork, 1996).

BRITISH STATE AND CATHOLIC NATION (1800-1920)

CHAPTER 26

THE EMERGENCE OF THE IRISH CATHOLIC NATION, 1750−1850

THOMAS BARTLETT

I

PERHAPS Lord John George de la Poer Beresford (1773–1862), Archbishop of Armagh, Chancellor of Trinity College Dublin, and scion of one of the greatest Protestant Ascendancy families in Ireland, summed it up best: 'when I was a boy', he wrote, shortly before his death, ' "the Irish people" meant the Protestants; now it means the Roman Catholics'.[1] During Beresford's lifetime, the Catholic people of Ireland became so identified with the Irish nation that it seemed that there could be neither room nor role for Protestants in it. Protestants, of course, might continue to describe themselves as Irish and very many did so; but the word 'Irish' was merely an adjective: as a collective noun, the term 'the Irish' was reserved for the Catholics. This startling transformation, from native sect to national body, from *a* people of Ireland to *the* people of Ireland, was to have dramatic consequences on Anglo-Irish relations, for it seemed axiomatic that a Catholic nation could never feel comfortable within a Protestant state. Accordingly, the last decades of the nineteenth century and the early decades of the twentieth were taken up with the struggle of this Catholic nation to win a state of its own.

II

It was in the late eighteenth century that the identification of the Catholics as 'the nation of the Irish' or 'the Irish people' became commonplace. In 1782, the earl of Clare, Lord Chancellor of Ireland, and the son of a convert to the Church of Ireland, rounded on his fellow peers for speaking of the Protestants as 'the People of Ireland'. The 'melancholy truth', he explained, was that the Catholics, 'the great body of the people', deserved that designation. The United Irishman, Theobald Wolfe Tone, engaged in promoting a French expeditionary force to Ireland in 1796, agreed: the Catholics were 'the Irish, properly so called'.[2]

Admittedly, in the seventeenth century, especially among Catholic clerical exiles in the Irish colleges in Douai, Salamanca, Paris, and elsewhere in continental Europe, there had been those who had promoted the synonymity of Irish and Catholic. Geoffrey Keating, for example, writing his history of Ireland, had revived *Éireannach*, a Gaelic word that had fallen into disuse, and given it a new meaning: formerly it had simply meant an Irish person, henceforward it would mean not just Irish but Catholic as well, the implication being that no Protestant could be *Éireannach*.[3] And it undoubtedly suited many Protestants to agree with him. Sir Richard Cox in his *Hiberniae Anglicana* (1689–90) commented that if the most natural-born Irishman was a Protestant, 'no man takes him for other than an English-man', whereas 'if a Cockny be a papist', he is reckoned as Irish 'as if he was born on Slevetogher'.[4] And yet these examples, and there are many more that could be given, did not at all signify the emergence of the Catholics of Ireland as the people of Ireland by the end of the seventeenth century. Rather, they belong to the pre-history of Irish nationalism (or Catholic consciousness) and would later be significant in associating Catholicism with victimhood. By 1700, the harsh reality was that, with crushing military defeat, catastrophic loss of land, and exile abroad for many potential leaders, the Catholics of Ireland in the decades after the Battle of the Boyne (1690) simply did not count. Jonathan Swift dismissed them as 'natives' or, on occasion, 'our savages' and he could do so because they were, or appeared to be, largely powerless, largely propertyless, and largely pauperized. With good reason, it was the Protestants that he memorably dubbed in the 1720s 'the Whole People of Ireland', and that was to remain the case until the end of the eighteenth century.[5]

III

In retrospect, it was the emergence of what became known as 'The Catholic Question' in the mid eighteenth century that heralded the rise of Catholic Ireland. In the first instance, there was not supposed to be a 'Catholic Question': that vexing problem had surely been solved by military victory at the Boyne, reinforced by the exile of potential Catholic leaders, and copper-fastened by a stringent series of penal laws that in effect denied the mass of Catholics ambition while offering inducements to their remaining social superiors to convert to the Established Church. For these reasons, the return of the Catholic Question to the political agenda was disquieting for Irish Protestants and it was also a cause for dismay to them that, beginning in the 1760s, successive British governments began to court Irish Catholics. Even more alarming was the speed with which the issue of civil and political rights for Irish Catholics came to dominate all others.[6]

The re-emergence of a question that was believed long settled can be explained by reasons that were both external and internal to the Catholic body. First, relations between successive British governments and the Irish Protestants had not been smooth during the early eighteenth century. In particular, a flat refusal to allow British ministers to define the constitutional relationship between Ireland and Britain, to the latter's advantage, had been productive of tension and occasional disputes. Irish Protestants were also persuaded that the London government was in effect plundering the resources of Ireland and discriminating against Irish Protestants in patronage matters. Exasperation at Protestant recalcitrance and protests may have been a factor in leading British ministers to look more favourably on Irish Catholics who, after all, had made a habit of proclaiming their loyalty to the British Crown.

Protestant division—the rivalry between members of the Church of Ireland and the Presbyterian Church—was also a factor in creating a certain space for Catholics to stand forward. After 1690, Irish Protestants were by no means content to share the fruits of the victory over Catholic Ireland with Presbyterians. Instead, certain penal laws were passed against them that had the effect of excluding Presbyterians from crown and municipal offices. True, Indemnity Acts (from 1719 on) had tempered their effects, but the laws remained on the statute books, and were a galling reminder to Presbyterians of their second-class status. Essentially, Irish Protestants kept Presbyterians in an inferior position because they could do so, and because they believed that, should a crisis arise in Ireland, they could count on them to stand fast alongside them as in 1688–90. Hence, they resisted any attempt to repeal the penal laws against Presbyterians and only did so as late as 1780. Protestant division between Anglican and Presbyterian, between Church and Kirk, was a source of weakness to the Protestant cause. In theory, it opened up the possibility of a choice of ally to British ministers, and it also held out the chance of Irish Presbyterians making common cause with Irish Catholics. True, neither prospect looked at all likely for most of the eighteenth century, but, when in 1791, in Presbyterian Belfast, the Society of United Irishmen was set up, it did make overtures to Irish Catholics to join with them in their assault on the Anglican political establishment. This set in train a series of events that was to lead to rebellion, the Anglo-Irish Union, and the end of the Protestants as the 'Irish nation'.

A further inducement for British ministers to re-examine their traditional hostility to Irish Catholics was the stark fact that the armed forces of the Crown were suffering a manpower shortage, because wars were both more intensive in terms of the numbers deployed to fight them and also more extensive in terms of potential theatres, ranging from India to North America, and many places in between. Irish Catholics had been barred from the British army and navy since the 1690s (though many served surreptitiously): but blind-eye turning was no substitute for open recruitment, and this was what was wanted. The Seven Years' War (1756–63) was crucial in this regard.

By 1763, Britain famously was possessed of an empire on which the sun never set, but the question was: would she be able to garrison and defend it? In 1767, a modest proposal to increase the number of soldiers paid for by Ireland—a proposal that itself was a product of imperial reform—had led to a major change in the way Ireland was governed. A system of direct rule, bypassing the local political magnates or undertakers, was installed. Additionally, in a sop to the *amour propre* of Irish politicians, an Octennial Act—allowing for general elections in Ireland every eight years instead of, as hitherto, on the accession of a new sovereign—was passed in 1768. Politicization in Ireland received a boost as a result. In theory, such a development could have no bearing on Irish Catholics for they could neither vote nor sit in the Irish parliament, but in the heightened political atmosphere produced by more frequent elections, Catholics might be emboldened to protest at their exclusion. In short, by the 1770s, the Irish political landscape had begun to change, and in ways that could only be to Catholic advantage.

And so, too, had the confessional context. By the mid-decades of the eighteenth century, western Europe generally was experiencing the growth of what might be called indifferentism in religious matters, at least at the elite level.[7] The furies aroused by the religious wars of the seventeenth century seemed remote; 'enthusiasm' was to be reprobated; the pope's temporal power seemed to be in permanent decline; the Stuart cause was finished; and penal laws against deviant religious communities were difficult to defend. To an extent, Irish Protestants—or some of them—shared in this disdain for religious discrimination: central to the emergence of the Catholic question was a growing embarrassment at the penal laws against Irish Catholics, and a gnawing anxiety that it might not be a good idea to let the British government take the credit for ending them.

And yet, for *a* Catholic Question to emerge, and then become *the* Catholic Question and remain the key issue in Irish politics for the next fifty years, it was necessary for Irish Catholics to be able to take advantage of the altered political context and the changed religious atmosphere and step forward with their own demands. By the early 1760s, a Catholic Committee had been set up in Dublin, in itself a startling development: heretofore, such assertiveness would have elicited a robust official response with allegations of conspiracy and plots being directed at it; now it was grudgingly accepted. Those historians who have investigated the Catholic Committee in the period up to 1790 have concluded that its achievements were very limited, for it was unduly deferential, even sycophantic toward the authorities, and it was beset by bitter divisions between lay and clerical members, and between the surviving Catholic aristocracy and leading members of the Catholic mercantile interest.[8] Such criticisms, while valid, ignore one salient point: the continuous existence of the Committee during these decades was its achievement; the Catholics had come in from the cold. That they were able to do so was a product of the changed political and military context noted above, but it was also the outcome of their wealth, their interest in land, and especially their numbers.

The penal laws had focused on keeping Catholics out of the professions (the army, the law, politics, the administration, though not medicine), and their object was to reduce further still the amount of land owned by Catholics. They had, however, little to say about Catholic involvement in commerce and during the eighteenth century considerable fortunes were made by Catholic merchants in Ireland as well as abroad. They took advantage of, and further extended, a network of Catholic merchants that stretched from Ireland to Spain and France, across the Atlantic to the British colonies of the North American mainland, and the West Indies. Catholic involvement in commerce was not in proportion to their numbers, but Catholic wealth was substantial and when the opportunity beckoned, as it did with Britain's American troubles in the 1770s, Catholics had the resources to step forward and seek recognition and the restoration of rights. For example, in September 1781, at the height of the American war, George Goold, a prominent Catholic merchant from Cork, offered to advance the sum of £6000 to help with recruitment to the British Army.[9]

Moreover, if Catholic wealth derived from commerce was sizeable, so, too, was the Catholic interest in Irish land. The penal laws had been directed against Catholic *land-owning* and this had certainly declined to single percentage points by the late eighteenth century, but the laws had had little to say about such matters as Catholic lease-holding, or lease-speculation—or indeed the collusive discovery of illegal land transactions by Catholics, a procedure by which a 'friendly' party brought the culprit to court and then in a sense 'minded' the property in his interest thereafter. By such stratagems, the sharp thrust of the penal legislation was blunted and its intention circumvented. As a result, it is possible to claim that the Catholic *interest* in land actually increased in the eighteenth century. The significance of this is clear: in the early modern period throughout the Atlantic world, land was vital; those who owned or had an interest in land possessed social authority and most had political authority; those without land had neither.

To Catholic mercantile wealth and interest in land can be added Catholic numbers. On the face of it, this seems improbable, for the clear majority that Irish Catholics held over Protestants had been, and would continue to be, a cogent reason to retain the penal laws against them. Not that Protestants appeared to be all that interested in the relative size of the various religious communities in Ireland. A half-hearted attempt was made in 1732–3 to take a religious census through the agency of the Hearth Tax collectors: when completed they estimated that Catholics were 1.4 million out of a population of nearly 2 million (when the figures are adjusted, between 72 and 82 per cent). But, beyond that attempt, no official effort was made to find out precisely how the rival religions broke down by numbers. In parenthesis, we might note that, by 1800, the Irish population can be put at around 5.4 million, and the percentage that was Catholic had crept up to 80 per cent, and this remained the case through to the 1840s.[10] For most of the eighteenth century, Irish Protestants had little interest in the precise breakdown of Catholics and Protestants, possibly because they well knew that they would come out badly in any such exercise, but also because numbers did not really matter. In Ireland, as in Europe generally, quality, not quantity, counted: Protestants were the quality, at least in terms of political power, landowning, and wealth.

For Irish Catholics, it was all rather different, and they were keen to stress their numbers, their loyalty, and their willingness to serve in the armed forces of the Crown. British ministers, tasked with defending the far-flung British Empire after 1763, found the prospect of large numbers of Catholic recruits irresistible and by the time of the American War of Independence (1775–83), a tentative policy of trading Catholic relief for Catholic recruits was in place. During the American War, two Catholic Relief Acts were passed, in 1778 and 1782, that effectively dismantled the key restrictions on Catholic worship, landowning, and access to the professions. Catholics, however, were still denied political rights, for they could neither vote in elections nor take a seat in the Irish parliament. This exclusion was partly breached in 1793 when, once again in a time of war, the restriction on

Catholics voting in the counties was removed. As before, the thinking behind this remark-able turnaround was to fix Catholic loyalty in the coming struggle with Revolutionary France, and especially to draw on Catholic manpower for the army and navy. In the early eighteenth century, war had meant danger for Irish Catholics, for they were viewed with suspicion and subject to harassment by the authorities; but long before the 1790s, war meant opportunity—to parade their loyalty and show off their numbers.

Catholics were not averse to displaying their numbers in other ways. In 1792, and in 1793, they took advantage of their numbers to draw up petitions to reinforce their claims for relief. Again, in 1792, the Catholic Committee had summoned a Catholic Convention to meet in Dublin to call for further Catholic concessions. The Convention consisted of over 230 delegates from twenty-five counties chosen by 'all the people' (that is the Catholics) and with the active support of the parish clergy. The petition that emerged from this gathering was speedily conveyed to George III, where it was repre-sented as 'the universal wish of EVERY Catholic in the nation', and played no small part in forcing the concession on the franchise. In 1795, in the aftermath of the recall of Earl Fitzwilliam, a pro-Catholic chief governor, Edward Hay, a Catholic activist, proposed a religious census of Ireland to be carried out by both the Catholic and Protestant clergy. Dublin Castle was alarmed and moved to head off this exercise. Hay's proposal had lit-tle scientific rationale and was, as Edward Cooke, Under-Secretary, claimed, clearly an attempt 'to enforce the power of numbers...representing the Catholics as the *People* of Ireland and their present political inferiority as tyranny'. Hay's proposal was rejected by the Catholic bishops, for they were anxious not to antagonize the Castle at a time when delicate negotiations were underway concerning the setting up, with government money, of a Catholic seminary in Maynooth, County Kildare.[11]

Lastly, it was to be of the utmost significance that, throughout the eighteenth century, the Catholic Church in Ireland had remained beyond the influence of Dublin Castle or the British government. It may have been the only major church in Europe to have escaped some degree of secular control, and it would be a frequent lament of British ministers in the early nineteenth century that in seeking (belatedly) to have some say in how the Catholic Church in Ireland conducted its affairs—the selection of bishops, for example—it sought no more, and sometimes less, than had been allowed to the govern-ments of France, Spain, or Prussia. In Ireland, the reality was that the Catholic Church—the church of the people—had flourished behind the penal laws, and when the time came, its clergy was able to take on a leadership role uncontaminated by contact with or payment from the civil establishment. In a real sense, it was under the carapace of the penal laws that the Catholic nation was incubated.

IV

Catholic advances during the eighteenth century threatened to be undone by their involvement in the rebellion of 1798. This rebellion can be traced directly to the setting up of the Society of United Irishmen in Belfast in October 1791, and in Dublin a month later. The Society was little more than a 'Presbyterian Committee' on the model of the Catholic Committee that had apparently enjoyed so much success in the previous thirty years. Its primary objective was parliamentary reform, needed nowhere more than in Belfast where wealthy Presbyterian merchants were 'represented' in the Irish parliament by the nominees of the absentee, Anglican, spendthrift, and occasional fugitive from justice, the earl of Donegall. To add traction to their campaign, it was evident that Catholic support was required: a previous campaign for parliamentary reform in the early 1780s had foundered because it had been based on much too narrow a sectarian base—Catholics had been comprehensively excluded.

Events in France helped in this respect. Since 1789, French Catholics had clearly been active in promoting liberty and had taken a lead in separating church and state and curbing the pretensions of the most powerful Catholic Church in the world. If French Catholics, so ran the argument of Theobald Wolfe Tone's pamphlet, could embrace freedom, then surely Irish Catholics—despite much historical evidence to the contrary—could do the same.[12] Accordingly, overtures were made to the Catholic Committee and encouraging answers were received. However, the Catholics were adept at playing a double game—flirting with the Presbyterian United Irishmen while simultaneously making doe eyes at the British government—and their strategy paid off. The major concession of the vote in 1793 can be explained by British alarm at the prospect of a Presbyterian-Catholic alliance. However, there was a danger here: the Catholic Relief Act of 1793 was railroaded through the Irish Parliament by a British government that was intent on buying off trouble through concession. Some Irish Protestants, understandably, were less than impressed with this empowerment of their long-standing enemies and grew alarmed at what next was in store for them.

Catholics, in effect, had got the vote—could the right to sit in parliament be long delayed? But, given Catholic numbers, wealth, and clerical leadership, it was axiomatic that they would soon command a majority in the Irish parliament. With that majority, they would seek to undo the land settlement of the seventeenth century and then move for independence. In its turn, this would trigger another English conquest of Ireland—as in Tudor times—because Ireland, unlike the American colonies, was too close to Britain and too weak and vulnerable to foreign predators to be allowed, so to speak, to sail off into the sunset. It was the Catholic Relief legislation of 1793, not the 1798 rebellion, that moved the object of a parliamentary union firmly onto the Anglo-Irish political agenda. The remaining concession, the right of Catholics to sit in parliament—now dubbed Catholic Emancipation—could only safely be conceded following a legislative union, not preceding it. This vital consideration goes far towards explaining the collapse of Earl Fitzwilliam's viceroyalty in 1795. Had Catholic Emancipation been conceded during his term in Ireland, the prospect of a parliamentary union would have faded.

The 1798 rebellion, of course, played its part, for it moved the question of union from the desirable to the practical, from distant aspiration to pressing reality. Savage cruelties, religious furies, and appalling massacres had terrified the Protestant parliamentary classes and they rushed to vacate the Irish House and to embrace the spacious British

Mansion, eager to experience, as William Knox, Protestant Bishop of Killaloe put it, the joy and relief of 'consider[ing] myself as one of fourteen Protestants to three Roman Catholics, instead of being as I now am, as one in three'.[13] Union, following some rather tepid debates, passed quietly in mid 1800 and came into effect on 1 January 1801.

The role played by the Catholics in the passing of the Act of Union remains a matter for debate. They commanded no seats in the Irish House of Commons, and therefore in strictly parliamentary terms their influence was very limited. Union, it has been argued, was carried by the normal methods of parliamentary management—the disbursement of the 'loaves and fishes' of place, pension, title, promotion, and even cash, in order to win over votes—and hence the support or otherwise of the Catholics was largely irrelevant to its fate.[14] Such a view, however, is much too narrow. Cornwallis and his chief secretary, Lord Castlereagh, were certainly eager to win Catholic support for Union and to secure pro-Union addresses from Catholic bodies. For its part, the Catholic hierarchy was anxious to oblige. The bishops had been alarmed at the voices describing the rebellion as a popish plot that demanded condign punishment—perhaps a confiscation of Catholic land, as in the seventeenth century, or even the return of the penal laws. Was it not clear, the Protestant zealot John Foster demanded, from, inter alia, the burning of Protestants at Scullabogue and the piking of Protestant prisoners on Wexford Bridge, that 'demons of every sort [had] escaped from their cells when the padlocks were taken off the Papists' fetters'? Perhaps the chains should be re-riveted? In this fevered and sectarianized atmosphere, the Catholic bishops, with the Archbishop of Dublin, Dr Troy, in the van rightly perceived that their true interests lay in accommodating themselves to the wishes of Dublin Castle and the British government. Accordingly, they pledged their loyalty to the Lord Lieutenant, Marquis Cornwallis, whom they regarded as almost a lone voice pleading for leniency and clemency in an Ireland where 'party and religious prejudice has literally made the Protestant part of the country mad'.[15]

Then again, the Catholic bishops might have mused, what had the Irish parliament ever done for Irish Catholics? If we ignore the so-called 'Patriot Parliament' of May to July 1689 on the grounds that it was an illegal assembly, no Catholic had sat in an Irish parliament since 1660. In the early eighteenth century, Irish Protestant M.P.s had sought to shackle Catholics with penal laws; later in the century, their successors in the Irish parliament, by and large, had resisted any attempt to free them. Why not support Union, and the end of that anti-Catholic institution?

Accordingly, Catholic pro-Union addresses were promoted: in all, eleven were secured out of a total of seventy-six for the pro-Union side, while not one of the fifty anti-Union addresses emanated from a Catholic body. Admittedly, there was some opposition among Dublin Catholics to the measure, perhaps because of anxieties for the future of their city. Famously, Daniel O'Connell, in what was essentially his first public appearance, came out against Union on national grounds: but his was a lone voice, and a relatively unknown one, and Catholic dissent in Dublin was easily contained. The stakes were high, as Lord Cornwallis recognized, and he was at all times attentive to the Catholics. They 'have been chiefly courted by him', wrote Edward Cooke, 'and he has always been of opinion that if they would act heartily in support, the Protestants would not resist the efforts of British government assisted by the population of the country.' Had the Catholic Church come out decisively against Union, it is hard to see how that measure could have passed.

However, if historians have debated the precise weight to be attached to the role played by the Catholic Church in the passing of the Act of Union, there has been general agreement on the importance of the *Catholic Question* in making Union a vital policy objective of the British government. Quite simply, without the pressure exerted by the emergence of the Catholic Question, there would have been little incentive for the British government to move for the union of the two parliaments, and of course, there would have been no inducement for the members of the Irish parliament to give up an institution that was so completely bound up with their identity as the 'Irish nation'. Union was seen to be the necessary gateway to the solution of the Catholic Question: hence, as noted above, emancipation must not precede Union. Were that to happen, wrote Cooke, then 'the great argument for an Union would be lost'.

Both Cornwallis and Castlereagh had strongly intimated to members of the Catholic hierarchy that emancipation would follow Union. An intimation was not, of course, a firm pledge, much less a binding promise, but then such a commitment was probably not sought by members of the Catholic hierarchy. The reality was that Union without emancipation made no sense, and on all sides there was a firm expectation, and in certain 'red-hot' or ultra-Protestant quarters a gloomy resignation, that emancipation would quickly follow the enactment of Union. When that failed to happen, and when it rapidly became clear that Union, so far from being a gateway to emancipation, was an apparently insuperable barrier to it, there was a sense of outrage among the Catholics of Ireland. 'The nation of the Irish' had been betrayed and insulted, and the stage was set for that nation to assert itself.[16]

V

It is tempting to speculate on what might have happened in Anglo-Irish relations had emancipation gone through as expected in 1801. Might the Union have bedded down, with two or three Catholic M.P.s (out of the hundred allowed for by the terms of Union) making the journey to the united parliament at Westminster? Or would the campaign for repeal of the Act of Union simply have been brought forward from the 1830s to the early years of the century? We cannot know the answer to these questions. This much is clear however: from the beginning, the Union would be on trial to see whether it could deliver on the hopes and aspirations held out for it; but the thirty years that would elapse before Catholic Emancipation was conceded blighted the entire promise of Union, and made it likely that movements to end it would emerge in Irish politics from time to time in the nineteenth century. Moreover, the huge effort required to press home the campaign for Catholic Emancipation, nothing less than the comprehensive mobilization of the Catholic people of Ireland, not only raised Catholic consciousness, but educated

Catholics to an awareness of their grievances and further empowered them to a due appreciation of their numbers. The struggle for emancipation would bring the Catholic people of Ireland into the political arena and lead them to the realization that they were 'emphatically the people of Ireland'. The consequences for the future of the Union were bound to be grave.

On one level, the first two decades after the Union were years of failure, so far as Catholic emancipation was concerned.[17] George III's steadfast refusal, his 'invincible repugnance', to the idea of Catholics in parliament had come as an unwelcome surprise to those in Ireland and in Britain who had believed that emancipation would easily be put through the united parliament. It was evident, however, that George III had his finger on the popular pulse, and that his action met with widespread approval in Britain. Largely as a result of the interminable wars with France, there was widespread revulsion in Britain against all innovation and there was a detestation of foreign religions, by which was meant Roman Catholicism.[18]

In quick order, the Prime Minister, William Pitt, and the Dublin Castle team of Cornwallis, Castlereagh, and Cooke, all resigned and were replaced by those firmly opposed to Catholic emancipation or resolved to keep that topic off the political agenda. At Dublin Castle, the anti-Catholic 'old guard' from the 1790s (John Foster, William Saurin) returned and was reinforced by an accession of new British talent such as Sir Robert Peel. In Britain, the Catholic issue was pronounced an 'open' question—don't ask, don't tell—but in Ireland, at least until 1818, only those with strong anti-Catholic credentials were considered for Irish office. Irish Catholics struggled to make headway against this inveterate opposition. A Catholic petition was organized in 1805 but was ineffective, and the next fifteen years saw a series of setbacks for the Catholic cause. Chief Secretary Sir Robert Peel (1812–8) proved to be a particularly able foe of the Catholics, and he ignored numerous Catholic petitions, harassed Catholic newspapers, and faced down various Catholic Boards.

Catholics themselves played a part in their failure. During most of the 1810s, they were distracted by a dispute over whether it would be permissible as a condition of emancipation to give the British government some say in the appointment of Irish bishops, or some supervision of the bishops' correspondence when appointed. The irony here was that those opposed to Catholic Emancipation were not at all prepared to drop their opposition if one or other of these conditions were met. The debate on the 'Veto question', as it was known, was largely internal to 'Catholic Ireland', with accusations of bad faith, lies, heresy, disloyalty, and even insanity being hurled around, much to the amusement of those opposed to the Catholic cause, and much to the bewilderment of those British friends who were well disposed towards the Catholics. Interestingly, the Catholic hierarchy, led by Troy, had tentatively agreed to some such control in 1799; but it was a sign of how matters had changed that, ten years later, no matter what the bishops might have thought privately, no such 'Veto' would be countenanced by the Catholic laity. The Irish Catholic bishops were prized precisely because they were beyond British government control; to place them, and thus the Irish Catholic Church, however remotely, under an obligation to British ministers would be to destroy their credibility and their national credentials. It mattered not a jot that similar provisions were in place in Prussia and France. As Daniel O'Connell put it, and his opposition to the proposed 'Veto' brought him to the leadership of the Catholic movement, Catholics opposed giving any say to British ministers 'because of the inveterate hatred which seven centuries of oppression has inspired in the Irish mind'. The question of a British 'Veto' was a national question for Irish Catholics, not really a religious one, and that was why it mattered so much to them.[19]

In the event, it was not until 1821 that all talk of a British 'Veto' was abandoned. The key point that emerged from what was often a tiresome and pointless dispute was that Catholic Ireland was determined to withhold the degree of legitimacy from the British government that it had been ready to concede in 1799. Within a few years of Union, Catholic alienation and, possibly, disaffection were becoming apparent.

And yet, while the first two decades of the nineteenth century witnessed little progress on the Catholic Question, at least at the national level, they were certainly not devoid of significance. Far away from the palace of Westminster, and remote from the increasingly jaded rhetoric of imminent victory, and the intricacies of the Veto issue, major changes were afoot in Irish society. A formidable process of politicization had begun; Catholic consciousness was rising appreciably and a Catholic nation was emerging, one shaped by history and a sense of the past but one also moulded by the realities of contemporary Irish life. Catholic emancipation would never be granted but it would be taken, and the Catholic nation that had arrived by 1820 and was mobilized in the 1820s, would, under the demonic leadership of O'Connell, eventually seize the prize.

The very fact of Union was of critical importance to this process, for the removal of the Irish parliament by laying bare the connection between Ireland and England provided the framework within which a new, a Catholic, nationalism could be fashioned. Fearful of the rise of Catholic Ireland, and terrified by the 1798 Rebellion—widely regarded as a Popish rebellion on the model of 1641—Protestants had abandoned their claim to be the Irish nation in 1800 and the way was clear for the Catholics to move in. Again, the early experience of Union, the frustrations and disappointments that accompanied it, and especially the rampant sectarianism that marked its operation—despite promises made during its passing—provided the overwhelming sense of grievance that fuelled the Catholic movement.

Economic change in the post-war period which led to widespread immiseration and famine conditions in 1816–17 also played a part in provoking a number of secret agrarian societies, as did demographic growth for an acute awareness of Catholic numbers, sharpening that vital sense of Catholic grievance. Perhaps four processes in mobilization can be identified. First, the intense sectarianization of Irish society which was a noted feature of the post-Union decades; second, the increased sociability in Irish life in this period, a product of a large increase of occasions at which Catholics could meet socially; third, the steady democratization, or knowledge of the political process, that the numerous petition-signings and various elections of delegates brought in their train; and finally, evidence in Ireland of a new 'militarization', the result of the unprecedented demand for recruits for the British armed services. These four developments were to an extent discrete, and will be considered separately, but they were all related and there was considerable overlap. In the 1820s, they fused to produce that nation that O'Connell would lead to victory in the Emancipation campaign.

Sectarianism was not a new phenomenon in Irish society in the period 1800–1820, and later.[20] It had long existed as a way of viewing the world through the prism of Catholic and Protestant enduring enmity and hatred. Given the numerous confessional wars, rebellions, and massacres that studded the history of early modern Ireland, this is not surprising. It can be argued, however, that in the late eighteenth century there had occurred something of a thaw in Catholic-Protestant relations. There had grown up a certain forbearance (tolerance is too strong), that revealed itself, for example, in disapproving of 'poaching' converts from the other side, or in shying away from public debate over the respective merits of each faith. The 'indifferentism' that was noted above also played a part, and so, too, did a general frowning on enthusiasm in religious matters. Overall, there appeared to be a reluctance to wave the bloody confessional shirt or stir up sectarian passions, at least at elite level.

By the 1790s, however, such restraint was in full retreat. Economic, ethnic, political, and religious rivalries came together in County Armagh where the Catholic Defenders battled the Protestant Peep of Day Boys and spread far beyond its borders. By 1795, the Peep of Day Boys had transformed themselves into the Orange Order, a Protestant fraternal society that quickly gained official countenance and spread rapidly, attracting many elite members and patrons. Just as the United Irishmen in their avowedly non-sectarian manner had appealed to the Irish of all denominations to forget about the past—'Are we forever to walk like beasts of prey over fields which these ancestors stained with blood?'—so in response the Orange Order, and those wedded to the notion of Protestant Ascendancy would retort that it was only through an examination of history and by drawing the correct lessons that the way forward could be charted. The central message from Irish history was that there could be no partnership or harmony between Catholic and Protestant, only enduring hostility; that if one rose, the other must fall, and that the prosperity of the one was predicated on the eclipse of the other. Such sentiments gained a massive boost when the excesses of the 1798 Rebellion were cried up and lovingly revealed in all their lurid detail.

In this respect, the key text was Sir Richard Musgrave's *Memoirs of the Different Rebellions in Ireland* (1801), a volume that detailed Catholic atrocities in the rebellion, ascribed them to the tenets of the Catholic religion—murder was mandated by their religion, he claimed—and then traced the whole rebellion back to the machinations of the Vatican. The volume enjoyed good sales, was warmly welcomed in anti-Jacobin circles in England, and, despite its great length, went through a number of editions. Musgrave's message was a simple one: how could anyone contemplate civil rights for such barbarians?[21]

Catholics were quick to offer a robust response, in itself an indication that they were no longer content to hold their silence in the face of such attacks. Edward Hay published his *History of Insurrection in the county of Wexford* in 1803, a volume which, complained a Castle official, 'abounded in matter which it were best was not published'. Far more alarming was the publication of Watty Cox's *Irish Magazine* in 1807, a journal, noted one observer, whose 'favourite object seems to be to prove that, in recent as well as in former times, the *English* government has been tyrannical and oppressive over the *Irish* people'. It devoted considerable space to the cruelties carried out by Crown forces during the rebellion. Protestant accusations over cruelties and atrocities elicited a Catholic response, and the sectarian atmosphere was duly heightened.

It was no accident that volumes such as these coincided with a religious revival in the early nineteenth century and this, too, helped intensify inter-denominational divisions.[22] An evangelical mission took hold in both the Church of Ireland and the Presbyterian Church, with missionaries, in a marked departure from previous practice, aggressively targeting Catholics. A Religious Tract and Book Society (1810) flooded the country with millions of pamphlets within a few years, and by 1816 some twenty-one Methodist missionaries were at work, primarily in the west of Ireland. It was noticeable, too, that the interdenominational education offered by the Kildare Place Society, under the pressure of the evangelical revival, was considerably diluted. The increased Protestant atmosphere in the schools led to the removal of Catholic children, and the withdrawal of Catholic board members such as O'Connell.

Catholic priests, in a noted departure from their previous docility, were quick to respond to what were seen as Protestant attacks and encroachments. Fr Hayes of Cork regaled his parishioners with stories of Protestant reformers such as Wyclif, Zwingli, and Luther enjoying intercourse with the devil, and Fr Burke of Roscarberry, County Cork, compared the current English rulers unfavourably with those of pagan Rome. For its part, the Catholic Committee set up a committee on grievances in 1809 and it began gathering evidence of Orange outrages and unfair treatment of Catholics at the hands of the army, the police, and in the courts. It was in the latter sphere that O'Connell made his reputation as an able, abrasive, and forthright defender of ordinary Catholics against the prejudiced 'Orange system'. Sensationally, the English Catholic Bishop, Charles Walmsley, writing under the pen name Pastorini, compiled a *General History of the Christian Church* (Dublin, 1805; Belfast, 1816; Cork, 1820). This book excited much comment because it forecast the destruction of Protestantism in either 1821 or 1825. The key passages of Walmsley's book were condensed into a short tract and distributed widely. The agrarian secret society, the Rockites, or the followers of Captain Rock, made much of this prophecy in their campaign of murder, mutilation, and incendiarism through most of Munster in the early 1820s.[23] By the early 1820s, Catholics and Protestants had drawn decisively apart: they no longer prayed together, rarely attended one another's funerals, refused to be godparents to each other's children, frequently brawled together (in and out of uniform), and engaged in a form of boycotting, known as 'exclusive dealing'. As a result, the 'Catholic mind of Ireland' had a heightened awareness of Catholic grievances at the hands of Protestants.

Separate from this intense sectarianism was the growing democratisation of the Catholic people of Ireland. It will be remembered that in 1793 Catholics had got the vote in the counties on the same terms as Irish Protestants. Inevitably, it took a number of years, and some electoral organisation for this concession to have an impact in the constituencies. However, as early as 1802 a Catholic interest was evident and had become much more widespread by 1807. It was noted, for example, that while the Catholic forty-shilling freeholders voted generally at the command of the landlord (though revolts were by no means unknown), their presence and their numbers tended to have an influence on the candidate put forward for election. By 1818, a large majority of Irish M.P.s (whatever their *private* views might be) were, *in public*, in favour of emancipation largely because electoral prudence left them with no other choice. By the early 1820s, a Catholic electorate had emerged, largely considered unworthy by Catholic elite figures, but it was disciplined and potentially formidable, and had been well schooled in the hurly-burly of Irish sectarian politics over the previous decades. Catholics were also equally experienced in the turbulent world of the various Catholic representative bodies.

Organizing the signing of petitions, electing delegates, drawing up agendas, identifying grievances, and conducting debates made a huge contribution to the democratization of the Catholic community in the early nineteenth century. The Catholic Convention of 1792–3, the elections that preceded it, and the pressure that it subsequently brought to bear on the British government remained the model for those Catholics who sought to win emancipation in the vastly changed circumstances of post-Union Ireland. In the early years of the new century, delegates were elected for the express purpose of preparing an address or a petition, and, in May 1806, Catholic addresses with several thousand signatures reached Dublin Castle. In 1807, the assistance of the Catholic bishops was sought, and was forthcoming, in a similar exercise. By 1809, the Catholic bishops sent Edward Hay, the Catholic body's secretary, lists of their parish priests so that he could approach them for help in what had become almost an annual petition. Priests also aided in the collection of money to defray the expenses of the petition. Catholic priests threw themselves into parliamentary election contests, and they were very active throughout the whole petitioning process in the first two decades of the nineteenth century. The addresses and the petitions may have fallen on deaf ears, and were sometimes regarded as shameful, but from the point of view of educating Catholics to the mechanics of politics, they offered invaluable and lasting lessons.

Alongside the democratization of Irish Catholics, through their attempts to elect representative committees and their involvement in parliamentary elections and petitioning, often aided by their priests, there was the phenomenon of sociability, the growing pressure to associate for various purposes. Between the 1790s and the 1820s, large segments of the Irish peasantry were brought to an awareness of their political weight and their numbers, and grew accustomed to acting together. People came together at wakes, funerals, executions, patterns, cockfights, sporting events, agrarian secret societies, fairs, and markets. None of these were new but what was striking in the three decades after 1790 was how frequently such hitherto politically neutral occasions of sociability took on a highly charged politicized character.

In the mid-1790s, the United Irishmen in rural Ulster organized 'potato diggings' on land held by members in prison. This could be seen as simply age-old communalism at work, but such activities enabled the United Irishmen to show their strength in the area, thus making a political point. At the same time, in Dublin, in the mid-1790s, their urban colleagues organized political funerals at which large numbers attended to show solidarity with the deceased, and to intimidate the authorities by their numbers. Nearly thirty years later, it was reported that '20 000' had turned up at the execution in 1823 of the Rockite leader John Marum, in Kilkenny, and 'a vast concourse' attended another execution. Similar estimates were given for the number of those who attended the burial (if the body was released) of those executed. We might note that there were many such occasions in the heavily sectarianized Rockite insurgency: between 1821 and 1824, up to one hundred murders can be attributed to Rockite violence and these led to around a hundred executions, with some six hundred transported to Australia.[24]

During the first two decades of the nineteenth century, many traditional gatherings were transformed into demonstrations in order to make political statements. In 1803, for example, perhaps as many as ten thousand people showed up at Balla, County Mayo, for what was billed as a local religious ceremony but was regarded by the authorities as 'a day of folly'. This was three times the number that had attended the previous year, and the authorities suspected that the gathering was a pretext for conspiracy. Again, in 1810, what was described as a large crowd assembled on the Hill of Alske, in the Wicklow mountains, to listen to one Doyle, a poet, recite his work. His poems seemed innocuous enough, but towards the end of the recitation two figures appeared on the platform, representing Napoleon and Josephine. And, in 1813, large crowds gathered at the grave of a Fr Nugent because the earth from his grave when mixed with local holy water was reputed to be a cure for various ailments. Local observers were suspicious, however, and concluded that the gathering was only a pretext for nightly meetings with a conspiratorial objective.

Sporting occasions also provided opportunities for large crowds to gather and, as ever, to make a political point. In the first few years of the century, crowds were reported to have come together in Leitrim, Tipperary, Meath, Cavan, and Dublin, variously 'under the pretence of hurdling [sic]', 'under the pretext of playing football' or 'for the purpose of playing at football as was said but for disaffected purposes as was suspected'. At one game in Dublin in 1804, fifty-four people were arrested. The authorities sought to stop such public displays, claiming that they were similar to those that had been held before the attempted insurrection of Robert Emmet in 1803.

Then there was the sociability offered by the secret societies. From the Whiteboys of the 1760s through to the Defenders of the 1790s and on to the Threshers, Caravats, Ribbonmen, and Rockites of the period 1800–1825, there were few years when Ireland was free of agrarian insurgency. With regard to sociability, these secret societies were important, for they provided their members with experience in organizing, acting together, and identifying grievances. They also brought them face to face with the power, or frequently the powerlessness, of the state, and thus showed them the strength of solidarity. It is worth stressing, too, how the perception of the forces of law and order as entirely sectarian instruments reinforced Catholic solidarity in the face of the 'Orange' foe. The Police, the Yeomanry, and even the regular army were all viewed as essentially Protestant forces deployed oppressively against Irish Catholics. Members of the Yeomanry, in particular, were widely hated for their use of excessive force, their Orange triumphalism, and their clear invulnerability to disciplinary charges. On occasion, occasions of rural sociability were the target of this force, for the Yeomanry were also notorious for dispersing country dancers, scattering mourners at wakes and funerals, and closing pubs.[25]

Lastly, we come to militarization as a factor in the politicization of Irish Catholic society in the early decades of the nineteenth century. For large numbers of adult males, perhaps as many as one in six during the Revolutionary and Napoleonic wars, a portion of their lives was spent in uniform; drilling, marching, parading, and taking orders from a superior officer. By 1810, nearly one million men had been recruited in the British Isles to fight the French, of which Ireland's share was out of proportion to her numbers. At least two hundred thousand Irish joined the army and navy and tens of thousands more served in the Militia and Yeomanry.[26] This huge recruitment had an enormous impact on Irish life.

As noted above, the manpower requirements of the British war machine played a major role in bringing about the repeal of a number of the penal laws in the late eighteenth century. Similarly, the ending of the wars in 1815 removed any pressure to make concessions to Irish Catholics, as Catholic recruits were not now crucial to success. Beyond these obvious points, it is clear that the recruitment of such large numbers gave something of a military flavour to Irish popular disturbances. Contemporaries were impressed with the drill and parade skills of societies such as the Shanavests, who turned out in Killenaule, County Tipperary, in 1810. Not surprisingly, their discipline and arms-bearing was attributed to the presence of deserters and ex-soldiers among them. Again, it was notorious that service in the British armed forces could pose problems for the conscientious Catholic. There was frequent pressure on them to attend Protestant services on Sunday, and a refusal might lead to charges. Edmund Burke in the 1790s, and Archbishop Troy and Daniel O'Connell in the new century, all intervened in defence of Catholic soldiers charged with disobeying orders to attend Protestant services. In humiliating contrast, Catholic worship in the armed services was not considered a priority, and some officers considered it bad for regimental discipline. All in all, those soldiers who served and who survived to re-enter civilian life almost certainly did so with memories of the lowly status of their religion and the frequency with which this was brought home to them. In O'Connell's 'army', such veterans found a home.

In short, the sectarianized, democratized, socialized and militarized masses that would bring O'Connell victory in the campaign for Catholic Emancipation in 1829 had not been called into existence by him. In fact, he may have been the principal beneficiary of a generation of politicization in Ireland that would result in the emergence of a Catholic nation.

At the same time, O'Connell's enormous contribution to the final outcome cannot be gainsaid or diminished.[27] Born in 1775, of strong farming stock in County Kerry, O'Connell's life until 1800 had been largely uneventful. He had been in Paris at the start of the revolution but, despite speculation to the contrary, there is no evidence that the scenes he witnessed there left him with a life-long commitment to non-violence or pacifism. He then trained as a lawyer in London but his experience there hardly filled him with affection for the English. Almost certainly he was a member of the United Irishmen in Dublin, but he took no part in the 1798 rebellion. What made an indelible impression on him was his religion, for he was an Irish Catholic and, as he never ceased to proclaim, he loved his religion because it was Irish and because it was Catholic. Irish Protestants, by contrast, are no better than 'foreigners to us because they are of a different religion'. O'Connell bestrode in equal measure the Gaelic-speaking world of deliverance, millenarian dreams, and vision poetry, and the English-speaking world of the political philosophers William Godwin and Jeremy Bentham. His mastery of both spheres rendered him an altogether new and immense force in Irish and English life; equally it offered him opportunities for deceit, deception, and dissembling that were denied to monocultural and monolingual individuals. No Englishman could understand him: he was clearly not a gentleman, for his 'word' seemed never to be a binding commitment; yet his command of the language of politics, and of the tactics of party politics, placed him recognizably within the British parliamentary tradition. Similarly, he was an enigma to his Irish subordinates (these were all he had, for he would brook no rival), displaying real warmth and generosity on many occasions, but proving merciless in debates, and vindictive in his enmities. Perhaps it was the masses who understood 'An Counsiléar'(the counsellor. or, lawyer) best, for they could see in him the incarnation of their dreams and aspirations. All—labourer, landless, cottier, or strong farmer, despite their furious rivalries that would manifest themselves in competing agrarian secret societies—could see themselves in him and they responded to his call. Not surprisingly, the Irish folklore archives are stuffed with tales and stories about O'Connell (Bonaparte comes a distant second), casting him in the role of a Gaelic Messiah or Gaelic hero, tracing his ancestry back to the earliest Gods and investing him with appropriate traits—boundless sexual energy, being one of the more notable, with none other than the young Queen Victoria reportedly succumbing to his charms. And in the anglophone world of popular music, O'Connell was to figure prominently, for he was to be the most 'ballad-ised' of all the Irish national leaders. He was a man driven—possessed, some claimed—by history, by religion, and by a sense of grievance, both personal and for his people. His target, for all that it might seem to shift from decade to decade, if not year to year, was ultimately the destruction of the Protestant Ascendancy.

VI

The turning point in Catholic fortunes came in 1823 with the setting up of the Catholic Association.[28] By that date, George III was dead, though any advantage this might have brought was to an extent set aside by his successor's desire to honour his father's memory by continued resistance to the Catholic claims. Moreover, the Catholic campaign had made good progress in the House of Commons, with a slight majority of M.P.s being in favour of a bill to remove Catholic disabilities. However, once again, this advantage was entirely offset because the House of Lords remained an apparently insuperable block to Catholic advance. Nonetheless, the ending of the 'Veto' controversy and, as well, the appointment of Marquis Wellesley in 1822 as Lord Lieutenant seemed to open up better prospects for Catholics, for he was known to be in favour of Catholic Emancipation, and his wife was an American Catholic widow. O'Connell was jubilant. He regarded these events as most auspicious and declared that Wellesley's appointment would be 'a harbinger of victory'. O'Connell was to be disappointed by Wellesley and in reaction he began to pursue a more aggressive strategy. In April 1823, O'Connell and Richard Lalor Sheil agreed to put their differences behind them and came together to set up the Catholic Association.

The new association differed from the Catholic Board which it replaced in that its primary task was not to organize yet another annual petition (now dubbed by O'Connell 'the annual farce'). Instead, its aims were much wider and encompassed the politicization of all Catholic grievances, and then while keeping within the law, to bring 'our cause to the attention of parliament'. Accordingly, all manner of Catholic grievances were brought forward, among them the proselytism of the Kildare Place Society, the lack of a Catholic chaplain at Newgate prison, disputes over graveyards, bias in the judiciary, grasping landlords, and the problem of tithes. The initial response to this new policy was rather halting and the upsurge in the Association's fortunes came nine months after it was set up with the establishment of a 'Catholic rent', set at 1d per month and to be levied throughout Ireland. Within a few months this development was being described as 'in truth, an Irish Revolution'.

The idea of collecting subscriptions from the Catholics was not a new one. Forty years earlier Lord Kenmare had called for a collection from the 2500 Catholic parishes to defray expenses incurred in petitioning. Nothing came of this, and there had been intermittent attempts since then to raise money, again with little success. This time it was different: by December 1824 some £7500 had been collected and by March 1825 a further £9000 had come in. The explanation for this turnaround lies almost entirely in the Association's new policy of taking up all sorts of Catholic grievances and in making available legal advice to Catholics who sought it. (O'Connell's expertise was vital here). The Catholic bishops were fully behind the collection of the Catholic rent, and the parish priests and the curates were active in promoting and in supervising the plan.

The year 1823–24 was a particularly fraught one throughout Ireland with sectarian consciousness at a high point. A 'Second Reformation' had been declared in 1822 by William Magee, the Protestant archbishop of Dublin, and there were furious arguments between Catholic priests and Protestant missionaries over the interpretation of the bible and over proselytism. In the countryside, Rockite depredations continued, many bearing a strong sectarian colouring, while at the popular level the excitement engendered by Pastorini's prophecy that Protestantism would end in 1825 kept the masses on edge. To sponsor the Catholic rent was to enter the fray, and few Catholic priests could resist.

Almost inevitably, the government prepared to ban the Catholic Association, and would have done so had it not dissolved itself first. The ensuing relief was short-lived for the New Catholic Association was formed and sought to continue the work of its predecessor. By 1826, Sir Robert Peel at the Home Office, and the duke of Wellington in the House of Lords, had concluded that resistance to the Catholic demands was not only futile but dangerous, for it might spark a civil war in Ireland. What was needed was an emergency in Ireland that would offer the necessary opportunity to grant emancipation, and to grant it, as Peel put it, 'in such a way as to preserve the Protestant interest in Ireland'.

In 1826, that necessary emergency began to unfold. In that year, in the Waterford county election, Thomas Wyse and other local Catholic activists decided to run a candidate against Lord George Beresford, a powerful sitting M.P., wholly opposed to Catholic Emancipation and a scion of one of the leading Ascendancy families. O'Connell reluctantly concurred, for he doubted whether the Catholic freeholder vote could be detached from their landlord, and he had even been prepared at one stage to concede an end to this franchise as a condition of emancipation. The result of the election, however, defied O'Connell's gloomy expectations and was never in doubt; the candidate sponsored reluctantly by O'Connell, and enthusiastically by Wyse and his associates, easily topped the poll. Elsewhere there were similar successes, as a number of sitting candidates were defeated, or nearly overturned. What had happened in the 1826 election was not the product of one man; nor was it the result of recent disappointments. What it represented was the outcome of long-maturing processes at work deep within Irish society over the previous sixty years and more. By 1826, politicization had reached a level at which a call for action would evoke a response and lead to mobilization. The events of 1826 revealed the existence of an aggressively politicized Catholic nation, one whose identity had been formed by hostility to Protestants and from Protestants.

Emancipation would almost certainly have been granted in the aftermath of the 'freeholder revolts' of 1826 but for ministerial instability in London which meant that some eighteen months elapsed before a government headed by the duke of Wellington as prime minister and Peel, once again as Home Secretary, took office. It was quickly confronted by a new (and in the event the final) crisis, for O'Connell declared himself a candidate for parliament in a by-election to be held in County Clare. Catholics could not take their seats because of the oaths that were required of all members: but there was nothing to stop a Catholic running for election. The result was not long in doubt. All the features of earlier freeholder revolts were quickly apparent. The Catholic clergy rowed in behind O'Connell's candidacy, the forty-shilling freeholders were urged, even ordered, to 'Vote for your religion', and O'Connell duly romped home. With the threat of violence heightening appreciably and with a prospect of Protestant resistance looming, Wellington and Peel resolved to act swiftly: the King was told firmly that concession was necessary to head off violence, and Wellington's influence in the House of Lords was sufficient to overcome opposition there. An Emancipation Bill was put through which met with O'Connell's approval: but in order to prevent wholesale electoral revolution, the forty-shilling freeholder franchise was raised to £10. The Emancipation Act came into effect in April 1829.

VII

The true significance of O'Connell's triumph in the struggle for Catholic Emancipation lies more in the means employed to bring it about than in the victory gained, for the right to sit in the united parliament could be exercised at that time only by a handful of Catholics. Under O'Connell's inspired leadership, the Catholic masses of rural Ireland were enlisted into the campaign for emancipation. This had proved no easy task, for furious tensions and raging rivalries concerning class, wealth, and land had long seethed just beneath (and sometimes above) the surface of Irish life. Nonetheless, by focussing on the single goal of emancipation, by appealing to a shared Catholic consciousness and by harping on historic and current grievances and resentments, O'Connell had managed to keep these divisions at bay. For the first time in Irish history, Catholic numbers—or in O'Connell's words, the 'electricity of public opinion'—had been devastatingly deployed in a political movement and, to the evident dismay of the governing class in both Ireland and England, the 'quantity' had carried the day over the 'quality'.

The campaign for Catholic Emancipation put a question mark against the future of the Union, and in many ways the outcome of that struggle determined the later political history of the nineteenth century. The Act of Union had once been heralded as the gateway to emancipation: instead, it had rapidly taken on the status of a grievance. Emancipation had been conceded only when civil war threatened, and this would strengthen the hand of those who argued that the Union could never offer good government to Ireland, and that only self-government would do that. In addition, just as the passing of the Act of Union had damaged the Protestant governing elite, so, too, the winning of Catholic emancipation marked a further grave erosion of its political power.

Lastly, it was ominous that the first peaceful mass movement in Irish, indeed in European history, had turned essentially on a religious question. True, Catholic Emancipation was ostensibly about Catholic access to politics, but the campaign to achieve it had been conducted along the lines of a religious revival with Catholic priests as cheerleaders, and no one could be in any doubt that this was a religious contest between the religion of the Irish and the religion of the English. Famously, O'Connell had confessed that he loved his religion because it was Irish and because it was Catholic; infamously, he had sneeringly dismissed Irish Protestants as 'foreigners'. There was, of course, much more to O'Connell than this sectarianism, but after 1829 the Catholics were indisputably the people of Ireland, and O'Connell was their leader.

VIII

It had frequently been claimed that Catholic Emancipation would mean an end to the Irish Question. Richard Lalor Sheil had forecast that once Catholics were eligible to sit in parliament no man would be able 'to draw huge convocations of men together in Ireland' no matter what his object was, while J.W. Doyle, the Catholic bishop of Kildare and Leighlin, predicted that 'the whole of the Catholic population would consider their grievances, as it were, at an end.' In the event, it was Peel who was proved correct, for he had claimed in 1829 that 'the settlement of the Catholic Question would not be the settlement of Ireland'. Campaigns for an end to tithes, for political and educational reform, and for repeal of the Union followed on relentlessly in the decades after 1830.

After Emancipation, Daniel O'Connell swiftly turned, or returned, to his long-term goal of repealing the Act of Union. Like the able politician that he was, O'Connell resolutely refused to spell out precisely what he meant by 'repeal'. On the face of it, he was demanding the repeal of the Irish Act of Union, but he surely could not have desired the return of the old Irish parliament, for that had been an entirely Protestant body. The members of the old Irish House of Commons had been elected under a variety of franchises, now no longer operative, and a majority had been returned from borough constituencies, most of which had since disappeared. As a slogan, 'Repeal' (or 'Repale' as O'Connell's opponents used to mock his accent) had the considerable merit of being both pithy and opaque, and O'Connell's adoring troops, eager for another struggle under his messianic leadership, duly fell in behind it. It is clear, even so, that the goal of ending the Act of Union did not engage the enthusiasm of his followers as much as Catholic Emancipation. Indeed, it is not even certain that O'Connell himself regarded it as anything other than an 'in terrorem' measure, that is, as a way of gaining leverage with the British government, for he was quite prepared to switch to conventional politics when the time seemed right. Thus, by the time the Liberator died in 1847 the movement for repeal had run out of steam.

The insurmountable problem that O'Connell encountered where repeal was concerned was one that lay athwart all later movements that sought to create, or re-create, a devolved legislative assembly in Ireland. No matter what protestations of loyalty to the British connection were made by those in favour of such a course, no matter how indignantly accusations of separatism were denied, the reality was that, until the 1880s, and after, in Britain and amongst Irish Protestants generally, the objective of Irish self-government, however described or circumscribed, was held to be completely illegitimate, wholly inadmissible, and utterly destructive to both countries. O'Connell might claim that repeal was both loyal and national, and that he himself was a firm monarchist, but it made no difference. In Britain, Irish self-government was viewed as a stepping-stone to Irish separatism and had, therefore, to be resisted at all costs up to, and including, war.

At the time of the Catholic Emancipation crisis, and faced with a choice between widespread public disorder or Catholic Emancipation, Peel had wisely opted for concession upon face-saving terms; but confronted with the options of civil war or repeal of the Act of Union, no British government would have hesitated to go to war to maintain the Union. In short, when O'Connell declared for repeal, his campaign could not but end in failure. Perhaps he sensed this?

Certainly, this suggestion might help explain quite why O'Connell from an early date was prepared to 'park' the repeal demand and seek an accommodation with the new Whig government in London. O'Connell dressed up this new strategy as 'testing the Union', the clear inference being that the Union would fail the test because no British government, no matter how well-intentioned towards Ireland, could possibly do for Ireland what self-government alone could achieve. That being said, O'Connell's determination to press the new prime minister, Lord Melbourne, and his Whig government to commit to reform in Ireland and to deliver on its promises in that regard, bore fruit throughout the 1830s. It helped that the Whig government of the 1830s was a self-consciously modernizing one, resolved to bring in much-needed reforms on a whole range of topics; and so O'Connell was pushing against an open door in advocating state action in Ireland. Whatever the springs of policy, by the end of the decade a transformation had taken place in the administration of Ireland, and O'Connell could point to his alliance with the Whigs as helping to influence, if not to direct, the shape of those changes.

Out of the many reforms that were brought in during the 1830s, those that purported to tackle the problems of tithe, municipal corporations, ignorance, and poverty were particularly noteworthy. The Catholic masses had long regarded the payment of tithe to an alien church in the same light as the denial of a seat in parliament had seemed to O'Connell's better-off supporters—an insupportable affront. Given their mean condition, O'Connell's army of peasants could have no realistic aspiration to parliamentary representation, but an end to tithe would constitute for them both a tangible reward for their role in winning emancipation and another victory over their Protestant masters. Following a brief but bloody 'tithe war', and a more effective 'tithe strike', tithe commutation was brought in by legislation in 1835. Henceforth, tithe was to be paid by the landlord (and recouped by him as a charge on rent), associated arrears were to be paid by the government, and, crucially, the poorest cultivators in the countryside—yearly tenants and tenants-at-will—were to be exempt from any payment. Tithe had not been abolished, but it was now made invisible, and another mass peasant protest had had its victory.

The sectarianism that accompanied much of the anti-tithe agitation was replicated in the debate over the future of Irish municipal corporations. Since Cromwellian times, these had been bastions of the Protestant Ascendancy, notionally tasked not with advancing urban improvement but, like the old Irish parliament, with furthering the Protestant interest, and promoting the Protestant religion. Whatever about their original, theoretical remit, by the 1830s their inefficiency, corruption, and utter lack of civic responsibility had become matters of public notoriety. Of course, Irish corporations were not unique in these respects, for their English counterparts were almost equally useless. However, when it came to reform, there was to be a marked difference in the approach adopted in both countries.

In Britain, the Municipal Reform Act of 1835 gave new powers to corporations, granted the franchise to all ratepayers, and allowed them to elect their own sheriff and control their local police. For Ireland, it was to be rather different. Five years of bitter and prolonged parliamentary debate resulted in the Municipal Corporation Act of 1840, a compromise measure which, far from rationalizing and making Irish corporations more responsible, in fact, abolished the vast majority, leaving only ten in place in the bigger urban centres. The key difficulty here was that any attempt to open up Irish municipal corporations to the breadth of public opinion meant inevitably that there would be a Catholic takeover of many, perhaps most, of them. As a result, rather than permit the 'enemy' to seize these Protestant redoubts, those opposed to any change—Irish Protestants, generally, and their Tory allies in Britain—preferred to see them destroyed. Protestant fears in this regard may not have been groundless. In 1841, O'Connell became the first Catholic lord mayor of Dublin since the seventeenth century, a triumph almost as symbolic as his earlier parliamentary one of a decade before.

Possession of the municipal franchise and the conduct of local government were, for the most part, matters of concern to a minority of Irish people; but it was different with the introduction of an Irish Poor Law.[29] Mass poverty was widely regarded in British government circles as a principal cause of Irish disaffection and 'agitation' and the solution adopted was the same as that for England. A network of workhouses was to be created and those seeking relief had to enter into them. Mass ignorance was also regarded as a source of Irish disaffection and to remedy this a national system of elementary education was set up, which was to be non-denominational. The various religious interests involved paid lip service to this notion of all-children-together and within a short period the guiding principle had been abandoned in the face of protests by the religious denominations. The result was emphatically not what the government had intended: a national system of publicly funded elementary education that was controlled by the Catholic Church, where it was in the ascendancy, by the Presbyterians where they dominated and by the Church of Ireland where its members were in a local majority. What had been envisaged as a system of religiously integrated education, one that would smooth away the rough edges of confessional enmity among the young, within a short time had become almost entirely sectarianized.

The replacement of the Whig administration of Lord Melbourne with a Tory one led by Sir Robert Peel in 1841 brought to a shuddering halt all co-operation or compact between O'Connell and the government, for between the two men there existed a deep-seated antipathy. O'Connell promptly announced the resumption of his repeal campaign, claiming that since even a sympathetic government such as that of Lord Melbourne had proved incapable of quenching the Irish thirst for self-government, there was no possibility, therefore, that a Tory government, headed by 'Orange' Peel, would be any more successful in this regard.

Peel's policy in the early 1840s, aptly described as one of 'iron-handed reconciliation', was considerably successful in the short term. In the face of the government's firm resolve, O'Connell's repeal campaign quickly ran into sand, and while he was able to attract large numbers to his 'monster meetings' to demand repeal, his bombast proved ineffective against Peel's determination. A particularly galling setback for O'Connell occurred when the government banned a planned monster meeting at Clontarf in October 1843 and, rather than risk disorder, he had to call it off. Previous meetings at

Trim in March and at Tara Hill in August of that year had reputedly attracted hundreds of thousands but had achieved precisely nothing. In 1844, Peel moved against O'Connell himself, and he was put on trial on charges of conspiracy for which he was duly convicted and sentenced to twelve months imprisonment. He was released after a few months, but it was evident that the repeal campaign was going nowhere.

In the struggle for Catholic emancipation, O'Connell had been the undisputed leader, almost entirely above criticism from his followers; but it was all rather different when he turned his attention to repeal in the 1840s. Here his leadership came under searching scrutiny from a group of largely Protestant repealers who clustered around the Trinity-educated journalist Thomas Davis, and who soon became known collectively as Young Ireland.[30] For O'Connell, the re-establishment of the Irish parliament was the first step in giving good government to Ireland. He viewed with equanimity, and probably with approval, the undoubted fact that any new parliament would be largely Catholic in membership. And he saw repeal as reversing the historic wrongs done to Catholic Ireland. For Davis and his colleagues—John Mitchel, Charles Gavan Duffy, William Smith O'Brien, and John Blake Dillon were the most prominent—it was all rather different, for they saw in repeal merely the first step in the regeneration of Ireland and they were appalled at the vista of a Catholic ascendancy replacing the Protestant one. Almost certainly, they found nauseating the blatant sectarianism that had accompanied and shaped the reforms of the 1830s. Certainly, O'Connell's clear understanding that 'Catholic' and 'Irish' were interchangeable, and that Catholic numbers necessarily meant that they must rule, offered them little comfort in this respect.

Davis and the others were in agreement with O'Connell that self-government was vital to a nation's well-being, but where they moved beyond him was in their mystical reverence for the very notion of the nation. To them, the nation was a product of history, language, and literature, and every nation had an undeniable right to self-rule. Ireland fitted all their criteria: the Irish or 'Celts' were racially distinct from the Saxon; they had a glorious history; and they had their own Gaelic language. Young Ireland's mission was to publicize these attributes. Hence, a weekly newspaper, Nation, edited by Charles Gavan Duffy, was brought out in 1842 and soon attained a circulation of 10 000. As well as current news items, its readers were regaled with stirring poems, rousing or sentimental ballads, and exciting stories, all designed to instil patriotic fervour. To that end, Irish heroism and resistance were highlighted while Saxon perfidy was denounced.

All that was missing, the Young Irelanders felt, was a genuine national literature, that is, a literature that would serve the needs of the nation. Literary merit was, of course, desirable in this national literature, but not essential. To meet this need, a Library of Ireland was instituted to bring cheap editions of inspiring works, historical and literary, to the widest readership (and, thanks to the national school system, there was now an expanding public for such books). O'Connell had no particular problem with much of this, though the constant harping on about battles and massacres, and the note of martial pride that infused much of Young Ireland's writings, would have caused him some unease, for he was resolutely committed to staying within the law in his campaign.

Essentially, where O'Connell and Young Ireland parted company, was over the role of religion. For O'Connell, with his belief that Catholic and Irish were merely two words for the one thing, it was natural that Catholics must rule, given that they were the clear majority in Ireland. Young Ireland, for its part, argued that confessional religion was a private matter, and that the public religion they espoused—nationalism—was the only true faith. As one of their poems put it:

'What matter that at different shrines we pray unto our God?
What matter that at different times our fathers won this sod?'

To which, of course, the answer was that it mattered a lot to a Catholic middle-class, convinced that its church was despised, and it also mattered a lot to Catholic tenant farmers, who believed that the land confiscations of the seventeenth century were quite simply a historic crime that demanded redress. It was all very well for Davis and his friends to claim that religion was a private affair, and to urge all Irish people to worship publicly at the altar of nationalism, eschewing all denominational advantage, but there can be little doubt that the fervour with which Young Ireland bowed down before an all-embracing, non-denominational nationalism was sharpened by a chilling recognition of the bleak future for the Protestants of Ireland if, and when, the Catholic 'quantity' would finally triumph (trample?) over the Protestant 'quality'.

It was probably inevitable that O'Connell and Young Ireland would quarrel: he was old and they young, by the mid-1840s he was tired, and they had grown impatient. He had never been comfortable with questioning of his leadership, much less criticism of his tactics; Young Ireland's profound distaste for O'Connell's continual flirtation with Westminster politicians and his involvement in their intrigues, compromises, and alliances swiftly led to open argument. There was also a sharp division of opinion between O'Connell and Young Ireland over the provision of university education for Ireland. Ultimately, O'Connell followed the majority of the Catholic bishops in their opposition to 'Godless colleges', while Young Ireland was in favour of the proposed institutions precisely because of their lack of religious affiliation. A breach between the two might have occurred over this matter. In the event, the proximate cause of the rupture between O'Connell and Young Ireland stemmed from a newspaper article written by John Mitchel that addressed the question of ambush tactics in a military conflict. O'Connell seized on this item as proof of Young Ireland's martial intentions and he issued them an ultimatum to disavow violence under all circumstances, or else. Rather than yield to such an ultimatum, and protesting that such a demand was extraordinary, even esoteric, since they had no plans for insurrection, the Young Irelanders seceded in a body from O'Connell's movement in July 1846.

O'Connell died in Genoa in 1847, appropriately enough while making a pilgrimage to Rome; for their part, the Young Irelanders went on to stage a futile insurrection in 1848, for which, happily, none of them was made to pay the ultimate price. Meanwhile, in the Irish countryside, as the debate on nationalism between Young and Old Ireland continued in the late 1840s, and the question of physical force versus moral force was canvassed, hundreds of thousands were starving to death, similar numbers were perishing from disease, and as many again were fleeing the island. The Catholic nation had more victims, but now it had gone global.

NOTES

1. Cited in Thomas Bartlett, *The Fall and Rise of the Irish Nation: the Catholic Question, 1690–1830* (Dublin, 1992), 343; and see the entry for Beresford in the *Dictionary of Irish Biography*, (9 vols, Cambridge, 2009) by Raymond Refaussé.
2. George Boyce, *Nationalism in Ireland* (3rd edition, London, 1995), 125.
3. See Bernadette Cunningham, *The World of Geoffrey Keating: History, Myth and Religion in Seventeenth-century Ireland* (Dublin, 2000).
4. Boyce, *Nationalism*, 85.
5. H. Davis (ed), Jonathan Swift, *The Drapier's Letters to the People of Ireland* (Oxford, 1935); and see also Boyce, *Nationalism*, 106–8.
6. Unless otherwise stated, I have drawn freely on my *Fall and Rise of the Irish Nation* (Dublin, 1992).
7. Nigel Yates, *The Religious Condition of Ireland 1770–1850* (Oxford, 2006), 29–30.
8. Gerard O'Brien (ed), *Catholic Ireland in the Eighteenth Century: the Collected Essays of Maureen Wall* (Dublin, 1989).
9. George Goold to General Irvine, 13 September 1781: TNA, State Papers 63/476/141.
10. S.J. Connolly, *Priests and People in Pre-Famine Ireland* (Dublin, 1982), 281–3.
11. Bartlett, *Fall and Rise*, 206.
12. Marianne Elliott, *Wolfe Tone, Prophet of Irish Independence* (New Haven, 1990).
13. Bartlett, *Fall and Rise*, 259.
14. Patrick Geoghegan, *The Irish Act of Union: a Study in High Politics* (Dublin, 1999); see also G.C. Bolton, *The Passing of the Irish Act of Union: a Study in Parliamentary Politics* (Oxford, 1966).
15. Bartlett, *Fall and Rise*, 258–9.
16. Bartlett, *Fall and Rise*, 259–61.
17. For these decades, see the chapters by S.J. Connolly in W.E. Vaughan, *A New History of Ireland, vol. 5: Ireland under the Union, 1801–1870* (Oxford, 1989).
18. See Linda Colley, *Britons: Forging the Nation, 1707–1837* (New Haven, 1992), passim; see also James Kelly, *Sir Richard Musgrave, 1746–1818: Ultra Protestant Firebrand* (Dublin, 2009), ch. 6.
19. For the Veto question, see Gerard O'Brien, 'The beginning of the veto controversy in Ireland', *Journal of Ecclesiastical History* (January 1987), 80–94.
20. See J.S. Donnelly, *Captain Rock: the Irish Agrarian Rebellion of 1821–24* (Wisconsin, 2009), a book much wider than its title suggests.
21. Kelly, *Musgrave*, passim.
22. See Irene Whelan, *The Bible War in Ireland: the 'Second Reformation' and the Polarisation of Protestant-Catholic Relations, 1800–1840* (Wisconsin, 2005).
23. Donnelly, *Captain Rock*, 122–127.
24. Donnelly, *Captain Rock*, 318, 323.
25. Donnelly, *Captain Rock*, 140.
26. See J.E. Cookson, *The British Armed Nation, 1793–1815* (Oxford, 1997).

27. Oliver MacDonagh, *The Hereditary Bondsman: Daniel O'Connell, 1775–1829* (London, 1988) and *The Emancipist* (London 1989) is the definitive biography for this generation. Patrick Geoghegan's two-volume study of O'Connell, *King Dan, the Rise of Daniel O'Connell* and *Liberator, the Life and Death of Daniel O'Connell, 1830–1847* (Dublin 2008, 2010) considers O'Connell in a wide perspective. The study by Gearóid Ó Tuathaigh in the *Dictionary of Irish Biography* (Cambridge, 2009) is succinct and exceptional.

28. In this section I have drawn freely on my *Fall and Rise*, chs. 13 and 14.

29. See Peter Gray, *The Making of the Irish Poor Law, 1815–43* (London, 2009).

30. For Young Ireland, see Boyce, *Nationalism*, 154–177.

SELECT BIBLIOGRAPHY

Bartlett, Thomas, *The Fall and Rise of the Irish Nation, 1690–1830* (Dublin, 1992).

Bergin, John, Magennis, Eoin, Ní Mhungaile Lesa, and Walsh, Patrick (eds), New perspectives on the penal laws: *Eighteenth century Ireland, Special issue no. 1* (Dublin, 2011).

Clark, Samuel and Donnelly, James, *Irish Peasants: Violence and Political Unrest, 1780–1870* (Manchester, 1993).

Connolly, Sean, *Religion, Law and power: the Making of Protestant Ireland, 1660–1760* (Oxford, 1992).

Corish, Patrick. *The Irish Catholic Experience: an Historical Survey* (Dublin, 1985).

Gray, Peter, *Famine, Land and Politics: British Government and Irish Society, 1843–50* (Dublin, 1999).

Keogh, Daire, 'The French disease': the Catholic Church and Radicalism in Ireland, 1790–1800* (Dublin, 1993).

McBride, Ian, *Eighteenth-century Ireland: the Isle of Slaves* (Dublin, 2009).

McDonagh, Oliver. *Daniel O'Connell* (2 volumes, London, 1988–9).

Power, T.P. and Whelan, Kevin (ed), *Endurance and emergence: Catholics in Ireland in the eighteenth Century* (Dublin, 1990).

Yates, Nigel, *The Religious Condition of Ireland, 1770–1850* (Oxford, 2006).

CHAPTER 27

FAMINE AND LAND, 1845–80

PETER GRAY

THE Great Famine of 1845–50 plays a central role in the historical narrative of modern Ireland, both as a profoundly traumatic event occurring at a key moment in the process of Irish nation-building, and as a motor for extensive social, economic, and demographic change within Ireland, and, through mass emigration, in the wider anglophone world. Despite a tendency in much Irish historical writing of the 1950s–70s to displace the Famine from the pivotal position it had acquired in popular understandings of the Irish past, more recent research has tended to re-emphasize its significance, albeit with due regard to longer-term socio-economic trends that were already promoting growing emigration and social change. Historians writing in recent years have also refocused attention on the controversial issue of state responsibility for the extensive mortality of the Famine, while tending to eschew the hyperbolic claims of 'genocide' advanced by some nationalist commentators from the 1840s through to the present.

In absolute terms, the Great Famine was a horrendous catastrophe for the people of the island. Of an estimated population of 8.5 million when the potato blight first struck in autumn 1845, demographic historians now tend to agree that about one million perished from famine-related disease and starvation, while another 0.4 million 'averted births' further reduced the population.[1] In addition to these 'excess deaths', around a million people emigrated during the Famine years, and the rate of exodus remained extraordinarily high through to the mid 1850s. Although imperfect in its methodology, the 1851 Irish census could not but flag the scale of the demographic disaster. The head-count indicated a 20 per cent decline since 1841, and suggested—assuming a 'natural' increase of 1 per cent per annum in line with 1821–41 averages—a shortfall of 2.47 million (27 per cent) of the anticipated 1851 total of just over nine million.[2] As historians seeking to locate the Famine in comparative context have observed, this placed the Irish experience at towards the top end proportionately, if not absolutely, of demographic catastrophes in modern times.[3]

The Great Famine was by no means the first major famine in Irish history, nor was it (in proportionate terms) necessarily the most devastating. The early eighteenth century had witnessed extensive loss of life with famines in the 1720s, climaxing in the 'year of the slaughter' in 1739–41, in which up to 20 per cent of the country's population may have perished.[4] Although the threat of famine subsequently receded, periods of economic growth were punctuated by occasional subsistence crises during which hunger-related fever epidemics took off sizeable numbers. Yet, despite the advancing impoverishment of the lower classes in the increasingly densely populated countryside, and the growing dependence on the potato as a subsistence foodstuff, the Great Famine of 1845–50 was not inevitable and few commentators foresaw its scale or duration. T.R. Malthus himself failed to predict an Irish famine and reductionist Malthusian explanations, which were applied retrospectively, now attract limited historical support.[5] Crucially also for its long-term impact, the Great Famine took place in a very different context from its predecessors, in a modernizing world in which the state could, and was expected to, take a more proactive role in social welfare, in which long-distance movement of large quantities of goods and people by sea was now practicable, and in which modern forms of nationalism were already well advanced within Ireland and its developing diaspora. Whereas the memory of 1741 survived only in the oral tradition of the rural poor, that of 1845–50 would take centre stage in the textual and political memory of the Irish nationalist community at home and overseas.[6]

Modern research tends to place great stress on the contingency and the potency of the ecological trigger, albeit impacting on a vulnerable society. The potato blight fungus *phytophthora infestans* had been active in North America for several years before 1845, but its arrival in Ireland in the autumn of that year was unexpected, perplexing, and ominous. Then unknown to botanical scientists—who pointed instead to vectors as various as minute insects, atmospheric miasmas, and the degeneracy of the potato—the blight spread quickly across Europe from its bridgehead in the potato-seed importing centres of the Low Countries and spelled ecological ruin for the potato fields it reached in that damp season.[7] Significant reports of blight in Ireland appeared in September, and by mid October the lord lieutenant was expressing serious concern about the subsistence crop in his correspondence with London.[8]

Most observers, from Dublin Castle to the inhabitants of the cottages and huts of the rural west, were conscious of what a serious potato failure might presage for Ireland, or for individual communities and families. Potatoes had supported rapid population growth from under 2.5 million in 1753 to 5 million by 1800 and at least 8.1 million by 1841. The combined pressures from the 1770s of praedial subdivision and the drive for increased grain production for export to Britain pushed much of the labouring and smallholding peasantry towards ever-increasing dependency on the root. By the early 1840s, it is estimated that more than half the population subsisted almost entirely on the potato, much of it raised by the rural poor themselves on smallholding or 'conacre' plots, rented from farmers or landowners in return for labour service. There was lower dependency on the crop in the 'oatmeal zone' in northeastern Ireland, where higher wages and tradition favoured a more mixed staple diet. However, with around 60 per cent of Irish agricultural output accounted for by the potato in the 1840s, and much of the remaining output priced beyond the reach of the poor and exported to fund farming profits and landlord rents, the country was acutely susceptible to any major loss of this crop.[9]

In 1845, the incidence of the disease appeared to be patchy, with early frosts impeding its progress in some places and estimates of loss varying wildly. Only when storage pits were opened over the winter did it become evident that the national loss was greater than many had feared, amounting to up to a third of the total harvest that year. This degree of loss was much less than that witnessed in parts of continental Europe in 1845–6, and in Ireland itself the following season, but was enough to impel the rural poor into adopting their traditional modes of surviving a hard year: selling their (potato-fed) pigs and poultry and pawning their clothing, farming, and fishing implements, and seeking relief employment from landowners and the state, and rent remittances from farmers and proprietors. These makeshifts, along with temporary resort to begging and to the newly opened workhouses, had seen most of the rural poor through seasons of dearth in the previous decades, and it is likely that many anticipated that this hungry year would be followed by painful recovery as the blight passed away.

The state's response to this and the following crop failures remains a topic of intense controversy. Sir Robert Peel's Conservative government mustered sufficient Irish experience to know that an extensive potato failure must lead to significant distress. The prime minister was also all too aware, however, of the acute political sensitivities associated with food policy in 1845. An Irish subsistence crisis would inevitably draw attention to the existing protectionist restrictions on the import of foodstuffs to the UK and provoke demands for reciprocity from British taxpayers (stirred up by the radicals of the Anti-Corn Law League) for any relief expenditure in Ireland. Having invested significant political capital since 1844 in seeking to decouple moderate Irish Catholic opinion from O'Connellite nationalism, he was also under pressure to be seen to be acting generously and promptly in the face of threatened Irish distress and noisy agitation on the danger by the Irish press and the Dublin Mansion House Committee. Mixed in with these calculations was a genuine perception, shared by his overtly evangelical Home Secretary, Sir James Graham, that the blight was a manifestation of divine providence, a 'visitation' issued to expose 'unnatural' and hence unsustainable elements in the economic and social constitutions of both Britain and Ireland.[10]

This combination of political and ideological considerations helps explain the government's response to the crisis of 1845–6—a reaction that arguably helped stave off starvation in the first year of Ireland's Great Famine, at the expense of splitting the ruling Conservative Party and virtually terminating Peel's political career. As soon as he was persuaded that the Irish crisis was sufficiently serious, the prime minister committed himself to tying relief to the repeal of the Corn Laws, and hence drew on himself the ire of the landed interest, including many of his own backbenchers. It is true that stimulating the import of cheap substitutes for the potato—principally maize and rice—might temporarily have been accomplished without repeal, but Peel combined an element of free-trade opportunism with a serious concern for what he hoped would be a long-term replacement of peasant potato subsistence with the consumption of imported grain (purchased in the marketplace by proletarianized wage-labourers), and a belief that the providential warning of the blight could not be ignored with impunity. As a committed free-trader, Peel ignored appeals from O'Connell and others in Ireland for a ban on distillation and temporary suspension of grain exports from Ireland, a policy his successors would also adhere to religiously.

The consequence was that Peel's relief policy for Ireland, greeted with a lack of enthusiasm by his own party, was accepted by the opposition radicals and Whigs. It featured a Relief Commission chaired by Sir Randolph Routh, head of the army commissariat—the supply agency best placed to implement relief logistics—which would coordinate the local relief committees and subsidize their voluntary charitable subscriptions. Legislation was passed to finance public relief works, principally on roads and drainage schemes, in collaboration with local landowners and county grand juries, and employing those deemed by the committees to be deserving of relief. This was a long-established policy in response to Irish food crises, albeit now undertaken on a larger scale. Peel's other principal measure was more innovative, but intended as a temporary expedient to pump-prime the as yet under-developed grain import trade. In early 1846, the government secretly purchased £100 000 worth of maize (Indian corn) on the New York market for transhipment to Ireland, where it was parcelled out to depots managed by the commissariat and coast guard. The purpose was not to feed the Irish directly, but to regulate the market price of grain and to accustom the peasantry to this new staple (the commissariat distributed numerous handbills to educate the people on the preparation of what was labelled 'Peel's brimstone' by his critics). As growing distress led to food and employment riots, the relief works and depots were gradually opened.[11]

Peel's measures are generally regarded by many historians as having been generally effective in preventing famine mortality in the first season of the crisis. However, the emphasis behind the policy was transitional and suffered from a number of flaws. Having intervened once in the international food trade, the government was evidently reluctant to do so again, and regarded the significant private importation of maize in summer 1846 as a vindication of this withdrawal from interference. In line with Conservative thinking, relief policy relied heavily on the voluntary contributions of local landed elites, and offered relatively generous grants and loan terms to support this. Both Dublin administrators and the chief civil servant at the Treasury in London, Charles Trevelyan, grew increasingly critical of what they regarded as the reluctance of these local elites to take a fair share of the relief burden, and their apparent readiness to exploit the relief works to improve their own estates at public expense, and abuse the relief ticket system to favour their own dependants and tenants rather than the truly needy. As the British press began to pick up these criticisms, a perception that Peel's system had been too generous took hold. At the same time, Peel's insistence on pressing a robust coercion bill on Ireland to deal with an upsurge in agrarian unrest provoked opposition from Catholic and nationalist interests in Ireland, and provided the opportunity for his parliamentary opponents to bring down his administration in June 1846.

There was widespread uncertainty, and a degree of complacency, respecting the prospective potato harvest for 1846. Previous potato diseases had rarely extended beyond one season, and the rural poor in any case had little choice but to gamble their hoarded potato seed on a revived crop. Demand for conacre plots remained high, and farmers, lacking the will or the means to pay cash wages, were still prepared to let them—some two million acres in total—to the labouring poor.

The shock of the second potato failure, when it came in early August 1846, was sudden and catastrophic. The blight re-emerged in endemic form in that damp mild summer and devastated the potato fields throughout the country, eliminating an unprecedented 80–90 per cent of the harvest. Perhaps inevitably, given the absence of any persuasive scientific explanation, observers turned to the supernatural: 'Divine Providence, in its inscrutable ways, has again poured out upon us the vial of its wrath', wrote the Irish Capuchin friar Theobald Mathew to Trevelyan on 7 August. His intention—evidenced in his following description of 'the wretched people...seated on the fences of their decaying gardens, wringing their hands and wailing bitterly the destruction that had left them foodless'—was to elicit sympathy for those who would be rendered destitute. Many in Britain and overseas were indeed to respond generously to appeals for charitable aid for Ireland (at least for a time), but providentialist readings of the blight could also provoke other, less sympathetic, interpretations. Ultra-Protestants tended to see the failure as an act of divine anger against Catholicism (and indirectly against British governments who had tolerated or compromised with it), and responded with an intensification of support for evangelical missions in the Irish west—whose 'souperist' activities would continue to spark sectarian controversy long after the Famine ended.[12] For other, and ultimately more influential, actors, the second visitation appeared designed to force attention to a profound cancer at the heart of Irish social relations and the Irish people's mentality, and to require a response calculated to transform both.

The task of responding to the renewed Irish catastrophe fell to the new Whig-Liberal administration of Lord John Russell, a weak minority administration dependent on the continuing division of its opponents for survival. Russell himself had been associated with Irish reforms in the 1830s and his lord lieutenant, the earl of Bessborough, was an old friend of O'Connell. For his part, the 'Liberator' broke with his Young Ireland critics in July 1846, ostensibly over the peace resolutions rejecting the principle of nationalist resort to armed action; in reality over his decision to restore the Whig alliance and work with the new administration. O'Connell's decision was denounced at the time by the *Nation* and subsequently by its contributors, Charles Gavan Duffy and John Mitchel, in their later incarnations as historians. His confidence in the reforming credentials of the Whig government was later to appear woefully misplaced, but in his defence O'Connell correctly identified the scale of the 1846 disaster (he predicted two million might perish if not assisted), and recognized that only the British parliament could command the food and logistical resources necessary to diminish its impact. Unfortunately for his tactics, his health collapsed from late 1846, his party machine fell apart following his death in May 1847, and appeals for sympathetic treatment of Ireland made limited inroads when confronted by political and ideological imperatives generated from within the British body politic as the famine progressed.[13]

The incoming Russell government quickly came under pressure in parliament and from the British press to terminate the perceived 'abuses' of Peel's policy. Corn merchants lobbied to ensure that there would be no repeat of the state's purchase of grain on the international markets, and were rewarded by Russell's assurance that the trade would be left to the free market. Depots with remaining stocks would be retained, but sales would henceforward be at market price and stocks would only be replenished in exceptional circumstances. Peel's Relief Commission was stood down (paving the way for direct Treasury control) and the public works system overhauled. At the same time, Russell announced publicly on 17 August that his government would use 'the whole credit of the Treasury and means of the country...as it is our bounden duty to use them...to avert famine and to maintain the people of Ireland'.[14] The contradictions between these imperatives would soon become more than evident.

In the absence of much experience in managing food crises in Ireland, the government placed heavy reliance on the guidance of Charles Trevelyan, who had held the assistant secretaryship at the Treasury since 1840. Trevelyan's role in the Great Famine remains highly controversial. For twentieth-century followers of his contemporary national-ist critics, he remains a 'Victorian Cromwell', the malevolent *eminence grise* of the fam-ine administration.[15] Taking an opposite tack, a recent detailed study seeks to exonerate him of such charges by stressing his non-political function as a civil servant, and (from a neo-liberal perspective) the reasonableness of the policy adopted in 1846–50.[16] The truth lies somewhere in between. Government policy was indeed circumscribed by fluctua-tions in British public opinion, parliamentary arithmetic, and a seriously deteriorating fiscal situation following the banking crash of autumn 1847; the cabinet also contained powerful and vociferous *laissez-faire* ideologues such as Charles Wood and Earl Grey. At the same time, Trevelyan was never a distant mandarin; closely related by marriage and politics with leading Whig figures such as T.B. Macaulay, his correspondence also reveals him to have been an ideologically driven workaholic with a clear conviction that the 'social revolution' he believed essential in Ireland was mandated by divine providence.[17]

Trevelyan strongly believed in the utility of non-interference in the food trade and had suitable extracts from Adam Smith's *Wealth of Nations* circulated to bolster the doubts of relief officials in Ireland on this head. However, his faith in the optimizing effects of the laws of supply and demand was misplaced: after summer 1846, private maize imports to Ireland dried up, and what was available on the international markets was drawn to countries where demand was most robust. Irish grain prices escalated steeply, peaking in February–March 1847 at more than double the normal average. Nationalists then, as later, asserted that famine could have been averted if Ireland's non-potato food output was retained in the country, and damned the administration for refusing to introduce an export embargo. Their claims that the famine was artificial were driven more by political rhetoric than economic reality, but did give vent to genuine moral outrage at continuing export from a starvation-racked country.[18] Exports undoubtedly did worsen the 'hunger winter' of 1846–7, but acted as a multiplier to the real food availability decline produced by the loss of the bulk of the subsistence potato crop. Moreover, retaining high-value grain and livestock products in Ireland would have done little for the rural labouring poor without some effective distribution mechanism (and indeed there is evidence that retained grain was as likely to be fed to cattle as to the destitute poor), and on this subject nationalists tended to be vague at best.

The government retained the principle of relief by public works from their predecessors, but revamped it under the 1846 Labour Rate Act. Designed to take a harder line against opportunism by local elites, this measure centralized administration under the Board of Works (itself answerable directly to the Treasury) and made the total cost repayable by the rates levied on the localities. Despite attempts by Dublin Castle officials to soften its impact, the underlying purpose of the new system was to introduce a more penal element to the public works, aimed at landowners and labourers alike. The Treasury sought to veto all useful or 'reproductive' works (thereby obliging landowners to borrow privately to improve their estates and avoid the ultimate costs of state relief works), while imposing 'piece work' payments on the labourers—a measure intended to stimulate work-discipline and reward effort, but which in practice pushed those least able to exert themselves, such as the ill and elderly, below the threshold of subsistence.

Despite its gross limitations, desperation led thousands to throw themselves on the public works relief in the harsh winter of 1846–7. The official head-count soared from 114 000 in late October to 441 000 by the end of the year and peaked at 714 390 in March 1847, with each labourer typically seeking to support a family of four or five on their meagre earnings. As numbers escalated, the Board of Works bureaucracy struggled to keep up. Works were disrupted by strikes or riots against petty tyrannies, delays in wage payments, and the imposition of piece rates, while food prices outran the wages deliberately pegged at low levels to encourage labourers to seek agricultural employment instead. Despite the vast costs of the relief works (which would account for some £5 million in 1846–7) the outcome of the system was almost certainly to augment rather than prevent excess mortality. Heavy labour, especially in the harsh winter conditions of 1846–7 placed extreme stresses on the bodies of the malnourished, who began to die in large numbers on the works in early 1847.[19] Social upheaval and distress created the ideal conditions for contagious fevers such as typhus and relapsing fever, which now also reached epidemic proportions. If a relatively low proportion of deaths in the Famine years were officially attributed to 'starvation', this was because either fevers or diseases associated with malnutrition, such as dysentery and marasmus, carried people off first.[20]

By early 1847, Irish and British press reports were replete with eyewitness accounts of mass mortality in western Ireland. The parish clergy—Protestant as well as Catholic— were frequently the most active in drawing attention to local suffering (the plight of the Skibbereen district in west Cork was first highlighted when its Anglican clergy toured England at the end of 1846). Their efforts were supplemented by organized humanitarian campaigns by the Society of Friends (Quakers) and the writings of philanthropic pamphleteers. By the time the popular *Illustrated London News* provided graphic visualizations of Skibbereen's sufferings in February in the form of James Mahony's lithographed engravings, a tide of humanitarian concern for Ireland was swelling in Britain, North America, and parts of continental Europe.[21] The government was not slow to react to this, supporting the establishment of the charitable British Association in London, instigating a 'Queen's Letter' to raise charitable funds at church doors and ultimately endorsing a 'National Day of Fast and Humiliation' on 24 March. Contrary to stereotype, Trevelyan himself was an active enthusiast for such semiofficial philanthropy, although he subsequently sought to channel the British Association's outlay so as not to conflict with public policy. In spring 1847, the popular response to these appeals was generous, raising upwards of £435 000 within the UK for distribution by the British Association, in addition to separate funds generated by the Quakers, American philanthropists, and the Vatican to meet Irish needs. For most contributors, however, Irish philanthropy was a passing fashion, rapidly ebbing from mid 1847 under the combined impacts of the UK industrial recession, anxiety about pauper Irish immigration, political upheaval in Europe, and a growing sense in Britain that Irish 'ingratitude' for the previous largesse should be punished rather than indulged.[22]

The sympathetic impulse of early 1847 combined with several factors to spur a radical turn in relief policy. Russell's government, ostensibly 'friendly' towards Ireland, was shamed by public exposures and lobbied by its own officials in Dublin into abandoning the failed public works regime. In addition, the costs of the system were becoming prohibitive and its consequences evidently demoralizing as well as largely ineffective. After debating various options, the government decided to follow the Quaker example and offer direct food aid to those most in need, through a network of state-sponsored soup kitchens. The prime minister observed that 'the pressing matter at present is to keep the people alive', but other ministers and Trevelyan noted other attractions to such a system—a cooked food test of destitution would prevent importunity (ever an obsession despite the evident collapse of much of Irish rural society), while transferring the repayment costs of the new scheme onto the poor law rates would (it was hoped) act as a more direct stimulus to proprietors to offer employment and pave the way for a permanent extension of the poor law system. While a temporary relief act was rapidly passed, establishing a new relief bureaucracy took an inordinate length of time, and staged lay-offs from the public works from March, while few soup kitchens were operational before late May or June, threw thousands into the grossly overcrowded workhouses, or onto the roads, with nothing but the erratic ministrations of private charities to support them.

Only when the soup kitchens came fully into operation, distributing free rations of a cheap 'stirabout' porridge of maize, rice, and oats, did the appalling mortality rates of 1847 begin to abate. Although far from flawless, most historians agree that the soup kitchen regime, issuing as many as three million daily rations by July, to over 90 per cent of the population of some western unions, demonstrated the capacity of the Victorian state to curb, if not to terminate, the horrors of the Famine. The initiative also was significantly cheaper than the public works to run, and was aided by a rapid fall in the market price of grain within Ireland in spring and summer. As if in belated vindication of Trevelyan's faith in the free market, massive US shipments of maize began to arrive in Irish ports, bringing down the price by August to half what it had been in February. Imports would continue at a slightly diminished scale for the rest of the Famine period, outweighing the continuing grain exports from Ireland. Paradoxically, this sudden influx of cheap grain had several unexpected effects, undermining (in some cases bankrupting) the Irish grain merchants who had profited from the inflated prices of 1846–7, and also reducing the winter feeding costs of 'strong' farmers in a position to shift (with their landlord's encouragement) into the cattle economy in these years.

All too quickly, the soup kitchen relief scheme was abandoned from September 1847 and replaced as the principal mode of relief by the extended poor law. Despite strong opposition from Irish landowners and their British Conservative allies, this policy shift had been agreed early in the year, in response to a growing conviction that 'Irish property must pay for Irish poverty'.[23] The Poor Law Extension Act of 1847 permitted (for the first time) outdoor relief funded from the rates for certain classes of paupers, and also for the 'able-bodied' if the workhouses were full, and required elected boards of guardians to relieve all those classed as destitute. As a concession to landowners, however, the Act also contained an amendment restricting relief to those still holding more than a quarter acre of land—a provision used by many proprietors to facilitate the permanent clearance of smallholding peasants from their estates.

In essence the extended poor law, while welcomed by many Irish Catholic clergymen (as well as much of British public opinion) as a well-merited punishment for the landed class who had created the social conditions triggering famine, transferred the full costs of relief from the UK Treasury to the Irish localities. Several developments made this expedient. Growing economic difficulties in Britain made raising Irish loans more difficult in the money-markets and stimulated middle-class demands for lower taxation, and the general election of summer 1847 returned a turbulent group of *laissez-faire* radicals, led by Richard Cobden, who held the parliamentary balance of power. The prime minister observed that 'we have in the opinion of Great Britain done too much for Ireland and have lost elections for doing so'.[24] Importantly, the potato did not fail in 1847 (although as few had been planted, the crop was still meagre). The apparent absence of a renewed 'visitation', along with low food prices and a good grain harvest, provided the illusion that the famine was now over, and Trevelyan's apologia, *The Irish Crisis,* published in early 1848, added to this impression.

As Ireland moved into the latter stages of the Famine, the crisis became more one of entitlements than absolute food shortage: the rural poor were still unable to cultivate their own food (potato blight ravaged the west again in 1848 and 1849), but also lacked access to the employment required to purchase what was now available in the markets.[25] Landowners and larger farmers by now envisaged the post-corn laws agricultural future of Ireland as being predominantly pastoral and especially cattle-exporting—a vision which held little or no place for the masses of spade-husbandry cottier peasants and labourers, now dismissed as a 'redundant population'. Mass evictions, stimulated in part by default of rents and by a desire to evade escalating poor rates, but also by a desire to clear land for larger-scale cattle farming, increased from the later months of 1847. A handful of landowners assisted their evicted tenants to emigrate; most did not—asserting that the cost should fall on the national exchequer and that they (in Lord Sligo's words) must evict or be themselves evicted. In some districts with a tradition of agrarian insurgency, the upsurge of clearances sparked retaliatory violence against landowners and their allies—the murder of Denis Mahon of Strokestown, County Roscommon being the most notorious and controversial. However such violence subsided in 1848 following the renewal of coercion.

For those unable to find the financial and psychological resources to emigrate, or who had no access to the remittances sent back by emigrant relatives, the workhouse, its auxiliaries, or outdoor relief in its immediate vicinity soon became the only resort. Private charitable resources were mostly exhausted by early 1848 (although the Quakers kept up their work with diminishing means for another year), and traditional modes of mutual assistance had largely broken down in much of Ireland. The 130 workhouses rapidly became swamped and additional accommodation was hired, more than doubling 'indoor' accommodation to 250 000 places by September 1849. 'Outdoor' relief numbers had reached 800 000 a year earlier and would remain very high for the next two years. Sufficient rates could never be raised to cover the escalating costs of housing and feeding so many in the unions, however, and with minimal state assistance forthcoming the system began to collapse into insolvency and chaos in the west. Although there is evidence that differing responses by boards of guardians made some difference to mortality levels in some unions, this was marginal—fever epidemics broke out in many workhouses and outdoor relief work-yards and excess mortality soared in the winters of 1847–8 and 1848–9. By early 1849, the weekly body-count within the workhouses was running at some 2500. Administrators in Ireland were more than aware of the consequences of adhering to 'sound doctrine'. Although a supporter of the poor law policy on his arrival in Ireland in June 1847, Lord Lieutenant Clarendon became a strong critic of the failure of London to deliver supplementary assistance to western unions or 'comprehensive measures' that might provide useful employment or assisted emigration, and warned in 1848 that those 'who had been feeding more on hope than on meal' would now 'die in swarms'.

It is perhaps not surprising that the radical nationalists of Young Ireland who so vociferously blamed the sufferings of the famine on British malevolence should have resorted to armed rebellion in 1848. However, closer analysis suggests that while anglophobia tended to unite this group, they lacked a shared socio-economic agenda and (beyond an export ban imposed by an independent Irish parliament) a coherent alternative famine policy. The most radical stance, adopted by John Mitchel and drawing on the journalism of the agrarian radical James Fintan Lalor, called from early 1847 for a peasant social revolution, confiscating and redistributing the landlords' estates and thereby repealing the conquest along with the Union. Mitchel proceeded to advocate a revolutionary strategy of catastrophe (informed by the apocalyptic world-view he shared with Lalor) of calling for a universal rent and rates strike. This was largely ignored and drew the opposition of not only the constitutionalist leader, John O'Connell, and the vast majority of the Irish Catholic clergy, but also of more moderate Young Irelanders. Himself of Protestant landed background, the movement's senior figure, William Smith O'Brien, continued to hope that alienation from British misgovernment would rally the 'patriotic gentry' to nationalism, and his reluctance to raise a peasant jacquerie was shared by the *Nation* editor Charles Gavan Duffy, who believed in a more ordered and staged form of land reform. The consequence was a damaging split in the newly founded Irish Confederation, with Mitchel and his allies launching rival papers, the *United Irishman* and later the *Irish Felon*.

The outbreak of revolutions in Europe from February 1848 restored Young Ireland's confidence and brought something of a rapprochement between its leaders, but did not resolve its underlying contradictions, nor do much to extend its appeal from the urban centres to the countryside—where clerical antagonism and famine-related exhaustion made organization virtually impossible. Hopes of French intervention were misplaced, and the authorities began to take the movement seriously, transporting Mitchel in May and preparing further coercive measures against the vacillating leadership. In late July, Smith O'Brien reluctantly took action and sought to raise the flag of independence in County Tipperary. The outcome, ridiculed as the 'battle of the widow McCormack's cabbage patch' was shambolic, and all but the most committed faded away as it became clear that the rebels had no food to distribute and disapproved of the seizure of private stocks.[26]

With the leaders arrested or fled abroad, the revolutionary moment (such as it was) passed. Young Ireland's principal impact would not be (*pace* the rhetoric and later US military career of T.F. Meagher) with the sword, but with the pen. Its exiled writers, principally Mitchel and Duffy, would shape the textual memory of the Great Famine for subsequent generations of nationalists. In the short term, however, the failed rising merely reinforced a widespread prejudice in Britain that the Irish were ungrateful brutes who should be abandoned to the workings of 'natural causes'. Ironically, given Mitchel's aspiration to reawaken the spirit of non-sectarian republicanism in the north, and the incorporation of a conciliatory orange bar into the tricolour unveiled by the Young Irelanders in 1848, the rising stoked up the dormant loyalist spirit of the Orange Order, a mobilization that led to a sectarian massacre at Dolly's Brae in County Down in July 1849.

Famine conditions began to dissipate in the recovering north and east of Ireland from 1848, but continuing potato blight, social dislocation, and clearance extended its impact in the west to 1850 and in some districts of Mayo and Clare to as late as 1852. Faced with continuing parliamentary hostility towards welfare transfers to Ireland, Russell resorted in spring 1849 to a 'rate in aid', essentially a levy on ratepayers in the north and east to assist the western unions. Whatever aid was generated was at the expense of alienating these areas, and called into question—as Isaac Butt observed—the very principle of the legislative union of 1801.[27] Edward Twisleton, chief commissioner of the Irish Poor Law, resigned in disgust at what he denounced as a policy amounting to 'extermination'. Russell and Clarendon, aware of the extent of their government's failure, lapsed into fatalism, while others, such as Wood and Trevelyan, continued to stress the purgative necessity of enforcing self-help on the feckless Irish.[28]

The government's only two significant initiatives in the latter stages of the Famine were to introduce an Encumbered Estates Act, a measure aimed at creating a 'free trade in land' and thereby inject British entrepreneurialism into the bankrupt land system of Ireland, and to facilitate a royal visit—the first by Queen Victoria—in the summer of 1849. The latter was intended to stimulate investment in the country as well as to impose a symbolic closure on the Famine era. While the Queen was received with some enthusiasm in the urban centres of Belfast, Dublin, and Cork, she did not visit the western countryside, which was still suffering from four years of acute distress.[29] In the end, only a few British capitalists purchased Irish estates. A large acreage was sold under the landed estates court and the weaker landed families (most with large pre-Famine debts) were winnowed out, and some Irish Catholic merchants and professionals bought small estates; but most of the purchases were by members of existing Irish gentry families, who took advantage of the system to clear their larger debts and extend their holdings.[30] Thus, the Irish landed class emerged stronger from the difficult years of the Famine, and were in a position to share with the emerging class of large 'grazier' farmers the profits of the developing cattle trade of the 1850s.

Just as the Famine's geographical and social impact was uneven, its legacy in the following decades was mixed. In much of rural Ireland the horrors of mass famine mortality, combined with the scale of depopulation through emigration and land clearance, left a traumatic legacy that was difficult to measure, but qualitatively observable to contemporaries, and lodged in the folk memory of the countryside.[31] Yet, while the famine years themselves had seen few unambiguous 'gainers' in Ireland, not all groups had suffered equally and those best placed to benefit from the export-led boom of the following decades had less reason to dwell on the past.

The Ireland of the early 1850s to later 1870s has been characterized as both 'mid Victorian' and 'post-Famine'. Assessing the two frames of reference, Vincent Comerford chose to place greater weight on the former, stressing the extent to which the country successfully escaped the famine syndrome through sustained economic growth, and moved towards social and political integration with its dynamic British neighbour.[32] There is much evidence to support this: commercial activity, railway communications, and literacy and newspaper consumption in English expanded rapidly. A farming middle class consolidated its place in society, and enjoyed rising levels of material consumption along with rising expectations. The agricultural labourers, whose numbers had already been devastated by the famine, continued to decline through heavy emigration, their services no longer demanded by the new agricultural system.

However, it would be a mistake to write off too completely the continuing shadow of the famine. Kevin O'Rourke has posited that the cattle economy was less a natural response to secularly changing commodity prices and British demand than a forced consequence of the collapse of potato cultivation, followed by a sustained depression of the crop's yield.[33] Other economic historians, such as Ó Grada and Turner, have questioned the conclusions of a previous generation that Ireland's farmers (rather than landowners) were the principal beneficiaries of the post-Famine boom and suggested a much more mixed economic picture.[34] This suggestion that there was greater economic uncertainty and landlord-tenant tension raises the probability that fear of vulnerability, and with it the spectre of a return to famine conditions, was never far from the consciousness of even the more prosperous farming families. These anxieties were naturally most acute in the west, where pre-Famine peasant social structures and potato reliance remained more common and where bitter memories of clearance and mass mortality remained entrenched.[35]

Irish politics of the 1850s–70s were dominated by two issues—religion and land. However, as Theo Hoppen has demonstrated, in the wake of the collapse of the O'Connellite movement during the Famine, political life in Ireland became fractured and localized, with organized nationalism being reduced to the margins. Reform of the

Irish franchise in 1850 gave the vote to large numbers of tenant farmers, but did so in the context of a revived and assertive Irish Toryism.[36] As the pre-eminent Catholic clergyman in the country, following his return from Rome in 1849, Paul Cullen was potentially in a position to deploy the church's reviving weight in politics, but for the most part chose not to do so consistently—prioritizing instead the promotion of the 'devotional revolution' in Catholic practice and seeking to curb what he regarded as the previous excessive political engagement of the clergy in secular politics. This is not to say that the church did not have political ambitions—especially the promotion of state-funded Catholic education and the dis-establishment of the Church of Ireland—but that its leadership tended to refrain from whole-hearted political engagement except when it considered its interests threatened.

The first such occasion, in 1850–2, was provoked by the virulent anti-Catholicism unleashed by the so-called 'Papal Aggression' of 1850, and Russell's ill-advised response in the 1851 Ecclesiastical Titles Act. The ensuing Catholic Defence League drained support from Irish liberalism and contributed to the electoral success of the Independent Irish Party at the 1852 general election, but as the threat faded Cullen's support lapsed, hastening the new party's collapse. A second excursus into electoral politics with the 1864 National Association was stimulated by concern at the rise of support for Fenianism, but made little headway before being absorbed into the Gladstonian campaign of 1868.

The politics of land also fluctuated in this period, and failed to find a stable political vehicle at national level. Agitation for land reform preceded the Famine, and had continued at local level among the stronger farmers in less devastated regions. Attempts by Young Irelanders to take control of this scattered movement in the south in 1847–8 had not been successful, while Presbyterian engagement with land reform was unsympathetic to nationalism.[37] Nevertheless, as virtually the sole surviving Young Ireland leader left in Ireland after 1848, Charles Gavan Duffy discerned in the land question the potential for a new political initiative that might unite north and south. The virulence of landlord clearances, pressure on farming incomes, and high levels of poor rates (falling on stronger farmers as well as proprietors) combined in the latter years of the Famine to promote the formation of tenant defence associations in much of the country. Insofar as these shared a coherent objective, it was the claim for legalization of 'tenant right', drawing heavily on the ideal of the 'Ulster custom' as a form of securing compensation for evicted tenants, that had been advocated for many years in press and parliament by the Ulster radical William Sharman Crawford.[38] Duffy's alliance with Crawford led to the formation of the Tenant League as a national body in August 1852 and its subsequent endorsement of the Independent Party. However, despite strong campaigning and the mobilizing of many Presbyterian clergymen in its support, Crawford and other Tenant League candidates were unsuccessful in Ulster.

Neither the Tenant League nor the Independent Party long survived their moment in the limelight in 1852. Parliamentary inertia and the lure of patronage led to a series of defection to the Liberals, and the party had ceased to exist by 1859. The rapid recovery in farming incomes—particularly stoked by strong demand during the Crimean War (1854–6)—the easing of evictions by landlords, and growing north-south tensions saw the dissolution of the League as an effective force, although local tenant associations remained and the aspiration to 'tenant right' became entrenched. Disillusioned, Duffy sold the *Nation* and transferred his talents to the colony of Victoria in 1855.

The politics of land went into abeyance for the remainder of the decade, marginalized by the scale of the agricultural boom (albeit starting from an abysmally low base) that appeared to many observers to have obscured, and perhaps even to have justified, the sufferings of the Famine. The optimism of these years shaded, in the writings of the liberal political economists of the Dublin Statistical Society, into a free-trade triumphalism. As if to place the capstone on the tomb of land agitation, the Palmerston government's 1860 Cardwell-Deasy land acts, placing land lord tenant relations solely on a contractual basis, were passed with little opposition.

In 1859–64, however, Ireland suffered a run of very poor harvests, a depression of agricultural prices and outbreaks of disease that devastated the pastoral economy. The threat of a return to famine conditions was exaggerated by some politicians, but the memory of 1845–50, still fresh in many minds, was revived. If the proliferation of small retail shops and massive imports of maize staved off the risk of starvation, it was at the cost of a credit nexus that left both small farmers and shopkeepers mired in debt.[39] The indicators of prosperity so lauded in the 1850s now pointed in a wholly different direction, and were readily grasped by both Conservative and nationalist critics; falling output and living standards and rising emigration seemed to give the lie to the idea that the Famine had permanently ushered in a new era.[40] Agricultural prosperity may have returned by the mid 1860s, but uncertainty—stimulated by well-publicized if unrepresentative events such as the Derryveagh evictions of 1860—could not be eradicated.

If recruitment into the ranks of the recently founded Irish Republican Brotherhood was promoted by the downturn of the early 1860s, that revolutionary movement continued to be hampered in the countryside by both the overt hostility of the bulk of the Catholic clergy, and by its own reluctance to engage with the land question. Instinctively hostile towards landlords, the movement nevertheless failed to develop a doctrine of land reform before 1870.[41] Its growing public impact did, nevertheless, focus the minds of others on popular grievances, including land reform.

Gladstone's 1870 Irish Land Act appears anomalous in being conceded at a time when there was no major land mobilization and when, as W.E. Vaughan has pointed out, Irish farming was at the peak of its post-Famine prosperity.[42] The explanation is in large part political—Gladstone's desire to pre-empt Fenianism by conceding something to the tenant lobby. But it is also, in part, ideological. The 1859–64 crisis had delivered a shock to the confidence of political economy in Ireland, and prompted a shift from Smithian orthodoxy towards a historicism that stressed Irish exceptionalism and valorized the official recognition of customary practice as the only means of dampening agrarian unrest. Searching for a meaningful concession to Irish tenants that did not undermine the fundamentals of property rights, Gladstone and his advisers identified legalizing the 'Ulster Custom', long advocated by Sharman Crawford as the key to the 'land question'; although even this was watered down to form 'compensation for disturbance' in the other provinces. While alarming many (although by no means all) Irish landowners over the principle of state intrusion, the 1870 Act did little to satisfy the raised expectation of tenants that a genuine 'fixity of tenure' would be introduced; nor did it touch on the issue of rent levels.[43]

These unresolved issues would form the basis of the great agitation that arose in the dual contexts of sustained agricultural recession and effective nationalist politicization of the countryside in the later 1870s. However, as Terence Dooley outlines in chapter six, above, the 'land war' that broke out in Ireland in 1879 did so in a highly radicalized context. Sustained waves of poor harvests and cattle disease (augmented in 1879 by the return of potato blight) combined with low export prices produced by American competition, to throw landowners and tenant farmers into a pitch of social confrontation not witnessed since the late 1840s. The revival of large-scale eviction as a landlord strategy appeared to many to threaten a restoration of the horrors of that earlier era. What led to an very different outcome was the development of a dynamic political leadership, combining revolutionary and constitutional elements, that provided the organization for a sustained agrarian campaign, and the availability of fighting funds to support it, largely garnered from the Irish Catholic diasporic communities that had been so enlarged and embittered by the Famine exodus.[44]

Notes

1. Cormac Ó Gráda, *Ireland: A New Economic History 1780–1939* (Oxford, 1994), 173–87; for a recent methodological discussion, see H.P.H. Nusteling, 'How many Irish potato famine deaths? Toward coherence of the evidence', *Historical Methods*, 42:2 (2009), 57–80.
2. The census commissioners sought to rationalize these bleak statistics by characterizing Ireland as a 'land of famine'; see Peter Gray, 'Accounting for catastrophe: William Wilde, the 1851 Irish Census and the Great Famine', in M. De Nie and S. Farrell (eds), *Power and Popular Culture in Modern Ireland* (Dublin, 2010), 50–66.
3. Cormac Ó Gráda, *Famine: A Short History* (Princeton, 2009).
4. David Dickson, *Arctic Ireland: The Extraordinary Story of the Great Frost and the Forgotten Famine of 1740–41* (Belfast, 1997).
5. L.M. Clarkson and E.M. Crawford, *Feast and Famine: A History of Food and Nutrition in Ireland 1500–1920* (Oxford, 2002); Cormac Ó Gráda, 'Malthus and the pre-famine economy' in A.E. Murphy (ed), *Economists and the Irish Economy from the Eighteenth Century to the Present Day* (Blackrock 1984), 75–95.
6. For the development of this memory, see James S. Donnelly Jr, *The Great Irish Potato Famine* (Stroud, 2001), 209–46.
7. For the European context, see C. Ó Gráda, R. Paping, and E. Vanhaute (eds), *When the Potato Failed: Causes and Effects of the 'Last' European Subsistence Crisis, 1845–1850* (Turnhout, 2007).
8. The scientific uncertainty over the blight is addressed in Austin Bourke, *The Visitation of God? The Potato and the Great Irish Famine* (Dublin, 1993).

9. Joel Mokyr, *Why Ireland Starved: A Quantitative and Analytical History of the Irish Economy, 1800–1850* (London, 1985); Ó Gráda, *Ireland*, 69–130.

10. For a more detailed account of Peel's policy in 1845–46, see Peter Gray, *Famine, Land and Politics: British Government and Irish Society, 1843–50* (Dublin, 1999), 95–141.

11. Andres Eriksson, 'Food supply and food riots' in C. Ó Gráda (ed), *Famine 150* (Dublin, 1997), 67–94.

12. For religious interpretations of the Famine, see Boyd Hilton, *The Age of Atonement: The Influence of Evangelicalism on Social and Economic Thought 1785–1865* (Oxford, 1988), Peter Gray, 'National humiliation and the great hunger: fast and famine in 1847', *Irish Historical Studies*, 32 (2000), 193–216; for 'Souperism', see M. Moffitt, *Soupers and Jumpers: The Protestant Missions in Connemara 1848–1937* (Stroud, 2008), Irene Whelan, 'The stigma of souperism', in Cathal Póirtéir (ed), *The Great Irish Famine* (Cork, 1995), 135–54.

13. For Irish politics during the Famine, see S.J. Connolly, 'The Great Famine and Irish politics', in Póirtéir (ed), *Great Famine*, 34–49.

14. *Hansard*, 3rd sen, lxxxviii, cols 766–99, 17 August 1846.

15. See, for example, J.M. Hernon, 'A Victorian Cromwell: Sir Charles Trevelyan, the Famine and the age of improvement', *Eire-Ireland*, 22 (1987), 15–29.

16. Robin Haines, *Charles Trevelyan and the Great Irish Famine* (Dublin, 2004).

17. For a fuller discussion of the ideology behind famine policy, see Peter Gray, 'Ideology and the Famine', in Póirtéir (ed), *Great Famine*, 86–103.

18. Few historians support the case advanced by John Mitchel that Ireland produced sufficient alternative foodstuffs to have filled the 'potato gap' in 1846–47, but for a partial exception based on the view that Irish exports were significantly under-recorded, see Christine Kinealy, *A Death-Dealing Famine: The Great Hunger in Ireland* (London, 1997), 77–91. For a balanced discussion of the import/export question, see Donnelly, *Great Irish Potato Famine*, 57–64.

19. For the failures of the public works system, see James S. Donnelly Jr, 'The administration of relief, 1846-7' in W.E. Vaughan (ed), *A New History of Ireland, V: Ireland under the Union, 1, 1801–70* (Oxford, 1989), 295–306.

20. Larry Geary, 'Famine, fever and bloody flux', in Póirtéir (ed), *Great Famine*, 74–85.

21. For Mahony's sketches, see E.M. Crawford, 'The great Irish famine, 1845-9: image versus reality', in B. Kennedy and R. Gillespie (eds), *Ireland: Art into History* (Dublin, 1995).

22. Gray, 'National humiliation'; Christine Kinealy, 'Potatoes, providence and philanthropy the role of private charity during the Irish famine', in Patrick O'Sullivan (ed), *The Meaning of the Famine* (London, 1997), 140–71; Tim O'Neill, 'The charities and famine in mid-nineteenth century Ireland', in J.R. Hill and C. Lennon (eds), *Luxury and Austerity: Historical Studies XXI* (Dublin, 1999), 137–59.

23. James S. Donnelly Jr. ' "Irish property must pay for Irish poverty": British public opinion and the great Irish famine', in C. Morash and R. Hayes (eds), *Fearful Realities: New Perspectives on the Famine* (Dublin, 1996), 60–76.

24. Russell to Clarendon, 2 August 1847, Clarendon Deposit Irish, box 43, Bodleian Library, Oxford.

25. For the applicability of Amartya Sen's entitlement theory of famine causation to Ireland, see Cormac Ó Gráda, *Black '47 and Beyond: The Great Irish Famine in History, Economy and Memory* (Princeton, 1999), 122–5.

26. A recent study credits the 1848 movement with greater revolutionary potential, but the historical consensus continues to stress its incoherence and disorganization, Christine Kinealy, *Repeal and Revolution: 1848 in Ireland* (Manchester, 2009); cf. James Quinn, *John Mitchel* (Dublin, 2009), Robert Sloan, *William Smith O'Brien and the Young Ireland Rebellion of 1848* (Dublin, 2000).

27. James Grant, 'The great famine and the poor law in Ulster: the rate-in-aid issue of 1849', *Irish Historical Studies*, 27 (1990), 30–47.

28. Gray, *Famine, Land and Politics*, 284–327.

29. See James Loughlin, 'Allegiance and illusion: Queen Victoria's Irish visit of 1849', *History*, 87 (2002), 491–513.

30. Ó Gráda, *Black '47*, 126–34.

31. Niall Ó Ciosáin, 'Famine memory and the popular representation of scarcity', in Ian McBride (ed), *History and Memory in Modern Ireland* (Cambridge, 2001), 95–117.

32. R.V. Comerford, 'Ireland 1850–70: post-famine and mid-Victorian; in W.E. Vaughan (ed), *A New History of Ireland V: Ireland under the Union, 1, 1801-70* (Oxford, 1989), 372–95.

33. Kevin O'Rourke, 'Did the Great Famine matter?', *Journal of Economic History*, 51 (1991), 1–22.

34. Ó Gráda, Ireland, 255–64; Michael Turner, *After the Famine: Irish Agriculture 1850–1914* (Cambridge, 1996); K.T. Hoppen, *Ireland since 1800: Conflict and Conformity* (Harlow, 1989), 90–94.

35. For a reassertion of the significance of the scale of famine clearances, and their long-term impact on landlord-tenant relations, see Tim P. O'Neill, 'Famine evictions', in C. King (ed), *Famine, Land and Culture in Ireland* (Dublin, 2000), 29–70.

36. K.T. Hoppen, *Elections, Politics and Society in Ireland, 1832–1885* (Oxford, 1984), 257; for Irish Toryism, see Andrew Shields, *The Irish Conservative Party 1852–1868: Land, Politics and Religion* (Dublin, 2007).

37. Gray, *Famine, Land and Politics*, 171–8.

38. Philip Bull, *Land, Politics and Nationalism: A Study of the Irish Land Question* (Dublin, 1996), 35–40.

39. James S. Donnelly, 'The Irish agricultural depression of 1859–64', *Irish Economic and Social History*, III (1976), 33–54.

40. Peter Gray, 'The making of mid-Victorian Ireland? Political economy and the memory of the Great Famine, 1847–80' in P. Gray (ed), *Victoria's Ireland? Irishness and Britishness 1837–1901* (Dublin, 2004), 151–166.

41. Bull, *Land*, 40–2.

42. W.E. Vaughan, 'Ireland c. 1870', in Vaughan (ed), *New History of Ireland*, V, 744–58.

43. Bull, *Land*, 45–53.

44. For a summary account of the land war, see R.V. Comerford, 'The Land War and the politics of distress, 1877–82' in W.E. Vaughan (ed), *A New History of Ireland VI: Ireland under the Union, 2, 1870–1921* (Oxford, 1996), 26–51.

SELECT BIBLIOGRAPHY

Bourke, Austin, *The Visitation of God? The Potato and the Great Irish Famine* (Dublin, 1993).
Bull, Philip, *Land, Politics and Nationalism: A Study of the Irish Land Question* (Dublin, 1996).

Clarkson, L.M. and E.M. Crawford, *Feast and Famine: A History of Food and Nutrition in Ireland, 1500–2000* (Oxford, 2002).

Dickson, David, *Arctic Ireland* (Belfast, 1997).

Donnelly, James S, *The Great Irish Potato Famine* (Stroud, 2001).

Gray, Peter, *Famine, Land and Politics: British Government and Irish Society, 1843–50* (Dublin, 1999).

Gray, Peter, *The Making of the Irish Poor Law, 1815–43* (Manchester, 2009).

Haines, Robin, *Charles Trevelyan and the Great Irish Famine* (Dublin, 2004).

Hilton, Boyd, *The Age of Atonement: The Influence of Evangelicalism on Social and Economic Thought, 1785–1865* (Oxford, 1988).

Hoppen, K. Theodore, *Elections, Politics and Society in Ireland, 1832–85* (Oxford, 1984).

Kinealy, Christine, *A Death-Dealing Famine: The Great Hunger in Ireland* (London, 1997).

Kinealy, Christine, *Repeal and Revolution: 1848 in Ireland* (Manchester, 2009).

Mokyr, Joel, *Why Ireland Starved: A Quantitative and Analytical History of the Irish Economy, 1800–50* (London, 1985).

Nusteleng, H.P.H., 'How many Irish potato famine deaths? Towards coherence of the evidence', *Historical Methods*, 42, 2 (2009), 57–80.

Ó Gráda, Cormac, *Ireland: A New Economic History, 1780–1939* (Oxford, 1994).

Ó Gráda, Cormac, *Black '47 and Beyond: The Great Irish Famine in History, Economy and Memory* (Princeton, 1999).

O'Rourke, Kevin, 'Did the Great Famine matter?', *Journal of Economic History*, 51 (1991), 1–22.

Póirtéir, Cathal (ed), The Great Irish Famine (Cork, 1995).

Shields, Andrew, *The Irish Conservative Party, 1852–68: Land, Politics and Religion* (Dublin, 2007).

Turner, Michael, *After the Famine: Irish Agriculture, 1850–1914* (Cambridge, 1996).

Vaughan, W.E. (ed), *A New History of Ireland V: Ireland under the Union 1, 1801–1870* (Oxford, 1989).

Vaughan, W.E. (ed), A New History of Ireland VI: Ireland under the Union, 2, 1870–1921 (Oxford, 1996).

CHAPTER 28

....

EMIGRATION, 1800–1920

....

DONALD M. MACRAILD

I. INTRODUCTION

....

DURING the nineteenth century, in what was an age of mass migration, Ireland sent a higher proportion of its population overseas than any other European nation.[1] Little wonder that emigration, migration, and the creation of what has latterly been called an Irish 'Diaspora', have been subjected to immense—occasionally encyclopaedic—scholarly attention.[2] Ireland's migrations, however, both pre-dated and post-dated the long nineteenth century. By 1800, as many as 200 000 Protestants from Ulster had settled in Britain's North American colonies.[3] Towards the end of the eighteenth century, the west coast of Scotland received a smaller but important flow of emigrants from the same province and the first shoots of what would become large communities of Irish-born had also begun to emerge in Manchester, Liverpool, and Newcastle.[4] Whilst the Irish in Britain, and those located in Canada and the infant republic of the United States, comprised only a small fraction of the millions who would emigrate in during the nineteenth century, the essential characteristics of Irish emigration had already taken shape before the population flows of the industrial age unfolded. Throughout the years after the French Wars (1792–1815), traditional pathways of Irish emigration to Britain and North America were retained, but new routes were also cut out as migrations became more truly global. By the 1820s, the Irish were heading to Australasia, South America, and the multiplicity of places encompassed under the umbrella of the British Empire. An understanding of the global reach of these migrations has begun, in recent times, to take a hold in scholarship and has been particularly illuminated in comparison with other countries that also sent forth large emigration populations.[5]

Pioneering Irish scholarship also examined the globalization of the Irish flows—not simply by studying isolated instances of emigration or by ignoring emigrants once they had left Ireland's shores, but by integrating the larger-scale dimensions and seeing Irish migration as creating myriad connected communities around the world. This is notable in Fitzpatrick's path-breaking studies of emigration which analyse population movements across our entire period;[6] in Akenson's innovative encapsulation of Ireland's global reach;[7] in Kenny's powerful assessment of both diasporic and comparative dimensions of Irish emigrant cultures;[8] in comparative studies such as Malcolm Campbell's analysis of American and Australian flows and Akenson's sophisticated examination of both Irish and Swedish migrations;[9] and in Campbell's and MacRaild's shorter considerations of, respectively, the Irish in the Pacific and Atlantic worlds;[10] and in intensively research-based comparative studies, such as Matthew Gallman's analysis of the famine and poor relief in Liverpool and Philadelphia.[11] More recently, Fitzgerald and Lambkin have brought diverse literatures together in their historiographical conspectus of the wide range of approaches to Irish migration studies.[12] Belchem has, however, questioned the validity of the amorphous, shifting concept of Diaspora, focusing on Liverpool, the hub of the Atlantic World traffic in people.[13]

Such studies reflect a continued interest in migration as a central theme in the modern history of Ireland. They also flag potential new directions and fresh methodological approaches. Equally, the weight of scholarship focuses in a conventional fashion on discrete, temporal spaces. As we move beyond Ireland's shores, to the places in which so many Irish people settled, there remains an almost dogmatic commitment to specific local studies. Against this assessment, however, must be set an opening up of the intellectual and methodological terrain by leading specialists, not least in the use of fresh concepts, such as Diaspora, with its stress upon a global community of Irish people connected by common origins,[14] and new sources, such as letters and other personal narratives. This chapter seeks to provide an overview of traditional approaches, the state of the art, and potential avenues for new and fresh thinking.

II. EMIGRATION IN IRISH HISTORY AND HISTORIOGRAPHY

The importance of emigration in Irish history is demonstrated by the stress historians have laid upon it. All the general accounts make mention of the great emigrations; some dedicate specific chapters to the phenomenon, usually focusing on the famine.[15] The 'Great Famine' (1845–52) has long been viewed as the turning point of Irish history: a series of events which, by promoting emigration, economic change, and population decline, destroyed traditional cultures and ushered in the modernization of Irish society. Although the emigrations from Ireland in the decades prior to the famine have yielded relatively little discrete historical analysis compared to the Famine exodus, some of the most important general studies have established the growing importance of emigration long before the 'Potato Blight' struck. W. F. Adams and later Raymond Crotty were among the first to suggest that the Famine, rather than setting new trends, actually enhanced demographic and economic patterns that were already noticeable in the generation after 1815, when the return to a peacetime economy ended a generation of relative rural prosperity for poorer Irish people.[16] At heart, the quickening pace of migration was spurred by contextual economic factors. Evidence for this view is provided by reference to the contrasting economic fortunes of the Irish during and after the French Wars. Whereas the period from 1780 to 1815 had been characterized by increases in tillage, potato cultivation, and sharp population growth, conditions thereafter became favourable for a return to less labour-intensive dairy and pasture farming.[17] This had a knock-on effect on the poorer population by reducing demand for landless rural workers. From 1815 to the 1840s, Ireland's agricultural economy was marred by falling prices, banking collapses, and failed speculations. The period also witnessed increasing pressure on the scant resources, especially of small farmers and farm labourers, with poverty becoming more marked. Despite the off-putting effects of war on the high seas between Britain and France, and legislative attempts (the Passenger Acts) to limit migrations to the former colonies of the fledgling United States, Fitzpatrick suggests up to 100 000 Irish people crossed the Atlantic in the three decades from the 1780s, while a further million left between the cessation of the French Wars in 1815 and the first signs of the 'Blight' in 1845.[18] Moreover, these migrants were new in important respects: they derived from provinces other than Ulster as the tendency to leave spread from the Protestant north to the Catholic south; and they increasingly included poorer workers rather than former tenant farmers and tradesmen. The class profile of emigrants generally remained higher in the run-up to the famine, but thereafter there was a broadening and deepening of the population susceptible to the attractions of leaving the homeland.

The timing of these economic problems, and the scale of sustained emigration, led Crotty to declare that 1815, not 1845, was the great 'watershed' of Irish history. Crotty's argument is controversial because it plays down the Famine's effects, which were by any measure horrific. Yet, we must recognize that many indicators of demographic and economic change were apparent in the generation between 1815 and 1845. The population continued to rise throughout the 1820 and 1830s, but the rate of increase was reduced. Moreover, emigration rates grew consistently in this period, with year-on-year growth in the migration flow to the United States as the young republic began to replace Canada as the main destination (other than Britain) to which Irish people emigrated.

The emigrations of the 1840s and 1850s have featured significantly in the scholarship on the Famine, dating from the early 1950s when the centenary volume, edited by R. Dudley Edwards and T. W. Moody, included an important essay by Oliver MacDonagh which examined the assisted emigrations of the period. The ultimate importance of the Famine as a driver for emigration is captured succinctly by Kerby Miller, who writes of the situation in Ireland during the Famine: 'more people left in just eleven years than during the preceding two and one-half centuries'.[19] Miller's wide-ranging Marxist account examines a wide vista on either side of the Famine, but in the case of the Famine, as more generally, he stresses the effects of political and structural forces as the cause of emigration. Although Miller uses more than 5000 emigrant letters to colour his deeply researched text, he stressed impersonal forces and English colonialism at the expense of the migrants' own role in the decision-making process. In short, he downplays human agency.

The nature of population loss was undoubtedly different during the Famine, as Delaney's fresh new account of the period shows.[20] For the first time, a majority of emigrants came from the poorer classes. Although the very poorest people in Ireland were much more likely to die of disease and the effects of hunger and privation, up to 90 per cent of those who left between 1851 and 1855 were recorded as labourers: in other words, landless, poor workers who left for survival and work. This inevitably helped to create the spectral images of pathetic, hungry people crowding the wharves and quays of the great Atlantic ports. Newspapers such as the *Cork Examiner* reported graphically on the poverty, disease, and death which were the Famine's yield for the unluckiest in Irish society. In addition, social reports, political tracts, and priests' writings spread around the anglophone world and reported the horrors of the Famine, helping to create a public consciousness which, while sympathetic to the suffering, also envisioned the Irish as a lower stratum of society. Such negative contemporary images also markedly shaped the historiography which professional historians later developed.[21] The Famine and the attendant social problems associated with a compressed, mass emigration fundamentally shaped generations of pioneering scholarship on the Irish abroad. For generations, there was little interest in Irish migration beyond the 1840s.[22]

Historians such as Swift and Gilley (on Britain),[23] Bayor and Meagher and Clark (on east-coast America),[24] and the works of O'Driscoll and Roberts on Canada,[25] reveal elements of similarity within the profiles of the Irish who landed and settled in the urban areas of Britain and North America during the crucial middle decades of the nineteenth century. The connections are clearest during the Famine flight, when poverty, indigence, Catholicism, and a shortage of industrial skills brought the Irish to the forefront of the minds of social critics, journalists, and local officials on both sides of the Atlantic. Such factors as overcrowding in dirty cities, a disproportionate link with crime and imprisonment, associations with diseases such as typhoid fever, and habits of hard drinking and the attendant social dislocation have all featured prominently in the historiographies of the countries of the Atlantic rim, just as they had influenced onlookers at the time.[26] Consequently, the 'Condition of England'[27] period in Britain, and the age of urban growth and Nativist anti-immigrant hostility in the US, yielded many studies granting the Irish a central place in immigrants' struggles for adjustment amidst social change.[28] This convergence in perspective occurred because, to some extent, countries on both sides of the Atlantic were sharing common experiences of rapid economic development and extensive social change. The negative commonalities were personified by the Irish immigrant: even in the United States, where new Irish citizens were traditionally of higher status, approximately three-quarters were drawn from the labouring class. The majority of these people were poor, hailing from Irish-speaking regions, and were Catholic. Such factors hardly smoothed their passage into the new communities. Cheap transport helped to prime the emigrant pump, and another significant lubricant was the development of chain migration through the system of remittances, whereby family members sent back cash or pre-paid tickets to assist relatives.[29]

Thus, emigration is rightly viewed as a central feature of Irish demographic and economic history.[30] For population historians, it is impossible to ignore the life-cycle impact of so many young Irish people leaving a country whose population halved during the half-century after the famine. For economic historians, emigration was vital to their explaining the structures of Irish society, particularly overpopulation in the countryside and low rates of urbanization, for these two elements contributed vitally to the sheer size of Ireland's emigrations. In all such considerations of Irish demographic and population history, the precedents of the first great population theorist, the Rev Thomas R. Malthus, loom large.[31]

Malthusianism influenced the most important demographic historian of the post-war period, K.H. Connell, author of the foundational text to which all historians of Irish population and emigration must first turn. Connell's approach adapted Malthusianism to the Irish situation by concentrating upon Irish conditions and responses: rural over-population, land tenure, famine, and emigration. Connell recounts how, for him, in the post-Famine period, land tenure, family structure, and emigration in Ireland came together to encourage primogeniture (inheritance by one offspring, usually a son) and increased celibacy. In Connell's analysis, Ireland responded to modernity by produc-ing generation after generation of landless, non-inheriting children, with a post-Famine tendency towards celibacy among increasing numbers of landowners, who protected their economic interests by not marrying. This, in turn, made the prospects of gen-erations of unmarried women particularly bleak, for this was increasingly a world of non-marrying men. Emigration encouraged primogeniture; for second and later sons, who would not inherit land, it encouraged the exodus. As a result of famine, falling fer-tility rates, and emigration, the population continued to fall, nearly halving between 1841 and 1891, from 8.2 to 4.5 million.

The most recent and influential national study of emigration and economy by Timothy W. Guinnane modifies Connell's argument by focusing on the economic choices of the people of Ireland whose decision created the population structure in the first place, and the massive emigration rates, which we associate with the country in the post-Famine period.[32] Guinnane drills down below the quantitative sources to the individual level in order to employ what he dubs (borrowing from Hammel) 'culturally smart microeconomics',[33] whereby population is analysed at the level of the household, not of the nation. Nevertheless, Guinnane still demonstrates the striking conflation of factors that made Ireland unique.

Fitzpatrick's essays on emigration essentially set the benchmark for scholarship and established our understanding of the complicated and diverse patterns of population loss from Ireland's shores.[34] Covering internal as well as external migrations, but also establishing the low rates of return migration, Fitzpatrick draws upon the overall trajec-tories of emigration: Britain dominated as a recipient of Irish migrants until the 1840s; Canada was an early destination whose importance as a receptor of the Irish had faded significantly by the 1860s; the United States established its ascendancy from Britain and held it until the 1930s, when Britain resumed primacy; Australia, New Zealand, Argentina, and South Africa became important destinations after the Famine, though the first of these had established a sustained demographic relationship with Ireland through convict and free migrations much earlier.[35]

III. Sources and Approaches

History is fundamentally shaped by the available sources, and the study of Irish emigration is no different. Generally, emigration data in the United Kingdom (which in our period included the whole of Ireland) is poorer than for other European countries. Places such as Germany and Norway were more assiduous and precise in collecting consistent emigration data from an earlier point in the century than was true of Ireland or Britain. Even where data are available to measure emigration and immigration, there are problems of standardization, compatibility, and comparison. For example, statistics do not align across national boundaries (censuses in the US were taken on the first year of the decade, for example, 1870, whereas British ones were counted a year later). More significantly, no agency directly or consistently measured Irish migration out of Ireland and into Britain. There was no legal border between the two major islands of the United Kingdom during the period of the Union. Thus, historians of the Irish in Britain are further hamstrung by the fact that migrants between the two islands were not counted in and out as they were when embarking overseas. The only way to capture these migrants is in the most important sources of emigration data for Ireland—the annual series of returns of the US immigration authorities, the Emigration Commissioners' returns, and (from 1876) the Returns of the Registrar General for Ireland—measure only aggregate overseas emigration.[36]

Historians such as Fitzpatrick and Ó Gráda have, however, sought to counteract such data problems by working creatively and intelligently with available evidence. Fitzpatrick measured outflows through an analysis of cohort depletion: that is, by taking the size of the age group 5–24 in one census and comparing it with the age group 15–34 at the next, and making allowances for depletion by mortality, to provide 'a useful proxy for net outwards migration'.[37] Ó Gráda tried to find ways of calculating migration rates to Britain by using Irish and American sources to distinguish between emigration to the USA and to other destinations.[38] However, he found that these sources produced a significant underestimation of the Irish-born population across the Irish Sea. As a result, the decennial population censuses for the UK remain our only reliable source of data.

Mass migration was a feature of European society in our period, with no country immune from its influences and effects. At the same time, particular regions and localities within national borders were more affected by migration than others. Emigration was driven by factors of economic development, agriculture change and decline, and by urbanization. Drawn together as a series of balances between home region and potential regions of settlement, known as 'push' and 'pull' factors, these forces acted differently upon individual regions at different times. Whilst Ireland corresponded to patterns of highly regionalized migration, it was also one of the countries in which all regions were affected by population loss of this type to some degree. Ulster featured prominently in pre-modern migrations, but continued to send emigrants in the nineteenth century: as well as farmers heading for the colonies, Ulster's migrants included industrial workers from the linen industry, shipbuilders, and engineers who were increasingly integrated into a trans-Irish Sea migratory network connecting the industrial regions of Britain with those in the north-eastern corner of Ireland. In Dundee, where flax and jute were milled, the Irish settled in large numbers; and in shipbuilding and metal manufacturing towns such as Workington and Barrow-in-Furness, large proportions of the Irish came from Ulster.[39] Whilst the major outflows from the west, where death rates during the Famine were highest, occurred at the end of our period, there were nevertheless emigrations from Mayo, Galway, and Clare to British towns and cities which predated the Famine.

The shock waves of emigration thus crossed townland, parish, and county lines. Universal factors such as chain migration, remittance payments by established migrants, gendered social relations, and class-inspired analyses of the iniquities of the home country, all added emigration pressures. Certain regions sent more migrants, but no county or town was immune. High peaks of emigration were influenced by structural and more immediate concerns; but, over time, the trend of emigration spread to every corner of Ireland. Overall, women left at approximately the same rate as men, though as with other countries, the young were more likely to leave than the old. In the early period, prior to the Famine, families migrated together; later, migration became mainly a young person's pursuit, though young married couples migrated as well as single folk. Occasionally, local studies illuminate still further reasons for spikes in emigration, for example in Robert Scally's compelling account of the mass local migration of the Famine era where an entire community migrated following defeat in a protracted legal battle between the tenantry and the Crown at Ballykilcline, Roscommon.[40]

Some of the most important recent works on Irish emigration have made use of qualitative sources. Personal narratives, such as letters and diaries, have been particularly usefully interpreted to provide an angle on the decision to leave Ireland and an idea of the experiences of settlement in different countries.[41] Miller's classic, *Emigrants and Exiles*, remains one of the most influential studies of Irish emigration, enforcing as it does the idea that a considerable number of Irish-Americans were freighted with feelings of exile from their homeland.[42] A path-breaking approach is taken in Fitzpatrick's study of Irish-Australian correspondence, which focuses on 111 letters sent by a series of families with Australian connections. Fitzpatrick discovered instances of loneliness, despair, and poverty alongside happiness, positivity, and the mundane. Yet, unlike Miller, he found nothing in the emigrants' letters to suggest that emigrants were bound by an exile mentality: indeed, the term 'exile' was not used.[43] His former doctoral student, McCarthy, used more than double the number of letters, which she grouped into thirty families' sets, to recreate something of the emotional narrative of Irish New Zealand. Rather than sequencing the letters, as Fitzpatrick does, she writes a thematic study of Irish New Zealand in which excerpts from the letters are woven into a general history of settlement, development, and experience.[44] Whilst a number of other scholars have made use of Irish letters,[45] the works of Miller, Fitzpatrick, and McCarthy provide a crucial comparison of different approaches to these types of personal narratives. All of these authors recognize the limits and selectiveness of emigrants' letters; but none goes as far as Gerber in stressing the positivist instrumentalism in emigrants' letters or in decon-structing the 'epistolary' framework of such writings.[46] In addition to letters, memoirs and autobiographies have long been reproduced with scholarly introductions because of what they tell us about the lives of their authors, and interesting cases such as that of Joseph Keating, the Welsh-Irish working-class writer, are fascinating for what they reveal about the cultural hybridity of those who grew up in Irish communities abroad; but, again, questions of selectivity and typicality rise up, for memoirists were not every-day people.[47]

At the other end of the scale is the tendency towards demographic analysis of immigrant communities, particularly those utilizing census enumerators' books. Such studies, pioneered by scholars during the 1970s when computer-aided mass data analysis methods first became widely available, have made a considerable mark on scholarship on the Irish in Britain.[48] With notable exceptions, studies of the Irish in America have not focused upon the provenance of Irish settlers, offer-ing only anecdotal evidence of specific place of origin; such studies have tended to overlook the demographic aspect, paying much less attention to issues such as household structure, family patterns, intermarriage, etc. In much Irish-American historiography, the implicit assumptions have been that Irish emigrants to America were mostly Catholic, bound together by the negative experiences of living in a coun-try dominated by the colonial apparatus of the British state; as such, the common features of Irish settlement have been stressed, with victimhood offering a shared bond, and with studies of ghettoized communities seemingly endorsing the view. In such approaches, questions of individual experience or divergence from the accepted norm, for example, presence of the middle classes or Protestants among the migrants, have attracted almost no attention. Since Stephan Thernstrom's important work on Newburyport, Massachusetts, pointed to low rates of social mobility among the Irish in America,[49] there have been countless local studies, many of them focus-ing primarily on the misery of the famine years. In contrast, R.A. Burchell's study of the San Francisco Irish shows that the Irish in the gold rush city rose up the social scale quickly across the generations, which runs counter to the impression gleaned from Thernstrom.[50] More recently, David Emmons' fine ethnic-labour history of the Irish in Montana has shown the extent to which Irish miners mixed their national interests with class politics; and Meagher's exhaustively detailed study of the Irish in Worcester, Massachusetts, points to the complexity of synchronic and diachronic pressures faced by the Irish in a multi-generational community.[51]

IV. Patterns of Emigration and Settlement

Patterns of Irish emigration are best understood as a manifestation of interregional connections between the lands sending and receiving emigrants. Munster and Ulster provided most emigrants to the Antipodes; Connacht provided a large proportion of those who went to America. All counties of Ireland were represented in the complex imperial hub Liverpool. The Irish-born population of the great Atlantic gateway city was exceeded only by the number in the metropolis.

The Irish who migrated to Britain followed a number of long-established pathways, traditional channels which, once established, were used by subsequent generations of movers. By the late nineteenth century, the north of England was part of a highly integrated interregional economy connecting it with eastern Ulster and the central belt of Scotland. Migration was only one manifestation of this fact; however, it was an important one, as the settlement patterns of not only Irish workers, but also English and Scots migrants, clearly shows. Each of the three countries in question—Ireland, Scotland, and England—provided notable communities of people who settled in each of the other two countries. Although the English migrations to Scotland and Ulster, and the migration of Scots to Ulster and England, have not been studied in any real depth, the interregional relationships that they represented are not in question.

Despite the confidence of these assertions, even the Irish, who are the most studied of these groups, still remain relatively little-known in the terms we describe. Very little has been written about the formation of pathways of connection between Ireland and Britain along which these migrants travelled. In one sense, we know they were founded essentially upon obvious geographical connections: ease of travel ensured connections between Ulster and western Scotland, or central Ireland (through Dublin) to Lancashire, and so on. Thus, in broad terms, Ulster migrants were not as likely to be found in south-east England as in western Scotland; Kerrymen were less common in Edinburgh than in London. Persons from Cork, following existing trade links to South Wales, or aided by direct steamer connections to Bristol, London, and other southern ports, were even more likely to be found in Wales or the south of England. This does not mean that individual Kerrymen did not find their way to Scotland, nor Ulstermen to the south of England; individuals confounding the general rules are not in themselves proof enough of an alternative thesis in which the Irish went from places in Ireland to all places in Britain. The general patterns are strongly regional, and so these form the fulcrum of our investigation.

Despite the great volume of research on the Irish in Britain over the past four decades, our knowledge of the interregional flow of migrants between the two islands does not extend much beyond rough general observations. What we learnt from the earliest studies, however, remains important and has not really been superseded. Three major arcs of migration were noted—between Ulster and Scotland; Connacht and central and east-central Ireland through Dublin to Liverpool; and from Munster and south and west Connacht to South Wales, the English south coast, and London, and these remain applicable in the broadest terms, though further case study research has added new layers of explanation below these regional or provincial patterns. Local analyses sometimes throw up examples of long-distance migration and secondary migration beyond ports of settlement which cloud this picture.

Illuminating the underpinning patterns of migration has been a feature of the historiography. Increasingly, microstudies have provided some of the most fascinating texture to the overall broadcloth, with detailed and exhaustive studies of the patterns of inter-regional migration from particular parts of Ireland to specific places overseas shaping the narratives. One of the exemplars of this approach is Bruce Elliott's.[52] Other studies also provide clear pictures of localized migrations and the factors which motivated them. Thus, Malcolm Campbell's careful study, *The Kingdom of the Ryans: The Irish in Southwest New South Wales, 1816–1890* (Sydney, 1997), shows how the eponymous clan formed a thriving community of Tipperary folk in New South Wales, Australia. Although not specifically an exercise in interregional migration, David Emmons's *The Butte Irish*, which reconstructs the social and labour history of the Irish copper miners in far-flung Montana, provides important insights into the patterns of migration from the copper-mining regions of Cork to the mining lands of the Rockies.[53]

For Britain, the establishment of such interregional connections has usually rested on an analysis of what the census tells us. This relies on the enumerators to have recorded a specific Irish county, town, or parish. However, one of the main problems confronting us is the fact that, in a majority of cases, the census enumerators failed to record specific counties or parishes of birth for Irish-born residents in England and Wales. Instead, as Smith and MacRaild have shown, in nearly 75 per cent of cases, they made use of the most general designation, 'Ireland'.[54] Historians such as Richardson, Dillon, Finnegan, and MacRaild have used censuses to demonstrate that, in Yorkshire, most Irish migrants came from central and western Ireland and that, in the far north-west of England, Ulster provided most migrants.[55] Such approaches have been used much more systematically, albeit on a small scale, in Herson's series of articles on the Irish in Stafford. One of the most impressive and sustained series of local studies shows the 'patterns' and 'chains' of migration—connections between localities and individuals—that caused a large minority of Irish in the Midlands town of Stafford to emanate from a clearly defined zone around Castlerea, which overlapped counties Galway, Roscommon, and Mayo. Herson's work thus provides evidence of the existence of specific sub-regional migrations between clearly defined sending and receiving areas; it also counsels against excessive generalization.[56]

As the historiography has evolved, the focus of study has gradually shifted from studies of *emigration* to studies of *immigration*. Whilst the effects of emigration on Irish society clearly continue to inspire historians, the volume of such work is now dwarfed by the quantity of local, regional, and national studies of how Irish people adapted to lives in new communities.

Irish settlement was primarily, though not exclusively, an urban phenomenon. In neither Britain nor America did more than a minority of Irish cross the physical and psychological frontier to a rural way of life. The big-city experience dominated Irish lives in both Britain and America. In 1841, over 40 per cent of the Irish in Britain were to be found in London, Liverpool, Glasgow, and Manchester; by 1871, this proportion was still one-third. In America, patterns of settlement were even more focused. In 1870, nearly 95 per cent of the Irish-born of America were concentrated in twenty states.[57] In the same year, only 15 per cent of the Irish-born population of the United States were engaged in agricultural work, compared with more than 50 per cent of the native-born. The two largest communities of Irish-born outside of Ireland were in New York and Liverpool.

Despite overwhelming focus on the urban Irish and on the experiences of the Irish in big cities of the industrial revolution period, not all of the Irish in the Atlantic World were to be found in cities. Akenson has counselled historians against excessive concentration on the urban sphere. Indeed, he has even pointed to the importance of agricultural pursuits and rural living to the Irish in America.[58] In addition to Akenson's pioneering work, Elliott, Toner, and others have demonstrated that, in Canada for example, the Irish experience was much more variegated, with rural pursuits and places continually important.[59] Although big cities and large towns from Halifax and New Brunswick in the Maritime Provinces to Toronto and the urban settlements of Ontario were important, the Irish were also to be found as farmers and agricultural labourers across Canada.[60] The Protestant Irish were, however, much more likely to be minor landowners than their Catholic counterparts; and Catholics were more likely than Irish Protestants, or the English or Scots settlers, to be found in unnamed trades; that is, labouring. However, in both cases, small towns and rural settings were just as important to the Canadian Irish experience as were towns and big cities. A similar desire to probe the variety of Irish immigrant experiences has also influenced the work on scholars working on the Irish in the United States, particularly Malcolm Campbell, in his innovative comparative work on the Irish in farming communities in Minnesota and New South Wales, Australia, and by Graham Davis in his work on the Irish in Texas.[61] Whilst David Gleeson's prizewinning study of the Irish across the southern states of America shows the importance of coastal cities and towns from Charleston to New Orleans, he, too, finds the Irish living in much less typical industrial, commercial, and classically nineteenth-century towns and cities.[62] More recent still, an ambitious study of the Irish in the American West by David M. Emmons explores the Irish in both rural and industrial settings. Although a significant break from the normal urban and northeastern focus of studies of Irish migration in the US, Emmons's work nevertheless finds the same issues of hostility, prejudice, hardship, and communal togetherness affecting the Irish out West as were inflicted on those in the big cities of the East.[63]

Whilst Australia captures many of the complexities of assessing the balance of rural and urban in the Irish emigrant experience, that destination also had its unique place in the shaping of the Diaspora. For one thing, it began as a distant penal colony and most of its early Irish emigrants were reluctant prisoners. If Irish convicts and pre-1840 free migrants are combined, the total Irish-born influx over Australia's first fifty years is likely to have been in the vicinity of 50 000.[64] Around 80 per cent of these were convicts borne to Australia in chains. Between 1840 and 1914, more than 300 000 emigrated from Ireland to Australia, either under their own steam, or, in the case of four-fifths of the total, under one of the many different assisted emigration schemes.[65] A large part of the Australian Irish were also drawn from a cluster of midlands counties, west of Dublin and out to northern Tipperary.[66] Apart from several thousand assisted emigrants, there was relatively little movement from Ireland to Australia during the Famine. The 1850s saw an upturn, and the heaviest migrations occurred in the early 1860s when the American Civil War dulled the point of migration to the USA. There was a final surge of emigration to Australia during the mid 1870s when economic depression was affecting Britain and North America. With the end of the convict trade in 1868, the free Irish community reflected many of the balances of rural, small-town and big-city life that comprised the mixed experience of the Irish in other colonies, such as Canada and New Zealand.

Emigration to New Zealand followed similar chronological patterns, though there was no convict settlement in the farthest outpost of Empire. Migrants made their way to New Zealand in only small numbers prior to 1850; during the 1860s, there was a significant upsurge with assisted migrants travelling there directly, with others, particularly fortune hunters arriving via California and Australia following news of gold strikes.[67] New Zealand's age of great migrations was in the 1870s when the colonial governments were pressing hard to build up their population stock and therefore engaged in systematically supporting assisted emigrants from Britain and Ireland, more than half of the latter being recruited in Ulster, with much of the remainder drawn from Munster. Numbering only tens of thousands, New Zealand emigration was relatively unimportant to the larger story of Irish emigration; but this was also true of the third of a million who went to Australia. Although dwarfed by flows to Britain and the United States, these migrants were vital to the sparsely populated, and late-developing colonial economies and societies of the Antipodes.

By the later nineteenth century, the drift towards towns and cities, both in Canada and across Australasia, was pronounced. Australia and New Zealand may, at this time, have been more associated with sheep and rural production than with cities and industrial manufacturing, but in New Zealand, despite the colony's importance as a source of cheap food for the mother country, most people lived in towns and cities by 1880. Despite pockets of industrial work, which attracted the Irish to cities such as Dunedin, a great portion of the Irish and other labour in New Zealand worked on the docks, as 'wharfies', or in the warehouses and processing outlets which turned agricultural production into an export trade. In the larger and more variegated Australia and Canada, rural and small-town life accounted for a more significant proportion of the population, but still cities and towns accounted for most people. Moreover, this pattern affected the Irish as much as the non-Irish.

V. Future Directions

The history of emigration has long been located within wider histories of social and economic change. Comparative or general studies of emigration trends have indicated awareness that emigration from Ireland—though unique in scale and persistence—was part of a wider process of modernization in Europe. Where scholars have focused on emigration as a result of colonialism, the exploitation of a weaker nation by a more powerful one, they, too, have recognized that other examples of this type exist in European history; that, in effect, emigration can be a political process enforced by issues of power and domination. Further research which compares Irish emigration with wider European emigrants would undoubtedly benefit scholars as they seek to understand the full extent to which emigration was an effect of modernization or, contrastingly, a pre-meditated policy resulting from British rule. Whilst the arguments in favour of a colonialist explanation may work for the nineteenth century, they have decreasing purchase after 1922, when the Free State was formed.

No survey of emigration can avoid the story of immigration, the settlement of Irish people in the destinations they chose or to which they were directed. The story of Ireland's Diaspora *after* its constituents had left Ireland is the one area where systematic new layers of research are needed. The shape of future research in these areas really needs to address one fundamental issue: the extent to which historians view, or do not view, immigrants as true parts of the host societies. The most lucid enunciation of this problem is David Feldman's important essay. Feldman focuses on the Irish in Britain in particular when arguing that immigrants still tend to be treated as a separate, disconnected stream within modern societies.[68] Therefore a current and remaining challenge for historians is to develop models for analyzing Irish immigrant communities by laying more stress on the interactions between hosts and immigrants. However, this will require more than simply studying ethnic tensions; most extant studies offer at least passing insights into the role of anti-Irish violence and prejudice, particularly during the mid nineteenth century. Instead, the focus will need to be upon the role which Irish men and women played in the societies in which they settled. This, in turn, will influence the types of issues, events, and expressions of the immigrant past on which historians will focus.

For one thing, there needs to be less stress on modes of ethnicity: those things which separate the Irish from other groups. Reflecting on the current state of the historiography, it is evidence that, apart from notions of anti-Irish victimization, the most common foci are religion and ethnic politics: social Catholicism and the vitality of the church which, in the overwhelmingly Protestant worlds of America and the British Empire, the Irish did so much to forge; and the great variety of nationalist politics, from Fenianism to organized Home Rule, which shaped the consciousness of the Irish Diaspora and its lynchpin. American ethnic history provides hints of the direction in which the history of the Irish in Britain and other anglophone countries might go. Historians need to address not so much the ethnic forms which endured among Irish communities, as the points of connection with host institutions through which the Irish became integrated into society. This is not to replace ideas of ethnic pluralism with an unproblematic assimilationist agenda in which Irish identity was a burden to be thrown off; but clearly the points at which identities blur are important and under-researched. Perspectives from anthropology suggest that the concept of cultural evolution may help us understand how, and when, the Irish ceased being Irish and became American, Australian, or British—new research on the declining usage of traditional Irish forenames, such as Patrick and Bridget, suggest one form of ethnic fade.[69] Perhaps others can be discovered.

A truer picture of the role and experience of the Irish in Britain, Canada, or America involves examination of the Irish role in the institutions they found in the new communities, such as political parties, churches, associations, clubs, societies, and a plethora of others. The relationship between Irish politics and British or American politics, from an immigrant point of view, is one of the best examples of this. Eric Foner and Steven P. Erie (for America) and Fielding (for England) laid markers for the study of how ethnic political organization served as a platform from which the Irish launched themselves into full participation in American working-class structures and the British Labour Party.[70] For Foner, the Land League provided a vehicle, not only for making sense of Irish politics in Ireland, but also for addressing the problems which Gilded Age capitalism presented to organized labour. Fielding, in one of the best discussions of the links between ethnicity and class, shows how Irish nationalist organizations provided a training ground for early Irish incursions into Liberal and then Labour politics.[71] American scholarship has long recognized how, in a nation of immigrants, ethnic politics was key to understanding what instances of class consciousness there were in a country where the political institutions of labour were weak. In Britain, however, the emergence of a culture of second-generation Irish support for Labour remains a very undercooked topic of study. Yet, the emergence of the modern Labour Party was one of the key developments in twentieth-century working-class British history, and the role of the Irish in its ranks has to be included in this narrative—as with the sketch-map laid down by T.W. Moody in his short study of the Labourite turn of the former Fenian and Parnellite warhorse, Michael Davitt, in the last few years of his life and career.[72] More work is needed here.

Janet Nolan and Hasia R. Diner led a new turn in the historiography in the 1970s and 1980s with major considerations of the gender dimensions of the Irish emigration story.[73] For Britain, one of the leading studies is Hickman's attempt to integrate social categories, such as ethnicity and gender, into a broader examination of state, church, and power relations as they worked out in the lives of the Irish in Victorian Britain.[74] Despite the growing interest in the gender aspect, and the appearance of a number of important studies, both the female side of emigration and gender dynamics of emigration and immigration remain fertile areas for further study. Pioneering works by Enda Delaney and Bronwen Walter have integrated women into their work, but these advanced studies examine the twentieth century.[75] In both Britain and America, there are also notable studies of Irish nuns which explore one of the most important occupations for Irish women;[76] whilst a certain amount has been written on women in other occupations.[77] There are, however, still relatively few distinct studies of Irish women in the new communities in the industrial age. Even if we prefer a new methodology in which women are integrated into general narratives, there are still relatively few studies which achieve this and much work remains to be done in this regard.

Dennis Clark pioneered the study of regional dimensions of Irish settlement in the United States, and the spirit of this can be seem in *The Encyclopaedia of the Irish in America*, which genuinely attempts to cover a wide geography, with major studies by region, state, and city.[78] The same is true of Gleeson's study of the Irish in America's southern states, which takes the narrative beyond the narrow confines of New England and the Middle Atlantic States.[79] However, too little of this work is comparative in nature. Similarly, the Irish in Britain are well served by local studies, but major cities such as London and Glasgow have still been inadequately served and little, if anything, has been done to integrate the Irish into a much wider story of varying regional performances and experiences in the age of urbanization and industrialization.

We can conclude overall that, while much exciting and important work has been done, there are still many topics, places, and angles to be covered. But perhaps the most telling omission thus far is the integration of Ireland and her emigrants into the larger narrative affecting all of the countries of Europe and peoples throughout the anglo-phone world and beyond.

NOTES

1. Marcus Lee Hansen, *The Atlantic Migration, 1607–1860: A History of the Continuing Settlement of the United States* (Cambridge, MA. 1940).
2. For example, the epic, collaborative treatment in Michael Glazier (ed), *The Encyclopedia of the Irish in America* (Notre Dame, IA, 1999).
3. E.R.R. Green, *Essays in Scotch-Irish History* (London, 1969); J.G. Leyburn, *The Scotch Irish: a Social History* (Chapel Hill, 1989); H.T. Blethen and C.W. Wood, Jr (eds), *Ulster and North America: Transatlantic Perspectives on the Scotch-Irish* (Tuscaloosa, 1997).
4. T.M. Devine (ed), *Irish Immigrants and Scottish Society in the Nineteenth and Twentieth Centuries* (Edinburgh, 1991); M.J. Mitchell, *The Irish in the West of Scotland, 1797–1848* (Edinburgh, 1998); idem (ed), *New Perspectives on the Irish in Scotland* (Edinburgh, 2008); D.M. MacRaild, *The Irish Diaspora in Britain, 1750–1939* (Basingstoke, 2010), ch.2.
5. See, for example, Lesley Page Moch, *Moving Europeans: Migration in Western Europe Since 1750* (Bloomington, 1992). For specific Irish comparisons with other Europeans, see: Jay P. Dolan, *The Immigrant Church: New York's Irish and German Catholics, 1815–1865* (South Bend, IA, 1992); Hasia R. Diner, *Hungering for America: Italian, Irish, and Jewish Foodways in the Age of Migration* (Cambridge, MA., 2001); and Donald H. Akenson, *Ireland, Sweden and the Great European Migration, 1815–1914* (Liverpool, 2011).
6. David Fitzpatrick, 'Emigration, 1801–70', in W.E. Vaughan (ed), *A New History of Ireland, VI* (Oxford, 1986), 562–622; idem, 'Emigration, 1870–1921', in Vaughan (ed), *New History of Ireland, VI*, 606–52, idem, *Emigration, 1801–1922* (Dublin, 1984). See also P. O'Sullivan (ed), *The Irish World-Wide*, 6 vols (Leicester, 1992–95): I: *Patterns of Migration*.
7. Donald H. Akenson, *The Irish Diaspora: A Primer* (Toronto and Belfast, 1996).
8. Kevin Kenny, 'Diaspora and Comparison: The Global Irish as a Case Study', *Journal of American History*, 90 (June 2003), 134–62.
9. Malcolm Campbell, *Ireland's New Worlds: Immigrants, Politics and Society in the United States and Australia, 1815–1922* (Madison, WI, 2008); Akenson, *Ireland, Sweden and the Great European Migration*.
10. Malcolm Campbell, 'Ireland's Furthest Shores: Irish Immigrant Settlement in Nineteenth-Century California and Eastern Australia', In *Pacific Historical Review* 71, no. 1 (2002), 59–90; Donald M. MacRaild, 'Crossing Migrant Frontiers: Comparative Reflections on Irish Migrants in Britain and the United States during the Nineteenth Century', *Immigrants and Minorities*, 18 (1999), 40–70; Alan O'Day, 'Imagined Irish

Communities: Networks of Social Communication of the Irish Diaspora in the United States and Britain in the Late Nineteenth and Early Twentieth Centuries', *Immigrants and Minorities*, 23 (2005), 399–424.

11. Matthew Gallman, *Receiving Erin's Children: Philadelphia, Liverpool and the Irish Famine Migration, 1845–1855* (Chapel Hill, NC, 2000).

12. Patrick Fitzgerald and Brian Lambkin, *Migration in Irish History, 1607–2007* (Basingstoke, 2008), which has a comprehensive bibliography.

13. J.C. Belchem, 'Hub and Diaspora: Liverpool and transnational labour', *Labour History Review*, 74, 4 (2009), 20–9.

14. For a discussion of the utility of the term when applied to the Irish, see 'Symposium: perspectives of the Irish Diaspora', *Irish Economic and Social History*, 33 (2006), 35–58, with contributions from Enda Delaney, Kevin Kenny, and Donald M. MacRaild.

15. J.C. Beckett, *Ireland, 1603–1972* (London, 2008 edn); F.S.L. Lyons, *Ireland Since the Famine* (London, 2009 edn); R.F. Foster, *Ireland, 1603–1988* (Harmondsworth, 1988), ch. 15; D.G. Boyce, *Nineteenth-Century Ireland: the Search for Stability* (Dublin, 2005 ed.); and Alvin Jackson, *Ireland, 1798–1998: Politics and War* (London, 1999).

16. W.F. Adams, *Ireland and the Irish Emigration to the New World from 1815 to the Famine* (New Haven, CT., 1932); Raymond Crotty, *Irish Agricultural Production: Its Volume and Structure* (Cork, 1966).

17. C. Ó Gráda, *Ireland Before and After the Famine: Explorations in Economic History 1800–1930* (Manchester, 1988).

18. Fitzpatrick, 'Emigration, 1801–70', 565; see also Adams, *Ireland and the Irish Emigration*, 410–28.

19. Kerby A. Miller, *Emigrants and Exiles: Ireland and the Irish Exodus to North America* (New York and Oxford, 1985).

20. Enda Delaney, *The Curse of Reason: The Great Irish Famine* (Dublin, 2012), especially ch. 10.

21. D.M. MacRaild, 'Irish Migration and the "Condition of England" Question: the roots of an historiographical tradition', *Immigrants and Minorities*, 14 (1995), 67–85.

22. See, however, the essays in D.M. MacRaild (ed), *The Great Famine and Beyond: Irish Migrants in Britain in the Nineteenth and Twentieth Centuries* (Dublin, 2000).

23. Roger Swift and Sheridan Gilley (eds), *The Irish in the Victorian City* (Beckenham, 1985); *The Irish in Britain, 1815–1939* (London, 1989); and *The Irish in Victorian Britain: The Local Dimension* (Dublin, 1999).

24. Ronald H. Bayor and Timothy J. Meagher (ed), *The New York Irish* (Baltimore, MD, 1996); Dennis Clark, *The Irish in Philadelphia: Ten Generations of Urban Experience* (Philadelphia, PA, 1973).

25. Robert O'Driscoll and Lorna Roberts, *The Untold Story: The Irish in Canada*, 2 Vols (Toronto, 1988).

26. E. Margaret Crawford (ed) *The Hungry Stream: Essays on Emigration and Famine* (Belfast, 1997).

27. A term coined by Thomas Carlyle, in his essay *Chartism* (London, 1839), to capture the dramatic and negative social change of the early industrial age.

28. Classically, in Tyler Anbinder's *Five Points: The 19th Century New York City Neighborhood That Invented Tap Dance, Stole Elections, and Became the World's Most Notorious Slum* (New York, 2002).

29. Sending back money and pre-paid tickets are common themes in the literature, for example, A. Schrier, *Ireland and the American Immigration, 1850–1900* (Minneapolis, 1958), 103–6. A useful summary is found in Fitzgerald and Lambkin, *Migration*, 31–33.

30. L. Kennedy and L.A. Clarkson, 'Birth, death and exile: Irish population history, 1700–1921' in B.J. Graham and L.J. Proudfoot (eds), *An Historical Geography of Ireland* (Dublin, 1993), 158–84.

31. There are many editions, but see: T.R. Malthus, *Essay on the Principles of Population*, ed. Patricia James (Cambridge, 2008).

32. T.W. Guinnane, *Vanishing Ireland: Households, Migration, and the Rural Economy in Ireland, 1850–1914* (NJ, 1997).

33. Guinnane, ibid., 17.

34. David Fitzpatrick: '"A peculiar tramping people": the Irish in Britain, 1801–70' and 'The Irish in Britain, 1871–1921', which appear in W.E. Vaughan (ed), *A New History of Ireland*, V (Oxford, 1986), 623–60 and VI (Oxford, 1996), 606–52.

35. Patrick O'Farrell, 'The Irish in Australia and New Zealand, 1791–1870' and 'The Irish in Australia and New Zealand, 1870–1990' in Vaughan (ed), *New History of Ireland*, V, 661–81; and VI, 703–24.

36. C. Ó Gráda, 'A Note on Nineteenth-Century Emigration Statistics', *Population Studies*, XXIX (1975) and his 'Some Aspects of Nineteenth-Century Irish Emigration', in L.M. Cullen and T.C. (eds), *Comparative Aspects of Scottish and Irish Economic and Social History, 1600–1900* (Edinburgh, 1977), 65–73; Donald M. MacRaild, *The Irish in Britain, 1800–1914* (Dundalk, 2007).

37. Fitzpatrick, 'Emigration, 1801–70', 565.

38. Ó Gráda, 'Note on Nineteenth-Century Emigration Statistics'.

39. MacRaild, *Culture, Conflict and Migration*.

40. Robert J. Scally, *The End of Hidden Ireland: Rebellion, Famine and Emigration* (Oxford, 1995).

41. Although it sits outside our period, perhaps the most remarkable study of this type is also one of the most recent: Miller, Schrier, Boling, and Doyle's *Irish Immigrants in the Land of Canaan: Letters and Memoirs from Colonial and Revolutionary America, 1675–1815* (Oxford, 2003). This monument of careful scholarship offers a history of Irish emigration, settlement, and experience from the late seventeenth to the early nineteenth century with each theme focused on the narratives of the emigrants themselves.

42. Miller, *Exiles and Emigrants*. He revisits this theme and analyses many others in his *Ireland and Irish America: Culture, Class and Transatlantic Migration, Field Day Files 3* (Dublin, 2008).

43. Fitzpatrick, *Oceans of Consolation* (Cork, 1994).

44. Angela McCarthy, *Irish Migrants in New Zealand, 1840–1937: 'The Desired Haven'* (Woodbridge, 2005).

45. C.J. Houston and W.J. Smyth, *Irish Emigration and Canadian Settlement: Patterns, Links and Letters* (Toronto and Belfast, 1990); O'Farrell, *Irish-Australian Letters; Annie O'Donnell, Your Fondest Annie* (Dublin, 2005), edited with an introduction by Maureen Murphy; *The Reynolds Letters: an Irish Emigrant Family in Late Victorian Manchester*, ed. L.W. McBride (Cork, 1999).

46. David A. Gerber, 'The Immigrant Letter between Positivism and Populism: The Uses of Immigrant Personal Correspondence in Twentieth Century American Scholarship', *Journal of American Ethnic History*, 16 (1997), 4–34; and his, 'Epistolary Ethics: Personal Correspondence and the Culture of Immigration in the Nineteenth Century', *Journal of American Ethnic History*, 18 (2000), 3–23.

47. Joseph Keating, *My Struggle for Life* (Dublin, 2005).

48. Lynn H. Lees, *Exiles of Erin: The Irish in Victorian London* (Manchester, 1979); Frances Finnegan, *Poverty and Prejudice: the Irish in York, 1840–1880* (Cork, 1982); Colin G. Pooley 'The residential segregation of migrant communities in mid-Victorian Liverpool', *Transactions of the Institute of British Geographers, New Series* 2(3), (1977), 364–82 and W.J. Lowe, *The Making of a Working-Class Community: The Irish in mid-Victorian Lancashire* (New York, 1989).

49. Stephan Thernstrom, *Poverty and Progress: Social Mobility in a Nineteenth-Century City* (Cambridge, MA, 1964).

50. R.A. Burchell, *The Irish in San Francisco, 1840–1880* (Manchester, 1979).

51. Meagher, *Inventing Irish America: Generation, Class, and Ethnic Identity in a New England City, 1880–1928* (Notre Dame, IA, 2001).

52. Bruce Elliott, *The Irish in Canada: A New Approach*, 2nd ed. (Toronto, 2004).

53. David Emmons, *The Butte Irish: Class and Ethnicity in an American Mining Town, 1875–1925* (Urbana, 1993).

54. Malcolm Smith and D.M. MacRaild, 'Nineteenth-century population structure of Ireland and of the Irish in England and Wales: an analysis by isonymy, '*American Journal of Human Biology*, 21 (2009), 283–89.

55. T. Dillon, 'The Irish in Leeds, 1851–1861', *Thoresby Society*, XVI (1974), 1–28; C. Richardson, 'Irish Settlement in Mid-Nineteenth-Century Bradford', *Yorkshire Bulletin of Economic and Social Research*, XX (1968), 40–57; idem,'The Irish in Victorian Bradford', *Bradford Antiquary, new series*, IX (1976), 294–316; F. Finnegan, *Poverty and prejudice: a study of Irish immigrants in York, 1840–1875* (Cork, 1982). MacRaild, *Culture, Conflict and Migration*, ch. 2.

56. J. Herson, 'Irish migration and settlement in Victorian Britain: a small town perspective', in R. Swift and Gilley, *The Irish in Britain, 1815–1939* (London, 1989); 'Migration, 'community' or integration? Irish families in Victorian Stafford' in Swift and Gilley (eds.), *The Irish in Victorian Britain: the Local Dimension* (Dublin, 1999), 156–89 and 'Irish immigrant families in the English West Midlands: a long-term view', in J.C. Belchem and K. Tenfelde (eds), *Irish and Polish Migration in Comparative Perspective* (Essen, 2003), 93–108.

57. A. Munslow, ' "Bigger, better and busier Boston". The pursuit of Irish political legitimacy: the Boston Irish, 1890–1920', in O'Sullivan (ed), *Irish World Wide*, I. See also K.A. Miller, 'Class, culture and immigrant group identity in the United States: the case of Irish-American identity', in Yans-McLaughlin (ed), *Immigration Reconsidered* (New York, 1990), 106–8, for a succinct overview of the importance of the urban Irish.

58. Donald H. Akenson, *Being Had: Historians, Evidence and the Irish in North America* (Port Credit, Ontario, 1985), ch. 3.

59. Elliott, *Irish in Canada*; P. Toner, *New Ireland Remembered: Historical Essays on the Irish in New Brunswick* (Fredericton, 1988).

60. O'Driscoll and Roberts, *Untold Story*.

61. Campbell, *Ireland's New Worlds*, ch. 3; G. Davis, *Land! Irish Pioneers in Mexican and Revolutionary Texas* (College Station, TX, 2002).

62. David T. Gleeson, *The Irish in the South, 1815–77* (Chapel Hill, NC, 2001).

63. David E. Emmons, *Beyond the American Pale: The Irish in the West, 1845–1890* (Norman, OK, 2010).

64. Robert Hughes, *The Fatal Shore* (London, 1988).

65. P. O'Farrell, 'The Irish in Australia and New Zealand, 1870–1990', in Vaughan (ed), *New History of Ireland*, VI, 703–24.

66. Fitzpatrick, *Oceans of Consolation*.

67. Two particularly valuable collections and the sources cited therein: B. Patterson (ed), *The Irish in New Zealand: Historical Contexts and Perspectives* (Wellington, 2002); Fraser, Lyndon (ed), *A Distant Shore: Irish Migration and New Zealand Settlement* (Dunedin, 2000). Also four important monographs: Richard Davis, *Irish Issues in New Zealand Politics, 1868-1922* (Dunedin, 1974) and D.H. Akenson, *Half The World From Home: Perspectives on the Irish in New Zealand, 1860-1950* (Wellington, 1990); L. Fraser, *To Tara via Holyhead: Irish Catholic Immigrants in Nineteenth-Century Christchurch* (Auckland, 1997); McCarthy, *Irish Migrants*; and J. Phillips and T. Hearn, *Settlers: New Zealand Immigrants from England, Ireland & Scotland 1800-1945* (Auckland, 2008).

68. 'Migration', in M. Daunton (ed), *The Cambridge Urban History of Britain, III: 1840-1950* (Cambridge, 2000), 185–206.

69. Smith and MacRaild, 'Paddy and Biddy no more: an evolutionary analysis of the decline in Irish Catholic forenames among descendants of nineteenth century Irish migrants to Britain', *Annals of Human Biology*, 2009.

70. Eric Foner, 'The Land League and Gilded Age Capitalism', *Marxist Perspectives*, 1 (1979), 6–55; Steven P. Erie, *Rainbow's End: Irish-Americans and the Dilemmas of Urban Machine Politics, 1840–1985* (Berkeley, 1990); Steve Fielding, *Class and Ethnicity: Irish Catholics in England, 1880-1939* (Buckingham, 1992).

71. Fielding, *Class and Ethnicity*, chs. 1 and 2.

72. T.W. Moody, 'Michael Davitt and the British Labour movement, 1882–1906', *Transactions of the Royal Historical Society*, VIII, 5th series (1958).

73. Hasia Diner, *Erin's Daughters in America: Irish Immigrant Women in the Nineteenth Century* (Baltimore, MD, 1984); Janet Nolan, *Ourselves Alone: Women's Emigration from Ireland, 1880–1920* (Lexington, KY, 1989).

74. Mary Hickman, *Religion, Class and Identity: The State, the Catholic Church and the Education of the Irish in Britain* (Avebury, 1995); idem, 'Migration and Diaspora', in *The Cambridge Companion to Modern Irish Culture*, Joe Cleary and Claire Connolly (eds) (Cambridge, 2005), 117–36.

75. E. Delaney, *State, Demography and Society* (Liverpool, 2000) and idem, *The Irish in Post-War Britain* (Oxford, 2007); B. Walter, *Outsider Inside: Whiteness, Place and Irish Women* (London, 2000).

76. Suellen Hoy, *Good Hearts: Catholic Sisters in Chicago's Past* (Urbana and Chicago, 2006). Important Irish context is found in an important work: Mary Peckham Magray, *The Transforming Power of the Nuns Women, Religion, and Cultural Change in Ireland, 1750-1900* (Oxford, 1998) and Barbara Walsh, *Roman Catholic Nuns in England and Wales: a Social History* (Dublin, 2002).

77. Diane Hotten-Somers, 'Relinquishing and reclaiming independence: Irish domestic servants, American middle-class mistresses, and assimilation, 1850–1920', *Eire-Ireland*, 36 (2001), 185–201; Bronwen Walter, 'Strangers on the inside: Irish Domestic Servants in England, 1881', *Immigrants and Minorities*, 27 (2009), 279–99.

78. Dennis Clark, *Hibernia America: The Irish and Regional Cultures* (Westport, CT., 1986); Michael Glazier (ed), *The Encyclopedia of the Irish in America* (Notre Dame, 1999).

79. David T. Gleeson, *The Irish in the South, 1815-1877* (Chapel Hill, 2001).

SELECT BIBLIOGRAPHY

Adams, W.F., *Ireland and the Irish Emigration to the New World from 1815 to the Famine* (New Haven, CT., 1932).

Akenson, D.H., *The Irish Diaspora: A Primer* (Toronto and Belfast, 1996).

——, *Ireland, Sweden and the Great European Migration, 1815–1914* (Liverpool, 2011).

Campbell, M., *Ireland's New Worlds: Immigrants, Politics and Society in the United States and Australia, 1815–1922* (Madison, WI, 2008).

Crawford, E.M. (ed.) *The Hungry Stream: Essays on Emigration and Famine* (Belfast, 1997).

Elliott, Bruce, *The Irish in Canada: A New Approach*, 2nd edn (Toronto, 2004).

Emmons, David M., *The Butte Irish: Class and Ethnicity in an American Mining Town, 1875–1925* (Urbana, 1993).

——, *Beyond the American Pale: The Irish in the West, 1845–1890* (Norman, OK, 2010).

Fitzgerald, P., and Lambkin, B. *Migration in Irish History, 1607–2007* (Basingstoke, 2008).

Fitzpatrick, David, 'Emigration, 1801–70', in W.E. Vaughan (ed.), *A New History of Ireland*, VI (Oxford, 1986), 562–622.

——, 'Emigration, 1870–1921', in Vaughan (ed), *New History of Ireland*, VI (Oxford, 1996), 606–52.

Gallman, M., *Receiving Erin's Children: Philadelphia, Liverpool and the Irish Famine Migration, 1845–1855* (Chapel Hill, NC, 2000).

Gleeson, D.T., *The Irish in the South, 1815–77* (Chapel Hill, NC, 2001).

Guinnane, T.W. *Vanishing Ireland: Households, Migration, and the Rural Economy in Ireland, 1850–1914* (NJ, 1997).

Houston, C.J. and Smyth, W.J., *Irish Emigration and Canadian Settlement: patterns, links and letters* (Toronto and Belfast, 1990).

Kenny, K., 'Diaspora and Comparison: The Global Irish as a Case Study', *Journal of American History*, 90 (June 2003), 134–62.

MacRaild, D.M., *The Irish Diaspora in Britain, 1750–1939* (Basingstoke, 2010).

Meagher, T., *Inventing Irish America: Generation, Class, and Ethnic Identity in a New England City, 1880–1928* (Notre Dame, IA, 2001).

Miller, K.A., *Emigrants and Exiles: Ireland and the Irish Exodus to North America* (New York and Oxford, 1985).

——, A. Schrier, B. Boling, and D.A. Doyle, *Irish Immigrants in the Land of Canaan: Letters and Memoirs from Colonial and Revolutionary America, 1675–1815* (Oxford, 2003).

O'Driscoll, R., and Roberts, L., *The Untold Story: The Irish in Canada*, 2 vols (Toronto, 1988).

O'Sullivan, P. (ed), *The Irish World-Wide*, 6 vols (Leicester, 1992–95): I: *Patterns of Migration*.

Schrier, A., *Ireland and the American Immigration, 1850–1900* (Minneapolis, 1958).

CHAPTER 29

....

HOME RULE AND ITS ENEMIES

....

MATTHEW KELLY

I. CONTEXTS

IRISH political history decisively entered a new phase in the early 1870s when the Home Rule idea began to be discussed. Home Rule dominated Irish politics until the First World War, generating a remarkably cohesive nationalist movement under the successive leaderships of Isaac Butt, Charles Stewart Parnell, Justin McCarthy, and John Redmond. Periodically, Home Rule was also the dominant question in British politics: Liberal support for Home Rule and Conservative opposition did more to define party political identity in late Victorian and Edwardian Britain than any other single issue.

Convinced Home Rulers did not seek Ireland's secession from the Union or complete separation, possibly under a republican system of government. Nor did Home Rulers demand the repeal of the Act of Union, which would create an Irish parliament under the Crown, parallel rather than subservient to the Westminster parliament. Instead, Home Rule prospected a form of devolved government within the Union, which would see Westminster voluntarily devolve certain responsibilities to an Irish executive formed from, and answerable to, an elected Irish parliament. In theory, the British government could use the legislative process to reverse or extend such act(s). Home Rule represented a more modest form of Irish self-government than Fenian separatism or O'Connellite repeal: successfully implemented, it would leave the Union intact with British sovereignty over Ireland uncompromised.

To understand the ramifications of Home Rule correctly, the constitutional context must be grasped. The Act of Union (1800) created a new state called the United Kingdom of Great Britain and Ireland. It did not absorb Ireland into Britain, and Ireland was never a part of Britain, as the name of the state then and today indicates. Instead, the Union unified the British and Irish parliaments, translating the Irish component from

College Green to Westminster. In doing so, the Union created a peculiar form of British government. Ireland was not governed through empowered local elites, as was the norm in Britain, but through an executive appointed by the government and based at Dublin Castle. Highly centralized, this was emphatically a form of imperial government, maintained by a mixture of state patronage and force.[1] Home Rule sought to replace 'Castle' government with a form of government accountable to an assembly representative of Irish public opinion. Technically, opposition to Home Rule was Unionist because it favoured the continuing unity of the Irish and British parliaments; polemically, Irish Unionists represented Home Rule as a revolutionary threat to the British-Irish connection.

The political logic of the Home Rule demand made it a form of constitutional nationalism wedded to a parliamentary political strategy. Under the leadership of Home Rule's principal originator, Isaac Butt, an Irish Protestant Tory, the party did not aim to become a mass-based or democratic organization, but an association of like-minded gentlemen M.P.s. Butt defined Home Rule in terms intended to appeal to Irish Protestant and British public opinion and he believed that the achievement of Home Rule would satisfactorily reconcile Irish nationality to the British Empire. The Home Rule idea achieved full coherence only when framed in an imperial context. Orthodox Home Rulers were convinced that to so reconstitute British-Irish relations represented not a pragmatic political compromise but the best possible outcome for Ireland. As such, they were no less idealistic than their separatist critics and, barring the ambiguous decade-long Parnellite interlude, they dominated the leadership of the Home Rule party throughout its fifty-year history.

The campaign's primary organizational manifestation was the Irish Parliamentary Party, which after 1879 nurtured and largely dominated a succession of subsidiary mass membership organizations such as the Land League, the Irish National League, the United Irish League, and the Ancient Order of Hibernians. The Party also had close links with partner organizations in the United States and the British Dominions, which were an important source of party income. Despite this, orthodox Home Rule thinking never achieved a comfortable ascendancy over the Home Rule movement. Many supporters, among them leading activists, either expressed their support for Home Rule in ambiguous terms, blurring the distinction between Home Rule and separation, leaving their ultimate aims obscure, or they participated in political organizations or campaigns, particularly focused on agrarian politics, which encouraged a rhetorical separatism and non-lawful political activism. Semi-autonomous, grass-roots activism was always a component of Home Rule politics, periodically energizing the movement while at the same time undermining the ability of the leadership to determine its meaning. After 1880, most Irish nationalists, often including those with Fenian antecedents or connections, identified as Home Rulers to some degree or another, enjoying the unity the term's ambiguity allowed.

British supporters, however, endeavoured to define Home Rule and were keen to emphasize its precise lineaments in order to demonstrate the moderate and workable nature of the demand. The most important exercises in definition were the three Liberal

Home Rule Bills placed before the House of Commons in 1886, 1893, and 1912. In contrast to the superficial clarity of O'Connellite repeal and Fenian separatism, Home Rule only took on clear meaning through the legislative process and the three bills revealed the extent to which a succession of Liberal governments believed Ireland should be self-governing.[2] As such, the appeal of Home Rule to British Liberals lay in the degree to which it allowed them to calibrate Irish self-government according to their sense of Ireland's fitness to receive this privilege.

As a consequence, although the relationship between Irish Home Rulers and their British sponsors could seem, as it was termed in the late 1880s, a Union of Hearts, the reception of the proposed settlements by Irish Home Rulers were shaped by rituals of scepticism and dissatisfaction. A Home Rule Bill which seemed equal to the expectations fostered by the Home Rule party was scarcely conceivable, while the accompanying parliamentary process, mired in detailed discussion of individual clauses and dogged by financial questions, could hardly write the exultant final chapter demanded by popular nationalist narratives of 'the Story of Ireland'.[3]

II. Irish Friends

Isaac Butt, in the 1830s and 40s one of the 'Orange Young Irelanders' of the *Dublin University Magazine* and, from 1836, Professor of Political Economy at Trinity College Dublin, was a harsh critic of British policy in Ireland. Butt condemned its centralizing tendencies and failure to address comprehensively the land and education questions to the satisfaction of the Irish majority.[4] Consequently, he saw Fenianism as symptomatic of the British misgovernment of Ireland and it was on this basis that he was willing to act for the defence in the Fenian trials of the late 1860s. Despite his populist touch, Butt believed not only that Home Rule would reconcile Irish nationalism to the realities of the British power, but that it would also help bring about the kind of Ireland he desired. And it was this Ireland that would prove the undoing of Butt's conception of Home Rule. As a Tory who saw the vote as a privilege, he looked to create a system of self-government for Ireland which would restore traditional social hierarchies, returning the landed and professional elite—Protestant and Catholic—to their proper places as the natural leaders of society. Butt believed that Castle government both denied Ireland its right to self-government and created an unhealthy dependency culture in which the privileged were not required to exercise their responsibilities. Home Rule, Butt hoped, would stymie the development of a more popular radical politics, rendering Fenianism impotent in the face of a benevolent patrician politics.

In practice, it was Home Rule that had to come to terms with the popular political impulses roused by Fenianism.[5] In the early 1870s, the Supreme Council of the Irish Republican Brotherhood agreed to suspend its revolutionary activities in order to give the Home Rule movement a chance to prove its efficacy and compatibility with its ideological integrity. Unconvinced that either condition was fulfilled, in 1877 the Supreme

Council forbade further Fenian cooperation with the movement. However, just as Butt found that the popular activism released by Fenianism would not be subdued, so many republicans found Home Rule party politics a congenial substitute for revolutionary plotting. John O'Connor Power and J. G. Biggar, both prominent IRB members and now M.P.s, refused to submit to the Supreme Council's authority and were expelled from the Brotherhood. As significant as the Irish liberals and conservatives, who opportunistically aligned themselves with Home Rule during its break-through general election of 1874,[6] were the IRB men who were elected as Home Rule M.P.s and the many more who worked for the movement despite the Supreme Council's opposition.[7] Butt may have been the most effective articulator of the Home Rule idea, but he did not represent the emergent Home Rule rank and file.

A more convincing representative of these popular passions was Charles Stewart Parnell. Parnell was also a Protestant but, in sharp contrast to Butt's political trajectory, his entry into parliament in 1875 was sponsored by a small group of radical nationalists.[8] Once in parliament, Parnell immediately associated with Biggar and the other obstructionists who disrupted parliamentary proceedings in order to heighten Home Rule's profile and give voice to their principled objection to British imperial policy.[9] Parnell's famous denial in parliament that the Manchester Martyrs had committed 'murder' brought him to the notice of the Fenian-influenced Home Rule Confederation of Great Britain, who in 1878 replaced Butt with Parnell as their president. Also observing Parnell, this time from afar, was John Devoy, Irish-American leader of the republican Clan na Gael. Devoy came to believe that Parnell could provide the figurehead for a form of Home Rule politics whose vigour was compatible with his republican ideals. On 24 October, he sent a telegram, simultaneously published in the Irish-American press, which laid out the conditions the Home Rule movement must meet if it were to attract republican cooperation. Often described as marking a New Departure in Irish nationalist politics, it stated:

> Nationalists here will support you on [the] following conditions: (1) abandonment of the federal demand [and] substitution [of] general declaration in favour of self-government; (2) vigorous agitation of land question on basis of peasant proprietary, while accepting conditions tending to abolish arbitrary eviction; (3) exclusion of all sectarian issues from platform; (4) [Irish] members to vote together on all imperial and home questions, adopt aggressive policy, and energetically resist all coercive legislation; (5) advocacy of all struggling nationalities in British empire and elsewhere.[10]

Parnell did not find it necessary to agree explicitly to Devoy's terms, though there would be considerable congruency between them and Parnell's future leadership of the movement.

If Devoy's telegram provided separatist ideologues cover for their work for the Home Rule movement, of greater significance was Parnell's decision in 1879 to adopt the cause of the Land League. As T.W. Moody argued in a classic thesis, the alignment of the socio-economic interests of the Irish tenantry, in the West of Ireland facing renewed distress, with this new nationalism marked a more significant New Departure.[11] The old demand for the three Fs—fair rents, fixity of tenure, the right to free sale—proved a more popular rallying cry than Devoy's strictures, and the creation of the Land League, under the presidency of the former Fenian, ex-convict, and radical Michael Davitt, triggered a period of intensive agrarian agitation against landlordism. Land League methods included official actions such as organized boycott, rent strike, and collective resistance to eviction, as well as acts of violent intimidation such as sending threatening letters, maiming livestock, and shootings. The government's response was two-pronged. Vigorous coercive measures, including the selective suspension of habeas corpus (which saw certain districts 'proclaimed'), were married to reforming legislation, notably the 1881 Land Act which guaranteed the three Fs.

By the winter of 1881/2, Parnell and much of the Land League leadership were in Kilmainham Jail and Ireland was often described as being in a state of anarchy. Alarmed by what he had helped unleash, Parnell let it be understood that, if released from jail, he would wind up the agitation and commit the movement to purely constitutional methods. The so-called 'Kilmainham Treaty', later criticized by Davitt as a counter-revolutionary betrayal of the Land War's radical potential, led to the release of Parnell and his colleagues in May 1882.[12] A day or two later, the new Chief Secretary of Ireland and the Under Secretary were murdered in Phoenix Park by a group of renegade separatists known as the Invincibles. This momentarily undermined Parnell's legendary poise and he offered his resignation, regarding the murders as having ruthlessly exposed the limitations of his authority. Gladstone insisted that Parnell stay on and such was the shock at these grisly murders throughout Ireland that they inadvertently strengthened Parnell's position, heightening the appeal of constitutional methods.

Thereafter, Parnell proved reluctant to countenance agrarian agitation and distanced himself from the Fenians: John O'Leary's dictum, that to succeed in Irish politics a leader needed either the support of the Fenians or the Catholic Church, carries more than a grain of truth for, as Parnell pulled back from the radicalism that had brought him to the leadership of the movement, he drew closer to the Church. By October 1884, the Party and the Church had reached a concordat, the Church satisfied that the Party could be relied upon to promote their educational interests at Westminster. Despite this, throughout the 1880s Parnell kept the radicals in view, peppering his speeches with suggestive phrases such as 'no man has the right to fix the boundary to the march of a nation'. His coalition, loose and unstable, was in place.

Parnell's career ended in spectacular failure. Exposed as an adulterer in late 1890, Gladstone and the Catholic Church both indicated that they would no longer back his leadership. Determined to hang on—some say wounded vanity drove him on, others that he wanted to avoid the Home Rule movement becoming excessively confessional—Parnell led a minority of loyal Home Rule M.P.s in a nine-month battle that culminated in his premature death in October 1891.[13] Thanks to his pandering to Fenian sentiment (the so-called 'appeal to the hillside men'), Parnell attracted the support of Dublin and much radical and urban opinion, but as the three by-elections of those months demonstrated, he did not have the support of the enfranchised

Catholic electors of rural Ireland. Parnell's Dublin funeral, the most important public event of late nineteenth-century Ireland, symbolically repudiated all talk of recon
ciliation. John Redmond, Parnell's successor as leader of a minority of loyal M.P.s,
was bequeathed a difficult legacy, his political survival dependent on maintaining a
Redmondite-Fenian nexus.[14]

The circumstances which saw Parnellites and anti-Parnellites reunited under
Redmond's leadership in 1900 were very different. Gladstonian hopes had been suppressed by a long period of Conservative government that saw no prospect of a Home
Rule Bill. As a consequence, the Party ceased to be a vehicle for popular political participation and donations dried up.[15] By contrast, grass-roots radicalism revived. Most significantly, William O'Brien established the United Irish League in 1898 and led a new
land agitation, while the separatists organized the 1798 centenary commemoration
movement, led opposition to the Boer War (1899–1902) and the royal visits of 1900 and
1903, and embarked on an anti-recruiting campaign.[16] Despite the Party's organizational
weakness, Redmond and other Home Rulers retained considerable personal authority and they proved adept at exploiting or aligning themselves with these new initiatives. Consequently, constitutionalists dominated proceedings at the major '98 events
and, through vigorous parliamentary interventions, made their opposition to the Boer
War clear, reminding the Liberals of their shared opposition to Tory foreign policy
adventurism.

Most remarkable, however, was the continued capacity of the party to mobilize
itself against agrarian radicalism and separatist enthusiasm. In the first years of the
new century, the United Irish League and the emerging Catholic-nationalist Ancient
Order of Hibernians were tamed, both brought firmly within the Home Rule fold,
while the neo-Fenianism of the '98 organizations that would feed the new Sinn Féin
movement were firmly marginalized: Party activists fulminated against factionists
driven by fanciful ideas who were determined to divide the national movement.
With some justification, the Party's reunification and reassertion of its authority has
been seen as reflecting the vested interests of middle class Catholics and their clerical allies.[17] Of equal importance was the simple fact that the prospect of the Liberals
returning to power promised to demonstrate the continuing efficacy of the parliamentary strategy. Over the longer term, the specific lineaments of Redmondite
politics became clear. It meant Empire loyalty and the conciliation of moderate
southern landlords, as emphasized by Paul Bew, but also, as James McConnel shows,
a thoroughgoing commitment to political centralism and hostility to localism,
socialism, and monocultural Gaelicism.[18]

III. British Friends

Indisputably, the most important British friend of Home Rule was William Ewart
Gladstone, Prime Minister 1868–74, 1880–5, 1886, and 1892–4. His decision in

December 1885 to fly the 'Hawarden Kite', which signalled that he intended to place a Home Rule Bill before the House of Commons, transformed British-Irish political relations. The importance of this stemmed not merely from its political ramifications, but from the justification Gladstone increasingly provided for his decision. If, on the one hand, he emphasized Irish readiness for self-government, with all that this implied about the right of Britain to make this decision, on the other, he made it clear that his commitment reflected his conviction that the means by which the Act of Union had been brought about were 'unspeakably criminal'.[19] This represented an extraordinary concession not only to the Irish Parliamentary Party but to Irish nationalism in general. The greatest British politician of the age had become more than a convert to Home Rule for Ireland; he had come to see the British connection as Irish nationalists did.

Gladstone's first Home Rule Bill provoked a split in the Liberal Party and it was defeated in the House of Commons, precipitating a new election which the Conservatives decisively won. When Gladstone returned to office in 1892, elected on a Home Rule platform, he could be sure the bill would pass relatively smoothly through the Commons but could only hope that the Lords would recognize the electoral mandate which Home Rule had attracted. When the Lords threw the bill out, Gladstone went into retirement. Lord Rosebery took over the Liberal leadership and in 1895 the British electorate returned the Conservatives to office. Resolutely anti-Home Rule Conservative governments followed, until the Liberals returned to power in 1906.

Gladstone's first Home Rule Bill outlined a system of devolved parliamentary government for Ireland in which two 'orders' would sit together in the same chamber. The first order would be composed of M.P.s elected under the existing householder franchise (as established by the 1884 Reform Act). The second order comprised the Irish peerage and a number of elected senators, men of property who would be returned through a more restricted £25 franchise. The two orders would sit together, each having the power of veto and the right to vote separately if so desired. Gladstone hoped this system would have the effect of elevating the Irish peerage in the eyes of the people, reviving respect for the 'natural rulers of Ireland' and diminishing 'the influence of nationalist agitators and ultramontane priests'.[20]

Under Home Rule, Westminster would retain control over policing, military defence, foreign affairs, and commerce, this last denying the Irish full control over trade policy and the sensitive question of tariffs. Crucially, under the first bill there would be no representation of Irish M.P.s at Westminster, raising the spectre of taxation without representation. Parnell later admitted to Cecil Rhodes that this 'exclusion may have given some colour to the accusations so freely made against the bill that it had a separatist tendency'.[21] The 1893 bill broadly adhered to the provisions of the first bill as regards Irish control over domestic matters, but it retained Irish representation at Westminster and proposed an Irish parliament consisting of two houses. The lower house would consist of the 103 M.P.s elected on the present franchise and the upper house would be composed of forty-eight members elected by voters, who owned or occupied land with an annual valuation of £200 or more.

The question of whether Gladstone's commitment to Home Rule was motivated by 'Irish ideas', according to which he had famously declared his intention to govern Ireland on first taking office in 1868, was the subject of immediate political controversy and much subsequent historiographical debate. The Tories accused Gladstone of opportunism, and it is indisputable that, by securing the support of the Irish Home Rule M.P.s, he was propelled into office in January 1886. More subtle is the proposition that Gladstone was motivated by what he perceived to be the needs of the Liberal party. Increasingly divided as it was between radicals headed by Joseph Chamberlain and Whigs associated with Lord Hartington, Gladstone came to believe that the integrity of the party and a proper conception of liberalism depended upon the maintenance of his leadership. A big bill predicated on sound liberal principles would restore unity to a fissiparous party threatened by the rising tide of 'Tory democracy'.[22] Cooke and Vincent, in the most ingenious reading of Gladstone's actions in 1886, infer a greater level of calculation still, suggesting that Gladstone intended to use the Home Rule Bill as cover for the passage of a Land Purchase Bill. They argue that Home Rule was intended to fail, whereas Land Purchase was to go through, providing the means by which the Land Question, the fundamental source of Ireland's ills, would be answered. By creating a nation of contented peasant proprietors, the demand for self-government would be exposed as symptomatic of socio-economic discontent rather than a more profound drive for national self-government.[23]

Although the explosive circumstances of 1885/6 cannot but fascinate the political historian, such narrowly 'high political' interpretations are now generally rejected. Also found wanting is the hagiographical view that Gladstone's commitment was predicated purely on *his* peculiar capacity to realize that Home Rule would deliver 'justice for Ireland'.[24] Gladstone's personal authority was certainly central to the acceptance of Home Rule by the 'non-conformist conscience' troubled by the Catholicity of Irish nationalism,[25] but recent work suggests this should be considered alongside what J.P. Parry describes as the 'deeper rhythms of Liberal politics'.[26] Parry and Eugenio Biagini are exponents of what might be considered the liberal idealist school of British historiography.[27] Both emphasize the way in which Home Rule came to be seen by some Liberals as the ideologically sound solution to the Irish Question, the only genuinely democratic and liberal alternative to coercion.[28] By their readings, Home Rule, whether intended to fulfil a nationalist agenda or deliver a just extension of local government, had had currency among liberals, particularly radicals, since the 1870s. Gladstone did not so much spring Home Rule on credulous Liberals innocent of the idea as place it unexpectedly at the top of the Liberal agenda.[29] Indeed, Biagini contends that an 'elective affinity' rooted in an anti-jingoistic, democratic politics had developed between British liberalism and Irish nationalism in the late 1870s. Stephen Ball complicates the picture, noting that the signals coming from Ireland indicated the possibility of the development of a more significant Irish separatist movement that could be forestalled by a significant act of devolution.[30] If the political and ideological intricacies of Gladstonian manoeuvre continue to perplex, it is nonetheless clear that mainstream British liberals took the view that the Irish Question was a British problem to be settled within the confines of the Union.

At the level of liberal political discourse things were clearer. If the democratic rights of the Irish people did not extend to secession, the democratic logic of the 1884–5 Reform and Redistribution of Seats Acts provided a powerful component of pro-Home Rule Liberal polemic.[31] As Gladstone argued after the 1886 defeat, the overwhelming support for Home Rule by the Irish electorate in the 1885 general election indicated that the 'settled opinion' of the Irish people was in favour of Home Rule. Allied to this was the view that the Irish, as a nation, comprised a distinct democratic unit within the United Kingdom. Its legitimate needs could only be met if the UK's non-Irish majority fulfilled its moral obligation to respond positively to these democratically expressed demands, overcoming a politics predicated on a crude parliamentary majoritarianism. Moreover, although Gladstone did not take Fenianism's separatism seriously, he judged its 'intensity' as symptomatic of legitimate socio-economic grievances. By contrast, the demand for Home Rule was legitimized by its apparently moderate, reasonable, and liberal characteristics.[32] Such thinking reflected the belief widespread among Britons that they were peculiarly favoured by Providence, forming the world's greatest, most progressive, and most fortunate nation. The logic that flowed from this premise was simple: a politics predicated on secession could only be the politics of a people ill-equipped for self-government, whereas a politics that sought to improve the system in a manner compatible with liberal principles must have reason and justice on its side. In sum, Liberal supporters of Home Rule recognized that Ireland was a distinct nation with distinct national rights and Home Rule represented an attempt not to subordinate but to align these rights with British interests. Liberal Home Rule reflected the limitations Britain imposed upon Ireland's right to self-determination. Rather than anticipating an Ireland governed according to 'Irish ideas', Gladstonian Home Rule sought to engineer an answer to the Irish Question rooted in British liberal ideas.

IV. British Enemies

It is all too easy to denounce British opponents of Home Rule as anti-Irish and anti-Catholic, as men and women who allowed sectarian prejudice, often expressed with a racist inflection, to dictate their politics. As Michael Bentley put it, as Tory opposition to Home Rule developed, 'Irish space became as distinct as Indian, as foreign, as colonial, as *unpleasant*'.[33] In addition, Home Rule's Tory opposition stands accused of defending the Union by encouraging loyalist extremism, seemingly licencing political violence and resistance to the Crown authorities. In one of the most notorious speeches given by a Conservative politician in response to Gladstone's first Home Rule Bill, Lord Randolph Churchill told an audience at the Ulster Hall, Belfast, on 22 February 1886, that they might find themselves having to act outside 'the lines of what we are accustomed to look upon as constitutional action'.[34] Churchill's words came at the end of a speech which had emphasized the shared history of religious struggle by Protestants on both sides of the Irish Sea, asserting that their English brethren would never betray their Ulster fellow Protestants. Several months later, Churchill used a phrase that would go down in history, telling a Scottish Liberal Unionist in a public letter that 'Ulster will fight; Ulster will be right'.[35] Bentley again provides a pithy summary: 'Once in place, "Irish" politics became a Tory language of resistance neither more or less'.[36]

Churchill's words were more carefully pitched than these isolated quotations suggest and his manner recalled Parnell's oratorical techniques, saying enough to imply that there were foreseeable circumstances in which the use of force would be justified. Lord Salisbury (prime minister 1886–1892, 1895–1902) was more provoking still. On 10 May 1886, in one of the most notorious political speeches of the period, he compared the Irish in racially disparaging terms to Hottentots and Orientals, suggesting that 'self-government... works admirably well when it is confided to the Teutonic race, but it does not work so well when people of other races are called upon to join in it'. Salisbury seemed to suggest that his answer to the Irish Question was coercion and mass emigration or, as John Morley memorably paraphrased it, 'manacles and Manitoba'.[37]

According to his biographer, the most notable section of Salisbury's major speech in opposition to Gladstone's second Home Rule Bill emphasized that thirty-eight Home Rule M.P.s had at one time or another been described by judges as being associated with organizations that mutilated cattle, withheld rents, and even murdered people.[38] The association of Parnellism with crime and the idea that the Irish were 'assassins' proved one of the most emotionally powerful aspects of British opposition to Home Rule, but it did not serve merely to confirm pre-existing prejudices. As news of the violence of the Land War came to dominate the press in 1879–82, A.V. Dicey, the eminent liberal jurist, went from being favourably disposed to staunchly opposed to Home Rule, believing Ireland's nationalist leadership had comprehensively demonstrated that they were unsuited to self-government.[39] In contrast to the Liberal view that Irish nationalists would learn how to act responsibly when faced with the realities of government,[40] Dicey believed the Land War proved that Irish self-government would prove disastrous.[41] In a string of writings throughout the 1880s and 1890s, he deployed his considerable intellectual powers to make 'England's Case Against Home Rule'. In essence, he argued that a minority sub-group (the Irish) had no right to dictate to the majority group (the English) a set of changes which would have the effect of 'revolutionizing the constitution of the whole United Kingdom'.[42] More than this, Dicey ruthlessly exposed the calculated obfuscations which underpinned the Home Rule campaign, arguing no less insistently than the orthodox separatists that 'A bona fide Home Ruler cannot be a bona fide Nationalist'.[43]

There can be little doubt that many British Unionists shared an affinity for Irish Unionism as a Protestant people under siege, their hard-won liberties apparently threatened by Catholic Ireland. As Salisbury put it, the securities offered by Gladstone's bills were no more than 'paper barricades' that would prove ineffectual as Dublin gradually assumed full independence. Home Rule would not answer the Irish Question for—again in Salisbury's words—there was 'no middle term between government at Westminster and independent and separate government at Dublin'.[44] Moreover, nationalism carried more than a whiff of a more socially radical politics, challenging the rights of property that all mainstream British politicians believed were the basis of a properly ordered society.

And yet, if in office the Liberals pursued the headline-grabbing political panacea of Home Rule, the Conservative record in Ireland was more substantial. Between 1885 and 1903, they passed legislation which accumulatively created a peasant proprietorship and democratized Irish local government, measures that radically reduced the social, economic, and political power of the old Unionist elite. Ireland's infrastructure was also improved, with harbour walls strengthened and light railways built, and agencies were established to enhance Ireland's economic potential, notably the Department of Agriculture and Technical Instruction. When, in 1906, the Liberals were returned to power after twelve years of Tory government, Ireland was more economically dynamic and more politically democratic than at any time in the period of the Union.

None of this was inevitable and explaining this 'constructive unionism'—in Gerald Balfour's famous phrase, the attempt to 'kill home rule with kindness'—is not straight-forward. Notwithstanding the intensity of his racial rhetoric in 1886, Salisbury con-sistently believed that Ireland's problems were material and he thought Ireland would benefit from a widening of the 'base of property'.[45] Similar thinking motivated Irish Chief Secretaries such as Arthur Balfour (1887–1891), Gerald Balfour (1895–1900), and George Wyndham (1900–05); also important was the presence in the Salisbury coali-tion of Liberal Unionists, often of a Chamberlainite turn of mind. They shared many commonplace anti-Irish prejudices, not least in seeing the Irish as 'childish', which description they applied almost as readily to Unionists as Nationalists.[46] Nonetheless, Chamberlain's radical defence of the Union was predicated on the notion that 'if poverty was to be reduced by state intervention, then what Britain required was not devolution and the weakening of Parliament, but the rational reconstruction and empowerment of the imperial executive at its centre'.[47]

G.K. Peatling argues that Unionist thinking fits into the broader context of late nineteenth-century imperial thinking. By the 1880s and 90s, the notion that large states and empires would break up along lines determined by ethnically based nationalisms, so powerfully influential in the 1850s and 60s, appeared outmoded. German unification and imperial expansion—the 'scramble for Africa'—suggested history would favour large expansionist states that were sufficiently resolute when facing down challenges to their authority. The optimistic rationalism of the mid-Victorian period had given way to this more conflictual understanding of international politics, which was sometimes expressed in neo-Darwinian terms. Consequently, although Conservative thinking was disturbed in the early twentieth century by debates about the possibility of a fed-eral future for the British Empire, stimulated in part by the grind of the South African War, generally speaking the prospect of Home Rule for Ireland appeared to endanger the fundamentals of Britain's global imperial ascendancy.[48] Indeed, Irish separatists and British Unionists alike maintained that Irish independence would begin the unravelling of the Empire: Unionists frequently asked how they could hope to retain control of India once it became clear that they could not hold Ireland, whereas separatists saw Home Rule as an attempt to stave off imperial dissolution.[49] Consequently, although there were circumstances in which British Unionists might grant the five million people of Ireland self-government, such an experiment could not be chanced if it might threaten the capacity of London to determine the British Empire's future.

V. Irish Enemies

Irish enemies of Home Rule fell into two main categories, Irish Unionists and Irish separatists.

Unionism was a political form of the broader phenomenon of Loyalism. Loyalism was a Protestant political creed that professed allegiance to the Crown and the permanency of the Protestant Act of Settlement (1701).[50] Unionism emerged from within Loyalism as a form of organized political opposition to Home Rule. At first glance, Unionism is a misnomer, signifying a political identity predicated on the false claim that orthodox Home Rulers sought to undo rather than recalibrate the Union. However, a fundamental feature of Unionist politics was the notion, sometimes sincerely held, sometimes deployed for political effect, that Home Rule was a Trojan horse for separation. Home Rule, Unionists insisted, was the latest Nationalist synonym for either separation, repeal, or Rome Rule. In effect, Unionists claimed that Irish nationalists were not nationalists at all but Romanists eager to hand the country over to the dictates of the Vatican. For example, Unionists claimed the violent hostility in the 1890s that greeted Protestant street preachers in southern Irish towns presaged the realities of a Home Rule Ireland,[51] while the Ulster feminist Isabella Tod feared that, if Ireland fell under a form of Catholic rule, women would be kept 'down permanently'.[52] Also apparently threatened was Ulster's dynamic industrial economy. Devolution risked a Dublin government disadvantaging Ulster's booming linen and shipbuilding industries by imposing tariffs thought to be in the interest of the country as a whole. Finally, Home Rule was projected as a humiliation, demoting Ireland from a partner state of the imperial power to a colony. The accumulated effect of these fears saw the Unionists re-imagine the Act of Union as the guarantor of the fundamental rights and liberties of the Irish Protestant just as the Irish nationalists had a tendency to imagine Home Rule as the solution to all their problems.

If British proponents or opponents of Home Rule made their case broadly in terms of British ideas, so Irish Unionism was fundamentally Irish. Unionists opposed Home Rule less because they were worried it would endanger British India than because they feared it would deliver government by Catholic Ireland. Such hostility was generalized, stemming from a political identity forged by the violent religious political conflict of the seventeenth century, the memory of which was sustained by the rituals of loyalist associationalism, and was highly personalized. Like the Tories, Irish Unionists were repulsed by the criminality and anarchy brought by the Land War and threatened by the Irish National League. Many Unionists loathed Parnell and his lieutenants, repelled by men they associated with the anarchy of the winter of 1881–2 and the Phoenix Park murders.

Unionists can be classified in broadly socio-economic and geographical categories. First were the members of the Anglo-Irish aristocracy and gentry, formed of landowners and often Trinity College- or Oxbridge-educated members of the higher professions. This old elite was increasingly joined by an emergent Protestant middle class, notably the product of Ulster's rapid industrial and commercial development in the nineteenth century but who were to be found in smaller numbers throughout the country. Finally, there were the Protestant working class and tenant farmers, both overwhelmingly concentrated in Ulster, but again present in significant numbers elsewhere in the country.

The concentration of the Protestant population in Ulster was of enormous political significance. For just as Home Rule was the nationalist politics of the new democracy, superseding the secret organization of the Fenians and the O'Connellite politics of the Catholic Whigs, so Unionism supplanted the old Irish loyalism of the elites with a democratic politics of the masses. As a consequence, the basis of Loyalist political power shifted, developing from an Irish Loyalism predicated on the shared interests of the landed elite throughout the British Isles to a distinct Ulster Unionism, rooted in an Ulster democracy projecting a specifically Ulster identity, which mirrored the cultural revivalism of late nineteenth-century Irish nationalism.[53] As a consequence, the Loyalist elite came to terms with the fact that, if they were to mount an effective resistance to Home Rule while retaining something of their socio-political pre-eminence, they needed to align with the democratic Loyalism of the Protestant working class, notably the form of popular Protestant associationalism known as Orangeism, however prone to intense and sometimes violent displays of sectarianism.

These realignments should not be seen as the manipulation of the masses by the old elite. Orangeism had a vitality of its own and Ulster Protestant democracy had distinct economic interests, often at odds with those of the old elite. For example, some Protestant tenant farmers had joined the Land League, while in the late 1890s Russellism, a radical reformist Unionism, developed a distinctly Unionist threat to the entrenched socio-economic interests of the landed elite.[54] Although Unionism's success was built on the successful integration of the Protestant classes, its capacity to present a united front was directly proportional to the degree of nationalist threat at any given moment.

Avatars of these general observations were the careers of the leading Unionists of the day. Colonel Edward Saunderson (1837–1906), in the 1870s an Ulster liberal and landlord, emerged as the leader of Irish parliamentary Unionism in the 1880s. Although his predominance reflected the ascendancy of Ulster Unionism within Unionism, he was dogged throughout his career by suspicions raised by his Liberal political origins. His declining authority in the 1890s, notwithstanding his personal inadequacies as a leader, reflected the passing of the immediate threat of Home Rule and his conservative stance on the Land Question and other social questions important to the Unionist rank and file.[55] Saunderson's successors, Edward Carson (1854–1935) and James Craig (1871–1940), reflected the complexity of the Unionist coalition which confronted the third Home Rule Bill of 1912. Carson, a Trinity-educated Dublin barrister, represented the old Loyalist elite but could speak the language of popular Protestantism, whereas Craig, the Belfast-born son of a whiskey distiller, provided Ulster ballast to that Carsonian grandeur.

Unionist unity was facilitated by the reforms of the Conservative governments of 1895–1906, not least Wyndham's Land Purchase Act of 1903, which apparently demonstrated that Unionism could deliver the reforms demanded by the grass roots. Constructive unionism did not wholly resolve the class tensions within Irish Unionism, but the Carson-Craig nexus was greatly eased by its ministrations.

Irish separatist opposition to Home Rule was predicated on the notion that British government in Ireland was a form of political despotism, whose local agents were an imperial settler class, their 'West Briton' accomplices to be found among Irish Catholics and state agents like the Royal Irish Constabulary and the courts. This power complex was reinforced by a deliberately nurtured sectarianism which succeeded in dividing the Irish people against themselves. Crucially, separatists rejected the idea that Ireland was a colony, arguing in rather more Victorian terms that Ireland was a nation under imperial rule.[56] Many Home Rulers agreed with this diagnosis, but whereas they believed devolution might legitimize the Union, separatists argued that the politics of devolution served to legitimize British power. Home Rule, the separatists maintained, would not reverse the conquest but would confirm Ireland in its servitude, seeing the representatives of the Irish people accede to a position in the British Empire. There is a peculiar congruency between this nationalist thinking and the Unionist idea that Home Rule would render Ireland a colony.

Separatist sentiment was not uncommon, but its political significance was undermined by the ability of the Home Rulers to blur ideological lines, presenting Home Rule as Fenianism by other means. Nonetheless, Irish Republican Brotherhood activity could be found throughout Ireland, not least in the Workmen's Clubs, and in the 1880s a renewed separatist presence surfaced in Irish public life through cultural nationalist organizations such as the Gaelic Athletic Association, the Young Ireland Societies, and various commemorative and friendly societies. Such advanced nationalist associations, with their secessionist tendencies, fed the 1798 centenary movement and stimulated wider pro-Boer sympathies during the second South African War (1899–1902). And while the significance of this activity should not be exaggerated—the police disparaged the separatists as marginal and socially insignificant—few Home Rule politicians could afford to ignore entirely the way separatist sentiment resonated with the wider population. Many platform orators, facing a rowdy outdoor crowd, found a little Fenian-speak went a long way.

By the turn of the twentieth century, the options for the aspirant separatist had expanded from Fenianism's republicanism to include Sinn Féin's 'Dual Monarchism'. Arthur Griffith, Sinn Féin's leading ideologue, rejected Fenianism's republican absolutism, arguing that the 1782–3 complex of legislation which created Grattan's parliament saw Ireland achieve full independence. Consequently, Griffith argued that Ireland need not embark on a foolhardy revolution, but should withdraw its representatives from parliament, set up an executive and assembly in Dublin, and assume the constitutional rights and liberties illegally confiscated by the British government through the Act of

Union. In this way, Griffith advocated not the radical break with the past demanded by the republicans, but the restoration to Ireland of her constitutional rights. Griffith's '82ism attempted to find common ground between the strict constitutionalists of the Home Rule party and the revolutionism of the IRB. Famously drawing inspiration from the Austro-Hungarian *Ausgleich* of 1867, Griffith's argument carried echoes of O'Connellite repeal and Parnellite articulations of Home Rule, despite despising the former and distancing himself from the latter. Alhough, as the home ruler Tom Kettle put it, Sinn Féin had a 'great capacity for getting itself talked about"; its electoral achievements were limited to a clutch of local government seats won in 1907–8 and lost by 1912.[57]

VI. The Ulster Crisis

The Liberal Party did not return to power in 1906 with any particular enthusiasm for Irish Home Rule. The Gladstonian commitment remained part of the party's agenda, but thanks to a strong majority, more immediately pressing concerns and the passing of a full decade since last they enjoyed power, Home Rule had ceased to be British liberalism's defining political question. The Home Rule Party had become an irritant and the Irish Councils Bill of 1908, which looked to strengthen Irish local government, was an attempt to neutralize the issue. Presented to the Home Rule Party as a reasonable compromise on their core demand, it provoked severe criticism in Ireland, reminding the Liberal and the Home Rule parties alike that Home Rule marked the extent of the compromise nationalists were willing to make. A similar outcry greeted Redmond's claim to an American audience in 1910 that Home Rule represented no greater measure of self-government than the federal structure gave each US state.[58]

It would take the greatest constitutional crisis of twentieth-century British politics to revive the half-dormant Liberal commitment to Home Rule. In 1909, Lloyd George presented a radical budget which, in defiance of all parliamentary tradition, was promptly thrown out by the House of Lords. In February 1910, the government went to the country, seeking a mandate for the budget. They were able to form a majority only owing to support from the Home Rule Party, yet still the Lords refused to bend to the will of the Commons. Now determined to win a clear mandate for the reform of the House of Lords, the government once more went to the country in December. The outcome again saw the Home Rule M.P.s hold the balance of power and Asquith committed his government to a new Home Rule Bill. Threatened with the creation of hundreds of Liberal peers, the Lords passed the Parliament Bill in August 1911. The removal of the Lords, power of veto over Commons legislation transformed the Irish Question, diminishing what seemed to be the principal obstruction to a Home Rule Bill. In April 1912, Asquith placed the third Home Rule Bill before the House of Commons.

The near certainty that a Home Rule Bill would pass into law saw the principal site of struggle pass from the Palace of Westminster to the towns and villages of Ireland. Ulster Unionism mobilized. On 28 September 1912, 471 414 Ulster men and women

signed the Ulster League and Covenant, pledging to resist by force the implementation of Home Rule. On 31 January 1913, the Ulster Volunteer Force was established
and eventually presented British and Irish observers with a well-organized force of
85 000 men. Nationalist Ireland did not take this mobilization very seriously, largely
retaining its faith in the parliamentary process. Michael Wheatley describes this as a
period of nationalist apathy, with time marked as they waited to see what shape the
long-promised Home Rule Bill would take once it had worked its way through the legislative process.[59] Nonetheless, separatists such as Patrick Pearse were excited by these
developments. Irish Unionists drilling and carrying arms suggested that Unionists
were shaking off their dependency on the British, which Pearse construed as their first
step towards realizing their true destiny as a part of the Irish nation.[60]

British politicians were less sanguine. The Liberal Party recognized that the UVF
offered a real threat to law and order in Ireland, while the Conservatives stoked up
Unionist defiance, arguing that the Liberals were abusing their power by threatening to
use the Parliament Act to push through the Lords a bill for which they had no distinct
mandate. Jeremy Smith suggests that much of this talk was 'bluff and bluster', arguing
that the Conservative strategy was to prolong the crisis until the Liberals were forced
to go to the country, at which point the electorate would reject the Liberals and Home
Rule would be sidelined.[61] However, the growing possibility of separate treatment for
Ulster—first raised in an amendment by a little-known backbencher in June 1912—
finally roused nationalist Ireland. Loyalist mobilization could be airily dismissed as
posturing but the possibility that this might lead to a Home Rule Bill that undermined
the geographical integrity of Ireland could not be lightly shrugged off. Consequently,
when the cultural nationalist Eoin MacNeill sounded the call in November 1913, many
nationalists without formal connections to the separatist movement readily joined the
Irish Volunteers. Although this mobilization was presented not as act of rebellion but as
a form of republican virtue, aimed at upholding the law in the face of Unionist anarchy,
the movement was strongly shaped by a new generation of separatists who were inspired
by the senior Fenian Tom Clarke and read *Irish Freedom*, a new separatist newspaper.[62]

Politicians on all sides were forced by the volunteering phenomenon to confront
the fact that to impose a Home Rule settlement based on a unitary Dublin government would demand the massive coercion of Ulster. The so-called Curragh Mutiny
of 20 March 1914 indicated that the army could not be relied upon, while the Larne
gunrunning of 24–5 April suggested the UVF's seriousness of intent. The army and
the UVF can only have been encouraged by the widespread Unionist activism of the
British League of Covenanters and the extremist British League for the Support of
Ulster and the Union.[63] Nationalist events, such as the landing of guns at Howth on
26 July, which led to several civilians being shot dead by the police at Bachelor's Walk
in Dublin later that day, were as much separatist propaganda exercises aimed at the
Home Rule leadership as threats to the Unionists or the British government. The violent threat that Unionism posed to any Home Rule settlement exposed horribly the
act of faith that had underpinned Home Rule since it had abandoned Butt's attempt
to win Protestant Ireland over to the cause.

War broke out in August, and in September the government passed a Home Rule Act accompanied by a suspending motion, aiming to settle any outstanding difficulties and implement the Act at the end of the European conflict. Redmond immediately committed the Irish National Volunteers—now a force some 180 000 strong—to the war effort, pledging their service to 'wherever the firing line extends', a confident gesture reflecting the continuing vitality of Home Rule.[64] Only 10 000 separatists under the leadership of MacNeill seceded from the movement to form the Irish Volunteers. It was an IRB minority of this volunteer minority, with support from James Connolly's socialist Irish Citizen Army, which occupied Dublin's General Post Office on Easter Monday 1916 and declared an Irish republic. The rising was suppressed—the leadership faced a British firing squad some weeks later—and the British crackdown, which included the internment without trial of thousands of men, dramatically undermined Irish nationalist support for continuing attempts by Home Rule politicians, Unionists, and the government to reach an agreement on the implementation of the 1914 bill.

The decline of Home Rule is shadowed by bleak ironies. A sophisticated Redmondite Home Ruler like Stephen Gwynn had hoped that under Home Rule Irish nationalism would be reconciled to the British Empire and the Irish people to each other.[65] Yet, when Northern Ireland was carved out of Ulster and granted a form of Home Rule in 1920, the state created was predicated on the maintenance of Protestant ascendancy. Ultimately, thanks to a British government neglectful of its responsibilities, Home Rule did not deliver Ireland over to Rome but Northern Ireland over to Protestant rule. Unionists, it seems, had been correct about the weakness of the safeguards Home Rule legislation offered minorities living under its provisions. For Ireland's remaining twenty-six counties, including the three Ulster counties excluded from Northern Ireland, a new set of constitutional arrangements inspired by the example of Britain's imperial Dominions were drawn up. This created one of the most religiously homogenous societies in modern Europe and few twentieth-century European societies would so suffer the effects of religious authoritarianism as the Irish Free State and subsequent Irish Republic. Home Rulers, at their most open-minded and progressive, articulated their politics in terms of pluralism and toleration. They did not have a monopoly on these themes, as anticlerical Fenians and progressive Unionists would have been quick to point out. But irrespective of whether Home Rule would have secured the Union or Ireland's secession, the failure of its adherents to undermine the religious determinants of mainstream Irish political identities was the people of Ireland's loss, Protestant and Catholic alike.

Notes

1. David Fitzpatrick, 'Ireland and Empire' in Andrew Porter (ed), *The Oxford History of the British Empire. The Nineteenth Century* (Oxford, 1999), 494–9.
2. Oliver MacDonagh, *States of Mind. A Study of Anglo-Irish Conflict 1780–1980* (London, 1983), 59–61.

3. R.F. Foster, *Telling Tales and Making It Up in Ireland* (London, 2002), 19.

4. The outstanding published work on Isaac Butt's political ideas is Joseph Spence, 'Isaac Butt and Irish nationality' in D. George Boyce and Alan O'Day (eds), *Defenders of the Union. A survey of British and Irish unionism since 1801* (London, 2001), 65–90.

5. Marta Ramón, 'National Brotherhoods and National Leagues: The IRB and its Constitutional Rivals during the 1860s' in James McConnel and Fearghal McGarry, *The Black Hand of Republicanism. Fenianism in Modern Ireland* (Dublin, 2009), 18–33.

6. David Thornley, *Isaac Butt and Home Rule* (London, 1964), 195–204.

7. On the significance of this strain of Fenian influence in later years, see James McConnel, 'Fenians at Westminster: the Edwardian Irish Parliamentary Party and the legacy of the new departure', *Irish Historical Studies*, 34:133 (May 2004), 42–64.

8. In brief, see F. S. L. Lyons, *Charles Stewart Parnell* (Dublin, 1977, 2005), 35–9. For detail, see Robert Kee, *The Laurel and the Ivy. The Story of Charles Stewart Parnell and Irish Nationalism* (London, 1993), 50–76.

9. For a pioneering assessment of this phase in the development of Home Rule politics, see Paul A. Townend, 'Between Two World's: Irish Nationalists and Imperial Crisis 1878–1880', *Past and Present*, 194 (February 2007), 139–74.

10. Quoted in T.M. Moody, *Michael Davitt and Irish Revolution, 1846–82* (Oxford, 1981), 250.

11. Moody, *Davitt*, 325–6.

12. Michael Davitt, *The Fall of Feudalism in Ireland: or the Story of the Land League Revolution* (London, 1904), 361–4.

13. The positions of Paul Bew, Philip Bull, Frank Callanan, and F. L. Lyons are summarized in M.J. Kelly, *The Fenian Ideal and Irish Nationalism, 1882–1916* (Woodbridge, 2006), 41–2.

14. Matthew Kelly, ' "Parnell's Old Brigade": The Redmondite-Fenian nexus in the 1890s', in *Irish Historical Studies*, 33:130 (November 2002), 209–32.

15. F. L. Lyons, *The Irish Parliamentary Party, 1890–1910* (1951).

16. Philip Bull, *Land, Politics and Nationalism: A Study of Irish Land Question* (Dublin, 1996); Senia Pašeta, 'Nationalist Responses to Two Royal Visits to Ireland, 1900 and 1903', in *Irish Historical Studies*, 31:124 (November 1999), 488–504; Terence Denman, ' "The Red Livery of Shame": The Campaign Against Army Recruitment in Ireland, 1899–1914' in *I.H.S.*, 29:114 (November 1994), 208–33.

17. Fergal McCluskey, 'A Period of Nationalist Flux: The IRB and the Growth of Devlinite Nationalism in East Tyrone, 1902–7' in McConnel and McGarry, *Black Hand of Republicanism*, 86–104.

18. Paul Bew, *Conflict and Conciliation in Ireland, 1890–1910: Parnellites and Radical Agrarians* (Oxford, 1987) and James McConnel, *The Irish Parliamentary Party and the Third Home Rule Crisis* (Dublin, 2013).

19. W.E. Gladstone, *Special Aspects of the Irish Question* (1886), 9.

20. As summarized in Jonathan Parry, *The Rise and Fall of Liberal Government in Victorian Britain* (Yale, 1993), 296.

21. Parnell to Rhodes, 23 June 1888 (NLI MS. 41,788/1–9). It was an admission that earned the Home Rule Party a £10 000 donation.

22. D.A. Hamer, *Liberal Politics in the Age of Gladstone and Rosebery: A Study in Leadership and Policy* (Oxford, 1972), 104–12.

23. A.B. Cooke and John Vincent, *The Governing Passion: Cabinet Government and Party Politics in Britain, 1885–86* (Hassocks, 1974), 54–6.

24. J.L. Hammond, *Gladstone and the Irish Nation* (London, 1938), ix: 'The more his career is examined, the higher will his reputation stand, for the clearer will it be that his great struggle for Ireland's freedom was unmixed with any personal ambitions of his own.'

25. D.W. Bebbington, *The Nonconformist Conscience. Chapel and Politics 1870–1914* (London, 1982), 85–7.

26. J.P. Parry, *The Politics of Patriotism: English Liberalism, National Identity and Europe, 1830–1886* (Cambridge, 2006), 27.

27. Eugenio Biagini, *British Democracy and Irish Nationalism 1876–1906* (Cambridge, 2007).

28. H.C. G. Matthew emphasized that Gladstone's commitment to Home Rule was part of an evolution in his thinking, which did not involve an 'inward struggle' or the 'resolution of contending tensions'. See his *Gladstone 1809–1898* (Oxford, 1997), 464ff.

29. T.A. Jenkins, *Gladstone, Whiggery and the Liberal Party 1874–1886* (Oxford, 1988), 277–8.

30. Stephen Ball, *Dublin Castle and the First Home Rule Crisis: The Political Diary of Sir George Fottrell* (Cambridge, 2008), 3.

31. In general, see K. Theodore Hoppen, 'The Franchise and Electoral Politics in England and Ireland, 1832–1885', *History*, 70 (1985), 202–17.

32. For an extended treatment of this argument, see W.E. Gladstone, *Special Aspects of the Irish Question* (1886).

33. Michael Bentley, *Lord Salisbury's World: Conservative Environments in Late-Victorian Britain* (Cambridge, 2001), 61.

34. R.F. Foster, *Paddy and Mr Punch: Connections in Irish and English History* (London, 1993), 255.

35. Quoted in Andrew Roberts, *Salisbury: Victorian Titan* (London 1999), 379.

36. Bentley, *Lord Salisbury's World*, 63.

37. Roberts, *Salisbury*, 383–5; David Steele, *Lord Salisbury: A Political Biography* (London, 1999), 200.

38. 5 September 1893. Roberts, *Salisbury*, 589.

39. Trowbridge H. Ford, 'Dicey's conversion to unionism', in *Irish Historical Studies*, 18:72 (September 1973), 552–82.

40. Parry, *Rise and Fall of Liberal Government*, 296.

41. For the similar starting points and different conclusions of pro- and anti-British Home Rulers, see G.K. Peatling, *British Opinion and Irish Self-government, 1865–1925. From Unionism to Liberal Commonwealth* (Dublin, 2001), 34–46.

42. A.V. Dicey, *England's Case Against Home Rule* (London, 1886), 17–18.

43. Dicey, *England's Case*, 33.

44. Roberts, *Salisbury*, 378, 382.

45. Allen Warren, 'Lord Salisbury and Ireland, 1859–87: Principles, Ambition and Strategies', *Parliamentary History*, 26, pt 2 (2007), 203–24.

46. As Alvin Jackson observes, 'Constructive Unionism was simply a more than usually expensive and progressive programme of colonial government; and it was partly the recognition of this which inspired resentment among loyalists.' See his *The Ulster Party: Irish Unionists in the House of Commons 1884–1911* (Oxford, 1989), 115–16.

47. Biagini, *British Democracy*, 221, 247.

48. E. H. Green, *The Crisis of Conservatism: The politics, economics and ideology of the British Conservative Party, 1880–1914* (London, 1995), 59–77, 194–206.

49. Indeed, Indian nationalists studied the progress of Irish Home Rule as a means of gauging the likely success of their own reform agendas. See James McConnel and Matthew Kelly,

'Devolution, federalism and imperial circuitry: Ireland, South Africa and India' in Duncan Tanner, Chris Williams, Wil Griffith, and Andrew Edwards (eds), *Debating Nationhood and Governance in Britain, 1885–1945: Perspectives from the 'Four Nations'* (Manchester, 2006), 171–91.

50. David Miller, *Queen's Rebels: Ulster Loyalism in Historical Perspective* (Dublin, 1978), 25ff.
51. Matthew Kelly, 'The politics of Protestant street preaching in the 1890s Ireland', *Historical Journal*, 48:1 (2005), 107–9.
52. Quoted in Biagini, *British Democracy*, 257.
53. James Loughlin, 'Creating "A Social and Geographical Fact": Regional Identity and the Ulster Question 1880s-1920s', *Past & Present*, 195 (May 2007), 159–96.
54. Alvin Jackson, 'Irish Unionism and the Russellite Threat, 1894–1906', *Irish Historical Studies*, 25:100 (November 1987), 376–404.
55. Alvin Jackson, *Colonel Edward Saunderson: Land and Loyalty in Victorian Ireland* (Oxford, 1995).
56. Matthew Kelly, 'Irish Nationalist Opinion and the British Empire in the 1850s and 1860s', *Past and Present*, 204 (August 2009), 127–54.
57. Kelly, *Fenian Ideal*, 176.
58. Michael Wheatley, 'John Redmond and Federalism in 1910', *Irish Historical Studies*, 32:127 (May, 2001), 343–64.
59. Michael Wheatley, ' "These quiet days of peace": Nationalist Opinion before the Home Rule Crisis, 1909–13' in D. George Boyce and Alan O'Day (eds), *Ireland in Transition, 1867–1921* (London, 2004), 62–7.
60. Ruth Dudley Edwards, *Patrick Pearse: The Triumph of Failure* (London, 1977), 179.
61. Jeremy Smith, 'Bluff, bluster and brinkmanship: Andrew Bonar Law and the Third Home Rule Bill', *Historical Journal*, 36:1 (March 1993), 161–78.
62. Matthew Kelly, 'The Irish Volunteers: A Machiavellian Moment?' in D. George Boyce and Alan O'Day (eds), *The Ulster Crisis 1885–1921* (Basingstoke, 2006), 64–85; Kelly, *Fenian Ideal*, 179–236.
63. Daniel Jackson, *Popular Opposition to Irish Home Rule in Edwardian Britain* (Manchester, 2009) and David Thackeray, 'Rethinking the Edwardian Crisis of Conservatism', *Historical Journal*, 54:1 (2011), 202–6.
64. For the complexities of Redmondite recruiting efforts, see James McConnel, 'Recruiting Sergeants for John Bull? Irish Nationalist MPs and Enlistment during the early months of the Great War', *War in History*, 14:4 (2007), 408–28.
65. Colin Reid, *The Lost Ireland of Stephen Gwynn: Irish Constitutional Nationalism and Cultural Politics, 1864–1950* (Manchester, 2011).

SELECT BIBLIOGRAPHY

Biagini, Eugenio *British Democracy and Irish Nationalism 1876–1906* (Cambridge, 2007).
Bew, Paul *Ideology and the Irish Question: Ulster Unionism and Irish Nationalism, 1912–1916* (Oxford, 1994).
Gailey, Andrew *Ireland and the Death of Kindness: The Experience of Constructive Unionism, 1890–1905* (Cork, 1987).
Boyce, D. George and O'Day, Alan (eds), *Defenders of the Union. A Survey of British and Irish Unionism since 1801* (London, 2001).

Foster, R.F., *Paddy and Mr Punch: Connections in Irish and English History* (London, 1993).

Jackson, Alvin, *Colonel Edward Saunderson: Land and Loyalty in Victorian Ireland* (Oxford, 1995).

Jackson, Daniel, *Popular Opposition to Irish Home Rule in Edwardian Britain* (Manchester, 2009).

Jalland, Patricia, *The Liberals and Ireland: the Ulster Question in British Politics to 1914* (Brighton, 1980).

Kelly, M.J., *The Fenian Ideal and Irish Nationalism, 1882–1916* (Woodbridge, 2006).

Loughlin, James, 'Creating "A Social and Geographical Fact": Regional Identity and the Ulster Question 1880s-1920s', *Past & Present*, 195 (May 2007).

Lyons, F.S.L., *Charles Stewart Parnell* (Dublin, 1977).

Matthew, H.C.G., *Gladstone 1809–1898* (Oxford, 1997).

Maume, Patrick, *The Long Gestation: Irish Nationalist Life, 1891–1918* (Dublin, 1996).

McConnel, James, *The Irish Parliamentary Party and the Third Home Rule Crisis* (Dublin, 2013).

Pašeta, Senia, *Before the Revolution: Nationalism, Social Change and Ireland's Catholic Elite, 1879–1922* (Cork, 1999).

Peatling, G.K., *British Opinion and Irish Self-government, 1865–1925: From Unionism to Liberal Commonwealth* (Dublin, 2001).

Smith, Jeremy, *The Lost Ireland of Stephen Gwynn: Irish Constitutional Nationalism and Cultural Politics, 1864–1950* (Manchester, 2011).

Smith, Jeremy, *The Tories and Ireland: Conservative Party Politics and Home Rule, 1910–1914* (Dublin, 2000).

Thornley, David, *Isaac Butt and Home Rule* (London, 1964).

Townshend, Charles, *Political Violence in Ireland: Government and Resistance Since 1848* (Oxford, 1983).

CHAPTER 30

....

IRELAND AND THE FIRST WORLD WAR

....

TIMOTHY BOWMAN

I. INTRODUCTION

....

WRITING in his important *Modern Ireland 1600–1972*, Roy Foster noted the importance of this conflict stating, 'The First World War should be seen as one of the most decisive events in modern Irish history'.[1] The war witnessed the service of 210 000 Irish men and a few hundred Irish women in the British armed forces (of whom around 40 000 were killed). It established the preconditions for the Easter Rising, the decline of the Irish Parliamentary Party, and the partition of Ireland in 1920. However, for intellectual and political reasons, the impact of the Great War on Ireland as a whole has not received the attention that it deserves, though some areas, such as recruitment and commemoration, have attracted considerable scholarly attention.

In intellectual terms, historians of Ireland have struggled to decouple the experience of the First World War from the experience of the Irish Revolution as a whole. This was particularly noticeable in Thomas Bartlett and Keith Jeffery's seminal *A Military History of Ireland,* where the events of the First World War, revolutionary period, and Irish participation in the South African War of 1899–1902 were unsatisfactorily combined in one short chapter.[2] The three edited collections, David Fitzpatrick (ed), *Ireland and the First World War*, Adrian Gregory and Senia Paseta (eds), *Ireland and the Great War,* and John Horne (ed), *Our War: Ireland and the Great War,* which by their titles suggest a comprehensive study of the subject, prove to be decidedly mixed bags.[3] *Ireland and the First World War* tends to concentrate on the important issues of recruitment and commemoration but to the exclusion of any meaningful discussion of the home front or experience of Irish soldiers serving in the British Army. *Ireland and the Great War* contains essays which are interesting in their own right but contributions such as Paseta's own 'Thomas Kettle: "An Irish soldier in the army of Europe"?' and Peter Martin's 'Dulce et Decorum: Irish nobles and the Great War, 1914–19' tell us little about the broader Irish experience of the war. *Our War* is based on the 2008 Thomas Davis lectures broadcast on RTE radio. In its attempts to address a mass audience, its editor shows a certain amount of confusion. Thus, David Fitzpatrick, Keith Jeffery, and Philip Orr provide what could be termed 'populist' précis based on their considerable published works on Ireland and the First World War. By contrast, there are important original contributions considering women, the labour movement, and veterans by Caitriona Clear, Niamh Puirseil, and Jane Leonard respectively. Few unifying themes emerge from these edited collections; *Ireland and the First World War* even lacks an introductory chapter and *Our War* includes an introduction that demonstrates a lack of knowledge concerning both recent scholarship on Ireland and the Great War and the place of the Irish regiments within the British Army. Some similar problems are evident in Keith Jeffery's important and thought provoking *Ireland and the Great War,* based on his Lees Knowles lectures delivered at Trinity College Cambridge in 1998 which, despite its comprehensive title, focuses on recruitment, the military experience of the war, cultural responses, and the collective memory of the war in Ireland.[4]

Historians of Britain have frequently failed to make any mention of the Irish experience of the war; perhaps, by implication, suggesting that there was definite Hibernian exceptionalism to the British norms. For example, Peter Dewey in his otherwise excellent study of British agriculture during the war makes very limited reference to Ireland, which seems curious given the importance of agriculture within the wartime Irish economy. Similarly, Jay Winter's important *Great War and the British People* fails to consider the case of Ireland in any meaningful way.[5]

For political reasons, the experiences of Irish people from Southern Ireland serving in the British armed forces were ignored for many years in a display of 'national amnesia'.[6] It was much more fashionable to claim that one had a relation who had fought in the GPO in 1916 than one who had served at Gallipoli or on the Western Front. This is a condition which has changed only in the past twenty years with the creation of the Royal Dublin Fusiliers, Royal Munster Fusiliers, and Connaught Rangers Associations and the development of the new National Museum gallery in Collins Barracks which gives recognition to those Irish men and women who served in the British forces.[7]

In Northern Ireland there was much myth-making regarding Ulster's role in the Great War. There existed—and, despite the work of professional historians, still continues to exist—a Unionist war myth which suggests that, within Ireland, only Protestant Ulster rallied to Britain in its hour of need, focusing attention, almost exclusively, on the actions of the 36th (Ulster) Division at the Battle of the Somme in July 1916.[8] The Irish experience of the Great War has continued to be used for political ends in Northern Ireland.

At one level there is what could be called the 'reconciliation' approach, which attempts to use the comradeship of the trenches to bring communities together.[9] The problem with this approach is that it, somewhat unwittingly, repeats an argument made by a number of Irish Parliamentary Party M.P.s in the First World War itself; namely, that Ulster Unionists would become reconciled to Home Rule if they served alongside Nationalists at the front.[10] This argument was, itself, a dubious one. There is really very little evidence to suggest that a particularly warm relationship grew up between Catholic Nationalists and Protestant Unionists serving in the 16th (Irish) and 36th (Ulster) Divisions. Lieutenant Colonel Rowland Feilding noted that, when the divisions played football against each other, 'a wag on the Ulster side was heard to say, "I wonder if we shall get into trouble for fraternising with the enemy."'[11] Denys Reitz related how he, as the commanding officer of the 7th Royal Irish Rifles, a unit with Nationalist political overtones serving in the 16th (Irish) Division, prevented a major outbreak of violence between the divisions when his battalion was sent bottles of soda water by the 36th (Ulster) Division with the legend 'Boyne Water' written on them (seen as a reference to the Battle of the Boyne of 1690 by his men but actually a perfectly innocent commercial label originating from the Boyne Bridge aerated water plant in Sandy Row, Belfast).[12] Lieutenant Witherow, an officer in the 36th (Ulster) Division was arrested by a sentry as a suspected spy when he strayed into the 16th (Irish) Divisional area.[13]

At another and much less laudable level, the experience of the Great War has been used by Loyalist paramilitaries to rehabilitate themselves and justify their previous nefarious activities. Keith Jeffery and, more particularly, Philip Orr may rejoice that former paramilitaries have decided to stop attempting to kill their fellow human beings and are reading the occasional military history book or organizing the odd cross-community battlefield tour or memorial exercise, but many of us will not see this as a particular contribution to the understanding of Ireland's experience of the Great War.[14]

The Somme Association and its Heritage Centre at Conlig in County Down manages to reflect both of these political strands. At one level it parades its cross-community credentials, extolling the virtues of Catholic and Protestant schoolchildren visiting its Heritage Centre. However, this same organization gives preferential membership rates to members of the Orange Order.[15] More important, it is hard to argue that the Heritage Centre gives proportionate coverage to Irish units as a whole, concentrating overwhelmingly on the experience of the 36th (Ulster) Division. The amateur nature of the Association means that some of the public lectures given by its staff have been based on minimal research and have tended to reinforce, rather than challenge, existing myths about Ulster's involvement in the Great War.[16]

II. EARLY WORKS

There was a flurry of writing concerning Ireland's role in the war during the First World War itself and in the immediate post-war period. The public interest in, and early disbandment of, the many Irish New Army units saw the publication of many histories concerning these formations.[17] Similarly, the disbandment of the Southern Irish infantry regiments of the British Army—the Royal Irish Regiment, Connaught Rangers, Leinster Regiment, Royal Dublin Fusiliers, and Royal Munster Fusiliers—with the establishment of the Irish Free State saw the production of commemorative histories of these units.[18] Most of these histories were antiquarian in nature and tended to focus on exploits in battle (replicating the material contained in the official war diaries) and the activities of the officer corps, glossing over recruiting and disciplinary problems. Nevertheless, these histories, most recently republished by the Naval and Military Press, can still be read with profit and in many cases provide important first-hand accounts written by officers who served in the units concerned through most of the war. For example, H.N. Jourdain, who wrote the history of the Connaught Rangers and a volume of memoirs after the war, commanded the 5th, 6th, and 3rd battalions of this regiment during the course of the war and was rarely away from regimental duty.[19] His works provide an interesting account of what it was like to be a regular officer confronted with raising a New Army battalion in 1914 and serving in both the Gallipoli campaign and on the Western Front.

Two of these formation histories merit special attention: the history of the Irish Guards written by Rudyard Kipling; and Cyril Falls's *History of the 36th (Ulster) Division*.[20] While most of the regimental histories written in the 1920s were compiled by retired or serving army officers, the Irish Guards managed to secure a major literary figure, in the shape of Kipling, as their historian. Kipling had used his influence to get his son John, 18 years old and with very poor eyesight, a commission in the army. Kipling's friendship with Field Marshal Lord Roberts, the Honorary Colonel of the Irish Guards, had secured a place for John Kipling in the then newly formed 2nd Irish Guards. John Kipling's death in action at Loos (1915) had a profound impact on his father and his questioning of many Irish Guardsmen in an attempt to discover the exact circumstances of his son's death led him into a very close relationship with the regiment.[21]

Cyril Falls's *History of the 36th (Ulster) Division* can be read on a number of levels. Falls was a distinguished military historian and later became the Chichele Professor of War at the University of Oxford. His work can hold some claims to be the most professionally researched and written divisional history of the Great War. At another level, Falls's work can be read as a soldier's memoir of the formation he served in. Falls was commissioned into the 11th Royal Inniskilling Fusiliers when the battalion was formed in 1914 on the basis of his having been a company commander in the Fermanagh Regiment of the Ulster Volunteer Force (UVF). He subsequently went on to be a staff officer in the division, intimately involved in the actions of which he writes. Falls' pre-war UVF membership is a key to understanding the other level on which his work can be read: a celebratory Ulster Unionist account of the service of the 36th (Ulster) Division. Writing at a time when the new Northern Ireland state was in its infancy and with the clear support of Edward Carson and James Craig (who both provided forewords to the book), Falls's work was also a piece of propaganda designed to remind both Ulster Unionists and the British government of the sacrifices that Ulster had made for the Empire.[22]

In the last twenty years, there has been much scholarly attention paid to Ireland and the First World War. This has tended to concentrate, however, on three narrow areas: Irish recruitment to the British Army, the experience of Irishmen in the British Army, and the commemoration of the Great War in Ireland. It is to a discussion of these areas that this chapter will now turn.

III. Irish Recruitment to the British Armed Forces

In terms of recruitment to the British armed forces, the Irish case was unusual in a British context as Irish recruitment was considerably more politicized and conscription was never introduced in Ireland, whereas it was brought in in Great Britain in 1916. There is some disagreement about the number of Irishmen who enlisted in the British Army. We will never have an exact figure on this as Irishmen who enlisted in Great Britain were generally not counted as Irishmen, whereas those from elsewhere in Great Britain who enlisted in Ireland or served in Irish units often were.[23] The problem was compounded by the propensity of officers of Irish units to 'poach' recruits in Great Britain.[24] The best estimates that we have to date come from David Fitzpatrick and Keith Jeffery. Fitzpatrick's figures are around 5000 men higher, suggesting a total of 144000 recruits during the war in addition to 58000 serving regulars or reservists at the outbreak of war.[25]

The most comprehensive study of Irish recruitment to the British Army in the Great War remains Patrick Callan's unfortunately unpublished doctoral thesis.[26] However, in a typically thought-provoking article, David Fitzpatrick provides detailed consideration of recruitment figures and patterns. Discounting conventional arguments that Irishmen who enlisted in the British Army were motivated by economic factors, religious affiliation, or loyalty to Britain, Professor Fitzpatrick goes on to suggest that it was men's membership of 'fraternities' such as sporting clubs which explained their decision to enlist. There are a number of problems with Fitzpatrick's calculations which mean that his figures should be treated with some caution; his decision to exclude those employed in agriculture from his calculations seems odd, given the importance of this sector in the Irish economy in this period. We should also be aware that the basis of many of Fitzpatrick's calculations is dubious. Government reports and ministers were quite clear that the figures released concerning recruitment in terms of religion, previous Irish National Volunteers (INV) or UVF membership, or the locality where men lived before their enlistment were little more than best estimates; given the number of enlistments in the early months of the war and the subsequent breakdown of the usual War Office recruiting system, we should not be surprised by this.[27]

Those who were members of the INV or UVF pre-war, the largest 'fraternities' identified by Fitzpatrick, provided a high proportion of the Irish recruits to the British Army. The most reliable government figures suggest that, up to 15 April 1916, 29 617 UVF members and 30 161 INV members had enlisted, whereas 57 863 men with no affiliation to either group had also joined up.[28] In absolute terms this did not mean that INV or UVF members were exactly rushing to the colours. The UVF had a strength of something in the region of 100 000 men in July 1914 and the INV probably as many as 180 000. This should not distract us from the point that UVF members were considerably more likely to enlist than those from the INV and clearly 'loyalty' played a role in the decision to enlist, a factor which Professor Fitzpatrick has been too ready to discount.[29]

Economic factors were clearly important in men's decisions to enlist. In his idiosyncratic work, T.P. Dooley, considering Waterford as a case study, notes that unskilled labourers stood to increase their earnings by 154 per cent by enlisting in the British Army.[30] Fitzpatrick has discounted economic motivations by noting the large numbers of skilled workers who enlisted in the British Army in the early months of the war. However, this fundamentally misconstrues the employment prospects of many skilled workers in this unusual period. In Belfast, uncertainty about future orders saw men laid off in both the shipbuilding and engineering industries during the early months of the war. That other great staple of industrial Belfast, the linen industry, was badly affected by the stoppage of flax imports from Belgium and Russia on the outbreak of war.[31]

Fitzpatrick's argument that 'fraternities' are the key to understanding recruitment patterns seems to be fundamentally flawed, particularly with his reference to sports clubs. Certainly the Irish Rugby Football Union formed 'D' company of the 7th Royal Dublin Fusiliers but beyond that one struggles to find other examples.[32] Attempts to form both 'University' and 'Sportsmen's' battalions in the 36th (Ulster) Division, on the pattern of the University and Public Schools and Sportsmen's battalions raised in the Royal Fusiliers, were stillborn.[33] Similarly, whilst in Scotland and England some football clubs served as the basis of 'Pals' battalions, there are no comparable examples in Ireland.

While historical debate regarding the importance of economic and political factors will clearly continue, some general points can safely be made with regard to Irish recruiting patterns, particularly given the detailed statistics published by the British government in 1916.[34] Up until early 1916, when conscription was introduced into Great Britain but not Ireland, Irish recruitment patterns followed those of the United Kingdom as a whole, though at a much lower base, well below Ireland's share of the UK population. As in the rest of the UK, Irish recruitment reached a peak in September 1914 and then went into a sharp, if uneven, decline.[35] Recruiting in Ireland was an urban rather than a rural experience. From the outbreak of war until 15 October 1916, 130 241 men enlisted in Ireland; of these, 38 543 were from Belfast, 21 412 from Dublin, and 8360 from Cork. While the relatively high percentage of UVF members who enlisted in the British Army suggests that Unionists were more likely to enlist than Nationalists, this figure is skewed by the propensity of citizens of Belfast to enlist. Indeed, rural recruitment in Ulster was not noticeably higher than in the rest of Ireland.

The role of politics in Irish recruitment is worth considering in some detail, given the extent to which the Irish experience differed from the situation in the United Kingdom as a whole. On the outbreak of war, both Nationalist and Unionist politicians pledged their support for the British war effort and members of the respective paramilitary armies, the INV and UVF, were encouraged to enlist, particularly in the 16th (Irish) and 36th (Ulster) Divisions respectively. However, political encouragement was not as proactive as was once assumed. James McConnel has shown that John Redmond was not acting in accordance with the views of the Irish Parliamentary Party as a whole when he delivered his famous speech to INV members at Woodenbridge in County Wicklow, encouraging his followers to 'go wherever the firing line extends'. Indeed, McConnel shows that many IPP M.P.s were very reluctant recruiting sergeants, shown most forcibly by the small numbers of M.P.s who personally served in the British forces.[36] Similarly, Edward Carson, while sincere in his support for Britain's war effort, was unable to carry all of his followers with him, some of whom expected British duplicity over the Home Rule issue.[37]

While the 10th (Irish) Division was largely formed by the War Office, utilizing a large number of recruits from Great Britain, the subsequently raised 16th (Irish) Division was largely identified with the IPP and the 36th (Ulster) Division with the UVF.[38] Lord Kitchener, as Secretary of State for War, had been reluctant to incorporate either of the political militias in Ireland wholesale into the British Army but poor recruiting rates in Ireland in the early weeks of the war led him to revise this opinion.[39] The 36th (Ulster) Division certainly had clear links with the UVF but it would be wrong to over-play these.[40] It appears that less than a third of the UVF enlisted during the Great War and rural battalions in the 36th (Ulster) Division particularly struggled to reach their established strength. Indeed, as the most extreme example, in early October 1914 when the Belfast-raised battalions of the 36th (Ulster) Division were practically complete, all with over one thousand men each, the 11th Royal Inniskilling Fusiliers, recruiting from Donegal and Fermanagh, had raised just 471 recruits.[41] Even in Belfast, with its comparatively impressive recruiting figures, UVF enlistment into the British Army did not proceed as smoothly as the Ulster Unionist leadership had hoped.

Edward Carson managed to secure some key concessions from the War Office which gave the 36th (Ulster) Division a particularly political complexion. The term 'Ulster' used in the divisional title had never been seen in the *Army Lists* before and battalion names served to connect battalions in the newly raised division to pre-war UVF regiments, thus, for example, the 9th (West Belfast Volunteers) and 14th (Young Citizen Volunteers) Battalions of the Royal Irish Rifles. More tangibly, retired or serving British Army officers who had served in the UVF were secured for the 36th (Ulster) Division and monopolized the senior command positions in the division. The benefit of UVF links to the 36th (Ulster) Division is debatable as some of the officers who had impressed by their loyalty to Ulster Unionism failed the test of military competence. This was most notable in the case of Brigadier General G.H. Couchman, who was rapidly removed from his command of the 107th (Belfast) Brigade shortly after it arrived in France, being held responsible for the poor training and discipline of this formation.[42] Elsewhere, UVF connections were a mixed blessing for the 36th (Ulster) Division. Despite the elaborate parades and propaganda and the success of the Larne gunrunning, the UVF was a poorly trained force whose members did not have a significant advantage over the Kitchener volunteers who flocked to recruiting offices in Great Britain. The firm identification of the 36th (Ulster) Division with Unionism possibly served to retard Catholic enlistment in rural Ulster. One benefit which the 36th (Ulster) Division did obtain from the UVF was the use of rifles and machine guns for instruction and training purposes at a time when the British Army had few to spare.

While the 36th (Ulster) Division was formed as a result of Ulster Unionist pressure, the 16th (Irish) Division was belatedly given a Nationalist identity when attempts to recruit it under the War Office had failed.[43] Contemporary Nationalist M.P.s were critical of how the War Office dealt with the 16th (Irish) Division in comparison to the 36th (Ulster) Division.[44] Complaints centred on the unwillingness of the War Office or Lieutenant General Sir Lawrence Parsons, the GOC of the division, to appoint Catholic, Nationalist officers to the division and on Parsons' unwillingness to accommodate Nationalist symbols. This debate was essentially between those who wanted a politically motivated officer corps and those who wanted a professionally trained officer corps. Parsons' unwillingness to appoint Irish Catholic officers seems reasonable given the lack of officer training corps units at Catholic schools or universities or, indeed, the lack of retired Catholic regular or militia and Special Reserve officers. Nevertheless, this removed an important form of patronage from IPP M.P.s. Parsons established a cadet company in the 7th Leinster Regiment, supposedly to enable Catholic middle-class recruits to gain commissions, but this did not meet the approval of the INV as membership was open to non-Catholics.[45] The role of the cadet company was somewhat frustrated by the War Office, who continued to post junior officers to the 16th (Irish) Division.[46]

On other political issues, Parsons's opposition to Nationalist demands seems unreasonable. Refusing to grant John Redmond's son, William Archer Redmond, M.P., a commission in the 16th (Irish) Division looked spiteful when M.P.s were easily obtaining commissions elsewhere. It was to look utterly ridiculous when William Archer Redmond was granted a commission in the Irish Guards and, furthermore, when he went on to win the DSO, clearly demonstrating his military abilities.[47] The desire of John Redmond to secure a special badge and INV battalion titles for its units, along the pattern adopted in the 36th (Ulster) Division, were surely matters which a less obstinate general would have found easy ways to accommodate.[48] It seems likely that John Redmond's inability to secure these concessions for the INV did much to reduce Irish Nationalist enlistment into the British Army and ultimately did much to damage the electoral prospects of the IPP itself.

The final aspect of Irish recruiting which deserves some consideration is the conscription crisis of April 1918. Given the collapse of Irish voluntary recruiting by early 1918, and the heavy losses incurred by the British Army in the German Spring Offensive, the decision was taken to apply conscription to Ireland, in line with the rest of the UK. This was despite widespread opposition to the application of conscription to Ireland amongst senior political and military figures. The Chief Secretary, H.E. Duke, Lieutenant General Sir Bryan Mahon, the GOC in Ireland, and Brigadier General Sir Joseph Byrne, the Inspector General of the RIC, believed that, militarily, nothing would be achieved. They suggested that at least 6000 extra British troops would be required to enforce conscription in Ireland and that the military utility of Irish conscripts would be very low. On a political front, they believed that attempts to enforce conscription in Ireland would meet with widespread opposition, including riots, and would turn Nationalist Ireland very firmly against the British war effort. Opposed to these doom-laden predictions was the view of Field Marshal Sir John French, Commander in Chief, Home Forces, and, from 5 May, Lord Lieutenant of Ireland. French believed that his Irish ancestry and occasional visits to Ireland gave him a unique insight into the political condition in Ireland. French maintained that a period of military government would enable him to completely defeat the Sinn Féin movement, allowing for the introduction both of conscription and ultimately a settlement based on Home Rule.

Adrian Gregory argues that senior British politicians understood the situation in Ireland, but they supported the extension of conscription to Ireland for wider British political purposes. Winston Churchill and David Lloyd George did not think a war-weary population in Great Britain would endorse another 'combing out' of essential industries and extension of the age groups liable for military service in Great Britain unless Ireland was expected to contribute her share of conscripts. It seems convincing to argue that Irish political concerns were neglected in the circumstances of total war, as the warnings of Byrne, Duke, and Mahon were all too accurate in terms of the rise of Sinn Féin and demise of the Irish Parliamentary Party.

The Military Service Amendment Act was passed on 16 April 1918. However, its provisions relating to Ireland were never implemented as Nationalist Ireland united against this legislation. The IPP M.P.s walked out of the House of Commons during the first reading on 10 April, essentially endorsing the Sinn Féin policy of abstentionism. The Irish Trades Union Congress called a one-day strike for 23 April and this was effective in most parts of Ireland, outside Unionist Ulster. Perhaps most importantly, the Roman Catholic Church entered the political fray as the Catholic bishops in Ireland called for a resistance pledge against conscription.[49]

IV. THE EXPERIENCE OF IRISHMEN IN THE BRITISH ARMY

The wartime service of Irishmen in the British Army has received considerable attention. Unfortunately, much of this has been by amateur historians who have produced unsophisticated works, very much in the tradition of the battalion and regimental histories produced in the 1916–28 period.[50] At their worst these have relied on little more than the older regimental histories, the readily available battalion war diaries, local newspapers, and some dubious local folklore masquerading as oral history. However, James Taylor's works on the Royal Irish Rifles make use of the recently released officers' personal files held at The National Archives, Kew, and Philip Orr's work on the 36th (Ulster) Division makes interesting use of oral evidence and some important privately held manuscript material.[51] Richard Grayson's important work makes systematic use of the recently released soldiers' files at Kew, along with newspaper archives, to build up a complex study of the experiences of men from West Belfast in the British Army during the Great War, pioneering what he terms 'military history from the street'.[52] In essence, the wartime experience of Irish soldiers was not that dissimilar to that of British soldiers as a whole. It should be stressed that Irish regiments were integral parts of the British Army and attempts to portray Irish soldiers as some sort of colonial force, with all that this implies, are deeply unconvincing.[53]

Where the Irish experience did diverge markedly from the British experience as a whole was in the shortage of Irish replacement troops and subsequent disbandment of many Irish units. Indeed, the supposedly poor performance of the 16th (Irish) Division during the German Spring Offensive of 1918 is largely explicable by the fact that most of its units were almost 50 per cent under strength. The British regimental system, based on localized recruiting and envisaging the need to replace casualties incurred in limited colonial wars, quickly broke down as a whole in the Great War, though this was particularly noticeable in the case of Irish regiments.[54] From March 1916 to the end of the war, most of the wartime-raised Irish battalions were successively reinforced with English conscripts, amalgamated, and ultimately disbanded, as Irish recruitment stalled and conscription failed to solve Britain's manpower problems. Indeed, by the end of the war, the 10th (Irish) Division had been Indianized and contained just three Irish battalions and the 16th (Irish) Division had been Anglicized in April 1918 and contained just one Irish battalion. The 36th (Ulster) Division had survived as an Irish formation, but only by incorporating the regular battalions of the Royal Inniskilling Fusiliers, Royal Irish Rifles, and Royal Irish Fusiliers.[55]

Whereas in most British regiments, when battalions had to be disbanded (as happened on a widespread basis in early 1918 when infantry brigades were reduced from four to three battalions), the most junior battalions were sacrificed, this was not the case in the Irish regiments. In the 36th (Ulster) Division, Major General Oliver Nugent was very careful to balance local representation, disbanding one Belfast battalion, rather than one from rural County Antrim, even though the Belfast battalion was senior. Nugent also disbanded the 14th Royal Irish Rifles, which he believed to be ill-disciplined, while retaining the more junior 16th Royal Irish Rifles.[56]

One important point to make regarding the wartime experience of Irish regiments is that there is very little evidence of sympathy for the Sinn Féin movement developing during 1917 and 1918. When 116 men of the 16th (Irish) Division mutinied in April 1918, this was due to orders to reduce their battalions to training cadres, with the intention of ultimately disbanding them. The 106 men found guilty served suspended sentences (that is, they continued to serve with their battalions) and the battalions were reprieved, suggesting that the High Command was sympathetic to their complaints.[57] Irish units serving in Ireland itself were seen as more susceptible to Sinn Féin infiltration, although the decision to post Irish reserve units to Great Britain in early 1918 had more to do with the likely need to use troops to enforce conscription in Ireland.[58]

V. COMMEMORATION OF THE FIRST WORLD WAR

The final area concerning the Irish experience of the war which has received considerable attention from historians is the commemoration of the war. Works on this topic have clearly been inspired by the work of Jay Winter and have struggled to push the debate beyond the parameters established by Keith Jeffery.[59] They have tended to concentrate on the building of war memorials or the politics of Remembrance Day. Curiously, such works have neglected to consider the foundation, membership, and activities of British Legion branches throughout the island of Ireland, which one would have thought would have been more indicative of popular attitudes to wartime service.[60]

Shortly after the Armistice, the memory of the Great War became politicized in Ireland on a national and regional basis. The Unionist-dominated Belfast City Corporation ensured that the peace celebration of 19 July 1919 and a civic reception and review of Ulster troops held on 9 August 1919 would identify Ulster's contribution to the war effort almost exclusively with the 36th (Ulster) Division and, by implication, with Ulster Unionism.[61] Similarly, the newly created Northern Ireland government was quick to erect a war memorial on the Somme, eager to highlight Britain's 'debt of honour' to Ulster in the difficult political situation of 1920–1. The Ulster Tower was erected at Thiepval with the use of UVF funds and Sir James Craig decided that it should be based on Helen's Tower at Clandeboye (where units of the 36th (Ulster) Division had trained) to prevent the delay which would otherwise be caused by holding a competition for a design. The Ulster Tower was the first British war memorial to be completed on the Somme and was dedicated by that staunch supporter of Ulster Unionism, Field Marshal Sir Henry Wilson, on 18 November 1921.[62] The decision to site the tower at Thiepval served to tie the Northern Ireland state's official memory of the Great War with the actions of the 36th (Ulster) Division at the Battle of the Somme.

Political considerations meant that it was to take a very long time before a Southern Irish war memorial was built. There was also, in Dublin, some debate as to whether the national war memorial should be practical or artistic, with many favouring the concept of a memorial club. A public appeal for funds quickly raised £42 000, meaning that finance was not a major problem, as it was to be for many local authority ventures. Eventually, the funds raised were spent on three commemorative projects. Around £5000 was spent on publishing *Ireland's Memorial Records* in 1923. One hundred copies of this eight-volume work were published and distributed free to major public libraries. Another £1500 was spent to erect stone crosses to the memory of the 16th (Irish) Division at Ginchy and Wytschaete and to the 10th (Irish) Division at Salonika. Original plans to build a permanent war memorial at Merrion Square came to naught in a Senate debate in 1927 and ultimately the memorial, designed by Sir Edwin Lutyens, was completed at Islandbridge, on the outskirts of Dublin, in spring 1938.[63]

Practical memorials to the war in Ireland, North and South, were built under the Irish Land (Provision for Sailors and Soldiers) Act of 1919. Under this, the British government made provision for up to 7600 houses to be let to ex-servicemen at preferential rents. These houses were built to a high standard and a large number still survive in Killester in north Dublin and in East Belfast. The British government was not entirely altruistic in building these homes, with senior politicians stressing the political benefits of this scheme, which they hoped would retain Irish ex-servicemen's loyalty to the British state.[64]

At the local level, one might have expected to see the same patterns played out as at the national level, with Unionist local authorities quick to commemorate their war dead and Nationalist areas reluctant to do so. However, this was not to be the case; the Belfast Cenotaph was not to be unveiled until 11 November 1929.[65] The debate as to whether memorials should be practical or artistic was played out at the local level, as at the national. In Newtownards, County Down, a proposal that a commemorative grammar school should be erected was rejected by the chairman of the Urban District Council, who argued that few of the relatives of the town's war dead would ever have an opportunity to attend such a school. In Enniskillen, a local landowner, J.P. Porter, put forward a scheme which would have seen a memorial tablet erected in the town hall and a memorial wing constructed on the county hospital. However, public pressure, mobilized by W.C. Trimble, editor of the *Impartial Reporter*, ensured that the money raised for a war memorial was spent on a sculpture. Trimble's objections to the hospital project had a firm political edge as he suggested that the then Nationalist-dominated County Council would ensure that only Catholics worked in the hospital and that Catholics had contributed very little to the memorial fund.[66]

Politics continued to cast a long shadow over commemoration in Ireland. When the Belfast Cenotaph was unveiled in 1929, the largely Catholic 16th (Irish) Division Ex-Servicemen's Association was not invited to lay a wreath, although this telling oversight was corrected at the 1930 Armistice Day ceremony.[67] Armistice Day continued to be a highly charged political event in Ireland with significant poppy stealing taking place and Trinity College Dublin students engaging in provocative acts of loyalty to Britain.[68] The IRA clearly identified commemoration of the war dead with Unionism in 1987 when their notorious 'Poppy Day' bombing killed eleven people at the Remembrance Sunday ceremony in Enniskillen.[69]

More recently, the memory of the Great War has been mobilized in the peace process. At a local level, senior Sinn Féin figures, particularly Alex Maskey and Tom Hartley in Belfast, started to take part in Remembrance Day ceremonies in attempts to reach out to the Unionist community, though cynics may have concluded that Sinn Féin politicians found it less problematic to engage with the Unionist dead than the Unionist living. At a national, and indeed international, level, the Island of Ireland Peace Tower was constructed at Messines/Mesen, in Belgium. It was dedicated on 11 November 1998 by Queen Elizabeth II, President Mary McAleese, and King Albert of Belgium. This is an imposing structure, in the form of a traditional Irish round tower constructed from limestone blocks taken from the demolished Mullingar Workhouse. Despite its laudable aims, purists have much to concern themselves about regarding this tower. Two politicians, Paddy Hart, a former Fine Gael TD, and Glenn Barr, a community activist and former loyalist paramilitary leader, were the instigators of this project and some may have been uneasy about Mr Barr's engagement in the 1970s with the Ulster Defence Association. Visitors to the Peace Tower will also find little to greet them, in sharp contrast to the Ulster Tower at Thiepval, where a memorial chapel, museum, and knowledgeable caretakers make visitors of all political persuasions welcome. Military historians may also wonder why the Peace Tower is built in an area over a mile from where the 16th (Irish) and 36th (Ulster) Divisions served, in an area where New Zealand troops fought and died.[70]

VI. FUTURE DIRECTIONS

With the centenary of the Great War and the recent release of soldiers' personal files and census materials online, a large number of publications on this topic can be expected over the next five years.[71] Undoubtedly, much of this will be by amateur historians (and the fear is that few of these will be gifted amateurs) content to reproduce material readily available in local newspapers or on the Commonwealth War Graves website.[72] However, this renewed public interest may see the publication of many important archival sources, a process which has already started.[73] In terms of the academic contribution, while we probably know more about recruitment and commemoration in Ireland than in the rest of the UK, these are still important areas of research, where debates will doubtless continue for many years to come. County studies of the Irish Revolution are now numerous and this approach has been usefully pioneered for the Great War experience by Colin Cousins in his study of County Armagh.[74] It is also to be hoped that the 'new' regimental histories by Mark Connelly and Helen McCartney will influence Irish historians and essentially lead to a regional approach to issues such as recruitment and wartime experience.[75] Just as there is a need to understand the local and regional contexts, so is there a need to understand the wider trans-national contexts, particularly Ireland's place within the wider UK experience. A start has been made on this by Catriona Pennell, but her argument that Irish 'war enthusiasm' can be located within a shared British experience remains unconvincing.[76] The 'war and society' approach to history which was so important in the 1980s and 1990s rather passed Irish history by and it is to be hoped that proper studies of issues such as the Irish economy and social change during the Great War will emerge in the near future.

NOTES

1. R.F. Foster, *Modern Ireland, 1600–1972* (London, 1988), 471.
2. David Fitzpatrick, 'Militarism in Ireland, 1900–1922' in Thomas Bartlett and Keith Jeffery (eds), *A Military History of Ireland* (Cambridge, 1996), 379–406.
3. David Fitzpatrick (ed), *Ireland and the First World War* (Dublin, 1988), Adrian Gregory and Senia Paseta (eds), *Ireland and the Great War: 'A War to unite us all'?* (Manchester, 2002), and John Horne (ed), *Our War: Ireland and the Great War* (Dublin, 2008).
4. Keith Jeffery, *Ireland and the Great War* (Cambridge, 2000).
5. P.E. Dewey, *British Agriculture in the First World War* (London, 1989), 45 and 231. J. M. Winter, *The Great War and the British People* (London, 1985), 26, 27, 95, 164.
6. This phrase was coined by F.X. Martin, '1916—myth, fact and mystery', *Studia Hibernica*, 7 (1967), 68.
7. Since 1997 the Royal Dublin Fusiliers Association has published an interesting journal *The Blue Cap*, and their website is available at http://www.greatwar.ie/. The Royal Munster Fusiliers Association maintains a website at http://www.rmfa92.org and the Connaught Rangers Association at http://www.connaughtrangersassoc.com/, all accessed 15 January 2009.

8. This is seen most vividly in the Loyalist Wall Murals in Ulster. See B. Graham and P. Shirlow, 'The Battle of the Somme in Ulster Memory and Identity', *Political Geography*, 21 (2002), 881–904

9. This is particularly evident in the Northern Ireland Common Curriculum where Key Stage 3 (that is, 13–14-year-olds) pupils are expected to consider the experience of Irishmen in the war as a conciliation exercise and the development of the Island of Ireland Peace Park at Messines; see Jeffery, *Ireland and the Great War*, 138–43.

10. Terence Denman, *A Lonely Grave: The Life and Death of William Redmond* (Dublin, 1995), 101–3.

11. Rowland Feilding, *War Letters to a Wife: France and Flanders, 1915–1919* (London, 1929), 170.

12. Denys Reitz, *Trekking On* (London, 1933), 182.

13. Liddle Collection, University of Leeds, The papers of Second Lieutenant[sic.] T. H. Witherow, 5. See also Timothy Bowman, *Irish Regiments in the Great War: Discipline and Morale* (Manchester, 2003), 154–5.

14. Philip Orr, *The Road to the Somme: Men of the Ulster Division tell their Story* (2nd ed., Belfast, 2008), 286–90 and Jeffery, *Ireland and the Great War*, 143.

15. Jeffery, *Ireland and the Great War*, 177.

16. See, for example, a lecture by Billy [sic] Ervine, 'Gone but not forgotten: The Somme' delivered to Ballymacarrett Arts and Cultural Society and subsequently published in Belfast by Island Publications, 1999.

17. Anon., *A Short Record of the Services and Experiences of the Fifth Battalion Royal Irish Fusiliers in the Great War* (Dublin., 1919), Bryan Cooper, *The Tenth (Irish) Division in Gallipoli* (London, 1918), Henry Hanna, *The Pals at Suvla Bay: being the Record of 'D' Company of the 7th Royal Dublin Fusiliers* (Dublin, 1916), H.F.N. Jourdain, *Record of the 5th (S.) Battalion the Connaught Rangers* (Oxford, 1916), A.P.I. Samuels and D.G.S[?]., *With the Ulster Division in France; A Story of the 11th Battalion Royal Irish Rifles (South Antrim Volunteers) from Bordon to Thiepval* (Belfast, no date [1918?]) and G.A. Cooper Walker, *The Book of the 7th Service Battalion, the Royal Inniskilling Fusiliers: from Tipperary to Ypres* (Dublin, 1920).

18. H.F.N. Jourdain, *History of the Connaught Rangers* (Whitehall, 1924–8), Stephen McCance, *The History of the Royal Munster Fusiliers, vol. II, From 1861 to 1922 (Disbandment)* (Aldershot, 1927), F.E. Whitton, *The History of the Prince of Wales' Leinster Regiment (Royal Canadians)* (London, no date [1926?]), H.C. Wylly, *Crown and Company, The Historical Records of the Second Battalion, Royal Dublin Fusiliers, vol.II, 1911–1922* (Aldershot, 1922) and H.C. Wylly, *Neill's 'Blue Caps', The History of the First Battalion, Royal Dublin Fusiliers, vol. III, 1914–1922* (Aldershot, 1925).

19. H.F.N. Jourdain, *Ranging Memories* (Oxford, 1932).

20. Rudyard Kipling, *The Irish Guards in the Great War: The Second Battalion* (London, 1923). Cyril Falls, *The History of the 36th (Ulster) Division* (Belfast, 1922).

21. The circumstances of John Kipling's service and death with the Irish Guards has recently been dramatized in David Haig, *My Boy Jack*, first as a play and then an ITV drama, first broadcast on 18/11/07. See also Francis Law, *A Man at Arms: Memoirs of Two World Wars* (London, 1983), 43 and 56 for a fellow officer's memories.

22. Personal file of Captain C.B. Falls, TNA, WO339/213 and Michael Howard, 'Cyril Bentham Falls', http://www.oxforddnb.com.chain.kent.ac.uk/view/article/310938, accessed 15 January 2009.

23. This is a problem when using government publications as a whole and the Irish National War Memorial, *Ireland's Memorial Records, 1914–1918* (Dublin, 1923). The destruction of around 50 per cent of British servicemen's records by enemy action in the Second World War means that it is impossible to calculate an exact figure.

24. Peter Simkins, *Kitchener's Army: The Raising of the New Armies, 1914–16* (Manchester, 1988), 70–1.

25. Jeffery, *Ireland and the Great War*, 7 and David Fitzpatrick, 'The Logic of Collective Sacrifice: Ireland and the British Army, 1914–1918', *Historical Journal*, XXXVIII, 4 (1995), 1017–30.

26. Patrick Callan, 'Voluntary Recruiting for the British Army in Ireland during the First World War', unpublished PhD thesis, University College Dublin, 1984. See also Patrick Callan, 'Recruiting for the British Army in Ireland during the First World War', *The Irish Sword*, XVII, 66 (1987), 42–56.

27. Letter, A.P. Magill to Matthew Nathan, 22/11/14, MS. Nathan, 457, f.155, Bodleian Library, letter, Nathan to The O'Mahony, 21/5/15, MS. Nathan, 463, f.337, Bodleian Library and 'Report on Recruiting in Ireland', Cd. 8168, 1916, 3–4.

28. Statement on enlistments in Joseph Brennan papers, Ms.26,154, NLI. Fitzpatrick suggests higher figures of 32 105 INV and 30 738 UVF recruits but continues his figures until the end of 1917, presumably using the RIC County Inspectors' reports in TNA, CO904 series.

29. For a detailed discussion of the role of the UVF during the war, see Timothy Bowman, *Carson's Army: The Ulster Volunteer Force, 1910–1922* (Manchester, 2007), 163–89.

30. T.P. Dooley, *Irishmen or English Soldiers? The Times and World of a Southern Catholic Irish Man (1876–1916) Enlisting in the British Army during the First World War* (Liverpool, 1995), 124.

31. Eric Mercer, 'For King, Country and a Shilling a Day': Recruitment in Belfast During the Great War, 1914–18', unpublished MA dissertation, Queen's University of Belfast, 1998, 13–16, and Michael Moss and J.R. Hume, *Shipbuilders to the World: 125 years of Harland and Wolff, Belfast, 1861–1986* (Belfast, 1986), 175–96.

32. Hanna, *The Pals at Suvla Bay*.

33. *The Northern Whig*, 7/9/14, 16/9/14, 21/9/14 and 22/9/14.

34. 'Report on Recruiting in Ireland', Cd. 8168, 1916 and 'Men of Military Age in Ireland', Cd. 8390, 1916.

35. Keith Grieves, *The Politics of Manpower, 1914–18* (Manchester, 1988), 8–17.

36. James McConnel, 'Recruiting Sergeants for John Bull? Irish Nationalist MPs and enlistment during the early months of the Great War', *War in History*, 14, 4 (2007), 408–28.

37. *Belfast News Letter* 7/8/14.

38. Terence Denman, 'The 10th (Irish) Division, 1914–15: A study in military and political interaction', *The Irish Sword*, XVII, 66 (1987), 16–25.

39. Simkins, *Kitchener's Army*, 94–5.

40. Timothy Bowman, 'The Ulster Volunteer Force and the formation of the 36th (Ulster) Division', *Irish Historical Studies*, XXXII, 128 (2001), 498–518.

41. *Belfast Evening Telegraph*, 3/10/14.

42. Bowman, *Irish Regiments in the Great War*, 111–17 and Nicholas Perry, *Major General Oliver Nugent and the Ulster Division 1915–1918* (London, 2007), 19.

43. Terence Denman, *Ireland's Unknown Soldiers: The 16th (Irish) Division in the Great War* (Dublin, 1992), 38.

44. Stephen Gwynn, *John Redmond's Last Years* (London, 1919), 173 and D.D. Sheehan, *Ireland since Parnell* (London, 1921), 286–8.

45. N.L.I., Ms.10,561/1–18, Moore papers, letter, Maurice Moore to Joseph Devlin, M.P., 7/11/14.

46. Denman, *Ireland's Unknown Soldiers*, 45, and letter, Parsons to Military Secretary, War Office, 29/11/14, Parsons papers, NLI, Ms. 21 278.

47. Denman, *Ireland's Unknown Soldiers*, 48 and Alan O'Day, 'William Archer Redmond', http://www.oxforddnb.com.chain.kent.ac.uk/view/article/65858?docPos=4, accessed 15 January 2009.

48. Bowman, *Irish Regiments*, 78–9.

49. R.J.Q. Adams and P.P. Poirier, *The Conscription Controversy in Great Britain, 1900–18* (Columbus, Ohio, 1987), 230–41, Adrian Gregory, ' "You might as well recruit Germans": British public opinion and the decision to conscript the Irish in 1918' in Gregory and Paseta (eds) *Ireland and the Great War*, 113–32, Grieves, *The Politics of Manpower*, 188–92, and Richard Holmes, *The Little Field Marshal: A Life of Sir John French* (London, 1981), 326–40.

50. W.J. Canning, *Ballyshannon, Belcoo, Bertincourt; The History of the 11th Battalion, The Royal Inniskilling Fusiliers (Donegal and Fermanagh Volunteers) in World War One* (privately published Antrim, 1996), W.J. Canning, *A Wheen of Medals: The History of the 9th (Service) Bn., The Royal Inniskilling Fusiliers (The Tyrones) in World War One* (Antrim, 2006), An Crann, *Donegal, Ireland and the First World War* (publisher and place of publication unknown, 1987), James McGuinn, *Sligo Men in the Great War 1914–1918* (Belturbet, 1994), Gardiner Mitchell, *Three Cheers for the Derrys! A History of the 10th Royal Inniskilling Fusiliers in the 1914–18 War* (Londonderry, 1991), and S.N. White, *The Terrors; 16th (Pioneer) Battalion, Royal Irish Rifles, 1914–19* (Belfast, 1996).

51. Orr, *Road to the Somme*, J.W. Taylor, *The 1st Royal Irish Rifles in the Great War* (Dublin, 2002) and J.W. Taylor, *The 2nd Royal Irish Rifles in the Great War* (Dublin, 2005).

52. R.S. Grayson, *Belfast Boys: How Unionists and Nationalists Fought and Died together in the First World War* (London, 2010). Grayson was also involved in, Various, *The 6th Connaught Rangers: Belfast Nationalists and the Great War* (Belfast, 2008).

53. Terence Denman, 'The Catholic Irish Soldier in the First World War: The "Racial Enviroment" ', *Irish Historical Studies*, XXVII, 108 (1991), 352–65.

54. Hew Strachan, *The Politics of the British Army* (Oxford, 1997), 206–9.

55. Bowman, *Irish Regiments*, 140–61 and Nicholas Perry, 'Nationality in the Irish infantry regiments in the First World War', *War and Society*, XII, I (1994), 65–95.

56. PRONI, MIC/571/10, Farren Connell papers, letter, Nugent to James Johnston, Lord Mayor of Belfast, 28/2/18, and PRONI, MIC/571/10, Farren Connell papers, letter, Nugent to the Adjutant General, 11/12/17.

57. Bowman, *Irish Regiments*, 170–1.

58. Ibid., 196–9.

59. Jay Winter, *Sites of Memory, Sites of Mourning: The Great War in European Cultural History* (Cambridge, 1995), Jeffery, *Ireland and the Great War*, 107–43, Keith Jeffery, 'Irish culture and the Great War', *Bullan*, 1, 2 (1994), 87–96.

60. N.C. Johnston, *Ireland, the Great War and the Geography of Remembrance* (Cambridge, 2003) is a particularly strange contribution to the debate, which has a chapter considering recruiting posters and another entitled 'Remembering the Easter Rebellion 1916'. See also Jane Leonard, 'The twinge of memory: Armistice Day and Remembrance Sunday in Dublin since 1919' in Richard English and Graham Walker (eds), *Unionism in Modern Ireland: New Perspectives on Politics and Culture* (Basingstoke, 1996), 99–114, James

Loughlin, 'Mobilising the sacred dead: Ulster unionism, the Great War and the politics of remembrance' in Gregory and Paseta (eds), *Ireland and the Great War*, 133–54, and Catherine Switzer, *Unionists and Great War Commemoration in the North of Ireland 1914–1939* (Dublin, 2007). Niall Barr, *The Lion and the Poppy: British Veterans, Politics and Society, 1921–1939* (London, 2005) includes no discussion of Ireland.

61. Loughlin, 'Mobilising the sacred dead', 138–41.
62. Jeffery, *Ireland and the Great War*, 108–9, Johnson, *Ireland, the Great War and the Geography of Remembrance*, 105–6, Loughlin, 'Mobilising the sacred dead', 144–5, PRONI, PM9/17, file concerning the Ulster Tower.
63. Jeffery, *Ireland and the Great War*, 109–28 and Johnson, *Ireland, the Great War and the Geography of Remembrance*, 84–94 and 108–11.
64. Murray Fraser, *John Bull's Other Homes: State Housing and British Policy in Ireland, 1883–1922* (Liverpool, 1996), 240–71.
65. Jeffery, *Ireland and the Great War*, 131–2.
66. Switzer, *Unionists and the Great War*, 68–71.
67. Jeffery, *Ireland and the Great War*, 132.
68. Leonard, 'The twinge of memory', 99–114.
69. Switzer, *Unionists and the Great War*, 154.
70. Jeffery, *Ireland and the Great War*, 138–43. These comments are also based on the author's visits to these two memorials in April and July 2008.
71. Most of The National Archive, Kew records relating to First World War soldiers (but not officers) are available at http://search.ancestry.co.uk/search/category.aspx?cat=39 (accessed, 14 December 2012). The 1911 Irish Census returns are available from the National Archives of Ireland at http://www.census.nationalarchives.ie/ (accessed 14 December 2012).
72. The Commonwealth War Graves Commission website is available at http://www.cwgc.org/ (accessed 14 December 2012).
73. David Truesdale (ed), *'Young Citizen Old Soldier' from Boyhood in Antrim to Hell on the Somme: The journal of Rifleman James McRoberts, 14th Battalion Royal Irish Rifles, January 1915–April 1917* (Solihull, 2012).
74. Colin Cousins, *Armagh and the Great War* (Dublin, 2011).
75. Mark Connelly, *Steady the Buffs! A Regiment, a Region, & the Great War* (Oxford, 2006) and H.B. McCartney, *Citizen Soldiers: The Liverpool Territorials in the First World War* (Cambridge, 2005).
76. Catriona Pennell, *A Kingdom United: Popular Responses to the Outbreak of the First World War in Britain and Ireland* (Oxford, 2012).

Select Bibliography

Bowman, Timothy, 'The Ulster Volunteer Force and the formation of the 36th (Ulster) Division', *Irish Historical Studies*, XXXII, 128 (2001), 498–518.
Bowman, Timothy, *Irish Regiments in the Great War: Discipline and Morale* (Manchester, 2003).
Callan, Patrick, 'Recruiting for the British army in Ireland during the First World War', *The Irish Sword*, XVII, 66 (1987), 42–56.
Cooper, Bryan, *The Tenth (Irish) Division in Gallipoli* (London, 1918).
Cousins, Colin, *Armagh and the Great War* (Dublin, 2011).

Denman, Terence, 'The 10th (Irish) Division, 1914–15: A study in military and political interaction', *The Irish Sword*, XVII, 66 (1987), 16–25.

Denman, Terence, *Ireland's Unknown Soldiers: The 16th (Irish) Division in the Great War* (Dublin, 1992).

Falls, Cyril, *The History of the 36th (Ulster) Division* (Belfast, 1922).

Fitzpatrick, David (ed), *Ireland and the First World War* (Dublin, 1988).

Fitzpatrick, David, 'The Logic of Collective Sacrifice: Ireland and the British Army, 1914–1918', *Historical Journal*, XXXVIII, 4 (1995), 1017–30.

Grayson, R.S., *Belfast Boys: How Unionists and Nationalists Fought and Died Together in the First World War* (London, 2010).

Gregory, Adrian and Paseta, Senia (eds), *Ireland and the Great War: 'A War to unite us all'?* (Manchester, 2002).

Horne, John (ed), *Our War: Ireland and the Great War* (Dublin, 2008).

Jeffery, Keith, *Ireland and the Great War* (Cambridge, 2000).

McConnel, James, 'Recruiting Sergeants for John Bull? Irish Nationalist MPs and enlistment during the early months of the Great War', *War in History*, 14, 4 (2007), 408–28.

Pennell, Catriona, *A Kingdom United: Popular Responses to the Outbreak of the First World War in Britain and Ireland* (Oxford, 2012).

Perry, Nicholas, 'Nationality in the Irish infantry regiments in the First World War', *War and Society*, XII, I (1994), 65–95.

Perry, Nicholas, *Major General Oliver Nugent and the Ulster Division 1915–1918* (London, 2007).

Switzer, Catherine, *Unionists and Great War Commemoration in the North of Ireland 1914–1939* (Dublin, 2007).

CHAPTER 31

···

THE IRISH REVOLUTION, 1912–23

···

NIALL WHELEHAN

I

···

THE dramatic events that took place in Ireland during the years 1912–1923 were part of the cycle of European and global violence characterized by war, labour militancy, and revolution. By 1923, Ireland was transformed, divided into the twenty-six-county Irish Free State and the six-county Northern Ireland, but the changes that people had reasonably expected in 1912 were the ones that had not come to pass. Chance and circumstance seemed to shape the Irish revolution and histories have long emphasized chronologies, how the sudden outbreak of European war in 1914 defused a likely civil war but also created opportunities for rebellion. At the same time, the Irish Revolution was rooted in long-standing structural factors and social and political tensions. The resolution of these tensions was not inevitably violent, but after 1912, actions increasingly spoke louder than words.

The historical interpretation of the Irish Revolution has changed radically in recent decades. Earlier histories followed the paper trail in the limited official sources available and typically focused on elite policy-making, the Anglo-Irish Treaty, and personalities like Éamon de Valera, Michael Collins, Lloyd George, Constance Markievicz, or Ernie O'Malley. Memoirs and autobiographies featured prominently. In the late 1970s, international trends in social history began to shape new approaches to the Revolution and, particularly in the 1990s and 2000s, scholarly writing shifted substantially to social and cultural approaches that incorporated detailed studies of the complexities of revolution at local level.[1] These approaches, coupled with the availability of important new sources since 2003, have transformed our understanding of the period. Revisionist controversies continue to attract scholarly attention, but to a lesser degree when compared to the 1980s and 1990s, which is in part due to the new questions that emerged from fresh approaches and sources, and also to the 1998 Good Friday Agreement and the post-Troubles environment. This chapter explores some of these new questions and approaches to the themes of republicanism, self-determination, and imperialism in the decade or so of the Irish Revolution.[2]

II

As Irish nationalists replicated the Ulster Volunteer Force (UVF) in 1913, social conditions in Dublin were among the worst in the United Kingdom. In 1911, 23 per cent of Dublin's population of over 300 000 people lived in one–roomed tenements in city slums, most of them semi- and unskilled workers. In 1914, a parliamentary investigation recognized the problem as acute and recommended the 'complete breaking up of the tenement house system as it exists'. The death rate in Dublin was around twenty-three per thousand, compared to about fifteen per thousand in London. The proportion of deaths that took place in public institutions was nearly two and a half times that in England.[3] Against this backdrop, the greatest labour dispute in Ireland's history unfolded in Dublin in August 1913, raising complicated issues on which many nationalists had hitherto preferred to keep silent.

Dublin's employers went on the offensive in 1913. Led by Cork-born businessman and former Home Rule M.P. William Martin Murphy, they locked out members of the Irish Transport and General Worker's Union (ITGWU) and employed blacklegs to take their place. In response, James Larkin organized a strike of Dublin's tram workers during the Dublin Horse Show, one of the busiest weeks in the city calendar. A number of clashes between workers and police followed, resulting in countless injuries and at least three fatalities, including the August riot that became known as Bloody Sunday. What Murphy called 'Larkinism' was an Irish variant of syndicalism, an international movement of revolutionary trade unionism that rejected parliamentary tactics as a dead end and advocated direct action and sympathetic strikes. Ireland's position in the United Kingdom was crucial to the ITGWU strike, which counted on sympathetic actions in British ports and cities and material support from the British Trades Union Congress (TUC) that came to over £106 000. Yet, personality and policy clashes between Larkin and British trade union leaders led to the withdrawal of support in December 1913 and ultimately the strike ended in January 1914 in defeat for the workers.[4]

The violence of the lockout discredited the Dublin police, the army, the courts, and the Irish administration more generally, weakening the state's legitimacy and giving impetus to separatism. Famously, the socialist James Connolly led the Irish Citizen Army, the workers' militia established during the lockout, in the 1916 Rising. The ITGWU became 'more aggressively nationalist' after 1913, which 'reinforced the interplay of republicanism and syndicalism'.[5] Witness statements have revealed that some 1916 rebels were politicized by clashes with the police during the lockout, and the question of how the use and perception of physical force during the lockout influenced later attitudes towards violence merits further exploration.[6] At the same time, 1913 is too frequently read in the historiography as no more than a curtain raiser for 1916. The leading role of Connolly and others in the fighting has folded the lockout into a nationalist narrative, obscuring a harder look at the limitations and bitter defeat of labour in 1913. The lockout is often portrayed in heroic terms, but Padraig Yeates's authoritative study argues that it was a 'more mundane affair' that could have been avoided had it not been for the uncompromising and divisive figures of Larkin and Murphy. The lockout also stirred nationalist and religious tensions within the ITGWU, and British help was 'often resented'.[7]

The events of 1913 raised awkward questions and contradictions for Irish nationalism. Many of the employers who orchestrated the violence against Dublin's working class were Catholic and nationalist, led by Murphy and counselled by the veteran parliamentary nationalist Tim Healy. Beyond Connolly's increasing centrality, in the aftermath of the lockout, the goals of the nationalist movement were not significantly restructured to accommodate ideas of social justice. Yeates has provocatively asked whether the working class gained anything at all from independence. In 1922, the new Irish government denied postal workers the right to strike, and, as Diarmaid Ferriter put it, 'the speed with which Cumann na nGaedheal...became associated with the "men of property" was telling'.[8] For many nationalists, Home Rule or republican, allaying the concerns of property and Catholic clerics was more urgent than allaying the concerns of people who lived in slums. The Catholic Church proved influential in ending the strike, successfully blocking a scheme to temporarily send the children of the worst-affected families to the homes of sympathetic workers in Britain for the duration of the strike, in the process further fuelling Unionist fears of 'Rome Rule'.[9] Concern for children's eternal souls was a political issue during the Irish Revolution, when Catholics sought to rescue them from heathen homes in Liverpool or Protestant orphanages in Galway. Throughout the lockout, the Catholic Church took the side of property and held the attitude that poverty was preordained and slum dwellers should be content with their lot. Exposure to 'satanic socialism' in Britain could have given the working class a sense of entitlement when they returned.[10] Many working-class families who did emigrate, however, didn't return.

The outbreak of the First World War changed the labour market in Ireland and calmed simmering tensions. It also temporarily defused the danger of civil war by removing the majority of volunteers, unionist and nationalist, to die on European battlefields. Yet a political solution to the aggressive divisions of 1913 was far from clear. The 1912 Home Rule Bill appeared to indicate a triumph for peaceful constitutional nationalism, as opposed to violent separatism, but in reality the two strands of Irish nationalism were inextricably interwoven. From the birth of the Irish Party in the 1870s, the Irish Republican Brotherhood (IRB) had seeped into its ranks. Although the IRB faded from view in the late 1880s, it did not disappear and had regained influence by 1914.[11] In 1915, Edward Carson and Andrew Bonar Law, who two years earlier had preached sedition and the use of force to resist the enactment of Home Rule, were not only tolerated, but found themselves in Asquith's coalition government. This did not create incentives for the IRB and Irish Volunteers to remain in the borders of legality, and, when conscription was introduced in Britain in 1916, the former was moving toward action.

The First World War was a catalyst of the Irish Revolution that shaped and accelerated change.[12] Britain was involved in a major European conflict for the first time since the

Crimean War, which itself had spurred the establishment of the IRB in 1858. The First World War, Charles Townshend has asserted, provided the 'the key context' for the 1916 Rising.[13] It produced circumstances more favourable to rebellion than Tom Clarke, an IRB activist since the late 1870s, had experienced in his lifetime. It created the prospect of military assistance from a foreign power, it allowed for the view that rebels might have a stake in a post-war peace conference, and it influenced the rebels' reverence for military values. The war also shaped the state's reaction to rebellion. The shelling of Dublin's city centre with artillery and the imposition of martial law befitted a war more than an insurrection. This disproportionate response was also suggestive of the colonial dimensions of Ireland's status and it would be 'difficult to envision the same tactics being so readily deployed in a British city'.[14]

The week-long rebellion in Dublin has been traditionally understood to be the key event of the Irish revolution, bringing in separatism from the margins to the centre of the nationalist movement and precipitating the War of Independence. The dimensions and meaning of this seminal event have at times been fiercely contested; anniversaries have come and gone that were marked by both celebration and uncomfortable commemoration.[15] In the approach to Ireland's 'decade of centenaries', interest in 1916 took a turn that surprised historians. The day after the €85 billion EU/IMF/ECB bailout of the collapsed Irish economy in 2010, the emotive front page of the *Irish Examiner* featured the 'Proclamation of Dependence', a parody of the 'Proclamation of Independence' delivered in 1916. On the same day, *The Irish Times*, a paper that, along with the *Irish Independent*, encouraged the execution of the rebels in 1916, asked, 'Was it this...the men of 1916 died for?'[16] The gravest charge one could direct at the Irish government, it seemed, was that they had dishonoured the 1916 rebels.

Our understanding of these rebels and what they aimed to achieve has changed since historians gained access to the files of the Bureau of Military History. Between 1947 and 1957, this Fianna Fáil-led project collected 'witness statements' from participants in the Irish Revolution, which were opened to the public in 2003 when the last recipient of a pension for service died.[17] Revisionist interpretations viewed the Rising primarily as a romantic gesture, designed by poets for symbolic but not pragmatic reasons.[18] Yet, Fearghal McGarry's study of the Rising 'from within and below' reveals a variety of expectations. Above a romantic or irrational commitment to self-immolation, many rebels simply preferred insurrection to inaction, as 'an act of propaganda', and were well aware of the minimal possibilities for military success. They believed themselves to be participating in a regular military enterprise, legitimized by adherence to the rules of war, exercise of restraint, and codes of chivalry.[19] Long-standing historical debates exist regarding the decision to stage an old-fashioned, '1848-style' insurrection in 1916. Rebellion was far from an inevitable course of action in 1916, and the volunteer leaders Bulmer Hobson and Eoin MacNeill both advocated 'hedge-fighting' or guerrilla tactics as the most realistic strategy.[20] Yet, the rebels chose a conventional style of warfare that appealed to gendered ideas of military honour and masculine identities that were shaped by the wartime context. During the Rising, female volunteers, organized in Cumann na mBan, were frustrated with the limited, subordinate roles the leaders were prepared to offer them. The Irish Citizen Army proved somewhat different and female members were assigned combatant roles at St Stephen's Green, though few were armed.[21]

Much writing on 1916 has centred on the magnetic Patrick Pearse and his legacy, but recent studies have emphasized the importance of the IRB leaders Tom Clarke and Seán MacDermott.[22] At the same time, the IRB held limited organizational capacity in 1916 and sought to act primarily as a leaven within the Irish Volunteers. Most of the 1916 leaders held no backgrounds in the IRB. They fought for an independent republic, but in comparison with the Irish republic declared by Fenians in 1867, the 1916 proclamation was less secular and less social in outlook. Owen McGee has argued that the 1916 generation represented the eclipse of the nineteenth-century Fenians' brand of progressive republicanism by the more Catholic, Irish-Ireland outlook of de Valera and Pearse. It was this Irish-Ireland generation of petit-bourgeois nationalists, memorably described by Tom Garvin, rather than the anti-clerical Fenians who predominated the republican movement from 1916 to 1923.[23]

The year 1918 was one of considerable transformation. In February, the Representation of the People Act extended the franchise to women over 30 (with property qualifications). This sweeping social change was overshadowed in Ireland by popular resistance to anticipated conscription. The execution of the 1916 leaders had proven to be unpopular, but it was the mass arrests and severe treatment in improvised prisons that stirred deep discontent with government. As in the nineteenth century, political prisoners played an important role in shaping British-Irish relations and created formidable problems for the authorities throughout the Irish Revolution, particularly when the hunger strike was used a means of protest.[24] Inflamed by the threat of the draft, popular disaffection energized Sinn Féin. With the support of the Catholic Church, the party consolidated its position in the December elections and replaced the Irish Party as the dominant expression of Irish nationalism. By 1918, the project for all-Ireland Home Rule had failed.[25] Sinn Féin abstained from the Westminster parliament and established Dáil Éireann in Dublin, the parliament of the Irish republic declared in 1916.

III

The War of Independence is generally understood to have begun on 21 January 1919, the day that the Dáil held its first session and, by coincidence, when two policemen were killed in an ambush at Soloheadbeg, County Tipperary, an attack undertaken at local initiative. Viewing these events as the starting point of war is somewhat misleading, as low-level violence was occurring in Ireland in the preceding years. In 1918, County Clare had been declared a special military area and attacks and arms raids on RIC barracks were relatively common. After the Tipperary ambush, attacks on RIC barracks and personnel, mostly Catholics, increased but violence remained limited. It was not until the summer of 1920 that a serious escalation in violence took place that lasted until the truce of July 1921.

In the aftermath of the First World War, the Irish administration's monopoly on violence dissolved. Writing in 1919, Max Weber described a 'monopoly of the legitimate use of physical force within a given territory' as an essential condition of the modern state. In this conception, rather than merely possessing the technological and military might to maintain internal peace, the state legitimizes the use of force through some form of consensus and integration of citizens into a national structure.[26] During the nineteenth century, the state's presence in Ireland was never monolithic and it frequently resorted to emergency legislation, but it was sufficient to prevent a permanent disruption of the social order, even during the pervasive unrest of the Land War. The response to the Ulster Volunteers, the repression of labour in 1913, and the 1916 Rising all weakened the state's legitimacy and it began to fade rapidly in the post-war years, which saw the mobilization of a democratic mass-movement in Ireland. This movement found widespread international sympathy and its goal of an independent nation was increasingly viewed as revolutionary but reasonable in the post-war context. Republicans sought to create an alternative state through the Dáil, the Irish Republican Police force, and the Dáil Courts, while at the same time enforcing a strict boycott of the RIC, the assize courts, and juries that led to mass resignations and effectively made the administration of civil justice and provision of some basic services impossible. By mid-1920, RIC officers were resigning at a rate of almost 200 per month. The British government's decision to introduce martial law and reinforce the RIC with paramilitary units, who at times engaged in excessive violence with free rein, fundamentally weakened the state's legitimate monopoly of force.

Over the past two decades, much writing on the War of Independence has followed the local approach pioneered by David Fitzpatrick in his groundbreaking study of County Clare and the social context of revolution.[27] County-based or regional studies of the War of Independence have flourished, illuminating diverse experiences across the island, the uneven distribution of violence, and the different relations between religious communities in each county.[28] Although they reveal diversity, national patterns have also emerged from county studies regarding the backgrounds of volunteers, the victims of warfare, and the nature of official reprisals. The most influential county study to emerge, and one that has energized debates on the period, is Peter Hart's innovative 1998 study of Cork, a county that, along with the cities Belfast and Dublin, bore the brunt of the violence. Hart drew from an admirably wide range of sources to reconstruct an expansive picture of the IRA and the targets of their attacks, to put a 'human face' on the violence of the War of Independence, the Civil War, and the significant period in between, from July 1921 to June 1922, when it was less clear than ever where and with whom authority and sovereignty rested.[29]

Hart expanded his research and interpretations of the conflict in Cork to the national level in subsequent studies. He found that the volunteers were 'Catholic almost without exception', were typically unmarried males, unpropertied, and 'urban, educated, skilled (and thus at least potentially socially mobile)'. The average age of membership was about 25, which Hart maintained brought a generational aspect to the fighting, a conflict of fathers and sons.[30] The predominance of young males in the IRA ranks has sometimes been explained by the closing off of emigration during the First World War which left, by 1918, a surplus of young, would-be emigrants in Ireland, contributing to the swell in ranks of republican movements. Hart contended, however, that more young men joined the British forces in 1914–18 than would have emigrated, leaving no surplus, and added that Irish emigrants were typically from a lower socio-economic background than the volunteers. This shared lower-middle class background and age cohort of the volunteers, he maintained, was key to consolidating the collective and sustaining their activism.[31] In this picture, men predominated the guerrilla operations and Cumann na mBan volunteers found a more chauvinist attitude toward their involvement than in 1916. Women participated in the war in multiple ways, however, including intelligence gathering, provision of safe houses, and smuggling arms.[32]

Numerous county studies reveal consistencies and divergences from Hart's pattern. A broad-ranging study of Tipperary, Wexford, Derry, Dublin, and Mayo demonstrated that IRA members' backgrounds unsurprisingly varied according to their environments, but in general their age and occupations reflected their status as integrated members of their communities, rather than marginalized and disaffected malcontents. The IRA 'appealed more to people who did have a stake in the country, if not necessarily the largest'. Members were mobilized by local traditions of resistance, familial connections to republicanism, and also opportunities for militant action, which most frequently occurred in heavily policed urban centres. By late 1920, IRA violence was increasingly motivated by intensified repression.[33] In Longford, the curtailment of emigration after 1916 most likely did influence the growth of the volunteers, many of whom hailed from rural areas. Marie Coleman has argued that Hart's nationwide profile rested predominantly on urban data, but in Longford the IRA was organizationally strongest in the countryside, as Fitzpatrick had previously observed in Clare.[34] In Galway, in contrast to Cork, Sinn Féin and the IRA were not from the middling classes, but comprised 'a coalition of the poorer classes', smallholders and labourers, who had the most to gain from expected redistribution of land. Their campaign of agrarian radicalism resulted in a social, as well as political, revolution in Galway.[35] The importance of ideology has often been neglected in studies that foreground statistical social analysis. John O'Callaghan has downplayed shared occupational or generational backgrounds in Limerick, instead emphasizing ideology as a key mobilizing factor, the 'organised attempt to defend and secure the Republic as declared in 1916 and again by the Dáil in 1919'.[36]

Traditional accounts of the war emphasized the IRA's flying columns ambushing the Crown forces, but the war also entailed much face-to-face killing and many victims were shot at close range. Bloody Sunday 1920 is perhaps the most notorious day of the war. That afternoon, British forces fired into a crowd of spectators at a Gaelic football match in Croke Park, killing twelve and injuring sixty. Three prisoners were also shot dead that evening. The killings were in revenge for the shooting of nineteen men in Dublin that morning, which left fourteen dead. The men, who were suspected British spies, were awoken by gunmen and shot in their beds. This style of violence was not unusual. In an important article, Anne Dolan has pointed out how it took its toll on some volunteers who struggled to reconcile the grim nature of their actions. Many had 'a sense of knowing that it was wrong, that there was something in it that was just not fair'.[37] The war was also characterized by what we might call invisible violence. People behaved in certain ways due to a state of permanent intimidation. Threatening letters, the fear of forgetting a boycott or to shun a certain member of your community shaped behaviour and mindsets, as did the dread of the nocturnal visit from the Black and Tans, whether it came to pass or not.

In Hart's picture of Cork, what was explicitly called revolutionary violence was implicitly about the settling of old scores, material interest, or ethnic tensions. Suspicions of informing to the authorities fell easily on Protestants and ex-soldiers, who the IRA sometimes shot, he maintained, 'not because of what they did but because of who they were'.[38] Protestants targeted by the IRA often felt their religion was a factor in the attacks in Cork, and evidence from County Monaghan also points to sectarian violence and the targeting of army veterans.[39] John Borgonovo has maintained that the IRA in Cork City had established a sophisticated intelligence gathering system and aimed for certainty when killing informers. As occurred in Longford and Clare, the IRA leaders in the city took action to prevent sectarian killings and sanctioned violence only against civilians who were 'actively anti-Irish', although local volunteers did not always seek formal approval before acting.[40]

The most heated debates about the War of Independence and Civil War concern the rules of military engagement and sectarian killing. In 1920, one week after Bloody Sunday, a group of IRA volunteers ambushed and killed seventeen Auxiliaries—an offensive, mobile corps of gendarmerie—at Kilmichael, near Macroom, in Cork. In his memoirs, the IRA leader Tom Barry maintained that some of the Auxiliaries staged a false surrender, and this led to the high number of fatalities. Hart, however, contended that the surrender was genuine and the volunteers gunned down Auxiliaries who had their hands up.[41] This controversial interpretation jarred with the traditional take on things, and a number of historians placed it under the microscope and found inconsistencies in Hart's evidence that have not been satisfactorily explained. Yet, the traditional version requires considerable faith in an account written by one man, Barry.[42] It is unlikely the matter will be resolved; both versions of events rest on volatile testimonies recorded decades after the event, factors that few contenders in the debate have properly addressed. All wars come to be defined in some way by flashpoints, but the extent of the debate surrounding this single event, albeit a very well known one, has absorbed much scholarly energy that might be better spent elsewhere. Was the Kilmichael ambush generally representative of the war? Hart's story is not provable but is plausible. For practical reasons the IRA usually took no political prisoners and sometimes killed men who surrendered. Prisoners were shot at Dromkeen in Limerick and drowned in Roscommon. Overall, however, one study of the encounters between the IRA and the British forces has maintained that, 'after successful ambushes, the volunteers usually chose to simply disarm their prisoners and let them go'.[43]

More controversy was generated by Hart's careless use of the term 'ethnic cleansing' when discussing the 'Protestant exodus' from southern Ireland in 1920–2. He stopped short of arguing that actual ethnic cleansing occurred in Ireland, nonetheless his use of the term was deliberately provocative.[44] Again, the debate largely revolved around a key flashpoint. In April 1922, an IRA commandant was shot dead by a Protestant civilian while he attempted to seize his car. Over the following two nights, thirteen Protestant civilians were killed in villages in the area surrounding Bandon, Cork. These were revenge killings, Hart argued, that targeted the victims simply because they were Protestant.[45] Some historians differ, maintaining that the IRA had discovered intelligence that indicated that the victims were informers and they were killed for military reasons. This debate has produced an antagonistic discussion between John Regan and David Fitzpatrick regarding Hart's interpretation and 'elision' of his sources.[46]

Leaving aside the vexed and unresolved question of whether the victims were informers, there are a number of factors that indicate the ethnic cleansing argument is not valid. Ethnic cleansing is not defined in international law, but it may be broadly described as the use of force or intimidation designed to remove people of a certain ethnic, racial, national, or religious group from an area. When Hart discussed ethnic cleansing, he conflated motivation and effect. Even if we accept his view that the Bandon killers acted out of a hatred for Protestants and a desire to teach them a lesson, the effect of the killings may have been for Protestants to leave the region in fear, but this is not necessarily what was intended, and there is no evidence to suggest that it was. Scale is also important. Ethnic cleansing in the former Yugoslavia, which took place when Hart was writing and influenced his choice of the term, entailed a 'widespread or systematic attack on a civilian population'.[47] In southern Ireland, the Bandon killings appear to have been exceptional and republican leaders took actions to prevent similar episodes reoccurring. Many Protestants who left the region later returned. Finally, research by David Fitzpatrick and Andy Bielenberg on Protestant communities in Cork indicates that, while some Protestants undoubtedly fled in fear, population decrease during the Irish Revolution was in line with long-term trends. There may have been an upturn in the numbers leaving in the years following the First World War, but a number of these were 'would-be' migrants who were unable to move during the war. When the period 1914–18 is taken into proper consideration, there are consistencies in the trend.[48]

Indicative of the rude health of public history in Ireland, key debates have taken place beyond the academy, in the magazine *History Ireland*, and in television and cinema, such as the RTÉ programme *Hidden History* and the feature film *The Wind that Shakes the Barley*. The latter, which won the 2006 Palme d'Or, received hostile criticism in some British newspapers for its favourable portrayal of the Irish War of Independence.[49] Yet Loach's film was no romanticized picture of Irish heroism. Benefitting from the presence of Donal Ò Drisceoil as historical advisor, the film explored state terrorism, but also conflicts within republican ranks and the devastating effects of divisions during the Civil War. The film also brought to the fore social conflicts and labour agitation which, some historians found overstated onscreen, but had been neglected in existing portrayals of the conflict in film and in text. In April 1920, a general strike was called in support of political prisoners on hunger strike in Mountjoy jail and the next month railwaymen refused to transport British forces or munitions, an embargo that lasted till December. The Crown forces also targeted labour newspapers and the halls and members of the ITGWU.[50]

IV

The IRA fought a guerrilla campaign designed to provoke the ugly side of the state, to draw their irreversibly stronger opponent into indistinct confrontations where routines of action were not clear and where strong-armed measures could become counter-productive. British forces could intervene decisively in crushing rebellion, but military superiority was not so effective in other situations. The IRA targeted the police force to a much greater extent than the army, because they were considered to be more effective intelligence gatherers and they were also more vulnerable. Attacks on barracks forced the constabulary to retreat to strongholds in towns, leaving no police presence in large parts of the countryside. To counter this strategy the British government reinforced the RIC with over 11 000 new recruits known as the Black and Tans and the Auxiliary Division. They were products of the integration of political and military decision-making during the First World War and their roles mixed the duties of soldier and policeman. Though only about one-sixth of the British forces in Ireland, these paramilitaries came to define the war in popular memory, representing British decadence and the worst of the war. They were typically viewed as a motley crew of war veterans, ex-convicts, and guns for hire recruited from the British urban underclass, their names a byword for brutality.

New studies have shed more light on who these paramilitaries were, arguing that they were not ex-convicts, but ordinary men 'looking for a new start in life' at a time of high unemployment. They were attracted to Ireland by high RIC salaries, which had more than doubled in 1920. The majority were war veterans who hailed from British cities; a disproportionate number were from London and the surrounding counties. The vast majority—80 per cent—were Anglicans. Just over half were semi- or unskilled workers, 35 per cent were skilled workers, and just 6 per cent were clerks/shopkeepers. This occupational profile holds some similarities with the Dublin IRA, though there were more clerks in republican ranks, but contrasts with the middle-class provincial IRA described by Peter Hart. Apart from rural/urban antipathies, the Black and Tans were likely considered to be social inferiors by their opponents, and also by the Irish-born RIC, who hailed mainly from farming backgrounds. The Auxiliaries were mainly ex-officers, though were not from elite backgrounds, many having climbed the ranks during the First World War.[51]

From the summer of 1920 the 'reprisals' of the Black and Tans, Irish-born policemen, and particularly the Auxiliaries, descended into state terrorism, comprising collective punishment, indiscriminate violence, and torture. Dwellings, businesses, and factories were destroyed, burnings and sackings took place in Mallow, Cork, Tuam, Balbriggan, and Tralee, among other towns, and civilians were targeted in numerous instances. Many nationalists' unease with IRA violence was frequently forgotten in outrage at the brutality of British reprisals, which forced people to take sides and increased civilian support for the Volunteers.[52] The disarray was facilitated by official policy that refused to fight a 'war' against rebels. The army was for external confrontations; internal security required a 'policeman's job' that involved a blind eye or unwillingness to enforce military discipline on paramilitaries. Transgressions were overlooked and the indisciplined Auxiliaries operated with almost free rein, frequently crossing the line of acceptable behaviour. Thresholds of violence broke down, creating a scenario where things easily got out of hand and all sides became caught up in a brutalizing cycle of violence.[53] People on each side sought to take the initiative, at times improvising new and spontaneous tactics without seeking approval from superior officers.

Men and women experienced war differently, and violence against women is relatively under-explored. In contrast to some contemporary paramilitary conflicts in post-war Europe, where rape was a weapon to assert dominance, few instances of sexual violence were recorded in Ireland. Speaking in 1921, the Irish Chief Secretary asserted there had 'never been one bit of evidence' that women were sexually assaulted by Crown forces, while the American Commission on Conditions in Ireland also commended paramilitaries for their honourable behaviour. Yet, Ann Matthews has argued that few reports of rape surfaced because families were extremely reluctant to report it due to the social consequences publicity might bring for the victims. Margaret Connory, a member of the Irish Women's Franchise League, investigated sexual assault in 1921 and maintained that 'women and children were in a constant state of depression and nervous breakdown … women know that it is during curfew hours attempts of a sexual nature have been made'.[54] Before female searchers were introduced in 1921, the Black and Tans' power to stop and search anyone on the street left women in vulnerable positions and in some rural areas women reportedly stopped walking the roads. The most common form of police violence against women was rough hair shaving, designed to humiliate abettors of the IRA and send a message to other transgressors. This tactic was also widely employed by the IRA against the girlfriends of policemen and soldiers, domestic servants who worked in barracks, and women who supplied provisions to the Crown forces. Arson attacks also targeted the wives and widows of constables. In 1920, the IRA issued orders that female spies were not to be executed, unlike their male counterparts, but some women were killed and as with men there were sometimes ambiguities as to whether they were informers. Overall, about 10 per cent of civilian casualties were female.[55]

Conventional explanations for the excesses of the Black and Tans' behaviour contended that they were victims of the experience of fighting in the First World War, which desensitized them to violence by the time they arrived in Ireland. Recent literature has nuanced this brutalization thesis. The war had not necessarily desensitized the veterans who came to Ireland, but it shaped their ideas of what war was. They had become used to fighting, but a different kind of fighting that entailed large battlefields where roughly symmetrical forces in uniform would engage according to rules of war, often in long distance artillery exchanges.[56] The War of Independence was an asymmetrical confrontation with no frontier, where distinctions between combatants and non-combatants were unclear and killing occurred at close proximity. The contrast bred frustrations that shaped the Black and Tans' perception of the IRA guerrillas as cowardly, dishonourable, and failing to adhere to the rules of warfare.[57] Yet there is also a danger of over-emphasizing the paramilitaries' backgrounds in the First World War. Leeson has argued that the reprisals and atrocities carried out by the Black and Tans and Auxiliaries are better explained by the confusing environment they found in Ireland, an environment where the roles of policemen and soldiers were blurred, where the enemy could be selling you cigarettes or painting your barracks wall. Irish-born RIC constables who did not fight in the war, he contends, instigated reprisals to a greater extent than has been traditionally acknowledged.[58]

One is tempted to then ask the question: if the First World War had never happened would the violence of the Irish War of Independence have been different? The war of 1914–18 undoubtedly triggered and shaped key events in the Irish Revolution, but was the violence more intense and ugly because of it? The First World War did not conclude a long period of regular warfare where battles were symmetrical affairs, fought according to codified rules of war. The irregular warfare of the post-war years was not new and transgressions of the line between combatants and non-combatants were common in European colonial conflicts during the nineteenth century. Collective reprisals and indiscriminate violence often characterized the actions of imperial armies because they were the 'only means these armies had to defeat elusive, highly mobile peoples who were adept practitioners of guerrilla warfare'.[59] In the 1880s, Britain was engaged in conflicts in Egypt and Sudan which were not symmetrical affairs. During the Second Boer War, which came between the 1899 and 1907 Hague Conventions to codify the rules of war, British forces met guerrilla tactics with extreme violence and collective punishment. The soldiers fighting in colonial wars were often reinforced by 'hordes of irregulars' and mercenaries. In the absence of vast numbers of unemployed war veterans, empires still found people to do their dirty work.[60]

The truce of July 1921 calmed the violence in Ireland, if not stopping it completely, and the war officially ended with the 1921 Anglo-Irish Treaty, the signing of which was hastened by Lloyd George's ultimatum of 'war within in three days'. From the beginning of 1917 to the end of 1921, 2141 people were killed in Ireland by political violence. Of that number, 898 were civilians. The war was intense in Dublin and Cork, two counties that accounted for 804 fatalities.[61] The treaty gave dominion status to the Irish Free State within the Commonwealth, but allowed Britain to retain some naval ports. Members of the new Irish parliament were required to take a diluted oath to the King of the United Kingdom. The boundary of Northern Ireland was discussed but partition itself was not negotiated as it had already been enforced by the 1920 Government of Ireland Act.[62]

A disproportionate amount of historical writing on the War of Independence and Civil War has focused on Cork, which saw high levels of violence in city and county, yet from mid 1920 to mid 1922 Belfast was the most violent place in the country. Over 460 people died in that city during this period, while 80 fatalities occurred elsewhere in Northern Ireland. Peter Hart acknowledged this in his comparison of north and south, observing that 'in either relative or absolute terms, northern Catholics were far worse off than their southern Protestant counterparts'. At the same time, while hotly contested in Cork, sectarian killing in Northern Ireland after 1920 is less explored and much less publically debated, reflecting what one study argues is a ' "partitionist" outlook, fueled by a distinct Southern progressiveness about the events of the revolutionary period'.[63]

Violence assumed different forms in the north of the island. There were few Black and Tans in northern counties, and while the IRA and Ulster Special Constabulary engaged in reprisals against each other and civilians, violence in Ulster was distinguished by higher instances of rioting, which held a comparatively longer tradition in the province. IRA flying columns operated with nothing resembling their effectiveness in the south, but after the truce recruitment almost doubled and activity intensified. The organization was demoralized, however, by active repression and internment in deplorable conditions aboard the ship *Argenta*. Some IRA attacks during the border campaign were successful in isolation, but they provoked fierce unrest in Belfast. In February 1922 a gunfight at the train station in Clones left one IRA man dead and killed four members of the Ulster Special Constables (USC), wounding many more. The attack triggered a deadly backlash in Belfast and in the following weeks forty-three people were killed, including six children who were killed by a bomb thrown into a Catholic schoolyard. During the month of March fifty-nine people were killed in the city; in May the number increased to seventy-five. Religious tensions were at play and inter-communal violence was more prevalent in Ulster in comparison with the rest of the country. Religion was also a factor in attacks and expulsions in rural communities close to both sides of the border, though the extent to which traditional agrarianism played a role requires further exploration.[64]

The Anglo-Irish Treaty was endorsed by the general election of June 1922, but the failure to achieve the republic and the presence of the oath of allegiance led to a Civil War that lasted from June 1922 to May 1923. Much historical writing on the Civil War has formed part of the local studies of the Irish Revolution and illuminated divergent experiences of the conflict. Some areas of intense activity during the War of Independence emerged relatively unscathed, such as Longford, while others, such as Sligo or south Wexford, were more violent during the Civil War than during 1919–21.[65] Stand-alone investigations of the conflict at the national level, however, have been rare since the publication of Michael Hopkinson's *Green Against Green* (1988). Indicative of this relative lacuna is how estimates of fatalities still vary widely, from 927 to over 3000.[66] The lack of attention afforded the Civil War is partly explained by the context of the Troubles, during which some historians viewed the anti-treaty republicans as anti-democratic and as precursors of the Provisional IRA. Yet, more recent studies have also asked questions about the democratic credentials of the Free State, considering that the fear of British violence was a factor in some people accepting it.

Writing on the Civil War has progressed substantially from the Collins versus de Valera paradigm. Bill Kissane's political science approach eschewed the personalization of the fighting in key figures and investigated the Civil War as a conflict about variant attitudes to self-determination and empire that started in 'the institutional vacuum' of 1922. The republicans' guerrilla campaign, similar to 1919–21, aimed to make the country ungovernable and provoke counter-productive repression, but their local rural bases were isolated from each other and by the autumn of 1922 resistance was restricted to pockets of the south-west. The republican side was fundamentally weak due to the absence of a constructive alternative to the Free State, serious difficulties in resource mobilization, and, above all, a war-weary public.[67] This was a war that nobody seemed to want. True, some republicans emphatically rejected the treaty and militantly opposed its implementation, yet there are difficulties in assessing grassroots opinion for either side. For example, the apparently outright vote against the treaty at the Cumann na mBan convention of February 1922 was unrepresentative of the countrywide membership, reflecting the Dublin leadership's views rather than those of the rank-and-file.[68]

During the Civil War the Provisional Government sought to self-consciously establish to the world Ireland's readiness for self-government. In doing so, they demonstrated they would not shirk methods of state terrorism to uphold central authority and law and order. In December 1922, four republican leaders were executed in an official but illegal act in response to the killing of one member of the Dáil. Within six months, the notorious number of seventy-seven people had been executed, more than during the War of Independence. Unofficial executions also occurred and, in March 1923, eight republican prisoners were brutally executed in an infamous act of revenge in Kerry when they were tied to a landmine that was then detonated. In the next four days, a further nine prisoners were killed in similar circumstances.[69] A key personality in these atrocities was Major-General Paddy Daly, a veteran of Michael Collins's 'Squad'. The following June he was involved in another incident known as the 'Kenmare Case' when, in a nocturnal visit, Daly and two soldiers dragged two women from their house, beat and flogged them with belts, then smeared their heads with axle grease. Reports as to whether they were also sexually assaulted vary. The case was reported, but Daly was not removed from his command by Richard Mulcahy.[70] These incidents were a grim indication of the indiscipline in the Free State army by the spring of 1923.

As in the War of Independence the south-west saw high levels of unrest, but the manner of violence often differed. Arson attacks on the 'big houses' of the Protestant gentry occurred in 1920–21, but they increased markedly during the Civil War, a development Hart linked to sectarian prejudice. In an alternative reading, James Donnolly has contended that big houses were targeted because they had billeted Crown forces, or had simply been inspected by soldiers for possible occupation, or the owners served as magistrates in local courts. Moreover, the 'big house' was symbolic of the old landed elite and 'agrarian considerations exercised considerable influence over the actions of the Cork IRA brigades', and arson attacks resembled the nineteenth-century tactics of moonlighters or Ribbonmen.[71] In the border counties there was 'certainly more than a hint of agrarianism' about attacks on the Protestant gentry. A number of Protestant families moved across the border from Monaghan to Fermanagh during the period 1919–23, yet attacks on big houses were not as intense as in Cork and there was no revolution in land-ownership. Vacated Protestant farms were typically incorporated by neighbouring Protestant farmers.[72]

The war ended in April 1923 and Cumann na nGaedheal began to concentrate on institution building in the 26 counties. The nature of official decision-making and repression during the Civil War, John Regan has argued, marked the beginning of a conservative counter-revolution that endured into the following decade and consolidated the power of the Catholic middle class.[73] Whether this was the case, the psychological impact of the manner of violence was immense in the aftermath of the Civil War. The snapping of the fraternal bonds forged during the War of Independence led to a bitter conflict that, in the words of Joe Lee, turned 'heart to stone'.[74] Throughout the twentieth century the divisions of the war were repeatedly evoked and shaped party politics, but the nature of the fighting itself was 'distorted, misunderstood', but most of all, 'ignored'.[75]

V

The historiography of the Irish Revolution is presently undergoing transformation thanks to the new availability of sources and digitization of archival material. The Bureau of Military History archive, which includes 1773 witness statements, has already started to filter through in publications.[76] The 285 000 detailed files in the Military Service Pensions Collection also promise to change our understanding of the period, lessening dependence on memoir literature and giving us new tools for reconstructing perspectives from grassroots participants. These sources are also revealing in terms of how the war was experienced on an everyday level in the years 1916 and 1919–23, but beyond these flashpoints, historians must also reconstruct the everyday experience of revolution during the more mundane years. Generational approaches also promise new vistas on the period by constructing group biographies of the revolutionary generation, examining their education, family relations, intellectual influences, travels, participation in clubs, reading groups, and militant political organizations.[77]

When looking back on the events of 1913, the founder of the Irish Citizen Army, Jack White, remarked that in Ireland 'real upheavals come in unison with worldwide movements'.[78] Historians have acknowledged the importance of external factors in Ireland during this period, yet accounts of the Revolution have typically adopted national or local frameworks. Emerging historiography has begun to situate the Irish Revolution in wider British, Atlantic, European, and imperial contexts, establishing an agenda for transnational research that contributes to reconfiguring our understanding of the period. Transnational history is best understood as a complement to national and local perspectives, rather than a replacement for them. To vary the scales of analysis—ranging from the local to the global—is at the heart of the approach, but the default scale is no longer the nation-state.[79] The Irish Revolution lends itself to transnational analysis in a threefold manner: first, by investigating how the movement and experiences of people outside Ireland before and during the years 1912–23 shaped actions when they returned; second, by tracing parallels or connections between the Irish and other cases of paramilitary violence in post-war Europe; and third, by considering how the conditions of globalization and news of far-off events influenced the thinking of government and resistance.

The syndicalist currents in the 1913 lockout found parallels in France, Italy, Britain, and the United States, while many of the personalities of 1913 spent considerable time outside Ireland.[80] Jack White was born in Antrim, attended an elite public school in England, then Sandhurst Academy, before fighting in the Second Boer War. Leaving the army, he travelled in Bohemia and Canada and lived on a Tolstoyan commune in England. He was active in Ireland 1913–16 and later fought with the anarchist CNT-FAI during the Spanish Civil War. Mobility was characteristic of the personalities of the Irish Revolution. James Connolly, another British Army veteran, was radicalized in Scotland before his involvement in New York with the Irish Socialist Federation and the Industrial Workers of the World (IWW), the syndicalist organization that the Cork-born Mary 'Mother' Jones helped to found. James Larkin became a labour agitator in Liverpool and in 1914 moved to the United States where he also joined the IWW. Interestingly, the key personality of the IWW, Bill Haywood, was in Paris in 1913 when he heard of the lockout in Dublin, and travelled to the city with 1000 francs collected for Irish workers. Haywood was heartened to see a large IWW sign when he entered Liberty Hall, but later discovered the letters represented the Irish Women Workers' Union.[81]

Individual mobility and connections with the Irish diaspora were an important factor in shaping revolutionary mentalities. Many key personalities of the period spent significant periods of time abroad and Fearghal McGarry has pointed out that five of the seven signatories of the 1916 Proclamation spent time in the United States. Tom Clarke, for example, returned to Ireland in 1907. He had originally joined the IRB in Tyrone before conspiring in Brooklyn in the early 1880s to bomb British cities, which led to 15 years' imprisonment in Britain. IRA leader Michael Collins' 'immersion in London's émigré nationalist community... was central to the making of Ireland's most important revolutionary career'.[82] Irish diaspora nationalism has been written about extensively in the context of how it developed in separate countries and how it provided material aid to the home movement, but transnational approaches seek, first, to integrate nationalist activity abroad with events at home and, second, to investigate how revolutionary lives and ideas were constructed in the movement back and forth between Ireland and emigrant communities, how the tensions of local situations in Boston, Glasgow, London, or Wellington shaped revolutionary mentalities in Ireland.[83] Beyond diasporic connections, studies have begun to trace the circulation and transfer, or failed transfer, of intellectual currents in Ireland and how they influenced thinking during this period.[84]

What happened in Ireland held its own peculiarities and idiosyncrasies, but the chronology of developments suggests parallels with other national and regional conflicts in post-war Europe, a period when things seemed to be up for grabs, when opportunities seemed poised to be taken by new movements. The Irish case has been somewhat neglected in seminal comparative studies of revolutionary violence and war by Tilly, Hobsbawm, or Kalyvas, yet new studies are addressing this gap. One study of the long twentieth century has identified five overlapping 'waves' of political violence in Europe, the second wave occurring from 1917 till the mid 1920s and distinguished by unprecedented levels of revolutionary violence. In post-war regimes that 'appeared to lack both solidity and legitimacy, the incentive to remain within the conventional boundaries of political legality had largely disappeared', and the resort to violence became less exceptional than before the First World War.[85] Historians are making inroads toward situating the Irish Revolution in this cycle of European violence, through paired comparison or, as in John Horne and Robert Gerwarth's collective project, through exploring parallels in paramilitary violence across disparate European cases in the context of 'revolution, imperial collapse and ethnic conflict'.[86]

In comparative light, the moderation of the Irish Revolution is striking. Joe Lee has drawn our attention to Finland, a country of comparable size to Ireland, which lost 36 000 people to civil war in six months in the winter of 1918, over 1 per cent of the population. The majority of combatants on both sides were not veterans of the First World War, but the conflict assumed its own brutalizing dynamics.[87] Tim Wilson's comparison of Upper Silesia and Ulster revealed that proportionately 'violent death was nearly three times more common' in the former region. In the larger countries of Italy, the Ukraine, and Poland, the scale of paramilitary violence against armed combatants and unarmed civilians between 1919 and 1922 prolifically exceeded that in Ireland.[88] Contrasting body counts is, however, a small aspect of comparative history which can reveal insights into why certain forms of violence flared up and then faded; how distinctions between military and civilian were eroded; how violence was influenced by issues of class, gender, and ethnicity; the place of labour unrest in the larger picture of political violence; how paramilitaries came to view themselves as pre-state armies of newly defined communities; and why some conflicts resulted in stable democracies but not others.

Paramilitary police were an important aspect of strategies to maintain the internal and external security of the British empire. Some members of the Auxiliaries served in Burma, Canada, and one in the Chinese Labour Corps before coming to Ireland, and in turn, lessons learned during the War of Independence transferred to other parts of empire. In 1922 over six hundred former Black and Tans joined the Palestinian Gendarmerie. In the 1930s, colonial officials in India drew parallels between the IRA's guerrilla war and revolutionary violence in Bengal.[89] The use of paramilitary police to contain strikes in Britain in the 1920s revealed a mechanism of maintaining order that was developed in the colonies and then circulated back to the metropole. The War Office saw a necessity for 'some efficient force of a semi military character' to face down the red threat posed by strikes in British cities.[90]

The conditions of globalization in the early twentieth century influenced the development of the Irish Revolution. Hopes and fears were shaped by the news of distant events, even when no concrete connections existed. The 1917 Russian Revolution generated palpable anxieties about threats to the political and social order. Bolshevism quickly became 'synonymous with the elusive threats and underhand enemies that menaced European post-war societies'.[91] The Bolshevik threat in Ireland was more speculation and propaganda than genuine; nonetheless, elements in the British forces perceived Ireland to be one battlefield in a transnational struggle that stretched across Liverpool, New York, Cairo, Calcutta, and Moscow. Henry Wilson believed 'he was fighting anarchy and Bolshevism in Ireland just as he was fighting anarchy and Bolshevism on the Liverpool docks and in the Lancashire mines, as sure as the *Union Civiques* were in France, as sure as the *Freikorps* or the White Army itself'.[92]

Transnational perspectives also open up paths to examining how the revolution was perceived externally. We know that the Bolsheviks came close to recognizing an Irish state in 1920 through the efforts and skill of republicans, and Ireland was included as one of the 'oppressed nations of the world', along with India, in an appeal to Wilson's fourteen points.[93] Exchanges also occurred where there was no direct communication. Michael Silvestri has revealed how Irish republican nationalism provided inspiration for Bengali nationalists in the 1930s, who admired the martyrdom of the 1916 rebels and viewed Dan Breen's *My Fight for Irish Freedom* as a model for revolutionary action, translating it into Hindi, Punjabi, and Tamil.[94] The role of the press was crucial in shaping how the Irish Revolution was perceived externally and how international developments influenced matters at home. The digitization of newspapers is far from complete, yet ongoing projects have enabled research that can investigate the significance of different provincial, national, British, and international newspapers during the Irish Revolution.

One key challenge when adopting a transnational approach to the Irish Revolution, it seems, is how to combine broad perspectives with the intricate, local detail that continues to be illuminated by the county study. There are legitimate concerns that local complexity may get lost in more wide-ranging vistas, but transnational history does not aim to erase the nation or the locality. It is possible to safeguard against the burial of the peculiarities of county experience beneath broader hypotheses. Utilizing a transnational lens provides a tangential perspective that, depending on the questions asked, can zoom in and out from large-scale questions to small-scale analyses of human agency. The local study or the biography can reveal how transnational processes play out at the micro-scale. To turn the tables, studies that are primarily local or national in scope also need to confront how experiences outside Ireland shaped the actions and thoughts of the individuals in their story, and how news of events in distant lands like Russia or America impacted on local situations.[95] Exploring the manifold aspects of the Irish Revolution necessitates some transnational frame of reference that balances larger contexts with the rich detail excavated by the county study. Alternating the scale of analysis—between local, regional, national, transnational, global—creates possibilities to achieve such a balance while working closely with primary sources.

Notes

1. David Fitzpatrick, *Politics and Irish Life: Provincial Experiences of War and Revolution*, Dublin, 1977. To coincide with the Irish 'Decade of Centenaries', the publisher Four Courts Press has recently commissioned thirty-two county studies for the series 'The Irish Revolution, 1912–1923', edited by Mary Ann Lyons and Daithí Ó Corráin. My thanks to Enda Delaney, David Fitzpatrick, and Fearghal McGarry for their advice while I wrote this chapter.
2. The Ulster question and the First World War have been treated elsewhere in the volume, Here attention turns principally to the years 1918–23 after some consideration of 1913 and 1916.

3. *Report of the departmental committee appointed by the Local Government Board for Ireland to inquire into the housing conditions of the working classes in the city of Dublin*, HC, Reports Of Commissioners, 1914, 20; *The Times* (London), 22 October 1913; Jacinta Prunty, *Dublin Slums, 1800–1925, a Study in Urban Geography*, (Dublin, 1998).

4. Francis Devine (ed), *A Capital in Conflict: Dublin City and the 1913 Lockout*, (Dublin, 2013); 'Lockout 1913: Special Issue', *History Ireland*, 21, (2013); Emmet O'Connor, *A Labour History of Ireland, 1824–2000*, (Dublin, 2011), 92–5; Donal Nevin (ed), *James Larkin: Lion of the Fold*, (Dublin, 2006); Padraig Yeates, *Lockout: Dublin, 1913*, (Dublin, 2001).

5. O'Connor, *A Labour History of Ireland*, 95–6; Adrian Grant, *Irish Socialist Republicanism, 1909–36*, (Dublin, 2012), 48–75.

6. Fearghal McGarry, *The Rising: Ireland: Easter 1916*, (Oxford, 2010), 38–9, 177–8.

7. Yeates, *Lockout*, xi, 75, 585.

8. Diarmaid Ferriter, *The Transformation of Ireland, 1900–2000*, (London, 2004), 256.

9. Karen Hunt, 'Women, solidarity and the 1913 Dublin Lockout: Dora Montefiore and the 'Save the Kiddies' scheme', in Devine, *A Capital in Conflict*, 107–128.

10. Yeates, *Lockout*, 312–13; Tom Garvin, *Nationalist Revolutionaries in Ireland, 1858–1928*, (Dublin, 2005) ed., 72.

11. Owen McGee, *The IRB: The Irish Republican Brotherhood from the Land League to Sinn Féin*, (Dublin, 2005); James McConnel, ' "Fenians at Westminster": The Irish parliamentary party and the legacy of the new departure', *Irish Historical Studies*, 34, (2004), 41–64.

12. Some historians argue that the First World War was a causal factor of the Irish Revolution; see David Fitzpatrick, *The Two Irelands, 1912–1939*, (Oxford, 1998), 44–114.

13. Charles Townshend, *Easter 1916: The Irish Rebellion*, (London, 2005), xvi; John Horne (ed), *Our War: Ireland and the Great War*, (Dublin, 2008); Keith Jeffery, *Ireland and the Great War*, (Cambridge, 2000).

14. McGarry, *The Rising*, 204.

15. Roisín Higgins, *Transforming 1916: Meaning, Memory and the Fiftieth Anniversary of the Easter Rising*, (Cork, 2013); Gabriel Doherty, 'The commemoration of the ninetieth anniversary of the Easter Rising' in Gabriel Doherty and Dermot Keogh (eds), *1916: the Long Revolution*, Cork, 2007, 376–407; Mary Daly and Margaret O'Callaghan (eds), *1916 in 1966: commemorating the Easter Rising*, (Dublin, 2007).

16. *Irish Examiner*, 18 November 2010; *The Irish Times*, 18 November 2010.

17. This important source has its drawbacks. The statements were recorded some three decades after the events, the project was not comprehensive, and not all veterans participated. See Eve Morrison, 'The Bureau of Military History and Female Republican Activism, 1913–23', in Maryann Gialanella Valiulis (ed), *Gender and Power in Irish History*, (Dublin, 2009), 59–83 (59–60).

18. Ruth Dudley Edwards, *Patrick Pearse: the Triumph of Failure*, (London, 1977).

19. McGarry, *The Rising*, 4, 176, 183.

20. *The Irish Volunteer*, 15 April 1916.

21. McGarry, *The Rising*, 162–165; Louise Ryan, ' "Furies" and "Die-hards": Women and Irish Republicanism in the Early Twentieth Century', *Gender & History*, 11, 1999, 256–75; Margaret Ward, *Unmanageable Revolutionaries: Women and Irish Nationalism*, (London, 1983).

22. Gerard MacAtasney, *Tom Clarke: Life, Liberty, Revolution*, (Dublin, 2013).

23. McGee, *The IRB*, 355–6. McGarry, *The Rising*, 135, 160; Garvin, *Nationalist Revolutionaries*, 127–33, 138–41.

24. Seán McConville, *Irish Political Prisoners 1848–1922: Theatres of War*, (London, 2003), 405–768.

25. Alvin Jackson, *Home Rule: An Irish History, 1800–2000*, (Oxford, 2004), 186, 200–2.

26. Max Weber, 'Politics as a Vocation', in *From Max Weber: Essays in Sociology*, (London, 1998), 77–128 (78).

27. Fitzpatrick, *Politics and Irish Life*.

28. Two important exceptions to the county approach are Michael Laffan, *The Resurrection of Ireland: the Sinn Féin Party, 1916–1923*, Cambridge, 1999; Ronan Fanning, *Fatal Path: British Government and Irish Revolution*, (London, 2013).

29. Peter Hart, *The I.R.A. and its Enemies: Violence and Community in Cork 1916–1923*, (Oxford, 1998), 18.

30. Peter Hart, *The I.R.A. at War 1916–1923*, (Oxford, 2003), 121, 131; Garvin, *Nationalist Revolutionaries*, 117–19.

31. David Fitzpatrick, 'Emigration, 1871–1921', in W.E. Vaughan, *A New History of Ireland: Volume VI: Ireland under the Union, II: 1870–1921*, (Oxford, 1989), 631–2; Laffan, *Resurrection of Ireland*, 188–9; Hart, *The I.R.A. at War*, 50–1.

32. Morrison, 'The Bureau of Military History and Female Republican Activism, 1913–23', 59–83; Cal McCarthy, *Cumann na mBan and the Irish Revolution, 1914–1923*, (Cork, 2007), 114–170; Ann Matthews, *Renegades: Irish Republican Women*, (Dublin, 2010), 238–265.

33. Joost Augusteijn, *From Public Defiance to Guerrilla Warfare: the Experience of Ordinary Volunteers in the Irish War of Independence 1916–1921*, (Dublin, 1996), 360; idem, 'Accounting for the Emergence of Violent Activism among Irish Revolutionaries, 1916–1921', *Irish Historical Studies*, 35, 2007, 327–44.

34. Marie Coleman, *County Longford and the Irish Revolution, 1910–1923*, (Dublin, 2003), 172–8; Fitzpatrick, *Politics and Irish Life*, passim.

35. Fergus Campbell, *Land and Revolution: Nationalist Politics in the West of Ireland, 1891–1921*, (Oxford, 2005), 226–285, 263, 302; Tony Varley, 'A Region of Sturdy Smallholders? Western Nationalists and Agrarian Politics during the First World War', *Journal of the Galway Archaeological and Historical Society*, 55, 2003, 127–50. Others have emphasized the socially conservative aspects to the Irish Revolution: see Fitzpatrick, *Politics and Irish Life*, 232; Laffan, *Resurrection of Ireland*, 315.

36. John O'Callaghan, *Revolutionary Limerick: the Republican Campaign for Independence in Limerick, 1913–1921*, (Dublin, 2010), 192.

37. Anne Dolan, 'Killing and Bloody Sunday, November 1920', *The Historical Journal*, 49, 2006, 789–810, (810).

38. Hart, *The I.R.A. and its Enemies*, 17.

39. Fearghal McGarry, *Eoin Duffy: a Self Made Hero*, (Oxford, 2005), 53–62.

40. John Borgonovo, *Spies, Informers, and the 'Anti-Sinn Féin Society': The Intelligence War in Cork City, 1920–1921*, (Dublin, 2007); Coleman, *County Longford*, 155–157.

41. Hart, *The I.R.A. and its Enemies*, 21–38.

42. Meda Ryan, 'The Kilmichael Ambush, 1920: Exploring the "Provocative Chapters"', *History*, 92, 2007, 235–249; B.P. Murphy and Niall Meehan, *Troubled History: 10th anniversary critique of Peter Hart's The IRA and Its Enemies*, (Cork, 2008); more recently see Eve Morrison, 'Kilmichael Revisited: Tom Barry and the "False Surrender"', in David Fitzpatrick, *Terror in Ireland 1916–1923*, (Dublin, 2012), 158–180; John Borgonovo, 'Review article: Revolutionary Violence and Irish historiography', *Irish Historical Studies*, 2012, 325–31; John Regan, 'West Cork and the Writing of History', *Dublin Review of Books*, 28, 2013.

43. D.M. Leeson, *Black and Tans: British Police and Auxiliaries in the Irish War of Independence*, Oxford, 2011, 148, 151, 261; O'Callaghan, *Revolutionary Limerick*, 139–49; Eichenberg, 'Paramilitary violence', 239.

44. Hart, *The I.R.A. at War, 1916–1923*, 237, 245–6.

45. Hart, *The I.R.A. and its Enemies*, 288.

46. John Regan, 'The "Bandon Valley Massacre" as a historical problem', *History*, 97, 2012, 70–98; idem, 'Dr Jekyll and Mr Hyde: "the Two Histories"', *History Ireland*, 20, 1, 2012; David Fitzpatrick, 'Ethnic Cleansing, Ethical Smearing and Irish Historians', *History*, 98, 2013, 135–44; idem, 'Dr Regan and Mr Snide', *History Ireland*, 20, 2, 2012, 12–13. For sectarian killing in Northern Ireland see Lynch, 'Explaining the Altnaveigh Massacre', passim.

47. Michael Mann, *The Dark Side Of Democracy: Explaining Ethnic Cleansing*, Cambridge, 2005, 353–427; Brian Hanley, 'Terror in Twentieth Century Ireland', in Fitzpatrick, *Terror in Ireland*, 10–25, (13).

48. David Fitzpatrick, 'The Spectre of "Ethnic Cleansing" in Revolutionary Ireland', *Bulletin of the Methodist Historical Society of Ireland*, 18, 2013, 5–70; Andy Bielenberg, 'Exodus: The Emigration of Southern Irish Protestants During the Irish War of Independence and the Civil War', *Past and Present*, 218, 2013, 199–233.

49. The historian Ruth Dudley Edwards claimed the film was a 'travesty of history' by a 'morally lazy' director. These criticisms were all the stranger for the fact that she had not seen the film and expressed no desire to do so, but still felt qualified to criticize it. Ruth Dudley Edwards, 'Why does Ken Loach loathe his country so much?', *Daily Mail*, 30 May 2006; 'What about making Black and Tans: the movie?' *The Guardian*, 6 June 2006.

50. Emmet O'Connor, *Syndicalism in Ireland, 1917–23*, Cork, 1988; Charles Townshend, 'The Irish Railway Strike of 1920: Industrial Action and Civil Resistance in the Struggle for Independence', *Irish Historical Studies*, 22, 1979, 265–82.

51. Leeson, *Black and Tans*, 75, 104–107; Anne Dolan, 'The British culture of paramilitary violence in the Irish war of independence', in John Horne and Robert Gerwarth (eds), *War in Peace: Paramilitary Violence in Europe after the Great War*, Oxford, 2012, 200–15; W. J. Lowe, 'The war against the RIC, 1919–21', *Éire-Ireland*, 37, 2002, 79–117; Charles Townshend, *The British Campaign in Ireland 1919–1921: the Development of Political and Military Policies* (Oxford, 1975).

52. James S. Donnelly Jr. '"Unofficial" British Reprisals and IRA Provocations, 1919–20: The Cases of Three Cork Towns', *Éire-Ireland*, 45, 2010, 152–97.

53. Leeson, *Black and Tans*, 223; Dolan, 'The British Culture of Paramilitary Violence', 202–4.

54. Quoted in Matthews, *Renegades*, 266, 269; T. K. Wilson, *Frontiers of Violence: Conflict and Identity in Ulster and Upper Silesia 1918–1922* (Oxford, 2010), 166. In Ulster some cases of sexual assault by B Specials were publicized. See Robert Lynch, 'Explaining the Altnaveigh Massacre, June 1922', *Eire-Ireland*, 45, 2010, 184–210, (196–201).

55. Matthews, *Renegades*, 269–79; Leeson, *Black and Tans*, 62; O'Halpin, Counting terror', 154; Anne Dolan, 'Ending a War in a "Sportsmanlike Manner": The Milestone of Revolution, 1919–23', in T. E. Hachey, *Turning Points in Twentieth Century Irish History* (Dublin, 2011), 21–38.

56. Roger Chickering and Stig Förster, *Great War, Total War: Combat and Mobilization on the Western Front, 1914–1918* (Cambridge, 2000).

57. Dolan, 'The British Culture of Paramilitary Violence', 205; Paul McMahon, *British Spies and Irish Rebels: British Intelligence and Ireland, 1916–1945* (Woodbridge, 2008), 165; Julia

Eichenberg, 'Soldiers to Civilians, Civilians to Soldiers: Poland and Ireland after the First World War', in Gerwarth and Horne, *War in Peace*, 184–99, 186–7.

58. Leeson, *Black and Tans*, 2.

59. Bruce Vandervort, 'War and imperial expansion', in R. Chickering, D. Showalter, and H. van de Ven (eds), *The Cambridge History of War*, IV (Cambridge, 2012), 69–93 (93).

60. Ibid., 84–5; Denis Judd and Keith Surridge, *The Boer War* (New York, 2003).

61. O'Halpin, 'Counting Terror', 152–3.

62. Nicolas Mansergh, 'The Government of Ireland Act 1920: Its Origins and Purposes—the Working of the 'Official' Mind' in Diana Mansergh (ed), *Nationalism and Independence: Selected Irish Papers by Nicolas Mansergh*, Cork, 1997, 64–92; Lee, *Ireland, 1912–1985*, 50–4.

63. Lynch, 'Explaining the Altnaveigh Massacre', 187; Hart, *The I.R.A. at War*, 243.

64. Robert Lynch, *The Northern I.R.A. and the Early Years of Partition, 1920–22*, Dublin, 2006, 107–28, 220; Wilson, *Frontiers of Violence*, 101; Hart, *The I.R.A. at War*, 249–50; Fitzpatrick, *The Two Irelands*, 118–23.

65. Michael Farry, *The Aftermath of Revolution: Sligo, 1921–23*, Dublin, 2000; Coleman, *County Longford*, 167.

66. Hart, *The I.R.A. at War*, 64–73; Sean Connolly (ed), *The Oxford Companion to Irish History* (Oxford, 2011) ed., 277.

67. Bill Kissane, *The Politics of the Irish Civil War*, Oxford, 2007, 232; David Fitzpatrick, *Harry Boland's Irish Revolution* (Cork, 2003), 306–20.

68. McCarthy, *Cumann na mBan*, 177.

69. Michael Hopkinson, *Green Against Green: The Irish Civil War*, Dublin, 2004 ed., 240–1.

70. *Dáil Éireann, Parliamentary Debates*, Vol. 8, 23 July 1924; *The Irish Times*, 24 July 2012.

71. James S. Donnolly Jr, 'Big House Burnings in County Cork during the Irish Revolution, 1920–21', *Éire-Ireland*, 47, 2012, 141–97.

72. Terence Dooley, *The Plight of Monaghan Protestants, 1912–26*, Dublin, 2000, 47, 58.

73. John Regan, *The Irish Counter Revolution 1921–1936* (Dublin, 1999).

74. Lee, *Ireland, 1912–1985*, 69.

75. Anne Dolan, *Commemorating the Irish Civil War: History and Memory, 1923–2000* (Cambridge, 2003), 2.

76. http://www.bureauofmilitaryhistory.ie/.

77. Roy Foster, 'Making a Revolutionary Generation in Ireland', *British Academy Review*, 21, 2013, 11–14.

78. Jack White, *Misfit: A Revolutionary Life* (Dublin, 2005) [1930], 98.

79. Niall Whelehan (ed), *Transnational Perspectives on Modern Irish History*, London, 2014.

80. Ralph Darlington, *Radical Unionism: The Rise and Fall of Revolutionary Syndicalism*, Chicago, 2013; Steven Hirsch and Lucian van der Walt (eds), *Anarchism and Syndicalism in the Colonial and Postcolonial World, 1870–1940* (Leiden, 2010).

81. Bill Haywood, *Bill Haywood's Book: the Autobiography of William D. Haywood* (New York, 1929), 273–4.

82. See the chapter by Fearghal McGarry in Whelehan, *Transnational Perspectives in Modern Irish History*; Gerard MacAtasney, *Tom Clarke: Life, Liberty, Revolution*, Dublin, 2013.

83. These themes are considered in some essays in Ruan O'Donnell (ed), *The Impact of the 1916 Rising: among the Nations*, Dublin 2008.

84. Garvin, *Nationalist Revolutionaries*, passim; Joost Augusteijn, 'Patrick Pearse: proto-fascist eccentric or mainstream European thinker?', *History Ireland*, 18, 2010; W. J. McCormack, *Dublin 1916: the French connection*, Dublin, 2012; MacAtasney, *Tom Clarke*.

85. Martin Conway and Robert Gerwarth, 'Revolution and counter-revolution', in Donald Bloxham and Robert Gerwarth (eds) *Political Violence in Twentieth-Century Europe*, Cambridge, 2011, 140–75, (153).

86. Robert Gerwarth and John Horne (eds), *War in Peace: Paramilitary Violence in Europe after the Great War*, Oxford, 2012, 7; Wilson, *Frontiers of Violence*; Julia Eichenberg, 'The Dark Side of Independence: Paramilitary Violence in Ireland and Poland after the First World War', *Contemporary European History*, 19, 2010, 231 248; Kissane, *Civil War*, 231.

87. Lee, *Ireland, 1912–1985*, 69, 527; Pertti Haapala and Marko Tikka, 'Revolution, Civil War, and Terror in Finland in 1918', in Horne and Gerwarth, *War in Peace*, 72–84.

88. Wilson, *Frontiers of Violence*, 5; Eichenberg, 'The Dark Side of Independence', 233; idem, 'Soldiers to Civilians, Civilians to Soldiers: Poland and Ireland after the First World War', in Gerwarth and Horne, *War in Peace*, 184–99; Gerwarth and Horne, *War in Peace*, 7.

89. Michael Silvestri, *Ireland and India: Nationalism, Empire and Memory*, Basingstoke, 2009, 46–75; A.D. Harvey, 'Who Were the Auxiliaries?' *The Historical Journal* 35, 1992, 665–9; Jane Leonard, ' "English Dogs" or "Poor Devils"? The Dead of Bloody Sunday Morning', in Fitzpatrick (ed), *Terror in Ireland*, 102–38; T. Bowden, *The Breakdown of Public Security; The Case of Ireland 1916–1921 and Palestine 1936–1939*, London, 1977.

90. Quoted in Keith Jeffery, 'The British Army and Internal Security 1919–1939', *The Historical Journal*, 24, 1981, 377–97, (394).

91. Robert Gerwarth and John Horne, 'Bolshevism as Fantasy: Fear of Revolution and Counter-Revolutionary Violence, 1917–1923', in Gerwarth and Horne (eds), *War in Peace*, 40–51.

92. Dolan, 'Paramilitary violence', 213; Richard Dawson, *Red Terror and Green: the Sinn Féin-Bolshevist Movement*, New York, 1920, 208–65.

93. Erez Manela, *The Wilsonian Promise: Self-Determination and the International Origins of Anticolonial Nationalism*, Oxford, 2007, 95–6.

94. Silvestri, *Ireland and India*, 46–75; Chiara Chini, 'Italy and the "Irish Risorgimento": Italian perspectives on the Irish War of Independence, 1919–21', in N. Carter, *Britain, Ireland and the Italian Risorgimento*, Basingstoke, 2014.

95. For a discussion of the interplay between the transnational and the local see Ian Tyrrell, 'Reflections on the Transnational Turn in United States History: theory and practice', *Journal of Global History*, 4, 2009, 453–74; Bernhard Struck, Kate Ferris, and Jacques Revel, 'Introduction: Space and Scale in Transnational History', *International History Review*, 33, 2011, 573–84.

Select Bibliography

Augusteijn, Joost, *From Public Defiance to Guerrilla Warfare: the Experience of Ordinary Volunteers in the Irish War of Independence 1916–1921*, Dublin, 1996.

Campbell, Fergus, *Land and Revolution: Nationalist Politics in the West of Ireland, 1891–1921*, Oxford, 2005.

Dolan, Anne, 'Killing and Bloody Sunday, November 1920', *The Historical Journal*, 49, 2006, 789–810.

Donnolly, James S, 'Big House Burnings in County Cork during the Irish Revolution, 1920–21', *Éire-Ireland*, 47, 2012, 141–97.

Fitzpatrick, David (ed), *Terror in Ireland 1916–1923*, Dublin, 2012.

Fitzpatrick, David, *Politics and Irish life 1913–1921. Provincial experience of war and revolution*, Cork, 1998 ed.

Garvin, Tom, *Nationalist Revolutionaries in Ireland, 1858–1928*, Dublin, 1987.

Hart, Peter, *The I.R.A. and its Enemies: Violence and Community in Cork 1916–1923*, Oxford, 1998.

Hart, Peter, *The I.R.A. at War 1916–1923*, Oxford, 2003.

Hopkinson, Michael, *Green against Green: the Irish Civil War*, Dublin, 1988.

Horne, John and Gerwarth, Robert (eds), *War in Peace: paramilitary violence in Europe after the Great War*, Oxford, 2012.

Kissane, Bill, *The Politics of the Irish Civil War*, Oxford, 2007.

Laffan, Michael, *The Resurrection of Ireland: The Sinn Féin Party 1916–1923*, Cambridge, 1999.

Leeson, D.M., *Black and Tans: British Police and Auxiliaries in the Irish War of Independence*, Oxford, 2011.

McGarry, Fearghal, *The Rising. Ireland: Easter 1916*, Oxford, 2010.

O'Connor, Emmet, *Syndicalism in Ireland, 1917–23*, Cork, 1988.

Townshend, Charles, *Easter 1916. The Irish Rebellion*, London, 2005.

Wilson, T.K., *Frontiers of Violence: Conflict and Identity in Ulster and Upper Silesia 1918–1922*, Oxford, 2010.

Yeates, Padraig, *Lockout: Dublin, 1913*, Dublin, 2001.

DOMINION, REPUBLIC, AND HOME RULE: THE TWO IRELANDS, 1920–2008

CHAPTER 32

....

SOUTHERN IRELAND, 1922–32

A Free State?

....

FEARGHAL MCGARRY

I. INTRODUCTION

THE Irish Free State came into being on 6 December 1922. The historic significance of this event—the culmination, at least in many people's eyes, of a long and sometimes violent struggle for political independence—was acknowledged by the *Irish Times*, then the most important organ of unionist opinion in the country:

> It is an almost bewildering moment of transition. Great and ancient institutions have vanished or are vanishing, and are replaced already, or soon will be replaced, by others that, in their turn, must dare the ordeal of time.... Today all things are made new. The Irish people, by their own deliberate choice, are left to their own resources. They will make their own laws, shape their own progress, establish their own traditions of government.[1]

Yet, the underwhelming nature of the occasion was also evident from the same newspaper's coverage. In contrast to the truce of July 1921, the inauguration of the Free State was not accompanied by any enthusiasm on the streets of Dublin: 'No heroic effort by railway engine-drivers to make their locomotives sound a paean of joy. No sound of revelry by night.... Very like any other night—except that there was an uncanny absence of shots. Not even the usual one or two per hour'. The cursory political ceremony that inaugurated the state—'a very dull affair'—also provoked little public interest: 'there was nothing to mark the change from the old to the new'.

This lack of excitement was partly a consequence of the ongoing Civil War, which had brought chaos to much of southern and western Ireland. The Dáil's public gallery remained closed for the ceremony, and Leinster House was ringed by uniformed and plain-clothes security forces. Leading government deputies wore military uniforms or, the *Irish Times* observed, appeared 'obviously ill-at-ease in civilian attire'.[2] Such precautions were warranted. The following day, the pro-treaty TD (and National Army officer), Seán Hales, was killed and the Deputy Speaker of the Dáil, Pádraic O'Máille, wounded in an attack by IRA gunmen as they made their way to the Dáil. This deliberate assault on the institutions of the state prompted the government's equally calculated decision to kill four prominent republicans 'without any pretence of legality' on 8 December.[3] The Irish Free State was baptized in blood.

The apathy which marked the birth of the Free State was also a consequence of the difficult compromises that had been required to secure British approval for the new state which, from the outset, called into question its legitimacy for many republicans (as was illustrated by the empty seats reserved for Sinn Féin's anti-treaty deputies). The first duty of those deputies who did attend the opening of the parliament was to swear an oath of fidelity to King George V, and the first speech recorded in the proceedings of the parliament was the protest of the Labour Party leader, Thomas Johnson, at the necessity for this. Foreshadowing the pragmatic stance adopted by de Valera's republican followers in 1927, Johnson described the taking of the oath as a temporary expedient:

> We recognise the 'Oath of Allegiance' as a formality, a condition of Membership of the Legislature, implying no obligation other than the ordinary obligation of every person who accepts the privileges of citizenship.... The terms of the Treaty...are accepted by us, as they are accepted by the people generally, under protest, having been imposed upon Ireland by the threat of superior force, and were not freely determined by the people of Ireland or their representatives.[4]

In his address to the Dáil, following his election as president of the Executive Council (or cabinet) of the Irish Free State, W.T. Cosgrave did not seek to play down the challenges confronting the new state. The most immediate of these was anti-treaty violence, which remained at alarming levels: 'Twelve months which might have been spent conserving the fruits of our struggle have been wasted in resisting the mad efforts of those who...took up arms in order that they might, by violence and tyranny, wrench from the people what they had won'. Contrasting the attitude of anti-treaty republicans—'who set their own narrowness or what they would call intellectualism against the broad good sense of the people'—with that of the British government, which had behaved 'with scrupulous and undeviating good faith' since the Treaty, Cosgrave insisted that the Free State represented the attainment of genuine independence. It would allow the Irish people 'to conduct their affairs as they shall declare right without interference, not to say domination, by any other authority whatsoever on this earth'. As for the connection with Britain, they had joined not the British Empire but the Commonwealth, a 'free partnership, in which all are equal'.

Although it has often been observed that Sinn Féin's leaders devoted little attention to the north, much of Cosgrave's inaugural speech concerned the position of Northern Ireland which, under the terms of the Treaty, was permitted to preserve its devolved status within the United Kingdom by opting out of the Irish Free State settlement. While making it clear that his government had no intention of coercing those parts of Ulster with unionist majorities, Cosgrave declared that, 'we must not, cannot, forget our solemn pledges to those great sections of the population in the Six Counties who *do* want us'. The Boundary Commission authorized by Article 12 of the Treaty would rectify such 'cases of obvious injustice' by transferring those areas with nationalist majorities, such as the counties of Fermanagh and Tyrone, to southern jurisdiction: 'Why there has ever been the slightest confusion about this part of the Treaty I could never understand'. Sadly, from the point of view of his party's nationalist credibility, future developments would make clear why there was grounds for more than confusion about how the Commission would 'determine in accordance with the wishes of the inhabitants, so far as may be compatible with economic and geographic conditions, the boundaries between Northern Ireland and the rest of Ireland.'[5]

Contemporary political and press responses make clear that the principal, and inextricably linked, issues that would shape the fate of the Irish Free State—determining how, in the words of the *Irish Times*, it would 'dare the ordeal of time'—were apparent from the outset. The most important of these were its contested legitimacy; the military and political threat posed by anti-treaty republicans; its ability to convincingly embody national sovereignty; and its relationship with Northern Ireland and the British Empire. Cosgrave's speech made equally clear his party's strategy from the outset: to identify the Free State with the attainment of an 'almost unlimited measure of freedom and independence'; to cast republican enemies of the state as the potential wreckers of that freedom; and to depict the state's connection with Britain as a benign and consensual relationship leading towards full equality. The strength of the Free State's position was that it was rooted in a measure of self-government that was substantial, popular, and, as constitutional developments over the next decade would demonstrate, capable of evolving towards greater sovereignty; its fatal weakness was that it fell significantly short of the republic for which Irish separatists had fought since 1916. The connection with Britain that Cosgrave sought to characterize as a free partnership was—as Thomas Johnson awkwardly pointed out—imposed by the threat of violence. With hindsight, the Executive Council's decision to dedicate itself to the long-term defence of the Treaty, by striving to develop Irish sovereignty only within the constitutional parameters of that settlement, can be seen to have played an important part in its fall from power in 1932 and the demise of the Free State itself only fifteen years after its inauguration.

The reputations of both the Irish Free State and Cumann na nGaedheal, the political party formed by the pro-treaty section of Sinn Féin in March 1923, have not fared well since. In contrast to the Easter Rising, and the establishment of the First Dáil, the inauguration of the Free State—tainted both by its association with the divisive violence of the Civil War and its constitutional ties to Britain—is seldom commemorated, while the term 'Free Stater' quickly became an insult in political discourse.[6] In contrast to the attention devoted to every shade of inter-war republicanism, Treatyite politics has remained a neglected topic, as demonstrated by the remarkable fact that the founding president of the Free State has yet to inspire a major scholarly biography. Cosgrave's decade in power has been characterized as a period of narrow, unimaginative—even counter-revolutionary—rule, while his party has been widely criticized for failing to fulfil the potential of independence.

Rather than marking the culmination of a political revolution, the establishment of the Irish Free State would later seem, to many people, to represent little more than a change of management, an interpretation powerfully conveyed in Ken Loach's depiction of the birth of the state in *The Wind that Shakes the Barley* (2006). The state's institutions—its bicameral political system, strong executive, hierarchical civil service, and remote legal system—appeared little different from those of the semi-colonial regime that republicans had fought to overthrow. In social and economic terms, the harsh economic realities endured by many people—including poverty, unemployment, and mass emigration—differed little from life under the Union. The bleak politics of the 1920s were shaped by the hatreds of the Civil War, and the rhetoric of many leading Cumann na nGaedheal politicians was increasingly characterized by disillusionment rather than the expectation or optimism that might have been expected of a period of state-building.[7]

This chapter surveys the major policies of the Cumann na nGaedheal government and their wider impact on Irish society, identifying some key points of consensus and disagreement, and highlighting where recent research has advanced some of these debates. It assesses the government's achievements within the context of the possibilities and constraints of the time, as well as the experiences of other European states. While many of the criticisms levelled at the Treatyite politicians are well founded, their substantial achievements have not always received sufficient recognition. The state-builders of the 1920s were overshadowed by the more dramatic successes of Fianna Fáil which, ironically, Cosgrave's decade in power did much to facilitate. De Valera's political triumph—and the failure and demise of Treatyite politics—further tarnished the memory of Cumann na nGaedheal, as did the success of republican propagandists in caricaturing it as a pro-British party of the wealthy.

II. State-Building

Aside from the constraints imposed by the Treaty and 1922 constitution, the formative influence on the institutions and politics of the Irish Free State was the Irish Civil War. In comparative terms, Ireland's civil war was not particularly violent but it produced substantially more deaths than the much longer War of Independence, and its impact was intensified by the fratricidal animosities to which it gave rise. Less easy to assess is the impact of the political divide brought about by the Treaty split and Civil War, and the death of leaders of the stature of Michael Collins and Arthur Griffith. The threat to the survival of the state compelled the government to resort to emergency measures from the outset, most controversially the execution of some seventy-seven republican prisoners, tainting 'the Cosgrave government with the image of being vindictive, mean spirited and spiteful'.[8] The fact that the war ended in a suspension rather than cessation of hostilities ensured the continued use of coercion throughout the decade, including the imprisonment of around twelve thousand republicans until 1924, and the implementation of a series of increasingly draconian public safety acts in 1923, 1927, and 1931. In the short term, these measures appeared to meet with public acquiescence, provoking far less opposition than did the much smaller number of British executions during the War of Independence. In time, however, the government's reliance on authoritarian legislation—however necessary—made it easier for republicans to question the democratic legitimacy of the state.

The Civil War, which witnessed a concerted campaign of economic sabotage by anti-treaty combatants, added greatly to the fiscal constraints on a government that was not predisposed to high levels of public expenditure. The war itself cost around thirty million pounds, while defence spending and compensation claims absorbed almost a third of government expenditure up to 1927.[9] It also necessitated the creation of a vast, expensive, and ill-disciplined National Army. In political terms, it is difficult to overstate the impact of the Civil War on the new state. On a practical level, it reinforced its conservatism, as many of the more innovative aspects of both the revolutionary Dáil and Free State constitution were abandoned in favour of greater centralization of state authority.[10] In terms of party politics, the Civil War polarized southern politics for several decades, turning in on itself the energies of a republican movement that would otherwise have focused on the pursuit of unification and national sovereignty.

The impact of the Civil War on the stability of southern democracy is less certain. Echoing Treatyite self-perceptions, some political scientists have interpreted the Civil War as a conflict between democratic pragmatists and anti-democratic idealists.[11] Jeffrey Praeger identified a struggle between the 'Irish-Enlightenment' and 'Gaelic-Romantic' traditions within modern Irish political culture that reflected fundamentally different aspirations about independence.[12] Tom Garvin has argued that the success of moderate Treatyites in prosecuting a ruthless civil war against unaccountable elitists resulted in an enduring victory for democratic civic nationalism.[13]

Although academic historians are also generally more sympathetic to the Treatyite position as a result of its greater claim to democratic legitimacy, they tend not to define the Civil War as a conflict between opposing political cultures, placing more emphasis on the role of personal rivalries, factional divisions, local issues, and social tensions in shaping the conflict. Biographies of leading revolutionaries demonstrate how aspects of both sides of the clash of political values discerned by political scientists were often expressed by individual politicians, and how the factors influencing the decision to support or oppose the treaty were sometimes more arbitrary than ideological. The passage of time has also increased awareness of how the hatreds engendered by the conflict served to mask a conservative consensus on both sides of the subsequent political divide. As with historical writing on the revolution more generally, the extent to which historiographical debates were influenced by the Northern Irish Troubles is also becoming more evident. What some might regard as a 'revisionist' consensus on the unjustifiable nature of anti-treaty violence has been challenged by recent studies. Bill Kissane, for example, has interpreted the Civil War as a conflict between 'rival claims of democracy and self-determination', while, less convincingly, Michael Collins has been accused of establishing a military dictatorship.[14]

Although it is difficult to envisage less propitious circumstances, the Irish Free State distinguished itself from almost every other post-war European 'successor state' by establishing a democracy that survived the political and economic instability of the inter-war era. This has generally been attributed to a combination of fortunate circumstances and the behaviour of the political elite on both sides of the Civil War divide.[15] The Irish Free State inherited a relatively modern society with a well-educated population and reasonable levels of urbanization and socio-economic development. Its high level of land ownership and the persistence of mass emigration also contributed to the conservatism and stability of the state. Although the source of intense political resentment, partition ensured that much of the potential for class and ethnic, or sectarian, conflict was exported north. The continued importance of the 'national question'—a legacy both of the Civil War and the unfinished nature of the revolution—also militated against the emergence of strong socialist or sectional parties, north and south, reinforcing what would, in the south, prove a durable two-party system.[16] Although nationalists fretted about the possibility of reoccupation by the British until the return of the 'Treaty ports' in 1938, the Free State proved fortunate in its sheltered geographical position, as the Second World War demonstrated. The experience of British rule—not least the skill with which generations of Irish nationalists had pursued political means to overthrow it—and its institutional legacy also contributed to the stability of Irish democracy. This stability, however, came at a cost. With hindsight, one of the most striking features of the outcome of the Irish revolution was the weakness of radical ideological impulses, such as feminism, socialism, and secular republicanism that had played a significant role within separatist politics before the Easter Rising. Among those who lost out from the contraction of political possibilities brought about by revolutionary violence and the emergence of two conservative states that prioritized stability over social reform were not just home rulers and southern unionists but progressives of different varieties, including feminists, socialists, liberals, and intellectuals.

Despite the conservatism of the era, the challenges facing the Free State government in 1922—vividly conveyed by Kevin O'Higgins—should not be underestimated:

> there was no State and no organized forces. The Provisional Government was simply eight young men in the City Hall standing amidst the ruins of one administration with the foundations of another not yet laid, and with wild men screaming through the keyhole. No police force was functioning through the country, no system of justice was operating, the wheels of administration hung idle battered out of recognition by the clash of rival jurisdictions.[17]

In seeking to restore law and order and reconstruct the machinery of government, pro-treaty politicians had to choose whether to create new forms of administration, adapt the existing British structures, or build on the republican institutions that had emerged during the War of Independence.[18] Again, the impact of the Civil War proved decisive: political divisions within the republican institutions (as well as their ad hoc nature) rendered them largely unsuitable for use, while the immediate threat to the state rendered the innovation of new structures less likely.

Although the government deployed all of the above strategies—the new police force, for example, comprised a new organization, the Civic Guard, alongside the old Dublin Metropolitan Police, and a 'Special Branch' which pragmatically amalgamated revolutionary and pre-revolutionary personnel—it relied most heavily on the existing British structures. While understandable, and perhaps inevitable, this much-criticized decision is often viewed as the principal reason for the disappointing conservatism of the new state. The most obvious example occurred within the civil service, where some 21 000 public servants were transferred from the authority of Dublin Castle to that of the Free State. That the administration of the central government was staffed by the same people, performing similar tasks, in much the same manner as before 'virtually eliminated the chance of radical structural change'.[19]

Although such continuity appears one of the most striking features of the new regime, it does not explain fully why the administration of the new state was so influenced by British practice. Highlighting the high level of disruption within the senior civil service brought about by a rapid purge of personnel and an exodus of voluntary retirements, one recent study instead attributes the failure of the new civil service to function as an effective agent of change to the Free State government's desire to construct a cheaper version of Whitehall: 'Whether that model was appropriate for the new State was not considered by the new government'.[20] The most important measure in terms of creating an administrative structure that stifled rather than facilitated the rapid decision-making that had characterized the revolutionary Dáil was the 1924 Ministers and Secretaries Act (designed by C.J. Gregg, an Irish-born senior British civil servant) which established the principle of ministerial responsibility for all actions undertaken by civil servants within a government department. The real purpose of this fiction, Joe Lee has argued, 'was to provide a façade for civil service, and particularly Finance, influence over government'.[21] It was certainly its outcome.

Senior civil servants and government ministers perceived a strong link between administrative continuity and the stability of the state. Ireland's revolutionaries, many of whom had worked within the British public service, were familiar with the British model of administration. Britain was a very successful state, and its public service was much admired. Such continuity also reflected the ideological inclinations of the Cumann na nGaedheal elite. Kevin O'Higgins remarked: 'we were probably the most conservative-minded revolutionaries that ever put though a successful revolution'.[22] O'Higgins may have been more accurately describing himself and some of his cabinet colleagues, rather than the republican movement as a whole, but it is clear that Sinn Féin's leadership had dedicated itself to achieving self-government more as an end in itself than as a means of effecting radical social and economic change.[23] The revolutionary ambitions of many leading republicans were confined to the sphere of culture, language, and identity. This conservatism was exacerbated by the Civil War split, as for reasons that are not obvious, many of the more socially progressive or economically interventionist figures ended up on the marginalized anti-treaty side of the political divide.

Strangely, then, one consequence of Irish independence was to substitute the Union's semi-colonial administration with structures that more closely resembled the UK's administration. For example, although often viewed as the most successful innovation of the new government, the creation of an unarmed and apolitical police force dedicated (at least rhetorically) to upholding civil law rather than the authority of the state clearly owed more to the British model of policing than the Royal Irish Constabulary. Consequently, one effect of the government's state-building efforts was to bring about the sort of administration that British officials had strived to create in Ireland: 'a centralised and hierarchical structure of departments under finance control and answerable to politicians'.[24] A similar tendency towards centralization and the dilution of local influence was evident in local government, the judiciary, and other key aspects of administration.

Although widely criticized, centralized administration was not without benefits, particularly in a country whose population, for historical reasons, lacked (and continues to lack) a strong sense of civic responsibility and tradition of ethical behaviour. Recruitment to the civil service—which, in the days of Dublin Castle, had been identified with sectarian discrimination and political patronage—became more meritocratic. One of the government's most important early reforms was the establishment of civil service and local government commissions to depoliticize public appointments. Just how successful these were remains a matter of debate. While Joe Lee has described the cultivation of ethical standards in public employment as 'one of the most remarkable achievements in the history of the state', others argue that the introduction of Irish language tests, preferential treatment for National Army veterans, and the dismissal of republican internees and suspects from the public service marked the beginning of a 'jobs for the boys' mentality.[25] But although appointments to many positions in the new public service were influenced by political considerations—whether to reward loyal supporters or reconcile potential opponents of the state—the apparent lack of corruption within the public service (until recent decades) and the continuity of personnel within the public service following the election of Fianna Fáil in 1932 suggest that the state did not become a crude instrument of patronage.[26]

III. SECURITY AND SOVEREIGNTY

In terms of state-building, the most sensitive area remained security. While largely bound up with self-interested factional rivalries, divisions within the defence forces also owed something to political and ideological tensions stemming from the Free State settlement. Since the split over the Treaty—and indeed for a considerable period before—the assertion of political authority over the military had been incomplete. Tensions within the military and between the military and civil government were compounded by the Civil War, which saw an unorthodox convergence of political and military power under Michael Collins, who was both Chairman of the provisional government and Commander-in-chief. Following his death, Richard Mulcahy continued his predecessor's practice of keeping a foot in both camps by combining his role as Commander-in-chief with his position as Minister for Defence during the Civil War, much to the irritation of some of his cabinet colleagues. The influence of the Irish Republican Brotherhood, the fraternal secret society to which many leading republicans had owed their first allegiance until the Treaty split, created further uncertainty, particularly as both Collins and Mulcahy utilized it as a means of reinforcing the loyalty of military officers to the army leadership.

The exercise of political authority over the military raised awkward questions: how much power should the army wield within the new state, and to what extent would it remain loyal to the aims of the revolution rather than the political interests of the government? Collins had alienated cabinet colleagues in 1922 by secretly authorizing collaboration between the pro-treaty and anti-treaty IRA as a means of staving off civil war, most notably by encouraging the destabilization of the northern state.[27] The resulting misgivings of other ministers were partly due to the fact that Collins appeared willing to subvert the Treaty in order to avoid a permanent break with his former comrades, but also reflected wider issues. Was the Treaty, as Collins had publicly insisted, a stepping-stone to the Republic or—as influential colleagues such as Griffith and O'Higgins appeared to accept—a settlement deserving of consolidation rather than subversion?

Cumann na nGaedheal remained divided between supporters of consolidation (who came to dominate the Executive Council) and advocates of a more republican interpretation of the Treaty settlement (who were better represented among party activists and military officers but divided among rival factions). These tensions were never entirely resolved, as the Blueshirt split in 1934 and Fine Gael's abandonment of the Commonwealth position in 1948 illustrated, but the consolidationists had gained the upper hand by the mid 1920s.[28] Their position was strengthened by Cumann na nGaedheal's reliance on the economic and political support of influential sections of opinion that were either indifferent or hostile to republicanism—most notably the principal losers of the Irish revolution, the Irish Parliamentary Party and Southern Irish Unionism—but backed the party as the lesser of two evils.

Inevitably, these tensions emerged more openly within the army and cabinet as the anti-treaty military threat receded in 1923. Reports of indiscipline within the National Army, and mounting cabinet dissatisfaction at the continued lawlessness of much of the country sparked open rows between Kevin O'Higgins—the deeply conservative Minister for Home Affairs (and the cabinet's acknowledged strong man) who advocated a hard line against subversion—and defence minister Richard Mulcahy who felt that his cabinet colleagues did not appreciate the fragility of the army's loyalty to the state. Against this background, the decision to reduce the size of the army led to insubordination on 6 March 1924 when a section of officers known as the 'IRA Organization' presented the Executive Council with an ultimatum demanding an end to demobilization and a more 'republican form of government'.[29] Although Mulcahy demanded an unequivocal stance against this outrageous repudiation of governmental authority, the convoluted chain of events that followed had led to his resignation and that of his Army Council comrades less than a fortnight later, when they were judged to have contravened the will of the Executive Council by arresting mutineers without the authority of the recently appointed general officer commanding and inspector general Eoin O'Duffy. Joe McGrath, the Minister for Industry and Commerce, who had made no effort to hide his sympathies with the mutineers, also fell victim to the political crisis.

The army mutiny, the first serious challenge to the authority of the Free State government since the Civil War, was a manifestation of a common problem in post-revolutionary states: the difficulty of imposing civilian control and professional standards over an army led by former volunteers whose revolutionary ideals had brought that government to power. It also illustrated a growing level of dissatisfaction about the outcome of the Irish revolution as it gradually dawned on senior officers 'that the Free State was the end for which we fought, not the means to that end'.[30] In political terms, the clear winner was Kevin O'Higgins who successfully presented his actions to the public as a decisive and principled defence of democratic government against militarist elites within the army and cabinet. The irony that O'Higgins had brought about Mulcahy's resignation only after persuading the Executive Council to adopt a more conciliatory approach to the mutineers' demands was lost on most people due to public disquiet at the revelation of the Army Council's manipulation of the IRB.

Nonetheless, the principle of civilian authority over the military had been asserted. The size of the army fell sharply from 48 200 (1923) to 11 600 (1927) to 5800 (1932), and the National Army never gained the prestigious status enjoyed by the military in other countries. However, by confirming the political ascendancy of those who advocated a conservative consolidation of the Free State over advocates of a more republican approach, the political fallout from the mutiny further diminished the appeal of Treatyite politics among nationalists. It also weakened the authority of W. T. Cosgrave (confined to his bed by illness throughout the crisis) who can be seen more as a mediator between pro-treaty factions than a visionary leader in the mould of de Valera.

The embarrassing Boundary Commission debacle in 1925 prompted similar tensions. The establishment of the Free State had coincided with a decisive shift from the policy of destabilization previously advocated by Collins, as was demonstrated by the end of the government's efforts to obstruct the setting up of the northern civil service and its withdrawal of financial support for the boycott of Northern Ireland's Department of Education by teachers in Catholic schools.[31] Although it appeared to run counter to its official objective of reunification, the southern authorities were the first to make partition an economic reality on the ground by erecting customs barriers along the border in April 1923. Throughout this period, the prospect that the Boundary Commission promised by Article 12 of the Treaty might significantly revise the border led the Free State authorities to encourage northern Catholics to demonstrate their opposition to the northern state. Delayed by the Civil War and the northern state's refusal to nominate a commissioner, the commission finally got underway in the autumn of 1924. However, nationalist hopes that it would interpret its ambiguous brief by transferring substantial territories with Catholic majorities to southern control were dashed when its findings were leaked to the press.

The revelation that the commission was to recommend only minor adjustments (including, embarrassingly, the transfer of some Free State territory in east Donegal) prompted the resignation of its southern representative, the Minister for Education, Eoin MacNeill. The government acted promptly to secure the agreement of the British and Northern Irish governments in quashing the report. The existing border was confirmed by a tripartite agreement which also scrapped the 'Council of Ireland' (originally intended to facilitate cross-border cooperation leading to potential unification) established by the 1920 Government of Ireland Act. In return for this humiliating debacle, some of the Free State's financial obligations to Britain under the Treaty were waived. Although partition would remain an important grievance, particularly during elections when it provided a valuable mobilizing issue for republicans, no southern government would begin to formulate a constructive policy on the north until the meetings between Seán Lemass and Terence O'Neill in 1965. The northern 'peace process' of recent decades inevitably involved revisiting the constitutional architecture of the Government of Ireland Act, and tackling key issues, such as representative policing and fair employment, that northern and southern politicians had attempted, but resoundingly failed, to address in the early 1920s.

The failure of the commission has been described as Cumann na nGaedheal's 'greatest disappointment'.[32] It may well have been for some of the Treatyite political class—it certainly exposed the hollowness of the government's claim that the Treaty would bring the freedom to achieve freedom—but the short-term political fallout, the resignation of three TDs from the party, was insignificant. The public response was also muted, the Garda Commissioner privately observing that 'the average citizen is sublimely indifferent to the Boundary Question'.[33] In the longer term, the crisis further tarnished the government's frayed nationalist credentials. It also brought home the inability of the abstentionist opposition to influence government policy, providing de Valera with further leverage to challenge his party's commitment to abstention from the Dáil. Failing to win the argument, de Valera and his supporters split from Sinn Féin in 1926 to establish Fianna Fáil, which would rapidly mount an effective political challenge to Cumann na nGaedheal.

In its ambition to assert the sovereignty of the state though diplomacy, the government met with more success, although the domestic political returns for this were modest. In September 1923, the Free State secured membership of the League of Nations at Geneva, where the Irish government further irritated Britain by registering the Treaty as an international agreement. By 1930 the Free State had secured membership of the council of the League, although the government failed to establish a high profile in Geneva until after de Valera's election as president in 1932. Irish sovereignty was further asserted by establishing diplomatic legations in Washington, Paris, Berlin, and the Vatican during the 1920s. The government also cooperated with other 'restless dominions' within the Commonwealth—notably Canada, South Africa, and Australia—in pursuit of equality with Britain.[34] The culmination of their collective efforts was the Statute of Westminster (1931) which recognized the equal status of the member nations of the Commonwealth, effectively ending British legislative supremacy over the dominion parliaments. As with many of Cumann na nGaedheal's subtle foreign policy achievements (a subtlety epitomized by the insertion of 'O'Higgins' comma' in the British monarch's official title in 1926), this advance provoked little in the way of domestic comprehension or enthusiasm. Indeed, Fianna Fáil propagandists successfully turned the government's obvious enthusiasm for Commonwealth gatherings against it by caricaturing its delegates as top-hat-and-tailed imperialists cravenly aping their social superiors.

IV. Society and Economy

Further evidence that the administrative continuity of post-independence Ireland should not be overemphasized as a cause of the government's conservatism is provided by the social and economic polices pursued by Cumann na nGaedheal during the 1920s. During the first decade of the Free State, fiscal policy was characterized by a determined commitment to retrenchment. Under the influence of a parsimonious Department of Finance, headed by the Ulster-born Presbyterian Ernest Blythe, government expenditure was slashed from £42 million (1923–4) to £32 million (1924–5) to £24 million (1926–7), thereby facilitating the reduction of income tax from 5 shillings (1924) to 3 shillings (1927–8) in the pound. This was achieved by minimizing public investment, increasing indirect taxation, and curtailing welfare expenditure, a regressive approach symbolized by the notorious, and characteristically politically counter-productive, reduction of the old-age pension to pre-independence levels.

The government's policies reflected a commitment to the economic status quo that necessitated the abandonment of Sinn Féin's ideological commitment to protectionism. Between 1923 and 1927, key committees of inquiry on fiscal policy, agriculture, and banking rejected radical alternatives in favour of a continued commitment to the link with sterling, the prioritization of agricultural exports to Britain, and the maintenance of free trade.[35] Other sectors of the economy remained underdeveloped and, aside from some notable exceptions (such as the Shannon hydro-electric scheme and the establishment of state-owned enterprises such as the Electricity Supply Board and Agricultural Credit Corporation), intervention in the economy remained limited. The rationale for these policies—which were much less politically appealing to a largely nationalist electorate than the promise of protectionism held out by Fianna Fáil—was the government's belief that the prosperity of the state could be most effectively pursued by prioritizing the needs of Irish agriculture. This policy, entailing support for cattle-raising graziers rather than more labour-intensive arable farming, and the strengthening of the export trade to Britain, earned agriculture minister Paddy Hogan the title of 'minister for green grass and emigration'. In contrast to Hogan's determined attempts to improve agricultural efficiency, no concerted effort was made to develop the limited industrial base of the economy, an objective that would have necessitated high public expenditure and the systematic imposition of import tariffs. As a result, living standards in rural Ireland continued to be effectively subsidized by mass emigration and a low standard of living for those without land who chose to remain.

Cumann na nGaedheal's economic policies have been widely criticized, but often for reasons that owe more to politics than economics. Under Cosgrave, the fortunes of the new state remained dependent on Britain, and it became clear that, contrary to the assumption of most nationalists, prosperity and economic independence would not automatically accompany political independence. Although this would also remain true during the 1930s, Cumann na nGaedheal, in contrast to Fianna Fáil, made little effort to challenge the state's economic subordination to Britain. Economic historians such as Liam Kennedy and Cormac Ó Gráda have been less critical of the first Free State government, a trend that has continued in recent years. This slightly more favourable re-evaluation of Cumann na nGaedheal is not a result of its policies being judged more coherent or effective than previously thought, but rather a greater awareness of the limited range of options open to the government at the time, and the poor economic performance of comparable states during this period.[36] Previously considered one of the most unsuccessful economies in Europe, one recent study has judged the southern state's inter-war (and twentieth-century) performance as 'a modal rather than a mediocre experience' in comparative European terms.[37]

The international context is important for other reasons. Cumann na nGaedheal's commitment to free trade reflected the prevailing economic orthodoxy of the 1920s, just as de Valera's policies coincided with a wider international shift towards protectionism in the 1930s. Cumann na nGaedheal's decision to prioritize agricultural output was a rational policy that was undermined by the international collapse in food prices and exports triggered by the Great Depression, the impact of which outweighed the limited ability of government policies to shape the Irish economy. Given different circumstances, Cormac Ó Gráda has concluded, Cumann na nGaedheal's 'conservative polices might have yielded dividends in due course'.[38] It was not only in Ireland but also in the UK and throughout much of Europe that export earnings failed to recover between 1929 and the Second World War. Moreover, unlike some European countries, the state avoided hyperinflation and maintained a positive credit rating. The failure to industrialize—if not perhaps the lack of effort to do so—must also be seen in context of the possibilities at the time. As the Fiscal Inquiry Committee of 1923 concluded, the state's relatively uncompetitive industries were not prepared for a decisive shift to protectionism, a judgement confirmed by the economically disastrous (if politically popular) consequences of Fianna Fáil's protectionist policies in the 1930s.

Perhaps more deserving of criticism were Cumann na nGaedheal's social policies. The government's austere opposition to the expansion of social welfare was partly rooted in Sinn Féin's self-reliant ethos. Despite the rhetoric of the Democratic Programme (1919), Sinn Féin's politics had long been characterized by hostility to organized labour, working-class interests, and socialism. Opposition to state intervention also reflected the strong influence of Catholic social thought on this generation of intellectuals (of whom there were a remarkable number among the Treatyite elite). The resulting scepticism about the potential of the state to transform society, illustrated by Desmond FitzGerald's comments, was reinforced by the disillusioning experience of civil war, and a growing awareness of the limitations of independence:

> Think of the passion that we put into the national struggle. To create a national Government, a national state. I can remember when people spoke of the wonderful things that would happen when we got Home Rule, and the ridiculous things that were expected to come with a Republic. Implicit in our intense nationalism was the supposition that with the coming of a national Government our lives would be radically changed. And how could that be unless the Government took possession of those lives...[39]

Admittedly, some Treatyite politicians took this attitude to extremes, particularly in comparison to the more reassuring paternalism that informed the policies of Fianna Fáil which, by extending social welfare to a large section of the population in the 1930s, had a significant impact on the lives of many people. The reactionary rhetoric of government ministers—who tended to regard themselves as principled statesmen rather than opportunistic politicians—amplified this austerity. Justifying the reduction of the old-age pension, P.J. Burke, the Minister for Local Government and Public Health, contrasted the increasing 'number of people who lead a parasitic existence' with those 'striving to make an honest living'. In 1924, Patrick McGilligan, the Minister for Industry and Commerce, notoriously warned that 'people may have to die in this country and may have to die from starvation'.[40] Such statements did little to indicate a sympathetic attitude towards the poor for whom emigration continued to provide one of the few means of economic survival. In 1925–6, for example, 30 000 people left the state, the only significant change from pre-independence days being the supplanting of the US by the UK as their principal destination.[41]

One area of policy where the governing party could not be accused of lacking ambition was in its aim of reviving a Gaelic Ireland. Republicans may not have agreed on the necessity for transforming the economy or the structure of society, but the one truly radical objective that united this generation of revolutionaries was the desire to create an Irish Ireland. The ideology of Sinn Féin owed more to the philosophy of cultural nationalism—the desire to reverse centuries of 'anglicization' that prompted the emergence of such organizations as the Gaelic League and Gaelic Athletic Association in the late nineteenth century—than republican political theory. The compromises imposed by the Treaty, and subsequent republican attempts to depict its supporters as pro-British, reinforced the impulse to define Irish identity in opposition to English culture.[42]

The principal means by which it was sought to Gaelicize the population was compulsion. Gaelic became a requirement for many jobs within the public service, and it was made an essential subject in the schools which were identified as the key to creating an Irish-speaking society. But while it proved possible to impart a rudimentary knowledge of Gaelic to most schoolchildren, the Irish remained stubbornly anglophone despite numerous incentives for Gaelic speakers. The focus on compulsion rather than voluntary means (which had met with considerable enthusiasm when deployed by the pre-revolutionary Gaelic League), and the relative neglect of other subjects in schools has also been criticized, while the imposition of language tests alienated the state's Protestant minority.[43] The few Irish-speaking regions of the country, moreover, continued to contract due to the unwillingness of policymakers to confront the underlying social and economic reasons for the decline of the number of Irish speakers. Despite its ineffectiveness, and the emergence of a '*cúpla focail*' culture in public life that gave rise to a certain degree of cynicism, the commitment to Gaelic would remain a bipartisan cornerstone of state policy due to its importance as a symbol of national identity.

The policy of Gaelicization may have been radical in its intent but it contributed to the socially conservative and introspective ethos of independent Ireland. Much has been written about the negative aspects of a post-independence sense of identity grounded in a chauvinistic commitment to Catholic and Gaelic values. This impulse was perhaps most clearly evidenced in the state's willingness to impose morality by legislative means. The demoralizing experiences of the Civil War, and the continued threat to the state posed by republican and left-wing subversives, predisposed church and state leaders to alarmist (and often self-serving) pronouncements about the threats posed by modern and foreign influences. The 1929 Censorship of Publications Act (a product of the evocatively titled Committee on Evil Literature) which resulted in the banning of books by most serious contemporary writers provided one example of how the politics of cultural defence—the prioritization of public order, morality, and a narrow conception of national identity over civil liberties and pluralist debate—disfigured the intellectual life of the nation.[44] It does not necessarily follow, though, that Irish society formed a kind of cultural wasteland, or that the Treatyite government received uniform support from the Catholic Church.[45] More research is required to assess the extent and significance of these cultural anxieties within a comparative European context, particularly given the tendency to attribute to Catholic nationalism aspects of Irish cultural life, such as censorship and opposition to modernism, that were prevalent throughout inter-war Europe.

Although all republicans agreed that partition had created a sectarian state in the north, few considered the potential corollary of this. The safeguards imposed by the 1922 constitution (such as the composition of the Senate to reflect minority interests and the retention of proportional representation) ensured a political voice for the ex-unionist minority, and their relatively privileged economic status went largely unchallenged by the government. Nonetheless, the new state was a cold house for Protestants. Republican propagandists and a popular Catholic press—whose excesses were epitomized by the entertaining fulminations of the *Catholic Bulletin*—made much of the purportedly sinister influence of 'freemasons' and unionists in Irish society. However, demographic and ideological factors ensured that southern Protestants faced less discrimination than northern Catholics. The size of the Protestant community (which had declined to 7 per cent of the state's population by 1926) ensured that, in contrast to northern Catholics, it could never threaten the southern state regardless of its level of dissatisfaction (which remains difficult to ascertain). Republican ideology, although irretrievably conjoined with Catholic nationalism, permitted a public role for Irish Protestants of the right cultural background that northern Catholics could never assume in the unionist state: it is difficult, for example, to envisage a Catholic head of state emerging in Northern Ireland (had such a position existed) as Douglas Hyde would under de Valera's 1937 constitution.

Both states enthusiastically identified with the values of their confessional majorities. The influence of the Catholic Church on matters impinging on public morality, health, education, and welfare went largely unchallenged by the state with some positive outcomes that were, nonetheless, far outweighed by the appalling consequences for vulnerable women and children that have only been comprehensively exposed in recent years.[46] Although the 1922 constitution granted women equal voting rights, they became increasingly inconspicuous in political life, except as the widows or mothers of the patriot dead. In addition, their status as citizens was eroded by their effective exclusion from civil service examinations (1925) and juries (1927), as well as the introduction of a 'marriage bar' for female teachers and civil servants. The commitment of Free State politicians to gender inequality, which transcended party affiliations, culminated in 1937 with the dispiriting, if largely symbolic, commitment of de Valera's constitution to safeguard the place of women 'within the home'.

Despite such grim facets of Irish society, it would be pointless to judge the past by present-day values. In Ireland, as throughout much of inter-war Europe, democracy was understood as reflecting the will of the majority rather than protecting the rights of minorities.[47] Many criticisms of the illiberal nature of the Free State could be directed at Irish society more generally rather than its politicians in particular. Moreover, the idea that an authoritarian clericalism was imposed from above by political and religious elites is contradicted by the popularity of sodalities, vigilance societies, and spectacles such as the Eucharistic Congress which illustrated how religious identity fulfilled important social and cultural needs for Irish Catholics. That many unpalatable aspects of society in the Free State—including the undermining of the status of women and the curtailment of individual liberties—were also features of inter-war Europe suggests that they should not be exclusively attributed to the widely held desire to construct a more Catholic Gaelic society.

Although Cosgrave, like many of the state's founding fathers, appears to have been deeply devout, his record in terms of preventing sectarian discrimination was reasonable, as was demonstrated by his willingness to confront Mayo County Council's refusal to employ a Protestant librarian (in the face of the support of the local clergy and Fianna Fáil for the council's stance).[48] His record on such matters was certainly superior to de Valera who described Ireland as a Catholic nation, and whose 1937 constitution explicitly identified the state with Catholic patriarchal values. Caution is also required in making assumptions about the degree to which the alarmist attacks of xenophobic cultural nationalists, pious politicians, or puritanical clerics on dance halls, 'nigger jazz', and the 'filthy press' reflected, or influenced, the views of ordinary people. Observing the existence of 'an almost underground resentment and resistance to excessive enforced piety', Diarmaid Ferriter has suggested that a preoccupation with what people were not allowed to do has overshadowed our knowledge of what they actually did: 'It is surely ironic, given the constant references to "alien influences", that the Irish population became one of the heaviest cinema-going populations in the world, and were keen to drink as much as possible and dance from one end of the country to the other'.[49]

V. New Directions in Historiography

Such issues highlight directions for future research. The opening of the archives of the Irish state and other public institutions, and the release of the papers of the state's founding generation of politicians in the 1980s and 1990s provided an abundance of primary sources which has resulted in valuable empirical studies of the state, its institutions, political parties, and leading figures. The deluge of new sources and the focus on political and constitutional history resulted, however, in a degree of what Ulrich Beck has termed 'methodological nationalism', the tendency to regard the nation-state as the natural unit of study, to downplay the influence of other agents of historical change, and to arbitrarily exclude frames of reference that lie beyond the island (or even the border). One example is the many histories of departments of the Irish state which drew heavily on the documents of civil servants and politicians to provide a highly detailed but ultimately rather narrow perspective on Irish history.

With the essential building blocks of the 'high politics' of the state now firmly in place, emerging scholars are tackling more interesting fields of research and embracing more challenging interpretative frameworks. New areas of social history—such as welfare, health, the family, and sexuality—have been pioneered, as the focus of historians shifts from state to society.[50] Intellectual history, however, remains underdeveloped. The importance of social class, particularly outside the cities, continues to be neglected, as does the history of business and consumerism, and economic history more generally.[51] Historians have also been slow to devote the same attention and originality of approach to cultural history as scholars from other disciplines.[52]

The history of women has long moved on from a narrow focus on a handful of 'great women' to less prominent historical figures;[53] its earlier focus on the status of women (involving, inevitably, a preoccupation with what was denied to women rather than their actual experiences) has been increasingly complemented by more research into the working and everyday lives of ordinary women. The approach of many historians in this field, particularly those interested in the construction of identity, is increasingly characterized by a broader interest in gender—rather than a more narrow focus on women—as a category of inquiry.[54] New areas of inquiry will continue to emerge: for example, there remains little research on masculinity, with the partial exception of the growing body of scholarship on sport, which has finally been recognized as a subject worthy of the serious research it has long received elsewhere.[55]

The application of new perspectives and methodologies will broaden the historiography of the Free State which remains dominated by a focus on post-revolutionary politics and state-building. There is no reason why the local study which, at its best, provided such a revealing anatomization of the dynamics of power during the Irish revolution, should not be applied to the study of the Free State, a period in which the coercive relationship between the powerful and powerless remains just as pressing a subject of inquiry.[56] At the other end of the methodological spectrum, there is a need to place the Free State in a broader context, as has been more effectively accomplished by historians of earlier periods. Transnational approaches, concerned with understanding the movement of people, material goods, and ideas across borders, will provide one means of achieving this;[57] comparative studies, particularly of other inter-war European societies, offer another means of approaching emotive, still unresolved debates—such as the extent of the Free State's repressive nature, its preoccupation with sexual morality, and its treatment of the vulnerable and minorities—in a measured and objective way.

In addition to rethinking the geographical borders of Irish history, there is a need to reconsider its temporal contours: essays such as this reflect a periodization that takes for granted that the struggle for independence and the history of the state form the central narrative of Irish history. Such an approach may reinforce simplistic or insular ideas about the forces responsible for historical change: de Valera becomes not just the personification but the cause of inertia, Lemass the heroic modernizer. Change appears to occur rapidly in the 1960s, more slowly in the 1930s, and hardly at all in the 1950s.[58] The role of international economic forces and wider cultural and technological developments is diminished. In reality, political events provide, at most, the backdrop to peoples' lives, whereas the forces which impact most on society transcend the dramatic conflicts and political ruptures with which historians are often preoccupied.

VI. Conclusion

The government's final years in power were characterized by declining public support and a corresponding alarmism about the revival of anti-treaty republicanism. After Fianna Fáil's election in 1932, prominent Treatyite politicians—including Cosgrave, a man of modesty and integrity—concluded that their party had failed in its mission. Certainly, Cumann na nGaedheal never inspired anything like the same devotion as Fianna Fáil. Throughout its decade in power, it failed to achieve the support of even two fifths of the electorate, its vote slumping from 39 per cent to 30 per cent between 1923 and 1933. In contrast, the rise in first preference votes for Fianna Fáil, once it shook off the millstone of abstention, was dramatic: from 26 per cent (June 1927) to 35 per cent (September 1927), 44 per cent (1932), and 50 per cent (1933).[59] Whereas Cumann na nGaedheal's commitment to the Treaty settlement prevented it from building on the divergent elements of support it had initially attracted in 1923, de Valera effectively exploited both socio-economic grievances and the government's nationalist shortcomings to mobilize a much broader section of the electorate.[60] De Valera was also fortunate that the Great Depression of 1929 undermined the credibility of the free trade orthodoxy to which Cumann na nGaedheal had committed itself, resulting in a global shift towards interventionist and protectionist economic policies.

Nonetheless, by integrating the anti-treaty opposition within the political structures of the state, the government could claim an enduring legacy. Following the shocking assassination of Kevin O'Higgins by IRA gunmen in July 1927, Cosgrave's government acted decisively to end the opposition's abstention from the Dáil, which it blamed for legitimizing republican violence. The introduction of a public safety bill, legislation to prevent Fianna Fáil from overturning the oath of allegiance, and a further act requiring parliamentary candidates to pledge to swear an oath of allegiance if elected, forced de Valera's hand. In August 1927 'the Chief' led the soldiers of destiny into the Free State parliament where they swore the oath as 'an empty political formula'. Whether this represented a noble act of political self-sacrifice by Cumann na nGaedheal is debatable: Cosgrave would have had reason to hope that the hypocrisy demonstrated by de Valera's decision to take the oath—fewer than five years after a Civil War had been fought on the issue—would have divided republicans and discredited Fianna Fáil. Regardless, Fianna Fáil's decision to enter the Dáil signalled its tacit acceptance of the legitimacy of the Free State and—as the peaceful transition of power in 1932 confirmed—marked the consolidation of democracy in Southern Ireland.

Cumann na nGaedheal's weaknesses as a political party could form an extensive list. It would include its inability to develop social and economic policies that were either popular or effective, its failure to construct a party organization as effective as its electoral opponents, and its leaders' preference for assertions of statesmanlike principle over the cultivation of grass-roots support. These shortcomings, particularly its authoritarian inclinations, became more evident in its final year in power, when the government responded to IRA violence by opportunistically exaggerating the existence of a communist threat to the state in order to secure clerical support for repressive public safety legislation. A principal weakness remained its political ineptitude: few governing parties would have introduced a supplementary budget that reduced public service pay and raised income tax prior to a general election. Even more than most governments, circumstances ensured that its most talented adherents devoted their energies to the executive and the state rather than the party. The fact that Cumann na nGaedheal had been established after the state, and had often been regarded as something of a nuisance by leading Treatyites, did not help. The party was also undone by the importance of symbols in a historical period dominated by nationalism. Its nationalist credibility was eroded by the imperial baggage inherited by the Free State—exemplified by the much resented office of the governor-general, the oath of allegiance, and the continued payment of land annuities to Britain (measures which de Valera's government quickly dispensed with)—while the legacy of the Civil War ensured that there was no possibility that Cosgrave's reforms (in contrast to those of de Valera) could legitimize the state in the eyes of a recalcitrant minority of the population.

A list of the Free State government's achievements would be far shorter but nonetheless impressive, particularly given the volatile international context. Its state-building achievements, notably the restoration of law and order, effective administration, and stable government against the background of the Civil War and a continued military and political challenge to the legitimacy of the state were considerable. It was largely due to the government's resolve that republican opponents of the state were forced to work within the Treaty settlement to change it: that de Valera's Ireland was essentially built on the foundations of the Free State provided all the more reason not to publicly acknowledge the value of Cosgrave's legacy. Cumann na nGaedheal successfully advanced Irish sovereignty on the international stage, even if its constructive rather than confrontational engagement with Britain and the Commonwealth won it little popularity at home, and proved less effective than Fianna Fáil's unilateral assault on the Treaty in the 1930s. The successful transition of power in 1932—less than a decade after the Civil War—marked another significant achievement with enduring consequences, particularly in light of the presence of authoritarian voices within the Irish security forces, and the unattractive alternatives pursued elsewhere in inter-war Europe. Ultimately, it was perhaps inevitable that the party's state-building achievements were not accompanied by electoral success. Scarred by the experience of the Civil War, and committed to the security of the state that emerged from that conflict, Cumann na nGaedheal could never resolve the inherent contradiction between its defence of the Treaty settlement and its aspiration to win as full as possible a measure of national freedom.

NOTES

1. *Irish Times*, 6 December 1922. Subsequent quotes derive from this source.
2. *Irish Times*, 7 December 1922.
3. Eunan O'Halpin, *Defending Ireland: The Irish State and its Enemies since 1922* (Oxford, 1999), 34.
4. Dáil Debates, 6 December 1922. Subsequent quotes derive from this source.
5. Michael Kennedy et al (eds), *Documents on Irish Foreign Policy Volume I, 1919–1922* (Dublin, 1998)
6. On Free State commemoration, see Anne Dolan, *Commemorating the Irish Civil War: History and Memory, 1923–2000* (Cambridge, 2003).
7. John M. Regan, *The Irish Counter-Revolution 1921–1936* (Dublin, 1999), 180–2.
8. Maryann Valiulis, *Portrait of a Revolutionary: General Richard Mulcahy and the Founding of the Irish Free State* (Dublin, 1992), 184.
9. R.F. Foster, *Modern Ireland 1600–1972* (London, 1989), 523.
10. Tom Garvin, *1922: The Birth of Irish Democracy* (Dublin, 1996), 178–9.
11. See, for example, Brian Girvin, *From Union to Union: Nationalism, Democracy and Religion in Ireland—Act of Union to EU* (Dublin, 2002), 63.
12. Jeffrey Praeger, *Building Democracy in Ireland* (Cambridge, 1986).
13. Garvin, *1922*, 141–5.
14. Bill Kissane, *The Politics of the Irish Civil War* (Oxford, 2005); John M. Regan, 'Michael Collins, General Commanding-in-Chief, as a Historiographical Problem', *History*, 92, no. 307, 318–46.
15. Bill Kissane, *Explaining Irish Democracy* (Dublin, 2002); J.J. Lee, *Ireland 1912–1985: Politics and Society* (Cambridge, 1989), 69–94.

16. Fearghal McGarry, 'Radical Politics in Interwar Ireland, 1923–1939' in Donal Ó Drisceoil and Fintan Lane (eds), *Politics and the Irish working class, 1830–1945* (Basingstoke, 2005).

17. Terence de Vere White, *Kevin O'Higgins* (Tralee, 1966), 83.

18. David Fitzpatrick, *The Two Irelands 1912–1939* (Oxford, 1998), 156.

19. Ibid., 157.

20. Martin Maguire, *The Civil Service and the Revolution in Ireland, 1912–38: 'Shaking the blood-stained hand of Mr Collins'* (Manchester, 2008), 227.

21. Lee, *Ireland*, 106; Garvin, *1922*, 179.

22. Michael Laffan, '"Labour Must Wait": Ireland's conservative revolution', in P.J. Corish (ed), *Radicals, Rebels and Establishments* (Belfast, 1985), 219.

23. David Fitzpatrick, *Politics and Irish Life 1913–1921: Provincial Experience of War and Revolution* (Cork, 1998 ed.), 192–230.

24. Maguire, *Civil Service*, 227.

25. Lee, *Ireland*, 107; Fitzpatrick, *Two Irelands*, 157–8.

26. Elaine Byrne, *Political Corruption in Ireland 1922–2010: A Crooked Harp* (Manchester, 2012).

27. Robert Lynch, *The Northern IRA and the Early Years of Partition, 1920–22* (Dublin, 2006).

28. John M. Regan, 'The politics of reaction: the dynamics of Treatyite government and policy 1922–33', *Irish Historical Studies* 30, no. 120 (November 1997), 563.

29. O'Halpin, *Defending Ireland*, 45–53; Lee, *Ireland*, 96–105.

30. Michael Brennan to Richard Mulcahy, 15 May 1923, quoted in Michael Hopkinson, 'Civil War and aftermath, 1922–4', in J.R. Hill (ed), *A New History of Ireland VII: Ireland 1921–1984* (Oxford, 2010), 49.

31. Fitzpatrick, *Two Irelands*, 137.

32. Eunan O'Halpin, 'Politics and the State, 1922–32', in Hill, *A New History*, 106.

33. Fearghal McGarry, *Eoin O'Duffy: A Self-Made Hero* (Oxford, 2005), 140.

34. Deirdre McMahon, 'Ireland, the Empire and the Commonwealth, 1886–1972', in Kevin Kenny (ed), *Ireland and the British Empire* (Oxford, 2004).

35. Mary Daly, *Industrial Development and Irish National Identity, 1922–39* (Dublin, 1992), 32.

36. See, for example, Brian Girvin's re-evaluation of his earlier criticism of the Free State government's economic policy (*From Union to Union*, 69).

37. D.S. Johnson and Liam Kennedy, 'The two economies in Ireland in the twentieth century', in Hill (ed), *A New History*, 453.

38. Cormac Ó Gráda, *A Rocky Road: the Irish Economy since the 1920s* (Manchester, 1997), 4–5, 144–8.

39. Desmond FitzGerald, cited in Garvin, *1922*, 149. See also McGarry, *Eoin O'Duffy*, 206–7.

40. Ó Gráda, *Rocky Road*, 91.

41. Enda Delaney, *Irish Emigration since 1921* (Dublin, 2002).

42. R.V. Comerford, *Ireland* (London, 2003).

43. Paul Bew, *Ireland: the Politics of Enmity 1789–2006* (Oxford, 2007), 482.

44. Peter Martin, *Censorship in the Two Irelands* (Dublin, 2006); Tom Garvin, *Nationalist Revolutionaries in Ireland 1858–1928* (Oxford, 1987).

45. Brian Fallon, *An Age of Innocence: Irish Culture 1930–1960* (Dublin, 1998); Patrick Murray, *Oracles of God: The Roman Catholic Church and Irish Politics, 1922–37* (Dublin, 2000).

46. Eoin O'Sullivan and Ian O'Donnell (eds), *Coercive Confinement in Ireland: Patients, Prisoners and Penitents* (Manchester, 2012).

47. Mark Mazower, *Dark Continent: Europe's Twentieth Century* (London, 1998).

48. Pat Walsh, *The Curious Case of the Mayo Librarian* (Cork, 2009).

49. Diarmaid Ferriter, *The Transformation of Ireland 1900–2000* (London, 2004), 334, 10, 336–7.
50. For recent research on the family and sexuality, see Lindsey Earner-Byrne, *Mother and Child: Maternity and Child Welfare in Ireland, 1920s-1960s* (Manchester, 2007); Susanna Riordan, 'A reasonable cause: the age of consent and the debate on gender and justice in the Irish Free State, 1922–35', *Irish Historical Studies*, 37, no. 147 (May 2011), 427–46; Diarmaid Ferriter, *Occasions of Sin: Sex and Society in Modern Ireland* (London, 2009); and Leanne McCormick, *Regulating Sexuality: Women in Twentieth-century Northern Ireland* (Manchester, 2010).
51. For intellectual history, see Bryan Fanning, *The Quest for Modern Ireland: the Battle of Ideas, 1912–1986* (Dublin, 2008). On class, see Fintan Lane and Donal Ó Drisceoil (eds), *Politics and the Irish Working Class, 1830–1945* (Basingstoke, 2005); Fintan Lane (ed), *Politics, Society and the Middle Class in Modern Ireland* (Basingstoke, 2010).
52. Nicholas Allen, *Modernism, Ireland and Civil War* (Cambridge, 2009).
53. See, for example, Leeann Lane, *Rosamond Jacob: Third Person Singular* (Dublin, 2010).
54. Maryann Gialanella Valiulis (ed), *Gender and Power in Irish History* (Dublin, 2008).
55. See, for example, Liam O'Callaghan, *Rugby in Munster. A Social and Cultural history* (Cork, 2011).
56. For a recent example of such an approach, see Una Newell, '*Evolution or Revolution? Politics and the Populace: County Galway 1922–1932*' (Dublin: UCD PhD, 2009).
57. Enda Delaney, 'Our island story? Towards a transnational history of late modern Ireland', *Irish Historical Studies*, 37, no. 148 (November 2011), 599–621.
58. Ibid., 'Modernity, the past and politics in Post-war Ireland' in Thomas Hachey (ed), *Turning Points in Twentieth-Century Irish History* (Dublin, 2010) 103–20.
59. Fitzpatrick, *Two Irelands*, 198.
60. Socio-economic rather than republican factors are emphasized in Richard Dunphy's *The Making of Fianna Fáil Power in Ireland 1923–1948* (Oxford, 1995).

SELECT BIBLIOGRAPHY

Cronin, Mike and John Regan. *Ireland: the Politics of Independence, 1922–1949* (Basingstoke, 2000).
Dolan, Anne. *Commemorating the Irish Civil War: History and Memory, 1923–2000* (Cambridge, 2003).
Dunphy, Richard. *The Making of Fianna Fáil Power in Ireland 1923–1948* (Oxford, 1995).
English, Richard. *Radicals and the Republic: Socialist Republicanism in the Irish Free State 1925–1937* (Oxford, 1994).
Ferriter, Diarmaid. *The Transformation of Ireland 1900–2000* (London, 2005).
——. *Judging Dev* (Dublin, 2007).
——. *Occasions of Sin: Sex and Society in Modern Ireland* (London, 2009).
Fitzpatrick, David. *The Two Irelands 1912–1939* (Oxford, 1998).
Garvin, Tom. *1922: The Birth of Irish Democracy* (Dublin, 1996).
Hanley, Brian. *The IRA 1926–1936* (Dublin, 2002).
Hill, J.R. (ed). *A New History of Ireland VII: Ireland 1921–1984* (Oxford, 2003).
King, Linda and Elaine Sisson (eds). *Ireland, Design and Visual Culture: Negotiating Modernity, 1922–1992* (Cork, 2011).
Kissane, Bill. *Explaining Irish Democracy* (Dublin, 2002).

Lee, J.J. *Ireland 1912–1985: Politics and Society* (Cambridge, 1989).

McGarry, Fearghal. *Eoin O'Duffy: A Self-Made Hero* (Oxford, 2005).

——. *Frank Ryan* (Dublin, 2010 ed.).

Meehan, Ciara. *The Cosgrave Party: a History of Cumann na nGaedheal 1923–1933* (Dublin, 2010).

Murphy, Brian. *Patrick Pearse and the Lost Republican Ideal* (Dublin, 1991).

Murray, Patrick. *Oracles of God: the Roman Catholic Church and Irish politics, 1922–37* (Dublin, 2000).

O'Halpin, Eunan. *Defending Ireland: The Irish State and its Enemies since 1922* (Oxford, 1999).

Regan, John M. *The Irish Counter-Revolution 1921–1936* (Dublin, 1999).

....

CHAPTER 33

DE VALERA'S IRELAND,
1932−58

....

DIARMAID FERRITER

THE success of Fianna Fáil in the Irish Free State general election of 1932 represented an extraordinary political comeback for its leader Eamon de Valera, who had been on the losing side during the Civil War less than ten years earlier. It also marked the inauguration of an era that witnessed Fianna Fáil evolve into one of the most successful political parties in the world. But while the political context changed considerably with the electoral triumph of Fianna Fáil in 1932, which enabled them to form a government with the support of the Labour Party, there was also much continuity; many of the issues associated with maximizing cultural and political sovereignty were in practice an extension of the state building of the 1920s by Cumann na nGaedheal.[1]

De Valera's domination of politics throughout these decades—Fianna Fáil was in power 1932–48, 1951–4 and he won his final election as leader of the party in 1957 before stepping down in 1959—has been the subject of numerous and contrasting assessments over the past twenty years. In his book *Ireland 1912–85: Politics and Society*, published in 1989, historian Joe Lee acknowledged the stability de Valera brought to Irish politics, his ability to lead Fianna Fáil with 'superb tactical judgement', his imaginative use of symbolism, and his capacity to be 'a marvellous manipulator of private and public minds, of individual and collective mentalities'. Arguably more significantly, he insisted 'de Valera did not abuse his trust as leader throughout his long public life. He revelled in the cult of "The Chief", but he used it primarily for party and national purposes.'[2] Alvin Jackson's two-hundred-year survey of Irish history, published in 1999, described de Valera as 'this self-appointed guardian of the national conscience', possessed of a 'highly calculating intelligence' and highlighted de Valera's skill during the Second World War in 'simultaneously coping with Irish patriotic sensitivities as well as well as macropolitical realities'.[3]

In contrast, Tom Garvin, the most prolific political scientist of his generation in Ireland, in his 2004 book *Preventing the Future: why was Ireland so poor for so long?* was scathing in his criticisms of the mindset that he believes was responsible for Ireland's chronic underdevelopment during the first few decades of independence. He placed de Valera and his stubborn longevity at the centre of his thesis:

> A bucolic quietus was to be the solution to Ireland's incoherent yearnings towards individual freedom, self-realisation, equality, individualism and authenticity as expressed dramatically in the writings and deeds of the revolutionaries and poets.

Furthermore, change only came about when 'de Valera as Fianna Fáil's lay Archbishop, mysterious and remote in demeanour, was replaced by men of a distinctly non-charismatic stripe, managerial in style, rather than romantic or pseudo-heroic'.[4] In the same vein, Henry Patterson's recent political history of Ireland after 1939 suggests de Valera ruled supreme 'as the philosopher king of Irish pastoralisms and frugal comfort',[5] while Paul Bew's extensive survey of modern Irish history is critical of Irish neutrality during the Second World War, and the persistence of the self-serving belief that 'the most oppressed people in Europe in the 1940s were to be found in Ireland'.[6] Tim Pat Coogan's biography of de Valera, published in 1993, concluded with a withering putdown: he did 'little that was useful and much that was harmful'.[7] Arguably, these more hostile assessments of de Valera involve the simplification of a man who maximized the sovereignty of the twenty-six counties with determination and often sophistication in the 1930s, enhanced the legitimation of democratic institutions, was determined to implement an independent foreign policy, and showed courage and consistency in resisting attempts to secure Irish entry to the Second World War on the side of the Allies.[8] The considerable thought given to foreign policy and its execution during this period has been extensively documented in the Documents on Irish Foreign Policy series published by the Royal Irish Academy in recent years.[9]

Notwithstanding, Fianna Fáil managed to dominate Irish politics during this period while failing to achieve most of its stated ambitions. The constitution of the Fianna Fáil party established by de Valera and his colleagues in Dublin in 1926 declared seven aims: to secure the unity and independence of Ireland as a republic; to restore the Irish language as the spoken language of the people and to develop a distinctive national life in accordance with Irish traditions and ideals; to make the resources and wealth of Ireland subservient to the needs and welfare of all the people of Ireland; to make Ireland, as far as possible, economically self-contained and self-sufficient; to establish as many families as practicable on the land; and, by suitable distribution of power, to promote the ruralization of industries essential to the lives of the people as opposed to their concentration in cities.[10]

Despite its frustrated ambitions, Fianna Fáil evolved into an exceptionally successful political party, not just in national, but international terms. In 2004, Peter Mair made the observation that Fianna Fáil's electoral record in almost eighty years of its existence, securing an average of 45 per cent of the vote over twenty-four general elections, is 'virtually without equal across the western democratic universe'.[11] An ideology that was 'petty bourgeois' has been accurately identified by Richard Dunphy as being the essence of its success, making it populist, but not a vehicle for the advancement of socialism despite the accusation by the Labour Party leader Thomas Johnston that it had drawn twelve of its fifteen 1932 manifesto pledges from earlier Labour programmes.[12] A snap general election in 1933 resulted in an increased majority of seats for Fianna Fáil, meaning it no longer needed the support of the Labour Party.

Fianna Fáil convincingly sold the Irish electorate a simple message about representing the interests of the 'men of no property' and, in external affairs, asserting the rights of small nations; in truth the party was a coalition of traditionalists, modernizers, visionaries, and conservatives, a party which denied it was a sectional grouping, asserting to the contrary that it was a national movement. While increased cultural sovereignty and a heightened sense of Irish identity may have gathered new momentum when the party gained power, the issues which dominated the politics of the 1920s—most notably stability and security—continued to be relevant. When deemed necessary, threats to the stability of the state were responded to forcefully.[13] There were new ideas on economics, on the role of the state, and the relationship with England, but equally, Ronan Fanning was accurate in asserting that the 1937 constitution, one of the significant legacies of this era, was a validation of values established over fifteen years of Irish independence, and not just the priorities of Fianna Fáil after taking office in 1932.[14]

In terms of domestic policy, the appeal of Fianna Fáil lay in its promises to cater for the needs of the small farmer and working classes. In presenting themselves as saviours of the less well-off, Fianna Fáil also managed to portray those who advocated class politics as champions of an exploitation that would hinder the development of a strong and autonomous trade union movement. Fianna Fáil, having broken the connection with the original Sinn Féin, also learned from the mistakes of that movement, particularly regarding Sinn Féin's lack of attention to social policy and the failure to devise a long-term strategy. Three other essential ingredients in its success were discipline within the ranks,[15] electioneering, and skilful leadership, which is why much attention has justifiably been given to the political tactics of de Valera.[16]

There were many indications that Fianna Fáil, while determined to experiment with new policies, was also pragmatic in emphasizing its commitment to a Catholic ethos for the Free State and its upholding of the law. The Eucharistic Congress in Dublin in 1932, in honour of the Blessed Sacrament, seemed to confirm that whatever divided Irish people politically, they were firmly united when it came to their Catholic faith, with a million devotees thronging the centre of Dublin. Fianna Fáil took full advantage of the Congress as an opportunity to demonstrate its Catholic credentials. The government also built on the legislation that had emerged in the 1920s to safeguard Irish Catholic morality by restricting the importation of foreign literature and culture as well as banning the sale and importation of contraceptives.

While many republican prisoners were released after Fianna Fáil assumed power, de Valera was keen in the 1930s to place distance between himself and the IRA and was quick to use emergency legislation that had been introduced in the 1920s in order to marginalize and proscribe militant republicans. A letter from IRA chief-of-staff Moss

Twomey to prominent Irish-American republican Joseph McGarrity, reveals the IRA's dilemma in the early 1930s:

> Will we stick by the Republic? Or tacitly submit to Free State and trust to evolution for a republic?...our difficulty today is that most things we do to maintain and strengthen ourselves is branded as obstructing FF and it is amazing the people who think so.

It also struggled against accusations of communism, was riven with splits and factions, and the government banned it in 1936.[17] This was another confirmation that democracy in Ireland had stabilized, as was the effective resistance offered to the Blueshirts, a proto-fascist group of disgruntled Cumann na nGaedheal supporters, who were the main victims of de Valera's economic war with Britain over the refusal to continue paying land annuities to the British government. Recent research on the Blueshirts and its leader Eoin O'Duffy by Fearghal McGarry challenges the lazy tendency to view O'Duffy's career as simply one of tragedy and farce. Rather, it focuses on 'his successful invention of a persona which reflected, if in a highly exaggerated and distorted form, the values of the society and times in which he lived', suggesting scholars need to answer difficult questions about the nature of Irish politics and society from the 1920s to the 1940s. O'Duffy's extremism was also a product of his and many others' fears about the effects of IRA violence. 'We do not want party politics and politicians' became O'Duffy's mantra, and there was much admiration for fascist forms within Ireland's pro-Treaty political class who saw initial toleration of the IRA and coercion of Blueshirts as a glaring double standard. In many respects O'Duffy personified the worst excesses of the 1930s, but he was not alone in dismissing the value of politics and politicians.[18]

Much attention has rightly been devoted to the stabilization of democracy in Ireland in the 1930s and the 1940s, but this was accompanied by an almost ruthless approach to the centralization of political power. How this power was structured and exercised needs more scholarly exploration. Fianna Fáil built up a formidable organizational network that was very much based on localism, but they were hostile to any sense of local power or devolution. Within two years of taking over the reins of power in 1932, the party effectively sought to abolish local government in Ireland. A memorandum on the necessity for reform of county administration in March 1934, for example, suggested:

> The existing system of local administration is defective and unsatisfactory...Local elected councils are a relic of British administration when the people sought for the control of popular bodies for the furtherance of national agitations rather than by reason of any intrinsic administrative merits possessed by such bodies.
>
> With the establishment of a central administration responsible to the people as a whole and with modern improvements in transport and communications, governmental intervention and supervision is now feasible in respect of all national activities. The retention of local government bodies is, therefore, gradually becoming an expensive anachronism.[19]

The significance of such sentiments transcends their obvious illustration of a government resentful of what it viewed as irksome and expensive local councils. At their core was a fundamental belief in the necessity of a powerful central state. Many contemporary Catholic intellectuals were gravely worried about the implications of such views, but were faced with the dilemma of pitching Catholic social theory, which called for as much decentralization as possible, against the actual practice of government in an infant state. It was a struggle the central government won decisively, a reminder of the dangers of exaggerating Fianna Fáil's subservience to the Catholic Church.[20]

Successive Fianna Fáil governments were in no mood to countenance surrendering even a fraction of their power. Fianna Fáil treated the report of the Commission on Vocational Organisation, which sat from 1939–43 and was chaired by Bishop Michael Browne of Galway, with contempt because it suggested a wholesale reorganization of the manner in which power in Ireland was distributed, with the emphasis on power from below. It was a report that irritated serving government ministers, and in the long term left the Church looking stubbornly idealistic. Perhaps there is truth in Joe Lee's assertion that the failure of the Catholic Church to counteract the power of bureaucratic centralization represented 'one of the great lost opportunities of Irish intellectual endeavour',[21] but this must be qualified by emphasizing that the opponents of bureaucracy met more than their intellectual match in the administrators and politicians who were determined to justify an excessively centralized state at a time of international economic and political instability.

Was there a meaningful commitment to improving welfare in de Valera's Ireland? Undoubtedly, one of the appeals of Fianna Fáil in the early years was its commitment to economic protectionism and welfare policies; indeed, throughout his career, Seán Lemass, de Valera's successor and one of his most important cabinet ministers, was fond of insisting that Fianna Fáil was the real Irish Labour party. Many high-profile members of Fianna Fáil during these years might have found a more natural home in the Labour Party if the civil war divisions had not tied them to de Valera. But how successfully did they deliver on the economic reform and welfare agenda?

The small amount paid under the Widows and Orphans Pensions Act of 1935 did not increase until 1942. David Fitzpatrick suggested that Fianna Fáil's appeal to the poor only lasted until 1938.[22] Notwithstanding, a commitment to an increase on social spending is revealed in the figures that show such spending rose from 36 per cent of the government's budget in 1929 to 40 per cent in 1939.[23] Brian Girvin's account of Fianna Fáil's economic policy during these years makes the point that by 1939 approximately fifty thousand new jobs had been created as a result of protection, a notable success at a time of international depression. The introduction of an unemployment assistance bill, although 'less radical and generous than originally proposed … complied with Lemass's view that a minimum income should be available for the genuinely unemployed'.[24] The government also demonstrated willingness in the 1930s to respond to trade union pressure, introducing the Workmen's Compensation Act in 1934 and the Conditions of Employment Act in 1936 to improve working conditions, guarantee paid holidays, and prevent exploitation of child labour. Fianna Fáil also angered many in the labour movement with the 1941 Trade Unions Act which limited the right of unions to negotiate and

strike; more positively received was the Industrial Relations Act of 1946 which established the Labour Court.

These various initiatives hardly amounted to a social revolution, but there were also
significant reforms in the context of pensions, hospital care, and the provision of labourers' cottages. There was a specific large-scale housing programme in the 1930s targeted
at agricultural labourers. As well as using legislation to empower the Land Commission
to expropriate land deemed suitable for redistribution among small farmers, Fianna Fáil
increased the government subsidy for cottage building from 36 per cent to 60 per cent of
the local authorities' loan repayments, and in 1936 the Labourers Act allowed for the sale
of cottages to labourers. Mary Daly suggests twenty thousand cottages were built between
1932 and 1940[25] and although their construction did not solve all the ills of rural Ireland,
they went some way to giving meaning to the professed desire to achieve 'frugal content-
ment' in 'cosy homesteads' in rural Ireland. De Valera dealt rigorously with local government bodies attempting to obstruct his schemes and castigated the 'red tape' that slowed
their construction.[26] Private individuals and public utility societies were responsible for
the building of an additional twenty-two thousand rural houses between 1932 and 1942.[27]

The urban housing programme initiated also yielded significant results, and economic historian Cormac O'Gráda has identified it as one of Fianna Fáil's most impressive achievements in the 1930s.[28] As Mary Daly points out, by 1931 there was an intensive
publicity campaign to highlight conditions in city slums and, with the active intervention of the Department of Finance, between 1932 and 1942 local authorities built
twenty-nine thousand urban houses and flats, while private individuals and public utility societies constructed eleven thousand urban houses. There was also a high level of
expenditure on grants for private houses that proved popular with the public, though
it is questionable whether enough government assistance went to those most in need.
Daly gives an approximate total of eighty-two thousand houses (rural and urban) built
in the decade 1932 to 1942.[29] This active housing programme, according to Joe Lee, combined social, economic, and political motives 'in a nice blend from a Fianna Fáil perspective. It led to a genuine improvement in horrific housing conditions for families,
provided employment for needy workers, profits for needy employers and in due course
subscriptions to a needy party.'[30]

Notable legislative developments in relation to health and child welfare included the
National Health Insurance Act and the Public Hospitals Act, both in 1933, and the 1944
Childrens' Allowance Act, introduced 'after a long internal party struggle' and despite
the opposition of Minister for Local Government and Public Health, Seán MacEntee,
who believed such an allowance 'would drive the unfit into matrimony' at the expense of
the taxpayer.[31] The possibility of a separate department of health was discussed during
the Second World War, and the new Department of Health was created in 1947 (formerly
health affairs had been the responsibility of the Department of Local Government and
Public Health). The 1947 Health Act, with provisions regarding the health of mothers
and children, was a response to growing concerns about the persistence of high levels of
child and maternal mortality and an indication that the new Minister for Health, Dr Jim
Ryan, 'lost no time in putting health at the centre of the government's agenda.'[32]

But there were notable failures also, including completely inadequate investment in education. As Tom Garvin trenchantly argues, the failure to develop different types of education and open up educational opportunity to more people was one of the main factors retarding the Irish economy. The decision not to raise the school leaving age from 14 to 16 was taken by an interdepartmental committee in 1936.[33]

Fianna Fáil's economic policies did not succeed in achieving the self-sufficiency that was promised in the agricultural and industrial sectors due to their reliance on imports for industrial raw materials and the dependence on Britain for export of agricultural produce. The Economic War of 1932–8, which came about as a result of the withholding of land annuities, and the imposition of tariffs on Irish exports in response, did more damage to Irish cattle traders than anyone else; it was eventually settled in 1938 and did not damage the overall popularity of Fianna Fáil. The irony of its economic policies, as pointed out by Garret FitzGerald, was that ultimately the protectionist industries became dependent on imported raw materials for industrial processing and the industrial workers came to spend an increasing portion of their wages on imported goods; by 1950 the share of external trade in Ireland's economy had risen by almost one third. In effect, industrialization was achieved 'with a reduction in self-sufficiency'.[34] As minister for Industry and Commerce in the 1930s, Seán Lemass was a key figure in the formulation of economic policy; he was a champion of private enterprise 'while having a radical streak in the form of respect for the worker'. As Minister for Industry and Commerce, he lost his initial enthusiasm for tariff-driven development at a relatively early stage, but the Second World War stymied his desire to engineer a new, free market approach.[35] The most recent biography of him challenges the uncritical historiography of him to date and focuses on his authoritarianism, cunning, and alleged impatience with democracy.[36]

New semi-state companies such as the Industrial Credit Corporation were considered successful, but despite nationalist rhetoric, Fianna Fáil governments allowed considerable monopoly powers to foreign companies. As Mary Daly has observed, while the policies resulted in a new economic elite, the existing elite did not suffer.[37] The poor performance of the Irish economy also explained the increase in the gap between British and Irish wages in the late 1930s and early 1940s, and a White Paper on national income and expenditure for the years 1938–44 revealed that roughly the top three thousand earners took 5 per cent of all income in 1943, suggesting little progress in narrowing the gap between the poor and wealthy.[38]

Irish writer Seán O'Faoláin, previously a sympathetic biographer of de Valera, penned a reassessment of him in the June 1945 issue of *The Bell* magazine and disputed the notion that Fianna Fáil was a party championing the poor, arguing that 'he is held in power by the conservative middle-part of the community'. He added that 'it is only in the thirteenth year of office that the present government introduces legislation to deal with tuberculosis ... as for the poor and the unemployed we all know what has happened to the latter. The poor he has kept afloat by every kind of state charity; he has no constructive policy for either.'[39] Disease and poverty remained rife; the overall infant mortality rate in Ireland in the 1930s was almost 7 per cent of births, which was very high by European standards.[40] Legislation to provide maternity and child welfare services was not mandatory, and departmental policy was to look to voluntary organizations to provide services of this nature. One indication of their success was that infant mortality showed a continuous decline in urban areas from the mid 1920s to the mid 1930s. Nonetheless, infant mortality in Dublin remained a significant problem. A Departmental survey of 1941 suggested that 60 per cent of Dublin mothers were unable to breastfeed due to their own malnourishment, a shocking statistic which forced the Department to begin to consider more seriously the whole question of maternal health. Gastro-enteritis was responsible for one third of infant deaths in 1942 and the following year a local government departmental committee, established to examine cases of gastro-enteritis and diarrhoea, drew attention to the link between non-breastfed babies and their death from gastro-enteritis.[41]

Poor living conditions meant that tuberculosis remained a serious problem until the 1950s. The early chapters of the acerbic memoir of Noel Browne (who was appointed Minister for Health in 1948) give some indication of the bleakness facing generations inflicted with TB, with often entire families succumbing to the disease. Reflecting on his older brother Jody, a TB victim who was crippled by the condition, Browne wrote 'It is impossible to imagine the awesome humiliation and desperation of his life. I have never understood the purpose of it.'[42] As late as 1945, a report of a TB committee established by the Department of Local Government noted that practical problems such as the preponderance of unpasteurized milk had still not been tackled and that crippled children blotted the Dublin slum landscape because they were drinking contaminated milk and enduring overcrowding, living at or below the poverty limit.[43]

Nor was there much success in relation to another core aim of Fianna Fáil—to make Irish a living, thriving language. For all the focus on the Irish language in education and administration (competence in Irish became compulsory in 1937 for entry to the civil service and the Gardaí), by 1931, 38 per cent of teachers had no formal qualifications in Irish, while only 30 per cent were qualified to use Irish as a medium of instruction.[44] The emphasis on written rather than spoken Irish continued to frustrate the quest for revival. Fine Gael's James Dillon suggested in the Dáil in 1936 that it was necessary to teach Irish and provide education at the same time.[45] The Supreme Court found the linking of salary increments to knowledge of Irish unlawful in 1940, but the fact that there were so few opportunities to use Irish outside of the schools continued to be ignored, as was the folly of the belief that schools alone could rescue the language.[46]

The Irish Constitution of 1937 was another significant legacy of Fianna Fáil's tenure in office. The most recent scholarship on its origins and drafting has been impressively detailed; de Valera closely supervised its construction by appointing a committee of civil servants that reported directly to him, consisting of John Hearne, the principal drafter, Maurice Moynihan, Philip O'Donoghue, and Michael McDunphy. European— and especially German—constitutional thinking, and the Weimar constitution of 1919, influenced Hearne, a legal adviser to the Department of External Affairs. This influence was reflected, for example, in articles concerning the presidency, equality before the law, the right of property, and the protection of marriage. Hearne's preferred tone did not always prevail; his more secular original draft was altered to include more Catholic influences. In relation to the religious article (44), de Valera rejected the demands of senior Catholic churchmen such as Cardinal Joseph MacRory and John Charles McQuaid, then President of Blackrock College and later Archbishop of Dublin (1940–72), for an exclusive recognition of the Catholic Church. The 'special position' conferred on the Catholic Church was a compromise, and the Constitution's explicit references to Protestant denominations and to Jews denied the Catholic Church the supremacy it would have preferred. McQuaid, and the Jesuit Fr Edward Cahill, another friend of de Valera, supplied documentation relating to papal encyclicals, philosophy, and theology. Some of this material influenced the articles of the constitution relating to personal rights, the family, education, and private property.[47] It was also clear that with the Constitution, de Valera's cutting of ties with the IRA was complete: as far as he was concerned, the moment it was enacted, treason had a new meaning.[48]

The Constitution attempted to combine the essence of a liberal secular democracy with an emphasis on family values and a sense of community. In articles 2 and 3, the Constitution maintained that the island of Ireland was a thirty-two-county one, rather than the twenty-six counties of the Free State. The Constitution was a document that endured partly because it contained scope for review and change through referendum and its commitment to human rights. It was also a demonstration that, officially, huge importance was attached to the family in twentieth-century Ireland; the most obvious manifestation of this was in the articles that afforded it the status of a moral institution with inalienable and imprescriptible rights as well as the articles that stipulated a woman's place was in the home. In practice, however, there was a gulf between the ideals and the reality and there is much scope for researchers and historians in elaborating on the implications of this. Although an emphasis on mothers staying in the home was not a philosophy unique to Ireland—the groundbreaking Beveridge Report in England which paved the way for the welfare state in post-war Britain emphasized that 'in the next 30 years housewives as mothers have vital work to do in ensuring the adequate continuance of the British race and of British ideals in the world'[49]—it angered Irish feminists.[50]

Those feminists were protesting in a hostile climate; in the same year that the Irish constitution was introduced, the supposedly liberal and Protestant *Irish Times* articulated its opposition to female participation in the labour force—'some day, Please heaven! the nation will be so organised that work will be available for every man, so that he may marry and assume the burdens of a home and for every woman until she embarks on her proper profession—which is marriage'.[51] Many trade unionists (including females) had similar views. Some of the recent research on women of this era has focused on groups that were more interested in improving the lot of women in the home[52] or active in voluntary work, rather than looking at issues that came to dominate the women's movement from the 1970s, such as political representation, access to paid employment, equal pay, divorce and contraception; subjects that did not regularly feature as part of the political and societal discourse of the 1930s and 1940s. Influential and vocal groups included the National Council of Women, the Joint Committee of Women's Societies and Social Workers, the Catholic Federation of Women's Secondary School Teachers, the Irish Countrywomen's Association, and the Irish Housewives Association.

Various terms have been used to describe their work, including 'maternalist' 'recreational welfare' or 'social feminism'.[53]

The main political parties failed to offer women a chance for involvement in politics and, with notable exceptions, there was also very little scope for trade union involvement, given the sometimes sexist outlook of the labour movement in Ireland. When Hanna Sheehy-Skeffington attempted in 1943 to get elected to the Dáil as a member of the Women's Social and Progressive League, she forfeited her deposit, which seemed indicative of a marginalization of radical female political activism. Her electoral address was based on the idea that women 'are responsible for the feeding, the clothing, and the nursing of the sick, the tending of the aged, the running of the home. They will play an immense part in the rebuilding of the world in the present chaotic condition.'[54] It was an appeal that fell on deaf ears, but the under-representation of women in politics was not unique to Ireland; 2.2 per cent of TDs in 1942 were female, compared to 1.5 per cent of M.P.s elected to Westminster in the same era.[55]

In the realm of social and cultural life, Terence Brown in 1981 referred to Ireland in the 1930s as experiencing 'an almost Stalinist antagonism to modernism ... combined with prudery and a deep reverence for the Irish past'.[56] Exploring that 'prudery' has revealed a more complex society than Brown allowed for; sexual morality and a whole host of 'hidden Irelands' are subject matters where the diligence, detailed research, and expository skills of young Irish historians in recent years have forced a reassessment of many long-held assumptions about the nature of Irish society in the 1920s and 1930s.

The idea that the political chaos of the early twentieth century had resulted in a moral crisis was shared on both sides of the border, as Peter Martin's perusal of a great variety of archival sources relating to censorship makes clear.[57] Sex, or 'the morals of the poultry yard', to use the memorable description of the Irish film censor, James Montgomery, was not the only concern; the censorship process was also about the interaction between church, state, and the power (often exaggerated and resented) of social reform movements and lobby groups. Much doubt, confusion, and resentment existed about how to define indecency. Current work on prostitution, illegitimacy, infanticide, abortion, and child abuse is beginning to unravel the complex webs of the relationship between sex and power in Ireland.[58] When he began editing his seminal journal *The Bell* in 1940, Seán O'Faoláin was determined that it would resist abstractions, discuss social issues 'clearly and faithfully', and 'have nothing to do with generalizations ... not capable of proof by concrete expression'.[59] This was particularly important in a country where, according to O'Faoláin, 'there could not be heard a frank public discussion of any three of the following subjects: birth control, Freemasonry, the Knights of Columbanus, unmarried mothers, illegitimacy, divorce, homosexuality, rhythm, lunacy, libel, euthanasia, prostitution, Venereal Disease or even Usury'.[60] He identified the Irish as ostriches when it came to open discussion of sex, though it became evident during these decades that there were those prepared to challenge this muteness, through public discourse and private reflection. The Carrigan Committee of 1930–1, established to investigate the operation of the criminal law and juvenile prostitution, had heard evidence from Garda Commissioner Eoin O'Duffy of 'an alarming amount of sexual crime increasing yearly, a feature of which was the large number of cases of criminal interference with girls and children from 16 years downwards, including many cases of children under 10 years'.[61] A memorandum compiled by the Department of Justice stated that the obvious conclusion to be drawn from the report was that 'decency and morality had faded'; that policing was the only remedy, and that 'It is clearly undesirable that such a view of conditions in the Saor Stát [Free State] be given wide circulation'.[62] The report highlighted the way the prevailing judicial processes operated to the detriment of children by not being victim-oriented, often seeing children as accomplices to crime, concluding: 'the frequency of assaults on children is to some degree attributable to the impunity on which culprits may reckon under this protection'.[63]

The prevailing view was that public debate on the morality of the country was out of bounds and inappropriate. Mark Finnane, a sociologist based in Brisbane, has argued convincingly that in the 1930s 'an obsession with the visibility of sex (in dance halls, on country lanes, or imagined in the motor vehicles parked along the roads) avoided a more considered attention to the contexts and harm of serious sexual offending'.[64] The reality of sexual abuse contrasted strongly with the picture Irish society wanted to paint of itself and present to others. Eamon de Valera's most quoted broadcast, the 1943 St Patrick's day 'Ireland that we dreamed of' speech, is often now seen as encapsulating a hopelessly unreal and romanticized articulation of an ideal rural family-centred existence. Its mention of 'cosy homesteads' and the 'laughter of comely maidens' has perhaps inevitably been the target of revisionism by a generation who paid the price for the failure of the Irish economy to be self-sufficient. But it also conjured up an image that every society needs to be healthy—'the romping of sturdy children'.

Joe Lee has suggested that this speech was important in terms of its emphasis on the links between generations and the dependent ages in society: childhood, youth, and old age, and because it stressed that rights in Irish society had to be balanced by responsibilities. He also suggested, no doubt accurately, that many family, social, and community relationships bore a broad similarity to this ideal.[65] But re-examining that speech in the light of what has been revealed in the last decade, by historians, journalists, and victims of a variety of abuse, one is now more drawn towards the phrase: 'the romping of sturdy children'. Many, as is now known, from the 1920s to the 1960s in particular, were failed by the contract between the dependent generations, had no rights recognized, and were burdened with responsibilities that should not have been theirs, often as a result of institutionalization. The harrowing treatment afforded to unmarried mothers and the abuse of children was an illustration of collaboration between state, church, and society in refusing to deal humanely with the deprived, or the so-called 'fallen' of Irish society and a determination to contain them out of sight.[66]

How Irish foreign policy was framed and executed in the 1930s is a subject that has received much attention from historians in recent years and the archival material relating to that policy provides some clues as to why the reputation of de Valera and Fianna Fáil in the 1930s has undergone something of a rehabilitation. The pursuit of sovereignty, including the abolition of the Oath of Allegiance, ending the payment of land annuities, which led to the Economic War with Britain, the abolition of the governor generalship, the Irish Nationality and Citizenship Act of 1935 which replaced British citizenship with Irish, the introduction of a new constitution, and the attempt to carve a niche for Ireland in international affairs dominated de Valera's political life after Fianna Fáil formed its first government. He assumed the position of Minister for External Affairs as well as President of the Executive Council. National Archives documents, alongside de Valera's own archival papers held in University College Dublin, which go to the heart of de Valera's quest to establish an independent role for Ireland in international affairs during a tumultuous decade, reveal a confidence and clarity of thinking that existed within government and the civil service about this matter.

De Valera and his colleagues involved in this exercise not only tore up the Anglo-Irish Treaty of 1921 but also manoeuvred themselves into a situation where they prepared the ground for the return of the ports controlled by Britain under the terms of the Treaty, in 1938, a prerequisite for Irish neutrality. It took an exceptionally able generation of independent-minded and ideologically driven public servants to make this possible.

When he addressed the League Assembly of the League of Nations in Geneva in 1932 when the Irish Free State held the presidency of the League Council, de Valera highlighted his disquiet about larger powers dominating international organizations, while as Taoiseach and Minister for External Affairs, and working closely with Joseph Walshe,[67] Secretary of the Department of External Affairs, he was mostly concerned with wresting control of foreign policy from the British government. All negotiations were heading towards one thing—for Walshe, as he put it in March 1932, that '"Ireland" will be our name, and our international position will let the world and the people at home know that we are independent'. Walshe gave de Valera crucial strategic advice regarding how to deal with Britain and urged him to take complete control. In June 1933 he wrote: 'In the trying years before us especially the same mind must directly control what are, really, only two facets—the external and the internal—of the same group of activities of our State life.' The real foreign policy successes lay in achieving complete independence from Britain and the declaration of neutrality; Walshe's optimism regarding an end to partition ('I believe you can achieve the unity of this country in seven years') was misplaced.[68]

Despite de Valera's foreign policy successes, or perhaps because of them, in particular the return of the Treaty Ports, he banged the anti-partition drum whenever possible. As pointed out by John Bowman, he always kept a map of the partitioned island close to hand to impress his views on visitors. But one of the most senior Irish diplomats with long experience of de Valera's attempts to interest London in the issue 'concluded that de Valera's error was that he believed that partition could be solved by logical argument'.[69]

While de Valera's upholding of the principle of neutrality during the Second World War commanded respect and widespread support at home, neutrality was conveniently ambiguous and allowed a great deal of co-operation with Britain. The recent survey of Irish neutrality by Brian Girvin rides roughshod over the traditional interpretation of neutrality as representing de Valera's finest hour. 'Every state has the right to be neutral, but has it the right to be indifferent to outcome?' is the question posed by Girvin and his emphatic answer is that Ireland could have joined the Allies after 1943 with relatively little cost, and a united Ireland could have been achieved in the process. Instead de Valera opted for a policy based on 'scepticism and indifference...the safer Ireland became the more emphasis the government placed on its insecurity', and in doing so exercised an extreme and at times farcical censorship. There was, as the author acknowledges, a genuine fear in Ireland that Britain would seek to reconquer Ireland. US president Roosevelt thought this was 'preposterous...absurd nonsense'.[70]

In the midst of all this, at least sixty thousand southern Irish citizens served in the British forces, and Girvin makes the point that some of them returned to an Ireland that did not want to know: 'for many Irish men and women who joined the battle there was a sense of disappointment that the Irish neutrality which they often defended could be used to ignore what they had achieved'.[71]

Despite his formidable research, Girvin's conclusions can be challenged. Granted, there was much Irish hypocrisy and self-interest on display, but the tendency to interpret all Irish rhetoric negatively is accompanied by an unwise willingness to take most of the British and American rhetoric and intentions at face value. For all his obduracy, de Valera was surely correct to bring the Irish independence struggle to its logical conclusion by implementing an independent foreign policy. Why should he have agreed to promises (such as a united Ireland) when he had no guarantee they would be honoured?

Girvin suggests that de Valera, in his dealings with Churchill, evaded any discussion on the rights or wrongs of Britain's war with Germany and that this reflected the 'worst aspects of nationalism'. This underestimates just how important sovereignty was for de Valera; after all, he had devoted the previous decade of Anglo-Irish negotiations to this very cause. Girvin's conclusions also underestimate the widespread pride in neutrality, insightfully observed by novelist Elizabeth Bowen, who compiled some reports for the British government while she was in Ireland. In November 1940 she noted: 'It may be felt in England that Eire is making a fetish of her neutrality. But this assertion of her neutrality is Eire's first free self-assertion: As such alone it would mean a great deal to her. Eire (and I think rightly) sees her neutrality as positive, not merely negative.'[72] The more information that has come to light about neutrality—in Clair Wills's book *That Neutral Island*, published in 2007, for example, or the account of wartime Ireland by the US minister in Dublin during the war, David Gray, published in 2012—the more one can appreciate and respect, in the words of Terence Brown, 'the way de Valera kept his nerve, when the fate of the country was an uncertain one and when he had great powers lined up against him'.[73] This could not have been done without paying a price, including countless accusations of treachery, the Irish response to which 'was about strident and confused in equal parts' and a difficulty in holding 'the moral questions at bay'. As Seán O'Faoláin put it in *The Bell* in July 1945, 'We emerge, a little dulled, bewildered, deflated. There is a great leeway to make up, many lessons to be learnt, problems to be solved which, in those six years of silence we did not even allow ourselves to state.'[74]

Any hope, however, that the post-war period would witness Ireland embracing the welfare state or imitating the social-democratic forms of government in vogue on the continent were soon dashed. It was significant that one of the electoral challenges facing Fianna Fáil in the immediate post-war period was from Clann na Poblachta (CNP), a political party formed in 1946 that promised a return to the 'welfarism' espoused by Fianna Fáil in the 1930s. But the experiences of CNP, which won ten seats in the 1948 election that forced Fianna Fáil out of power, and participated in coalition government 1948–51, were chastening. Part of the problem was that there were too many disparate elements to satisfy in the party, and it was unclear what exactly it stood for. The party had made a film showing the need for political change in Ireland which made it clear that Civil War issues would no longer dominate election campaigns—the film put a spotlight on the tenement slums, highlighting forced emigration and uncontrolled tuberculosis. But how would these issues be tackled and what middle-class sensibilities would have to be trampled on the process? Answering that satisfactorily was part of the problem for CNP. In reflecting on those early days of the party, Noel Browne, who was elected a TD for CNP in 1948 and appointed Minister for Health, castigated the party's 'utopian wooliness'.[75]

Nonetheless, its emergence enabled the ousting of Fianna Fáil from government. The 1948 election also salvaged the electoral future of Fine Gael and healed divisions in the Labour party. The coalition government was presided over by Fine Gael Taoiseach John A. Costello who had to endure not only a coalition of five political parties and independents, an unusually large cabinet, a wide range of cabinet committees (sixteen in 1950) but also brazen and regular breaches of collective responsibility; though in this regard, the historian of that government, David McCullough, exonerates Costello from this charge in relation to the premature announcement in Canada that Ireland was to be declared a Republic.[76] Although it was deeply divided on economic issues, the introduction of capital budgets by this government was a turning point in Irish economic planning; there was much progress made on housing and state-led investment, and despite balance of payment problems and unemployment, and the Labour party's failure to push through their desired social welfare reforms, the arrival of Marshall Aid funds was significant in forcing Irish economists to think internationally. McCullough is perceptive in recognizing that it was Fianna Fáil who in many ways benefited from the new departures in economic thinking by taking subsequent advantage of new economic discourses and philosophies later in the 1950s. The experiences of this coalition government have also been amplified with the publication of a lengthy biography on the individual who kept this remarkably motley crew together, John A. Costello.[77]

In the post-war period there was a general re-evaluation of the role of the state, and by extension local authorities, in relation to public health. As a result, the need to be more interventionist, with a concentration on the principles of preventative rather than curative medicine, was recognized. This new recognition had important implications for the welfare of mothers and children. The conflict over improved maternity and child welfare spearheaded by the state—the Mother and Child Scheme controversy that led to the resignation of Noel Browne and contributed to the demise of CNP and the coalition government—was a class conflict as much as anything else. The interests of the medical profession prevailed, particularly the view expressed by Catholic extremist Dr James McPolin, that the scheme had to be defeated 'on the grounds that it obliterated a whole section of private practice for doctors'.[78] The Catholic hierarchy was also brought on board and wrote to the Taoiseach stating it 'cannot approve of any scheme which, in its general tendency, must foster undue control by the state in a sphere so delicate and intimately concerned with morals.'[79] John Charles McQuaid, Archbishop of Dublin from 1940 to 1972, in a private meeting with Taoiseach John A. Costello in April 1951, 'took occasion at once to explain to the Taoiseach that the phrase "Catholic social teaching" used by the Bishops meant "Catholic moral teaching in regard to things social".[80] The correspondence of McQuaid, held in his remarkably voluminous archive, is very revealing, often spiky, occasionally sinister, and sometimes funny, and exposes much about his *modus operandi*, mindset, and power during this period. Although some of these letters have been published, there is still much scope for historians to deepen an understanding of his episcopacy, its impact, and legacy.[81]

The unfortunate reality was that the 1950s was a decade in which the response of the middle-class establishment to Ireland's social and economic malaise was entirely ineffectual. This was partly a product of scaremongering about socialist politics, sponsored by the Catholic Church, the larger political parties, and the middle-class professions, and involved a denial that Ireland was a very poor country. For example, in 1951, a contributor to the Jesuit publication *Studies*, insisted

> Poverty fifty years ago was real, now it is comparative . . . the poor are still with us, but actual destitution if it is still to be found in Ireland is rare and avoidable . . . unless we are deliberately determined to drift into communist slavery let us strop repeating the stupid propaganda of the calamity mongers who, day in day out, declare that we were never so badly off as we are now, when, in actual fact, we are more fortunate than most nations and have the power to continue advancing if we have the will.[82]

It would be difficult to find a more blatant example of middle-class denial, although it needs to be acknowledged that 'both the conservative and liberal wings of the Catholic bourgeois who dominated politics and academia set out their thinking in *Studies*'.[83]

Those intent on invoking class politics were depicted by established politicians as foreign-influenced and dangerous radicals, and when it returned to power, the Fianna Fáil hierarchy seemed more concerned with American dollars than with the sufferings of an Irish underclass. In the 1950s, borrowed American dollars were of crucial importance to the post-war Irish economy, but they came at a price, and those who paid the biggest penalty were the poorest. Seán MacEntee, Minister for Finance in 1953, blamed the huge unemployment problem in Ireland on foreign borrowing: 'It would be very much better if these people were employed, but when the first demand on the economy was to meet interest owed to the US, some elements of the population were bound to suffer', he was quoted as saying in the *Dublin Evening Mail* newspaper.[84]

Much more research needs to be done on the social history of the 1950s and the experience of groups such as The Dublin Unemployed Association, which revealed individual cases of extraordinary hardship:

> One such case was that of a mother of 3 children who had approached the association for help. Her husband was suffering from acute heart trouble and had been removed

to St Kevin's hospital in a dying condition. She had been in receipt of 37 shillings 6 pence home assistance. The relieving officer had heard of her husband going into hospital, had come to the house and told her she would be cut down to 35 shillings as she had one less mouth to feed. The woman was distraught—the cut was a deathblow. She paid 6 shillings rent, 2 shillings insurance, 4 shillings gas, 4 shillings bus fare to visit her husband and brought cigarettes and tea to him. She was left with 19 shillings a week to feed and clothe herself and 3 children. She had never bought coal.[85]

Hopes of a new political dawn had been well shattered by the early 1950s. A second inter-party government was in office from 1954–7 and in many respects, in the words of Alvin Jackson, 'looked very much like a continuation of the first'. Balance of payments crises abounded, and despite some 'daring' new economic thinking and a long overdue questioning of economic nationalism, the government did not last long enough to give effect to these new ideas.[86]

The obvious alternative to enduring Irish poverty was to emigrate. Between 1951 and 1961, half a million people emigrated from Ireland. In 1957 alone, the figure was sixty thousand, at a time when the population of the Republic was under four million people. While it is true that these figures caused alarm, there was far too much attention devoted to the supposed moral and spiritual threats that existed to Irish people once they left, than to the impact it was having at home. *The Report of the Commission on Emigration and Other Population Problems* (1956)[87] was a worthy exercise but there was not enough attention given to the impact of emigration as a form of exclusion at familial and national level. Many of the dispossessed Irish found an enjoyable anonymity and little preoccupation with their class background once they were abroad. One such emigrant, Bernadette Fahey, who fled abuse in an Irish orphanage, summed this feeling up well:

> I left Ireland for several reasons, chief amongst which was the feeling that I didn't belong to anyone, anything or anywhere. I was also sick and tired of being asked where I came from and who I was. In common with hundreds of others who were raised in orphanages, I was ashamed of my past and did all in my power to hide it. England was a useful place to evade these issues. It was less parochial. People were happy enough to know which country you came from and leave it at that. For that reason alone it became the safe haven of thousands of orphans who couldn't bear the daily pressures that Irish society put on them. We were constantly confronted with our lack of roots and identity. This was extremely painful in a society that laid so much emphasis on one's family pedigree, place of birth and religious persuasion. These were the barometers by which individuals, families and groups were acceptable or not.[88]

As Enda Delaney has illustrated, emigrants were often depicted as somewhat feckless and easily led, which amounted to a tendency to blame the emigrants themselves rather than the society they left. This is particularly relevant in relation to the exodus of women; for every 1000 Irish men who emigrated between 1946 and 1951, 1365 Irish women emigrated. In 2007, when Mary Muldowney published the first book to date on the experiences of Irish women during the Second World War, it included an interview with a woman who volunteered for the armed forces and recalled being proud of her service in a British uniform: 'I wasn't anybody's wife or anybody's daughter or sister, I was me and it was really marvellous. It's nice to be yourself once in a while.'[89] Caitríona Clear has provocatively and convincingly demolished the myth that all female emigrants were victims, and sees low marriage rates and high rates of permanent celibacy as reflecting the fact that 'women were rejecting men'. One young woman, who spoke to Seán O'Faoláin, left him in no doubt of the reasons for her choice: 'I saw what my mother went through—not for me, thank you.'[90]

Despite the exodus, Ireland during these years was not a cultural wasteland. There were many achievements in arts and creative writing, thriving theatres, the inauguration of many enduring festivals including the Cork Opera and the Dublin Theatre festivals, and Irish short story writers, novelists, and poets continued to produce exceptional work.[91] There also emerged a critical questioning of the persistence of underdevelopment, as the 1950s was the decade in which emigration damaged the national psyche and the rural hinterland and placed under strain much of the rhetoric concerning the ideal rural life and the merits of self-sufficiency. Historian Dermot Keogh has also highlighted aspects of the 1950s that need further research, particularly the growth of the voluntary disability sector and the extent to which people were forming organizations to respond to unmet needs. There was much despair in 1950s Ireland, but there was also restlessness, questioning, and creativity.[92] Advances in the historiography of sport in Ireland have also created a new framework for an analysis of the success of the GAA in Irish life, despite emigration and other social pressures, a reminder that an analysis of sport and Irish society can go a long way towards revealing insights into that society's social and cultural fabric and value systems. The GAA demonstrated an ability to adapt to changed environments, and ultimately created a unique blend of the traditional and the modern.[93]

An unquestioning acceptance of clerical domination was also under some strain, as the unifying thread it provided after the political divisions of the earlier part of the twentieth century became less relevant. Towards the end of the 1950s, Ireland was also increasingly exposed to outside influence and the development of Keynesian economics, exemplified by the Programmes for Economic Expansion, begun in 1958, finally put paid to any lingering attachment to the virtues of economic and cultural isolationism.

The prosperity that accrued in the 1960s and the decline in unemployment and development of a robust export trade indicated the merits of a more open economy and Ireland engaged in a successful game of catch-up with many of the economies of Western Europe. What remained constant was the exceptional electoral appeal of Fianna Fáil, underlining the significance of the legacy of de Valera.

Notes

1. Ciara Meehan, *The Cosgrave Party: A History of Cumann na nGaedheal, 1923–33* (Dublin, 2010).

2. Joe Lee: *Ireland 1912–85: Politics and Society* (Cambridge, 1989), 340–1.

3. Alvin Jackson, *Ireland 1798–1998* (Oxford, 1999), 288–301.

4. Tom Garvin, *Preventing the Future: Why was Ireland so Poor for so Long?* (Dublin, 2004), 38–45.

5. Henry Patterson, *Ireland Since 1939: the Persistence of Conflict* (Dublin, 2006), 72–7.

6. Paul Bew, *Ireland: The Politics of Enmity 1789–2006* (Oxford, 2007), 464–79.

7. Tim Pat Coogan, *De Valera: Long Fellow, Long Shadow* (London, 1993), 693–705.

8. See Diarmaid Ferriter, *Judging Dev: A Reassessment of the Life and Legacy of Eamon de Valera* (Dublin, 2007).

9. Catriona Crowe, Michael Kennedy, Eunan O'Halpin, Ronan Fanning and Dermot Keogh (eds), *Documents on Irish Foreign Policy Vol.IV, 1932–36* (Dublin, 2004), *Vol.V, 1937–39* (Dublin, 2006) and *Vol.VI, 1939–41* (Dublin, 2008).

10. Ferriter, *Judging Dev*, 70ff.

11. Peter Mair, 'De Valera and democracy' in Tom Garvin, Maurice Manning and Richard Sinnott (eds) *Dissecting Irish Politics: Essays in honour of Brian Farrell* (Dublin, 2004), 31–48.

12. Donal O'Drisceoil, The 'Irregular and Bolshie situation': Republicanism and Communism 1921–36 in Fearghal McGarry (ed) *Republicanism in Modern Ireland* (Dublin, 2003), 45 and Henry Patterson, *Ireland since 1939*, 18.

13. Ferriter, *Judging Dev*, 183–95.

14. Ronan Fanning, *Independent Ireland* (Dublin, 1983), 116–8.

15. Eunan O'Halpin, 'Parliamentary party discipline and tactics; the Fianna Fáil archives, 1926–32', *Irish Historical Studies*, Vol.xxx, no.120, November 1997, 581–91.

16. Ferriter, *Judging Dev*, 99–121; for a more critical view see Tim Pat Coogan, *De Valera: Long Fellow, Long Shadow* (London, 1993), 693–705.

17. Brian Hanley, *The IRA, 1926–36* (Dublin, 2002) and ibid., *The IRA: A Documentary History 1916–2005* (Dublin, 2010), 79–83.

18. Fearghal McGarry, *Eoin O'Duffy: Self-made Hero* (Oxford, 2007).

19. National Archives of Ireland (NAI) Department of the Taoiseach (DT) S 4964, April 1933.

20. See Dermot Keogh, *Ireland and Europe 1919–39* (Dublin, 1988) and Diarmaid Ferriter, *Lovers of Liberty? Local Government in Twentieth Century Ireland* (Dublin, 2001).

21. Joe Lee, 'Centralisation and community', in Joe Lee (ed) *Ireland: Towards a Sense of Place.* (Cork University Press, 1985), 84–106.

22. David Fitzpatrick, *The Two Irelands 1912–1939* (Oxford, 1998), 197.

23. Ferriter, *Transformation*, 398.

24. Brian Girvin, *Between Two Worlds: Politics and Economy in Independent Ireland* (Dublin, 1989), 93.

25. Mary E. Daly, *The Buffer State: The Historical Roots of the Department of the Environment* (Dublin, 1997), 215–21.

26. Ann Marie Walsh, 'Root them in the land' Cottage schemes for agricultural labourers' in Joost Augusteijn (ed) *Ireland in the 1930s: New Perspectives* (Dublin 1999), 47–67.

27. Daly, *Buffer State*, 221.

28. Cormac O'Gráda, *Ireland: A New Economic History 1780–1939* (Oxford, 1994), 439–41.

29. Ibid.

30. Joe Lee, 'Squaring the economic and social circles' in Philip Hannon and Jackie Gallagher (eds), *Taking the Long View: 70 Years of Fianna Fáil*, (Dublin, 1996), 54–64.

31. Richard Dunphy, *The Making of Fianna Fáil Power in Ireland* (Oxford, 1995), 260 and Tom Feeney, *Seán MacEntee: A Political Life* (Dublin, 2008).

32. Joseph Robbins (ed), *Reflections on Health: Commemorating 50 years of the Department of Health 1947–1997* (Dublin, 1997) p.vii.
33. Garvin, *Preventing the Future* 140–5.
34. Garret FitzGerald, 'Eamon de Valera: the Price of his achievement' in Garret FitzGerald, *Ireland in the World: Further Reflections* (Dublin, 2005), 68–91.
35. Tom Garvin, *Judging Lemass: the Measure of the Man* (Dublin 2009).
36. Bryce Evans, *Seán Lemass: Democratic Dictator* (Cork, 2011).
37. Mary Daly, *Industrial Development and Irish National Identity* (Dublin, 1992), 171.
38. Ferriter, *Transformation*, 372.
39. Seán O'Faoláin, 'Eamon de Valera' *The Bell*, v.10, no.1, April 1945, 1–18.
40. Ferriter, *Transformation*, 394–5.
41. NAI, *Report of Department of Local Government and Public Health, 1942*; Lindsey Earner-Byrne, *Mother and Child Welfare in Dublin, 1922–60* (Manchester, 2007), 24–120.
42. Noel Browne, *Against the Tide* (Dublin, 1986), 58.
43. Earner Byrne, *Mother and Child*, 24–120.
44. Adrian Kelly, 'Cultural imperatives: The Irish language revival and the education system' in Augusteijn (ed), *Ireland in the 1930s*, 29–47.
45. Maurice Manning, *James Dillon: A Biography* (Dublin, 1999), 58–9.
46. Ferriter, *Transformation*, 350–1.
47. Dermot Keogh and Andrew J. McCarthy, *The Making of the Irish Constitution 1937* (Cork, 2007) and Gerard Hogan, *The Origins of the Irish Constitution, 1928–41* (Dublin, 2012).
48. See Seán MacBride, *That Day's Struggle: a memoir 1904–51* (Dublin, 2005).
49. Finola Kennedy, *Cottage to Creche: Family Change in Ireland* (Dublin, 2001), 5.
50. Ferriter, *Judging Dev*, 235–51.
51. Kennedy, *Cottage to Creche*, 82.
52. Caitriona Clear, *Women of the House: Women's Household work in Ireland, 1926–61* (Dublin, 2000), Alan Hayes (ed), *Hilda Tweedy and the Irish Housewives Association* (Dublin, 2012).
53. Mary Daly, '"Oh, Kathleen Ní Houlihán, your way's a thorny way!" The Condition of Women in Twentieth Century Ireland' in Anthony Bradley and Maryann Valiulis (eds), *Gender and Sexuality in Modern Ireland* (Massachusetts, 1997), 102–27.
54. Margaret O'Callaghan, 'Women and politics', in Angela Bourke et al (eds) *Field Day Anthology, Volume V*, 168.
55. Daly, 'Oh, Kathleen ní Houlihan', 102–27.
56. Terence Brown, *Ireland: a Social and Cultural History 1922–79* (London, 1981), 147.
57. Peter Martin, *Censorship in the Two Irelands, 1922–39* (Dublin, 2006).
58. Siobhán Kilfeather, 'Sexuality, 1685–2001' in Angela Bourke et al (eds) *The Field Day Anthology of Irish Writing, Volume IV: Irish Women's Writing and Traditions* (Cork, 2002); Maria Luddy, 'Sex and the single girl in 1920s and 1930s Ireland', *The Irish Review*, no.35, Summer 2007, 79–92; Diarmaid Ferriter, *Occasions of Sin: Sex and Society in Modern Ireland* (London, 2009); Maria Luddy, *Prostitution and Irish Society* (Cambridge, 2007) Sandra McAvoy 'Before Cadden: Abortion in Mid-Twentieth-Century Ireland' in Dermot Keogh, Finbarr O'Shea and Carmel Quinlan (eds) *The Lost Decade: Ireland in the 1950s* (Cork, 2004), 147–164, Rattigan, Cliona, 'Crimes of Passion of the worst character': Abortion cases and gender in Ireland, 1925–50 in Maryann Valiulis (ed), *Gender and Power in Irish History* (Dublin, 2008), 115–140, Mary Raftery and Eoin O'Sullivan, *Suffer the Little Children: The Inside Story of Ireland's Industrial Schools* (Dublin, 1999), Cliona Rattigan, *What else could I do? Single Mothers and Infanticide, Ireland 1900–1950* (Dublin, 2011).

59. Seán O'Faoláin, 'Answer to a Criticism', *The Bell*, Vol. 1 no.3, December 1940, 5–7. See also Bill Kirwin, 'The social policy of The Bell', *Administration*, Vol.37, 1989, 99–119.
60. Seán O'Faoláin, 'The Mart of Ideas', *The Bell*, Vol. 4 no.3, June 1942, 153–8.
61. National Archives of Ireland (NAI) Department of Justice (DJUS), H247/41 A, November 1932.
62. NAI, Department of the Taoiseach (DT) S 5998, November 1932.
63. *Report of the Committee on the Criminal Law Amendments Acts (1880–1885) and Juvenile Prostitution* (Dublin, 1931), 26.
64. Mark Finnane, 'The Carrigan Committee of 1930–31 and the 'moral condition of the Saorstát'. *Irish Historical Studies*, xxx11, no.128 (November 2001), 519ff.
65. Quoted in Harry Bohan and Gerard Kennedy, *Are We Forgetting Something?* (Dublin, 1999), 30–4.
66. See James M. Smith, *Ireland's Magdalen Laundries and the Nation's Architecture of Containment* (Notre Dame, 2007), Ferriter, *Occasions of Sin*, 407–547, *Report of the Commission to Inquire into Child Abuse* (Dublin, 2009).
67. Michael Kennedy, 'Joseph Walshe, Eamon de Valera and the execution of Irish foreign policy, 1932–8' *Irish Studies in International Affairs*, V.14, 2003, 165–85.
68. Catriona Crowe, Ronan Fanning, Michael Kennedy, Dermot Keogh and Eunan O'Halpin (eds) *Documents on Irish Foreign Policy Volume IV*, (Dublin, 2004), 229.
69. John Bowman, *De Valera and the Ulster Question, 1917–73* (Oxford, 1982), 308.
70. Brian Girvin, *The Emergency: Neutral Ireland 1939–45* (London, 2006), 60ff.
71. Ibid., and Richard Doherty, *Irish Men and Women in the Second World War* (Dublin, 2009), Brian Girvin and Geoffrey Roberts, *Ireland and the Second World War: Politics, Society and Remembrance* (Dublin, 2000), Neil Richardson, *Dark Times, Decent Men: Stories of Irishmen in World War II* (Dublin, 2012).
72. Girvin, *The Emergency*, 320ff.
73. Terence Brown 'Responses to the Emergency', *Irish Times*, 17 March 2007. Clair Wills, *That Neutral Island: A Cultural History of Ireland in the Second World War* (London, 2007), Paul Bew (ed), *The Memoir of David Gray: A Yankee in De Valera's Ireland* (Dublin, 2012).
74. Wills, *That Neutral Island*, 391–417.
75. Noel Browne, *Against The Tide* (Dublin, 1986), 98.
76. David McCullagh, *A Makeshift Majority: The First Inter-party Government 1948–51* (Dublin, 1998), 110.
77. David McCullagh, *The Reluctant Taoiseach: John A.Costello* (Dublin, 2010).
78. Kennedy, *Cottage to Creche*, 198.
79. Dublin Diocesan Archives (DDA), Papers of John Charles McQuaid, Government Box 5, AB8/B, 5 April 1951.
80. Ibid., 6 April 1951, McQuaid to his Grace, Archbishop of Armagh.
81. John Cooney, *John Charles McQuaid: Ruler of Catholic Ireland* (Dublin, 1999), Louise Fuller, *Irish Catholicism since 1950: The Undoing of a Culture* (Dublin, 2002), Margaret O hOgartaigh and Clara Cullen (eds) *His Grace is Displeased: Selected Correspondence of John Charles McQuaid* (Dublin, 2012).
82. Séamus O'Farrell 'The changing pattern of Irish life' *Studies*, vol.40, December 1951, 428–36.
83. Bryan Fanning (ed), *An Irish Century: Studies 1912-2012* (Dublin, 2012), 1–21.
84. Evanne Kilmurray, *Fight, Starve or Emigrate* (Dublin, 1988), 9–30.
85. Ibid.
86. Jackson, *Ireland 1798–1998*, 314–5.

87. See Mary E Daly, *The Slow Failure: Population Decline and Independent Ireland* (Wisconsin, 2006).
88. Bernadette Fahey, *Freedom of Angels: Surviving Goldenbridge Orphanage* (Dublin, 1999), 194.
89. Mary Muldowney, *Irish Women and the Second World War: An Oral History* (Dublin, 2007), vi.
90. See Keogh et al (eds), *The Lost Decade* and John O'Brien (ed) *The Vanishing Irish* (London, 1954), 113.
91. Brian Fallon, *An Age of Innocence: Irish Culture 1930–1960* (Dublin, 1998), 263–5.
92. Dermot Keogh, 'Introduction: The Vanishing Irish' in Keogh et al (eds), *The Lost Decade*, 11–20.
93. See Mike Cronin, William Murphy and Paul Rouse (eds) *The GAA: 1884–2009: A History* (Dublin, 2009), William Nolan, *The GAA in Dublin* (Dublin 2005), Mike Cronin, Mark Duncan and Paul Rouse, *The GAA: A People's History* (Cork, 2009).

SELECT BIBLIOGRAPHY

Bew, Paul, *Ireland: The Politics of Enmity 1789–2006* (Oxford, 2007).
Bourke, Angela (ed), *The Field Day Anthology of Irish Writing, Volume IV: Irish Women's Writing and Traditions* (Cork, 2002).
Clear, Caitriona, *Women of the House: Women's Household work in Ireland, 1926–61* (Dublin, 2000).
Cronin, Mike, William Murphy, and Paul Rouse (eds), *The GAA: 1884–2009: A History* (Dublin, 2009).
Crowe, Catriona, Michael Kennedy, Eunan O'Halpin, Ronan Fanning and Dermot Keogh (eds), *Documents on Irish Foreign Policy Vol.IV, 1932–36* (Dublin, 2004), *Vol.V, 1937–39* (Dublin, 2006) and *Vol.VI, 1939–41* (Dublin, 2008).
Earner-Byrne, Lindsey, *Mother and Child: Maternity and Child Welfare in Dublin 1922–60* (Dublin, 2007).
Evans, Bryce, *Seán Lemass: Democratic Dictator* (Cork, 2011).
Fallon, Brian, *An Age of Innocence: Irish Culture 1930–1960* (Dublin, 1998).
Fanning, Bryan, (ed), *An Irish Century: Studies 1912–2012* (Dublin, 2012).
Ferriter, Diarmaid, *The Transformation of Ireland 1900–2000* (London, 2004).
Ferriter, Diarmaid, *Judging Dev: A Reassessment of the Life and Legacy of Eamon de Valera* (Dublin, 2007).
Ferriter, Diarmaid, *Occasions of Sin: Sex and Society in Modern Ireland* (London, 2009).
FitzGerald, Garret, *Ireland in the World: Further reflections* (Dublin, 2005).
Fitzpatrick, David, *The Two Irelands 1912–1939* (Oxford, 1998).
Fuller, Louise, *Irish Catholicism since 1950: The Undoing of a Culture* (Dublin, 2002).
Garvin, Tom, *Preventing the Future: Why was Ireland so Poor for so Long?* (Dublin, 2004).
Garvin, Tom, *Judging Lemass: The Measure of the Man* (Dublin 2009).
Girvin, Brian, *Between Two Worlds: Politics and Economy in Independent Ireland* (Dublin, 1989).
Girvin, Brian, *The Emergency: Neutral Ireland 1939–45* (London, 2006).
Hanley, Brian *The IRA, 1926–36* (Dublin, 2002).
Hayes, Alan (ed), *Hilda Tweedy and the Irish Housewives Association* (Dublin, 2012).
Hogan, Gerard, *The Origins of the Irish Constitution, 1928–41* (Dublin 2012).

Jackson, Alvin, *Ireland 1798–1998* (Oxford, 1999).

Keogh, Dermot, and Andrew J. McCarthy, *The Making of the Irish Constitution 1937* (Cork, 2007).

Lee, Joe, *Ireland 1912–85: Politics and Society* (Cambridge, 1989).

Luddy, Maria, *Prostitution and Irish Society* (Cambridge, 2007).

Martin, Peter, *Censorship in the Two Irelands, 1922–39* (Dublin, 2006).

McCullagh, David, *The Reluctant Taoiseach: John A.Costello* (Dublin, 2010).

McGarry, Fearghal, *Eoin O'Duffy: Self-made Hero* (Oxford, 2007).

O'Gráda, Cormac, *Ireland: A New Economic History 1780–1939* (Oxford, 1994).

Patterson, Henry, *Ireland Since 1939: the Persistence of Conflict* (Dublin, 2006).

Rattigan, Cliona, *What Else Could I Do? Single Mothers and Infanticide, Ireland 1900–1950* (Dublin, 2011).

Richardson, Neil, *Dark Times, Decent Men: Stories of Irishmen in World War II* (Dublin, 2012).

Wills, Clair, *That Neutral Island: A Cultural History of Ireland in the Second World War* (London, 2007).

CHAPTER 34

··

UNIONISM, 1921–72

··

HENRY PATTERSON

BEFORE the late 1960s, writing on Unionism was a project largely indulged by what Gramsci would have termed the organic intellectuals of the Unionist political project.[1] It was, to use a helpful distinction, Unionist history as opposed to the history of Unionism written by historians.[2] Although Unionism originated as an all-Ireland movement to resist Home Rule, the necessity of constructing a movement with a mass popular following meant an Ulsterization not simply of political strategy but also of ideology. The result was a narrative of the 'Ulsterman' and his historical, regional, and psychological distinctiveness. James Loughlin[3] has argued the development of notions of the 'Ulsterman' need to be seen in terms of theories of racial categorization which were current in Victorian times. The Northern Irish version had the 'Ulsterman' as the embodiment of honesty, hard work, resolution, and resourcefulness as compared to the Catholic Irish who were portrayed as, at best, dreamy and impractical and, at worst, feckless and lazy.

Unionists had also emphasized the progressive impact of Protestant settlements in modernizing what was portrayed as the archaic structures of Gaelic Ulster and making north-east Ulster the only part of Ireland to industrialize successfully. Much of the Unionist propaganda during the Home Rule period had emphasized those personal and moral characteristics of the Protestant population which had been conducive to economic development and which any all-Ireland parliament dominated by Irish Catholics would be sure to destroy. Thus the Trinity historian W. Alison Phillips alleged that the native Irish were incapable of ruling themselves: 'the Celtic race, by virtue of its inherent qualities is incapable of developing unaided a high type of civilization.'[4]

This racial theme was not the only, or in fact the determinant, element in Unionist explanations of Irish economic and social backwardness, which more often featured an emphasis on the institutionalized power of Catholicism and a long-standing political culture of lawlessness. A key characteristic of Unionist thought and politics which carried over into the new state was a conviction of the insularity and economic backwardness of Catholic Ireland. Although Unionist self-confidence would decline in the inter-war period as the staple industries of the north suffered major contraction, it was reborn in the 1940s along with a continuing concern to point out the superiority of

economic and social conditions in the north to those in the south. But while there was
a hard substratum of materialism in Unionist arguments against Home Rule, and after
1921 Unionists would continue to defend partition in terms of its economic benefits,
arguments about the economy were often linked to religious and sectarian themes. Paul
Bew has underlined the central role played by issues of religious freedom and Ulster
Protestant concerns about the power of the Catholic Church in any Irish legislature in
the mass mobilization against the third Home Rule Bill: 'there really is no denying the
specifically religious or sectarian tone of much of the controversy'. He points out how
fear of the pretensions of the Catholic Church and the associated threat to Protestants'
civil and religious liberty in a Home-Rule parliament were not simply the concern of
working-class Orangemen but an impelling consideration for many of Belfast's liberal
Presbyterian bourgeoisie.[5] After 1923 Ulster Unionists had, in the experiences of southern Protestants during the revolutionary period and as a minority in the new Free State,
a plentiful source of examples of the religious and cultural travails which partition had
saved them from enduring. Dennis Kennedy has demonstrated how Unionist attitudes
were seriously affected not only by the nationalist violence directed against southern
Protestants in the period 1920–2 but also by their subsequent treatment as Dublin
moved more explicitly towards the adoption of a constitution in 1937 which was heavily
influenced by Catholic religious and social teachings.[6]

The academic study of Unionism by those without a Unionist political identity has
a relatively recent history and also one which was deeply affected from its origins by
political events. The expansion of higher education from the 1960s and the burgeoning Northern Irish Troubles produced a major expansion of work on Unionist politics,
ideology, and identity. The first serious works, Patrick Buckland's two-volume history
of Irish and Ulster Unionism and John Harbinson's history of the Ulster Unionist Party
(UUP), were published in the early 1970s as Northern Ireland was shattered by unprecedented levels of terrorist and inter-communal violence.[7] Both Buckland's study of the
Ulster Unionist movement and the formation of the Northern state and Harbinson's
history of the UUP appeared just five years after the civil rights movement had organized its first marches and the attendant irruption of the 'Ulster Crisis' on to British and
international television screens and leader columns. At this stage not only most labour
and liberal opinion, but also a significant sector of conservatism, sympathized with the
critics of what was seen as a regime which was, at best, characterized as somnolent and
third-rate and, at worst, actively sectarian and discriminatory. The result was a tendency to focus on Unionism as a problem, the roots of whose inadequacies needed to
be explored. Unionism was defined by its failure to measure up to liberal democratic
norms and by what was seen as a spiritual and cultural regression. The research agenda
was therefore to explain this anomalous regime and its purblind followers. The syndrome was well summed up by Sarah Nelson in a pathbreaking study of some Protestant
working class communities in Belfast during the 1970s:

> Who are the loyalists of Ulster? To many outsiders they are 'the voice of unreason, the
> voice of illogicality'. They are loyal to Britain yet ready to disobey her ... they refuse to
> do the rational, obvious thing.[8]

Harbinson, a former research officer for the Northern Ireland Labour Party[9], provided the explanation which had been in the stock-in-trade of Irish socialists and labourites for decades:

> After 1920 their objective was to maintain the Union. The strategy they employed was simple, short-term and effective. They maintained themselves in power by banging the big drum, waving the flag, and playing upon the emotions of the Protestant population.[10]

John Whyte in his survey of the political and academic debates aroused by Northern Ireland's conflicted history pointed out the problem with this approach to Unionism with its emphasis on elite manipulation: its underestimation of the popular roots of Unionism.[11] When Harbinson wrote, there was no existing work on popular Unionism. Before the introduction of the thirty-year rule he was also dependent on the Unionist Party for any access to the organization's papers held in the Public Record Office of Northern Ireland. He was also unable to access the departmental and cabinet papers of Unionist administrations. This contributed to the overly monolithic picture painted and the tendency to identify the Unionist Party as an Orange version of toryism.

Patrick Buckland provided a relatively sympathetic account of the origins of the organized Unionist movement from the 1880s, stressing its twin roots in Protestantism and uneven economic development, a theme which would become central to the first serious Marxist analysis of Unionism which was produced by Peter Gibbon in 1975.[12] But, writing in the early 1970s, it was hard not to read the history of Unionism through the prism of armed insurrection, sectarian assassinations, and above all the peremptory and demoralizing humiliation of direct rule. Thus he concluded:

> The roots of the Northern Ireland trouble that began in 1968–69 thus lay in the origins of Northern Ireland. In the early years, 1921–22, the tenor of the new state was determined...the Protestant community was defensively minded and anti-Catholic...its political leaders who had lively memories of the early years and shared these apprehensions were unable or unwilling to alter this mentality and to broaden Ulster unionist outlooks...The 1920s mentality produced a 1920s situation.[13]

Andrew Gailey noted the problems of writing about Unionism's past from the standpoint of the 1970s: 'Not surprisingly, perhaps, our appreciation of the past has been overwhelmed by the awfulness of the present.' Gailey was attempting to recapture the post-1945 history of Northern Ireland and the unprecedented sense of progressive optimism on the part of mainstream Unionism. This post-war world had, he believed, been almost obliterated from public memory by the descent into catastrophe after 1968: 'The tendency to judge is instinctive in us all, and after more than twenty years of Troubles post-war Ulster has been judged harshly.'[14]

The idea that it was the fraught conditions in which the state was created that determined an inflexible, partisan, and sectarian *mentalité* was given a revived Marxist inflection in one of the most influential works of the Troubles: Michael Farrell's *Northern*

Ireland: The Orange State.[15] The book's proclaimed leftism meant that it portrayed Unionism as a counter-revolutionary movement led by the Protestant bourgeoisie and large landowners which used a mixture of religious sectarianism and appeals to the 'marginal privileges' of the Protestant proletariat to enlist mass support. But the student leftism of the 1968 generation also generated a critique of this type of 'anti-imperialist' analysis of Unionism with its emphasis on the sectarianism and irrationality of popular Unionism. Here the publications of a small Marxist sect, the Irish Communist Organization, later the British and Irish Communist Organization (BICO), were seminal. It was in their substantial pamphlets, *The Two Irish Nations* and *The Economics of Partition*[16] that Ulster Unionism's material foundations in the uneven development of Irish capitalism and the hegemonic role in opposition to the demand for Home Rule played by the Protestant bourgeoisie of Belfast were established.

The BICO were clearly an influence on Peter Gibbon's historical sociology of the origins of Ulster Unionism. Published in 1975, it emphasized the dominant role of a modernizing Belfast bourgeoisie within the Unionist bloc. Gibbon's analysis has been criticized for exaggerating the role of the Belfast bourgeoisie in hegemonizing the leadership of Unionism and Jackson has emphasized the importance of a shared leadership involving the landed interest.[17] Gibbon was also prone to urban-centrism and a vision of Unionism which had little to say of rural Ulster. Although he made a serious attempt to investigate the role of Belfast's Protestant working class within the Unionist bloc, his analysis was too indebted to the Leninist idea of 'labour aristocracy' as the material basis for conservative and Orange sentiments amongst the Protestant proletariat.

Gibbon's depiction of Unionism as a form of Ulster nationalism was one of the earliest academic forays into the analysis of the nature of Unionist identity. The influence of Marxism on studies of Unionism and nationalism in the decade or so after 1968 was not conducive to the exploration of what has subsequently become a dominant theme in the study of Unionism. But there was one extremely influential work published in this area in the 1970s: David Miller's *Queen's Rebels*.[18] Miller's work was inspired by one of the most significant manifestations of popular Unionist militancy since the 1880s: the Ulster Workers' Council Strike of 1974 which overthrew the recently formed power-sharing government. How did those who emphasized their loyalty justify their defiance of the will of the government of the day? The answer lay, he argued, in the contractarian tradition of the Protestant settlers in Ulster during the seventeenth century. Ulster Protestants' loyalty was a 'pre-modern' one with little in common with modern notions of nationality and nationalism. Its focus was not on the 'imagined community' of the British nation but on a contractual relationship with the Crown which was obliged to defend its Protestant subjects in Ireland. If that obligation was not fulfilled then Protestants would turn to a centuries-old tradition of the 'public band' through which they would organize to defend and rule themselves. The 'conditional loyalty' of Ulster Protestants has produced one of the most important debates in academic studies of Unionism in and it rightly highlighted the importance of taking the ideological dimension of Unionism seriously. However, it was also prone to an essentialism which did not sufficiently register the diversity of Unionist ideology and of exaggerating the

Unionist capacity to go its own way in defiance of critical material and security depend-
ences on the British state.

Buckland's most important work on Unionism had to await the availability of the
archives of the Northern Ireland state which were made available for the first time in
January 1977. Although under the thirty-year rule this documentary treasure trove was
available up to 1947, Buckland chose to terminate his study in 1939 on the basis that
'During these years the pattern of government and politics was so firmly established
that by the late 1930s it was unlikely to be fundamentally altered except by political or
economic revolution.' The picture of Unionist government and administration painted
by Buckland is a powerful indictment not of partition but of legislative devolution,
which he argued produced a government which, whatever Sir James Craig's declaration
in 1921 that his government would be 'absolutely honest and fair in administering the
law', turned out to be disfigured by its Protestant populism and ethnic partisanship.[19]
This book was one of two published in 1979 which used official sources to investigate
the political and administrative practices of Unionism in power. *The State in Northern
Ireland*, like Buckland's, gave a central emphasis to divisions and fractures within
Unionism as the overriding concern of successive administrations who, in their relationship with the Catholic population were more impelled by fears of intra-Unionist
schism than by an active sectarian animus.[20] In its analysis of the governmental records
for the inter-war period it claimed to have discovered 'an unexpected picture of the politics of the ruling class in Ulster'. This involved a departure from the Farrellite view of a
monolithic 'Orange state' and instead a view of intra-state conflict between two identifiable groups:

> One group centred around Sir James Craig; the Minister of Labour, John Andrews
> and the Minister of Home Affairs, Dawson Bates. Broadly speaking, this group
> sought to generalise to the state as a whole the relation between Protestant classes
> epitomised in the B Specials…characterised by a combination of sectarian and
> 'democratic' practices, and by a high consumption of public funds…Another group,
> centred on two of the regime's Ministers of Finance, Hugh Pollock and John Milne
> Barbour, and the head of the Northern Ireland Civil Service, Sir Wilfred Spender,
> opposed this tendency. They strove instead to press the state along a *via Britannica* of
> a pre-Keynesian kind.[21]

The 'populist/anti-populist' division was traced over a set of issues including the
employment of Catholics in the Northern Ireland Civil Service, and strongly conflicting
views of the financial relations with the Treasury where populists were undeterred by
Treasury rebuffs over demands for more generous treatment, seen as 'spongeing' while
anti-populists believed firmly that Northern Ireland should adopt the prudent house-
keeping rules that would allow it to live within the constraints of the revenue generated
within the Province. At the root of the division was the populists' acute awareness of the
fissiparous nature of Unionism as a political alliance of divergent classes and interest
groups and the perceived danger this represented to Unionist control of the Province.
The emphasis on intra-Unionist conflict, particularly stemming from class antagonisms,

has proved to be one of the most fruitful foci of recent scholarship, with important work on Harry Midgley and the Northern Ireland Labour Party by Graham Walker,[22] on the unemployment issue by Christopher Norton, and on independent Unionism by Colin Reid.

After partition, the new government was from the start seriously concerned by the threats to Unionist unity posed by the independent tradition whether in the secular form of the NILP or the muscular Protestant populism of independents like Tommy Henderson, MP for Shankill, and John Nixon, the former District Inspector of the RUC who was sacked by the Minister of Home Affairs in 1924 after he had made a series of militant speeches at Orange Order meetings. He became M.P. for Woodvale, a Belfast constituency which, like its neighbouring constituency of the Shankill, was a heartland of working-class Protestants.[23] Reid points out the broader political significance of the independent Unionists and their impassioned attacks on the government and UUP in the inter-war period:

> Lord Craigavon headed a government which was guided by Protestant populism and was extremely sensitive to unrest within the Unionist bloc. In the 1930s in particular, his rhetoric was more 'Protestant' than 'Unionist', partly cultivated by the UUP's reliance on electioneering on loyalist principles. This was fostered by the need to confront independent Unionism and to provide an agenda behind which all Unionists could fall.[24]

These intra-bloc tensions are crucial for resolving a central question in the historiography of Unionism. If the stridently Protestant tone of the Northern state in the inter-war period can, in substantial part, be explained by the vivid memories and resentments that stemmed from the violent conditions in which the state was created, why were the constitutionally more secure conditions of the post-war years and the much improved material position of the North, particularly in comparison with the Republic, not the basis for a serious attempt to reform the state?

In this context, the role of Basil Brooke, later Lord Brookeborough, has been subject to much critical comment. Leading members of Sinn Féin still refer to his 1933 speech at an Orange Order demonstration in Newtownbutler when he had boasted that 'he had not a Roman Catholic about his own place' because 'the Roman Catholics were endeavouring to get in everywhere and were out with all their force and might to destroy the power and constitution of Ulster'.[25] Condemned as the 'Colebrooke Hitler' by another Fermanagh landowner, Brooke would later try to justify the speech and several more in which he had defended it, as a reflection of the intense strain which he, as a founding member of the Ulster Special Constabulary in 1921/22 had been under living in one of the parts of Fermanagh most vulnerable to IRA attacks in the early 1920s: 'What they forget is that I lived through one of the most terrible times in this country. Therefore I am not as ecumenical as the others.'[26] As M.P. for Lisnaskea at Stormont, he was representing a constituency where the Protestant population co-existed with a Catholic community which contained a militant republican element which, in the disturbed conditions of the early 1920s, was reinforced by IRA flying squads from the border counties of the Free State,

Cavan and Monaghan. In order to understand many of those aspects of Brooke's period as prime minister which infuriated his more liberal colleagues, the importance of the distinctive features of Unionism in border areas of Northern Ireland needs to be taken into account in any attempt to grasp the dilemmas of post-war Unionism.

It is also important to register the fact that Brooke began his prime ministerial career tasked with reinvigorating a government which, under a decrepit Craigavon and the short-lived successor regime of John Andrews, had singularly failed to mobilize Northern Ireland's economy and society for the challenge of war. A number of high-profile by-election defeats for official Unionist Party candidates from 1940 generated a crisis in the parliamentary party and forced Andrews's resignation. Brooke cleared out some of the most aged and incompetent members of the government and succeeded in giving his government a clear sense of purpose and in generating tangible results in terms of economic mobilization.[27] Politically, he was acutely attuned to the threat from the discontent amongst working-class Protestants which had been manifest in the by-election defeats. This meant making it clear that, despite the opposition of much of the party, he would implement the recommendations of the Beveridge Report in Northern Ireland. The challenge from the Left was a real one, particularly as by the end of the war the North's war economy had been losing momentum for more than a year. The Unionist Party fought the Stormont elections on a strong anti-socialist and private enterprise platform although it also stated that it would introduce whatever social reforms were introduced in Britain. Labour parties of various shades won 32 per cent of the vote in Northern Ireland and five Stormont constituencies, while in Belfast the 'non-nationalist Left' which included the NILP, the Commonwealth Labour Party, and the Communist Party, won 40 per cent of the vote.[28] The labourist upsurge convinced Brooke that his government had to embrace the welfare state no matter how much this enraged Unionism's middle-class supporters. However, the money to support the welfare state and attract new industries to replace the declining staples of shipbuilding, textiles, and agriculture could only come from London and that would mean intensifying dependence on the British Treasury in the post-war period. Here, Unionist leaders made much of the debt of gratitude which they claimed Britain owed the Province because of its role in the fight against Hitler.

The Ireland Act of 1949 reflected the moral capital accumulated by Northern Ireland's involvement in the war in contrast to the Free State's policy of neutrality and its subsequent refusal to join NATO because of Partition. For a period at least, stalwarts of the new Labour government like Herbert Morrison were enthusiastic defenders of partition. One indication of pro-Stormont attitudes in London was the fact that Hugh Massingham, an *Observer* journalist, whose father had founded the *Nation* and been an ardent Home Ruler, was now writing to Brookeborough urging him to appoint a press officer in London to respond to attacks from Hugh Delanty, Eire's High Commissioner.[29] The more sympathetic attitude towards Stormont in Westminster and Whitehall encouraged Unionist self-confidence and the belief that the government, secure constitutionally and strengthened materially by the arrival of the welfare state in the North, could expect more 'sensible' Catholics to see that the anti-partitionist project was dead and that they should make their peace with the regime. At the same time Brookeborough and some of the more perceptive of his ministers were concerned that the new international context and its themes of decolonization and the defence of human rights would be exploited by the Irish state and Irish nationalism. This meant a desire that, as far as possible, the state should avoid policies or actions which enabled its opponents to label it sectarian and intolerant. Thus when a Unionist candidate in the 1950 Westminster general election finished his oration by declaring 'To hell with the Pope!' he was quickly repudiated by the government and the party.[30] Similarly, when resolutions came before the executive of the UUP for possible debate at the annual conference, those demanding that government and public bodies favour loyalists in their appointments, were returned noting that such discussion would provide fertile ground for propaganda by 'the enemies of Ulster'.[31] The Prime Minister's bruising encounters with opponents of alleged 'romanizing' and 'appeasement' policies over education and public order policies seem to have convinced him that glacial change was all that was compatible with the maintenance of Unionist unity. This immobilism was encouraged by the upsurge in militant anti-partitionism that culminated in the IRA's campaign from 1956–62. This served to emphasize the differences between Unionists in border areas which were seriously affected by the campaign and those East of the Bann who enjoyed largely tranquil conditions. It was here and in the greater Belfast area in particular where dissatisfaction with what was seen as the somnolent conservatism of Brookeborough's regime was most threatening. It ranged from the electorally significant threat of a resurgent Northern Ireland Labour Party to the populist Protestantism of the emerging scourge of the 'appeasing' Unionist establishment, Ian Paisley, but it also included younger members of the Unionist Parliamentary Party, like William Craig, M.P. for Larne, who as Chief Whip made regular visits to the home of the Westminster M.P. for Londonderry, Robin Chichester-Clark, to ask advice on how to get rid of Brookeborough 'with his antediluvian views' and replace him with the Minister of Finance, Terence O'Neill.[32]

However, it is important to realize that those like O'Neill and Craig and those in the top ranks of the civil service who may have despaired of the regime's conservative and reactive style of government were not proponents of significant reforms in the relationship between the state and its Catholic population. Jack Sayers, who as editor of the *Belfast Telegraph*, would be an enthusiastic supporter of liberalization, sketched out the choice facing Unionism in the mid 1950s. He pointed to Brookeborough's support for the Education Act of 1948 which had outraged significant sections of Protestant and Orange opinion due to the substantial increase in financial support for Catholic schools:

> The measure stands as an example of liberal policy, but it remains to be decided whether the Unionist Party is prepared to make it a precedent for appeals to the minority on an even broader front.[33]

Yet, if Brookeborough's government failed the challenge, then it needs to be recognized that very few senior figures in the government, even of the most modernizing variety, were thinking of the sort of reforms which might have forestalled the crisis of the 1960s. The most advanced liberal, and someone who paid a high price for his views, was Brian Maginess, who, as Minister of Home Affairs in the early 1950s, had blighted a promising political career by banning an Orange parade. But at the core of Maginess's reformism was the desire for the incorporation of influential sections of the Catholic population into a redefined Unionist project which emphasized a common regional identity built around shared material interests in the continuation of the British connection.[34] This would involve certainly: a playing down of the more muscularly Protestant inflections of government and party; respect for 'traditional' that is, non-republican, manifestations of Irish national identity; accommodation of the interests of the Catholic Church in the fields of education and health; and, most immediately controversial, the encouragement of Catholics to become members of the Unionist Party. Although Maginess's travails were evidence of the powerful pressures from traditional Protestant and Orange sources, it is important to register the degree which much post-war public policy in the fields of economic development, social policy, and education transcended communal criteria in helping to improve the welfare and opportunities for all citizens of the state but particularly for the working class. The period from 1945 to the mid 1960s was defined by the degree to which concerns about issues of economic development, industrial diversification, and the potentialities of economic planning dominated not simply the agenda of government departments but much of the most significant political debate.

The arrival of the welfare state in the Province, while an unmitigated benefit for the Unionist cause providing as it did a qualitative leap in the material advantages of partition, opened up potential fissures in Unionism as a cross-class alliance. Many M.P.s, councillors, and constituency chairmen were instinctive conservatives on economic and social issues and castigated the government and Stormont administration for acting as a conveyor belt for legislation passed by the Labour government at Westminster and adopted with only minor modifications by Stormont. There was considerable support for the idea of dominion status through which Northern Ireland would become effectively independent and thus be able to resist the implementation of 'socialistic legislation'. The Unionist Party had fought the Stormont 1945 elections on a strongly anti-socialist and pro-private enterprise manifesto, although being careful to qualify this by stating that it would introduce whatever social reforms which were brought in in the rest of the UK. The election witnessed the defection of a substantial minority of the Protestant working class to the NILP and convinced the Prime Minister that, no matter how repugnant the welfare state might be to bourgeois members of the party, the government had no choice but to embrace it fully. The shift towards welfarism and a substantial increase in the size and role of government was the basis for an under-researched aspect of Northern Ireland in the post-war period: the increase in the weight of an increasingly self-confident 'banal' Unionism which took the unquestioned superiority of northern standards of well-being and life chances to those in the south for granted. While it is customary to decry the supposed 'supremacist' aspects of the Unionist *mentalité* it is necessary to register the degree to which a northern sense of superiority to the 'backward', priest-ridden and insular Irish Republic was shared by many in the rest of the UK where the Republic's refusal to countenance membership of NATO because of partition was coolly received. Thus it was not difficult for Unionists to find useful ammunition even in unexpected quarters. The *Catholic Herald* denounced Dublin for its refusal to see that, in the light of the need to defend the West against the 'anti-God East', 'the old issues of separation and conflicting loyalties had largely lost their *raison d'être*'. Whilst deploring discrimination against Catholics in Northern Ireland, it added that 'It is only fair to point out that the Northern Ireland majority can hardly fail to see the minority as a menace to itself. Indeed the whole Catholic Irish attitude to Partition obviously constitutes an avowed menace to the present popularly supported regime in the Six Counties.'[35]

Although Unionist concern with the anti-partition threat would not recede in the post-war period, the idiom of its response did register an important shift away from the strident tones of the 1949 election and its emphasis in what a critical review of Unionist strategy called 'the Big Drum'. There was an increasing awareness of the fact that the economic and social benefits of the British link were more obvious than at any time since Unionists had boasted of Belfast being the 'industrial capital of Ireland' during the struggle against Home Rule. As the government's director of publicity set out the case to be made against the raising of partition at the United Nations by the recently admitted Irish delegation:

> What we should always remember is that, to quote Nicolas Mansergh 'In 1921 the romance of Irish independence was over, its history had begun'. That history has considerably tarnished the romance, particularly in comparison with our progress in Ulster. In agriculture, the social services, education, industrial development, in our standard of living and in many other ways, we are streets ahead of Eire, and are strengthening our lead every day.[36]

This sort of argument allowed those Unionists interested in expanding the state's appeal beyond the Protestant population to develop a new version of the 'constructive Unionism' which had at the beginning of the twentieth century attempted to undermine the appeal of Irish nationalism through policies of land reform and industrial development. To its critics it appeared a strategy of avoidance of dealing with those features of Unionist political culture and practice which most alienated northern Catholics. Yet, its most important proponent did push the agenda beyond lauding the economic and social case for the Union.

The failure of Unionism in power to develop a more inclusive philosophy of government cannot be discussed adequately without acknowledging the profound obstacle represented by the official ideology of the Irish State, the suspicious hostility of the northern nationalism, and continued appeal of physical-force republicanism, especially in the border counties. It was therefore unsurprising that dominant modernizing agenda focused more on the development of the North's economic and social conditions, which was seen as a means of shifting popular horizons away from zero-sum conflicts over issues of political power and identity towards a common project of material betterment and increased opportunities for economic and social advance independent of religious/political affiliation. Although some politicians and civil servants would decry the post-war 'degeneration' of devolution into the marginal amendments of policies decided in Westminster and Whitehall, the senior ranks of the Northern Ireland Civil Service contained a number of officials who seized the opportunities of the post-war social democratic consensus to develop progressive policies in a range of fields, including education, industrial diversification, health, housing, and transport. The NICS remains largely under-researched and we are indebted to a retired senior official in the Department of Education, the late Arthur Green, for a powerful and eloquent registering of the importance of this group, a substantial number of whom were English, recruited through Whitehall's competitive examinations. Though not immune to the local parochial, sectarian pressures, the leadership of the NICS was far from acting as the representatives of the 'Orange state'.[37] These officials had to be aware of broader UK developments in their policy areas and of the increasing complexities of policy formation and implementation. Unlike many Unionist M.P.s and ministers who regarded politics and administration as part-time duties, they were impatient with the constraints of a provincial political culture and it was to some of them that Brookeborough's successor would look for his main support of his self-proclaimed modernization project.

The period ushered in by Terence O'Neill's unelected succession to Brookeborough was characterized by an accelerating pace of political change and increasing unease and instability in the Unionist party. It continues to be understood in the terms within which its tensions and conflicts were framed at the time by critics of the regime. As much of the impetus for change came from actual or feared 'interference' from Westminster, this early understanding of the dialectic between what were seen as the twin poles of 'reform' and 'reaction' was unsympathetic or even hostile to Unionism. An early example was Robert Kee's programme on Northern Ireland shown on ITV's *This Week* in December 1964. Although impressed by the government's advanced factory provision, he noted the contrast between 'the highly impressive industrial developments now taking place under government inspiration all over Northern Ireland' and 'the backward forces on both sides'.[38] Interviewing Brian Faulkner, who as Minister of Commerce had responsibility for the industrial development drive, Kee raised the awkward issue of 'a certain contradiction' between 'the wish to create a modern industrial society...and some of the political and social features of Ulster' amongst which he mentioned the restriction of local council voting to ratepayers, the gerrymandering of electoral wards in Derry, and discrimination in the allocation of council housing. Faulkner, visibly uncomfortable during this part of the interview, would have been less than pleased with the broadcast version where, as the camera focused on his face, the soundtrack featured the Orange anthem 'The Sash My Father Wore'.[39]

Anti-Catholic discrimination and the massed ranks of Orangemen decked out in exotic regalia would become the staple of much UK and international media 'analysis' of the Northern Irish crisis as it unfolded over the next decade. Faulkner's embarrassment on television was an early example of the difficulty which even the most intelligent and accomplished defenders of the government would have in persuading an uncomprehending external audience that they were not running a supremacist state. The party's relationship with the Orange Order, which was structurally inscribed in the constitution of the Ulster Unionist Council from its origins, was a rich mine for anti-regime propaganda and academic coverage of the Order. Despite this, the Order's role in Unionism has, until recently, lacked serious analysis. There has been a tendency to portray it in crudely instrumentalist terms: the Unionist elite using the Order's links with working-class Protestants to maintain its electoral hegemony. The price of this Faustian pact was seen to be the imposition of a sectarian flavour to many aspects of public policy, from recruitment to public employment to public order policy. The recent availability of the internal records of both the Unionist Party and the Orange Order has shown a more complex picture. There are certainly more than enough examples of Orange pressure against the employment of 'disloyalists', for the Northern Ireland Housing Trust to allocate housing on a sectarian basis, and against any attempt to regulate Orange marches which interfered with their customary routes. However, what the records demonstrate is that the Order in the post-war period became riven by the broader tensions within the Unionist bloc and that in particular it was increasingly marked by a contest between the 'traditional' elite group of landlords and clergymen, who saw the Order's role as the maintenance of the existing Unionist regime taking into account unwelcome but unignorable pressures for change and an 'independent' populist opposition with strong roots in the Orange rank and file, particularly the urban working-class members, that increasingly criticized the elite for a willingness to compromise with 'romanism' and 'ecumenism'.[40]

The earlier academic analyses of O'Neillism tended to echo the dismissive approach to his reformist programme adopted by the more radical elements of the civil rights movement. Bew, Gibbbon, and Patterson emphasized that in the initial years of his regime his main aim was to promote a modernization strategy to 'steal the thunder of the NILP'. His professed commitment to improving community relations and building bridges to the Catholic community were dismissed as largely cosmetic, raising expectations of change that he was incapable of fulfilling. However, since the publication of Marc Mulholland's impressive analysis of the O'Neill years, the discussion of O'Neillism has become more nuanced. Mulholland argues that the modernization strategy had implicit in it 'an entire reconfiguration of politics in Northern Ireland. A reformed Ulster Unionist Party would slough off its bigoted ultra-Protestant wing and attract a substantial Catholic vote on the basis of technocratic modernity.'[41] But even if the genuineness of O'Neill's commitment to transforming the state's relationship to Catholics is accepted, there remains the fact, acknowledged by his strongest supporters like Jack Sayers of the *Belfast Telegraph*, that he lacked a political strategy for achieving his reformist objectives. Some of O'Neill's critics tend to assume that his failure was one of will and personal inadequacies—his patrician and aloof political style in contrast with the common touch and easy charm of Brookeborough or his failure to grasp that Catholic alienation was 'structural' rather than 'behavioural'.[42] However, the core problem for him and his successors went deeper than this and reflected the fact that woolly expressions of the need for change and transforming the face of Ulster were inevitably seen as highly suspect by a much broader section of the Unionist community than the strident minority who supported Paisley. It is best summed up in Andrew Gailey's perceptive comment on the limitations of the vision of one of O'Neill's most important supporters, Jack Sayers:

> Sayers's liberal constituency was in spirit too professional middle class, too sub-urban, and too east of the Bann...he failed to appreciate the fears of ordinary Protestants...his sharp retort during the West affair that the Unionist Party should not be run at the behest of Fermanagh starkly reflected the contempt shown by those for whom 'civilisation ended at the Finaghy crossroads'.[43]

O'Neill largely ignored his party, seeing it a force of conservatism and devoting no thought or effort to how to win the case for reform within it. This would not have been an easy task but the fact that he did little to hide his low opinion of his backbenchers and most of his cabinet colleagues did not help.[44] His failure to consult his cabinet before his historic meeting with the Irish Taoiseach, Seán Lemass, in January 1965 was symptomatic and did much to build up grass-roots suspicion of his leadership.

His plans for reorganizing and centralizing the planning system and the decision to build the new city of Craigavon just thirty miles from Belfast stoked the fears of border Unionists that they were being neglected by Stormont.[45] In April 1967, O'Neill fired Harry West, his Minister of Agriculture and MP for Enniskillen, over a land deal which he claimed broke the ministerial code he had introduced to govern ministers' business interests. In Fermanagh, many party members saw the sacking as the victimization of a politician whose real crime was to defend their interests from O'Neill's reformist agenda and in particular from the feared reform of local government; as one prominent Fermanagh Unionist put it: 'if this (one-man one-vote) is granted, Tyrone, Fermanagh and Londonderry will fall to our opponents'.[46] In 1970, the then Minister of Development, Brian Faulkner, charged with introducing local government reform, made a spirited defence of its necessity for placating an implacable British government but also of its unthreatening nature, as even if nationalists controlled Fermanagh, Tyrone, and Derry, the 'sheet-anchor' of the Union would remain in unionist control of Stormont. Of course this was not an argument that Faulkner recognized as a rising star of the Unionist right in the late 1950s when he was happy to argue that loss of these counties would be a major blow to Unionist control of the Province and would embolden nationalism to press on for more radical political changes.[47] In 1959, when he opposed franchise reform, the IRA's assault on Northern Ireland had clearly failed and in the Westminster elections the Sinn Féin vote slumped dramatically. At the time revisionist voices were beginning to demand a more positive engagement of Catholics with the state and there were some signs of a mellowing of communal relations, at least east of the Bann. By 1968, with a new mass Catholic militancy manifested in the civil rights marches and an impatient British prime minister demanding serious reforms, Unionist leaders would struggle to convince their followers that concessions would lead to pacification and not radicalization of the Catholic population.

The profound difficulty of Unionist reformism has not been adequately registered in existing accounts, which have tended, like British policy-makers at the time, to ignore the profundity of popular fears and resentments. At the centre of mobilizing these forces was the Rev Ian Paisley. He has too often been understood in terms of his religious fundamentalism and the Manichean world view which has been seen as appealing to grassroots Unionism unnerved and disorientated by the acceleration of political changes.[48] Christopher Farrington has suggested that such an approach fails to register Paisley's active role as an agent of political transformation, arguing that the religious dimension of his appeal has been exaggerated and that it was his ability to portray events like the widespread Catholic participation in the 1916 commemoration parades in 1966 as evidence of a mass republican threat to Protestant ethnic interests that put him in a position to mobilize grassroots Unionist resentment with the trend of political events, particularly when the civil rights movement took to the streets in the late summer of 1968.[49] A new generation of scholars are beginning to think about the period from O'Neill's accession to the imposition of direct rule in terms that emphasize the importance of specifically political triggers of crisis and a more state-centric analysis. This approach challenges notions of the inevitability of the descent into violence, whether based on republican or cruder Marxist analyses.

Our understanding of the enveloping crisis post-1968 has also suffered from lack of serious studies of either of O'Neill's successors which could rank with Marc Mulholland's substantial political biography of Terence O'Neill.[50] James Chichester-Clark and Brian Faulkner still await serious attention and their role has suffered from the partisan and journalistic accounts which have dealt with them.[51] Chichester-Clark's premiership in particular demands more attention than it has received.[52] It is true that while he had a much better relation with his Cabinet than O'Neill, his public performances were 'shaky' and his television appearances could appear 'bumbling'.[53] This may have hindered his effectiveness in selling a deepening process of reform to the Unionist grassroots. However, the main problems of his premiership were so profound that deficiencies in projecting the reform project were, at most, a secondary issue. The eruption of violence in Derry and Belfast in August 1969 produced a fundamental shift in power to Westminster as Harold Wilson and his Home Secretary, James Callaghan, used Stormont's request for British troops to impose a set of major reforms which included the disarming of the RUC and the disbandment of the 'B' Specials. A new UK representative, a senior Foreign Office official sent to ensure Chichester-Clark's government pressed on with reforms, made clear he did not want to be sullied by physical location at Stormont, choosing instead an hotel on the outskirts of west Belfast so that he could be an effective channel for nationalist grievances and demands, a incitement to radicalization of nationalist perspectives on the possibilities of change.[54] Too much focus has been given to the failures of Unionist leaders and the reactionary pressures of Unionist grassroots and not enough attention paid to the increasing radicalization of the opposition's demands and the ham-fisted nature of many of the new policies introduced at Westminster's behest. Graham Walker praises Chichester-Clark for 'a series of courageous declarations of a civic-minded unionism...and a raft of reforms the commendable and forward-looking character of which was in effect neutered by the mayhem in the streets'.[55] With 'no-go' areas controlled by paramilitaries, an IRA offensive gathering pace, and a new policing chief, Sir Arthur Young, surplus to requirements in Britain but thought good enough for the challenging tasks of policing Northern Ireland's riot- and murder-spattered streets,[56] the burdens on Chichester-Clark were soon to prove overwhelming.

Although the arrival of a Conservative government in June 1970 was claimed by nationalists to herald a pro-Unionist shift in London's policies, recent research has undermined this[57] and points to a continuity of British pressure for reform and impatience with Chichester-Clark's increasing emphasis on the need to deal with intensifying levels of IRA violence. Even the Ardoyne IRA's brutal killing of three young British soldiers, lured to their deaths during an evening's drinking, was not thought sufficient cause to heed the demand for a substantial increase in troop numbers and a more activist set of security policies. The resultant resignation brought Brian Faulkner to office but, although he had long desired the job and had a not-unjustified belief in his superior capacities to those of his two predecessors, his premiership was destroyed by the twin incubi of apparently uncontainable IRA violence and a British government that was advised by its representative in Belfast that Faulkner 'does not well understand that there is no military solution. There must be the prospect of progress which dispels the sense of hopelessness amongst the Roman Catholics upon which the IRA depends'.[58] This criticism came less than a month after leading opposition politicians had welcomed enthusiastically a package of proposals to enable the opposition to play a more meaningful role at Stormont through a committee system, half of which would have been chaired by opposition M.P.s. The package was not seen by Faulkner as a final offer but rather the initiation of a process of what the political scientist Robin Wilson has called, following Gramsci, *transformismo*—the formation of an ever more extensive ruling class.[59] That within a month the SDLP had withdrawn from Stormont to set up an alternative assembly reflected not the inadequacies of Faulkner's reformism but the shooting dead of two Catholics in Derry by the army, something which was the responsibility of the Ministry of Defence and the British government, not Stormont. The SDLP's radicalization was a direct product of IRA strategic calculations as they intensified a bombing campaign aimed at enraging the Unionist community and forcing the introduction of internment, an eventuality which republicans correctly calculated would usher in the final crisis of the Northern Ireland state.

Unionism would be politically expropriated by Direct Rule and suffer a deepening process of fractionalization. It would also continue to be pilloried for its 'supremacist' past and its incoherent and conservative resistance to change after 1972. Ignored within this conventional wisdom was one fundamental fact: by the time Chichester-Clark became prime minister, the civil rights phase of Catholic mobilization had begun transforming into a more traditional agenda which, after August 1969 when Stormont lost the capacity to police and secure its rule and the new British presence prioritized reform over security, left substantial parts of the North's territory near to a state of nature. In 1921, Ulster Unionism had the capacity to form a state and force a reluctant British government to recognize and support it; by the 1960s in a context of economic dependence and an international context where repression by what was perceived as a right-wing regime was ruled out, Unionism appeared to have lost any effective autonomy apart from that of implementing or frustrating the initiatives of other more powerful forces.

Notes

1. Antonio Gramsci, 'The Formation of Intellectuals' in his *The Modern Prince and Other Writings* (New York, 1971), 118–25.
2. Alvin Jackson, 'Irish Unionism' in D. George Boyce and Alan O'Day (eds) *Modern Irish History Revisionism and the Revisionist Controversy* (London and New York, 1996), 121.
3. James Loughlin, ' "Imagining Ulster": the North of Ireland and British national identity, 1880–1921' in S.J. Connolly (ed), *Kingdoms United? Great Britain and Ireland since 1500: integration and diversity* (Dublin, 1999).
4. Gillian McIntosh, *The Force of Culture Unionist Identities in Twentieth-Century Ireland* (Cork, 1999), 21.
5. Paul Bew, *Ideology and the Irish Question: Ulster Unionism and Irish Nationalism 1912–1916* (Oxford, 1994), 29–34.
6. Dennis Kennedy, *The Widening Gulf: Northern Attitudes to the Independent Irish State 1919–1949* (Belfast, 1988).
7. Patrick Buckland, *Irish Unionism: One: The Anglo-Irish and the New Ireland 1882–1922* (Dublin and New York, 1972), and *Ulster Unionism and the Origins of Northern Ireland 1886–1922* (Dublin and New York, 1973); J.F. Harbinson, *The Ulster Unionist Party, 1882–1973 Its Development and Organisation* (Belfast, 1973).
8. Sarah Nelson, *Ulster's Uncertain Defenders: Loyalists and the Northern Ireland Conflict* (Belfast, 1984), 1.
9. Aaron Edwards, *A History of the Northern Ireland Labour Party: Democratic Socialism and Sectarianism* (Manchester, 2009), 46.
10. Harbinson, *The Ulster Unionist Party*, 166.
11. John Whyte, *Interpreting Northern Ireland* (Oxford, 1991), 175–7.
12. P. Gibbon, *The Origins of Ulster Unionism* (Manchester, 1975).
13. Buckland, *Ulster Unionism and the Origins of Northern Ireland*, 178.
14. Andrew Gailey, *Crying in the Wilderness Jack Sayers: A Liberal Editor in Ulster 1939–69*, (Belfast, 1995), ix.
15. Michael Farrell, *Northern Ireland The Orange State* (London, 1976).
16. British and Irish Communist Organization, *The Economics of Partition*, Revised and extended edition (Belfast, 1972).
17. Alvin Jackson, *The Ulster Party: Irish Unionists in the House of Common 1884–1911* (Oxford, 1989), 5–6.
18. David Miller, *Queen's Rebels: Ulster Loyalism in Historical Perspective* (Dublin, 1978). Reprinted with an introduction by John Bew (Dublin, 2007).
19. Patrick Buckland, *The Factory of Grievances: Devolved Government in Northern Ireland 1921–39* (Dublin, 1979), 1.
20. P. Bew, P. Gibbon, and H. Patterson, *The State in Northern Ireland 1921–1972: Political Forces and Social Classes* (Manchester, 1979).
21. Ibid., 76.
22. Graham Walker, *The Politics of Frustration: Harry Midgley and the NILP* (Manchester, 1985) and 'The Northern Ireland Labour Party 1924–45' in Fintan Lane and Donal O Drisceoil

(eds), *Politics and the Irish Working Class, 1830–1945* (Basingstoke, 2005); Christopher Norton, 'Creating jobs, manufacturing unity: Ulster Unionism and mass unemployment, 1922–34', *Contemporary British History*, 15 (2001); Colin Reid, 'Protestant Challenges to the "Protestant State": Ulster Unionism and Independent Unionism in Northern Ireland, 1921–1939', in *Twentieth Century British History*, 19: 4, 2008.

23. Reid, 'Protestant challenges', 431.
24. Ibid., 445.
25. Brian Barton, *Brookeborough: The Making of a Prime Minister* (Belfast, 1988), 78.
26. Ibid., 87.
27. The most authoritative work on Northern Ireland during the war is Philip Ollerenshaw, *Northern Ireland in the Second World War: Politics, Economic Mobilisation and Society 1939–1945* (Manchester, 2013).
28. H. Patterson and E. Kaufmann, *Unionism and Orangeism in Northern Ireland since 1945* (Manchester, 2007) 19–20.
29. Letter from Hugh Massingham, *The Observer*, to Basil Brooke, 12 February 1949, in Public Record Office of Northern Ireland (PRONI), Cabinet Publicity Committee, 2 March 1949, CAB4A/26/33
30. Henry Patterson, 'Party versus Order: Ulster Unionism and the Flags and Emblems Act', *Contemporary British History*, 13: 4, 1999.
31. Patterson and Kaufmann, *Unionism and Orangeism*, 49.
32. Notes on Sir Edward Heath's autobiography by Sir Robin Chichester Clark, courtesy of the author.
33. Thomas Wilson (ed), *Ulster under Home Rule* (Oxford, 1955), 75.
34. Henry Patterson, 'Brian Maginess and the Limits of Liberal Unionism', *The Irish Review*, 25, 1999/2000, 95–112.
35. Cabinet Publicity Committee, 24 May 1949, CAB 4A/26/34.
36. Memorandum on publicity in US by Eric Montgomery, Director of Information, Cabinet Publicity Committee, CAB4A/26/75, 7 April 1956.
37. Arthur Green, 'Bureaucracy for Belfast: A Historiography', a paper presented to the Belfast Literary Society, January 10 2005. Available on website of The Cadogan Group: www.cadogan.org/articles/bureaucracy.htm
38. John Hill, *Cinema and Northern Ireland: Film, Culture and Politics* (London, 2006), 138.
39. Ibid., 139.
40. Eric P Kaufmann, *The Orange Order: A Contemporary Northern Ireland History* (Oxford, 2007), 38.
41. Marc Mulholland, 'Modernizing Conservatives: The Northern Ireland Young Unionist Movement in the 1960s', *Irish Political Studies*, 25: 1, 2010, 72.
42. Fergal Cochrane, 'Meddling at the Crossroads: The Decline and Fall of Terence O'Neill within the Unionist Community', in Richard English and Graham Walker, *Unionism in Modern Ireland* (Basingstoke and London, 1996), 148.
43. Gailey, 164–5.
44. Andrew Gailey, 'The destructiveness of constructive unionism: theories and practice, 1890s–1960s', in D. George Boyce and Alan O'Day (eds), *Defenders of the Union* (London, 2001), 238.
45. Henry Patterson, 'In the Land of King Canute: the Influence of Border Unionism on Unionist Politics 1945–63', *Contemporary British History*, 20: 4, December 2006, 511–32, and Martin Joseph McCleery, 'The Creation of the "New City" of Craigavon: A Case Study

of Politics, Planning and Modernisation in Northern Ireland in the Early 1960s', *Irish Political Studies*, 27: 1, 2011, 89–109.

46. Patterson and Kaufmann, *Unionism and Orangeism*, 78.
47. Ibid., 57.
48. Steve Bruce, *For God and Ulster: The Religion and Politics of Paisleyism* (Oxford, 1986)
49. Christopher Farrington, 'Mobilisation, State Crisis and Counter-Mobilisation: Ulster Unionist Politics and the Outbreak of the Troubles', *Irish Political Studies*, 23: 4, December 2008, 524–9.
50. Marc Mulholland, *Northern Ireland at the Crossroads: Ulster Unionism in the O'Neill Years* (Basingstoke and London, 2000).
51. A recent and fairer assessment can be found in Graham Walker, *A History of the Ulster Unionist Party* (Manchester, 2004).
52. See Clive Scoular, *James Chichester-Clark, Prime Minister of Northern Ireland* (Antrim, 2000) and C.D.C. Armstrong, 'James Dawson Chichester-Clark', *Dictionary of National Biography*, www.oxford.dnb.com/view/article/76880
53. Robert Ramsay, *Ringside Seats: An Insider's View of the Crisis in Northern Ireland* (Dublin, 2009), 60.
54. Henry Patterson, 'The British State and the Rise of the IRA 1969–1971: The View from the Conway Hotel', *Irish Political Studies*, 23: 4, December 2008, 496–8.
55. Walker, *A History of the Ulster Unionist Party*, 189.
56. 'It was only after he was long gone that the officials in the Home Office admitted to us the background story: in the planning of senior appointments in GB Young had been considered, inconveniently "surplus to requirements" and it had been Callaghan's personal brainwave to offload him on the RUC.' Ramsay, *Ringside Seats*, 61–2.
57. Thomas Hennessey, *The Evolution of the Troubles 1970–72* (Dublin, 2007), 343.
58. Howard Smith to Home Secretary, 10 June 1971, quoted in Patterson, 'The British State and the Rise of the IRA', 507–8.
59. Robin Wilson, 'Ethnonationalist Conflicts, Consociational Prescriptions and the Travails of Politics in Northern Ireland', PhD, Queen's University Belfast, November 2008, 119.

Select Bibliography

Boyce, D. George and Alan O'Day, *Defenders of the Union: A Survey of British and Irish Unionism since 1801* (London, 2001).
Bruce, Steve, *God Save Ulster! The Religion and Politics of Paisleyism* (Oxford, 1989).
Edwards, Aaron, *A History of the Northern Ireland Labour Party* (Manchester, 2009).
English, Richard and Graham Walker, *Unionism in Modern Ireland* (Basingstoke & London, 1996).
Gailey, Andrew, *Crying in the Wilderness: Jack Sayers: A Liberal Editor in Ulster 1939–69* (Belfast, 1995).
Hennessey, Thomas, *The Origins of the Troubles* (Dublin, 2004).
Hennessey, Thomas, *The Evolution of the Troubles 1970–72* (Dublin, 2007).
Kaufmann, Eric P., *The Orange Order: A Contemporary Northern Irish History* (Oxford, 2008).
McCleery, Martin Joseph, 'The Creation of the "New City" of Craigavon: A Case Study of Politics, Planning and Modernisation in Northern Ireland in the Early 1960s', *Irish Political Studies*, 27:1, 2011.

Miller, David W. *Queen's Rebels: Ulster Loyalism in Historical Perspective* (Dublin, 2007).

Mulholland, Marc, *Northern Ireland at the Crossroads: Ulster Unionism in the O'Neill Years, 1960–69* (Basingstoke and London, 2000).

Mulholland, Marc. 'Modernising Conservatism: The Northern Ireland Young Unionist Movement in the 1960s', *Irish Political Studies*, 25:1, 2010.

Patterson, Henry. 'In the Land of King Canute: the Influence of Border Unionism on Ulster Unionist Politics 1945–63', *Contemporary British History*, 20: 4, December 2006.

Patterson, Henry and Eric Kaufmann. *Unionism and Orangeism in Northern Ireland since 1945* (Manchester, 2007).

Walker, Graham. *A History of the Ulster Unionist Party* (Manchester, 2004).

CHAPTER 35

....

THE SECOND WORLD WAR
AND IRELAND

....

EUNAN O'HALPIN

I. Introduction

THE Irish experience of the Second World War presents a number of problems for historians, as it did at the time for the Irish people and their nearest neighbours. 'Irish', in this context, refers to the independent Irish state and its people (including those who chose to participate in some way in the war, whether through military service in the Allied armed forces, through civilian work in the United Kingdom, or through intrigue with Britain's enemies). The experience of Northern Ireland is not addressed, save insofar as problems of border security, north/south relations, and transport ties are concerned. Some reference is also made to the experience of other aspirant neutral states, which formed the great majority of the independent countries of Europe, Asia, and the Americas in 1939.

Ireland's policy during the Second World War had a profound impact on her sense of sovereignty, on her international standing, and on her experience during the years of European economic, political, and social reconstruction which followed. What is less clear, though much debated, is the consequence of wartime neutrality for relations with what many regarded as the lost province and people of Northern Ireland, for Anglo-Irish and for Irish-American relations. Some have argued that, in staying out of the war in defiance of strategic logic in 1940 and in refusing defence facilities to Britain—her sole strategic guarantor and only economic partner—independent Ireland placed parochial, half-imagined grievances above the need to defend civilization itself against the Nazi onslaught. Such arguments, combining moral and practical elements, came particularly easily to the government of the United States (despite America's own neutrality until December 1941). There was a sense that, whatever their residual differences, particularly partition, the United Kingdom and Ireland shared sufficient democratic and internationalist values to require the Irish to stand together with Britain in her hour of greatest need (especially as, if Britain fell, so inevitably would Ireland). Given what we now know and given how the Second World War in Europe is largely explored, we must note that during the conflict the greatest moral issue of all—the fate of European Jewry—was never adduced as a reason to fight Hitler.

Irish neutrality became a practical proposition only in April 1938, when the Irish and British governments agreed a number of economic and financial measures which, it was hoped, would put an end to the friction which had characterized Anglo-Irish relations since de Valera took office in March 1932. Amongst these was a British agreement to relinquish her Irish defence rights under the 1921 Anglo-Irish Treaty which had brought independent Ireland into being. Although war with Germany seemed increasingly likely, British strategic planners reasoned that the ports, coastal defence forts, moorings, and associated facilities detailed in the 1921 treaty were run-down and unsuitable for modern warfare; furthermore, because of their location they could not be operated in wartime without Irish assistance, which would not be forthcoming. In reality, however obsolete the installations themselves, in wartime they would have provided a foot in the Irish door, and they would have made Ireland a legitimate target for attack by Britain's most likely enemy, as was Northern Ireland. In 1938 it was generally assumed in London that, when war came, de Valera would row in; yet he made it crystal clear to the Dáil that, while Ireland would be particularly mindful of Britain's legitimate defence and security interests in a future war, Ireland would stay out of such a conflict unless herself attacked.

When war came, no one save a handful of pro-German republicans made any kind of case for joining in. On the contrary, all the evidence points to widespread cross-party support for the policy of staying out at all costs; the later ascendancy of the Allies, so far from undermining neutralist sentiment, reinforced it, particularly in the face of British and American hectoring. Germany, by contrast, was content to see Ireland remain neutral, although irked by de Valera's public denunciation of her invasion of the neutral Low Countries in May 1940. De Valera chose to endure British brickbats rather than suffer German bombs in the first years of the war, on the calculations that Britain would prevent a German invasion, that Britain could be appeased by effective covert security cooperation, and that she would not risk alienating American opinion by armed action against Ireland; in the latter phase of the war, he adopted a holier-than-thou public approach to neutrality which many saw as reflecting purblind pedantry, and which fostered delusions about how Ireland's defence interests had actually been secured during the conflict, obscuring the strategic lessons to be drawn.

The first full treatment of Irish neutrality was Joseph Carroll's *Ireland in the War Years* (1975). This disclosed the extensive range of covert Anglo-Irish cooperation in wartime defence and security matters and linked this to de Valera's overall aim of saving Ireland from the ravages of war, containing the internal threat posed by the IRA, and maintaining the forms of neutrality, while quietly accommodating Britain's legitimate security concerns so as not to give her a *casus belli*. Carroll emphasized that de Valera also pursued correct relations with the Axis powers, long after the outcome of the conflict—and the bestial nature of the Nazi regime in particular—were in any doubt. In Carroll's view, as in that of de Valera's authorized biographers, this was the only logical and consistent line for a small state to take.

However, absolute consistency and *realpolitik* proved uncomfortable bedfellows. As the Allies' stock rose remorselessly, most of the world's remaining neutral states outside Europe had, with varying degrees of reluctance, clambered onto the Allied bandwagon so as to be on the winning side and to protect their interests in the post-war world. Those European countries which still lay within range of German retribution, whether the exemplary democracies of Sweden and Switzerland or the Fascist powers of Spain and Portugal, gradually trimmed towards the Allies while more slowly reducing their economic ties with Hitler. Germany protested violently in 1943 when Portugal agreed to allow the Allies to use bases in the Azores, but was silenced by the Portuguese response that any German economic or military reprisals would inevitably lead to a rupture of diplomatic and trade relations vital to Germany's interests.[1] Even Franco's Spain, which in October 1940 appeared poised to throw in its lot with the Axis, had adopted a quietly conciliatory tone towards the western Allies by the summer of 1942. In South America, Argentina, whose political elite were strongly pro-German, was nevertheless coerced into joining the Allied camp in 1944. Similarly, in Asia, Turkey gradually wound down her important trading ties with Germany, and eventually joined the Allies early in 1945 without the necessity of firing a shot.

Robert Fisk's groundbreaking study *In Time of War: Ireland, Ulster and the price of neutrality* (1983) addressed the particular question which de Valera faced in the early years of the war: whether to trade neutrality for the promise of eventual Irish unity. That the British Prime Minister Winston Churchill had twice invited de Valera to make such a choice—in June 1940 and in December 1941—had long been known. Fisk's work produced a mass of detail on the origins and limitations of those offers, and on de Valera's calculations in resisting these overtures.

The progressive release of relevant records over the last two decades in Britain, Ireland, and America has seen the publication of useful archives-based studies on specific aspects of wartime Ireland, including Mark Hull's authoritative analysis of German intelligence and Ireland, *Irish Secrets* (2003), two detailed studies of British intelligence concerning Ireland—Paul McMahon's *British Spies and Irish Rebels* (2008) and Eunan O'Halpin's *Spying on Ireland* (2008)—and Michael Kennedy's *Guarding Neutral Ireland* (2008), an innovative study of Irish coastal surveillance. In *Irish Women and the Second World War* (2006), Mary Muldowney examined the experiences both of women who were 'in' the war by choice or circumstance in Northern Ireland and in Britain, and women who remained in neutral Ireland. Enda Delaney's *Demography, State and Society* (Liverpool, 2000) described the state-assisted phenomenon of Irish migration to Britain during the war years. The thorny question of Irish policy towards European war refugees of varying ideological persuasions was examined particularly in Dermot Keogh's *Jews in Twentieth Century Ireland* (1998), and more recently in Daniel Leach's *Fugitive Ireland* (2009), while Peter Rigney's *Trains, Coal and Turf: Transport in neutral Ireland* (2010) cast much light on the near-paralyzing effects of wartime conditions and supplies on the Irish transport system, the stark limits of import substitution and technical improvisations, the importance of informal links between the Dublin-based and Belfast-based railway companies, and the extent of quiet Anglo-Irish interdependence even in the midst of what Churchill intended as a rigorous British economic blockade in 1940–1.

On a broader plane, Brian Girvin's *The Emergency* (2005) advanced a challenging analysis of the consequences of neutrality for economic and social development as well as for relations with the United Kingdom (and more particularly Northern Ireland). By contrast, T. Ryle Dwyer produced a trenchant defence of Irish policy and a critique of British and American attitudes towards Irish neutrality in *Behind the Green Curtain* (2008), arguing that Ireland's 'Phoney Neutrality' should have received more gracious Allied acknowledgement because of covert security cooperation—although after the war, and for varying reasons, the British, American, and Irish governments all wished to keep such matters strictly secret—while in *That Neutral Island* (2007) Clair Wills explored the psychological impact of neutrality on the Irish psyche and on opinion in Northern Ireland and Britain. This cast light on the moral awkwardness of neutrality in the midst of total war when, even before the details of the Holocaust became widely known, it was obvious that the ethical balance lay unequivocally with the Allies and with those many European would-be neutral states ruthlessly attacked by Germany and Italy. On the other hand, recent works such as Roy Douglas's *Architects of the Resurrection* (2009) and David O'Donoghue's *The Devil's Deal* (2009) serve as a reminder of the unsavoury intersection at that time between strands of Irish nativist republicanism and far-right ideology.

In terms of wider foreign policy, Ireland, like other neutrals, sought simply to stay out of harm's way as war engulfed much of the world. There was no bloc of like-minded neutrals and no role for it had one existed. De Valera carefully avoided various diplomatic hazards arising from the course of the war, maintaining relations with the same states on the same basis as prior to September 1939. This was well understood and accepted by the British government and other British dominions, Canada in particular. Ireland did not crow at the sweeping away of European colonial regimes in Asia; the claim of Subhas Chandra Bose that de Valera had recognized his Japanese-sponsored 'Indian Provisional Government' was simply untrue. British ministers were, however, discomfited and irritated when the Dáil approved a grant of £200 000 for famine relief in Bengal in 1943 because it placed British government in India in a bad light.[2]

Such relative public generosity towards suffering in India may be contrasted with Irish attitudes towards the fate of European Jewry. On this the government, which had been markedly unsympathetic towards Jewish immigration in the years leading up to the war, remained silent throughout the conflict, although, in common with other European and Asian neutrals and sometimes at Vatican prompting, occasional ineffectual diplomatic efforts were made to succour individual groups of Jews destined for oblivion after 1942. In 1995, Taoiseach John Bruton stated that 'Ireland's doors were not freely open to those families and individuals fleeing from persecution and death. Some people did find refuge and comfort in Ireland, but their numbers were not very great. We must acknowledge the consequences of this indifference.'[3] Bruton was broadly right in characterizing Irish immigration policy towards European Jews before and during the war as, at best, uncaring and legalistic; he might, however, usefully have gone on to observe that the public record indicates that anti-Semitic prejudice had been more freely and vehemently expressed in the 1930s and 1940s by members of his own party, Fine Gael, than by de Valera's supporters. This continued even after unequivocal knowledge of the Holocaust emerged in 1945, when very limited plans to succour Jewish children while, supposedly, ignoring the plight of German and Polish Christian orphans were raucously attacked by Opposition politicians.

II. Anglo-Irish Relations in Time of War

It is essential to differentiate between the immediate and the long-term consequences of Irish neutrality for Anglo-Irish relations. In the first phases of the war, and particularly during the fraught year following the fall of France, Irish neutrality caused acute worry in London for strategic reasons, especially, though not exclusively, to Churchill; once the likelihood of a German invasion of the British Isles had more or less disappeared, apprehension at the consequences of Ireland's policy was succeeded by anger and resentment. Yet, for all the popular antagonism against Irish shirkers, and Churchill's idiosyncratic belief that 'their conduct in this war will never be forgiven by the British people . . . we must save these people from themselves', at a practical level, British policy was characterized by a quiet pragmatism even as the prime minister huffed, puffed, and encouraged President Roosevelt to join him in putting the squeeze on de Valera.[4]

Churchill's nurturing of Roosevelt's particular animus towards neutral Ireland succeeded, perhaps beyond what was intended. Irish neutrality left a far more sour taste in Washington than it did in London, where the challenges of reconstruction and social reform facing the Attlee government in 1945 precluded any efforts to punish Ireland retrospectively. The rancorous course of wartime American-Irish diplomacy left Dublin more fearful and mistrustful of the United States than of Britain, resulting in an extraordinarily hesitant and half-hearted Irish response to the opportunities for economic and social development offered by the Marshall Plan. It was unarguably in his clumsy transatlantic diplomacy, not helped by the inadequacies of the respective Irish and American envoys, that de Valera's foreign policy was most damaging to Ireland's long-term interests and international reputation.

III. The War, Neutrality, and North/South Relations

The need for close cooperation between the police forces north and south of the border, particularly in respect of the movement of people between jurisdictions, was quietly recognized both in Dublin and Belfast. We know little of such matters below the headquarters level, although it can be shown that in adjoining areas along the border the police forces had long-established informal understandings. The same undoubtedly held good for the respective Customs and Excise services. The Royal Ulster Constabulary Inspector General Sir Charles Wickham constantly deprecated the tendency of his own government to play up the security threat arising from Irish neutrality and the highly permeable border, instead insisting as early as October 1940 that the Garda Siochána had the IRA firmly under control. Liaison between the respective police special branches was carefully nurtured, while Irish army intelligence worked very closely with the British security service, MI5.[5]

At the political level, however, there was no contact at all between north and south and no desire in either Dublin or Belfast to seek any. The Belfast government was unwilling under any circumstances to bargain away the Province's position within the United Kingdom in return for independent Ireland's participation in the war. De Valera, who anyway dreaded the consequences of aerial bombardment for his unprepared state, had no intention of bringing Ireland, united or not, into the war. Neither Dublin nor Belfast believed that Churchill had either the intention or the capacity to bring about a united Ireland by agreement, whatever transpired during the war.

IV. DOMESTIC POLITICS DURING THE CRISIS YEARS

It has been argued that the maintenance of neutrality copper-fastened de Valera's political pre-eminence. The same cannot be said for his party: Fianna Fáil did not fare very well in the two wartime elections of 1943 and 1944, due to widespread dissatisfaction with economic conditions and a general weariness with politics, and the party was evicted from office in the first post-war election in 1948 (albeit in rather odd circumstances, as its vote held up well). Political debate was considerably constrained by two novel factors: the very tight press censorship imposed in the name of state security; and the clear consensus amongst the political class, bitterly divided though the main parties otherwise remained, on the importance of staying neutral. Donal O'Drisceoil has contrasted the rigorousness of Irish press censorship with the relative freedom of debate seen in neutral Sweden and Switzerland, arguing convincingly that at times censorship served the interests of the ruling party rather than of the state as a whole. On the other hand, contiguity ensured the relatively liberal media regimes in Sweden and Switzerland did little to hamper close economic and intelligence cooperation between these democratic neutrals and Germany until very late in the war.[6]

The war also had a profound impact on Irish radical politics; in particular, the crushing of the republican movement within the state. The IRA's pretensions to being an army-in-waiting, poised to overthrow de Valera in combination with their German allies, were shown to be a pathetic delusion as well as an ideological embarrassment. The tiny all-island communist movement, which took its lead from its British comrades in opposing the war as a capitalist folly in 1939 and 1940, was, like them, thrown into confusion as events unfolded and the Soviet Union, from being an adamantine neutral, became Hitler's nemesis after 22 June 1941.

V. Defence and Security

In 1945, the forceful Army Chief of Staff Dan McKenna, who had had an outstandingly 'good war'—or, rather, non-war—was crystal clear about the key lessons of the previous six years. If Ireland wished in future to pursue a policy of military neutrality during a major war involving Britain and the United States, she would have to develop defence forces and doctrine capable of acting as a credible deterrent to any likely attacker. In addition to sustained investment in equipment and weaponry on a scale not seen since the civil war, including the development of a functional air arm and a naval service capable of patrolling Ireland's territorial waters, this would require the implementation of compulsory military service along the lines operated in most European states, belligerents and neutrals alike. His views were studiously ignored.[7]

The defence forces performed surprisingly well, particularly in terms of internal security, counterespionage, coastal surveillance, and discreetly managing relations with the British and American armed forces and intelligence agencies, but they were never tested in serious combat. The army did not have sufficient anti-aircraft weapons, searchlights, or expertise to do more than mount a token defence against air attack, as was demonstrated during occasional and possibly accidental German bombings in 1940 and 1941. McKenna made clear that his forces had neither the equipment, the weapons, the vehicles, the aircraft, nor the experience to mount more than limited resistance to a modern battle-hardened opponent, whether it be Britain, the United States (which by 1942 had many thousands of men in Northern Ireland), or Germany.

VI. Economy and Society

The war years brought home to many the disagreeable reality that neutrality, far from preventing, if anything, ensured economic stagnation and privation. For all the nationalist pride in Ireland's ability to produce enough food to feed herself unaided, agriculture suffered alongside industry due to the chronic shortage of imported materials and fuel needed for food production and distribution on a mass scale.

The task of keeping Ireland running was entrusted on the outbreak of war to Seán Lemass, widely recognized as the most dynamic and innovative minister. Lemass had been the enthusiastic architect of industrialization through protection in the 1930s; now his temporary Department of Supplies was charged with acquiring and distributing whatever resources were needed to keep the economy moving. Bryce Evans' *Seán Lemass: Democratic Dictator* (2011) questions the efficacy, propriety, and long-term consequences of Lemass's management of his Supplies brief.

Transport was a key and problematic element of Lemass's task. Because of petrol and diesel shortages, and the wartime hazards for even coastal shipping, most bulk goods in Ireland had to be moved by train. In common with other countries who met their fuel needs through imports in peacetime, trains got slower and slower as the war years passed and imported supplies diminished. To the uninitiated, turf seemed a logical and viable alternative, but vast quantities were required in order to generate sufficient steam to drive a locomotive. In consequence, the movement of goods for both domestic and export purposes became an arduous and uncertain undertaking.

Despite efforts to safeguard Irish vessels through conspicuous markings, and close cooperation with the British naval authorities, Irish-flagged shipping suffered considerable losses caused by mines and submarine and air attacks. The worst period was between April 1940 and March 1941, when nine vessels were lost. In the course of the war, a total of sixteen vessels of various kinds were sunk, and about 170 crew were lost.

Domestic industries, developed in the years leading up to the war as Ireland embraced protectionism, relied on imported goods, equipment, and fuel which became progressively harder to obtain. Supplies of oil, rubber, and other industrial commodities were subject to the hazards of wartime shipping, the competing demands of the combatant nations of the British commonwealth and, until 1942, the vagaries of the British policy of selective economic blockade of Ireland (although in matters such as food supplies where Irish cooperation and goodwill was essential, individual British ministries bent the rules in order to help out individual Irish producers and the railway and shipping companies). In response, the state became a shameless scavenger: officials were constantly on the lookout for whatever usable detritus of war might float ashore. Despite greatly increased demand from Britain, Irish agricultural production suffered considerably during the war years. It became almost impossible to import phosphates for fertilizer, and experiments with indigenous alternatives such as seaweed proved a disappointment. The handful of Irish diplomatic and consular staff in Canada, the United States, Spain, and Portugal became ad hoc trade officials and shipping agents as the state tried desperately to get the commodities it needed to keep the country ticking over, from wheat to binder twine.[8]

In contrast to the United Kingdom, no discernible societal benefits arose from the state's increased role as provider, regulator, and distributor of food, fuel, clothing, and other essential supplies. Rationing was primarily an instrument for the distribution of scarce imported commodities or for restricting domestic demand for produce needed for export to Britain, not a device for the systematic provision of a balanced basic diet equitably across the population. Visitors from the United Kingdom were dazzled at the amount of fresh food available in shops and restaurants—fresh butter, milk, bacon, beef, and other commodities which had disappeared from the British market could all be easily and legally bought by anyone with the money, but this apparent plenitude disguised the fact that many Irish people, particularly in urban areas, could not afford to feed themselves properly. It does not follow that Ireland would necessarily have fared any better as a belligerent: Iran suffered acute food shortages under Anglo-Soviet occupation after 1941, while in British India perhaps as many as three million Bengalis perished through famine between 1942 and 1944, a catastrophe accentuated, if not caused, by British policy and callousness at the highest level. Churchill constantly bridled at the warnings of the Viceroy of India and Secretary of State about the unfolding calamity, regarding the Bengal famine as a tragedy India had brought upon herself.[9]

In the related area of public health, the story was much the same. Food safety regulations were largely placed in abeyance in the face of increased domestic and export demand, thereby ensuring the spread, particularly amongst disadvantaged children, of the pernicious milk-borne disease tuberculosis. Its spread was compounded by poor living conditions, exacerbated by shortages of fuel for domestic heating other than home-produced—and generally reviled—turf.

The limited and haphazard infrastructure of health provision remained just that: there was not enough money or will at central or local government level to maintain what was there, let alone to finance modernization and expansion and to plan for tomorrow. Ireland had no indigenous pharmaceutical industry, and sophisticated medicines were in short supply, even for those who could afford to pay for them. The widespread public debate in the United Kingdom on the future provision of comprehensive social and health services—which began in 1942 following the publication of the Beveridge report—attracted considerable notice in Ireland, but it inspired no comparable exercise: no great social contract was drafted to mobilize public aspirations for a brighter future. The 1944 report of the Commission on Vocational Organisation offered only an eccentric blueprint for remodelling Irish society which would not have been out of place in 1920s Fascist Italy. There were a few minor innovations, notably the introduction of children's allowances on a national basis in 1944, but no grand design emerged during these years for that better tomorrow (although some serious thinking did take place behind the closed doors of the policy system, resulting in the crucial 1947 Health Act).

The state's difficulties in maintaining economic activity were accentuated, if not instigated, by continued emigration of the young and the fit. The national consensus on neutrality was matched by universal acceptance of the legitimacy of individuals travelling to the United Kingdom to work in the war economy. Between 1939 and 1945, something like a sixth of the adult population of working age went to work in the United Kingdom as civilians or in the fighting services. This was despite the risk of death or injury, from July 1940 a very real hazard for anyone within range of the German air force. The state assisted rather than resisted the departure of this stream of Irish talent, facilitating British recruitment of civilian workers; as Brian Girvin observed, such 'private collusion ... suited both sides ... and worked to the advantage of the Irish in providing an outlet for surplus Irish labour at high wages at a time when Irish industry could not hope to keep output at pre-war levels'.[10] There was also considerable daily or weekly migration of labour across the border, particularly between Donegal and the booming port city of Derry and its associated British and Canadian naval bases. The state also turned a blind eye to the embarrassing fact that a large number of young men and women left Ireland in order to join the British fighting services. Not all were civilian: by 1942, desertion from the defence forces had become a serious problem, particularly in border areas where soldiers attracted by the prospect of active combat and much better pay could simply walk into Northern Ireland and make their way to recruiting stations in the nearest towns. Wartime emigration became a source of widespread dissatisfaction, particularly in poorer rural areas, as became clear in the 1943 general election in which both the main political parties fared badly. The emigrants themselves seem generally to have had limited regrets, either then or in the post-war era, at exchanging the privations of a neutral state for those of one at war, and few returned to live in Ireland once peace came.

VII. Fundamental Freedoms and the Maintenance of Neutrality During the War Years

The deadening impact of press censorship is captured in the observation of the British director of naval intelligence John Godfrey on the 'dull and insipid' character of Irish newspapers. This was reflected both in the deadpan, limited, and self-consciously even-handed reportage of war news and in the absence of informed press debate on war issues, especially on Irish policy towards the belligerents. The government had valid reasons for operating a strict censorship. One was that it allowed the state to manage its relations with the belligerents far from the public gaze. This was particularly useful in dealing with the host of issues and incidents that inevitably arose from Ireland's contiguity with two war zones, the United Kingdom and the Atlantic, which could most easily be dealt with in secret. Another straightforward reason for strict censorship was that constantly stressed by the British authorities: to ensure that no sensitive war news leaked out through Ireland. A related reason for censorship was prevention of the dissemination of both pro-Axis and pro-IRA opinion and argument. This ensured that the public (other than those who had access to the underground *War News*, a crude production in which standard anti-British diatribes were intermingled with toxic nativist, xenophobic, and pro-Axis argument) learned very little about the IRA's reasoning and intentions. Another justification, which even two such incisive critics as O'Drisceoil and Wills overly discount, was the fear that foreign powers would seek to manipulate the Irish media for their own ends. Both sets of belligerents attempted to do precisely that.

Critics of the way Irish censorship operated are, however, surely right in pointing out that it had a clear impact on domestic party political discourse. That in turn benefitted the government of the day, which, in the name of national unity in the face of peril, was able to suppress perfectly legitimate criticism of its own performance across all spheres of national life.

The operation of a system of postal censorship was arguably less damaging to the democratic fibre of the Irish state precisely because it was overt and visible. A letter sent from Cork to New York would pass through not one but three national postal censorship systems—the Irish, the British, and the American—before delivery. The principal reason for Irish censorship was straightforward: to prevent the passage of war information or subversive material, and to demonstrate to belligerent states that Ireland was being duly rigorous in that regard. Strict postal censorship in itself discouraged use of the postal system for espionage or subversive purposes. In practice, the postal censorship also provided a virtual rolling opinion poll on a host of issues, great and small, arising from wartime circumstances and conditions. The same was true for the British authorities: in 1941 Churchill was struck by the extent of resentment amongst Irish people in Britain, disclosed by postal censorship, at Britain's failure to acknowledge the voluntary contributions of Irish men and women to the war effort. His efforts to address this through the development of military and air units with a specific Irish identity were, however, soon lost in the quicksands of interdepartmental consultations.[11]

Legal as well as practical obstacles to free movement between the islands of Ireland and Britain were put in place by June 1940, although cross-border traffic was recognized as being impossible to control. The cross-channel movement controls were a British initiative, but Dublin had no objections despite the difficulties which it caused for the public.

Media and postal censorship impacted on the public generally, but more draconian aspects of the state's emergency powers were directed at small subsets of Irish life. The IRA and the broader republican movement were singled out for rigorous attention. Repression had been stepped up well before the outbreak of war, in response to the IRA's 'S-Plan' bombing campaign in Britain which began in January 1939. The use of internment as a tool to control the IRA, thrown into doubt in December 1939 when existing legal provisions were found to be unconstitutional, was hastily validated through a constitutional amendment. In June 1940, in the midst of an invasion scare and just a few days after the first evidence of a serious German/IRA link had been discovered in a police raid, about five hundred republicans were arrested and interned.

This action, arguably overdue, proved decisive. A thorough history of Irish internment has yet to be written, not least because the relevant records in the Department of Justice are still closed to research (not for security reasons but on grounds of personal confidentiality).[12] What can be said is that, in the aggregate, the individual records of the thousand or so men, and fifty or so women who were either jailed or interned (or both) for subversive activities are a very rich source. They show that the Justice minister Gerry Boland took his responsibilities very seriously and that, his remorseless public persona notwithstanding, he used internment in a sophisticated and humane way. A former subversive and political prisoner, he understood that people became involved with the republican movement to different degrees and through a range of circumstances and motivations, and he had a shrewd idea of the types of young people concerned. On occasion he refused Garda requests for internment orders, or revoked them, on the grounds that the individuals concerned were of little account or were callow youths who should first be given a stern warning. Imprisonment and internment were also used in a few cases as a calculated short, sharp shock against individuals involved in amateurish pro-British activities, such as attempts to encourage enlistment in British forces and efforts to collect intelligence on pro-Axis elements. Secret records indicate that Boland kept individuals locked up for as brief a period as possible, that he and his officials were ingenious in transforming emergency release for family, compassionate, or medical reasons into graduated extended parole, and that he was uneasy concerning cases where people ostensibly involved in IRA activities were in fact simply pursuing family or land feuds. His clear intention was to deprive individuals of their liberty only for as long as was absolutely necessary, and he prided himself on the discrimination with which he exercised his powers.

Unfortunately, this material is not yet in the public domain. It qualifies the dominant standard republican narratives of internment. These tend, not surprisingly, to stress the arbitrary nature of internment without trial, along with the negative and dispiriting aspects of being locked up in a draughty camp for an indefinite period, without any indication of when the gates might be opened, and living on notoriously poorly prepared rations (ironically, precisely the same food as enjoyed by the soldiers guarding the camp).[13] Individual internment files record a rather different picture, showing many people who came into custody malnourished and run-down whose general health improved during incarceration.

The Emergency years saw the execution of eight IRA men for political crimes, seven for murder, and one (Richard Goss) for attempted murder. It can be argued to differing extents in each instance that this was rough justice—particularly in the case of the veteran gunman George Plant, who was tried twice for the same crime by different courts—but the rules of the game had been changed by the circumstances of the war and by the IRA's attacks on the state and its servants (the last IRA man executed, Charlie Kerins, had been involved in the assassination of a Special Branch detective two years earlier). British and American observers could not help but note the *sangfroid* with which de Valera's government executed IRA men, including one well-known 1916 veteran, in contrast with their near-hysterical response to the hanging in Britain of the Coventry bombers Barnes and McCormack for the deaths of five civilians in 1940, and of the IRA's Thomas Williams for his part in the killing of an RUC constable in Belfast in 1942.

State repression of the republican movement, viewed in isolation, may appear severe. Its justification lay not simply in the IRA's own actions against the state—including killing seven policemen and wounding others—but in republicanism's alliance with Nazi Germany.

VIII. The Costs of Neutrality in Comparative Terms

We may speculate about the likely consequences had Britain and the United States occupied Ireland or as much of it as they felt they needed. This is not a military question, but an ethical and reputational one.

The consequences of a successful British occupation in 1940–1 have been well canvassed. After organized Irish defence had been overcome—presumably in a matter of days—it is likely that the government would have had to surrender in order to prevent needless civilian casualties (and possibly to avoid the arrival of unwelcome German assistance). This would have probably put an end to all military resistance. Elements of the republican movement might well have tried to attack the invader, but the IRA had been severely crippled by the decisive action taken against it in Britain in 1939 and in Ireland in 1940 and even with substantial German aid could have achieved little.

What lessons can be drawn from the experience of neutrals which were occupied by the Allies, or effectively coerced by them to abandon full neutrality? In the Middle East, Britain attacked and occupied Iraq in April 1941. The proximate reason was to counteract a pro-Axis coup, but that was essentially a pretext for Churchill to strengthen Britain's hand in the region. Iraq's neutral neighbour, Iran, soon suffered a similar fate: in August 1941 she was invaded jointly by the British and the Soviets, on the flimsy excuse that she harboured hundreds of German spies and saboteurs (the Iranian government had initiated somewhat dilatory efforts to reduce the number of Axis civilians). In due course occupied Iraq and Iran both formally joined the war on the Allied side. Although she remained a neutral, Egypt was not fully sovereign because of the presence of British forces to defend the Suez Canal; in 1942, the king was forced to change his prime minister at the point of British guns, a public humiliation never forgotten. Although the course of war allowed these Middle Eastern states fortuitously to emerge more or less on the right side of history, none of them benefitted conspicuously from their forced involvement in the conflict.

IX. Conclusion

In September 1939, neutrality appeared the only rational policy choice for the Irish government. After June 1940, it seemed the state's only hope if, as expected, Hitler succeeded in conquering Britain. De Valera was unwilling to trade neutrality for British support for a post-war united Ireland, not simply because of the inherent implausibility of Churchill being able to deliver on his offers, but because he saw neutrality as the ultimate proof of the sovereignty for which Irish nationalists had fought between 1916 and 1921. The entry of the United States into the war in December 1941 changed the geopolitics of the war, but Irish policy on neutrality never wavered, and attitudes in Dublin hardened as the war turned in favour of the Allies.

Independent Ireland undoubtedly benefitted materially through neutrality. The state never became a battleground, and the internal threat posed by the IRA was confronted and defeated with surprising ease. The economy limped along, although acutely hampered at one remove by the impact of the war at sea on supplies. For a variety of social, economic, and political reasons, Irish men and women voluntarily joined the British war effort in very large numbers, yet anecdotal evidence suggests that they also supported their state's neutrality. So significant was their contribution that the British security service MI5 concluded 'it is at least arguable that Eire neutral was of more value to the British war effort than Eire belligerent would have been', since Ireland at war would have kept her people at home for defence purposes and would have had to be provided by Britain with weapons for defence 'at a time when supplies were practically non-existent, particularly at the period of greatest danger after the fall of France; all this to an accompaniment of minor guerrilla warfare by the IRA and their supporters'.[14]

In practical terms, in the immediate post-war years the memory of neutrality damaged Ireland's standing with the United States more than it did relations with Britain. But even in Washington it appears that no one knew or cared much about Ireland. The true post-war consequence of neutrality was not that Ireland was punished in the new world order, but that she was ignored.

Notes

1. O'Halpin, *Spying on Ireland*, 230. For a useful comparative survey of European neutrals, see Neville Wylie (ed), *European Neutrals and Non-Belligerents during the Second World War* (Cambridge, 2002).

2. Kate O'Malley, *Ireland, India and Empire: Indo-Irish Radical Connections, 1919–1964* (Manchester, 2008), 144–7.

3. Extract from Taoiseach Bruton's speech on Yom Ha Shoah, 26 April 1995, accessed at http://www.hetireland.org/index.php?page=ireland_YOM-HA-SHOAH On anti-Semitism within the political mainstream, see Keogh, *Jews in Twentieth Century Ireland*.

4. Churchill to Attlee (Dominions Secretary), 5 May 1943, quoted in O'Halpin, *Spying on Ireland*, 240.

5. Eunan O'Halpin, *Defending Ireland: the Irish State and its Enemies since 1922* (Oxford, 1999), 225–31.

6. On such relationships see Christian Leitz, *Sympathy for the Devil: Neutral Europe and Nazi Germany during the Second World War* (New York, 2001).

7. Michael Kennedy and Victor Laing, *The Irish Defence Forces 1940–1949: the Chief of Staff's Reports* (Dublin, 2011), 411.

8. TNA, HW12/281: Decode of Irish legation, Ottawa, to Dublin, 7 October 1942.

9. The diaries of Leo Amery, Secretary of State for India, are particularly telling on Churchill's antagonism towards Indians. Churchill College Cambridge Archives, Amery diaries, AMEL 7/34-8.

10. Brian Girvin, 'The republicanisation of Irish society, 1932–1948', in J.R. Hill (ed), *A New History of Ireland: VII Ireland 1921–84* (Oxford, 2003), 153; Wills, *That Neutral Island*, 309–33.

11. Quoted in O'Halpin, *Spying on Ireland*, 195.

12. The author has had sight of these records as a member of the Department of Justice, Equality and Law Reform Archives Advisory Group established in 2006 to help frame policy on the release of security records. Kennedy and Laing, *The Irish Defence Forces 1940–1949*, 411.

13. Wills, *That Neutral Island*, 337.

14. Eunan O'Halpin (ed), *MI5 and Ireland, 1939–1945: the Official History* (Dublin, 2003), 31.

SELECT BIBLIOGRAPHY

Carroll, Joseph, *Ireland in the War Years* (Newton Abbott, 1975).

Douglas, Roy. *Architects of the Resurrection: Ailtirí na hAiséirghe and the Fascist 'New Order' in Ireland* (Manchester, 2009).

Evans, Bryce, *Séan Lemass: Democratic Dictator* (Cork, 2011).

Fisk, Robert, *In Time of War: Ireland, Ulster and the Price of Neutrality* (London, 1983).

Girvin, Brian, *The Emergency: Neutral Ireland, 1939–1945* (London, 2006).

Hull, Mark, *Irish Secrets: German Espionage in Wartime Ireland 1939–1945* (Dublin, 2003).

Kennedy, Michael and Victor Laing, *The Irish Defence Forces 1940–1949: the Chief of Staff's Reports* (Dublin, 2011).

Leach, Daniel, *Fugitive Ireland: European Minority Nationalists and Irish Political Asylum 1937–2008* (Dublin, 2009).

Leitz, Christian, *Sympathy for the Devil: Neutral Europe and Nazi Germany during the Second World War* (New York, 2001).

McMahon, Paul. *British Spies and Irish Rebels: British Intelligence and Ireland, 1916–1945* (Woodbridge, 2008).

Muldowney, Mary, *The Second World War and Irish Women: an Oral History* (Dublin, 2007).

O'Drisceoil, Donal, *Censorship in Ireland 1939–1945: Neutrality, Politics and Society* (Cork, 1996).

O'Halpin, Eunan, *Defending Ireland: the Irish state and its Enemies since 1922* (Oxford, 1999).

O'Halpin, Eunan (ed), *MI5 and Ireland, 1939–1945: the Official History* (Dublin, 2003).

O'Halpin, Eunan, *Spying on Ireland: British Intelligence and Irish neutrality during the Second World War* (Oxford, 2008).

O'Malley, Kate, *Ireland, India and Empire: Indo-Irish Radical Connections, 1919–1964* (Manchester, 2008).

Rigney, Peter, *Trains, Coal and Turf: Transport in Emergency Ireland* (Dublin, 2010).

Wiley, Neville (ed), *European Neutrals and Non-Belligerents During the Second World War* (Cambridge, 2002).

Wills, Clair, *That Neutral Island: a Cultural History of Ireland during the Second World War* (London, 2007).

....

CHAPTER 36

THE LEMASS LEGACY
AND THE MAKING OF
CONTEMPORARY IRELAND,
1958–2011[1]

....

BRIAN GIRVIN

I. Introduction

....

THERE is general agreement that Ireland has changed dramatically over the past fifty years, but there is some uncertainty concerning the nature of the change and its consequences. In this regard, the study of contemporary issues poses special problems for the historian. There is the limited availability of archives and personal papers, restrictions imposed by the thirty-year rule. Even when appropriate materials are available, it is difficult to assess their comprehensiveness. In addition, historians have to compete with journalists who at their best have access to key public figures on a day-to-day basis. Social scientists also challenge the historian by utilizing other sources and applying sophisticated methodologies to contemporary questions. In contrast to the relative paucity of archival sources, historians have to pay attention to other sources such as memoirs, diaries, and documentaries as well as radio and television interviews. Moreover, use can be made of formal public inquiries, as well as utilizing oral history and focus groups. Thus, Foster cautiously insists, 'It should be possible for a historian to look at the latest period in Irish history from a historical standpoint, as opposed to that of a sociologist, or an economist, or a political scientist—though the insights of all these disciplines must be employed.'[2] This is certainly the path that will be pursued in this chapter but the historian's subjectivity also has to be confronted. If all historical analysis is potentially revisionist, this will be even more the case with contemporary history.

If journalism is the first draft of history and social science provides the second, then hopefully historians will produce a third and more nuanced assessment. However, the historian is as prone to bias and subjectivity as the journalist or the social scientist, but may not be as aware of this when dealing with contemporary questions. Direct experience of events can provide insight, but can also affect the historian's research strategy. This problem may be even greater if an individual has been an activist-participant in the events (s)he is describing. This can lead to an over-emphasis on the significance of what one has experienced and a neglect of other factors. Most importantly, the historian may reflect the concerns of society in which (s)he is working. Thus, Lee was concerned with the consequences of slow growth and economic instability, among other matters, when working in the 1980s. By way of contrast, when writing in the early 2000s, Ferriter celebrated the achievements and successes of a prosperous state. Foster emphasized 'Luck', a contentious term in itself, but perhaps anticipating a new uncertainty about Ireland at the end of the decade.[3] The point at this stage is not to adjudicate between these three approaches but to note the extent to which the society's preoccupations can inform what will be focused on. In his classic and innovative study of contemporary history, Barraclough acknowledges the need to stand apart from events when studying the contemporary issues. He recognizes that this is difficult, but the attempt must be made. Barraclough emphasizes the novel nature of contemporary history: 'it remains true that unless we keep our eyes alert for what is new and different, we shall all too easily miss the essential—namely, the sense of living in a new period'.[4] This is indeed what many contemporary historians engage in and do so with skill and sophistication. However, without losing sight of the new and novel, it is also important to recognize that the new is often framed and indeed constrained by the past. To focus on continuity in a time of change can provide important insights into the new period and present a more nuanced appreciation of the tensions between continuity and change.[5]

II. The Lemass Era: 1959–66

The transfer of leadership from de Valera to Lemass in July 1959 did not in itself herald a transformation in Ireland. Lemass had worked closely with de Valera and retained most of his predecessor's cabinet. In the short run at least, it is difficult to detect change. Despite this, Lemass's short period as Taoiseach (1959–66) is rightly considered to be the beginning of contemporary Ireland and more controversially it is possible to detect the origins of the Celtic Tiger in decisions taken during this time.[6] The Lemass period is well served historiographically; there is a comprehensive biography by Horgan and the scholarly literature has produced significant studies on economic development, Northern Ireland, Europe, and church and state.[7] Lemass's greatest achievements were to reconfigure Fianna Fáil's political rhetoric, abandon protectionism, and persuade the country that pursuit of economic growth and membership of the EEC were patriotic goals. What is remarkable is that he did so without serious internal opposition in Fianna Fáil and maintained the party's dominant position in the political system. Lemass and his immediate successor, Jack Lynch, adapted to the pressures of the new Ireland in the

1960s, while managing change in a way that benefited Fianna Fáil electorally. In 1965, Lemass was rewarded with a majority in the election, a position maintained by Lynch in 1969.

Nonetheless, this successful management of political change can obscure other achievements. It is arguable that Lemass's most important contribution was psychological. He inspired confidence in his colleagues, encouraged fresh initiatives, and his mind sought out innovative solutions to problems.[8] Lemass also promoted a number of younger Fianna Fáil members to senior positions in the party and cabinet, including Charles Haughey, Patrick Hillery, and Brian Lenihan. He was also a conscious modernizer who mastered the latest Keynesian economic thinking. In contrast to de Valera, Lemass had little time for agriculture or farmers, recognizing that rural Ireland could contribute little to economic development or modernization. He had little patience with James Dillon, the leader of Fine Gael, who believed that agriculture should remain the main focus for Irish policy making.[9] Lemass recognized that economic change would have significant social consequences. He told journalist Desmond Fisher that contraception and divorce would be legal by the end of the century and that Ireland would be both materialist and prosperous. He encouraged the Supreme Court to promote a more active attitude to the 1937 Constitution and supported the establishment of an 'Informal Committee' to review the Constitution itself. When he retired as Taoiseach in 1966, he joined the committee and some of its recommendations in 1967 bear the stamp of his influence. Lemass was a risk taker in politics and at times impetuous, an aspect of his personality that worried many of his colleagues.[10]

Lemass's impact on Irish policy making was significant. In economic policy he worked closely with T.K. Whitaker, the secretary of the Department of Finance, who was an ardent advocate of free trade and economic modernization. They were unlikely allies, but Lemass supported Whitaker in his battle against the protectionists in his old department, Industry and Commerce. Lemass actively promoted the use of the state as an active agent of economic development. He also believed that the state had a responsibility to the citizens to achieve these goals.[11] On Northern Ireland, Lemass broke with the traditional nationalist position and sought to engage actively and positively with Unionism as well as Britain. His visit to Belfast (with Whitaker) in January 1965 remains a significant event, as does O'Neill's return visit. Lemass's hope that closer cooperation between north and south would improve the prospects for unity was short-lived and the breakdown of order in 1969 postponed that prospect indefinitely.[12] The most significant departure of the Lemass period was the decision to apply for membership of the EEC in 1961. In the short term, it transformed Irish foreign policy, and marked the end of economic nationalism and the policy victory for free trade. It also committed Ireland to a process of integration within Europe that continues to have an impact on its politics and society into the 21st century.

Lemass provided political support for educational reform, though Donogh O'Malley pre-empted his government colleagues by announcing the introduction of 'free-education' without discussion in cabinet. The Commission on Higher Education 1960–7 provided the stimulus for the expansion and transformation of the third-level system.[13] The introduction of a national television service was a major innovation with significant long-term social consequences.[14] Overall, the historiography agrees that Lemass's achievement was considerable. His governments broke the cycle of crisis and stagnation that had plagued Ireland during the 1950s and he positioned Ireland to apply successfully to join the EEC. This positive evaluation is justified and it would be difficult to challenge the view that Lemass kick-started the most recent modernization of Ireland.

However, there are a number of issues that require further attention. The first is the extent to which Lemass's policies were successful. By the time he retired in 1966, the economy was performing poorly, while special interests were undermining the state's efforts to coordinate policy, especially planning. Moreover, while emigration had been cut back significantly, employment creation remained well below predictions or expectations. A re-evaluation of the strategic decisions taken between 1958 and 1966 is now overdue. In particular, research needs to be focused on how effective policy was and to what extent objectives were achieved. Thus, Garvin's assertion that 'the late 1950s very-belated Irish dash for growth... actually worked' requires at the very least more justification. Garvin has noted more realistically that 'by 1987 Ireland, although her performance had improved considerably, was actually relatively poorer than in 1957'.[15] Thus, it is necessary to ask if the 'dash for growth' actually failed or, if not, why Ireland fared so poorly in comparative terms from the 1950s to the 1990s.[16] Part of this answer can be obtained by analyzing why Ireland fell behind in the 1950s and was then unable to 'catch up' with Europe until the 1990s. A further consideration here is that Ireland was not poor in comparative terms in 1945 but was decidedly so when compared with Europe by the 1960s. There is a tendency to view the economic changes in the 1960s positively, because the performance was better than in the 1950s, but not enough attention has been paid to policy weaknesses and to the obstacles to growth and development. One way forward in this respect will involve a more critical assessment of the role of T.K. Whitaker and the advice provided by the Department of Finance for the government. Whitaker clearly won the critical debate over Europe and free trade, yet the consequence of this outcome requires careful consideration. Such a review would involve an evaluation of Jack Lynch as Minister for Finance and new assessments of the role of the Departments of Agriculture and Industry and Commerce in the developmental process. The absence of a major study of the importance of farming and its influence on policy making is a significant gap in the literature for this period.[17]

Surprisingly, work on Ireland's relationship with Europe lacks sophistication and historians have adopted uncritically the dominant political consensus that Irish membership has been uniformly positive. There is an over-dependence on the official position taken by the Department of Foreign Affairs and such work is rarely comparative. As a result, there is a failure to appreciate fully the political consequences of Irish membership or to assess the benefits and losses to specific sections of society. Recent research has uncovered considerable unease among the public, prior to joining the EEC, concerning potential benefits, especially among the working class. However, the polling evidence was effectively suppressed by the Department of Foreign Affairs and the Minister involved was, to say the least, 'economical with the truth' when questioned in the Dáil on the matter.[18] A more rounded assessment of the period can also be obtained when a comprehensive history of Fianna Fáil is available and detailed examination of the activities of the Departments of Education, Justice, and Health on a variety of issues.

III.   Jack Lynch and the Failure of Irish Modernization 1966–79

The period after 1966 is less well served by the historical literature, although there is a biography of Jack Lynch based on his private papers and an important biography of Patrick Hillery. Collins' study provides important insights, but is not based on archives for the most part.[19] Dooley's examination of the Land Commission and land policy concentrates on the period up to the 1950s, but is slighter on the later period. Nevertheless, the study does provide important insights into the interaction between rural Ireland and government policy making in this field during a period of significant change for the former. However, one must turn to non-historical studies to gain significant insights into the impact of these changes on farming communities.[20] John Whyte's account of church–state relations remains the main scholarly study of this complex issue. More recently, Ó Corráin focused primarily on the Church of Ireland's relationship with the Irish Republic and that of the Catholic Church with the government of Northern Ireland. The discussion is taken up to 1973 and there is considerable detail and insight on the 1960s and early 1970s, as well as an important assessment of inter-church relations and ecumenism. Ferriter has provided a detailed account of Irish sexuality, which contains important insights into this period.[21]

Puirséil's study of the Labour Party since 1922 contains a substantial and well-researched section on the period since 1966. She traces how the party responded to pressures to shift to the left but also to liberal and progressive changes in urban Ireland. She provides a critical re-assessment of the opportunities available to Labour in this new environment, its success in attracting new members, but also a realistic assessment of the party's limited electoral appeal. There is a sympathetic and balanced evaluation of the significance of Brendan Corish who became leader in 1960. Frequently seen as a traditional and conservative politician, Corish emerges from this study as a more complex individual and one who was more radical than his critics claimed.[22] Corish is on record as expressing intolerant remarks in the 1950s, yet had become a liberal by the late 1960s. It is possible that the deliberations of the Second Vatican Council influenced him and others. Ó Corráin suggests that the impact was dramatic and stimulated ecumenism among Catholics. Lemass referred to the Council's documents on civil liberty and conscience when considering possible changes to the Constitution, as did the informal Committee on the Constitution. The 'Just Society' document produced for Fine Gael by Declan Costello expressly refers to the discussions at the Council. It is probable that the discussion on toleration and ecumenism reinforced liberal trends among Irish Catholics. However, a systematic study is required. Cooney's biography of John Charles McQuaid, the Archbishop of Dublin, provides some detail on this period and there is an extensive study of McQuaid's response to the Vatican Council.[23]

The period between 1966 and 1979 was a dramatic one and important questions remain concerning Lynch, his governments, and the extent to which Ireland changed. Lynch was an unusual choice for leader of Fianna Fáil. He did not have a personal or family connection with the independence era, as was the case with many of his colleagues. He was a celebrity politician and had been an uninspiring Minister who owed his position to Lemass's support and to fears that a struggle between Charles J. Haughey and George Colley would seriously divide the party. One legacy was that Lynch never seems to have fully commanded the support of Haughey, Boland, or Blaney, even before the 'arms crisis' of 1969–70. While Lynch, Hillery, and Haughey have often been described as modernizers, it is more appropriate to see them as cautious reformers within Fianna Fáil. This does not mean that they were opposed to more traditional aspects of party policy, as proved to be the case in the 1970s. However, they agreed on the need for a more dynamic economy, to prepare the country for Europe, and to limited reform when vested interests were not affected. This response was essentially cautious and conservative in policy terms. When Fianna Fáil recommended constitutional change in 1968, it was to abolish proportional representation and benefit the party at elections. This in turn brought about a successful counter-mobilization that defeated the proposal.

Notwithstanding this setback, Fianna Fáil was remarkably successful in managing change in its own interests between 1966 and 1969. This was a time of some instability, especially in urban Ireland. There was considerable industrial unrest, new left-wing social movements gained in influence, and the IRA adopted a Marxist programme that led to activism on social issues. In these circumstances the traditional parties appeared out of step and conservative. Surprisingly, Fianna Fáil managed this better than Fine Gael. In 1967, Brian Lenihan, the Minister for Justice, reformed the censorship laws, effectively undermining the original intention of the legislation. In the same year, the government issued a White Paper on EEC membership that demonstrated a new professionalism in respect of Ireland's position in relation to Europe.

Two events pushed Fianna Fáil in a more conservative direction. The first of these was the move to the left in Irish politics and especially the threat from the Labour Party at the 1969 election. Fine Gael was also re-formulating its programme to take account of the Vatican Council's emphasis on social justice and to position itself to the left of Fianna Fáil for the first time. Some of Fine Gael's changes were cosmetic and Declan Costello failed to have his 'Just Society' document accepted as party policy. Nevertheless, Fine Gael was able to attract liberal non-socialist professionals into the party at this time, leading in the 1970s to a significant change in emphasis.[24] These were clear political threats to Fianna Fáil after twelve years in government and following their defeat at the 1968 referendum on PR. Fianna Fáil attacked Labour as extremist and anti-national in ideology, especially when leftist intellectuals such as Conor Cruise O'Brien joined the party. This 'red scare' was a conservative response by a party on the defensive. While most of the Labour pro-gramme was moderate, some of it was naive and utopian. Yet, the party was attempting a difficult task (one that all three parties were faced with) in attempting to retain tra-ditional voters while pursuing new policies. Labour's refusal to discuss coalition with Fine Gael weakened the anti-Fianna Fáil vote, but it was also an attempt to forge a new left-wing force in Irish politics. Labour had already performed well at the 1965 general election, more than doubling its vote in Dublin. Puirséil points out that this success pro-vided the focus for the confrontation with conservative Ireland and the 1969 slogan that 'The Seventies would be Socialist'. On the other hand, Keogh is dismissive of Labour in 1969, characterizing the party as inept and naive, but this fails to appreciate the chang-ing political climate that Labour activists were responding to.[25] Labour's move to the left was reinforced by the radical political mood in Europe and the United States in 1968 and also by the emergence of the civil rights movement in Northern Ireland. Change was in the air and Labour clearly thought that it could channel some of these energies into the party and at the election.

Fianna Fáil also redrew the electoral boundaries to maximize its vote–seat ratio. While these two factors are important, not enough attention has been placed on Fianna Fáil's conscious development of a modern conservative response to change. Kevin Boland feared that the party was moving to the right, yet this misses the essential point. The period 1967–70 involved a realignment of politics in much of the democratic world. Fianna Fáil's remaking of itself as a moderate conservative party with a catch-all but tra-ditional appeal can be compared to the political success of Richard Nixon in the United States, de Gaulle in France in 1968, and Edward Heath in Britain in 1970. All three con-fronted radical challenges by invoking electoral majorities to neutralize this threat to the system. Fianna Fáil argued that it would assure continuity, order, and prosperity with-out the uncertainties that radicalism and socialism would bring. Keogh has described Lynch's style in 1969 as 'strongly populist, highly ideological and accusatory', and he might have added extremely successful. While there was a left surge in Dublin and to a lesser extent in urban Ireland, the rest of the electorate provided Lynch with a significant political victory.[26]

The second contribution to Fianna Fáil's conservative stance was not as easy to deal with. Despite the opening to the North by Lemass, events there were largely outside the control of the Irish government and as the situation deteriorated, traditional responses reappeared quickly. Whitaker prepared a memorandum for Lynch on Northern Ireland in late 1968 that emphasized the need to pursue a moderate and cautious policy and advised the Taoiseach to view unity as a long-term strategy. Whitaker also predicted that 'Force will get us nowhere; it will only strengthen the fears, antagonisms and divi-sions that keep North and South apart'.[27] While Whitaker's rational analysis was influ-ential and he continued to provide advice to Lynch, his moderate voice was ignored as political order collapsed in 1969. At the 1969 Fianna Fáil Ard Fheis, Lynch followed the position suggested by Whitaker while emphasizing the need for Irish unity. Keogh has suggested that Lynch lost control of Northern Ireland policy in early 1969, perhaps because he underestimated the extent and nature of the crisis. He was also concerned for much of this period with the forthcoming general election in June. What no Irish gov-ernment could control was the reaction of sections of the Unionist population to what they considered to be a threat to their sovereignty. Historically, the key weakness of Irish policy in respect of Northern Ireland was a failure to appreciate the fears of the Unionist community. The government was certainly unprepared for the crisis that erupted in August 1969. When it did occur, Ministers and party members placed Lynch's moderate position under considerable pressure by demanding a more active policy in response to Northern Ireland.

The breakdown of order in Northern Ireland opened up serious divisions in the party on how to respond. The important point is that it was no longer politics as usual; the violence in Northern Ireland touched an emotional cord in Fianna Fáil and seriously divided the party. For some it was an opportunity to end partition; for others it opened the possibility of a change in leadership; and for yet others it offered the prospect of per-sonal advancement. The pressure within Fianna Fáil pushed Lynch to take a more tradi-tional position on the North and one that was possibly more militant than he intended. In the short term, Lynch resisted the pressure for a more interventionist policy and there is no evidence that he actively considered invading Northern Ireland. However, some of his rhetoric and that of other Fianna Fáil members may have given Unionists the idea that he did.[28] While Hillery's negotiations at the United Nations defused some of this pressure in the short term, as did British military intervention in the north, Haughey, Blaney, and others were subverting public funds to acquire weapons for northern nationalists and engaging in discussions with sections of the IRA on tactics and strategy in respect of partition. This in turn led to the dismissal of Haughey and Blaney and the resignation of Boland and others from the cabinet. The trial of those charged with con-spiracy to import arms proved to be a disaster for Lynch as all the accused were found not guilty. Though Lynch asserted control of the party in 1970 and 1971, the escalating violence in Northern Ireland increased pressure on his government to adopt a more militant position in respect of partition. Close study of Lynch's speeches between 1970 and 1975 highlights his attempt to balance the moderate with the militant. In practice, Lynch pursued a vigorous anti-IRA policy while in office, so much so that the IRA Army Council discussed the possibility of assassinating the Minister for Justice Desmond O'Malley. However, Lynch was unable to maintain the balance between these two posi-tions and when Fianna Fáil went into opposition after the 1973 election, his moderate policy was put under pressure. Lynch was also weakened by the return of Haughey to the centre of the party after the 1973 election. By 1975, the party had decided to adopt a policy that called for an 'ordered withdrawal' by Britain from Northern Ireland and Lynch was forced to endorse this against his better judgement.

There are a number of unanswered questions concerning the period 1969 to 1973, which, in the absence of Garda and intelligence files, it is difficult to address. Keogh has provided new documentation from Lynch's personal papers and challenges one of the key sources for the period. This is the so-called Berry diaries published in *Magill* magazine and for some time the only direct source on the background to the arms cri-sis. Keogh is dismissive of Berry's recollections and rejects his contention that he had warned Lynch of the conspiracy to import arms in late 1969. Lynch argued persistently that he was not made aware of this situation until April 1970, a view that Keogh endorses. Keogh's discussion is credible, if not entirely convincing, and certainly poses important questions concerning Berry's reliability at the time. This is clearly an area for further analysis, as the discrepancy between the two positions is considerable.[29]

Fianna Fáil's decision to occupy the conservative ground in Irish politics was reinforced in the course of the 1970s as Ireland changed. Political demands were made for change in the Constitution, on social and moral issues and on Northern Ireland. Fianna Fáil was well placed to mobilize conservative and centrist opinion for its moderate conservatism, as proved to be the case in 1977, but could also lose the crucial floating vote as occurred during the electoral cycle of 1981–2. However, public opinion changed during the 1970s and opinion polls detected a new liberal constituency in urban Ireland, but these polls also identified the continuing strength of a traditional majority among the electorate. Mac Gréil's study of Dublin in 1972 describes a society no longer homogeneous and a population with complex and pluralistic views on a wide range of issues. Some of these express dramatic dissent from traditional attitudes on Northern Ireland, sexual morality, and civil liberties. Mac Gréil's work suggests that in Dublin opinion had changed and in some cases quite dramatically. Liberals and conservatives were contesting Ireland's future and arguing about its past. The dichotomy between Dublin and the rest of Ireland in the 1970s requires further attention and later polls confirm that liberalism remained weak outside Dublin. However, in political terms, it helps to explain why Fianna Fáil and to a lesser extent Fine Gael continued to support conservative policy options on moral issues such as contraception. Younger voters, those living in urban areas, and the better educated were more likely to take liberal positions in the 1970s, but older voters, women, those living in rural Ireland and with less education identified closely with the conservative and traditional positions adopted by Fianna Fáil.[30]

The election of the Fine Gael/Labour Coalition government in 1973 cemented the image of a conservative–liberal realignment in Irish politics, although that could be exaggerated. Attitudes to Northern Ireland were especially polarized and the Minister for Posts and Telegraphs, Conor Cruise O'Brien, probably the most formidable intellectual in Ireland at the time, became a figure of intense dislike for Fianna Fáil and traditional nationalists. In contrast to his cabinet colleague and Minister for Foreign Affairs, Garret FitzGerald, O'Brien aggressively challenged many of the foundation myths of Irish nationalism, questioning the irredentist nationalism of the Irish state. O'Brien argued that the very demand for Irish unity was mistaken and provided legitimacy for IRA violence. O'Brien also challenged the position of the Catholic Church from a liberal-humanist perspective, criticizing its influence on the Irish state. While O'Brien's position was never a representative one, it was the first time that an Irish cabinet minister engaged in such heated controversy with nationalism and religion.[31] These controversies accompanied and reinforced a growing sense of crisis by the mid 1970s. The Dáil voted to declare a national emergency in response to the IRA campaign of violence in September 1976, in addition to the curtailment of certain civil rights and media freedoms. The benefits from membership of the EEC were short-lived for most sections of the community and economic expansion quickly stalled. In addition, the government was unpopular and often divided on major issues of reform. The most notable example of this was the decision by the then Taoiseach, Liam Cosgrave, to vote against his own government's legislation to legalize the importation and sale of contraceptives in July 1974. The Supreme Court had declared that married couples could import contraceptives for their personal use at the end of 1973 and this liberalized the environment significantly. While Cosgrave's vote has attracted most attention, what is sometimes overlooked is that the overwhelming majority of Fine Gael and Labour deputies voted for a reform that was criticized by the Catholic hierarchy and was opposed by many of their constituents.[32]

In the run-up to the 1977 general election, Fianna Fáil played very successfully on the fears of the electorate on a number of levels, but especially on unemployment and the economy. Its election manifesto promised full employment and benefits for most of the electorate, a strategy rewarded with a landslide majority. Despite its twenty-seat majority and the establishment of the Department of Economic Planning and Development to oversee expansion through a Keynesian stimulus, the government failed to reverse the serious economic situation and may indeed have made it worse. By 1979, the Fianna Fáil government in turn was unpopular, the party was divided on Northern Ireland, and the economic situation continued to deteriorate. It is arguable that Lynch made a serious misjudgement when he decided to resign as leader of the party. He believed that George Colley would succeed him easily, but Haughey had assiduously cultivated grassroots opinion in the party and his views on Northern Ireland, the economy, and moral issues were closer to the now-dominant conservative mood of the party. In the event he was successful, but the divisions between Colley and the moderate minority and Haughey's supporters remained a characteristic feature of Fianna Fáil politics for nearly twenty years.

IV. Crisis and the Birth of the Celtic Tiger 1979–97

Notwithstanding Lemass's achievements, and subsequent progress, considerable economic difficulties continued to plague policy makers until the 1990s. It could be argued that in many respects the Irish economy performed no better under free trade and EEC membership than under protection and this requires explanation. The structure of the economy, the composition of exports, and the nature of investment changed, yet in terms of employment, income, and living standards, Ireland was not comparatively better off in 1987. It also raises questions concerning the contribution of free trade, foreign direct investment, and EEC membership to development. It may be that the situation would have been worse without the changes and a critical engagement with these issues may clarify the situation. Ireland seems to have experienced growth in output without significant employment increase. The labour force was approximately the same size in 1986 as it was in 1961, but Ireland had a much larger population in 1986 and the unemployment rate was considerably higher. When account is taken of the virtual exclusion of women from the workforce, emigration, and unemployment, the results of thirty years of economic development were disappointing. For this period, Lee's pessimistic analysis is more justified than later optimistic views, and it remains a warning that economic convergence for small open states is difficult to achieve.[33]

If the changes introduced by 1966 do constitute a turning point, then why did it take over thirty years to achieve growth with prosperity? Foster has argued that the period should not be conceived as a 'great leap forward' but 'a series of interconnected crises, whose outcome must remain unknown'.[34] If this is so, then the question of how these crises were resolved has to be persuasively answered. I would suggest that one way towards an explanation will involve focusing on continuity and constraints that maintained existing attitudes and interests while blocking innovative departures. While continuity is not necessarily a constraint on change, in the Irish case it is possible that the cumulative impact of continuity was to do so. Continuity is evident in constitutional and institutional arrangements and in the denominational aspects of educational and medical policy, despite the growth of liberalism. The continuing political strength of Fianna Fáil and the traditional political system also contributed to continuity, as did the importance of nationalism as a focus for political mobilization and party competition.

The 1980s can be characterized as the decade when Irish modernization and progressive change were effectively blocked by conservative mobilization. As Minister for Health in the Lynch government, Haughey had successfully piloted the Health (Family Planning) Act 1979 through the Dáil. This legalized the importation and sale of contraceptives and was commended by Haughey as a conservative (if moderate) resolution of the issue. Despite this, the legislation promoted a counter-mobilization by traditional and conservative opinion in opposition to what was considered to be the erosion of traditional Irish values, a view reinforced by the visit of Pope John Paul II in 1979. Conservatives feared that the legislature or the Supreme Court would defy majority opposition and liberalize laws on abortion, homosexuality, and pornography. The political tool chosen to meet this challenge was the referendum, in the belief that moral issues should only be decided by majority vote. This method was used most decisively in the case of the 'right to life' amendment in 1983 and the defeat of the proposal to remove the prohibition on divorce in 1986.[35] The votes on abortion and divorce demonstrated the extent to which traditional appeals could be politically successful, even as sections of the electorate were becoming more liberal. It draws attention to the illiberal, but democratic, strain in Irish political culture that gave priority to majoritarian outcomes over toleration or individualism, a theme that requires further attention. Ireland proved to be the most conservative state in the European Community in 1980 and remained so for the rest of that decade. The moderate nationalist Garret FitzGerald misjudged the mood of the country when he announced the need for a 'constitutional crusade' to reform aspects of the constitution and social legislation in order to address the crisis in Northern Ireland. Sustained opposition from Fianna Fáil reflected wider unease and conservatism among the electorate and his proposals came to naught. The conservative backlash weakened liberalism further and more directly the liberal wing of Fine Gael who actively supported FitzGerald.

The New Ireland Forum was initially promoted as a liberal opening to Unionism, but offered little new and was eventually undermined by Haughey's reassertion of traditional nationalism. The failure of the Forum provided FitzGerald with the opportunity to engage in direct and successful bilateral negotiations with Margaret Thatcher and the British Government. The surprising outcome of this engagement was the Anglo-Irish Agreement in 1985, which transformed the relationship between Britain and Ireland if not between north and south. This agreement weakened Ulster Unionism within the UK and also challenged traditional nationalism in the Irish Republic. Haughey opposed the agreement, but dissident members of Fianna Fáil, Desmond O'Malley and Mary Harney, formed the Progressive Democrats in response to Haughey's position on the Agreement, and to Fianna Fáil's heavy-handed dealing with dissent and to the party's illiberalism. At the 1987 election, the new party won fourteen seats, attracting significant support from the middle classes on a programme that emphasized liberal social policy and neo-liberal economic policies. The Progressive Democrats took votes from Fianna Fáil and from Fine Gael and it is probable that this deprived Fianna Fáil of an overall majority in 1987. However, Fianna Fáil's poor performance during the election campaign led to a fundamental reappraisal of policy. Haughey was forced to reverse his opposition to the Anglo-Irish Agreement, even while the party's reservations remained in place. He also backtracked on economic policy, effectively adopting the regressive fiscal and monetary policies established by the previous government, which he had promised to remove. Moreover, Haughey also abandoned the party's traditional commitment to single-party government when he formed a coalition with the Progressive Democrats in 1989. The new coalition government changed the nature of Irish politics and ushered in a dramatically new period for Ireland generally.

The coalition with the Progressive Democrats imposed serious constraints on Haughey and eventually weakened him to the extent that the party abandoned him in early 1992 and elected Albert Reynolds as leader and Taoiseach. It is possible to argue that 1989 is the crucial dividing line between the continuation of traditional Ireland (and its poor economic performance) and the emergence of a new modern Ireland (if not as yet the Celtic Tiger). It is unlikely that a social partnership would have been agreed without Haughey's input and support; certainly Fine Gael, Labour, or the Progressive Democrats would not have actively done so. This was reinforced after the 1987 election by the political consensus on the response to economic crisis, effectively ratified by the new leader of Fine Gael, Alan Dukes, in the so called Tallaght strategy. If these developments stabilized the economy and provided a stimulus for expansion in the 1990s, public opinion was also moving beyond the constraints of the 1980s on moral issues and Northern Ireland. The election of Mary Robinson as President in 1990 demonstrated that it was possible for a candidate to pursue an openly liberal programme in the face of Catholic and right-wing opposition. The 'X' case in 1992 effectively unravelled the 'right to life' amendment and successive attempts to return to the 1983 status quo failed.

Opinion became more liberal between 1980 and 1990 and appreciably so by 2000.[36] The positive result of the second divorce referendum in 1995, while close, led to the introduction of divorce and remarriage. This liberal trend had an impact on Fianna Fáil after Haughey's departure when it was defeated in the 1992 general election. Reynolds negotiated an unprecedented coalition with the Labour Party and agreed an ambitious reform programme. However, this programme was never delivered and after the collapse of this coalition an alternative was negotiated on more liberal grounds between Fine Gael, Labour, and the Democratic Left, which lasted to 1997. The successful negotiation of the Good Friday Agreement and the subsequent amendment of articles 2 and 3 of the Constitution provide further evidence for change in Irish society.

V. POLITICAL CONSENSUS, THE CELTIC TIGER, AND CRISIS, 1997–2011

Lemass predicted that Ireland would be significantly changed by the end of the century and his view was borne out by events. Ireland entered the twenty-first century in optimistic mood and the pessimism, violence, and decline of the previous thirty years was quickly left behind. By 2000, there was peace in both parts of the island, the Irish Republic had a high and rising standard of living shared by most people, and public opinion was converging with European attitudes as never before. In a remarkable turnaround, Ireland generated one million new jobs over a fifteen-year period and for the first time since independence there was full employment and its human capital was utilized to the full (especially women and emigrants). An important by-product of this process was the growth of a more complex and pluralist society made up of diverse ethnic and religious groups.[37] Fianna Fáil was the main political beneficiary of this transformation. Led by Bertie Ahern, the party returned to government in 1997 and was rewarded electorally by further success in 2002 and 2007. Ahern was closely associated with social partnership, considered by many to be a major contribution to economic and social stability. Furthermore, coalition government with Fianna Fáil at the centre now became the preferred governmental option. Ahern and Fianna Fáil exhibited considerable flexibility in choosing coalition partners, though the main objective of the strategy was to maintain the party in government.

Ireland seemed to have discovered a successful growth and developmental model that became the envy of other states in Europe and elsewhere. However, important questions remain unanswered concerning the nature of the 'Celtic Tiger' and economic success itself. Was Ireland 'lucky' in the sense that a number of factors converged to create the conditions for growth and prosperity?[38] How important was the state's engagement with European integration and globalization and how did these engagements contribute to success? Was the primary cause of economic success domestic (due to a successful policy mix) or determined by factors over which the state had little influence? What

requires further explanation is the extent to which traditional norms and special interests constrained Irish development between 1973 and 1995 and how these constraints
were removed or weakened.[39]

These questions become more important in the context of the current crisis of capitalism and the future of Irish economic growth is closely linked to how these questions
are answered. The collapse of the Celtic Tiger has been as impressive as its original
appearance. In the case of the economic crisis, it was a self-inflicted wound that might
have been avoided if, as Whelan suggests, intervention as late as 2005 'could have prevented the upcoming meltdown'. Policy decisions based on electoral considerations,
an overoptimistic belief that recession was impossible, and a failure to take seriously
well-intentioned advice undermined the competitive growth model that had been so
successful after 1987. Low tax, preferential treatment for property speculation, and a
poorly regulated banking system provide the domestic origins of Ireland's latest depression. Given its openness, Ireland would have been challenged by the global downturn
after 2007, but the severity of its experience is a consequence of policy errors on the part
of the political elite.[40] This was compounded by short-term electoral considerations and
a belief that Ireland had found a 'magic formula' that made it immune to crisis. This led
the Taoiseach in 2007 to suggest that critics should commit suicide.

The depression, however, disguises a deeper crisis in the system. Growing scepticism
towards Europe was expressed in the initial rejection of the Nice and Lisbon referendums and public opinion was much cooler towards further integration than heretofore.
Independent tribunals uncovered extensive corruption and tax evasion among the elite.
Financial irregularities eventually forced the Taoiseach, Bertie Ahern, to resign in May
2008 after a decade of successful political and economic management. This was compounded by the revelations of extensive clerical abuse against vulnerable young people
over a long period. What this also highlighted was collusion between church and state
and a refusal to acknowledge the extent of the abuse. These issues raise serious questions
concerning the nature of consensus, the dominance of a single political party in the state
institutions, and the power of private interests in a small homogeneous society.

The most remarkable change in the last decade has been the outcome of the 2011 general election. Fianna Fáil became the main victim of the economic crisis and its support plummeted to an all-time low. The Fine Gael/Labour coalition that formed the
new government has been implementing the rescue package agreed with the EU/IMF
though this does not disguise the real loss of sovereignty suffered by the state as a consequence of virtual collapse of the banking system in 2008. What is not clear is whether
Fianna Fáil's setback in 2011 is a short-term rejection due to poor economic management or an indication of more fundamental changes in the political system. In the circumstances, many questions remain unanswered, especially in the absence of archival
material. These developments raise a deeper question for the historian. Are the changes
we see only surface ones or do strong patterns continue underneath that reflect deeply
embedded norms and values? It is not difficult to locate continuity in Irish institutions
and especially in the Constitution as a normative document. That Ireland has changed
is indisputable; perhaps what needs further attention is the extent to which this change

has been accompanied by continuity in terms of Irish national identity and the political culture's self-image, in Europe and the world.

NOTES

1. I would like to thank the Carnegie Trust for the Scottish Universities for financial support while researching this chapter. Rona Fitzgerald read and commented on an earlier version with her usual skill and insight.
2. R. F. Foster, *Luck and the Irish: A Brief History of Change 1970–2000* (London, 2007), 1.
3. J. J. Lee, *Ireland 1912–1985: Politics and Society* (Cambridge, 1989); Diarmaid Ferriter, *The Transformation of Ireland 1900–2000* (London, 2004); Foster, *Luck and the Irish*.
4. Geoffrey Barraclough, *An Introduction to Contemporary History* (Harmondsworth, 1967; original edition 1964), 13–14.
5. Brian Girvin, 'Continuity, Change and Crisis in Ireland: An Introduction and Discussion' *Irish Political Studies* 23: 4 (December 2008), 457–74.
6. Brian Girvin and Gary Murphy, 'Whose Ireland? The Lemass Era' in Brian Girvin and Gary Murphy (eds) *The Lemass Era: Politics and Society in the Ireland of Seán Lemass* (Dublin, 2005), 1–11; we concluded 'Seán Lemass is one of the most impressive figures in Irish politics during the twentieth century. More so than Eamon de Valera, contemporary Ireland bears the stamp of Lemass.'
7. John Horgan, *Seán Lemass: The Enigmatic Patriot* (Dublin, 1997); Paul Bew and Henry Patterson, *Seán Lemass and the Making of Modern Ireland 1945–66* (Dublin, 1982) provides a challenging interpretation of this period; for the most recent research see Girvin and Murphy (eds), *The Lemass Era*.
8. William Roche, 'Social Partnership: From Lemass to Cowen' *The Economic and Social Review* 40: 2, (Summer, 2009), 183–205, who describes Lemass as a 'corporatist visionary and pragmatist'.
9. Maurice Manning, *James Dillon: A Biography* (Dublin, 1999), 315.
10. Horgan, *Seán Lemass*, op.cit., 225; 210–11; 202; Trinity College Dublin: Erskine Childers Papers, MS 9959/17 notes for obituary of Lemass 16 May 1971.
11. Horgan, *Seán Lemass*, 213–51; Gary Murphy, *Economic Realignment and the Politics of EEC Entry: Ireland 1948–72* (Dublin, 2003), 47–90; 157–92; see also John F. McCarthy (ed) *Planning Ireland's Future: The Legacy of T. K. Whitaker* (Sandycove, Co. Dublin, 1990).
12. Maurice FitzGerald, *Protectionism to Liberalisation: Ireland and the EEC, 1957–1966* (Aldershote, 2000), 237–302.
13. John Walsh, 'The Politics of educational expansion' in Girvin and Murphy, *The Lemass Era*, 146–65; John Walsh, *The Politics of Expansion: The Transformation of Educational Policy in the Republic of Ireland 1957–72* (Manchester, 2009).
14. Robert Savage, *A Loss of Innocence? Television and Irish Society 1969–72* (Manchester, 2010).
15. Tom Garvin, *Preventing the Future: How was Ireland so Poor for so Long?* (Dublin, 2004), 199, 119; Bryce Evans, *Seán Lemass: Democratic Dictator* (Cork, 2011), 207–59 provides a more critical assessment.
16. D. S. Johnson and L. Kennedy, 'The Two Economies in Ireland in the Twentieth Century' in J. R. Hill (ed) *A New History of Ireland VIII: Ireland 1921–1984* (Oxford, 2003), 452–86.
17. Murphy, *Economic Realignment*, provides an important discussion of trade union and farmer attitudes to Europe but does not discuss in detail other aspects of policy.

18. Gary Murphy and Niamh Puirséil, ' "Is It a New Allowance?" Irish Entry to the EEC and Popular Opinion' *Irish Political Studies* 23: 4 (December 2008), 533–54: Michael J. Geary, *An Inconvenient Wait: Ireland's Quest for Membership of the EEC 1957–73* (Dublin, 2009).

19. Dermot Keogh, *Jack Lynch: A Biography* (Dublin, 2008); John Walsh, *Patrick Hillery* (Dublin, 2008); Stephen Collins, *The Power Game: Fianna Fáil since Lemass* (Dublin, 2000).

20. Terence Dooley, 'The Land for the People' *The Land Question in Independent Ireland* (Dublin:, 2004); Damien F. Hannan and Patrick Commins, 'The Significance of Small-scale Landholders in Ireland's Socio-economic Transformation' in J. H. Goldthorpe and C. T. Whelan (eds) *The Development of Industrial Society in Ireland* (Oxford, 1992), 79–104.

21. Daithí Ó Corráin *Rendering to God and Caesar! The Irish Churches and the Two States in Ireland 1949–73* (Manchester, 2006); J. H. Whyte, *Church and State in Modern Ireland 1923–1979* (Dublin: 1980, second edition); Diarmaid Ferriter *Occasions of Sin: Sex and Society in Modern Ireland* (London, 2009).

22. Niamh Puirséil *The Irish Labour Party 1922–73* (Dublin, 2007), 211–307.

23. Brian Girvin, 'Church, state, and society in Ireland since 1960' *Éire/Ireland* 43: 1–2 (2008), 74–99; John Cooney *John Charles McQuaid: Ruler of Catholic Ireland* (Dublin, 1999); Francis Xavier Carty *Hold Firm: John Charles McQuaid and the Second Vatican Council* (Dublin, 2007).

24. Garret FitzGerald *All in a Life* (Dublin, 1992).

25. Puirséil, *The Labour Party*, op.cit., 246; Keogh, *Jack Lynch*, 154–5.

26. Neither Keogh nor Walsh provides a satisfactory discussion of Fianna Fáil's electoral tactics in 1969, nor does Collins.

27. Keogh, *Jack Lynch*, 141–6.

28. Eunan O'Halpin, ' "A Greek Authoritarian Phase"? The Irish Army and the Irish Crisis' *Irish Political Studies* 23: 4 (December 2008), 475–90.

29. Keogh, *Jack Lynch*, 218–220; 240–261; The 'Berry Diaries' appeared in *Magill* June 1980.

30. Mícheál Mac Gréil *Prejudice and Tolerance in Ireland* (Dublin, 1977), 410–6; 377–8; the survey work for this research was carried out in 1972; Michael Fogarty, Liam Ryan and Joseph Lee, *Irish Values and Attitudes* (Dublin: Dominican Publications, 1984) which reports on the European Values Study carried out in 1981.

31. *Conor Cruise O'Brien, States of Ireland* (London, 1972); for an evaluation of O'Brien see Diarmuid Whelan, *Conor Cruise O'Brien: Violent Notions* (Dublin, 2009).

32. Brian Girvin, 'Contraception, Moral Panic and Social Change in Ireland, 1969–79' *Irish Political Studies* 23: 4 (December 2008), 555–76.

33. Rona FitzGerald and Brian Girvin, 'Political culture, growth and the conditions for success in the Irish economy' in Brian Nolan, Philip J. O'Connell and Christopher T. Whelan (eds) *Bust to Boom? The Irish Experience of Growth and Inequality* (Dublin, 2000), 268–85.

34. Foster, *Luck and the Irish*, 6.

35. Girvin, 'Church, State, and Society in Ireland since 1960', 74–98.

36. Tony Fahey, Bernadette C. Hayes, Richard Sinnott, *Conflict and Consensus: A Study of Values and Attitudes in the Republic of Ireland and Northern Ireland* (Dublin, 2005).

37. Tony Fahey, Helen Russell and Christopher T. Whelan (eds.) *Best of Times? The Social Impact of the Celtic Tiger* (Dublin, 2007).

38. *The Economist*, 'The Luck of the Irish', 4 October 2004 (Survey on Ireland).

39. Fitzgerald and Girvin, 'Political culture, growth and the conditions for success in the Irish economy'.

40. Karl Whelan, 'Policy Lessons from Ireland's Latest Depression' *The Economic and Social Review* 41:2 (2010) 225–54.

Select Bibliography

Bew, Paul and Henry Patterson. *Seán Lemass and the Making of Modern Ireland 1945–66* (Dublin, 1982).

Collins, Stephen, *The Power Game: Fianna Fáil since Lemass* (Dublin, 2000).

Daly, Mary E., *Sixties Ireland: Reshaping the Economy, State and Society, 1957–1973* (Cambridge, 2016).

Ferriter, Diarmaid, *The Transformation of Ireland 1900–2000* (London, 2004).

FitzGerald, Garret, *All in a Life* (Dublin, 1992).

Foster, R. F., *Luck and the Irish: A Brief History of Change 1970–2000* (London, 2007).

Garvin, Tom, *Preventing the Future: How was Ireland so Poor for so Long?* (Dublin, 2004).

Girvin, Brian, *Union to Union: Nationalism, Democracy and Religion in Ireland* (Dublin, 2002).

Girvin, Brian and Gary Murphy (eds), *The Lemass Era: Politics and Society in the Ireland of Seán Lemass* (Dublin, 2005).

Girvin, Brian and Gary Murphy (eds), *Continuity, Change and Crisis in Ireland: New Perspectives, Research and Interpretation* (London, 2009).

Girvin, Brian (guest editor) 'The Origins of Contemporary Ireland: New Perspectives On The Recent Past', Special Issue *Irish Historical Studies* xxxviii, 151 (May 2013).

Goldthorpe, J. H. and C. T. Whelan (eds), *The Development of Industrial Society in Ireland* (Oxford, 1992).

Horgan, John, *Seán Lemass: The Enigmatic Patriot* (Dublin, 1997).

Keogh, Dermot, *Jack Lynch: A Biography* (Dublin, 2008).

Lee, J. J., *Ireland 1912–1985: Politics and Society* (Cambridge, 1989).

Mac Gréil, Mícheál, *Prejudice and Tolerance in Ireland* (Dublin, 1977).

Murphy, Gary, *Economic Realignment and the Politics of EEC Entry: Ireland 1948–72* (Dublin, 2003).

Murphy, Gary, *Electoral Competition in Ireland Since 1987: The Politics of Triumph and Despair* (Manchester, 2016).

Ó Corráin, Daithí, *Rendering to God and Caesar! The Irish Churches and the Two States in Ireland 1949–73* (Manchester, 2006).

Puirséil, Niamh, *The Irish Labour Party 1922–73* (Dublin, 2007).

Walsh, John, *Patrick Hillery* (Dublin, 2008).

Walsh, John, *The Politics of Expansion: The Transformation of Educational Policy in the Republic of Ireland 1957–72* (Manchester, 2009).

Whyte, J. H., *Church and State in Modern Ireland 1923–1979* (Dublin, 1980, second edition).

CHAPTER 37

....

THE LONG WAR AND ITS
AFTERMATH, 1969–2007

....

PAUL ARTHUR

I. INTRODUCTION

IN 1914, George Bernard Shaw described a putative Ulster entity as 'an autonomous political lunatic asylum' with Sir Edward Carson as 'the chief keeper'. If indeed that was to be in any way an accurate reflection on what became known as Northern Ireland, it was in the interests of its 'chief keeper' to ensure that this condition was withheld from the rest of the world. One of the successes of successive Unionist governments was that capacity to make Northern Ireland the Albania of the western world, hermetically sealed from outside intervention. In effect the Ulster Unionist Party (UUP) had become a 'party of regional defence' whose 'strategic strength has lain in its capacity to represent and nurture an alliance between "Ulster" and the English Conservative Party, or certainly a blocking section of it'.[1] This sense of isolation was encouraged by British politicians eager to keep their distance from Belfast.

This condition fitted in with the structure of power in the United Kingdom (UK) which has been called the Dual Polity—'a structure of territorial politics in which Centre and periphery had relatively little to do with each other', whereby 'until recently the Centre sought not to govern the United Kingdom but to manage it'.[2] In that respect Unionists were ideal collaborators, 'stable, quiescent, efficient, and yet fundamentally weak in their relations with the Centre . . . sustained by the Centre's indifference, not by peripheral strength'.[3] Once London began to scrutinize Northern Ireland's affairs, the house of cards began to collapse. In 1966, one observer noted a change in Catholic attitudes from one of 'a mere hopeless antagonism' to 'a more active self-respect. It is not ridiculous to envisage a Catholic civil rights movement in the not too far distant future.'[4]

The period from 1968 onwards witnessed a fundamental shift not only in relations between the two communities within Northern Ireland, but equally in relationships within the British/Irish archipelago, and ensured that the Northern Ireland conflict attracted international attention. In the previous four decades, the Northern Ireland political system had produced no more than three scholarly books. Yet, by 1990, it was described as 'perhaps the most heavily researched area in the world': a research output which bore very limited pickings—'... there is still only partial agreement on the nature of the problem and none at all on the nature of the solution.'[5]

Given the intensity and the intractability of the violence during this time, it wasn't surprising that solutions were thin on the ground. In that respect, Northern Ireland serves as a model of the life cycle of a conflict that went through three phases of analysis, negotiation, and implementation. It is a period marked by nihilism, devastation, and by profound constitutional uncertainty that was mirrored in the party system. What had been a one-party regime since its inception collapsed after 1972 into a welter of parties competing across and within ethnic divisions for the simulacrum of power. Indeed, the period after 1972 is denoted as one of extended direct rule from Westminster where Northern Ireland politicians enjoyed virtually no control over their own destiny. When the opportunity arose to cede some power back from Westminster in 2007, that became possible only because the two perceived 'extreme' parties at opposite ends of the sectarian divide—the Democratic Unionist Party (DUP) and Sinn Féin (SF)—were prepared to enter into government together. By any standards in the western world this was a remarkable turnaround and needs some explanation.

Part of that explanation can be found in changes in the international community. The Cold War dominated until the collapse of the Soviet Union at the end of the 1980s. Europe's initial response to the devastation of two World Wars had been to create a form of functional cooperation that would replace the dominant Franco-German animosity—hence a coal and steel community blossomed into a European Economic Community (EEC) of six European states, through a European Community (EC), towards a European Union (EU) of 27 states, that transcended many of the divisions that had crippled the continent. In doing so, Europe turned its back on a Hobbesian model of perpetual power struggles and strived after Kantian perpetual peace.[6] Equally, the end of the Cold War created the conditions for a paradigm shift in confronting conflict as South Africa removed itself from its pariah status. The Irish conflict eventually moved in a similar direction.

It is in this context that John Whyte's pessimism of 1990 can be contrasted with the uplifting rhetoric of President Bill Clinton when he declared in Belfast on 3 September 1998 that 'in the early days of the American Republic the Gaelic term for America was Inis Fail—Island of Destiny. Today Americans see you as Inis Fail and your destiny is peace.'[7] His comments were particularly pertinent because they followed the obscenity of the Omagh bomb on 15 August, when the Real IRA killed twenty-nine people—men, women, children, even the unborn, and Spanish as well as British and Irish citizens. And that carnage had followed the killings of three young Catholic brothers on 12 July after their house had been petrol-bombed by loyalists protesting against the standoff over an Orange march.

How do we explain this resort from naked sectarianism and the deadly technology of a deluded ideology to the sunny uplands of Ireland's destiny of peace? That is the remit of this chapter.

II. ANALYSIS

(a) Frozen Violence

Shortly after the People's Democracy—a student left-wing civil rights movement—was formed in October 1968 at Queen's University Belfast, Conor Cruise O'Brien addressed a student body at Queen's on the topic of 'Civil Disobedience'. He spoke of the 'subordination of Catholic to Protestant in Derry' as a result of force and the threat of force: 'The condition of Derry may be thought of as one of frozen violence: any attempt to thaw it out will liberate violence which is at present static.'[8] These were prophetic words.

It was not that there existed already well armed and mobilized groups. The IRA in Belfast had no more than twenty-four members in 1962 and had grown only to 120 by 1969. By February 1970, there was complacency inside the British cabinet that it was only 'professional anarchists' making trouble.[9] The Ulster Volunteer Force (UVF) had been active since 1966 but had been proscribed, and the Ulster Defence Association (UDA) had not yet emerged. To understand why there was a rapid transition to protracted violence we need to examine attitudes rather than armoury.

In a survey of political developments after the Belfast Agreement was signed in 1998, Aughey refers to a political culture that fostered 'a discourse of grievance, a style of politics that had a long pedigree in Irish politics', a discourse based on self-pity and self-righteousness. Its outcome was that Unionists and nationalists had 'sought to allocate historical blame rather than to seek present compromise'.[10] Both sides indulged in 'victimhood', the political economy of helplessness, through a highly selective reading of history. As Bowyer Bell noted, 'the whole process was so *natural* as to be beyond comment... Nothing had to be imported, nothing fashioned by ideologues, nothing sold to the people, nothing secretly arranged because of events. All that was needed was to exploit the existing reality',[11] a reality manufactured out of a civil rights movement based on extra-parliamentary protest with the wide support of Catholic opinion. Hence throughout the conflict an area like the Bogside remained a 'community, not a war zone'.[12] Equally, the IRA would insist that their legitimacy rested on the fact that their historical and organizational origins emerged from the Easter Rising of 1916 but that the 'circumstances which shaped the support for the IRA today are above all the experience of the barricade days from 1969–72 ... because they saw the development of tremendous communal solidarity...'.[13]

Their only reason for engaging in armed struggle, they asserted, would be that there would be no hope of getting the required changes without it. They had to convince the ghetto that 'IRA volunteers are actually civilians, political people who decide for short periods in their lives to take part in armed action [because it is] a political necessity'.[14] In short, the IRA were less a revolutionary vanguard than a people's army in the same mould as the ANC and the PLO. It removed them from the charge of elitism and placed them at the heart of their own community. This sense of communal solidarity sustained them through the years of the long war and reinforced their sense of moral certitude.

Loyalist paramilitarism indulged in similar sentiments. The UVF self-perception was of a long tradition of 'public banding' whereby public order was derived more from the Protestant community's exertions than from the activities of the sovereign authority, a tradition that went back to the seventeenth century.[15] It was demonstrated most forcefully and courageously at the Battle of the Somme in 1916 when so many of their ancestors paid the ultimate price to protect democracy. This sense of timeless patriotism carried itself into the post-1968 era and is encapsulated in the phrase: 'Their only crime was loyalty'. The Ulster Defence Association (UDA) could not claim a similar lineage. It was formed in September 1971, dedicated to defending its territory from the IRA. In that respect it saw itself as a 'counter-terrorist organisation', to quote from its Supreme Commander. That *raison d'être* enabled it to maintain that, so long as the IRA remained in business, it would not disband.

What all of these had in common was that they believed that they were representatives of their respective communities and had political as well as defensive roles to play. The intensity of their activity meant that they muddied conventional wisdom and they made the search for a political solution even more complicated. The IRA in particular set out to demonstrate that 'their opponents had no exit, no opportunity simply to ignore acts of violence and thus to escape the communicative frame'.[16] They set out to persuade their own community that violent acts could have substantive political consequences. Adams was convinced that the tactic of armed struggle was necessary to provide a vital cutting edge: 'Without it, the issue of Ireland would not even be an issue. So, in effect, the armed struggle becomes armed propaganda.'[17]

(b) Endogenous Contradictions

The 'Agreement Reached in the Multi-Party Negotiations' in Belfast on Good Friday 1998—to give its official title, its place of birth, and the (religious) date of its signature (since all three titles, the 'Agreement', the 'Belfast Agreement' and the 'Good Friday Agreement' were used as forms of ethnic shorthand)—has been compared to an archaeological site that 'can be read as a brief constitutional summary of the Troubles...', and as 'an institutionalized holding operation whilst the forces of unionism and nationalism regrouped and repositioned themselves'.[18] That is a neat summary of an incredibly complex process that indicates an acknowledgement that a peace agreement may represent no more than the lowest common denominator. Implementation carries its own health warnings.

If the 1998 Agreement contains within itself 'the reworked remnants of failures' (to quote Aughey) a starting point might be the Downing Street Declaration of 19 August 1969 signed by the UK and Northern Ireland governments. At one level it can be read as a firm indication of Stormont's subordinate status to the sovereign authority in terms of implementing civil rights reforms. But its true significance lies in its assertion that 'Northern Ireland is entirely a matter of domestic jurisdiction. The United Kingdom Government will take full responsibility for asserting this principle in international relationships.' That was to be official UK policy until the 1980s.

The context for the signing of the Declaration is important. It followed very seri-ous sectarian rioting in Belfast and elsewhere in which the police were involved and a number of civilians were killed. It forced the government into establishing the Scarman Commission to inquire into particular acts of violence between March and August 1969. The report (published in 1972) makes the interesting point that in a 'very real sense our inquiry was an investigation of police conduct' (para. 3.1). Earlier, the Hunt Commission (1969) inquired into the structure of the indigenous security forces. It led to the (tempo-rary) disarmament of the RUC and the disbandment of the B. Specials. Incidentally, it led to the first serious rioting between loyalists in which a police officer was killed by loyalists protesting on the side of law and order.

Both Reports highlighted the confusion which arose between the army and the RUC and between Westminster and Stormont over the division of control of security mat-ters. It hampered the security effort and added to London's embarrassment internation-ally when forced to explain itself after the introduction of internment in August 1971 and Bloody Sunday 1972 when thirteen unarmed civilians were killed by paratroop-ers in Derry—a fourteenth was to die five months later. The response of Lord Saville of Newdigate who conducted a second official enquiry into Bloody Sunday nearly thirty years later was to conclude that '[W]hat happened on Bloody Sunday strengthened the Provisional IRA, increased nationalist resentment and hostility towards the Army and exacerbated the violent conflict of the years that followed. Bloody Sunday was a tragedy for the bereaved and the wounded, and a catastrophe for the people of Northern Ireland.' A similar sentiment was expressed by the Prime Minister, David Cameron, when he told the Commons on 15 June 2010 that 'you do not defend the British Army by defending the indefensible... what happened on Bloody Sunday was both unjust and unjustifia-ble'.[19] The official title of the security response was known as 'Operation Banner' (1969–2007). During that period more than 250 000 armed personnel had served in Northern Ireland, the largest peacetime operation ever undertaken by the UK, when 651 service personnel were killed and 6307 wounded.

Resentment was compounded at official level when two senior Whitehall officials were dispatched to Stormont with a remit to report directly to London and joint work-ing parties of officials were established to examine the extent and pace of a proposed reform package. This was the context in which Northern Ireland was ruled until direct rule was imposed in March 1972. It was direct rule *by proxy* and was a tacit acknowledge-ment that there was no repository of knowledge in the Whitehall machine concerning Northern Ireland. There were tensions with the Home Office in the period prior to the imposition of direct rule, and within the Northern Ireland civil service in the period fol-lowing direct rule.[20] Instead it dithered—although radical solutions were not discounted outright. For example, a report to the Heath government from the Central Policy Review Staff (CPRS) in September 1971 contemplated joint administration of Northern Ireland by London and Dublin.[21]

It was the apparently uncontrollable spiral of violence which led the Prime Minister, Edward Heath, to transfer the control for law and order to Westminster. In response the Northern Ireland premier, Brian Faulkner, resigned and direct rule was established, with William Whitelaw appointed the first Secretary of State for Northern Ireland. Faulkner was convinced that 'after three years of the most strenuous efforts to reform our society on a basis at once fair and realistic', his government had earned the right to the confidence and support of the UK government.[22] It was not to be—internment and Bloody Sunday had seen to that. A new democratic deficit had been created.

These were the circumstances in which the Northern Ireland Office (NIO) was created when direct rule came into operation on 30 March. In the following fourteen months, the Commons debated forty-four pieces of Irish legislation and had five full-scale debates on a Green and White Paper: 'Indeed the legislative workload since "direct rule" has been such that the small and new Northern Ireland Office stands at fourth place in the House of Commons league tables of hours consumed in Parliamentary business....[23] It was not a conventional department within the Whitehall machine. It was to be a temporary arrangement to enable Northern Ireland politicians to reach a political accommodation. But it faced massive administrative and political problems from the outset. The NIO had to be constructed incrementally and be sensitive to inherited animosities. Its creation was a triumph over adversity and an exercise in crisis management. It was unlike any other territorial ministry in the UK because so much of its energy was consumed by security matters and (initially) constitutional innovation.

(c) An Adventure Playground for Constitutional Innovators?

In keeping with the ethos of the 1969 Downing Street Declaration, policy-makers pursued an endogenous approach over the following decade. There were no less than four attempts to find a solution within UK parameters—the power-sharing executive of 1974, the Northern Ireland Constitutional Convention of 1975–6, the Atkins initiative of 1980–1, and rolling devolution (1982–6)—although the first introduced the fated and fateful concept of the Irish dimension. The incumbent secretary of state attached his authority to each of these initiatives. Two of these were genuinely innovative (those of 1974 and of 1982–6) and the other two were merely holding operations.

The 1974 power-sharing experiment broke the stranglehold of one-party rule in Northern Ireland and deviated from the Westminster model of government. The executive, which was created on 1 January 1974, drew together a group of comparatively moderate Unionists under Brian Faulkner (who became Chief Executive), the SDLP, and the Alliance Party, but lasted less than five months. Many Unionists were resolutely opposed to sharing power with nationalists. Before the executive had had time to prove itself, anti power-sharing Unionists in the United Ulster Unionist Council (UUUC) won eleven of the twelve Northern Ireland seats at the February 1974 general election. The UUUC claimed that the result was a clear vote of no confidence in Faulkner's executive. It took particular exception to the establishment of a Council of Ireland which gave Dublin a formal—if only consultative—role in Northern Ireland's political process. The UUUC's electoral success legitimized loyalist protest—the Ulster Workers' Council (UWC) strike of May 1974, which brought the province to a virtual standstill. The strike was described by the prominent Conservative spokesman Lord Hailsham as 'a conspiracy against the state'.[24] It raised questions once again about the nature of loyalty within the UK. It demonstrated too that monolithic Unionism was redundant and that the resort to violence and intimidation was not simply the exclusive property of the IRA.

In an attempt to return to some kind of normality, a Constitutional Convention was established in 1975 to consider what 'provision for the government of Northern Ireland is likely to command the most widespread acceptance throughout the community there'.[25] Needless to say it did not succeed. Perhaps its real merit was that it dissipated loyalists' euphoria. During the UWC stoppage, UVF car bombs killed twenty-seven people in the Republic in a single day. The collapse of power-sharing and the failure of the Convention occurred under Merlyn Rees's tenure. He was to devote most of the rest of the time to the security question.

Rees was succeeded in September 1976 by Roy Mason who also placed great emphasis on security results and eschewed grand constitutional initiatives. He made a concerted effort to revive the Northern Ireland economy with very mixed results. During his time he managed to alienate constitutional nationalists, whom he dismissed as 'greens', and satisfy the Unionists when Northern Ireland representation at Westminster increased from twelve to seventeen seats—a bargain struck to keep the minority Labour government in office a little longer. Indeed, one insider, senior policy advisor to the prime minister, suggested that 'he has become spokesman of the Protestants...offhand about the Catholics and scathing about the Republic'.[26] The two nationalist M.P.s, Gerry Fitt and Frank Maguire, exacted their revenge in a vote of confidence in March 1979 and the Labour government fell.

Following the Conservative general election victory in May, Margaret Thatcher appointed Humphrey Atkins as Secretary of State. He initiated a Conference to look at a narrow range of political options from power-sharing to a system of majority rule with a minority blocking mechanism. It was damned from the outset because the UUP refused to participate on the grounds that it abandoned the Conservative Party manifesto of closer integration. In any case, he was engrossed in the hunger strikes of 1980–1. He was removed to the Foreign Office in September 1981. But he left a significant legacy when he stated that the 'geographical and historical facts of life obliges us to recognise the special relationship that exists between the two component parts of the British Isles...we do improve our chances of success by recognising that the Republic is deeply interested in what happens in Northern Ireland'.[27] That was the theme that was to dominate from the 1980s onwards.

However, not before a final attempt at an internal solution: rolling devolution. This was the brainchild of the new Secretary, James Prior, who was considered to be ideologically 'wet' and the prime minister's primary rival. He had come to Northern Ireland reluctantly since he realized that it would remove him from the centre of power in Westminster. His response was to see an end to the 1981 hunger strike and to launch rolling devolution whereby power would be devolved incrementally once the parties demonstrated that they could work across the sectarian divide at departmental level. Its primary assumption was that politicians yearn for power. It was doomed from the outset. Mr Prior received little support from his own party. The 1982 Assembly elections resulted in significant gains for Sinn Féin, who boycotted Assembly proceedings. The SDLP followed suit and the Assembly turned into a Unionist talking shop (with opposition being provided by the Alliance Party). There could be no rolling devolution in the absence of one community from the Assembly.

Above all, the hunger strikes had cast an ominous pall on political progress. Since 1976, republicans had been demanding the restoration of special category status inside the prisons. They considered themselves to be prisoners of war and resented greatly the appellation of criminality which the authorities imposed upon them. Their protest took various forms and culminated in staging a hunger strike in 1980. That ended in December when, with some of their number at the point of death, they thought that they had extracted concessions on prison reform. Their sense of betrayal led to a second strike the following year. This was a turning point in the armed struggle. It fell back on the religion of nationalism first invoked by Patrick Pearse in 1916.[28] It was based on a powerful religious and political symbolism that called on Christian martyrology. Its very theatricality attracted enormous international publicity and inverted the nature of political discourse. It was Mrs Thatcher who now appeared to be in the dock. International sentiment moved against her.[29] It resulted in an even deeper sectarianism within Northern Ireland.

III. Negotiation

(a) The International Dimension

In retrospect, we can say that the impact of the hunger strikes altered the existing realities. Firstly, it rejuvenated the republican campaign and diverted them into a political reassessment. In an attempt to persuade Mrs Thatcher to meet their demands, the hunger strike leader, Bobby Sands, succeeded in being elected to Westminster in a by-election. She was unmoved and he died shortly afterwards. In an effort to maintain supremacy, Sinn Féin adopted the strategy of the 'ballot box and the Armalite' at its 1982 Ard Fheis—in future, the armed campaign would be reinforced by a political strategy that, while not everybody could plant a bomb, everyone could cast a vote. But it was flawed in that it challenged the democratic credentials of republicans—while Sinn Féin was making political progress in Northern Ireland throughout the 1980s, it was gaining only about 2 per cent of the vote in the Republic. In these circumstances, it was difficult to maintain the fiction that they were fully representative of the Irish people. It was to lead to a profound reappraisal of its campaign, so that by the end of the decade Sinn Féin was in tentative discussions with its political opponents.

Secondly, the hunger strikes accelerated interaction between the British and Irish governments begun soon after Mrs Thatcher became prime minister in 1979. That election brought the direct intervention of prominent US politicians who demanded that urgent action be taken in Northern Ireland to remove nationalist alienation. It led to a series of British-Irish summits that began to explore means by which there could be much closer cooperation between both states. The conflict was being moved out of the narrow ground of Northern Ireland and placed in its proper temporal and spatial context. Despite several setbacks, the process culminated in the signing of the Anglo-Irish Agreement at Hillsborough Castle on 15 November 1985.

The significance of the agreement is explained in two contrasting views. The first comes from the chief British negotiator, Cabinet Secretary Robert Armstrong, that 'we were now adding a new chapter to a long history, and that we had the possibility of creating an opportunity for a profound, beneficial and lasting change in that relationship'.[30] The second comes from the IRA's Christmas message to its supporters in 1985 when they described it as a 'highly sophisticated, counter-revolutionary plan' designed to isolate republicans and as the 'most elaborate and determined of schemes yet contrived by Britain in the past 16 years'. In short, it had both profound political *and* security implications. It gave the Irish government a formal role in the governance of Northern Ireland. And it gave republicans much food for thought.

The agreement signalled the third change in the new dispensation—the internationalization of the process. Officials had already begun to turn their attention to the international dimension: 'Hunt (Cabinet Secretary) became very interested in Ireland, above all from a NATO point of view. What would happen to Ireland and to NATO if Ulster left the UK? This was his big interest…'.[31] As the agreement was being signed at Hillsborough Castle—and Unionist politicians were protesting impotently outside the grounds—it was being recognized in the Oval Office by President Reagan and Speaker O'Neill, and endorsed by many international leaders. US influence on Mrs Thatcher had been huge.[32] Perhaps the real significance lay in the precedent American pressure set for a future president. In this instance the State Department's traditional dominance of Northern Ireland policy had been undermined: 'The potentialities of such bypassing of ordinary channels, small in effect in 1985, were large and decisive under the next Democratic president.'[33]

Equally, the EC had been providing a watching brief as the 1980s unfolded. As early as 1972 the French Foreign Minister raised issues about the impact of Northern Ireland on the new Europe.[34] In 1973, a Brussels think tank, Pro Mundi Vita, had stressed the embarrassment that the Northern Ireland conflict was causing in a modernizing and more secular Europe—this long before the Balkans exploded. Europe responded through a series of reports and initiatives concerned with socio-economic improvements to the Northern Irish infrastructure. A potentially more political intervention came in the form of a report presented by a Danish politician, Nils Haagerup, to the European Parliament in 1984. Whereas Haagerup eschewed any overtly political role for Europe, its very publication was a political act—it called for increased economic aid and British-Irish co-operation to bring about a 'political system with an equitable sharing of Government responsibilities'. It illustrated too how the European dimension was used in managing the conflict through EU policies and reports on Northern Ireland, the

EU in Northern Ireland, the EU as a political arena, and the EU as a model of negotiated governance.[35] Northern Ireland was no longer hermetically sealed.

(b) The Primacy of the Political

When John Hume became SDLP leader in 1979, he set out to challenge the political orthodoxy of one-party rule by broadening his constituency. He had made his mark already in the US when he established a powerful alliance with four prominent Democrats.[36] When the Democrats lost office in 1979, this group widened their influence through the creation of the Friends of Ireland, a bipartisan Congressional group. They were to have a telling influence on President Reagan. Equally, Hume challenged Irish republican orthodoxy by questioning the efficacy and morality of armed struggle and this was to lead eventually to bringing Sinn Féin in from the cold and negotiation with the British government.

Now for the first time in its history Unionism could not rely on any British political party to protect its interests. Their initial response was to fall back on 'public banding', organizing massive demonstrations, refusing any contact with the government, and withdrawing from parliament to force a series of by-elections that would serve to demonstrate Unionism's unanimous rejection of the Agreement. They failed in all of these. While mass demonstrations produced a sense of solidarity (and continuity with 1974 and 1912) they were unpredictable and often degenerated into mindless delinquency. Their slogan of 'Ulster Says No' reinforced British prejudices that 'all Ulster politicians were died-in-the wool oppositionists'.[37] Their attempt to turn the Assembly into a forum to challenge the Agreement led to its suspension by the British cabinet. The by-elections fell short of the figure predicted by the UUP leader, James Molyneaux, and they lost one seat to the SDLP. Their policy of abstention from Westminster collapsed in March 1987. Eventually they were to realize that their internal exile was counterproductive. Reluctantly, they entered into talks about talks before they were to engage in formal negotiations from the early 1990s.

The first indication that the game was up came in January 1987 when the New Ulster Political Research Group (NUPRG)—the UDA's think tank—published *Common Sense*. It argued that an exclusivist mentality was counterproductive and that the Agreement could act as a catalyst. It displayed sensitivity towards minorities and sought an agreed process for the governance of Northern Ireland. It was a remarkable document and one can say, with hindsight, that it marked the demise of traditional resistance to constitutional reform. It was followed in July by a UUP/DUP task force report, *An End to Drift*, that recognized the 'inadequacies of the existing protest campaign' and the 'limits of Unionism's negotiation strength'. The sum total was an acknowledgement that the tactics which had been employed for a century were now redundant.

We have noted, too, that republicans were reconsidering their tactics. The futility of the Armalite and ballot box strategy was exposed by the Enniskillen bomb in 1987 when eleven innocent people were killed by an IRA bomb at a Remembrance Day ceremony. It was a public relations disaster. Hume seized the psychological moment to challenge the armed struggle. In a letter to Gerry Adams on the following St Patrick's Day, he exposed the contradictions in their role as *soi-disant* defenders of their community; and that in fact the IRA 'methods and their strategy have actually become more sacred than their cause'.[38] There followed a series of meetings between the two parties which ran until September. The significance of such talks was that republicanism had started the long journey away from being a sect, towards becoming a political party. It enabled direct talks between Hume and Adams which culminated in a joint statement that was submitted to the Dublin government on 25 September 1993. Its impact was felt in the US: 'The document "sanitized" Irish republicanism. It indicated that Sinn Féin...took seriously the unarmed ballot-box strategy long-advocated by the SDLP'.[39]

Evidence has emerged that in any case Sinn Féin had been pursuing a political strategy for some time. A back channel had been established between them and the government from the early 1970s.[40] It was there in its 1992 discussion paper, *Towards a Lasting Peace in Ireland,* when it acknowledged Unionist fears and accepted that British withdrawal would only be brought about by a process of cooperation between both governments and in consultation with all Northern Ireland parties. And it is patently there in its pamphlet *Setting the Record Straight* (January 1994), whose sub-title accurately reflects its contents: 'A record of communication between Sinn Féin and the British government October 1990–November 1993'. All of this was to be a backdrop for the republican and loyalist cessations of violence in August and October 1994, respectively.

(c) Intergovernmental Cooperation

The essence of the 1985 Agreement was that it 'provided institutional machinery for the cultivation of a mature diplomatic rapport between Britain and Ireland'.[41] But that is not to say that there were those who still supported a security response. As late as 1991 a senior British army officer was putting the case for internment to break up the IRA's command structure: '...we can deliver, given a favourable or at least not unhelpful climate in the south; and if you can keep the Americans off our backs, and deal with the EC and the human rights people and so on...'. That was an unwitting, but accurate, reflection of how the game was changing. Two years later, when news broke of the secret contacts with the IRA, and the Head of Government Information Services received an urgent call, he assumed that internment was being reintroduced and that he had been called in to deal with the consequences.[42]

By this stage 'mature diplomatic rapport' had become personalized in the hands of the two Prime Ministers, John Major and Albert Reynolds, who launched their Joint Declaration in December 1993. It was to establish the basis for a comprehensive and lasting peace. That wasn't obvious at the outset because it was a (deliberate) piece of tortuous syntax that defies textual exegesis. Its essence was described as 'a minor diplomatic masterpiece...[which] is not a formal agreement or treaty setting the framework for a comprehensive constitutional settlement; it is a political statement of attitude and intent directed primarily at the IRA. The two heads of government have carefully shelved all the difficult longer term issues...in order to make a bid for an IRA ceasefire.'[43] The use of coded language and of constructive ambiguity was to cause problems further down the line. But for the present it led to intense political and diplomatic activity, beginning with the granting of a forty-eight-hour visa to Gerry Adams to visit the US the following January. This caused an immediate *frisson* in Anglo-American relations, but it was a crucial decision because it placed Adams in thrall to the US agenda.

After extensive consultations the IRA announced its cessation of violence—but refused to use the word 'permanent'—on 31 August 1994, to be followed by the UDA and UVF on 13 October. While there was no expectation of a sudden return to war, there was a sense of realism of proper timescales. In November 1995, John Hume spoke of 'the real healing process [which] will take place and *in a generation or two* a new Ireland will evolve' (italics added). To add impetus to the process, President Clinton made a historic visit to Britain and Ireland that month, after both governments announced the 'launch of a "twin track" process to make progress in parallel on the decommissioning [of arms] issue and on all-party negotiations'. Republicans had become convinced that too much emphasis was put on the former in an attempt to stall the latter. The Irish government sought to have Sinn Féin involved in democratic politics from October 1994 through the creation of a Forum for Peace and Reconciliation in Dublin. But the IRA considered that there was insufficient alacrity on the part of the British authorities and responded with the Canary Wharf bomb on 9 February 1996. It did enormous financial damage to the City of London (besides killing two innocent civilians) and was a classic example of the communicative frame of violence—'this is what we do best and will continue to do so unless we get a place at the negotiations'.

That was unlikely to happen because Prime Minister Major's majority was paper-thin and was dependent on the support of the UUP. Even before Canary Wharf, an enquiry chaired by former US Senator George Mitchell produced a report that decoupled decommissioning through the enunciation of six principles with the need for confidence-building measures during inclusive negotiations, and made the stark point that 'success in the peace process cannot be achieved solely by reference to the decommissioning of arms' (para. 51). The government responded by calling elections for a Northern Ireland Peace Forum to be held on 30 May, in which Sinn Féin attained its highest-ever poll. A surreal elective process enabled some of the smaller parties to have representation. Hence the Northern Ireland Women's Coalition (NIWC), the Progressive Unionist Party (PUP), and the Ulster Democratic Party (UDP) (both of whom had connections with loyalist paramilitarism) were to be involved in formal negotiations. They were to make a significant contribution in those talks.

The stalemate was broken when Labour won the May 1997 election with a majority of 179. On 19 July, the IRA announced 'a complete cessation of military operations'. In the meantime, Prime Minister Blair set the multi-party talks' deadline for one year later. They were chaired by George Mitchell who displayed remarkable patience and diplomacy throughout the process. Sinn Féin's entry in September made them more inclusive but led to a DUP walkout. On 28 March 1998, Mitchell set 9 April as the date for agreement, and on 7 April he published his own draft paper. Agreement was finally reached early on 10 April, and was endorsed by 71.1 per cent in Northern Ireland, and 94.39 per cent in the Republic in two separate referendums on 22 May.[44] The stage was set for implementation.

IV. IMPLEMENTATION

In her comparative study of peace agreements Christine Bell asserts that 'peace agreements are best understood as a *form of transitional constitution*'.[45] Peace Agreements are usually points of transition where it is imperative to 'establish realistic expectations about how much and how quickly a weak and tentative peace agreement can alter the basic nature of a long and profoundly bitter conflict...needs and priorities change, interests must be redefined or revisioned, and a joint learning process must be institutionalised and accelerated.'[46] A plateau had been reached. The comparison with the 1973 Sunningdale Agreement is apt: 'The Belfast Agreement offers a fuller recognition of the right of the people of Northern Ireland to determine their constitutional future. It is much more inclusive of the range of political opinion and more supportive of equality and human rights. Crucially, it offers something Sunningdale could not: a complete end to political violence. These differences reflect profound differences in the contexts of the two agreements.'[47]

The agreement in principle to a complete end of violence and its deliverance in practice are, of course, two different things. The Omagh bomb demonstrates this but it is remarkable that the mainstream IRA and Sinn Féin remained intact. One reason was that they too engaged in constructive ambiguity. Sinn Féin's consistent denial of any relationship with the IRA prolonged the implementation period but ensured that peace held. On the assumption of the DUP–Sinn Féin-led Executive in 2007, the lowest number of security-related deaths was recorded since records began in 1969. To reinforce the sense of normality, the Independent International Commission on Decommissioning (established in August 1997) was dissolved in February 2010.

If the journey was arduous, the reasons were complex and based on an absence of trust. The Agreement had simply stated that all participants reaffirm their total commitment to the complete disarmament of all paramilitary organizations and 'to use any influence they may have, to achieve the decommissioning of all paramilitary arms' by May 2000. Since Sinn Féin was not the IRA, its influence was, *ipso facto*, limited. Indeed the IRA didn't begin to decommission all its weapons until November 2001; and it wasn't until 28 July 2005 that the IRA leadership formally ordered an end to its armed campaign and instructed all IRA units to dump arms. The IICD confirmed the completion of IRA decommissioning on 26 September 2005. It gave them cover to make progress on other security-related and human rights matters.

Republicans wanted to place these affairs in a wider context. They preferred to speak of 'disarmament' of *all* weapons. Policing had to be reformed root-and-branch and the whole security technology had to be dismantled. With the diminution of paramilitarism it was easier to justify the removal of troops. The reform of policing was more challenging. Five hundred and nine RUC and auxiliary personnel had died during the conflict. There was an emotional Unionist attachment to 'our' police. Further, given that both governments were committed to 'an accelerated programme for the release of prisoners' belonging to organizations committed to a total and unequivocal ceasefire and to their reintegration into the community, it was going to be difficult to persuade a 'law and order' community to buy into both concessions. And yet policing reform was one of the major successes of the peace process.

This was achieved by taking it out of the political realm—'An Independent Commission on Policing for Northern Ireland' was established in June 1998 under the terms of the Agreement to seek a 'new beginning to policing in Northern Ireland with a police service capable of attracting and sustaining support from the community as a whole'. It reported in September 1999 with 175 recommendations, the vast majority of which have been accepted. The Police Service of Northern Ireland (PSNI) replaced the RUC; a recruitment policy to attract more Catholics succeeded (and overcame initial hostility from many Unionists). By the time Sinn Féin took its seats on the Policing Board in 2007, there could no longer be said to be an exclusive association between Protestants and policing.

There was further evidence of the attenuation of Protestant/Unionist domination. One was the position of the Orange Order and its relationship to Unionism. The Order had always been seen as a barometer of Protestant fears with numbers rising in times of crisis. Yet 'Kaufmann's (2007) study of the Orange Order shows that its influence has been in steady decline since 1960'.[48] Insofar as that is the general trend over the past half-decade, the explanation may lie in the general decline of Unionist political power. Direct rule gradually eroded the Order's nepotistic influence; a more assertive Catholic community challenged its control of the public space; and some controversies over parade rerouting signalled public relations disasters. When there was a formal separation between the Order and the UUP in 2005, it passed with little notice. Truly a new political order was emerging.

A possible explanation lies in the 'success' achieved through the 1998 Agreement. Firstly, it replaced the hated 1985 Agreement. Secondly, republicans had signed up to the doctrine of consent, had disbanded the IRA, and had taken their places inside a British political dispensation. Thirdly, the Irish Government had removed its irredentist claims on Northern Ireland. In 2007, the Northern Ireland Life and Times Survey reported that 57.5 per cent of Protestant participants felt that 'the Good Friday/Belfast Agreement was a good thing for Northern Ireland'. The results 'signal greater Protestant investment in power sharing and a willingness to rely less heavily on external British support'.[49] One individual who can take credit for this turnaround is David Trimble. The man who had taken on the UUP leadership in 1995, allegedly with the support of the Order, was the leader who was prepared to take a leap in the dark in 1998. The DUP, who had not signed up to the Agreement, enjoyed the luxury of being *in* government but not *of* government;

that is, they controlled their own ministerial portfolios without accepting responsibility for the out-workings of government. In a series of post-1998 elections conducted in an atmosphere of uncertainty, the DUP outstripped the UUP to become the largest party in Northern Ireland.

In a careful analysis of the 1914 crisis, with that which unfolded after 1968, Jackson asserts that Trimble 'has not only modified the strategies of Unionism, he has also shifted its historical paradigms' by adopting James Craig's fraught diplomacy in 1920–5.[50] It was Trimble's fraught diplomacy (with the overwhelming support of both governments) that carried the Agreement through its early precarious years. There the analogy ends. James Craig died in bed in 1940 while still Prime Minister. As First Minister, David Trimble presided over an Assembly and Executive that was suspended four times on issues of decommissioning and IRA trustworthiness. Trimble's position became more precarious and he resigned as UUP leader in May 2005. The same fate awaited the SDLP, and the 'Strong Centre' that had delivered the 1998 Agreement was pushed to the margins of political power. The trend was confirmed at the May 2005 general election and, once IRA decommissioning had been confirmed, the position for a new political configuration was in place.

To create this reconfiguration the governments convened talks in Scotland in October 2006 to reach agreement for a timetable to restore the institutions. The Assembly elections in March 2007 reiterated the new DUP/Sinn Féin dominance and led the way for a new dispensation. When Albert Reynolds became Taoiseach in 1992, he asked an intermediary to see whether Ian Paisley would be prepared to talk to him. '"The answer's in two parts", he said. "One—don't be wasting your time. Two—not until he is number one!"'.[51] Once he became number one all things became possible. In May, Ian Paisley and Martin McGuinness took up their positions as First Minister and Deputy First Minister of a new Northern Ireland Executive.

The genius of the 1998 Agreement can be traced to how it deals with identity when it confirms 'the birthright of all the people of Northern Ireland to identify themselves and be accepted as Irish or British, *or both*, as they may so choose, and accordingly confirm that their right to hold both British and Irish citizenship is accepted by both Governments and would not be affected by any future change in the status of Northern Ireland' (emphasis added). At a stroke, the Ulster question had been liberated from the deadening hand of history. One of the more stimulating interpretations of the Agreement comes from a literary critic who invokes the ghost of Oscar Wilde when he maintains that much of the language of the Agreement 'is vague, even "poetic". That is because it offers a version of multiple identities, of a kind for which no legal language yet exists. The Wilde who suggested that the only way to intensify personality was to multiply it would have approved: but where is the lawyer who can offer a constitutional definition as open rather than fixed, as a process rather than a conclusion?'[52]

It can be asserted that it was the gift of the poetic that enabled the prosaic—security reform, decommissioning, justice and human rights, and so on—to be implemented in the fullness of time.

V. Conclusion

Declan Kiberd is a fitting reference with which to end because his influential *Inventing Ireland* (1995) calls into play the incredible invective surrounding the debate about the nature of modern Irish nationalism and cultural theory, ranging from traditional to neo- to post-nationalism and the ferocity of the debate attached to revisionists, anti-revisionists, and post-revisionists.[53] It transferred into the political sphere when deciding how to commemorate 1916 with the triumphalism of the 50th anniversary followed by the downgrading of the 75th anniversary in the light of northern violence and the Irish government's attempt to reassert its authority against the growth of Sinn Féin in the Republic. In the less trying circumstance of political life in the Republic, historians and other academics entered into the debate—and not necessarily in an enlightened manner.

Consider the situation in Northern Ireland. Here we contemplate the dilemma *in extremis* concerned with the nature of contemporary history, the impact of 'noises in the street', and diverging intellectual fads. A good starting point is to revert to one of the gurus:

> Contemporary history embarrasses a writer not only because he knows too much, but also because what he knows is too undigested, too unconnected, too atomic. It is only after close and prolonged reflection that we begin to see what was essential and what unimportant, to see why things happened as they did, and to write history instead of newspapers.[54]

Collingwood's strictures are well taken and have a particular redolence in the historiography of the contemporary history of Ireland where, it might be argued, some went beyond writing newspapers and drifted towards polemic. One of our most eminent historians, A.T.Q. Stewart, 'deplored the habit of Irish historians (including some very distinguished ones) of introducing the current Irish troubles into their work'. Admittedly, that was difficult for those of us whose stock in trade was the current troubles and especially those of us who had been engaged in protest in our student days. But if your chosen period was well removed from the present, then you had, you believed, the advantage of keeping out of trouble: 'Like Carlyle, I believed that the beauty of the past was precisely that it had none of the problems of the present in it. Unfortunately, where Ireland was concerned this was notoriously not true.' And so, as the troubles unfolded, 'I felt as a French historian might have felt in the Paris of 1789, distracted by noises in the street as he toiled over a history of the monarchy'.[55]

For many it was difficult not to get carried away by the noises in the street and, in that respect, much of the historiography reflected the current political dynamic. Like many in the Unionist professional class, Stewart was outraged by the signing of the Anglo-Irish Agreement 1985. In an article anticipating its first anniversary he wrote: 'The road to reform, and indeed even to the recovery of basic democratic freedom, has been firmly closed. The hour for determined resistance is passed, yet an implacable British Government is driving [unionists] towards violence as inexorably as a sheepdog driving a flock of sheep'.[56] One cites Stewart *because* he was acutely aware of the pitfalls. Others were similarly aware and endorsed G.R. Elton's hostility to 'present-centred history and his plea for the ideal of the 'professional sceptic'.

But scepticism can present its own problems. Hence a study of contemporary Unionism opens with a claim that this is 'a book about a tradition which has often been disparaged and has lent itself easily to caricature and to misrepresentation'. The volume sets out to set the record straight and to challenge important features of Irish nationalist thinking where the editors detect a certain complacency and bland relativism. In doing so, the editors suggest 'that key aspects of existing nationalist thought have been opened to intellectual scrutiny in such a way as to require a serious reappraisal of the philosophy as it stands in its various guises'.[57] The book was published at a time of great uncertainty for Unionism. It was as if only one tradition could be defended at the cost of the other. Yet in more potentially benign times, Richard English went on to produce distinguished studies of the IRA and of Irish nationalism.[58] What was particularly interesting about the former was the access he got to key players in the republican movement, access that may not have been granted in the previous decade. In a post-peace process period, the protagonists are anxious to have a favourable light shone upon them.

This recalls the sage advice of E.H. Carr that one should not only look at the name of the author and the title of the book but also at the date of publication. Carr's dictum can be applied in at least two other instances. Arthur Aughey's *Under Siege* is an angry tirade on the Anglo-Irish Agreement whereas his *Politics of Northern Ireland* is a considered and sophisticated analysis of the dispensation created by the 1998 Agreement.[59] The contrast is not only one of mood but that of a quieter optimism. The second instance concerns intellectual fads. Compare and contrast, for example, *The State in Northern Ireland, 1921–1972: Political Forces and Social Classes* (1979) with *Northern Ireland 1921–1996: Political Forces and Social Classes* (1996). Besides the fact that both books carry the same subtitle, they were also written by the same authors (Paul Bew, Peter Gibbons, and Henry Patterson). The former is garnished with the dense and interminable internal debates of the Marxist gurus Althusser and Poulantzas; the latter is not.[60]

The Marxist analysis (alongside those of traditional Nationalist, traditional Unionist, and internal-conflict interpretations) are dealt with painstakingly and dispassionately in John Whyte's magisterial study in 1990,[61] that is, in the period immediately after the collapse of the Iron Curtain. In the intervening years, Marxist analysis has lost much of its redolence in the academic literature. One might argue that an uneasy truce has broken out in a discussion of the other three interpretations through a communal sense of shame as we contemplate what we have done to each other over three decades.[62] The dilemma for the present generation (including the academic community) is how we deal with this immediate past. That much was recognized at the outbreak of the conflict by the playwright Stewart Parker in an article he wrote in the *Irish Times* (7 April 1970) in which he considered the heritage of his grandfather who had been in the original UVF and had participated in gunrunning in 1914:

> Nearly every day now in the North, the plea goes out to 'forget the past'. Such advice is both impracticable and pernicious. On the one hand, you can't forget a nightmare while you are still dreaming it. On the other, it is survival through comprehension that is healthy, not survival through amnesia. Besides, the past is not a dead letter. The past is explosive cargo in everybody's family dresser. Your grandfather is the past.[63]

The nature of the historiographical debate should allow us to pause and ponder and to embrace a degree of self-scrutiny and humility. The 'Troubles' forcibly removed many of us from the Ivory Tower: 'We live in a human condition, so we cannot through politics grasp for an absolute ideal...'.[64] For 'politics', substitute the 'study of history'.

NOTES

1. Harvey Cox, *Establishing Northern Ireland: Some Features of the Period 1912–25* (A paper presented at the Conference on Conflict in Northern Ireland, Lancaster University, December 1971).
2. J.G. Bulpitt, *Territory and Power in the United Kingdom: An Interpretation* (Manchester, 1983), 160.
3. Ibid., 146.
4. John McCrae, *Polarisation in Northern Ireland: A Preliminary Report* for the Lancaster Peace Research Centre, July 1966, 14.
5. John Whyte, *Interpreting Northern Ireland* (Oxford, 1990), 246.
6. See Robert Kagan, *Paradise and Power: America and Europe in the New World Order* (London, 2003).
7. Martina Purdy, *Room 21: Stormont behind Closed Doors* (Belfast, 2005), 54.
8. Conor Cruise O'Brien, *States of Ireland*, (London, 1972), 158.
9. Henry Patterson, *Ireland Since 1939: The Persistence of Conflict*, (Dublin, 2006), 199, 216.
10. A. Aughey, *The Politics of Northern Ireland: Beyond the Belfast Agreement*, (London, 2005), 9–11.
11. J. Bowyer Bell, 'Aspects of the Dragonworld; Covert Communication and the Rebel Ecosystem', *Intelligence and Counterintelligence*, 3, 1 (1990), 15–43.
12. David Apter, 'A View from the Bogside' in Hermann Gilomee and Janie Ganiano (eds), *The Elusive Search for Peace: South Africa, Israel and Northern Ireland*, (Capetown, 1990), 164.
13. Gerry Adams, *The Politics of Irish Freedom*, (Dingle, 1986), 52.
14. Ibid., 64–5.
15. The concept of 'public banding' is explored in David W. Miller, *Queens Rebels: Ulster Loyalism in Historical Perspective*, (Dublin, 1978).
16. David Moss, 'Analysing Italian Political Violence as a Sequence of Communicative Acts: The Red Brigades 1970–1982', *Social Analysis*, 13, (May 1983), 86.
17. Gerry Adams, *Free Ireland: Towards a Lasting Peace*, (Dingle, 1995), 64.
18. Aughey, *op. cit.*, 85 and 105.

19. Both the Saville and Cameron remarks are taken from a debate in the House of Lords on 15 October 2010 at cols. 556 and 739–40.

20. See the memoirs of two former Northern Ireland civil servants: Patrick Shea, *Voices and the Sound of Drums: An Irish Autobiography*, (Belfast, 1981); and John A. Oliver, *Working at Stormont: Memoirs*, (Dublin, 1978).

21. Brendan O'Duffy, *British-Irish Relations and Northern Ireland: From Violent Politics to Conflict Regulation*, (Dublin, 2007), 82–3.

22. Cited in Kenneth Bloomfield, *A Tragedy of Errors: The Government and Misgovernment of Northern Ireland*, (Liverpool, 2007), 28–9.

23. Roger Darlington, *Fortnight*, 8 June 1973.

24. Robert Fisk, *The Point of No Return: The Strike which Broke the British in Ulster*, (London, 1975), 202.

25. Northern Ireland Act 1974, ch. 28, s. 2.

26. Bernard Donoghue, *Downing Street Diary Volume Two: With James Callaghan in Number 10*, (London, 2008), 298.

27. *HC Deb*. Vol. 998, col.557 (9 July, 1980).

28. This is discussed in Oliver MacDonagh, *States of Ireland: A Study of Anglo-Irish Conflict 1780–1980*, (London, 1983), 71–89.

29. See Paul Arthur, ' "Reading" Violence: Ireland' in David Apter (ed), *The Legitimization of Violence* (London, 1997), 234–91.

30. Cited in a letter from one of the Irish negotiators, Michael Lillis, in The Irish Times, 27 May 2011.

31. Ion Trewin (ed), *The Hugo Young Papers: Thirty Years of British Politics—Off the Record* (London, 2008), 113. Young was quoting Harold Wilson's press secretary, Joe Haines, 1 June 1977.

32. See Paul Arthur, *Special Relationships: Britain, Ireland and the Northern Ireland Problem* (Belfast, 2001), 116–59.

33. Timothy J. Lynch, *Turf War: The Clinton Administration and Northern Ireland* (Aldershot, 2004), 21.

34. See Robert Ramsay, *Ringside Seats* (Dublin, 2009), 102–5.

35. Brigid Laffan and Jane O'Mahony, *Ireland and the European Union* (London, 2008), 201–18.

36. They—Senators Edward Kennedy and Daniel Patrick Moynihan, Speaker 'Tip' O'Neill, and Governor Hugh Carey of New York—were known as the 'Four Horsemen'. They exerted considerable leverage in Congress from 1977 onwards. See Arthur, op.cit., 135–43.

37. US Ambassador Raymond Seitz quoted in Trewin (ed), op.cit., 399.

38. On that last point Hume quoted (tellingly) Wolfe Tone, the secular saint of Irish republicanism, on the distinction between objectives and means. The five-page letter is remarkably prescient.

39. Lynch, *op. cit.*, 46.

40. See Peter Taylor, *Talking To Terrorists: Face To Face With The Enemy* (London, 2011), 1–48.

41. Richard Bourke, *Peace in Ireland: The War of Ideas* (London, 2003), 281.

42. Niall O'Dochartaigh, ' "The Contact": Understanding a Communication Channel' in Joseph J. Popiolkowski and Nicholas J. Cull (eds), *Public Diplomacy, Cultural Interventions and the Peace Process in Northern Ireland* (Los Angeles, 2009), 67.

43. David Goodall, 'Terrorists on the spot', *Tablet*, 25 December 1993/1 January 1994, 1676. Goodall was one of the architects of the 1985 Agreement.

44. See George J. Mitchell, *Making Peace* (London, 1999), passim.

45. C. Bell, *Peace Agreements and Human Rights* (Oxford, 2000), 9 (italics added).

46. Robert Rothstein, 'After the Peace: The Political Economy of Reconciliation', Inaugural Rebecca Meyerhoff Memorial Lecture (Jerusalem, 1996), 7.

47. Joseph Ruane and Jennifer Todd, 'The Belfast Agreement: Context, Content, Consequences' in Ruane and Todd (eds), *After the Good Friday Agreement: Analysing Political Change in Northern Ireland* (Dublin, 1999), 1.

48. Lee A. Smithey, *Unionists, Loyalists, and Conflict Transformation in Northern Ireland* (Oxford, 2011), 137. The author cites different reports which paint a similar picture.

49. Ibid., 67

50. Alvin Jackson, 'Militant opposition to Home Rule: the after-life' in Sabine Wichert (ed) *From the United Irishmen to Twentieth Century Unionism: A Festschrift for A.T.Q. Stewart* (Dublin, 2004), 184–5.

51. Albert Reynolds, *My Autobiography* (London, 2009), 199.

52. Declan Kiberd, *Irish Classics* (London, 2000), 636.

53. See for example, Ciaran Brady (ed), *Interpreting Irish History* (Dublin, 1994), Sean Hutton and Paul Stewart (eds), *Ireland's Histories: Aspects of State, Society and Ideology* (London, 1991; and R. F. Foster, *Luck and the Irish: A Brief History of Change 1970–2000* (London, 2007).

54. R. G. Collingwood, *Speculum Mentis: The Map of Knowledge* (London, 1924), 236.

55. A. T. Q. Stewart, *The Narrow Ground: The Roots of Conflict in Ulster* (London, 1989), 1–2.

56. A. T. Q. Stewart, 'Strikes may mark first anniversary of pact', *Irish Times*, 8 November 1986.

57. Richard English and Graham Walker (eds), *Unionism in Modern Ireland: New Perspectives on Politics and Culture* (Dublin, 1996) Ix, 220–1.

58. Richard English, *Armed Struggle: the History of the IRA* (London, 1st edn, 2003); and *Irish Freedom: The History of Nationalism in Ireland* (London, 2006).

59. A. Aughey *Under Siege: Ulster Unionism and the Anglo-Irish Agreement* (Belfast, 1989), vii and passim; *The Politics of Northern Ireland: Beyond the Belfast Agreement* (London, 2005).

60. Published respectively by Manchester University Press and Serif. It is interesting to follow the intellectual trajectory of these authors either singly or in co-authored books to see how they have responded to noises in the streets. The 1985 Agreement appears to have marked a landmark in their analysis. If one were to seek a similar example from the political science literature a useful exemplar would be Rupert Taylor (ed), *Consociational Theory: McGarry and O'Leary and the Northern Ireland Conflict* (London, 2009).

61. John Whyte, *Interpreting Northern Ireland* (Oxford, 1990).

62. The best source for examining the abysmal horror of the period is David McKittrick, Seamus Kelters, Brian Feeney and Chris Thornton (eds) *Lost Lives: The Stories of the Men, Women and Children Who Died as a Result of the Northern Ireland Troubles*, (Edinburgh, 2000). The essence of their message lies in the subtitle because it removes us from the statistical and abstract to the deeply personal.

63. Cited in Marilyn Richtarik, *Stewart Parker: A Life* (Oxford, 2012), 84.

64. Bernard Crick, *In Defence of Politics*, (Harmondsworth, 1968), 15.

Select Bibliography

Adams, Gerry, *The Politics of Irish Freedom* (Dingle, 1986).

Arthur, Paul, ' "Reading" Violence: Ireland' in David Apter (ed), *The Legitimization of Violence* (London, 1997), 234–91.

Arthur, Paul, *Special Relationships: Britain, Ireland and the Northern Ireland Problem* (Belfast, 2000).

Aughey, Arthur, *The Politics of Northern Ireland: Beyond the Belfast Agreement* (London, 2005).

Bourke, Richard, *Peace in Ireland: The War of Ideas* (London, 2003).

Bulpitt, J.G., *Territory and Power in the United Kingdom: An Interpretation* (Manchester, 1983).

Dixon, Paul, *Northern Ireland: The Politics of War and Peace* (London, 2008).

Elliott, M. (ed.), *The Long Road to Peace in Northern Ireland* (Liverpool, 2007).

Kagan, Robert, *Paradise and Power: America and Europe in the New World Order* (London, 2003).

Lynch, T. J., *Turf War: The Clinton Administration in Northern Ireland* (Aldershot, 2004).

MacDonagh, O., *States of Ireland: A Study of Anglo-Irish Conflict 1780–1980* (London, 1983).

Miller, D.W., *Queen's Rebels: Ulster Loyalism in Historical Perspective* (Dublin, 1978).

Mitchell, George, *Making Peace* (London, 1999).

O'Brien C.C. *States of Ireland* (London, 1972).

Pocock, J.G.A., 'The Limits and Divisions of British History: In Search of an Unknown Subject', *American Historical Review*, 87, 2, (1982).

Ramsay, Robert, *Ringside Seats* (Dublin, 2009).

Rothstein, R. (ed). *After the Peace—Resistance and Reconciliation* (Boulder Colo., London, 1999).

Stewart, A.T.Q., *The Narrow Ground: The Roots of Conflict in Northern Ireland* (London, 1989).

Townshend, C., *Political Violence in Ireland: Government and Resistance since 1848* (Oxford, 1983).

Whyte, John, *Interpreting Northern Ireland* (Oxford, 1990).

INDEX

Lightning Source UK Ltd.
Milton Keynes UK
UKOW07f0517170317
296846UK00001B/1/P